Angela Feagan

UNDERSTANDING THE TIMES

THE RELIGIOUS WORLDVIEWS OF OUR DAY AND THE SEARCH FOR TRUTH

DAVID A. NOEBEL

HARVEST HOUSE PUBLISHERS
Eugene, Oregon 97402

First printing, July 1991
Second printing, December 1991
Third printing, August 1992
Fourth printing, July 1993
Fifth printing, October 1993
Sixth printing, August 1994

Published by Harvest House Publishers
Eugene, Oregon 97402

Library of Congress Catalog Card Number: 91-065741
ISBN 1-56507-268-5

Printed in the United States of America.

This textbook is dedicated to every student who attended the Summit Ministries two-week program over the past 30 years. May this volume be used by our great God to more firmly establish you in the faith, and may it encourage you to continue to fight the good fight (2 Timothy 4:7).

ACKNOWLEDGMENTS

The story behind this Story began over 30 years ago in a chapel service at Hope College in Holland, Michigan. The chapel speaker was Dr. Fred Schwarz, and he was speaking about communism—its atheism, dialectical materialism, and economic determinism.

Following the chapel service I told Dr. Schwarz how much I enjoyed his chapel message. Dr. Irwin Lubbers, our college president, overheard my comments, and asked me if I would like to lead a study group about communism. Talk about the blind leading the blind! Despite my reservations, however, I accepted—and so as a junior at Hope College, I began studying communism and leading discussions about it. From that day till now, my interest in the subject has only deepened. I noticed that communism had a theology, a philosophy, an ethics, a politics, and an economics. Why, communism had a total religious worldview! Could Christianity hope to match the comprehensive worldview of communism? Were other religious worldviews in competition with my beliefs? The answer took years to sort out. This book represents the finished product of the sorting-out process. Thank you Dr. Lubbers, thank you Dr. Schwarz, for starting me on such a rewarding study.

Over the years others have had a part in the development of this text. James Orr's *The Christian View of God and the World*, the writings of Francis A. Schaeffer, Norman L. Geisler, and Carl F. H. Henry (especially *God, Revelation and Authority*) all had a tremendous impact on my worldview analysis.

The most important part, however, was played by Summit Ministries, a ministry I have presided over for 30 years. During this time, thousands of students have listened to our lectures and said they understood—realizing that the Biblical Christian worldview is consistent and comprehensive and under attack from every conceivable direction. To all the students, staff, faculty, and supporters of the Summit: Thank you for your inspiration and encouragement. Thank you for taking the lessons you learned here back to your colleges and universities and city council meetings and family Bible studies. The battle for the mind, heart, soul, and body of each person is a real battle—and you fight it well.

Many others have played a significant role in bringing this project to a fitting conclusion. Though fearful I will not be able to thank everyone, I must mention and thank John Hannah, Ron Jensen, Randy Rodden, J. P. Moreland, and the Campus Crusaders who helped sort and label categories for our studies. Thank you Carl Henry for looking over our outline and saying, "I've always wanted to do something like that." Thank you Ron Nash, for your time at one of our Society for Christian Philosophers meetings. Thank you John A. Stormer, Herb Titus, Virginia Armstrong, Duane Gish, Mark Hartwig, Mike McGuire, Connie Willems, and Cal and Debbie Beisner (Cal did a great job editing and expanding on some of our ideas, and Debbie was helpful designing the text). Thank you Jim and Carole Bowers, Jay Butler, Clark Bowers, and Ken Gasper for reading and re-reading and suggesting and re-suggesting.

Special thanks to Jeff Baldwin, a Summit graduate and Westmont College alumnus, who was willing to interrupt his graduate studies to help me research and write this text—later laying out the text camera-ready for the printer.

To one and all mentioned—and unmentioned—an unqualified "thank you" for a job well done. Even before this English edition is printed, we have received requests to translate into Romanian, Polish, Russian, and Lithuanian. May this project, in that capacity, ignite a renaissance of interest in the Christian worldview. May our Lord Jesus Christ bless this work to that end.

CONTENTS

INTRODUCTION

Every individual bases his thoughts, decisions and actions on a worldview. A person may not be able to identify his worldview, and it may lack consistency, but his most basic assumptions about the origin of life, purpose, and the future guarantee adherence to some system of thought.

Because worldviews are pertinent to every person's life—the way we think and the way we act—and because virtually all worldviews promise salvation or utopia, the study of worldviews is of critical importance. Indeed, personal integrity requires each of us to examine various worldviews and then adopt the one that is most persuasive—that seems to answer life's searching questions best in the context of the physical world, human events, and each individual's mind and heart.

This study will discuss the three fundamental worldviews of Western civilization: Biblical Christianity, Marxism/Leninism, and Secular Humanism. An emerging Eastern worldview known as the New Age movement, or Cosmic Humanism, is making sufficient gains in the West to merit close attention and is examined in Appendix A.

By the time students complete this study, they should have a comprehensive grasp of the major ideas, issues, and personalities that shaped the twentieth century and will shape the twenty-first. Further, they should understand how certain ideas comprise a worldview's content and give it form. Students should be able to recognize whether these ideas are growing in acceptance (e.g., Is Secular Humanism's brand of atheistic evolution gaining or losing popular support?); whether these ideas are systemic to the overall worldview (e.g., Is the idea of private property a fundamental part of Biblical Christianity, and would its denial adversely affect the Christian worldview?); and how many ideas foundational to a worldview must be changed or negated before the worldview itself is altered. Recently, Marxism/Leninism has

Notes
and
Asides

undergone sweeping changes in Eastern Europe and the Soviet Union. Which of these changes are systemic, and which are peripheral? Which speak to the heart of the worldview, and which affect only the fringes?

This study, designed especially for Christian high school and college students (but of significant interest to any concerned person), emphasizes the importance of understanding the Christian worldview's relevance in an academic environment. It is no secret that Biblical Christianity faces difficult times in academia. Most subjects taught in the social sciences and humanities, for example, are taught from a distinctly non-Christian perspective. Some are taught from an anti-Christian perspective.[1] This study looks at the worldviews being taught under the banners of "education," "academic freedom," "scholarship," and "truth."

Often Christian parents, after spending years and tens of thousands of dollars raising their children, see their precious investment of time, heartache, and money go down the drain, thanks to university courses based on non-Christian worldviews. Family values are trashed in favor of co-ed dorm "new morality," "safe-sex" kits, trial marriage arrangements, feminist and homosexual values. Religious values are attacked by atheism, agnosticism, nihilism and despair, and social values are replaced by radical politics, Marxism, socialism, etc.

Out of this confrontation and resultant value erosion, four things become obvious:

(1) Christian young people are not intellectually well grounded in their faith and therefore do not recognize the truth and power inherent in their worldview.

(2) Parents have a premonition something is wrong, but cannot put their finger on it. Rarely do they realize their child is being seduced out of one worldview (Christianity) into another (Secular Humanism or Marxism).

(3) The deck is stacked against Christians by hostile or lukewarm educators. The traditional family values and the Christian point of view seldom are justly represented. A 900-page biology textbook, for example, may contain 200 pages about evolution and only a line or two admitting that some "fundamentalist" Christians believe God created the heavens and the earth.

(4) Christian parents are paying the salaries of Secular Humanist professors (through taxes and tuition) for the seduction of their own children! "Professors, whose salaries are paid by the taxes and tuition subsidies of millions of hard-working Americans,"

Used by permission of the *Colorado Springs Sun*

say James Dobson and Gary Bauer, "ridicule capitalism, attack family values, and rewrite American history, so that if it is taught at all, America is always the villain."[2] This is perhaps the cruelest irony. While Christians in the United States clearly outnumber their worldview rivals (192 million Americans claim to be Christians while Isaac Asimov, president of the American Humanist Association, admits that there are only 7.3 million Humanists in the United States), taxpayers' school children are taught almost exclusively the Secular Humanist religious worldview.

This study is intended to encourage Christians to reclaim the classroom. If Secular Humanism is a religious worldview (as we demonstrate in this text), it has, by present interpretation of the "separation of church and state" doctrine, no place in the public school system. We do not, of course, expect Biblical Christianity to be the only worldview taught in America's schools. But we do expect fair representation. At the very least, this study should "level the playing field" so

Notes and Asides

"Education makes a people easy to lead, but difficult to drive; easy to govern, but impossible to enslave."

—Lord Brougham

that Christian students and their parents will recognize worldview bias and understand how to take effective countermeasures to preserve their point of view. Dobson and Bauer refer to the battle for the next generation's allegiance as the "Second Great Civil War." Christian young people need to know where the battlefields are and what armies are involved.

We know Christian young people will fight the good fight of faith, finish the course, and keep the faith (2 Timothy 4:7) if they understand the truth of their worldview and know who and where the enemy is. David W. Breese wrote in *Seven Men Who Rule the World from the Grave*, "The seven [Charles Darwin, Karl Marx, Sigmund Freud, John Dewey, John Maynard Keynes, Julius Wellhausen, and Søren Kierkegaard] . . . ruled the world more permanently because they and their ideas became gods of the mind rather than masters of real estate. For them, the battle for the minds of men was the ultimate thing."[3] Tim LaHaye said this very thing in *Battle for the Mind*, and the Bible said it much earlier: "As a man thinketh in his heart, so is he" (Proverbs 23:7).

This course of study will not only inform Christian young men and women about various intellectual battlefields and the armies arrayed against them during their academic years, but also train them for a productive and Christ-centered life.

After years of atheism at work in America and abroad ("Men Have Forgotten God," the title of Alexander Solzhenitsyn's acceptance speech when he won the Nobel Prize, expresses the cry from Eastern Europe), the world yearns for a revival of soul and spirit—that is, a revival of truth. The Biblical Christian worldview forms the basis for such a revival. This text aims to set forth that worldview in contrast with its chief competitors and to show that it deserves, morally and intellectually, to triumph over them.

[1]See Roger Kimball, *Tenured Radicals* (New York: Harper and Row, 1990), Charles J. Sykes, *The Hollow Man* (New York: National Book Network, 1990), and Dinesh D'Souza, *Illiberal Education: The Politics of Race and Sex on Campus* (New York: The Free Press, 1991). According to D'Souza, the people on campus who are targeted for censorship are "the white, male, heterosexual, able-bodied, Christian, middle-class norm" (p. 214). The only white European males not "deconstructed" arc Karl Marx and Charles Darwin. For the first time, says D'Souza, "Harvard and Yale have assembled Curriculum Committees to explore course material on 'Gay, Lesbian and Bisexual Studies'" (p. 214). Stanford University is replacing the (mostly Christian) authors who influenced Western civilization with the likes of *I, Rigoberta Menchu*, a book narrated by an illiterate from Guatemala who just happens to be a feminist and a Marxist. For further insight into what is transpiring on our campuses we recommend: William J. Bennett, *The De-Valuing of America* (New York: Simon and Schuster, 1992), Charles J. Sykes, *A Nation of Victims* (New York: St. Martin's Press, 1992), Martin Anderson, *Impostors in the Temple: American Intellectuals Are Destroying Our Universities and Cheating Our Students of Their Future* (New York: Simon and Schuster, 1992), Page Smith, *Killing the Spirit* (New York: Penguin Books, 1990), and Thomas Sowell, *Inside American Education: The Decline, the Deception, the Dogma* (New York: The Free Press, 1993).

[2]James C. Dobson and Gary L. Bauer, *Children at Risk* (Dallas, TX: Word, 1990), p. 182.

[3]David W. Breese, *Seven Men Who Rule the World from the Grave* (Chicago: Moody Press, 1990), p. 20.

CHAPTER

1

THE BATTLE FOR HEARTS AND MINDS

"Nothing short of a great Civil War of Values rages today throughout North America," say James Dobson and Gary Bauer. "Two sides with vastly differing and incompatible worldviews are locked in a bitter conflict that permeates every level of society."[1]

This book is an in-depth account of this "Second Great Civil War"—an account of the war for our children and grandchildren. The war, as Dobson and Bauer put it, is a struggle "for the hearts and minds of people. It is a war over ideas."[2]

To be more precise, it is a battle between worldviews. On one side is the Christian worldview. On the other is the Humanist worldview divided into three easily definable branches: Secular Humanism, Marxism/Leninism, and Cosmic Humanism or the New Age movement. While the latter three don't agree in every detail, there is one point on which they unanimously concur—their opposition to Biblical Christianity. It is in this context that we will seek to understand all three while

Notes and Asides

presenting a strong, honest, truthful, intelligent defense of the Biblical Christian worldview.

"Someday soon," Dobson and Bauer say, ". . . a winner [in the battle for our children's hearts and minds] will emerge and the loser will fade from memory. For now, the outcome is very much in doubt."[3] In order to emerge victorious, Christians must quickly arrive at an understanding of the times and take action (I Chronicles 12:32).

The Heart of a Worldview

Worldview is any ideology, philosophy, theology, movement, or religion that provides an overarching approach to understanding God, the world, and man's relations to God and the world.

The term *worldview* refers to any ideology, philosophy, theology, movement, or religion that provides an overarching approach to understanding God, the world, and man's relations to God and the world. Specifically, a worldview should contain a particular perspective regarding each of the following ten disciplines: theology, philosophy, ethics, biology, psychology, sociology, law, politics, economics, and history.

If Biblical Christianity contains a specific attitude toward all ten disciplines it is, by our definition, a worldview. And, since it contains a theology, it is by implication a religious worldview.

Secular Humanism and Marxism/Leninism are also religious, as this study will show. Both have theologies. There is a Secular Humanist theology; there is a Marxist/Leninist theology. Further, both are worldviews, because they speak directly to each of the other nine disciplines. The New Age movement (Cosmic Humanism) on the other hand, is an emerging worldview, because it has something to say about some of the categories (e.g., theology, politics, and biology), but little to say about others (e.g., law and sociology).

"A worldview is a way of viewing or interpreting all of reality. It is an interpretive framework through which or by which one makes sense of the data of life and the world."

—Norman Geisler, William Watkins

Each worldview offers a particular perspective from which to approach each discipline. Conversely, each discipline is value laden with worldview implications. Christian students must understand that these various disciplines are not value free. Each discipline demands basic assumptions about the nature of reality in order to grant meaning to specific approaches to it.

This text analyzes the three worldviews' perspectives on each of the ten disciplines, but it does so without losing sight of how each system of thought integrates its various presuppositions, categories, and conclusions. We are not out to "over-analyze." Rather, we are attempting to understand each discipline and how it fits into each worldview. Dissecting is artificial; integration is the real world. No discipline stands alone. Each affects all others in one way or another. The line separating theology and philosophy is fragile; the line separating theology, philosophy, ethics, law, and politics is more so. In fact, there is no ultimate

Notes and Asides

line, only a difference in emphasis and perspective.[4]

Thus, the arrangement of the categories is, to some degree, arbitrary; but we have tried to place them in their most logical sequence (See Figure 1:1, p. 10). It is clear that theological and philosophical assumptions color every aspect of one's worldview and that disciplines such as sociology and psychology are related; but other relations and distinctions are less recognizable. Therefore, one reader may feel that we have done law an injustice by distancing it from ethics, and another may feel history to be almost as foundational to a worldview as philosophy. There is no correct order according to which these chapters must be read. Our format is a logical suggestion; it is not binding. Readers are encouraged to adhere to any study method or outline with which they feel comfortable. Further, the Christian worldview may require one arrangement and the Secular Humanist or Marxist worldview another.

"All the branches of knowledge are connected together, because the subject matter of knowledge is intimately united in itself, as being the acts and the work of the Creator."
—John H. Newman

Worldview Advocates, Past and Present

The contention that Biblical Christianity, Marxism/Leninism, and Secular Humanism are worldviews is supported by some of the most important representatives of each system of thought.

Over one hundred years ago (1890-1891), James Orr presented the Kerr Lectures in Edinburgh, Scotland. He entitled his series *The Christian View of God and the World* and argued forcefully for the proposition that Christianity possesses a *Weltanschauung* or *Weltansicht*—"a view of the world." While some Christians may consider the Christ of Christianity relevant only to matters of the heart, Orr argues His relevance for both heart and head. "If there is a religion in the world," says Orr, "which exalts the office of teaching, it is safe to say that it is the religion of Jesus Christ."[5]

In other words, one who says he believes with his whole heart that Jesus is the Son of God "is thereby committed to much else besides."[6] What else? "He is committed," says Orr, "to a view of God, to a view of man, to a view of sin, to a view of redemption, to a view of the purpose of God in creation and history, to a view of human destiny, found only in Christianity."[7]

To name the name of Christ is to desire to grow in His grace—to be more like Christ, to exemplify his qualities, to walk as he walked (Ephesians 4); but to name the name of Christ is also to desire to grow in His knowledge and to allow this knowledge to influence our creative/redemptive life. This creative/redemptive life involves body, soul, and spirit; home, church, and state; love, power, and justice, etc. Such is certainly the desire of St. Paul in his prayer "that ye might be filled with the knowledge of his will in all wisdom and spiritual understanding;

FIGURE 1:1

	SECULAR HUMANISM	MARXISM/ LENINISM	BIBLICAL CHRISTIANITY
SOURCE	*HUMANIST MANIFESTO I & II*	*WRITINGS OF MARX & LENIN*	*BIBLE*
THEOLOGY	ATHEISM	ATHEISM	THEISM
PHILOSOPHY	NATURALISM	DIALECTICAL MATERIALISM	SUPERNATURALISM
ETHICS	ETHICAL RELATIVISM	PROLETARIAT MORALITY	ETHICAL ABSOLUTES
BIOLOGY	DARWINIAN EVOLUTION	DARWINIAN/ PUNCTUATED EVOLUTION	SPECIAL CREATIONISM
PSYCHOLOGY	MONISTIC SELF-ACTUALIZATION	MONISTIC PAVLOVIAN BEHAVIORISM	DUALISM
SOCIOLOGY	NON-TRADITIONAL WORLD STATE ETHICAL SOCIETY	ABOLITION OF HOME, CHURCH AND STATE	HOME CHURCH STATE
LAW	POSITIVE LAW	POSITIVE LAW	BIBLICAL/NATURAL LAW
POLITICS	WORLD GOVERNMENT (GLOBALISM)	NEW WORLD ORDER	JUSTICE FREEDOM ORDER
ECONOMICS	SOCIALISM	SOCIALISM/ COMMUNISM	STEWARDSHIP OF PROPERTY
HISTORY	HISTORICAL EVOLUTION	HISTORICAL MATERIALISM	HISTORICAL RESURRECTION

Notes and Asides

that ye might walk worthy of the Lord unto all pleasing, being fruitful in every good work, and increasing in the knowledge of God; strengthened with all might, according to his glorious power, unto all patience and long-suffering with joyfulness; giving thanks unto the Father, which hath made us meet to be partakers of the inheritance of the saints in light" (Colossians 1:9-12).

Orr went on to summarize nine specific areas covered by "the Christian view of the world," stating that this view affirms:

(1) the existence of a personal, ethical, self-revealing God;

(2) the creation of the world by God, involving His holy and wise government of it for moral ends;

(3) the spiritual nature and dignity of man as created in the image of God;

(4) the fall of man into sin;

(5) the historical self-revelation of God to the patriarchs and in the line of Israel;

(6) the incarnation of Jesus Christ as the eternal Son of God, yes, as God manifest in flesh;

(7) the redemption of the world through the atoning death, burial, and resurrection of Jesus Christ;

(8) the founding of the Kingdom of God on earth, which includes the spiritual salvation of individuals and a new order of society ("the result of the action of the spiritual forces set in motion through Christ"); and

(9) history has a goal, including resurrection, judgment, and separation of the righteous and the wicked, the righteous to eternity with God and the wicked to eternal suffering excluded from his presence.[8]

Much of Orr's approach centers on five categories: theology, philosophy, ethics, biology, and history. Our approach expands the Christian worldview by incorporating psychology, sociology, economics, politics, and law. We take courage in doing so from Orr's own statement:

Notes and Asides

> I recognize therefore to the full the need of growth and progress in history. Bit by bit, as the years go on, we see more clearly the essential lineaments of the truth as it is in Jesus; we learn to disengage the genuine truths of Christ's gospel from human additions and corruptions; we apprehend their bearings and relations with one another, and with new truths, more distinctly; we see them in new points of view, develop and apply them in new ways.[9]

"The task of Christian leadership is to confront modern man with the Christian world-life view . . ."
—Carl F. H. Henry

Notre Dame professor Alvin Plantinga also defends the existence of a Christian worldview. He insists that there is a Christian philosophy as well as a Christian biology, psychology, sociology, and economics. He declares, "All these areas need to be thought anew from an explicitly Christian and theistic perspective. They're typically not done that way at all, of course, and the results are usually antithetical or irrelevant to Christianity."[10] Plantinga echoes Orr's observation: "I conclude, therefore, that it is legitimate to speak of a Christian 'Weltanschauung,' and that we are not debarred from investigating its relations to theoretic knowledge."[11]

Joining Plantinga and Orr in their call for a Christian worldview is theologian Carl F. H. Henry. In his six-volume *God, Revelation and Authority*, he wrote,

> The task of Christian leadership is to confront modern man with the Christian world-life view as the revealed conceptuality for understanding reality and experience, and to recall reason once again from the vagabondage of irrationalism and the arrogance of autonomy to the service of true faith. That does not imply modern man's return to the medieval mind. It implies, rather, a reaching for the eternal mind, for the mind of Christ, for the truth of revelation, for the Logos as transcendent source of the orders and structures of being, for the Logos-incarnate in Jesus Christ, for the Logos as divine agent in creation, redemption and judgment, for the Logos who stands invisibly but identifiably as the true center of nature, history, ethics, philosophy and religion.[12]

Logos means "word" in Greek. **Logocentrism** is the expression that best summarizes a Christ-centered, common-sense worldview.

Clearly, Christian scholars recognize the need for every Christian to embrace a Christ-centered, common-sense worldview.

Marxists also understand their system of thought to be an all-encompassing worldview. Karl Marx used the language of worldview when he wrote, "I shall therefore publish the critique of law, ethics, politics, etc., in a series of distinct, independent pamphlets, and afterwards try in a special work to present them again as a connected whole

Notes and Asides

showing the interrelationship of the separate parts."[13] Marx would not have attempted this had he not understood his view to be far more than simply an economic or political perspective.

Likewise, Humanists recognize that their beliefs form a comprehensive worldview. While Paul Kurtz at one point in *The Humanist Alternative* insisted that Secular Humanists should not be expected "to offer a total worldview,"[14] he later admits,

> The humanist thus attempts to make some kind of generalized sense of reality. . . . Using physics, astronomy, and the natural sciences, we can develop some cosmologies that explain the expanding universe. Using biology and genetics we can try to interpret the evolution of life. We can use psychology to understand human behavior, and we can draw upon anthropology, sociology, and the other social sciences to develop appropriate theories about sociocultural phenomena.[15]

This is unquestionably the language of worldview.

Why These Three Worldviews?

Marxist/Leninists, Secular Humanists, and Biblical Christians understand that their fundamental presuppositions create an all-encompassing view of reality. But other philosophies and religions also form worldviews; why concentrate on Christianity, Marxism and Humanism? Let's justify our choices one at a time.

The Christian Worldview

First, this text will focus on Christianity because it is the only worldview that provides a consistent explanation of all the facts of reality with regard to theology, philosophy, ethics, economics, or anything else. As Carl Henry says, "The Christian belief system, which the Christian knows to be grounded in divine revelation, is relevant to all of life."[16]

This relevance results from the fact that Christianity is, we believe, the one worldview based on truth. "Christianity is true," says George F. Gilder, author of *Wealth and Poverty*, "and its truth will be discovered anywhere you look very far."[17] Gilder (who is not only an outstanding economic philosopher but also a sociologist) found Christ while seeking sociological truth. Says Gilder, "My discovery that the essential themes of Christian teaching about marriage and family were true led me to the church, rather than the other way around."[18]

"Truth will ultimately prevail where there is pains taken to bring it to light."
—George Washington

Notes and Asides

Philosopher C. E. M. Joad found Christ and Christianity because he was seeking ethical truth. "I now believe," he wrote, "that the balance of reasoned considerations tells heavily in favour of the religious even of the Christian view of the world."[19] Joad's comments regarding Christianity and truth are also worth pondering:

> The central core of the Christian faith is either absolute truth or it is nonsense. Being absolute, the truths which it proclaims also claim to be eternal. If they were not absolute, if they were not eternal, they would not be worth believing. Scientific knowledge, on the other hand, is relative, relative to what at any given moment happens to have been found out about the natural world. A religion which is in constant process of revision to square with science's ever-changing picture of the world might well be easier to believe, but it is hard to believe it would be worth believing.[20]

"If Christianity is untrue, then no honest man will want to believe it, however helpful it might be: if it is true, every honest man will want to believe it, even if it gives him no help at all."
—C. S. Lewis

The truth of the Christian worldview is reinforced by the fact that it is a common-sense perspective that avoids the pitfalls of extremist worldviews. Writes Charles F. Baker,

> The Bible avoids all of the extremes and lopsided views of life and the world. Idealistic philosophy denies the existence of matter, holding that only mind is a reality. Materialism holds just the opposite extreme view. The Bible teaches the objective reality of both mind and matter, but points out the ephemeral character of the physical and the abiding character of the spiritual (2 Corinthians 4:18). The pantheist denies the transcendence of God and the deist denies His immanence. The Bible teaches both: God is all in all and God over all (1 Corinthians 15:28; Romans 9:5). Secularism places all of the emphasis upon the present life; fanaticism ignores the present and concerns itself only with the life to come. Buddhism would suppress all human desire; Hedonism would do nothing but fulfill human desire. Manicheanism held that the human body is evil; Hinduism teaches caste; Confucianism ignores God and the future. The Bible, on the other hand, brings all of these extremes into sharp focus and presents a well-rounded, common-sense world view.[21]

Further, the spiritual values contained in Biblical Christianity (honesty, integrity, purity, love for God, respect for oneself and others, etc.) are the values that make for strong lives, strong families, strong

Notes and Asides

churches, and strong societies. We agree with economist Warren Brookes' observation that, even though Christmas and Hanukkah come only once a year,

> the spiritual values they celebrate are universal and fundamental, and without them, even the most conceptually efficient economic system will fail. Democracy itself could disappear into tyranny. After all, economic activity is about the adding of value. But in its essence, value is spiritual, the expression of qualities of thought: self-discipline, order, self-respect, honesty, integrity, purity, loyalty, principle, genuine pride, love and respect for others. The list is infinite. Societies with strong spiritual values tend to generate economic value and expand. Societies with too materialistic values ultimately fall into disrepair and decay. Those that have tried to abandon religious or theological support for moral values, which are the key to self-government, have generally declined into despotic deprivation.[22]

"I believe Christianity is the only logical, consistent faith in the world."
—Mortimer Adler

Christianity is the embodiment of Christ's claim that he is "the way, the truth, and the life" (John 14:6). When we say "this is the Christian way," we mean "this is the way Christ would have us act in such a situation." It is no small matter to think and act as Christ instructs. The Christian agrees with Humanist Bertrand Russell's admission that "What the world needs is Christian love or compassion."[23]

America is often described as a Christian nation. Over one hundred and fifty years ago, Alexis de Tocqueville wrote, "There is no country in the whole world, in which the Christian religion retains a greater influence over the souls of men than in America; and there can be no greater proof of its utility, and of its conformity to human nature, than that its influence is most powerfully felt over the most enlightened and free nation of the earth."[24] Unfortunately, however, America is turning its back on its heritage. It is eradicating large chunks of Christianity from the public square.

"What the world needs is Christian love or compassion."
—Bertrand Russell

"America is great because she is good, and if she ever ceases to be good, she will no longer be great." -A.T.

We contend that America should be moving in the opposite direction—embracing the Christian worldview rather than pushing it away. Francis Schaeffer blames America's drift toward secularism and injustice on the Christian community's failure to apply its worldview to every facet of society: "The basic problem of the Christians in this

Notes and Asides

country in the last eighty years or so, in regard to society and in regard to government, is that they have seen things in bits and pieces instead of totals."[25] He goes on to say that Christians have very gradually

> become disturbed over permissiveness, pornography, the public schools, the breakdown of the family, and finally abortion. But they have not seen this as a totality—each thing being a part, a symptom of a much larger problem. They have failed to see that all of this has come about due to a shift in the world view—that is, through a fundamental change in the overall way people think and view the world and life as a whole. This shift has been *away* from a world view that was at least vaguely Christian in people's memory (even if they were not individually Christian) *toward* something completely different—toward a world view based upon the idea that the final reality is impersonal matter or energy shaped into its present form by impersonal chance.[26]

This study is a wake-up call for America. A country seeking to promote human rights and liberty must adhere to the only worldview that can account for their existence.

Even such unlikely commentators as James Reston and Walter Lippman understood the inconsistency of the American nation turning her back on Christianity. Lippman wrote,

> The liberties we talk about defending today were established by men who took their conceptions of man from the great central religious tradition of Western civilization [Christianity], and the liberties we inherit can almost certainly not survive the abandonment of that tradition. The decay of decency in the modern age, the rebellion against law and good faith, the treatment of human beings as things, as mere instruments of power and ambition, is without a doubt the consequence of the decay of the belief in man as someone more than an animal animated by highly conditioned reflexes and chemical reactions. For unless man is something more than that, he has no rights that anyone is bound to respect, and there are no limitations upon his conduct which he is bound to obey. This is the forgotten foundation of democracy.[27]

Reston likewise pointed out the vital relationship between religious tradition and the public square:

> The political life and spirit of this country were based on religious convictions. America's view of the individual was

Notes and Asides

> grounded on the principle, clearly expressed by the Founding Fathers, that man was a symbol of his Creator, and therefore possessed certain unalienable rights which no temporal authority had the right to violate. That this conviction helped shape our laws and sustained American men and women in their struggle to discipline themselves and conquer a continent even the most atheistic historian would defend. And this raises a question which cannot be avoided: If religion was so important in the building of the Republic, how could it be irrelevant to the maintenance of the Republic? And if it is irrelevant for the unbelievers, what will they put in its place?[28]

What unbelievers in the West most often put in its place is either Secular Humanism or Marxism/Leninism. In and of itself, this makes these worldviews worthy of study. As we shall see, many other reasons exist as well.

The Marxist/Leninist Worldview

Marxism/Leninism is a well-developed atheistic worldview. In some ways it is more consistent than Secular Humanism. Marxist/Leninists have developed a perspective regarding each of the ten disciplines—usually in great detail. Often, Marxism produces a "champion" of its perspective in the various fields (for example, I. P. Pavlov in psychology or T. D. Lysenko in biology). All these things make Marxism worthy of study—but the main reason why it is crucial for Christians to understand Marxism is that Marxism is one of Christianity's most vocal detractors and persecutors.

This fact becomes all the more sinister when one realizes that some Christian groups have attempted to combine their Christianity with Marxism. Evangelical voices, sometimes referred to as the "Christian Left," have been known to support the Marxist position.[29] The World Council of Churches, "an instrument of Soviet policy since 1966,"[30] saw no inconsistency in holding its meetings behind the Iron Curtain before it disintegrated (although one WCC leader did apologize for not criticizing the Communist empire more). Say the editors of *National Review*, "In Eastern Europe, the Christian church has been a powerful force acting to speed the disintegration of communism. Substantial parts of various American churches, however, have been active on the side of communist insurrection. The Maryknoll priests, the liberation theologians, Episcopal and Methodist groups and Jesuits have placed themselves in direct alliance with totalitarianism. . . . With an enormous Christian rebirth taking place in Eastern Europe, it is ironic that so much

> "Substantial parts of various American churches . . . have been active on the side of communist insurrection."
>
> —*National Review*

Notes and Asides

of the American church is decadent."[31]

The liberal American churches' position regarding Marxism does not, of course, take into account what Alexander Solzhenitsyn describes as the profound incompatibility of their faith with the Marxist worldview:

> The Soviet Union [under Marxist rule] is a land where churches have been leveled, where triumphant atheism has rampaged uncontrolled for two-thirds of a century, where the clergy is utterly humiliated and deprived of all independence, where what remains of the Russian Orthodox Church as an institution is tolerated only for the sake of propaganda directed at the West, where even today, people are sent to labor camps for their faith, and where, within the camps themselves, those who gather to pray at Easter are clapped into punishment cells.[32]

Mikhail Gorbachev's apology for the way the Bolsheviks treated believers "in the 1930s and subsequent years"[33] certainly seems to substantiate Solzhenitsyn's claims and demonstrate that liberal (and some evangelical) voices have been deceiving the West. Obviously, there is a need for a text that delineates the insurmountable differences between Marxism and Christianity. This study, by addressing both worldviews, highlights their incompatibility.

Some might raise the objection that the Marxist/Leninist worldview has already been proved to be a failure and completely incompatible with reality, as witnessed by the downfall of communist countries all over the world. Why, in light of these events, need one study the Marxist/Leninist perspective? Isn't Marxist ideology dead?

To begin with, *Time* magazine's Man of the Decade for the 1980s, Mikhail Gorbachev, remains a staunch Marxist/Leninist: "The works of Lenin, and his ideals of socialism," says Gorbachev, "remain for us an inexhaustible source of dialectical creative thought, theoretical wealth and political sagacity."[34] "I am now just as I've always been, a convinced communist."[35] "Those in the West who expect us to give up socialism will be disappointed. . . . I . . . hold a firm trust in socialist democracy and socialist humanism [atheism]."[36]

"I am now just as I've always been, a convinced communist."
—Mikhail Gorbachev

And even if one were to grant that Marxism/Leninism is being abandoned by the Eastern European countries, some of the republics within the Soviet Union, and other early advocates (a phenomenon that admits of other explanations),[37] Marxism retains its obdurate grip on the People's Republic of China,[38] and new support for it has arisen in too many other places to declare it dead. In some African and Latin American countries (under the guise of Liberation Theology)[39] and, incredibly, on many American university campuses, Marxism/Lenin-

Used by permission of the *Colorado Springs Gazette Telegraph*

ism is chic. "Marxism may be dying as a philosophy in Eastern Europe, and even in the Soviet Union," say Dobson and Bauer, "but it is alive and well in many faculty centers in our universities."[40] Malachi Martin speaks of the "rising tide of Marxist interpretation of history, law, religion and scientific inquiry." He says, "the complexion of education in everything from genetics to sociology and psychology became decidedly, and often exclusively, materialistic."[41]

In an article titled "Marxism in U.S. Classrooms,"[42] *U. S. News and World Report* reported that there are ten thousand Marxist professors on America's campuses. Georgie Anne Geyer says that "the percentage of Marxist faculty numbers can range from an estimated 90 percent in some midwestern universities."[43] She quotes Jean Francois Revel, author of *How Democracies Perish*, that he "can't find any French Marxists" and instead has to "import American intellectuals;" Arnold Beichman that "Marxist academics are today's power elite in the universities;" and Marxist professor Bertell Ollman that "A Marxist cultural revolution is taking place today in American universities."

"The strides made by Marxism at American universities in the last

Notes and Asides

"The society of unbelievers makes Faith harder even when they are people whose opinions, on any other subject, are known to be worthless."

—C. S. Lewis

two decades are breathtaking," says New York University's Herbert London.

> Every discipline has been affected by its preachment, and almost every faculty now counts among its members a resident Marxist scholar. There are more than 400 courses offered today on American campuses in Marxist philosophy; in the 1960s only a handful were being taught. In addition, two self-declared Marxist historians, Eugene Genovese and William A. Williams, were elected president of the Organization of American Historians in successive elections, and Louis Kampf, a radical with Marxist predilections, was elected president of the Modern Language Association.[44]

Dr. Arnold Beichman and Professor John P. Diggens agree with London's assessment: "The field of American history has come to be dominated by Marxists and feminists."[45] Duke University Slavic Languages professor Magnus Krynski described increasing Marxist presence on his campus—a presence actively encouraged by the university administration, which, he says, is "faddishly" luring Marxist literary critics to Duke with large salaries. In fact, in March 1987 Duke University hosted the Southeast Marxist Scholars Conference. Dr. Malcolm Gillis, vice provost of Duke University, thanked some one hundred Marxist professors, graduate students, and activists for gathering at Duke and said, "When I left this campus twenty years ago, there were very few Marxists here. When I returned in 1984, I saw Marxists in many parts of the social science faculty."[46] The conference was sponsored by the Marxist Educational Press (based at the University of Minnesota) and Duke's own Program on Perspectives in Marxism and Society.

John LeBoutillier, president of Accuracy in Academia and author of *Harvard Hates America*, said he entered Harvard as a moderate but left a confirmed conservative. One of his first professors at Harvard, a Marxist sympathizer, advocated a 100 percent inheritance tax as a way of eliminating inequality of wealth. LeBoutillier soon learned that the professor maintained an opulent lifestyle supported by his wife, the heiress to the Singer sewing machine company fortune. LeBoutillier said that "this was typical of the hypocrisy routinely practiced by leftists at Harvard."[47]

The Marxist influence (or, as it is now referred to, the "Left Eclecticism") has reached its most alarming heights in American universities' humanities departments. "With a few notable exceptions," says former Yale professor Roger Kimball, "our most prestigious liberal arts colleges and universities have installed the entire radical

Notes and Asides

menu at the center of their humanities curriculum at both the undergraduate and the graduate level."[48] The influential humanities quarterly *October*, for example, was named in celebration of the Bolshevik revolution of October 1917 and the 1928 film *October*. Kimball provides more evidence that Duke University is in the forefront of academia's move toward Marxism, noting that it has "recently conducted a tireless—and successful—campaign to arm its humanities department with the likes of the Marxist literary critic Frederic Jameson, Barbara Herrnstein Smith, Frank Lentricchia, Stanley Fish (and his pedagogically like-minded wife, Jane Tompkins), and other less well known souls of kindred intellectual orientation."[49]

The Marxist worldview is alive and well in the American classroom. Since this is true, one would be wise to heed the words of Dr. Fred Schwarz:

> The colleges and universities are the nurseries of communism. The ranks of the communists are replenished every year by the equivalent of the "college draft" that maintains the supply of professional football, baseball and basketball players. In every country, the leader of the communist forces is almost always one who was recruited as a student.[50]

Alert Christian students who understand Marxism should not be caught up in these nurseries.

The Secular Humanist Worldview

Marxism, however, is not the only worldview that threatens to take the classroom hostage. Secular Humanism also vies for total control of education—which brings us to why we have included the Secular Humanist worldview in this study.

Secular Humanism is the dominant worldview in our secular colleges and universities. It has also made gains in some Christian colleges and universities. Christians considering a college education must be well versed in the Humanistic worldview or risk losing their own Christian perspective by default. Why? Because Humanist professors are unwilling to present the Christian perspective accurately, while many Christian educators feel duty bound to give fair representation to the Humanist viewpoint. This is especially true with regard to the creation/evolution controversy. Most evolutionists adamantly oppose allowing any hints of creationism into the classroom.[51] Humanists are particularly guilty of this one-sided approach. For example, on "November 9, 1989, the California State Board of Education . . . adopted

Notes and Asides

new guidelines for teaching science in the public schools. . . . [T]he document was substantially prepared at the request of School Superintendent Bill Honig by scientists affiliated with the American Humanist Association."[52] Creationism was ruled out of the physical sciences classroom by decree.[53]

Humanists recognize the classroom as a powerful context for indoctrination. They understand that many worldviews exist and believe Humanists must use the classroom to flush out "unenlightened" worldviews and encourage individuals to embrace their worldview. Thus, R. M. Lauer and M. Hussey state,

> We aim to have students make explicit their own and others' implicit ideas about the way the world is or should be. Like artisans creating a mold out of the earth's supplies, we learn that our minds put the infinite mass of what is going on into an order; we relate parts to each other and create a whole structure. Thereafter, we use this structure like a template that forever determines what we perceive and how we evaluate, decide, and act upon it. By focusing educational content upon our ordering, relating, and structuring processes, we can expose the templates, making them available for restructuring as we evolve into better artisans.[54]

You can be sure that the templates these professors want to evolve are not based on the Christian perspective, especially when you consider that Humanists perceive Christianity as a backward superstition. In light of what he calls the "conservative Christian resurgence" in our

Humanist Manifesto I Signatories

J. A. C. F. Auer	Albert C. Dieffenbach	R. Lester Mondale	V. T. Thayer
E. Burdette Backus	John H. Dietrich	Charles Francis Potter	Eldred C. Vanderlaan
Harry Elmer Barnes	Bernard Fantus	John H. Randall, Jr.	Joseph Walker
L. M. Birkhead	William Floyd	Curtis W. Reese	Jacob J. Weinstein
Raymond B. Bragg	F. H. Hankins	Oliver L. Reiser	Frank S. C. Wicks
Edwin Arthur Burtt	A. Eustace Haydon	Roy Wood Sellars	David Rhys Williams
Ernest Caldecott	Llewellyn Jones	Clinton Lee Scott	Edwin H. Wilson
A. J. Carlson	Robert Morss Lovett	Maynard Shipley	
John Dewey	Harold P. Marley	W. Frank Swift	

Notes and Asides

times, Edmund D. Cohen asks, "How is it that the relatively enlightened condition of American society in our time does not seem to work to prevent such a thing?"[55]

It is not an exaggeration to say that Humanism is constantly working to aid America to "prevent such a thing," especially in the classroom. Christianity has been deliberately, some would say brilliantly, erased from America's educational system. The direction of America's education can be seen as a descent from Jonathan Edwards (1750) and the Christian influence, through Horace Mann (1842) and the Unitarian influence, to John Dewey (1933) and the Humanist influence.

But we contend that Jonathan Edwards has more to say than John Dewey, and that Christianity should get back into the public square and influence educational policy. The Christian worldview is a fitting competitor to Dewey's religious view as summarized in *A Common Faith.* But since most Christian teenagers accept their older, "wiser" professors' teachings uncritically and may therefore find themselves subject to Humanistic viewpoints, this study becomes necessary to equalize the battle for the mind. Hosea's statement, "My people are destroyed for lack of knowledge" (4:6), applies in spades to Christian college-bound students. Many never recover from their educational befuddlement, lapsing instead into atheism, materialism, new morality, evolutionism, globalism, etc. Others suffer for years from their near loss of faith. Those prepared, however, survive and flourish.

> Christianity is a "religion for losers."
> —Ted Turner

America's colleges and universities are not the only areas of Secular Humanist influence, however. The mass media continually publish and broadcast the Humanist worldview. The 1990 Humanist of the Year was Ted Turner, chief executive officer of Turner Broadcasting System, which now owns TBS SuperStation, CNN, CNN Headline News, and Turner Network Television (TNT). In 1985 Turner founded the Better World Society;[56] presently he is willing to present $500,000 to anyone able to invent a new worldview suitable for the new, peaceful earth. According to Turner, Christianity is a "religion for losers"[57] and Christ should not have bothered dying on the cross. "I don't want anybody to die for me," said Turner. "I've had a few drinks and a few girlfriends, and if that's gonna put me in hell, then so be it."[58] Turner also maintains that the Ten Commandments are "out of date." He wants to replace them with his Ten Voluntary Initiatives, which include the statements: "I promise to have love and respect for the planet earth and living things thereon, especially my fellow species—humankind. I promise to treat all persons everywhere with dignity, respect, and friendliness. I promise to have no more than two children, or no more than my nation suggests. I reject the use of force, in particular military force, and back United Nations arbitration of international disputes. I

Notes and Asides

support the United Nations and its efforts to collectively improve the conditions of the planet."[59]

Cal Thomas regards Turner's attempt to replace the Ten Commandments and start a new calendar by replacing B.C. and A.D. with B.P. and A.P. (Before Peace and After Peace) as "attempting to take on God." But then that is what Secular Humanism is all about. *The Humanist* states, "He [Turner] then unveiled his ten 'voluntary initiatives'—a humanistic alternative to the 'obsolete' biblical Ten Commandments. . . . Humanists everywhere are watching the ratings."[60] Which makes obvious the importance of watching the Humanists.

Still another reason for examining the Humanist worldview is that many Humanists besides Turner have gained positions of considerable influence in our society. B. F. Skinner, Abraham Maslow, Carl Rogers, and Erich Fromm, all former Humanists of the Year, have powerfully affected psychology. Carl Sagan, another Humanist of the Year, preached his Humanism on a widely heralded television series. Norman Lear has produced and otherwise influenced a number of the shows on television today. Ethical decisions are made for our young people by Humanist of the Year Faye Wattleton, director of Planned Parenthood. Humanist Isaac Asimov writes tirelessly for his cause. Clearly, Humanists are willing to support their worldview—often more faithfully than Christians.

> "As ten millions of circles can never make a square, so the united voice of myriads cannot lend the smallest foundation to falsehood."
> —Oliver Goldsmith

Their commitment has paid off. As Dobson observes, "The humanistic system of values has now become the predominant way of thinking in most of the power centers of society."[61] Dobson specifically mentions the universities, news media, entertainment industry, judiciary, federal bureaucracy, business, medicine, law, psychology, sociology, arts, public schools, and Congress. None of this is exaggerated—Humanists have made strides in each of these realms.

But as admirable as the Humanists' initiative is, and as far-reaching as their impact has been, their efforts will only serve a destructive purpose if their fundamental belief system is wrong. Good intentions are not enough: these intentions must be based upon truth. The Christian, believing that Humanists are leading society in the wrong direction, has a duty to provide leadership according to the worldview he believes is based on truth. We can learn from the Humanists' dedication and aspirations; but we must show them the error of their ways, "speaking the truth in love" (Ephesians 4:15). This text is designed to provide the basis for such leadership by exposing the fallacies and flaws of Marxism and Humanism and elaborating on the truthfulness and consistency of the Christian view.

Notes and Asides

Conclusion

Therefore, it is appropriate to examine all three worldviews—Biblical Christianity, Marxism/Leninism, and Secular Humanism—in this text. Throughout this study, it should become clear that Marxism and Humanism are similar in a number of ways. The body of this work will demonstrate that this relationship is not casual or peripheral. The two are family. Secular Humanism is the mother (Humanists trace their heritage to the Greeks four hundred years before Christ), and Marxism is the daughter. Secular Humanism is the root, Marxism the branch. At the heart of both worldviews are atheism, materialism, spontaneous generation, and evolution. From a comprehensive point of view, their differences are minor. Both Karl Marx and Humanist Paul Kurtz recognize the truth of these assertions. Marx said it like this: "Communism, as fully developed naturalism, equals humanism."[62] And Kurtz says Marx "is a humanist because he rejects theistic religion and defends atheism."[63]

The significance of this cannot be overstated. While we watch Marxism crumble in Eastern Europe—and, we hope, all over the world—America's public schools are immersed in these same values, under a different name and with a slight change in emphasis. Only when the emphasis has completely shifted to a Christian perspective can young people flourish in light of the true worldview. And this dramatic shift in emphasis can be brought about best through the leadership of a few well-grounded, confident Christian students.

This, then, is our most fundamental reason for preparing *Understanding the Times*: too many Christian young people are ill prepared to lead. The vast majority have no concept of the components of their worldview and stand intellectually naked before left-wing professors. Carl F. H. Henry says that evangelical students know more about God than their secular counterparts, but "with some few gratifying exceptions, neither home nor church has shaped a comprehensive and consistent faith that stands noon-bright amid the dim shadows of spiritual rebellion and moral profligacy."[64]

Christ's teachings impart just such a noon-bright faith to all Christians who master their worldview, who "understand the times." This book's foundational verse, 1 Chronicles 12:32, announces that just two hundred individuals who "understood the times" provided the leadership for an entire nation. We believe that a comprehensive knowledge of the Christian worldview and its rivals will provide today's young people with the understanding necessary to become Christian leaders.

[1]James C. Dobson and Gary L. Bauer, *Children at Risk: The Battle For the Hearts and Minds of Our Kids* (Dallas, TX: Word, 1990), p. 19.
[2]Ibid., pp. 19-20.
[3]Ibid., p. 20.
[4]For example, today's discussion about abortion is largely political, whereas thirty years ago it was primarily theological.
[5]James Orr, *The Christian View of God and the World* (Edinburgh: Andrew Elliot, 1897), p. 20.
[6]Ibid., p. 4.
[7]Ibid.
[8]Ibid., pp. 32-34.
[9]Ibid., p. 25. Our approach is just one of the "bits" Orr was talking about. This study certainly does not replace Biblical theology, systematic theology, philosophical theology, historical theology, covenant theology, dispensational theology, etc. In fact, worldview study could be termed comparative theology—a theology concerned with the day-by-day implications of the gospel of Christ in the total makeup of the Christian's creative/redemptive life.
[10]Religious News Service, April 3, 1989. Printed in *The Christian News*, April 10, 1989, p. 11.
[11]Orr, *The Christian View of God and the World*, p. 31.
[12]Carl F. H. Henry, *God, Revelation and Authority*, six volumes (Waco, TX: Word, 1976), vol. 1, p. 43.
[13]Karl Marx and Frederick Engels, *Collected Works*, forty volumes (New York: International Publishers, 1976), vol. 3, p. 231.
[14]Paul Kurtz, ed., *The Humanist Alternative* (Buffalo: Prometheus, 1973), pp. 182-3.
[15]Paul Kurtz, *Eupraxophy: Living Without Religion* (Buffalo: Prometheus, 1989), pp. 31-2.
[16]Carl F. H. Henry, *Toward a Recovery of Christian Belief* (Westchester, IL: Crossway Books, 1990), p. 113.
[17]L. Neff, "Christianity Today Talks to George Gilder,"*Christianity Today*, March 6, 1987, p. 35.
[18]Ibid.
[19]C. E. M. Joad, *The Recovery of Belief* (London: Faber and Faber, 1955), p. 22.
[20]Ibid., p. 240.
[21]Charles F. Baker, *A Dispensational Theology* (Grand Rapids, MI: Grace Bible College Publications, 1971), pp. 53-4.
[22]Warren Brookes, "The Key to Well-Being,"*The Washington Times*, December 25, 1989, p. D1.
[23]Bertrand Russell, *Human Society in Ethics and Politics* (New York: Mentor, 1962), p. viii.
[24]Alexis de Tocqueville, *Democracy in America*, two volumes (New Rochelle, NY: Arlington House, n.d.), vol. 1, p. 294. Elsewhere he declared, "The Americans combine the notions of Christianity and of liberty so intimately in their minds, that it is impossible to make them conceive the one without the other" (p. 297).
[25]Francis A. Schaeffer, *A Christian Manifesto* (Westchester, IL: Crossway, 1981), p. 17.
[26]Ibid.
[27]James Reston, "'Faith of Our Fathers, Living Still'?"*The New York Times*, April 2, 1969, p. 46.
[28]Ibid.
[29]See Ronald H. Nash, ed., *Liberation Theology* (Milford, MI: Mott Media, 1984), for material on *Sojourners* magazine and its editor, Jim Wallis. See also Nash's *Social Justice and the Christian Church* (Milford, MI: Mott Media, 1983), p. 158: "One evangelical who can hardly restrain his enthusiasm for Marxism is Jim Wallis, editor of the journal, *Sojourners*. Wallis writes longingly of the day when 'more Christians will come to view the world through Marxist eyes.'" Franky Schaeffer in *Is Capitalism Christian?* (Westchester, IL: Crossway, 1985), p. xxii, notes: "The Roman Catholic Church is not alone in its problems. Within the evangelical community, too, leaders have emerged whose gullibility is made dangerous by their popularity." The Evangelical "Christian Left" finds its home in Evangelicals for Social Action.
[30]Malachi Martin, *The Keys of This Blood* (New York: Simon and Schuster, 1990), p. 304. Martin also notes that the Pontifical Commission for Justice and Peace "has been taken over by converts to Marxism" (p. 305).
[31]"No One Here But Us Church Mice,"*National Review*, December 31, 1989, p. 15.
[32]Reed Irvine, "Soviet Religious Propaganda,"*The Washington Times*, April 3, 1984, p. 9A.
[33]*Isvestia*, May 1, 1988, cited in Paul Kurtz, "Militant Atheism Versus Freedom of Conscience," *Free Inquiry*, Fall 1989, p. 30.

[34]Mikhail Gorbachev, *Perestroika: New Thinking for Our Country and the World* (New York: Harper and Row, 1987), p. 11.
[35]"Gorbachev Interview: 'I am an Optimist,'" *Time*, June 4, 1990, p. 31.
[36]"In His Words," *U.S. News and World Report*, November 9, 1987, p. 74.
[37]For a different but defensible opinion—that the apparent breakdown of communism in the Soviet Union and most eastern European countries is a pretense orchestrated by the KGB to lull the West into complacency before a major ideological and possibly even military offensive—see Anatoliy Golitsyn, *New Lies for Old: The Communist Strategy of Deception and Disinformation* (New York: Dodd, Mead and Co., 1984; rpt. Atlanta, GA: Clarion House, 1990).
[38]The entire government in the People's Republic of China is based on "the four Cardinal principles:" (1) the leadership of the Communist Party, (2) Marxism/Leninism and Mao Zedong's theories, (3) people's democratic dictatorship, and (4) adherence to the socialist road. For a more thorough discussion of these principles see Robert Morris, *Detente or Deception: Should the US Disarm in a Dangerous World?* (New Rochelle, NY: America's Future, 1990). This pamphlet can be obtained from America's Future, 514 Main Street, New Rochelle, NY 10801.
[39]See the following works for important information regarding Liberation Theology: Malachi Martin, *The Jesuits: The Society of Jesus and the Betrayal of the Roman Catholic Church* (New York: Simon and Schuster, 1987); Nash, ed., *Liberation Theology*; Raymond C. Hundley, *Radical Liberation Theology: An Evangelical Response* (Wilmore, KY: Bristol, 1987); David W. Balsiger, ed., *Liberation Theology: Will it Liberate or Enslave People?* (Costa Mesa, CA: Family Protection Scoreboard, 1989).
[40]Dobson and Bauer, *Children at Risk*, p. 182.
[41]Martin, *The Keys of This Blood*, p. 262.
[42]David B. Richardson, "Marxism in U. S. Classrooms," *U.S. News and World Report*, January 25, 1982, pp. 42-5.
[43]Georgie Anne Geyer, "Marxism Thrives on Campus," *The Denver Post*, August 29, 1989, p. B7.
[44]Herbert London, "Marxism Thriving on American Campuses," *The World and I*, January 1987, p. 189.
[45]*Accuracy in Academia Campus Report*, July/August 1987.
[46]*Accuracy in Academia Campus Report*, April 1987, p. 1.
[47]*Accuracy in Academia Campus Report*, July/August 1987. One should note the similarities between what LeBoutillier observed at Harvard and the opulent lifestyles of the recently deposed Communist leaders in Eastern Europe.
[48]Roger Kimball, *Tenured Radicals* (New York: Harper and Row, 1990), p. xiii. Christian young people should read Kimball's book, then Allan Bloom's *The Closing of the American Mind: How Higher Education has Failed Democracy and Impoverished the Souls of Today's Students* (New York: Simon and Schuster, 1987), and finally Ronald Nash's *The Closing of the American Heart* (Brentwood, TN: Wolgemuth & Hyatt, 1990) to grasp what Christian students face in America's colleges and universities.
[49]Kimball, *Tenured Radicals*, p. xiv.
[50]Newsletter of the Christian Anti-Communist Crusade, P. O. Box 890, Long Beach, California 90801; February 1, 1988.
[51]Cornell University's William Provine is a notable exception to this rule. Wendell R. Bird, in *The Origin of Species Revisited*, two volumes (New York: Philosophical Library, 1989), vol. 1, p. 8, quotes Provine: "Creationism should be taught along with evolutionism in grade school and high schools . . . in the science classroom. . . . Creationism is a viable, understandable and plausible theory." Bird quotes other evolutionists to the same effect (p. 9): "Solomon agrees that both explanations should be taught because 'nothing is so unscientific as . . . seeking to suppress or conceal dissent rather than grappling with it.' Alexander concurs that 'a comparison of the two alternatives can be an excellent exercise in logic and reason.' Anderson and Kilbourn agree that at least 'an argument for teaching special-creation can be made.'" Bird also quotes John Scopes himself, who said, "I believe in teaching every aspect of every problem or theory."
[52]*Acts and Facts*, vol. 19, no. 1 (January 1990). *Acts and Facts* is published by the Institute for Creation Research, P. O. Box 2667, El Cajon, CA 92021.
[53]This was a most unpopular decision. Even forty-two Jewish college and high school teachers, physicians, and other professionals—mostly in the Brooklyn, New York, area—protested California's decision. In a petition

sent to Mr. Honig they said, "We condemn Bill Honig for his bigoted narrow-minded injustice." And again, "Creationism is the only rational explanation of all the natural phenomena." See *Acts and Facts*, vol. 19, no. 1 (January 1990), for a more detailed discussion.

[54]R. M. Lauer and M. Hussey, "A New Way to Become Educated,"*The Humanist*, Jan./Feb. 1986, p. 5.

[55]Edmund D. Cohen, "The Psychology of the Bible-Believer,"*Free Inquiry,* Spring 1987, p. 22.

[56]The Better World Society's international board of directors includes Jimmy Carter, Georgiy Arbatov (Soviet Politboro member), and Zhou Boping (Chinese ambassador to America).

[57]Cal Thomas, "Turner's Takeover Tender,"*The Washington Times*, November 6, 1989, p. F2.

[58]Ibid.

[59]Julie Lanham, "The Greening of Ted Turner,"*The Humanist*, Nov./Dec. 1989, p. 6.

[60]Ibid., p. 30.

[61]Dobson and Bauer, *Children at Risk*, p. 22.

[62]Marx and Engels, *Collected Works*, vol. 3, p. 296.

[63]Paul Kurtz, *The Fullness of Life* (New York: Horizon Press, 1974), p. 36.

[64]Carl F. H. Henry, *Twilight of a Great Civilization* (Westchester, IL: Crossway, 1988), p. 94.

CHAPTER

2

RELIGIOUS WORLDVIEWS IN CONFLICT

Many people believe that when Christians confront other worldviews and attempt to speak to such "worldly" disciplines as politics, economics, biology, and law, they are overstepping their bounds. "Mind your own business," we are told. Jesus taught His followers, "you do not belong to the world, but I have chosen you out of the world" (John 15:19).

How, then, can the Christian justify his claim to a worldview that speaks to every facet of life? Shouldn't he stick to spiritual matters and allow the Humanists and Marxists to concentrate on the practical matters of running the world?

In short, isn't there a difference between the secular and the sacred?

Not according to Dietrich Bonhoeffer, who says we should not distinguish between the two:

Notes and Asides

> There are not two realities, but only one reality, and that is the reality of God, which has become manifest in Christ in the reality of the world. . . . There are not two spheres but only the one sphere of the realization of Christ, in which the reality of God and the reality of the world are united.[1]

From the Biblical Christian perspective, the ten disciplines addressed in this text reflect various aspects of God and His creative or redemptive order. God created mankind with theological, philosophical, ethical, biological, etc. dimensions. We live and move and have our being (our very essence and existence) within and about these categories. We are humanly definable and possess our human value within these categories. Why? Because that is the way God created us.

Such being the case, these categories are, from the Christian perspective, sacred and not secular. They are sacred because they are imprinted in the creative order. Both the early record of Genesis and the life of Jesus Christ reflect this truth.

For example, Genesis 1:1—"In the beginning God created the heavens and the earth"—is value laden with theological and philosophical ramifications. Genesis 2:9—"knowledge of good and evil"—contains ethical ramifications; Genesis 1:21—"after their kind"—biological; Genesis 2:7—"a living soul"—psychological; Genesis 1:28—"be fruitful, and multiply, and fill the earth"—sociological and ecological; Genesis 3:11—"I commanded thee"—legal; Genesis 9:6—"whoso sheddeth man's blood"—political and legal; Genesis 1:29—"it shall be for food"—economic; Genesis 3:15—"enmity between thee and the woman"—historical. All ten disciplines are addressed in just the first few chapters of the Bible because they manifest and accent certain aspects of the creative order.

Further, God manifests Himself in the form of Christ in such a way as to underline the significance of each discipline. In theology, for example, Jesus Christ is "the fullness of the Godhead" (Colossians 2:9); in philosophy, Christ is the Logos of God (John 1:1); in ethics, Christ is "the true light" (John 1:9; 3:19-20); in biology, Christ is "the life" (John 1:4; 11:25; Colossians 1:16); in psychology, Christ is "Savior" (Luke 1:46-47; Titus 2:13); in sociology, Christ is "Son" (Luke 1:30-31; Isaiah 9:6); in law, Christ is lawgiver (Genesis 49:10; Isaiah 9:7); in politics, Christ is "King of kings and Lord of lords" (Revelation 19:16; 1 Timothy 6:15; Isaiah 9:6; Luke 1:33); in economics, Christ is Owner of all things (Psalm 24:1; 50:10-12; 1 Corinthians 10:26); and in history, Christ is the "fullness of times" (Galatians 4:5). The integration of these various categories into society has come to be known as Western Civilization.

> "Christianity is a world and life view and not simply a series of unrelated doctrines. Christianity includes all of life. Every realm of knowledge, every aspect of life and every facet of the universe find their place and their answer within Christianity. It is a system of truth enveloping the entire world in its grasp."
> —Edwin H. Rian

The Bible and the life of Jesus Christ provide the Christian with the basis for a complete worldview. Indeed, the Christian gains a perspec-

Notes and Asides

tive so comprehensive that he is commanded to "take captive every thought to make it obedient to Christ" (2 Corinthians 10:5).

Once we have captured all thoughts and made them obedient to Christ, we are to use these thoughts, ideas, and truths to "demolish arguments and every pretension that sets itself up against the knowledge of God" (2 Corinthians 10:4-5). When nations and men forget God (see Psalm 2) they experience what mankind has experienced in the twentieth century. Nazism and Communism, two major movements bereft of the knowledge of God, cost the human race millions of lives. Whittaker Chambers says that Communism's problem is not a problem of economics, but of atheism: "Faith is the central problem of this age." Solzhenitsyn echoes him: "Men have forgotten God."

The Apostle Paul insists in Colossians 2 that those who have "received Christ Jesus the Lord" (Colossians 2:6) are to be rooted and built up in him, strengthened in the faith as they were taught (Colossians 2:7). While the Christian works to strengthen his faith or worldview, he must see to it that no one takes him "captive through hollow and deceptive philosophy, which depends on human tradition and the basic principles of this world rather than on Christ" (Colossians 2:8). From the Christian point of view Secular, Cosmic and Marxist Humanism fall within the confines of "the basic principles of this world." They are based on the wisdom of this world, and not upon Christ.

> "Faith is the central problem of this age."
> —W. Chambers

This wasn't mere doctrine for Paul. He practiced what he preached. In Acts 17, Paul confronted the vain and deceitful philosophies of the atheistic Epicureans and pantheistic Stoics—the professional Humanists of his day (the Epicureans "were materialistic monists" and the Stoics "were also materialistic monists but of a less thoroughgoing type."[2]). The Apostle countered their ideas with Christian ideas, he reasoned and preached, and he accented primarily three Christian truths—the resurrection of Jesus Christ (Acts 17:18), the creation of the universe by God (Acts 17:24), and the judgment to come (Acts 17:31).

Can we do less? We, too, must fearlessly proclaim the good news of the gospel (God created the universe and all things in it, mankind rebelliously smashed the image of God by sin, Jesus Christ died for our sin, was raised from the dead, and is alive forevermore (1 Corinthians 15:1-4]), and we must stand fast in the context of the same worldview as Paul—creation, resurrection, and judgment.

The Religion of Marxism/Leninism

Paul recognized that man cannot compartmentalize aspects of his life into boxes marked "sacred" and "secular." He understood not only that Christianity was both a worldview and a religion, but also that all worldviews are religious by definition. Indeed, he went so far as to tell

Notes and Asides

the Epicureans and Stoics that they still worshiped—but were worshiping an "Unknown God."

The same applies to Humanism and Marxism today. These worldviews, like all other worldviews, are at bottom religious. All are religious because all contain a theology—that is, all begin with a religious declaration. Christianity begins with "In the beginning God." Marxism/Leninism and Secular Humanism begin with "In the beginning no God." Cosmic Humanism begins with the declaration "Everything is God."

The Marxist view demonstrates itself to be religious in a number of other ways, as well. Marxism's philosophy of dialectical materialism grants matter God-like attributes, as Gustav A. Wetter acknowledges in *Dialectical Materialism*:

> [T]he atheism of dialectical materialism is concerned with very much more than a mere denial of God. . . . [I]n dialectical materialism . . . the higher is not, as such, denied; the world is interpreted as a process of continual ascent, which fundamentally extends into infinity. But it is supposed to be matter itself which continually attains to higher perfection under its own power, thanks to its indwelling dialectic. As Nikolai Berdyaev very rightly remarks, the dialectical materialist attribution of "dialectic" to matter confers on it, not mental attributes only, but even divine ones.[3]

Religion is "the thing a man does practically believe; the thing a man does practically lay to heart, and know for certain, concerning his vital relations to this mysterious Universe, and his duty and destiny there, . . . that is his religion."
—Thomas Carlyle

We will discuss this further in Marxist Philosophy. For now, it is enough to understand that Wetter perceives communism as religious in character.[4]

Even Secular Humanists such as Bertrand Russell recognize the religiosity of Marxism: "The greatest danger in our day comes from new religions, Communism and Nazism. To call these religions may perhaps be objectionable both to their friends and to their enemies, but in fact they have all the characteristics of religions. They advocate a way of life on the basis of irrational dogmas; they have a sacred history, a Messiah, and a priesthood. I do not see what more could be demanded to qualify a doctrine as a religion."[5]

The Religion of Secular Humanism

Secular Humanism is even more openly religious than Marxism. The first *Humanist Manifesto* described the agenda of "religious" Humanists. The 1980 preface to the *Humanist Manifestoes I & II*, written by Paul Kurtz, says, "Humanism is a philosophical, *religious*, and moral point of view."[6] John Dewey, a signatory of the 1933 *Manifesto*, wrote *A Common Faith*, in which he said, "Here are all the elements for a religious faith that shall not be confined to sect, class or race. . . . It remains to make it explicit and militant."[7]

While the *Humanist Manifesto II* (written primarily by Paul Kurtz and published in 1973) drops the expression "religious humanism," it nevertheless contains religious implications and even religious terminology, including the statement that "no deity will save us; we must save ourselves."[8]

Further, in its decision in *Torcaso* v. *Watkins* (June 19, 1961), the U.S. Supreme Court stated, "Among religions in this country which do not teach what would generally be considered a belief in the existence of God are Buddhism, Taoism, Ethical Culture, Secular Humanism and others." A few years later (1965) the Supreme Court allowed Daniel Seeger conscientious objector status because of his religious beliefs. He claimed to be a Secular Humanist.[9]

In a guest editorial for the *Journal of Church and State* entitled "Issues That Divide: The Triumph of Secular Humanism," Leo Pfeffer insists that Secular Humanism will triumph over its religious competitors—Protestantism, Catholicism, and Judaism. Says Pfeffer, "In [the college arena], it is not Protestantism, Catholicism, or Judaism which will emerge the victor, but secular humanism, a cultural force which in many respects is stronger in the United States than any of the major religious groups or any alliance among them."[10]

In *The Humanist* for January/February 1983, John J. Dunphy admitted that Secular Humanism's opposition is Christianity, not a particular political party. Says Dunphy,

> These [Humanist] teachers must embody the same selfless dedication as the most rabid fundamentalist preachers, for they will be ministers of another sort, utilizing a classroom instead of a pulpit to convey humanist values in whatever subject they teach, regardless of the educational level—preschool day care or large state university. The classroom must and will become an area of conflict between the old and the new—the rotting corpse of Christianity, together with its adjacent evils and misery and the new faith of Humanism, resplendent in its promise of a world in which the never-realized Christian idea of 'Love Thy Neighbor' will finally be achieved.

What Dunphy doesn't understand is that the so-called "new faith of Humanism" is older than Christianity by about four hundred to six hundred years. He is correct, however, in noting that Christianity and Humanism are religious antagonists.

Notes and Asides

See Also: *Commentary* August 1991, p.22f; Charles Francis Potter's *Humanism: A New Religion* (New York: Simon and Schuster, 1930); Lloyd and Mary Morain's *Humanism as the Next Step* (Boston: The Boston Press, 1954); and the *Harvard Gazette* July 3, 1993 article featuring Harvard's Humanist Chaplain.

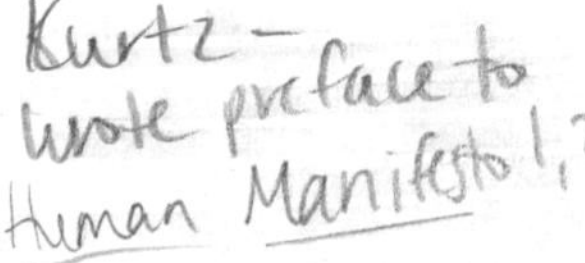
Kurtz—
wrote preface to
Human Manifesto 1,2

Auburn University's Student, Faculty and Staff Directory contains a section entitled "Auburn Pastors and Campus Ministers." Included in the listing is a Humanist Counselor, Delos McKown, who also happens to be the head of Auburn's philosophy department. This is not an isolated example—the University of Arizona also lists Humanism under religious ministries.

In fact, the American Humanist Association "certifies humanist counselors who enjoy the legal status of ordained priests, pastors, and rabbis."[11] In its preamble, the Association states that one of its functions is to extend its principles and operate educationally. Toward this end it publishes books, magazines, and pamphlets; engages lecturers; selects, trains, and "accredits humanistic counselors as its ordained ministry of the movement."[12]

Kurtz—who has written a book that denies that Humanism is a religion throughout its first half and, in the last half, encourages the establishment of humanist churches, calling them Eupraxophy Centers[13]—admits that the organized Humanist movement in America is put in a quandary over whether Humanism is a religion. Why? Simply because the "Fellowship of Religious Humanists (300 members), the American Ethical Union (3,000 members), and the Society for Humanistic Judaism (4,000 members) consider themselves to be religious. Even the American Humanist Association," says Kurtz, "has a [501(c)3] religious tax exemption."[14] Isaac Asimov, a confirmed atheist, [15] is President of the AHA.

In a chapter entitled, "The Myth of Neutrality," Christian author Richard A. Baer says,

> The claim that secular humanism is not a religion is wrong. . . . [I]t is essential to recall that John Dewey and a whole generation of nontheistic humanists maintained that their nontheistic beliefs were "religious." Only in our day, when this claim has been seen to carry with it certain obligations as well as privileges, has it been dropped and discounted by most nontheistic humanists.[16]

Elsewhere Baer states,

> I consider the distinction between the religious and the secular—as it functions in most school debates today—to be false. Or, more precisely, the secular in education typically becomes secularism, and takes on a kind of "religious" life of its own. John Dewey said of his own atheistic, humanistic philosophy and morality: "Here are all the elements for a religious faith that shall not be confined to sect, class or race." Atheistic humanists

Notes and Asides

with considerable frequency referred to their own philosophical beliefs as "religious" up until the post-World War II period. Perhaps it is more than coincidence that this is the same period during which the Supreme Court began to push religious practices out of government schools.[17]

Baer's observation that Humanists have begun to refrain from calling their position religious seems generally true, and the reason for this retreat is both obvious and extremely significant. If Secular Humanism is a religion with counselors treated on a par with ministers, priests, and rabbis, then what is it doing in the public schools? If Christianity is thrown out of secular schools under the guise of separation of church and state, why shouldn't we banish Secular Humanism as well? Paul Kurtz understands this, admitting that if Secular Humanism is a religion, "then we would be faced with a violation of the First Amendment to the United States Constitution."[18]

Christians who have seen their worldview effectively eliminated from the public schools are rightfully outraged by the Marxists' and

Used by permission of the *Colorado Springs Gazette Telegraph*

Notes and Asides

Humanists' violations of the present interpretation of the First Amendment. They are angered that a mere 7.3 million Humanists[19] can control the content of public schooling while the country's 192 million Christians[20] provide the lion's share of the students, and that the Humanists add insult to injury by making the 192 million Christians bear the majority of the cost for such discrimination through their tax dollars. It makes no sense for Christian parents to spend their lives and their fortunes (a university education can cost $40,000 to $100,000) raising their children with Christian values, only to find these values under constant attack at the college level. Indeed, it is a national scandal to see Christian values, which undergird the society (as Mikhail Gorbachev is finally discovering),[21] replaced by values that destroy society via hedonism, sexual revolutions, AIDS, drug revolutions, and anarchy.

Humanists attempt to downplay their violation of the present interpretation of the First Amendment by claiming that they present a neutral viewpoint. But no educational approach is neutral, as Richard A. Baer notes:

> Education never takes place in a moral and philosophical vacuum. If the larger questions about human beings and their destiny are not being asked and answered within a predominantly Judeo-Christian framework [worldview], they will be addressed with another philosophical or religious framework—but hardly one that is "neutral." The arrogance and philosophical implausibility of secular humanism are demonstrated by the insistence of many humanists that their position possesses such neutrality, lack of dogma, and essential rationality. It is an arrogance that also quickly becomes coercive and imperialistic, as is clearly seen in the widespread opposition among such educators toward genuine choice in education, for instance, the kind of choice that would be possible through a system of education tuition vouchers.[22]

Clearly, both Humanism and Marxism are religious worldviews. Trying to separate the sacred from the secular is like trying to sever the soul from the body—a deadly experiment. Thus, in order to provide a just educational system for our young people, we must recognize that all worldviews have religious implications and that it is discriminatory to bar some worldviews and not others from the classroom. As Baer says, "Within the context of a functional definition of religion, it is just as improper for the state to promulgate nontheistic or secular humanistic answers to the Big Questions—such as those that underlie Values Clarification or sex education curricula—as it is for it to recommend traditional Christian or Jewish beliefs. The claim that secular human-

Notes and Asides

ism is not a religion is wrong. It is essential to discredit this claim if we are to achieve justice in public education."[23]

It is also essential to discredit this claim and Marxism's similar denial in order to empower Christians to form a coherent worldview. Once we realize that no distinction between the sacred and the secular exists, we understand that Biblical Christianity, as the worldview grounded in truth, speaks most adequately to and forms the strongest foundation for law, politics, history, and all disciplines.

Even-Handed Approach

After many years of study, contemplation, and teaching, we honestly believe that the Biblical Christian worldview is spiritually, intellectually, emotionally, and practically far superior to all other worldviews. Christianity is something that, as C. S. Lewis said, mankind "could not have guessed," but that, once revealed, is recognizable as indisputable truth. Therefore, we believe that if students are given the opportunity to study and seriously think through creation versus evolution, for example, the vast majority will choose the creationist or Christian position.

This book represents an effort to allow individuals such opportunities by comparing the doctrines of three dominant worldviews. We have presented these views and their approach to the ten disciplines (theology, philosophy, biology, ethics, etc.) as accurately as possible. Occasionally, we will comment on an inconsistency inherent to the Marxist or Humanist view, but for the most part we will refrain from introducing a bias to the body of the text (reserving our critical comments for the conclusion). Put simply, we allow the worldviews to speak for themselves.

We have not represented Marxists or Humanists as either stupid or insane, despite their tendencies to describe Christians in such unflattering terms. While Humanists such as Albert Ellis call Christians "emotionally disturbed: usually neurotic but sometimes psychotic,"[24] this text resists such name-calling and treats Humanists and Marxists simply as individuals who have not yet recognized the inconsistent and erroneous nature of their worldviews.

No Marxist or Humanist, upon reading this text, should feel that we misrepresented his position. We quote the exact words of adherents to each worldview in their corresponding chapters, so that Humanists describe the Humanist position, Marxists the Marxist position, and Christians the Christian position. When we say Secular Humanism is atheistic, we believe the student should hear what the Secular Humanists say about the issue themselves. When we contend that Marxism/

> "Under the phony canopy of what is deceptively described as value-free education, public school students are being . . . indoctrinated in--all kinds of value-charged ideas. The only thing we can know for certain is that only one set of values is deemed out of bounds in this process, and that is the values of the Christian worldview."
>
> —Ronald H. Nash

Notes and Asides

Leninism relies biologically on punctuated equilibrium, the student should hear that from the Marxist. Further, no quote has purposely been taken out of context. We have, in the best tradition of Christian scholarship, allowed the competing non-Christian worldviews to have their say as they wish to say it.

We contend that by seeing the worldviews contrasted, the student will understand his own worldview and the alternatives better and be able to enunciate and defend his position more persuasively and intelligently. Many young people don't have the foggiest notion what they believe; it is the Christian's duty to share his faith with such a spiritually and intellectually rootless generation. The Apostle Peter says as much when he exhorts believers in Jesus Christ to "be ready always to give an answer to everyone that asketh you a reason of the hope that is in you with meekness and reverence" (1 Peter 3:15).

A Word About Sources

There is no lack of sources or resources for each worldview we have chosen to analyze, and we have focused on the best of these materials. When we describe the Marxist position, for example, we will quote its ideological leaders, not a small band of neo-Marxists from Duke.

The primary publishing house of the Secular Humanists is Prometheus Books, located in Buffalo, New York. Their leaders include John Dewey, Roy Wood Sellars, Corliss Lamont, Paul Kurtz, Isaac Asimov, Sidney Hook, Carl Sagan, Julian Huxley, and Erich Fromm. The list of signatories of the *Humanist Manifestoes* includes scores of men and women who endorse that position. Those chosen as "Humanist of the Year" also provide a rich source of Humanistic viewpoints, as do contributing authors in *The Humanist* and *Free Inquiry* magazines. Through strict adherence to these resources, we are able to capsulize Secular Humanism without distortion.

Marxism/Leninism is even easier to document. None deny the major roles Karl Marx, Frederick Engels, V. I. Lenin, and Joseph Stalin have played in formulating the Marxist position. International Publishers, in New York City, prints and distributes hundreds of books from the Marxist/Leninist point of view. English translations of works published in the Soviet Union are easily accessible, thanks to various distribution centers located in the United States.

The Bible, of course, is the primary source for the Christian worldview. Christian writers provide a rich variety of commentary. Our interpretation of the Bible is admittedly from an evangelical perspective, but then many skeptics who have converted—St. Augustine, C. S. Lewis, C. E. M. Joad, Mortimer Adler—have converted to evangelical

Notable Signatories of *Humanist Manifesto II*

Isaac Asimov
Paul Blanshard
Francis Crick
Miriam A. deFord
Edd Doerr
Paul Edwards
Albert Ellis
Joseph Fletcher
Antony Flew
Betty Friedan
Sidney Hook
Julian Huxley
Lester A. Kirkendall
Paul Kurtz
Corliss Lamont
Floyd W. Matson
Lester Mondale
Herbert J. Muller
Kai Nielsen
John H. Randall, Jr.
Jean-Francois Revel
Herbert W. Schneider
Roy Wood Sellars
B. F. Skinner
V. M. Tarkunde
Herbert A. Tonne
Edwin H. Wilson
Marvin Zimmerman

Christianity, not liberal Christianity.[25]

Strangely, the Bible often receives better print outside Christianity than inside liberal "Christian" circles. For example, Will Durant, an agnostic, writes in *Caesar and Christ*, "After two centuries of Higher Criticism the outlines of the life, character, and teachings of Christ remain reasonably clear, and constitute the most fascinating feature in the history of Western man."[26] Elsewhere Durant says, "That a few simple men [Matthew, Mark, Luke, John] should in one generation have invented so powerful and appealing a personality, so lofty an ethic, and so inspiring a vision of human brotherhood, would be a miracle far more incredible than any recorded in the Gospels."[27]

As evangelicals, we believe there's a logical reason for the miraculous nature of the Bible: it was written by men guided by Divine inspiration. The Christian worldview explains the facts of reality better than any other worldview because it relies not only on the words of credible men, but also on the words of God. If the Bible is truly God's special revelation to man, as we believe it is, then the only completely accurate view of the world must be founded on Scripture.

Further, the divine inspiration of Scripture explains not only its miraculous coherency but also the incredible power of the figure of Christ. Atheist historian W. E. H. Lecky admits that the character of Jesus "has been not only the highest pattern of virtue but the strongest incentive to its practice; and has exercised so deep an influence that it may be truly said that the simple record of three short years of active life has done more to regenerate and to soften mankind than all the disquisitions of philosophers, and all the exhortations of moralists."[28] We believe the reason for this is that when Christ told the woman who spoke of the Messiah, "I who speak to you am he" (John 4:26), He was telling her the most fundamental truth of all. Biblical Christianity is essentially the ways of Christ—the most special revelation of God's

Notes and Asides

entire revelation in Scriptures. What Christ said concerning life and death, the saved and lost condition of mankind, body and soul, and truth constitutes the central precepts of the Christian worldview. Christ is its cornerstone. He is the way, the truth, and the life (John 14:6).

When presenting the Christian worldview, then, we take the Bible at face value. Call it "literal" interpretation if you wish, but it is difficult to see how else the writers of the Old and New Testaments meant to be taken.[29] Figures of speech, yes; typologies, yes; analogies, yes; but overall they wrote in simple, straightforward terms. When a writer says, "In the beginning God created the heavens and the earth," we understand him to say that there is a God, there was a beginning to creation, that heaven and earth exist, and that God made them. When a writer says, "God so loved the world that he gave his only begotten Son that whosoever believeth on him shall not perish but have everlasting life," we understand him to say that there is a God, that God loves, that God sent His Son, and that those who believe Him shall not perish but have everlasting life.

It does not take a Ph.D. or a high IQ to comprehend the basic message of the Bible. God's special revelation is open to everyone. This point is expressed well by John W. Montgomery:

> The issue of scriptural clarity is not hard to test. Take a passage such as "there went out a decree from Caesar Augustus, that all the world should be taxed" (Luke 2:1); could it legitimately be construed as referring to the banana crop of Tanganyika? . . . English actor Alec McCowen, whose solo recitations of St. Mark's Gospel have electrified audiences on both sides of the Atlantic, maintains that the ordinary meaning of that book would be plain to us even if the book were unearthed for the first time yesterday.[30]

The major criticism leveled against the Bible is that it is either prescientific or unscientific. This does not hold water. The science of archaeology has by no means "demolished" the Bible. William F. Albright, a world class archaeologist, declares, "Modern scholarship, instead of discrediting the Bible, is furnishing striking confirmation of its accuracy."[31] Further (as we shall explain in the text), the sciences of physics, paleontology, chemistry, and biology do not "demolish" the Bible either. In fact, they often lead scientists to the inescapable conclusion that the Bible is a historical document. Wendell R. Bird develops eighteen categories of hard scientific evidence that are specifically supportive of the Bible, including abrupt appearances in the fossil record, systematic gaps in the fossil record, information theory (which involves the vast amount of information content of all living

Notes and Asides

forms), genetic limits on viable change, etc.[32] Historian Werner Keller concludes, "In view of the overwhelming mass of authentic and well-attested evidence now available, as I thought of the skeptical criticism which from the eighteenth century onward would fain have demolished the Bible altogether, there kept hammering in my brain this one sentence: 'The Bible is right after all.'"[33]

Perhaps, however, after reading this text the student will decide that the Bible is not right, and that Humanism or Marxism is the worldview that most conforms to the truth. If the facts support such a conclusion, personal integrity demands that the student adopt that view. But we contend that such a conclusion is not possible. We have examined the facts and wrestled with the possibilities, and we have found that intellectual integrity demands adherence to Biblical Christianity. We believe Harvard psychiatrist Robert Coles hit on a profound truth when he said,

> Nothing I have discovered about the make-up of human beings contradicts in any way what I learn from the Hebrew prophets such as Isaiah, Jeremiah and Amos, and from the Book of Ecclesiastes, and from Jesus and the lives of those he touched. Anything I can say as a result of my research into human behavior is a mere footnote to those lives in the Old and New Testaments.[34]

"The Christian and the Materialist hold different beliefs about the universe. They can't both be right. The one who is wrong will act in a way which simply doesn't fit the real universe."

—C. S. Lewis

Most social ills, problems, and sins[35] are ultimately matters of the mind, soul, and spirit. Materialistic worldviews are unable to solve these ills; rather, they contribute more problems. Only the worldview based on Jesus Christ—a worldview that promotes and sustains the proper attitudes toward family, church, and state—can effectively speak to these areas. However, we cannot force this conclusion on others. All we can do is encourage individuals to "Taste and see that the Lord is good." We believe the Lord is good and His ways are good, and in this study His ways and teachings form a consistent, truthful, well-rounded Christian worldview.

Study Procedures

Students wishing to build a foundation for approaching this text would do well to read James Orr's *A Christian View of God and the World*, along with James W. Sire's *The Universe Next Door*[36] and four significant manifestoes: *The Christian Manifesto* by Francis Schaeffer, *The Communist Manifesto* by Karl Marx and Frederick Engels, and *The*

Notes and Asides

Humanist Manifestoes I and II by Roy Wood Sellars and Paul Kurtz respectively. These works make a fitting introduction to this study by preparing the student to think in terms of worldviews and enforcing the notion that ideas have consequences—even logical consequences that proceed from prior beliefs.

However, reading such books is not mandatory for the student approaching this text—nor does the student need to be well-versed in worldview study. This work paints the various categorical positions of each worldview with broad and general strokes, adhering to Einstein's dictum: "Everything should be made as simple as possible, but not simpler." Each chapter of a section, we know, could consume hundreds of pages by itself. In fact, millions of pages and billions of words have been written on Christian theism alone. We have attempted, therefore, not to address every subtlety of each approach, but rather to capture the "kernel" of each worldview's perspective on each discipline. We follow C. S. Lewis's formula, striving to capture "mere Christianity," as well as mere Humanism and mere Marxism. For example, the heart of Christian theology will always be theism, just as the heart of Humanist ethics will always be relativism and the heart of Marxist biology will always be evolution. Thus, we examine the core, the foundational approach, of each worldview. In this way, we assure the reader a text that will never be outdated. Even should Marxism/Leninism fall from political power in the Soviet Union and the People's Republic of China, the worldview will not change. Marxism/Leninism will still be atheistic, materialistic, etc.

There are two possible approaches to this text. A student could focus on one section at a time, thereby concentrating on each discipline, or he could focus on a specific worldview and examine its approach to each of the ten disciplines before moving on to study a second worldview and then a third. Whichever approach he chooses, the final result will be the same—the student will have gained insight by contrasting the various ideas central to each point of view. He or she will have engaged in comparative analysis.

A few decades ago (1925), evolutionists were bemoaning the fact that they were not given the opportunity to teach their viewpoint to American students. Dudley Field Malone, John Scopes's attorney argued, "For God's sake, let the children have their minds kept open—close no doors to their knowledge; shut no door from them."[37] Today the situation is completely reversed. University of Missouri professor of biology and science education A. Thompson says that Scopes would have difficulty recognizing the battle lines of today: "*Creationists are now espousing* one of the arguments of Clarence Darrow's ardent defense of Scopes; that one theory of the beginning should not be taught

Notes and Asides

to the exclusion of another. In short, perhaps creationism should be considered along with the evolutionary theory."[38]

Bird explains the injustice of such discrimination:

> Academic freedom is often more honored in the breach than in the observance in regard to controversial viewpoints. Widespread discrimination actually exists against discontinuitist [creationist] scientists, teachers, and students. Most self-designated civil libertarians conveniently overlook this phenomenon, although they would be uncontrollably exercised if the situation were reversed. True civil liberty involves the right to hear all alternatives on controversial subjects in governmental schools, rather than to suffer indoctrination in what a high or petty official or teacher has determined to be orthodox in science.[39]

We mention this injustice not just because it demands correction, but also because it serves as a reminder of the need to teach by contrast. Discrimination against a certain viewpoint or worldview can only hinder academic freedom and responsible decision making by our young people. Bird provides the Christian student with an excellent chapter on the importance of teaching by contrast.[40] Although Bird specifically is referring to the creationism/evolutionism controversy, nearly everything he says can be applied to our attempt to contrast the Christian worldview with the Marxist and Secular Humanist worldviews.

For example, Bird states, "Many educational theorists state or imply the benefit of contrasting explanations. 'Comparative analysis' is stressed as the first of twenty-two instructional considerations in curriculum development, by Wiles and Bondi."[41] He goes on to quote Wiles and Bondi: "Comparative analysis—A thought process, structured by the teacher, that employs the description, classification, and analysis of more than one system, group, or the like in order to ascertain and evaluate similarities and differences."

Bird quotes other educators to the effect that by supplying students with "contrasting positions," "multiple working hypotheses," or "a number of solutions" to a problem or a question, we are teaching students how to think. Karl Popper says we should "construct alternative theories"—even to "compellingly established theories."

This course of study is based on the belief that by learning to contrast worldviews, the student improves his overall conceptual skills. Perhaps some people feel that Christians should be shielded from Humanist or Marxist views. We disagree. Such studies are essential to prepare Christians to face the real world, including the university.

"True civil liberty involves the right to hear all alternatives on controversial subjects in governmental schools, rather than to suffer indoctrination in what a high or petty official or teacher has determined to be orthodox in science."

—W. R. Bird

Notes and Asides

Some Christians need to be in secular colleges, jobs, etc. We can't shield ourselves from the world and still spread the message of christ.

Facing the Challenge

As the Apostle Paul faced the religious humanists of his day (Acts 17), so the faithful and aware Christian must, if he is truly to follow Christ, face the religious Humanists of our day. In the West this means facing the Secular, Cosmic, and Marxist varieties. It also means—a lot of hard work.

This study requires work. But the student need not be disheartened by the effort required. The ideas of theism, atheism, supernaturalism, teleology, naturalism, materialism, dialectics, spontaneous generation, evolution, Biblical morality, class morality, new morality, freedom, totalitarianism, private property, socialism, globalism, mind, soul, spirit, self-actualization, sin, and law make the world turn. Those willing to struggle with such ideas earn an invaluable reward: "an all-encompassing belief system, grander than the individual and larger than the family, to explain disparate facts and to furnish meaning in life."[42]

We believe the Christian worldview is the only proper "all-encompassing belief system"—larger than both the individual and the family, but destroying neither. Christianity furnishes meaning in life and best fits the facts of experience. Thus, it is time once again to offer the Christian worldview as a fitting alternative to the Marxist/Leninist system (which appears to be crumbling)[43] and the Secular Humanist system (which cannot replace its ideological offspring).

Why do people choose lives of suffering + pain when they could have the joy of christ for nothing?

"The greatest question of our time is not communism versus individualism, not Europe versus America, not even the East versus the West," says Will Durant, "it is whether man can live without God."[44] This text attempts to demonstrate the impossibility of survival on such terms by delineating a theistic worldview so comprehensive that it renders all questions of atheism obsolete. Christianity is so consistent and so faithful to the truth that we should ask instead why man would *want* to live without God.

It is our prayer that this study will assist each Christian student to see the value, truthfulness, and superiority of the Christian worldview, as he grows in the grace and knowledge of his Lord and Savior, Jesus Christ.

In a world that wants everything we have, even the breath we breathe - God offers his love and joy, with no strings attached.
- Angie Feagan

[1]H. Burtness, "Bonhoeffer, Dietrich," in *Baker's Dictionary of Christian Ethics*, ed. Carl F. H. Henry, (Grand Rapids, MI: Baker, 1973), p. 67.
[2]Louis Trenchard More, *The Dogma of Evolution* (Princeton, NJ: Princeton University Press, 1925), p. 67. Cited by Henry Morris, *The Long War Against God* (Grand Rapids, MI: Baker Book House, 1990), p. 211.
[3]Gustav A. Wetter, *Dialectical Materialism* (Westport, CT: Greenwood Press, 1977), p. 558.
[4]Ibid.
[5]Bertrand Russell, *Understanding History* (New York: Philosophical Library, 1957), p. 95.
[6]Paul Kurtz, ed., *Humanist Manifestoes I and II* (Buffalo: Prometheus, 1980), p. 3, emphasis added.
[7]John Dewey, *A Common Faith* (New Haven: Yale University Press, 1934), p. 87.
[8]Kurtz, ed., *Humanist Manifestoes I and II*, p. 16.
[9]*United States v. Seeger*, 380 U.S. 163. Also see *Welsh v. United States*, 398 U.S. 333 (1970).
[10]Leo Pfeffer, *Journal of Church and State*, vol. 19, no. 2 (Spring 1977), p. 211.
[11]See *American Education on Trial: Is Secular Humanism a Religion?* (Cumberland, VA: Center for Judicial Studies [zip code 23040], 1987), p. 34.
[12]Ibid., p. 34.
[13]Paul Kurtz, *Eupraxophy: Living Without Religion* (Buffalo: Prometheus, 1989).
[14]Paul Kurtz, "Is Secular Humanism a Religion?"*Free Inquiry*, Winter 1986/87, p. 5.
[15]Isaac Asimov, "An interview with Isaac Asimov on Science and the Bible," *Free Inquiry*, Spring 1982, p. 9: "I am an atheist, out and out. It took me a long time to say it. I've been an atheist for years and years. I don't have the evidence to prove that God doesn't exist, but I so strongly suspect he doesn't that I don't want to waste my time."
[16]Ken Sidey, *The Blackboard Fumble* (Wheaton, IL: Victor Books, 1989), p. 59.
[17]Richard A. Baer, Jr., "Character Education and Public Schools: The Question of Context," Proceedings of a Symposium Sponsored by the National Council on Educational Research, April 24, 1986.
[18]Kurtz, *Eupraxophy*, p. 80.
[19]Isaac Asimov says in his July 1989 letter to the American Humanist Association, "I estimate there are 7.3 million of us right here in America."
[20]A 1988 Gallup Poll found that 84% of the people in America believe Jesus to be God or the Son of God. George Gallup, Jr. and Jim Castelli, in *The People's Religion: American Faith in the 90s* (New York: Macmillan, 1989), write of the "enduring popularity of religion" in America, noting that "the baseline of religious belief is remarkably high—certainly, the highest of any developed nation in the world" (p. 20). The authors found that 90 percent of the American people believe in life after death; 80 percent believe in miracles; etc. They also found, contrary to Secular Humanist expectations, that religious faith is not eroded by a high level of education. College graduates participate in the life of churches and seek religious education for their children. Contrary to John Dewey and his disciples, at least in America, secularism is not replacing religious faith as the basis for Western Civilization. According to a *New York Times* report of August 29, 1982, 44 percent of the Americans polled held to the Genesis account of creation and 38 percent to a theistic evolution position. Only 9 percent held an atheistic evolutionary position on origins. An AP/NBC poll (November 24, 1981) found 86 percent of the public favoring teaching the theory of creation in public schools rather than only the theory of evolution. For more data on similar polls see Wendell R. Bird, *The Origin of Species Revisited*, two volumes (New York: Philosophical Library, 1987, 1988, and 1989), vol. 1, p. 8.
[21]Mikhail Gorbachev, "Gorbachev, God and Socialism,"*Time*, December 11, 1989, p. 37: "We need spiritual values, we need a revolution of the mind. This is the only way toward a new culture and new politics that can meet the challenge of our time. We have changed our attitude toward some matters—such as religion—which, admittedly, we used to treat in a simplistic manner [the Bolsheviks systematically slaughtered millions of Christian believers]. . . . [W]e also say that the moral values that religion generated and embodied for centuries can help in the work of renewal in our country, too."
[22]Richard A. Baer, "They Are Teaching Religion in Public Schools," *Christianity Today*, February 17, 1984, p. 15.
[23]Sidey, *The Blackboard Fumble*, p. 59.
[24]Albert Ellis, "The Case Against Religiosity," from a section reprinted in "Testament of a Humanist," *Free Inquiry*, Spring 1987, p. 21.

[25]Some present examples of liberal Christianity include Liberation Theology, in which Christ is portrayed as a socialist revolutionary, and feminist theology, in which the male Savior is replaced with a female "Christa," a "crucifix with a nude female body sculpted in 1975 by Edwina Sandys" (see *Newsweek*, February 13, 1989). Perhaps the best single source for getting a grasp on Protestant liberal Christianity is C. Howard Hopkins, *The Rise of the Social Gospel in American Protestantism 1865-1915* (New Haven: Yale University Press, 1940). Liberal Christianity came out of a Unitarian background (Unitarians denying the Deity of Jesus Christ and the Tri-unity of the Godhead of Father, Son, and Holy Spirit) and stressed "the dignity and divine possibilities of man, the achievement of salvation through character culture, the unity and immanence of God, and the importance of the present life" (p. 4). Nearly every facet of present-day Liberation Theology can be traced to Liberal Theology, including the distaste for private property, a heaven on earth in a collectivist society, etc.
[26]Will Durant, *The Story of Civilization*, ten volumes, (New York: Simon and Schuster, 1944), vol. 3, *Caesar and Christ*, p. 557.
[27]Ibid.
[28]W. E. H. Lecky, *History of European Morals (from Augustus to Charlemagne)*, two volumes (New York: George Braziller, 1955), vol. 2, pp. 8-9.
[29]We are not attempting to shortchange the importance of hermeneutics or the proper understanding or interpretation of Scripture, but such a study is beyond the scope of this work. We recommend S. Lewis Johnson, Jr., *The Old Testament in the New* (Grand Rapids, MI: Zondervan, 1980), followed by Milton S. Terry, *Biblical Hermeneutics: A Treatise on the Interpretation of the Old and New Testaments* (New York: Phillips and Hunt, 1883; rpt. Grand Rapids, MI: Baker, 1979), Earl D. Radmacher and Robert D. Preus, *Hermeneutics, Inerrancy, and the Bible* (Grand Rapids, MI: Zondervan, 1984), and Bernard Ramm, *Protestant Biblical Interpretation: A Textbook of Hermeneutics* (Grand Rapids, MI: Baker, 1970). Most Christians certainly wish to understand Scripture according to Biblical principles of hermeneutics. Unfortunately, most divisions among Christians ultimately can be traced to differences of opinion regarding hermeneutics. Therefore, it probably is best to restate that our approach to Scripture is evangelical in character as over against liberal, liberation, feminist, etc.—but realizing that even among evangelicals there are differences between the dispensational and reformed hermeneutic.
[30]John Warwick Montgomery, *Human Rights and Human Dignity* (Dallas, TX: Probe Books, 1986), p. 163.
[31]William F. Albright, *The Archaeology of Palestine*, (Baltimore: Penguin Books, 1960), pp. 123-4. G. Ernest Wright, *Biblical Archaeology* (Philadelphia: Westminster Press, 1970), "It can now be said that the text of no other work from antiquity is so well attested by manuscript tradition as that of the New Testament" (p. 242). Nelson Glueck, *Biblical Archaeologist*, XXII (December 1959), p. 101: "It may be stated categorically that no archaeological discovery has ever controverted a biblical reference."
[32]Bird, *The Origin of Species Revisited*, vol. 2, p. 462.
[33]Werner Keller, *The Bible as History* (New York: William Morrow, 1964), p. xviii.
[34]P. Yancey, "The Crayon Man,"*Christianity Today*, February 6, 1987, p. 20.
[35]Karl Menninger's *Whatever Became of Sin?* (New York: Hawthorn Books, 1973) is an important book on this topic because Menninger, an unbeliever, recognizes that society's denial of the existence of sin has led to many psychological problems. It is clear to the Christian man or woman that sin exists in every human heart and cannot be ignored.
[36]James W. Sire, *The Universe Next Door* (Downers Grove, IL: InterVarsity Press, 1976).
[37]Bird, *The Origin of Species Revisited*, vol. 2, p. 367.
[38]Ibid., p. 377.
[39]Ibid., p. 366. Christian parents are urged to make Bird's *The Origin of Species Revisited* available to their children.
[40]Ibid., Chapters 17-19, beginning on page 367 of volume 2.
[41]Ibid., vol. 2, p. 369.
[42]Ken Adelman, "Beyond Ideology,"*The Washington Times*, December 25, 1989, p. D4.
[43]The collapse of the Marxist/Leninist worldview in Eastern Europe creates a vacuum that can be filled adequately only by Christianity. With people-power revolutions calling for "freedom" and "democracy" in Eastern Europe and abandoning Marxism, it is important for freedom-loving peoples to understand that freedom is, in the final analysis, a gift of God and comes from spiritual values originating in Biblical truths. Western

values, though many times ignored and even denied by the West, are basically Biblical values. The Christian worldview does not encourage or end in totalitarianism. It is the true base for actual political, economic, and religious freedom. The relationship between freedom and the need for moral principles, conscience, reason, softening of prejudices, and calming of passions speaks volumes for the necessity of studying Christianity as a worldview.

[44]Cited in Charles Colson, *Kingdoms in Conflict* (Grand Rapids, MI: Zondervan, 1987), p. 225.

SECTION ONE

THEOLOGY

THEOLOGY [Greek: *theos* (God) + *logos* (word)]: The study of the existence (or non-existence), nature, and attributes of God.

	SECULAR HUMANISM	MARXISM/ LENINISM	BIBLICAL CHRISTIANITY
SOURCE	*HUMANIST MANIFESTO I & II*	*WRITINGS OF MARX & LENIN*	*BIBLE*
THEOLOGY	ATHEISM	ATHEISM	THEISM
PHILOSOPHY	NATURALISM	DIALECTICAL MATERIALISM	SUPERNATURALISM
ETHICS	ETHICAL RELATIVISM	PROLETARIAT MORALITY	ETHICAL ABSOLUTES
BIOLOGY	DARWINIAN EVOLUTION	DARWINIAN/ PUNCTUATED EVOLUTION	SPECIAL CREATIONISM
PSYCHOLOGY	MONISTIC SELF-ACTUALIZATION	MONISTIC PAVLOVIAN BEHAVIORISM	DUALISM
SOCIOLOGY	NON-TRADITIONAL WORLD STATE ETHICAL SOCIETY	ABOLITION OF HOME, CHURCH AND STATE	HOME CHURCH STATE
LAW	POSITIVE LAW	POSITIVE LAW	BIBLICAL/NATURAL LAW
POLITICS	WORLD GOVERNMENT (GLOBALISM)	NEW WORLD ORDER	JUSTICE FREEDOM ORDER
ECONOMICS	SOCIALISM	SOCIALISM/ COMMUNISM	STEWARDSHIP OF PROPERTY
HISTORY	HISTORICAL EVOLUTION	HISTORICAL MATERIALISM	HISTORICAL RESURRECTION

CHAPTER

3

SECULAR HUMANIST THEOLOGY

"There is no place in the Humanist worldview for either immortality or God in the valid meanings of those terms. Humanism contends that instead of the gods creating the cosmos, the cosmos, in the individualized form of human beings giving rein to their imagination, created the gods."[1]

—Corliss Lamont

"Humanism cannot in any fair sense of the word apply to one who still believes in God as the source and creator of the universe."[2]

—Paul Kurtz

SUMMARY

The theological foundation of Secular Humanism is atheism. The present head of the American Humanist Association, Isaac Asimov, said, "I am an atheist, out and out." The Humanists' major publications, *The Humanist* and *Free Inquiry* magazines, are atheistic. Paul Kurtz, editor of *Free Inquiry*, argues that the term *Humanism* cannot apply to one who believes in God. Corliss Lamont, author of *The Philosophy of Humanism*, insists that atheism is the cornerstone of the Secular Humanist worldview. According to Lamont, the science of biology has conclusively shown that life, including man, is the result of a long process of evolution stretching out over three billion years. Such a scenario makes supernatural creation by God superfluous. Humanists view God as the creation of man. "It is said that men may not be the dreams of the gods," said Carl Sagan in *Cosmos*, "but rather that the gods are the dreams of men." Other outspoken Humanists, including John Dewey, Bertrand Russell, Julian Huxley, and Erich Fromm, are published atheists. The major *Humanist Manifestoes* are atheistic. The major Humanist publishing arm—Prometheus Books—is a publisher of atheistic literature. Humanists argue that science and the scientific process have rendered God obsolete. They believe that only nature exists, that it has always existed, that man is a conscious speck of nature, and that nature requires neither supernatural explanation nor God.

Introduction

After thinking about religion and the supernatural for three years, Bertrand Russell abandoned the notion of God. He later admitted, "I believed in God until I was just eighteen."[3] Russell, one of Secular Humanism's international voices (along with Julian Huxley), maintained that the whole idea of God was a conception derived from the ancient Oriental despotisms, and therefore concluded, "I am not a Christian . . . I do not believe in God and in immortality; and, . . . I do not think that Christ was the best and wisest of men, although I grant Him a very high degree of moral goodness."[4]

While eighteen may seem a tender age to determine whether or not God exists, Miriam Allen deFord, an American Humanist, had by age

Notes and Asides

thirteen already concluded that there was sufficient evidence for denying the existence of all gods. Furthermore, she was convinced that man possessed no soul or immortality (life after death). "To put it bluntly and undiplomatically," deFord says, "Humanism, in my viewpoint, must be atheistic or it is not Humanism as I understand it."[5]

According to nearly fifty years of *The Humanist* magazine and numerous articles and books by recognized Humanists, deFord's understanding of Humanism differs little from that of most other Humanists. The weight of evidence is so overwhelmingly in favor of atheism as the theological foundation of Secular Humanism that whatever non-atheistic Humanists there may be must be viewed as anomalies, even self-contradictions.

Corliss Lamont, author of *The Philosophy of Humanism*, insists that Humanism, "rejecting supernaturalism" and "seeking man's fulfillment in the here and now of this world," has a long and honored tradition starting with Democritus and Aristotle in ancient Greece and Lucretius in ancient Rome and continuing with Spinoza in the seventeenth century, Diderot and Voltaire in the eighteenth century, and John Dewey and Bertrand Russell in the twentieth century. Although Aristotle, Spinoza, and Voltaire were not atheists, there is little doubt that Lamont is correct about Dewey and Russell.

Atheism [Greek: *a* (no) + *theos* (God)] is the belief that God does not exist.

Lamont's definition of the theological basis of Secular Humanism is consistently atheistic—with one exception, found in his introduction to the sixth edition (1982) of *The Philosophy of Humanism*. There he maintains that while Humanists find no adequate proof for a supernatural God functioning on this earth and guiding the human race to a divine future, "The immensity of the universe makes [Humanists] cautious about absolutely denying the existence of a God among the billions of galaxies billions of light-years away. . . . Humanists are awe-struck by the fathomless mystery of the origin, size, and destiny of the whole mighty cosmos."[6] Apart from this one admission of doubt, this one crack in his atheistic armor, Lamont rigidly maintains a militant atheistic stance.

Humanist Jean-Paul Sartre, who for most of his life proclaimed a "heroic atheism," experienced a similar moment of doubt. Toward the end of his life he admitted, "I do not feel that I am the product of chance, a speck of dust in the universe, but someone who was expected, prepared, prefigured. In short, a being whom only a Creator could put here; and this idea of a creating hand refers to God."[7] In the main, however, Humanists rigorously ignore the existence of the supernatural.

Notes and Asides

Humanist Response to the Supernatural

What are the basic principles of Humanism that define its position and distinguish it from other worldviews? Lamont states the fundamental principle: "Humanism . . . considers all forms of the supernatural as myth."[8] The supernatural—that is, anything outside nature, "does not exist."[9] "Humanism," says Lamont, "in its most accurate philosophical sense, implies a worldview in which Nature is everything, in which there is no supernatural."[10]

Lamont asserts that "intellectually, there is nothing to be gained and much to be lost for philosophy by positing a supernatural Creator or First Cause behind the great material universe."[11] There is no place in the Humanist worldview for God and, insists Lamont, instead of the gods creating the cosmos, "the cosmos, in the individualized form of human beings giving rein to their imagination, created the gods."[12]

Some years earlier than Lamont's first edition of *The Philosophy of Humanism* (1949), the Humanists, including Dewey, Roy Wood Sellars, John H. Randall, Jr., E. A. Burtt, and Edwin H. Wilson, published *The Humanist Manifesto* (1933). It described the universe "as self-existing and not created." Further, the *Manifesto* declared, "the time has passed for theism. . . ."[13]

Since Dewey's name has been associated so closely with the 1933 *Manifesto*, it is important to mention his approach to the supernatural. In his work *A Common Faith*, Dewey distinguishes between the words *religion* and *religious*. He reserves the term *religion* for the supernatural while maintaining the term *religious* for the world of the natural (especially as it involves human relations, welfare, and progress). Dewey rejects the supernatural and the supernatural God. He accepts only evolving nature, with all of its "religious" ramifications: "I cannot," says Dewey, "understand how any realization of the democratic ideal as a vital moral and spiritual ideal in human affairs is possible without surrender of the conception of the basic division to which supernatural Christianity is committed."[14] For Dewey, democracy cannot ingest the Christian notions of *saved* and *lost, sheep* and *goats*, etc. He considers such notions "spiritual aristocracy" and contrary to the ideals of democracy. A democratic church must include believer and unbeliever.

Dewey makes it clear that he believes science has largely discredited Biblical Christianity. "Geological discoveries," he says, "have displaced Creation myths which once bulked large."[15] Biology, says Dewey, has "revolutionized conceptions of soul and mind which once

Notes and Asides

occupied a central place in religious beliefs and ideas."[16] He also says that biology has made a "profound impression" on the ideas of sin, redemption, and immortality. Anthropology, history, and literary criticism have furnished a "radically different version of the historic events and personages upon which Christian religions have built."[17] And psychology is already opening up "natural explanations of phenomena so extraordinary that once their supernatural origin was, so to say, the natural explanation."[18] For Dewey, science and scientific method have exiled God and the supernatural to the dustbins of history.

Indeed, for Dewey, faith in God and the supernatural is "sapping the religious life itself."[19] Ronald Nash, in *The Closing of the American Heart*, quotes Dewey to the effect that "faith in the prayer-hearing God is an unproved and outmoded faith. There is no God and there is no soul. Hence, there are no needs for the props of traditional religion. With

CLOSE-UP

John Dewey (1859-1952)

John Dewey's academic career was relatively uninspired until, at the University of Vermont, he read a physiology textbook by T.H. Huxley. Dewey was convinced by Huxley's claim that man is the result of natural evolutionary processes, and credited the book with being responsible for his "intellectual awakening." Building on this evolutionary perspective throughout his life, Dewey arrived at a form of naturalism known as pragmatism. His career as a professor began at the University of Michigan in 1884, and by 1894 he was the head of the philosophy, psychology, and pedagogy department at the University of Chicago. At Chicago, he began an experimental school to test his educational theories. This led to a conflict with the university's president, and Dewey wound up moving to Columbia University in 1904. His fame spread, and many of his Humanistic educational theories found their way into America's public school system. Many of his books, including *Experience and Nature* and *Liberalism and Social Action*, have also impacted the academic world. Dewey's influence on modern society is further manifested in the American Civil Liberties Union, which he helped found. He also served as the first president of the American Humanist Association.

Notes and Asides

dogma and creed excluded, then immutable truth is also dead and buried. There is no room for fixed, natural law—or moral absolutes."[20]

Forty years after the 1933 *Manifesto*, the Humanists published *Humanist Manifesto II* and reiterated, "We find insufficient evidence for belief in the existence of a supernatural; it is either meaningless or irrelevant to the question of the survival and fulfillment of the human race. As non-theists, we begin with humans not God, nature not deity." Again, ". . . we can discover no divine purpose or providence for the human species. While there is much that we do not know, humans are responsible for what we are or will become. No deity will save us; we must save ourselves."[21] Hundreds of Humanists signed this declaration of atheism.

> "Among religions in this country . . . [is] . . . Secular Humanism"
> —**Supreme Court Justice Black**

In 1960, the United States Supreme Court considered the issue of Secular Humanism's stance regarding the supernatural in a case involving a Humanist, Mr. Roy R. Torcaso. Torcaso was refused his commission as a Notary Public under Maryland law, which required all public officers in the State to believe in God. The Maryland statute was struck down as unconstitutional under the First Amendment. Justice Hugo L. Black wrote, "Among religions in this country which do not teach what would generally be considered a belief in the existence of God are Buddhism, Taoism, Ethical Culture, Secular Humanism and others."[22]

> "No deity will save us; we must save ourselves."
> —*Humanist Manifesto II*

The Supreme Court considered Secular Humanism not only atheistic but also a religion in the same sense that Buddhism and Taoism are religions. Humanism, by implication, was granted status as a worldview complete with its own theology.

Sellars, a long-time Humanist and co-signer of the 1933 *Humanist Manifesto I*, recognized that Humanism's atheism might inhibit acceptance of its worldview. Says Sellars, "Humanism is naturalistic and rejects the supernaturalistic stance with its postulated Creator-God and cosmic Ruler. . . . Nontheism is a neutral term and may be preferable to atheism."[23]

Other Humanists have no such problems with the term *atheism*. Gora, for example, boldly declares, "Humanists reject faith in God, soul and after life, since science shows them unverifiable." After stating that atheism is the principal feature of Humanism, Gora insists that "Atheism activates Humanists" and that vigilant Humanism is the need of the hour and "atheism supplies the need."[24]

Notes and Asides

While these statements may shock the casual observer of Humanism, they can in no way be disregarded as the radical views of fringe Humanists. Bold atheism is proclaimed by the most orthodox of Humanists, including Paul Kurtz. He declares, "Humanism cannot in any fair sense of the word apply to one who still believes in God as the source and creator of the universe. Christian Humanism would be possible only for those who are willing to admit that they are atheistic Humanists. It surely does not apply to God-intoxicated believers."[25]

For Kurtz, "God himself is man deified."[26] Such theology, of course, is quite close to the Marxist point of view. In fact, Kurtz refers to Marx as "one of history's great humanist thinkers." Kurtz says Marx is a Humanist because "he rejects theistic religion and defends atheism."[27]

Humanistic Theological Literature

Secular Humanism's primary publishing arm is Prometheus Books, located in Buffalo, New York. Among other things, Prometheus publishes atheistic children's books, including *What About Gods?* by Chris Brockman. This book is designed to indoctrinate children with dogmatic atheistic sentiments like, "Many people say they believe in a god. Do you know what a god is? Do you know what it means to believe in a god? A god is a mythical character. Mythical characters are imaginary, they're not real. People make them up. Dragons and fairies are two of many mythical characters people have made up. They're not real. . . ."[28]

Prometheus also publishes atheistic literature geared toward adult audiences. Paul Blanshard's *Classics of Free Thought* was published "to keep atheism before the public." *Critiques of God* contains 371 pages supporting Humanist theology's denial of the existence of God. *Critiques* editor Peter Angeles says,

> There is no anthology in the philosophy of religion that exclusively presents the case against God. This one does. . . . The themes being criticized throughout this anthology are: The universe owes its original and continued existence to an immaterial, omnipotent, omniscient, omnipresent and omnibenevolent God. . . . God is a cosmic mind as evidenced in the design and purposiveness of all things. . . . This God created the universe for a particular purpose. . . . God's purpose is to create

> Karl Marx is "one of history's great humanistic thinkers."
> —Paul Kurtz

Notes and Asides

> in His own image a creature who will glorify and stand in awe of Him as a sacred and mysterious object and will, only with His assistance, become a moral creature capable of receiving the gift of eternal immortality bestowed by His grace.[29]

Angeles explains that belief in the supernatural has all but vanished from our culture. He says that God has lost His spatial location as a monarch in heaven and His temporal precedence to the universe as its Creator *ex nihilo*. "It is not that God is being relegated to a remote region," Angeles insists. "It is not that God has become a bodiless abstraction (a sexless It). It is the realization that there is no God left to which to relate. Without God, what is left? Man and the Universe. That should be enough. That has to be enough because that is all there is."[30]

The Humanist theologians listed on the front cover of the book include: Ernest Nagel, Sidney Hook, Paul Edwards, Wallace I. Matson, Michael Scriven, Richard Robinson, Walter Kaufman, Sigmund Freud, Erich Fromm, Dewey, H. J. McCloskey, Antony Flew, Kai Nielsen, Lamont, Kurt E. M. Baier and Russell—all orthodox Humanists, all opposed to mankind clinging to unenlightened theistic beliefs.

Critiques of God finds all arguments in favor of the existence of God unconvincing. The cosmological argument[31] is considered weak, since if everything requires a cause then God must also need a cause. If one answers that God is self-caused, the Humanist counters with the question, why can't the world also be self-caused? To the more sophisticated answer that the cosmological argument does not say that *everything* has a cause, only that every *effect* has a cause, and that there cannot be an infinite regress of causes so there must be a First Cause, the Humanist rightly points out that even if the argument is sound, it doesn't prove that the First Cause is all-powerful, all-good, or in any sense personal.

The ontological argument (we have the idea of the absolutely Perfect; existence is an attribute of perfection; therefore the absolutely Perfect must exist) is considered weak since ideas do not demand the existence of their objects in reality. And the teleological argument, based on design and purpose in nature, is believed to have been shattered by Charles Darwin's theory of evolution. As one Humanist put it, "The danger posed to traditional theism by Darwinism was more fundamental: it lay in the undermining of the design axiom."[32] The existence of complex living organisms as proof of the existence of a supreme designer is denied since, according to the Humanist, living organisms are better explained by Darwinian biology (chance variations).

Notes and Asides

The mathematical structure of the universe, such as the precise mathematical configuration of the atomic chart, can also be explained without reference to God or any divine mathematician. This aspect of the teleological argument is dismissed by Ernest Nagel as follows: "The success of mathematical physics in giving us some understanding of the world around us does not yield the conclusion that only a mathematician could have devised the patterns of order we have discovered in nature."[33] Humanists believe that there would be some order even in a universe with only chaotic origins. They must believe in an ordered universe so that they may continue to trust science as the ultimate means of discerning truth. Ironically, the Humanist's incredible faith in science causes him to disbelieve anything that cannot be studied by the scientific method. Thus, Wallace I. Matson bases his atheism on his assumptions about science: "A creation out of nothing, by an infinite Being if you like, is a hypothesis that cannot be ruled out by the physical evidence presently available. But neither is it in any degree confirmed by that evidence, nor is it the only possible hypothesis."[34]

Matson and all other Humanists, with their rigid faith in science, place themselves in the position of Doubting Thomas—declaring, "Unless I see the nail marks in [Christ's] hands and put my fingers where the nails were, and put my hand into his side, I will not believe it" (John 20:25). One chapter in *Critiques of God*, "The Meaning of Life," by Kurt E. M. Baier, summarizes the Humanist's scientific rationale for denying the existence of God and draws the inescapable conclusion. Says Baier,

> The scientific approach demands that we look for a natural explanation of anything and everything. The scientific way of looking at and explaining things has yielded an immensely greater measure of understanding of, and control over, the universe than any other way. And when one looks at the world in this scientific way, there seems to be no room for a personal relationship between human beings and a supernatural perfect being ruling and guiding men. Hence many scientists and educated men have come to feel that the Christian attitudes towards the world and human existence are inappropriate. They have become convinced that the universe and human existence in it are without a purpose and therefore devoid of meaning.[35]

The existence of evil in the world is also cited by the Humanists as proof that an omnipotent, omniscient, and omnibenevolent God does not exist. If such a God existed, there would be no "superfluous" evil. The unvarnished facts of human existence rule against the existence of such a Creator, says one Humanist, and another contends, "We must conclude from the existence of evil that there cannot be an omnipotent, benevolent God."[36] Because the Humanist is strictly concerned with scientific, physical evidence, he weights the existence of evil more heavily than all the testimonies of individuals who have experienced God's saving power in their lives.

> " . . . the universe and human existence . . . are without a purpose and therefore devoid of meaning."
> —Kurt E. M. Baier

Theological Beliefs of Leading Humanists

Isaac Asimov served as the director of the American Humanist Association for 1989. Writing in *Free Inquiry*, Asimov leaves no doubt regarding his personal theology: "I am an atheist, out and out. It took me a long time to say it. I've been an atheist for years and years, but somehow I felt it was intellectually unrespectable to say one was an atheist, because it assumed knowledge that one didn't have. Somehow it was better to say one was a humanist or an agnostic. I finally decided that I'm a creature of emotion as well as reason. Emotionally I am an atheist. I don't have the evidence to prove that God doesn't exist, but I so strongly suspect he doesn't that I don't want to waste my time."[37] Other Humanists have likewise publicly reported their theological preference.

Julian Huxley said, "I disbelieve in a personal God in any sense in

Notes and Asides

which that phrase is ordinarily used."[38] He went on to say, "For my own part, the sense of spiritual relief which comes from rejecting the idea of God as a supernatural being is enormous."[39]

Arthur E. Briggs said, "[A] Humanist is one who believes in man as center of the universe."[40]

Humanist Arthur Davison Ficke wrote, "Humanism's central ideas, if I understand correctly, are . . . that nature alone, out of its infinite evolutionary complexity, gave rise to man, and that there exists no supernatural powers."[41]

Norman Mailer admits, "I suppose that I would have to list myself under 'atheistic humanism.'"[42]

Wendell Thomas confided, "As one endeavoring to work out a humanistic naturalism, I agree with the humanist belief in continuous emergent evolution, in the creative life for all, in a socialized and cooperative economic order. With humanists I protest against dualism and supernaturalism."[43]

"I propose to meet the issue squarely," says Harold R. Rafton, "by fostering Humanism, a rationalistic religion based on science, centered in man, rejecting supernaturalism but retaining our cherished moral values."[44]

Harvard's J. A. C. F. Auer defined Humanism as men who sit in judgment of God. "Man would worship God if man felt that he could admire God. But if not, if God fell below the level of moral excellence which he, man, set up, he would refuse his worship. That is Humanism—Man the measure of all things, including religion."[45]

Harold H. Titus says that Humanism is a "religion without God,"[46] adding, "Humanistic naturalists regard the universe as 'self-existing and not created.' They have abandoned all conceptions of a supernatural and all forms of cosmic support. Consequently, man must give up all teleological conceptions and realize that the world order is nonpurposive and neutral in its relation to human values."[47]

"Supernaturalism," says Read Bain, "in all its forms, is dying out. Science replaces revelation and tradition as the source of knowledge and the means of using it."[48]

According to John A. Hutchinson and James A. Martin, Jr., "Humanists hold belief in God to be scientifically untenable."[49] And Blanche Sanders insists, "A Humanist has cast off the ancient yoke of supernaturalism, with its burden of fear and servitude, and he moves on the earth a free man, a child of nature and not of any man-made gods."[50]

"I am an atheist, out and out."
—Isaac Asimov

Notes and Asides

Sagan's *Cosmos*—A Humanist Bible

While the Secular Humanist would certainly deny his adherence to any specific dogmatic theological text, Carl Sagan's *Cosmos* encapsulates the theological assumptions of orthodox Humanism so well it is not unfair to suggest that he has provided the world with a Humanist "Bible." Unfortunately, this Bible has been embraced by both Humanists and non-Humanists—in fact, no Humanist work in recent times has had greater influence. Both the public television series by the same name and the book proclaim atheistic assumptions to all who will listen—and sometimes to those who have no choice. The thirteen-hour-long TV presentation is required viewing for many public high school biology courses.

Such statements as "The Cosmos is all that is or ever was or ever will be,"[51] or Sagan's favorable quotation of Democritus to the effect that "Nothing exists but atoms and the void," present the Humanist theological position that only the cosmos—nature or the physical universe—is real. For Sagan all reality is explainable in material terms. "We are in the most profound sense, children of the Cosmos,"[52] says Sagan. He then says that our ancestors worshiped the Sun and that their worship was not foolish, since "It makes good sense to revere the Sun and the stars because we are their children." For Sagan the Cosmos is god. After describing the Hindu doctrine of the universe resulting from a divine dream, Sagan says, "These great ideas are tempered by another, perhaps still greater. It is said that men may not be the dreams of the gods, but rather that the gods are the dreams of men."[53] Instead of the Christian Bible's "In the beginning God," we have "In the beginning Man." Man created God in his own image.

Cosmos refers to the universe considered as a harmonious and orderly system.

The idea that Sagan wishes to get across in *Cosmos* is that it is possible to know the world "without the god hypothesis." According to Sagan, God, religion, and superstition are confined to minds tinged with fanaticism and bigotry. Religion represents the suppression of ideas while science represents the freeing of man from such suppression. And, from Sagan's point of view, the natural sciences "prove" his Humanistic theological interpretation of reality. *Cosmos* presents the Humanistic perspective unashamedly, declaring that the physical world is the ultimate reality and the natural sciences are the only means of understanding it. This doctrine is the foundation of Humanist theology and consequently the foundation for the entire Secular Humanist worldview.

Notes and Asides

Conclusion

The Secular Humanists' latest declaration (1980) does not diverge significantly from their orthodox theological views. Written by Kurtz and published in *Free Inquiry*, it contends that "Secular Humanists may be agnostics, atheists, rationalists, or skeptics, but they find insufficient evidence for the claim that some divine purpose exists for the universe. They reject the idea that God has intervened miraculously in history or revealed himself to a chosen few, or that he can save or redeem sinners."[54]

Agnosticism [Greek *a* (no) + *gnostic* (knowledge)] is the belief that the human mind cannot know whether or not there is a God.

Humanist theology, start to finish, is based on the denial of God and the supernatural. This denial, however, leads the Humanist to another necessary theological conclusion: man is the Supreme Authority. Of course, it is possible that Humanism's deification of Man may have preceded its atheistic assumptions, since the existence of God becomes a decided nuisance after one has declared one's self sovereign.

At bottom, it is of little importance whether atheism or the deification of man was Humanism's first theological presupposition; the crux of their theology remains anti-God. This is the heart and soul of Secular Humanism: man setting himself in opposition to God. Thus, the Humanist may declare with William Ernest Henley: "I am the master of my fate; I am the captain of my soul."[55] Unfortunately for the Humanist, this theology often strips him of all sense of purpose. As Ernest Nagel explains, atheism "can offer no hope of personal immortality, no threats of divine chastisement, no promise of eternal recompense for injustices suffered, no blueprints to sure salvation. . . . A tragic view of life is thus an uneliminable ingredient in atheistic thought."[56]

Isn't it better to live a life at least believing that there is a better future for us, that we didn't live our lives only to die and shrivel up?

[1]Corliss Lamont, *The Philosophy of Humanism* (New York: Frederick Ungar Publishing, 1982), p. 145.
[2]Paul Kurtz, "Is Everyone a Humanist?" in *The Humanist Alternative*, ed. Paul Kurtz (Buffalo: Prometheus Books, 1973), p. 177.
[3]Bertrand Russell, "My Mental Development," in *The Basic Writings of Bertrand Russell*, ed. Robert E. Egner and Lester E. Denonn (New York: Simon and Schuster, 1961) p. 40.
[4]Russell, "Why I Am Not A Christian," in *Basic Writings of Bertrand Russell*, p. 586.
[5]Miriam Allen deFord, "Heretical Humanism," in *The Humanist Alternative*, p. 82.
[6]Lamont, *Philosophy of Humanism*, pp. xviii, xix.
[7]Jean-Paul Sartre, cited by Thomas Molnar in *National Review*, June 11, 1982, p. 677.
[8]Lamont, *Philosophy of Humanism*, pp. 12, 13.
[9]Ibid., p. 14.
[10]Ibid., p. 22.
[11]Ibid., p. 123.
[12]Ibid., p. 145.
[13]*Humanist Manifesto I* (Buffalo: Prometheus Books, 1980), p. 8.
[14]John Dewey, *A Common Faith* (New Haven, CT: Yale University Press, 1934, renewed 1962), p. 84.
[15]Ibid., p. 31.
[16]Ibid.
[17]Ibid.
[18]Ibid.
[19]Ibid., p. 30.
[20]Ronald Nash, *The Closing of the American Heart* (Dallas, TX: Probe Books, 1990), p. 91.
[21]*Humanist Manifesto II* (Buffalo: Prometheus, 1980), p. 16.
[22]Supreme Court case 367 U.S., at p. 495. The Torcaso case was decided June 19, 1961.
[23]Roy Wood Sellars, "The Humanist Outlook," in *The Humanist Alternative*, p. 135.
[24] Gora, "Humanism and Atheism," in *The Humanist Alternative*, pp. 148, 149, 150.
[25]Kurtz, "Is Everyone a Humanist?" *The Humanist Alternative*, p. 177.
[26]Paul Kurtz, *The Fullness of Life* (New York: Horizon Press, 1974), p. 19.
[27]Ibid., pp. 35, 36.
[28]Chris Brockman, *What About Gods?* (Buffalo: Prometheus Books, 1978).
[29]Peter Angeles, ed., *Critiques of God* (Buffalo: Prometheus Books, 1976), pp. xi-xii.
[30]Ibid., p. xiii.
[31]See the Christian Philosophy section for elaborations on the cosmological, ontological, and teleological arguments.
[32]Wallace I. Matson, "The Argument from Design," in *Critiques of God*, p. 69.
[33]Ernest Nagel, "Philosophical Concepts of Atheism," in *Critiques of God*, p. 10.
[34]Matson, "The Argument from Design," in *Critiques of God*, p. 81.
[35]Kurt E. M. Baier, "The Meaning of Life," in *Critiques of God*, p. 296.
[36]H. J. McCloskey, "God and Evil," in *Critiques of God*, p. 223.
[37]Isaac Asimov, "An Interview with Isaac Asimov," *Free Inquiry*, Spring 1982, vol 2, no. 2, p. 9.
[38]Julian Huxley, *Religion Without Revelation* (New York: Mentor, 1957), pp. 17-8.
[39]Ibid., p. 32.
[40]Arthur E. Briggs, cited in "The Third Annual Humanist Convention," *The Humanist*, Spring 1945, p. 53.
[41]Arthur Davison Ficke, "It Depends on Definition," *The Humanist*, Autumn 1942, p. 107.
[42]Norman Mailer, cited in Warren Allen Smith, "Authors and Humanism: A Classification of Humanism, and Statements," *The Humanist*, no. 5, 1951, p. 201.
[43]Wendell Thomas, "*The Humanist Manifesto* Re-examined," *The Humanist*, Winter 1947, p. 118.
[44]Harold R. Rafton, "Released Time or Democracy," *The Humanist*, Spring 1947, p. 204.
[45]J. A. C. F. Auer, "Religion as the Integration of Human Life," *The Humanist*, Spring 1947, p. 161.
[46]Harold H. Titus, "Humanistic Naturalism," *The Humanist*, no. 1, 1954, p. 33.
[47]Ibid., p. 30.
[48]Read Bain, "Scientific Humanism," *The Humanist*, no. 3, 1954, p. 116.

[49]John A. Hutchison and James A. Martin, Jr., "The Humanist Faith Today," *The Humanist*, no. 4, 1954, p. 179.
[50]Blanche Sanders, *The Humanist*, no. 5, 1954, p. 226.
[51]Carl Sagan, *Cosmos* (New York: Random House, 1980), p. 4.
[52]Ibid., p. 242.
[53]Ibid., p. 258.
[54]"A Secular Humanist Declaration," *Free Inquiry*, vol. 1, no. 1 (Winter 1980/81), p. 5.
[55]William Ernest Henley, *Invictus* (1875; 1888), as cited in *The Victorian Age: Prose, Poetry, and Drama*, ed. John Wilson Bowyer and John Lee Brooks (Englewood Cliffs, NJ: Prentice-Hall, 1954), p. 754.
[56]Nagel, "Philosophical Concepts of Atheism," in *Critiques of God*, p. 17.

CHAPTER

4

MARXIST/ LENINIST THEOLOGY

"Our propaganda necessarily includes the propaganda of atheism. . . ."[1]

—V. I. Lenin

"Religion is opium for the people. Religion is a sort of spiritual booze. . . ."[2]

—V. I. Lenin

SUMMARY

Karl Marx (1818-1883) became an atheist while studying at the University of Berlin. His atheistic convictions predated his socialistic beliefs and were based not on the plight of oppressed masses but on Ludwig Feuerbach's philosophical conclusion pertaining to the existence of God. Marx's doctoral dissertation in the field of philosophy emphasized his "hatred of all the gods." He grew to perceive belief in God as a narcotic. His criticism and elimination of religion formed the foundation for all other criticisms; that is, Marx felt that atheism in practice consisted of the "forcible overthrow of all existing social conditions." Frederick Engels and V. I. Lenin agreed that religion was a drug or "spiritual booze" and must be combated. "Every idea of God," insisted Lenin, "is unutterable vileness." The Marxist/Leninist movement has not deviated from its founding fathers' attitude toward God specifically nor toward religion in general. *The Atheist's Handbook* declares, "The Communist Party has always taken and continues to take a position of militant atheism and of an implacable aggressive ideological struggle against religious befuddlement." Under the direction of the Council of Religious Affairs, the Central House of Scientific Atheism, the Institute for Scientific Atheism and its publication *Science and Religion*, the doctrine of atheism has maintained its foundational role in Communist ideology. Only in the sixth era of glasnost and perestroika has the Soviet Union taken a less aggressive stance toward religion, but these concessions are in no way a rejection of the basic tenets of Marxist/Leninist theology, which is still unapologetically atheistic.

Introduction

"We Communists are atheists,"[3] declared Chou En-lai at the Bandung Conference in April, 1955. This Chinese Communist leader captured the fundamental theological ingredient of Marxism/Leninism in one word: *atheism*. Today, Marxist/Leninists prefer two words: *scientific atheism*.

From the university days of Karl Marx to the present, official spokesmen for Marxism have been consistent about the content of their theology—God, a Supreme Being, a Creator, a Ruler, does not, can not, and must not exist.

Notes and Asides

God is considered an impediment, even an enemy, to a scientific, materialistic, socialistic world outlook. The idea of God, insists Lenin, encourages the working class (the proletariat) to drown its terrible economic plight of slavery and misery "in a sort of spiritual booze" of some mythical heaven ("pie in the sky by and by"). Even a single sip of this intoxicant decreases the revolutionary fervor necessary to exterminate the oppressing class (the bourgeois) and its perpetuation of inhuman miseries, thus causing the working class to forfeit their only chance of creating a truly human heaven on earth: global Communism.

Influences Affecting Marx's Theology

Religion as the opium of the masses, however, was a later development in the mind of Karl Marx. His atheism was conceived in the heady arena of philosophy, not economics or sociology. When Marx became an atheist at the University of Berlin, he was not thinking about surplus value or the dictatorship of the proletariat. He was thinking about the philosophies of Prometheus, Georg W. F. Hegel, and Ludwig Feuerbach.

"Philosophy makes no secret of it," said Marx. "Prometheus's admission: 'In sooth all gods I hate' is its own admission, its own motto against all gods, heavenly and earthly, who do not acknowledge the consciousness of man as the supreme divinity. There must be no god on a level with it."[4]

In a circle of radical Young Hegelians that included Ludwig Feuerbach, Arnold Ruge, Max Stirner, Moses Hess, and eventually Frederick Engels, Marx became an atheist. Atheism was embraced by the group, with Feuerbach proclaiming, "It is clear as the sun and evident as the day that there is no God; and still more, that there can be no God."[5]

"It is clear as the sun and evident as the day that there is no God; and still more, that there can be no God."
—Ludwig Feuerbach

"My atheism," Feuerbach further declared, "[is] merely the unconscious and actual atheism of modern humanity and science, made conscious, untwisted and openly declared."[6] Marx accepted Feuerbach's thesis: that the turning point of history will be the moment man realizes that the only god of man is man himself.

Feuerbach believed that the notion of God emerges from man's projection of his human attributes (consciousness, intelligence, love) into an imaginary heaven and wrapping such attributes around a nonexistent heavenly figure. For example, the concept of spirit emerges by projecting human intelligence or understanding into an imaginary heaven. The idea of God as spirit, therefore, is merely man's intelligence in abstract form. Projecting human love into the heavens creates the concept of God as love. According to Catholic theologian Hans

Notes and Asides

Küng, this view implies that "God appears as a projected, hypostatized reflection of man, behind which nothing exists in reality."[7]

Accepting Feuerbach's conclusion that God is a projection of man writ large, Marx boasted, "Man is the highest being for man." Indeed, Marx explains that this view signals the demise of all religion: "The criticism of religion ends with the teaching that man is the highest being for man. . . ."[8]

For Marx, then, man is God. Man created God in his own image. Man created religion in order to worship himself. The notion that God is merely a projection of man is contained in Marx's assertion that man "looked for a superhuman being in the fantastic reality of heaven and found nothing there but the reflection of himself."[9]

In 1841, Marx completed his doctoral dissertation on atheistic philosophy among the ancient Greeks. He titled it *The Difference between Democritean and Epicurean Philosophy of Nature*, prefacing it with a profession of atheism, a proclamation that human consciousness was the supreme deity.

> "The first requisite for the happiness of the people is the abolition of religion."
> —Karl Marx

By 1844 Marx had published his *Critique of Hegel's Philosophy of Law*. The *Critique* opened with the assertion, "For Germany the criticism of religion is in the main complete, and criticism of religion is the premise of all criticism. The profane existence of error is discredited after its heavenly speech of altars and hearths has been rejected. . . . The basis of irreligious criticism is: Man makes religion, religion does not make man. . . . The abolition of religion as the illusory happiness of the people is required for their real happiness."[10]

Marx's emphasis on his belief that criticism of religion (i.e., atheism) is the premise of all criticism reveals the importance Marx placed on denying God. "Absolute criticism," he wrote, "still regards the abolition of religion, atheism, as the condition for civil equality."[11] Atheism is the cornerstone of Marx's thought and life, and atheism is today the theological cornerstone of the Marxist/Leninist worldview. Atheism is the "premise of all criticism." Marxism is atheism in theory and practice. The abolition of religion is the theory of atheism in practice.

Marx observes, "The philosophers have only interpreted the world, in various ways; the point, however, is to change it."[12] Since the institutions of society rested on a foundation of theism, Marx determined to change all social institutions and re-establish them on atheistic foundations. To this end, Marx and Engels, in *The Communist Manifesto*, called for the "forcible overthrow" of all existing social conditions.

Notes and Asides

Significance of Theology in Marxist Theory

While some attempts have been made to minimize atheism's role in Marxist theory (especially in recruiting naive Christians and other religious people to participate in Marxist/Leninist activity[13]—such as the Liberation Theology movement[14]), Marxists are privately aware of their fundamental need for an atheistic foundation. Vincent Miceli, in *The Gods of Atheism*, sums up the reason Marxism must be built upon atheistic assumptions: "If, according to Marx, 'the criticism of religion is the premise of all criticism,' then atheism is established by him as the major premise, the seminal proposition for a communist humanism. And if in the beginning is the revolution against God as man's first creative work, then the communist program must progress from this initial liberation to the final self-glorification of man."[15]

Marx's search for "scientific truths" to bolster his atheism led him to conclusions that shaped his communist theory. As he moved from the philosophical basis for his atheism into the socio-economic realm, he reached the conclusion (based upon his atheistic assumptions) that religion is merely an anti-depressant for the oppressed working class. His summary of this explanation has been quoted throughout the world, even though it was not his original basis for atheism. "Religion," said Marx, "is the sigh of the oppressed creature, the sentiment of a heartless world, as it is the spirit of spiritless conditions. It is the opium of the people."[16] Eventually, when the whole world has embraced communism (as it is destined to do[17]), no one will be oppressed, and therefore no one will cling to the unscientific fairy tales of religion. Marx explains, "Communism is that stage of historical development which makes all existing religions superfluous and supersedes them."[18]

Marx's friend and fellow atheist, Engels, declared, "We want to sweep away everything that claims to be supernatural and superhuman, for the root of all untruth and lying is the pretension of the human and the natural to be superhuman and supernatural. For that reason we have once and for all declared war on religion and religious ideas and care little whether we are called atheists or anything else."[19]

In a famous passage in a letter to Eugene Dühring, Engels set down his position on the origin of the idea of God. He did this in an effort to explain humanity's faith and religious convictions in a materialistic way. Pursuing the origins of religion from an "evolutionary conception of the universe" in which there is no room for a Supreme Being, Engels explains that early man created the concept of God. This concept was initially based on external forces of Nature and later the social forces

> "Religion . . . is the opium of the people."
>
> —Karl Marx

Notes and Asides

"[R]eligion, and not atheism, is the true remedy for superstition."
—Edmund Burke

surrounding mankind. Experiencing Nature's great power, for example, drove early man to believe in some supernatural power. Ultimately man projected the attributes of both Nature and Society into "one almighty god," and monotheism was born. "All religion," says Engels, "is nothing but the fantastic reflection in men's minds of those external forces which control their daily life, a reflection in which the terrestrial forces assume the form of supernatural forces. In the beginning of history it was the forces of Nature which were at first so reflected, and in the course of further evolution they underwent the most manifold and varied personification among the various people. . . . But it is not so long before side by side with the forces of nature, social forces begin to be active, forces which present themselves to man as equally extraneous and at first equally inexplicable, dominating them with the same apparent necessity as the forces of nature themselves. . . . At a still further stage of evolution, all the natural and social attributes of the innumerable gods are transferred to one almighty god, who himself once more is only the reflection of the abstract man. Such was the origin of monotheism, which was historically the last product of the vulgarized philosophy of the later Greeks and found its incarnation in the exclusively national god of the Jews, Jehovah."[20]

As with Marx, Engels foresaw a time when all religion would cease. He contended that when society adopts socialism, i.e., when society takes possession of all means of production and uses them on a planned basis (thus eliminating the working class's economic bondage), religion itself will vanish.[21]

Lenin's Theological Contributions to Marxism

Some years later, V. I. Lenin, whom biographer Robert Payne portrays as one with an undisguised hatred of Christ,[22] commented on Engels' letter to Dühring, writing, "The philosophical basis of Marxism, as Marx and Engels repeatedly declared, is dialectical materialism . . . a materialism which is absolutely atheistic and positively hostile to all religion. Let us recall that the whole of Engels' Anti-Dühring, which Marx read in manuscript, is an indictment of the materialist and atheist Dühring for not being a consistent materialist and for leaving loopholes for religion and religious philosophy."[23] Elsewhere, Lenin made it clear that fighting religion was an essential ingredient in a materialistic reality. "We must combat religion," he said, "that is the ABC of all materialism, and consequently of Marxism."[24]

In his "Socialism and Religion" address, Lenin insists that the Communist program is based on the scientific, materialistic world outlook and therefore "our propaganda necessarily includes the propa-

Notes and Asides

ganda of atheism."[25] Lenin went on to urge his fellow communists to follow Engels' advice and translate and widely disseminate the atheistic literature of the eighteenth-century French Enlightenment.

Lenin admired the staunch atheism of the eighteenth-century French Encyclopaedists and called for Marxists to follow their example. "Marxism is materialism," he wrote. "As such, it is as relentlessly hostile to religion as was the materialism of the eighteenth-century Encyclopaedists or the materialism of Feuerbach."[26]

Exactly how hostile Lenin felt fellow Marxists should be toward religion can be seen in a letter he wrote to Maxim Gorky in 1913. Lenin had criticized Gorky for being a "god-builder," since Gorky was attempting to turn socialism into a form of religion. Lenin made it clear that any idea of God was taboo, claiming, "Every religious idea, every idea of God, even flirting with the idea of God, is unutterable vileness . . . vileness of the most dangerous kind, 'contagion' of the most abominable kind. Millions of sins, filthy deeds, acts of violence and physical contagions . . . are far less dangerous than the subtle, spiritual idea of a God decked out in the smartest 'ideological' customes. . . . Every defense or justification of the idea of God, even the most refined, the best intentioned, is a justification of reaction."[27]

> **"We must combat religion, that is the ABC of . . . Marxism."**
> **—V. I. Lenin**

Clearly, Lenin's theology unerringly corresponds with that of Marx and Engels. Together they established the foundations for future communist declarations of atheism. "For Marx and the classical Marxist authors," wrote Küng, "in their personal life, in their culture, in their system and in their practice—atheism was and remained of central importance and essentially connected with their theory of society and history."[28]

Manifestations of Atheism in the Soviet Union

Marxist theology has remained consistent throughout the history of Communism. From Marx's time to the present, Communists everywhere have vehemently denied the existence of God. The *Great Soviet Encyclopedia*, published in Moscow in 1950, called on the Communist Party to oppose religion and "to fight for the 'full victory' of atheism."[29]

The Young Communist League's list of Ten Commandments contains the declaration "If you are not a convinced atheist, you cannot be a good Communist. . . . Atheism is indissolubly bound to Communism."[30]

Notes and Asides

In 1955, Soviet premier Nikita Khrushchev said, "Communism has not changed its attitude of opposition to religion. We are doing everything we can to eliminate the bewitching power of the opium of religion."[31] Khrushchev's antireligious campaign from 1959 to 1964 was responsible for reducing the 20,000 Russian Orthodox churches by half. The number today, according to James Thrower, is about 7,000.[32]

Also in 1955, an article by M. T. Iovchuk entitled "The Role of Socialist Ideology in the Struggle against the Survivals of Capitalism" was published. The article declares that the Communist Party aims at "doing away with the remnants of the old order, including the religious remnant. An intensification of scientifico-atheistic propaganda is needed in order to raise the cultural level of Soviet citizens and to further their education for communism."[33]

The Atheist's Handbook was published in Moscow in 1959 in conjunction with Khrushchev's campaign to eliminate the remaining traces of religion in the U.S.S.R. This text attacks the Bible, the Koran, Christianity and Islam. "Science," says the *Handbook*, "has long since established that Jesus Christ never existed, that the figure of the alleged founder of Christianity is purely mythical."[34] The Apostle Paul, too, turns out to be "a mythical figure."[35]

This type of unfounded criticism of the Bible was described by Richard Wurmbrand in his work *My Answer to the Moscow Atheists*: "But Bible criticism as practiced by our atheist opponents is of an entirely different type. They deny the most important events of Bible narrative and relegate the principal Biblical personalities to the realm of myth."[36]

These denials, however, are never wholly successful—many people living in a communist state ignore the propaganda and continue to worship God. Thus, Marxists must take more drastic measures. They must discourage theism by destroying the classes that cling to such "superstitions." *The Atheist's Handbook* openly proclaims,

> As a result of the victory of socialism in our country, the exploiter classes which spread and supported religion and religious and ecclesiastical organizations were destroyed. In this way, the social roots of religion were undermined. As a result of the cultural revolution which has taken place in our country and the spread of scientific atheist propaganda, the overwhelming majority of the population of the Soviet Union has made a complete break with religion and has adopted the position of atheism.[37]

This "cultural revolution" led to the destruction of a ghastly number of men, women, and children. Russian author Alexander Solzhenitsyn

Notes and Asides

places the figure at 60 million, "not counting war casualties."[38] First-hand testimonies from inside the Soviet Union have recently confessed "mass arrests, deportations, tortures, imprisonments and executions that befell millions [probably fifty million] of innocent citizens in the

CLOSE-UP

Karl Marx (1818-1883)

Karl Marx has had more influence on the modern world than any other 19th century figure (with the possible exception of Charles Darwin). His theories, refined by Frederick Engels and later by V. I. Lenin, form a worldview which has directly influenced the lives of millions of people. And yet Marx lived his life in relative obscurity. After choosing to believe that God does not exist and later accepting much of Ludwig Feuerbach's materialistic philosophy, Marx spent a number of years writing radical newspaper articles and being exiled from various countries. He finally settled in London in 1849, and lived there the rest of his life, attempting to support his family by writing articles and books. This, however, proved impossible--indeed, Marx once admitted, "*Das Kapital* will not even pay for the cigars I smoked writing it." Thus, Marx found himself relying on Marxism's co-founder, Frederick Engels, to support him and his family. Engels did so by selling his partnership in his father's textile business, allowing Marx to live off the proceeds of the sale from 1869 till his death. This measure of independence should have freed Marx to become a prolific writer, but he was constantly hampered by illnesses, including hereditary liver derangement, frequent outbreaks of carbuncles and furuncles, toothaches, lung abscesses, and eye inflammations. He published only five books while he was alive. Two of these, the *Communist Manifesto* (co-written with Engels) and *Das Kapital*, are generally described as forming the basic foundation for Marxism. However, both *Critique of Political Economy* and *The German Ideology* (published posthumously) also make significant contributions to Marxist theory, as does an essay entitled "Critique of the Gotha Programme." Marx died as he had lived, in obscurity. Six people attended his funeral.

Notes and Asides

USSR and throughout its satellite nations."[39]

People are killed or persecuted for their religious beliefs because religion is inimical to the communist social order, and the Communist Party is said to continue to take a position of "militant atheism" and an "implacable aggressive ideological struggle against religious befuddlement."[40] It is this "militant atheism" that is being totally overlooked in the West, according to Solzhenitsyn, and especially being downplayed by recent Soviet emigres who "do not even blame the Soviet system for the sixty million lives it destroyed, or reproach it for its militant atheism."[41]

The objective of the Marxist/Leninists is to destroy religion. The *Handbook* states, "Communism does not leave a place for any kind of religion."[42] The text goes on to delineate the means of accomplishing this task: (1) eliminate the exploiter class, (2) establish a dictatorship of the proletariat, and (3) build a Communist society. To build a Communist society, each Party member must "be an atheist and conduct active anti-religious propaganda among those not belonging to the party."[43] "Atheistic propaganda must occupy a paramount place in all our ideological work," insists the *Handbook*.

When *The Atheist's Handbook* was published, the Society for the Dissemination of Political and Scientific Knowledge was in charge of propagating atheism. That activity is now the responsibility of the Central House of Scientific Atheism and the Institute for Scientific Atheism (which publishes *Science and Religion*). Established in 1963, both organizations seek to show religious believers "the illusions of religious points of view" and to "spread the atheistic world view"—which is "a communistic world view for the people."

"Atheistic propaganda must occupy a paramount place in all our ideological work."
—*The Atheist's Handbook*

The Central House and Institute outline three main reasons Marxists must adhere to atheism: (1) clergy are anti-communist, (2) religion is philosophically wrong, thereby giving believers a false sense of reality, and (3) atheism supports the workers.[44]

The Institute is headquartered in Moscow as a division of the Academy of Social Sciences, and one of its most important tasks is to design the curriculum for the required university course on scientific atheism. The Institute for Scientific Atheism has close ties with the Soviet Museum of the History of Religion and Atheism located in the former Kazan Cathedral in Leningrad.[45]

Dr. Charles J. McFadden had the opportunity to visit the Kazan Cathedral (built in the early 1800s as a monument to the defeat of Napoleon), which is now a Museum of Atheism. Says McFadden, "Every conceivable device is used to ridicule religion as a crude superstition. A poster boasts that in 1917 there were 466 churches in

Notes and Asides

Leningrad, while there are now only 14; in 1917, there were 4,214 members of the clergy, while there are now only 63."[46]

Education and Atheism in the Marxist State

Dr. Victor D. Timofeyev of the Institute for Scientific Atheism says the main purpose of the Institute is to "spread the atheistic world view, the atheistic behavior pattern, the atheistic way of understanding life, understanding ethics, and so on. Beginning in school, we work to bring up all the people in the atheistic world view."[47]

Atheism is preached in the classrooms of the Marxist state. Regarding the role of atheism in the classroom, Sinaida Vetschenko says that although there are no special teachers of atheism in the Soviet Union, "incorporated into every subject is education in the spirit of Marxism, of which atheistic ideas are a part. . . . Besides their regular classes, there is also a program after school when children attend a special study club. Here the teachers utilize movies and slides and lectures on atheism."[48]

Yevgenia Ossipova, a professor of atheism at the Institute of Culture, describes how the subject is handled at the university level: "The study of atheism is incorporated into the philosophy course. We teach this subject at the Institute of Culture for just one semester. This is done through lecture-study classes and seminars. The students write special papers and then they have an exam. Atheism and science, atheism and morals, atheism and art, atheism and religion in the socialist society—these are typical sub-subjects of this course."[49]

In the 1930s the chairman of the Communist Party USA, William Z. Foster, wrote a book entitled *Toward Soviet America*. In it he insisted that in the Soviet Union "religion is being liquidated," and furthermore, in a Soviet America, "Science will become materialistic" and "God will be banished from the laboratories as well as from the schools."[50]

Marxists also seek to indoctrinate youth through extra-curricular activities. Thus, in communist Russia in 1925, the League of Militant Godless was established to unite all anti-religious propaganda work under the general directions of the Party. It organized atheist lectures and within ten years had five million members. "Children eight to fourteen," says Humanist Paul Kurtz, "were enrolled in groups of 'Godless Youth.' These were disbanded before the war [World War II], though the League of Communist Youth (Komsomol) continues its atheist indoctrination to this day."[51] Clearly, the official religion forced on youth in a communist state is atheism.

Notes and Asides

The Role of the Church in Marxist Theology

Although the July 10, 1918 Constitution of the U.S.S.R. recognized freedom of both "religious and anti-religious propaganda" as the right of every citizen, the Soviet state has kept religion at arm's length and has constantly worked to suppress it. Article 65 of the 1918 Constitution declared priests and clerics to be "servants of the bourgeoisie" and disfranchised. This meant, among other things, that priests were denied ration cards and their children were barred from schools above the elementary grade. Kurtz points out that from 1918 to 1921 "religious persecution continued unabated. . . . All church property was nationalized, and it is estimated that tens of thousands of bishops, clerics, and laymen were killed or imprisoned."[52]

By May 1929, Article 18 of the Constitution was amended to read "freedom of religious worship and anti-religious propaganda." At the same time the Commissioner of Education replaced a policy of nonreligious teaching in the schools to one calling for "definitely antireligious instruction."[53] According to Robert Conquest, the Central Committee held a special conference on anti-religious matters in the summer of 1929. In June came the All-Union Congress of Militant Atheists. "And through the next year, all over the USSR, the attack on religion sharpened from month to month."[54] During the drive toward collectivism in late 1929, the suffering of hundreds of thousands "was not the result of their social status but of their religious belief."[55] A Law of Religious Associations was also enacted in 1929. According to Kurtz, "it banned the religious instruction of children by anyone except their parents. To convene a Sunday-school or catechism class was a criminal offense. All religious groups had to be registered."[56] Leonard Schapiro writes in *The Communist Party of the Soviet Union*, "In practice the Church was from the start placed under a handicap, since it was the Vecheka [the Soviet Secret Police] which in the last resort had the power of determining what was 'religious propaganda' and what was 'counter-revolutionary propaganda.'"[57]

In the Soviet Union, church after church has been declared counterrevolutionary and shut down. The Holy Trinity Monastery in the village of Demydivka (Poltava Province) was turned into a library and in 1930 was demolished. Its materials were used to build barns and a tobacco store on the Petrovsky collective farm.

The tenth-century Desyatynna church in Kiev and the Mykhaylivsky and Bratsky monasteries were destroyed. St. Sophia Cathedral and other churches in Kiev were turned into museums or anti-religious centers. Churches were turned into cinemas, radio stations, granaries, machine repair shops, etc. According to Robert Conquest, before the revolution Moscow had 460 Orthodox churches. On January 1, 1930,

Notes and Asides

the number was down to 224, and by January 1, 1933, the figure was about 100.

Even though the 1936 Constitution again guaranteed "freedom of religion," Conquest notes that the Old Believers or Evangelicals would try to register at the village Soviet only to be told to collect fifty signatures. Upon collection, "all fifty would be arrested as members of a secret counter-revolutionary organization."[58]

The churches allowed to remain in existence in Russia are restricted to inconsequential roles and given no freedom. Yevgenia Ossipova says, "In our country, the church is separated from the government and so there is no religious upbringing in the schools or on television. The Church has the right to function in the rank of a cult. There is no mass media advertising of the church and there is no church propaganda. But atheists have the right to propagate and use all television and all mass media for atheistic propaganda."[59]

> "[I]t is estimated that tens of thousands of bishops, clerics, and laymen were killed or imprisoned."
>
> —Paul Kurtz

The resulting atheistic influence on the church was identified by Solzhenitsyn when he wrote to the Russian Orthodox Patriarch Pimen in 1972 and told him, "A church dictatorially ruled by atheists is a sign not seen in two thousand years. Also under their control is the church economy and the use of church resources, those coins deposited by the fingers of the devout."[60]

Present Trends in Marxist Theology

Of course, our discussion of the prevalence of atheistic influence in the modern Soviet state has focused exclusively on the USSR prior to the advent of glasnost and perestroika. Have these policies, which appear to soften Soviet adherence to hard-line Marxist doctrine, eradicated the need for an atheistic stance at the base of Marxist worldview?

Not at all. Regardless of Soviet policy, atheism must always serve as the cornerstone for the dialectical materialism central to Marxist thought (as demonstrated throughout this chapter). Further, the Soviet Marxist/Leninist party still espouses atheism, albeit in a less militant manner.

The 1991 Director of the Institute of Scientific Atheism, Viktor Garadza, called only for a change of direction in atheistic propaganda, maintaining that previous methods were ineffective and that "today no one disputes the necessity of restructuring the entire system of atheistic education."[61] This new approach, according to Garadza, should "break established dogmas which prevent a sober new look at the theory and practice of atheism, its history, methods of propaganda, and the system of atheistic education."[62]

Since Soviet theists are now looked upon as necessary partners in

Notes and Asides

the task of salvaging the bankrupt economy, the 27th Party Congress program called for atheistic programs that would respect the beliefs of theists. Accordingly, "the time of bulldozer and dynamite atheism has passed."[63] Theoretically, this attitude displays the new-found understanding that terrorist tactics toward the church are counterproductive at best.

Still, atheism is a central state doctrine. Glasnost and perestroika have only rendered Soviet atheistic propaganda more subtle. It is every bit as determined. For example, a 1989 book directed at the Soviet military contends, "in the area of people's existence, religious traditions, customs, and norms manifest their own power. And they cause enormous injury to people. . . . Religion causes huge damage even to a person's psychology."[64]

Lowering the volume of atheistic rhetoric does not mean Marxism is giving up its theological base. It simply means that the hostility toward religion in general and God in particular will be better channeled and controlled. This is summarized by A. James Melnick, a critic of Marxism: "It remains clear that 'atheistic upbringing' will continue under the political reforms. While the process of 'dialogue' takes place on one level, atheistic socialization or 'atheistization' will continue on another. There are numerous examples. Targeting foreign students in the USSR for atheism is one: 'Atheistic work with foreign students demands maximum tact. . . .' Further, the reforms are intended to raise 'scientific atheism' and 'atheistic upbringing' to new levels of sophistication. Nevertheless, the 'old' characteristics have not yet disappeared entirely and still manifest themselves on occasion. A 1989 work directed at atheistic work in the military stated that, among Pentecostals, the occurrences of parents killing their babies 'are far from rare.' Such commentary is reminiscent of some of the crudest propaganda of the 'pre-glasnost' past."[65]

Conclusion

Solzhenitsyn revealed the practical conclusions of Marxist/Leninist Scientific Atheism in his 1980 book *The Mortal Danger*. He writes:

> For those who genuinely love Russia no reconciliation with communism has ever been possible or ever will be. That is why communism has always been most ruthless of all in its treatment of Christians and advocates of national rebirth. In the early years this meant wholesale execution; later the victims were left to rot in the camps. But to this very day the persecution continues inexorably. Vladimir Shelkov was done to death by

Notes and Asides

> twenty-five years in the camps, Ogurtsov has already served thirteen years and Osipov twelve; this winter the completely apolitical "Christian Committee for the Defense of Believer's Rights in the U.S.S.R." was smashed: the independent priests Father Gleb Yakunin and Father Dimitri Dudko have been arrested, and the members of Ogorodnikov's Christian seminar have been hauled off to prison. The authorities make no attempt to hide the fact that they are crushing the Christian faith with the full force of their machinery of terror.[66]

And while today some Marxists are seeking "a common language with believers"[67]—even to the extent of allowing the Campus Crusade "Jesus" film in many of their churches and schools—an editor of the journal *Science and Religion*, published by the Institute for Scientific Atheism, told a group of American Humanists that the Communist Party "had not abandoned its belief in atheism"[68] but rather that Soviet society will become fully atheistic "only after true socialism is achieved in the future."[69]

> "They that deny a God destroy man's nobility . . . "
> —Sir Francis Bacon

In theory and practice, therefore, Marxism/Leninism reflects its atheistic base. To be a Marxist/Leninist demands adherence to atheism. To be a good Marxist/Leninist entails being a propagator of atheism. To be the best Marxist/Leninist is to see atheism as part of the scientific, materialistic, socialistic world outlook and to strive to eradicate all religious sentiment.

Theists everywhere recognize, as did Feodor Dostoevski, that "The problem of Communism is not an economic problem. The problem of Communism is the problem of atheism."[70]

[1]V. I. Lenin, *Complete Collected Works*, forty-five volumes (Moscow: Progress Publishers, 1978), vol. 10, p. 86.
[2]Ibid., p. 83.
[3]See James D. Bales, *Communism: Its Faith and Fallacies* (Grand Rapids: Baker Book House, 1962), p. 37.
[4]Karl Marx and Frederick Engels, *On Religion* (New York: Schocken Books, 1974), p. 15.
[5]See Richard Wurmbrand, *My Answer to the Moscow Atheists* (New Rochelle, NY: Arlington House, 1975), p. 16.
[6]Ludwig Feuerbach, *Nachgelassene Aphorismen*, in *Sämtliche Werke*, ed. Bolin and Jodl (Stuttgart: 1911), vol. 10, p. 345. Cited in Hans Küng, *Does God Exist?* (Garden City, NY: Doubleday and Company, 1980), p. 211.
[7]Küng, *Does God Exist?*, p. 200.
[8]Marx and Engels, *Karl Marx—Frederick Engels: Collected Works*, 40 volumes (New York: International Publishers, 1976), vol. 3, p. 182.
[9]Ibid., vol. 3, p. 175.
[10]Ibid. Marx's reference to Germany and the completion of the criticism of religion refers to Feuerbach's critique of religion and his conclusion that God is a reflection of man.
[11]Ibid., vol. 4, p. 89.
[12]Marx, *Theses on Feuerbach*, in Marx, *On Historical Materialism* (New York: International Publishers, 1974), p. 13.
[13]Marx admits in *The Communist Manifesto*, "Nothing is easier than to give Christian asceticism a Socialist tinge. . . . Christian Socialism is but the Holy Water with which the priest consecrates the heart-burnings of the aristocrat."
[14]For an excellent discussion of Liberation Theology, see Malachi Martin, *The Jesuits* (New York: Simon and Schuster, 1987).
[15]Vincent P. Miceli, *The Gods of Atheism* (Harrison, NY: Roman Catholic Books, 1971), p. 102.
[16]Marx and Engels, *Collected Works*, vol. 3, p. 175.
[17]See the Marxist Politics chapter.
[18]Marx and Engels, *Collected Works*, vol 6, p. 103.
[19]Ibid., vol. 3, p. 463.
[20]Frederick Engels, *Anti-Dühring*, in Marx and Engels, *On Religion*, pp. 147-8.
[21]Ibid., p. 149.
[22]Robert Payne, *The Life and Death of Lenin* (New York: Simon and Schuster, 1964), p. 550.
[23]Lenin, *Collected Works*, vol. 15, p. 402.
[24]Ibid., p. 405.
[25]Ibid., vol. 10, p. 86.
[26]Ibid., vol. 15, p. 405.
[27]Ibid., vol. 35, p. 122.
[28]Küng, *Does God Exist?* p. 257.
[29]*The Great Soviet Encyclopedia* (Moscow: 1950), cited in Bales, *Communism: Its Faith and Fallacies*, p. 163.
[30]Young Communist League's "Ten Commandments of Communism," cited in Bales, *Communism: Its Faith and Fallacies*, p. 37.
[31]Nikita Khrushchev, speech, September 22, 1955, cited in Bales, *Communism: Its Faith and Fallacies*, pp. 165-6.
[32]James Thrower, "Some Reflections on Religion in the U.S.S.R.," *The Humanist*, January/February 1987, p. 23.
[33]M. T. Iovchuk, "The Role of Socialist Ideology in the Struggle Against the Survivals of Capitalism," cited in Gustav A. Wetter, *Dialectical Materialism* (Westport, CT: Greenwood Press, Publishers, 1977), pp. 245-6.
[34]*The Atheist's Handbook*, [Sputnik Ateista], (Moscow: 1959), reproduced in English by U.S. Joint Publications Research Service (Washington, D.C.), p. 117.
[35]Ibid., p. 69.
[36]Wurmbrand, *My Answer to the Moscow Atheists*, p. 70.
[37]*The Atheist's Handbook*, p. 201.

[38]Alexander Solzhenitsyn, *The Mortal Danger* (New York: Harper and Row, 1980), p. 58.
[39]Malachi Martin, *The Keys of This Blood* (New York: Simon and Schuster, 1990), p. 177.
[40]*The Atheist's Handbook*, p. 204.
[41]Solzhenitsyn, *The Mortal Danger*, p. 23.
[42]*The Atheist's Handbook*, p. 33.
[43]Ibid., pp. 222, 225.
[44]Boris M. Marjamov, cited in "A Face-to-Face Interview with Soviet Atheist Leaders," ed. Frederick Edwords, *The Humanist*, January/February 1987, p. 9.
[45]Robert M. Hemstreet, "Religious Humanism Meets Scientific Atheism," *The Humanist*, January/February 1987, p. 6.
[46]Charles McFadden, *The Philosophy of Communism* (Kenosha, WI: Cross Publications, 1963), p. 121.
[47]Victor D. Timofeyev, cited in "A Face-to-Face Interview with Soviet Atheist Leaders," ed. Edwords, *The Humanist*, January/February 1987, p. 9.
[48]Sinaida Vetschenko, cited in "A Face-to-Face Interview with Soviet Atheist Leaders," p. 9.
[49]Yevgenia Ossipova, cited in Ibid., p. 10.
[50]William Z. Foster, *Toward Soviet America* (Balboa Island, CA: Elgin Publications, 1961), pp. 113, 317.
[51]Paul Kurtz, "Militant Atheism Versus Freedom of Conscience," *Free Inquiry*, Fall 1989, p. 28.
[52]Ibid.
[53]Robert Conquest, *The Harvest of Sorrow* (New York: Oxford University Press, 1986), p. 203.
[54]Ibid.
[55]Ibid., p. 204.
[56]Kurtz, "Militant Atheism Versus Freedom of Conscience," *Free Inquiry*, Fall 1989, p. 28.
[57]Leonard Schapiro, *The Communist Party of the Soviet Union*, rev. ed. (New York: Random House, 1971), p. 346.
[58]Conquest, *Harvest of Sorrow*, p. 209. Many of the facts concerning the closing of the churches are found in Conquest's chapter "The Churches and the People."
[59]Yevgenia Ossipova, cited in "A Face-to-Face Interview with Soviet Atheist Leaders," p. 10.
[60]Solzhenitsyn, cited in James Thrower, "Some Reflections on Religion in the USSR," *The Humanist*, January/February, 1987, p. 23.
[61]Viktor L. Garadza, *Nauka i religija*, 1 (1989), p. 2. Cited in A. James Melrick, *Studies in Soviet Thought* 40:223-229, 1990, p. 223.
[62]Ibid.
[63]A. Cudakov, *Komsomol'skaja pravda*, October 11, 1988, p. 2. Cited in Ibid.
[64]I. S. Iscenko and S. I. Iscenko, "Iz plena sueverii: zametki ob ateisticeskom vospitanii vojnov," M. Voenizdat, 1989, pp. 8-9. Cited in Ibid., p. 225.
[65]*Studies in Soviet Thought* 40: 1990, p. 227.
[66]Solzhenitsyn, *The Mortal Danger*, pp. 34-5.
[67]Kurtz, "Militant Atheism Versus Freedom of Conscience," p. 30.
[68]Ibid.
[69]Ibid., the editor quoted by Kurtz.
[70]Whittaker Chambers, *Witness* (New York: Random House, 1952), p. 712.

CHAPTER

5

BIBLICAL CHRISTIAN THEOLOGY

"In the beginning God created the heavens and the earth."

—Genesis 1:1

"In the beginning was the Word, and the Word was with God, and the Word was God."

—John 1:1

"Theism, the belief that God is, and atheism, the belief that God is not, are not simply two beliefs. They are two fundamental ways of seeing the whole of existence. The one, theism, sees existence as ultimately meaningful, as having a meaning beyond itself; the other sees existence as having no meaning beyond itself."[1]

—Stephen D. Schwartz

"Belief in God is the heart and center of the Christian religion—as it is of Judaism and Islam."[2]

—Alvin Plantinga

SUMMARY

Christian theology affirms the existence of an intelligent, powerful, loving, just God. From the Christian perspective, "In the beginning God" (Genesis 1:1) is the foundation for all meaning. It explains why there is something rather than nothing. The vastness and orderly integrity of the universe reflect the infinite nature of God's mind (John 1:1-3) and power (Psalm 19:1f; Romans 1:20). The Christian sees purpose and design throughout the universe—from the smallest subatomic particle to the farthest island universe. Chance—a series of pure accidents, mindless natural processes and random mutations—cannot explain a universe manifesting mathematical precision (Sir James Jeans referred to God as "The Great Mathematician"), principles of order or disorder (like the laws of thermodynamics), and effects of intelligence and information (like DNA) necessary for life itself. Facing evidences of a cosmic blueprint everywhere, the Christian reaches the only reasonable conclusion: he posits a powerful, intelligent Designer—God. Christianity further proclaims that this powerful, intelligent God who created all things in heaven and earth is the same God who took upon Himself human form in the person of Jesus Christ and died for our sins. Christianity proclaims a God who is both Mind and Heart—who not only created the world, but also loves it so much that He sent His only begotten Son to die for it (John 3:16). The Christian sees God's handiwork not only as he observes the intricacies of a gold-edged maple leaf, as he views the birth of a newborn child, or contemplates his own earth, moon, sun, stars, and galaxies, but also as he sees an individual saved from a meaningless existence and reborn as a productive, loving, purposeful child of God. Christian theism declares in large letters, "God is," "God created," "God loves," and "God judges." The Christian finds his highest fulfillment of worship in the declaration, "I believe in God, the Father Almighty, maker of Heaven and Earth," and in the challenge to love this God of creation and salvation with all his heart, soul, mind, and strength (Mark 12:30). The Christian echoes James Orr, who believes "everything becomes an insoluble mystery" without a Designer to explain its existence.

Introduction

Christian theism rests primarily on two foundations: special revelation (the Bible) and general revelation (the created order). While the Bible reveals the character and personality of God page after page, the "whole

Notes and Asides

workmanship of the universe," according to John Calvin, reveals and discloses God day after day. James Orr explains that the theistic position is established not by any single clue or evidence, but by "the concurrent forces of many, starting from different and independent standpoints."[3] The beginning of the universe, for example, and the individual conscience are two forces that strengthen the notion of the existence of God. Life itself, mind, and personality are other forces pointing in the same direction. Is it not reasonable to conclude that life, mind, and personality have their source in something living with a mind and personality? The Bible says this living, personal divine mind is the triune God.

Christians see evidences of God everywhere. "Belief in God," says Alvin Plantinga, "is the heart and center of the Christian religion." It is the Christian position that history,[4] theology,[5] philosophy,[6] science,[7] mathematics, and logic[8] all point to the existence of God. And while some (for example physicist Steven Weinberg) view the universe as "pointless,"[9] we agree with physicist Paul Davies, who feels that Weinberg and others like him are "unable to see the wood for the trees."[10]

> "That the universe is ordered seems self-evident."
> —Paul Davies

The Bible's opening statement proclaims, "In the beginning God" (Genesis 1:1). As a matter of course, the Bible continually points readers to the "natural order" as being *God's order*. "The heavens declare the glory of God," says the psalmist David, "and the firmament sheweth his handiwork" (Psalm 19:1).

God asked Job, "Where were you when I laid the earth's foundation?" (Job 38:4). Today scientists still search to understand the beginning of the universe, and the emerging answers are consistent with belief in the God whom Christians believe created it. While Davies accepts the notion of the "big bang" theory to explain the creation and believes the universe continues to be creative, he also acknowledges that there is "something going on behind it all."[11] Physicist Robert Jastrow believes astronomical evidence "leads to a biblical view of the origin of the world"[12] and that three lines of evidence—the motions of the galaxies, the laws of thermodynamics, and the life story of the stars—all point to one conclusion: "all indicate that the Universe had a beginning."[13]

God directs Job to the heavens and asks, "Can you bind the beautiful Pleiades? Can you loose the cords of Orion? Can you bring forth the constellations in their seasons or lead out the Bear with its cubs? Do you know the laws of the heavens?" (Job 38:31-33). Twentieth-century science (especially physics) is moving ever closer to discovering "the laws of the heavens," and again the conclusions are far from being anti-God. "That the universe is ordered seems self-evident," says Paul Davies in *God and the New Physics*. "Everywhere we look, from the

Notes and Asides

far-flung galaxies to the deepest recesses of the atom, we encounter regularity and intricate organization. . . . Moreover, the behaviour of physical systems is not haphazard, but lawful and systematic." Davies concludes, "Scientists frequently experience a sense of awe and wonder at the subtle beauty and elegance of nature."[14] It should come as no surprise, therefore, when Christians not only experience this same sense of awe and wonder at the beauty and elegance of nature, but also experience awe and wonder in worshiping the Creator of such elegance.

From the time of David a thousand years before Christ to the present, the heavens constantly declare the power, beauty, elegance and "awesome majesty" (Job 37:22) of the Almighty, the Creator of the heavens and the earth.

St. Paul makes it clear that mankind cannot ignore God's handiwork as evidenced throughout creation: "For the invisible things of Him from the creation of the world are clearly seen, being understood by the things that are made, even his eternal power and Godhead; so that they are without excuse" (Romans 1:20). Paul understands that the created order reflects the power of God and believes that such a display of power renders men "without excuse" for ignoring God's existence. To paraphrase the apostle, "Nature demands a supernature." Years later one of modern science's founders, Francis Bacon, said, "I had rather believe all the fables in the Legend, and the Talmud and the Koran, than that this universal frame is without a mind. And therefore God never wrought miracles to convince atheism, because his ordinary works convince it." Bacon went on to say that "a little philosophy inclineth man's mind to atheism; but depth in philosophy bringeth men's minds about to religion."[15]

Still, some people insist that Charles Darwin made the existence of God meaningless by proving that mindless natural processes can account for all reality. Many claim that natural explanations exist for every phenomenon, every wonder of creation. But even these confirmed doubters recognize the insufficiency of natural explanations at present and are hesitant to abandon all notions of a supernatural Being. Thus, Humanists like Corliss Lamont acknowledge that "the immensity of the universe makes [Humanists] cautious about absolutely denying the existence of a God among the billions of galaxies billions of light-years away, and all containing billions of stars."[16]

Christianity declares that all of nature has a supernatural explanation. It views the natural order as powerful evidence for the existence of God. The universe and its inherent laws (both scientific and ethical) provide mankind with general revelation of God's existence.

Notes and Asides

Design and General Revelation

Theologian Lewis S. Chafer states, "the term revelation is restricted to the divine act of communicating to man what otherwise man would not know."[17] Christian theists believe that God has revealed Himself to mankind in a general way through creation and in a special (personal) way evidenced by His divine words and acts contained in the Bible and especially in the person of Jesus Christ. Millard Erickson defines the two forms of revelation this way: "On the one hand, general revelation is God's communication of Himself to all persons, at all times, and in all places. Special revelation on the other hand, involves God's particular communications and manifestations which are available now only by consultation of certain sacred writings."[18]

General revelation has been viewed consistently throughout church history by a variety of Christian theists as a necessary but insufficient means for providing knowledge about the Creator and His character. Thus, it is preferable to begin with special revelation when seeking to understand God, rather than with empirical nature and attempting to derive a reasonable concept of God from His works. It is better theology and philosophy to begin with the God of the Bible to explain the universe than to begin with the universe to explain God.[19] The Christian should trust ultimately in special revelation for his understanding of God and should not feel threatened by changing public perception of general revelation. As Carl F. H. Henry says,

General revelation refers to God's means of revealing Himself to man through the physical universe and the moral order.

> Christianity fears nothing from public reason; it is neither fideistic nor empiricistic nor rationalistic. . . . Christianity has no less right to affirm its ultimate explanatory principles than do other world-and-life-views. . . . As revelationally grounded, intelligible faith, Christianity sets out from the ontological priority of the living God and the epistemological priority of divine revelation. From these basic postulates it derives and expounds all the core doctrines of the Christian religion.[20]

Fideism is the belief that faith is the basis for all knowledge, and that reason is irrelevant.

Special revelation, then, is the linchpin of Christianity, while general revelation serves as a prod that encourages man to recognize the ultimate truths set down in Scripture and embodied in Jesus Christ. Dutch Reformed theologians like G. C. Berkouwer, Cornelius Van Til, Abraham Kuyper, Benjamin Warfield, and others believe that God's revelation of Himself through nature and history is objectively conclusive but subjectively convincing only to regenerate people because only

Notes and Asides

they are capable of understanding it (just as musical notes are comprehensible only to those who are not tone-deaf).[21] Other great Christian thinkers, such as Martin Luther, John Calvin, Charles Hodge, and Matthew Henry, believe that general revelation conveys objectively sufficient evidence of God's reality but that it does not show men how to be saved from God's judgment or how to know God personally. On the same note, Lewis S. Chafer states, "the revelation of God through nature has its limitations" because "it does not reveal a way of salvation by which a sinner can be reconciled to a Holy God."[22]

Although God's revelation through nature, in and of itself, fails to bring men to a saving knowledge of God, it is capable of bringing men to a general knowledge of God. A great majority of intellectuals agree that the concepts of purpose and design, for example, have validity in regard to the question of the existence of God. "In the world," writes Immanuel Kant, "we find everywhere clear signs of an order which can only spring from design—an order realized with greatest wisdom, and in a universe that is indescribably varied in content and in extent infinite."[23] At the close of a long life of atheism, existentialist philoso-

CLOSE-UP

Carl F. H. Henry (1913-)

Carl F.H. Henry is one of the leading Christian theologians of our time. As such, he fully understands the need for Christians to study the Bible in an effort to develop a Christian worldview. His contributions to Christian worldview analysis are diverse: addressing the realm of politics, he wrote *Twilight of a Great Civilization*; toward a Christian sociology, he wrote *Christian Countermoves in a Decadent Culture*; and his work *Christian Personal Ethics* shines as one of the most important studies in Christian ethics. Further, his mammoth six-volume *God, Revelation and Authority* provides the Christian with one of the most comprehensive studies of the Bible, Christ's life, and their significance for mankind. His books and lectures are always grounded firmly on biblical teaching, and thus his message has consistently refreshed Christians seeking truth in a relativistic world.

Notes and Asides

pher Jean Paul Sartre confessed, "I do not feel that I am the product of chance, a speck of dust in the universe, but someone who was expected, prepared, prefigured. In short, a king whom only a Creator could put here; the idea of a creating hand refers to God."[24] Ironically, even Darwin observes, "The impossibility of conceiving that this grand and wondrous universe with our conscious selves arose through chance seems to me the chief argument for the existence of God."[25]

Anglican clergyman William Paley argued in *Natural Theology* (a book about which Darwin admitted, "I do not think I hardly ever admired a book more . . .") that a man chancing upon a watch in the wilderness could not conclude that the watch had simply always existed; rather, the obvious design of the watch—not only its internal makeup but also the fact that it clearly exists for a *purpose*—would necessarily imply the existence of its designer. Paley went on to substitute the universe for the watch and contended that a mechanism so obviously designed as the universe necessitated the existence of a grand Designer. He further contended that the argument could not be weakened by claims such as (a) we had never seen a watch made; (b) the watch sometimes did not work exactly right; (c) some parts of the watch did not appear purposeful to me; (d) the watch was just a possible combination of forms already existing in matter; (e) life naturally tends to be orderly; (f) the watch was just a trick to make man think a watchmaker existed; (g) the watch had arisen due to laws of metallic nature; and finally, (h) man does not know enough about design to reason to a Designer. In the end, Paley said, we are still stuck with a watch and the question of its origin.[26] In the same way, we are stuck with a universe that exudes design.

Davies writes, "In his book *Natural Theology* William Paley (1743-1805) articulated one of the most powerful arguments for the existence of God: 'In crossing a heath, suppose I pitched my foot against a stone, and were asked how the stone came to be there: I might possibly answer, that, for anything I knew to the contrary, it had lain there forever; nor would it, perhaps, be very easy to show the absurdity of this answer. But suppose I found a watch upon the ground, and it should be inquired how the watch happened to be in that place. I should hardly think of the answer I had given before—that, for anything I knew, the watch might always have been there. Yet why should not this answer serve for the watch as well as for the stone?'"[27] Davies believes that someone who had never seen a watch with its intricate and delicate organization and each component dovetailing accurately would conclude that "this mechanism was devised by an intelligent person for a purpose."[28]

Sir Fred Hoyle, British mathematician and astrophysicist, was an atheist for much of his life. In 1981 he wrote a book with Chandra Wickramasinghe entitled *Evolution from Space*. Both Hoyle and Wick-

Notes and Asides

ramasinghe came to the conclusion that the high degree of order and specificity in the universe demanded a pre-existing intelligence:

> Once we see, however, that the probability of life originating at random is so utterly minuscule as to make it absurd, it becomes sensible to think that the favourable properties of physics, on which life depends, are in every respect deliberate. . . . It is, therefore, almost inevitable that our own measure of intelligence must reflect higher intelligences . . . even to the limit of God.[29]

Hoyle's *New Scientist* article on chance and living organisms contained the following observation: "I don't know how long it is going to be before astronomers generally recognize that the combinatorial arrangement of not even one among many thousands of biopolymers on which life depends could have been arrived at by natural processes here on the earth."[30] Hoyle argued that there are two thousand complex enzymes required for a living organism, but not a single one of these could have formed on earth randomly even in 20 billion years.

James Orr also believes that chance cannot possibly explain our ordered reality. He claims that the very materials of the universe "show by their structure, their uniformity, their properties, their mathematical relations, that they must have a Creator; that the Power which originated them, which weighed, measured and numbered them, which stamped on them their common characters, and gave them definite laws and relations, must have been intelligent."[31]

Evolutionist Paul Amos Moody acknowledges that the more he studies science, the more he is impressed with the thought that this world and universe "have a definite design—and a design suggests a designer." Moody says that evidences of design are everywhere, from the starry heavens to the electrons swirling in orbit around the atomic nuclei. What happens when we seek the natural laws that perfect such design? "There we find the Creator," says Moody.[32]

Clearly, the universe forces its sense of design (and thus a Designer) on all men open to such a possibility. Many discover God through the general revelation of a structured universe; many more encounter God in the general revelation of the purposeful nature of reality. C. E. M. Joad, a gifted philosopher and contemporary of Bertrand Russell, expresses this sense of purpose in the universe:

> We grow up, mate, bring children into the world, satisfy our desires, pursue our careers, gratify, so far as we are able, our ambitions, and then we die without knowing why we have lived. What, we wonder, has been the point of it all? Why was life

Notes and Asides

Recommended Reading for Advanced Study

James Orr, *The Christian View of God and the World* (Grand Rapids, MI: Kregel, 1989).

Norman L. Geisler and William E. Nix, *A General Introduction to the Bible* (Chicago: Moody, 1968).

Carl F. H. Henry, *God, Revelation and Authority,* six volumes (Waco, TX: Word, 1983).

Roy Abraham Varghese, ed., *The Intellectuals Speak Out About God* (Dallas, TX: Lewis and Stanley, 1984).

J. P. Moreland and Kai Nielsen, *Does God Exist?* (Nashville: Thomas Nelson, 1990).

William Lane Craig, *The Existence of God and the Beginning of the Universe* (San Bernardino, CA: Here's Life, 1979).

> given us? Has the whole affair, which has meant so much to us, been of no cosmic account, been in fact, an accident without point or purpose, of no significance to anything or anybody? But that, surely, is intolerable.[33]

Joad, who was an atheist for much of his professional career, wrote a book entitled *The Recovery of Belief* shortly before his death. This book traces his gradual advance to God and Jesus Christ. "I now believe," said Joad, "that the balance of reasoned considerations tells heavily in favor of the religious, even of the Christian view of the world."[34]

Still another twist on the argument for the general revelation of God's existence is presented by C. S. Lewis. Suppose there were no intelligence behind the universe, says Lewis. In that case nobody

Notes and Asides

designed my brain for the purpose of thinking. Thought is merely the by-product of some atoms within my skull. "But if so, how can I trust my own thinking to be true?" asks Lewis. "But if I can't trust my own thinking, of course, I can't trust the arguments leading to atheism, and therefore have no reason to be an atheist, or anything else. Unless I believe in God, I can't believe in thought; so I can never use thought to disbelieve in God."[35]

Science, as well as much of philosophy, has proven a valuable ally for Christian theism. Indeed, the more we learn from science, the more the wondrous design of the universe emerges. Scientist Henry Margenau says simply, "It is absolutely unreasonable to reject the notion of a Creator by appealing to science. Science has definitely shown the non-contradiction of Creation out of nothing."[36]

It was Margenau who challenged us to ask "really good scientists," that is, men who have made significant contributions to science—Sir John Eccles, Eugene Paul Wigner, Werner Heisenberg, Erwin Schroedinger, Albert Einstein—what they thought of God. Says Margenau, "If you take the top notch scientists, you find very few atheists among them."[37]

In the book *The Intellectuals Speak Out About God*, Stephen D. Schwarz notes that until recently it was thought by many people that science supports atheism. In fact, some even consider science the rational alternative to theism. But, says Schwarz,

> It is now clear that science not only does not support atheism, but even lends rational support for Theism. There is strong scientific evidence for God . . . [including] (1) The Second Law of Thermodynamics, (2) The impossibility of spontaneous generation of life from non-life, (3) Information theory (DNA) and (4) The Anthropic Principle [which maintains that the earth was tailored for the sake of man's existence].[38]

A generation ago other scientists were also stating that science and God were not in conflict. Arthur Compton in *The Freedom of Man* notes that far from being in conflict, "science . . . has become an ally of religion." He argues that "By increased knowledge of nature we become better acquainted with the God of nature."[39] He also states that few men of science were willing to defend an atheistic attitude.[40]

Sir Arthur Eddington in his *New Pathways in Science* said, "The new conception of the physical universe puts me in a position to defend religion against a particular charge, viz., the charge of being incompatible with physical science."[41]

"The God of science," said Robert Millikan in *Science and the New Civilization*, "is the spirit of rational order, the integrating factor in the

Notes and Asides

world of atoms and of ether and of ideas and of duties and of intelligence. Materialism is surely not a sin of modern science."[42] In *Science and Religion*, Millikan states quite matter-of-factly, "Science began to show us a universe of orderliness and of the beauty that goes with order, a universe that knows no caprice, a universe that behaves in a knowable and predictable way, a universe that can be counted upon; in a word, a God who works through law."[43]

Writes Sir James Jeans,

> If the universe is a universe of thought, then its creation must have been an act of thought. Indeed, the finiteness of time and space almost compel us, of themselves, to picture the creation as an act of thought. . . . Modern scientific theory compels us to think of the creator as working outside time and space, which are part of his creation, just as the artist is outside his canvas.[44]

So many conditions are essential to the very existence of life on our earth, observes scientist A. Cressy Morrison in *Seven Reasons Why a Scientist Believes in God*, that it would be mathematically impossible for all of them, in all of their necessary relationships, to exist by mere chance. For example, Morrison points out that the surface temperature of the sun is 12,000 degrees Fahrenheit. The sun is distanced just enough to warm us. Any closer and we would roast. Any farther and we would freeze or, at best, starve. He also points out that if our sun were as large as some stars, the whole orbit of the earth would be millions of miles below its surface. He notes that the earth travels around the sun at eighteen miles per second. "If the rate of revolution had been say, either six miles or forty miles each second, we would be too far from the sun or too close for our form of life to exist."[45] Not only does the design of the world impress Morrison, but he also feels that life itself, the mind of man, animal wisdom, etc. all declare the glory and wisdom of God. He finds no contradiction between being a scientist and believing in God.

The more science progresses, explores, and discovers, the more we see a cosmos that is uniform, consistent, and designed. Scientist Sir John Eccles admits that "we come to exist through a divine act, that divine guidance is a theme throughout life; at our death the brain goes, but that divine guidance and love continues. Each of us is a unique, conscious being, a divine creation. It is the religious view. It is the only view consistent with all the evidence."[46] And the evidence points to what Christians believe—that a personal God has revealed Himself through a created world, and that He has a plan and ultimate destiny for that world.

> "Each of us is a unique, conscious being, a divine creation. It is the religious view. It is the only view consistent with all the evidence."
>
> —Sir John Eccles

Notes and Asides

Special Revelation

According to the Christian view, the destiny of created mankind involves both salvation and judgment. It is not general revelation but special revelation (the Bible) that answers such questions as: How can mankind be saved? What must mankind be saved from? Why will judgment occur? Special revelation, then, is "special" because it is the key that opens the door between heaven and earth. Carl F. H. Henry writes, "Special revelation is redemptive revelation. It publishes the good tidings that the holy and merciful God promises salvation as a divine gift to man who cannot save himself (O.T.) and that He has now fulfilled that promise in the gift of his Son in whom all men are called to believe (N.T.)."[47]

Special revelation refers to God's specific means of revealing Himself to man, through the Bible and in the person of Jesus Christ.

One of the most basic tenets of Christian belief is the divine inspiration of the Bible. When the individual accepts Scripture as the Word of God, the teachings and events described in the Bible become the most important basis for understanding all reality. As Henry proclaims, "The Word of God remains no less critically decisive for man's destiny today than at the beginnings of human history."[48] Without faith that the Bible is God's Word, mankind is left floundering—forced to trust his own (unfounded) thought processes as his ultimate criteria for discerning truth. Henry notes, "To deny the rational intelligibility of divine revelation is to forego the connection between authentic faith in God and any necessary adherence to particular beliefs."[49]

No one can deny the Bible's divine inspiration and still claim to be a Biblical Christian, for the simple reason that Scripture proclaims itself to be God-breathed. Second Timothy 3:16-17 declares, "All Scripture is God-breathed and is useful for teaching, rebuking, correcting and training in righteousness, so that the man of God may be thoroughly equipped for every good work." If one believes the Bible to be a true and accurate document, then one must accept its claim to be divinely inspired.

What, specifically, does this claim entail? Norman Geisler and William Nix define inspiration as "that mysterious process by which the divine causality worked through the human prophets without destroying their individual personalities and styles, to produce divinely authoritative writings."[50] That is, " . . . God *revealed* and man *recorded* His word. The Bible is God's word in the sense that it originates with Him and is authorized by Him, even though it is articulated by men."[51]

The evidence for the Christian's belief in the divine inspiration of the Bible is powerful. For example, the unity of teaching in the Bible is startling in light of the fact that its books were authored by different men faced with very different circumstances. Geisler and Nix point out that

Notes and Asides

"the Bible contains hundreds of themes, written in several languages, by nearly forty writers, over a period of about fifteen hundred years, in several different countries, by men of various occupations. Yet, amid all this diversity there is a sustained unity of subject, teaching, and solution to man's problem of sin. . . . The probability of such unity being accidental is infinitely less than that it is providential."[52]

Further, the astounding ability of the Bible to metamorphose the lives of individuals who accept its authority also strengthens its claim to be special revelation from God. Geisler and Nix write,

> The transforming power of the Scriptures has always been one of the strongest evidences of its own divine origin. Untold thousands of individuals down through the centuries have been converted, and societal reforms have resulted from the application of biblical teachings.[53]

Geisler and Nix also believe the degree of moral truth contained in the Bible supports its divine inspiration: "There are flashes of high moral teaching in the Koran, Bhagavad-Gita (Hindu), Tripitaka (Buddhist), and other writings, but the floodlight of all these truths *and more* shines forth from the Bible alone."[54] All these arguments support the belief that the Bible is God's Word; however, the most convincing witness for divine inspiration is the Bible itself. Those hesitant to accept Scripture as God's special revelation are most often convinced by a thorough, open-minded study of the Bible.

In studying the Bible, the reader meets God's most direct form of special revelation: the person of Jesus Christ. "In Jesus of Nazareth," writes Henry, "the divine source of revelation and the divine content of that revelation converge and coincide."[55] Thus, Christ's teachings and actions as revealed in the Bible provide the cornerstone for special revelation and a solid foundation for Christian theism.

> "In darkness there is no choice. It is light that enables us to see the differences between things; and it is Christ that gives us light."
> —J. C. & A. W. Hare

The purpose of divine revelation lies in its communication to the Christian of the significance of Christ's teachings and actions. The third member of the Trinity, the Holy Spirit, plays an important role in this dialogue. Henry explains: "Scripture itself is given so that the Holy Spirit may etch God's Word upon the hearts of his followers in ongoing sanctification that anticipates the believer's final, unerring conformity to the image of Jesus Christ, God's incarnate Word."[56] This is the ultimate reason God chose to reveal Himself and His plan for mankind in the Bible.

God's special revelation to mankind, however, is not yet complete. We do not yet fully understand God. That is, "The revelation given to man is not exhaustive of God. The God of revelation transcends his creation, transcends his activity, transcends his own disclosure."[57]

Notes and Asides

Thus, the Christian trusts that God will more fully reveal Himself in the future. In Matthew 10:26, Jesus promises, "There is nothing concealed that will not be disclosed, or hidden that will not be made known." This special revelation will culminate in a final Day of Judgment, when all mankind will face God. Henry states, "God's progressive disclosure will climax in the final eschatological judgment of the unrepentant, and in a full and glorious sharing of himself with believers. Although God has already revealed himself, both universally and particularly, in an amazing variety of ways his consummatory disclosure still lies before us."[58]

Until that final day, the Christian relies on the Bible as God's special revelation. This reliance should be profound and constantly renewed—the Christian doesn't read the Bible once and set it aside; rather, he studies it as the Word of God and works constantly to conform himself to its teachings. He spends his life striving to understand the powerful unity of the Bible. Francis A. Schaeffer says, "The whole Bible's teaching gives us a series of balances that no one verse can give. This takes a lifetime of careful study."[59] It is through this faithful commitment to special revelation that the Christian can grow toward understanding the nature and attributes of God.

God Is Personal

Since the beginning of recorded history, mankind has consistently believed in a creator, first cause, supreme ruler, and/or heavenly father. Plato's Timaeus portrayed the cosmos or universe "as an artifact modeled after an ideal archetype by an ungrudging agent." Throughout the centuries, serious thinkers including Aristotle, Augustine, Anselm, Aquinas, Pascal, Kant, Leibniz, Whitehead, Lonergan, and Plantinga have attempted to prove the existence of God through various rational exercises. In the present era, scientists like Einstein have confessed belief in "a spirit [that] is manifest in the laws of the universe—a spirit vastly superior to that of man, and one in the face of which we with our modest powers must feel humble."[60] This belief is crucial; for, as Hebrews 11:6 states, "anyone who comes to God must believe He exists." Christian theism, however, takes the "God concept" beyond the absentee God of Deism, the unmoved mover of Aristotle and the unknowable, unrelated, indescribable God of other philosophers and theologians,[61] and dares to claim that one can encounter God personally and begin to comprehend His divine character and nature. William Craig notes that while many people believe there is a God, they really do not know Him personally, for, "if they did, their lives would be different."[62]

This can apply to "Christians" too that don't try to live Christ-centered lives.

Notes and Asides

The Christian is concerned not only with the existence of God in general, but also with the relationship that exists between God and man, and particularly with the redemption of all mankind. While Humanists declare in the *Humanist Manifesto II* that no God can save us—"we must save ourselves"—Christian theism echoes Thomas—who referred to Jesus as "My Lord and My God" (John 20:28)—and with Peter, who said to Jesus, "You alone have the words of eternal life" (John 6:68). God, as revealed throughout the Bible and especially in the person of Christ, is clearly knowable and desires to be known.

To say that God is knowable is also to say that God "relates" or has personality—that He is "personal." James W. Sire writes, "God is not mere force or energy or existent 'substance,' God is personality." And "personality requires two basic characteristics: (1) self-reflection and (2) self-determination." "In other words," says Sire, "God is personal in that He knows Himself (He is self-conscious and He possesses the characteristics of self-determination), He 'thinks' or 'acts.'"[63] God's self-awareness, His emotions, and His self-determining will make up the core of His divine personality. The Bible is emphatic in describing God as a person aware of Himself. In Isaiah 44:6, God says, "I am the first and I am the last, and there is no God besides me." In Exodus 3:14, God says to Moses, "I Am Who I Am."

Besides possessing a sense of self-awareness, the God of the Bible (like man) has sensibilities. At times God is portrayed as being sorrowful (Genesis 6:6), angry (Deuteronomy 1:37), compassionate (Psalm 111:4), jealous (Exodus 20:5), and able to show satisfaction (Genesis 1:4). Theologians do not feel that such scriptures suggest that God is limited, but rather that God is willing to reveal Himself in an anthropomorphic, personal way to mankind.

Characteristics of the Personal God

Besides believing that God is a personal God and has communicated His nature to mankind, Christians believe that God is self-determining, that is, sovereign in regard to His will. J. I. Packer writes, "the God of the Bible does not depend on His human creatures for His well being (see Psalm 50:8-13; Acts 12:25), nor now that we have sinned is He bound to show us favor. He is not obliged to pity and pardon; if He does so it is an act done, as we say, 'of His own free will,' and nobody forces His hand."[64] In the book of Daniel God's self-determination is more than evident: "And all the inhabitants of the earth are accounted as nothing, but he does according to His will in the host of heaven and among the inhabitants of the earth; and no one can ward off His hand or say to Him, 'what hast Thou done?'" (Daniel 4:35).

Notes and Asides

In addition to being self-determining, the God of the Bible is moral. Proverbs 15:3 warns us that God distinguishes between good and evil, and that He is concerned with our morality (also see Proverbs 5:21). God's uncompromisingly moral character is one of the most crucial aspects of His being. A true understanding of God's absolute goodness leads the individual unerringly to the conclusion that every man has an acute need for a Redeemer. Lewis writes,

> If the universe is not governed by an absolute goodness, then all our efforts are in the long run hopeless. But if it is, then we are making ourselves enemies to that goodness every day, and are not in the least likely to do any better tomorrow, and so our case is hopeless again. We cannot do without it, and we cannot do with it. God is the only comfort, He is also the supreme terror: the thing we most need and the thing we most want to hide from. He is our only possible ally, and we have made ourselves His enemies. Some people talk as if meeting the gaze of absolute goodness would be fun. They need to think again. They are still only playing with religion."[65]

Long-suffering patience and faithfulness are also personality traits of God. God's willingness to delay His judgment upon the Israelites when they worshipped the golden calf (Exodus 32:11-14) and His faithful promise to save the believer from eternal judgment (John 10:28) are prime examples of His patience and faithfulness.

Perhaps the most astounding characteristic of God's personality is that He is triune. The Christian believes that God is three co-existent, co-eternal persons in one, who are equal in purpose and in essence, but differ in function. In regard to God's triune nature, Sire writes, "the Trinity confirms the communal, 'personal' nature of ultimate being. God is not only there—an actually existent being—he is personal and we can relate to Him in a personal way. To know God, therefore, means knowing more than that he exists. It means knowing him as we know a brother or, better, our own father."[66]

Creation *ex nihilo* is the doctrine which asserts that God created the cosmos out of nothing.

The God of the Christian is also a God of power, evidenced by His works in creation and providence. Hebrews 1:10 declares, "In the beginning, O Lord, you laid the foundations of the earth, and the heavens are the works of your hands." Christian theology asserts that God is the source of all things and that He created the cosmos *ex nihilo* (out of nothing). Concerning creation *ex nihilo*, Sire writes, "God is not the source of the cosmos in that he made it out of himself. Rather, God spoke it into existence."[67] Therefore, creationism rejects such dualistic

Notes and Asides

notions as matter co-existing eternally with God. Stephen Charnock defines the conditions of creation simply: "before the heavens and the earth there was nothing absolutely created and therefore no matter in being before the act of creation passed upon it."[68]

Creation was of divine intention and divine will, and is the ultimate manifestation of God's wisdom and power. The act of creation should be of importance to man because he sits at the apex of God's creative work. Genesis provides a number of evidences that man was to be the most valuable and cherished aspect of God's handiwork: (1) Man was created on the last day, (2) God told man to subdue the earth and to rule over it (Gen. 1:28), (3) Every plant, animal, and bird was given to man and was under his dominion (Gen. 1:29-30), (4) God created man differently from other creatures—man was created as a complex being with personhood, self-awareness, and individuality,[69] (5) Man was created perfect, with a free will, and had the ability to reason and discern, and (6) Man also had the capacity to choose between good and evil, between right and wrong, and between harmony with God and rebellion against Him.

"Some people talk as if meeting the gaze of absolute goodness would be fun. They need to think again."
—C. S. Lewis

Unfortunately, man spurned the special role God had prepared for him, so that since the Fall, God's power has been manifested through His preservation of humanity. H. C. Thiessen provides a concrete definition of this doctrine: "By preservation we mean that God sovereignly, by a continuous agency, maintains in existence all the things which He has made, together with all their properties and powers."[70] Paul, in his letter to the Colossians, tells us that God is before all things, and in Him all things hold together (Colossians 1:17). Hebrews 1:3 states that Christ is "the radiance of His glory and the exact representation of His nature, and upholds all things by the word of His power."

God also demonstrates His power by moving His world to its purposeful end. Each created thing has an appointed destiny—God has a plan for His world, and nothing takes Him by surprise. The Bible is emphatic on this point. Romans 9:25-26 says, "I will call those who were not my people, My people, and her who was not beloved, beloved. And it shall be that in the place where it was said to them 'you are not my people,' there they shall be called sons of the living God." Scripture makes it clear that God manifests His power by a sovereign and Holy plan—a plan which often collides with the plans of men. This is not to say that God is constrictive or oppressive, but that God has a divine and perfect plan and an ultimate destiny for His creation. James Orr describes the manifestations of God's power when he states, "The universe itself is a law-connected whole; there is order and plan, organization and system, utility and beauty, means and ends."[71]

Jeremiah 29:11

CLOSE-UP

Saint Augustine (354-430)

Saint Augustine, quite possibly the greatest Christian theologian, arrived at the conclusion that Christianity was true in a very roundabout way. While studying rhetoric in Carthage at the age of sixteen, Augustine abandoned the Christianity infused in him by his mother, and took a mistress. Shortly thereafter, he converted to Manichaeism, a Persian religion which portrayed the soul as good and the physical realm as evil. Then, while teaching rhetoric at Rome in 383, Augustine became sympathetic toward the skeptical viewpoint, believing that one could not be certain of any truth. This belief faded when he moved to Milan the following year and came under the influence of Christian Platonists. Still, Augustine did not embrace Christianity until he had a conversion experience later the same year, triggered by reading Romans 13:13-14. After his full recognition of the truth of Christianity, Augustine put his faith into action with a zeal that is unsurpassed. Ordained in 391, he founded a religious community in Hippo, and presided as bishop over the community from 396 until his death. During this period of his life he wrote a number of important theological works, exposing the bankruptcy of skepticism, Manichaeism, and a host of other false worldviews. His most famous work, *The City of God*, is every bit as timely today as it was 1500 years ago—a strong testimony to the truth of Christianity.

God as Judge

The judgment of God is not a popular subject—even among Christians. A great majority of people abhor the thought that the "God of love" could also be the "God of wrath." However, one cannot read the Bible without encountering the judgment of God, nor can one read a theologian without encountering long expository essays on the holiness, righteousness, and wrath of God. Augustus Strong insists that a God who is not a judge of sin is no God at all. In his *Systematic Theology*,

Notes and Asides

Strong writes, "God can cease to demand purity and to punish sin only when He ceases to be holy, that is when He ceases to be God."[72]

The holiness of God necessitates the judgment of God. Christian theists agree that God must be a judge because His holy nature is antithetical to sin. A. W. Tozer writes, "God's first concern for His universe is its moral health. To preserve His creation God must destroy whatever would destroy it."[73] Such acts in the Bible as the great flood (Genesis 6:17-7:24), the destruction of Sodom and Gomorrah (Genesis 19), the smiting of Nadab and Abihu (Leviticus 10:1-7), the fall of the Canaanites (Leviticus 18-20), and indeed the fall of Israel (2 Kings 17) and Judah (2 Chronicles 36) are all demonstrations of God's judgment as motivated by His holy nature.

Christianity teaches that God is fair and always right, because His nature is perfect. In his *Basic Theology*, Charles Ryrie has stated that "God is righteous, there is no law, either within His own being or His own making, which is violated by anything in His own nature."[74] God is not a giant bully or a cosmic killjoy brooding in the heavens, waiting for every opportunity to spoil man's fun. The Bible teaches that God is truly interested in good winning over evil, and in holiness being the victor over moral depravity. In short, God is the judge of men because men are sinners. The Bible is clear in communicating that God does not take pleasure in the judgment of the wicked (Ezekiel 33:11), but the wicked must be judged because God is holy (Jude 15).

A second reason God judges mankind lies in the fact that the Bible portrays God as one who is wise, discerning, and able to know what should be judged. A prime example of the Lord's use of discernment in judgment of His people occurs in Genesis 18:20. God says, "Because the cry of Sodom and Gomorrah is great, and because their sin is very grievous, I will go down now, and see whether they have done altogether according to the cry of it, which is come unto me; and if not, I will know." The Christian believes that God is all-wise, all-knowing, and stands alone as the One qualified to discern truth from deceit.

God acts as judge for a third reason as well: He is the universe's ultimate authority. God created us, sustains us, and, as Packer says, "He owns us, and as our owner, He has the right to dispose of us," or "reward us."[75] None may question God's authority to judge the actions of His own creations, because all exist only due to God's great mercy and power. God described the immeasurable gap between His right and man's right to judge when He asked Job, "Where were you when I laid the earth's foundation? Tell me, if you understand. Who marked off its dimensions? Surely you know! Who stretched a measuring line across it? On what were its footings set, or who laid its cornerstone—while the morning stars sang together and all the angels shouted for joy?" (Job 38:4-7).

Notes and Asides

A final reason God judges lies in His desire to place a restraint on man's inhumanity to man. Richard Wurmbrand, who was tortured for his faith in God while in Communist prisons, says,

> The cruelty of atheism is not hard to believe when man has no faith in the reward of good or the punishment of evil. There is no reason to be human. There is no restraint from the depths of evil which is in man. The Communist torturers often said, "There is no God, no hereafter, no punishment for evil. We can do what we wish." I have heard one torturer even say, "I thank God, in whom I don't believe, that I have lived to this hour when I can express all the evil in my heart." He expressed it in unbelievable brutality and torture inflicted on prisoners.[76]

God as Redeemer

In His mercy, God has provided an advocate for every individual—an advocate so righteous that He washes away the sin that should condemn man. God as the Redeemer, in the person of Christ, saves mankind from His wrath on the Day of Judgment.

The central theme of redemption is the love of God. John 3:16 informs us, "God so loved the world, that He gave His only begotten Son, that whoever believes in Him should not perish, but have eternal life." Using John 3:16 as a text for portraying God's love, theologian Floyd Barackman points out the following characteristics of this love:

"Here we have the triune God standing with His arms open telling us that even though we are sinners He has provided a way through which 'whosoever will' may come."
—Francis Schaeffer

1. *God's love is universal*. God loves every nation, tribe, race, class, and gender equally. There were no social prejudices when God offered His Son. Christ died for the rich and for the poor; for the free and for the enslaved; for the old and for the young; for the beautiful and the ugly. In reference to God's "universal love," Schaeffer writes, "Here we have the triune God standing with His arms open telling us that even though we are sinners He has provided a way through which 'whosoever will' may come."[77]

2. *God's love is gracious*. God loves sinners even when they hate Him and are undeserving of His love. Romans 5:8 clearly outlines the nature of God's love: "But God demonstrates His own love toward us, in that while we were yet sinners, Christ died for us." The Bible defines the sinner as one who is dead in his sins (Ephesians 2:1); one who is unrighteous and suppresses the truth in unrighteousness (Romans 1:18); one who walks according to the course of this world, according to the prince of the power of the air, and who is controlled by the spirit

Notes and Asides

that is now working in the sons of disobedience (Ephesians 2:2). Such descriptions of the unredeemed sinner spotlight man's intense need as well as the awesome nature of God's grace.

How could God love the sinner? This question is answered by the Christian doctrine of grace. Christianity declares that God's love and mercy are so awesome that He can love the sinner while hating the sin. Packer writes, "once a man is convinced that his state and need are as described, the New Testament gospel of grace cannot but sweep him off his feet with wonder and joy, for it tells how our Judge has become Savior."[78] Nothing sums up the wonder of God's love and mercy better than the first verse of John Newton's best-loved hymn: "Amazing grace, how sweet the sound, that saved a wretch like me! I once was lost, but now am found, was blind but now I see."

3. *God's love is sacrificial*. God did not send His only Son to earth just to be a good example or simply to be a teacher, but to be a perfect and atoning sacrifice for sin. Christ's substitutionary death was sacrificial and closely resembles the Old Testament concept of atonement. Chafer, in *Major Bible Themes*, says that sin can be cured only through the shed blood of the Son of God. This was as true for those who anticipated the death of Christ by animal sacrifices as it is now for those who look back to that death by faith.[79] The main difference between the Old Testament concept of atonement and the New Testament concept is that atonement in the Old Testament was temporary, whereas in the New Testament Christ atoned for sins once and for all. Hebrews 9:11-12 states: "But when Christ appeared as a high priest of the good things to come, He entered through the greater and more perfect tabernacle, not made with hands, that is to say not of this creation, and not through the blood of goats and calves, but through His own blood, He entered the holy place once for all, having obtained eternal redemption." Christ's death is perfectly sufficient in God's eyes. Through the death of Christ, God has reconciled the world to Himself, and offered a way for His wrath to be appeased (Colossians 1:20)—man now must be reconciled to God through faith in Christ (2 Corinthians 5:20). God's sacrificial love is best summed up in John's statement: "In this is love, not that we loved God, but that He loved us and sent His Son to be the propitiation for our sins." (1 John 4:10).

A **propitiation** is a representative which appeases, or regains the good will of, someone.

4. *God's love is beneficial*. For all those who receive Christ (John 1:12), for all those who are born from above (John 3:3), for all those who believe (John 3:16), there await certain eternal benefits given by God. Scripture declares that through God's grace, the believer will not be condemned (Romans 3:24) and will not be captive to sin (Romans 6:11). Further, the believer is a new creation (2 Corinthians 5:17) who

Notes and Asides

has been declared righteous (2 Corinthians 5:21), redeemed (1 Peter 1:18), forgiven (Ephesians 1:7) and the recipient of the gift of eternal life (John 3:16).

Conclusion

Christian theology is Christ-centered. The power and wisdom of God manifests itself in the creative order. The love and justice of God are exhibited by His redemptive provision for sin. The God who "so loved the world that He gave His only Son" has allowed for a personal relationship between Himself and fallen man. Theoretical atheistic possibilities belittle the God who has revealed Himself propositionally through His creation and His word and has sacrificed His incarnate and holy Son. If the story be true, then the world that lives in unbelief should be fearful, for it sits under the judgment of God until it recognizes and experiences the ever-faithful promise of Jesus: "Behold, I stand at the door and knock; if anyone hears My voice and opens the door, I will come in to him, and will dine with him, and he with Me" (Revelation 3:20).

Christian theism may be summarized thus:

We don't have to worry about theories.

> God existed as Father, Son, and Holy Spirit before His creative acts; God created the heavens and the earth; God created mankind along with the rest of his creation, and placed mankind in charge of the environment; God loved mankind in spite of man's sinful, rebellious attitude toward God; God provided a Savior in the person of Jesus Christ, who said, "I am the way, and the truth, and the life; no one comes to the Father, but through Me" (John 14:6); and God's purpose for redeemed mankind involves a New Heaven, New Earth, and New Jerusalem—an eternity with the triune God.

[1] Stephen D. Schwartz, "Introduction—Philosophy," *The Intellectuals Speak Out About God*, ed. Roy Abraham Varghese (Dallas, TX: Lewis and Stanley, 1984), p. 98.
[2]Alvin Plantinga, "Reason and Belief in God," in *The Intellectuals Speak Out About God*, ed. Varghese, p. 185.
[3]James Orr, *The Christian View of God and the World* (Edinburgh: Andrew Elliot, 1897), p. 111.
[4]For example, consider the role of Jesus Christ in history, even as portrayed in skeptic Will Durant's *Caesar and Christ* (New York: Simon and Schuster, 1944), and in Christian historian John Warwick Montgomery's *History and Christianity* (Downers Grove, IL: InterVarsity Press, 1964).
[5]For example, the Bible.
[6]C. E. M. Joad turned to Christ when he was convinced that the Christian explanation for the existence of evil was superior to all others. He wrote of his conversion in *The Recovery of Belief* (London: Faber and Faber Limited, 1955).
[7]See Paul Davies, *God and the New Physics* (New York: Simon and Schuster, 1983).
[8]Consider, for example, causation: "In the Christian view, God's mind and will are the source of all truth of mathematics, of logic, of law, and of cosmic order." Carl F. H. Henry, *Toward a Recovery of Christian Belief* (Westchester, IL: Crossway Books, 1990), p. 70.
[9]Paul Davies, *Superforce* (New York: Simon and Schuster, 1984), p. 222.
[10]Ibid., p. 223.
[11]Paul Davies, *The Cosmic Blueprint* (New York: Simon and Schuster, 1988), p. 203.
[12]Robert Jastrow, *God and the Astronomers* (New York: W. W. Norton, 1978), p. 14.
[13]Ibid, p. 111.
[14]Davies, *God and the New Physics*, p. 145.
[15]Francis Bacon, "Of Atheism," reprinted in *Selected Writings of Francis Bacon*, ed. Hugh G. Dick (New York: Random House, 1955), p. 44.
[16]Corliss Lamont, *The Philosophy of Humanism* (New York: Frederick Ungar Publishing, 1982), p. xviii.
[17]Lewis Sperry Chafer, *Systematic Theology*, seven volumes (Dallas: Dallas Seminary Press, 1947), vol. 1, p. 48.
[18]Millard J. Erickson, *Christian Theology*, three volumes (Grand Rapids, MI: Baker Book House, 1983), vol. 1, p. 153.
[19]This does not mean, however, that one cannot point to general revelation as sound evidence for the existence of God. Both the teleological argument and the moral argument, as we will see, are logical attempts to reason from the physical universe to God. See also Dallas Willard, "Language, Being, God, and the Three Stages of Theistic Evidence," in *Does God Exist? The Great Debate*, by J. P. Moreland and Kai Nielsen (Nashville: Thomas Nelson, 1990), pp. 197-217; Willard provides another fine example of such reasoning.
[20]Henry, *Toward a Recovery of Christian Belief*, p. 59. Clearly, Henry sees no reason to compromise the Christian message to make Christian theism more palatable for non-believers. "Christian theism," Henry says, "does not depend on whether unbelievers find its presuppositions [God exists and He revealed Himself in the Bible] acceptable, or upon espousing only those beliefs that dissenting philosophers approve" (p. 66).
[21]For an excellent explanation of this view, see Benjamin B. Warfield, "On Faith in Its Psychological Aspects," in *Works of Benjamin B. Warfield*, ten volumes (Grand Rapids, MI: Baker Book House, 1981), in vol. 9.
[22]Chafer, *Systematic Theology*, vol. 1, p. 32.
[23]Immanuel Kant, quoted in Orr, *The Christian View of God and the World*, p. 98.
[24]Jean Paul Sartre, quoted in *The Intellectuals Speak Out About God*, ed. Varghese, p. 122.
[25]Charles Darwin, quoted in Richard Wurmbrand, *My Answer to Moscow's Atheism* (New York: Arlington House, 1975), p. 16.
[26]William Paley, *Natural Theology* (Houston: St. Thomas Press, 1972), reprint.
[27]Davies, *God and the New Physics*, p. 164.
[28]Ibid.
[29]Fred Hoyle and Chandra Wickramasinghe, *Evolution from Space* (London: J. M. Dent and Company, 1981), pp. 141, 144.
[30]Fred Hoyle, "The Big Bang in Astronomy," *New Scientist*, vol. 92, no. 128 (Nov. 19, 1981), p. 521.
[31]Orr, *The Christian View of God and the World*, p. 102.
[32]Paul Amos Moody, *Introduction to Evolution* (New York: Harper and Row, 1970), pp. 497, 8.

[33]Joad, *The Recovery of Belief*.
[34]Ibid, p. 22.
[35]C. S. Lewis, *Broadcast Talks* (London: 1946), pp. 37-8.
[36]Henry Margenau, quoted in *The Intellectuals Speak Out About God*, ed. Varghese, p. 6.
[37]Henry Margenau, "Modern Physics and the Turn to Belief in God," in *The Intellectuals Speak Out About God*, pp. 43-44.
[38]Stephen D. Schwarz, "Introduction—Philosophy," in *The Intellectuals Speak Out About God*, pp. 101-2.
[39]Arthur Compton, *The Freedom of Man* (New Haven: Yale University Press, 1935), p. xi.
[40]Ibid, p. 73.
[41]Arthur Eddington, *New Pathways in Science* (New York: Macmillan, 1935), p. 308.
[42]Robert Millikan, *Science and the New Civilization* (New York: Macmillan, 1930), p. 83.
[43]Robert Millikan, *Science and Religion* (New Haven: Yale University Press, 1930), p. 79.
[44]Sir James Jeans, *The Mysterious Universe* (New York: Macmillan, 1930), pp. 154-5.
[45]A. Cressy Morrison, *Seven Reasons Why A Scientist Believes in God* (Old Tappan, NJ: Fleming H. Revell, 1945), pp. 12-13.
[46]John Eccles, "Modern Biology and the Turn to Belief in God," in *The Intellectuals Speak Out About God*, ed. Varghese, p. 50.
[47]Carl F. H. Henry, ed. *Evangelical Dictionary of Theology* (Grand Rapids, MI: Baker Book House, 1984), p. 946.
[48]Carl F. H. Henry, *God, Revelation and Authority*, six volumes (Waco, TX: Word Books, 1976ff), vol. 2, pp. 8-9.
[49]Ibid, p. 12.
[50]Norman L. Geisler and William Nix, *A General Introduction to the Bible* (Chicago: Moody Press, 1980), p. 29.
[51]Ibid, p. 28.
[52]Ibid, p. 118.
[53]Ibid, p. 116.
[54]Ibid, p. 120.
[55]Henry, *God, Revelation and Authority*, vol. 2, p. 11.
[56]Ibid., p. 15.
[57]Ibid, p. 9.
[58]Ibid, p. 16.
[59]Francis A. Schaeffer, *Basic Bible Studies*, in *The Complete Works of Francis A. Schaeffer*, five volumes (Westchester, IL: Crossway Books, 1984), vol. 2, p. 322.
[60]Albert Einstein, quoted in *The Intellectuals Speak Out About God*, ed. Varghese, p. 45.
[61]J. Oliver Buswell, Jr., "Theism," in *Baker's Dictionary of Theology*, ed. Everett F. Harrison, Geoffrey W. Bromiley, and Carl F. H. Henry (Grand Rapids, MI: Baker Book House, 1966), p. 516.
[62]William Lane Craig, *The Existence of God and the Beginning of the Universe* (San Bernardino, CA: Here's Life Publishers, 1979), p. 96.
[63]James W. Sire, *The Universe Next Door* (Downers Grove, IL: InterVarsity Press, 1988), p. 26.
[64]J. I. Packer, *Knowing God* (Downers Grove, IL: InterVarsity Press, 1973), p. 119.
[65]C. S. Lewis, quoted in *A Mind Awake*, ed. Clyde S. Kilby (New York: Harcourt Brace Jovanovich, 1968), p. 84.
[66]Sire, *The Universe Next Door*, p. 27.
[67]Ibid., p. 28.
[68]Stephen Charnock, *The Existence and Attributes of God*, two volumes (Grand Rapids, MI: Baker Book House, 1979), p. 37.
[69]Floyd H. Barackman, *Practical Christian Theology* (Old Tappan, NJ: Fleming H. Revell, 1984), pp. 191-2.
[70]Henry C. Thiessen, *Lectures in Systematic Theology* (Grand Rapids, MI: Eerdmans, 1975), p. 174.
[71]Orr, *The Christian View of God and the World*, p. 55.
[72]Augustus H. Strong, *Systematic Theology* (Old Tappan, NJ: Fleming H. Revell, 1907), p. 293.
[73]A. W. Tozer, *The Knowledge of the Holy* (London: Harper and Row, 1961), p. 113.

[74]Charles C. Ryrie, *Basic Theology* (Wheaton, IL: Victor Books, 1986), p. 42.
[75]Packer, *Knowing God*, p. 128.
[76]Richard Wurmbrand, *Tortured for Christ* (London: Hodder and Stoughton, 1967), p. 34.
[77]Francis A. Schaeffer, *Basic Bible Studies*, in *The Complete Works of Francis A. Schaeffer*, vol. 2, p. 331.
[78]Packer, *Knowing God*, p. 120.
[79]Chafer, *Systematic Theology*, vol. 1, p. 182.

SECTION TWO

PHILOSOPHY

Chapter 6: *Secular Humanism*
Chapter 7: *Marxism/Leninism*
Chapter 8: *Biblical Christianity*

PHILOSOPHY [Greek: *philo* (love) + *sophia* (wisdom)]: The love of wisdom; the attempt to discover an explanation for the whole of existence or reality.

	SECULAR HUMANISM	MARXISM/ LENINISM	BIBLICAL CHRISTIANITY
SOURCE	*HUMANIST MANIFESTO I & II*	*WRITINGS OF MARX & LENIN*	*BIBLE*
THEOLOGY	ATHEISM	ATHEISM	THEISM
PHILOSOPHY	NATURALISM	DIALECTICAL MATERIALISM	SUPERNATURALISM
ETHICS	ETHICAL RELATIVISM	PROLETARIAT MORALITY	ETHICAL ABSOLUTES
BIOLOGY	DARWINIAN EVOLUTION	DARWINIAN/ PUNCTUATED EVOLUTION	SPECIAL CREATIONISM
PSYCHOLOGY	MONISTIC SELF-ACTUALIZATION	MONISTIC PAVLOVIAN BEHAVIORISM	DUALISM
SOCIOLOGY	NON-TRADITIONAL WORLD STATE ETHICAL SOCIETY	ABOLITION OF HOME, CHURCH AND STATE	HOME CHURCH STATE
LAW	POSITIVE LAW	POSITIVE LAW	BIBLICAL/NATURAL LAW
POLITICS	WORLD GOVERNMENT (GLOBALISM)	NEW WORLD ORDER	JUSTICE FREEDOM ORDER
ECONOMICS	SOCIALISM	SOCIALISM/ COMMUNISM	STEWARDSHIP OF PROPERTY
HISTORY	HISTORICAL EVOLUTION	HISTORICAL MATERIALISM	HISTORICAL RESURRECTION

CHAPTER

6

SECULAR HUMANIST PHILOSOPHY

"Humanism is naturalistic and rejects the supernaturalistic stance with its postulated Creator-God and cosmic Ruler."[1]

—Roy Wood Sellars

"Naturalistic Humanism . . . is the Humanism that I have supported through the written and spoken word for some forty years."[2]

—Corliss Lamont

SUMMARY

Humanism's atheism is foundational not only to its theology but also to its philosophy, which is naturalistic. Naturalism declares that only nature exists—thus, God, heaven, angels, Satan, hell, mind, spirit, soul, and all other hints of the supernatural are relegated to the realm of fantasy.

This ontological aspect of Humanist philosophy—that is, their assumption that matter is ultimate reality—is based on their epistemology. Secular Humanism's theory of knowledge claims to be rationalistic (using reason as its ultimate source for discerning truth). Thus, Ernest Nagel proclaims, "Human reason is not an omnipotent instrument for the achievement of human goods; but it is the only instrument we do possess, and it is not a contemptible one."[3] Such statements might cause one to assume that Humanists really do base their epistemology on rationalism, but this assumption would be mistaken. Humanists discount miracle stories (such as the virgin birth and Christ's resurrection) and the claims of mystics not because they are unreasonable but because the Humanists themselves did not observe and have never observed supernatural events.

In reality, Humanistic epistemology is a form of scientism. The Humanist trusts the scientific method as the only sure method of arriving at knowledge. If something cannot be observed, tested, and experimented on, it cannot exist. Only what is empirically testable is meaningful and so can be true or false; all else is unreal. The logical extension of scientism is the conclusion that the material world is ultimate reality. In other words, since God is not laboratory tested, the supernatural does not exist.

A necessary corollary to the "scientific" conclusion reached by naturalists is the denial of mind and soul. Because nothing exists that cannot be observed and tested, ideas, imagination, and rationality are all viewed by the Humanist as side effects of the physical brain. No neurosurgeon has ever surgically removed and observed an idea, so ideas cannot be "real" in any meaningful sense. This is the monistic view of man. According to the Humanist, it is the only rational, scientific way to perceive man and his thoughts. Corliss Lamont declares that "Science . . . refutes dualistic psychology."[4] Humanists do not think that men's imagination and ideas refute their dogmatic scientific naturalism. Rather, their commitment to scientific naturalism forces them to see ideas and imagination as nothing more than the cause-and-effect based chemical firing of synapses in the human brain, brought about by brute force as part of the whole random physical process that comprises reality; they are not the product of reason. Unfortunately, if ideas are mere chemical firings of synapses rather than the product of real reasoning, then Humanistic ideas are also chemical firings of synapses and hence are neither better nor worse than Christian ideas. It is difficult to speak of reason and truth under such circumstances. Yet Humanists certainly believe their worldview is true. (At least relatively speaking! There are, of course, no absolutes in Humanist philosophy.)

Notes and Asides

Introduction

Humanists, as a rule, reject dogmatism and attempt to portray their worldview as a general philosophy optimistic about the future of man. Paul Kurtz says, "Although Humanism presents a critique of transcendental supernaturalistic theories of the universe, it is not necessarily committed to a specific metaphysical doctrine, except in the broadest sense. It could incorporate, for example, scientific materialism, evolutionary naturalism, organicism or some other metaphysical account based upon science. The point is that it is opposed to metaphysical theories grounded solely on faith or mystery, but it is open to alternative metaphysical explanations."[5] Philosophical terms unclear to the reader will be explained later in this chapter—what is important to understand from this quote is Kurtz's attempt to avoid dogma in his interpretation of Humanism. He stresses that there are a number of philosophies a person could believe and still be a Humanist. What he does not acknowledge is that all the philosophies he names hold the same basic tenet: the material world is all that exists. In fact, each philosophy Kurtz lists is really little more than a synonym for naturalism, which is the philosophical view Secular Humanists hold.

In truth, Kurtz himself states a strictly naturalistic view when he writes in *Humanist Manifesto II*: "Nature may indeed be broader and deeper than we now know; any new discoveries, however, will but enlarge our knowledge of the natural."[6] This belief is the essence of Naturalism: whatever exists can be explained by natural causes; the supernatural cannot exist. This belief is the very foundation of Humanism, regardless of the terminology describing it. Some Humanists prefer to call themselves materialists (or "scientific" materialists)—the name makes little difference. As Corliss Lamont notes, "Materialism denotes the same general attitude toward the universe as Naturalism."[7] He goes on to say:

Naturalism is a philosophical view which acknowledges only natural elements and forces, denying the existence of the supernatural.

> Closely related to Naturalism in its basic world-view and similarly a strong bulwark for Humanism is the philosophy of Materialism, holding that the foundation stone of all being is matter in motion. Like Naturalism, Materialism relies first and foremost on scientific method, believes in the ultimate atomic structure of things, and finds in Nature an order and a process that can be expressed in scientific laws of cause and effect.[8]

Indeed, naturalism and materialism are so closely related they are inseparable. Roy Wood Sellars, author of the first *Humanist Manifesto*, points out the similarities this way: "Like naturalism, modern materialism is opposed to any other criterion of human value and policy than human needs and aspirations. It combats all forms of authoritarianism

Notes and Asides

in morals and arts, opposes reduction of ethics to mere formalism, and rejects the appeal to any supposed extranatural source of experience. With the removal of a supernatural perspective, man must stand consciously on his own feet."[9] The bottom line is the same: Humanist philosophy believes matter is all that exists. For our purposes we shall call this view naturalism, since it is the title most often used by the Humanists to describe their philosophy.

The list of Humanists embracing naturalism is almost endless. For some, naturalism preceded their Humanism. Sellars writes, "My philosophical thinking led me to a physical naturalism. I had to fit man into the picture and the development of human culture. The result was an outlook which I called Humanism."[10] For others, the terms are complementary and virtually synonymous. Lamont writes, "naturalistic Humanism . . . is the Humanism that I have supported through the written and spoken word for some forty years."[11]

Julian Huxley also treats the terms as synonymous:

> I use the word 'Humanist' to mean someone who believes that man is just as much a natural phenomenon as an animal or a plant, that his body, his mind, and his soul were not supernaturally created but are all products of evolution, and that he is not under the control or guidance of any supernatural Being or beings, but has to rely on himself and his own powers.[12]

Miriam Allen deFord writes, "My own tentative general definition of Humanism as a whole would be that it is a philosophical system based on the concept that the universe, life and consequently mankind are the result of natural evolutionary processes alone, and hence that our view of them must be monistic. In other words, there is nothing in existence except random, fortuitous forces which eventually—in the manner of the famous example of the monkeys pounding typewriters who finally emerge with the works of Shakespeare—bring together consonant elements from which under favourable circumstances, galaxies, planetary systems, bacteria and human beings gradually issue and evolve."[13] It is important to note that the naturalistic philosophy is implicit to deFord's very definition of Humanism—that naturalism is the foundation for her beliefs. This is true for most Humanists; therefore, throughout this chapter the term "Humanism" will imply a naturalistic view, and vice versa.

Denial of the Supernatural

The key tenet of naturalism is its denial of the supernatural. People either believe that some supernatural things exist or that only natural

Notes and Asides

things exist. By "supernatural," philosophers mean things that are immaterial, such as the soul, personality, or God. Naturalists deny everything that is not made up of matter, that does not exist in nature. Lamont writes, "Humanism . . . believes in a naturalistic cosmology or metaphysics or attitude towards the universe that rules out all forms of the supernatural and that regards nature as the totality of being and as a constantly changing system of events existing independently of any mind or consciousness. There is no room in this picture for a properly defined Divine Providence."[14] Indeed, there is no room for anything supernatural. This is the consistent Secular Humanist worldview.

Lamont states elsewhere,

> The adjective "naturalistic" shows that Humanism, in its most accurate philosophical sense, implies a world-view in which Nature is everything, in which there is no supernatural and in which man is an integral part of Nature and not separated from it by any sharp cleavage or discontinuity. This philosophy, of course, recognizes that vast stretches of reality yet remain beyond the range of human knowledge, but it takes for granted that all future discoveries of truth will reveal an extension of the natural and not an altogether different realm of being, commonly referred to as the supernatural.[15]

> "There is no room in [the Humanistic] picture for a properly defined Divine Providence."
> —Corliss Lamont

He sums up his position:

> The nonreality of the supernatural means, on the human level, that *men do not possess supernatural and immortal souls*; and, on the level of the universe as a whole, that *our cosmos does not possess a supernatural and eternal God.*[16]

This current of thought runs throughout Humanist beliefs. Sellars writes, "Christianity, for example, had a supernaturalistic framework in a three-tier universe of heaven, earth and hell. . . . The Humanist argues that the traditional Christian outlook has been undercut and rendered obsolete by the growth of knowledge about man and his world."[17] Humanists rely on this "growth of knowledge" to provide a more accurate worldview. Sidney Hook states,

> The existence of God, immortality, disembodied spirits, cosmic purpose and design, as these have been customarily interpreted by the great institutional religions, are denied by naturalists for the same generic reasons that they deny the existence of fairies, elves, and leprechauns. There are other conceptions of God, to be sure, and provided they are not self-contradictory in meaning, the naturalist is prepared in principle to consider their

Notes and Asides

> claims to validity. All he asks is that the conception be sufficiently definite to make possible specific inferences of the determinate conditions—the how, when, and where of His operation.[18]

Naturalism calls for the object to be observable and measurable to be believable.

Naturalists are especially unwilling to believe in a universe that exudes too much design, because this design could be construed as evidence for a Designer. They avoid the teleological problem by holding to the view that "Nature is a principle intelligible in all its parts, but it cannot be explained as a whole. For this would presumably require reference to a natural cause, and outside nature as a whole there are no natural causes to be found. Or else it would require reference to a nonnatural object, but such reference is never explanatory."[19]

The naturalist can accept no Designer and no personal First Cause. Sellars writes, "the naturalist is skeptical of any other assignment of value to the universe. There is no central, brooding will which has planned it all."[20] Henry Miller is even more vehement in his denial of God: "To imagine that we are going to be saved by outside intervention, whether in the shape of an analyst, a dictator, a savior, or even God, is sheer folly."[21]

Naturalistic Humanism, then, is the denial of the supernatural. But it is more than that—it is a complete philosophy. Lamont puts it this way: "To define naturalistic Humanism in a nutshell: it rejects all forms of supernaturalism, pantheism, and metaphysical idealism, and considers man's supreme aim as working for the welfare and progress of all humanity in this one and only life, according to the methods of reason, science and democracy."[22] This definition is important from a philosophical perspective, because it outlines both the metaphysics and epistemology of naturalism. This chapter will focus on the metaphysics (specifically the cosmology) of naturalism first, and then explore naturalism's epistemology.

Metaphysics is the branch of philosophy that examines first principles, and includes ontology and cosmology.

Cosmology/Metaphysics

Cosmology refers to the philosophical study of the universe, especially its origin. Secular Humanists believe that the physical universe came to exist by accident and that it is all that exists. Obviously, this belief relies on their denial of God and the supernatural. Lamont states,

> The central pillar in the Humanist metaphysics is that the underlying and continuing foundation of the universe is not

Notes and Asides

> mind or consciousness, but matter in its multiple and changing modes. The truth of this position is not dependent upon the definition of matter in terms of any particular stuff. Our position is based simply on the proposition that objective reality—an external world—call it matter, energy, substance, events, electricity or what you will, exists antecedent to and independent of the human mind, a Divine Mind, or any other conceivable mind.[23]

That is, matter spontaneously generated life and ultimately the human mind through evolution.

Cosmology is the branch of metaphysics concerned with the origin, elements or being, and laws of the cosmos.

The cosmology of naturalism is best summed up by Carl Sagan, 1981 Humanist of the Year: "The Cosmos is all that is or ever was or ever will be."[24] The Humanist belief is simple: the universe is all that exists, the supernatural is a fairy tale. Lamont says, "For Humanism the

CLOSE-UP

Roy Wood Sellars (1880-1973)

Roy Wood Sellars never achieved the level of popularity of John Dewey or Erich Fromm, but his work as a pioneer in modern Humanistic thought is second to none. As the major force behind *Humanist Manifesto I* (published in 1933), Sellars provided the first significant attempt to synthesize the Humanist worldview. Further, he contributed a great deal to Humanist philosophy, especially in his work *Evolutionary Naturalism*. His belief that knowledge is ultimately nothing more than the adjustment of the organism to its environment perfectly integrates the evolutionary viewpoint with naturalism, and provides a foundation for all Humanist epistemology. On this foundation, Sellars drew the conclusion that "life is not a nonnatural force coming from outside, but a term for the new capacities of which nature has found itself capable." This conclusion allows the Humanists to abandon the notion of God. Sellars believed firmly in man's capacity to evolve into higher life forms, and trusted that a society based on democratic socialism would encourage such progress. The influence of these beliefs shows clearly in Secular Humanistic thought today.

Notes and Asides

universe of Nature is all that exists; and man's greater good within this Nature is man's be-all and end-all. This-earthly human achievement is a worthwhile goal in itself and not a means to salvation in another life. Whatever salvation man can find from evil must be in this world."[25] This attitude about the universe naturally leaves man without hope of supernatural salvation; therefore, as the *Humanist Manifesto II* explains, "man must save himself."

For the Humanist, no personal First Cause exists; only the cosmos. "Nature is but an endless series of efficient causes. She cannot create but she eternally transforms. There was no beginning and there can be no end."[26] Of course, there is no need for a God to explain a beginning that didn't happen.

Humanists assign a different basis for reality, a non-sequential group of first causes, to the universe to avoid God as the First Cause. Lamont calls these the "ultimate principles of explanation and intelligibility," stating,

> Metaphysics, then, deals with the lowest common denominators of everything that exists, whether it be animate or inanimate, human or nonhuman. These lowest common denominators, such as substance and activity, supplement one another and must be consistent with one another; but they cannot be deduced from one another or from any conception common to some or all of them. We can find no intelligible explanation of why these particular generic traits exist; they simply are. Precisely because they are ultimate principles of explanation and intelligibility, they themselves are not susceptible of explanation. To demand a reason for them is like asking the cause of causality.[27]

Ontology is the branch of metaphysics concerned with the nature of ultimate reality or substance.

This realm of metaphysics, which deals with the nature of ultimate reality or substance, is known as ontology. The naturalistic ontology is summed up in the statement, "the physical realm [nature] is the locus of efficient causality."[28] Ontology and cosmology both are aspects of metaphysics, and in naturalistic terms they are grounded, as Lamont previously noted, in an "attitude towards the universe that rules out all forms of the supernatural. . . ."

Epistemology

Epistemology is a theory of knowledge. That is, epistemology answers the question, "How much can one know about the world, and how does one obtain this knowledge?" Naturalism answers that everything in the physical world (which means *everything*) is knowable, and science is

Notes and Asides

the proper means of knowing it. Sellars writes, "What, then, can we know about the external world? Essentially what science has worked out—structure, relative dimensions, relative mass, energy-content, behavior. Theory of knowledge does not so much dictate to science as interpret it."[29] In fact, Sellars goes so far as to state, "The spirit of naturalism would seem to be one with the spirit of science itself."[30]

Sellars elaborates by integrating science and epistemology so that they are virtually inseparable:

> Knowledge of the physical world is a comprehension of the characteristics of things by means of subjective contents. An idea, or judgment, is said to be a case of knowledge when it makes a claim to reveal something about things, and its claim is granted. This definition permits the usual belief that there are degrees in the completeness of our knowledge of things as we pass from ordinary perception to science. It is not that careful perception is wrong—for it is the right sort of response to the stimuli—but that the methods of science use perception, that is, observation to carry us further in our comprehension of things.[31]

Epistemology is the theory of the origin, nature, and boundaries of knowledge.

That is, science is the highest degree of perception, and therefore the most accurate means of obtaining knowledge.

Most Humanists agree with Sellars. The *Humanist Manifesto II* states, "Any account of nature should pass the tests of scientific evidence . . .,"[32] which, of course, supernatural explanations could never do, since they are not measurable or observable. Refer back for a moment to Hook's statement that he would be open to a supernatural Being if only he could learn the "how, when, and where of his operation." This statement calls for a god that could be seen and poked and prodded to discover His characteristics; i.e., a god that is not supernatural. Hook, as a naturalist, will only believe what he sees with his eyes—that is, the physical—and so anything supernatural cannot exist. Hook further says that naturalists are united in "the wholehearted acceptance of scientific method as the only reliable way of reaching truths about the world of nature, society, and man."[33]

Lamont also believes this: "The Humanist insists that his inclusive philosophy must be consistent throughout with the established facts and laws of science."[34] Kurtz echoes him: "Using the powerful critical tools of science and logical analysis, modern man now recognizes that the universe has no special human meaning or purpose and that man is not a special product of creation."[35]

Clearly, Humanists' naturalistic epistemology shapes their metaphysics. Because Humanists believe that science tells us we are products of chance and have evolved over billions of years, they must act on

Notes and Asides

"[S]cience has itself become a kind of religion . . . "

—Carl Sagan

that knowledge and formulate a worldview consistent with it—a worldview in which the universe is all that exists and ever will exist, because science (according to their view) has no means of obtaining knowledge about the supernatural (and therefore the supernatural must not exist). But doesn't this grounding of belief in science as the ultimate means of perception require faith, just as the supernatural does? Doesn't Sagan's statement that "science has itself become a kind of religion"[36] admit that very self-contradiction?

Lamont acknowledges the charge as valid and answers it this way:

> It is sometimes argued that since science, like religion, must make ultimate assumptions, we have no more right to rely on science in an analysis of the idea of immortality than on religion. Faith in the methods and findings of science, it is said, is just as much a faith as faith in the methods and findings of religion. In answer to this we can only say that the history of thought seems to show that reliance on science has been more fruitful in the progress and extension of the truth than reliance on religion.[37]

John Herman Randall, Jr., also admits the need for faith in the Humanist's philosophical position, noting, "Assuredly, the antinaturalists are right: our world is perishing for want of faith. The faith we need, the faith that alone promises salvation, is the faith in intelligence."[38]

Indeed, the Humanist tells us that this was Christ's biggest flaw. Edwin Arthur Burtt writes,

> Jesus had no appreciation of the value of intelligence as the most dependable human faculty for analyzing the perplexities into which men fall and for providing wise guidance in dealing with them. Simple and childlike trust in the Heavenly Father and humble obedience to his will was the sum and substance of life's wisdom to him. His theory of the world, which to his mind justified this confident faith, is squarely opposed to the scientific naturalism that a frank assessment of experience increasingly compels modern men to accept. Far from thinking of nature as an objective, law-abiding order, to which man must patiently learn how to adjust himself while assuming responsibility intelligently to transform those parts of it that are amenable to human control, he believed it to be directly subject in all its details to the purposive care of a personal being.[39]

Mankind must learn more faith in intelligence and science and abandon its faith in God, according to naturalism.

Notes and Asides

Humanists impatiently await this abandonment of God for the religion of science. John Dewey believes that this must happen before the science of philosophy can be made complete. He states, "Until the dogma of fixed unchangeable types and species, of arrangement in classes of higher and lower, of subordination of the transitory individual to the universal or kind had been shaken in its hold upon the science of life, it was impossible that the new ideas and method should be made at home in social and moral life. Does it not seem to be the intellectual task of the twentieth century to take this last step? When this step is taken the circle of scientific development will be rounded out and the reconstruction of philosophy be made an accomplished fact."[40] For the naturalist, science is the ultimate means of perception, and therefore the ultimate means of gaining knowledge, and it should be applied to every aspect of life (including the social and moral) so that we can have a better understanding of our world. The epistemology of the naturalist is inseparable from science and, indeed, requires faith in science as the only means of knowing the world around us.

The Mind-Body Problem

The epistemology and metaphysics of naturalism present a very specific problem for the Humanist philosophy. This dilemma is traditionally referred to as the mind-body problem, because it asks, "Does the mind exist solely within nature, just as the body does, or is the mind more than matter?" Sellars admits, "No problem is more crucial for a naturalistic view of the world than the mind-body problem."[41] He goes on to say, "Man cannot know himself unless he has an answer to the question whether he is literally, and in all respects, a child of this earth, or has a dual nature which unites him by one of its parts with that which transcends the visible world."[42] Lamont concurs:

> For Humanism, as for most philosophies, the most important and far-reaching problem connected with the nature and destiny of man is what sort of relationship exists between the physical body and the personality, which includes the mind in its every aspect.[43]

Naturally, Humanists believe that the mind (or consciousness, or personality, or soul—for the sake of continuity we shall refer to this phenomenon as the mind) is simply a manifestation of the brain—just an extension of the natural world, and easily explainable in purely physical terms. This belief arises from their epistemology in the sense that science is our best way of obtaining knowledge, and the knowledge

Notes and Asides

it has obtained (according to Humanists) supports their metaphysical belief that life arose spontaneously and has evolved to its present state. Since this view of the cosmos allows only for the existence of matter, the mind must somehow be a strictly physical phenomenon. This view is commonly referred to as monism, while the opposing view is called dualism.

Lamont defines *dualism* this way: "Those thinkers who have emphasized the distinction between body and personality, and the personality's power over the body, have insisted that the personality is a substance of a different order, an immaterial or non-physical soul that inhabits the body and uses it as its instrument. When the body dies, this soul departs and may go on existing elsewhere; and, according to some, it existed before its earthly body came into being at all. In philosophical and psychological terminology this theory of the personality's independence has been called dualism or Platonism."[44] He goes on to define *monism*: "Other thinkers, while admitting a distinction between body and personality, have claimed that the personality is the life or function or activity of the body. It is the body acting, the body living; and, to be exact, the body acting and living in certain definite ways closely associated with the brain and the rest of the central nervous system. For purposes of convenience we talk and write about an abstraction, personality; but it can in actuality no more be abstracted from the human body than can the activities of breathing and digestion. This personality is, then, a quality of the body, not an independently existing thing, just as redness is an inseparable quality of a red rose."[45]

Dualism is a philosophical doctrine that affirms the existence of both the natural and the supernatural. When applied to the mind-body debate, it describes human personality as both spiritual and natural.

It is important to note that Humanists consistently affirm the unique character of the mind. Apparently, they have no problem with the seemingly contradictory views regarding the mind as unique and yet a material phenomenon. Lamont writes, "Unsurpassed among the glories of man is his mind."[46] Sellars notes, "If, then, any psychologist comes to me and says that there is no such thing as consciousness, I simply reply that he does not know what he is saying."[47] Gora claims, "Humanists respect human personality,"[48] and Mathilde Niel sums up: "For the Humanist faith, conscience does not constitute an isolated phenomenon in the universe; it is an integral part of man and life. Conscience, far from being a void which we attempt to fill . . . constitutes a creative drive to synthesis, which, if not hindered by absolutist aspirations and messianic aspirations, tends to connect the individual to life, to the world and to the infinite."[49]

Monism is the philosophical doctrine that claims all reality is one substance, either natural or supernatural. Naturalism presupposes a monistic view.

From whence did this incredibly unique consciousness, this amazingly complex mind, arise? According to the naturalist philosophy, it evolved. Lamont says, "naturalistic Humanism . . . take[s] the view that the material universe came first and that mind emerged in the

Notes and Asides

animal man only after some two billion years of biological evolution upon this material earth."[50] Huxley echoes Lamont: "Humanist beliefs are based on human knowledge, especially on the knowledge-explosion of the hundred years since Darwin published *The Origin of Species*, which has revealed to us a wholly new picture of the universe and of our place in it. We now believe with confidence that the whole of reality is one gigantic process of evolution. This produces increased novelty and variety, and ever higher types of organization; in a few spots it has produced life; and, in a few of those spots of life, it has produced mind and consciousness."[51] The *Humanist Manifesto II* concurs, stating, "science affirms that the human species is an emergence from natural evolutionary forces. As far as we know, the total personality is a function of the biological organism transacting in a social and cultural context."[52]

Once naturalists have explained where mind and consciousness came from, they must explain the mind's relationship with the body in a way that keeps it firmly grounded in the physical. Sellars believes he accomplishes this by referring to the mind and body together as the "living organism," and then presents his "thesis of evolutionary naturalism": "The living organism, when properly and adequately conceived, includes consciousness and is the sole source of that differential behavior which distinguishes it from less integrated bodies."[53] He states this premise a little more coherently when he says, "evolutionary naturalism suggests that the brain may include consciousness in a unique way because consciousness is a novel quality of the tensionally functioning brain."[54] Consciousness is an extension of our purely physical brain—one might say it is a trick that our brain plays on us every day.

Lamont describes the relation between mind and body this way: "Mind, like digestion and respiration, is not a separate agent or thing-in-itself, but it is a particular type of doing, of activity on the part of a human being. Thought always signifies thinking; reason is always reasoning."[55] Therefore, the mind is just a function of the material brain.

Dewey also believes the mind to be a purely natural phenomenon, an attribute of the brain:

> Some bodies have souls preeminently as some conspicuously have fragrance, color, and solidity. To make this statement is to call attention to properties that characterize these bodies, not to import a mysterious non-natural entity or force. . . . To say emphatically of a particular person that he has soul or a great soul is not to utter a platitude, applicable equally to all human

HUMANISTS OF THE YEAR

1953: Anton J. Carlson
1954: Arthur F. Bentley
1955: James P. Warbasse
1956: C. Judson Herrick
1957: Margaret Sanger
1958: Oscar Riddle
1959: Brock Chisholm
1960: Leo Szilard
1961: Linus Pauling
1962: Julian Huxley
1963: Hermann J. Muller
1964: Carl Rogers
1965: Hudson Hoagland
1966: Erich Fromm
1967: A. H. Maslow
1968: Benjamin Spock
1969: R. Buckminster Fuller
1970: A. Philip Randolph
1971: Albert Ellis
1972: B. F. Skinner
1973: Thomas Szasz
1974: Joseph Fletcher
Mary Calderone
1975: Henry Morgentaler
Betty Friedan
1976: Jonas E. Salk
1977: Corliss Lamont
1978: Margaret E. Kuhn
1979: Edwin H. Wilson
1980: Andrei Sakharov
1981: Carl Sagan
1982: Helen Caldicott
1983: Lester A. Kirkendall
1984: Isaac Asimov
1985: John Kenneth Galbraith
1986: Faye Wattleton
1987: Margaret Atwood
1988: Leo Pfeffer
1989: Gerald Larue
1990: Ted Turner

> beings. It expresses the conviction that the man or woman in question has in marked degree qualities of sensitive, rich and coordinated participation in all the situations of life.[56]

That is, when one speaks of his soul, one is simply speaking of his ability to participate in life.

Regardless of which method naturalists use to answer the mind-body problem, they must always support monism and reject dualism in order to be consistent with their worldview. A philosophy that believes all of existence is grounded in nature cannot allow for mind or

Notes and Asides

consciousness to exist in the supernatural. Thus the *Humanist Manifesto I* states, "Holding an organic view of life, humanists find that the traditional dualism of mind and body must be rejected."[57] Lamont expounds on this idea,

> It is obvious that the Humanist metaphysics or theory of the universe, in line with the traditional naturalisms and Materialisms, leaves no room for world-views in which supernaturalism plays any part. Thus it rules out the metaphysical Dualisms which divide the universe into two separate realms, a material one and a spiritual one; and which also divide man himself into two separate entities, hence making inevitable a dualistic psychology and a dualistic ethics.[58]

Implications of the Monistic View

Just as the naturalistic epistemology and metaphysics necessitates a monistic view, this view, in turn, implies two more necessary conclusions for the Humanist. The first answers the question, "Is man immortal?" Lamont recognizes this question, noting that the answer lies "in the relationship between body or the physical organism on the one hand and personality or soul on the other."[59] He later faces the only conclusion open to the naturalist: "If, on the other hand, the monistic theory of psychology is true, as Naturalism, Materialism, and Humanism claim, then there is no possibility that the human consciousness, with its memory and awareness of self-identity intact, can survive the shock and disintegration of death. According to this view, the body and personality live together; they grow together; and they die together."[60]

For the Humanist, there can be no life after death. In fact, the denial of the after-life is inherent to the Humanist worldview, so much so that the belief in mortality is seen by Lamont as the first step in becoming a Humanist. He writes, "The issue of mortality versus immortality is crucial in the argument of Humanism against supernaturalism. For if men realize that their careers are limited to this world, that this earthly existence is all that they will ever have, then they are already more than half-way on the path toward becoming functioning Humanists. . . ."[61]

"The issue of mortality versus immortality is crucial in the argument of Humanism against supernaturalism."
—Corliss Lamont

The second necessary conclusion for Humanists results from their belief that mind evolved through natural processes. According to this view, there is no guarantee that mind is anything special at all—some better mutation of mind could occur any day. In truth, some Humanists believe this more efficient mind is being created today. Victor J. Stenger, author of *Not By Design*, writes,

Notes and Asides

> Computers obviously do not think quite like humans, and I do not claim that the computer of today is necessarily a valid model of the human brain. But computers process data and make decisions based on that data, which is all that the human brain does under the label of thinking. A prime area of study today is artificial intelligence (AI), and its practitioners harbor few doubts that someday computers will be made to do all the operations normally associated with human intelligence, and many more. If the intelligence that results is not strictly human, that is not to say that it will necessarily be inferior. Perhaps artificial intelligence will be superior, with characteristics and capabilities the human mind can not even imagine.[62]

Artificial Intelligence is a branch of computer science concerned with developing systems which mirror or surpass human intelligence.

But, humans program computers!

Stenger goes on to claim, "Future computers will not only be superior to people in every task, mental or physical, but will also be immortal." He believes it will become possible to save human "thoughts which constitute consciousness" in these computer memory banks, as well as program computers in such a way as to give them the full range of human thought. After all, he says, "If the computer is 'just a machine,' so is the human brain. . . ." So why shouldn't the computer become the next step in the evolutionary chain, the new, higher consciousness? Stenger sees this as a real possibility, and concludes, "Perhaps, as part of this new consciousness, we will become God."[63]

Sound like science fiction? Far from it. In a naturalistic, monistic worldview, it is not only a logical possibility, but a likely one. Evolution created the human mind strictly out of matter; evolution and natural selection are still at work to improve that mind; and the computer is really nothing more than an incredibly efficient material mind, perhaps the inevitable next step in the evolutionary chain.

Scary!!

Conclusion

Naturalism, with its denial of the supernatural and its reliance on science as its source of knowledge, necessitates not only specific conclusions about the mind and mortality, but also implies a distinct worldview. This view, as adopted by the Humanists, tends to elevate man in terms of his abilities to control his fate, but at the same time has immense difficulty in overcoming pessimism. Burtt believes "the ultimate accommodation necessary in a wise plan of life is acceptance of a world not made for man, owing him nothing, and in its major processes quite beyond his control."[64]

Lamont focuses more on the abilities of man and looks toward the future for hope, stating,

Notes and Asides

> Humanism is the viewpoint that men have but one life to lead and should make the most of it in terms of creative work and happiness; that human happiness is its own justification and requires no sanction or support from supernatural sources; that in any case the supernatural, usually conceived of in the form of heavenly gods or immortal heavens, does not exist; and that human beings, using their own intelligence and cooperating liberally with one another, can build an enduring citadel of peace and beauty upon this earth.[65]

where do they base their Standards/values?

Obviously, this citadel has not yet been attained and will require a superhuman effort from man, if we are to believe it can happen at all. Lamont alludes to this need for greater efforts from mankind, stating, "Humanism assigns to man nothing less than the task of being his own savior and redeemer."[66] Algernon D. Black says, "Man stands on his own feet without fear of punishment or promise of reward. Man makes his own Hell and his own Heaven, and he makes it here and now."[67]

"All good and moral philosophy, as was said, is but a hand-maid to religion."
—Sir Francis Bacon

These are bold statements, speaking of the triumphant nature of life for the Humanist. However, they are at best idealistic. The real purpose of life consistent with the naturalistic philosophy adopted by Humanists is summed up by Clarence Darrow: "The purpose of man is like the purpose of the pollywog—to wiggle along as far as he can without dying; or, to hang to life until death takes him."[68]

If there is no afterlife... what is man saving + redeeming himself for?

[1]Roy Wood Sellars, "The Humanist Outlook," in *The Humanist Alternative*, ed. Paul Kurtz (Buffalo: Prometheus, 1973), p. 135.
[2]Corliss Lamont, as cited in *The Best of Humanism*, ed. Roger E. Greeley (Buffalo: Prometheus, 1988) p. 149.
[3]Ernest Nagel, "Naturalism Reconsidered," in *American Philosophy in the Twentieth Century*, ed. Paul Kurtz (New York: Macmillan, 1967), p. 555.
[4]Corliss Lamont, *The Philosophy of Humanism* (New York: Frederick Ungar, 1982), p. 91.
[5]Paul Kurtz, "Is Everyone a Humanist?" in *The Humanist Alternative*, ed. Kurtz, p. 178.
[6]*Humanist Manifesto II* (Buffalo: Prometheus, 1980), p. 16.
[7]Lamont, *The Philosophy of Humanism*, p. 28.
[8]Ibid., pp. 37-8.
[9]Roy Wood Sellars, Marvin Farber, and V. J. McGill, "The Quest of Modern Materialism," in *American Philosophy in the Twentieth Century*, ed. Paul Kurtz, p. 504.
[10]Sellars, "The Humanist Outlook," p. 137.
[11]Lamont, as cited in *The Best of Humanism*, ed. Greeley, p. 149.
[12]Julian Huxley, as cited in *The Best of Humanism*, pp. 194-5.
[13]Miriam Allen deFord, "Heretical Humanism," in *The Humanist Alternative*, ed. Kurtz, p. 81.
[14]Corliss Lamont, *Voice in the Wilderness* (Buffalo: Prometheus, 1975), p. 18.
[15]Lamont, *The Philosophy of Humanism*, p. 22.
[16]Ibid., p. 116, emphases added.
[17]Sellars, "The Humanist Outlook," p. 133.
[18]Sidney Hook, "Naturalism and Democracy," in *Naturalism and the Human Spirit*, ed. Y. H. Krikorian (New York: Columbia University Press, 1944), p. 45.
[19]Arthur C. Danto, "Naturalism," in *The Encyclopedia of Philosophy*, eight volumes, ed. Paul Edwards (New York: Macmillan and Free Press, 1967), vol. 5, p. 448.
[20]Roy Wood Sellars, *Evolutionary Naturalism* (Chicago: Open Court, 1922), p. 343.
[21]Henry Miller, as cited in *The Best of Humanism*, ed. Greeley, p. 144.
[22]Corliss Lamont, as cited in *The Best of Humanism*, ed. Greeley, p. 149.
[23]Lamont, *The Philosophy of Humanism*, pp. 145-6.
[24]Carl Sagan, *Cosmos* (New York: Random House, 1980), p. 4.
[25]Lamont, *The Philosophy of Humanism*, p. 176.
[26]Robert Green Ingersoll, as cited in *The Best of Humanism*, ed. Greeley, p. 162.
[27]Lamont, *The Philosophy of Humanism*, pp. 170-1.
[28]Sellars, *Evolutionary Naturalism*, p. 264.
[29]Roy Wood Sellars, "Critical Realism," in *American Philosophy in the Twentieth Century*, ed. Kurtz, p. 367.
[30]Sellars, *Evolutionary Naturalism*, p. 5.
[31]Ibid., p. 35.
[32]*The Humanist Manifesto II*, p. 16.
[33]Hook, "Naturalism and Democracy," p. 45.
[34]Lamont, *Voice in the Wilderness*, p. 5.
[35]Kurtz, *The Humanist Alternative*, p. 5.
[36]Carl Sagan, *UFO's—A Scientific Debate* (Ithaca, NY: Cornell University Press, 1972), p. xiv.
[37]Corliss Lamont, *The Illusion of Immortality* (New York: Frederick Ungar, 1965), pp. 124-5.
[38]John Herman Randall, Jr., "The Nature of Naturalism," in *Naturalism and the Human Spirit*, ed. Krikorian, p. 382.
[39]Edwin Arthur Burtt, *Types of Religious Philosophy* (New York: Harper and Brothers, 1939), pp. 359-60.
[40]John Dewey, "The Scientific Factor in Reconstruction of Philosophy," in *Philosophy in the Twentieth Century*, ed. William Barrett and Henry D. Aiken (New York: Random House, 1962), vol. 1, p. 309.
[41]Sellars, *Evolutionary Naturalism*, p. 286.
[42]Ibid.
[43]Lamont, *The Philosophy of Humanism*, p. 81.
[44]Lamont, *The Illusion of Immortality*, p. 27.
[45]Ibid., pp. 27-8.

[46]Ibid., p. 276.
[47]Sellars, *Evolutionary Naturalism*, p. 46.
[48]Gora, "Humanism and Atheism," in *The Humanist Alternative*, ed. Kurtz, p. 147.
[49]Mathilde Niel, "Contribution to a Definition of Humanism," in *The Humanist Alternative*, ed. Kurtz, p. 145.
[50]Lamont, *Voice in the Wilderness*, p. 82.
[51]Julian Huxley, as cited in *The Best of Humanism*, ed. Greeley, p. 195.
[52]*Humanist Manifesto II*, p. 17.
[53]Sellars, *Evolutionary Naturalism*, p. 298.
[54]Ibid., p. 55.
[55]Lamont, *The Illusion of Immortality*, p. 107.
[56]John Dewey, *Experience and Nature* (New York: Norton, 1929), pp. 293-4.
[57]*Humanist Manifesto I* (Buffalo: Prometheus, 1980), p. 8.
[58]Lamont, *The Philosophy of Humanism*, p. 131.
[59]Lamont, *The Illusion of Immortality*, p. 24.
[60]Lamont, *The Philosophy of Humanism*, pp. 81-2.
[61]Ibid., p. 82.
[62]Victor J. Stenger, *Not By Design* (Buffalo: Prometheus, 1988), p. 187.
[63]Ibid., pp. 188-9.
[64]Burtt, *Types of Religious Philosophy*, p. 353. Clearly, the Humanist has no patience with the Anthropic Principle, which contends that the world was tailored for man's existence. For an excellent defense of this principle, see Roy Abraham Varghese, ed., *The Intellectuals Speak Out About God* (Dallas, TX: Lewis and Stanley, 1984), pp. 102ff.
[65]Lamont, *The Philosophy of Humanism*, p. 14.
[66]Ibid., p. 283.
[67]Algernon D. Black, "Our Quest for Faith: Is Humanism Enough?" in *The Humanist Alternative*, ed. Kurtz, p. 77.
[68]Clarence Darrow, as cited in *The Best of Humanism*, ed. Greeley, p. 154.

CHAPTER

7

MARXIST/ LENINIST PHILOSOPHY

"The real unity of the world consists in its materiality, and this is proved . . . by a long and protracted development of philosophy and natural science. . . . But if the . . . question is raised: what then are thought and consciousness, and whence they come, it becomes apparent that they are products of the human brain and that man himself is a product of nature, which has been developed in and along with its environment."[1]

—Frederick Engels

"Dialectics reveals that development proceeds by a process, in which the given situation—or thing, or idea, always gives birth to its exact antithesis, opposite; and in so doing creates a tension, a struggle, which becomes the motive power for change, progress, as the antithesis struggles with its mother, the thesis, until out of the struggle a new stage in history—be it of the situation, of the thing, or of the idea—is reached, namely the synthesis—and this, in turn, becomes the starting point of another round, by giving birth once more to its opposite."[2]

—V. I. Lenin

SUMMARY

Marxist philosophy, known as dialectical materialism, attempts to explain all of reality—including inorganic matter (the molecular, atomic, and subatomic), the organic world (life and, according to materialism, mind or consciousness), and social life (economics, politics, etc.). All of nature reflects, illuminates, and illustrates communist dialectical philosophy. Modern physics was even in travail, thought Lenin, "giving birth to dialectical materialism." Marxist philosophy insists that the material universe is infinite, that matter is eternal (negating, of course, the need for a beginning), uncreated (negating the need for a Creator), indestructible, and dialectical (the clash between opposites, for example, explains the self-motion of matter, which eliminates the need for a Mover outside of matter or nature). Marxism also perceives matter's motion as upward and evolutionary. Matter is not static or at rest, but actively in process, progressive. Matter dialectically viewed explains its own nature and progress from its inorganic state through its development into life, onward to animal consciousness, and ultimately to human mind and consciousness and social institutions.

Matter can move upward from the inorganic to the organic, from the organic to the human, and from the human to the social level because of its dialectical nature—a nature responding to certain laws including: (a) the unity and struggle of opposites, (b) the transformation of quantity into quality, and (c) the negation of the negation. The dialectical laws manifest a threefold rhythm of equilibrium (thesis), disturbance (antithesis) and re-establishment of equilibrium (synthesis). Because the dialectic is a progressive process, each synthesis becomes not merely a *new* thesis but a *higher* one. In reality, what Darwin's theory of natural selection is to evolution, the dialectic is to matter. Marxist philosopher G. V. Plekhanov came to regard Marxism as "Darwinism in its application to social science."[3] Marx and Engels acknowledge that Darwin's theory of natural selection served them well as the basis for their theory of the class struggle. From Darwin's point of view, in Gustav A. Wetter's words, "insignificant quantitative changes in plants and animals eventually lead by accumulation and inheritance to the formation of new species,"[4] i.e., changes in quantity lead ultimately to changes in quality. The present clash between socialism and capitalism, for the Marxist, is similar in kind to the clash among biological creatures "struggling for existence" and the clash between positive and negative charges in electricity. And the evolution of mankind from spontaneous generated life (the first speck of life from non-living matter) serves as an example of the progress of matter through many minute quantitative changes (due to natural selection) to great qualitative changes (new species). For better or worse, the Marxist's philosophy of dialectical materialism is built primarily on the "science" of Darwinian evolution.

Notes and Asides

Introduction

Virtually every individual professing to be a Marxist/Leninist believes dialectical materialism is the proper philosophy for understanding and changing the world. Indeed, what dialectical materialism is to the Marxist, God is to the Christian. Virtually all the ways Christians describe God—eternal, infinite, uncreated, indestructible, lawgiver, life, mind, etc.—Marxists assign to dialectical matter. Making matter the essence of all things is called metaphysical materialism. This philosophy affirms matter as ultimately real and denies the reality of God. It is a "sort of godless theology."

All true Marxists, therefore, affirm their faith in materialism as the only true reality. Karl Marx, in a letter to Frederick Engels, wrote, "as long as we actually observe and think, we cannot possibly get away from materialism."[5] Along this same epistemological line, Engels wrote, "The materialist world outlook is simply the conception of nature as it is. . . . "[6] In other words, what you see of nature is all there is, and because nature appears to be made up of matter of some sort, that is all there is to the real world. This perspective has been maintained by Marxists throughout their history, and, as we shall see, it is imperative that one believe in the materialistic interpretation of the world if he is to be a Marxist/Leninist in the true sense of the word.

Materialism is a philosophical school virtually indistinguishable from naturalism. It also assumes matter or nature to be all that exists, denying the supernatural.

The *Political Dictionary*, published in Moscow in 1940, defines materialism as a "philosophical trend which correctly maintains that at the basis of the entire world lies matter—nature, existing independently of the consciousness of man. Materialism is opposed to [metaphysical] idealism which erroneously views idea, spirit, consciousness as the basis of life and all nature. Materialism, said Vladimir Lenin, views nature as primary, spirit as secondary; existence is in the first place, thinking is second. . . . The highest stage of the development of materialism is dialectical materialism."[7] Of course, putting the choice this way ignores the Christian alternative, metaphysical dualism, which affirms the reality of both matter and spirit (mind), thus avoiding the pitfalls of both materialism and idealism.

The belief that matter is the basic ingredient of reality—indeed, the only ingredient—underlies all Marxist philosophy. Maurice Cornforth, a noted Marxist philosopher, reaffirms this idea:

> However much particular materialist theories may be falsified by events, we can remain sure that the right explanation is along materialist lines; and however well particular idealist theories may evade falsification, we can remain sure that they are nevertheless mere fancies. That is why Marxism rejects every idealist theory about human affairs.[8]

Notes and Asides

Metaphysical materialism is the supreme test of orthodoxy in Marxist philosophy. "Matter is," wrote Lenin "primary nature. Sensation, thought, consciousness, are the highest products of matter organized in a certain way. This is the doctrine of materialism, in general, and Marx and Engels, in particular."[9] Elsewhere, Lenin contended that matter is a philosophical category denoting objective reality—i.e., people, plants, animals, stars, etc. "Matter is the objective reality given to us in sensation."[10] Our seeing the physical world, the material world, was proof enough for Lenin that only matter existed, that it was eternal, uncreated, indestructible, and dialectical. Being eternal and uncreated, and obeying dialectical law, however, is not exactly obvious to everyday sense perception. In this case, presumption determines and even takes precedence over observation.

Engels clarifies the significance of choosing between materialism and supernaturalism by writing, "Did God create the world or has the world been in existence eternally? The answers which the philosophers gave to this question split them into two great camps. Those who asserted the primacy of spirit to nature, and, therefore, in the last instance, assumed world creation in some form or other . . . comprised the camp of idealism. The others, who regarded Nature as primary, belong to the various schools of materialism."[11]

Before we turn to Marxist epistemology, we need to comprehend the full significance of what is at stake between a materialist and a dualist (e.g., Christian supernaturalist) cosmology. When Lenin says that matter is primary, he is saying that matter is eternal and uncreated and that billions of years into this eternity life spontaneously emerged from non-living, non-conscious matter. He is also stating that not only life but also mind, thinking, and consciousness developed or evolved out of this matter. In other words, out of this material universe evolved the mental; out of the unconscious material universe emerged the conscious; out of the non-living evolved the living and ultimately man himself.

Marxist Epistemology

Science plays a crucial role in the Marxist theory of knowledge. "The fundamental characteristic of materialism," says Lenin, "arises from the objectivity of science, from the recognition of objective reality, reflected by science."[12] Leading Soviet philosophers, in *The Fundamentals of Marxist-Leninist Philosophy*, state,

> It was the discovery of the law of the conservation of energy, of the unitary cellular structure of all living organisms, and Dar-

Notes and Asides

> win's theory of the evolution of biological species that provided the foundation on which Marx and Engels built dialectical materialism.[13]

These philosophers go on to describe science as the basis of all fact and religion as the basis of all fantasy: "All knowledge, including scientific knowledge, is regarded by Marxism as reflection of nature and social existence. . . . Religion gives a fantasy reflection of reality, whereas science, taken as a whole, provides a true reflection of nature and society. . . . Religion is hostile to reason, whereas science is the highest achievement of human reason, the embodiment of its strength and effectiveness."[14]

Like Humanism, Marxist epistemology professes faith in science and just as much faith that all religious claims are untrue. This faith in science as a virtually infallible source of all knowledge results from Marxism's ideas about reality. Writes Lenin, "Perceptions give us correct impressions of things.—We directly know objects themselves."[15] These objects, of course, are strictly material: "Matter is . . . the objective reality given to man in his sensations, a reality which is copied, photographed, and reflected by our sensations."[16] Of course, since something supernatural is not an objective, materialist reality, according to Marxism, then we have no means of perceiving it and, therefore, no means of obtaining knowledge about it.

For this reason, Marxists deny the supernatural. They distinguish between knowledge and what they term *true belief* in an attempt to allow for scientific speculation while ignoring speculation about God: "What we call 'knowledge' must also be distinguished from 'true belief.' If, for example, there is life on Mars, the belief that there is life on Mars is true belief. But at the same time we certainly, as yet, know nothing of the matter. True belief only becomes knowledge when backed by some kind of investigation and evidence. Some of our beliefs may be true and others false, but we only start getting to know which are true and which are false when we undertake forms of systematic investigation. . . . For nothing can count as 'knowledge' except in so far as it has been properly tested."[17] Therefore, we can never know belief in the supernatural to be "true belief," because it can never be properly (i.e., empirically, scientifically) tested. Only speculations about the material can ever be found to be true beliefs, since only they can be investigated systematically. Knowledge can apply only to the material world.

> "Truth is the object of philosophy, but not always of philosophers."
>
> —Churton Collins

Marxists, however, rely on more than science and general perception for their epistemology. They believe that *practice,* that is, testing knowledge throughout history, is a valuable aid to gaining knowledge as well. "Marxism has solved the problem of the criterion of truth by

Notes and Asides

showing that it lies ultimately in the activity which is the basis of knowledge, that is, in social historical practice."[18] In other words, Marxists believe that we can test knowledge by applying it to our lives and to society and that this application will eventually determine the truth or falsity of that knowledge. Therefore, by examining history, we can determine better which knowledge is correct and which is not.

This does not make Marxist epistemology unscientific, according to Cornforth; rather, it heightens its scientific stature: "Dialectical materialism, the philosophy adopted by Marxist parties, is a truly scientific world outlook. For it is based on considering things as they are, without arbitrary, preconceived assumptions (idealist fantasies); it insists that our conceptions of things must be based on actual investigation and experience, and must be constantly tested and re-tested in the light of practice and further experience."[19] That is, testing knowledge through practice is simply an extension of the scientific nature of Marxist epistemology.

The power of using practice to test knowledge is espoused by every Marxist philosopher. M. N. Rutkevich states simply, "Practice is the foundation of the entire knowing-process, from beginning to end."[20] And when practice is used scientifically, there is nothing that Marxist philosophy cannot know about the material universe. "Marxist dialectical materialism proceeds from the fact that the world of nature, proved by experience and practice, is valid knowledge having the significance of objective truths; that there are no unknowable things in the world, but rather only things not yet known which will be revealed and known through the power of science and practice."[21] Of course, this circular argument depends on a materialist assumption: there are no unknowable things because everything is material and therefore testable. How do we know? By empirical testing, which we know is the only valid way of knowing because only matter is real.

Marxist epistemology is inextricably tied to the Marxist dialectic. In fact, it is virtually impossible to separate Marxist materialism, dialectics, and epistemology. This is true largely because Marxists claim that dialectics operates in the place of metaphysics in their philosophy and makes metaphysics and epistemology even more interdependent.

Marxist Dialectics

The notion of dialectical process was modified and polished into a broad-based philosophy by Georg Wilhelm Friedrich Hegel, who died when Marx was thirteen years old. The dialectical process was not a creation of Marxist philosophy. Rather the Marxist use of it in conjunc-

Notes and Asides

tion with materialism creates a unique hybrid philosophy. Marx and Engels simply adopted Hegel's ideas, which were built on an idealistic foundation (that is, the dialectic was thought to be a mental construct), and redesigned them to fit into a materialistic scheme of reality. Thus Lenin could write of "The great Hegelian dialectics which Marxism made its own, having first turned it right side up."[22] Indeed, says Marx, "In Hegel's writings, dialectic stands on its head. You must turn it right way up again if you want to discover the rational kernel that is hidden away within the wrappings of mystification."[23] In turning the dialectic "right way up," Marx denied everything supernatural and adopted a materialistic viewpoint. He writes,

> My own dialectic method is not only different from the Hegelian, but is its direct opposite. For Hegel . . . the thinking process is the demiurge (creator) of the real world, and the real world is only the outward manifestation of "the Idea." With me, on the other hand, the ideal is nothing else than the material world reflected by the human mind and translated into terms of thought.[24]

Modern Marxist philosophers, like Cornforth, echo this belief: "The difficulty in Hegel . . . results from his idealism."[25]

Gustav A. Wetter summarizes the Hegelian dialectic as follows: "In Hegel's sense of the term, dialectic is a process in which a starting-point [a thesis, e.g., Being] is negated [the antithesis, e.g., Non-Being], thereby setting up a second position opposed to it. This second position is in turn negated i.e., by negation of the negation, so as to reach a third position representing a synthesis [e.g., Becoming] of the two preceding, in which both are 'transcended,' i.e., abolished and at the same time preserved on a higher level of being. This third phase then figures in turn as the first step in a new dialectical process [i.e., a new thesis], leading to a new synthesis, and so on."[26] Hegel believed the Absolute worked in such a way before creating the universe. He further believed that the created universe behaved in similar fashion. Marxists totally disagree with Hegel's first point regarding the inner workings of the Absolute, but they readily accept his second point regarding the outworking of the dialectic in nature.

The **dialectic** is a progressive process in which the thesis (the status quo) clashes with its antithesis and forms a synthesis, which becomes the new, more advanced thesis.

The fundamental perspective with regard to dialectics is best summed up by Engels: "The world is not to be comprehended as a complex of ready-made [i.e., created] things, but as a complex of [evolutionary] processes."[27] This notion is inherent to the dialectic, which views all of life as a constant evolving process resulting from the clash of opposing forces.

Notes and Asides

> The dialectic draws attention to the opposing tendencies, revealed in every evolving phenomenon; in the mutable it distinguishes the permanent, and in what seems stable it remarks the germ of changes to come.[28]

This development is not always gradual, but it is constantly self-improving. Engels viewed nature as in a constant process of attraction and repulsion, action and reaction, combinations and dissociations (atoms), pluses and minuses, positives and negatives, heredity and adaptations, for and against, light and darkness, hot and cold, life and death, haves and have-nots (class struggle), etc. "Dialectics," says Engels, "is only the reflex of the movement in opposites which asserts itself everywhere in nature, and which by the continual conflict of the opposites and their final merging into one another, or into higher forms, determines the life of nature."[29] V. Afanasyev, author of *Marxist Philosophy*, writes, "Marxist dialectics regards development as movement from the lower to the higher, from the simple to the complex, as a revolutionary process advancing by leaps from one stage to another."[30]

The exact nature of the dialectic, and its tendency to make those who believe in it look for conflict and tension rather than harmony and peace in society, are best summed up by Lenin:

> Dialectics reveals that development proceeds by a process, in which the given situation—or thing, or idea—always gives birth to its exact antithesis, opposite; and in so doing creates a tension, a struggle, which becomes the motive power for change, progress, as the antithesis struggles with its mother, the thesis, until out of the struggle a new stage in history—be it of the situation, of the thing, or of the idea—is reached, namely the synthesis—and this, in turn, becomes the starting point of another round, by giving birth once more to its opposite.[31]

In the dialectical process, the thesis must always attract an antithesis, and this tension must always result in a synthesis, which in turn becomes a new thesis. This new thesis is always more advanced than the last thesis, because dialectics perceives the developmental process as an upward spiral (See Figure 7-1). To simplify: dialectics sees change or process due to conflict or struggle as the only constant—bearing in mind that this change and conflict always lead to more advanced levels.

Marxists believe the proof for dialectics is all around us. Engels notes, "When we reflect on Nature, or the history of mankind, or our own intellectual activity, the first picture presented to us is an endless maze of relations and interactions."[32] These interactions, of course, are

Notes and Asides

always in the process of thesis/antithesis/synthesis. This constant development, or process, or evolution implies that the world (indeed, the universe) is always in motion—always moving, always changing. In fact, Engels says, "Motion is the mode of existence of matter. Never anywhere has there been matter without motion, nor can there be. . . . Matter without motion is just as unthinkable as motion without matter."[33]

Now we can begin to see how dialectics affects the materialist view. For the Marxist, matter can only be understood when one understands that it is constantly going through an eternal process. This idea is best illustrated in the theory of evolution—for, according to this theory, life on earth underwent subtle changes throughout time beginning with simple living forms slowly evolving onward and upward through natural selection to achieve their more advanced states of existence. "Nature is the proof of dialectics," Engels writes. ". . . An exact representation of the universe, of its evolution, of the development of mankind, and of the reflection of this evolution in the minds of men, can only be obtained by methods of dialectics."[34] Engels thought that the seed-grain which fell into the ground and brought forth the plant which in turn produced new seed-grains was an example of dialectical materialism in action. Lenin even went so far as to exclaim, "In a word, not only do oats grow according to Hegel, but the Russian Social-Demo-

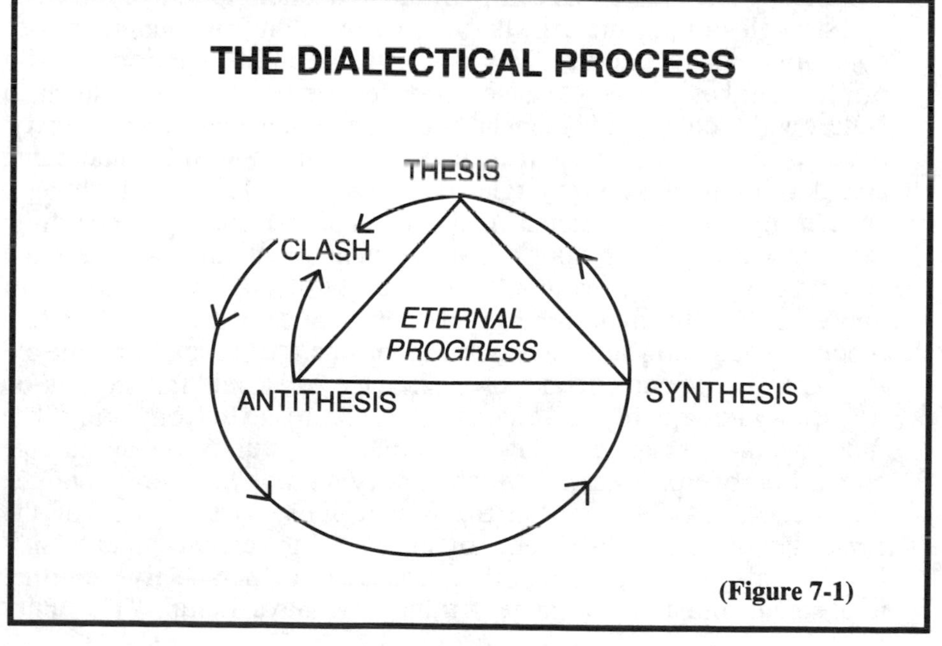

(Figure 7-1)

Notes and Asides

crats wage war among themselves according to Hegel."[35]

Engels also ties in dialectics with Marxist epistemology, noting that "it must be said for modern science that it has furnished this proof with very rich materials increasing daily, and thus has shown that, in the last resort, nature works dialectically."[36] Indeed, the scientific aspect of Marxist epistemology is crucial to dialectics. "Dialectics is not just a matter of asserting that everything develops. What we have to do is to understand the mechanism of this development scientifically."[37]

Alternately, epistemology must be thought of dialectically. Lenin says, "In the theory of knowledge, as in every other sphere of science, we must think dialectically, that is, we must not regard our knowledge as ready-made and unalterable, but must determine how knowledge emerges from ignorance, how incomplete, inexact knowledge becomes more complete and more exact."[38] Engels, too, looked upon human knowledge as a process with no final or eternal truths:

> Truth lay now in the process of cognition itself, in the long historical development of science which mounts from lower to ever higher levels of knowledge without ever reaching, by discovering so-called absolute truth, a point at which it can proceed no further, where it would have nothing more to do than to fold its hands and gaze with wonder at the absolute truth to which it had attained.[39]

Engels listed three basic laws of the dialectic: the law of the unity and struggle of opposites, the law of the transition from quantitative to qualitative change, and the law of the negation of negation.[40] Stalin offered four basic laws: the general connection between phenomena in Nature and society, movement and development in Nature and society, development as a transition from quantitative changes into qualitative, and development as a struggle of opposites.[41] And Lenin thought sixteen ingredients sufficient to understand the concept, including: interconnection of all things; development of all things; internally contradictory tendencies in all things; unity of opposites; conflict of opposites; transformation of every degree, quality, feature, etc.; endless process of deducing new aspects, relationships, etc.; reversion to the old form; conflict of content and form, and vice versa; and transformation of quantity into quality and vice versa.[42] According to Cornforth, "The fundamental concept of dialectics is that of the unity or inseparable connection of opposites,"[43] which is very similar to Lenin's beliefs. "Dialectics," said Lenin, "in the proper sense is the study of the contradiction in the very essence of objects . . . the essence of things."[44] It should also be remembered that, from Lenin's perspective, conflict is absolute, but unity is merely transitory. Says Lenin, "The unity

Notes and Asides

(coincidence, identity, resultant) of opposites is conditional, temporary, transitory, relative. The struggle of mutually exclusive opposites is absolute, just as development and motion are absolute."[45] Development is the struggle of opposites.

The notion of the "unity of opposites" means that any idea, situation, or thing will create or attract its own opposite, and these opposites will necessarily clash. Thus, a thesis will naturally bring about an antithesis, and they will war with each other until a synthesis is reached, which, in turn, will become a new and higher thesis that will bring about its own antithesis, and so on *ad infinitum*. This idea is expressed in *The Fundamentals of Marxist-Leninist Philosophy*: "the struggle of opposites [thesis and antithesis] naturally results in the disappearance of the existing object as a certain unity of opposites and the appearance of a new object [synthesis] with a new unity of opposites inherent in the particular object."[46] This simply means that both thesis and antithesis disappear when they struggle, since they reappear in slightly different form as synthesis or new thesis. The synthesis or new thesis inevitably elicits a new antithesis, and the process continues.

"Dialectics in the proper sense is the study of the contradiction in the very essence of objects . . ."
—V. I. Lenin

The dialectical law of the transition from quantity to quality is best illustrated in the theory of evolution. According to Darwin, natural selection of numerous small quantitative changes in plants and animals through competition for survival leads eventually to the formation of new species of higher quality. Engels saw this law at work in all fields of study at all levels, including chemistry, biology, and physics.

The negation concept is primarily the reference to the antithesis uniting with and struggling with the thesis. In the ensuing struggle, the thesis and its antithesis (negation) are transformed or transcended into a different and newer quality. The synthesis is the negation of the negation. The third aspect (synthesis) negates the negation of the second aspect (antithesis), which in turn negated the first aspect (thesis). The synthesis, i.e., the negation of the negation, in turn becomes the new starting point or new thesis (slightly improved and developed), which elicits its new antithesis as the eternal process continues. Engels believed he saw examples of this process in nature and history. The seed-grain (thesis) falls into the soil and passes away (negation or antithesis) and brings forth the new plant (synthesis or negation of the negation), which in turn produces new seed-grain. With each new generation of the triad (thesis/antithesis/synthesis), improvements, development, and evolution occur by minute changes, just as plants and animals slowly evolve upward into new species. Engels saw history likewise evolving from its original state of primitive communism (thesis) to private property (antithesis or negation) to a new type of communism or common ownership of property (synthesis or negation of the negation). Since the dialectical process is eternal, it follows

What a confusing cycle!!!

Notes and Asides

(and should be noted) that there is never a resolution, even after the establishment of a worldwide classless communist society. Every synthesis (including the classless society) becomes a new thesis, and the historical process continues on into the future as dictated by the eternal laws of the dialectic.

It should be obvious by now that what Darwin taught in biology the Marxists have fixed into a universal law for the whole universe—organic and inorganic. Engels makes this clear: "All nature, from the smallest thing to the biggest, from a grain of sand to the sun, from the protista [the primary living cell] to man, is in a constant state of coming into being and going out of being, in a constant flux, in a ceaseless state of movement and change."[47]

Wetter's observation on this point is critical for understanding exactly what is entailed in making a biological principle germane to the inorganic and social spheres:

> Dialectical materialism attributes to the whole of Nature, and ultimately to the whole of reality, a state of affairs established in the field of biology (and here indeed we must leave open the question whether the formation of new species by way of natural selection and inheritance is actually proved; the prevailing opinion is in fact against it); but as to this it must be observed that in Darwin's postulated transition from chance to law "necessity" does not come about by a simple repetition of accidents, for contingency is transformed, rather, into necessity by natural selection and inheritance, and chance is supplemented in the process, not only by the element of frequency, but also by that of stability; but this is only possible in the realm of organic Nature and not in that of Nature as a whole.[48]

"Nowadays, in our evolutionary conception of the universe, there is absolutely no room for either a creator or a ruler."

—Karl Marx

Dialectics Opposed to Metaphysics

Dialectics is a means of understanding the processes of life. Marxism took this method and applied it to its philosophy, which is foundational for its entire worldview. In making this application, Marxists have hastened to point out that dialectics is a method directly opposed to metaphysics, claiming that metaphysics is an outdated mode of viewing the world.

In making this claim, however, Marxists define metaphysics in a peculiar way. As normally understood, metaphysics is "the branch of philosophy that deals with first principles and seeks to explain the

CLOSE-UP

Frederick Engels (1820-1895)

As a young man, Frederick Engels came in contact with a radical group known as the Young Hegelians and became enchanted with their ideas, especially the materialist philosophy of Ludwig Feuerbach. Engels readily adopted this materialistic outlook, which caused him to be sympathetic toward another young radical, Karl Marx, and in 1844 they began a lifelong friendship. This friendship gave rise to Marxism, one of the twentieth century's most dominant worldviews. Oddly enough, the vital role that Engels played in co-founding Marxism is often overlooked. Marx, looming larger than life, seems to overshadow Engels' contributions. But the fact remains: Marxism would not have gained the ascendency of a dominant worldview without Engels. Not only did he co-write the *Communist Manifesto* with Marx, but he also edited and coordinated volumes 2 and 3 of *Das Kapital.* Further, his own works, such as *Anti-Duhring, Socialism, Utopian and Scientific*, and *Dialectics of Nature*, vastly influenced the fledgling theory of Marxism. Perhaps Engels' most significant contribution to Marxism, however, came from his pocketbook. Because Marx chose not to work and his writings never provided a substantial income, his family would have been constantly penniless, were it not for the financial support provided by Engels. Ironically, the support for these two champions of the proletariat was provided by a bourgeois enterprise--namely, Engels' father's textile business. From 1869 until their deaths, Engels and Marx developed Marxist theory while living off the proceeds of that business.

Notes and Asides

nature of being or reality (*ontology*) and of the origin and structure of the world (*cosmology*)"[49]—and every philosophy must confront these questions sooner or later. Marxists, however, attempt to dodge this branch of philosophy by claiming that metaphysics assumes that nature and being are stagnant and unchanging while dialectics views life as a constant process, and that metaphysics views reality as unconnected parts while dialectics views reality as an interconnected whole.

For example, Engels writes, "The metaphysical mode of thought consists in the habit of considering objects and processes in isolation, detached from the whole vast interconnection of things; and therefore not in their motion, but in their repose; not as essentially changing, but as fixed constants. . . ." Therefore, "in considering individual things it loses sight of their connections; in contemplating their existence it forgets their coming into being and passing away; in looking at them at rest it leaves their motion out of account."[50]

Cornforth views the Marxist problem with metaphysics this way: "All such philosophers thought they could sum up 'the ultimate nature of the universe' in some formula. Some have had this formula, some that, but all have been metaphysicians. Yet it has been a hopeless quest. We cannot sum up the whole infinite changing universe in any such formula. And the more we find out about it, the more is this evident."[51] In fact, according to Afanasyev, metaphysics of any kind is a hindrance to progress: "Since metaphysics does not recognize progressive development, the struggle of the new against the old and the inevitable victory of the new, it serves the interests of reaction and is used in the struggle against everything progressive."[52]

Indeed, most Marxist philosophers attempt to present metaphysics as the direct opposite of dialectics. Writes Cornforth, "The materialist approach, as recommended by Marxism, has to be dialectical. While opposing 'materialism' to 'idealism,' Marx and Engels opposed 'dialectics' to what they called 'metaphysics.' This means that the necessary approach for working out informative theory is that of material dialectics—in opposition to the idealist error of false abstraction, and also to the sort of error denoted by the word 'metaphysics.'"[53] And Afanasyev writes, "The method which is the antithesis of dialectical materialism is metaphysics."[54]

If we grant the Marxists their definition of metaphysics, then we cannot argue with their conclusion that dialectics is directly opposed to it. However, in the proper sense of the word *metaphysics*, Marxists most definitely do maintain a metaphysics, and they are not shy about putting it into words. Since understanding a philosophy's beliefs about the nature of being and the origin and structure of the universe is crucial to understanding the philosophy as a whole, we will now examine Marxist metaphysics (in the traditional sense of the word), beginning with its cosmology and moving on to its ontology.

Notes and Asides

Marxist Metaphysics

As noted elsewhere, Marxist theology and philosophy have no room for the supernatural. The universe is all that exists and all that ever will exist. "Materialism gives a true picture of the world, without any irrelevant adjuncts in the shape of spirits, of god who created the world, and the like. The materialists do not await the help of supernatural powers, they believe in man, in his capacity to transform the world by his own hand."[55]

Engels declares, "the last vestige of a Creator external to the world is obliterated."[56] Marx denies the supernatural, stating, "The ideal [soul, consciousness, etc.] is nothing else than the material world reflected by the human mind and translated into forms of thought."[57] Cornforth proclaims, "For materialism, then, there is nothing outside the material world. There is no separate or independent spiritual world, no mind or spirit separate from matter."[58] Afanasyev explains, "Contemporary science has proved that consciousness is a product of the prolonged evolution of matter. Matter, nature have always existed, while man is a result of a relatively later development of the material world."[59]

Obviously, whether Marxists choose to admit it or not, their philosophy includes a metaphysical cosmology. They are far from bashful about declaring the absence of a God or anything supernatural in the universe, just as they are more than willing to proclaim that the material universe is all that exists and that it has always existed and always will.

At least one Marxist recognizes the importance of a cosmology in Marxist philosophy. M. S. Eigenson writes, "The Marxist-Leninist doctrine of the infinitude of the universe is the fundamental axiom at the basis of Soviet cosmology. . . . The denial or abandonment of this thesis . . . leads inevitably to idealism and fideism, i.e., in effect, to the negation of cosmology, and therefore has nothing in common with science."[60] In other words, without the belief that the universe is infinite, eternal, and all that exists, the Marxist philosophy has abandoned its cosmology and made its philosophy meaningless. There can be no doubt that philosophy requires a cosmology and that Marxism relies on a specific view of the universe, whether one chooses to label it cosmology or not.

> "[T]he last vestige of a Creator external to the world is obliterated."
>
> —Frederick Engels

Marxist philosophy relies on a specific ontology, as well. For Marxists, the ultimate substance and the ultimate cause is ever-changing dialectical matter. Perhaps this is why they choose to avoid metaphysics—it is difficult, in the face of modern physics, to argue that matter is the ultimate substance. (We examine this issue in the chapter on Christian philosophy.) Nonetheless, Marxist philosophy holds tenaciously to the view that matter is all that exists, it is eternal, and it is the ultimate substance or reality.

Notes and Asides

Alexander Spirkin, a modern Marxist author, writes that "matter is the only existing objective reality: the cause, foundation, content and substance of all the diversity of the world."[61] Certainly this is an ontological statement. M. M. Rozental and P. Yudin, authors of the *Short Philosophical Dictionary*, also write ontologically: "For Marxist philosophical materialism, substance, i.e., essence, the ground of all things, consists in self-moving and eternally developing matter."[62] Engels says we know from experience and theory "that both matter and its mode of existence, motion, are uncreatable."[63] Elsewhere he says, "We have the certainty that matter remains eternally the same in all its transformations, that none of its attributes can ever be lost. . . ."[64]

The eternal nature of matter is also proclaimed in *The Fundamentals of Marxist-Leninist Philosophy*: "One result of the historical development of science and social historical practice has been to prove the materiality of the universe, its uncreatability and indestructibility, its eternal existence in time and infinity in space, its inexhaustible self-development, which necessarily leads, at certain stages, to the emergence of life and of sentient beings. Through them matter becomes capable of knowing the laws of its own existence and development."[65] Despite all its protests, dialectical materialism does have some concrete ideas about the nature of ultimate reality. Even Lenin, who was extremely wary of ontology after the new discoveries in physics that occurred in his lifetime, speaks of "eternally developing matter"[66] and says that when you study the relation of the atom to the electron, you are seeing "matter throughout infinite in depth."[67]

Lenin attempts to dodge the problems presented to Marxist ontology by the new physics (which seems to be concluding that ultimate reality is not material), stating, "The 'essence' of things, or 'substance,' is also relative; it expresses only the degree of profundity of man's knowledge of objects; and while yesterday the profundity of this knowledge did not go beyond the atom, and today does not go beyond the electron and ether, dialectical materialism insists on the temporary, relative, approximate character of all these milestones in the knowledge of Nature gained by the progressing science of man. The electron is as inexhaustible as the atom, Nature is infinite. . . ."[68] In his admission that the ultimate substance may change, however, Lenin is unwilling to give up the idea that the ultimate substance will always be material. This is an ontology in itself: the ultimate substance, by whatever name one chooses to call it, is definitely matter. It is Nature that is infinite, so from Nature the ultimate substance must rise. "Dialectics," as we quoted Lenin earlier, "is the study of the contradiction within the very essence of things."[69]

While Lenin did not know what the basic ingredients of matter consisted of, and while he knew that modern physics was searching and

Notes and Asides

digging deeper and deeper into the subject, he was satisfied that whatever the composition, it would act according to the laws of the dialectic. One could almost say that at the heart of matter is law—eternal dialectical law.

Marxist dialectics, then, is not opposed to metaphysics in the traditional sense of the word. In truth, Marxist philosophy relies on its metaphysics (ontology and cosmology), which it assumes in its entirety without rational defense, to provide a basis and explanation for being, the nature of the universe, and ultimately man himself.

The Mind-Body Problem

Like every philosophy, dialectical materialism must face the mind-body problem. The key word Marxists rely on when addressing this problem is *reflect*. It is their contention that the human mind reflects matter in a way that makes perception accurate for us. For Marx, "the ideal is nothing else than the material world reflected by the human mind, and translated into forms of thought."[70] Lenin echoes him: "The existence of the mind is shown to be dependent upon that of the body, in that the mind is declared to be secondary, a function of the brain, or a reflection of the outer world."[71]

In this way, Marxists attempt to avoid the whole problem of perceiving thought as material (since no one can ever claim to have seen a thought or an idea), thus maintaining a strictly materialistic worldview. For example, in *The Fundamentals of Marxist-Leninist Philosophy*, the authors admit, "It is a great mistake to identify consciousness with matter." But they hasten to add, "Consciousness is not a special essence divorced from matter. But the image of the object created in the human brain cannot be reduced to the material object itself, which exists outside the subject, the knower. Nor can it be identified with the physiological processes that occur in the brain and generate this image. Thought, consciousness are real things. But they are not objective realities; they are something subjective, ideal."[72]

Marxism uses the notion that consciousness is just a subjective reflection of objective reality to avoid calling consciousness supernatural. The question still arises, however: from whence did this ideal arise?

For the Marxist, everything evolves from matter. Afanasyev, using a subtly veiled form of the post hoc fallacy, writes, "Natural science, for instance, has indisputably proved that the Earth had existed many millions of years before man and life in general appeared on it. This shows that matter and nature in general are objective and independent of man and his consciousness, and that consciousness itself is merely a product of the prolonged evolution of the material world."[73] (*Even if* the

Earth existed millions of years before man's consciousness, it would not necessarily follow that consciousness is merely a product of the Earth, any more than my washing my car before it rains proves that the washing caused the rain.)

Most Marxist philosophers even believe the precursors for human consciousness can be seen in the animal world. Cornforth writes, "When animals develop a nervous system and begin actively to relate themselves to their environment by conditioned connections, then the nervous process becomes a conscious process, a process of sensation and, in man, of thinking. Hence sensations and thoughts are the peculiar products of the nervous process."[74] And *The Fundamentals of Marxist-Leninist Philosophy* proclaims, "The high level of development of mental activity in animals shows that man's consciousness has its biological preconditions and that there is no unbridgeable gap between man and his animal ancestors; in fact, there is a certain continuity."[75] For the Marxist, evolution "creates" consciousness, the beginnings of which are evident even in the higher animals. Man is an evolving animal with consciousness.

> "Whether or not the philosophers care to admit that we have a soul, it seems obvious that we are equipped with something or other which generates dreams and ideals, and which sets up values."
>
> —John Erskine

This evolution is not just physical, however. According to Marx, consciousness requires social evolution as well: "It is not the consciousness of men that determines their being, but, on the contrary, their social being that determines their consciousness."[76] For Marx, social relationships actually shape men's consciousness. This is true for all Marxists. Spirkin says, "Dialectical materialism showed that consciousness arises, functions and develops in the process of people's interaction with reality, on the basis of their sensuously objective activity, their socio-historical practice. Since it reflects the objective world in its content, consciousness is determined by natural and social reality."[77]

The authors of *The Fundamentals of Marxist-Leninist Philosophy* hold this to be a crucial aspect of their philosophy: "Dialectical materialism proceeds from the fact that consciousness is an attribute not of any matter but of highly organized matter. Consciousness is connected with the activity of the human brain, with the specifically human, social way of life."[78] Elsewhere they write, "Man himself is the most complex of all known material systems and all manifestations of his activity, including the higher forms of mental reflection and creation, have a material origin and depend on social relations."[79] In fact, they view human society as "the highest stage in the development of matter on earth."[80]

Do they believe that their "evolution" just stopped?

Obviously, society plays a big role in the evolution of consciousness for the Marxist—but we must remember that society itself is simply a stage in the development of matter. For the dialectical materialist, everything must have proceeded from matter, even societal interrelationships and the mind. Cornforth writes, "Mental functions

Notes and Asides

are functions of highly developed matter, namely, of the brain. Mental processes are brain processes, processes of a material, bodily organ."[81] It is convenient for the Marxist to refer to thought as the "reflection" of objective reality, but in the final estimation he must admit that the mind is simply a function of matter. Again, Cornforth proclaims, "The mental functions, from the lowest to the highest, are functions of the body, functions of matter. Mind is a product of matter at a high level of the organization of matter."[82] This is in direct opposition to any philosophy that claims that a Divine Mind preceded matter, or that anything supernatural exists. "In contrast to these various idealist beliefs materialism proceeds from the fact that consciousness is a function of the human brain the essence of which lies in the reflection of reality."[83]

(While Marx was a dyed-in-the-wool materialist, he certainly noted the primacy of mind to matter in one situation. Seeking to identify what distinguishes the most incompetent architect in the world from the best of bees, Marx concluded, "The architect has built a cell in his head before he constructed it in wax."[84] A non-materialist cosmologist would likewise contend that God built the universe in His mind before He constructed it in matter.)

Conclusion

Dialectical materialism, the philosophy of Marxism, contains an epistemology, a cosmology, an ontology, and an answer to the mind-body problem. For the Marxist, science and practice refine knowledge, the universe is infinite and all that will ever exist, matter is eternal and the ultimate substance, life is a product of this non-living matter, and mind is a reflection of this material reality. But the Marxist philosophy embraces an even broader view of the world than is generally meant by the term *philosophy*. In truth, dialectical materialism is an entire method for viewing the world—it colors the Marxist perception of everything from ethics to history. "The dialectical materialist theory of matter and its forms of existence is the foundation of Marxist-Leninist philosophy, the basis of its integrated monistic world outlook. It is of great importance as a method for modern science and helps us to integrate the sciences and evolve an integral conception of the world as moving and developing matter."[85]

In fact, Marxist philosophy as a worldview must be understood by anyone who claims to support the Marxist cause. "One cannot become a fully conscious, convinced Communist without studying Marxist philosophy. This is what Lenin taught."[86] Why? Because, according to Marxism, the dialectic can explain every process and change that

Notes and Asides

occurs. Marxist philosophy is process philosophy. This process is written not only in the metaphysical make-up of the matter, but also, and equally large, in the evolution of man and the evolving social and historical context of man's existence. It is this materialist belief that affects the Marxist view of history and causes Marxists to view the bourgeoisie and the proletariat as thesis and antithesis, clashing to form a synthesis. "The history of all hitherto existing society is the history of class struggles," say Marx and Engels in the first chapter of the *Manifesto of the Communist Party*. If one does not understand dialectics, and therefore does not understand that the proletariat must naturally struggle against the oppressing bourgeoisie, then one cannot truly understand Marxism. "Materialist dialectics . . . helps to reveal the inner contradictions of the present epoch, contemporary economic, socio-political and intellectual processes and to work out a scientifically based strategy and tactics for the Marxist-Leninist parties, who are leading the struggle of the working people [antithesis] against the forces of imperialism [thesis]."[87]

"One cannot become a fully conscious, convinced Communist without studying Marxist philosophy. This is what Lenin taught."
—*The Fundamentals of Marxist-Leninist Philosophy*

Marxist philosophy, as a worldview, is also a philosophy of revolution. The clash of the proletariat with the bourgeoisie is an evolutionary struggle. The interworkings of nature itself decree the outcome. Joseph Stalin goes so far as to claim that dialectical materialism "is the doctrine of the proletarian masses, their banner; it is honored and 'revered' by the proletarians all the world over. Consequently Marx and Engels are not simply the founders of a philosophical 'school' . . . they are the living leaders of the living proletarian movement, which is growing and gaining strength every day."[88]

While evolutionists believe that animals evolved certain physical characteristics to aid in their survival, Marxists believe their philosophy of dialectical materialism evolved to meet the needs of the proletariat. "Marxist philosophy was brought into being by the fundamental needs of the revolutionary struggle of the working class, whose goal is to put an end to the system of capitalist relations and build classless communist society. It has become a powerful theoretical instrument of scientific cognition and the revolutionary transformation of the world."[89]

Cornforth echoes this sentiment, saying, "A revolutionary working-class party needs a revolutionary working-class philosophy, and that philosophy is dialectical materialism."[90] Elsewhere he notes, "Dialectical materialism is a theoretical instrument in the hands of the people for use in changing the world."[91] Marxism requires a devotion to the revolution; inherent in its philosophy is the call for constant struggle toward synthesis. It is important to note that Marxist political activity is based on what Marxists believe is the true interpretation of the true activity of ultimate reality. All reality reflects dialectical materialism: thesis and antithesis in conflict, bringing about synthesis.

Notes and Asides

The universe operates according to the same principles at all levels, from the sub-atomic world to the organic world and finally to the political world.

Every Marxist recognizes this and is prepared to act in accordance with dialectical materialism. While many philosophies are chiefly theoretical, Marxism is concerned with theory *and practice*. Dialectical materialism is a worldview and a philosophy of *evolution and revolution*—the call to action is implicit in its makeup. Every good Marxist understands his philosophy and is prepared to act on it, because Marx himself requires it: "The philosophers have only interpreted the world in various ways; the point, however, is to change it."[92]

For Marxists, the change includes moving from a theistic theology to an atheistic theology; from a supernatural philosophy to a materialistic philosophy; from a Christian or religious-oriented ethic to a class morality ethic; from a creation-oriented biology/anthropology to an evolutionary biology; from a capitalist economics to a socialist and classless society economics; from a multitude of nation states to a single worldwide soviet state or world government, etc. The theoretical and practical basis of bringing about this world change is dialectical materialism.

Unfortunately from a Marxist point of view, all such change is merely transitory, since each new synthesis (including the long-anticipated communist classless society) inevitably becomes a new thesis in the never-ending process of dialectical materialism. As Engels says,

> All successive historical situations are only transitory stages in the endless course of development of human society from the lower to the higher. Each stage is necessary, therefore justified for the time and conditions to which it owes its origin. But in the newer and higher conditions which gradually develop in its own bosom, each loses its validity and justification. It must give way to a higher form which will also in turn decay and perish.[93]

> "Many talk like philosophers and live like fools."
> —H. G. Bohn

Even the victorious dictatorship of the proletariat will be but a brief moment in evolutionary history. Communist dialectics decrees that communism itself is transitory. The synthesis of communism today will become the new thesis of tomorrow, and new struggles will evolve. Thus is it written in the laws of dialectical materialism.

[1]Frederick Engels, *Anti-Dühring*, cited in V. I. Lenin, *The Teachings of Karl Marx* (New York: International Publishers, 1976), p. 14.
[2]V. I. Lenin, *Collected Works* (Moscow: Progress Publishers, 1977), vol. 38, p. 358; cited in *A Lexicon of Marxist-Leninist Semantics*, ed. Raymond S. Sleeper (Alexandria, VA: Western Goals, 1983), p. 89.
[3]Gustav A. Wetter, *Dialectical Materialism* (Westport, CT: Greenwood Press, 1977), p. 107. Marxism for Plekhanov "is the application to social development of the Darwinian theory of the adaptation of biological species to the conditions of the environment."
[4]Ibid., p. 323.
[5]Karl Marx, Letter to Engels, December 12, 1866, cited in Lenin, *The Teachings of Karl Marx*, p. 15.
[6]Engels, cited in Joseph Stalin, *Dialectical and Historical Materialism* (New York: International Publishers, 1977), p. 15.
[7]*Political Dictionary* (Moscow: 1940), p. 335. Cited in *A Lexicon of Marxist-Leninist Semantics*, ed. Sleeper, p. 167.
[8]Maurice Cornforth, *The Open Philosophy and the Open Society* (New York: International Publishers, 1968), p. 48.
[9]V. I. Lenin, *Materialism and Empirio-Criticism* (New York: International Publishers, 1927), p. 34.
[10]Ibid., p. 145.
[11]Frederick Engels, *Ludwig Feuerbach* (New York: International Publishers, 1974), p. 21.
[12]Lenin, *Materialism and Empirio-Criticism*, p. 252.
[13]*The Fundamentals of Marxist-Leninist Philosophy*, chief ed. F. V. Konstantinov (Moscow: Progress Publishers, 1982), p. 61.
[14]Ibid., pp. 366-7.
[15]Lenin, *Materialism and Empirio-Criticism*, p. 81.
[16]Ibid., p. 102.
[17]Cornforth, *The Open Philosophy and the Open Society*, p. 82.
[18]*The Fundamentals of Marxist-Leninist Philosophy*, ed. Konstantinov, p. 166.
[19]Maurice Cornforth, *Materialism and the Dialectical Method* (New York: International Publishers, 1968), p. 120.
[20]M. N. Rutkevich, *Practice as the Foundation of Knowledge and Criterion of Truth* (Moscow: 1952), p. 125. Cited in Wetter, *Dialectical Materialism*, p. 507.
[21]*Political Dictionary*, pp. 173-4. Cited in *A Lexicon of Marxist-Leninist Semantics*, ed. Sleeper, p. 89.
[22]Lenin, *Collected Works*, vol. 7, p. 409.
[23]Karl Marx, *Capital* (London: Dent and Sons, 1930), vol. 2, p. 873.
[24]Ibid.
[25]Cornforth, *The Open Philosophy and the Open Society*, p. 68.
[26]Wetter, *Dialectical Materialism*, p. 4.
[27]Engels, *Ludwig Feuerbach*, p. 44.
[28]*Fundamentals of Marxism-Leninism* (Moscow: 1959), p. 84. Cited in *A Lexicon of Marxist-Leninist Semantics*, ed. Sleeper, p. 88.
[29]Frederick Engels, *Dialectics of Nature* (New York: International Publishers, 1976), pp. 206-7.
[30]V. Afanasyev, *Marxist Philosophy* (Moscow: Foreign Languages Publishing House, 1963), p. 85.
[31]Lenin, *Collected Works*, vol. 38, p. 358.
[32]Engels, *Anti-Dühring*, p. 27.
[33]Ibid., p. 70.
[34]Frederick Engels, *Socialism: Utopian and Scientific* (New York: International, 1935), p. 48.
[35]Lenin, *Collected Works*, vol. 7, p. 409.
[36]Engels, *Socialism: Utopian and Scientific*, p. 48.
[37]*The Fundamentals of Marxist-Leninist Philosophy*, ed. Konstantinov, p. 101.
[38]Lenin, *Materialism and Empirio-Criticism*, p. 103.
[39]Engels, *Ludwig Feuerbach*, p. 11.
[40]Engels, *Dialectics of Nature*, p. 26.
[41]Stalin, *Dialectical and Historical Materialism*, pp. 7-11.

[42]Lenin, *Collected Works*, vol. 38, pp. 220-222.
[43]Cornforth, *The Open Philosophy and the Open Society*, p. 101.
[44]Lenin, *Collected Works*, vol. 38, pp. 251-2.
[45]Ibid., p. 358.
[46]*The Fundamentals of Marxist-Leninist Philosophy*, ed. Konstantinov, p. 111.
[47]Engels, *Dialectics of Nature*, p. 13.
[48]Wetter, *Dialectical Materialism*, p. 392.
[49]Jean L. McKechnie, et al., ed., *Webster's New Twentieth Century Dictionary of the English Language*, 2d ed., unabridged (USA: Collins & World, 1977), p. 1132.
[50]Engels, *Anti-Dühring*, cited in Cornforth, *The Open Philosophy and the Open Society*, p. 60.
[51]Cornforth, *Materialism and the Dialectical Method*, p. 60.
[52]Afanasyev, *Marxist Philosophy*, p. 15.
[53]Cornforth, *The Open Philosophy and the Open Society*, p. 60.
[54]Afanasyev, *Marxist Philosophy*, p. 14.
[55]*Fundamentals of Marxism-Leninism*, p. 15. Cited in *A Lexicon of Marxist-Leninist Semantics*, ed. Sleeper, p. 168.
[56]Engels, *Anti-Dühring*, p. 18.
[57]Karl Marx, introduction to *Capital* (London: 1889), vol. 1. Cited in Cornforth, *The Open Philosophy and the Open Society*, p. 118.
[58]Cornforth, *The Open Philosophy and the Open Society*, p. 45.
[59]Afanasyev, *Marxist Philosophy*, p. 71.
[60]M. S. Eigenson, "On the Problem of Cosmogony," in *Circular*, No. 30, (1955), p. 10. Cited in Wetter, *Dialectical Materialism*, p. 436.
[61]Alexander Spirkin, *Dialectical Materialism* (Moscow: Progress Publishers, 1983), p. 66.
[62]M. M. Rozental and P. Yudin, *Short Philosophical Dictionary*, 4th ed., (Moscow: 1955), p. 467. Cited in Wetter, *Dialectical Materialism*, p. 292.
[63]Engels, *Dialectics of Nature*, p. 337.
[64]Ibid., p. 54.
[65]*The Fundamentals of Marxist-Leninist Philosophy*, ed. Konstantinov, p. 59.
[66]Lenin, *Collected Works*, vol. 19, p. 24.
[67]V. I. Lenin, *Philosophical Notebooks*, in *Lenin's Selected Works* (Moscow and London: 1936-9), vol. 11, p. 29. Cited in Wetter, *Dialectical Materialism*, p. 291.
[68]Lenin, *Materialism and Empirio-Criticism*, p. 271.
[69]Lenin, *Collected Works*, vol. 38, pp. 251-2.
[70]Marx, introduction to *Capital* (London: 1889), vol. 1.
[71]Lenin, *Materialism and Empirio-Criticism*, p. 66.
[72]*The Fundamentals of Marxist-Leninist Philosophy*, ed. Konstantinov, p. 83.
[73]Afanasyev, *Marxist Philosophy*, p. 53.
[74]Maurice Cornforth, *The Theory of Knowledge* (New York: International Publishers, 1963), p. 25.
[75]*The Fundamentals of Marxist-Leninist Philosophy*, ed. Konstantinov, p. 91.
[76]Karl Marx, *A Contribution to the Critique of Political Economy*, preface, cited in Wetter, *Dialectical Materialism*, p. 38.
[77]Spirkin, *Dialectical Materialism*, p. 153.
[78]*The Fundamentals of Marxist-Leninist Philosophy*, ed. Konstantinov, p. 80.
[79]Ibid., pp. 75-6.
[80]Ibid., p. 70.
[81]Cornforth, *The Theory of Knowledge*, p. 22.
[82]Ibid., pp. 10-11.
[83]*The Fundamentals of Marxist-Leninist Philosophy*, ed. Konstantinov, p. 80.
[84]Karl Marx, *Capital* (London: E. and C. Paul, 1930), vol. 1, pp. 169-70.
[85]*The Fundamentals of Marxist-Leninist Philosophy*, ed. Konstantinov, p. 78.
[86]Ibid., p. 480.

[87]Ibid., p. 478.
[88]Joseph Stalin, *Anarchism or Socialism?* in *Works* (London: 1953), vol. 1, p. 351. Cited in Wetter, *Dialectical Materialism*, p. 55.
[89]*The Fundamentals of Marxist-Leninist Philosophy*, ed. Konstantinov, p. 478.
[90]Cornforth, *Materialism and the Dialectical Method*, p. 7.
[91]Ibid., p. 15.
[92]Karl Marx, *Theses on Feuerbach*, in *Collected Works*, forty volumes (New York: International, 1976), vol. 5, p. 8.
[93]Engels, *Ludwig Feuerbach*, p. 12.

CHAPTER

8

BIBLICAL CHRISTIAN PHILOSOPHY

"In the beginning was the Word, and the Word was with God, and the Word was God."

—John 1:1

"In whom [the mystery of God, and of the Father, and of Christ] are hid all the treasures of wisdom and knowledge."

—Colossians 2:3

"A little philosophy inclineth man's mind to atheism, but depth in philosophy bringeth men's minds about to religion."[1]

—Francis Bacon

SUMMARY

The philosophical quest that most appeals to Christians is the attempt to obey 2 Corinthians 10:5—"Overthrowing reasonings and every high thing [scientism, dialectical materialism, evolutionism] that exalteth itself against the knowledge of God, and bringing into captivity every thought to the obedience of Christ." What makes philosophy unchristian, what the Bible refers to as "vain and deceitful philosophy," is basing philosophy on the "traditions of men, after the basic principles of the world, and not after Christ" (Colossians 2:8). In Christ are hid all the treasures of wisdom and knowledge (Colossians 2:3)—as Carl F. H. Henry says, "God's mind and will are the source of all truth."

The single most important philosophical truth in the Bible is that Jesus Christ is the Logos of God. Christian philosophy, especially metaphysics, is grounded in John 1:1-4. Christian philosophy posits Christ the Logos as the explanation for the universe and all things therein. "In the beginning was the Word [Logos]" is the starting point of Christian philosophy, just as "In the beginning God" is the starting point of Christian theology. John l:1-4 teaches mind before matter, design before creation, and life from life—all crucial philosophical points. As Paul the Apostle stood in the midst of the philosophical capital of the world—Mars Hill in Athens (Acts 17:15ff)—he reiterated three points: (a) "God that made the world and all things therein, seeing that he is Lord of heaven and earth, dwelleth not in temples made with hands" (v. 24); (b) "Jesus and the resurrection" (vv. 18, 32); and (c) "he [Christ] will judge the world in righteousness" (v. 31).

Just as the professional philosophers—the atheistic Epicureans and pantheistic Stoics—of Paul's day rejected the heart of the Christian philosophy, so the Marxists and Humanists today reject God, creation, resurrection, and judgment. The major charge against Christianity in general and Christian philosophy in particular is that it is unscientific. Marxists and Humanists claim that only their philosophy, their metaphysics (ontology/cosmology), and their epistemology are scientific. Christians reject the charge and argue that modern science was founded in the Biblical Christian tradition and that science is an ally of Christian philosophy. Christians also claim that the Christian doctrines of God, creation, Logos, design, purpose, law, order, and life are much more consistent with the findings of science, history, and personal experience than the vain and deceitful philosophies of dialectical materialism and philosophical naturalism (which are pre-scientific positions). In fact, modern science could not have been founded and nurtured on a diet of Marxism and Humanism. The Christian philosophical tradition is rich and satisfying. Christian young people are invited to see how Christ is the key to Christian philosophy and asked to put into practice the Biblical admonition to "attain knowledge, learning, understanding, and wisdom" (Proverbs 1). After all, philosophy literally means "love of wisdom" (*philos*: love, *sophia*: wisdom).

Notes and Asides

Introduction

After an examination of Marxist and Humanist philosophies, one might assume that the Christian worldview cannot possibly have a philosophy of its own, since it requires faith in Biblical revelation, while naturalism and materialism are, theoretically, grounded firmly in modern scientific methodology and enlightened human experience. How can the Christian, who is required to postulate existence or reality outside the material realm, ever hope to prove his beliefs true, reasonable, rational, and worth living and dying for?

Unfortunately, some Christians adopt just such an attitude—conceding that their faith is indefensible. They attempt to avoid the whole problem by stating that what they believe is "beyond reason." These Christians point to Colossians 2:8, where Paul writes, "See to it that no one takes you captive through hollow and deceptive philosophy . . .," and from this they draw the conclusion that God does not want us to meddle in such a vain and deceitful discipline as philosophy. However, people who point to this verse as a warning against philosophy often omit the rest of the verse, in which Paul describes the kind of philosophy he is warning against, viz., philosophy "which depends on human tradition and the basic principles of this world rather than on Christ."

Clearly, the Bible does not ask the Christian to abandon reason in accepting its truth. "Come now," records Isaiah, "and let us reason together, saith the Lord: though your sins be as scarlet, they shall be white as snow" (Isaiah 1:18). In fact, 1 Peter 3:15 encourages Christians to understand and be able to present logical, compelling reasons for their hope in Christ. But is this possible? Is Christian faith and, more specifically, Christian philosophy defensible?

Many well-known philosophers throughout history have believed that their faith in Christ is both defensible and rational. This has been true of St. Augustine, St. Anselm, Thomas Aquinas, John Scotus, Nicolas Malebranche, St. Bonaventure, Rene Descartes, Gottfried von Leibniz, Blaise Pascal, William of Ockham, Francis Bacon, Francisco Suarez, Immanuel Kant,[2] George Berkeley, John Locke, Soren Kierkegaard, Jonathan Edwards, Josiah Royce, and on through modern philosophers C. S. Lewis, Bernard Lonergan, Frederick Copleston, William P. Alston, George I. Mavrodes, Stanley Jaki, Elton Trueblood, Dallas Willard, Norman Geisler, J. P. Moreland, and Alvin Plantinga.

C. E. M. Joad, who lived most of his life believing that the concept of God was unacceptable, finally concluded, "It is because . . . the religious view of the universe seems to me to cover more of the facts of experience than any other that I have been gradually led to embrace it."[3] He concluded his long personal pilgrimage by admitting, "I now believe that the balance of reasonable considerations tells heavily in

Notes and Asides

favor of the religious, even of the Christian view of the world."[4] This is the same Joad who appeared on BBC radio with Humanist Bertrand Russell attacking Christianity.

Many who finally begin to reflect on the deeper things of life—"How did I get here? Why am I here? Where am I going?" simply discover that Christianity answers more questions more completely than any other worldview. John Baillie counted among his friends a rather "remarkable number of men of high intellectual distinction" who returned to the full Christian outlook after years of defection, and in practically every case "the renewed hospitality of their minds to Christian truth came about through their awakening to the untenability of the alternative positions, which previously they had been attempting to occupy."[5] This notion that non-Christian views are simply not rational enough or do not explain reality is echoed by Norman L. Geisler, who says that in recent times there has been "a collapse of the intellectual grounds for holding an atheist position."[6] Atheism just cannot explain the orderliness and beauty of the universe. Neither can it explain the origin of life or give any hope that the Second Law of Thermodynamics can be reversed. If it can't be reversed, all philosophy is vanity, including Christian philosophy. Romans 8:19-23 gives Christians hope that the Second Law will indeed be reversed.

"Thou hast formed us for Thyself, and our hearts are restless till they find rest in Thee."
—St. Augustine

William Lane Craig also accepts Christian philosophy because it seems to him more believable than opposing philosophies. He found it intellectually easier to believe in a God who is the cause of the universe than in a universe that came into existence uncaused out of nothing or has existed from eternity without a beginning. "For me," says Craig, "these last two positions are implausible intellectually, and it would take more faith for me to believe them than to believe that God exists."[7]

Bernard J. F. Lonergan, who (according to *Time* magazine) "is considered by many intellectuals to be the finest philosophic thinker of the 20th century," believes,

> There lies within [man's] horizon a region for the divine, a shrine for ultimate holiness. It cannot be ignored. The atheist may pronounce it empty. The agnostic may urge that he finds his investigation has been inconclusive. The contemporary humanist will refuse to allow the question to arise. But their negations presuppose the spark in our clod, our native orientation to the divine.[8]

In other words, man is religious by nature and craves a God. Lonergan is saying nothing more than what St. Augustine said some fifteen

Notes and Asides

hundred years before him, in the opening paragraph of his *Confessions*: "Thou hast formed us for Thyself, and our hearts are restless till they find rest in Thee."

Unfortunately, if man does not worship the one true God of the Bible, he will worship the sun, the state, sex, stones, insects, etc. (Romans 1:23). It is all well and good to debate whether God exists, but for the average person the debate is a moot point—people are aware of His existence in their very souls. Even today the vast majority of human beings in the world (some polls place the figure as high as 95 percent) believe in a God. Paul found this to be true also in Athens (Acts 17:23).

Alvin Plantinga recognizes this phenomenon: "I don't think argument for the existence of God is necessary any more than argument for the existence of other persons, the past, and material objects. Belief in God, like belief in these other things, is properly basic."[9] However, Plantinga is not implying that Christians can thus safely ignore philosophy—on the contrary, Plantinga has devoted most of his career to reinforcing the truthfulness of the Christian faith. His belief that its truth and reasonableness are basic is the result of years of inquiry, and Plantinga undoubtedly would agree with Lonergan's remark, "I do not think it difficult to establish God's existence. I do think it a life-long labor to analyze and refute all the objections that philosophers have thought up against the existence of God."[10]

Obviously many serious thinkers view Christianity as containing a rational, reasonable, true philosophy. But can the same be said for the common man? Perhaps only men of genius can grasp the rationality of the Christian faith, and the average individual must shy away from reason and philosophy.

This attitude is entirely unfounded. Geisler speaks to this issue by insisting that most men do not live by leaps of faith into the absurd. Rather, they live and move on the sufficiency of the evidence. And what is true of their everyday life, says Geisler, is not entirely untrue of their religious life. "Theists have not usually come to believe that there is a God because they think this is the most unreasonable view they could hold. On the contrary, theists almost always believe their position is most reasonable."[11] This is true for every man. People tend to believe the most likely solution to a problem. The idea of a God has always been a given for the vast majority of the world's residents. That's why most people tend to believe, "In the beginning God created the heavens and the earth" (Genesis 1:1) and "all things therein" (Acts 17:24). It makes more (common) sense to believe Genesis 1:1 than to believe that a series of cosmic accidents brought about the orderly, beautiful, meaningful cosmos.

Notes and Asides

Faith and Epistemology

The basic tenets of Christian philosophy can be demonstrated to be rational, for they are held by average, rational men and women. But surely, Christianity must still run into an epistemological problem—how does the Christian "know" without clashing with science and experience? How can the knowledge we gain through faith in Biblical revelation compare to knowledge gained by a scientific investigation of the universe?

The answer is not as difficult as one might imagine. When all is said and done, all knowing requires faith. "[Max] Planck and Albert Einstein, like Isaac Newton, were strongly motivated by faith in the orderliness of nature."[12] Faith precedes reason or, as W. J. Neidhardt puts it, "Faith correctly viewed is that illumination by which true rationality begins."[13] Thus faith is "an inescapable element of all human understanding," says Carl F. H. Henry, "not excluding that of scientists who may be tempted to categorize it as unpardonable ignorance."[14]

While Marxists and Humanists like to portray science as primary knowledge and faith in Biblical revelation as some blind second-class epistemology or even superstition, the fact remains that all methods of knowing ultimately rely on certain assumptions. Edward T. Ramsdell writes, "the natural man is no less certainly a man of faith than the spiritual, but his faith is in the ultimacy of something other than the Word of God. The spiritual man is no less certainly a man of reason than the natural, but his reason, like that of every man, functions within the perspective of his faith."[15]

Warren C. Young reconciles faith with reason in much the same way. He doesn't find the basic problem of philosophy to be the old problem of faith versus reason. "The crucial problem is that some thinkers place their trust in a set of assumptions in their search for truth, while other thinkers place their trust in a quite different set of assumptions."[16] That is, Humanists and Marxists place their trust in certain findings of science and experience, neither of which can be rationally demonstrated to be the source of all truth. Christians also put some faith in science, history, and personal experience, but they know such avenues for discovering truth are not infallible. Christians know that men of science make mistakes and scientific journals can practice discrimination against views considered dangerous.[17] Christians know that history can be perverted, distorted or twisted, and that some personal experiences are not a good source of fact or knowledge. On the other hand, Christians believe that Biblical revelation is true and that God would not fool or mislead His children. Each day's newspaper more than confirms to any unbiased person, for example, that the heart of man is "deceitful and desperately wicked" (Jeremiah 17:9; Romans 3:23).

Notes and Asides

But having said this, Christian philosophy does not throw out reason or tests for truth. Christianity says the New Testament is true because its truths can be tested. "Christianity," says John Warwick Montgomery, "declares that the truth of its absolute claims rests squarely on certain historical facts open to ordinary investigation. These facts relate essentially to the man Jesus, His presentation of Himself as God in human flesh, and His resurrection from the dead as proof of His deity."[18]

Christians aren't asking the non-believer to believe a revelation of old wives' fables, but instead to consider certain historical evidences that reason itself can employ as an attorney building a case uses evidences "in the law to determine questions of fact."[19] Christian epistemology at this level comes down to one single question: "How reliable are the New Testament records?" In answering this question Montgomery observes the following: (1) The New Testament documents "fulfill the historian's requirements of transmissional reliability."[20] He reports that Simon Greenleaf (Harvard's greatest nineteenth-century authority on the law of evidence in the common law world) "concluded that the competence of the New Testament documents would be established in any court of law."[21] (2) If one compares the New Testament documents with universally accepted secular writings

CLOSE-UP

Alvin C. Plantinga (1932-)

Born in Michigan on November 15, 1932, Alvin Plantinga is now the leading philosopher to champion a comprehensive Christian worldview. Plantinga received his PhD from Yale University in 1958, and worked as a philosophy professor at Wayne State University and Calvin College before accepting a position at the University of Notre Dame in 1982. About the time he moved to Notre Dame, he served as president of the Western Division of the American Philosophical Association. His work in the realm of philosophy has convinced him that belief in the existence of God is rational, and further that faith in Biblical Christianity demands adherence to a specific worldview. His works include *God and Other Minds: A Study of the Rational Justification of Belief in God* and *God, Freedom, and Evil.*

Notes and Asides

of antiquity "the New Testament is more than vindicated."[22] (3) The accuracy of the writers can be checked "scientifically." Says Montgomery, "Modern archaeological research has confirmed again and again the reliability of New Testament geography, chronology, and general history."[23] (4) The resurrection of Jesus Christ is "contained in the very New Testament documents whose historical reliability we have confirmed."[24]

Christian epistemology, therefore, is based on special revelation, which in turn is based on history, the law of evidence, and the science of archaeology. Henry says that the Christian religion "champions rationality over against the pervasive irrationalism of our age, and that it promotes rather than evades the demand for verification and tests for truth."[25]

"Philosophy is the highest music."
—Plato

Indeed, faith in reason must precede all other faiths. James Oliver Buswell, Jr., notes, "Speaking of logical (not chronological) priority, I believe the first step in any knowledge process must be faith in reason. It can be shown that faith is necessary in abstract reason. It can be shown that faith is necessary in abstract mathematics, in formal logic, and in the physical and biological sciences just as truly as faith is necessary in the acceptance of Christianity."[26]

It would be unrealistic ever to speak of philosophy as excluding faith. Philosophy, like all of life, is grounded on basic assumptions that man must trust implicitly. The writer of Hebrews says, "he that cometh to God must believe that God exists, and is a rewarder of them that diligently seek him" (Hebrews 11:6). This does not imply that an individual can (in good conscience) accept any ridiculous proposition. Rather, the Christian philosopher must use his faith and reason together to arrive at a comprehensive, true worldview.

Philosophical naturalists also make assumptions that they necessarily accept on faith. All naturalists agree that there is no supernatural. "This point," says Young, "is emphasized by the naturalists themselves without seeming to be at all troubled by the fact that it is an emotional rather than a logical conclusion."[27] The naturalist (and the materialist) accept on faith the non-existence of the supernatural. This assumption provides the whole framework for their philosophy. Again, Young observes that it is not methodology that rules out the possibility of the supernatural, "but rather the basic assumption with which the naturalistic thinker begins, namely, that there is no supernatural."[28] There is nothing in history or science to disprove the supernatural. In fact, most argue that the supernatural, by definition, is outside the scope of the scientific method.[29]

Of course, the naturalist claims that the supernatural can be ruled out rationally by appealing to science—the supernatural has never been empirically observed, measured, and experimented on; therefore we

Notes and Asides

have no evidence that it exists. Indeed, the naturalist claims, the supernatural need not exist to explain the existence of the universe or anything in it, because the theory of evolution has demonstrated the way in which life develops.

We will answer this charge only in passing at present, because the compatibility of all philosophy and science will be examined later, and the entire evolution/creation debate will be covered in another chapter. For now, suffice it to say that science has in no way proven that man evolved from non-life; in fact, science seems capable of disproving this theory. However, the theory of evolution is crucial to the naturalist's philosophy, and this colors his whole perception of truth. As D. Gareth Jones says, "The reliance placed upon the assumptions and speculations of the general theory of evolution depends upon the philosophical presuppositions of those making them. For humanists, these assumptions and speculations are essential if they are to acquire a coherent and unified picture of the world. Hence evolutionary theory within a humanist framework almost invariably undergoes a mutation to become evolutionism. Christians, holding a more supernaturalistic view of the world, are free to accept or reject such assumptions."[30]

Faith is critical in every philosophy. The individual developing a philosophy must be extremely careful to base his case on the most truthful assumptions—otherwise, should one of the assumptions be demonstrated to be untrue (as it appears the assumptions of the theory of evolution will be), the whole philosophy will crumble. If evolution crumbles (which is quite possible—Dr. Karl Popper doesn't even believe evolution fits the definition of "a scientific theory"), Marxism and Humanism are intellectually dead.

Up to this point we have established two things regarding Christian philosophy: many hold it to be the most rational of all worldviews, and it requires virtually no more faith than any other philosophy. Indeed, one could argue that it takes a great deal more faith to believe in the spontaneous generation doctrine of Marxism and Humanism or the randomness of all nature (i.e., that the universe happened by accident) than it does to accept the Christian doctrine of Creator/Creation.

Metaphysics: Ontology/Cosmology

The Christian view of metaphysics—of ultimate reality (ontology and cosmology)—is part of what C. S. Lewis termed "Mere Christianity." There are certain things virtually all Christians believe, and one is that God is the supreme source of all being and reality. He is the ultimate reality and because He is, we are. Behind physical reality there is the ultimate reality that gives meaning to the physical order. The entire

Notes and Asides

"Since God is supreme being . . . it follows that He gave being to all that He created out of nothing."
—St. Augustine

space-time creation, says Henry, depends on the Creator-God "for its actuality, its meaning and its purpose."[31] This creation is intelligible because God is intelligent, and we can understand the creation and Creator because He made us in His image with the capacity to understand Him and His intelligent order. The Christian bases his metaphysics on Biblical revelation, so the difficulty lies not so much in developing a Christian metaphysics as in defending its rationality and implications. Therefore, we will posit the Christian metaphysics and then concentrate on reinforcing the truth of these claims.

J. M. Spier, reiterating the idea that philosophy requires faith, describes Christian metaphysics this way: "All philosophy has a religious starting point. Christian philosophy, based upon the regenerate heart of the believer, which is enlightened by the light of the divine revelation of the Word of God, is constructed upon the distinction between God and the cosmos."[32] This foundational assumption is summed up by C. S. Lewis: "No philosophical theory which I have yet come across is a radical improvement on the words of Genesis, that 'In the beginning God made Heaven and Earth.'"[33]

For the Christian, matter exists but it is not the ultimate substance. It is real, but it is not ultimate reality. It is not eternal. Rather, the material universe was created on purpose out of the mind of the living Logos (John 1:1-4), and all the cosmos, existing independently of God, relies on God for its very existence and explanation. In other words, the Christian explanation for the world of matter or nature is that the supernatural created the natural. And since the supernatural God of the Bible is a rational, purposeful, powerful God, the created universe itself contains such qualities. It is no accident that at every level of the cosmos—sub-atomic, atomic, organic, inorganic, sub-human, human, earth, moon, sun, stars, galaxies—all things manifest amazing order and rationality that can be reasonably explained only as the result of a deliberate, creative act of God. Christianity considers entirely irrational the notion that the orderly cosmos is the result of a series of accidents, chance, or random happenings. Such a position is tantamount to having a bridge, an airplane, an automobile, or a skyscraper, without an architect, plan, or engineer. It doesn't happen that way in the real world; only in the minds of those who lack faith in the supernatural and in the Bible. No part or piece of a Boeing 747 airplane ever occurred by chance or accident. Every item was designed to function in a certain way, and apart from its design and construction there would be no functioning whole.

The early verses of John 1 contain the Christian's metaphysics in a nutshell. "In the beginning [of the cosmos] was the Word [Logos, mind, reason, thought, wisdom, intelligence, idea, law, order, purpose, design], and the Word was with God, and the Word was God. The same

[Word] was in the beginning with God. All things were made by him; and without him was not anything made that was made. In him was life; and the life was the light of men" (John 1:1-4).

The flow of this passage sets forth the parameters of Christian philosophy: mind before matter; God before man; plan and design before creation; life from life; and enlightenment from the Light. The orderly universe was conceived in the orderly and rational mind of God before it was created (as Disneyland was conceived in the mind of Walt Disney before it was created). The creation is the thought of God in praxis. Without the Logos there would be no cosmos. From the Christian perspective it is no surprise to see philosophers and scientists refer to the universe as a manifestation of mathematical law, order, design, beauty, etc. This is the way it was created "in the beginning." Physicist Paul Davies asks, "If the world's finest minds can unravel only with difficulty the deeper workings of nature, how could it be supposed that those workings are merely a mindless accident, a product of blind chance?"[34]

Then, too, as modern science (especially physics) pushes deeper and deeper into the sub-atomic world, the nature or essence of the atom seems to take on almost spiritual/mental qualities. Matter, for example, is losing much of its material substantiality, while the spiritual/mental nature of the atom is being writ in larger and larger letters. "It is difficult for the matter-of-fact physicist," says Sir Arthur Eddington, "to accept the view that the substratum of everything is of mental character."[35] Further, he says, to put the conclusion of the matter crudely—"the stuff of the world is mind-stuff."[36] But Eddington doesn't even stop here. First he says that "time" is far more typical of physical reality than "matter" and openly states, "physics may as well admit at once that reality is spiritual."[37]

Both Sir James Jeans and Davies insist on the mathematical character of ultimate reality. Jeans refers to God as "The Great Mathematician," and Davies believes the physical universe was once a mere mathematical point. Mathematics is a mental construct. Carl F. H. Henry argues not only that "mathematics comes from God"[38] but also that the laws of logic are grounded in God's very being. Says Henry, "The laws of logic are the 'architecture' or organization of the divine mind. They are the systematic arrangement of God's mind or the way God thinks. The laws of logic, therefore, have an ultimate ontological reality."[39]

Davies, in *God and the New Physics* and *Superforce*, makes it very clear that the sub-atomic level is a world of rational principles, law, order and design. He says that "the universe is seen to be a product of *law* rather than *chance*,"[40] and further,"The new physics and the new cosmology reveal that our ordered universe is far more than a gigantic

Notes and Asides

Praxis refers to practice specifically distinguished from theory.

"'Logocentrism,' so contemptuously assaulted in the academy, ignored in the media, undermined in the marketplace, is the West's only means of restoring sanity."
—*National Review*

Philosophers and Scientists Affirming the Supernaturalist Position

Immanuel Kant (1724-1804): *"In the world we find everywhere clear signs of an order which can only spring from design—an order realized with the greatest wisdom, and in a universe which is indescribably varied in content and in extent infinite."* [41]

John Stuart Mill (1806-1873): *"[T]he adaptations in Nature afford a large balance of probability in favor of creation by intelligence."* [42]

Albert Einstein (1879-1955): *"Everyone who is seriously involved in the pursuit of science becomes convinced that a spirit is manifest in the laws of the universe—a spirit vastly superior to that of man, and one in the face of which we with our modest powers must feel humble."* [43]

David Hume (1711-1776): *"The whole frame of nature bespeaks an intelligent author; and no rational enquirer can, after serious reflection, suspend his belief a moment with regard to the primary principles of genuine theism and Religion."* [44]

Jean Paul Sartre (1905-1980), a life-long atheist philosopher,[45] said at the close of his hedonistic life: *"I do not feel that I am the product of chance, a speck of dust in the universe, but someone who was expected, prepared, prefigured. In short, a king whom only a Creator could put here; the idea of a creating hand refers to God."* [46]

Sir James Jeans (1877-1946): *"If the universe is a universe of thought, then its creation must have been an act of thought. Indeed, the finiteness of time and space almost compel us, of themselves, to picture the creation as an act of thought. Modern scientific theory compels us to think of the creator as working outside time and space, which are part of his creation, just as the artist is outside his canvas."* [47]

Sir Arthur Eddington (1882-1944): *"The idea of a universal Mind or Logos would be, I think, a fairly plausible inference from the present state of scientific theory; at least it is in harmony with it."* [48]

Paul Davies (1946-): *"The laws which enable this universe to come into being spontaneously seem themselves to be the product of exceedingly ingenious design. If physics is the product of design, the universe must have a purpose, and the evidence of modern physics suggests strongly to me that the purpose includes me."* [49]

Notes and Asides

accident. I believe that a study of the recent revolution in these subjects is a source of great inspiration in the search for the meaning of life."[50] Elsewhere he expands on this belief:

> Every advance in fundamental physics seems to uncover yet another facet of *order*. The very success of the scientific method depends upon the fact that the physical world operates according to rational principles which can therefore be discerned through rational enquiry. Logically, the universe does not have to be this way. We could conceive of a cosmos where chaos reigns. In place of the orderly and regimented behavior of matter and energy one would have arbitrary and haphazard activity. Stable structures like atoms or people or stars could not exist. The real world is not this way. It is ordered and complex. Is that not itself an astonishing fact at which to marvel?[51]

These remarks by Davies are all the more extraordinary when one considers that just a few years ago he was arguing that science did not support the religious picture of a creator.[52]

Clearly, Christian metaphysics does not have to apologize to modern science or modern philosophy. Joad sees the universe as two orders of reality:

> The natural order, consisting of people and things moving about in space and enduring in time, and a supernatural order neither in space nor in time, which consists of a Creative Person or Trinity of Persons from which the natural order derives its meaning and in terms of which it receives its explanation.[53]

Young says, "Christian realists are contingent dualists but not eternal dualists. They hold that there are two kinds of substance: Spirit (or God) and matter which was created by God ex nihilo as Augustine suggested. Matter is not spirit, nor is it reducible to spirit, but its existence is always dependent upon God Who created it out of nothing."[54] Young chooses to use the term *Christian realism* to represent the Christian philosophy. In an effort to stress the existence of something other than the material, we employ the term *supernaturalism*. Regardless of the name, true Christian philosophy requires a metaphysics consistent with Biblical teaching. Buswell sums up this position when he writes, "In metaphysics we believe that God is the supreme personal Intelligence, Creator of the finite universe. We hold that the created universe exists, not independently, or as something unrelated or apart;

Supernaturalism is a philosophical term which describes people who affirm the existence of both the natural and the supernatural.

Notes and Asides

but it is a distinct thing, not part of, or an emanation of, or a thought or act of, but numerically other than its Creator or His thoughts or acts."[55]

Christian Epistemology

The Christian theory of knowledge includes the belief that knowledge is attainable not only through personal experience, history, and science, but also through divine revelation. Christians view the Bible as a fountainhead of heavenly wisdom and find nothing in human history or science to discredit what it says about God ("God created the heavens and earth"), the universe (the "heavens declare the glory of God"), or man (man was created "in the image of God").

This epistemology does not (as some suppose) exclude science, history, or experience as methods of obtaining knowledge. In fact, the Christian recognizes all three, with reservations of course, as additional ways of discovering God's methods and handiwork in the universe. The Christian's reservations with regard to science are summed up by Henry, who says the scientific method "may explain a great deal," but it cannot establish "the meaning of events and relationships." He adds, "The fact is that empirical science has no firm basis whatever on which to raise objections to Christianity, not because scientific and historical concerns are irrelevant to revelation and faith, but because scientists must allow for possible exceptions to every rule they affirm, and for the empirical vulnerability of the rules themselves."[56]

Christian epistemology hinges on the belief that truth exists independent of man, but because man was created in the image of a moral, loving, rational God (Genesis 1:27), man is capable of recognizing and understanding truth. St. Augustine suggested an analogy for the nature of truth, which is described by Gordon H. Clark: "The teacher in the classroom does not give his students ideas. The ideas or truths are discovered by the student in his own mind; and as he contemplates the truth within, he judges whether the teacher has taught the truth. But though the truth is discovered within the mind, it is not a product of the student. Truth is not individual, but universal; truth did not begin when we were born, it has always existed."[57]

"Truth is not individual, but universal; truth did not begin when we were born, it has always existed."
—Gordon H. Clark

This universal nature of truth requires the philosopher to be open to it no matter how it is presented. That is, the philosopher cannot throw away divine revelation simply because it may be considered pre- or extra-scientific. "What is characteristic of the Augustinian method as such is its refusal to blind reason systematically by closing its eyes to anything faith points out. Whence the corresponding ideal of a Christian philosophy which is true philosophy to the extent that it is Christian; for while allowing each knowledge its proper order, the

Notes and Asides

Christian philosopher considers revelation a source of light for his reason."[58] For the supernaturalist, reason (in order to be reasonable) must not prejudice itself against faith; e.g., believing that God has provided his children with a revelation concerning Himself and things about which His children could not otherwise obtain knowledge.

In fact, for the supernaturalist, epistemology *must* take into account matters of faith, because the theory of knowledge relies to an extent on experience, and through faith the Christian has had experiences that imply the existence of the supernatural. Young states, "The Christian realist stands on the basis of experience just as much as do the naturalist and the idealist. He would be most incoherent if he did not take into account his supernatural experience for it is the most real and most essential element of his philosophy of life."[59]

Geisler believes that the totality of human experience favors the Christian belief in God:

> Unless it is true that no man in the history of the world has ever really been truly critical of his religious experience, then it follows that the reality of God has been critically established from human experience. Experience—hard, critical experience—indicates that men are not being totally deceived. There is a reality basis for at least some religious experience. And hence, there is a God . . . to fulfill men's need to transcend.[60]

Indeed, experience is crucial for the average man's epistemology—the times the Christian experiences God's truth are the most meaningful for his faith.

Even the Bible appeals to experiential evidence. Buswell states that the one epistemological trait characteristic of the Biblical writers is "the appeal to empirical evidence in verification of the divine authority of the message."[61] Buswell points to John 10:37-38, in which Jesus asks the Pharisees to judge His works to determine the truth of His claims, stating, "Do not believe me unless I do what my Father does. But if I do it, even though you do not believe me, believe the miracles, that you may learn and understand that the Father is in me, and I in the Father." Christ is asking the Pharisees to believe their own experience, just as the Christian today counts his experience as important to his knowing process.

The Christian believes both that truth is universal and knowable and that experience is a proper mode of discovering that truth. However, contrary to both Humanists and Marxists, who seek to paint the Christian as a believer in superstition, the Christian is willing to include science in his epistemology. Christianity is not afraid of personal experience, history, philosophy, or science. Christianity welcomes all

Notes and Asides

four, but always in light of the Bible. Buswell describes the entire Christian theory of knowledge when he writes,

> In epistemology, we believe that God, the supreme personal Intelligence, has created us to be in some measure capable of intelligent apprehension of truth. We regard the basic laws of logic as derived from the character of God's intelligence. . . . We believe it profitable to formulate our ideas of discovered truth in verifiable propositions, and we believe that such propositions may be made more and more accurate and comprehensive by the scientific method, that is, by the assiduous application of careful observation, experimentation, and analytical, discriminating thought.[62]

Notice that Buswell accepts the scientific method into the Christian epistemology. This is true of almost every Christian. Indeed, science supports Christian philosophy more than it does evolutionary naturalism or dialectical materialism. The following will address the scope of science and its relation to philosophy.

Science and Christianity

Regardless of what Humanists and Marxists believe, science cannot act as the sole foundation for a theory of knowledge. Science, operating within the framework of the scientific method including observation, hypothesis, experimentation, falsification, predictability, and law, can only describe reality that is observable and measurable. It is necessarily limited in its examination of anything imperceptible to the five senses. It is also limited with regard to the past, since it cannot measure and observe anything that does not exist in the present. Since all history, for example, is a one-time event, history is outside the scientific method. As Young points out, "when the naturalist limits himself to the scientific or experimental method, his conclusions must necessarily be limited to the area from which his data is [sic] gathered—namely, the world of sense perception."[63]

If the mind, for example, is only a brain process, then the scientist will be able to explain it. But if the mind exists in the supernatural realm, science, by definition, cannot *know* anything about it. Joad notes, "Yet if the mind has no 'physical connections,' I do not see how a scientist, in so far as he follows the classical methods of science, can hope to give an account of it."[64] No brain surgeon has yet seen an idea, much less dissected one!

Therefore, the conclusion may be drawn, as Joad says, that "though

Notes and Asides

science may succeed in increasing our knowledge of the nature of the constitution of the physical world, it can have no contribution to make to the religious interpretation of the universe."[65] Science, by its very nature, cannot pass judgment on the supernatural interpretation thesis.

As Lewis puts it, "Supposing science ever became complete so that it knew every single thing in the whole universe. Is it not plain that the questions, 'Why is there a universe?' 'Why does it go on as it does?' 'Has it any meaning?' would remain just as they were?"[66] It is not science's role to discover the meaning of life—only to describe the methods the physical universe employs to sustain life.

Young describes the mainstream Christian attitude toward science when he says that for the Christian realist there is no quarrel with the findings of science. For the Christian, all truth is God's truth and should be accepted. "Yet the Christian does not feel obliged to accept as truth all the theories propounded by scientists. Theories are constantly being shown to be inadequate. The Christian is quite willing to accept all the truth about the nature of things that science is able to discover."[67]

The Origin of Science

An examination of the history of modern science reaffirms the supernaturalist's premise that science is not hostile to his position. This examination will demonstrate, again, that Christian philosophy is not hostile toward science, but rather relies on science to reveal one dimension of God's handiwork.

Modern science was founded by men who viewed the world from a Christian perspective. Neither the Marxist nor the Humanist worldview, with their corresponding beliefs that the universe was brought about by a series of accidents, could serve as a fitting base for modern science. Francis Schaeffer writes, "Since the world had been created by a reasonable God, [scientists] were not surprised to find a correlation between themselves as observers and the thing observed—that is, between subject and object. This base is normative to one functioning in the Christian framework, whether he is observing a chair or the molecules which make up the chair. Without this foundation, modern Western science would not have been born."[68] Elsewhere he clarifies this position, stating that the early scientists believed the world was created by a reasonable God, and therefore "they were not surprised to discover that people could find out something true about nature and the universe on the basis of reason."[69]

> Christianity was "the mother of modern science."
> —Francis Schaeffer

Christianity was "the mother of modern science."[70] Norman L. Geisler and J. Kerby Anderson's *Origin Science* contains a chapter titled "The Supernatural Roots of Modern Science." Both Alfred North

Notes and Asides

Whitehead and J. Robert Oppenheimer defended this view. Whitehead contended, "The faith in the possibility of science, generated antecedently to the development of modern scientific theory, is an unconscious derivative from medieval theology."[71] Philosopher and historian of science Stanley L. Jaki notes that historically the belief in creation and the Creator was the moment of truth for science. "This belief formed the bedrock on which science rose."[72] Jaki has powerfully defended this position in *The Origin of Science*[73] and *The Savior of Science*.

What does the history of science have to do with supernaturalism? One must remember that the difficulty for the Christian philosopher lies not in developing a consistent metaphysics or epistemology (these are presented most coherently in the Bible) but in defending the rationality of such a philosophy. For us, this defense may take at least two forms: we can endeavor to demonstrate the rationality of believing in the existence of God through philosophic proofs, or we can show that science, the very basis for most secular philosophies, not only does not detract from the rationality of supernaturalism but actually bolsters the veracity of its claims.

Re-examine the statements by Schaeffer, Jeans, and Jaki for a moment. Notice that each claim is grounded on the fact that science assumed an orderly universe. If man believed the universe to be disorderly or chaotic, he never would have bothered with science, which relies on matter to behave in certain meaningful ways under controlled conditions. On earth, we always expect an apple to fall down rather than up, because we believe in a consistent Law—the Law of Gravity. Lewis says men became scientific because they expected Law in Nature, and "they expected Law in Nature because they believed in a Legislator."[74] In other words, the origin of modern science itself provides grounds for the teleological argument—the argument from design to Designer.

Science and Teleology

Humanists and Marxists would have us believe that science is their own special domain. In reality, Christians have had a great deal to do with the development of modern science. "Most early scientists worked out their scientific views from within this theistic Christian belief in a supernatural creator and the doctrine of creation,"[75] write Geisler and Anderson. Some of these early men of science were Johannes Kepler, Pascal, Robert Boyle, Nicolaus Steno, Isaac Newton, Michael Faraday, Charles Babbage, Louis Agassiz, James Simpson, Gregor Mendel, Louis Pasteur, William Thomson (Lord Kelvin), Joseph Lister, James

Notes and Asides

C. Maxwell, and William Ramsay. But is science still amassing evidence for an orderly, cleverly designed universe today?

The answer is certainly an unqualified *yes* if we listen to F. R. Moulton:

> To the astronomer the most remarkable and interesting thing about that part of the physical universe with which he has become acquainted is not its vast extent in space, nor the number and great masses of its stars, nor the violent forces that operate

Recommended Reading for Advanced Study

Warren C. Young, *A Christian Approach to Philosophy* (Grand Rapids, MI: Baker, 1975).

James Oliver Buswell, Jr., *A Christian View of Being and Knowing* (Grand Rapids, MI: Zondervan, 1960).

J. P. Moreland, *Scaling the Secular City* (Grand Rapids, MI: Baker, 1987).

C. E. M. Joad, *The Recovery of Belief* (London: Faber and Faber, 1955).

Alvin Plantinga, *God, Freedom, and Evil* (Grand Rapids, MI: Eerdmans, 1983).

Sir James Jeans, *Physics and Philosophy* (Cambridge: University Press, 1948).

Norman L. Geisler and Winfried Corduan, *Philosophy of Religion*, 2nd ed. (Grand Rapids, MI: Baker, 1988).

Stanley L. Jaki, *The Road of Science and the Ways to God* (Chicago: University of Chicago Press, 1978).

Notes and Asides

> in the stars, nor the long periods of astronomical time; but that which holds him awe-struck is the perfect orderliness of the universe and the majestic succession of the celestial phenomena. From the tiny satellites in the solar system to the globular clusters, the galaxy, and exterior galaxies, there is no chaos, there is nothing haphazard, and there is nothing capricious. The orderliness of the universe is the supreme discovery in science; it is that which gives us hope that we shall be able to understand not only the exterior world but also our own bodies and our own minds.[76]

In truth, the more science discovers, the more orderly the universe appears. And this orderliness is true at the other end of the universe—the sub-atomic level, and everything between the sub-atomic and the galaxies. An unprejudiced observer would certainly conclude that the universe is based on a blueprint only God could draft.

The **teleological argument** is an attempt to reason from design in the physical universe to a cosmic Designer/Creator.

As Joad puts it, "Scientists have often expatiated upon the majesty of nature and upon the imposing regularity of natural processes. Precisely what one would expect of processes that God ordained!"[77] Indeed, Young says, "Apart from the idea of design and purpose it seems impossible to understand this universe of which we are a part."[78] Again, the dependence of science on an orderly universe is stressed by D. Elton Trueblood: "It is important to realize that this entire scientific enterprise would be impossible if the actions of the various constituents of the universe which we study were arbitrary. Only upon the supposition that the natural world is fundamentally ordered is science possible at all."[79]

Clearly, science relies on an orderly universe, which implies the question, From whence did the order come? Even more significantly, How is it that humans are capable of recognizing orderly processes? That is, Why do minds perceive order? As Albert Einstein says, "the very fact that the totality of our sense experiences is such that by means of thinking . . . it can be put in order . . . is a fact which leaves us in awe, but which we shall never understand."[80] How did man evolve a mind that is capable of ordering an orderly universe? The answer, of course, is that our mind did not evolve at all—rather, it was created by the Ultimate Mind, the Mind that put order in Nature and then granted us the ability to perceive order. Jaki writes, "It was this belief [in a personal rational Creator], as cultivated especially within a Christian matrix, which supported the view for which the world was an objective and orderly entity investigatable by the mind because the mind too was an orderly and objective product of the same rational, that is, perfectly consistent Creator."[81] This argument, an offshoot of the teleological

Notes and Asides

argument, postulates God as the Cause behind the human mind and is often referred to as the mental proof.

Reconciling Science and Christian Philosophy

At the outset of this chapter, it appeared that reconciling supernaturalism with science would be difficult. However, in light of the previous discussion, little reconciliation, if any, is necessary.

In fact, the wise Christian philosopher recognizes the scientific method as a limited but valuable ally.[82] In addition to lending support for the teleological argument, science also shores up the cosmological argument (as we will see later), and modern physics is raising serious questions about the materiality of the atom (which doesn't bode well for either naturalism or materialism).

Joad reinforces the idea that science does not threaten Christianity, stating, "It has often been represented that the conclusions of science are hostile to the tenets of religion. Whatever grounds there may have been for such a view in the past, it is hard to see with what good reason such a contention could be sustained today."[83] Stephen D. Schwarz agrees:

> For until recently, it was thought by many people that science supports atheism, that science is even the rational alternative to theism. It is now clear that science not only does not support atheism, but even lends rational support for theism. There is strong scientific evidence for God. Scientists, without presupposing God or creation, without trying to prove them, have come up with findings that strongly support God, His creation of the universe and man, and a supernatural purpose for the world we live in.[84]

Schwarz goes on to cite four specific scientific discoveries that support the conclusion that God exists: the Second Law of Thermodynamics, the impossibility of spontaneous generation of life from non-life, genetic information theory (DNA), and the Anthropic Principle.

For the Christian, then, science need not be an enemy—indeed, science should be accepted as a somewhat successful method of obtaining knowledge about God's design in the universe. Max Planck, one of the greatest scientific minds of all time, believes that "Religion and natural science are fighting a joint battle in an incessant, never relaxing crusade against skepticism and against dogmatism, against disbelief and against superstition, and the rallying cry in this crusade

The **Anthropic Principle** asserts that the parameters of the Earth were specifically tailored to foster human life.

Notes and Asides

has always been, and always will be: 'On to God!'."[85] Doubtless, God must be at the center of the Christian philosophy—indeed, the whole Christian worldview. Lewis places Him there eloquently when he writes: "In science we have been reading only the notes to a poem; in Christianity we find the poem itself."[86]

Mind-Body Problem and the Mental Proof

The supernaturalist believes that the mind, or consciousness, exists as a separate entity from the purely physical. As mentioned earlier, the Christian believes that his mind is a reflection of the Universal Mind that created the universe ex nihilo, and he sees the mind as an additional proof for the existence of the supernatural.

Most men perceive their thinking process as something different from the material world. Young says that the concept of the mind and the brain interacting is "the most widely accepted theory of the relation of mind and body. It is true to experience. By thinking about an act one can deliberately carry it out in the body. When the body is affected in some way, a sensation is produced in the mind. In thousands of ways every day we experience mind-body interactions."[87] Put more simply, Young says, "Man is so made that his spirit may operate upon and influence his body, and his body is so made that it may operate upon his mind or spirit."[88] Buswell echoes him, stating, "There are mental events and there are material events and it is a daily experience that purposes in the mind release energy in the body and produce effects in the material world, just as events in the material world, through the sensory organs, produce events in the mental world."[89]

This distinction between brain and mind implies a distinction about the whole order of things: matter exists, and something other than matter exists. "We find in the created universe an important difference between beings which think, and beings which are spatially extended, or spiritual beings and material beings. . . . In the body and mind of man we see integrated interaction between the spiritual thinking being, and the material extended being."[90]

The **mental proof** asserts that mind is a supernatural entity distinct from the brain, and that its existence implies the existence of a Higher Mind—i. e., God.

Many Christian thinkers believe this distinction between the brain and the mind is intuitively obvious, and this is the beginning of the mental proof for the existence of a Higher Mind responsible for our minds. Buswell writes,

> It is my suggestion that elementary intuitive experiences lead to the theory that there are ontologically existing substantive entities which occupy space, entities with which we have to do. At the same time elementary intuitive experiences lead to the

Notes and Asides

> inference that there are thinking beings with whom we have to do, and who, like ourselves, have to do with each other and with extended things in the world. It is my opinion that our process of coming to believe in ourselves as thinking beings, and in others as thinking beings, is implied in the elementary intuitive experience, and is developed by a process of inference from effects to causes.[91]

Other Christian thinkers begin with the untenability of the materialist position that the mind is only a material phenomenon and draw the conclusion that since the materialist explanation is irrational, the supernatural explanation must be the acceptable position. Again, science aids the Christian philosopher in undermining the materialist worldview. Writes Buswell,

> The mind is not the brain. The "brain track" psychology has failed. If the brain were identical with the mind, a monkey trained to perform a certain trick with his right hand would be unprepared to perform the trick with his left. But this does not prove to be the case. It is a known fact that if certain parts of the brain are destroyed, and the functions corresponding to those parts impaired, the functions may be taken up by other parts of the brain. There is no exact correspondence between mind and brain.[92]

"There is something which is directing the universe, and which appears to me as a law. . . . I think we have to assume it is more like a mind . . . you can hardly imagine a bit of matter giving instructions."

—C. S. Lewis

Sir John Eccles has made a voluminous contribution to this discussion in recent years. His three works, *The Self and Its Brain* (with Karl Popper), *The Human Mystery*, and *The Human Psyche* are considered classics in the field. Eccles maintains that having a mind means one is conscious, and that consciousness is a mental event, not a material event. He further contends that there are two distinct, different orders, i.e., the brain is in the material world and the mind is in the "world of subjective experience."[93]

Explaining this world of mental experience, Eccles says,

> Thoughts, of course, do eventually find expression in language, that is what one does in the ordinary business of talking, thoughts converted into language. So that part of the story is fairly clear: that we do have mental events before they are converted into brain events. The monist materialist thinks that the mental events are simply derivative of aspects of the nerve endings. But there is no evidence for this whatsoever. It's part of a hypothesis. But they think that, therefore, they are escaping from the difficulties of physics. But they just create a worse

Notes and Asides

> difficulty in physics, namely, there is no such thing in physics as mental events, mental happenings. The world of mind is not recognized by the physicist at all. They invented something which they superimposed upon physics simply to escape from the difficulties of having mental events as distinct from material events.[94]

Lewis cuts to the heart of the materialist and naturalist dilemma when he writes, "The Naturalists have been engaged in thinking about Nature. They have not attended to the fact that they were thinking. The moment one attends to this it is obvious that one's own thinking cannot be merely a natural event, and that therefore something other than Nature exists. The Supernatural is not remote and abstruse: it is a matter of daily and hourly experience, as intimate as breathing."[95] For Lewis, too, the non-physical nature of thought is intuitively obvious.

Regardless of whether the Christian philosopher chooses a positive or negative approach to proving the separate nature of the mind, once people are convinced of the truth of this premise, they are only a step away from accepting the logical existence of God. Bruce Milne writes that the mental proof "argues that pure materialism is unable to explain the capacity of the mind to move logically from premises to conclusions; only the existence of a transcendent Mind explains the effective operation of our human intelligence, or indeed of other non-material qualities of the mind and imagination. If there is no divine intelligence, it asks, how can we trust our thinking to be true, and hence, what grounds can there be for trusting any argument advanced in support of atheism?"[96]

In fact, Trueblood believes that supernaturalism is unavoidable. He believes that a boldly accepted naturalism leads directly to supernaturalism! "How can nature include mind as an integral part unless it is grounded in mind? If mind were seen as something alien or accidental, the case would be different, but the further we go in modern science the clearer it becomes that mental experience is no strange offshoot. Rather it is something which is deeply rooted in the entire structure."[97] Implied, then, is the existence of a God that could create an entire structure with mind as an integral part. Once an individual grants the existence of an orderly mind separate from the physical universe, belief in the Ultimate Mind becomes the only rational option.

God and the Philosophers

For many Christian thinkers, there is no need to go beyond the mental proof—the existence of the mind is intuitively obvious, and therefore

Notes and Asides

supernaturalism must be the rational conclusion. However, the mental proof, since it simply requires the assumption of one premise, cannot be viewed as a philosophical proof in the strict sense of the word. Using the term *philosophy* in a narrow sense, only three arguments for the existence of God are generally held to be plausible. The first, the teleological argument, has been examined both in this chapter and in the Christian theology chapter. The second of these is the cosmological argument.

The cosmological argument was first formulated by Thomas Aquinas, and although many have attempted to improve upon it, the argument has not been revised significantly since his time. His presentation is still a model of clarity:

> We find in nature things that are possible to be and not to be, since they are found to be generated and to be corrupted, and consequently, it is possible for them to be and not to be. But it is impossible for these always to exist, for that which can not-be at some time is not. Therefore, if everything can not-be, then at one time there was nothing in existence. Now if this were true then even now there would be nothing in existence, because that which does not exist, begins to exist only through something already existing. Therefore if at one time nothing was in existence, it would have been impossible for anything to have begun to exist; and thus now nothing would be in existence—which is absurd. Therefore, not all beings are merely possible, but there must exist something the existence of which is necessary. But every necessary thing either has its necessity caused by another, or not. Now it is impossible to go on to infinity in necessary things which have their necessity caused by another, as has already been proved in regard to efficient causes. Therefore, we cannot but admit the existence of some being having of itself its own necessity, and not receiving it from another, but rather causing in others their necessity. This all men speak of as God.[98]

The **cosmological argument** distinguishes between necessary beings and contingent beings, and asserts that God is the necessary being which explains the existence of men and all other contingent beings

A specific version of this argument that has gained popularity in recent years is the Kalam cosmological argument. William Lane Craig believes this to be the strongest of the "proofs" for the existence of God, and he concludes his study of the argument by stating,

> Since everything that begins to exist has a cause of its existence, and since the universe began to exist, we conclude, therefore, the universe has a cause of its existence. We ought to ponder long and hard over this truly remarkable conclusion, for it

CLOSE-UP

Saint Thomas Aquinas (ca. 1224-1274)

Saint Thomas Aquinas provided leadership in two important realms of Christian thought: the division between the sacred and the secular, and the integration of faith and reason. Thomas recognized early in life that it is wrong for the Christian to withdraw from the world, that "a city on a hill cannot be hidden" (Matthew 5:14). His parents intended for him to become abbot of a prestigious monastery, but Thomas came to believe that the Christian must champion the cause of the sacred in the realm of the secular. Thus, he focused much of his later career on lecturing in universities, and writing treatises regarding the integration of faith and reason. Thomas rightly recognized that if the Christian view is true, it applies to every aspect of reality, and must be treated as a systematic worldview. His ideas, referred to as the Thomist synthesis, were an attempt to integrate philosophy with theology--specifically, Aristotelian thought with Biblical Christianity. Thomas' most important work is the *Summa theologica*, an impeccable defense of the Christian faith.

> means that transcending the entire universe there exists a cause which brought the universe into being ex nihilo. If our discussion has been more than a mere academic exercise, this conclusion ought to stagger us, ought to fill us with a sense of awe and wonder at the knowledge that our whole universe was caused to exist by something beyond it and greater than it.[99]

Every serious philosopher must grapple with Craig's conclusion—if his argument is without flaw, the only further question that should concern us is how we should lead our lives in the most proper accordance with this great First Cause.

Again, science testifies to the rationality of the Christian faith—this time specifically in support of the cosmological argument. Trueblood notes, "The Second Law of Thermodynamics [the movement from order to disorder in a closed system] thus points directly to theism as an explanation of the world, and the reasoning based upon it provides a modern counterpart to the cosmological argument."[100]

Notes and Asides

The third philosophical "proof" for the existence of God is the ontological argument. This is generally the favorite argument for Christian philosophers—Milne calls it "the most important philosophically,"[101] and Plantinga states, "What I claim for [the ontological] argument, therefore, is that it establishes, not the truth of theism, but its rational acceptability."[102] A simplified version of the ontological argument is described by Milne:

> The classical statement, given by Anselm (1033-1109), has two steps. First: God is 'a being than which nothing greater can be conceived' ('greater' = 'more perfect'). Second: something which exists only in the mind is distinct from something which exists in the mind and in reality. Put the two steps together: if God does not exist (i.e. exists only in the mind but not in reality), it is possible to conceive of a more perfect being than the most perfect being; that is an impossible contradiction. Hence we must accept the alternative; the most perfect being exists in reality as well as in the mind.[103]

The **ontological argument** asserts that the perfect being, as conceived by man, must actually exist.

While this argument may seem like little more than a play on words to the beginning philosophy student, one must only consider that it has been around more than eight hundred years to understand that it has lasting philosophical implications.

God Is More Than First Cause or Ultimate Mind

The various arguments for the existence of God have obvious merit. However, they can become stumbling blocks to developing a consistent Biblical Christian worldview. One can easily become enchanted by these "proofs" and forget that they are only the first step in knowing the personality and attributes of God. Even if someone accepted the cosmological argument, he might still need to be convinced of the truth of Christianity. One can use the cosmological argument to postulate a First Cause without allowing that First Cause to be omniscient, all-powerful, or holy—and such proofs certainly do not necessitate a loving God who is concerned about His creative and redemptive order.

Most Christian philosophers argue that the notion of God is meaningless unless God be a personal Mind. Trueblood writes,

> The central point is that, if God is not personal, in a literal sense, then God is not the ultimate explanation of that which most requires explanation. What baffles the materialist is the emergence of personal character in a world of chemical reactions.

Notes and Asides

> Only one who is supremely personal can be the Ground for the emergence of even the finite personality which we see in our fellows and know intimately in ourselves. If God is only an impersonal force, then the stream has risen higher than its source, for we can at least be certain that personality appears in us.[104]

Schwartz argues along the same lines:

> Such a Being, the Creator of the universe, must be a Personal Being, the Absolute Person, the Absolute Consciousness, the Absolute Knowledge, Will, and Love. For if He is the Ground of our being He cannot be less than what we are, personal beings. If God were an impersonal force, we would be higher than God, as conscious persons, which is absurd. And the act of intending the universe to be, of creating it into actual being, essentially requires a Conscious Person.[105]

The proper Christian attitude toward integrating "proofs" of God's existence with sharing the gospel with non-Christians is summed up by Milne:

> The God of the Bible is undoubtedly a far greater concept than the God of natural theology. Since the way God is known can be properly discussed only in the light of who he is, Christians will best serve those they hope to see awakened to faith by setting forth, as adequately as possible, the God of the Bible in all his transcendent majesty and greatness, beauty and power, grace and holiness, and by demonstrating something of his reality in their personal lives and in their Christian community.[106]

The God of rational "proofs" alone is unworthy of worship—only the Christian God, in all His power and holiness, elicits awe and love in their proper proportion.

Conclusion

Matthew Arnold suggested that philosophy is the attempt to see life steadily and to see it whole. Others, says Young, have suggested that philosophy is the attempt to give a coherent account of all of one's experience. "The basic question of human experience is not philosophy versus no philosophy," says Young, "but good philosophy versus bad

Notes and Asides

philosophy. Everyone has a philosophy of life, a worldview, no matter what form it may take. Our problem is not to get rid of philosophy, but to find the right philosophy, and, having found it, to present it to others with a conviction that grows out of the assurance that one has found the truth."[107]

Just like evolutionary naturalism and dialectical materialism, supernaturalism is more than a philosophy in the narrow sense. Christian philosophy represents an entire worldview, a view that is consistent with the Bible throughout. In the end, everyone must choose basically between a materialist/naturalist worldview and a supernaturalist worldview—and the choice will create repercussions throughout every aspect of the individual's life.

"The Christian and the Materialist hold different beliefs about the universe," says Lewis. "They can't both be right. The one who is wrong will act in a way which simply doesn't fit the real universe. Consequently, with the best will in the world, he will be helping his fellow creatures to their destruction."[108] The choice that leads a person to either Christianity or materialism results from the individual's answer to one simple question:

> Is existence ultimately meaningful, or is it ultimately absurd? If God is, He represents the ultimate meaning of existence, the sufficient reason why it [the universe] came into existence and the final end towards which it [the universe] moves as its destiny. If God is not, existence is an accident, a momentary flicker of light between an infinite darkness and void before, and after.[109]

"Natural philosophy, next to the word of God, is the surest medicine for superstition."
—Sir Francis Bacon

The Christian philosophy embraces the meaningful, purposeful life, a life in which each of us shapes his beliefs according to a coherent, reasonable, truthful worldview. We believe a Christian young person with such a worldview will not be tossed to and fro by every secularist doctrine. "In the same way," says Dr. Young, "it can be said that the Christian philosopher and theologian must be acquainted with the contending world-views of his age. Philosophy after all is a way of life, and the Christian believes that he has the true way—the true pattern for living. It is the task of the Christian leader to understand the ideologies of his day so that he may be able to meet their challenge. The task is a never-ending one, for, although the Christian's worldview does not change, the world about him does. Thus the task of showing the relevance of the Christian realistic philosophy to a world in process is one which requires eternal vigilance. To such a task, to such an ideal, the Christian leader must dedicate himself."[110]

In closing this chapter on Christian supernaturalism we would ask

Notes and Asides

each Christian student to ponder the following challenge by Carl F. H. Henry:

> Metaphysics tomorrow will be either Christian or non-Christian, but metaphysics there will be. While Christians hesitate to expound an authentic worldview, Marxists [and Secular Humanists] will continue to expound an artificial one. If modern man, the conqueror of outer space, does not make up his mind, he will vacillate intellectually to a gypsy's grave. The task of Christian leadership is to confront modern man with the Christian world life view as the revealed conceptuality for understanding reality and experience, and to recall reason once again from the vagabondage of irrationalism and the arrogance of autonomy to the service of true faith. That does not imply modern man's return to the medieval mind. It implies, rather, a reaching for the eternal mind, for the mind of Christ, for the truth of revelation, for the Logos as transcendent source of the orders and structures of being, for the Logos-incarnate in Jesus Christ, for the Logos as divine agent in creation, redemption and judgment, for the Logos who stands invisibly but identifiably as the true center of nature, history, ethics, philosophy and religion.[111]

[1]*Select Writings of Francis Bacon*, ed. Hugh G. Dick (New York: Random House, 1955), p. 44.
[2]Kant argued that it was impossible to disprove the existence of God and admitted that "belief in God and in another world is so interwoven with my moral sentiment that as there is little danger of my losing the latter, there is equally little cause for fear that the former can ever be taken from me." *Critique of Pure Reason*, B 857, cited by Dallas Willard in J. P. Moreland and Kai Nielsen, et al., *Does God Exist? The Great Debate* (Nashville: Thomas Nelson, 1990), p. 211.
[3]C. E. M. Joad, *The Recovery of Belief* (London: Faber and Faber Limited, 1955), p. 16.
[4]Ibid., p. 22.
[5]John Baillie, *Invitation to Pilgrimage* (New York: Scribner, 1942), p. 15.
[6]*The Intellectuals Speak Out About God*, ed. Roy Abraham Varghese (Dallas, TX: Lewis and Stanley, 1984), p. 129.
[7]William Lane Craig, *The Existence of God and the Beginning of the Universe* (San Bernardino, CA: Here's Life Publishers, 1979), p. 84.
[8]Bernard J. F. Lonergan, *Method in Theology* (New York: The Seabury Press, 1972), p. 103.
[9]*The Intellectuals Speak Out About God*, ed. Varghese, pp. 166-7.
[10]Ibid., p. 180.
[11]Norman L. Geisler, *Philosophy of Religion* (Grand Rapids, MI: Zondervan, 1974), p. 94. This important work has been updated: Norman L. Geisler and Winfried Corduan, *Philosophy of Religion*, 2d ed. (Grand Rapids: Baker Book House, 1988).
[12]Carl F. H. Henry, *God, Revelation and Authority*, six volumes (Waco, TX: Word Books, 1976), vol. 1, p. 169. Henry mentions W. J. Neidhardt's work "Faith, the Unrecognized Partner of Science and Religion" as the source for his comments.
[13]Ibid.
[14]Ibid.
[15]Edward T. Ramsdell, *The Christian Perspective* (New York: Abingdon-Cokesbury Press, 1950), p. 42.
[16]Warren C. Young, *A Christian Approach to Philosophy* (Grand Rapids, MI: Baker, [1954] 1975), p. 37.
[17]Stanley L. Jaki, *The Savior of Science* (Washington, D.C.: Regnery Gateway, 1988), p. 206. States Jaki, "The third charge [that should be pressed against materialist evolutionists] derives from a close look at the nature or composition of that human, indeed very human authority. It is made up of leading departments of biology, zoology, and genetics, of leading publishers, of the publishers of most university presses, of editors of most periodicals, weeklies, and newspapers. They come close to constituting a monopoly over information. Almost invariably they give good riddance to manuscripts whose authors question, however learnedly, the shibboleths of the academic establishment which, while making profuse references to bygone inquisitions, reopens daily its own inquisitorial tribunals."
[18]John Warwick Montgomery, *Human Rights and Human Dignity* (Dallas, TX: Probe Books, 1986), p. 133.
[19]Ibid.
[20]Ibid., p. 137.
[21]Ibid., p. 137.
[22]Ibid., p. 139.
[23]Ibid., p. 144.
[24]Ibid., p. 151.
[25]Henry, *God, Revelation, and Authority*, vol. 1, p. 225.
[26]James Oliver Buswell, Jr. *A Christian View of Being and Knowing* (Grand Rapids, MI: Zondervan, 1960), p. 198.
[27]Young, *A Christian Approach to Philosophy*, p. 182.
[28]Ibid., p. 40.
[29]Howard VanTill, et. al., *Science Held Hostage* (Downers Grove, IL: InterVarsity Press, 1988), part 1, chapters 1 and 2. While VanTill and his colleagues, Davis A. Young and Clarence Menninga, find much fault with the credentials of creationists—"it is very difficult to regard these people as professional, practicing scientists. They do not demonstrate the marks of integrity," Carl Sagan, on the other hand, who is hiding his religious humanism under the cloak of science, receives this from the writers: "Sagan has excellent credentials as a knowledgeable practicing scientist." Apart from this obvious bias, their critique of Sagan's *Cosmos* is excellent.

[30]D. Gareth Jones, *Horizons of Science*, ed. Carl F. H. Henry (San Francisco: Harper and Row, 1978), p. 44.
[31]Henry, *God, Revelation and Authority*, vol. 5, p. 336.
[32]J. M. Spier, *An Introduction to Christian Philosophy* (Nutley, NJ: The Craig Press, 1966), p. 30.
[33]*A Mind Awake: An Anthology of C. S. Lewis*, ed. Clyde S. Kilby (New York and London: Harcourt, Brace & World, 1968), p. 81.
[34]Paul Davies, *Superforce* (New York: Simon and Schuster, 1984), p. 236.
[35]Sir Arthur Eddington, *The Nature of the Physical World* (Ann Arbor, MI: University of Michigan Press, 1968), p. 281.
[36]Ibid., p. 276.
[37]Ibid., p. 275.
[38]Henry, *God, Revelation and Authority*, vol. 5, p. 389.
[39]Ibid., vol. 5, p. 334.
[40]Davies, *Superforce*, p. 9.
[41]Immanuel Kant, *Critique of Pure Reason*, as cited in James Orr, *The Christian View of God and the World* (Edinburgh: Andrew Elliot, 1897), p. 98.
[42]John Stuart Mill, *Three Essays on Religion*, as cited in Orr, *The Christian View of God and the World*, p. 100.
[43]*The Intellectuals Speak Out About God*, ed. Varghese, p. 45.
[44]David Hume, *The Natural History of Religion*, as cited by Dallas Willard in Moreland and Nielsen, et al., *Does God Exist?* p. 211.
[45]See Paul Johnson, *The Intellectuals* (New York: Harper and Row, 1988), pp. 225-251, for the life and times of existentialist Jean Paul Sartre.
[46]*The Intellectuals Speak Out About God*, ed. Varghese, p. 136.
[47]Sir James Jeans, *The Mysterious Universe* (New York: Macmillan, 1930), p. 154.
[48]Eddington, *The Nature of the Physical World*, p. 338.
[49]Davies, *Superforce*, p. 243.
[50]Ibid., p. 9.
[51]Ibid., p. 223.
[52]Paul Davies, *The Edge of Infinity* (New York: Simon and Schuster, 1981), p. 170.
[53]Joad, *The Recovery of Belief*, p. 182.
[54]Young, *A Christian Approach to Philosophy*, p. 84.
[55]Buswell, *A Christian View of Being and Knowing*, p. 8.
[56]Henry, *God, Revelation and Authority*, vol. 1, p. 175.
[57]Gordon H. Clark, *A Christian View of Men and Things* (Grand Rapids, MI: Baker Book House, 1952), p. 321.
[58]Etienne Gilson, *The Christian Philosophy of St. Augustine* (New York: Vintage Books, 1960), p. 242.
[59]Young, *A Christian Approach to Philosophy*, p. 58.
[60]Geisler, *Philosophy of Religion*, p. 82.
[61]Buswell, *A Christian View of Being and Knowing*, pp. 169-70.
[62]Ibid., pp. 8-9.
[63]Young, *A Christian Approach to Philosophy*, p. 39.
[64]Joad, *The Recovery of Belief*, p. 188.
[65]Ibid., p. 45.
[66]*A Mind Awake*, ed. Kilby, p. 235.
[67]Young, *A Christian Approach to Philosophy*, p. 80.
[68]Francis A. Schaeffer, *How Should We Then Live?* (Old Tappan, NJ: Fleming H. Revell, 1976), p. 134.
[69]Ibid., p. 133.
[70]Ibid., p. 134.
[71]Alfred North Whitehead, *Science and the Modern World* (New York: The Free Press, 1925), p. 13.
[72]Stanley L. Jaki, *The Road of Science and the Ways to God* (Chicago: University of Chicago Press, 1978), p. 143.
[73]Stanley L. Jaki, *The Origin of Science* (South Bend, IN: Regnery Gateway, 1979).
[74]*A Mind Awake*, ed. Kilby, p. 234.
[75]Norman L. Geisler and Kerby Anderson, *Origin Science* (Grand Rapids, MI: Baker Book House, 1987), p. 39.

[76]F. R. Moulton, *The Nature of the World and of Man* (Chicago: University of Chicago Press, 1927), p. 30.
[77]Joad, *The Recovery of Belief*, p. 110.
[78]Young, *A Christian Approach to Philosophy*, p. 82.
[79]D. Elton Trueblood, *Philosophy of Religion* (Grand Rapids, MI: Baker Book House, 1957), p. 206.
[80]Albert Einstein, *Physics and Reality*, cited in Jaki, *The Road of Science and the Ways to God*, p. 259.
[81]Jaki, *The Road of Science and the Ways to God*, p. 242.
[82]J. P. Moreland says that a number of scientific discoveries are "favorable to Christianity (e.g., the Big Bang theory and information DNA)." J. P. Moreland, *Christianity and the Nature of Science* (Grand Rapids, MI: Baker Book House, 1989), p. 248.
[83]Joad, *The Recovery of Belief*, p. 107.
[84]Stephen D. Schwarz, "Introduction—Philosophy," in *The Intellectuals Speak Out About God*, ed. Varghese, p. 100.
[85]Max Planck, *Scientific Autobiography and Other Papers* (London: Williams and Norgate, 1950), in the lecture "Religion and Natural Science."
[86]*A Mind Awake*, ed. Kilby, p. 240.
[87]Young, *A Christian Approach to Philosophy*, p. 119.
[88]Ibid., p. 120.
[89]Buswell, *A Christian View of Being and Knowing*, p. 128.
[90]Ibid., p. 8.
[91]Ibid., p. 184.
[92]Ibid., p. 142.
[93]*The Intellectuals Speak Out About God*, ed. Varghese, p. 49.
[94]Ibid.
[95]*A Mind Awake*, ed. Kilby, p. 205.
[96]Bruce Milne, *Know the Truth* (Downers Grove, IL: InterVarsity Press, 1982), p. 55.
[97]Trueblood, *Philosophy of Religion*, p. 101.
[98]Thomas Aquinas, *Summa Theologica*, Ques. 3, Art. 3.
[99]William Lane Craig, *The Kalam Cosmological Argument* (New York: Barnes and Noble, 1979), p. 149.
[100]Trueblood, *Philosophy of Religion*, p. 104.
[101]Milne, *Know the Truth*, p. 53.
[102]Alvin Plantinga, *God, Freedom, and Evil* (Grand Rapids, MI: William B. Eerdmans, 1974), p. 112.
[103]Milne, *Know the Truth*, p. 53.
[104]Trueblood, *Philosophy of Religion*, p. 270.
[105]*The Intellectuals Speak Out About God*, ed. Varghese, p. 109.
[106]Milne, *Know the Truth*, p. 58.
[107]Young, *A Christian Approach to Philosophy*, p. 200.
[108]C. S. Lewis, *God in the Dock*, ed. Walter Hooper (Grand Rapids, MI: William B. Eerdmans, 1970), p. 110.
[109]*The Intellectuals Speak Out About God*, ed. Varghese, p. 110.
[110]Young, *A Christian Approach to Philosophy*, pp. 228-9.
[111]Henry, *God, Revelation and Authority*, vol. 1, p. 43.

SECTION THREE

ETHICS

Chapter 9: *Secular Humanism*
Chapter 10: *Marxism/Leninism*
Chapter 11: *Biblical Christianity*

ETHICS [Greek: *ethikos* (custom)]: custom, usage, character, conduct. The study of conduct, moral values, duties, actions, and ends.

	SECULAR HUMANISM	MARXISM/ LENINISM	BIBLICAL CHRISTIANITY
SOURCE	*HUMANIST MANIFESTO I & II*	*WRITINGS OF MARX & LENIN*	*BIBLE*
THEOLOGY	ATHEISM	ATHEISM	THEISM
PHILOSOPHY	NATURALISM	DIALECTICAL MATERIALISM	SUPERNATURALISM
ETHICS	ETHICAL RELATIVISM	PROLETARIAT MORALITY	ETHICAL ABSOLUTES
BIOLOGY	DARWINIAN EVOLUTION	DARWINIAN/ PUNCTUATED EVOLUTION	SPECIAL CREATIONISM
PSYCHOLOGY	MONISTIC SELF-ACTUALIZATION	MONISTIC PAVLOVIAN BEHAVIORISM	DUALISM
SOCIOLOGY	NON-TRADITIONAL WORLD STATE ETHICAL SOCIETY	ABOLITION OF HOME, CHURCH AND STATE	HOME CHURCH STATE
LAW	POSITIVE LAW	POSITIVE LAW	BIBLICAL/NATURAL LAW
POLITICS	WORLD GOVERNMENT (GLOBALISM)	NEW WORLD ORDER	JUSTICE FREEDOM ORDER
ECONOMICS	SOCIALISM	SOCIALISM/ COMMUNISM	STEWARDSHIP OF PROPERTY
HISTORY	HISTORICAL EVOLUTION	HISTORICAL MATERIALISM	HISTORICAL RESURRECTION

CHAPTER

9

SECULAR HUMANIST ETHICS

"The fundamental question of ethics is, who makes the rules? God or men? The theistic answer is that God makes them. The humanistic answer is that men make them. This distinction between theism and humanism is the fundamental division in moral theory."[1]

—Max Hocutt

"No inherent moral or ethical laws exist, nor are there absolute guiding principles for human society. The universe cares nothing for us and we have no ultimate meaning in life."[2]

—William Provine

SUMMARY

Humanist ethics means human ethics—ethics of man, by man, and for man. Since Humanists reject the existence of God, there are no God-ordained ethical guidelines for man to acknowledge or follow. There is no revealed or heavenly truth concerning human behavior, no manufacturer's manual. Man writes his own manual out of the context of his own experience and the scientific method. Only human beings can devise their standard of behavior. However, as with other relativistic ethics, Humanists must decide whose standard to accept. Since there is no absolute standard of right and wrong, Humanism has had to propound an ethic described as ethical relativism, situation ethics, cultural relativism, new morality, etc. While some Humanists feel that there are some principles or standards gained from scientific inquiry and historical experience that might entail an ethical ought, others find no basis for such an ought. Still others are uninhibited in asserting the ideals, values, and standards mankind should follow.

Then, too, some Humanists view their ethics as part of the biological evolutionary process. "Ethics," say Michael Ruse and Edward O. Wilson, "is an illusion fobbed off on us by our genes to get us to cooperate. . . . Ethical codes work because they drive us to go against our selfish day to day impulses in favor of long-term group survival and harmony. . . . Furthermore, the way our biology forces its ends is by making us think that there is an objective higher code, to which we are all subject."[3]

While the Christian ethic states, "Thou shalt not commit adultery," the Humanist ethic responds, "Practice the ethics of marriage with freedom," or "Thou shalt not commit adultery . . . ordinarily."

Introduction

The theology of Humanism is atheism. This theology presents a special problem for Humanists, namely, what code of ethics should Humanism embrace? Humanists reject the strict moral codes posited by religion—in fact, Paul Kurtz, author of *Humanist Manifesto II*, states, "The traditional supernaturalistic moral commandments are especially repressive of our human needs. They are immoral insofar as they foster illusions about human destiny [heaven] and suppress vital inclinations."[4] Humanists find religious ethical codes, such as the Ten Com-

Notes and Asides

mandments, too restrictive to allow the human race to achieve fulfillment of the good life. They believe that the evils resulting from the removal of strict moral codes from society will be overshadowed by the good that comes about because of their removal.

Corliss Lamont describes the Humanist attitude toward the eradication of ethical codes this way:

> Humanist ethics is opposed to the puritanical prejudice against pleasure and desire that marks the Western tradition of morality. Men and women have profound wants and needs of an emotional and physical character, the fulfillment of which is an essential ingredient in the good life. Contempt for or suppression of normal desires may result in their discharge in surreptitious, coarse, or abnormal ways. While it is true that uncontrolled human desires are a prime cause of evil in the world, it is equally true that human desires directed by reason toward socially useful goals are a prime foundation of the good.[5]

Humanists are working toward a science of ethics that is specifically in keeping with their system of beliefs in atheism, naturalism, and evolution. Kurtz, in *The Humanist Alternative*, calls for Secular Humanism to be "interpreted as a moral point of view."[6] Indeed, in the preface to the *Humanist Manifestoes I & II*, Kurtz defines Humanism "as a philosophical, religious, and moral point of view."[7] He points out that, in keeping with this perspective, certain assumptions are to be made about what man's eventual moral goals are:

> If man is a product of evolution, one species among others, in a universe without purpose, then man's option is to live for himself and to discover new areas of significance and achievement.[8]

Kurtz is quick to add, however, that Humanists are not calling for the abandonment of all ethical principles. "Humanists do not wish to undermine the role of the family, as critics contend. They do advocate basic moral virtues—fairness, kindness, beneficence, justice, and tolerance."[9]

While Kurtz's assurances seem straight-forward enough, it is difficult to reconcile them with the general view of Humanists toward personal sexual ethics. Kurtz himself writes in *Humanist Manifesto II*, "Short of harming others or compelling them to do likewise, individuals should be permitted to express their sexual proclivities and pursue their life-styles as they desire."[10] This permissiveness calls for being open to the acceptability of pre-marital intercourse, extra-marital

Notes and Asides

affairs, homosexuality, and bisexuality, according to *A New Bill of Sexual Rights and Responsibilities*, by Lester Kirkendall, signed by Kurtz. This *New Bill* states, "Although we consider marriage, where viable, a cherished human relationship, we believe that other sexual relationships also are significant."[11] This new concept of sexual freedom necessitates a certain attitude about morals: "In order to realize our potential for joyful sexual expression, we need to adopt the doctrine that actualizing pleasures are among the highest moral goods. . . ."[12] We will return to this aspect of Humanist ethics after we consider the more theoretical basis of Humanism's ethical view.

"There is no significant example in history, before our time, of a society successfully maintaining moral life without the aid of religion."
—Will Durant

This basis seeks to answer the question, Can morality be achieved without the foundation of religious beliefs? Will Durant writes in *The Humanist*, "There is no significant example in history, before our time, of a society successfully maintaining moral life without the aid of religion."[13] Later in his career, Durant reiterated this belief, saying that it would be difficult for Humanists "to mold a natural ethic strong enough to maintain moral restraint and social order without the support of supernatural consolations, hopes, and fears."[14]

The need for a consistent Humanist stand on ethics to supplant supernaturalistic morality gave rise to a book edited by Morris B. Storer, titled simply *Humanist Ethics*. Storer summed up the multitude of Humanist views regarding ethics in his preface:

> Humanists are largely united in emphasizing human fulfillment, a measured freedom, the dignity of the individual, a factor of situational relativity, and a broad spectrum of human rights as cornerstones of humanist ethics. But it is clear that, beyond these essentials, we differ widely. Is personal advantage the measure of right and wrong, or the advantage of all affected: Humanists differ. Is there truth in ethics? We differ. Are "right" and "wrong" expressions of heart or head? Do people have free wills? Do you measure morality by results or by principles? Do people have duties as well as rights? We have our differences on all these and more.[15]

Kurtz agrees with Storer that a Humanist consensus would be ideal, but he doubts that this could ever occur. "There are always new problems to face, hence there is continued need to revise principles and values in light of altered social conditions. . . . Perhaps I am overly pessimistic. But I believe that there is little guarantee of getting a consensus of thought or action, other than in the broadest terms. . . . Humanism thus does not represent a fixed program or platform, but rather is a general outlook, a method of inquiry, an ethic of freedom, and it is committed to a limited number of basic values and principles."[16]

Notes and Asides

The Foundation of Humanist Ethics

This conflict of ethical concepts among Humanists results largely from their disagreement over the foundation of morality. Kurtz is quick to state that he believes in "a limited number of basic values and principles,"[17] but he does not point to a specific foundation for these principles, saying only that they are "naturalistic and empirical phenomena."[18]

Mihailo Markovic, another Humanist writing in Storer's collection of essays, takes exception to Kurtz's assumption about the origin of these principles, pointing out Kurtz's theoretical inconsistencies:

> It is not clear what is the theoretical status of those principles. At first they are construed as flexible, violable, approximate guides for conduct, as conditional obligations, the fulfillment of which is contingent upon an examination of the given situation. Furthermore, they are regarded as mere "empirical phenomena." . . . From here Professor Kurtz makes a jump and asserts that these are not merely duties but principles, "because we can generalize various kinds of action and recognize that these are general prescriptions, rules, and policies that we ought to observe." It remains quite unclear where this "ought" comes from. It is one thing to describe a variety of actual historical patterns of conduct and moral habits. It is a completely different thing to make a choice among them and to say that we "ought" to observe some of them. Why some and not others?[19]

Markovic has cut to the heart of the problem Humanists face when discussing ethics. If man is going to decide what he "ought" to do, then he must refer to a moral code, or foundation, which dictates this "ought." Kurtz, when challenged by Markovic, admitted, "I can find no ultimate basis for 'ought.'"[20] If there is no ultimate basis for "ought," then there is no basis for determining right or wrong, which means the Hitlers, Stalins, and Maos of the world are innocent of any wrongdoing.

"Of all the systems of morality, ancient or modern, which have come under my observation, none appear to me so pure as that of Jesus."
—Thomas Jefferson

This difference over foundation causes Humanists to be divided regarding the "absolute" nature of ethics. Hocutt says that he suspects "the 'humanist consensus' will reduce in the end to agreement that God does not exist." The problem, Hocutt continues, is that "The nonexistence of God makes more difference to some of us than to others. To me, it means that there is no absolute morality, that moralities are sets of social conventions devised by humans to satisfy their need. To [Alastair] Hannay, it means that we must postulate an alternative basis for moral absolutism."[21]

This debate over the foundation of ethics is fundamental to the

Notes and Asides

whole concept of Humanist ethics. Without a God who sets down an absolute moral code, Humanists must believe either that the code is subjective and should be applied differently to each changing situation, or that an absolute code exists, somehow outside of man, but within the whole evolutionary scheme of things.

Hocutt maintains that an absolute moral code cannot exist without God, and there is no God. "Furthermore, if there were a morality written up in the sky somewhere but no God to enforce it, I see no good reason why anybody should pay it any heed, no reason why we should obey it. Human beings may, and do, make up their own rules. All existing moralities and all existing laws are human artifacts, products of human society, social conventions. Morality is not discovered; it is made."[22]

This view is more consistent with the Humanist view that life evolved by chance—otherwise, the Humanist has a difficult time explaining where an absolute code outside of man originated. If man is the highest being in nature and did not develop the absolute moral code himself, then what creature in nature did? Frederick Edwords writes in *The Humanist*, "So we can see that without living beings with needs there can be no good or evil. And without the presence of more than one such living being, there can be no rules of conduct. Morality, then, emerges from humanity precisely because it exists to serve humanity."[23] This view is consistent with the idea that all ethics must be determined by man.

Joseph Fletcher, author of *Situational Ethics*, writes: "We have to validate happiness and moral concern humanly, not theistically. There are good gods and bad gods and we have to choose among them according to whether they pass our moral tests. We approve or disapprove of any particular divine command by a prereligious criterion."[24] Ultimately, decisions about morality rest with mankind in general and the individual specifically. Fletcher sums up the nature of ethics by saying, ". . . right and wrong are humanly perceived, not religiously revealed. In a word, ethics is humanist."[25]

Some Humanists have gone so far, however, as to cast doubt on the idea that man can even perceive what is right or wrong. Kai Nielsen, who signed the *Humanist Manifesto II*, proposed a "no-truth thesis" that states that no question of the truth or falsity of moral values can sensibly arise. This raises a serious problem for Humanists, because "there is still the haunting suspicion that if we press real moral disputes sufficiently, we will quite naturally get to a moral terrain where conflicting fundamental moral principles will be brought into play. Our 'moral truths' will be dependent on them and they will conflict and we will have no idea of how their truth or falsity is to be established. Even when we agree on the facts we will find such disputes intractable, since, for such deeply embedded moral beliefs, the no-truth thesis applies."[26]

Notes and Asides

Nielsen's statement would appear to be the proper conclusion for Humanists, since most are unwilling to grant the existence of an absolute moral code. Without this code, what standard does mankind have for judging its actions right or wrong, or its moral beliefs true or false? Humanists, however, recognize the dilemma of being unable to determine the difference between right and wrong and have attempted to explain away the "no-truth thesis" in a number of ways.

Hocutt claims that "even though there is no such thing as an absolute, divinely instituted morality, there is nevertheless a distinction between truth and falsity in ethics. Saying 'Honesty is a good policy' is saying something either true or false. Like other judgments, moral judgments have truth values. Furthermore, since moral judgments can be false as well as true, we can make mistakes. We can think to be good, practices that are in fact bad."[27] Hocutt does not explain how we will know when we have made mistakes, since there is no code to which to refer.

Fletcher, too, understands the threat that Nielsen's ideas pose toward Humanist ethics—he claims that Nielsen is saying right and

CLOSE-UP

Corliss Lamont (1902-)

Corliss Lamont graduated from Harvard in 1924 and earned his PhD in philosophy at Columbia in 1932. After completion of his doctorate, he taught at Columbia for fifteen years. During that time, and throughout the rest of his life, he worked as a tireless spokesman for Humanism. His book *The Philosophy of Humanism* is the definitive outline of Secular Humanist thought. He has also long been fascinated with Marxism, having visited the USSR in 1932 and 1938 and having returned with the impression that the Soviets were "making great economic and social progress." Much of his work implies belief that a synthesis between Marxism and Humanism would be desirable if only Marxism embraced the concept of democracy. Lamont has also attempted to reconcile Humanism with the concept of free will, going so far as to write *Freedom of Choice Affirmed* in an effort to refute the deterministic viewpoint of fellow Humanists like B.F. Skinner.

Notes and Asides

wrong exist outside of man, and that ethics may be discovered, but not determined by man. This belief, Fletcher says, "fits the religious ethic, based as it is on the objective, transcendental 'will of God' or 'divine imperative,' but it does not fit a humanistic ethic in which human beings must, as moral agents, themselves choose and freely posit or assert the ideals and values and standards of mankind."[28]

It would seem, however, that Humanism requires more than man "choosing" and "asserting." Konstantin Kolenda, another noted Humanist, says, "The assurance [that mankind will conform to a set of ethics] . . . cannot rest just on scientific or psychological facts; it must also involve an assumption of a commitment to a moral principle. The humanist cause rests on this assumption."[29] Empirical exploration of values is not enough for Kolenda—there must exist some real principles that all mankind recognizes as binding. Without these, conformity can never be assured.

Still, the majority of Humanists claim that ethics needs no foundation outside of man and that man himself must constantly rework his ethical ideas. The *Humanist Manifesto II* states, "We affirm that moral values derive their source from human experience. Ethics is autonomous and situational, needing no theological or ideological sanction."[30] Kurtz wrote those words in 1973, and despite the controversy over "situation ethics" (both within and outside Secular Humanism), he reaffirmed their truth in 1980, stating, "Humanists . . . are committed to free thought and to the view that ethical values are relative to human experience and needs. This means that ethics need not be derived from any theological or metaphysical propositions about the nature of ultimate reality, that it can be autonomous, and that ethical judgments to some extent may be grounded in reflective inquiry."[31] Today, the phrase *situation ethics* has been largely replaced by *ethical relativism*—but both phrases approximate the ideas of Kurtz and the majority of Humanists. For them, ethical decisions must be made in the context of each new situation so that man does not rely on dogma to dictate his moral decisions. "Relativism" refers to the idea that certain moral actions can be more or less right relative to the specific situation in which they are used.

Ethical relativism is the belief that no absolute moral code exists, and therefore man must adjust his ethical standards in each situation according to his own judgment.

Most Humanists believe reason is the key element for determining right or wrong in the context of ethical relativism. A general statement of policy issued by the British Humanist Association states, "Humanists believe that man's conduct should be based on humanity, insight, and reason. He must face his problems with his own moral and intellectual resources, without looking for supernatural aid. . . . We make no claims to special knowledge or final answers, since we regard the search for understanding as a continuing process."[32]

Humanists stress the importance of experience in making ethical

Notes and Asides

decisions also. Kurtz says, "Ethical judgments should have autonomous grounding in moral experience, and we would expect people to be truthful, honest, sincere, generous, whether or not they believe in God."[33]

Many other Humanists echo this call for the use of reason and experience as a guide for moral conduct. Lamont says that as long as man "pursues activities that are healthy, socially useful, and in accordance with reason, pleasure will generally accompany them; and happiness, the supreme good, will be the eventual result."[34]

However, there are those Humanists who claim that irrationality, rather than reason, is the real guide for an individual's moral conduct. Lucia K. B. Hall writes,

> Traditional religious belief has assumed that a deity was both the source and enforcer of the only possible right ethical system. As secular humanists, however, we need to discover a naturalistic explanation for the ethical impulse. Since the source of this impulse cannot be found in reason, we need to look to an irrational, emotional response that has evolved as part of the human species.[35]

This view is consistent with the Humanist beliefs that man evolved and that somehow morality must exist within mankind, but it is contrary to the stand taken by Lamont and the British Humanist Association regarding reason. Hall accepts it as intuitively obvious that the ethical impulse could not exist within reason, so she seeks it in irrationality. Hall claims that humans have evolved what she calls the "empathic response," which means that we naturally feel empathetic toward someone who is in pain or who is treated unjustly. This response, Hall claims, will automatically cause man to act morally toward his fellow man, once we allow our irrationality to be our guide for moral standards.

Many other Humanists share Hall's views on the evolution of ethics, if not her ideas on the irrational controlling the moral. In fact, the evolution of ethics could be referred to accurately as the view most consistent with Humanism, since it best explains whence ethics comes, assuming that morals do not arise from God or exist independently of nature. V. M. Tarkunde, who signed the *Humanist Manifesto II*, firmly believes in the evolution of ethics—in fact, he believes an "absolute" code of ethics evolved. He states, "Moral values, since they have been derived from the biologically inherited altruistic impulses, contribute to cooperative social existence. They are therefore as absolute and permanent as human society itself."[36]

Tarkunde goes on to clarify his stand on evolution, hinting that he

Notes and Asides

believes morality is actually a positive trait encouraged by natural selection:

> Struggle for existence is the basic characteristic of the entire biological world. In the course of that struggle, different biological species have developed marvelous adaptations which serve the primary purpose of survival. It is not surprising that in the animal world such adaptations are mental as well as physical. In the long history of biological evolution, the ancestors of homo sapiens and homo sapiens himself must have developed appropriate adaptive mental attributes. Man's will as well as man's reason are thus the products of biological evolution.[37]

Some Humanists, however, object to the view that ethics evolved along with man. Alastair Hannay responds to Tarkunde,

> The evolutionary perspective forces the facts of human society into too narrow a mold. Once it is allowed that rudimentary moral behavior exists in higher (nonhuman) animals, and can even be traced to "lower forms of life," it is difficult to admit that evolved morality contains anything essentially new. I think it obviously does, not least in virtue of what is specific to human powers of cognition and reason, and compassion.[38]

That is, Hannay cannot accept the notion that lower animals had the initial moral impulses; therefore he must discard the idea of moral evolution.

Hocutt is even more abrupt with Tarkunde's ideas regarding evolution. He writes,

> I agree . . . that human biology is relevant to morality, but I have not yet seen convincing proof that either egoism or altruism is "instinctive," and seeing purposes in biological evolution sounds suspiciously like claiming that God does have something to do with morality after all.[39]

The slightest hint of teleology, of course, is intolerable to all Humanists, so Hocutt protests Tarkunde's whole theory.

The more serious problem created by Humanism's desire to wed ethics to biology, however, is that this view allows Darwin's concept of the struggle for existence to become the absolute on which moral decisions are based. Such a morality allows men like Friedrich Nietzsche to declare, "A good war sanctifies every cause,"[40] and Friedrich von Bernhardi, in his work *Germany and the Next War*, to insist, "War is a

Notes and Asides

biological necessity; it is as necessary as the struggle of the elements of Nature; it gives a biologically just decision, since its decisions rest on the very nature of things."[41] Most Humanists would rather not open this can of worms, but it lurks in the background under the guise of social or ethical Darwinianism.

Ethical Relativism

By rejecting any kind of purpose behind the existence of a code of ethics, one necessarily finds himself rejecting any code that may exist outside of man. This done, all ethics are relative to man's interpretation of them in any given situation. As a result, Humanists must fall back on ethical relativism, which consists of little more than experimenting with ethics in every new scenario. Mason Olds describes it: "Of course, humanism has no single ethical theory, therefore ethical theory and moral subject must be chosen, examined, and even debated."[42] Olds does not tell us on what theory we should rely while Humanists reach a consensus.

We are warned, however, that perhaps we are expecting too much from ethics. Howard B. Radest states, "Once we humanize, as it were, moral activity, we cease to have perfectionist expectations of ethics. We come to understand that moral judgments like other human judgments are going to be partial, temporary, changeable, etc."[43] Since there is no absolute standard of ethics to which to refer, we must not expect Humanist ethics to meet such a standard.

> "One may go wrong in many different ways, but right only in one, which is why it is easy to fail and difficult to succeed—easy to miss the target and difficult to hit it."
>
> —Aristotle

It is important to note that these ideas about Humanist ethics are not just the radical ideas of a few Humanists on the fringe. Rather, *ethical relativism is the generally accepted morality for Humanists.* "The morality or immorality of any behavior," says Dr. Arthur E. Gravatt, "including sexual behavior, has been put in the context of 'situation ethics.' In this approach moral behavior may differ from situation to situation. Behavior might be moral for one person and not another or moral at one time and not another. Whether an act is moral or immoral is determined by 'the law of love'; that is the extent of which love and concern for others is a factor in the relationship."[44]

Joseph Fletcher says that "rights and wrongs are determined by objective facts or circumstances, that is, by the situations in which moral agents have to decide for the most beneficial course open to choice."[45] Herbert W. Schneider calls morality "an experimental art," saying it is the "basic art of living well together. Moral right and wrong must therefore be conceived in terms of moral standards generated in a particular society."[46] Kurtz says "moral principles should be treated as hypotheses," tested by their practical worth and judged by what they

Notes and Asides

cause to happen.[47]

Such thinking leads us into another area where Humanists cannot reach a consensus. Humanists disagree as to what the best consequences of a moral action could be—they are uncertain as to the aim of morality. Should utilitarianism (the greatest good for the greatest number) be considered the measure for the ethical value of an action? Or should we focus on fulfilling our desires? Or should the goal be something more futuristic, such as a global village? And whatever the end-based standard is, *why* should we pursue *that* end rather than some other? With no transcendent standard to appeal to, there seems to be no way to answer that question other than a faint-hearted, "Do your own thing," which amounts to no ethic at all.

The Aim of Morality

The problem with determining the aim of morality is summed up by Kolenda: "What we do not know is how to harmonize legitimate preferences, interests, and styles of life when they interfere with one another."[48] If one man can be made happy or be fulfilled by causing my unhappiness (say, by stealing my car), then how do we judge the morality of his action? Was he not just fulfilling his desires?

The *Humanist Manifesto II* answers the problem of the aim of morality this way:

> Ethics stems from human need and interest. To deny this distorts the whole basis of life. Human life has meaning because we create and develop our futures. Happiness and the creative realization of human needs and desires, individually and in shared enjoyment, are continuous themes of humanism. We strive for the good life, here and now. The goal is to pursue life's enrichment despite debasing forces of vulgarization, commercialization, bureaucratization, and dehumanization.[49]

Utilitarianism is an ethical doctrine that treats the greatest happiness of the greatest number of people as the ultimate aim of morality.

This particular aim of morality should not be confused with utilitarianism, which has been rejected by some Humanists for its unmeasurable nature. Kurtz says, "The greatest happiness principle [utilitarianism], though relevant in some contexts, is too general to be of much help."[50]

Hocutt simplifies the *Manifesto's* propositions about the aims of morality, stating, "If there is no earthly morality laid up in heaven, by what yardstick will we measure earthly moralities? The answer, of course, is that we should use the same yardstick we use to evaluate any other human artifact: satisfaction of our needs."[51] By using the term "yardstick," Hocutt seems to imply that Humanists can have a standard

Notes and Asides

by which to measure ethics. Later in his essay, however, he admits that this is not the case.

> How should that problem [of justice] be solved? I know no answer which could satisfy everybody. Having different, perhaps even incompatible, interests, we all wish to see the problem solved in the way that is best calculated to maximize the achievement of our own ends. Therefore, if I told you how the problem ought to be solved, if I laid down my ideas of "justice," I would be doing no more than trying to get you to accept a set of principles that would maximize my interests. Instead of putting out that kind of dishonest propaganda, I prefer to engage in open and forthright negotiations: let me have things partly my way, and I won't stand in the way of your having them partly your way. The alternative is to fight, and I'm a coward.[52]

Hocutt does not expand on what might occur if he were negotiating with someone who wasn't a coward.

Of course, not all Humanists like Hocutt's simplification. Tarkunde still insists that there is an absolute standard for ethics, saying, "I cannot fully share Prof. Hocutt's statement that the yardstick for evaluating ethical rules is the 'satisfaction of our needs.' . . . This approach has led Prof. Hocutt to conclude that there is no absolute right or wrong. . . ."[53]

Kirkendall attempted to clarify the aim of morality by expounding on its goals, actually creating a set of guidelines. He writes, "In considering these [ethical] issues I arrived at some assumptions, which in turn raised baffling, perhaps insoluble questions. . . . I assumed there should be an ethical/moral system and that it: 1. Should serve to insure the survival of humankind. . . . 2. Must rest upon a logical, rational, openly-acknowledged framework. Ethical decision making must have an authoritative basis. Otherwise it is likely to be capricious and inconsistent, often contradictory. . . . 3. Should be applicable universally. . . . 4. Should rest upon the basic need for enhancing altruistic experience, both in giving and receiving."[54]

Some Humanists would say that point 3 of Kirkendall's guidelines is the most crucial—that the universality of a moral code must be achieved. The *Humanist Manifesto II* calls for each person becoming a "citizen of a world community."[55] And Kurtz, in what he called *The Declaration of Interdependence* (which was signed by Isaac Asimov and Fletcher, among others), wrote, "We need to draw on the best moral wisdom of the past, but we also need to develop a new, revisionary ethics that employs rational methods of inquiry appropriate to the world of the future, an ethics that respects the dignity and freedom of each person but that also expresses a larger concern for humanity as a

Notes and Asides

whole."[56] This idea of universality is quite consistent with the Humanist worldview, which holds firm the belief that every individual has intrinsic value. In fact, Humanists not holding this view are dangerously close to denying one of their key precepts.

Still, the problems with this concept of universally pleasing everyone using some relative ethical ideals is obvious to most Humanists. Kurt Baier responds to essays by Kolenda and Schneider regarding the universality of morals, "Both papers draw from this the conclusion, which also seems plausible to me, that the humanist ideal of a morality for mankind as a whole is for the time being no more than an aspiration if not an illusion. Yet both authors appear to regard this aspiration as somehow attainable if it is worked for in certain ways. There remain, however, large questions in my mind about how this worldwide morality is to be achieved."[57]

It is obvious even Humanists will admit that there are problems with their ideas about the aim of morality. They also reluctantly acknowledge the weaknesses of ethical relativism.

Problems with Ethical Relativism

The first problem Humanists recognize is the effect ethical relativism might have on average men and women. Humanists generally call for avoiding all dogma, since they believe it unnecessarily restricts man in his pursuit of happiness. But how will the common man react to a society without rules and corresponding penalties? Kurtz writes,

> Nevertheless, the humanist is faced with a crucial ethical problem: Insofar as he has defended an ethic of freedom, can he develop a basis for moral responsibility? Regretfully, merely to liberate individuals from authoritarian social institutions, whether church or state, is no guarantee that they will be aware of their moral responsibility to others. The contrary is often the case. Any number of social institutions regulate conduct by some means of norms and rules, and sanctions are imposed for enforcing them. Moral conduct is often insured because of fear of the consequences of breaking the law or of transgressing moral conventions. Once these sanctions are ignored, we may end up with [a man] concerned with his own personal lust for pleasure, ambition, and power, and impervious to moral constraints.[58]

While Humanists refuse to give credence to the religious doctrine of original sin (because it is part of the religious myth), they recognize

Notes and Asides

the folly of untempered optimism with regard to mankind. Most Humanists would admit that there is no guarantee man will behave responsibly if all laws and dogma are removed. Kurtz says,

> Some utopian anarchists maintain that human nature is basically beneficent; it is restrictive societal laws that corrupt human beings, and not the contrary. Their solution is to emancipate individuals from them; this they believe will untap a natural propensity for altruism. Regretfully, there is no guarantee that this will occur. . . . Thus we have no guarantee that individual moral beneficence will reign once all institutional sanctions are removed. Moreover, even if the world were only full of people with good intentions, they might still differ in their interpretation or application of their moral convictions, and this can be a further source of conflict.[59]

Kurtz does not consider, in this context, the problem of how to define such terms in his own statement as *beneficence*, *altruism*, and *good* without reference to some transcendent standard, a reference inconsistent with Secular Humanism's philosophical and theological foundations.

In the end, however, the biggest problem with ethical relativism is still that basically anything can be construed as "good" or "bad" under the assumption that it is all relative to the situation in which a man finds himself. Even if individuals are striving to do the right thing, they may honestly disagree about what is the right thing, since there is no absolute standard. Baier writes,

> Plainly, it is not easy to determine in an objective way what conduct is morally ideal. Hence even among people of good will, that is, among people perfectly willing to do what is morally ideal, there may be sincere disagreement. But if people are to have the assurance that others will by and large do what is morally ideal, it is desirable that such conduct should be publicly recognized and taught to the next generation. For that will apprise people of good will what exactly will be generally regarded as morally ideal. The problem, of course, is that if there is likely to be disagreement on this score even among people of good will, it is also likely that some will disagree with at least some of what is regarded as morally ideal, and indeed sometimes rightly so.[60]

Like Kurtz, Baier avoids the problem of defining the *good* in *good will*, but he inadvertently raises another problem: Why should it even be

Notes and Asides

considered a mark of "good will," whatever that is, to be "willing to do what is morally ideal"? Why shouldn't "good will" be marked instead by the determination to do only what is morally anti-ideal? Is any answer to this question possible that will be consistent with Humanism's philosophical and theological foundations?

Hocutt understands the problems with ethical relativism so well that he attempts to deny relativism's relevance to humanist ethics. "[D]enying that there is an absolute right and wrong laid up in heaven does not require us to subscribe to the confused doctrine usually mislabeled 'ethical relativism'; it does not require us to believe that right and wrong are mere 'matters of opinion.' On the contrary, the latter doctrine . . . is as objectionable as theological absolutism. Thinking something true doesn't make it true, either in ethics or in anything else. Thinking the earth to be flat doesn't make the earth flat, and thinking a practice right doesn't make it right."[61] Hocutt, however, does not bother to explain how thinking the "satisfaction of our needs" is moral, as he states earlier in this chapter, makes it moral.

Hocutt goes on to create a new problem for Humanist ethics. He writes, "Does the end justify the means? Of course. If not what does? In order to adopt a means, what more reasons does one need than knowledge that it will help one to achieve one's ends?"[62] This is his way of avoiding the pitfalls of relativism—as long as something ultimately brings about some good (which may be any one of Humanism's stated aims of morality), then the act itself is good, regardless both of its other consequences and of its inherent moral constitution (if there is such a thing).

> "Does the end justify the means? Of course."
>
> —Max Hocutt

The problems with this idea are evident to most Humanists. Tarkunde responds, "If the question 'Does the end justify the means?' is properly formulated, it is in my view not capable of being answered in an emphatic affirmative as Prof. Hocutt has done. The question really is, Is it right to try to achieve a morally good end by recourse to morally bad means? The answer as a general rule must be in the negative, because the quality of the means normally affects the quality of the end. In other words, it is usually not possible to attain a good end except by good means."[63]

Lamont says it more succinctly: "No responsible person really believes that any object justifies any price any more than he believes that any end justifies any means."[64]

But immediately after Lamont attempts to clarify the Humanist position on ethics, he adds one final twist to ethical relativism which creates another problem:

> The irrational impulses of human beings have played an enormous role in bringing recurrent disasters upon mankind and remain a

Notes and Asides

> sinister danger in contemporary affairs. For the Humanist, stupidity is just as great a sin as selfishness; and "the moral obligation to be intelligent" ranks always among the highest of duties.[65]

Lamont seems to imply that only intelligent people are really capable of making the correct moral choices, which logically leads to the assumption that Lamont expects intelligent people to be the moral guides for the rest of society. Isn't this giving the power to a select few to create a dogma that others must follow? And isn't this precisely what Humanists have been trying to avoid all along by ignoring religious codes of ethics?

Moral Education and the Justice System

Still, most Humanists contend that these problems with their foundation for ethics, their aim of morality, and their ethical relativism can be overcome through education. This is a crucial aspect of Humanism's agenda—morality must somehow be passed on to each succeeding generation through education. Kurtz says this type of education happens whether we like it or not: "Nonetheless, I believe that the schools need to engage in moral 'instruction'—a better term than 'indoctrination'—of some kind; they do it anyway. In one sense virtually all education is moral. In so far as education strives to expand the horizons of the person, even his intellectual understanding, there is some modification, however subtle, and reconstruction of values going on."[66]

Kurtz thinks that a Humanistic ethical education would solve the problems of moral freedom:

> As I have said, moral freedom is a central humanist value: the freeing of individuals from excessive restraints so that they may actualize their potentialities and maximize free choice. However, such a normative value is hardly sufficient unless a moral growth takes place. It is not enough to release individuals from authoritarian institutions, for some individuals may degenerate into hedonistic fleshpots or amoral egoists; thus we need also to nourish the conditions for moral development, in which an appreciation for the needs of others can emerge; and this is dependent upon moral education.[67]

What if moral education doesn't work? Kurtz says the justice system must do everything in its power to encourage moral activity, but

Notes and Asides

he admits that Humanists don't have enough data right now to know what to do with hardened criminals.

> Some sociobiologists believe that moral turpitude may be in part genetic and that some individuals, particularly hardened criminals, are incorrigible. How, for example should the penal system deal with repeated offenders? By coddling or punishing them? Should the legal system be rehabilitative or retributive in its approach? The humanist does not wish to give up in his constant effort to reform the institutions of society so that the best that human beings are capable of will emerge. Konrad Lorenz and others, however, maintain that aggression is innate in the human species. Human vices, such as selfishness, laziness, vindictiveness, hatred, sloth, pride, jealousy are so widespread in human behavior that we are all capable of their temptations at times. Perhaps humanists have been overly optimistic about the full reaches of human nature. Perhaps "original sin"—in natural and biological terms—is present in some individuals, who are immune to our efforts at amelioration. What we need is a deeper empirical understanding of human nature, without reading in what our values demand.[68]

Again, for the Humanist there are no concrete answers about the right thing to do.

From Theory to Practice

We have outlined the theoretical base of humanist ethics—now we will examine how their relativistic ethics translates into practice, specifically in human sexuality.

Earlier we acknowledged Kurtz's contention that supernatural ethics are immoral since they: (a) foster illusions about human destiny (i.e., heaven), and (b) "suppress vital inclinations." What are these vital inclinations?

Some are described by Kirkendall in *A New Bill of Sexual Rights and Responsibilities*. They include homosexuality, bisexuality, pre- and extra-marital sexual relations, and something called "genital association."

The *Humanist Manifesto II* supports Kirkendall's conclusions, stating, "We believe that intolerant attitudes, often cultivated by orthodox religions and puritanical cultures, unduly repress sexual conduct. . . . The many varieties of sexual exploration should not in themselves be considered 'evil.' . . . individuals should be permitted to

Notes and Asides

"Humanists have had an important role in the sexual revolution."

—Lester Kirkendall, *A New Bill of Sexual Rights and Responsibilities*, p. 1.

express their sexual proclivities and pursue their life-styles as they desire."[69]

Legitimate alternative lifestyles include homosexuality, for the Humanist, because it has been "scientifically" proven that some men are born homosexual. Alfred Kinsey concluded that homosexuality was a biologically determined lifestyle from birth. The next two lifestyles that Humanists are studying to see if they are biologically determined are pedophilia (man/boy sex) and incest.[70] Humanist Vern Bullough, historian of the homosexual movement, is involved in the move to declare pedophilia "biologically determined."

Humanists act in accordance with their desire to further the sexual revolution by becoming involved in agencies like Planned Parenthood. Three Humanists of the Year—Margaret Sanger, Mary Calderone, and Faye Wattleton—have served in key positions in that organization. Wattleton, a president of Planned Parenthood, argues that the organization's focus is not to stop teenage sexual activity through education, but to stop "teenage pregnancy."[71] She champions easier access to condoms for teens and more school-based health clinics "that provide contraceptives as part of general health care."[72] The goal of Planned Parenthood, according to one staffer, is to help "young people obtain sex satisfaction before marriage. By sanctioning sex before marriage, we will prevent fear and guilt."[73] The Planned Parenthood publication *You've Changed the Combination* states, "There are only two kinds of sex: sex with victims and sex without. Sex with victims is always wrong [an absolute?]. Sex without is always right."[74]

When Wattleton accepted her Humanist of the Year award, she paid special tribute to the founder of Planned Parenthood, Margaret Sanger. To a great extent Sanger epitomizes the Humanist sexual ethic. Few things in her teaching or lifestyle fall outside of Humanist ethics in theory and practice. For example, she founded the publication *The*

Notes and Asides

Woman Rebel, whose slogan was "No Gods! No Masters!" Her first edition denounced marriage as a "degenerate institution" and sexual modesty as "obscene prudery."[75] Sanger's hero was Havelock Ellis. Upon reading his massive seven-volume *Studies in the Psychology of Sex*, she told her husband that she needed to be liberated from the strict bonds of their marriage vows. She ultimately deserted her husband to practice free love in Greenwich Village.

Mary Calderone, a founder of the organization Sex Information and Educational Council of the United States (SIECUS) and former Planned Parenthood medical director, said, "Mere facts and discussion are not enough. They [teens] need to be undergirded by a set of values."[76] Whose values? The answer becomes obvious when we examine SIECUS literature.

SIECUS Study Guide 5 deals with pre-marital sexual standards. It was written by Ira L. Reiss, one of the thirty-seven "leading authors and sexologists" who endorsed Kirkendall's *A New Bill*. According to Reiss, "The choice of a premarital sexual standard is a personal moral choice, and no amount of facts or trends can 'prove' scientifically that one ought to choose a particular standard."[77]

SIECUS Study Guide 9, written by Harold T. Christensen, proclaims, "The strict Judeo-Christian codes inherited from the past, in which chastity is prescribed, are being challenged. Rational enquiry is replacing blind faith. A so-called 'new morality' is being ushered in." Christian morality is, by implication, outdated; it is further described as "A morality of commandment, based upon the assumption that transcendental powers and eternal truths exist." Christensen sees the "relativistic position on sexual morality" as the rational one, backed up by research; it is this approach that seems to offer the most hope for consensus under modern conditions. This position does not see right or wrong "as eternal entities," but rather attempts to understand morality in the context of the scientific method.[78]

Before we conclude this chapter, it is important that we note how Lamont combines theory and practice. In *The Philosophy of Humanism*, Lamont argues that the chief end of Humanistic ethics is "happiness for all humanity in this existence," as contrasted with salvation for the soul in a future existence. Lamont sees Humanism adhering "to the highest ethical ideals." This requires him to oppose the "puritanical prejudice against pleasure and desire that marks the Western tradition of morality."[79] According to Lamont, "Men and women have profound wants and needs of an emotional and physical character, the fulfillment of which is an essential ingredient in the good life."[80]

In making ethical decisions, says Lamont, the Humanist relies upon the use of reason and the scientific method "instead of upon religious revelation or any sort of authority or intuition."[81] Applying the scien-

Notes and Asides

tific method to premarital sexuality, Lamont concludes that an experimental period of living together "for at least six months," with strict birth control in effect, would be desirable for all who are formally engaged or seriously contemplating matrimony.[82]

Applying this attitude to extramarital relations, Lamont agrees with Calderone's statement in *Playboy*: "An extra-marital affair that's really solid might have some good results."[83] Says Lamont,

> Yet since it is clear that one can be sincerely in love with at least two persons at the same time, a husband or wife should feel free to go the whole way with another person whom he or she truly loves. Many married couples find a certain monotony in monogamy; what they may need, as a sort of safety value, is some diversity in love-making. To limit the supreme sexual experience to just one member of the opposite sex for an entire lifetime represents an unreasonable restraint and a killjoy ethics.[84]

"An extra-marital affair that's really solid might have some good results."
—Mary Calderone

Lamont refers to this type of sexual activity as "The ethics of Marriage with Freedom."[85]

The "science" that makes Lamont's scientific ethics possible is that of birth control and abortion. Says Lamont, "Historically, a primary reason for the enormous importance given to genital faithfulness and unfaithfulness was the lack of reliable birth-control techniques. Now that those techniques, including abortion, are generally available, this importance has more and more diminished."[86] The scientific approach has placed the matter of faithfulness/unfaithfulness into a new dimension.

Conclusion

With all the squabbling among Humanists, it is difficult to pin down their ethical ideals enough to present them as a body of facts. It is safe to say that most Humanists are ethical relativists, and in fact must be if they are to be consistent with their philosophy and theology. It is difficult, however, to standardize what ethical relativism entails. It may be easier to say what it is not. Most Humanists ultimately resort to this type of definition. Nielsen says it best:

> It is not the case that morality is simply a matter of the heart, though it is that too, and it is not a matter of "you pays your money and you takes your choice" in which decision and simple desire is king. What is good is determined by what answers to human interests, what satisfies human needs, and what furthers

Notes and Asides

> human self-realization. But morality is not simply what is a person's interest, the interest of a ruling class, what is desired by an agent or approved of in his tribe. [Immanuel] Kant and [Henry] Sidgwick were far too rationalistic in thinking that morality is a "dictate of reason" but all the same it is none of the above-mentioned things and it is not an irrational response in an absurd world not of our own making.[87]

Still, overwhelmingly, Humanists insist that the loosely defined Humanist ethic is the proper means of achieving a better world. The picture of this better world is generally unclear, although it does involve the freedom of every man to choose his own ideals. John Herman Randall, Jr., probably paints the more realistic picture:

> It is man's power to use the vision of Good to achieve a moral perspective that will enable him to deal with and rise above the facts of evil and sin. It is clear that there will always be some limits to what human nature can become. At the same time, it is likewise clear that no specific limit can be found in human nature that is immutable and cannot be pushed back. The prospects seem to be for bigger and better sins; or rather, if we are very optimistic, for more refined, and perhaps for that very reason, more corrosive sins.[88]

[1]Max Hocutt, "Toward an Ethic of Mutual Accommodation," in *Humanist Ethics*, ed. Morris B. Storer (Buffalo: Prometheus Books, 1980), p. 137.
[2]William Provine, "Scientists, Face It! Science and Religion are Incompatible," *The Scientist*, September 5, 1988, p. 10.
[3]Michael Ruse and Edward O. Wilson, "Evolution and Ethics," *New Scientist*, October 17, 1985, pp. 51-2.
[4]Paul Kurtz, ed., *The Humanist Alternative* (Buffalo: Prometheus, 1973), p. 50.
[5]Corliss Lamont, *The Philosophy of Humanism* (New York: Frederick Ungar, 1982), pp. 229-30.
[6]Kurtz, ed., *The Humanist Alternative*, p. 179.
[7]Paul Kurtz, ed., *Humanist Manifestoes I & II* (Buffalo: Prometheus, 1980), p. 3.
[8]Kurtz, ed., *The Humanist Alternative*, p. 179.
[9]Paul Kurtz, "Humanism and Ethics," *Free Inquiry*, Spring 1981, p. 48.
[10]*Humanist Manifesto II*, p. 18.
[11]Lester Kirkendall, *A New Bill of Sexual Rights and Responsibilities* (Buffalo: Prometheus, 1976), p. 5.
[12]Ibid., p. 23.
[13]Will Durant, "Humanism in Historical Perspective," *The Humanist*, Jan./Feb. 1977, p. 26.
[14]Will Durant, "Humanism in Historical Perspective," in *Humanist Ethics*, ed. Storer, p. 8.
[15]Storer, "Preface," *Humanist Ethics*, ed. Storer, p. 3.
[16]Paul Kurtz, "Does Humanism Have an Ethic of Responsibility?" in *Humanist Ethics*, ed. Storer, p. 13.
[17]Ibid.
[18]Ibid., p. 22.
[19]Mihailo Markovic, "Comment by Mihailo Markovic on Kurtz," in *Humanist Ethics*, ed. Storer, p. 33.
[20]Ibid., p. 35.
[21]Max Hocutt, "Comment by Max Hocutt on Hannay Article," in *Humanist Ethics*, ed. Storer, p. 191.
[22]Hocutt, "Toward an Ethic of Mutual Accommodation," p. 137.
[23]Frederick Edwords, "The Human Basis of Laws and Ethics," *The Humanist*, May/June 1985, p. 13.
[24]Joseph Fletcher, "Humanist Ethics: the Groundwork," in *Humanist Ethics*, ed. Storer, p. 254.
[25]Ibid.
[26]Kai Nielsen, "Morality and the Human Situation," in *Humanist Ethics*, ed. Storer, pp. 58-60.
[27]Hocutt, "Toward an Ethic of Mutual Accommodation," p. 138.
[28]Fletcher, "Comment by Joseph Fletcher on Nielsen Article," in *Humanist Ethics*, ed. Storer, p. 71.
[29]Konstantin Kolenda, "Comment by Konstantin Kolenda on Baier Article," in *Humanist Ethics*, ed. Storer, p. 95.
[30]*Humanist Manifesto II*, p. 17.
[31]Kurtz, "Does Humanism Have an Ethic of Responsibility?" p. 11.
[32]Annual General Meeting of the British Humanist Association, July 1967.
[33]Kurtz, "Does Humanism Have an Ethic of Responsibility?" p. 14.
[34]Lamont, *The Philosophy of Humanism*, p. 253.
[35]Lucia K. B. Hall, "The Irrational Basis of Ethics," *The Humanist*, July/Aug. 1986, p. 20.
[36]V. M. Tarkunde, "Comment by V. M. Tarkunde on Hocutt Article," in *Humanist Ethics*, ed. Storer, p. 148.
[37]V. M. Tarkunde, "Towards a Fuller Consensus in Humanist Ethics," in *Humanist Ethics*, ed. Storer, p. 155.
[38]Alastair Hannay, "Comment by Alastair Hannay on Tarkunde Article," in *Humanist Ethics*, ed. Storer, pp. 168-9.
[39]Hocutt, "Comment by Max Hocutt on Tarkunde Article," p. 172.
[40]Cited in T. Walter Wallbank and Alastair M. Taylor, *Civilization Past and Present*, 4th ed. (New York: Scott, Foresman, 1961), vol. 2, p. 362.
[41]Cited in Bolton Davidheiser, *Evolution and Christian Faith* (Philadelphia, PA: Presbyterian and Reformed, 1969), p. 352.
[42]Mason Olds, "Ethics and Literature," *The Humanist*, Sept./Oct. 1985, p. 36.
[43]Howard B. Radest, "Relativism and Responsibility," in *Humanist Ethics*, ed. Storer, p. 229.
[44]Arthur E. Gravatt, cited in William H. Genne, "Our Moral Responsibility," *Journal of the American College Health Association*, vol. 15 (May 1967), p. 63.
[45]Fletcher, "Humanist Ethics: the Groundwork," p. 255.

[46]Herbert W. Schneider, "Humanist Ethics," in *Humanist Ethics*, ed. Storer, pp. 99-100.
[47]Kurtz, ed., *The Humanist Alternative*, p. 55.
[48]Kolenda, "Comment by Konstantin Kolenda on Schneider Article," p. 102.
[49]*Humanist Manifesto II*, p. 17.
[50]Kurtz, "Does Humanism Have an Ethic of Responsibility?" p. 21.
[51]Hocutt, "Toward an Ethic of Mutual Accommodation," p. 138.
[52]Ibid., p. 143.
[53]Tarkunde, "Comment by V. M. Tarkunde on Hocutt Article," p. 148.
[54]Lester Kirkendall, "An Ethical System for Now and the Future," in *Humanist Ethics*, ed. Storer, pp. 194-5.
[55]*Humanist Manifesto II*, p. 23.
[56]Paul Kurtz, "A Declaration of Interdependence: A New Global Ethics," *Free Inquiry*, Fall 1988, p. 6.
[57]Kurt Baier, "Comment by Kurt Baier on Schneider Article," in *Humanist Ethics*, ed. Storer, p. 102.
[58]Kurtz, "Does Humanism Have an Ethic of Responsibility?" p. 15.
[59]Ibid.
[60]Baier, "Freedom, Obligation, and Responsibility," in *Humanist Ethics*, ed. Storer, p. 81.
[61]Hocutt, "Toward an Ethic of Mutual Accommodation," pp. 138-9.
[62]Ibid., p. 143.
[63]Tarkunde, "Comment by V. M. Tarkunde on Hocutt Article," p. 149.
[64]Lamont, *The Philosophy of Humanism*, p. 236.
[65]Ibid., p. 248.
[66]Kurtz, "Does Humanism Have an Ethic of Responsibility?" p. 19.
[67]Ibid., p. 17.
[68]Ibid., p. 20.
[69]*Humanist Manifesto II*, p. 18.
[70]Judith A. Reisman and Edward W. Eichel, *Kinsey, Sex and Fraud* (Lafayette, LA: Huntington House, 1990), pp. 197-214.
[71]Faye Wattleton, "Reproductive Rights for a More Humane World," *The Humanist*, July/Aug. 1986, p. 7.
[72]Ibid.
[73]Lena Levine, "Psycho-sexual Development," *Planned Parenthood News*, Summer 1953, p. 10.
[74]Sherri Tepper, *You've Changed the Combination* (Denver, CO: Rocky Mountain Planned Parenthood, 1974).
[75]George Grant, *Grand Illusions* (Brentwood, TN: Wolgemuth and Hyatt, 1988), p. 49.
[76]Mary S. Calderone and Eric W. Johnson, *The Family Book About Sexuality* (New York: Bantam Books, 1983), p. 226.
[77]Ira L. Reiss, *SIECUS Study Guide 5: Premarital Sexual Standards*, October 1967.
[78]Harold T. Christensen, *SIECUS Study Guide 9: Sex, Science and Values*, February 1969.
[79]Lamont, *The Philosophy of Humanism*, p. 229.
[80]Ibid., p. 229.
[81]Ibid., p. 231.
[82]Lamont, *Voice in the Wilderness* (Buffalo, NY: Prometheus Books, 1974), p. 91.
[83]"Playboy Interview: Dr. Mary Calderone," *Playboy*, April 1970, p. 63.
[84]Lamont, *Voice in the Wilderness*, p. 94.
[85]Ibid., p. 97.
[86]Ibid., p. 97.
[87]Nielsen, "Morality and the Human Situation," p. 69.
[88]John Herman Randall, Jr., "What is the Temper of Humanism?" in *The Humanist Alternative*, ed. Kurtz, p. 60.

CHAPTER

10

MARXIST/ LENINIST ETHICS

"Is there such a thing as communist morality? Of course, there is. It is often suggested that we have no ethics of our own; very often the bourgeoisie accuse us Communists of rejecting all morality. This is a method of confusing the issue, of throwing dust in the eyes of the workers and peasants."[1]

—V. I. Lenin

"In what sense do we reject ethics, reject morality? In the sense given to it by the bourgeois, who based ethics on God's commandments. On this point we, of course, say that we do not believe in God."[2]

—V. I. Lenin

SUMMARY

Communist or class morality can be understood best within the context of dialectical and historical materialism. Marxists see their ethics proceeding out of the movement in history that will ultimately assure the destruction of all classes or forces opposing the classless or communist society. Each act is considered ethically good if it assists the flow of history toward a communist end. Killing, raping, stealing, and lying are not outside the boundaries of communist morality *if they help produce the classless communist society*. Marxist/Leninists believe that killing evolving human beings infected with the concepts of God and bourgeois capitalism is as morally justified as a farmer killing a cow afflicted with hoof-and-mouth disease. The killing fields of Cambodia, the Ukraine and the rest of the Soviet Union were the practical results of class morality. The mass murders in China came under the banner of class morality. "From the viewpoint of communist morality," says V. N. Kolbanovskiy, "that is moral which promotes the destruction of the old, exploiting society, and the construction of the new, communist society. Everything that hinders this development is immoral or amoral. To be a moral man, in our understanding means to devote all his forces and energy to the cause of the struggle for a new communist society."[3]

By definition, therefore, whatever advances the cause of communism is morally good; whatever hinders its advance in human and social evolution is morally evil. If the rest of the world looks on such activity as wicked or evil, the world's condemnation is a small price to pay to advance the flow of history toward a synthesis resulting in the creation of the new moral man—a man untainted by belief in a mythological God or exploitative capitalism.

Introduction

Marxist ethics proceeds out of Marxist theology, philosophy, biology, economics, and history. Whereas Humanists have a difficult time reaching a consensus regarding their ethical beliefs, Marxists do not face such problems—mainly because of their single-minded approach to all five aforementioned disciplines. Their approach is rooted in dialectical materialism and the class struggle. While there is no absolute morality for Marxism's ethical ideals, most Marxists believe the

Notes and Asides

absolute dialectical view of the class struggle is foundation enough.

"The principal ethical foundation of socialism can be completely understood only in the context of the dialectical materialist theory of man and history," states Prof. T. M. Jaroszewski. Building on this theory, Jaroszewski says the concept of man is no abstraction "with an invented, once and for all given 'essence.'" In Marxist ethics, he says, the concept denotes concrete, living people, acting in economic class and historical circumstances and having definite desires and interests. "From this it follows that man, each real, specific individual, is the main social value. This does not refer to any select groups or classes, but to the mass of the working people. The source of moral values is not the individual withdrawn into himself; moral values are produced by men in concrete work communities."[4]

According to the Marxist dialectic, everything in the universe, including society, is in a state of flux or constant change. This change in society is a move upward toward the elimination of all social and economic class distinctions, because evolution encourages more advanced civilizations. The next social advance in history will be the move from capitalism to socialism. This will inevitably result in a change in society's ideas about morals. The dialectical view of history dictates the clash of thesis and antithesis—in this historical context, the relentless clash between the proletariat and the bourgeoisie. Marxist/Leninists believe that the morality of these two classes is totally different, and when the proletariat finally destroys the bourgeoisie, a new morality will reign—a new morality for the new man.

Frederick Engels believed this interpretation of history was "destined to do for history what Darwin's theory has done for biology," explaining ". . . the whole history of mankind (since the dissolution of primitive tribal society, holding land in common ownership) has been a history of class struggles, contests between exploiting and exploited, ruling and oppressed classes; . . . the history of these class struggles forms a series of evolution in which, nowadays, a stage has been reached where the exploited and oppressed class—the proletariat—cannot attain its emancipation from the sway of the exploiting and ruling class—the bourgeoisie—without, at the same time, and once and for all, emancipating society at large from all exploitation, oppression, class-distinctions and class struggles."[5]

Engels blamed a large part of this exploitation and oppressive behavior on the morals inflicted upon the proletariat by the bourgeoisie. According to this view, the old religious moral codes must be abandoned so as to eliminate class distinctions. For Engels, "Thou shalt not steal" establishes a society in which some have property and some don't; such an establishment is the root of the problem.

Karl Marx, in *The German Ideology*, reasons this way:

Notes and Asides

> Morality, religion, metaphysics, all the rest of ideology and their corresponding forms of consciousness, thus no longer retain the semblance of independence. They have no history, no development; but men, developing their material production and their material intercourse, alter, along with this their real existence, their thinking and the products of their thinking. Life is not determined by consciousness, but consciousness by life.[6]

Thus, morality cannot exist independently of man and the course of history, for this is not in keeping with the philosophy of the dialectic. Moral codes are simply the result of man's perception of the state of things, and this perception is always changing since history is always changing. For this reason there can be no moral absolutes.

"It must be constantly borne in mind," says Howard Selsam, "that Marx and Engels denied that moral ideals, moral considerations, are central in human life and social evolution."[7] Rather, it is the biological and social evolution that dictates and determines morality. What is moral, what is right or wrong, is determined by what is best for such evolution. If the bourgeois class hinders either biological or social evolution, nature dictates the removal of that class.

V. I. Lenin also recognized that the ethics of Communism hinged on their historical and biological factors. He writes, "One therefore cannot deny the justice of Sombart's remark that 'in Marxism itself there is not a grain of ethics from beginning to end'; theoretically, it subordinates the 'ethical standpoint' to the 'principle of causality'; in practice it reduces it to the class struggle."[8] That is, ethics can be seen as the result of a specific event in history. In the Marxist view, this cause for the moral code stems directly from the course of history and man's participation in it. For Marxists "morality is not sanctioned by nature but created by history."[9]

The Evolution of Morality

The inevitability of change is the cornerstone for the Marxist ethical code. Marx writes in the *Manifesto of the Communist Party*, "Does it require deep intuition to comprehend that man's ideas, views and conceptions, in one word, man's consciousness, changes with every change in the conditions of his material existence, in his social relations and in his social life?"[10] This belief is echoed in the *History of the Communist Party of the Soviet Union*: "It was not ideas that determined the social and economic status of men, but the social and economic status of men that determined their ideas."[11] Because this social and economic status is, by Marx's definition, always changing according to

Notes and Asides

the laws of the dialectic, mankind's ideas about morality must also be in a state of change, or process of evolution.

It is useless for man to resist this change. Lenin states,

> The idea of determinism, which postulates that human acts are necessitated and rejects the absurd tale about free will, in no way destroys man's reason or conscience, or appraisal of his actions. . . . Similarly, the idea of historical necessity does not in the least undermine the role of the individual in history: all history is made up of the actions of individuals, who are undoubtedly active figures. The real question that arises in appraising the social activity of an individual is: what conditions ensure the success of his actions, what guarantee is there that these actions will not remain an isolated act lost in a welter of contrary acts?[12]

A man who is not acting in harmony with the changes occurring in society is like a man trying to swim upstream against a surging river. His actions are in vain. The course of history is set, and man's actions must be in keeping with that course if they are to accomplish anything.

This inevitability of change, in both history and ethics, causes some to question the existence of a moral code in Marxist philosophy. Lenin answers,

> "Is there such a thing as communist morality? Of course there is."
> —V. I. Lenin

> . . . is there such a thing as communist ethics? Is there such a thing as communist morality? Of course there is. It is often suggested that we have no ethics of our own; very often the bourgeoisie accuse us Communists of rejecting all morality. This is a method of confusing the issue, of throwing dust in the eyes of the workers and peasants.
>
> In what sense do we reject ethics, reject morality?
>
> In the sense given to it by the bourgeoisie, who based ethics on God's commandments. On this point we, of course, say that we do not believe in God, and that we know perfectly well that the clergy, the landowners and the bourgeoisie invoked the name of God so as to further their own interests as exploiters. Or, instead of basing ethics on the commandments of morality, on the commandments of God, they based it on idealist or semi-idealist phrases, which always amounted to something very similar to God's commandments.
>
> We reject any morality based on extra-human and extra-class concepts. We say that this is deception, dupery, stultification of the workers and peasants in the interests of the landowners and capitalists.[13]

Notes and Asides

Morality for the communists has evolved beyond what it was as used by the "exploiting classes," and a new morality will emerge from the working class. Because of this evolution, Marxists necessarily reject the old morality as a worthless tool of the oppressive classes. God's commandments are considered an outdated myth concocted by the exploiting class to suppress the exploited class. Says Lenin,

> We say that our morality is entirely subordinate to the interests of the proletariat's class struggle. Our morality stems from the interests of the class struggle of the proletariat.
>
> The old society was based on the oppression of all the workers and peasants by the landowners and capitalists. We had to destroy all that, and overthrow them but to do that we had to create unity. That is something that God cannot create. That is why we say that to us there is no such thing as a morality that stands outside human society; that is a fraud. To us morality is subordinated to the interests of the proletariat's class struggle.[14]

"Morality without religion is only a kind of dead reckoning,—an endeavor to find our place on a cloudy sea."
—H. W. Longfellow

Due to the dialectical evolutionary nature of ethics, there can be no unchanging ethical foundation. Ironically, it would be accurate to say that historical change is the foundation for Marxist ethics. It would also be accurate to say that class morality is ethical relativism with a vengeance.

Engels put it even more bluntly:

> We . . . reject every attempt to impose on us any moral dogma whatsoever as an eternal, ultimate, and for ever immutable moral law on the pretext that the moral world too has its permanent principles which transcend history and the differences between nations. We maintain on the contrary that all former moral theories are the product, in the last analysis, of the economic stage which society had reached at that particular epoch. . . .[15]

In contrast to bourgeois ethics, says A. Shishkin, Marxism rejects "any dogmatic system of morality which would fit all times and all nations and does not conceal the class origin of its ethics and does not substitute moral views for class struggle."[16] When all class distinctions are erased, however, the Marxist moral view necessarily must change again—because promoting class struggle will no longer be the immediate moral necessity. We say "immediate" because the dialectic is an eternal process that entails a continuing thesis/antithesis struggle. The ever-changing nature of history will dictate a new moral view for the Marxists. When Marxists say there is no system of morality that fits all

Notes and Asides

times, they include the future in their philosophy, realizing that history will change man's perceptions of life again after their present aims are attained. Something can only be morally right in its context in history. Today the morally right is the action necessary to attain the victory of the proletariat over the bourgeoisie.

So how will the new morality of the future be determined? The author of *Socialism as a Social System* believes that "socialist social relations determine the nature of moral change, the emergence of new moral standards, and the substance of socialist ideological-educational practice."[17] The new classless society itself will determine the new morality, just as this move toward a classless society is dictating the morality for today. For Marxists, morality is that conduct which is in harmony with history as it flows in the direction of a classless society.

Old Morality

Marxist/Leninists wholeheartedly reject moral codes with foundations in religious beliefs, including traditional universal moral ideals of our time. They reject such ideals as "old morality" as the products of the bourgeoisie, codes invented and used by that propertied class to oppress the propertyless proletariat. G. L. Andreyev, in *What Kind of Morality Does Religion Teach?* states,

> In the reigning morality under capitalism that act is considered moral which promotes the preservation and strengthening of the system of exploitation and the acquirement of profits. Religion merely justifies this unjust and oppressive, bloody, and inhuman system in the name of God. In our socialist society that act is considered moral which promotes the successful movement towards communism. Immoral is everything which hinders this.[18]

It is important to understand that Marxists perceive what is generally regarded by society as moral to be in direct contradiction to the Marxist goal of a classless society. Nikita Khrushchev states,

> We must introduce clarity into the question of humanism, into the question of what is good for whom and what is bad for whom. We approach this question, as we do all other questions, from the class standpoint, from the standpoint of defending the interests of the working people. So long as classes exist on the earth, there will be no such thing in life as something good in the absolute sense. What is good for the bourgeoisie, for the

Notes and Asides

> imperialists, is disastrous for the working class, and, on the contrary, what is good for the working people is not admitted by the imperialists, by the bourgeoisie.[19]

This, then, is the whole problem with the old morality as perceived by the Marxist. The old morality has simply been a tool for the oppressing classes to maintain their position in society. Christian ethics, for the Marxist, is just the means by which the rich control the working class poor.

Marx says that, for the proletariat, "Law, morality, religion, are . . . so many bourgeois prejudices, behind which lurk in ambush just as many bourgeois interests."[20] Lenin agrees with Marx: "The old society was based on the principle: rob or be robbed; work for others or make others work for you; be a slave-owner or a slave."[21]

Marxists have no use for Christian ideas about ethics. "[T]he age-old claim that nature and man are intrinsically or inherently evil and that only through supernatural intervention is man capable of good," says Selsam, "ignores the concrete fact that men judge things to be good or evil in so far as they promote or hinder the satisfaction of the needs and desires of the society or the special social classes or groups to which they belong."[22] The Marxist doesn't need the explanation of Original Sin or belief in a Creator—these are myths perpetuated by the bourgeoisie. The central problem with old morality is that "respect for the human being, his dignity and worth, [is] incompatible with the oppression and alienation of the human personality under capitalism. . . ."[23]

"The [bourgeois] is not a human being with individual traits, but a social abstraction, a creature devoid of virtue or free will and without the right to live."
—Jacques Barzun

Class Morality

For the present historical period, from the Marxist point of view, the proper morality to adopt is a class morality—specifically, the morality of the proletariat, the propertyless masses. "The morality which the revolutionary working class brought with itself into the world contains the nucleus of the future universal morality . . . Communist ethics is the science of the obligation of a worker towards socialist society, toward Soviet state, toward the socialist country and the mutual obligations of people to one another."[24]

According to *Scientific Communism: A Glossary*, "Devotion to the cause of the working class, collectivism, mutual aid, comradely solidarity, hatred toward the bourgeoisie and toward traitors to the common cause, internationalism, and stoicism in struggle are traits which not only define the content of proletarian ethics, but also characterize the moral image of the typical representatives of the working class."[25] This is precisely the code of ethics that all Marxists believe must be adopted.

Notes and Asides

It is interesting to note that included in this code is the call for hatred of the bourgeoisie. Robert Conquest's *The Harvest of Sorrow*, a documentation of the inhumanity of applied Marxist theory, contains illustration after illustration of "class hatred" or communist class morality in practice.[26] Hatred can be moral, according to the Marxist, as long as it is directed toward the proper institution, class, or enemy. When the communists, for example, decided to liquidate the bourgeois class of kulaks, E. H. Carr points out, even poor farmers were determined to

CLOSE-UP

V. I. Lenin (1870-1924)

Vladimir Ilich Lenin led Marxism from the theoretical realm to the practical, and as such is rightly included in the descriptive title of the Marxist/Leninist worldview. The son of nobility, Lenin reaped the benefits of an upper class education, and then rebelled. In 1897 he was arrested and exiled to Siberia for three years. Upon his release, he moved to Europe, where he stayed for most of the next seventeen years. He returned to Russia to stay in 1917, just prior to the October Revolution. Much of the credit for the success of that revolution rightfully belongs to Lenin, but it is also true that the czarist state was so decrepit that political power virtually fell into Lenin's lap. As the state crumbled, Lenin and the Bolsheviks—a majority party that had split with other Marxists at a 1903 Russian Marxist congress—seized power and created the USSR, expecting to escort the proletariat into the golden age of communism. Instead, civil war broke out, lasting from 1918 to 1921. Lenin and his party won the war, using it to more firmly establish their regime, but in the process the Soviet economy was ruined. Thus, Lenin had to resort to the New Economic Policy, which allowed for a great deal more capitalism than he would have liked, and which sorely hampered the move toward communism. Lenin died a few years later, having never realized his goal of establishing a communist state. He left behind a voluminous amount of theoretical writing, including *Materialism and Empirio-criticism* and *The State and Revolution*.

Notes and Asides

be kulaks if they were "devoted churchmen."[27]

Hatred becomes a necessary ingredient in the clash between the proletariat and the bourgeoisie. "The values of the various classes are determined by the relations of each to the other in the production process, and, when the relations of one class to the other are antagonistic ones, their values will not only be different, but in opposition."[28] It follows, then, that society's generally accepted moral principles (which Marxists claim are bourgeois tools) are in direct opposition to the moral principles of the proletariat. If this is the case, could any member of the bourgeoisie do anything right (short of giving all his possessions to the communist cause and becoming a proletarian) in the Marxist's eyes? Apparently not. Marx says, "A part of the bourgeoisie is desirous of redressing social grievances, in order to secure the continued existence of bourgeois society."[29] It would seem that unless a member of the propertied class could somehow become a proletarian, anything he does, no matter how moral by his standards, will be greeted with contempt by Marxists. In fact, the proletariat is called to rebel against the moral code long recognized by popular, capitalist society.

Justification of the Means

According to the Marxist, the acceptable form of conduct in class morality is whatever it takes to accomplish the ultimate goal—namely, a classless communist society. In other words, the end justifies the means. Regardless of what you do, it is moral if it brings the world closer to eradicating social classes. Selsam writes,

> Marxists believe, therefore, that the working class is supremely right in its struggle to defeat fascism [fascism in this context is used to define anyone or anything in opposition to communism], and in its struggles to create the necessary conditions for its own emancipation—so right, in fact, that its actions cannot be judged by the criteria that are the ethical expression of the capitalist class. This is not because the goals of the working class are good in and of themselves, but rather because they are the sole means to general human progress and the widest human good. Thus the Marxist does not examine each strike, each labor struggle, or each revolutionary uprising of workers, farmers, or colonial people to see whether in every particular case the ethical canons of the bourgeoisie are observed. He examines them only in terms of whether they will or will not advance the cause of the oppressed masses.[30]

Notes and Asides

An action is moral when it helps overthrow the bourgeoisie.

Selsam justifies this way of thinking: "the struggle for freedom . . . itself is moral or right because freedom is the highest good and that alone by which all acts and institutions can be judged."[31] According to Marxism, freedom can only truly be achieved when all class barriers are erased, and therefore anything that serves that end can be judged as moral. "Ethics, in short," says Selsam, "is good only as anything else is good, for what it can accomplish, for the direction in which it takes men."[32]

The problem, of course, is that man can justify mistreating his fellow man by claiming that it will serve in the long run a "higher good." Ivan Bahryany, a Ukrainian citizen who estimates that the Soviets killed 10 million of his countrymen between 1927 and 1939, states the problem this way: "The party clique which follows the slogan expressed by the saying 'the end justifies the means' is actually always ready to use any means."[33] In the case of the Ukrainians, the "means" included shooting, starvation, and slave labor in Siberia.[34] Joseph Stalin referred to such action as the liquidation of the kulak class.[35] Lenin admitted that the proletariat would be willing to work with the "petty bourgeois proprietors" as long as it furthered the Marxist cause, "But after that our roads part. Then we shall have to engage in the most decisive, ruthless struggle against them."[36]

This practical application of the "end justifying the means" is best summed up by Lev Kopelev:

> With the rest of my generation I firmly believed that the ends justified the means. Our great goal was the universal triumph of Communism, and for the sake of that goal everything was permissible—to lie, to steal, to destroy hundreds of thousands and even millions of people, all those who were hindering our work or could hinder it, everyone who stood in the way. And to hesitate or doubt about all this was to give in to "intellectual squeamishness" and "stupid liberalism," the attribute of people who "could not see the forest for the trees."[37]

Moral Revolution

What are the most efficient means for creating a society without class distinctions? According to Marxists, revolution is unavoidable—it is the only way to overthrow the bourgeoisie and lift up the proletariat. V. N. Kolbanovskiy, author of *Communist Morality*, writes,

Notes and Asides

> At the root of the communist morality, V. I. Lenin teaches, "lies the struggle for strengthening and achieving communism." This is why, from the viewpoint of communist morality, that is moral which promotes the destruction of the old, exploiting society, and the construction of the new, communist society. Everything that hinders this development is immoral or amoral. To be a moral man, in our understanding, means to devote all his forces and energy to the cause of the struggle for a new communist society.[38]

Communist revolution is unquestionably moral. "From the point of view of communist morality the struggle against everything which hinders the cause of communist construction is moral and humane," says Andreyev, "and for this reason we consider the struggle against the enemies of communism to be of a moral nature."[39] Nechayev's *The Revolutionary Catechism*, which influenced Lenin's thinking, contended that the revolutionary "hates the existing social morality in all its manifestations. For him, morality is everything which contributes to the triumph of the revolution. Immoral and criminal is everything that stands in the way."[40]

This class struggle is definitely not peaceful—but then the struggle for survival in nature is not peaceful. According to the Marxists, those who criticize the elimination of the bourgeoisie for social evolutionary reasons fail to remember the cost in death and suffering caused by biological evolution. Nature accumulates the good and disposes of the bad. The fit must survive both biologically and socially. The unfit, along with their social institutions, must perish.

Marx states, "The Communists disdain to conceal their views and aims. They openly declare that their ends can be attained only by the forcible overthrow of all existing social conditions."[41] This forcible overthrow, however, is perceived as morally right. It is right because it destroys the hindrances to a communist society:

> When you fight capitalism you are doing what is right and just and lawful from the point of view of your class interests and of the future of humanity. You are not 'outlaws' the way the capitalist world brands revolutionary fighters. You are fighting for a higher morality and a higher law that will forever abolish exploitation—the morality and the law of the social revolution.[42]

Morally speaking, it is not just okay to work for the forcible overthrow of capitalism—it is the communist's ethical duty, and he is morally wrong if he shirks that duty.

Notes and Asides

Does this obligation to overthrow the bourgeoisie include killing? Khrushchev answers,

> Our cause is sacred. He whose hand will tremble, who will stop midway, whose knees will shake before he destroys tens and hundreds of enemies, he will lead the revolution into danger. Whoever will spare a few lives of enemies, will pay for it with hundreds and thousands of lives of the better sons of our fathers. . . .[43]

How will an individual always know if his actions are the proper ones for accomplishing the Marxist goal? He won't. And he will make mistakes. Lenin says, "Even if for every hundred correct things we committed 10,000 mistakes, our revolution would still be—and it will be in the judgment of history—great and invincible. . . ."[44]

The Marxist revolution is morally right even if mistakes are made and even when it involves mass killings. Joseph Stalin took this philosophy to heart, stating, "To put it briefly: the dictatorship of the proletariat is the domination of the proletariat over the bourgeoisie, untrammelled by the law and based on violence and enjoying the sympathy and support of the toiling and exploited masses."[45] For this reason Stalin announced on December 27, 1929, "the liquidation of the kulaks as a class."[46] British journalist D. G. Stewart-Smith estimates that international communism has been responsible for 83 million deaths between 1917 and 1964.[47] From a Marxist/Leninist perspective, if 83 million died to abolish social classes and private property, it was worth the price—even morally just. Marxists judge the result, not the methods; the consequences, not the act.

> "Even if for every hundred correct things we committed 10,000 mistakes, our revolution would still be—and it will be in the judgment of history—great and invincible . . ."
>
> —V. I. Lenin

Of course, from mankind's general ethical standpoint, Stalin was morally decadent, to put it mildly. Milovan Djilas, a former admirer of Stalin, states, "If we assume the viewpoint of humanity and freedom, history does not know a despot as brutal and as cynical as Stalin was. He was methodical, all-embracing, and total as a criminal. He was one of those rare terrible dogmatists capable of destroying nine tenths of the human race to 'make happy' the one tenth."[48]

Stalin, however, acted always within the Marxist/Leninist ethical code. He used means that he assumed would serve his ends—the destruction of the class enemy—and should those ends ever be accomplished, Marxists would have to applaud Stalin as an individual with the proper ideas about morality. But Stalin was not alone in his morality; Lenin, too, advocated the elimination of the kulaks as a class, insisting that they were "not human beings"[49] and that it was necessary to have recourse to "economic terror."[50]

Notes and Asides

The Socialist/Communist Man

But what exactly are the ends Marxists are trying to accomplish? Obviously, they are attempting to abolish all elements of the bourgeois class and create world communism, but these objectives are really only more means to a further end. This further end involves the creation of a "new man." The reason man will become "new" is that the Marxist economic system (socialism) is morally superior to capitalism. "The socialist human ideal is finding embodiment in people's conduct to an ever greater extent. Socialism is superior to capitalism in that it provides the conditions for the emergence of a new, superior morality, the morality of the new man, with his new moral wants."[51]

Indeed, Marxists claim, socialism has already accomplished this in Soviet Russia. "The Great October Socialist Revolution raised the morality of all the people of Russia to a higher plane, the highest plane in human society,"[52] said M. I. Kalinin. The Soviet citizen's new morality is explained more fully by the authors of *The Fundamentals of Marxist-Leninist Philosophy*:

> One of the most important results of the development of Soviet society since the October Revolution of 1917 is the formation of a new type of person, a builder of the new society, a Soviet patriot and internationalist, who combines ideological conviction with vital energy, culture, knowledge and the ability to apply them. This person lives in a truly free society, in the morally healthy atmosphere of collectivism and comradeship, friendship between peoples and nations, and socialist humanism that characterise the way of life of the builders of communism—*the Soviet way of life*.[53]

Of course, these statements imply that there is a measure for morality after all, other than the abolition of enemy classes. In fact, Leonid I. Brezhnev states, "In socialist society a man is valued by his work, knowledge and spiritual qualities. The decayed morality of the old world with its exploitation and national discord, its desire for personal enrichment, its egoism, is entirely alien to us. We have rejected that morality finally and completely."[54] While it's true that Communists have rejected the so-called "old morality," it is hard to discover the ethical code on which they base their new morality. If, as they say, history and its social forces dictate man's morality, and history is always changing, how can a moral code be grounded in anything outside of history? How can a new morality be discovered to create a new man, since history could render that morality obsolete in a matter

Notes and Asides

of moments?

Roger Garaudy faced this dilemma and concluded,

> When we ask ourselves what we must do if we are to act rightly, we are not seeking to conform to a pre-existing law or to a being that is already "given": we are asking ourselves what must be brought into existence which is not yet existing.
>
> This ethic, which is history in process of being made, a specifically human history and one whose scenario has not been written by any god or any fate, nor by any abstract dialect, . . . this ethic is the continued creation of man by man.[55]

Man somehow working to hasten his own evolution into a higher being—that is the standard by which good can be measured. But no one really knows what will work best to bring this evolution about. Therefore, no one can be sure what actions could actually be considered moral.

Marxists are convinced that the abolition of social classes is the first step necessary in hastening dialectical social evolution. After this is accomplished, however, Lenin says it is up to this new society to discover new morals:

> When people talk to us about morality, we say: for the Communist, morality lies entirely in this solid, united discipline and conscious mass struggle against the exploiters. We do not believe in an eternal morality, and we expose the deceit of all the fables about morality. Morality serves the purpose of helping human society to rise to a higher level and to get rid of the exploitation of labour.[56]

Still, Marxists remain hopeful that the new man created by a classless society will discover a new, higher morality. Garaudy believes, "It helps us to understand that man is a creator, that he is his own creator, and it provides us with the means of overcoming alienation, which is the opposite of creation—of overcoming it for all of us: it enables us, that is, to base an indivisibly social and personal ethic not simply on its theoretical justification but on its practical realisation: an ethic whose ultimate end creates the conditions which will make it possible for every man to become effectively a man, that is to say a creator."[57] So, for some Marxists, man's becoming a creator will be the next moral good after a classless society is achieved. Still, a Marxist would have to believe that history could change this idea about morals at any time.

Notes and Asides

Conclusion

Many uncertainties surround Marxist ethics. While virtually all Marxists agree on the dialectical materialist foundation for their morality and the inevitability of change involved in moral precepts, these same Marxists would have difficulty predicting the ethics of a classless society. They are quick to label Christian ethics "immoral" because these ethics theoretically maintain the dominion of the bourgeoisie over the proletariat, but they cannot conceive of a moral scheme of their own other than the vague idea of "creation of a new moral man."

Marxists believe a classless society will render many of our moral ideals obsolete. Engels writes,

> From the moment that private property in movable objects developed, in all societies in which this private property existed, there must be this moral law in common: Thou shalt not steal. Does this law thereby become an eternal moral law? By no means. In a society in which the motive for stealing has been done away with, in which therefore at the very most only lunatics would ever steal, how the teacher of morals would be laughed at who tried solemnly to proclaim the eternal truth: Thou shalt not steal.[58]

Marxists believe that socialism will make it impossible for many moral evils to be committed—since property is everyone's, it makes no sense to steal.

However, this is not the case in socialist societies today. In Soviet Russia, home of the "new man" with morality on "the highest plane in human society," theft is still a very real problem. One Russian citizen, quoted by Lowell Blankfort, states,

> You have to understand our economic system. In Russia, everything is Socialist property. And what is Socialist property? Is it my property? No. Is it my neighbor's property? No. Is it anybody's property? No. So naturally everybody steals it. And with a clear conscience.
>
> Except it is not really stealing. It is what we call here, having a little business on the side. In Russia, everybody has a little business on the side.[59]

"Truth forever on the scaffold, Wrong forever on the throne."
—J. R. Lowell

This type of ethical ideology, including the belief about the inevitability of change and the evolutionary nature of morals, leaves Marxists free to abandon today's generally accepted moral standards in pursuit of a greater good—the creation of a communist society. This

Notes and Asides

pursuit requires the Marxist to dedicate his life to the cause and to use whatever action he believes will eventually result in a classless society. Therefore, his course of action, no matter how immoral it appears to a world that believes in an absolute or at least a universal moral standard, is determined by a dialectically driven history and is perceived as moral by the Marxist/Leninist.

[1]V. I. Lenin, *Collected Works*, forty-five volumes (Moscow: Progress Publishers, 1982), vol. 31, p. 291.
[2]Ibid.
[3]V. N. Kolbanovskiy, *Communist Morality* (Moscow: 1951), p. 20.
[4]T. M. Jaroszewski and P. A. Ignatovsky, eds., *Socialism as a Social System* (Moscow: Progress Publishers, 1981), pp. 249-50.
[5]Karl Marx and Frederick Engels, *The Communist Manifesto* (Chicago: Henry Regnery, 1954), p. 5.
[6]Karl Marx, *Selected Works* (Moscow: Foreign Languages Publishing House, 1962), vol. 1, pp. 14-15. Cited in James Bales, *Communism and the Reality of Moral Law* (Nutley, NJ: The Craig Press, 1969), p. 45.
[7]Howard Selsam, *Socialism and Ethics* (New York: International Publishers, 1943), p. 92.
[8]Lenin, *Collected Works*, vol. 1, pp. 420-1.
[9]Roger Garaudy, *Marxism in the Twentieth Century* (New York: Charles Scribner's Sons, 1970), p. 77.
[10]Karl Marx and Frederick Engels, *Collected Works*, forty volumes (New York: International, 1977), vol. 6, p. 503.
[11]*History of the Communist Party of the Soviet Union*, p. 14, cited in Bales, *Communism and the Reality of Moral Law*, p. 46.
[12]Lenin, *Collected Works*, vol. 1, p. 159.
[13]Lenin, *Collected Works*, vol. 31, p. 291.
[14]Ibid., pp. 291-2.
[15]Cited in R. N. Carew Hunt, *The Theory and Practice of Communism* (Baltimore: Penguin Books, 1966), p. 113.
[16]A. Shishkin, *Foundations of Communist Morality* (Moscow: 1955), p. 76.
[17]Jaroszewski and Ignatovsky, eds., *Socialism as a Social System*, p. 253.
[18]G. L. Andreyev, *What Kind of Morality Does Religion Teach?* (Moscow: 1959), cited in *A Lexicon of Marxist-Leninist Semantics*, ed. Raymond S. Sleeper (Alexandria, VA: Western Goals, 1983), p. 174.
[19]Nikita Khrushchev, "The Great Strength of Soviet Literature and Art," Soviet Booklet no. 108, March 1963 (London: Farleigh Press Ltd., 1963), p. 30. Cited in Bales, *Communism and the Reality of Moral Law*, p. 5.
[20]Marx and Engels, *Collected Works*, vol. 6, p. 494.
[21]Lenin, *Collected Works*, vol. 31, p. 293.
[22]Selsam, *Socialism and Ethics*, p. 72.
[23]*World Marxist Review*, August 1962, p. 43.
[24]*Bolshevik*, Moscow, 15 May 1948, p. 31.
[25]*Scientific Communism: A Glossary*, (Moscow: 1975), pp. 131-2, cited in *A Lexicon of Marxist-Leninist Semantics*, ed. Sleeper, p. 106.
[26]Robert Conquest, *The Harvest of Sorrow: Soviet Collectivization and the Terror-Famine* (New York: Oxford University Press, 1986).
[27]Ibid., p. 119.
[28]*Philosophy in Revolution* (New York: International, 1957), p. 136. Cited in Bales, *Communism and the Reality of Moral Law*, p. 4.
[29]Marx and Engels, *Collected Works*, vol. 6, p. 513.
[30]Selsam, *Socialism and Ethics*, p. 96.
[31]Ibid., p. 214.
[32]Ibid., p. 98.
[33]S. O. Pidhainy, ed., *The Black Deeds of the Kremlin* (Toronto: The Basilian Press, 1953), p. 14. Robert Conquest in *The Harvest of Sorrow*, p. 305, places the figure at 14.5 million.
[34]Conquest, *The Harvest of Sorrow*.
[35]Ibid., pp. 115, 117.
[36]Lenin, *Collected Works*, vol. 36, pp. 255, 265.
[37]Lev Kopelev, *The Education of a True Believer* (New York: 1977), pp. 11-12.
[38]Kolbanovskiy, *Communist Morality*, p. 20.
[39]Andreyev, *What Kind of Morality Does Religion Teach?*, cited in *A Lexicon of Marxist-Leninist Semantics*, ed. Sleeper, p. 175.
[40]Robert Payne, *The Life and Death of Lenin* (New York: Avon Books, 1964), p. 27.

[41]Marx and Engels, *Collected Works*, vol. 6, p. 519.
[42]M. J. Oglin, *Why Communism?* (New York: Workers' Library Publishers, 1935), p. 62.
[43]Nikita Khrushchev, *Ukrainian Bulletin*, August 1-August 15, 1960, p. 12. Cited in Bales, *Communism and the Reality of Moral Law*, p. 121.
[44]Lenin, *Collected Works*, vol. 28, p. 72.
[45]Joseph Stalin, speech delivered April 24, 1924 (New York: International Publishers, 1934).
[46]Conquest, *The Harvest of Sorrow*, p. 117.
[47]Eugene Lyons, *Workers' Paradise Lost* (New York: Paperback Library, 1967), p. 354.
[48]Cited in Bales, *Communism and the Reality of Moral Law*, p. 20.
[49]Cited in Conquest, *The Harvest of Sorrow*, p. 129.
[50]Ibid., p. 60.
[51]Jaroszewski and Ignatovsky, eds., *Socialism as a Social System*, p. 259.
[52]Bales, *Communism and the Reality of Moral Law*, p. 8.
[53]F. V. Konstantinov, chief ed., *The Fundamentals of Marxist-Leninist Philosophy* (Moscow: Progress Publishers, 1982), p. 347.
[54]Leonid I. Brezhnev, speech at the opening of the Lenin Boarding School, Havana, 31 Jan. 1974.
[55]Garaudy, *Marxism in the Twentieth Century*, p. 77.
[56]V. I. Lenin, *On Socialist Ideology and Culture* (Moscow: Foreign Languages Publishing House, n.d.), p. 55.
[57]Garaudy, *Marxism in the Twentieth Century*, p. 105.
[58]Frederick Engels, *Anti-Dühring* (New York: International, 1935), pp. 108-9.
[59]*Congressional Record*, Feb. 2, 1961, p. A660.

CHAPTER

11

BIBLICAL CHRISTIAN ETHICS

"Let love be sincere and without hypocrisy. Abhor that which is evil; cleave to that which is good."

—Romans 12:9

"Hate the evil and love the good, and establish judgment in the gate."

—Amos 5:15

"To judge the moral order spurious, or, conversely, valid, is at the same time to pass a verdict upon the whole of reality and, unavoidably to define the nature of man himself."[1]

—Carl F. H. Henry

SUMMARY

God's moral nature is absolute and unchanging. God always hates the evil and loves the good. The Bible is of supreme importance because it tells us the difference between good and evil, providing a framework on which a completely unambiguous ethic must be built. Using general revelation, God has granted every man a sense of right and wrong in the form of a conscience (John 1:9; Romans 1:20, 26-27; 2:14); however, the special revelation of Scripture and, especially, the life of Christ provide mankind with an unshakable foundational understanding of morality. On this foundation stand two fundamental precepts: God expects man to discern between good and evil (Hebrews 5:14) and to choose the good and avoid the evil (Romans 12:9).

Biblical Christianity's ethics are absolute and unchanging. Because God is a holy, righteous God, He demands consistent righteousness from His human creation. Indeed, reality itself is such that actions not conforming with God's nature are hopelessly counterproductive. God's moral order is as important as His physical order, because breaking God's moral laws results in consequences just as severe as breaking nature's physical laws. As G. K. Chesterton once noted, "There is an infinity of angles at which one falls, only one at which one stands."[2]

Of course, both Secular Humanists and Marxist/Leninists scoff at the existence of an all-encompassing moral order. They deny the concept of an absolute, holy God and conclude that moral absolutes cannot exist. But according to Biblical Christianity, ethical relativism leads to destruction (Matthew 7:13). Societies based on relativistic ethics cannot help but be victims of "the permissiveness syndrome," a syndrome which, according to Boris Sokoloff, "was present in various forms and

Introduction

Christian ethics is inseparable from theology because Christian ethics is grounded in the character of God. "One of the distinctions of the Judeo-Christian God," says Francis Schaeffer, "is that not all things are the same to Him. That at first may sound rather trivial, but in reality it is one of the most profound things one can say about the Judeo-Christian God. He exists; He has a character; and not all things are the same to Him. Some things conform to His character, and some are opposed to His character."[5] *The task of Christian ethics is determining what conforms to God's character and what does not.*

degrees during previous civilizations. As a rule it developed in nations which were in decline, in disintegration, or in serious troubles."[3]

The Christian believes that societies and individuals that choose ethical relativism incur God's wrath (Isaiah 5:20). The ethical relativist's code, which appears to be tolerant, twists in on itself and produces intolerance. Charles Colson points out that relativistic tolerance declares that "everyone has a right to express his or her own views," but it has an unspoken prejudice: "as long as those views do not contain any suggestion of absolutes that would compete with the prevailing standard of relativism."[4]

Ethical relativists claim that their stance against Christian ethics is justified because the Christian view denies free will, forcing every person to act in a specific, preordained way. The Christian, however, understands that sin, not an ethical code, destroys free will (and eventually the soul). The Apostle Paul, addressing Christians, speaks of a time before they knew Christ when they were "slaves to sin" and asks, "What benefit did you reap at that time from the things you are now ashamed of? Those things result in death" (Romans 6:20-21). Ignoring God's will chains the individual to a demanding, destructive master—sin. But true freedom is offered to all who accept Christ as their liberator: "For sin shall not be your master" (Romans 6:14). The Christian, choosing to trust in Christ to break the bonds of sin, becomes free to act in accord with God's will, living a joyfully productive life. Christianity's ethical order is not a grey, lifeless prison; rather, it is the key to a community in which each individual seeks to love and serve God and his fellow man instead of his own radically self-centered, tyrannical whims.

While Marxists and Humanists rely almost exclusively on their economic or naturalistic philosophy to determine ethics, the Christian places ethics in a moral order revealed by the Divine Creator. Rather than believing in some passing fancy bound to society's ever-changing whims, the Christian answers to a specific moral order revealed to man both through general revelation and through special revelation of the Bible.

The Christian knows this ethical order to be the only true source of morality. "The human mind," says C. S. Lewis, "has no more power of inventing a new [moral] value than of imagining a new primary colour, or, indeed, of creating a new sun and a new sky for it to move in."[6] Those

Notes and Asides

talking about establishing a new moral order are talking nonsense. This is no more possible than establishing a new physical order. Both are givens. They simply are. For the Christian, the moral order is as real as the physical order—some would say more real. The Apostle Paul says the physical order is temporary, but the order "not seen" is eternal (2 Corinthians 4:18). This eternal moral order is a reflection of the character of God.

Revelation and Our Common Moral Heritage

Christian ethics in one sense is simply an expansion on a moral order that is generally revealed to all men. Despite some disputes regarding the morality of certain specific actions, comments Calvin D. Linton, "there is a basic pattern of similarity among [ethical codes]. Such things as murder, lying, adultery, cowardice are, for example, almost always condemned. The universality of the ethical sense itself (the 'oughtness' of conduct), and the similarities within the codes of diverse cultures indicate a common moral heritage for all mankind which materialism or naturalism cannot explain."[7]

"Ethics is based on ethical laws that reflect the very nature of God."
—Norman Geisler

This common moral heritage could be defined as anything from an attitude to a conscience, but however one defines it, one is left with the impression that some moral absolutes exist outside of man. Joseph Butler, a Christian preacher and Bishop, believed that man's moral heritage manifests itself in the emotion we call shame, saying that "a man can as little doubt whether it was given him to prevent his doing shameful actions, as he can doubt whether his eyes were given him to guide his steps."[8] Philosopher D. Elton Trueblood believes that this heritage is evident whenever man assumes an attitude of judgment:

> Every person who engages in moral judgment implies by his judgment the existence of an objective moral order. This is because the relationship called judging involves at least three terms: the person who judges, the action that is judged, and the standard of judgment by which the judged action is measured. This last, if moral experience is to make sense at all, must be something independent of both of the other terms.[9]

According to this concept, whenever man judges he is relying upon a yardstick that measures actions against an absolute set of standards. Without a standard, there could be no justice; without an ethical absolute, there could be no morality.

This absolute standard outside of man is apparent throughout all of mankind's attitudes toward morality. "Although dismissing the non-

Notes and Asides

secular [Christian ethic] in theory," says Carl Henry, "the secular man betrays in his practice a self-awareness that incorporates and acknowledges the nonsecular; his everyday life mirrors a dimension of the ultimate that gives meaning to those very religious symbols he has professedly discarded. His conduct, moreover, reflects private assumptions about personal interrelationships and the given character of external reality that sharply contradict the naturalistic framework."[10] Secular man should, according to his own philosophy, lead a life that treats all morals as relative—but in practice, secular man treats some abstract values (such as justice or fairness, love, and courage) as consistently moral. How can this phenomenon be explained unless we accept the notion that certain value judgments are universal and inherent to all mankind?

Christian morality is founded on this belief in an absolute moral order existing outside of, and yet somehow inscribed into, man's very being. It is a morality flowing from the nature of the Creator through the nature of created things, not a construction of the human mind. It is part of God's general revelation to man. Butler believed that, even without the benefit of special revelation,

> man cannot be considered as a creature left by his Maker to act at random, and live at large up to the extent of his natural power, as passion, humour, wilfulness, happen to carry him; which is the condition brute creatures are in: but that from his make, constitution, or nature, he is in the strictest and most proper sense a law to himself. He hath the rule of right within: what is wanting is only that he honestly attends to it.[11]

This rule of right, this moral light, is what the Apostle John refers to as having been lit in the hearts of all men and women—"That was the true Light, which lighteth every man that cometh into the world" (John 1:9). It is what St. Paul referred to as "the work of the law written in their hearts, their conscience" (Romans 2:15). Dave Breese acknowledges this, saying, "To some degree, man has the law written in his heart and possesses, until he successfully destroys it, a conscience that brings guilt to his soul, which violates that law."[12]

> "To some degree, man has the [moral] law written in his heart and possesses, until he successfully destroys it, a conscience that brings guilt to his soul, which violates that law."
> —David Breese

Therefore, Christians have no qualms about acknowledging that Jesus Christ did not demand a new code of ethics. Writes Lewis,

> The idea (at least in its grossest and most popular form), that Christianity brought a new ethical code into the world is a grave error. If it had done so, then we should have to conclude that all who first preached it wholly misunderstood their own message: for all of them, its Founder, His precursor, His apostles, came

Notes and Asides

> demanding repentance and offering forgiveness, a demand and an offer both meaningless except on the assumption of a moral law already known and already broken. It is far from my intention to deny that we find in Christian ethics a deepening, an internalization, a few changes of emphasis, in the moral code. But only serious ignorance of Jewish and Pagan culture would lead anyone to the conclusion that it is a radically new thing.[13]

At the core of the Christian ethic is a moral order based on the character of God, which is revealed to man both through general and

CLOSE-UP

C. S. Lewis (1898-1963)

C. S. Lewis never strayed far from the halls of academia. Despite some unpleasant experiences in his early school years, his enthusiasm for learning and encouraging others to learn never dimmed throughout his life. By age 27 he was awarded a Fellowship at Magdalen College, and from that point forward he directed his energies toward teaching. For Lewis, however, teaching meant far more than academic instruction; it meant challenging all those around him to think critically and to live with their eyes open. Upon his conversion from atheism to Christianity in 1931, Lewis' drive to teach took on the added dimension of encouraging men and women to treat the Christian worldview as a viable option—as, indeed, the only option which explained the real world. Lewis often relied on the moral argument to demonstrate that experience points toward an eternal Creator. Two of his most important books, *Mere Christianity* and *The Abolition of Man*, provide impressive insights into the subtleties of the moral argument. But his skill as a teacher was not restricted to the realm of non-fiction. Some of his best-loved books, including the Narnia series, *The Screwtape Letters*, and *The Great Divorce* used symbolism and a sharp wit to convey the deeper truths of Christianity. Lewis' books reflect the rich complexity of his character and his passionate desire to better know, appreciate, and love God.

Notes and Asides

special revelation. "The Moral Law . . . this Rule of Right and Wrong, or Law of Human Nature, or whatever you call it," writes Lewis, "must somehow or other be a real thing—a thing that is really there, not made up by ourselves. And yet it is not a fact in the ordinary sense, in the same way as our actual behaviour is a fact. It begins to look as if we shall have to admit that there is more than one kind of reality; that, in this particular case, there is something above and beyond the ordinary facts of men's behaviour, and yet quite definitely real—a real law, which none of us made, but which we find pressing on us."[14] There is an order outside the empirical or five senses of man, and this order, by its very nature, must be treated as an absolute. A voice of conscience echoes down the corridors of time, imploring man to respect life, to love parents, to love God and his neighbor. People know in their hearts that worshiping idols, practicing homosexuality (male or female), fornication, wickedness, covetousness, maliciousness, envy, murder, deceit, whisperers, backbiters, haters of God, proud, boasters, inventors of evil things, disobedience to parents, covenant breakers, those without natural affection, and the unmerciful (Romans 1:23-32) are contrary to the eternal moral order.

This morality is not arbitrarily handed down by God to create difficulties for mankind. God does not make up new values according to any whim. Rather, God's very character is holy and cannot tolerate evil or moral indifference—what the Bible calls *sin*. Therefore, if we wish to please God, we must act in accordance with His moral order so as to prevent sin from separating us from Him. As Waldo Beach and H. Richard Niebuhr put it,

> What gives the ethical teaching of Jesus its special character, is not simply the strength of the conviction that God's rule will be made wholly manifest; it is even more his certainty that the God who rules nature and history is holy love. God, indeed, is just; he judges every man by his own standards: "With the judgment you pronounce you will be judged, and the measure you give will be the measure you get" (Matt. 7:2). He is just in that he makes up the unfair inequalities between men, granting to the poor, the meek, the hungry, the mourners what they have lacked (Matt. 5:3-11). His justice is the holy justice of one who demands complete, inner integrity (Matt. 5:17-6:6). But what the just God demands is what he gives before making any demands: love, mercy, forgiveness, kindness.[15]

Justice, holiness, love, faith, hope, mercy, forgiveness, kindness, and truth are all characteristics of the moral order because all are characteristics of the nature of God.

Notes and Asides

Christians are assured of these truths about God's nature and judgment as a result of special revelation. Whereas general revelation has informed all of mankind of the existence of a moral order, special revelation—the Bible—reveals specifics regarding such an order. "The Hebrew-Christian ethic is transcendently revealed," writes Henry. "Its source is a special Divine disclosure to man. In contrast with the ethics of human insight and speculative genius, Christian ethics is the ethic of revealed religion. In the preface to the Ten Commandments stands a dramatic and momentous phrase that is characteristic of revelational ethics: 'And God spake all these words' (Exodus 20:1). From this source it gains an eternal and absolute quality."[16] Christian ethics, in the final analysis, relies on God and His Word for the full explanation of the moral order.

The Christian Response to Secular Ethics

When one accepts the idea that there is a true moral order grounded on an absolute foundation—the nature of God—all other ethical codes show themselves to be mere imitations. Henry believes that Biblical ethics shows secular ethics to be less than trustworthy in its interpretation of the moral scene. "Secular ethics is not an exposition of general revelation; it reflects the distortion that is the result of human sin."[17] As a result of the Fall, mankind has an imperfect and even twisted understanding of the moral order and the supernatural. He sees through a glass darkly. This faulty knowledge is sometimes reflected in man's desire to create his own ethical systems. Although man has some knowledge of ethics thanks to general revelation, his understanding is clouded by his fallen nature. Rousas J. Rushdoony says that man wants and needs a world of blessings and prohibitions. "Everything in his nature, because it is God-created, demands a world of consequence and causality. However, because man has fallen and is in rebellion against God, he wants those curses and blessings to be meted out on his terms, in relationship to his demands and his estimate of justice."[18]

Secular ethics represents an effort by man to become God. Today, children are encouraged to take part in this effort through "values clarification"—a program that teaches that there are no moral absolutes and each child is his or her own standard of right and wrong. Instead of teaching such moral absolutes as Honor your parents or Do not murder, our public schools presently teach "values clarification," which makes the individual the source of all ethical wisdom, even encouraging children to make decisions about which lives are worth sustaining and which lives should be terminated for the good of the community.[19]

It is important for the Christian to be able to recognize secular ideas

Notes and Asides

regarding ethics and the flaws inherent in these ideas. For the Christian, morality is a lifestyle for glorifying God, and it is crucial for man's moral health to stay away from the hazy thinking that creates less-than-absolute moral values. The so-called "new morality" is nothing but an excuse to do as one pleases under the banner of morality. Mankind should have learned from its history that the consequences of such a morality is death. Instead, thousands today are dying as a direct consequence of their immoral behavior.

One interesting problem faced by "secular" ethical codes is their inability to postulate anything really new. "New moralities can only be contractions or expansions of something already given," says Lewis. "And all the specifically modern attempts at new moralities are contractions. They proceed by retaining some traditional precepts [thou shalt not murder] and rejecting others [thou shalt not commit adultery]: but the only real authority behind those which they retain is the very same authority which they flout in rejecting others."[20]

Therefore, secular moralities fall back on believing men's ideas about morality to be enough for an ethical code. This leaves man without a standard for judging actions with regard to his morality. Francis A. Schaeffer, author of *A Christian Manifesto*, insisted that there must be an absolute if there is to be a moral order and real values. "If there is no absolute beyond man's ideas, then there is no final appeal to judge between individuals and groups whose moral judgments conflict. We are merely left with conflicting opinions."[21]

This is the Achilles' heal of ethical relativism—it leaves mankind with no standards, only conflicting opinions or subjective value judgments that translate into no morality. This ethical vacuum created by relativism allows leaders to misuse their power without having to answer to a specific moral code. "Those who stand outside all judgments of value cannot have any ground for preferring one of their own impulses to another except the emotional strength of that impulse," wrote Lewis.

> We may legitimately hope that among the impulses which arise in minds thus emptied of all "rational" or "spiritual" motives, some will be benevolent. I am very doubtful myself whether the benevolent impulses, stripped of that preference and encouragement which the Tao [moral order] teaches us to give them and left to their merely natural strength and frequency as psychological events, will have much influence. I am very doubtful whether history shows us one example of a man who, having stepped outside traditional morality and attained power, has used that power benevolently.[22]

"He that would sing, but hath no song,/ Must speak the right, denounce the wrong."
—George MacDonald

Notes and Asides

Obviously, Christians cannot feel comfortable with an amoral government. But such an amoral government is more than unpleasant for Christians—it is a threat to their whole way of life. Schaeffer warns, "If we as Christians do not speak out as authoritarian governments grow from within or come from outside, eventually we or our children will be the enemy of society and the state. No truly authoritarian government can tolerate those who have a real absolute by which to judge its arbitrary absolutes and who speak out and act upon that absolute."[23]

There are other problems posed for Christians by relativism, as well. John Warwick Montgomery, in debating Joseph Fletcher over his brand of new morality, said,

> The insurmountable difficulty is simply this: there is no way, short of sodium pentothal, of knowing when the situationist is actually endeavoring to set forth genuine facts and true opinions, and when he is lying like a trooper. Why? Because deception is allowed on principle by the new morality, as long as the ultimate aim is love.[24]

Still another related problem is outlined by Lewis. He says you hardly can open a periodical without coming across the statement that "what our civilization needs is more 'drive,' or dynamism, or self-sacrifice, or 'creativity.' In a sort of ghastly simplicity we remove the organ and demand the function. We make men without chests [i.e., we deprive the younger generation of moral truths] and expect of them virtue and enterprise. We laugh at honour and are shocked to find traitors in our midst. We castrate and bid the geldings be fruitful."[25] The state, in this instance the U.S. Supreme Court, demands that America's public schools remove the Ten Commandments from school property and prohibits the teaching of "a supernatural God,"[26] encourages the teaching of Secular Humanist ethics under the guise of separation of church and state, shuns Christian ethics, and then is baffled by the gross immorality of the next generation.

"Morality, when vigorously alive, sees farther than intellect."

—J. A. Froude

The reason for this immorality is simple: trusting our impulses as moral truths does not work. Pitirim Sorokin argues that no law-abiding society is possible when a large number of its members are selfish nihilists preoccupied with pleasure. The reason is obvious.

> For inevitably such men and women come into conflict with one another, and are led to chronic violation of moral and legal imperatives and to endless transgression of the vital interests of each other. There results a progressive undermining of the existing legal and moral order, and a perennial war among members of the collectivity seeking a maximum share of

Notes and Asides

> material possessions and gratifications. In this struggle the established code of the society is repeatedly broken; standards of conduct are increasingly trespassed, and ultimately they lose their authority and control over individual behaviour. The society drifts closer and closer to a state of moral anarchy in which everyone regards himself as law giver and judge entitled to juggle all moral and legal standards as he pleases.[27]

For the Christian, God is the ultimate source of morality, and it is nothing short of blasphemy when we place ourselves in His role. And yet, if one does not submit his nature entirely to the moral absolutes founded in God's character, logically the only ethical authority residing over mankind is our own impulses. It is important for the Christian to understand the fallacies of secular ethics, so that he can avoid the inconsistencies of unfounded ethical ideals. All secular ethical codes are an aberration of God's code and should be recognized as such.

It is true, of course, for Christians and non-Christians alike, that their worldviews affect their ideas about morality. This difference in perspective between Christians and non-Christians is fundamentally irreconcilable, for, as Lewis says,

> where the Materialist would simply ask about a proposed action "Will it increase the happiness of the majority?", the Christian might have to say, "Even if it does increase the happiness of the majority, we can't do it. It is unjust." And all the time, one great difference would run through their whole policy. To the Materialist things like nations, classes, civilizations must be more important than individuals, because the individuals live only seventy odd years each and the group may last for centuries. But to the Christian, individuals are more important, for they live eternally; and races, civilizations and the like, are in comparison the creatures of a day.[28]

The "secular" perspective can only lead to ruin, a claim resoundingly confirmed by the history of the twentieth century. Alexander Solzhenitsyn, in his Templeton Address in 1983, said,

> More than half a century ago, while I was still a child, I recall hearing a number of older people offer the following explanation for the great disasters that had befallen Russia: "Men have forgotten God; that's why all this has happened."
>
> Since then I have spent well-nigh fifty years working on the history of our Revolution; in the process I have read hundreds of books, collected hundreds of personal testimonies, and have

Notes and Asides

already contributed eight volumes of my own toward the effort of clearing away the rubble left by that upheaval. But if I were asked today to formulate as concisely as possible the main cause of the ruinous Revolution that swallowed up some sixty million of our people, I could not put it more accurately than to repeat: "Men have forgotten God; that's why all this has happened."[29]

Modern man offers no solid basis for ethical norms, says Henry, and this path "leads to nihilism, to the loss of the worth and meaning of human existence."[30] Indeed, adopting this perspective is tantamount to rejecting God, since in the final analysis, "all human ethical systems are a willful rebellion against the Almighty God. They attempt to allow man to live a life not controlled by God and his law, but still justify himself as an ethical and moral being. In the Scriptures we have an ethical system that is perfectly balanced and that will meet all the needs of the human heart."[31]

Nihilism is the denial of the existence of any foundation for truth; thus, it is a philosophy which embraces meaninglessness.

Secular Arguments Against Christian Ethics

Some critics of Christian ethics argue that they cannot accept the Christian's view regarding morality because such views leave no room for freedom. The complaint is based on the idea that an absolute moral order presided over by an absolutely holy God dictates our actions. Given a moral order and a Judge so restrictive, how can man truly be said to have free will? This argument is best described by Lewis, when he writes about his own atheistic position before his conversion to Christianity. Lewis admitted that what mattered most of all was his deep-seated hatred of authority, his monstrous individualism, and his lawlessness.

> No word in my vocabulary expressed deeper hatred than the word Interference. Yet Christianity placed at the center what then seemed to me a transcendental Interferer. If its picture were true then no sort of "treaty with reality" could ever be possible. There was no region even in the innermost depth of one's soul (nay, there least of all) which one could surround with a barbed wire fence and guard with a notice of No Admittance. And that was what I wanted; some area, however small, of which I could say to all other beings, "This is my business and mine only."[32]

Lewis's disdain for an "Interferer" followed naturally from his belief that his life belonged to him alone—but as soon as one understands his life as a gift God has given, one recognizes that he cannot

Notes and Asides

possess it in some ultimate way that excludes God. When we recognize this and accept it, paradoxically, we are more free than we had ever been—freed, as it were, "from the awful gulf of sin." Theologian Roger R. Nicole argues that a rational agent's obedience to God is not to be viewed as renouncing free agency. He insists,

> True liberty and conformity to law, far from being mutually exclusive, are in fact complementary: it is only when man walks along the path delineated by God's commandments that he can realize true fulfillment of his personality. The law is not a tyrannical imposition, confining man and cramping his opportunity to enjoy life: on the contrary, it is God's gracious revelation of the structure of the spiritual universe, which teaches man to move along the cosmos' lines of force rather than at cross-purpose with his true destiny.[33]

This is the Christian's answer to the secular man's complaint about the lack of freedom in Christianity: "ye shall know the truth, and the truth shall make you free" (John 8:32).

Another objection raised against the Christian ethic is the apparent discrepancy between the moral commands of the Old Testament and those of the New Testament. This is often referred to as the dichotomy of ethics inherent in the Bible. Critics claim that the Old Testament portrays a vengeful, holy God and the New Testament describes a loving God. They argue, for example, that the God of the New Testament would never have called for the destruction of the Canaanites, as did the God of the Old Testament. Frank E. Gaebelein, in *Baker's Dictionary of Christian Ethics*, answers that there are many passages in the Old Testament that speak of God's love for His people, and His mercy is one of the great concepts of Hebrew religion.

> To be sure, the OT places great emphasis on God's justice and the judgment aspect of his dealings with men. And it was Jesus who revealed most fully the Fatherhood of God and who made known in his teachings and, supremely, in his redemptive work the Father's love for humanity. Yet no OT leader or prophet spoke stronger words of judgment than Jesus in his excoriation of the scribes and Pharisees (cf. Matt. 23) or taught more specifically about the drastic nature of eternal punishment than he did (e.g., "the unquenchable fire . . . where their worm does not die, and the fire is not quenched," Mark 9:43-48), and also the solemn close of the parable of the rich man and Lazarus, in which "a great chasm has been fixed" between those in paradise and the lost (Luke 16:19-31). The doctrine of God is progres-

Notes and Asides

sively revealed in Scripture. But progressive revelation must never be confused with discrepant views of God.[34]

Old Testament morality and New Testament ethics can be viewed as complementary, clarifying and deepening the significance of one specific ethical code. I. Howard Marshall says, "The basis of ethics thus becomes the two-fold command upheld and restated by Christ, to love God and to love one's neighbor (Mark 12:30f; John 13:34). These two commandments, however, represent the summing up of the OT law (Rom. 13:8-10) at a deeper level (Matt. 5:21-48), and hence they can and must be broken down into individual commandments: "this is love, that we follow his commandments" (II John 6)."[35]

Christian Ethics and Special Revelation

Christians emphatically embrace the concept of moral absolutes and believe they should be taught to our children. But what specific absolutes make up the moral order professed in Christian ethics? What ought we to do? How should we live?

Absolutes are revealed to man in the Bible. While it is impossible for every situation requiring moral decisions to be contained in the Bible, the Christian is given enough specific values and guidelines to have a sense of what is right and what is wrong in all situations. The most obvious absolutes, of course, are the Ten Commandments—the Decalogue.

Henry says, "The New Testament as a whole, as do Moses and the prophets and Jesus Christ, views the Decalogue as being a peak in ethical revelation. Jesus is not alone in his insistence that the Torah has a permanent duration. It has, in fact, a basis firmer than the stability of the space-time universe (Mt. 5:18)."[36]

Likewise, Dave Breese notes that God has revealed "the rules by which man is required to live if civilization is to continue."[37] And Henry M. Morris comments: "The Ten Commandments have long been regarded as the basis of civil morality in this country, as well as the minimum measure of Christian righteousness. Honesty, truthfulness, industry, unselfishness, respect for others, and willingness to forgive others are all implied in these commandments, as is integrity towards God and family."[38] Morris points out that these virtues have been largely replaced in modern society. If lying or stealing brings personal gain, then no outmoded Biblical ethic is going to stand in the way. Even murder has been legalized in the case of the unborn. Concludes Morris, "Though most scholars recognize that biblical laws, especially the Ten Commandments, originally formed the basis of our common-law

THE TEN COMMANDMENTS

(Exodus 20:1-17)

And God spoke all these words: I am the Lord your God, who brought you out of Egypt, out of the land of slavery. You shall have no other gods before me. You shall not make for yourself an idol in the form of anything in heaven above or on the earth beneath or in the waters below. You shall not bow down to them or worship them; for I, the Lord your God, am a jealous God, punishing the children for the sin of the fathers to the third and fourth generation of those who hate me, but showing love to thousands who love me and keep my commandments. You shall not misuse the name of the Lord your God, for the Lord will not hold anyone guiltless who misuses his name. Remember the Sabbath day by keeping it holy. Six days you shall labor and do all your work, but the seventh day is a Sabbath to the Lord your God. On it you shall not do any work, neither you, nor your son or daughter, nor your manservant or maidservant, nor your animals, nor the alien within your gates. For in six days the Lord made the heavens and the earth, the sea, and all that is in them, but he rested on the seventh day. Therefore the Lord blessed the Sabbath day and made it holy. Honor your father and your mother, so that you may live long in the land the Lord your God is giving you. You shall not murder. You shall not commit adultery. You shall not steal. You shall not give false testimony against your neighbor. You shall not covet your neighbor's house. You shall not covet your neighbor's wife, or his manservant or maidservant, his ox or donkey, or anything that belongs to your neighbor.

system and even our federal constitution, the courts have now banned mention of the Ten Commandments in our schools and indirectly removed their controlling guidelines from our lives."[39]

Since the moral order resides in God's character and God intended for all men to be aware of this moral order, it should come as no surprise to learn that God revealed the Decalogue to man before Moses. "All Ten Commandments," says Walter Kaiser, "had been part of the Law of

Notes and Asides

God previously written on hearts instead of stone, for all ten appear, in one way or another, in Genesis."[40] What Moses received was not a new moral order. Cain knew long before Moses that murdering his brother was wrong.

The Decalogue, on which the Christian ethic is built, is the framework resting on the absolute foundation of God and His holiness. "The Ten Commandments," says Rushdoony, "are not therefore laws among laws, but are the basic laws."[41] The Christian believes these absolutes and their various Biblical examples to be more than enough. However, critics complain that the morality taught in the Bible is too general to be of any use in daily life. Henry answers this charge fittingly:

> [W]ho cannot sense at once what a morally refreshing world this would be, were human relations restored to the closely knit affection of children and parents; were there no murder of human beings, with the accompanying grief and hardship in the lives of men; were the world of marital affairs immune from the triangle of illicit love, and homes unbroken by divorce and strained affections; were the theft of goods and money an unknown phenomenon; were false witness touching another person unthinkable; were the coveting of another's things resisted with might and main; were only the living God worshipped, and never false gods and graven images; were men to labor creatively six days and give their day of freedom from work in unrestricted devotion to the claims of the spiritual world? And lest it be thought that such external conformity alone comports fully with the commandments, let the issue be posed with larger fidelity to biblical ethics. Who can but acknowledge that the imagination itself is staggered in attempting to weigh the moral force of a world in which the ethical inwardness sought by the Decalogue would be realized, and in which all men would love God with their whole being and their neighbors as themselves? Once the commandments find a hold in the lives of sinful men, and are fulfilled, not merely externally—which of itself would mark an astonishing change in human conduct—but internally, then it will be time enough for skeptics and rationalists to scoff the Decalogue.[42]

After outlining the moral order, the Bible introduces us to God Incarnate, Jesus Christ, and describes His ministry and teachings so that Christians might better understand the implications of this order. The apex of Christ's ethical teaching is encapsulated in the Sermon on the Mount, found most comprehensively in Matthew 5-7. "The Sermon remains an 'ethical directory' for Christians. It contains the character

Notes and Asides

and conduct which Jesus commends to his followers, the demand which the nature and will of God make upon men, the fundamental law of the Kingdom, and the ideal and perfect standard. It is the ultimate formula of ethics for which ideal human nature was fashioned by creation and is destined in eternity. Fallen nature is justified in Christ in conformity to it, and redeemed nature approximates it by the power of the indwelling Spirit of God."[43]

For the Christian, the ethical exhortations in the Sermon on the Mount, coupled with the ethical pronouncements of the Old Testament, create a very specific ethical order. And, as if this code were not enough, Christians have the perfect role model to dictate the proper moral course of action: Jesus Christ, as revealed to mankind in the Bible. W. E. H. Lecky, who never claimed to be a Christian, admitted,

> The character of Jesus has not only been the highest pattern of virtue, but the strongest incentive to its practice, and has exerted so deep an influence, that it may be truly said, that the simple record of three short years of active life has done more to regenerate and to soften mankind, than all the disquisitions of philosophers and than all the exhortation of moralists.[44]

In fact, the call to follow Jesus is the simplest summation of Christian ethics, and at the same time, the most difficult thing for man to do. Dietrich Bonhoeffer, a Christian martyr, notes, "On two separate occasions Peter received the call, 'Follow me.' It was the first and last word Jesus spoke to his disciple (Mark 1:17, John 21:22)."[45] Christ really asks but one thing of Christians: follow Me!

The Bible gives us a further delineation of the moral order in the writings of the Apostle Paul:

> For by the grace given to me I bid every one among you not to think of himself more highly than he ought to think, but to think with sober judgment, each according to the measure of faith which God has assigned him. For as in one body we have many members, and all the members do not have the same function, so we, though many, are one body in Christ, and individually members one of another. . . .
>
> Let love be genuine; hate what is evil, hold fast to what is good; love one another with brotherly affection; outdo one another in showing honor. Never flag in zeal, be aglow with the Spirit, serve the Lord. Rejoice in your hope, be patient in tribulation, be constant in prayer. Contribute to the needs of the saints, practice hospitality.
>
> Bless those who persecute you; bless and do not curse them.

"The character of Jesus has not only been the highest pattern of virtue, but the strongest incentive to its practice . . . "
—W. E. H. Lecky

Notes
and
Asides

> Rejoice with those who rejoice, weep with those who weep. Live in harmony with one another; do not be haughty, but associate with the lowly; never be conceited. Repay no one evil for evil, but take thought for what is noble in the sight of all. If possible, so far as it depends upon you, live peaceably with all. Beloved, never avenge yourselves, but leave it to the wrath of God; for it is written, "Vengeance is mine, I will repay, says the Lord." No, "if your enemy is hungry, feed him; if he is thirsty, give him drink; for by so doing you will heap burning coals upon his head." Do not be overcome by evil, but overcome evil with good. . . .
>
> Owe no one anything, except to love one another; for he who loves his neighbor has fulfilled the law. The commandments, "You shall not commit adultery, You shall not kill, You shall not steal, You shall not covet," and any other commandment, are summed up in this sentence, "You shall love your neighbor as yourself." Love does no wrong to a neighbor; therefore love is the fulfilling of the law (Romans 12:3-5; 9-21; 13:8-10).

As a result of the special revelation given to us in the Bible, man can never excuse himself for doing wrong because he has not been told what is morally correct. Throughout the Bible, the question of ethics is specifically addressed; in truth, it cannot be separated from the Christian faith.

Responsibility in Christian Ethics

Christians are called to "love the Lord your God with all your heart and with all your soul and with all your strength and with all your mind, and love your neighbor as yourself" (Luke 10:27). This command, like all of the other commands in the Bible, implies that Christians have responsibilities. Among these responsibilities is the duty for the Christian to respect himself. Norman L. Geisler writes,

> [M]en ought to love themselves (1) for their own sakes as God's creatures, (2) for the sake of others as responsible creatures, (3) for God's sake and because God loves them and has provided redemption for them through Christ. And when there is a conflict between any of these levels of love, then the latter transcend the former. They must be arranged in an ascending order of priority. For many persons (viz., others) are of more

Notes and Asides

value than one person (viz., oneself) and the infinite Person (God) is of more value than finite persons (men).[46]

The call to self-love is not stressed in the Bible, however, because self-love follows naturally from understanding that one is a part of God's creative order. What is stressed is the responsibility of the Christian to love his neighbor as himself. "The epistles of the New Testament," Geisler says, "abound with exhortations to Christians to care for one another and for others. Paul wrote, 'Let each of you look not only to his own interests, but also the interest of others' (Phil. 2:4). Again, 'Bear one another's burdens, and so fulfill the law of Christ' (Gal. 6:2; cf. verse 10). The first epistle of John is very explicit about the Christian's responsibility to love others (cf. 3:17-18), as is James (cf. 1:27). In brief, man is morally responsible for other men. He is his brother's keeper."[47]

"[H]usbands ought to love their wives as their own bodies. He who loves his wife loves himself. After all, no one ever hated his own body, but he feeds and cares for it, just as Christ does the church."

—St. Paul

This responsibility to love others calls for an attitude not merely compassionate but servantlike. If we love God, we demonstrate it through serving our fellow man. It is our duty. "The Apostle John," says Henry, "appeals to the explicit teaching of the Redeemer to show the inseparable connection between love of God and love of neighbor: 'If a man say, I love God, and hateth his brother, he is a liar: for he that loveth not his brother whom he hath seen, how can he love God whom he hath not seen? And this commandment have we from him, that he who loveth God love his brother also' (1 John 4:20f.). 'God is love, and he that dwelleth in love dwelleth in God, and God in him' (4:16). The love of God is the service of man in love."[48]

This duty toward our fellow man requires more than serving his spiritual needs. "What sometimes escapes Christians," says Geisler, "is the fact that the responsibility to love other persons extends to the whole person. That is, man is more than a soul destined for another world; he is also a body living in this world. And as a resident of this time-space continuum man has physical and social needs which cannot be isolated from spiritual needs. Hence, in order to love man as he is—the whole man—one must exercise a concern about his social needs as well as his spiritual needs."[49] He continues,

> Briefly stated, the Bible teaches that it is morally wrong to exploit the poor and morally right to help the poor. Whether their need is food, clothes, or shelter, the believer is morally obliged to help fill it. In fact, what one does for the poor he is doing to Christ. "Truly, I say to you, as you did it to one of the least of these my brethren, you did it to me," for "I was hungry and you gave me food, I was thirsty and you gave me drink, I

Notes
and
Asides

Recommended Reading for Advanced Study

Carl F. H. Henry, *Christian Personal Ethics* (Grand Rapids, MI: Eerdmans, 1957).

C. S. Lewis, *The Abolition of Man* (New York: Macmillan, 1973).

Francis A. Schaeffer, *How Should We Then Live?* (Old Tappan, NJ: Fleming H. Revell, 1976).

Dietrich Bonhoeffer, *The Cost of Discipleship* (New York: Macmillan, 1963).

Boris Sokoloff, *The Permissive Society* (New Rochelle, NY: Arlington House, 1977).

Carl F. H. Henry, *The Christian Mindset in a Secular Society* (Portland, OR: Multnomah, 1984).

was a stranger and you welcomed me, I was naked and you clothed me . . ." (Matt. 25:40, 35-36).[50]

The Christian cannot claim that his faith in God and resulting perspective on life and ethics exempt him from concerns about worldly matters. Just the opposite is true. Because a person is a Christian, he must be concerned with working to achieve God's will for the world. God commands it. Bonhoeffer says,

> [S]ince the beginnings of Christian ethics after the times of the New Testament the main underlying conception in ethical thought, and the one which consciously or unconsciously has determined its whole course, has been the conception of a

Notes and Asides

> juxtaposition and conflict of two spheres, the one divine, holy, supernatural, and Christian, and the other worldly, profane, natural, and un-Christian. . . . It may be difficult to break the spell of this thinking in terms of two spheres, but it is nevertheless quite certain that it is in profound contradiction to the thought of the Bible and to the thought of the Reformation, and that consequently it aims wide of reality. There are not two realities, but only one reality, and that is the reality of God, which has become manifest in Christ in the reality of the world. . . . There are not two spheres but only the one sphere of the realization of Christ, in which the reality of God and the reality of the world are united.[51]

It is our duty as Christians to work always to glorify God in our world. Schaeffer insists that "as Christians we are not only to know the right world view, the world view that tells us the truth of what is, but consciously to act upon that world view so as to influence society in all its parts and facets across the whole spectrum of life, as much as we can to the extent of our individual and collective ability."[52]

In examining Christians' various obligations, including self-love, neighbor-love, and a consistent worldview, one finds a common basis for each duty: the Christian's love for God. "The moral end, or highest good, is the glory of God," writes William Young. "In declaring by word and deed the perfections, especially the moral perfections of the most High, man finds true happiness."[53] Our duty toward God is inextricably tied up with our other duties as Christians; it is accurate to state, as Henry does, "Hebrew-Christian ethics unequivocally defines moral obligation as man's duty to God."[54] This is the heart and soul of the Christian ethic.

"Man is a moral creature, created in God's image, and we have certain absolute moral obligations toward all men."
—Norman Geisler

The Inevitability of Sin

The Bible does not concern itself only with outlining the moral order, however. It also speaks of a time when God will judge man for his character and conduct. Revelation 22:11-15 warns that at that time many will be left outside the city of God: the unjust, the morally filthy, sorcerers, whoremongers, liars, murderers, etc. This has, of course, staggering implications for humanity. "Christianity declares that God is more than the ground and goal of the moral order," explains Henry.

> Unequivocally it lays stress on the reality of God's judgment of history. It affirms, that is, the stark fact of moral disorder and rebellion: "the whole world lieth in wickedness" (1 John 5:19).

Notes and Asides

> By emphasis on the fact of sin and the shattered moral law of God, on the dread significance of death, on the wiles of Satan and the hosts of darkness, Christian ethics sheds light on the treacherous realities of moral decision.[55]

The reality, of course, is that we "all have sinned and fall short of the glory of God" (Romans 3:23). This is another unique aspect of the Christian ethical system. "When a person makes up his own ethical code," D. James Kennedy says, "he always makes up an ethical system which he thinks he has kept. In the law of God, we find a law which smashes our self-righteousness, eliminates all trust in our own goodness, and convinces us that we are sinners. The law of God leaves us with our hands over our mouths and our faces in the dust. We are humbled before God and convinced that we are guilty transgressors of his law."[56]

This conviction of guilt is crucial for a Christian to understand the incredible sacrifice God made when He sent His Son to die for us. Lewis says, "Moral Law, and a Power behind the law, and that you have broken that law and put yourself wrong with that Power—it is after all this, and not a moment sooner, that Christianity begins to talk. When you know you are sick, you will listen to the doctor. When you have realised that your position is nearly desperate you will begin to understand what the Christians are talking about."[57] The Christian ethical code calls for perfection, and no man other than Christ has ever achieved that. Thus, it is the ethical code itself that points man first to his own sinful nature and then to the realization that the only One who can save him is the Man who has not stepped outside the moral code, Jesus Christ. The absolute moral code shows us our absolute dependence on Him. Put more simply, "The law is given to convince us that we fail to keep it."[58] And on realization of this truth, we are driven for salvation to the One who has not failed.

The real Christian cannot, however, simply rely on Christ to save him, and then continue in his sinful ways. Rather, once the Christian understands the ultimate sacrifice God made for him, he cannot help but respond with a grateful desire to please God by adhering to His moral order. This does not mean it becomes *easier* for a Christian to do what is morally right—it simply means that he is willing to strive to do God's will. This willingness to choose the morally right action is crucial for the Christian truly concerned with pleasing God. As Lewis says, "There is nowhere this side of heaven where one can safely lay the reins on the horse's neck. It will never be lawful simply to 'be ourselves' until 'ourselves' have become sons of God. It is all there in the hymn—'Christian, seek not yet repose.'"[59] Christian ethics requires a firm commitment to and an unflagging zeal for what is right and good in the

Notes and Asides

Lord's sight. As Paul said, Christians must "abhor that which is evil; cleave to that which is good" (Romans 12:9).

Conclusion

The Christian ethical system is both like and unlike any other system ever postulated. Every ethical system contains some grain of the truth found in the Christian code, but no other system can claim to be the whole truth, handed down as an absolute from God to man. As such, certain benefits are inherent to Biblical morality. The most obvious, of course, is its timelessness.

Even today, Christian ethics is the solution for a troubled world. Henry states, "Biblical ethics boldly and clearly addresses the abyss of immorality engulfing our technological civilization; it speaks to greed for money, to lust for sexual pleasure, to crime, murder, terrorism, arson, and other hallmarks of our warped society. It confronts all of modern life—its perverted sense of the good, its banalities and superficialities, its mythology of technocratic utopianism, its triumphal evils."[60]

"[A]bhor that which is evil; cleave to that which is good."
—St. Paul

Christian ethics also grants man more freedom than any other ethical code. "Either we are rational spirit obliged for ever to obey the absolute values of the Tao [the moral order]," says Lewis, "or else we are mere nature to be kneaded and cut into new shapes for the pleasures of masters who must, by hypothesis, have no motive but their own 'natural' impulses. Only the Tao provides a common human law of action which can over-arch rulers and ruled alike. A dogmatic belief in objective value is necessary to the very idea of a rule which is not tyranny or an obedience which is not slavery."[61] Mankind is either a slave to a tyrant, a slave to his own sinful impulses, or freed in the person of Jesus Christ.

A third aspect of Christian ethics that makes it still more attractive is its guarantee of ethical equality, by definition, for all men. "That Man is made in the image of God gives many important answers intellectually, but it also has had vast practical results, both in the Reformation days and in our own age," says Schaeffer. "For example, in the time of the Reformation it meant that all the vocations of life came to have dignity. The vocation of honest merchant or housewife had as much dignity as king. This was strengthened further by the emphasis on the biblical teaching of the priesthood of all believers—that is, that all Christians are priests. Thus, in a very real sense, all people are equal as persons."[62] Many other ethical codes claim to be striving to achieve such equality, but only Christianity makes men and women equal due to their very heritage as God's creations. Further, under the Christian

Notes and Asides

moral order there is an equality of responsibilities. It is wrong for the rich to steal, but it is equally wrong for the poor to steal. It is wrong for the ruler to lie, and it is also wrong for the ruled to lie.

One final strength of Christian morality is its powerful capacity for creating good results. When the Christian ethical code is put into practice, it has a regenerative power for both the individual and the society. This happens due to the very nature of Christian ethics. "The biblical message is truth and it demands a commitment to truth," writes Schaeffer. "It means that everything is not the result of the impersonal plus time plus chance, but that there is an infinite-personal God who is the Creator of the universe, the space-time continuum. We should not forget that this was what the founders of modern science built upon. It means the acceptance of Christ as Savior and Lord, and it means living under God's revelation. Here there are morals, values, and meaning, including meaning for people, which are not just a result of statistical averages. This is neither a utilitarianism, nor a leap away from reason; it is the truth that gives a unity to all of knowledge and all of life. This second alternative means that individuals come to the place where they have this base, and they influence the consensus. Such Christians do not need to be a majority in order for this influence on society to occur."[63]

No, Christians do not need to be a majority for this to occur. But they do need to be dedicated mind, body, and soul to serving God. This dedication has become far too rare in present-day society. "Who stands fast?" asks Bonhoeffer. "Only the man whose final standard is not his reason, his principles, his conscience, his freedom, or his virtue, but who is ready to sacrifice all this when he is called to obedient and responsible action in faith and in exclusive allegiance to God—the responsible man, who tries to make his whole life an answer to the question and call of God. Where are these responsible people?"[64]

"Be sure you are right, then go ahead."
—Davy Crockett

Where are they? Wherever Christians are willing to treat God's moral order with the same respect they show His physical order; wherever God is loved with an individual's whole body, soul, spirit, mind, and strength. They may be found in the halls of government, standing firm against tyranny and slavery, or in the mission field, sacrificing everything for the sake of the gospel. More often, these people are quite ordinary Christian men and women living extraordinary lives, showing the world that Christ can be believed and His standards lived. It is our Christian duty to join the ranks of these morally responsible people.

[1]Carl F. H. Henry, *Christian Personal Ethics* (Grand Rapids, MI: Eerdmans, 1957), p. 22.
[2]Cited in Charles Colson, *Against the Night* (Ann Arbor, MI: Servant Publications, 1989), p. 149.
[3]Boris Sokoloff, *The Permissive Society* (New Rochelle, NY: Arlington House, 1971) pp. 13-14.
[4]Colson, *Against the Night*, p. 47.
[5]John Warwick Montgomery, *Human Rights and Human Dignity* (Dallas, TX: Probe Books, 1986), p. 113.
[6]C. S. Lewis, *The Abolition of Man* (New York: Macmillan, 1973), p. 56-7.
[7]Calvin D. Linton, "Sin," in *Baker's Dictionary of Christian Ethics*, ed. Carl F. H. Henry (Grand Rapids, MI: Baker, 1973), p. 620.
[8]A. I. Melden, *Ethical Theories* (Englewood Cliffs, NJ: Prentice-Hall, 1959), p. 223.
[9]D. Elton Trueblood, *Philosophy of Religion* (Grand Rapids, MI: Baker, 1975) p. 111.
[10]Carl F. H. Henry, *God, Revelation and Authority*, six volumes (Waco, TX: Word, 1976), vol. 1, p. 149.
[11]Melden, *Ethical Theories*, p. 229.
[12]Dave Breese, *Seven Men Who Rule the World from the Grave* (Chicago, IL: Moody Press, 1990), p. 114.
[13]Ibid.
[14]C. S. Lewis, *Mere Christianity* (London: Geoffrey Bles, 1953), p. 16.
[15]Waldo Beach and H. Richard Niebuhr, *Christian Ethics* (New York: Ronald Press, 1955), p. 33.
[16]Henry, *Christian Personal Ethics*, p. 188.
[17]Ibid., p. 161.
[18]Rousas J. Rushdoony, *The Institutes of Biblical Law* (Nutley, NJ: Craig Press, 1973), p. 663.
[19]See Phyllis Schlafly, ed., *Child Abuse in the Classroom* (Alton, IL: Marquette Press, 1985), and James C. Dobson and Gary Bauer, *Children at Risk* (Dallas: Word, 1990).
[20]C. S. Lewis, *Christian Reflections* (Grand Rapids, MI: Eerdmans, 1967), p. 53.
[21]Francis A. Schaeffer, *How Should We Then Live?* (Old Tappan, NJ: Fleming H. Revell, 1976), p. 145.
[22]Lewis, *The Abolition of Man*, p. 78.
[23]Schaeffer, *How Should We Then Live?* p. 256.
[24]Joseph Fletcher and John Warwick Montgomery, *Situation Ethics: Is It Sometimes Right to Do Wrong?* (Minneapolis: Bethany Fellowship, 1972), p. 31.
[25]Lewis, *The Abolition of Man*, p. 35.
[26]Henry M. Morris, *The Long War Against God* (Grand Rapids, MI: Baker, 1990), p. 51, "Speaking for the 7-2 majority, Justice Brennan said: 'The preeminent purpose for the Louisiana legislature was clearly to advance the religious viewpoint that a supernatural being created humankind.' The law was thrown out primarily on this basis—that belief in a supernatural God is nothing but a 'religious viewpoint' and, as such, is to be excluded from our public institutions. To all intents and purposes, the Court's decision officially designates the United States of America to be, like Communist Russia, an atheistic nation, at least as far as the education of the young in public schools is concerned. Evolution is now the law of the land."
[27]Pitirim Sorokin, *The American Sexual Revolution* (New York: Porter Sargent, 1956), pp. 88-9.
[28]C. S. Lewis, *God in the Dock* (Grand Rapids, MI: Eerdmans, 1972), pp. 109-10.
[29]Alexander Solzhenitsyn, "Men Have Forgotten God," The Templeton Address, 1983, in *National Review*, July 22, 1983, p. 873.
[30]Carl F. H. Henry, "Preface," in *Baker's Dictionary of Christian Ethics*, ed. Henry, p. v.
[31]D. James Kennedy, *Why I Believe* (Waco, TX: Word Books, 1980), p. 89.
[32]C. S. Lewis, *Surprised By Joy* (New York: Harcourt, Brace and World, 1955), p. 172.
[33]Roger R. Nicole, "Authority," in *Baker's Dictionary of Christian Ethics*, ed. Henry, p. 47.
[34]Frank E. Gaebelein, "Bible," in *Baker's Dictionary of Christian Ethics*, ed. Henry, p. 60.
[35]I. Howard Marshall, "Personal Ethics," in *Baker's Dictionary of Christian Ethics*, ed. Henry, p. 505.
[36]Henry, *Christian Personal Ethics*, p. 329.
[37]Breese, *Seven Men Who Rule the World from the Grave*, p. 115.
[38]Morris, *The Long War Against God*, p. 137.
[39]Ibid.
[40]Walter C. Kaiser, Jr., *Toward Old Testament Ethics* (Grand Rapids, MI: Zondervan, 1983), p. 82.
[41]Rushdoony, *The Institutes of Biblical Law*, pp. 10-11.
[42]Henry, *Christian Personal Ethics*, pp. 336-7.

[43]Ibid., p. 22.
[44]W. E. H. Lecky, *History of European Morals (from Augustus to Charlemagne)*, two volumes (New York: George Braziller, 1955), vol. 2, pp. 8-9.
[45]Dietrich Bonhoeffer, *The Cost of Discipleship* (New York: Macmillan, 1963), p. 48.
[46]Norman L. Geisler, *Ethics: Alternatives and Issues* (Grand Rapids, MI: Zondervan, 1979), p. 156.
[47]Ibid., p. 179.
[48]Henry, *Christian Personal Ethics*, pp. 221-2.
[49]Geisler, *Ethics: Alternatives and Issues*, p. 179.
[50]Ibid., p. 184.
[51]Cited in James H. Burtness, "Dietrich Bonhoeffer," in *Baker's Dictionary of Christian Ethics*, ed. Henry, p. 67.
[52]Schaeffer, *How Should We Then Live?* p. 256.
[53]William Young, "Moral Philosophy," in *Baker's Dictionary of Christian Ethics*, ed. Henry, pp. 432-3.
[54]Henry, *Christian Personal Ethics*, p. 209.
[55]Ibid., p. 172.
[56]Kennedy, *Why I Believe*, p. 91.
[57]Lewis, *Mere Christianity*, pp. 24-5.
[58]Kennedy, *Why I Believe*, p. 90.
[59]Lewis, *God in the Dock*, p. 286.
[60]Carl F. H. Henry, *The Christian Mindset in a Secular Society* (Portland, OR: Multnomah Press, 1984), p. 37.
[61]Lewis, *The Abolition of Man*, pp. 84-5.
[62]Schaeffer, *How Should We Then Live?* p. 87.
[63]Ibid., p. 252.
[64]Joan Winmill Brown, ed., *The Martyred Christian* (New York: Macmillan, 1985), p. 157.

SECTION FOUR

BIOLOGY

BIOLOGY [Greek *bios* (life) + *logos* (word)]: The study of living organisms.

	SECULAR HUMANISM	MARXISM/ LENINISM	BIBLICAL CHRISTIANITY
SOURCE	*HUMANIST MANIFESTO I & II*	*WRITINGS OF MARX & LENIN*	*BIBLE*
THEOLOGY	ATHEISM	ATHEISM	THEISM
PHILOSOPHY	NATURALISM	DIALECTICAL MATERIALISM	SUPERNATURALISM
ETHICS	ETHICAL RELATIVISM	PROLETARIAT MORALITY	ETHICAL ABSOLUTES
BIOLOGY	DARWINIAN EVOLUTION	DARWINIAN/ PUNCTUATED EVOLUTION	SPECIAL CREATIONISM
PSYCHOLOGY	MONISTIC SELF-ACTUALIZATION	MONISTIC PAVLOVIAN BEHAVIORISM	DUALISM
SOCIOLOGY	NON-TRADITIONAL WORLD STATE ETHICAL SOCIETY	ABOLITION OF HOME, CHURCH AND STATE	HOME CHURCH STATE
LAW	POSITIVE LAW	POSITIVE LAW	BIBLICAL/NATURAL LAW
POLITICS	WORLD GOVERNMENT (GLOBALISM)	NEW WORLD ORDER	JUSTICE FREEDOM ORDER
ECONOMICS	SOCIALISM	SOCIALISM/ COMMUNISM	STEWARDSHIP OF PROPERTY
HISTORY	HISTORICAL EVOLUTION	HISTORICAL MATERIALISM	HISTORICAL RESURRECTION

CHAPTER

12

SECULAR HUMANIST BIOLOGY

"Evolution is a fact amply demonstrated by the fossil record and by contemporary molecular biology. Natural selection is a successful theory devised to explain the fact of evolution."[1]

—Carl Sagan

"Man is the result of a purposeless and natural process that did not have him in mind. He was not planned. He is a state of matter, a form of life, a sort of animal, and a species of the Order Primates, akin nearly or remotely to all of life and indeed to all that is material."[2]

—George Gaylord Simpson

SUMMARY

Without the theory of evolution there is no Secular Humanism. Humanists believe: (a) that 3 to 4 billion years ago the first speck of life came into existence by a series of accidental combinations of chemicals and energy (probably lightning); (b) that this first speck of life survived and reproduced itself; (c) that this reproduction continued and, by continuing, improved this life until ultimately a cell was produced. Some evolutionists believe the time required to move from the first life, spontaneously generated, to the first cell is equal to the amount of time required to progress from the first cell to man. From the first cell and by natural processes alone—including natural selection, mutations, etc.—cells evolved into other cells, simple plants (seaweeds and algae) and animals, more complex forms, and then fish. Fish slowly evolved into amphibians, amphibians into reptiles, reptiles into mammals, and then mammals into tree shrews and primates—monkeys, apes, and man. Charles Darwin in *Origin of Species* insisted that natural selection "acts solely by accumulating slight, successive, favourable variations, it can produce no great or sudden modifications; it can act only by short and slow steps."[3] Most Humanists implicitly trust Darwin's explanation, although some believe Stephen Jay Gould's more radical theory of punctuated equilibrium, an approach that portrays the evolutionary process as long periods of stasis (no change) punctuated by short spurts of rapid change.

Humanists further believe that science has proven the theory of evolution to such an extent that it is no longer a theory but a scientific fact. They also regard spontaneous generation (the view that life originated from non-living matter) as scientific, despite Francesco Redi's and Louis Pasteur's findings to the contrary. Others have referred to spontaneous generation as a "philosophical necessity," since Humanism has an atheistic theology and therefore God cannot be part of the equation of life.

The Secular Humanist worldview, in this respect, is consistent: God does not exist, only nature exists, life arose from dead or inorganic nature by natural, random means and evolved through a series of random processes over billions of years until man finally emerged to become nature's most formidable animal. Humanists argue that such a scenario is scientific fact and therefore should be the only view allowed in public school science classrooms. They claim that all other interpretations are "religious" and teaching them in public schools would violate the doctrine of separation of church and state. At the same time, they interpret the separation doctrine in such a way as to sanction the teacing of the religion of Secular Humanism in public schools.

Notes and Asides

Introduction

Belief in evolution is as crucial to Humanism's worldview as are its atheistic theology and naturalistic philosophy. In fact, the Humanist's ideas about the origin of life can be considered a special dimension of their theology and philosophy. Without the theory of evolution, the Humanist would have to rely on God as the explanation for life, which would necessarily destroy his atheism and hence his Humanism. Therefore, every Secular Humanist embraces the theory of evolution.

The *Humanist Manifesto I* states, "Humanism believes that man is a part of nature and that he has emerged as the result of a continuous process."[4] This belief is echoed in the *Humanist Manifesto II*, which claims that "science affirms that the human species is an emergence from natural evolutionary forces."[5]

"What distinguishes [John] Dewey," says Will Durant, "is the undisguised completeness with which he accepts the evolution theory."[6] Durant says that for Dewey mind and body evolved via the struggle for existence "from lower forms." In 1910, Dewey wrote *The Influence of Darwin on Philosophy*, in which he applauds the logic of modern man, "the logic of which Darwin's *Origin of Species* is the latest scientific achievement."[7]

Humanists rely on the theory of evolution with a tenacity bordering on religious zeal. Kurt E. M. Baier writes,

> Biology teaches us that the species man was not specially created but is merely, in a long chain of evolutionary changes of forms of life, the last link, made in the likeness not of God but of nothing so much as an ape.[8]

Roy Wood Sellars says simply, "Man is becoming aware that he is living on a little planet on which he has evolved step by step. . . ."[9]

Biologist Julian Huxley devoted most of his life to integrating evolution and the Humanist worldview. He states,

> I use the word "Humanist" to mean someone who believes that man is just as much a natural phenomenon as an animal or a plant, that his body, his mind, and his soul were not supernaturally created but are all products of evolution, and that he is not under the control or guidance of any supernatural Being or beings, but has to rely on himself and his own powers.[10]

"I use the word 'Humanist' to mean someone who believes that man . . . his body, his mind, and his soul were not supernaturally created but are all products of evolution."
—Julian Huxley

For the Humanist, atheistic evolution is not one option among many, but rather the only option compatible with their worldview. Creationism is considered an enemy of science, despite the fact that the

Notes and Asides

Christian worldview of creation had far more to do with the founding of modern science than did Humanism.[11]

The Role of Science

Humanism relies on science as its major source of knowledge. Its interpretation of science excludes any supernatural explanation for any event occurring in nature, including the origin of life. "The scientific approach," says Baier,

> demands that we look for a natural explanation of anything and everything. The scientific way of looking at and explaining things has yielded an immensely greater measure of understanding of, and control over, the universe than any other way. And when one looks at the world in this scientific way, there seems to be no room for a personal relationship between human beings and a supernatural perfect being ruling and guiding men.[12]

For Humanists the lesson of science is that whatever takes place in nature is "natural" not supernatural. Humanists believe that, for science, *supernatural* is a meaningless word.

Corliss Lamont writes,

> The development, over the past four centuries, of a universally reliable method for attaining knowledge is a far more important achievement on the part of science than its discovery of any single truth. For once men acquire a dependable method of truth-seeking, a method that can be applied to every sphere of human life, then they have an instrument of infinite power that will serve them as long as mankind endures. Scientific method is such an instrument. And not only does it constantly revise and render more precise our present body of knowledge, but it also steadily improves upon itself. It is a method that is self-corrective and self-evolving.[13]

Obviously, when one assumes that science is the best method of obtaining knowledge and that science must exclude the supernatural, one cannot accept the supernatural as a possible explanation for the origin of life. The only other possibility is evolution beginning with spontaneous generation. Julian Huxley sums it up: "the naturalist who notes the constant correspondence between structure and inborn behaviour on the one hand and environment and way of life on the other—

Notes and Asides

one has only to think of sloth and owl, anteater and flamingo, angler fish and whalebone whale—must believe either in purposive creation or in adaptive evolution. . . ."[14] Huxley goes on to make it clear which option he chooses: "How has adaptation been brought about? Modern science must rule out special creation or divine guidance."[15]

And why must "modern" science rule out creation? Because, as we have noted, science cannot observe or measure the supernatural and therefore is incapable of obtaining any knowledge about it. But by this definition science cannot render judgment on the theory of evolution, either. One-time-only historical events fall outside the scientific method because such events cannot be repeated, observed, tested, or falsified. Accordingly, neither creationism nor evolution is strictly "scientific." As Colin Patterson, longtime evolutionist and senior paleontologist at the British Museum of Natural History, states:

> If we accept [Karl] Popper's distinction between science and non-science, we must ask first whether the theory of evolution by natural selection is scientific or pseudo-scientific (metaphysical). . . . Taking the first part of the theory, that evolution has occurred, it says that the history of life is a single process of species-splitting and progression. This process must be unique and unrepeatable, like the history of England. This part of the theory is therefore a historical theory, about unique events, and unique events are, by definition, not part of science, for they are unrepeatable and so not subject to test.[16]

"[C]reationism seems like a bad dream . . ."
—Isaac Asimov

Still, Humanists insist that evolutionary theory is scientific and creation is not. Just how closed-minded the Humanists are toward creation is summed up by Isaac Asimov: "To those who are trained in science, creationism seems like a bad dream, a sudden reliving of a nightmare, a renewed march of an army of the night risen to challenge free thought and enlightenment."[17] This attitude is echoed by Robert Green Ingersoll: "The statement that in the beginning God created the heaven and the earth, I cannot accept."[18]

So where does this unwillingness to accept creation lead? Naturally, to the only other available option: evolution. Huxley says, "if we repudiate creationism, divine or vitalistic guidance, and the extremer forms of orthogenesis, as originators of adaptation, we must (unless we confess total ignorance and abandon for the time any attempts at explanation) invoke [Darwinian] natural selection."[19] This assumption that evolution (especially as described by natural selection) is the only viable explanation leads most Humanists to the next logical assumption: evolution is not a theory, but a fact. It must be a fact, because it is the only possible alternative that has not been disqualified by evoking

Notes and Asides

science as the end-all in epistemology.

Carl Sagan states simply, "Evolution is a fact, not a theory."[20] Huxley claims, "The first point to make about Darwin's theory is that it is no longer a theory, but a fact. . . . Darwinianism has come of age so to speak. We are no longer having to bother about establishing the fact of evolution."[21] Antony Flew is scandalized by the notion that there was a time "unbelievably" when the Vatican questioned "the fact of the evolutionary origin of the species."[22] Asimov says, "Today, although many educators play it safe by calling evolutionary ideas 'theory' instead of 'fact,' there is no reputable biologist who doubts that species, including Homo sapiens, have developed with time, and that they are continually, though slowly, changing."[23]

"Evolution is a fact, not a theory."
—Carl Sagan

These statements would not be quite so alarming if the Humanists were simply claiming that evolution within a species (microevolution) is a fact; unfortunately, each of these statements was made by an individual who believes that macroevolution, or the transmutation of species, is a scientific fact. Humanists are not just claiming that science has proved that dogs can change or evolve into faster or bigger breeds; rather, they are claiming that all dogs, indeed all mammals, evolved from reptiles, that reptiles evolved from amphibians, that amphibians evolved from fish, and so backward to the first speck of life. They wholeheartedly believe Darwin's conclusion that since microevolutionary changes occur among species (Darwin bred pigeons and saw such changes; dog and cattle breeders likewise see such changes), these changes can accumulate until macroevolution occurs. "I can see no limit to the amount of change," says Darwin, "to the beauty and complexity of the co-adaptations between all organic beings, one with another and with their physical conditions of life, which may have been affected in the long course of time through nature's power of selection, that is by the survival of the fittest."[24]

Microevolution refers to evolution within a species; **macroevolution** refers to speciation—that is, evolution across species.

However, macroevolution can only be embraced as a fact by those who have enough faith to deny all possibility of the supernatural. Science has never observed macroevolution, and there is no indication of such a series of "miracles" occurring in the fossil records. Therefore, the evolutionist must (just as the Christian does) "live by faith, not by sight" (1 Corinthians 5:7). Indeed, Thomas Henry Huxley's "conversion" to belief in evolution reads much like a Damascus Road experience. He says that Darwin's theory was a "flash of light, which to a man who has lost himself in a dark night, suddenly reveals a road which, whether it takes him straight home or not, certainly goes his way."[25]

Ironically, it was T. H. Huxley who voiced concern that science must remain totally outside the realm of faith and concentrate only on the facts: "[T]here is not a single belief that it is not a bounden duty with [scientists] to hold with a light hand and to part with cheerfully, the

Notes and Asides

moment it is really proved to be contrary to any fact, great or small."[26] Humanism, however, cannot accept this concept—evolution is too much an integral part of its worldview to be held lightly. Indeed, Humanist biology clings dogmatically to a number of ideas that are not grounded in scientific fact. The following discussion will outline these ideas; the major problems posed by them will be explained in the chapter on Christian biology and in the Conclusion of this book.

Spontaneous Generation

The first idea Humanist biology accepts is that life arose spontaneously from non-living matter by natural, random processes. No Humanist would disagree with George Gaylord Simpson's statement that life arose "from the inorganic spontaneously, that is, without supernatural intervention and by the operation of material processes, themselves of unknown origin, sometime during the first billion years or so of the earth's existence."[27] Without this concept, Humanism would have to postulate a supernatural force to explain the existence of the first life form on earth. Any supernatural force would be in direct contradiction with Humanism's atheistic theology and naturalistic philosophy. Therefore, Humanists are left with the pre-scientific theory of spontaneous generation, a theory so fraught with difficulties that few scientists consider it science at all. Humanists defend this doctrine because, as J. W. N. Sullivan says,

> It became an accepted doctrine that life never arises except from life. So far as actual evidence goes, this is still the only possible conclusion. But since it is a conclusion that seems to lead back to some supernatural creative act, it is a conclusion that scientific men find very difficult of acceptance.[28]

Spontaneous generation is the theory that non-living matter is, or at least was, capable of producing life. This theory is a philosophical necessity for anyone embracing atheism.

Lloyd and Mary Morain describe the Humanist belief in life arising from non-life this way: "Here we are, evolved through uncounted ages from the interreaction of chemicals and energies. Is this not the most awe-inspiring, downright spine-tingling drama that can be conceived?"[29] Chris McGowan is a little more cautious: "We do not claim to be able to document the evolution of living organisms from non-living ones, but the evidence we have presented makes a convincing case that such an evolution was possible."[30] Victor J. Stenger is even more cautious: "The universe, including its current orderly state, can have appeared spontaneously out of nothingness."[31]

Carl Sagan, however, throws caution to the wind, and in the name of science describes the actual process of spontaneous generation:

Notes and Asides

> The first living things were not anything so complex as a one-celled organism, already a highly sophisticated form of life. The first stirrings were much more humble. In those early days, lightning and ultraviolet light from the Sun were breaking apart the simple hydrogen-rich molecules of the primitive atmosphere, the fragments spontaneously recombining into more and more complex molecules. The products of this early chemistry were dissolved in the oceans, forming a kind of organic soup of gradually increasing complexity, until one day, quite by accident, a molecule arose that was able to make crude copies of itself, using as building blocks other molecules in the soup.[32]

Asimov agrees with Sagan: "Simple forms of life came into being more than three billion years ago, having formed spontaneously from nonliving matter."[33] Asimov's boldness here is puzzling in light of his having devoted a large part of the first chapter of his book *The Wellsprings of Life* to demonstrating that the theory of spontaneous generation was bad science. In that chapter he wrote, "Life comes only from life in the case of every animal man herds and of every plant man cultivates."[34] Later he noted, "It was the living creatures that caused life, and if they were kept out of any dead material, that dead material would stay very dead very permanently."[35] Asimov even uses the Bible to support this point, stating, "In fact, the Bible seems to speak out clearly against the notion of spontaneous generation. I would like to go into detail about this, not because the Bible is, or ever was intended to be, a scientific textbook, but because the Bible has so often been used to combat some of the ideas of modern science, that I think it would be refreshing to show that it can also be used to support some of these ideas."[36]

"Simple forms of life came into being more than three billion years ago, having formed spontaneously from nonliving matter."
—Isaac Asimov

Apparently, Asimov sees no contradiction between the notion that spontaneous generation has been disproved by modern science and the belief that spontaneous generation could have occurred three billion years ago. Indeed, by the end of *The Wellsprings of Life* he has drawn the conclusion that the origin of life can be explained thus:

> Once upon a time, very long ago, perhaps two and a half billion years ago, under a deadly sun, in an ammoniated ocean topped by a poisonous atmosphere, in the midst of a soup of organic molecules, a nucleic acid molecule came accidentally into being that could somehow bring about the existence of another like itself—
>
> And from that all else would follow![37]

Obviously, faith in spontaneous generation is essential for the theory of evolution as described by the Humanist. Ironically, however,

Notes and Asides

not even Darwin was willing to postulate a theory that hinged on spontaneous generation. Rather, he wrote, "Probably all the organic beings which have ever lived on this earth have descended from some one primordial form, into which life was first breathed."[38] Darwin himself felt the need to rely on some supernatural force to explain the existence of life—but the Humanist cannot afford such a concession. The existence of the supernatural has disastrous affects on the entire Secular Humanist worldview.

Natural Selection

The second idea Humanists embrace in biology is natural selection. Natural selection is the mechanism proposed by Darwin that, through competition and other factors such as mutations, predators, geography, and time, naturally and randomly allows only those life forms best suited to survive to live and reproduce. By reproducing, slight variations emerge that ultimately make it possible for the molecule, cell, plant, or animal to literally self-create new molecules, cells, plants, and animals. Tied up in this theory are the notions of the "survival of the fittest" and the struggle for existence, which we will examine shortly. Sagan insists that "Natural selection is a successful theory devised to explain the fact of evolution."[39]

Darwin relied on natural selection as the mechanism for his theory of evolution largely because he felt that it was something man had already observed artificially through breeding. When one breeds horses to create faster offspring, Darwin believed, one is artificially selecting a beneficial trait for that horse and therefore engaging in a microevolutionary process. Darwin was convinced that, given enough time, nature can use the process of selection to evolve all forms of life from the single original life form:

> Slow though the process of selection may be, if feeble man can do so much by his powers of artificial selection, I can see no limit to the amount of change, to the beauty and infinite complexity of the co-adaptations between all organic beings, one with another and with their physical conditions of life, which may be effected in the long course of time by nature's power of selection.[40]

Indeed, Darwin believed that "natural selection is daily and hourly scrutinizing . . . every variation, even the slightest; rejecting that which is bad, preserving and adding up all that is good; silently and insensibly working . . . at the improvement of each organic being. . . ."[41] While a breeder purposely (i.e., not randomly) controls selection so that each

Notes and Asides

generation of animal contains the best improvements, Darwin believed the jump to the assumption that random variations were responsible for such improvements in nature was logical.

Humanists are also willing to make the extrapolation from artificial selection to natural selection. Sagan writes,

> But if humans can make new varieties of plants and animals, must not nature do so also? This related process is called natural selection. That life has changed fundamentally over the aeons is

CLOSE-UP

Charles Darwin (1809-1882)

Charles Darwin was awarded his bachelor's degree in theology by Cambridge in 1831, and began the most important journey of his life that same year. As a naturalist for the H.M.S. *Beagle*, he circumnavigated the globe in a five-year period, and was thus afforded a unique opportunity to study a vast array of organisms and their habitats. His time on the ship also allowed him to thoroughly reflect on his observations and synthesize his views. Darwin did not discover the concept of evolution at that time; indeed, the concept of evolution was suggested at least as early as in classical Greece. What Darwin did begin to formulate during his time at sea was a theory about the mechanism which caused species to evolve. He eventually described this mechanism as "natural selection," and began writing a text which explained in great detail one possible way evolution might occur. Meanwhile, another naturalist, Alfred Russel Wallace, was independently developing a theory quite similar to Darwin's. This caused Darwin to rush ultimate completion of his text, which was published in 1859 as *On the Origin of Species by Means of Natural Selection, or the Preservation of Favoured Races in the Struggle for Life*. He tinkered with this book for the rest of his life, producing six editions in all, each edition more conciliatory than the previous one. He attempted other books, as well, but they were all overshadowed by *Origin of Species*. Growing more and more despondent, Darwin died April 19, 1882, never to know if the fossil record proved his theory correct.

Notes and Asides

> entirely clear from the alterations we have made in the beasts and vegetables during the short tenure of humans on Earth, and from the fossil evidence.[42]

Elsewhere he says, "If artificial selection can make such major changes in so short a period of time, what must natural selection, working over billions of years, be capable of? The answer is all the beauty and diversity of the biological world."[43]

Julian Huxley accepts natural selection as the mechanism used by evolution. "Darwin's special contribution to the evolution problem was the theory of natural selection. . . . To-day we . . . can demonstrate that natural selection is omnipresent and virtually the only guiding agency in evolution."[44] Elsewhere he is more bold: "So far as we know, not only is Natural Selection inevitable, not only is it an effective agency of evolution, but it is the only effective agency of evolution."[45] McGowan agrees with him: "We have seen that the basic mechanism of evolution is that there is variability among individuals, and that this variability, under the direction of natural selection, can lead to the origin of a new species."[46]

Julian Huxley relies on natural selection for a number of reasons—two of which are especially interesting: "Indeed, the net result of the last quarter century's work in biology has been the re-establishment of natural selection as the essential method of evolution, and its re-establishment not merely where Darwin left it, but on a far more secure footing. For one thing, the alternative explanations have ceased to be plausible."[47] His first reason results from the process of elimination—every theory is implausible except for natural selection (because, of course, Humanism has already ruled out the supernatural). His second reason for believing natural selection is the same one Humanists cite when accepting spontaneous generation as possible: the incredible length of time available. Huxley claims, "With the length of time available, little adjustments can easily be made to add up to miraculous adaptations; and the slight shifts of gene frequency between one generation and the next can be multiplied to produce radical improvements and totally new kinds of creatures."[48] Enough micro-changes within a species can be translated into macroevolution between species—over time.

Natural selection, a mechanism suggested by Charles Darwin and Alfred Wallace, postulates the survival and reproductive success of species better adapted to their environment as an explanation for the apparent progressive nature of evolution.

Struggle For Existence and Survival

Inherent in the notion of natural selection is the idea that those life forms best equipped to survive will win the struggle for existence. This allegedly explains why life forms have become better equipped to

Notes and Asides

survive as time passes. The concept comes from Darwin's statement quoted earlier: "I can see no limit to the amount of change to the beauty and complexity of the co-adaptations between all organic beings, one with another and with their physical conditions of life, which may have been affected in the long course of time through nature's power of selection, that is by the survival of the fittest."[49]

Humanist biologists accept this concept, although they are usually careful about acknowledging it. Lamont, however, is not bashful: "The processes of natural selection and survival of the fittest, with the many mutations that occur over hundreds of millions of years, adequately account for the origin and development of the species."[50] Baier is even willing to draw the conclusions that necessarily follow from the acceptance of such a precept:

"'The unfit die—the fit both live and thrive.'/ Alas, who say so? They who do survive."
—Sarah N. Cleghorn

> Evolution, to whose operation the emergence of man is due, is a ceaseless battle among members of different species, one species being gobbled up by another, only the fittest surviving. Far from being the gentlest and most highly moral, man is simply the creature best fitted to survive, the most efficient if not the most rapacious and insatiable killer.[51]

Baier has touched on the whole distasteful problem raised by survival of the fittest: the only moral good becomes survival. The only value evolved in the struggle is existence itself. Norman Macbeth (who is not a Humanist) sums up the problem: "Survival of the fittest has suffered the same blight as its companion . . . struggle-for-existence. It is politically unacceptable. It smells of Hitler, of the laissez-faire economists, of savage competition and devil take the hindmost."[52]

However, there is another problem with survival of the fittest that the Humanists recognize. Asimov describes it this way: "In the first place, the phrase 'the survival of the fittest' is not an illuminating one. It implies that those who survive are the 'fittest,' but what is meant by 'fittest'? Why, those are 'fittest' who survive. This is an argument in a circle."[53] In other words, when you say "survival of the fittest," you really aren't saying anything of consequence. It is a tautology—an explanation that includes its own definition.

A **tautology** is a repetition that does not clarify—often an explanation that refers back to itself in an unsuccessful attempt to define.

Obviously, the Humanist biologist would like to avoid discussing the struggle for existence whenever possible—but at the same time, he needs it to explain natural selection as a mechanism for evolution.

Mutations

Still another idea on which the theory of evolution relies is the concept of beneficial mutations. In fact, this is one of the precepts that has been

Notes and Asides

added to the theory of natural selection to create a more coherent mechanism for evolution.

Asimov adds three ingredients to natural selection to create his mechanism—one of which we have already stressed (the evolutionists' reliance on vast stretches of time). The other two are tied to the notion of mutation:

Today, when do we call mutations good?!

> . . . to account for the facts of evolution, randomness of gene shuffling as proposed by Mendel is all that is needed, provided it is combined with the natural selection postulated by Darwin, the mutation theory suggested by DeVries and the eons of time put forward by Hutton.[54]

Both Julian Huxley and Sagan also rely heavily on mutations. Huxley says that "it would seem that gene-mutation, together with the 'pseudo-mutation' due to position effects, is the most important source of evolutionary change."[55] Later he claims, "Gene-mutation, though a rare event, appears to account for most that is truly new in evolution. . . ."[56] Sagan agrees: "Accidentally useful mutations provide the working material for biological evolution. . . ."[57] Elsewhere he incorporates mutation with survival of the fittest: "Mutations—sudden changes in heredity—breed true. They provide the raw material of evolution. The environment selects those few mutations that enhance survival, resulting in a series of slow transformations of one lifeform [sic] into another, the origin of new species."[58]

Mutations are changes in the genetic information in individual members of species.

Adaptations

Combining mutations with the theory of natural selection provides an explanation for adaptation, yet another theory that Humanists accept. Adaptation helps explain why life forms seem to have evolved specialized abilities that allow them to survive better in their particular niches in the environment.

"The origin of adaptability in organisms is the thing to be explained, not the premise to start with," says Herman J. Muller. "The modern theory of gene mutation, coupled with Darwin's basic concept of natural selection, provides the basis for a process of evolution in which such adaptability will come into existence by the operation of natural processes."[59] For Muller, both natural selection and beneficial mutations must be fact to explain any part of the mechanism of evolution. This is true also for Julian Huxley: "Neither did the automatic process of natural selection 'know' anything about the mechanisms of evolution. Luckily this did not prevent it from achieving a staggering degree of evolutionary transformation, including miracles of adaptation and

Notes and Asides

improvement."[60]

Of course, in accepting adaptation as part of the mechanism of evolution, the Humanist must overlook (or explain away) all the apparently meaningless adaptations existing in our world. Darwin admits, "I did not formerly consider sufficiently the existence of structures which, as far as we can . . . judge, are neither beneficial nor injurious, and this I believe to be one of the greatest oversights as yet detected in my work. This led to my tacit assumption that every detail of structure was of some special though unrecognized service."[61] Even Julian Huxley must confess ". . . the display-characters may even be clearly disadvantageous to the individual in all aspects of existence other than the reproductive, as in the train of the peacock, the wings of the argus pheasant, or the plumes of some birds of paradise."[62]

Huxley gamely goes on to attempt what Darwin had tried so long ago—to explain seemingly harmful or meaningless adaptations in such a way that they could rightly be labeled beneficial. His attempt becomes absurd, however, when he tries to describe schizophrenia as a useful adaptation. He claims that "genetic theory makes it plain that a clearly disadvantageous genetic character like this cannot persist in this frequency in a population unless it is balanced by some compensating advantage. In this case it appears that the advantage is that schizophrenic individuals are considerably less sensitive than normal persons to histamine, are much less prone to suffer from operative and wound shock, and do not suffer nearly so much from various allergies."[63] Huxley does not say whether he would rather be a schizophrenic or suffer from allergies.

The Fossil Record

The final plank on which the theory of evolution rests is the claim that the fossil record gives an accurate account of the process of transmutation of the species or macroevolution. "Evolution is a fact," says Sagan, "amply demonstrated by the fossil record."[64] The fossil record is crucial for the evolutionist because it is the only means available to the scientist to observe steps in the evolutionary process. In Darwin's day, the actual evidence was missing. There was no fossil evidence that any of the major divisions of nature (fish, amphibians, reptiles, mammals) had been crossed gradually. Commented Darwin,

> The geological record is extremely imperfect and this fact will to a large extent explain why we do not find intermediate varieties, connecting together all the extinct and existing forms of life by the finest graduated steps. He who rejects these views

Used by permission of the *Colorado Springs Gazette Telegraph*

on the nature of the geological record, will rightly reject my whole theory.[65]

Without convincing evidence from fossils, the theory of evolution would have no basis for grounding itself in the scientific method and would be left in the realm of faith. Therefore, we find McGowan stating, "Much of my evidence is based on fossils and the rocks in which they are found, because the fossil record is the most concrete source of documentation for the slow process of evolution."[66]

Likewise, Sagan claims, "The fossil record speaks to us unambiguously of creatures that once were present in enormous numbers and that have now vanished utterly. Far more species have become extinct in the history of the Earth than exist today; they are the terminated experiments of evolution."[67] Julian Huxley also relies on the fossil record: "Most of evolution is thus what we may call short-term diversification. But this kaleidoscopic change is shot through with a certain proportion of long-term diversification in the shape of the long-range trends revealed in fossils by the paleontologist . . ."[68] This notion was espoused

"I will lay it on the line—there is not one such [transitional] fossil for which one could make a watertight argument."
—Colin Patterson

Notes and Asides

Paleontology is a branch of geology concerned with studying fossils to understand prehistoric life forms.

by Thomas Huxley decades earlier. He says, "Now, Mr. Darwin's hypothesis is not, so far as I am aware, inconsistent with any known biological fact; on the contrary, if admitted, the facts of . . . Geographical Distribution, and of Paleontology, become connected together, and exhibit a meaning such as they never possessed before. . . ."[69]

From these claims it would seem that the fossil record provides indisputable proof for macroevolution. This, however, is not the case. McGowan confesses,

> Darwin was perfectly correct, then, in blaming some of his problems on the incompleteness of the fossil record, but most of his problems arose because he was trying to use it to document the origins of new species. As we will now see, the fossil record lacks the fine resolution needed to chronicle such small-scale evolutionary changes.[70]

That is, while microevolution is observable in selective breeding and in some of the fossil record, no fossils exist that conclusively demonstrate evolution from one species to another. The only method science has available for demonstrating macroevolution through direct observation cannot prove or even hint at it.

"The evolutionists seem to know everything about the missing link except the fact that it is missing."
—G. K. Chesterton

Punctuated Equilibrium

If the fossil record is the only means available for employing the scientific method to "observe" macroevolution, and if that record provides nothing observable that corresponds with the theory, then the evolutionist is left holding a theory based largely on faith. This is intolerable for the Humanist—so a theory has been proposed that forces the fossil record to fit into the evolutionary mold. This theory is referred to as punctuated equilibrium. *Equilibrium* refers to the fact that species manifest a stubborn stability (stasis) in nature and *punctuated* refers to the dramatic changes deemed necessary to explain how the gaps are bridged in the fossil record between the major divisions in nature.

McGowan, after admitting that the fossil record does not contain evidence of macroevolution, jumps to the conclusion that a theory that allows for evolution and gets around the dilemma presented by the fossil record must be the scientific solution:

> Species remain unchanged (except for minor fluctuations) over long periods of time, for tens of thousands of years and perhaps for several millions of years. New species probably evolve only when a segment of the population becomes isolated from the

Notes and Asides

> rest. Speciation occurs relatively rapidly, probably in a matter of only a few thousand years and possibly less. This concept of long periods of stasis interspersed with periods of rapid change is often called "punctuated equilibrium."[71]

That is, punctuated equilibrium claims that science cannot discover the links between species in the fossil record because the change from one species to another occurs too rapidly to leave accurate fossil documentation.

McGowan claims that "most evolutionists share" this view—which is logical, since it is the only evolutionary view that can be construed as consistent with the fossil record. This view is basically a restatement of the "hopeful monster" theory, which suggests that evolution occurred not gradually but suddenly as the result of a monster, or missing link, born into one species but possessing numerous characteristics of another species. These monsters would become the original ancestors of a new species. Of course, none of the missing links were cooperative enough to leave evidences of their existence in the fossil record.

How does punctuated equilibrium mesh with the theory of evolution as presented by Darwin? Not as well as one might expect—in fact, it clashes directly with Darwin's ideas. He writes, "If it could be demonstrated that any complex organ existed, which could not possibly have been formed by numerous, successive, slight modifications, my theory would absolutely break down."[72] Apparently, evolutionists are willing to "break down" Darwin's theory in an effort to make some form of evolution fit the facts.

Punctuated equilibrium, in the strict sense, is a description of the fossil record. The term also is used to describe a class of theories that view evolutionary history as a series of periods of stasis interrupted by relatively abrupt change.

What else can they do? The problem of the non-existence of proof for gradual evolution has been around as long as the theory itself. Alfred Russell Wallace, co-founder of the theory of evolution as proposed by Darwin, recognized it in his lifetime: "Natural Selection could only have endowed the savage with a brain a little superior to that of the ape, whereas he actually possesses one very little inferior to that of the average member of our learned societies."[73] Obviously, there is a need for missing links to explain the jump from ape to man, or any species to any other species—and that is precisely where the theory of punctuated equilibrium steps in, causing Darwin's theory to "absolutely break down."

Conclusion

Secular Humanist biology rests its case for evolution on six specific planks: spontaneous generation, natural selection, struggle for existence, beneficial mutations, adaptations, and the observable nature of

Notes and Asides

Reality for a S.H.

"The vast majority of the known phyla of plants and animals (over 95%) appear as fossils within a very short period, geologically speaking. . . Any theory of life's origin must explain how all the major body plans for living things appeared so quickly when life began."

—Percival Davis, Dean H. Kenyon

evolution through the fossil record. In recent times, because the fossil record has only hindered their attempts to prove the "fact" that macroevolution occurs, evolutionists have been forced to abandon the most important parts of Darwin's theory and postulate punctuated equilibrium. In the context of every idea, the Humanist is forced to rely on the extrapolation of the observable through enormously long periods of time to account for apparent contradictions and to create miraculously varied forms of life.

Obviously, accepting such ideas and believing vehemently in the theory of evolution affects the Secular Humanist's entire worldview. Not only does it create a world without God; it also paints a radical picture of that world. Johann Bojer describes it this way: "We are flung by an indifferent law of the universe into a life we cannot order as we would; we are ravaged by injustice, by sickness and sorrow, by fire and flood. In our own home we are but on a visit."[74]

Lamont explains how belief in evolution affects Humanist philosophy:

> Humanism holds that the race of man is the present culmination of a time-defying evolutionary process on this planet that has lasted billions of years: that man exists as an inseparable unity of mind and body, and that therefore after death there can be no personal immortality or survival of consciousness.[75]

Algernon D. Black speaks of the evolutionary view's effect on ethics: "But in the evolution of human life, there is a consciousness and emerging conscience. The key question is whether human beings can rise to a level of awareness of the values and the choices which are within human control."[76]

The evolutionary perspective powerfully affects Humanism's ideal for the future, as well. Julian Huxley believes, "The next major step must be for the scientific method to be brought into the core of the psychosocial sphere. Man must take a scientific look at his values, at his ethics, at his art and aesthetics, at his social and economic organization, and at his religion."[77] Indeed, he foresees a new religion being created by man as he develops:

> The emergent religion of the near future could be a good thing. It will believe in knowledge. It will be able to take advantage of the vast amount of new knowledge produced by the knowledge-explosion of the last few centuries in constructing what we may call its theology—the framework of facts and ideas which provide it with intellectual support: it should be able, with our increased knowledge of mind, to define man's sense of right and

Notes and Asides

wrong more clearly, so as to provide a better moral support, and to focus the feeling of sacredness on fitter objects.[78]

Precisely what are those "fitter objects"? Lamont seems to believe it possible that man, or his descendants, will someday be worthy of worship: "Furthermore, if we take seriously the lessons of evolution, it would appear that God as a great cosmic Mind and Purpose, if he did exist, would have to be the end-product of a very long evolutionary process rather than its initiator and overseer."[79]

Humanism relies on evolution for much more than a theory about the origin of life. The Secular Humanist trusts evolution as a "fact" worthy of use as a foundation for many of his ideas about theology, philosophy, ethics, and even his social and political ideals for the future. In truth, the Humanist considers evolution the correct foundation for every individual's worldview and believes that the world can be properly understood only from this perspective. For this reason, Humanists encourage teaching evolution as "fact" throughout our educational system—thereby relegating the supernatural, especially God, to the world of mythology. The Humanist does not just expect evolution to be taught as a theory in the biology classroom, but rather believes, in the words of Julian Huxley, that "it is essential for evolution to become the central core of any educational system, because it is evolution, in the broad sense, that links inorganic nature with life, and the stars with earth, and matter with mind, and animals with man. Human history is a continuation of biological evolution in a different form."[80]

If man is only a part of nature, how can he know anything? He is only part of a material world.

[1]Carl Sagan, *The Dragons of Eden* (New York: Random House, 1977), p. 6.
[2]George Gaylord Simpson, *The Meaning of Evolution* (New Haven: Yale University Press, 1971), p. 345.
[3]Charles Darwin, *The Origin of Species*, 6th ed., (New York: Collier Books, [1872] 1962), p. 468, cited in Michael Denton, *Evolution: A Theory in Crisis* (Bethesda, MD: Adler and Adler, 1985), p. 57.
[4]*Humanist Manifesto I* (Buffalo: Prometheus Books, [1933] 1980), p. 8.
[5]*Humanist Manifesto II* (Buffalo: Prometheus Books, [1973] 1980), p. 17.
[6]Will Durant, *The Story of Philosophy* (New York: Simon and Schuster, 1927), p. 568.
[7]John Dewey, *The Influence of Darwin on Philosophy* (New York: 1910), p. 8. Cited in Ibid.
[8]Kurt E. M. Baier, "The Meaning of Life," in *Critiques of God*, ed. Peter Angeles (Buffalo: Prometheus Books, 1976), p. 315.
[9]Roy Wood Sellars, "The Humanist Outlook," in *The Humanist Alternative*, ed. Paul Kurtz (Buffalo: Prometheus Books, 1973), p. 133.
[10]Julian Huxley, as cited in Roger E. Greeley, ed., *The Best of Humanism* (Buffalo: Prometheus Books, 1988), pp. 194-5.
[11]See Norman L. Geisler and J. Kerby Anderson, *Origin Science* (Grand Rapids, MI: Baker, 1987), pp. 37-52. Geisler and Anderson quote M. B. Foster: "What is the source of those un-Greek elements in the modern theory of nature by which the peculiar character of the modern science of nature was to be determined? The answer to the first question is: The Christian revelation, and the answer to the second: The Christian doctrine of creation." They also quote Alfred North Whitehead's *Science and the Modern World*: "The faith in the possibility of science, generated antecedently to the development of modern scientific theory, is an unconscious derivative from medieval theology."
[12]Baier, "The Meaning of Life," in *Critiques of God*, ed. Angeles, p. 296.
[13]Corliss Lamont, *The Philosophy of Humanism*, rev. ed. (New York: Frederick Ungar, [1949] 1982), p. 197.
[14]Julian Huxley, *Evolution: The Modern Synthesis* (New York: Harper and Brothers Publishers, 1942), p. 413.
[15]Ibid., p. 457.
[16]Colin Patterson, *Evolution* (London: British Museum of Natural History, 1978), pp. 145-6, cited in Luther D. Sunderland, *Darwin's Enigma* (San Diego: Master Books, 1984), pp. 26-7.
[17]Isaac Asimov, in *Science and Creationism*, ed. Ashley Montagu (Oxford: Oxford University Press, 1984), p. 183.
[18]Robert Green Ingersoll, as cited in *The Best of Humanism*, ed. Greeley, p. 163.
[19]Huxley, *Evolution: the Modern Synthesis*, p. 473.
[20]Carl Sagan, *Cosmos* (New York: Random House, 1980), p. 27.
[21]Julian Huxley, "At Random", a television preview on Nov. 21, 1959. Also, Sol Tax, *Evolution of Life* (Chicago: University of Chicago Press, 1960), p. 1.
[22]Antony Flew, "Scientific Humanism," *The Humanist Alternative*, ed. Kurtz, p. 110.
[23]Isaac Asimov, *The Wellsprings of Life* (London: Abelard-Schuman, 1960), p. 56.
[24]Darwin, *The Origin of Species*, 6th ed., p. 48.
[25]T. H. Huxley, cited in Sagan, *Cosmos*, p. 28.
[26]T. H. Huxley, *Darwiniana* (1893), pp. 468-9, cited in Norman Macbeth, *Darwin Retried* (Boston: Gambit, 1971), p. 7.
[27]Simpson, *Meaning of Evolution*, p. 341.
[28]J. W. N. Sullivan, *The Limitations of Science* (New York: Mentor, 1963), p. 94.
[29]Lloyd Morain and Mary Morain, "Humanism: A Joyous View," in *The Humanist Alternative*, ed. Kurtz, p. 125.
[30]Chris McGowan, *In the Beginning . . .* (Buffalo: Prometheus Books, 1984), p. 53.
[31]Victor J. Stenger, *Not By Design* (Buffalo: Prometheus Books, 1988), p. 8.
[32]Sagan, *Cosmos*, pp. 30-1.
[33]Asimov, *Science and Creationism*, p. 182.
[34]Asimov, *The Wellsprings of Life*, p. 14.
[35]Ibid., p. 20.
[36]Ibid., p. 21.
[37]Ibid., pp. 224-5.
[38]Darwin, *The Origin of the Species*, cited in Sagan, *Cosmos*, p. 23.

[39]Sagan, *The Dragons of Eden*, p. 6.
[40]Charles Darwin, *The Origin of the Species* (London: John Murray, 1859), p. 109.
[41]Ibid., p. 84.
[42]Sagan, *Cosmos*, p. 27.
[43]Ibid.
[44]Julian Huxley, *Man in the Modern World* (New York: Mentor, 1944), p. 175.
[45]Julian Huxley, *Evolution in Action* (New York: Mentor, 1957), p. 35.
[46]McGowan, *In the Beginning . . .*, p. 34.
[47]Huxley, *Man in the Modern World*, p. 163.
[48]Huxley, *Evolution in Action*, p. 41.
[49]Darwin, *The Origin of Species*, 6th ed., pp. 114-15.
[50]Lamont, *The Philosophy of Humanism*, p. 120.
[51]Baier, "The Meaning of Life," in *Critiques of God*, ed. Angeles, p. 315.
[52]Norman Macbeth, *Darwin Retried*, p. 62. This problem is spelled out in detail by Jacques Barzun in "The Uses of Darwinism," a chapter in *Darwin, Marx, Wagner* (Garden City, NY: Doubleday, 1958).
[53]Asimov, *The Wellsprings of Life*, p. 57.
[54]Ibid., p. 73.
[55]Huxley, *Evolution: the Modern Synthesis*, p. 93.
[56]Ibid., p. 51.
[57]Sagan, *The Dragons of Eden*, p. 27.
[58]Sagan, *Cosmos*, p. 27.
[59]Herman J. Muller, *Genetics in the Twentieth Century*, ed. L. C. Dunn (New York and London: Macmillan, 1951), p. 92.
[60]Julian Huxley, *Essays of a Humanist* (New York: Harper & Row, 1964), p. 273.
[61]Charles Darwin, as cited in Macbeth, *Darwin Retried*, p. 73.
[62]Huxley, *Evolution: the Modern Synthesis*, p. 427.
[63]Huxley, *Essays of a Humanist*, p. 67.
[64]Sagan, *The Dragons of Eden*, p. 6.
[65]Charles Darwin, *The Origin of Species*, 6th ed. (London: John Murray, 1902), pp. 341-2, cited in Sunderland, *Darwin's Enigma*, p. 9. Sunderland observes, "Now, after over 120 years of the most extensive and pains-taking geological exploration of every continent and ocean bottom, the picture is infinitely more vivid and complete than it was in 1859. Formations have been discovered containing hundreds of billions of fossils and our museums now are filled with over 100 million fossils of 250,000 different species. The availability of this profusion of hard scientific data should permit objective investigators to determine if Darwin was on the right track" (p. 9).
[66]McGowan, *In the Beginning . . .*, p. xii.
[67]Sagan, *Cosmos*, p. 27.
[68]Huxley, *Man in the Modern World*, p. 168.
[69]T. H. Huxley, *Man's Place in Nature* (Ann Arbor: University of Michigan Press, 1959), p. 127.
[70]McGowan, *In the Beginning . . .*, p. 93.
[71]Ibid., p. 29.
[72]Darwin, *Origin of the Species*, p. 189, cited in Macbeth, *Darwin Retried*, p. 76.
[73]Alfred Russell Wallace, cited in Loren Eiseley, *Darwin's Century* (Garden City, NY: Doubleday, 1961), pp. 310-14.
[74]Johann Bojer, in *The Best of Humanism*, ed. Greeley, p. 144.
[75]Lamont, in *The Best of Humanism*, ed. Greeley, pp. 149-50.
[76]Algernon D. Black, "Our Quest for Faith: Is Humanism Enough?" in *The Humanist Alternative*, ed. Kurtz, p. 75.
[77]Huxley, *Essays of Humanist*, p. 52.
[78]Ibid., p. 88.
[79]Lamont, *The Philosophy of Humanism*, p. 121.
[80]Julian Huxley, "At Random," a television preview on Nov. 21, 1959.

CHAPTER

13

MARXIST/ LENINIST BIOLOGY

"Darwin's [Origin of Species] is very important and provides me with the basis in natural science for the class struggle in history."[1]

—Karl Marx

"Without a natural scientific basis, class struggle could not be properly understood: without its natural-historical foundation, the whole of Marxist theory is built on sand."[2]

—John Hoffman

SUMMARY

Marxism/Leninism depends on the theory of evolution. Karl Marx made it very clear that Charles Darwin's *Origin of Species* contained the scientific basis for his views on the class struggle. Some even defined Marxism as "Darwinism applied to human society." Just as the theory of evolution explained how man arrived on the scene from a molecule, so the theory also explained how society evolves. The major trouble with Darwin, from the Marxist perspective, is Darwin's slow, gradual process of natural selection. Marxist dialectical materialism called for something more than just gradual progression. The dialectic needs a theory with clashes (thesis against antithesis) and leaps (synthesis). While the struggle for existence may answer to the clash of the dialectic, nothing in Darwin answered to the leap. The recent theory of punctuated equilibrium, however, seems to satisfy the dialectical demand. Punctuated equilibrium posits a natural world that manifests species stability for great periods of time but occasionally ruptures or leaps from one species to another. The mechanics of such abrupt leaps in nature are still being sought. Some suggest a reptile laying an egg in which a bird emerges as a starting point for discussion, but few defend such a suggestion. Recently, Marxist biologists have stressed the power of beneficial mutations to create the jump in evolutionary development. Not surprisingly, Marxist biologists are using the inability of the fossil record to sustain the weight of the Darwinian theory to bolster their theory of punctuated equilibrium.

Then, too, with an atheistic base the subject of origins calls for the self-generation of nonliving matter. Marxist biology defends spontaneous generation despite the fact that it is a pre-scientific concept dating back to the Egyptians, Babylonians, and Greeks. Engels says he will "believe" in spontaneous generation no matter what Louis Pasteur and other scientists say or do to disprove it. In fact, Engels sees no scientific experiments capable of disproving the theory. The Marxist attitude is simple: given time, carbon, hydrogen, oxygen, and energy from the sun, matter is obligated to create life. According to the Marxist, we are the practical result of just such a materialistic matrix.

Introduction

While Karl Marx and Frederick Engels were developing their communistic worldview, Charles Darwin was presenting his theory of evolution and creating quite a stir among the intellectuals of the nineteenth century. Many people perceived Darwin's theory as providing the foundation for an entirely new materialistic perspective on life. Indeed,

Notes and Asides

Marx and Engels were among those who recognized the usefulness of Darwin's theory of evolution as just such a foundation.

In a letter to Engels, Marx writes, "During . . . the past four weeks I have read all sorts of things. Among others Darwin's work on Natural Selection. And though it is written in the crude English style, this is the book which contains the basis in natural science for our view."[3] Marx expresses the same sentiment in a letter to Lassalle, claiming that *The Origin of Species* "is very important and serves me as a natural scientific basis for the class struggle in history."[4] John Hoffman tells us that Marx so admired Darwin's work that he "sent Darwin a complimentary copy of Volume I of *Capital* and tried unsuccessfully to dedicate Volume II to him."[5]

Marxists are well aware that Marx depended on Darwin's theory of evolution for his materialistic and social/historical worldview. F. V. Konstantinov, in *The Fundamentals of Marxist-Leninist Philosophy*, states, "It was the discovery of the law of the conservation of energy, of the unitary cellular structure of all living organisms, and Darwin's theory of the evolution of biological species that provided the foundation on which Marx and Engels built dialectical materialism."[6] Theodosius Dobzhansky gave a paper in 1974 entitled "The Birth of the Genetic Theory of Evolution in the Soviet Union in the 1920s." In this paper Dobzhansky made it clear that while some scientists in the U.S.S.R. have reservations about certain aspects of Darwinian theory, they "still accepted evolution as part of the new gospel." He further said, "Evolution was accepted not only as a scientific theory but also as a part of the liberal worldview. . . . [S]tandard bearers of the radical youth proclaimed that a valid personal philosophy must rest on a solid base of natural science, and evolution was a pivotal part of that."[7]

"During . . . the past four weeks I have read all sorts of things. Among others Darwin's work on Natural Selection. . . . [T]his is the book which contains the basis in natural science for our view."
—Karl Marx

Why do Marxists embrace the theory of evolution so readily? Partially because it provides a picture of man's origin that is largely consistent with the Marxist dialectic and supports the Marxist notion that man's social history is a constant and continuing process. In fact, the Marxist theory of history and society is merely an extension and distortion of Darwin's theory of evolution.

Darwin, Marx, and Society

Marx believed that Darwin's evolutionary theory could be extended naturally to answer questions about human society. He felt that society, like life itself, had gone through an evolutionary process and must continue to undergo such a process until a classless society evolved. Marx integrated this notion of evolution into the his worldview, writing, "Darwin has interested us in the history of Nature's technol-

Notes and Asides

ogy, i.e. in the formation of the organs of plants and animals, which organs serve as instruments of production for sustaining life. Does not the history of the productive organs of man, of organs that are the material basis of all social organization, deserve equal attention?"[8] Engels makes the claim even more straight-forward: "Just as Darwin discovered the law of evolution in organic nature, so Marx discovered the law of evolution in human history."[9]

This claim has been reaffirmed throughout Marxism's development. V. I. Lenin echoes the founding fathers, stressing the scientific nature of their theory:

> Just as Darwin put an end to the view of animal and plant species being unconnected, fortuitous, "created by God" and immutable, and was the first to put biology on an absolutely scientific basis by establishing the mutability and the succession of species, so Marx put an end to the view of society being a mechanical aggregation of individuals which allows of all sorts of modification at the will of the authorities (or, if you like, at the will of society and the government) and which emerges and changes casually, and was the first to put sociology on a scientific basis by establishing the concept of the economic formation of society as the sum-total of given production relations, by establishing the fact that the development of such formations is a process of natural history.[10]

"Logically Marx's inquiry begins precisely where Darwin's inquiry ends."
—G. V. Plekhanov

Leon Trotsky says that "taken in the broadly materialist and dialectical sense, Marxism is the application of Darwinism to human society."[11] G. V. Plekhanov sees Marxism as "Darwinism in its application to social science."[12] Obviously, virtually all Marxists perceive Darwin's theory of evolution as an essential pillar in their communist worldview. This is due largely to the fact that it complements their social and historical theory so well; but of course, there is another, more important reason.

Darwin and Teleology

Just as the notion of God destroys the Humanist theology, the slightest hint of God is directly opposed to the Marxist theology. Atheism, as we have seen in Marxist/Leninist theology, is the very core of Marxist theory—their worldview is only consistent and coherent without God in the picture. As soon as one acknowledges the existence of God, or even of the supernatural, Marxism crumbles. Therefore, Marx and his followers eagerly embraced a theory that makes God unnecessary for the origin of life.

Notes and Asides

Marx proclaims, "Darwin's volume is very important . . . not only is the death-blow dealt here for the first time to 'teleology' in the natural sciences but their rational meaning is empirically explained."[13] Engels is especially aware of the ramifications of Darwin's theory: "Darwin must be named before all others. He dealt the metaphysical conception of nature the heaviest blow by his proof that all organic beings, plants, animals, and man himself, are the products of a process of evolution going on through millions of years."[14] And elsewhere he writes, "nowadays, in our evolutionary conception of the universe, there is absolutely no room for either a creator or a ruler."[15] Konstantinov, in *The Fundamentals of Marxist-Leninist Philosophy*, echoes him: "Darwin's theory of evolution is the third great scientific discovery that took place in the middle of the 19th century. Darwin put an end to the notion of the species of animals and plants as 'divine creations', not connected with anything else, providential and immutable, and thus laid the foundation of theoretical biology. . . ."[16]

This "great scientific discovery" is crucial. Without the theory of evolution, the design of the universe could be explained only by postulating a rational, purposeful, powerful God, and this is inconceivable for the Marxist. Engels demonstrates his awareness that teleology must be explained either by evolution or by the existence of God when he cites Darwin's theory and concludes:

> Thereby not only has an explanation been made possible for the existing stock of the organic products of nature, but the basis has been given for the prehistory of the human mind, for following all its various stages of evolution from the protoplasm, simple and structureless yet responsive to stimuli, of the lower organisms right up to the thinking human brain. Without this prehistory, however, the existence of the thinking human brain remains a miracle.[17]

Of course, there is no room for miracles in a materialistic worldview, so Marxism must accept evolution unreservedly. This willingness to accept evolution is also partially due to the fact that, on the surface, Darwin's theory seems to mesh perfectly with Marx's interpretation of dialectics. Next we will compare Darwin's theory with Marx's dialectics; then we will note some of the conflicting tenets of the two theories.

Darwin and Dialectics

Marx writes, "You will see from the conclusion of my third chapter . . . that in the text I regard the law Hegel discovered . . . as holding good both in history and natural science."[18] But if nature is dialectical and

Notes and Asides

Darwin's notion about the mechanism employed by nature to create species is correct, then Darwin's theory must be dialectical.

Engels is more than willing to accept this conclusion. He states, "Nature is the proof of dialectics. . . . An exact representation of the universe, of its evolution, of the development of mankind, and of the reflection of this evolution in the minds of men, can only be obtained by methods of dialectics."[19] And we read in *The Fundamentals of Marxist-Leninist Philosophy* that "Marx and Engels assessed Darwin's evolutionary theory as dialectical-materialist in its essence. . . ."[20]

Darwin's theory of evolution appeared especially dialectical to the Marxists for the specific reason that it portrays development as a process. For example, Engels writes,

> Precisely the infinite, accidental differences between individuals within a single species, differences which become accentuated until they break through the character of the species, and whose immediate causes even can be demonstrated only in extremely few cases, compelled [Darwin] to question the previous basis of all regularity in biology, viz., the concept of species in its previous metaphysical rigidity and unchangeability.[21]

Elsewhere, Engels discusses the work of Darwin and discoveries regarding the nature of protoplasm and cells, concluding: "The new outlook on nature was complete in its main features; all rigidity was dissolved, all fixity dissipated, all particularity that had been regarded as eternal became transient, the whole of nature was shown as moving in eternal flux and cyclical course."[22] This eternal flux is important for the Marxist worldview, for as Engels says, "The world is not to be comprehended as a complex of ready-made things, but as a complex of processes."[23]

Another reason why Darwin's theory seemed to reinforce dialectics was that it called for the evolution of the simple to the more complex. Marxist dialectics states that process is always spiraling upward—that the synthesis is always a more advanced stage than the previous thesis. Apparently, Darwin's theory of natural selection calls for the same thing—more advanced species better suited to live in their environment, nature accumulating the good and disposing of the bad. Thus, when Joseph Stalin says "that the process of development should be understood, not as movement in a circle, not as a simple repetition of what has already occurred, but as an onward and upward movement, as a transition from an old qualitative state to a new qualitative state, as a development from the simple to the complex, from the lower to the higher,"[24] he seems to echo precisely how Darwin described the

Notes and Asides

evolutionary development of the species.

At first glance Darwin's theory appears to fit perfectly with Marx's notions about dialectics. Closer inspection, however, shows otherwise. Lenin hints at a problem when he places Marx's theories separate from and above Darwin's, claiming,

> Still, this idea, as formulated by Marx and Engels on the basis of Hegel's philosophy, is far more comprehensive and far richer in content than the current idea of [Darwinian] evolution is. A development that repeats, as it were, stages that have already been passed, but repeats them in a different way, on a higher basis ("the negation of negation"), a development, so to speak, that proceeds in spirals, not in a straight line; a development by leaps, catastrophes, and revolutions; "breaks in continuity"; the transformation of quantity into quality; inner impulses towards development, imparted by the contradiction and conflict of the various forces and tendencies acting on a given body, or within a given phenomenon, or within a given society; the interdependence and the closest and indissoluble connection between all aspects of any phenomenon (history constantly revealing ever new aspects), a connection that provides a uniform, and universal process of motion, one that follows definite laws—these are some of the features of dialectics as a doctrine of development that is richer than the conventional one.[25]

Obviously, Lenin feels that there is a distinction between Darwinian evolution and the dialectic applied to nature. We will expand on this distinction after examining some of the more general facets of the theory of evolution that all Marxists accept.

More Reasons Why Marxism Embraces Evolution

Evolutionary theory can be interpreted in many different ways to bolster the Marxists' claim that their worldview is scientific. Various Marxists have cited the theory of evolution as a basis for the inevitability of revolution, the need for individuals to form collectives, the Marxist view of labor's role in the economy, and the materialist philosophy.

Stalin claims, "Evolution prepares for revolution and creates the ground for it; revolution consummates the process of evolution and facilitates its further activity."[26] Apparently he draws this conclusion from the doctrine of the survival of the fittest, perceiving the victors in the revolution as the fittest leaders in the evolution of human society.

"[Darwinian] Evolution prepares for revolution and creates the ground for it . . ."
—Joseph Stalin

Notes
and
Asides

Otto Rühle stresses the importance of the evolutionary view of mankind as a species, stating,

> Mankind will only be able to pursue its emancipatory ascent successfully, when it becomes competent to make every individual willing and able to bring his subjective scheme of life into harmony with the objective evolutionary scheme of society—when the private individual is wholly merged in the member of the species.[27]

For Rühle, evolution indicates that classes and private ownership must be abolished to further the development of mankind.

Labor's role in evolution is stressed as well by the Marxists, specifically when Hoffman writes, "When Marx enthusiastically championed Darwin's *Origin of Species*, he did so because the work drew specific attention to importance of pre-human labour, a dialectical practice before man, and referred ingeniously to the natural organs of plants and animals as having 'different kinds of work to perform.'"[28] This statement, of course, stresses the economic factor's influence on life, which is precisely what Marx postulated.

Finally, evolutionary theory supports Marxist philosophy as well. Obviously, a philosophy that insists on matter as the only mode of existence needs a theory that describes the origin of life from a material perspective. Thus, Engels recognizes that, thanks to Darwin, "The materialist conception of nature, therefore, stands today on very different and firmer foundations than in the last century."[29]

Just how firm is this foundation? Not so firm as to avoid undergoing drastic change since Darwin's theory was first accepted by Marx and Engels. Because Darwin's evolutionary mechanism does not mesh perfectly with the dialectic, Marxists are constantly fine-tuning their evolutionary model. In fact, throughout time, only two aspects of any theory of evolution have been embraced consistently by Marxists, and only one of these aspects has Darwinian roots.

Spontaneous Generation

The theory of spontaneous generation is the only offshoot of specifically Darwinian thought that is accepted unreservedly by Marxists. This is largely due to the Marxist need for a strictly materialist explanation for the origin of life. Marx uses spontaneous generation to back both his philosophy and his theology, stating, "the idea of the creation of the earth has received a severe blow . . . from the science which portrays the . . . development of the earth as a process of

Notes and Asides

spontaneous generation;" then he adds, "*generatio aequivoca* [spontaneous generation] is the only practical refutation of the theory of creation."[30]

Engels is equally willing to accept spontaneous generation, extolling "the proof which Darwin first developed in connected form, that the stock of organic products environing us today, including mankind, is the result of a long process of evolution from a few originally unicellular germs, and that these again have arisen from protoplasm or albumen, which came into existence by chemical means."[31] Elsewhere he reiterates, "With regard to the origin of life, therefore, up to the present, science is only able to say with certainty that it must have arisen as a result of a chemical action."[32] In fact, Engels uses spontaneous generation to support the dialectical notion of progress occurring in leaps: "In spite of all intermediate steps, the transition from one form of motion to another always remains a leap, a decisive change. . . . This . . . is . . . clearly the case in the transition from ordinary chemical action to the chemistry of albumen which we call life."[33] (This notion of evolution occurring in leaps is the second facet of evolutionary theory universally accepted by Marxist biology, and will be examined shortly.)

Spontaneous generation "is the only practical refutation of the theory of creation."
—Karl Marx

Marxists continue to embrace spontaneous generation long after Marx and Engels. A. I. Oparin, a Marxist scientist, "was the first to enunciate the theory of abiogenic origin of life."[34] Oparin claimed,

> We have every reason to believe that sooner or later, we shall be able practically to demonstrate that life is nothing else but a special form of existence of matter. The successes scored recently by Soviet biology hold out the promise that the artificial creation of the simplest living beings is not only possible, but that it will be achieved in the not too distant future.[35]

Almost a quarter of a century after Oparin first suggested his theory, M. A. Leonov affirmed his ideas, stating,

> Marxist philosophical materialism remains beyond all doubt, that at some time or other in the remote past life must have arisen from non-living matter, from inanimate structures in Nature, on the basis of the natural laws of their development, without the intervention of any forces of an immaterial, spiritual or "divine" character.[36]

Even modern Marxist textbooks embrace the theory of spontaneous generation. M. V. Volkenshtein, author of *Biophysics*, declares that Oparin "presumed that the origin of life had been preceded by chemical

Notes and Asides

evolution. . . . Today these ideas are widely accepted."[37] How widely can be seen from the fact that some American textbooks on biology consider Oparin an authority on the subject of spontaneous generation. For example, in *Biology*, by Karen Arms and Pamela S. Camp, we are told, "The events necessary for the beginnings of life were extremely unlikely. Given enough time, however, the occurrence of even very improbable events is inevitable. . . . Geological evidence indicated that the earth formed about 4.6 billion years ago, and the earliest known fossils of prokaryotic cells are found in rocks formed about 1.1 billion years later. So, as unlikely as living systems are, they had such a long time to arise that their evolution was probably inevitable."[38]

It is clear that Marxists can never abandon the theory of spontaneous generation, since it is the only theory that conforms with their atheism and materialism. "Aspects of evolutionism are perfectly consistent with Marxism," says Robert Young in *Marxism Today*.

> The explanation of the origins of humankind and of mind by purely natural forces was, and remains, as welcome to Marxists as to any other secularists. The sources of value and responsibility are not to be found in a separate mental realm or in an immortal soul, much less in the inspired words of the Bible.[39]

It is interesting to note, however, just what kind of proof it would take to convince the "scientific" Marxist that spontaneous generation is unscientific. Louis Pasteur (1822-1895) disproved the theory of spontaneous generation,[40] but apparently not to Engels's satisfaction:

> Pasteur's attempts in this direction are useless; for those who believe in this possibility [of spontaneous generation] he will never be able to prove their impossibility by these experiments alone. . . .[41]

In fact, the impossibility of spontaneous generation can never be proven to one like Engels, since proving the impossibility of an event in one situation does not preclude the possibility of that event under any given situation. The key phrase from Engels, of course, is "for those who believe;" Engels has faith in the possibility of spontaneous generation occurring sometime, somewhere, and his faith will always shield him from proofs of impossibility—scientific or not.

Every Marxist/Leninist accepts the theory of spontaneous generation on faith and relies on it to support his theology, philosophy, and biology. The only other facet of evolutionary theory that virtually every

Notes and Asides

Marxist agrees on is the theory of punctuated equilibrium—a theory opposed to Darwin's perception of natural selection.

Punctuated Equilibrium

Marxists expounded the theory of punctuated equilibrium long before other biologists found themselves forced to embrace it because of an uncooperative fossil record (gaps in the fossil record were not filled with the transitional forms required by gradual Darwinian theory).

According to dialectical materialism, whenever thesis and antithesis clash, the new synthesis created occurs rapidly, in the form of a jump, rather than in the form of a long, gradual process. Thus,

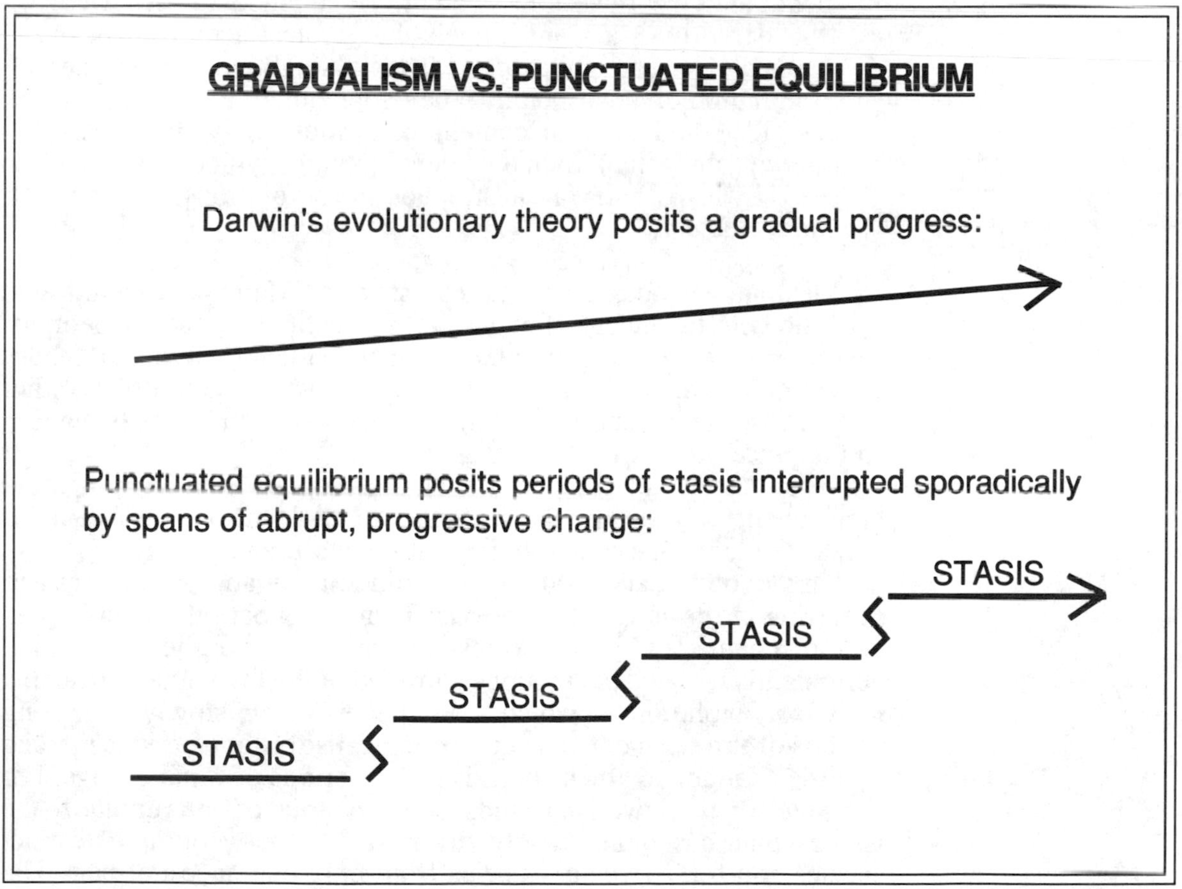
GRADUALISM VS. PUNCTUATED EQUILIBRIUM
Darwin's evolutionary theory posits a gradual progress:
Punctuated equilibrium posits periods of stasis interrupted sporadically by spans of abrupt, progressive change:
STASIS
STASIS
STASIS
STASIS

Notes and Asides

according to this view, both evolution and revolution are necessary in the social sphere to move from a capitalist society to a classless society; the change must occur rapidly, as did the overthrow of the Russian government. When thesis (bourgeoisie) and antithesis (proletariat) clash (through revolution), the resulting synthesis is a necessary leap resulting from the nature and flow of the dialectic. Darwin's slow, gradual natural selection theory does not fit well with the Marxist requirements of progress—either natural or social.

Therefore, Marxists expect evolution to work according to the dialectic: when thesis (a species) and antithesis (some aspect of the environment) clash, the synthesis (a new species) occurs rapidly. Lenin notes,

> As the most comprehensive and profound doctrine of development, and the richest in content, Hegelian dialectics were considered by Marx and Engels the greatest achievement of classical German philosophy. They thought that any other formulation of the principle of development, of evolution, was one-sided and poor in content, and could only distort and mutilate the actual course of development (which often proceeds by leaps, and via catastrophes and revolutions) in Nature and in society.[42]

Plekhanov echoes this sentiment, stating, "Many people confound dialectic with the theory of evolution. Dialectic is, in fact, a theory of evolution. But it differs profoundly from the vulgar [Darwinian] theory of evolution, which is based substantially upon the principle that neither in nature nor in history do sudden changes occur, and that all changes taking place in the world occur gradually."[43]

Punctuated equilibrium, however, does contain room for jumps and rapid change. It speaks the language of dialectical materialism. It speaks the language of revolution within evolution.

This evolutionary model sees evolution "as an episodic process occurring in fits and starts interspaced with long periods of stasis [i.e., lack of change]."[44] New species are said to rise rapidly "in small peripherally isolated populations." Instead of the Darwinian gradualist model of evolution in which new species occur slowly over long periods of time, punctuated equilibrium calls for long periods marked by little change, and then short, isolated periods of rapid change. For example, on the Hawaiian Islands there is a group of birds unique to the islands that has quite rapidly diversified into twenty-two distinct species and forty-five sub-species from only one ancestral pair. The change did not occur slowly over time, but rapidly.[45]

Notes and Asides

"According to this scheme," says Christian creationist Dr. Duane Gish,

> once a species has developed, it proliferates into a large population and persists relatively unchanged for one, two, five, or ten million years, or even longer. Then for some unknown reason a relatively small number of the individuals of the population become isolated, and by some unknown mechanism rapidly evolve into a new species (by rapid is meant something on the order of some tens of thousands of years). Once the new species has evolved, it then either becomes rapidly extinct or proliferates into a large population. This large population then persists for a million or more years. The long period of stasis [no change in the species] is the portion of the process referred to as the period of equilibrium, and the interval characterized by rapid evolution is the punctuation—thus the term, punctuated equilibrium.[46]

The idea that new species manifest themselves suddenly and by modifications appearing at once is not a new theory. Darwin himself addressed the issue in *The Origin of Species*. He rejected the idea and defended his theory of gradualism. He felt that domestic races may occasionally change abruptly while "entirely disbelieving" that natural species evolved according to such a mechanism.[47]

In this century, however, more attention has been directed toward the non-gradualism thesis. Hugo DeVries felt that new species could arise from time to time through a series of sudden or abrupt changes. O. H. Schindewolf, a German paleontologist, taught that evolution had proceeded by sudden jumps. In the 1930s he "proposed that a reptile laid an egg and hatched out a full-fledged bird as an explanation of the reptile-to-bird gap."[48]

In the 1940s, Richard Goldschmidt, in *The Material Basis for Evolution*, stated that a new theory of evolution was necessary since the required transitional forms in the fossil record were not being discovered. Goldschmidt hypothesized the "Hopeful Monster Theory," which suggested that occasionally a two-legged sheep or a two-headed turtle is born, and that two such monsters could mate and create something new. The similarity of the "Hopeful Monster Theory" to the punctuated equilibrium theory becomes obvious upon reading Stephen Jay Gould's article in *Natural History* entitled "The Return of the Hopeful Monsters."[49]

Today's version of the approach suggested by DeVries, Schindewolf, and Goldschmidt is called punctuated equilibrium. Those Ameri-

Notes and Asides

cans most closely associated with this theory are Gould, Richard Levins, and Richard Lewontin (Harvard University), Niles Eldredge (American Museum of Natural History), and Steven Stanley (Johns Hopkins University). "In 1972," says Gould, "my colleague Niles Eldredge and I developed the theory of punctuated equilibrium. We argued that two outstanding facts of the fossil record—geologically 'sudden' origin of new species and failure to change thereafter (stasis)—reflect the predictions of (this new) evolutionary theory, not the imperfections of the fossil record."[50]

Eldredge argued that if the conventional Darwinian evolutionary picture were true paleontologists should find a slow, gradual pattern of change in the fossil record. Instead, the record shows the sudden appearance of species that exist almost unchanged for millions of years. Instead of taking these abrupt appearances of fully formed animals and plants in the fossil record as a mark of creation (as creationists do), Eldredge sought to explain the sudden appearance of such animals as the result of sudden change in an isolated environment.

"To Frederick Engels, who got it wrong a lot of the time but who got it right where it counted."

—dedication in *The Dialectical Biologist,* by Levins and Lewontin

Stanley attacks Darwin's gradualism in *Macroevolution: Patterns and Process* (1979) and argues for (a) sudden appearances of species and (b) stability of species. Both points have been part of the Christian biology armory for many years.

Incredibly, these points have now been interpreted in a way that supports Marxist theory. Both Gould and Eldredge admit that their theory of punctuated equilibrium coincides with the Marxist interpretation of biology:

> Alternative conceptions of change have respectable pedigrees in philosophy. Hegel's dialectical laws, translated into a materialist context, have become the official "state philosophy" of many socialist nations. These laws of change are explicitly punctuational, as befits a theory of revolutionary transformation in human society. In light of this official philosophy, it is not at all surprising that a punctuational view of speciation, much like our own, but devoid (so far as we can tell) of references to synthetic evolutionary theory and the allopatric model, has long been favored by many Russian paleontologists. It may also not be irrelevant to our personal preferences that one of us [Gould][51] learned his Marxism, literally, at his daddy's knee.[52]

Notes and Asides

Gould, of course, has been criticized by other evolutionists for his Marxism. Edward O. Wilson complains, "He's willing to denigrate his own field of evolutionary biology in order to downgrade the enemy, sociobiology, which is a small but important branch of evolutionary biology. When Darwin conflicts with Marx, Darwin goes."[53] Michael Ruse says we are being offered the fossil record through the "lens of Marxism:"

> Quite openly, one of the leading punctuated equilibrists, Stephen Jay Gould, admits to his Marxism, and lauds the way in which his science is informed by his beliefs, and how conversely his beliefs are bolstered by his science. In short, what I argue is that through and through Gould produces and endorses a view of paleontology which is molded by, and conversely supports and proclaims a view of the world he holds dear. We are offered the fossil record as seen through the lens of Marxism.[54]

Lewontin co-authored a book on Marxist biology, *The Dialectical Biologist*, published by Harvard University press. In a review of the book David L. Hull writes,

> Richard Levins and Richard Lewontin are two of the most knowledgeable and innovative evolutionary biologists working today. They also view themselves as Marxist revolutionaries. As Marxists, Levins and Lewontin insist that the economic substructure of a society strongly influences its ideational superstructure, including science.[55]

Commenting on the situation at Harvard, where Darwinists refer to their biological opponents as "reds" and "revolutionaries," Christian creationist Henry M. Morris says,

> "Scientists, like other intellectuals, come to their work with a worldview, a set of preconceptions that provides the framework for their analysis of the world."
> —Richard Levins
> Richard Lewontin

> A very substantial number of other Harvard evolutionary scientists are also active Marxists in philosophy. Among these are: Richard Lewontin, a professor of population genetics; Jonathan Beckwith, a professor of microbiology; and Richard Levins, a professor of population biology. At sister institution [Massachusetts Institute of Technology], there are Jonathan King, associate professor of biology; Noam Chomsky, professor of linguistics; and others. All of these are recognized as top scientists, and there are many others around the country, all committed to Marx-style evolution. Many are members of a radical organization called "Science for the People," which grew out of the campus rebellions and anti-war protests of the 1960s.[56]

Notes and Asides

Clearly Marxists are pleased with the theory of punctuated equilibrium and how it affirms their worldview. Volkenshtein actually uses the fossil record as proof for the veracity of Marxist biology, claiming, "Whereas it was believed earlier that evolution occurs slowly, by way of gradual accumulation of small changes, at present biology takes into account a multitude of facts indicating that macroevolution occurred in a jumpwise manner and was not reduced to microevolution. The absence of transient forms in the paleontological records points, in a number of cases, not to a deficiency but to the absence of such forms. Small changes are often not accumulated at all."[57] In other words, since evolution across species is not observable in the fossil record, and since the theory of evolution cannot be wrong, the theory of the mechanism of evolution must be revised to fit the facts. Volkenshtein cites other "proof" for punctuated equilibrium as well, pointing out that "No gradual transition can take place between feathers and hair, etc."[58] Creationists have cited these facts for years in criticizing evolutionary theory, but they take on new importance for Marxists when they can be used as "proof" for a new theory of evolution better designed to account for the lack of real evolutionary proof in the fossil record!

Marxists are delighted that punctuated equilibrium is now considered a viable scientific explanation for the origin of the species, since it is more closely aligned with Marxist dialectics. However, Marxists will embrace virtually any idea about evolution as long as it fits their worldview and disallows the existence of anything supernatural. In fact, Marxism has undergone its own evolution in its views on the origin of life.

Evolution as Interpreted By Marx and Engels

While Darwin's theory was still in its infancy during the Marxist founding fathers' lifetimes, Marx and Engels were not bashful about declaring evolutionary theory to be a concrete fact. Indeed, in this way, Marxist biology has not changed since its inception. From the beginning, we find Engels claiming, "However numerous the modifications in details this theory [of evolution] will yet undergo, it nevertheless, on the whole, already solves the problem [of origins] in a more than satisfactory manner."[59] It is significant that, even before Engels was convinced of the difficulties Darwin's theory posed for the dialectic, he was willing to concede any modifications to the theory of evolution—so long as it effectively destroyed the concept of a supernatural Creator. Engels recognizes the firm foundation evolution provides for materialism and therefore unhesitatingly accepts Darwin's theory as law, declaring that "it is a fact that man sprang from the beasts."[60] In this way

Marxist biology has remained consistent throughout its history.

Marxist biology has also remained essentially unchanged in the area of accepted methods of "proof" for the theory of evolution. Marx and Engels relied heavily on paleontology and geology. Marx states, "Strata are our means of discovering about the epochs"[61] and "paleontology" just required skeptics "to see the things which lie in front of their noses."[62] Engels describes the revelation provided by the fossil record, noting that "More and more the gaps in the paleontological record were filled up, compelling even the most reluctant to acknowledge the striking parallelism between the history of the development of the organic world as a whole and that of the individual organism. . . ."[63] However, Engels was perceptive enough to understand the shortcomings of geology: "We are even worse off in geology, which by its nature is concerned chiefly with events which took place not only in our absence but in the absence of any human being whatever. This winning of final and absolute truths in this field is therefore a very troublesome business, and the crop is extremely meagre."[64] Therefore, Engels pointed to other sciences as well to bolster the theory of evolution. These sciences are still used as "proofs" today.

Engels relied on embryology, claiming that "there is in fact a peculiar similarity between the gradual development of organic germs [embryos] into mature organisms, and the succession of plants and animals following each other in the history of the earth. And it is precisely this similarity which has given the theory of evolution its most secure basis."[65] He also relied on comparative physiology, which he says "gives one a withering contempt for the idealistic exaltation of men over the other animals."[66] And in his most cohesive defense of evolution, Engels cites, among other scientific discoveries, geology, paleontology, Darwin and Lamarck's work, comparative anatomy, and embryology, then draws the conclusion that "The old teleology has gone to the devil, but it is now firmly established that matter in its eternal cycle moves according to laws which at a definite stage—now here, now there—necessarily give rise to the thinking mind in organic beings."[67]

Insofar as Marx and Engels accepted evolution as fact and relied on the same proofs as modern Marxists for the theory of evolution, Marxist biology has not changed since Darwin's theory was first introduced. But with regard to Marxist biology's interpretation of Darwin's theory, Marxism's views have changed drastically. For example, Marxist biology began by denying the very principle on which Darwin's theory hinged: natural selection, and its corollary, the struggle for existence. Engels says, "But it is absolutely childish to desire to sum up the whole manifold wealth of historical evolution and complexity in the meagre and one-sided phrase 'struggle for life.' That says less than nothing."[68]

Notes and Asides

"[I]t is a fact that man sprang from the beasts."
—Frederick Engels

Notes and Asides

Why is Engels so hostile toward the notion of natural selection? He provides us with the clue to the answer when he states,

> Darwin's mistake lies precisely in lumping together in "natural selection" or the "survival of the fittest" two absolutely separate things: 1. Selection by the pressure of over-population, where perhaps the strongest survive in the first place, but where the weakest in many respects can also do so. 2. Selection by greater capacity of adaptation to altered circumstances, where the survivors are better suited to these circumstances, but where this adaptation as a whole can mean regress just as well as progress (for instance adaptation to parasitic life is always regress).[69]

The fundamental points in this statement are the words *progress* and *regress* and Engels's concern that the weakest can also survive in natural selection. Engels is bothered by the fact that natural selection, as postulated by Darwin, does not always result in a more advanced, higher form of existence—a prerequisite demanded by Marxist dialectics. As demonstrated earlier, Marxist dialectics claims that all of life is progressive, and change is always for the better—but this is not necessarily the case in natural selection. Therefore, Engels must abandon the model and discover one more in keeping with his dialectics. We find him doing exactly that when he claims, "Haeckel's 'adaptation and heredity' also can determine the whole process of evolution, without need for [natural] selection and Malthusianism."[70]

Engels himself may have sensed the inaccuracy of his suggestion,[71] for elsewhere we discover him championing a theory that sounds suspiciously like natural selection: "This 'predatory economy' of animals plays an important part in the gradual transformation of species by forcing them to adapt themselves to other than the usual food, thanks to which their blood acquires a different chemical composition and the whole physical constitution gradually alters, while species that were once established die out. There is no doubt that this predatory economy has powerfully contributed to the gradual evolution of our ancestors into men."[72] And still elsewhere Engels shows himself willing to use Darwin's struggle for existence to make a point:

> Darwin did not know what a bitter satire he wrote on mankind, and especially on his countrymen, when he showed that free competition, the struggle for existence, which the economists celebrate as the highest historical achievement, is the normal state of the animal kingdom. Only conscious organization of social production, in which production and distribution are carried on in a planned way, can lift mankind above the rest of

Notes and Asides

> the animal world as regards the social aspect, in the same way that production in general has done this for mankind in the specifically biological aspect.[73]

Engels's waffling aside, the founding fathers of Marxism generally regarded Darwin's theory of natural selection as somewhat of a threat to the dialectic. This view was a logical response, because Darwin's theory of natural selection did not prove progress[74] or postulate abrupt leaps, as the dialectic insisted it should. However, Marxist biology has since been forced to change its views. This change did not occur, though, until Marxist biology had struggled through another phase, one due largely to the activity of one man, T. D. Lysenko.

Lysenko and Mendel

During World War II, Darwin's notions about struggle for existence and survival of the fittest were still unpopular with Marxists. Howard Selsam calls survival of the fittest "a social and logical perversion of Darwin's principle of natural selection. . . . It is what we have called a social perversion because it takes a principle from the non-human world of nature and attempts to apply it without qualification to the whole history of man and his societies, as if there were no features or elements in human society not reducible to those of the animal world."[75] However, Marxist biology was too concerned with attacking a different aspect of evolutionary theory to concentrate on the contradictions between the dialectic and Darwin's not-always-progressive evolution.

This attack was spearheaded by Lysenko, the leading Soviet biologist from the early 1930s into the 1950s and President of the Academy of Sciences during the height of his prestige (1936-45). Lysenko claimed that Gregor Mendel's discoveries about genetics were inconclusive, declaring, "it is time to eliminate Mendelism in all its varieties from all courses and textbooks."[76] With full support from the Russian Marxist government (indeed, most Soviet biologists who disagreed with Lysenko either repented or met untimely deaths), Lysenko began to preach a biology strictly denying Mendel's genetics:

> In our conception, the entire organism consists only of the ordinary body that everyone knows. There is in an organism no special substance apart from the ordinary body. But any little particle, figuratively speaking, any granule, any droplet of a living body, once it is alive, necessarily possesses the property of heredity, that is, the requirement of appropriate conditions for its life, growth, and development.[77]

Notes and Asides

Naturally, Lysenko's notions about heredity eventually led him to embrace Lamarckism, a theory that states that acquired characteristics can be passed from one generation to the next through heredity. He did not publicly admit his Lamarckian views, however, until it came to light that Stalin, years earlier, had supported neo-Lamarckism.[78] Once it became clear that both Stalin and Lysenko supported some form of Lamarckism, Marxist biology had no choice but to embrace this theory of acquired characteristics unreservedly. And on the surface, Lamarckism did seem to complement Marxist dialectics better, since it called for a more consistently progressive view of evolution than Darwin's theory.

CLOSE-UP

Trofim Lysenko (1898-1976)

Marxism claims to be the only scientific worldview. The life of one man, T. D. Lysenko, revealed that Marxism is just the opposite: a worldview ready to manipulate science to further its own cause. Lysenko was a Russian geneticist who became a full member of the Soviet Academy of Sciences in 1935. From there, he gained scientific credibility quickly, attaining the presidency of the Academy the following year. The Marxist government of the USSR embraced Lysenko so willingly largely because he attacked the conclusions of Gregor Mendel (the founder of genetics) and promoted a form of Lamarckism (a theory that claims acquired characteristics may be passed from parent to offspring). Such ideas meshed more readily with Marxism, because they allowed for a more consistently progressive form of evolution, which is demanded by the dialectic. Charles Darwin's mechanism of natural selection did not guarantee progress in every generation, whereas Lysenko's brand of Lamarckism could. Thus, Marxists were anxious to label Lysenko's conclusions "scientific" and to label legitimate scientists who supported Mendel "enemies of the people." This policy seriously hampered scientific discovery in the USSR, and eventually Soviet biology lagged years behind the rest of the world. Lysenko then fell from grace, and the effects of Lysenkoism were finally shaken off by Soviet scientists around 1965.

Notes and Asides

Unfortunately for Lysenko and the Marxists, they could only hide their heads in the sand so long before they had to face two facts the rest of the world had accepted long ago: Mendel's ideas about genetics were correct, and Lamarck's idea of acquired characteristics was absurd. Indeed, by 1981 Volkenshtein freely admitted that the "entire course of development of evolution theory is directly associated with Darwinism and genetics."[79] With these facts accepted and Lysenko discredited, Marxist biology was ready to move into its third phase: its modern interpretation of evolution.

Lamarckism is a theory that suggests that acquired characteristics are inheritable.

Present Marxist Interpretation of Evolution

Today, Marxism no longer can avoid the fact that natural selection is a crucial premise of the theory of evolution. But in order to cause natural selection to mesh with their dialectics, Marxist biologists have had to present a modified version of the theory. Natural selection is seen as occurring in leaps, according to punctuated equilibrium. The mechanism for such evolution is achieved by adding the notion of dramatic mutations to the theory of natural selection, thus creating a directionality better suited to fit the Marxist dialectic. Volkenshtein says, "The successful operation of natural selection does occur and is possible owing to the high individualization of biological systems. The evolution cannot repeat itself precisely because these systems are individual and any problem posed by the environmental conditions has numerous solutions. The presence of this multitude of solutions implies that the state of a system undergoing evolution is unstable. Mutations cause a transition of the system to one of the relatively stable states. The instability determines the directional, irreversible character of evolution."[80]

Of course, the addition of mutations seems to go against the dialectic in one sense, since mutation theory calls for randomness, but Volkenshtein hastily denies this possibility, stating, "The random, chance appearance of mutations does not imply the absence of directionality in evolution. Such directionality arises in a natural way, since selection through the survival of the fittest is a directional rather than an accidental factor."[81] Volkenshtein stresses directionality throughout his text, claiming that it is "the most important feature" of evolution.[82] This emphasis results from Marxism's need to interpret natural selection as compatible with dialectics, whatever the cost. Volkenshtein also attempts to tie the theory of evolution to dialectics when he writes, "Each new stage of evolution is the result of the instability of the preceding state of the system."[83] In other words, synthesis results from the clash (or instability) between thesis and antithesis.

Despite the Marxist move full circle from attacking natural selection to embracing it, some aspects of Marxist biology, as we have noted, remain constant. Volkenshtein relies basically on the same "proofs" for the theory of evolution that Marx and Engels relied on a century ago. He is especially dependent on the fossil record, as is evident when he writes, "How did evolution progress in time? Geology and paleontology provide a wealth of information on this problem."[84] Elsewhere he claims, "The modern conceptions of the origin of life are intimately connected with the results obtained by the study of geological evolution."[85]

In fact, the only new "proof" that Volkenshtein is able to offer is one unheard of in Marx and Engels's time—the breakthroughs made in molecular biology:

> In the last several decades the situation has changed owing to a deeper general understanding of the evolution of the Universe and to the successes achieved in genetics and molecular biology. Though no strict quantitative theory of evolution is available, we can give positive answers to the question indicated: yes, both the time and material were sufficient [for natural selection to direct the evolution of the species].[86]

Conclusion

The Marxist interpretation of evolution has undergone a number of changes since Marx first embraced Darwin's theory. These changes have been emphasized throughout this chapter to stress the willingness of Marxism to revise and distort the theory of evolution in an effort to make it more compatible with their dialectic. When natural selection can be discarded to avoid conflict with the dialectic, the Marxist will discard it. When natural selection must be embraced as a basic premise of evolutionary theory, the Marxist will twist it until it fits with the dialectic. Marxism will interpret the theory of evolution in any way that allows it to support the dialectic and still retain the use of the theory as a "scientific" answer to anyone suggesting the existence of the supernatural.

Also stressed throughout this chapter was the fact that Marxist biologists rely on the same "proofs" for the theory of evolution as the Secular Humanists (and indeed, all evolutionists)—namely, paleontology, geology, embryology, comparative anatomy, and molecular biology. These disciplines supply the "scientific" base for the theory of evolution. How well these disciplines provide support for evolutionary theory will be discussed in the chapter on Christian biology and in the

Notes and Asides

Conclusion of the book.

Regardless of how scientific or unscientific the theory of evolution is, however, we can be certain of one thing: Marxist biology will consistently declare it as factual and grounded in science. As we have seen, evolution provides a basis for both Marxist theology and Marxist philosophy, and without this foundation, Marxists are unable to explain the teleology of our universe and the phenomena of the human mind. As Engels says, "in our evolutionary conception of the universe, there is absolutely no room for either a creator or a ruler."[87] But without evolution, there can be no avoiding a Creator. And the Marxist must avoid a Creator at all costs.

[1]Karl Marx and Frederick Engels, in a letter to Lassalle dated Jan. 16, 1861, *Selected Correspondence* (New York: International Publishers, 1942), p. 125.
[2]John Hoffman, *Marxism and the Theory of Praxis* (New York: International Publishers, 1976), p. 69.
[3]Karl Marx, cited in Charles J. McFadden, *The Philosophy of Communism* (Kenosha, WI: Cross, 1939), pp. 35-6.
[4]Karl Marx, *Selected Correspondences*, p. 125.
[5]Hoffman, *Marxism and the Theory of Praxis*, p. 56.
[6]F. V. Konstantinov, ed., *The Fundamentals of Marxist-Leninist Philosophy* (Moscow: Progress Publishers, 1982), p. 61.
[7]Ernst Mayr and William B. Provine, *The Evolutionary Synthesis* (Cambridge: Harvard University Press, 1980), p. 229. Cited in Luther D. Sunderland, *Darwin's Enigma* (San Diego, CA: Master Books, 1984), pp. 109-10.
[8]Karl Marx, *Capital* (Lawrence and Wishart, 1970), vol. 1, p. 341.
[9]Frederick Engels, *Selected Works* (1950), vol. 2, p. 153, cited in R. N. Carew Hunt, *The Theory and Practice of Communism* (Baltimore: Penguin Books, 1966), p. 64.
[10]V. I. Lenin, *Collected Works*, forty-five volumes (Moscow: Progress Publishers, 1977), vol. 1, p. 142.
[11]Leon Trotsky, *Culture and Revolution* , p. 113, cited in David McLellan, *Marxism and Religion* (New York: Harper and Row, 1987), p. 107.
[12]G. V. Plekhanov, *In Defence of Materialism* (London: 1947), p. 244. Cited in Gustav A. Wetter, *Dialectical Materialism* (Westport, CT: Greenwood Press, 1977), p. 107.
[13]Marx, *Selected Correspondence*, p. 125.
[14]Frederick Engels, *Anti-Dühring* (New York: International 1935), p. 36.
[15]Frederick Engels, *Socialism: Utopian and Scientific* (New York: International, 1935), p. 21.
[16]Konstantinov, ed., *Fundamentals of Marxist-Leninist Philosophy*, p. 42.
[17]Frederick Engels, *Ludwig Feuerbach* (New York: International, 1974), p. 67.
[18]Karl Marx, *Gesamtausgabe*, sect. 2, vol. 3, p. 396, cited in McFadden, *The Philosophy of Communism*, p. 36.
[19]Engels, *Socialism: Utopian and Scientific*, p. 48.
[20]Konstantinov, ed., *Fundamentals of Marxist-Leninist Philosophy*, p. 43.
[21]Frederick Engels, *Dialectics of Nature* (New York: International, 1976), p. 234.
[22]Ibid., p. 13.
[23]Engels, *Ludwig Feuerbach*, p. 54.
[24]Joseph Stalin, *On Dialectical and Historical Materialism* , p. 107, cited in Wetter, *Dialectical Materialism*, p. 329.
[25]Lenin, *Collected Works*, vol. 24, pp. 54-5.
[26]Joseph Stalin, *Works* (Moscow and London: 1952/3), vol. 1, p. 304. Cited in Wetter, *Dialectical Materialism*, p. 325.
[27]Otto Rühle, *Karl Marx: His Life and Works* (New York: The Viking Press, 1928), pp. 66-7.
[28]Hoffman, *Marxism and the Theory of Praxis*, p. 69.
[29]Engels, *Ludwig Feuerbach*, pp. 67-8.
[30]Karl Marx, *Economic and Philosophical Manuscripts*, cited in Francis Nigel Lee, *Communism Versus Creation* (Nutley, NJ: The Craig Press, 1969), p. 68.
[31]Engels, *Ludwig Feuerbach*, p. 352.
[32]Engels, *Anti-Dühring*, p. 85.
[33]Ibid., p. 78.
[34]M. V. Volkenshtein, *Biophysics* (Moscow: Mir Publishers, 1983), p. 565.
[35]A. I. Oparin, *The Origin of Life* (Moscow: Foreign Languages Publishing House, 1955), p. 101.
[36]M. A. Leonov, *Outline of Dialectical Materialism* (Moscow: 1948), p. 494. Cited in Wetter, *Dialectical Materialism*, p. 496.
[37]Volkenshtein, *Biophysics*, p. 565.
[38]Karen Arms and Pamela S. Camp, *Biology*, 2d ed. (New York: CBS College Publishers, 1982), p. 293. Arms and Camp then turn to Oparin and Haldane for confirmation of spontaneous generation: "In 1924 a Russian, Alexander Oparin, published a theory of how life could have arisen from simple molecules on the early earth. An Englishman, J. B. S. Haldane, published a paper in 1929 that said essentially the same thing. . . . Research

since then has largely borne out the predictions made by Oparin and Haldane. Scientists have simulated prebiotic (before life existed) conditions in their laboratories; surprisingly, the nonliving systems formed in these artificial environments exhibit many properties that we consider characteristic of life" (p. 294). Haldane , wrote the preface and notes for Engels' *Dialectics of Nature*, 1940 edition. See Frederick Engels, *Dialectics of Nature* (New York: International Publishers, 1976).
[39]Robert M. Young, *Marxism Today*, vol. 26 (April 1982), p. 21. Cited in Sunderland, *Darwin's Enigma*, p. 109.
[40]*The World Book Encyclopedia* (Chicago: Field Enterprises Educational Corp., 1970), vol. 15, p. 169: "[Pasteur] was the first to show that living things come only from living things. Before that, many scientists believed in spontaneous generation, a theory that life could come from things that are not alive, such as dirt."
[41]Engels, *Dialectics of Nature*, p. 189.
[42]Lenin, *Collected Works*, vol. 24, p. 53.
[43]G. Plekhanov, *Fundamental Problems of Marxism* (London: Lawrence, 1929), p. 145.
[44]Michael Denton, *Evolution: A Theory in Crisis* (Bethesda, MD: Adler and Adler, 1985), pp. 192-3.
[45]Ibid., p. 84. Of course, the key problem for adherents to punctuated equilibrium theory is not answered by this scenario. These birds have changed, but they have not evolved into an entirely new species—they are still Hawaiian honeycreepers.
[46]Duane T. Gish, *Evolution: The Challenge of the Fossil Record* (El Cajon, CA: Creation-Life, 1985), p. 248.
[47]Charles Darwin, *The Origin of Species* (New York: Mentor Books, 1958), p. 224-5, cited in Sunderland, *Darwin's Enigma*, p. 97.
[48]Sunderland, *Darwin's Enigma*, p. 97.
[49]Stephen Jay Gould, "The Return of the Hopeful Monsters," *Natural History*, vol. 86 (June/July 1977), pp. 22-30.
[50]Stephen Jay Gould, *Discover*, May 1981, p. 36, cited in Sunderland, *Darwin's Enigma*, p. 98-9.
[51]Sunderland, *Darwin's Enigma*, pp. 108-9: "At least once under oath in a court deposition for the trial regarding the constitutionality of the Louisiana Balanced Treatment Law, he [Gould] acknowledged that he was a Marxist."
[52]Niles Eldredge and Stephen J. Gould, *Paleobiology*, vol. 3 (Spring 1977), pp. 145-6, cited in Sunderland, *Darwin's Enigma*, p. 108. According to Sunderland, punctuated equilibrium theory's success is mixed: "Regardless of the well-known objections, both social and scientific, to the theory of punctuated equilibrium evolution, it has within the last decade virtually swept aside all competition and become accepted by the vast majority of evolutionists in the United States. Stephen Jay Gould was chosen as 'Man-of-the-Year in Science' by *Discover* magazine and appeared on the cover of *Newsweek*. The educational system is slow to be turned from a pervasive course, however, and few textbooks even mention punctuated equilibrium theory a decade after it was first widely publicized" (pp. 110-11).
[53]Edward O. Wilson, *Bioscience* (June 1979), p. 342, cited in Henry Morris, *The Long War Against God* (Grand Rapids, MI: Baker, 1990), p. 88.
[54]E. Geisler and W. Scheler, ed., *Darwin Today* (Berlin: Akademie-Verlag, 1983), p. 246, cited in Morris, *The Long War Against God*, p. 89.
[55]David L. Hull, *Nature* (March 6, 1985), p. 23, cited in Morris, *The Long War Against God*, pp. 89-90.
[56]Morris, *The Long War Against God*, p. 88.
[57]Volkenshtein, *Biophysics*, p. 617.
[58]Ibid., p. 618.
[59]Engels, *Ludwig Feuerbach*, pp. 66-7.
[60]Engels, *Anti-Dühring*, p. 213.
[61]Marx, *Capital*, p. 172.
[62]Marx, *Selected Correspondence*, p. 235.
[63]Engels, *Dialectics of Nature*, pp. 12-13.
[64]Engels, *Anti-Dühring*, p. 101.
[65]Ibid., p. 85.
[66]Engels, *Selected Correspondence*, p. 114.
[67]Engels, *Dialectics of Nature*, p. 187.
[68]Ibid., p. 208.

[69]Ibid., p. 236.
[70]Ibid., p. 235.
[71]The theory of inherited acquired characteristics has been all but abandoned by science.
[72]Ibid., p. 286.
[73]Ibid., p. 19.
[74]Although Darwin believed natural selection did select the good traits for survival and dispatch the bad.
[75]Howard Selsam, *Socialism and Ethics* (New York: International, 1943), p. 90.
[76]T. D. Lysenko, *Iarovizatsiia* (1939), No. 1, cited in David Joravsky, *The Lysenko Affair* (Cambridge, MA: Harvard University Press, 1970), p. 211.
[77]T. D. Lysenko, *Agrobiologiia* (1949), p. 486, cited in Joravsky, *The Lysenko Affair*, p. 210.
[78]Joseph Stalin, *Collected Works* , vol. 1, pp. 301, 303, 309, cited in Joravsky, *The Lysenko Affair*, pp. 132, 231.
[79]Volkenshtein, *Biophysics*, p. 618.
[80]Ibid., p. 587.
[81]Ibid., pp. 586-7.
[82]Ibid., p. 618.
[83]Ibid., p. 589.
[84]Ibid., p. 587.
[85]Ibid., p. 565.
[86]Ibid., p. 585.
[87]Engels, *Socialism: Utopian and Scientific*, p. 21.

CHAPTER

14

BIBLICAL CHRISTIAN BIOLOGY

"And God created great whales, and every living creature that moveth, which the waters brought forth abundantly, after their kind, and every winged fowl after his kind."

—Genesis 1:21

"But from the beginning of the creation God made them male and female."

—Jesus Christ, Mark 10:6

"No one in all human history has ever observed one species evolve into a more complex and better adapted species by natural selection or any other mechanism. No one has seen evidence of any mechanism that would make evolution work. In the fossil record of the past, with billions of fossils preserved in the earth's sedimentary crust, no one has ever found any fossils showing incipient or transitional structures leading to the evolution of more complex species."[1]

—Henry M. Morris

SUMMARY

How does one prove that special creation, not evolution, accounts for all life on earth? Evolutionists claim that there is no scientific evidence for the Christian creationist explanation of biology. But what evidence would they accept? Presumably, they would acknowledge the validity of the creation model if we invented a time machine and transported them back in time to observe God creating the universe. But short of that, how might the creationist convince the evolutionist? How else can one demonstrate that God acted to create all reality?

There are at least two methods. First, the creationist could support his position by demonstrating that its only alternative—macroevolution—is false, either because it is impossible or because the preponderance of empirical evidence is against it, or both. If he can do that, then the creationist model wins by default. Second, the creationist may promote his position by presenting the vast number of scientific discoveries that evidence design, thereby suggesting a Designer. Only creationism adequately accounts for design in nature, since only it postulates a Designer, while materialist evolutionism postulates only chance.

Since the creationist cannot take the skeptic back to the beginning of the universe, these two approaches are all we can offer. By the same token, however, the evolutionist cannot observe and test the evolutionary process; he therefore is in no position to ignore the creationist's conclusions without examination.

Thus, we will concern ourselves in this chapter primarily with dismantling the evidence alleged to prove evolution and outlining some of the more startling scientific suggestions of design in nature. This will show why we believe the creation model fits the facts of science better than the evolution model.

Introduction

Perhaps no other aspect of Christianity has troubled believers more in the last century than the question of origins. Because many biologists treat evolution as a scientific fact, Christians have struggled to reconcile their faith in the Bible with the "fact" that man and all living things evolved from a single speck of life.

This reconciliation is impossible from a rational perspective. Christians who believe that God created the first glimmer of life on earth and then directed its evolution to generate man (the belief known as theistic evolution) must take substantial liberties in interpreting the Bible, and

Outstanding scientists like Michael Denton demythologize evolution by pointing out, "Neither of the two fundamental axioms of Darwin's macroevolutionary theory . . . have been validated by one single empirical discovery or scientific advance since 1859."[2] Uncanny instincts and other evidences of intelligent design in mammals (such as the sloth), insects (the *Odynerus*, or hunting wasp), fish (the *Tilapia macrocephala*), and birds (the water ouzel)[3] support the creationist claim that all was designed by an intelligent Creator. Science, when used as a means for discerning truth rather than as a vehicle for propagating atheistic dogma, corroborates Biblical revelation. This chapter presents the case for a belief that science and Genesis are allies, not enemies.

The Christian believes that Scripture is a historical account of origins. Christianity trusts the authority of Genesis and declarations concerning creation such as Mark 10:6 and Colossians 1:16. It was none other than Jesus Christ who said, "But from the beginning of the creation God made them male and female" (Mark 10:6). The Christian more quickly places his faith in the Bible than in science, which is certainly not infallible and is limited in its application.[4] But the Christian also recognizes that science, when earnestly seeking after truth, is a valuable ally. This chapter, therefore, is as concerned with challenging the unfounded belief that religion and science are enemies as it is with supporting creationist arguments. We will demonstrate that science and Christianity are compatible, declaring in unison that God "created all things" (Ephesians 3:9). Science gives us information about God's universe; the Bible gives us information about God's universe and God Himself.

they face most of the same arguments Christians use against atheistic evolution.

Genesis 1:1 clearly states, "In the beginning God created the heavens and the earth." Genesis 1:27 proclaims, "So God created man in his own image, in the image of God he created him; male and female he created them." This bold claim is unreservedly affirmed in the New Testament, as well. Paul, in Ephesians 3:9, speaks of "God, who created all things." And Jesus Christ declares in Mark 10:6, "But at the beginning of creation God 'made them male and female.'"[5]

Notes and Asides

Theistic evolutionists have, through semantic acrobatics, managed to interpret these verses so that they appear to support the evolutionary position. Theistic evolutionists contend that the term *creation* simply means that God created the first spark of life and then directed His creation through the vehicle of evolution.[6] Thus, some Christians believe that the Bible does not necessarily deny evolutionary theory as an explanation for origins. This may appear to be a tenable position when discussing only verses concerned strictly with the question of origins; however, when one examines the entire message of the Bible, the doctrine of theistic evolution severely undermines the Christian understanding of God and man's place in His universe.

For example, while it is true that God is capable of anything that is logically possible, so that He *could* have used evolution to generate all species, why would He employ such an inefficient (and often totally ineffective) mechanism? If God designed the world to operate according to specific natural laws requiring minimal routine interference, why would He use an evolutionary mechanism that would require His constant meddling with the development of life? Further, such a mechanism seems an especially cruel method for creating man. As Jacques Monod notes, natural selection is the "blindest and most cruel way of evolving new species."[7] Secular Humanist Bertrand Russell is shocked that any Christian could justify a theistic evolutionary position: "We are told that 'evolution is the unfolding of an idea which has been in the mind of God.' It appears that during those ages when animals were torturing each other with ferocious horns and agonizing stings, Omnipotence was quietly waiting for the ultimate emergence of man, with his still more widely diffused cruelty. Why the Creator should have preferred to reach His goal by a process, instead of going straight to it, these modern theologians do not tell us."[8]

More important, if evolution is true, then the story of the Garden of Eden and original sin must be viewed as nothing more than allegory, a view that undermines the significance of Christ's sinless life and sacrificial death on the cross. Why? Because the Bible presents Jesus as analogous to Adam. The condemnation and corruption brought on us by Adam's sin are the counterparts of the justification and sanctification made possible for us by Christ's righteousness and death (Romans 5:12-19). If Adam was not a historical individual, and if his fall into sin was not historical, then the Biblical doctrines of sin and of Christ's atonement for it collapse. Walter Brown, Jr., sums up the theistic evolutionist's predicament: "If evolution happened, then a tremendous amount of death occurred before man evolved. But if death preceded man and was not a result of Adam's sin, then sin is a fiction. If sin is a fiction, then we have no need for a Savior."[9] Of course, this conclusion is unacceptable for the Christian. Thus, it is our contention that the

Notes and Asides

proper Christian worldview requires a belief in the Creator as He is literally portrayed in the book of Genesis.

For a Christian to have believed in creation forty, thirty, or even twenty years ago might have seemed radical because, until recently, evolution appeared to be unassailable scientifically. Understandably, many Christians turned to theistic evolution as the only means of reconciling their reason with their faith.

Today, however, the scientific objections to evolution are so strong that Christians who wish to integrate faith and reason would do well to abandon evolution as a rational explanation for the origin of species. Indeed, today it is fair to declare creationism not only more reasonable but also more scientific than evolution. Henry Morris states,

> The scientific creationists themselves are men and women who have acquired all the standard credentials of the scientist, but who maintain that creation explains the facts of science better than evolution does. To them it is not primarily a question of religion (after all, people can be religious and moral while still believing in evolution), but of science. They are convinced that the creation model correlates the scientific data more effectively.[10]

The increasingly shaky scientific grounds for evolutionism are spelled out by David Raup, whose Field Museum of Natural History has one of the largest fossil collections in the world: "[W]e are now about 120 years after Darwin and the knowledge of the fossil record has been greatly expanded. We now have a quarter of a million fossil species but the situation hasn't changed much. The record of evolution is still surprisingly jerky and, ironically, we have even fewer examples of evolutionary transition than we had in Darwin's time."[11]

"[I]ronically, we have even fewer examples of evolutionary transition than we had in Darwin's time."
—David Raup

In the same vein, Michael Denton admits,

> The overriding supremacy of the myth [that Darwin discovered an indisputable truth] has created a widespread illusion that the theory of evolution was all but proved one hundred years ago and that all subsequent biological research—paleontological, zoological and in the newer branches of genetics and molecular biology—has provided ever-increasing evidence for Darwinian ideas. Nothing could be further from the truth. The fact is that the evidence was so patchy one hundred years ago that even Darwin himself had increasing doubts as to the validity of his views, and the only aspect of his theory which has received any support over the past century is where it applies to microevolutionary phenomena. His general theory, that all life on earth had

Notes and Asides

> originated and evolved by a gradual successive accumulation of fortuitous mutations, is still, as it was in Darwin's time, a highly speculative hypothesis entirely without direct factual support and very far from that self-evident axiom some of its more aggressive advocates would have us believe.[12]

For the Christian, this is a cause for much rejoicing. While it seemed for many years that a natural, normal interpretation of the Bible could not be reconciled with science, today this view should be reinstated as a guide for all scientific enterprises. Emphasis must be placed on the word *reinstated*, because for hundreds of years most scientists *did* rely on a strict understanding of God as Creator and Designer, and only recently has science turned away from its Christian heritage.

Christianity and Science

Modern science's roots are grounded in a Christian view of the world. This is not surprising, since science is based on the assumption that the universe is orderly and can be expected to act according to specific, discoverable laws. An ordered, lawful universe would seem to be the effect of an intelligent Cause, which was precisely the belief of many early scientists. The concept that "God is the builder of everything" (Hebrews 3:4) and that Christ "made the universe" (Hebrews 1:2) did not frighten the likes of Isaac Newton and other great early scientists.

According to Francis A. Schaeffer, "The rise of modern science did not conflict with what the Bible teaches; indeed at a crucial point the Scientific Revolution rested upon what the Bible teaches."[13] Renowned philosopher and historian of science Stanley L. Jaki specifies that "from Copernicus to Newton it was not deism but Christian theism that served as a principal factor helping the scientific enterprise reach self-sustaining maturity."[14]

"For the world was built in order/ and the atoms march in tune . . ."
—R. W. Emerson

Inherent to this early scientific dependence on the orderliness of the world was the belief that the world was ordered by a Divine creator. As Langdon Gilkey points out, "The religious idea of a transcendent creator actually made possible rather than hindered the progress of the scientific understanding of the natural order. In a real sense the modern conviction that existence is good because it is intelligible to scientific inquiry finds some of its most significant roots in the Christian belief that God created the world."[15] Norman L. Geisler and J. Kerby Anderson echo this belief: "Most early scientists worked out their scientific views from within this theistic Christian belief in a supernatural creator and the doctrine of creation."[16]

Today, too, scientists recognize the importance of orderliness in the

Notes and Asides

universe. Physicist Paul Davies writes,

> Science is possible only because we live in an ordered universe which complies with simple mathematical laws. The job of the scientist is to study, catalogue and relate the orderliness in nature, not to question its origin. But theologians have long argued that the order in the physical world is evidence for God. If this is true, then science and religion acquire a common purpose in revealing God's work.[17]

These last two sentences are especially significant from the Christian biologist's perspective. The argument that order and design in the universe help prove the existence of God (known as the teleological argument) can and should be used most effectively by Christian biologists to bolster the case for fiat creationism.

Before noting some teleological aspects of the universe, we must scrutinize the consequences of choosing (as most evolutionists do) to reject Christianity while still trusting in the validity of science. China is a fine example of a culture that denied Christianity during the development of modern science—and as a result, science in China has suffered. Jaki believes "the predicament of China, both ancient and modern, is an eloquent though tragic witness to the need of natural theology if science is to flourish."[18] Without a belief in order, science has no foundation.

Fiat creationism refers to the belief that God created the universe and everything in it in six days.

It is precisely this belief in order that was undermined by Charles Darwin more than one hundred years ago. Rather than relying on a Creator, Darwin postulated natural forces controlled by chance to explain the origin of man. Douglas Spanner views this as another form of idolatry:

> Now man has had, ever since his primal act of disobedience, a sad but understandable reluctance to meet God. However, he cannot help being a religious animal; so what does he do? He makes his own gods, of a sort which won't impose unacceptable demands on him and which he can manipulate. The mysterious and unknown, of course, must enter into their constitution, or they would hardly be gods. So he looks around for suitable material, and Chance suggests itself as an eligible candidate. It accordingly becomes deified, an active agency in its own right.[19]

This reliance on chance rather than order has severely shaken the cornerstone of scientific thought.

Indeed, when this belief in chance as the explanation for man's

CLOSE-UP

James Orr (1844-1913)

Perhaps at no other point in history was it more unfashionable to speak of a Christian worldview than in the late 19th century. Charles Darwin, Karl Marx and Friedrich Nietzsche had just finished burying God, and those people who still clung to Christianity were viewed as anti-intellectuals who had best worship God behind closed doors, apart from normal society. It was at this time, during the most unfavorable conditions, that James Orr published *The Christian View of God and the World*, a work which boldly called for an uncompromisingly biblical worldview. Most Christians will never know the debt they owe to this humble Scottish minister and professor who would not be swayed by popular opinion. Orr, a single light in a sea of darkness, championed the Christian worldview when many theologians were backpeddling and making concessions. The wisdom of such a stand is made clear in relevant modern events. Darwinism and Marxism are crumbling and Nietzsche's concept of superman has long been abandoned, but the power of the cross shines forth undimmed. Orr understood this power last century, and remains one of the clearest voices in a hazy age.

origin is carried to its logical conclusion, rationality and thought lose all meaning. "If life is ultimately the result of random chance, then so is thought," insists Brown. "Your thoughts—such as what you are now thinking—would, in the final analysis, be a consequence of accidents. Therefore, your thoughts would have no validity, including your thoughts that life is a result of chance or natural processes."[20] This, of course, is the ultimate problem facing a science that abandons all notions of God and an orderly, rational creation. Why should anyone believe anything emanating from an accidental mind constructed accidentally from accidental parts?

In a sense, this is a problem of perspective. The evolutionist (from this point forward, references to evolution will mean specifically atheistic evolution unless otherwise noted) does not view man in his

Notes and Asides

proper place in the universe, and therefore his view of science is distorted. C. S. Lewis speaks to the problem of perspective when he writes: "In modern, that is, in evolutionary, thought Man stands at the top of a stair whose foot is lost in obscurity; in [medieval thought] he stands at the bottom of a stair whose top is invisible with light."[21]

This problem of perspective causes many evolutionists to lose sight of the marvels that abound in our universe. Because the evolutionist sees the whole universe as nothing more than the product of chance processes, nothing can appear as "fearfully and wonderfully made." Whereas earlier scientists accepted Christianity and therefore were able to recognize the order of their world as a reflection of the Creator's omniscience, evolutionists must now view everything as fortunate accidents (with emphasis on chance instead of cosmos).

Davies writes, "Science itself cannot reveal whether there is a meaning to life and the universe, but scientific paradigms can exercise a strong influence on prevailing thought."[22] Unfortunately, in the last one hundred years most biological science has been influencing people to believe there is no meaning to life—that pure chance directs our universe. Only recently has science re-acknowledged the orderliness of the universe and begun to recognize that this orderliness speaks boldly in favor of creationism (and life as meaningful). Davies goes on to declare that the new model of the universe constructed by very recent science "paints a much more optimistic picture for those who seek a meaning to existence."[23] This picture, of course, is one of order and design—which leads us to the teleological argument and its relation to the creationist position.

Teleology Supports Creationism

The argument from teleology, or design in nature, as a proof for the existence of God was discussed in the Christian philosophy chapter. Here, we will emphasize (1) the scientific community's recent affirmations of teleology and (2) the implications for origins theory of the existence of design in nature. "Teleology," says Alan Hayward, "is creeping back into biology. . . . Hard-line unbelievers are clearly rattled by the trend."[24]

As previously noted, William Paley presented the most famous version of the teleological argument—that of the watch and the watchmaker. Since the nineteenth century, however, it has been widely believed that Paley's argument for a universal Designer was effectively answered by the philosopher David Hume. Hume claimed that Paley's analogy between living things and machines was unfounded and unrealistic and, therefore, that life does not need an intelligent designer,

Notes and Asides

as machines do. Hume's reply to Paley caused many people to discredit the teleological argument in all its forms, which also contributed to science's willingness to ignore design in nature and suggest that all life arose by chance.

But science can no longer ignore teleology. Indeed, science has recently discovered that life really is analogous to the most complex of machines, thereby reinforcing Paley's argument. Denton, a molecular biologist, states,

> It has only been over the past twenty years with the molecular biological revolution and with the advances in cybernetic and computer technology that Hume's criticism has been finally invalidated and the analogy between organisms and machines has at last become convincing. . . . Paley was not only right in asserting the existence of an analogy between life and machines, but was also remarkably prophetic in guessing that the technological ingenuity realized in living systems is vastly in excess of anything yet accomplished by man.[25]

Science is re-learning an old lesson: the more one discovers about the universe, the more one discovers design. Many notable scientists inadvertently support Paley nowadays as they describe the design in nature revealed to them through science. Davies is perhaps the most vocal of these modern teleologists. He affirms that science needs an orderly universe in order for scientists to draw meaningful conclusions, then points out the incredible degree of design present:

"Every advance in fundamental physics seems to uncover yet another facet of order."
—Paul Davies

> Every advance in fundamental physics seems to uncover yet another facet of order. The very success of the scientific method depends upon the fact that the physical world operates according to rational principles which can therefore be discerned through rational enquiry. Logically, the universe does not have to operate this way. We could conceive of a cosmos where chaos reigns. In place of the orderly and regimented behaviour of matter and energy one would have arbitrary and haphazard activity. Stable structures like atoms or people or stars could not exist. The real world is not this way. It is ordered and complex. Is that not in itself an astonishing fact at which to marvel?[26]

Elsewhere, Davies wonders at the order extant in living creatures: "Another distinguishing characteristic of life is, of course, the teleological quality of organisms. It is hard to see how these can ever be reduced to the fundamental laws of mechanics."[27] All of these discoveries of teleology by science lead Davies to a conclusion reached

Notes and Asides

hundreds of years ago by most early scientists: "The universe is seen to be a product of law rather than chance."[28]

At first, this seems to be an obvious conclusion of little significance. But strict evolution demands chance rather than a Law-maker as the guiding force. When a world-class non-Christian scientist like Davies declares that the universe cannot be viewed as a product of chance, it is a severe blow to materialistic evolutionary theory. It is also a severe blow to Secular Humanism and Marxism/Leninism. Both have staked their worldviews on chance, accident, and randomness.

Davies understands the conclusion demanded by his teleological findings, but he approaches it with a pantheistic attitude:

> The very fact that the universe *is* creative, and that the laws have permitted complex structures to emerge and develop to the point of consciousness—in other words, that the universe has organized its own self-awareness—is for me powerful evidence that there is "something going on" behind it all. The impression of design is overwhelming.[29]

> "The universe is seen to be a product of law rather than chance."
> —Paul Davies

Paul Amos Moody, a theistic evolutionist, is likewise overwhelmed by the teleological nature of the universe: "The more I study science," says Moody, "the more I am impressed with the thought that this world and universe have a definite *design*—and a design suggests a *designer*. It may be possible to have design without a designer, a picture without an artist, but my mind is unable to conceive of such a situation."

He continues:

> Evidences of design are everywhere about us; the forces producing the design are the so-called "laws of nature," many of which science has disclosed to us and many of which still await discovery. The greatest aspect of design visible to us is in the ordered movement of the stars and planets in this solar system and in other solar systems extending on and on through space—a design almost incomprehensibly large. At the other extreme we find all matter composed of invisible atoms, each of which in turn is a solar system almost inconceivably small, with electrons swinging in orbits around the atomic nuclei somewhat as planets circle about the sun. . . . And so it goes—everywhere there is design. Everything is conforming to definite forces acting upon it, is obeying natural laws applicable to its particular state. Whence come these natural laws? There we find the Creator.[30]

Christians have an answer to how the world began.

Why this need for a Creator as an explanation? Because the order

Notes and Asides

present in our universe exceeds the order of all objects designed by man. Denton provides an impressive example:

> Molecular biology has shown that even the simplest of all living systems on earth today, bacterial cells, are exceedingly complex objects. Although the tiniest bacterial cells are incredibly small, weighing less than 10(-12) gms, each is in effect a veritable micro-miniaturized factory containing thousands of exquisitely designed pieces of intricate molecular machinery, made up altogether of one hundred thousand million atoms, far more complicated than any machine built by man and absolutely without parallel in the non-living world.[31]

As Paley pointed out almost two centuries ago, this type of design requires an intelligent mind—chance processes cannot produce such intricate order. Many Christian biologists would carry this line of thinking one step further and claim that evolution is not a satisfactory explanation for the existence of such astonishing design, even if one postulates God directing the mechanism. This is a reasonable conclusion, because the evolutionary mechanism calls for gradual, transitional steps between species, and much of the design evident in living creatures would be useless, even a hindrance, in its developmental stages. Indeed, much of the design discovered in the animal world is still beyond human understanding—how could one help but conclude that a higher intelligence specifically created it?

Take, for example, the case of *Eumenes amedei*, a wasp-like insect found in southern Europe and northern Africa. Soon after mating, the female insect prepares a house where her young can develop and sufficient food can be stored. Building her house out of small stones (flint, limestone, even polished quartz) and mortar (she mixes her own saliva with flint dust), she constructs her walls in a circular fashion. As the walls grow higher she begins to slope them toward the center so as to construct a dome-like mosque. A hole is left open at the top. It will ultimately be filled with a constructed plug.

The insect's next task is to fill her house with fresh food for the future grub. The food she chooses consists of half-inch caterpillars. These are partially paralyzed by the insect's stinger (dead caterpillars would rot) and stored on the floor of the newly constructed house.

Eumenes amedei does not lay her egg among the partially paralyzed caterpillars. Instead she suspends it over the food by a tiny thread of silk fastened to the roof of the house. When the grub emerges from the egg it first eats the eggshell and then proceeds to spin a silken thread in

Notes and Asides

which it is enfolded tail-up with head hanging down. It can then lower itself down to its fresh meal and retreat when necessary. Only when the grub grows in size and strength does it lower itself down among its wriggly caterpillar food.

While all the houses this insect creates look alike, there is one significant difference. Some houses may contain five caterpillars and some ten. Why? Because female grubs eat twice as much as males. "But," writes Norman Macbeth, "note that the cells are stocked before the eggs are laid, and that biologists generally believe that the sex is already determined when an egg is laid. How does the *Eumenes* know the future sex of her eggs? How is it that she never makes a mistake?"[32] Indeed, how could evolution, a chance process, "teach" this insect to recognize the sex of her unborn offspring and provide for it accordingly? What did these insects do when their instincts were in a transitional stage? How could any instinct, other than the present, completely developed instinct, be viewed as beneficial to the insect?

Hayward's favorite example of teleology is the bombardier beetle. After examining its explosive chemicals (hydroquinone and hydrogen peroxide), its separate glands, its storage tank areas (to keep the two chemicals apart until they're ejected, lest the beetle blow itself up), and its perfect detonator, Hayward concludes, "natural forces alone could never have produced a bombardier beetle . . . there must be Somebody behind nature who designed and built the strange weaponry."[33]

> "The celestial order and the beauty of the universe compel me to admit that there is some excellent and eternal Being, who deserves the respect and homage of men."
>
> —Cicero

Teleology speaks powerfully in favor of fiat creationism in another way, as well. Evolution, even theistic evolution, cannot sufficiently explain the remarkable similarity between many forms that should have evolved apart from one another, whereas fiat creationism expects similarity in a universe created in a six-day span by one specific Designer. Denton sums up this aspect of the evolutionist's dilemma: "There is no doubt that in terms of evolution the fore- and hindlimbs must have arisen independently, the former supposedly evolving from the pectoral fins of a fish, the latter from the pelvic fins. Here is a case of profound resemblance which cannot be explained in terms of a theory of descent."[34]

Of course, the atheistic evolutionist's predicament is infinitely worse than that of the evolutionist who postulates a God. The evolution of all the universe's design guided entirely by natural processes can only be described as a theory in crisis. Darwin himself became suspicious that teleology might prove to be his theory's downfall:

> I remember well the time when the thought of the eye made me cold all over, but I have got over this stage of the complaint, and

Notes and Asides

now small trifling particulars of structure often make me very uncomfortable. The sight of a feather in a peacock's tail, whenever I gaze at it, makes me sick![35]

Darwin had every right to be sickened by evidences of design in nature. These evidences will cry out in favor of fiat creationism long after Darwin's theory of evolution is abandoned. The revolutionary change in scientific thought that is the prelude to the abandonment of Darwinism is occurring today. S. Lovtrup declares, "I believe that one day the Darwinian myth will be ranked the greatest deceit in the history of science. When this happens many people will pose the question: How did this ever happen?"[36] Fred Hoyle and Chandra Wickramasinghe, two individuals who, until recently, denied the existence of God, find Darwin's theory unacceptable and Paley's explanation of teleology most plausible:

"I believe that one day the Darwinian myth will be ranked the greatest deceit in the history of science."

—S. Lovtrup

> The speculations of *The Origin of Species* turned out to be wrong, as we have seen in this chapter. It is ironic that the scientific facts throw Darwin out, but leave William Paley, a figure of fun to the scientific world for more than a century, still in the tournament with a chance of being the ultimate winner.[37]

Teleology speaks loudly in favor of creationism. The order of our universe could not have arisen through chance processes. The failure of evolution as an explanation for man's origin will become even more evident as we examine evolution's irreconcilable clash with established facts of science and the flawed nature of evolutionary mechanisms.

DNA: Created or Evolved?

The existence and properties of deoxyribonucleic acid (DNA) support fiat creationism both through the teleological argument and by demonstrating evolutionary theory's inability to explain crucial aspects of life. DNA contains the genetic information code and is a crucial part of all living matter, yet evolutionary theory is powerless to explain how it came into existence, let alone why DNA evidences such phenomenal design.

This teleological quality of DNA is overwhelming. Charles Thaxton believes DNA is the most powerful indicator of intelligent design: "Is there any basis in experience for an intelligent cause for the origin of life? Yes! It is the analogy between the base sequences in DNA and alphabetical letter sequences in a book. . . . there is a structural identity between the DNA code and a written language."[38] That is, we can

Notes and Asides

assume DNA is the product of intelligence because it is analogous to human languages, which are, without exception, products of intelligent minds.

Brown expands on the wondrous design evident in DNA: "If all the DNA in your body were placed end-to-end, it would stretch from here to the moon over 100,000 times! If all this very densely coded information were placed in typewritten form, it would completely fill the Grand Canyon forty times! And yet, all of your DNA would not fill two teaspoons. The discovery and understanding of DNA is just one small reason for believing that you are 'fearfully and wonderfully made' (Psalm 139:14)."[39]

Clearly, to the Christian biologist, DNA speaks volumes about the existence of an intelligent Designer. But even excluding the teleological nature of DNA, its very existence severely undermines evolutionary theory. Brown points out, "DNA can only be produced with the help of at least 20 different types of proteins. But these proteins can only be produced at the direction of DNA. Since each requires the other, a satisfactory explanation for the origin of one must also explain the origin of the other. Apparently, this entire manufacturing system came into existence simultaneously. This implies Creation."[40]

This implication becomes even more plausible when one considers that DNA is not now capable of evolution, nor does it show signs of ever having evolved. Brown writes, "Since macroevolution requires increasing complexity through natural processes, the organism's information content must increase. But since natural processes cannot increase the information content of a system such as a reproductive cell, macroevolution cannot occur."[41] Denton hints at much the same thing:

> Apart from artificial language used in computers and human language itself, the genetic code, or the language of life as it has been called, is without any analogue in the physical universe. Like cilia and like so many of the characteristics found in living things on earth, the genetic code is not led up to gradually through a sequence of transitional forms.[42]

Denton also maintains that it is "an affront to reason" to believe that "a thousand million bits of information containing countless thousands of intricate algorithms controlling, specifying and ordering the growth and development of billions of cells into the form of a complex organism were composed by a purely random process."[43]

DNA obviously presents one of the most pressing problems for evolutionists. It is an intensely complex substance, yet it must be present in the very earliest forms of living matter. How can evolutionists explain this? Luther D. Sunderland, a leading creationist, believes

Notes and Asides

they cannot. He points out that "no one has yet shown how the enormous amount of genetic intelligence in a single-celled organism could have come spontaneously from non-living chemicals."[44]

In fact, no one has shown how life itself could arise from non-living chemicals, let alone such a complex aspect of life as DNA. This inability to demonstrate spontaneous generation (the development of life from non-life) is another key weakness in evolutionary theory.

Spontaneous Generation

For the atheistic evolutionist's belief to be rational, the major problem biology must overcome is the impossibility of spontaneous generation. In order for life to have arisen due to random processes, at some point in time non-living matter must have come alive. Yet this postulate of atheistic evolution runs contrary to everything science has discovered about life. "Spontaneous generation (the emergence of life from non-living matter)," says Brown, "has never been observed. All observations have shown that life only comes from life. This has been so consistently observed that it is called the Law of Biogenesis. The [materialistic] theory of evolution conflicts with this law by claiming that life came from non-living matter through natural processes."[45]

This denial of the scientific nature of spontaneous generation is echoed by Christian and non-Christian scientists alike. A. E. Wilder-Smith declares that "the chance formation of stable amino acids is good, the chances of polypeptide formation less good, while the chances of the random formation of a protein molecule complicated enough to function as an enzyme and bear life are, at our present state of knowledge of mathematical thermodynamics, negligible."[46] This assertion is backed by Hoyle, who, Sunderland tells us, "wrote in the 19 November 1981 *New Scientist* that there are 2,000 complex enzymes required for a living organism but not a single one of these could have formed on Earth by random, shuffling processes in even 20 billion years. . . ."[47]

Many evolutionists point to the work of Alexander Oparin in defense of spontaneous generation. Oparin described a theory that supposedly allowed for chance processes working in a prebiotic soup to give rise to life.

Unfortunately for evolutionists, this theory is rapidly being refuted by science. Charles B. Thaxton, Walter L. Bradley, and Roger L. Olsen write, "It is becoming clear that however life began on earth, the usually conceived notion that life emerged from an oceanic soup of organic

Notes and Asides

chemicals is a most implausible hypothesis. We may therefore with fairness call this scenario 'the myth of the prebiotic soup.'"[48] Elsewhere they reiterate this point, claiming that "the undirected flow of energy through a primordial atmosphere and ocean is at present a woefully inadequate explanation for the incredible complexity associated with even simple living systems, and is probably wrong."[49]

In fact, the further science progresses, the more unlikely spontaneous generation seems. Dean Kenyon, a biochemist and a former chemical evolutionist, now writes, "When all relevant lines of evidence are taken into account, and all the problems squarely faced, I think we must conclude that life owes its inception to a source outside of nature."[50] He bases this conclusion on four premises: (1) the impossibility of the spontaneous origin of genetic information, (2) the fact that most attempts to duplicate the conditions necessary for chemical evolution yield non-biological material, (3) the unfounded nature of the belief (necessary for the chemical evolutionist) that prebiotic conditions encouraged a trend toward the formation of L amino acids, and (4) the geochemical evidence that O_2 existed in significant amounts in the Earth's early atmosphere (organic compounds decompose when O_2 is present).[51] Brown also believes the existence of O_2 creates an insurmountable problem for chemical evolutionists:

> If the earth, early in its alleged evolution, had oxygen in its atmosphere, the chemicals needed for life to begin would have been removed by oxidation. But if there had been no oxygen, then there would have been no ozone in the upper atmosphere. Without this ozone, life would be quickly destroyed by the sun's ultraviolet radiation. The only known way for both ozone and life to be here is for both to have come into existence simultaneously—in other words, CREATION![52]

The concept of spontaneous generation is so questionable, even atheistic evolutionists feel compelled to abandon it. Francis Crick, a Nobel Prize winner and evolutionist, admits, "An honest man, armed with all the knowledge available to us now, could only state that in some sense, the origin of life appears at the moment to be almost a miracle, so many are the conditions which would have had to have been satisfied to get it going."[53] Of course, Crick is unwilling to accept the miraculous as an explanation, which forces him to postulate a third alternative that dodges the issue. He suggests the theory of Directed Panspermia which, according to Sunderland, claims that "the first living cell must have been transported by rocketship on a 10,000-year voyage from some

Notes and Asides

other planet outside our solar system."[54] The unscientific nature of this theory is eloquently summarized by Sunderland:

> This shatters the very foundation of arguments for the evolution of life on Earth. If first life could not have evolved spontaneously on Earth, then that definitely removes the question from the realm of science. We can't even observe a single planet outside our solar system, much less examine evidence that life evolved there.[55]

"Since science has not the vaguest idea how life originated on earth . . . it would be honest to admit this to students . . ."
—H. P. Yockey

It is clear that atheists must clash with science in presenting a theory that accounts for the origin of life from non-life. Unfortunately, many schools' science departments encourage this clash with science by treating some abiogenesis (life from non-life) theories as viable. H. P. Yockey, a leading biologist, calls for the end of such deception:

> Since science has not the vaguest idea how life originated on earth . . . it would be honest to admit this to students, the agencies funding research, and the public. Leaders in science . . . should stop polarizing the minds of students and younger creative scientists with statements for which faith is the only evidence.[56]

That is, the scientific community should accept the conclusions forced on it by its own discipline. Once it is willing to do that, it will recognize another point at which naturalistic evolutionary theory clashes with science: the second law of thermodynamics.

The Second Law of Thermodynamics

In order to understand the clash between evolution and the second law of thermodynamics, we must first understand a few of the implications of the second law. A. E. Wilder-Smith explains, "The second law of thermodynamics states that, although the total energy in the cosmos remains constant, the amount of energy available to do useful work is always getting smaller."[57] He goes on to clarify the meaning of this law:

> Let us use water as a symbol for energy. If we have water on top of a mountain, it possesses kinetic energy which we can put to use as it descends the mountain by passing it through turbines to generate electricity. However, once the water has reached sea level, no more kinetic energy is available to develop current. The mass of water theoretically remains the same, whether it is

Notes and Asides

> on top of the mountain or at sea level. But the available kinetic energy does change and diminishes as the water loses altitude. Thus the *total* energy in the cosmos remains the same, but the available energy is constantly diminishing. The available energy is continually approaching the position of "sea level," as it were, where nothing more is obtainable in the way of work.[58]

What does this law imply about the effect of time on the orderliness of the universe? Wilder-Smith answers:

> Order is improbable and order tends to disintegrate into disorder, just as water tends to flow down the mountain rather than up to the mountaintop. Order descends to chaos, just as a city with no cleaning, repair and disposal services descends to chaos with the passage of time. If one doubts this universal fact, it is only necessary to place one's shiny new car under a tree in a forest and leave it there for twenty years with no attention. Chaos will certainly have overtaken the once orderly car by then.[59]

The evolutionist, however, is moving in the opposite direction. His theory calls for life to become more complex (from amoeba to man) as time progresses. Wilder-Smith puts the contrast clearly:

> The theory of evolution teaches, when all the frills are removed, just the opposite to this state of affairs demanded by the second law of thermodynamics. Evolutionists assume that nonliving carbon atoms, hydrogen atoms, nitrogen atoms, etc., as they "fluttered down" through the ages since the beginning of time,

THE LAWS OF THERMODYNAMICS

1) Energy in a system cannot be created or destroyed.

2) In a system, the amount of disorder, or entropy, must increase and the amount of useful energy must decrease.

Notes and Asides

> have slowly ordered and organized themselves into more complex, more energy-rich, less chaotic forms. They believe that entropy, with respect to biogenesis, has not increased but spontaneously decreased during the passage of the ages.[60]

This is in flat contradiction to the second law of thermodynamics.

A theory contradicting a proven scientific law should be abandoned. Wilder-Smith challenges the evolutionists to do just that:

> The normal laws of thermodynamics, physics and biochemistry explain the functioning of the world, as we know it, quite well. As we have pointed out before, chemical and physical properties of the chemical elements must have remained unchanged from the beginning, if life has been continuous from the beginning. This being the case, why does the Darwinist not bow to these known laws of thermodynamics in his theories about the origin and development of life on this planet? If the laws of thermodynamics make the Darwinist's explanation of biogenesis and evolution by chance untenable, why does he not reject his views and admit that he has been wrong on sound theory all the time?[61]

The second law of thermodynamics doesn't just contradict evolution, either—it also reinforces the creationist explanation of man's origins. First, it suggests that the universe had a beginning. "If the entire universe is an isolated system, then, according to the Second Law of Thermodynamics," says Brown, "the energy in the universe that is available for useful work has always been decreasing. However, as one goes back in time, the amount of energy available for useful work would eventually exceed the total energy in the universe that, according to the First Law of Thermodynamics, remains constant. This is an impossible condition. Therefore, it implies that the universe had a beginning."[62]

Second, it suggests that the universe began as a highly ordered system, which, according to Davies, implies the existence of a Designer:

> Though the spontaneous appearance of order will not conflict with the second law of thermodynamics so long as compensatory disorder is generated elsewhere, it is clear that no order at all could exist unless the universe as a whole started out with a considerable stock of negative entropy. If total disorder always

> increases, in accordance with the second law, then the universe must, it seems, have been created in an orderly condition. Does this not provide strong evidence in favour of a creator-designer?[63]

The Christian biologist, of course, would argue that it does.

Indeed, many Christian biologists argue not only that evolution is bankrupt, but also that the facts of science, including the second law of thermodynamics, better fit the creationist model. The second law meshes far more appropriately with the Biblical account than with evolutionary theory. Wilder-Smith notes, "The second law of thermodynamics seems thus to describe the whole situation of our present material world perfectly and the Bible very clearly confirms this description. For example, Romans 8:22-23 teaches us that the whole creation is subjected to 'vanity' or to destruction. Everything tends to go downhill to chaos and destruction as things stand today."[64]

The creationist position, then, is more in sync with science than evolutionary theory. Also, it can be demonstrated that the creationist explanation for the existence of species is more rational than the mechanism propounded by evolutionists.

The Evolutionary Mechanism

According to Darwinian evolutionists, species evolve because the process of natural selection perpetuates mutations that cause life-forms to be better equipped (or adapted) for survival in their environment. These mutations are termed "beneficial," and viewed by evolutionists as the building blocks through which natural selection "creates" new species.

The first problem with the evolutionary mechanism becomes evident when one attempts to define "natural selection." Macbeth reveals the faulty reasoning inherent in this evolutionary concept:

> If we say that evolution is accomplished largely by natural selection and that natural selection consists of differential reproduction, what have we done? Differential reproduction means that some species multiply by leaving more offspring than one-for-one, while others leave one-for-one and remain stable, and others leave less than one-for-one and dwindle or die out. Thus we have as Question: Why do some multiply, while others remain stable, dwindle, or die out? To which is offered

Notes and Asides

> as Answer: Because some multiply, while others remain stable, dwindle, or die out. The two sides of the equation are the same. We have a tautology. The definition is meaningless.[65]

Even apart from the problem presented by the definition of natural selection, however, the evolutionary mechanism is hopelessly crippled. The reliance on beneficial mutations as the essential ingredients for new species leaves evolutionists searching for ghosts—for the simple reason that, as Brown notes, "Rarely, if ever, is a mutation beneficial to an organism in its natural environment."[66] C. P. Martin supports this claim: "Mutations are more than just sudden changes in heredity; they also affect viability, and to the best of our knowledge, invariably affect it adversely."[67] Sunderland sums up the matter by observing that there "has never been a case established where a living organism was observed to change into a basically different organism with different structures. No observed mutation has ever been demonstrated to be more beneficial to the overall population out in nature."[68]

Obviously, the evolutionary mechanism is in trouble. Since the phrase used by evolutionists to explain the process that encourages new, improved species is tautological, and since the "building blocks" for evolution have never provided any real material for change, it is easy to understand why evolutionists dislike discussing the mechanics of their theory. What is difficult to comprehend is why some Christians believe theistic evolution is more rational than creationism. This untenability of the evolutionary explanation will become even more apparent as we examine more evidence pertinent to origins theory.

The Gene Pool and the Limits to Change

Something else to examine when questioning evolutionary theory and studying the viability of creationism is the breeding limits observed by science. Evolutionists believe that no limits exist, since a vast amount of change must occur for the first spark of life to evolve to man. Indeed, evolutionists see beneficial mutations as breaking all barriers to change, since these mutations supposedly can produce a vast array of structures, even a human eye, given enough time.

Unfortunately for evolutionists, however, science simply has not been able to demonstrate that any mutations break these limits to change. Pierre Paul Grasse, after studying mutations in bacteria and viruses, concludes, "What is the use of their unceasing mutations if they do not change? In sum, the mutations of bacteria and viruses are merely hereditary fluctuations around a median position; a swing to the right, a swing to the left, but no final evolutionary effect."[69] This conclusion

Notes and Asides

meshes with the claims previously mentioned that a beneficial mutation has never been observed—how could a mutation, or any series of mutations, be termed beneficial if it was incapable of breaking the limits that must be broken for new species to evolve?

If indeed such limits exist, then evolution is a meaningless explanation. If a species can only evolve so far before it hits a barrier and is forced to remain the same species, then no macroevolution occurs. This notion of the gene pool limiting the possible variation of species has troubled a great number of evolutionists, including Alfred Russell Wallace, one of the founders of the theory of natural selection. Wallace grew to doubt his theory later in life, largely because he became aware of Gregor Mendel's genetic laws, and could not reconcile the apparent limits to change with evolution's need for boundless development. Wallace writes, "But on the general relation of Mendelism to evolution I have come to a very definite conclusion. This is that it has no relation whatever to the evolution of species or higher groups, but is really antagonistic to such evolution."[70]

Science today confirms Wallace's suspicions. Brown writes,

> Mendel's laws of genetics and their modern day refinements explain almost all of the physical variations that are observed within life, such as in the dog family. A logical consequence of these laws is that there are limits to such variation. Breeding experiments and common observations have also confirmed that these boundaries exist.[71]

These breeding experiments have proven to be a fatal blow to the theory of evolution, because every experiment has eventually hit a barrier, at which point no more change in the specific direction can be induced in the species. If this barrier truly exists, macroevolution cannot have occurred. William R. Fix notes that these experiments make evolutionists uncomfortable: "All competent biologists acknowledge the limited nature of variation breeders can produce, although they do not like to discuss it much when grinding the evolutionary ax."[72]

Evolutionists avoid discussing these limitations for good reason. Denton explains:

> . . . while breeding experiments and the domestication of animals had revealed that many species were capable of a considerable degree of change, they also revealed distinct limits in nearly every case beyond which no further change could ever be produced. Here then was a very well established fact, known for centuries, which seemed to run counter to [Darwin's] whole case, threatening not only his special theory—that one species

"[B]reeding experiments . . . revealed distinct limits in nearly every case beyond which no further change could ever be produced."
—Michael Denton

Notes and Asides

> could evolve into another—but also the plausibility of the extrapolation from micro to macroevolution, which, as we have seen, was largely based on an appeal to the remarkable degree of change achieved by artificial selection in a relatively short time. If this change was always strictly limited then the validity of the extrapolation was obviously seriously threatened.[73]

Luther Burbank, one of the most famous breeders of all time, supports the conclusion that limitations to change exist in every species:

> Experiments carried on extensively have given us scientific proof of what we had already guessed by observation; namely, that plants and animals all tend to revert, in successive generations, toward a given mean or average. Men grow to be seven feet tall, and over, but never to ten; there are dwarfs not higher than 24 inches, but none that you can carry in your hand. . . . In short, there is undoubtedly a pull toward the mean which keeps all living things within some more or less fixed limitations.[74]

Incredibly, Edward S. Deevey, Jr., also recognizes these limitations, and yet remains an evolutionist:

> Some remarkable things have been done by crossbreeding and selection inside the species barrier, or within a larger circle of closely related species, such as the wheats. But wheat is still wheat, and not, for instance, grapefruit; and we can no more grow wings on pigs than hens can make cylindrical eggs.[75]

How can Deevey remain an evolutionist in the face of such evidence? How can one believe in virtually unlimited change when limits abound within species? Rationally, one cannot. The creationist believes the evolutionary position is opposed to reason, and therefore rejects it. Macbeth believes much the same thing, despite his unwillingness to accept the creationist model. He challenges the evolutionist to give in to reason, noting that all biologists

> recognize the limits of variability, the curse of sterility, the dangers of extrapolation, the hopelessness of trying to convert bears into whales or of breeding winged horses, and the strong inertia of genetic homeostasis. I do not see how these points can be reconciled with Darwin's position, and I suggest that the time has come for a retreat.[76]

Notes and Asides

It would seem that the case against evolutionists and in favor of creationism is quite formidable—indeed, retreat appears to be the only option available to the evolutionist. Incredibly, this conclusion seems justifiable even without reference to what many consider the most powerful refutation of evolutionary theory: the gaps in the fossil record and the absence of transitional forms. A brief examination of this evidence should leave few doubts as to the bankruptcy of evolutionary theory.

Fossil Gaps and Intermediate Forms

So far each of our arguments has focused on whether evolution is theoretically possible. Now we turn to the question of whether the empirical evidence suggests that it happened.

Over one hundred years ago, Darwin wrote, "The geological record is extremely imperfect and this fact will to a large extent explain why we do not find intermediate varieties, connecting together all the extinct and existing forms of life by the finest graduated steps. He who rejects these views on the nature of the geological record, will rightly reject my whole theory."[77] When Darwin made this claim, he was correct in asserting that the geological record, as scientists knew it then, was imperfect. Could this claim still hold true today? After more than one hundred years of new discoveries, could one still chalk up the lack of transitional forms to the imperfection of the fossil record?

One reason the fossil record seems to condemn evolutionary theory is that many complex life forms appear in the very earliest rocks without any indication of forms from which they could have evolved. Sunderland writes,

> Most of the museums classify the deepest rocks which contain fossils of multi-celled organisms as Cambrian rocks. Dr. Preston Cloud, writing in *Geology* magazine in 1973, stated that not a single indisputable multi-cellular fossil had been found anywhere in the world in a rock supposedly older than Cambrian rocks. But in the Cambrian rocks is found a multitude of highly complex creatures with no ancestors.[78]

Creatures without ancestors cannot help but imply special creation. They certainly undermine the force of the evolutionary argument. "The evolutionary tree has no trunk," says Brown.

Notes and Asides

> There is a sudden explosion of complex species at the bottom of the fossil record. Complex species, such as fish, worms, snails, corals, trilobites, jelly fish, sponges, mollusks, and brachiopods appear suddenly in the lowest (Cambrian) layers that contain multicellular life. These layers contain representatives of all plant and animal phyla, including flowering plants, vascular plants, and animals with back bones. Insects, a class comprising four-fifths of all known animals (living and extinct), have no evolutionary ancestors. The fossil record does not support evolution.[79]

This explosion of complex life is not the only way in which the fossil record condemns evolution. The lack of fossils supporting the transitional phases between species is perhaps the single most embarrassing topic for evolutionists. And yet, this absence of transitional fossils is undeniable. Brown declares, "The gaps in the fossil record are well-known. A century ago evolutionists argued that these gaps would be filled as knowledge increased. Most paleontologists will now admit that this prediction failed."[80] J. K. Anderson and H. G. Coffin agree: "The search for these transitional forms (missing links) by paleontologists has not been very successful. Each major group of organisms appears abruptly in the fossil record without any transitions."[81]

This fact is grudgingly recognized by leading evolutionists. Raup, a geologist, admits,

> [W]e are now about 120 years after Darwin and the knowledge of the fossil record has been greatly expanded. We now have a quarter of a million fossil species but the situation hasn't changed much. The record of evolution is still surprisingly jerky and, ironically, we have even fewer examples of evolutionary transition than we had in Darwin's time. By this I mean that some of the classic cases of Darwinian change in the fossil record, such as the evolution of the horse in North America, have had to be discarded or modified as a result of more detailed information—what appeared to be a nice simple progression when relatively few data were available now appears to be much more complex and much less gradualistic.[82]

The problem for evolutionists unable to produce transitional fossils is made clear by Brown:

> If [Darwinian] evolution happened, the fossil record should show continuous and gradual changes from the bottom to the

Notes and Asides

> top layers and between all forms of life. Actually, many gaps and discontinuities appear throughout the fossil record. Many fossil links are missing among numerous plants, between single cell forms of life and invertebrates, invertebrates and vertebrates, fish and amphibians, amphibians and reptiles, reptiles and mammals, reptiles and birds, and between primates and other mammals. The fossil record has been studied so thoroughly that it is safe to conclude that these gaps are real; they will never be filled. The hypothetical evolutionary tree has no branches.[83]

An evolutionary tree with no trunk (no life forms earlier than the already very complex ones in Cambrian rocks) and no branches (no transitional forms) can hardly be called a tree at all.

Stephen Jay Gould, an ardent evolutionist, also recognizes this problem and candidly admits that evolutionists are often afraid to confront it:

> The extreme rarity of transitional forms in the fossil record persists as the trade secret of paleontology. The evolutionary trees that adorn our textbooks have data only at the tips and nodes of their branches; the rest is inference, however reasonable, not the evidence of fossils. . . . We fancy ourselves as the only true students of life's history, yet to preserve our favored account of evolution by natural selection we view our data as so bad that we never see the very process we profess to study.[84]

"The extreme rarity of transitional forms in the fossil record persists as the trade secret of paleontology."
—Stephen Jay Gould

This problem presented by the lack of transitional forms in the fossil record also extends to the lack of transitional forms observable in nature or even conceivable in the human mind. Evolutionists are unable not only to point to a specific form observed by science as an indisputable transitional form, but also to present a reasonable explanation for the survival of any hypothetical transitional forms in nature, since many forms would be useless until fully developed.

Let's begin by addressing the first half of the problem: the existence of transitional phases actually observable in living forms. Brown states, "There are many single-cell forms of life, but there are no forms of animal life with 2, 3, 4, . . . , or even 20 cells. If organic evolution happened, one would expect to find these forms of life in great abundance. Actually, none have been found."[85] The absence of observable transitional multi-cellular creatures strikes another blow against evolution, as do the recent findings of molecular biology, according to Denton:

Notes and Asides

> It is now well established that the pattern of diversity at a molecular level conforms to a highly ordered hierarchic system. . . . Thus molecules, like fossils have failed to provide the elusive intermediates so long sought by evolutionary biology. . . . At a molecular level, no organism is "ancestral" or "primitive" or "advanced" compared with its relatives. Nature seems to conform to the same non-evolutionary and intensely circumferential pattern that was long ago perceived by the great comparative anatomists of the nineteenth century.[86]

The second part of the evolutionist's paleontological problem—the fact that many forms exist in nature today that could not have been led up to through intermediate phases—is equally troublesome. Denton explains,

> And as far as the individual defining characteristics are concerned, one could continue citing almost ad infinitum complex defining characteristics of particular classes or organisms which are without analogy or precedent in any other part of the living kingdom and are not led up to in any way through a series of transitional structures. Such a list would include structures as diverse as the vertebral column of vertebrates, the jumping apparatus of the click beetle, . . . the wing of a bat, . . . the neck of the giraffe, the male reproductive organs of the dragonfly, and so on until one had practically named every significant characteristic of every living thing on earth.[87]

This leads us into the heart of the evolutionist's problem with transitional forms: not only are they non-existent in both the fossil record and the observable living world (a fact admitted even by evolutionists—Colin Patterson writes, "If I knew of any [evolutionary transitions], fossil or living, I would certainly have included them [in my book]."[88]), transitional forms are not even explicable by evolutionary mechanisms. That is, evolution demands that mutations be beneficial to cause them to be reproduced and become dominant in nature, and yet half-developed transitional forms provide no clear advantage; on the contrary, they are more likely to be handicaps. Brown elaborates: "All species appear perfectly developed, not half-developed. They show design. There are no examples of half-developed feathers, eyes, skin, tubes (arteries, veins, intestines, etc.), or any of thousands of other vital organs. For example, if a limb were to evolve into a wing, it would become a bad limb long before it became a good wing."[89] Again, underneath the whole current of debate, we find the teleological argument to be among the best answers to evolutionists and the

Notes and Asides

strongest support for creationism. It is clear that God as Designer provides a much better explanation for the design evidenced by life than does a theory that requires transitional forms guided by natural selection.

Wilder-Smith supports this claim, while providing another fine example of teleology that cannot be explained by gradual natural selection:

> There are also grave difficulties in the more general application of the idea of intermediate forms. It is often impossible to account for a complex organ and its derivation. It is only understandable in its fully developed form. The halfway stages in its evolution would serve no purpose, being completely useless. As an example take the complex structure possessed by the female whale for suckling its young under the water without drowning the suckling. No halfway stage of development from an ordinary nipple to that of the fully developed whale nipple, adapted for underwater feeding, is conceivable. Either it was completely developed and functional, or it was not. To expect such a system to arise gradually by chance mutations upward is to condemn all suckling whales during the development period of thousands of years to a watery grave by certain drowning.[90]

"It is interesting to note that in his book, *The Descent of Man*, Darwin did not cite a single reference to fossils in support of his belief in human evolution."
—Percival Davis
Dean H. Kenyon

Gould also recognizes this flaw in evolutionary theory, although (as we will see) he is still unwilling to abandon the concept of macroevolution:

> Even though we have no direct evidence for smooth transitions, can we invent a reasonable sequence of intermediate forms, that is, viable, functioning organisms, between ancestors and descendants? Of what possible use are the imperfect incipient stages of useful structures? What good is half a jaw or half a wing?[91]

It would seem, then, that some forms exist in nature that could not have been led up to through gradual, transitional phases. The fossil record, the observation of living organisms, and the teleological nature of numerous forms testify to the impossibility of gradual change. Yet gradual change is absolutely critical to traditional evolutionary theory. Darwin himself admits, "If it could be demonstrated that any complex organ existed, which could not possibly have been formed by numerous, successive, slight modifications, my theory would absolutely break down."[92]

Hello! Hasn't it been done?

This is precisely what creationists have claimed for years—that

Notes and Asides

Darwin's evolutionary theory is bankrupt. Reason requires the biologist to abandon evolution and embrace the more rational explanation: creation. Of course, creationism is untenable for all atheists; therefore, even if the atheist recognizes the irrationality of traditional evolutionary theory, he must postulate an equally indefensible theory to circumvent the notion of God.

Punctuated Equilibrium

Thus, evolutionists have suggested recently the theory of punctuated equilibrium. This theory allows the materialistic evolutionist to escape some of the inconsistencies of neo-Darwinian evolution while ignoring the possibility of the existence of God.

Actually, the theory of punctuated equilibrium is an old theory with a new coat. Nearly forty years ago, R. B. Goldschmidt suggested a

Recommended Reading for Advanced Study

W. R. Bird, *The Origin of Species Revisited*, two volumes (New York: Philosophical Library, 1989).

Norman Macbeth, *Darwin Retried: An Appeal to Reason* (Boston: The Harvard Common Press, 1971).

Luther D. Sunderland, *Darwin's Enigma* (Santee, CA: Master Book, 1988).

Michael Denton, *Evolution: A Theory in Crisis* (Bethesda, MD: Adler and Adler, 1986).

Henry Morris, *The Long War Against God* (Grand Rapids, MI: Baker, 1990).

Charles B. Thaxton, Walter L. Bradley, and Roger L. Olsen, *The Mystery of Life's Origin* (New York: Philosophical Library, 1984).

Notes and Asides

"hopeful monster" theory, in which he hypothesized, "When a new phylum, class, or order appears, there follows a quick, explosive (in terms of geological time) diversification so that practically all orders or families known appear suddenly and without any apparent transitions."[93] That is, one hopeful monster somehow "appears" and gives rise to a whole new species in a very short period of time.

Macbeth describes Goldschmidt's reasoning and the typical evolutionist's reaction to it:

> After observing mutations in fruit flies for many years, Goldschmidt fell into despair. The changes, he lamented, were so hopelessly micro that if a thousand mutations were combined in one specimen, there would still be no new species. This led him to propose the hypothesis of the "hopeful monster," whereby a huge change might have occurred all at once and been preserved by a favoring environment. His colleagues rejected this proposal as unsound, but they seem to escape Goldschmidt's despair only by an act of faith.[94]

Why does Macbeth speak of the desperate position of the evolutionist? Because the absence of transitional forms calls into question the veracity of Darwinian evolutionary theory. Duane T. Gish writes,

> . . . why did Goldschmidt feel forced to propose such an incredible mechanism in the first place? Goldschmidt felt forced to propose this mechanism because transitional forms between basic types cannot be found, each type appearing in the fossil record fully formed. Intense searching of the fossil record during the past quarter century has produced nothing that would have caused Goldschmidt to change his mind.[95]

Goldschmidt's faith in his "hopeful monster" theory is the only thing that allows him to avoid the problem of transitional forms and yet keep God out of the picture.

As noted above, Goldschmidt's theory was ridiculed until very recently. It was resurrected by a new generation of evolutionists who had also become acutely aware of the bankruptcy of strict Darwinian theory. The "hopeful monster" theory was touched up here and there and re-introduced as *punctuated equilibrium.* This theory basically claims that evolution occurs in spurts, in relatively short periods of time, which supposedly accounts for the absence of transitional forms. Gould is the theory's leading proponent, largely because he recognizes the untenability of any evolutionary theory that requires gradual, intermediate change, but is still unwilling to abandon the theory of evolu-

Notes and Asides

tion. He attacks Darwinian theory as vehemently as any creationist:

> The fossil record is full of gaps and discontinuities, but they are all attributed to the notorious imperfection of the fossil record. The fossil record is imperfect, but I think that is not an adequate explanation . . . one thing it does show that cannot be attributed to its imperfection is that most species don't change. . . . They may get a little bigger or bumpier but they remain the same species and that's not due to imperfection and gaps but stasis. And yet this remarkable stasis has generally been ignored as no data. If they don't change, it's not evolution so you don't talk about it.[96]

Yet, in the face of the mounting evidence against evolution, Gould still cannot bring himself to consider creationism as a viable option. This forces him to postulate an alternate evolutionary theory custom-built to fit the facts.

Gould's disillusionment with neo-Darwinian theory is one of the loudest proclamations of the death of traditional evolutionary thinking. From the weight of evidence presented in this chapter, it would seem that the evolutionary perspective needs to be completely abandoned. But perhaps we are drawing our conclusion too hastily. Might Goldschmidt's or Gould's solution be the most plausible theory of origins?

Not likely. The plausibility of punctuated equilibrium rapidly diminishes when one realizes that the theory, as it is most often stated, still relies on the Darwinian mechanisms of natural selection and survival of the fittest (albeit at a much faster pace and in isolated segments of a species' population). The problem with this reliance on Darwinian mechanisms, even if the mechanisms themselves were viable, is that Darwin explicitly declared that they must work gradually, imperceptibly. He writes, "As natural selection acts solely by accumulating slight, successive, favourable variations, it can produce no great or sudden modifications; it can act only by short and slow steps."[97] The punctuated equilibrium theorist's attempt to graft a plodding, deliberate mechanism onto his theory—a theory that requires an exceedingly quick mechanism—is doomed from the beginning. Sunderland writes,

> The theory of punctuated equilibria is causing much turmoil among evolutionists. They know that there is no actual mechanism that would explain large rapid jumps from one species to another and yet they also know the fossil record doesn't support gradualism. They are left on the horns of a dilemma.[98]

Notes and Asides

Another problem with the notion of punctuated equilibrium is outlined by Gish:

> Furthermore, this notion is without empirically observable scientific evidence. The only evidence for it is the absence of transitional forms. According to the punctuationist, since obviously one form did not slowly and gradually evolve into another, then just as obviously it must have rapidly evolved into the new form.[99]

But this is an illogical assumption—the lack of evidence for one proposed method of evolution does not necessarily prove the veracity of another proposed method. It might, instead, be interpreted as evidence that evolution itself did not occur. Patterson, an evolutionist, recognizes the flaw in the reasoning behind punctuated equilibrium:

> Well, it seems to me that [proponents of punctuated equilibrium] have accepted that the fossil record doesn't give them the support they would value so they searched around to find another model and found one. . . . Once you start applying that reasoning to the fossil record, you are doing what these people (creationists) are saying you are doing. When you haven't got the evidence, you make up a story that will fit the lack of evidence.[100]

Exactly what evolutionists are doing!

Obviously, an origins theory that cannot postulate a satisfactory mechanism but rather is based on the absence of evidence is no better than its parent theory, neo-Darwinism. Further, the speculations of punctuated equilibrium may avoid the problem of transitional forms, but they still are faced with the insurmountable problems presented by spontaneous generation, the lack of observed beneficial mutations, the tautology of natural selection, and evolution's contradiction of the second law of thermodynamics.

Punctuated equilibrium, then, is every bit as faulty as traditional evolutionary theory. Indeed, creationism proves to be a much better explanation of man's origin, when one takes into account evidences of intelligent design throughout the universe, a living God creating life, the complexity and ingenuity of DNA, the fossil record showing no transitional forms but rather "kind begetting kind," the extinction of species rather than new species evolving through natural selection or punctuated equilibrium, the law of biogenesis, and the second law of thermodynamics. "The biblical world outlook," says Morris, "is the scientific world outlook—namely, that the universe had a beginning

Notes and Asides

and that its processes and systems are reliable and intelligible, operating in accordance with fixed laws that can be discovered and used."[101]

Conclusion

Evolutionary theory has come full circle—from an assumption of the gradual appearance of all species to an assumption of the virtually instantaneous (geologically speaking) appearance of all species. From the Christian biologist's perspective, this is an interesting turn of events. Gish writes,

> . . . it cannot be emphasized too strongly that even evolutionists are arguing among themselves whether these major categories [phyla, classes, orders, etc.] appeared *instantaneously* or not! It is precisely the argument of creationists that these forms *did* arise *instantaneously* and that the transitional forms are not recorded because they never existed.[102]

Of course, the explanation Gish would give for the instantaneous appearance of all species is quite different from any explanation offered by an evolutionist. It is our contention, however, that Gish's explanation of creationism is far more scientific than any evolutionary explanation. If the science of biology cannot produce a new species by either natural selection or punctuated equilibrium, then why should we believe it can be done or has been done? The fruit fly was put through the equivalent of many millions of years of mutations and evolution, according to Jeremy Rifkin, but "scientists have never been able to come up with anything other than another fruit fly."[103] The sciences of geology and paleontology have not produced one fossil out of billions in existence to prove the upward evolutionary thrust of plant, animal or man.

"If by evolution we mean macroevolution," says Wolfgang Smith, "then it can be said with the utmost rigor that the doctrine is totally bereft of scientific sanction. . . . [T]here exists to this day not a shred of *bona fide* scientific evidence in support of the thesis that macroevolutionary transformations have ever occurred."[104] Patterson agrees:

> No one has ever produced a species by mechanisms of natural selection. No one has ever gotten near it and most of the current argument in neo-Darwinism is about this question: how a species originates[,] and it is there that natural selection seems to be fading out and chance mechanisms of one sort or another are being invoked.[105]

Notes and Asides

Not only has evolution been discredited at nearly every turn, but also creationism is being found to fit the conclusions of various disciplines, including comparative morphology, comparative anatomy, comparative biochemistry, information content analysis, probability argument (including probability of symbiosis of organism), and paleontology.

For example, Wendell R. Bird, in *Origin of Species Revisited*, quotes evolutionists who admit that when it comes to the fossil record "the creationists seem to have the better of the argument."[106] Indeed, Bird argues that there are basically "seven kinds of affirmative scientific evidence"[107] for creationism "involving fossils, information content, probability, genetics, and comparative biology."[108] The strength of Bird's arguments rests in the fact that he quotes evolutionists, rather than creationists, to support his assertions. Bird, like others before him, makes it very clear that scientific fact is not hurting the concept of creationism, but is hurting the theory of evolution—so much so that one evolutionist (Mark Ridley) admits that "no real evolutionist, whether gradualist or punctuationist, uses the fossil record as evidence in favor of the theory of evolution."[109]

Granted, the belief that God created all things, including man in His own image, requires faith. But evolutionary theory requires faith as well. This is largely because evolution has never been observed. Denton writes, "Even today, the origin of a new species from a pre-existing species has never been directly observed."[110]

"Even today, the origin of a new species from a pre-existing species has never been directly observed."
—Michael Denton

L. Harrison Matthews recognizes the dimension of faith required for evolution. In an introduction to Darwin's *The Origin of Species*, he writes, "The fact of evolution is the backbone of biology, and biology is thus in the peculiar position of being a science founded on an unproved theory—is it then a science or a faith? Belief in the theory of evolution is thus exactly parallel to belief in special creation—both are concepts which believers know to be true but neither, up to the present, has been capable of proof."[111] Karl Popper, a prominent philosopher of science, says much the same thing: "I have come to the conclusion that Darwinism is not a testable scientific theory, but a metaphysical research programme—a possible framework for testable scientific theories."[112] Smith agrees:

> The point, however, is that the doctrine of evolution has swept the world, not on the strength of its scientific merits, but precisely in its capacity as a Gnostic myth. It affirms, in effect, that living beings create themselves, which is, in essence a metaphysical claim. This in itself implies, however, that the theory is scientifically unverifiable (a fact, incidentally, which has often enough been pointed out by philosophers of science). Thus, in the final analysis, evolutionism is in truth a metaphysi-

Notes and Asides

cal doctrine decked out in scientific garb.[113]

Indeed, belief in evolutionary theory would require more faith than belief in creationism, since evolution runs contrary to reason. Still, many evolutionists hold desperately to their theory, simply because it is the only explanation of origins that excludes God. The scientist who believes that everything can be explained in natural terms cannot tolerate the concept of a supernatural Being. But for the Christian biologist, the world is only comprehensible in light of God's existence. This is especially true when one considers the question of origins.

Robert Jastrow accurately summarizes the clash between the materialistic scientist and the Christian with regard to origins:

> [A]t this moment it seems as though science will never be able to raise the curtain on the mystery of creation. For the scientist who has lived by his faith in the power of reason, the story ends like a bad dream. He has scaled the mountains of ignorance; he is about to conquer the highest peak; as he pulls himself over the final rock, he is greeted by a band of theologians who have been sitting there for centuries.[114]

On the basis of the evidence, it appears that this "band of theologians" has the ultimate answer for those seeking to understand the mystery of origins: creationism.

Of course, creationism is unacceptable for all materialistic scientists. It is unfortunate that these scientists stake their faith on the shaky evolutionary position in an effort to avoid facing God. Ironically, it was Darwin's wife who eloquently verbalized the creationists' remonstrance to evolutionists. In a letter to her husband, she wrote, "May not the habit in scientific pursuits of believing nothing till it is proved, influence your mind too much in other things which cannot be proved in the same way, and which if true, are likely to be above our comprehension?"[115]

[1]Henry M. Morris, *The Long War Against God* (Grand Rapids, MI: Baker, 1990), p. 256.
[2]Michael Denton, *Evolution: A Theory in Crisis* (Bethesda, MD: Adler and Adler, 1986), p. 345.
[3]See Fred John Meldau, *Why We Believe in Creation, Not in Evolution* (Denver, CO: Christian Victory Publishing, 1972).
[4]See J. P. Moreland, *Christianity and the Nature of Science* (Grand Rapids, MI: Baker, 1989) for a full discussion of science and its methods and limitations.
[5]This explanation beats the evolutionary explanation hands down when put to the test of Occam's razor. The creationist explanation is ingenious in its simplicity, whereas the evolutionist must struggle with questions such as, How did the first male and female humans evolve at the same time and in the same place?
[6]Richard T. Wright, *Evolution Through the Eyes of Faith* (San Francisco: Harper and Row, 1989) is an example of the Christian attempt to integrate evolutionary theory with Biblical doctrine. Unfortunately, this book is endorsed by the Christian College Coalition (consisting of eighty-three colleges and universities).
[7]Australian Broadcasting Co., June 10, 1976. Cited in Morris, *The Long War Against God*, p. 58.
[8]Bertrand Russell, *Religion and Science* (New York: Oxford, 1961), p. 73. Cited in Morris, *The Long War Against God*, pp. 58, 59.
[9]Walter T. Brown, Jr., *In the Beginning* (Phoenix: Center for Scientific Creation, 1986), p. 42.
[10]Henry M. Morris, *The Scientific Case for Creation* (San Diego: Creation-Life Publishers, 1977), p. 2.
[11]David Raup, "Conflicts Between Darwin and Paleontology," *Field Museum of Natural History Bulletin*, January 1979, p. 25.
[12]Denton, *Evolution: A Theory in Crisis*, p. 77.
[13]Francis A. Schaeffer, *How Should We Then Live?* in *The Complete Works of Francis A. Schaeffer*, six volumes (Westchester, IL: Crossway Books, 1982), vol. 5, p. 157.
[14]Stanley L. Jaki, *The Road of Science and the Ways to God* (Chicago: The University of Chicago Press, 1980), p. 11.
[15]Langdon Gilkey, *Maker of Heaven and Earth* (Garden City, NY: Doubleday, 1959), p. 110.
[16]Norman L. Geisler and J. Kerby Anderson, *Origin Science* (Grand Rapids, MI: Baker, 1987), p. 39. God, then, need not be automatically ruled out of scientific exploration. Moreland, in *Christianity and the Nature of Science*, p. 224, says, "Scientists of other generations recognized that God was a legitimate actual or hypothetical source of explanation in science (and some do today, including some who are not theists)."
[17]Paul Davies, *God and the New Physics* (New York: Simon and Schuster, 1983), p. 144.
[18]Jaki, *The Road of Science and the Ways to God*, pp. 14-15.
[19]Douglas Spanner, *Biblical Creation and the Theory of Evolution* (Greenwood, SC: Attic Press, 1987), p. 47.
[20]Brown, *In the Beginning*, p. 5.
[21]Clyde S. Kilby, ed., *A Mind Awake: An Anthology of C. S. Lewis* (New York: Harcourt Brace Jovanovich, 1980), p. 237.
[22]Paul Davies, *The Cosmic Blueprint* (New York: Simon and Schuster, 1988), p. 197.
[23]Ibid.
[24]Alan Hayward, *God Is* (Nashville, TN: Thomas Nelson, 1980), p. 113.
[25]Denton, *Evolution: A Theory in Crisis*, p. 340.
[26]Paul Davies, *Superforce* (New York: Simon and Schuster, 1984), p. 223.
[27]Davies, *The Cosmic Blueprint*, p. 148.
[28]Davies, *Superforce*, p. 9.
[29]Davies, *The Cosmic Blueprint*, p. 203.
[30]Paul Amos Moody, *Introduction to Evolution* (New York: Harper and Row, 1970), pp. 497-8.
[31]Denton, *Evolution: A Theory in Crisis*, p. 250.
[32]Norman Macbeth, *Darwin Retried* (Boston: Gambit, 1971), p. 72.
[33]Hayward, *God Is*, p. 107.
[34]Denton, *Evolution: A Theory in Crisis*, p. 152.
[35]Macbeth, *Darwin Retried*, p. 101 n.
[36]S. Lovtrup, *Darwinism: the Refutation of a Myth* (London: Croom Helm, 1987), p. 422.
[37]Fred Hoyle and Chandra Wickramasinghe, *Evolution from Space* (London: J. M. Dent and Co., 1981), p. 96.
[38]Charles Thaxton, "In Pursuit of Intelligent Causes: Some Historical Background," an unpublished essay

presented at an Interdisciplinary Conference in Tacoma, Washington, June 23-26, 1988, p. 13.
[39]Brown, *In the Beginning*, p. iii.
[40]Ibid., p. 6.
[41]Ibid., p. 20.
[42]Denton, *Evolution: A Theory in Crisis*, p. 109.
[43]Ibid., p. 351. Denton claims there is a growing likelihood that a genome may well contain one hundred thousand million bits of information.
[44]Luther D. Sunderland, *Darwin's Enigma* (San Diego, CA: Master Books, 1984), p. 149.
[45]Brown, *In the Beginning*, p. 1.
[46]A. E. Wilder-Smith, *Man's Origin, Man's Destiny* (Wheaton, IL: Harold Shaw, 1968), pp. 58-9.
[47]Sunderland, *Darwin's Enigma*, p. 60.
[48]Charles B. Thaxton, Walter L. Bradley, and Roger L. Olsen, *The Mystery of Life's Origin: Reassessing Current Theories* (New York: Philosophical Library, 1984), p. 66. This book is considered by many to be the authoritative study of spontaneous generation—students with questions pertaining to the origin of life are urged to consult it.
[49]Ibid, p. 186.
[50]Dean Kenyon, "Going Beyond the Naturalistic Mindset in Origin-Of-Life Research," *Origins Research*, Spring/Summer 1989, p. 15.
[51]Ibid.
[52]Brown, *In the Beginning*, p. 5.
[53]Francis Crick, *Life Itself* (New York: Simon and Schuster, 1981), p. 88.
[54]Sunderland, *Darwin's Enigma*, p. 55.
[55]Ibid.
[56]H. P. Yockey, "Self Organization Origin of Life Scenarios and Information Theory," *Journal of Theoretical Biology*, vol. 91 (1981), p. 29.
[57]Wilder-Smith, *Man's Origin, Man's Destiny*, p. 55.
[58]Ibid., pp. 55-6.
[59]Ibid., pp. 56-7.
[60]Ibid., pp. 57-8.
[61]Ibid., p. 81.
[62]Brown, *In the Beginning*, p. 9.
[63]Davies, *God and the New Physics*, p. 166.
[64]Wilder-Smith, *Man's Origin, Man's Destiny*, p. 72.
[65]Macbeth, *Darwin Retried*, p. 47.
[66]Brown, *In the Beginning*, p. 1.
[67]C. P. Martin, "A Non-Geneticist Looks at Evolution," *American Scientist*, January 1953, p. 102.
[68]Sunderland, *Darwin's Enigma*, p. 148.
[69]Pierre Paul Grasse, *Evolution of Living Organisms: Evidence for a New Theory of Transformation* (New York: Academic Press, 1977), p. 87.
[70]Alfred Russel Wallace, cited in Wendell R. Bird, *The Origin of Species Revisited*, two volumes (New York: Philosophical Library, 1989), vol. 1, p. 89.
[71]Brown, *In the Beginning*, p. 1.
[72]William R. Fix, *The Bone Peddlers: Selling Evolution* (New York: Macmillan, 1984) pp. 184-5. Two men who *will* discuss the limits of variation are Lane P. Lester and Raymond G. Bohlin, in *The Natural Limits to Biological Change* (Grand Rapids, MI: Zondervan, 1984).
[73]Denton, *Evolution: A Theory in Crisis*, pp. 64-5.
[74]Luther Burbank, cited in Macbeth, *Darwin Retried*, p. 36.
[75]Edward S. Deevey, Jr., "The Reply: Letter from Birnham Wood," *Yale Review* vol. 61, p. 636.
[76]Macbeth, *Darwin Retried*, p. 38.
[77]Charles Darwin, *The Origin of Species*, reprint of sixth edition (London: John Murray, 1902), pp. 341-2.
[78]Sunderland, *Darwin's Enigma*, p. 44.
[79]Brown, *In the Beginning*, p. 3.

[80]Ibid., p. 7.
[81]J. K. Anderson and H. G. Coffin, *Fossils in Focus* (Grand Rapids, MI: Zondervan/Probe, 1977), p. 16.
[82]Raup, "Conflicts Between Darwin and Paleontology," p. 25.
[83]Brown, *In the Beginning*, p. 3.
[84]Stephen J. Gould, "Evolution's Erratic Pace," *Natural History*, vol. 86 (May 1977), p. 14.
[85]Brown, *In the Beginning*, p. 3.
[86]Denton, *Evolution: A Theory in Crisis*, p. 290.
[87]Ibid., p. 107.
[88]Colin Patterson, letter to Luther Sunderland, 10 April 1979. Cited in Sunderland, *Darwin's Enigma*, p. 89.
[89]Brown, *In the Beginning*, p. 2.
[90]Wilder-Smith, *Man's Origin, Man's Destiny*, p. 144.
[91]Stephen J. Gould, "The Return of the Hopeful Monsters," *Natural History*, 1977, 86(6): 22-30.
[92]Charles Darwin, *The Origin of Species* (London: John Murray, facsimile printed by Harvard University Press, 1966), p. 189.
[93]R. B. Goldschmidt, cited in Duane T. Gish, *Evolution: The Challenge of the Fossil Record* (El Cajon, CA: Creation-Life, 1985), p. 235.
[94]Macbeth, *Darwin Retried*, p. 33.
[95]Gish, *Evolution: The Challenge of the Fossil Record*, p. 235.
[96]Stephen J. Gould, "Is a New and General Theory of Evolution Emerging?" a lecture at Hobart and William Smith College, 14 February 1980.
[97]Charles Darwin, *The Origin of Species*, 6th ed., (New York: Collier Books, 1962), p. 468.
[98]Sunderland, *Darwin's Enigma*, p. 104.
[99]Gish, *Evolution. The Challenge of the Fossil Record*, p. 249.
[100]Sunderland, *Darwin's Enigma*, p. 100.
[101]Morris, *The Long War Against God*, p. 304.
[102]Gish, *Evolution: The Challenge of the Fossil Record*, p. 231.
[103]Jeremy Rifkin, *Algeny* (New York: Viking Press, 1983), p. 134.
[104]Wolfgang Smith, *Teilhardism and the New Religion* (Rockford, IL: Tan Books, 1988), p. 5.
[105]Colin Patterson, "Cladistics," Interview on BBC, March 4, 1982. Cited in Morris, *The Long War Against God*, p. 159. Steven M. Stanley, a paleontologist at Johns Hopkins University, also agrees with Smith and Patterson: "The known fossil record fails to document a single example of phyletic evolution accomplishing a major morphological transition." Steven M. Stanley, *Macroevolution: Pattern and Process* (San Francisco, CA: W. M. Freeman, 1979), p. 39. Cited by Morris, p. 27.
[106]Bird, *The Origin of Species Revisited*, vol. 1, p. 50.
[107]Ibid., p. 39.
[108]Although we have summarized most of Bird's major points in this section, students interested in 1,000 more pages of excellent material are advised to read his powerful presentation.
[109]Mark Ridley, cited in Bird, *The Origin of Species Revisited*, vol. 1, p. 2.
[110]Denton, *Evolution: A Theory in Crisis*, p. 81.
[111]L. Harrison Matthews, "Introduction" to Charles Darwin, *The Origin of Species* (London: J. M. Dent and Sons, Ltd., 1971), p. x.
[112]Karl Popper, *Unended Quest* (La Salle, IL: Open Court, 1990), p. 168.
[113]Smith, *Teilhardism and the New Religion* , p. 2.
[114]Robert Jastrow, *God and the Astronomers* (New York: W. W. Norton, 1978), p. 116.
[115]N. Barlow, *Autobiography of Charles Darwin* (London: Collins, 1958), pp. 235-7.

SECTION FIVE

PSYCHOLOGY

PSYCHOLOGY [Greek: *psyche* (soul) + *logos* (word)]: The study of the soul, mind, and spirit.

	SECULAR HUMANISM	MARXISM/ LENINISM	BIBLICAL CHRISTIANITY
SOURCE	*HUMANIST MANIFESTO I & II*	*WRITINGS OF MARX & LENIN*	*BIBLE*
THEOLOGY	ATHEISM	ATHEISM	THEISM
PHILOSOPHY	NATURALISM	DIALECTICAL MATERIALISM	SUPERNATURALISM
ETHICS	ETHICAL RELATIVISM	PROLETARIAT MORALITY	ETHICAL ABSOLUTES
BIOLOGY	DARWINIAN EVOLUTION	DARWINIAN/ PUNCTUATED EVOLUTION	SPECIAL CREATIONISM
PSYCHOLOGY	MONISTIC SELF-ACTUALIZATION	MONISTIC PAVLOVIAN BEHAVIORISM	DUALISM
SOCIOLOGY	NON-TRADITIONAL WORLD STATE ETHICAL SOCIETY	ABOLITION OF HOME, CHURCH AND STATE	HOME CHURCH STATE
LAW	POSITIVE LAW	POSITIVE LAW	BIBLICAL/NATURAL LAW
POLITICS	WORLD GOVERNMENT (GLOBALISM)	NEW WORLD ORDER	JUSTICE FREEDOM ORDER
ECONOMICS	SOCIALISM	SOCIALISM/ COMMUNISM	STEWARDSHIP OF PROPERTY
HISTORY	HISTORICAL EVOLUTION	HISTORICAL MATERIALISM	HISTORICAL RESURRECTION

CHAPTER

15

SECULAR HUMANIST PSYCHOLOGY

"Everything depends on what you believe man is like." [1]

—Sidney M. Jourard

"For myself, though I am very well aware of the incredible amount of destructive, cruel, malevolent behavior in today's world—from the threats of war to the senseless violence in the streets—I do not find that this evil is inherent in human nature." [2]

—Carl Rogers

SUMMARY

Consistent adherence to atheistic theology and naturalistic philosophy should cause the Secular Humanist to champion behavioristic psychology. If the supernatural—including mind and spirit—does not exist, then every decision made by humans should be nothing more than the natural results of synapses firing in the brain. Thus, all human actions should be determined by purely natural causes, and Humanist psychologists should work within a behavioristic framework.

Some Humanist psychologists recognize the logical consequences of their theology and philosophy. B. F. Skinner, Humanist of the Year in 1972, was perhaps the most famous behaviorist in the world. But most Humanists are unwilling to embrace behaviorism. Why? Because it denies individual freedom.

Humanists believe that personal freedom is one of the greatest goods because they trust that truly free men will be able to get in touch with their inherent perfection and create a utopian world civilization. For this reason, most Humanists ignore their naturalistic assumptions when studying psychology. Wayne L. Trotta says bluntly, "It may be prudent to assume that all behavior is governed by causal laws. But reducing human conduct to a set of mechanistic . . . formulae would ultimately reduce therapy to nothing more than a set of techniques."[3] Humanists turn their backs on the logical consequences of their theology and philosophy for convenience.

Rejecting both behaviorism and Freudianism, Humanists embrace "third force" psychology—which is based almost exclusively on the work of Abraham Maslow, Rollo May, Erich Fromm, and Carl Rogers. This psychology focuses on man's inherent goodness and predicts that every individual can achieve mental health simply by getting in touch with his "real self." Humanists call for individuals to become "self-actualized" by meeting all their personal needs. Put bluntly, this psychology helps troubled individuals learn to worship their perfect selves.

Of course, a person seriously striving for self-esteem must abandon all feelings of inferiority, including guilt. Humanist psychologists believe guilt is forced on individuals by society and, as such, is unnecessary baggage. Christianity, according to the Humanist, is one of the chief sources of individual guilt and therefore is a serious hindrance to collective mental health. Peter Breggin declares, "it is certainly not hard to show that authoritarian religions create guilt. . . ."[4]

In fact, many Humanists explain away religious belief as a symptom of mental illness. People who subscribe to the notions of guilt and moral accountability, since they cannot be self-actualized, must be psychologically unbalanced. James J. D. Luce warns that "the fundamentalist experience can be a serious mental health hazard to perhaps millions of people."[5] The only means of coping with this hazard and healing all psychological wounds is provided by the Humanistic perspective. Humanism decrees that human nature is good and all mankind (once freed from supernatural superstition and the institutions based on it) can become self-actualized, perfect world citizens fit for a new world order.

Notes and Asides

Introduction

Humanist psychology, like all aspects of the Humanist worldview, is strongly influenced by its theology, philosophy, and biology. Leading Humanist psychologists begin with the assumption that a personal God is a myth. Erich Fromm says simply, "I am not a theist."[6] Abraham Maslow's perspective is summarized by Warren Bennis:

> For Abe each man's task is to become the best "himself." What Abe has done is to make natural what was religious, mystical, or supernatural. He has helped to give man ownership over his human potentials, rather than let them be arrogated by the temporal, nonhuman institutions that, at times, science, business, and the church have been.[7]

Next, Humanists assume that man is simply a product of spontaneous generation and billions of years of evolution. This perspective will become obvious throughout this chapter, especially when we examine the Humanist idea of "emerging conscience."

A naturalistic philosophy logically follows from these first two assumptions. Maslow declares, "Humanists for thousands of years have attempted to construct a naturalistic, psychological value system that could be derived from man's own nature, without the necessity of recourse to authority outside the human being himself." He goes on to admit that all these attempts have failed, but he does not allow this poor track record to discourage him, proclaiming, "certain developments in the science and art of psychology, in the last few decades, make it possible for us for the first time to feel confident that this age-old hope may be fulfilled if only we work hard enough."[8]

> "[H]umanists find that the traditional dualism of mind and body must be rejected."
>
> —*Humanist Manifesto I*

Of course, this naturalistic philosophy implies another assumption. The *Humanist Manifesto I* states, "Holding an organic view of life, humanists find that the traditional dualism of mind and body must be rejected."[9] This final assumption has severe ramifications for the psychological realm of Humanism that become obvious when one examines *Webster's New World Dictionary*'s first definition of *psychology*: "the science dealing with the mind and with mental and emotional processes. . . ."[10]

One cannot engage in too much study of the mind and its processes if one believes the mind to be no more than a series of physical/chemical responses to stimuli. In fact, strict adherence to the view that the mind is simply an extension of the body allows for only one type of psychology: behaviorism. We will examine behaviorism in the Marxist psychology chapter; for now, it will suffice to understand that Humanism declares itself to be a "third force" in the realm of psychology, falling somewhere between behaviorism and Freudianism.

Notes and Asides

The fact that a monistic psychology logically must embrace the behaviorist view does not seem to bother Humanists. Virtually all Humanist psychologists shun behaviorism, largely because it destroys the concepts of freedom and free will. Fromm writes, "Radical humanism considers the goal of man to be that of complete independence, and this implies penetrating through fictions and illusions to a full awareness of reality."[11] Behaviorism does not accept the notion that the individual can achieve complete independence, thus alienating most Humanists. Humanism, therefore, turns its back on the only branch of psychology consistent with its theology, biology, and philosophy, in an effort to allow for the existence of freedom. The presumptive preeminence of freedom is reiterated by Carl Rogers: "The direction which constitutes the good life is that which is selected by the total organism, when there is psychological freedom to move in any direction."[12]

Behaviorism is a branch of psychology which rejects the concept of mind, and describes human behavior as strictly determined by physical influences.

Only one leading Humanist psychologist, Fromm, seems willing to abandon the monistic position to create a more consistent science. He writes often of a "conscience" that seems to be more than physical response to stimuli. But this other-than-physical entity still is considered a result of the evolutionary process. We will examine Fromm's scrambled dualism shortly.

It is important to understand that Humanists call their psychology the "third force" in this discipline because they are unwilling to embrace behaviorism or Freudianism. On the one hand, Humanists reject behaviorism because it destroys their necessary concept of freedom. On the other hand, they reject Freudianism because it focuses too much on the individual apart from society. Fromm sums up the Humanist complaint against Freudianism:

> We believe that man is primarily a social being, and not, as Freud assumes, primarily self-sufficient and only secondarily in need of others in order to satisfy his instinctual needs. In this sense, we believe that individual psychology is fundamentally social psychology or, in Sullivan's terms, the psychology of interpersonal relationships; the key problem of psychology is that of the particular kind of relatedness of the individual toward the world, not that of satisfaction or frustration of single instinctual desires.[13]

Third force psychology assumes the inherent goodness of man and encourages individuals to discover their perfect selves through self-oriented pursuits.

The Humanist, unsatisfied with the two existing branches of psychology, created a third branch. In theory, this branch seems Humanistic. In reality, the Humanist must either abandon his philosophy or accept behaviorism as the proper view of man and his mental processes.

Thus, Humanists try to redefine psychology so as to avoid the dilemma of attempting to study a free mind made up only of synapses

Notes and Asides

responding to stimuli. Fromm says, "Human nature, though being the product of historical evolution, has certain inherent mechanisms and laws, to discover which is the task of psychology."[14] He does not bother to guess the origin of these inherent laws, leaving the definition vague enough to avoid the mind/body problem facing the psychologist.

With the inherent inconsistencies propounded by Humanist psychology, it is difficult to label their discipline as psychology at all, let alone as a science. Small wonder that James B. Klee admits, "Humanistic psychology offers no answers, and indeed few if any methods."[15] Still, Humanist psychology does make a consistent claim to understand mankind's mental problems, and it generally relies on a consistent framework built on its uncertain foundation.

Is Man Good or Evil?

Whereas Christianity believes man to be a fallen creation, Humanist psychology, consistent with Humanism itself, emphatically declares the innate goodness of man. This is a fundamental level on which Christianity and Humanism clash, as Fromm points out: "The position taken by humanistic ethics that man is able to know what is good and to act accordingly on the strength of his natural potentialities and of his reason would be untenable if the dogma of man's innate natural evilness were true."[16]

The Humanist is unwilling to view man as a fallen creature. Maslow writes, "As far as I know we just don't have any intrinsic instincts for evil. If you think in terms of the basic needs; instincts, at least at the outset, are all 'good'—or perhaps we should be technical about it and call them 'pre-moral,' neither good nor evil."[17] And elsewhere he declares, "I am saying that these basic needs are good, and that careful study of them will provide the values we need by which better societies can evolve."[18] Rogers says much the same thing: "I see members of the human species, like members of other species, as essentially constructive in their fundamental nature, but damaged by their experience."[19] Paul Kurtz views man as "a perfectible human being."[20]

This view of man is so incompatible with the Christian view that Humanists feel compelled to attack the notion of original sin. Floyd W. Matson writes, "The old reactionary doctrine of Original Sin, of innate depravity, has lately been enjoying a very popular and large-scale revival." He believes this revival is due to "mass failure of nerve" and says he does not "believe that humanistic psychologists will accept that cop-out."[21]

Obviously, they have not accepted this "cop-out." Rather, some have tried to reinterpret the Bible so as to distort the concept of man's

Notes and Asides

fall. Fromm claims, "The Christian interpretation of the story of man's act of disobedience as his 'fall' has obscured the clear meaning of the story. The biblical text does not even mention the word 'sin'; man challenges the supreme power of God, and he is able to challenge it because he is potentially God."[22] In other words, Fromm sees the Garden of Eden as a story allegorizing man's move to freedom, not as a true explanation for his sinful nature.

Still other Humanistic psychologists choose to attack the whole Christian view in an effort to avoid the concept of original sin. Wendell W. Watters writes,

> The true Christian is running furiously on a treadmill to get away from whole segments of his or her human nature which he or she is taught to fear or about which he or she is taught to feel guilty. The Christian is brainwashed to believe that he or she was born wicked, should suffer as Christ suffered, and should aspire to a humanly impossible level of perfection nonetheless.[23]

According to Watters, all this confusion and guilt heaped on the Christian helps promote mental illness: "A true Christian must always be in a state of torment," he says, "since he or she can never really be certain that God has forgiven him or her for deeply felt negative feelings—in spite of the Catholic confessional and the fundamentalist trick of self-deception known as being saved or born again."[24] Still elsewhere he declares that even the most lukewarm Christians have a faith that "could have side effects that are deleterious to their mental health and that of their children."[25] "Christianity has been not only steadfastly anti-pleasure but pro-suffering throughout its history," he insists.[26]

> "Men's minds are too ready to excuse guilt in themselves."
> —Titus Livius Livy

Clearly, Humanistic psychologists are uneasy with the whole Christian concept of original sin. This is largely because this doctrine provides an explanation for the existence of man-caused evil in the world, whereas Humanist psychology (on the surface) does not. However, Humanism has devised a theory to go hand-in-hand with the idea of man's innate goodness; a theory designed to explain the existence of wars, crime, etc. This theory is also crucial to the Humanistic psychological framework.

Societal and Cultural Influences

The good impulses within people, says Maslow, "are easily warped by cultures—you never find them in their pure state. The people within a culture may, deep within themselves, hold the universal constant of

Notes and Asides

justice. Within the framework of a bad culture it can be twisted into an instrument of evil."[27] Virtually every Humanistic psychologist shares this view of culture as the force responsible for the evil in mankind. It is the only means available for explaining the odd fact that man can be inherently good and still show such a tendency to commit evil acts.

Thus, Rogers notes that "experience leads me to believe that it is cultural influences which are the major factor in our evil behaviors."[28] And Lawrence K. Frank says,

> The "evil" in man becomes increasingly explicable as a product of what is done to and for the child and youth who, faced with these threats, these humiliations and denials, attempts to protect and maintain himself by distorted patterns of belief, action and feeling. These disturbances of personality appear, like disease, to be the efforts of the organism-personality to maintain itself in the face of a menacing environment, efforts that may be self-destructive as well as anti-social.[29]

> "Sick people are made by a sick culture . . ."
> —Abraham Maslow

And again Maslow declares, "Sick people are made by a sick culture; healthy people are made possible by a healthy culture."[30]

Fromm is a little less hard on society, noting that it is capable of the best as well as the worst: "The most beautiful as well as the most ugly inclinations of man are not part of a fixed and biologically given human nature, but result from the social process which creates man."[31] Still, Fromm's implication is clear: society shapes the individual, and in this shaping causes him to develop evil tendencies. This Secular Humanist view is a concerted effort to explain away man's evil nature and place the burden of evil elsewhere.

Humanist psychologist Rollo May, however, is unwilling to accept this premise. In response to claims by Rogers, May cuts to the heart of the matter when he writes, "But you say that you 'believe that it is cultural influences which are the major factor in our evil behaviors.' This makes culture the enemy. But who makes up the culture except persons like you and me?"[32] Indeed, how could culture or society ever have become evil if there were no tendency within man toward evil? Viewing society as a force operating separately from the individual is far more difficult than the Humanist would have us believe.

In practice, Humanists acknowledge this innate relation between society and the individual, despite the fact that once one assumes the individual to be perfectible and society to be the negative influence, the next logical step should be to change the culture first and then change the individual. For example, Lawrence Frank says, "Once we are convinced that we make up social order, and constitute the cultural world by what we believe and assume, we will recognize that social

Notes and Asides

advance can occur only in and through persons. Moreover it becomes clear that each member of the cultural group is participating in its perpetuation or in its change by and through his individual selection and rejection of beliefs and expectations."[33] Thus these Humanist psychologists put the emphasis on the individual's getting in touch with his "real self," that innate goodness that underlies whatever corruption might have been forced on him by culture and that will, when he has discovered (or actualized, or realized) himself, shine forth and make society better.

A Self-centered Worldview

Every Humanist psychologist believes the secret to better mental health lies in getting in touch with the unspoiled, inner self. When man strips himself of all the evil forced on him by society, he will become a positive agent with virtually unlimited potential. Just how much potential man is assumed to have is reflected by the title of one of Fromm's most important works, *You Shall Be as Gods*. Frank demonstrates how the Humanist view of potentialities meshes with its philosophy and biology: "We begin to grasp the full potentialities of human nature only when we can take that last step and see that what man has done and can do is possible because he derives all his potentialities from nature and therefore must believe in nature and human nature as the sources of his strength and of his difficulties."[34]

The Humanist emphasis, then, is on self-reliance, even self-centeredness. Harold P. Marley states, "To know Humanism, first know the self in its relation to other selves. Trust thyself to stand alone; learn of others, but lean not upon a single saviour."[35] This call to trust yourself and your natural inclinations is voiced powerfully by Maslow: "Since this inner nature is good or neutral rather than bad, it is best to bring it out and to encourage it rather than to suppress it. If it is permitted to guide our life, we grow healthy, fruitful, and happy."[36] We must focus on our own self, our own will and desires, for only then can we become good.

Ellis G. Olim describes what this person who listens to his real self is like: "[T]he fully functioning person has an acute sense of his own personal identity. As a consequence, he has also an awareness of his own powers to relate effectively to the world. He changes the world. He exercises mastery over it and over himself. The locus of evaluation of himself rests within himself."[37] It is important to notice that Olim calls for the self to be the center, or "locus," for one's experience. This self-centeredness is desirable, according to Humanist psychology.

In fact, self-centeredness is believed by Humanists to be the wave

Notes and Asides

of the future—an entirely new philosophy of life. Rogers, when considering what the philosophy of the future will be like, guesses, "It will stress the value of the individual. It will, I think, center itself in the individual as the evaluating agent."[38]

Humanist psychologists perceive this self-centered attitude as crucial for the mental health of the individual as well as for the eventual restructuring of society. Only when mankind accepts the need for the individual to be completely in control can we tap the unlimited potential of being human. Said Fromm, "The achievement of well-being is possible only under one condition: if we put man back into the saddle."[39]

Self-actualized Man

The immediate goal of man's self-centeredness, according to Humanist psychology, is for each individual to get in touch with his real, creative self—in Maslow's words, to become self-actualized. Maslow categorizes this drive to know the real self as a need that can be attended to only after the individual has satisfied his lower needs—namely, physiological, safety, social, and ego needs (see Figure 15:1). The individual must satisfy these needs as well as the need for self-actualiza-

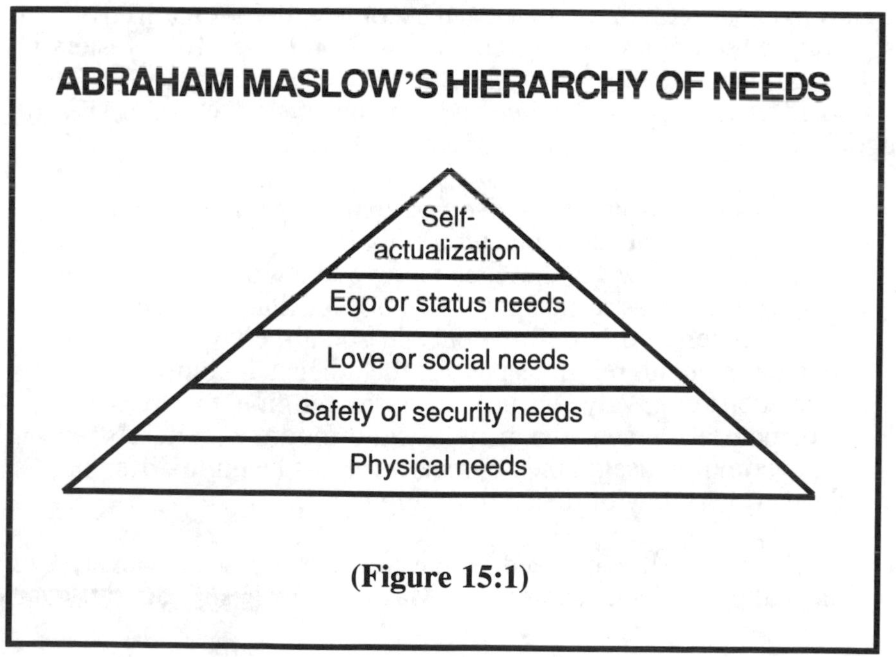

(Figure 15:1)

Notes and Asides

tion before he can truly be declared mentally healthy.

According to Maslow, few people in modern society are self-actualized. This probably means that most people are, by definition, mentally ill. Thus, when attempting to study self-actualized individuals, he relied to some extent on historical figures as models. Mother Teresa might be an excellent candidate, except she's a Christian. Maslow feels "fairly sure" that Abraham Lincoln "in his last days" and Thomas Jefferson were self-actualized. He also singles out Albert Einstein, Eleanor Roosevelt, Jane Addams, William James, Albert Schweitzer, Aldous Huxley, and Benedict de Spinoza as "highly probable" examples of self-actualization.[40]

What character traits mark these historical figures as more in tune with their real, creative selves? What are the characteristics of the self-actualized individual? Maslow says that self-actualization "stresses 'full-humanness,' the development of the biologically based nature of man. . . ."[41] This emphasis relies, as does all Humanist psychology, on the assumption of man's innate, evolved goodness. Elsewhere Maslow emphasizes the evolutionary perspective again, this time in an effort to demonstrate the need for a less restrictive culture: "The so-called spiritual, transcendent, or axiological life is clearly rooted in the biological nature of the species. It is a kind of 'higher' animality whose precondition is a healthy 'lower' animality and the two are hierarchically-integrated rather than mutually exclusive. However, the higher, spiritual 'animality' is timid and weak. It is so easily lost, easily crushed by stronger cultural forces, that it can become widely actualized only in a culture which approves of human nature and, therefore, fosters its fullest growth."[42]

Self-actualization, the highest need in Abraham Maslow's hierarchy of needs, occurs when the individual achieves full development of his or her abilities and ambitions.

In *Motivation and Personality*, Maslow becomes more specific about the individual who has achieved full growth:

> A few centuries ago these [self-actualized people] would all have been described as men who walk in the path of God or as godly men. A few say that they believe in a God, but describe this God more as a metaphysical concept than as a personal figure. If religion is defined only in social-behavioral terms, then these are all religious people, the atheists included. But if more conservatively we use the term religion to stress the supernatural element and institutional orthodoxy (certainly the more common usage) then our answer must be quite different, for then very few of them are religious.[43]

Just because self-actualized people are not religious, however, does not mean they are bad, according to Maslow. "[T]hese individuals are

Notes and Asides

strongly ethical, they have definite moral standards, they do right and do not do wrong. Needless to say, their notions of right and wrong and of good and evil are often not the conventional ones."[44]

This type of individual is exactly what we need for the future, according to Olim: "We do have a new conception of man. It is a conception that enables us to go forward into the future instead of trying to hold back the course of human development. This new conception is that man is constantly becoming. . . . What we want, then, is not to encourage a static type of personality based on traditional notions of right and wrong, but the kind of person who is able to go forward into the uncertain future. The man of the future should be self-actualizing. This means that he should ever be moving toward a greater realization of his human potential and, equally important, that he be constantly transcending himself."[45]

Fromm echoes this belief, claiming that society is presently failing due to the lack of people in touch with their real selves:

> The failure of modern culture lies not in its principle of individualism, not in the idea that moral virtue is the same as the pursuit of self-interest, but in the deterioration of the meaning of self-interest; not in the fact that people are too much concerned with their self-interest, but that they are not concerned enough with the interest of their real self; not in the fact that they are too selfish, but that they do not love themselves.[46]

"[M]an is in a constant process of evolving into higher and higher forms of humanness . . . "
—Ellis G. Olim

This belief in the need to tap the individual's virtually limitless potential is basic to Humanism. The *Humanist Manifesto I* states, "Religious humanism considers the complete realization of human personality to be the end of man's life and seeks its development and fulfillment in the here and now."[47] Olim sums up the specifically psychological position when he writes, "man is in a constant process of evolving into higher and higher forms of humanness, . . . his self is constantly going beyond previous selves. Man's human potential is not finite; it is infinite. There are no limits to the process of becoming. Thus, Maslow (1955) talks of the 'self-actualized' person; Rogers (1959) of the 'fully functioning' individual. . . ."[48]

The task for the Humanistic psychologist, then, is simply to unlock the potential creativity and goodness inherent in every human being. Mental health can be achieved worldwide, as soon as each individual's self-actualization needs are met. Specifically, as soon as each individual learns to love and nurture his real self, the mission of Humanism will be fulfilled.

Notes and Asides

Man-centered Values

Why will this unlocking of potential erase all mental illness? Again, the answer is tied into the notion of man's innate goodness. Once an individual becomes self-actualized, he will be capable of acting in harmony with his true self, and his true self always desires good. Therefore, the man who listens to his real inner nature will always act morally. For the Humanist, ethics is inseparable from psychology.

At the most basic level, Humanists assume self-actualization to be right and self-denial to be wrong. Fromm explains,

CLOSE-UP

Erich Fromm (1900-1980)

Erich Fromm, born in Germany in 1900, was the descendant of a long line of rabbis, but he chose to abandon Judaism at the age of 26. He declared, "I gave up my religious convictions and practices because I just didn't want to participate in any division of the human race, whether religious or political." This attitude shaped much of Fromm's Humanist vision, and was based on his trust that the inherent goodness of man would lead mankind away from the constraints of imperfect society to a united world community. One of Fromm's most popular works, *The Sane Society*, describes his belief that modern capitalist society is too consumption-oriented, and provides guidelines for establishing a society in which man's goodness can flourish. Fromm came to rely heavily on Marxist economic theory as a means of achieving this goal. As such, he was one of the leading Humanist proponents of socialism. Fromm saw little distinction between the Marxist and the Humanist worldviews, which drew the ire of some Humanists. Still, he was influential enough to earn Humanist of the Year honors in 1966, largely due to his contributions to Humanist psychology. Other important books by Fromm include *You Shall Be As Gods* and *Man for Himself*.

Notes and Asides

> I shall attempt to show that the character structure of the mature and integrated personality, the productive character, constitutes the source and basis of "virtue," and that "vice," in the last analysis, is indifference to one's own self and self-mutilation. Not self-renunciation nor selfishness but the affirmation of his truly human self, are the supreme values of humanistic ethics. If man is to have confidence in values, he must know himself and the capacity of his nature for goodness and productiveness.[49]

Robert Roessler agrees: "I have come to feel that people are neither innately good nor innately bad; they are either fully aware of themselves or, so to speak, divorced from themselves. If their own deepest feelings are available to them, they generally behave in ways we label 'good'; if they have come to deny themselves, they sometimes behave in ways we label 'bad.'"[50]

Secular Humanist psychology views ethics as inherently related to the individual and his mental health. Indeed, for the Humanist, ethics cannot exist outside of man. Fromm believes that "values are rooted in the very conditions of human existence; hence that our knowledge of these conditions—that is, of the 'human situation'—leads us to establishing values which have objective validity; this validity exists only with regard to the existence of man; outside of him there are no values."[51]

Therefore, man must turn his eyes inward to determine what is right. He needn't worry about helping others; rather, he should simply concentrate on creating a good self. Maslow describes this view succinctly: "In general, it looks as if the best way to help other people grow toward self-actualization is to become a good person yourself. Trying to help other people can be a way of avoiding our own troubles. I can deny that I am hostile, for example, by going and helping everybody else not to be hostile. A more humble approach is better. Clean your own doorstep first."[52] Again, the Humanist embraces self-centeredness in an effort to create a better world.

When one gets in touch with his innermost nature, his feelings become an accurate guide for choosing what is moral, according to Humanist psychologists. Roessler proclaims,

> Personal morality is defined in positive terms. Feelings become a reliable guide to action which enhances and enriches both self and others. Feelings are prescriptions for action rather than inaction. By contrast, codified moralities are most often preponderantly prohibitions, because they are frequently based on a pessimistic view of man's nature; and, as John Dewey has

Notes and Asides

> observed, ". . . morals cut off from positive roots in man's nature are bound to be mainly negative."[53]

Man must rely on his own feelings to live accurately according to his own nature.

This reliance on the self and its feelings causes Humanist psychologists to mistrust unselfishness. Fromm writes,

> "Don't be selfish" is a sentence which has been impressed upon millions of children, generation after generation. Its meaning is somewhat vague. Most people would say that it means not to be egotistical, inconsiderate, without any concern for others. Actually, it generally means more than that. Not to be selfish implies not to do what one wishes, to give up one's own wishes for the sake of those in authority. . . . Aside from its obvious implication, it means, "don't love yourself," "don't be yourself," but submit yourself to something more important than yourself, to an outside power or its internalization, "duty." "Don't be selfish" becomes one of the most powerful ideological tools in suppressing spontaneity and the free development of personality. Under the pressure of this slogan one is asked for every sacrifice and for complete submission: only those acts are "unselfish" which do not serve the individual but somebody or something outside himself.[54]

This call for the individual to be true to his feelings and innermost nature obviously allows for a great deal of experimentation. If an individual feels like his innermost nature is calling for him to act in a specific way, who has the authority to tell him he is misinterpreting his feelings? Humanism affirms man's freedom to experiment with values, to test which aspects of morality truly mesh with his inner nature. This is especially true with regard to Humanist psychology's attitude toward sexual relations. Robert N. Whitehurst writes,

> In the exploration that follows, it will be suggested that marriage is not a healthy institution for many people today, but it is not about to die; further, the future of alternatives is simply not predictable, given the status of current political winds and economic uncertainties. Given certain conditions, however, some probable options might come to fruition. . . . These involve modified open marriage, post-marital singlehood, triads, a variety of cooperatives, urban collectives and urban communes, extended intimate networks, rural communes, and finally swinging, cohabitation, and part-time marriage.[55]

Humanist psychologists believe that society's attitude toward sex is far too stuffy. At this level of discussion, Humanists make good Freudians. This is made clear by the authors of *Humanistic Psychology*, who "invite the readers to consider how harsh the controls on human sexual activity have been in the past, and continue to be in the present, and to decide whether we wish to continue to maintain an oppressive and harmful individual and societal attitude toward human sexuality."[56]

Humanist psychologists perceive self-actualized man as the final authority for ethics, regardless of how much scientific experimentation it requires to discover "the good." Unfortunately, "the good" discovered is only "the good" for that individual. Others may decide something else is "good." Then again some may decide there is "no good," there are "no rules," "no laws." In the final analysis, multiple rapist-murderer Ted Bundy could turn out to be, Humanistically speaking, a self-actualized person. After all, he did not allow any outside codes or books to influence him, and he was certainly in touch with his vital inclinations.

Humanist psychologists are quick to put a halt to this line of thinking, however, by arguing that few people are self-actualized, and the non-self-actualized must look to the self-actualized for guidance. According to Maslow, people not yet self-actualized can learn what is right by watching those who already are in touch with their true selves. Thus, the Humanists must look to mentally healthy (self-actualized) people to determine "scientifically," for example, if pedophilia (man/boy sex) is biologically determined and hence moral.[57] Maslow says, "It is certainly true that mankind, throughout history, has looked for guiding values, for principles of right and wrong. But he has tended to look outside of himself, outside of mankind, to a God, to some sort of sacred book perhaps, or to a ruling class. What I am doing is to explore the theory that you can find the values by which mankind must live, and for which man has always sought, by digging into the best people in depth. I believe, in other words, that I can find ultimate values which are right for mankind by observing the best of mankind."[58] And elsewhere he reiterates, "I propose that we explore the consequences of observing whatever our best specimens choose, and then assuming that these are the highest values for all mankind."[59]

The Role of the Conscience

This idea that a proper sense of values is inherent in every individual's nature seems to imply the existence of a conscience, or at the very least a mind, that is something more than physical impulses. Naturally, this implication is what one would expect from a psychology that avoids

Notes and Asides

behaviorism and emphasizes freedom. However, as previously mentioned, Humanism embraces a naturalistic philosophy and therefore denies the existence of a supernatural mind or conscience. Few Humanists recognize the inconsistency in their view, and very few allow for the existence of the conscience in an effort to create a more coherent psychology.

Fromm is the only notable Humanistic psychologist willing to openly describe man's innate goodness as a "conscience." He is careful to stress however, that this conscience is strictly human in origin and does not necessarily imply the existence of a Creator:

> In this assumption we are on dangerous ground theoretically. It would be easy if we could fall back on religious and philosophical assumptions which explain the existence of such trends by a belief that man is created in God's likeness or by the assumption of a natural law. However, we cannot support our argument with such explanations. The only way in our opinion to account for this striving for justice and truth is by the analysis of the whole history of man, socially and individually. We find then that for everybody who is powerless, justice and truth are the most important weapons in the fight for his freedom and growth. . . . We arrive therefore at the fact that, although character development is shaped by the basic conditions of life and although there is no biologically fixed human nature, human nature has a dynamism of its own that constitutes an active factor in the evolution of the social process.[60]

Obviously, Fromm is trying to create a coherent Humanist psychology while still clinging to Humanism's theological, philosophical and biological assumptions. He realizes that conscience is necessary for a psychology that is more true to the human condition than behaviorism, but he also is aware that belief in a conscience logically implies belief in the supernatural, which is dangerously close to affirming the existence of God. Still, Fromm tries valiantly to reconcile Humanist psychology with Humanist theology and philosophy.

> "He that loses his conscience has nothing left that is worth keeping."
> —Caussin

Thus, Fromm stresses the humanness of conscience, claiming, "Humanistic conscience is not the internalized voice of an authority whom we are eager to please and afraid of displeasing; it is our own voice, present in every human being and independent of external sanctions and rewards."[61] In this way Fromm believes he can factor God out of the equation and leave the approval or disapproval of our actions strictly in our own hands. "Actions, thoughts, and feelings which are conducive to the proper functioning and unfolding of our total personality produce a feeling of inner approval, of 'rightness,' characteristic

Notes and Asides

of the humanistic 'good conscience.'"[62] Like other Humanist psychologists, Fromm stresses the belief that any action that feels right for the individual must be right. He accepts the precepts of Humanist psychology and tries to make them compatible with a warped monism.

How did this mysterious conscience get inside man, assuming there is no God to place it there? The Humanist must believe it evolved, along with all other aspects of man. "But in the evolution of human life," declares Algernon D. Black, "there is a consciousness and emerging conscience. The key question is whether human beings can rise to a level of awareness of the values and the choices which are within human control."[63] Black, too, is attempting to allow for the existence of a conscience while remaining consistent with the Humanist belief that matter is all that exists.

Is Humanist Psychology Scientific?

Humanists have long attempted to redefine science to make it broad enough to include Humanist psychology. They justify their new definitions by pointing to the failure of the existing science to help the individual understand his nature. May complains, "Today we know a great deal about bodily chemistry and the control of physical diseases; but we know very little about why people hate, why they cannot love, why they suffer anxiety and guilt, and why they destroy each other. As we stand beneath the fateful shadow of the H-bomb, however, we have become vividly aware that there can be desperate perils in a scientifically one-sided study of nature and man."[64] Rogers says much the same thing: "It is quite unfortunate that we have permitted the world of psychological science to be narrowed to behaviors observed, sounds emitted, marks scratched on paper, and the like. In an attempt to be ultra-scientific, psychology has endeavored to walk in the footsteps of a Newtonian physics."[65]

What May and Rogers are concerned about is what philosopher Paul Weiss has been talking about for many years. Scientific knowledge, by definition, depends on measurables. It is quantifiable. The question is, can the mind be quantified? Can spirit be measured? Weiss argued that if you put electrical instruments to the nervous system and the brain, you "get only electrical answers." If you use chemical detectors, "you get chemical answers." Instead of concluding from this that the mind cannot exist because our scientific instruments cannot locate or measure it, Weiss suggests, "perhaps we have not yet found the particular kind of instrument that tells us the next unknown."[66] The Humanist, however, fears that this "next unknown" may be supernatural, so he suggests that psychology (rather than the subject it studies)

Notes and Asides

must be redefined.

After pointing out the deficiencies in science's restriction of psychology, the Humanists offer definitions of "scientific" psychology that will include their "third force" or Humanist ideas. Rogers believes a new trend will occur in science, a trend that "will attempt to face up to all of the realities in the psychological realm. Instead of being restrictive and inhibiting, it will throw open the whole range of human experiencing to scientific study. It will explore the private worlds of inner personal meanings, in an effort to discover lawful and orderly relationships there. In this world of inner meanings it can investigate all the issues which are meaningless for the behaviorist—purposes, goals, values, choice, perceptions of self, perceptions of others, the personal constructs with which we build our world, the responsibilities we accept or reject, the whole phenomenal world of the individual with its connective tissue of meaning."[67] Unfortunately for the Humanists, definitions of "scientific" studies such as these allow not only Humanist psychology to be termed scientific, but also every major religion, including Christianity. After all, isn't every major religion an attempt to explore "inner personal meanings"? Doesn't Christianity offer meaningful purposes, values, etc.?

Humanists, of course, will not stand for the treatment of Christianity as a viable option, so they continue to restructure their definition of the new science in an effort to include Humanist psychology and exclude religion. It is unlikely they will ever succeed, since their psychology requires more leaps of faith than most religions.

Conclusion

The Secular Humanists admit that they begin their study of the self, mind, and mental processes with certain assumptions. Adrian L. VanKaam believes that every psychologist of every school "always makes an ultimate and absolute judgment about what is called the nature of man and about the way in which man can be understood. These assumptions of psychologists are not arrived at by psychological research. On the contrary, the assumptions of the psychologist are the point of departure for the kind of research that he will perform and for the evaluation of the results of this research."[68]

The *three major assumptions* of Humanist psychology are: man is good by nature and therefore perfectible; society and its social institutions are responsible for man's evil acts; and mental health can be restored to everyone who gets in touch with his real "good" self. Marxists agree with the first two, Christians deny all three. Christians think individuals should face up to their own sinful nature and take

Notes and Asides

responsibility for their immoral actions instead of blaming someone or something else. Humanists merely give intellectual ammunition to those who never can accept blame and moral responsibility.

Humanists need to keep May's observation in mind: If man is so good, why is society so evil? Perhaps this is what Rogers was thinking about when he wrote, "I should like to make a final confession. When I am speaking to outsiders I present Humanistic psychology as a glowing hope for the future. But within the bosom of our family I have been trying to say that we have no reason whatsoever for feeling complacent as we look toward the future."[69]

[1] Sidney M. Jourard, in *Humanistic Psychology*, edited by I. David Welch, George A. Tate, and Fred Richards (Buffalo: Prometheus Books, 1978), p. 153.
[2]Carl Rogers, "Notes on Rollo May," *Journal of Humanistic Psychology*, Summer 1982, p. 8.
[3]Wayne L. Trotta, "Why Psychotherapy Must Be, and Cannot Be, a Science," *The Humanist*, Sept./Oct. 1989, p. 42.
[4]Peter Breggin, "Mental Health Versus Religion," *The Humanist*, Nov./Dec. 1987, p. 13.
[5]James J. D. Luce, "The Fundamentalists Anonymous Movement," *The Humanist*, Jan./Feb. 1986, p. 11.
[6]Erich Fromm, *You Shall Be as Gods* (New York: Holt, Rinehart and Winston, 1966), p. 7.
[7]Warren Bennis, "A Tribute to Abe Maslow," *The Humanist*, Jan./Feb. 1971, p. 35.
[8]Abraham Maslow, *Toward a Psychology of Being* (New York: Van Nostrand Reinhold, 1968), p. 149.
[9]*Humanist Manifesto I* (Buffalo: Prometheus Books, 1980), p. 8.
[10]*Webster's New World Dictionary*, ed. David B. Guralnik (New York: Simon and Schuster, 1982), p. 1147.
[11]Fromm, *You Shall Be as Gods*, p. 13.
[12]Carl Rogers, "A Therapist's View of the Good Life," *The Humanist*, Sept./Oct. 1957, p. 293.
[13]Erich Fromm, *Escape from Freedom* (New York: Holt, Rinehart and Winston, 1972), p. 290.
[14]Ibid., p. 15.
[15]James B. Klee, in *Humanistic Psychology*, ed. Welch, Tate, and Richards, p. 11.
[16]Erich Fromm, *Man for Himself* (New York: Holt, Rinehart and Winston, 1964), p. 118.
[17]Abraham Maslow, in *Humanistic Psychology*, ed. Welch, Tate, and Richards, p. 190.
[18]Ibid., p. 188.
[19]Rogers, "Notes on Rollo May," p. 8.
[20]Paul Kurtz, et al., "Credo," *The Humanist*, July/Aug. 1968, p. 18.
[21]Floyd W. Matson, in *Humanistic Psychology*, ed. Welch, Tate, and Richards, p. 32.
[22]Fromm, *You Shall Be as Gods*, p. 23.
[23]Wendell W. Watters, "Christianity and Mental Health," *The Humanist*, Nov./Dec. 1987, p. 32.
[24]Ibid., p. 10.
[25]Ibid., p. 5.
[26]Ibid., p. 11.
[27]Maslow, in *Humanistic Psychology*, ed. Welch, Tate, and Richards, p. 189.
[28]Rogers, "Notes on Rollo May," p. 8.
[29]Lawrence K. Frank, "Potentialities of Human Nature," *The Humanist*, April 1951, p. 65.
[30]Maslow, *Toward a Psychology of Being*, p. 6.
[31]Fromm, *Escape from Freedom*, p. 12.
[32]Rollo May, "The Problem of Evil: An Open Letter to Carl Rogers," *Journal of Humanistic Psychology*, Summer 1982, p. 12.
[33]Frank, "Potentialities of Human Nature," p. 68.
[34]Ibid., p. 67.
[35]Harold P. Marley, "First Know the Self," *The Humanist*, Nov./Dec. 1954, p. 258.
[36]Maslow, *Toward a Psychology of Being*, p. 4.
[37]Ellis G. Olim, in *Humanistic Psychology*, ed. Welch, Tate, and Richards, p. 223.
[38]Rogers, in *Humanistic Psychology*, ed. Welch, Tate, and Richards, p. 44.
[39]Erich Fromm, *On Disobedience and Other Essays* (New York: The Seabury Press, 1981), p. 15.
[40]Abraham Maslow, *Motivation and Personality* (New York: Harper & Row, 1987), pp. 127-8.
[41]Maslow, *Toward a Psychology of Being*, p. vi.
[42]Abraham Maslow, "The Good Life of the Self-Actualizing Person," *The Humanist*, July/Aug. 1967, p. 139.
[43]Maslow, *Motivation and Personality*, p. 141.
[44]Ibid., pp. 140-1.
[45]Olim, in *Humanistic Psychology*, ed. Welch, Tate, and Richards, p. 219.
[46]Fromm, *Man for Himself*, p. 139.
[47]*Humanist Manifesto I*, p. 9.
[48]Olim, in *Humanistic Psychology*, ed. Welch, Tate, and Richards, p. 219.
[49]Fromm, *Man for Himself*, p. 17.

[50]Robert Roessler, "A Psychiatrist's View of Morality," *The Humanist* Nov./Dec. 1958, p. 333.
[51]Fromm, *On Disobedience and Other Essays*, p. 1.
[52]Mildred Hardeman, "A Dialogue with Abraham Maslow," *Journal of Humanistic Psychology*, Winter 1979, p. 25.
[53]Roessler, "A Psychiatrist's View of Morality," p. 336.
[54]Fromm, *Man for Himself*, pp. 126-7.
[55]Robert N. Whitehurst, in *Humanistic Psychology*, ed. Welch, Tate, and Richards, pp. 207, 210.
[56]Welch, Tate, and Richards, ed., *Humanistic Psychology*, p. 48.
[57]Judith A. Reisman and Edward W. Eichel, *Kinsey, Sex and Fraud* (Lafayette, LA: Huntington House Publishers, 1990), pp. 197-214. Humanist historian Vern Bullough is deeply involved in this "scientific" quest. As the authors note: "Pedophilia and incest appear to be following in the footsteps of homosexuality" (p. 207).
[58]Maslow, in *Humanistic Psychology*, ed. Welch, Tate, and Richards, p. 188.
[59]Maslow, *Toward a Psychology of Being*, p. 169.
[60]Fromm, *Escape from Freedom*, pp. 288-9.
[61]Fromm, *Man for Himself*, p. 158.
[62]Ibid., p. 159.
[63]Algernon D. Black, "Our Quest for Faith," *The Humanist Alternative*, ed. Paul Kurtz (Buffalo: Prometheus Books, 1973), p. 75.
[64]Rollo May, *Psychology and the Human Dilemma* (Princeton: D. Van Nostrand Company, 1967), p. 188.
[65]Carl Rogers, in *Humanistic Psychology*, ed. Welch, Tate, and Richards, p. 322.
[66]Arthur Koestler and J. R. Smythies, ed., *Beyond Reductionism* (New York: Macmillan, 1970), p. 252.
[67]Ibid., pp. 322-3.
[68]Adrian L. VanKaam, "Assumptions in Psychology," in *Humanistic Viewpoints in Psychology*, ed. Frank T. Severin (New York: McGraw Hill, 1965), p. 177.
[69]Rogers, in *Humanistic Psychology*, ed. Welch, Tate, and Richards, p. 45.

CHAPTER

16

MARXIST/ LENINIST PSYCHOLOGY

"For the construction of a thoroughly scientific and materialist psychology there are two absolutely essential guiding principles: one, that mental activity is a function of the brain; and two, that it is a reflection of objective reality."[1]

—Harry K. Wells

"Only science, exact science about human nature itself, and the most sincere approach to it by the aid of the omnipotent scientific method, will deliver man from his present gloom, and will purge him from his contemporary shame in the sphere of interhuman relations."[2]

—Ivan P. Pavlov

"Psychology cannot be viewed as a neutral science, unaffected by class interests."[3]

—Joseph Nahem

SUMMARY

Karl Marx, Frederick Engels, and V. I. Lenin all describe the mind and mental activity as nothing more than reflections of the brain. This conclusion follows logically from their materialist philosophy. Unfortunately, it leaves Marxism with very little to study in psychology—for them, the "study of the mind" is reduced to the "study of the reflections of the brain." Such a position is called psychological or ontological monism.

Marxist psychology discovered its champion in Ivan P. Pavlov, a Russian physiologist. Pavlov, in his famous experiments with dogs, stressed the primacy of the nervous system in influencing the mental activity of the individual. He believed that two material factors could account for all mental activity: the individual's physiology and the environmental influence on the individual's nervous system. He writes that the "behaviour of man or animal is conditioned not only by the inborn properties of the nervous system, but also by the influences which have always acted on the organism during its individual existence."[4] This meshes beautifully with the Marxist worldview, in which man is approached from a strictly materialistic standpoint and is described as basically good, with his moral failings caused by oppressive societies.

Marxism accepts Pavlov's conclusions and therefore appears to embrace strict behaviorism. However, this is not the case. Marxism cannot accept a completely deterministic explanation of man, because Marxist theory calls for the working class to consciously decide to support the communist revolution. If every man's actions are determined, how can any individual consciously choose to revolt? "Choosing,"

Introduction

Marxist psychologists, it would seem, are tied even more inextricably than Humanists to the behaviorist view of man, since Marxism describes man's development as an inevitable march toward communism. This notion of a determined development of man seems to exclude free will, thereby supporting the behaviorist view that man's decisions and actions are simply the result of his brain's response to environmental stimuli.

Further, Marxist philosophy and biology are consistent with behaviorism. Marxism accepts evolution as fact and perceives materialism to be the only proper means of understanding the world. These beliefs, in

according to the behavioristic view, becomes a meaningless activity. Thus, the Marxist must water down his behaviorism to encourage the worker to actively, consciously strive for communism.

Pavlov provides the escape for the Marxist psychologist. He speaks of a "second stimuli" that only human beings have evolved the capacity to be influenced by: language. That is, Pavlov believes man's "mind" is shaped by his nervous activity and his environment, an environment that uniquely includes the stimulus of words. This belief allows the Marxist to claim that man's actions are largely determined but that the individual can obtain a measure of freedom in his use of and response to the stimulus of language. In this way, Marxism is able to cling to its behavioristic assumptions and still claim that the worker may choose to join the revolution.

Of course, all of Marxism's psychotherapy reflects its behavioristic, materialistic assumptions. Whereas the Marxist may give lip service to freedom of will, he treats mentally ill patients as automatons that require only a little physical/chemical fine tuning to become model citizens again. One day, according to the Marxist, all mankind can be made mentally healthy simply through manipulation of their environment and nervous activity. K. I. Platonov declares, "We have undoubtedly not yet fully mastered the methods of influencing the higher nervous activity of man by suggestion. This is the task of further research."[5] When and if further research grants the Marxist this ability, be assured he will use it in the name of scientifically sculpting the perfect society.

turn, affect the Marxist view of the mind/body relationship. The Marxist, like the Humanist, believes the mind is no more than the purely physical activity of the brain. Mind and brain are two words describing the same thing or entity.

V. I. Lenin states, "The existence of the mind is shown to be dependent upon that of the body, in that the mind is declared to be secondary, a function of the brain, or a reflection of the outer world."[6] Elsewhere he says, "Matter is primary nature. Sensation, thought, consciousness, are the highest products of matter organized in a certain way. This is the doctrine of materialism, in general, and Marx and Engels, in particular."[7]

As noted in the Humanist psychology chapter, psychology is the

Notes and Asides

study of the mind and its processes, and a philosophy that denies the mind as a supernatural phenomenon necessarily confines one to the behaviorist school of thought. Thus, when Lenin declares the mind to be strictly organized matter, he forces Marxism to accept the behaviorist position in order to be consistent with Marxist philosophy. Joseph Nahem digs the same hole for Marxism:

> Marxism is rooted in the philosophy of dialectical materialism. Its materialist viewpoint excludes religious, supernatural or idealist views. Thus, in psychology, it excludes the idea of a supernatural soul as explanatory of human behavior.[8]

Nahem uses the term *soul*, but it is clear from his statement that any notion of a supernatural mind is excluded as well.

This materialist philosophy presented a serious problem for Marxist psychology prior to the development of the behaviorist theory. Ivan P. Pavlov sums up the problem when he declares, "I cannot understand how the present conceptions of psychology, which have no relation to space, can be fitted into a material structure such as the brain."[9] Pavlov spent much of his life reconciling this conflict; in fact, he paved the way for behavioral theorists.

"The soul alone renders us noble."
—Lucius Seneca

Nahem, a modern Marxist psychologist, sums up this reconciliation between materialism and psychology and acknowledges Marxism's indebtedness to Pavlov:

> The fundamental propositions set forth by this materialist epistemology are: that matter is primary and that mind and consciousness are secondary and derivative; that mental processes and consciousness itself are products of specially organized matter in the form of the brain and nervous system. Thus, Marxist materialism holds that psychological theories which separate the mind from the brain, or which deny the primacy of the brain and nervous system are unscientific. The work of Pavlov and others in physiology is viewed as a confirmation of materialist epistemology since it confirms the reliance of mental processes on physiological processes.[10]

From this statement, it seems obvious that the Marxist must embrace behaviorism.

Indeed, behaviorism seems to be all that the Marxist can embrace while remaining consistent with his worldview. This is especially likely since Marxism categorically rejects Freudian psychology. L. P. Bueva writes, "In essence, psychoanalytic conceptions present a pessimistic evaluation of man whose life is presumed to consist of an eternal

Notes and Asides

struggle against a society that is inherently inimical and his instinctive nature consisting of wild and untamed human attractions and passions."[11] If the Marxist rejects Freudianism, rejects the supernatural mind, and believes mankind is destined to embrace communism (a clear-cut denial of free will), then he apparently has no choice other than accepting behaviorism.

Before we examine Marxist psychology's tendencies toward behaviorism further, we must understand precisely what this theory entails. This can be accomplished best by studying the thought of behaviorism's most vocal modern supporter, B. F. Skinner.

Behaviorism Defined

Behaviorism perceives man as simply a stimulus receptor, a creature capable of responding only one predetermined way to any given set of circumstances in his environment. Skinner believes this is the only truly scientific means of approaching psychology: "A scientific analysis of behavior dispossesses autonomous man and turns the control he has been said to exert over to the environment. The individual . . . is henceforth to be controlled by the world around him, and in large part by other men."[12]

Skinner roots this behaviorist view of man in an evolutionary perspective of the world: "The environment not only prods or lashes, it selects. Its role is similar to that in natural selection, though on a very different time scale. . ."[13] Obviously, when the environment does the selecting, man can no longer be perceived as a free agent. So Skinner declares, "The hypothesis that man is not free is essential to the application of scientific method to the study of human behavior."[14]

However, if man is not free, then his actions may be determined by anyone who knows how to pull the right strings. Skinner affirms this as well: "If we are to use the methods of science in the field of human affairs, we must assume that behavior is lawful and determined. We must expect to discover that what a man does is the result of specifiable conditions and that once these conditions have been discovered, we can anticipate and to some extent determine his actions."[15] Thus, Skinner admits, we face a seeming contradiction: man "plays two roles: one as a controller, as the designer of a controlling culture, and another as the controlled, as the product of a culture."[16]

"The hypothesis that man is not free is essential to the application of scientific method to the study of human behavior."
—B. F. Skinner

Skinner, however, does not view this as a real contradiction. Indeed, he believes, now that we have discovered the truth about human nature, we can create a perfect world here on earth: ". . . there is no reason why progress toward a world in which people may be automatically good should be impeded. . . . "[17]

Notes and Asides

The essence of behaviorism is the belief that man is controlled by stimuli from the environment and never makes a decision in which he exercises free will. This view of man as a receptor for outside stimuli is consistent with the materialist belief that man's brain is no more than a bundle of nerves and synapses ready to respond in a determined way to the environment. Clearly, Marxist psychology should embrace this view as the logical conclusion suggested by an evolutionary, materialistic perspective.

Marxist Affirmations of Behaviorism

On the surface, Marxist psychologists appear to embrace behaviorism as the only scientific approach to mental processes. In fact, virtually every leading Marxist psychologist accepts basic premises inherent in behaviorism as true.

Nahem faces the problem presented by a psychology that denies a supernatural mind and seems to draw the conclusion that a behaviorist view is the solution: "Psychology is the science which studies the human mind. . . . The human mind is based upon and produced by the brain and the central nervous system, which function according to certain physical, chemical, biological, and physiological laws. Particularly important for psychology is the study of the physiological laws relating to neurological activity."[18] This perspective appears to be exactly the kind Lenin had in mind when he described the "scientific psychologist" as someone who "has discarded philosophical theories of the soul and set about making a direct study of the material substratum of psychical phenomena—the nervous processes—and has produced, let us say, an analysis and explanation of some one or more psychological processes."[19]

A. R. Luria seems to embrace behaviorism as well, although he stops short of suggesting that behaviorism is the only explanation for mental processes:

> We begin with the view that in the organisation of behaviour there are some general laws operative, dependent upon the inclusion of some special vital forces. The organisation of adult human behaviour is the product of a fairly complicated and long development.[20]

Bueva bases his psychology on the assumption that "Man's needs represent a motivating force for his activities. They include basic needs relating to his livelihood as well as diverse specific social, socio-political, moral and cultural forms of his labour."[21] These needs, for

Notes and Asides

Bueva, are the forces that react to stimuli and shape behavior—a notion that has very behavioristic tendencies.

> It is not only the determining role of external and internal conditions, but rather the creative role of consciousness and man's activities that manifest themselves in people's needs. This refers both to the material and spiritual needs which determine individual's behaviour and stimulate his activity.[22]

When Bueva speaks of man's behavior as determined, he is moving dangerously close to the behaviorist denial of free will.

Marxist psychologists also seem to accept Skinner's premise that once we understand behavior, we may take the necessary steps to control it for the better. Thus, Bueva claims, "In providing an integrated view of the world dialectical-materialistic philosophy assists man in mastering the forces within his own nature and contributes to a realization of the humanistic function of not only perceiving the world but also transforming it in accordance with man's interests and objectives."[23] Nahem agrees: "Marxism links knowledge and freedom by calling for the utilization of natural, social and psychological laws discovered by science to achieve mastery over nature, society and ourselves. Knowledge thus is power—power to be free by utilizing knowledge."[24] Nahem, of course, uses the term *freedom* in an effort to shroud his theory in positive rhetoric, but notice what kind of freedom he is describing—the freedom to control other people and oneself. Skinner envisions this same type of freedom.

Marxist psychology, then, appears to accept behaviorism. Indeed, many Marxists make it sound as if behaviorism is the only scientific approach to psychology. Harry K. Wells declares, "Only by viewing mental activity as a function of higher nervous activity, can psychology be transformed into an objective science on a par with other sciences."[25]

Pavlov's Role in Marxist Psychology

Much of the reason Marxist psychologists often sound like behaviorists lies in the fact that one of the earliest Russian theorists, Pavlov, concentrated on the physiological aspect of psychology. That is, Pavlov believed much of mankind's mental processes could be described as the result of purely physical causes, just as the behaviorists believe today.

Pavlov concentrated his studies, for the most part, in animal psychology. He is perhaps most famous for experiments in which he induced salivation in dogs simply by ringing a bell. These experiments are significant, of course, because they led Pavlov to propose a theory

Notes and Asides

of conditioned reflexes that claimed that animals can learn to respond in a specific, predetermined way when exposed to certain stimuli. Pavlov's dogs originally salivated when a bell was ringing because they were eating food at the same time, but soon they "learned" the conditioned reflex that caused them to salivate simply because they were exposed to the stimulus of a ringing bell.

Pavlov describes the concept of conditioned reflexes this way:

> Thus, you see, that it is necessary to recognise the existence of two kinds of reflexes. One group of reflexes—ready from the time of birth—are purely conducting reflexes; but the other group—continually and without interruption being formed during the life of the individual, and just as regular as the first group—rest on the basis of another property of the nervous system, viz., its ability to make connections. . . . The congenital, generic, constant, stereotyped one we term unconditioned; the other, because it depends upon a multitude of conditions and constantly fluctuates in correspondence with many circumstances, we called conditioned. . . . The conditioned reflex is also determined and therefore inevitable, and so it belongs, like the unconditioned reflex, entirely to the domain of physiology.[26]

Conditioned reflexes are learned responses to secondary stimuli repeatedly associated with the primary stimuli.

Put more succinctly, Pavlov is declaring that all of an animal's activities can be accounted for in purely behavioristic terms. Elsewhere he spells it out, declaring that "the whole complicated behaviour of animals" is based on "nervous activity."[27]

Pavlov is willing to make the next logical step as well. As an avowed evolutionist, he does not hesitate to apply his conclusion to the highest animal, man: "I trust that I shall not be thought rash if I express a belief that experiments on the higher nervous activities of animals will yield not a few directional indications for education and self-education in man."[28]

Indeed, Pavlov believed (just as Skinner and other behaviorists believe today) that man can be educated and controlled so that he only does good. Shortly before his death, he told his laboratory assistants,

> Now we can and must go forward. . . . All of you physiologists should be acquainted with genetics in order to create an ideal type of the higher nervous activity of the dog—the strong, balanced, alert type—in order that we may use all of the experimental material for the investigation of the human being, striving to perfect the human race of the future.[29]

Notes and Asides

Of course, Pavlov believed this perfection would be relatively easy to achieve, since he held the Lamarckian view that acquired characteristics could be inherited by offspring. He declares, "It can be accepted that at a later stage some of the newly formed conditioned reflexes are transformed into unconditioned reflexes by heredity."[30] Today, this hypothesis has been abandoned by every competent scientist.

CLOSE-UP

Ivan Petrovich Pavlov (1849-1936)

On September 26, 1849, I.P. Pavlov was born in Ryazan, Russia. His father, a poor parish priest, infused in him a love of learning that drove him to excel in academics. In 1870 Pavlov began studying at the University of St. Petersburg (Leningrad), and upon graduation attended the Medico-Chirurgical Academy (renamed the Military Medical Academy in 1881). After completing his thesis in 1883, he received the degree of doctor of medicine. From that point forward he rarely strayed from the academy, eventually serving as chair of physiology from 1896 to 1925. Most of Pavlov's early work focused on the nerves directing the digestive glands. He discovered the secretory nerves of the pancreas in 1888, and received the Nobel Prize in 1904. From about 1902 to the end of his career, Pavlov began to concentrate on the realm of physiology which would make him famous: the study of conditioned reflexes. His experimentation with dogs and their response to stimuli is well-documented, as is his conclusion that all mental processes can be explained physiologically. It was this conclusion which caused Marxists to embrace Pavlov's work unreservedly, recognizing how well it complemented a materialist approach to psychology. Ironically, Pavlov was every bit as unimpressed with Marxism as the Marxists were impressed with him. After the October Revolution of 1917, Pavlov declared, "If that which the Bolsheviks are doing with Russia is an experiment, for such an experiment I should regret giving even a frog." Perhaps Pavlov's attitude toward Marxism was tempered in his later life, but he never allowed his interest in science to be distracted by a concern with Marxist ideology.

Notes and Asides

Regardless of the questionable aspects of Pavlov's worldview, however, Marxists still rely on his work with conditioned reflexes. Many times, it appears, they use his work to support a behaviorist view. Nahem echoes Pavlov, claiming the importance of animal nervous system activity for understanding human psychology:

> Since human beings are a product of evolutionary development, as Darwin demonstrated, the study of animal behavior sheds important light on human psychological functioning. Animal psychology, therefore, is allied to the science of human psychology.[31]

Marxism's Rejection of the Behaviorist View

It would seem obvious after reviewing Pavlov's impact on Marxist psychology and coupling this with the Marxists' own statements affirming the behaviorist view and the fact that behaviorism is the only psychology consistent with the Marxist worldview, that Marxism embraces behaviorism. However, Marxism can only embrace behaviorism to a limited extent. In fact, the Marxist must reject many of the logical conclusions that flow from behaviorism.

Thus, Nahem writes, "From this dialectical viewpoint, behaviorism in psychology, such as the theories of J. B. Watson or B. F. Skinner, must be criticized as mechanical, as the reduction of the psychological process of human functioning to the physiological process of behavior alone."[32] Later he states, "Throughout his work, Skinner has ignored or brushed aside fundamental laws of psychological development. He has reduced animal and human functioning to mechanical responses to rewards and punishments."[33]

For Nahem, as for all Marxist psychologists, behaviorism cannot be accepted wholeheartedly as an all-inclusive view of psychology. Instead, Marxism tries to pick and choose the bits of behaviorism it wants to accept, and abandon the rest. Nahem sums up: "Skinner reduces all human psychology to behavior in response to environmental rewards and punishments. Scientific psychology considers behavior only one among numerous features and categories of psychological life."[34]

Why can't Marxism accept behaviorism as a coherent psychological view? Why must the Marxist only tentatively support the notion that man is simply a receptor for environmental stimuli? Nahem hints at the reason:

> Marxism maintains that there are laws of social development which will lead, through conscious struggle, to a better society, socialism. Skinner believes that his "Behavioral Engineering"

Notes and Asides

will make for a better society. What kind of society will Skinner produce?[35]

This is the bottom line. The Marxists fear that a behaviorist psychology might not encourage the development of a *communist* society, since it denies the possibility of man's making a "conscious struggle" to achieve such a society. Free will is, after all, crucial for Marxist psychology. Marxism faces the same dichotomy it created for itself in economics: it declares communism to be inevitable, but it requires the willed revolt of the people to bring about its occurrence. Therefore, the Marxist must avoid a strict behaviorism that denies the free will of the proletariat to revolt and overthrow the oppressive upper classes.

Marxism's Reliance on Free Will

Karl Marx, prior to the existence of the behaviorist school of thought, recognized the inconsistency of a materialist philosophy and the notion of free will. He attempted to resolve the problem by claiming, "The materialist doctrine that men are the product of circumstances and education—forgets that circumstances are changed precisely by men."[36]

More than one hundred years later, Marx's followers are still trying to resolve the conflict, which has been made more obvious since the inception of the behaviorist school of thought. Bueva attempts to circumvent the problem this way: "Man's activity differs qualitatively from the activity of other living creatures, for it is directed not merely to passive adaptation to prevailing conditions of existence but to the creation and transformation of his conditions of existence and to the development of a specifically human world."[37]

Later, Bueva speaks more bluntly: "If man is formed by circumstances, then circumstances, too, are changed precisely by man and [to cite Marx] 'the coincidence of the changing of circumstances and of human activity or self-change can be conceived and rationally understood only as revolutionary practice.'"[38] Man, according to the Marxist view, must be free to revolt, to instigate change. Therefore behaviorism cannot be all true. Behaviorism does not allow for conscious struggle, which is a basic premise of Marxist dialectics.

Nahem sums up the Marxist position, describing precisely why Marxist psychologists can never accept all the logical conclusions of behaviorism:

> Above all, working people seek to rise from the indignity and lack of freedom that exist under capitalism. They hunger for and will seek freedom and dignity. They cannot achieve them

Notes and Asides

> through Skinner's scheme. Freedom and dignity will be achieved through their conscious struggles.[39]

Perhaps once a communist world is achieved, Marxist psychologists will be willing to accept behaviorism unreservedly. However, while revolution is still required to bring about the perfect society, free will is a more important psychological concept than deterministic behaviorism.

Speech and Stimuli

How, then, can the Marxist embrace so many aspects of behaviorism and still deny the final conclusion—the non-existence of free will? How can Marxist psychologists ground themselves in Pavlovian thought and ignore his behavioristic conclusions? Ironically, the answer for the Marxists comes from Pavlov himself.

Nahem tells us that "Pavlov identified the qualitative difference between humans and animals in the possession by humans of a second signal system, i.e., speech, which was 'the latest acquisition in the process of evolution.'"[40] Wells says that, according to Pavlov, this means "Animals could react to any sensory stimulation from the environment which might become connected with vital needs. Man not only had that same capacity to form temporary connections on the basis of sense stimulation, but in addition could react to words which had become signs standing for sense stimulations and sense objects."[41] That is, man differs from the rest of the animal world because he is capable of responding to word stimuli as well as the common environmental stimuli.

The **second signal system** refers to man's evolved ability to react to the stimulus of language.

Pavlov's own description of the importance of speech stimuli is less articulate, but still significant: "In this way, a new principle of nervous activity arises—abstraction and at the same time generalization of the countless signals of the first signaling system which is again accompanied by analysis and synthesis of the new generalized signals (words)—a principle which ensures unrestricted orientation in relation to the surrounding world and ensures the highest degree of adaptation, namely, science, both in the form of human universal empiricism and in specialized forms."[42] For Pavlov, man evolved the art of language, which became a new form of stimulus.

Marxist psychologists view this concept of speech as a "second signal system" as the key to synthesizing behaviorism with free will. Nahem says simply, "A . . . devastating refutation of Skinner is Pavlov's profound contribution to psychology by his analysis of speech and language as a second signal system."[43] This concept of speech as

Notes and Asides

another stimulus allows the Marxist to perceive man as shaped by environmental stimuli but also shaped by (and able to shape) his society. That is, speech is instrumental in defining and maintaining society, and it is a tool for man to shape the stimuli acting upon him, to a large extent, by shaping his own society.

The Role of Society in Man's Behavior

For the Marxist psychologist, speech—especially in the societal context—affects the individual's behavior. Indeed, according to Luria, the individual longs for this type of control, actually creating society so as to produce more external stimuli. He writes, "Our researches convince us that such a control comes from without, and that in the first stages of the control the human creates certain external stimuli, which produce within him definite forms of motor behaviour. The primordial voluntary mechanism evidently consists in the external setting, the production of cultural stimuli mobilising and directing the natural forces of behaviour."[44]

Nahem describes this notion of society as a major factor in determining behavior in layman's terms:

> Most decisive in its influence on our thoughts, feelings, and behavior is society and social relations. As Marx stated, "In its reality, it (the human essence) is the ensemble of the social relations." Human beings are distinguished from animals by their social labor, their social communication, their social groupings, by their social acquisition and use of language, and by their involvement in the ideas, attitudes, morality and behavior of their society.[45]

Indeed, this emphasis on the role of cultural influences in determining behavior is what makes Marxist psychology unique, according to Bueva. He writes, "In effect behaviouristic interpretations of the determination of the behaviour of individuals ignore the basic features of social determination which identify the dependence of social behaviour of individuals on trends that originate in principles governing the functioning and development of social systems of various types, laws of development of material production, social structure, and the political organization and culture of a particular society."[46] Elsewhere, Bueva sums up the Marxist position, stating simply, "Social interaction represents one of the essential factors within the complex process of social determination of man's behaviour."[47]

Clearly, Marxist psychologists stress the importance of society in

Notes
and
Asides

determining the individual's behavior. In fact, some Marxists believe cultural influences even determine the type of psychology extant in each society. Thus, the *Short Dictionary-Reference Book for the Political Informer and the Agitator* declares,

> A Socialist psychology is formed both as a result of the reflection of a socialist way of life in the consciousness of people and under the influence of the ideological activity of the communist party.[48]

That is, some societies are better designed to encourage the proper behavior in individuals.

The next logical step is obvious. Marxists declare the socialist society to be far superior to the capitalist society in terms of encouraging desirable behavior. In fact, we are told that capitalism has failed dramatically; only socialism can provide the proper setting for psychologically healthy individuals.

Capitalism's Failure and Socialism's Success

The major problem with capitalist society, according to the Marxist, is the divisive nature of classes. According to Bueva,

> Class affiliation predetermines to a definite extent the fate of a person, his typical way of life, and type of professional activity and hence the development of his abilities; the stimuli, motives for labour activities and nature of needs and level of their realization; and the rights and obligations of individuals and their social guarantees. Naturally, since in an antagonistic class society the position of individuals belonging to various classes differs and is even in opposition to each other, so does their development, their social direction and the level of their activity.[49]

Obviously, the abolition of classes (as required for the communist society) would be viewed by the Marxist as having a positive impact on personal development.

Another disadvantage of capitalism (one that will be eradicated by a socialist society) is the unfair system of labor. According to Nahem, "workers are estranged from their true nature as human beings because their work and its product are alien to them. They cannot feel a oneness with nature and society. Alienation is, therefore intrinsic to capitalism and the private ownership of the means of production. Hence, the basis

Notes and Asides

for its elimination, in the long run, is the replacement of capitalism by socialism."[50]

Bueva sums up *how the stimuli of capitalist society shape individuals' behavior negatively*:

> The development of capitalism destroys integral man: the social division of labour and the division of society into hostile classes lead to a separation and juxtaposition of types and forms of human activities, to a "creation of private individuals" and to a one-sided development of personalities. Private property and the transformation of products of human behaviour and of man himself into a commodity alienate from man his own actual and potential powers and abilities which in the form of capital are then directed against man.[51]

According to the Marxist, a system as flawed as capitalism must create a flawed psychology. Religious faith, for example, is one of the intolerable results of a capitalist society. "The essence of man is presented in a mystical way," says Bueva of bourgeois psychology; "the idea of the primacy of the spirit and of a full non-acceptance of objectivity, a rejection of the real world in favour of God, the idea of 'a revolution within man' through his spiritual renaissance based on religious faith—these are all ideological expressions of the crisis of capitalism's social system and of the contemporary bourgeois world's values."[52] The "crisis," of course, occurs when man turns to God for assistance.

What will save mankind from psychologically unsound societies? Only socialism as presented by Marxists! In fact, Marxist society will encourage only mentally healthy individuals. Bueva declares, "Socialist social relations develop an ability of the individual for self-regulation, control over his social behaviour and for developing an active attitude in relation to life."[53] For the Marxist, society can only shape an individual's behavior positively when it is socialist.

Dialectics and Marxist Psychology

This Marxist perception of the individual as determined by both society and typical environmental stimuli meshes well with Marxism's dialectical view. According to Marxist psychology, the forces of man's freedom to create whatever society he chooses clash with the forces of society and other environmental factors in determining man's behavior. The individual's freedom (thesis) attracts to itself and struggles with man's behavioristic tendencies (antithesis).

Notes and Asides

Thus, Bueva speaks of "the dialectical character and social roots of the contradiction between man's creative nature and his freedom, and the determination of his behaviour by real objective relations and laws of nature and of history."[54] This concept is built on the foundation set down by Marx in the declaration that "men make their own history, but they do not make it under circumstances chosen by themselves, but under circumstances directly encountered, given and transmitted from the past."[55]

For the Marxist, one can only understand the behavior of the individual in the context of his abilities and needs, as determined by society. "Accordingly," writes Bueva, "the principal source of determination of social behaviour of individuals and of the laws according to which they form and develop should be sought in the dialectical character of the mutual interaction of society and individuals and in historically concrete forms of social relations. It is on this basis that each person is engaged in a system of social activities that determines the development of his abilities (in relation to specific types of activities) and needs (motivating forces that encourage activities of individuals)."[56]

This dialectical relationship between man's freedom and behavioristic tendencies comprises the whole of Marxist psychology. According to N. P. Antonov, "Psychology is the science of the laws of development and formation of the psyche, man's consciousness, as a property of highly-organized matter, as a product of social development, and as a subjective reflection of the objective world in the human brain."[57] Bueva sums up: "A revolution within man presupposes a transformation of the entire social system. The development of society and of man are characterized by an integral dialectical unity."[58]

In the final estimation, the Marxist psychologist uses dialectics as his support for rejecting both strict behaviorism and Freudianism. Regarding strict behaviorism, Nahem states, "Skinner abandons freedom and dignity and espouses a rigidly determinist view, a view that Marxism calls mechanical materialism. It was only with the development of Marxism that the full relationship between freedom and determinism could be explained. Materialism needed dialectics to delineate the true meaning of freedom."[59] "Scientific psychology must reject the general theories of both Behaviorism and Freudianism. It must seek to show the dialectical relationship between social and individual reality, between thought, consciousness, unconscious processes, emotion, attitude and behavior."[60]

For the Marxist psychologist, the dialectical view of behavior and freedom is the only truly scientific view. It can be worded so that it appears to be consistent with Marxism's over-all worldview, and it seems to explain the urgency and inevitability of establishing world communism while still allowing for some concept of freedom.

Conclusion

Unfortunately, the term *freedom* does not mean the same thing to Marxist psychologists as it does to the rest of mankind. For the Marxist, freedom is simply the opportunity for the individual to choose what type of society will determine his behavior; it does not mean choosing his behavior himself. Consequently, whenever the individual is not exercising his freedom in selecting a society, he is controlled by his particular situation. This is at best a stunted concept of freedom—man is free to select the society that will determine his every action.

Marxists cloak this notion of a controlling society in vague descriptions of society's responsibility to "regulate" man. In reality, this "regulation" involves exposing individuals to the proper stimuli to elicit the proper behavior. "A mature socialist society cannot develop harmoniously unless all spheres of social life are based on principles of oriented development and scientific regulation," Bueva insists.[61] That is, development of man can only occur in a society "regulating" this development. Naturally, Bueva points out, the socialist society is best equipped for such regulation:

> The harmonious development of man cannot take place spontaneously, but must be the subject of special scientific regulation by society. In a socialist society the necessary conditions that are required exist and their realization depends on the conscious activities of individuals.[62]

This conscious activity refers only to the development of socialist society. Once the society is perfected, freedom will be unnecessary.

Pavlov agrees with this sentiment, claiming that man could be perfected, under the proper conditions (in society). He writes,

> Man is of course a system—roughly speaking, a machine—like every other system in nature subject to the inescapable and uniform laws of all nature; but the human system, in the horizon of our contemporary scientific view, is unique in being most highly self-regulatory. . . . But our system is self-regulatory in the highest degree—self-maintaining, repairing, readjusting, and even improving. The chief, strongest, and ever-present impression received from the study of the higher nervous

Notes and Asides

> activity by our method is the extreme plasticity of this activity, its immense possibilities: nothing remains stationary, unyielding; and everything could always be attained, all could be changed for the better, were only the appropriate conditions realised.[63]

This idea of man as self-regulatory is just another way of describing man as controlled by the society he establishes.

Nahem, too, believes society plays the chief role in human development (relegating human freedom to the role of selecting the proper society): "Marxism sees the science of psychology as playing an important role in advancing human development. The uncovering of laws of human psychological development can be of great value to education, to human personality, to the formation of character, and to the expansion of human abilities."[64]

What type of character will socialist society develop? Bueva minces no words in telling us: "Measures to influence the development of personality within a system of collective relations seek to encourage the appearance of socially typical traits and qualities of personality such as a purposefulness in activities, collectivism, internationalism, and patriotism, an orientation on communist ideals [the communist worldview], and a creative approach to practical tasks."[65]

As yet, not even socialist society has advanced enough to consistently develop these traits in its citizens. However, Luria does report that Marxist psychologists are able "to provoke definite conflicting processes, and by the help of them artificially to obtain certain concentrated symptoms of disorganised behavior."[66] Marxist psychology is capable of provoking disorganized behavior; apparently Luria believes this to be a good indication that they will soon develop organized behavior.

> "Trust that man in nothing who has not a Conscience in everything."
> —Laurence Sterne

Whether the behavior they discuss is organized or disorganized, Marxists clearly operate on the assumption that society determines behavior. In such a context, freedom means virtually nothing. When the Marxist speaks of a society scientifically "regulating" human development, it is obvious that freedom plays little role in his view of psychology; rather, he envisions a society much like the one described by George Orwell in *1984*. According to Marxist psychologists, man is merely an animal in need of some chemical fine tuning before heading on to perfection in the coming world order—an order in which all mankind will be stimulated to perfection. Unfortunately, this new order will deprive human beings of the same two things Skinner and all other materialists ultimately eradicated: freedom, and dignity.

[1] Harry K. Wells, *Ivan Pavlov: Toward a Scientific Psychology and Psychiatry* (New York: International Publishers, 1956), p. 72.
[2]Ivan P. Pavlov, *Lectures on Conditioned Reflexes* (New York: International Publishers, 1963), p. 41.
[3]Joseph Nahem, *Psychology and Psychiatry Today: A Marxist View* (New York: International Publishers, 1981), p. 13.
[4]I. P. Pavlov, *Twenty Years of Objective Study of the Higher Nervous Activity (Behaviour) of Animals* (Medgiz Publishing House, 1951), p. 458.
[5]K. I. Platonov, *The Word as a Physiological and Therapeutic Factor* (Moscow: Foreign Languages Publishing House, 1959), p. 12.
[6]V.I. Lenin, *Materialism and Empirio-Criticism* (New York: International Publishers, 1927), p. 66.
[7]Ibid., p. 34.
[8]Nahem, *Psychology and Psychiatry Today: A Marxist View*, p. 9.
[9]Pavlov, *Lectures on Conditioned Reflexes*, p. 224.
[10]Nahem, *Psychology and Psychiatry Today: A Marxist View*, p. 10.
[11]L. P. Bueva, *Man: His Behaviour and Social Relations* (Moscow: Progress Publishers, 1979), pp. 24-5.
[12]B. F. Skinner, *Beyond Freedom and Dignity* (New York: Bantam Books, 1972), p. 96.
[13]Ibid., p. 16.
[14]B. F. Skinner, *Science and Human Behavior* (New York: Macmillan, 1953), p. 447.
[15]Ibid., p. 6.
[16]Skinner, *Beyond Freedom and Dignity*, p. 197.
[17]Ibid., p. 63.
[18]Nahem, *Psychology and Psychiatry Today: A Marxist View*, p. 5.
[19]V. I. Lenin, *Collected Works*, forty-five volumes (Moscow: Progress Publishers, 1977), vol. 1, p. 144.
[20]A. R. Luria, *The Nature of Human Conflicts* (New York: Grove Press, 1960), p. 9.
[21]Bueva, *Man: His Behaviour and Social Relations*, p. 56.
[22]Ibid., p. 206.
[23]Ibid., pp. 10-11.
[24]Nahem, *Psychology and Psychiatry Today: A Marxist View*, p. 47.
[25]Wells, *Ivan Pavlov: Toward a Scientific Psychology and Psychiatry*, p. 67.
[26]Pavlov, *Lectures on Conditioned Reflexes*, p. 267.
[27]Ibid., p. 42.
[28]Ibid., p. 391.
[29]Ivan Pavlov, in a statement to his assistants on Feb. 21, 1936, according to W. H. Gantt in the introduction to *Conditioned Reflexes and Psychiatry* (New York: International Publishers, 1963), p. 34.
[30]I. P. Pavlov, *Complete Works* (Moscow, 1951/2), vol. 3, p. 217.
[31]Nahem, *Psychology and Psychiatry Today: A Marxist View*, p. 5.
[32]Ibid., p. 11.
[33]Ibid., p. 41.
[34]Ibid., p. 45.
[35]Ibid., p. 48.
[36]Karl Marx, "The Third Thesis on Feuerbach," *Gesamtausgabe* (Frankfurt, 1927-1932), sec. 1, vol. 5, p. 534. Cited in Charles J. McFadden, *The Philosophy of Communism* (Kenosha, WI: Cross, 1963), p. 68.
[37]Bueva, *Man: His Behaviour and Social Relations*, p. 51.
[38]Ibid., p. 43, citing Karl Marx, *Theses on Feuerbach*, in *Collected Works*, forty volumes (New York: International, 1976), vol. 5, p. 4.
[39]Nahem, *Psychology and Psychiatry Today: A Marxist View*, p. 49.
[40]Ibid., p. 9, citing Pavlov's *Selected Works* (Moscow: Foreign Languages Publishing House, 1955), pp. 536-7.
[41]Wells, *Ivan Pavlov: Toward a Scientific Psychology and Psychiatry*, p. 70.
[42]Ivan Pavlov, *Selected Works* (Moscow: Foreign Languages Publishing House, 1955), p. 537.
[43]Nahem, *Psychology and Psychiatry Today: A Marxist View*, pp. 43-4.
[44]Luria, *The Nature of Human Conflicts*, pp. 401-2.

[45]Nahem, *Psychology and Psychiatry Today: A Marxist View*, p. 45, citing Marx's *Theses on Feuerbach*, p. 84.
[46]Bueva, *Man: His Behaviour and Social Relations*, p. 170.
[47]Ibid., p. 133.
[48]*Short Dictionary-Reference Book for the Political Informer and the Agitator* (Moscow, 1973), p. 199, cited in *A Lexicon of Marxist-Leninist Semantics*, ed. Raymond S. Sleeper (Alexandria, VA: Western Goals, 1983), p. 227.
[49]Bueva, *Man: His Behaviour and Social Relations*, p. 175.
[50]Nahem, *Psychology and Psychiatry Today: A Marxist View*, p. 11.
[51]Bueva, *Man: His Behaviour and Social Relations*, p. 49.
[52]Ibid., p. 28.
[53]Ibid., p. 179.
[54]Ibid., p. 20.
[55]Karl Marx, "The Eighteenth Brumaire of Louis Bonaparte," *Collected Works* (New York: International Publishers, 1979), vol. 11, p. 103.
[56]Bueva, *Man: His Behaviour and Social Relations*, p. 174.
[57]N. P. Antonov, *Dialectical Materialism as the Theoretical Foundation of Psychology* (1953), vol. 1, p. 201, cited in Gustav A. Wetter, *Dialectical Materialism* (Westport, CT: Greenwood Press, 1958), p. 481.
[58]Bueva, *Man: His Behaviour and Social Relations*, p. 70.
[59]Nahem, *Psychology and Psychiatry Today: A Marxist View*, p. 46.
[60]Ibid., p. 11.
[61]Bueva, *Man: His Behaviour and Social Relations*, p. 220.
[62]Ibid., p. 246.
[63]Pavlov, *Conditioned Reflexes and Psychiatry*, p. 144.
[64]Nahem, *Psychology and Psychiatry Today: A Marxist View*, p. 19.
[65]Bueva, *Man: His Behaviour and Social Relations*, pp. 158-9.
[66]Luria, *The Nature of Human Conflicts*, p. 239.

CHAPTER

17

BIBLICAL CHRISTIAN PSYCHOLOGY

"So God created man in his own image, in the image of God created he him; male and female created he them."

—Genesis 1:17

"He breathed into his nostrils the breath of life and man became a living soul."

—Genesis 2:7

"We maintain the dualism of nature [brain] and spirit [mind] as strenuously as we maintain the dualism of God and the world, and in the same degree we regard the body and the spirit of man as being of a distinct nature."[1]

—Franz J. Delitzsch

SUMMARY

The greatest psychologists and the finest psychological methods ever devised still have not surpassed the insights into human nature provided by one ancient document: the Bible. Some people believe Christianity, based on such an old collection of teachings, has become outdated. Nothing could be further from the truth. William Kirk Kilpatrick believes that the Bible provides mankind with "a more profound understanding of human nature than psychology has yet arrived at."[2] This is precisely what one would expect from the special revelation of God, especially because God made us—body, soul, and spirit—and therefore knows us better than we know ourselves.

Both the Marxist and the Humanist believe that human nature is perfectible and that only our faulty societies and social institutions have hindered man's reach for flawless morality. Hence, these worldviews' psychological theories stress the inherent goodness of man and strive to build societies and develop methods that will better encourage man to get in touch with his "real self." The Christian, however, recognizes that getting in touch with oneself is not a final solution to psychological problems.

Indeed, Christian psychology helps people get in touch with their real selves only because it allows them to recognize their own sinfulness and consequently their need for a Savior (Romans 3:23; 6:23). The individual with psychological problems must recognize, as Boris Sokoloff says, that inherent in his own nature is "a desire for and drive toward unlimited freedom . . . a protest, often violent and vicious, against any limitation or restriction of freedom in any possible way."[3] It is this very aspect of human nature, this rebellion, that places the most strain on mind and spirit. While individuals want only to be free to follow their own whims, they really need to be freed from their sin nature by the redeeming work of Christ. People's greatest need is not self-esteem; it is the realization that they are sinners in rebellion against God.

Introduction

Christian psychology appears, at first glance, to be a contradiction in terms. After examining both Marxist and Humanist psychology and touching on still other theories of "secular" psychology, the Christian is tempted to conclude that psychology is a discipline unworthy of his attention. William Kirk Kilpatrick boldly declares, "if you're talking about Christianity, it is much truer to say that psychology and religion

"Christianity starts off," says Kilpatrick, "by saying that we're not OK the way we are. There is something wrong with us—a twist in our natures. And the twist is not removed by liking yourself, but by starting to live in Christ."[4] Only after accepting Christ as Savior can people begin to understand their value as creations in God's image and lead triumphant lives.

In this way, Christianity provides a much more realistic approach to one of mankind's deepest psychological problems: guilt. Whereas other worldviews insist that the individual need not feel guilty (because *objective* guilt is illusory, *subjective* guilt—the *feeling* that one is guilty—must be a delusion), the Christian view proclaims that (as every man senses) guilt feelings are justified because they are the symptom of objective guilt for objective sin. Every man is equipped by God with a conscience that constantly reminds him when he makes poor moral choices. Rather than demanding that the individual ignore his conscience, the Christian faith calls for him to face his guilt and repent. Biblical Christianity teaches moral responsibility, whereas Humanism and Marxism blame individual moral failings on society or the environment.

Christianity is superior to materialistic worldviews in a still more fundamental way. Marxists and Humanists, as *ontological monists*, must view the mind and the spirit as nothing more than reflections of the physical brain. Ideas, imagination, conscience, altruism, and other "supernatural" concepts are largely ignored by these worldviews. How can such a view mend the spirit when it denies its very existence? Only Christianity, with its emphasis on the spiritual and its understanding of man's fallen condition (Romans 1—3), can truly address the innermost concerns of the individual. And only Christ, who offered mankind "a spring of water welling up to eternal life" (John 4:14), can cleanse and constantly replenish men's troubled souls.

are competing faiths. If you seriously hold to one set of values, you will logically have to reject the other."[5] Psychology seems to be a brand new religion. Paul Vitz contends, "Today many are describing psychology in categories indistinguishable from those used for religious cures and conversions."[6]

Judging from these statements, it seems both Vitz and Kilpatrick would have us declare Christianity and psychology incompatible and close this chapter right now. Yet both men earn their livings as Christian

Notes and Asides

psychologists! How can these professionals declare psychology to be the rival of Christianity, and still dedicate their lives to integrating the two?

The answer is that both Vitz and Kilpatrick are contrasting the strictly "secular" views of psychology with Christianity. When they declare psychology to be setting itself up as an alternate religion, they are referring to the "secular" religious views. Unfortunately, these supposedly secular but really religious schools of psychology (based on the work of men like Sigmund Freud, B. F. Skinner, I. P. Pavlov, Carl Rogers, Abraham Maslow, and Erich Fromm) comprise virtually all of modern psychology.

Rousas J. Rushdoony sums up the Christian position regarding present-day psychology: "In psychology, therefore, the Christian Church faces a rival plan of salvation. This does not mean that all psychologists are non-Christian; it does mean that the modern schools of psychology [Behaviorism, Freudianism, Self-Actualism, etc.] are not only non-Christian but in essence have a rival doctrine of man and his salvation."[7] The Christian's task is to develop a Christian psychology based unequivocally on God's Word, diligent study and prayer, and Christian experience. This doesn't mean there is no room for the scientific method, but it does mean Christians do not have to accept the methods and standards of naturalistically based science. The Christian understands that true salvation can be found only in Christ and that any psychological theory must center on the One who said He was the way, the truth, and the life (John 14:6).

Contrary to secular assumptions, this does not tie the hands of Christian psychologists. Rather, it frees them to summon the wealth of wisdom recorded in the Bible and apply that wisdom to the spiritually needy. The world is starved for this kind of wisdom today. "The increasing prominence of psychology is an important sign of the times," says Rushdoony.

> When man becomes a problem to himself, psychology comes into its own. As man's inner problems grow, his ability to cope with the outer world and its problems declines. Thus, a psychology-oriented age is an age in decline, unsure of itself, and incompetent in the face of its responsibilities. It is significant that modern man talks so much about "alienation"; his position of modernity isolates him from God and man and leaves him a prisoner of his isolated ego.[8]

Only the Christian psychologist properly understands the source of man's "alienation." This understanding, coupled with the wisdom imparted by the Holy Spirit, causes the Christian to be the best-

Notes and Asides

equipped psychologist for a troubled mankind. Kilpatrick says, "In short, although Christianity is more than a psychology, it happens to be better psychology than psychology is."[9]

Christianity and psychology, therefore, are compatible for the simple reason that the worldview of Biblical Christianity contains a psychology. As Franz Delitzsch noted in *A System of Biblical Psychology* over one hundred years ago, psychology is "one of the oldest sciences of the church." *Psychology*, after all, deals with the *psyche*, the *soul*, an aspect of man that Christianity affirms but "secular" psychology says doesn't even exist. "Secular" *psychology*, then, is a self-contradiction. But Christianity, as Charles L. Allen so aptly points out, is tailor-made for psychology: "the very essence of religion is to adjust the mind and *soul* of man. . . . Healing means bringing the person into a right relationship with the physical, mental and spiritual laws of God."[10] Man created "in the image of God" (Genesis 1:27) requires a worldview that recognizes the significance of the spiritual.

The Supernatural Mind

Christianity, as we have demonstrated in the Christian theology and philosophy chapters, acknowledges the existence of the supernatural, including a consciousness within man that is more than an epiphenomenon[11] of the brain. Christians, in the main, do not equate mind and brain.[12] Reducing the spiritual mind of man to his material brain is called reductionism, which Christians avoid.[13] The fact that Christianity recognizes the existence of a supernatural mind is one reason this worldview is so well adapted to helping people psychologically. Whereas the Humanists and Marxists believe consciousness is strictly dependent on the brain's activity, the Christian views consciousness as a supernatural phenomenon that will continue after the death of the brain. Clearly, if it can be demonstrated that the mind or consciousness is more than a reflection of reality as perceived through the brain, then a psychology that acknowledges this reality will be better equipped to solve psychological problems.

> "Do not be afraid of those who kill the body but cannot kill the soul. Rather, be afraid of the One who can destroy both soul and body in hell."
>
> —Jesus Christ

The Bible's statements regarding body, breath of life, soul, spirit, and mind suggest a dualist ontology, that is, the view that human nature consists of two fundamental kinds of reality: physical (material or natural) and spiritual (supernatural). Christ's statement about fearing the one who could put "both soul and body" in hell (Matthew 10:28), and Paul's statement regarding body, soul, and spirit (1 Thessalonians 5:23), and our being told that the Word of God pierces to the point of dividing asunder soul and spirit, joints and marrow (Hebrews 4:12) all enforce the distinction between man's material and spiritual qualities.

Notes and Asides

The Bible does not deny body; it simply says man is more than body. St. Paul speaks about being absent from the body and present with the Lord (2 Corinthians 5:8) and about a man who presumably left his body and was caught up to the third heaven (2 Corinthians 12:2). These and other passages consistently lead to the conclusion defended by Delitzsch: "We maintain the dualism of nature and spirit as strenuously as we maintain the dualism of God and the world, and in the same degree we regard the body and the spirit of man as being of a distinct nature."[14]

Sir John Eccles, one of the world's most respected neuro-physiologists, believes dualism is the only explanation for many of the phenom-

CLOSE-UP

Jonathan Edwards (1703-1758)

A humble pastor in colonial New England, Jonathan Edwards was nonetheless one of the greatest intellects in American history. His whole life reflects a zeal to learn, based on a more fundamental drive to glorify God. Edwards graduated from Yale College in 1720, stayed for two years as a theology student, and then—before he was 19 years old—became minister of a church in New York. After returning to Yale to teach from 1724 to 1726, he moved to Northampton to work as an assistant for the church he would eventually lead from 1729 to 1750. During this period, Edwards ignited a number of revivals, playing an instrumental role in the Great Awakening, which began in 1740. He also authored some of his most important works during this era, including *The Distinguishing Marks of a Work of the Spirit of God* and *A Treatise Concerning Religious Affections* (a classic work on religious psychology). Edwards was dismissed from his ministerial position at Northampton on July 1, 1750, largely because of his unwillingness to compromise biblical precepts. He moved to Stockbridge, Massachusetts the following year, and began working both as a minister and as a missionary to the Indians. Edwards continued to produce scholarly books, examining difficult issues such as free will and original sin. In 1758 he became president of the College of New Jersey (now Princeton), but he died just two months after taking office. He left a legacy of well-reasoned, impassioned works dedicated to the glory of God.

Notes and Asides

ena of consciousness. Arthur Custance says Eccles concluded "that mind was not an emergent out of brain but somehow an independent observer and user of it. He speaks of the mind as manipulating the brain, of being its master not its servant. The mind searches the brain's store of engrammed information and integrates what it extracts from that store."[15]

Eccles sees the mind and brain "as a clear-cut dichotomy and goes so far as to equate self-conscious mind with an entity called soul."[16] Karl Popper, who wrote *The Self and Its Brain* with Eccles and is not a Christian, admits that his study of the subject has led him to "believe in the ghost in the machine." Says Popper, "That is to say, I think that the self in a sense plays on the brain, as a pianist plays on a piano or as a driver plays on the controls of a car."[17] And Popper apparently does not disagree with Eccles's conclusion: "the self-conscious mind exercises a superior interpretative and controlling role upon the neural events."[18]

In *The Human Psyche*, Eccles develops another powerful argument for the distinction between mind and brain, namely, unity of identity. "It has been shown in these lectures," says Eccles, "that dualist-interactionism has great explanatory power in respect of many phenomena that have otherwise not been explained. For example the unity of conscious experience cannot be derived from brain activities in themselves, which remain disparate unless brought together in the mental synthesis."[19]

Paul Weiss agrees, noting that "even though I know I am constantly changing—all molecules are changing, everything in me is being turned over substantially—there is nevertheless my identity, my consciousness of being essentially the same that I was 20 years ago. However much I may have changed, the continuity of my identity has remained undisrupted."[20] Weiss refers to this as "the unity which is my greatest experience." The point, of course, is that since the physical substance of the brain is constantly changing, no unity of identity could exist if consciousness were a condition wholly dependent on the physical brain. Something more than the physical brain, something supernatural, must exist.

Unity of identity refers to our intuitive awareness that identity remains undisrupted throughout the course of development.

Human memory is another facet of the unity-of-identity argument that supports the existence of a supernatural mind. Custance writes,

> What research has shown thus far is that there is no precise one-to-one relationship between any fragment of memory and the nerve cells in which it is supposed to be encoded. These cells can little by little be replaced by new cells (as happens throughout life), or they can be destroyed in large numbers or at least have their interconnections severed (as in Ralph Gerard's experi-

Notes and Asides

> ments with rats), or the whole cortex can be deliberately put out of action (as in experimental decerebrated dogs), and yet apparently "memory lingers on."[21]

Again, it appears that the brain is a less-than-acceptable explanation for some of our mental processes.

Along this same line Custance mentions Canadian neurosurgeon Wilder Penfield's work[22] and his observation that the history of the mind's development during life and the history of the brain's development are different. If one plots a curve, says Custance, "showing the excellence of human performance, one sees that the body's performance (and the brain's) improves with time as maturing takes place, until after a certain stage in life when a decline begins to set in and ultimately senility. By contrast, the mind reveals no characteristic or inevitable decline. In fact, in old age it reaches toward its fullest potential of understanding and judgment, while the body and the brain are slowing and sometimes failing to perform."[23]

Clearly, the materialist view of the mind and its mental processes presents more problems than it solves. Without any concept of a supernatural mind, the Humanist and the Marxist have difficulty explaining unity of identity, memory, and the inexorable maturation of the intellect. Still another problem arose in both the Humanist and Marxist psychology chapters: how can the materialist position account for free will? As Eccles says,

> Finally the most telling criticism of all materialist theories of the mind is against its key postulate that the happenings in the neural machinery of the brain provide a necessary and sufficient explanation of the totality both of the performance and of the conscious experience of a human being. For example the willing of a voluntary movement is regarded as being completely determined by events in the neural machinery of the brain, as also are all other cognitive [thinking] experiences.[24]

Not only is free will an issue, but also the very nature and credibility of ideas. Eccles and Daniel N. Robinson call "the denial of the reality of mental events . . . an easy cop-out. It must be an embarrassing belief to acknowledge publicly when it is recognized as negating even one's own conscious belief and experiences!"[25] Why should anyone accept the conclusions of someone who denies the existence of mental events and ideas? If one's beliefs are merely the result of atoms randomly smashing together in the head, then one's beliefs are changing constantly. If such were the case, of course, no ideas would be safe—including Humanist and Marxist ideas. If all ideas are in constant flux,

Notes and Asides

there is no value in any ideas. Such a view renders nonsensical not only the idea of God but also *all* ideas—including atheism, materialism, and evolution. If ideas are merely matter in motion, then all intellectual and spiritual concerns grind to a halt.[26]

The self-defeating nature of psychological naturalism (the belief that the mind is only an epiphenomenon of the brain) is no new discovery. As long ago as St. Augustine (A.D. 354-430) it was thought obvious that crediting ideas to the chance occurrences of nature was intellectual suicide. Augustine wrote of those "who think that all things are driven to and fro by chance accidents, and yet contend that this their wisdom and assertion is not of chance rashness, but of ascertained reason. What madness then is it, to lay to reason their discussions, and to make their actions subject to accidents!"[27] Claim that chance rules all and then claim rationality for your claim? Madness indeed!

For the Christian dualist, however, ideas are neither madness nor meaningless. Neither are there problems explaining free will, unity of identity, memory, etc. Christian dualism provides a better foundation for psychology because it defends the integrity of the mind and doesn't reduce spirit to matter or vice-versa. It also avoids the trap of nihilism. "I conclude," says Penfield, "that it is easier to rationalize man's being on the basis of two elements [mind and brain] than on the basis of one."[28]

Another key fact Christianity best explains is man's extraordinary mental superiority to the animals. Late-nineteenth-century evolutionist philosopher John Fiske wrote, "while for zoological man you can hardly erect a distinct family from that of the chimpanzee and the orang; on the other hand, for psychological man you must erect a distinct kingdom; nay, you must even dichotomise the universe, putting man on one side and all things else on the other."[29] If the mind were truly just an epiphenomenon of the brain, this dichotomy should not exist. Indeed, James Orr calls this the "chief point of weakness" in monistic theories and says that these theories

> . . . do nothing, really, to meet the proof, derived from the simple fact of man's susceptibility for education and progress, that there are barriers in their nature impassable between animal and human intelligence; which, accordingly, involve a distinction, not in degree only, but in quality and kind, between the two, and place man essentially in an order and kingdom by himself.[30]

Clearly, the Christian attitude toward the mind allows for a psychology consistent with reality—a psychology more consistent than any based on monism. As Orr says, "Mind, in brief, must be interpreted

Notes and Asides

through study of itself. When this is done, the facts of intellect, of moral freedom, of religious aspiration, which Monism would overthrow, will be found reinstated in more than their former honour. The Biblical view stands unharmed by monistic speculations."[31]

Calvin Seminary's professor of philosophical theology, John W. Cooper, has come to the same conclusion:

> Souls, spirits, minds, or persons might be able to exist without organisms, although they would be deprived by the loss. Let's call what I have been describing here "functional holism." My point is that it affirms phenomenological, existential, and functional unity, but does not conceptually entail monism or personal extinction at death.[32]

In other words, mind is not reduced to brain or brain activity. And while mind and brain are closely related, they are not identical. The mistake being made today is to expect the scientific method to give a full accounting of the mind/brain issue when the scientific method lacks the tools to do the job.

Weiss agrees:

> Maybe our concept of our nervous system is equally inadequate and insufficient, because so long as you use only electrical instruments, you get only electrical answers; if you use chemical detectors, you get chemical answers; and if you determine numerical and geometrical values, you get numerical and geometrical answers. So perhaps, we have not yet found the particular kind of instrument that tells us the next unknown.[33]

Instead of being led by faulty scientific methodology or instrumentation to throw away the mind or reduce it to matter, it would be far better to trust the Bible's statements regarding mind, especially in light of the fact that the dualism suggested in the Bible best explains man as he really exists.

Man's Origin

A worldview's perception of man's origin affects its beliefs about human nature. "The questions of the origin and of the nature of man are inseparably connected," writes Orr.

> Theories of origin, it is soon discovered, control in practice the view taken of man's essential constitution, and need to be

Notes and Asides

> checked and corrected by careful consideration of what man is—this being into whose origin we are inquiring. Conversely, the study of man's nature is speedily found to be implicated with theories of man's mental and moral evolution, which drive us back on considerations of origin.[34]

Obviously, the atheistic evolutionary perspective of man leads to a view of human nature different from one derived from the belief that man is the creation of an omniscient, loving God. For example, the evolutionary view leads to monism, which, as demonstrated above, is Biblically and intellectually untenable. In fact, evolutionary theory can be seriously questioned strictly on the grounds that it logically leads to psychological monism. Eccles and Robinson write, "It will be realized that the modern Darwinian theory of evolution is defective in that it does not even recognize the extraordinary problem presented by living organisms' acquiring mental experiences of a nonmaterial kind that are in another world from the world of matter-energy, which heretofore was globally comprehensive."[35]

The belief that mankind's origin can be explained by evolution has done a poor job of fitting the facts of experience, especially in the psychological arena. Custance sums up this position: "If man is part of Nature, as evolutionary philosophy insists he is, then how has it come about that a method which is so successful in dealing with the one part of Nature, the world outside of man, has failed so miserably in dealing with the other part of Nature, that which lies within him?"[36] The answer, of course, is that the evolutionary explanation is incorrect and therefore provides an inaccurate picture of human nature.

The Christian psychologist believes that man was created by God. This view has specific ramifications for human nature as well, and it is the Christian contention that this resultant view of human nature is more consistent with experience. Orr writes,

> Man, in virtue of this endowment, allying him with his Maker, is, as the animals are not, a personal, self-conscious being; capable of conceptual thought, of rational speech, of education, of development, of progress; capable also, therefore, of moral, self-regulated life. The enormous difference of potentiality involved in all this points to a distinct cause, and puts a gulf between man and the animals which no evolutionary theory has proved itself capable of bridging.[37]

If we accept the Christian view of origins as the correct view, we perceive man as a being who must answer to God's moral judgment. Custance puts it this way:

Notes and Asides

> But if [man] is something more than merely a mechanism, then his failure must be judged as something worse than the break-down of a machine. And by and large, most people in their quieter moments do admit to an uneasy feeling that we ought indeed to judge our own failures and those of other people as something much more serious. The Christian does so because he knows that there is a purpose in life which extends beyond and rises above mere biochemical mechanism, mere survival.[38]

This view grants man responsibility for his moral actions, something which the evolutionary perspective does not. As will be demonstrated, this belief in man's moral responsibility is fundamental for Christian psychology.

Man Created in the Image of God

Inherent in the Christian view of man's origin is the belief that man was created *in God's image* (Genesis 1:27). This belief also has important ramifications for the Christian's over-all understanding of human nature. In fact, Christian psychologists understand this point to be vital. As Francis Schaeffer says, "If you deal with a man merely as a structural machine, you miss the point; and if you deal with a man merely as a set of psychological conditionings, you miss the central point. Consequently, as Christians begin to deal with psychological problems, they must do so in the realization of who man is. I am made in the image of God."[39]

Exactly what does it mean, however, to be created in the image of God? Christians have debated this point for centuries. Orr sums up the orthodox position:

> [T]his image, or resemblance to God, must be supposed to lie primarily in man's nature, and secondarily, in the relation which through that nature he sustains to the lower creation, and to the world as a whole. As respects his nature, the resemblance cannot be looked for, as just said, in his body, nor in the animal functions of his soul. It must be looked for, therefore, in that higher constitution of his being which makes him spiritual. It is in the powers and activities of man as personal spirit that we are to seek his affinity to God and resemblance to Him. The image of God intended in Scripture, in other words, is a mental and moral image.[40]

Notes and Asides

For the Christian psychologist, man as created in God's image again implies moral responsibility and, furthermore, the existence of spirit within man. The Christian view of this supernatural facet of man's identity obviously has an impact on the Christian's psychology.

Custance describes man as consisting of three elements. He believes, "Man is a body-spirit entity, the union of the two resulting in the emergence of soul, or self. The body without the spirit is dead."[41] Orr seems to agree with Custance, stating, "Spirit, we have just seen, is not something distinct from soul as a third separable element, but denotes the higher, self-conscious activities of the soul. . . . "[42]

Martin and Deidre Bobgan also perceive man as comprised of body, soul, and spirit. They write, "The body, soul, and spirit are intimately related and interact with one another. However, according to the Christian position, the spirit has pre-eminence. It is through the spirit that we find the highest level of human existence."[43] According to this view, man possesses not only a supernatural mind (the soul) but also a higher, morally discerning element (the spirit) that is the vehicle or focus of communion with God.

Not all Christian thinkers agree that soul and spirit are distinct parts of man, however. Some, like Athanasius, Augustine, and most of the Church Fathers; Luther, Calvin, and most of the Reformers; and more recently Charles Hodge, Louis Berkhof, and James Oliver Buswell, Jr., believe that the terms *spirit* and *soul*, when used of the nonphysical part of man (often *soul* refers to the whole man, physical and nonphysical alike), denote the same thing, arguing that any distinction between them is one of function rather than identity.[44] Others, like J. Gresham Machen, hold that in most such uses in Scripture *soul* and *spirit* are interchangeable but that in some instances *soul* denotes the nonphysical part of man while *spirit* denotes the Spirit of God indwelling the believer.[45] Still others, like Delitzsch, teach that *soul* and *spirit* denote the same part of man so far as nature goes (the nonphysical as opposed to the physical) but emphasize different functions or aspects of that nature (usually saying that *spirit* emphasizes man's capacity for communion with God while *soul* emphasizes man's rational, emotive, and volitional abilities).[46]

"When Jesus had tasted it, he said, 'It is finished,' and bowed his head and dismissed his spirit."
—John 19:30

Regardless of whether Christians conceive of man as trichotomous (body, soul, and spirit) or dichotomous (body and soul [=spirit]), all Christians recognize that it is the nonphysical component of man that was made in God's image. Man's spiritual element is his very essence and the element of man that proper psychology should focus upon. A psychology that ignores the existence of the spirit cannot hope to deal with the deepest, most profound problems experienced by man. As the

Notes and Asides

Bobgans state, "The cornerstone of good total health is good spiritual health. A healthy physical life is related to a positive and stable mental-emotional life, which in turn is influenced by a sound spiritual life centered in Christ."[47] The recipe for a sound spiritual life is summed up in the command, "Love the Lord your God with all your heart and with all your soul and with all your mind and with all your strength" (Mark 12:30).

Original Sin

A proper understanding of man's nature does not, however, end with affirming the existence of a spirit within man. The Christian position goes on to define man's nature as inherently evil because of man's decision to disobey God in the Garden of Eden. This understanding of man's sinful bent is critical for understanding man's nature and mental processes. Rushdoony says, "Man is God's creature, and man and his nature can only be truly understood in terms of man's creation by God and man's revolt against God."[48]

This revolt by man against God has caused a dramatic, reality-shattering change in the relationship of man to the rest of existence and even to himself. Schaeffer describes the change this way:

> So sinful man takes his place among the lower circles of existence; he moves down from being man into the lower existence of the animals and the machines. Man is thus divided against, and from, himself in every part of his nature. Think of it in any way you will—he is divided from himself in his rebellion: in rationality, in morality, in his thinking, in his acting, in his feeling.[49]

Clearly, this kind of change has severe ramifications for all aspects of reality, including psychology. In fact, man's sinful nature, his desire to rebel against God, is the source of all psychological problems, according to the Christian view. Schaeffer sums up: "The basic psychological problem is trying to be what we are not, and trying to carry what we cannot carry. Most of all, the basic problem is not being willing to be the creatures we are before the Creator."[50] For the Christian, the existence of sin effectively explains all psychological problems, as we shall see. It also explains man's failings as a whole; John H. Hallowell believes, "The recognition of this inherent predisposition to sin helps to explain why the best laid plans of men never quite succeed."[51]

Notes and Asides

Human Nature and Sin

The existence of sin plays a pivotal role in Christian psychology. While both the Humanists and the Marxists assume human nature to be inherently good, the Christian sees man as rebelling against God. Orr claims, "Hereditary sin is a deep, dark strain in the history of our race, not to be explained away."[52]

This view is crucial for Christian theology because it allows us to understand our tremendous need for Christ's saving power. Orr says our conception of sin "vitally affects our conception of the Gospel, for it is a truism that, with defective and inadequate views of sin, there can never be an adequate doctrine of redemption."[53]

This conception of sin is crucial on a lesser level, as well, for Christian psychology. In order to properly understand human nature,

CLOSE-UP

C. E. M. Joad (1891-1953)

C. E. M. Joad authored only one book of importance to Christian worldview analysis, but that book, *The Recovery of Belief*, represents his life work, and as such is an invaluable contribution to Christian literature. The book, Joad's last, describes the evolution of his philosophy from Rationalist to Christian, and provides evidences for his new-found faith. *The Recovery of Belief* is extremely important because it allows insight into the mind of a man caught up in the Humanist worldview of his day—before his conversion, Joad was a socialist and a conscientious objector during World War I—and explains how, in earnestly seeking truth, Joad came to recognize the veracity of the Christian worldview. Much of the book is concerned with human nature, expounding on the fact that the Christian view of man is the only perspective which adequately explains why man behaves the way he does. Joad's conclusions shocked many of his atheistic and agnostic contemporaries, and he was shunned by some philosophers after his conversion. But he held fast to his convictions; he was a man swayed not by popular opinion, but by truth.

Notes and Asides

the psychologist must understand that man has a natural tendency to revolt against God and His laws. This revolt is a form of egoism. Orr writes that sin "is the exaltation of self against God: the setting up of self-will against God's will: at bottom, Egoism."[54] Custance says simply, "The real problem is in the will, not in the mind."[55]

If Custance's claim is correct—that is, if the Christian view of man's nature is the proper view—then only Christianity can develop a true, meaningful, and workable psychology, since only Christianity recognizes the problem of the will in relation to God. Again, we come back to the concept of moral responsibility. Only Christianity provides a framework in which man is truly held responsible for his thoughts and actions. "The great benefit of the doctrine of sin," says Vitz, "is that it reintroduces responsibility for our own behavior, responsibility for changing as well as giving meaning to our condition."[56]

Remarkably, some non-Christian psychologists are beginning to see the need to recognize the existence of sin in man's life. Karl Menninger, one of the greatest American psychiatrists and author of *Whatever Became of Sin?*—and certainly no orthodox Christian—declares,

> I have pursued the possible usefulness of reviving the use of the word "sin"—not for the word's sake, but for the reintroduction of the concepts of guilt and moral responsibility. Calling something a "sin" and dealing with it as such may be a useful salvage or coping device. It does little good to repent a symptom, but it may do great harm not to repent a sin. Vice versa, it does little good to merely psychoanalyze a sin. . . .[57]

Why have some secular psychologists attempted to revive the notion of sin? Because empirical science cannot provide an adequate description of human nature and therefore is failing to meet man's innermost needs. Historian Arnold Toynbee writes, "So far, however, science has shown no signs that it is going to be able to cope with man's most serious problems. It has not been able to do anything to cure man of his sinfulness and his sense of insecurity, or to avert the painfulness of failure and the dread of death.[58] Above all, it has not helped him to break out of the prison of his inborn self-centeredness into communion or union with some reality that is greater, more important, more valuable, and more lasting than the individual himself. . . ."[59]

Only the Christian psychologist perceives man's nature in a way that is consistent with reality and capable of speaking to man's most difficult problems. The Christian psychologist sees man as not only physical but also spiritual, as morally responsible before God, as created in God's image, and as having rebelliously turned away from

Notes and Asides

his Creator. Only Christianity is prepared to face the problem that necessarily arises out of man's nature: the existence of guilt.

Guilt: Psychological or Real?

Both Humanists and Marxists speak only of psychological guilt because, for them, only society is evil—man has done nothing individually which would make him actually guilty. For the Christian, however, each time a man rebels against God he is committing a sin, and the feeling of guilt that results from this rebellion is entirely justified. "Psychological guilt is actual and cruel," writes Schaeffer. "But Christians know that there is also real guilt, moral guilt before a holy God. It is not a matter only of psychological guilt; that is the distinction."[60]

Because only Christian psychology acknowledges the existence of real, objective guilt, only it can speak to a person who is experiencing such guilt. As Schaeffer says,

> When a man is broken in these [moral and psychological] areas, he is confused, because he has the feelings of real guilt within himself, and yet he is told by modern thinkers that these are only guilt-"feelings." But he can never resolve these feelings, because while there are merely guilt-feelings, he also has true moral awareness and the feeling of true guilt. You can tell him a million times that there is no true guilt, but he still knows there is true guilt. You will never find a person who does not still find these movings somewhere in his conscience.[61]

> "Every one of us, whatever our speculative opinions, knows better than he practices, and recognizes a better law than he obeys."
> —J. A. Froude

Christianity understands man's nature enough to know why this guilt arises and how to deal with it. While other schools of psychology must invent fancy terms to explain away the existence of real guilt as a result of real sin, Christian psychology deals with the problem at its roots.

Mental Illness

Modern secular psychologists often speak of "mental illness." Yet many Christian psychologists deny the existence of a large proportion of mental illnesses. Jay Adams writes, "Organic malfunctions affecting the brain that are caused by brain damage, tumors, gene inheritance, glandular or chemical disorders, validly may be termed mental illnesses. But at the same time a vast number of other human problems have been classified as mental illnesses for which there is no evidence that they have been engendered by disease or illness at all."[62]

Notes and Asides

Why is Adams so suspicious of problems that cannot be directly linked to organic causes being termed "mental illness"?

> To put the issue simply: the Scriptures plainly speak of both organically based problems as well as those problems that stem from sinful attitudes and behavior; but where, in all of God's Word, is there so much as a trace of any third source of problems which might approximate the modern concept of "mental illness"?
> . . . . What, then, is wrong with the "mentally ill"? Their problem is autogenic; it is in themselves. The fundamental bent of fallen human nature is away from God. . . . Apart from organically generated difficulties, the "mentally ill" are really *people with unsolved personal problems.*[63]

This view follows logically from the Christian perception of human nature: man has rebelled against God, he has real guilt feelings about this rebellion, and so he must reconcile himself with God or face unsolved personal problems.

Perhaps this denial of most mental illness seems harsh. But this is precisely the view that some "secular" psychologists are reluctantly embracing! Again, Menninger inadvertently backs the Christian position:

> I do not believe anyone would seriously classify [most sins] as either crime or disease. I'm aware that psychological jargon can be employed which relates many of them to peculiarities of conditioning, special inhibitions, interactional incompatibilities, and a dozen other technical constructs. I wouldn't dispute these; I just don't think they lead to the proper steps for correction.[64]

Indeed, throughout his book, Menninger argues for replacing the notion of many "mental illnesses" with the notion of sin.

This view is necessary for the Christian psychologist. It not only follows from his picture of human nature but also accurately describes the powerful effect sin has on people's lives. Lawrence Crabb, Jr. writes, "An appreciation of the reality of sin is a critically necessary beginning point for an understanding of the Christian view of anything. A psychology worthy of the adjective 'Christian' must not set the problem of sin in parallel line with other problems or redefine it into a neurosis or psychological kink."[65]

Notes and Asides

The Realistic Approach to Sin and Guilt

If the Christian psychologist denies the existence of most mental illnesses, what good is his psychology? That is, how can the Christian psychologist propose to help people if he views their mental problems as spiritual problems caused by alienation from God? Doesn't this view just place too much guilt on people and avoid any real therapy?

If by the word *therapy* one means consciousness-raising seminars or primal scream workshops, then it is true the Christian psychologist does away with therapy. However, the Christian psychologist still offers solutions for the troubled person. And, as noted earlier, these solutions begin with human nature and a concept of real guilt.

Because man has a conscience, and because he rebelled and continues to rebel against God, he is bound to experience real guilt. The Marxist and the Humanist deny the existence of this real guilt feeling. But the Christian psychologist acknowledges it and begins to treat the individual at that point, at the root of the problem. The real guilt is acknowledged, and the individual is reminded of Christ's sacrifice for mankind, so that real guilt can be handed over to Him. "To say that there is no real guilt is futile," says Schaeffer, "for man as he is knows that there is real moral guilt. But when I know the real guilt is really met by Christ, so that I do not need to fear to look at the basic questions deep inside myself, then I can see that the feeling of guilt that is left is psychological guilt and only that."[66]

The Christian psychologist, then, must stress personal moral responsibility. Without this responsibility, the individual may deny any real guilt caused by his sins and thereby avoid the heart of his problem—his alienation from God. Only through recognizing one's sinful nature and guilt before God can anyone reconcile his guilt feelings with reality. "Looking for the cause of an internal emotional problem in an external circumstance," writes Crabb, "strips the individual of responsibility for his problems and flatly contradicts the Lord's teaching that it is not what enters into a man that defiles him but what proceeds from within."[67] The Christian psychologist does not look for someone or something to blame, such as parents or society—he understands that the blame lies in every man's inherently evil nature.

> "[F]or all have sinned and fall short of the glory of God . . . "
> —Romans 3:23

Each man must take responsibility for this nature. Adams declares, "Contrary to much contemporary thought, it is not merciful to be nonjudgmental. To consider such counselees victims rather than violators of their conscience, to consider their behavior as neutral, or as not blameworthy only enlarges their lie and increases the load of guilt."[68]

This may seem like a rather insensitive approach to helping some

Notes and Asides

people with very sensitive problems. But what could be more cruel than treating just a symptom of the problem and ignoring the actual sickness? Who would fault a doctor for giving his patient a shot to fight a disease rather than a cough drop to mask a symptom? As Adams puts it,

> It is important for counselors to remember that whenever clients camouflage, whenever they hide to avoid detection, whenever they purport to be ill when they are not, sick treatment only makes them worse. To act as if they may be excused for their condition is the most unkind thing one can do. Such an approach only compounds the problem.[69]

Rather, the individual must be made to take personal responsibility for his actions so that he can be personally reconciled with himself and with God. Again, Menninger backs up the Christian position: "If the concept of personal responsibility and answerability for ourselves and for others were to return to common acceptance, hope would return to the world with it!"[70]

The first step for the Christian psychologist in dealing with many mental and spiritual problems is to hold each client personally responsible for the sin in his life. The remainder of the healing for the client hinges on this responsibility. Crabb writes, "Hold your client responsible: for what? For confessing his sin, for wilfully and firmly turning from it, and then for practicing the new behavior, believing that the indwelling Spirit will provide all the needed strength."[71]

This is the key for all Christian healing of "mental illnesses" that are not organically caused: confession of sin, forgiveness of sin through Christ (1 John 1:9), reconciliation with God (2 Corinthians 5:17-21), and sanctification through the disciplining work of God's Spirit (1 Thessalonians 5:23; Hebrews 12:1-11). Christian psychology, for all its fascination with human nature and the existence of guilt, leads to one simple method, summarized in James 5:16: "Therefore confess your sins to each other and pray for each other so that you may be healed. The prayer of a righteous man is powerful and effective." This same method is voiced in Galatians 6:1-2 by St. Paul, with the implication that any true Christian can act as a psychological counselor: "Brothers, if someone is caught in a sin, you who are spiritual should restore him gently. But watch yourself, or you also may be tempted. Carry each other's burdens, and in this way you will fulfill the law of Christ."

> "Sell not your conscience; thus are fetters wrought./ What is a Slave but One who can be Bought?"
> —Arthur Guiterman

Christian psychologists still find this method to be most effective today. "Only one thing lifts the depressed spirit crushed by a load of sin," writes Adams: "confession and forgiveness of sin."[72] "Sin and morality are not only involved in developing mental-emotional disor-

Notes and Asides

ders; they are also involved in the way to mental-emotional restoration as sin is confessed and new ways of behaving are adopted," the Bobgans insist.[73]

It should be stressed here that confession of sin does not automatically alleviate every problem faced by mankind. But it is the first step. Immediately after this step, the individual must decide to abandon the patterns of sin and focus on serving God's will rather than his own. "Spelling out and getting commitments to biblical patterns of behavior after an acknowledgment of and repentance for sin seemed to bring relief and results," Adams reports.[74] Crabb says much the same thing: "After counseling has identified wrong beliefs and taught right beliefs, the next step involves the client's decision to put off the practice of sin and to put on the practice of righteousness. Without this step, exhortations to change will produce surface, temporary results."[75] Confession of sin must be marked by true repentance and a turning toward God.

Remarkably, Menninger comes to virtually the same conclusion as the Christian psychologist. In fact, he chides the Christian clergy for not reaching the conclusion more rapidly and declaring it more vociferously: "Yet few clergymen nowadays venture to call for repentance, as did the prophets and John the Baptist. . . . They fear the public reproach of having reverted (as some extremists have) to threats of fire-and-brimstone damnation. They dread this accusation so much that they don't speak out even what they believe should be heard and heeded by the man in the pew."[76] Menninger's accusation should be heeded by all in the Christian community. Christian psychology better meets the facts of experience even for some secular psychologists, and still many Christians borrow their psychological concepts and methods from secular schools. The impropriety of this situation will become more apparent as we examine two other aspects of Christian psychology that make it superior to secular views.

The Problem of Suffering

Most secular psychologies attempt to alleviate all suffering for the individual. Psychologists speak of methods of "successful living" that are supposed to eradicate most pain and anguish. Vitz says this "selfist" psychology "trivializes life by claiming that suffering (and by implication even death) is without intrinsic meaning. Suffering is seen as some sort of absurdity, usually a man-made mistake which could have been avoided by the use of knowledge to gain control of the environment."[77]

In contrast, Christian psychology believes that God can use suffering to bring about positive changes in the individual. The Bobgans write, "The spiritual counselor believes in his heart that God is faithful

Notes and Asides

in all circumstances and that God allows circumstances, even adverse ones, for a person's growth."[78] Custance says much the same thing: "I mean only that handicaps do not, in themselves, prevent achievement: indeed,a case may almost be certainly made for the thesis that the absence of hindrances of some kind is more likely to lead to failure than their presence is."[79]

This difference between "secular" and Christian psychology has serious implications. Anyone who believes that suffering is more than an absurd reality of life, devoid of meaning, can only find affirmation in the Christian view. Writes Vitz,

> A final profound conflict between Christianity and selfism centers around the meaning of suffering. The Christian acknowledges evil—with its consequent pain and ultimately death—as a fact of life. Through the Christian's losing of his ordinary self in discipleship, in the imitation of Christ, such suffering can serve as the experience out of which a higher spiritual life is attained.[80]

No such meaning can be attached to suffering in the secular view. Meaning in suffering is a feature unique to Christian psychology. Thus we find Kilpatrick concluding, "The real test of a theory or way of life, however, is not whether it can relieve pain but what it says about the pain it cannot relieve. And this is where, I believe, psychology lets us down and Christianity supports us, for in psychology suffering has no meaning, while in Christianity it has great meaning."[81] Again, Christian psychology more adequately meets the needs of the individual.

Society and the Individual

Christian psychology's view of human nature grants the individual moral responsibility, works to reconcile the individual with God, and gives meaning to suffering. An offshoot of this perspective is that the Christian views society as the result of individuals' actions—that is, the individual is seen as responsible for the evils in society. This view is in direct contradiction to the Marxist and Humanist view that man is corrupted by evil societies.

As always, these opposing views have logical consequences. For Marxists and Humanists, society must be changed, and then man can "learn" to do right. For the Christian, however, the individual must change for the better before society can. Custance states this position well:

Recommended Reading for Advanced Study

Paul Vitz, *Psychology as Religion* (Grand Rapids, MI: Eerdmans, 1985).

William Kirk Kilpatrick, *Psychological Seduction* (Nashville: Thomas Nelson, 1983).

Jay E. Adams, *Competent to Counsel* (Grand Rapids, MI: Baker, 1970).

Arthur Custance, *Man in Adam and in Christ* (Grand Rapids, MI: Zondervan, 1975).

> [T]he malaise of society is but a reflection of the sickness of the individual. And a great part of the sickness of the individual stems from unforgiven sin, sin that poisons both the conscious and the unconscious part of his memory. In the final analysis the ills of society cannot be cured except through the individual.[82]

Hallowell agrees: "It is pride, self-righteousness, greed, envy, hatred and sloth that are the real evils and the ones from which social evils spring. When man is thwarted in his attempts to realize justice it is because he is thwarted by his own sinful predisposition."[83]

Thus, the Christian believes that each individual must abandon his sinful nature and serve God, which in turn will make society morally healthy. When individuals turn away from God, the society becomes morally bankrupt. Writes Custance,

> No society, with the possible exception of the Chinese, ever before felt itself able to perform so many of its functions, both individual and corporate, with such complete indifference to God. Consequently, our society is probably less concerned with sin than any society in history. Unfortunately, since the reality of sin remains and since the effect of sin is a sense of guilt, our society is plagued by a dis-ease with which it is totally unable to cope. And this dis-ease, which is personal, soon becomes a

Notes and Asides

social disease exhibiting itself in behavior that is completely without moral constraints.[84]

For the Christian, blaming individual sins on society is a cop-out. Menninger again affirms the Christian position: "If a group of people can be made to share the responsibility for what would be a sin if an individual did it, the load of guilt rapidly lifts from the shoulders of all concerned. Others may accuse, but the guilt shared by the many evaporates for the individual. Time passes. Memories fade. Perhaps there is a record, somewhere; but who reads it?"[85]

The Christian, of course, knows there is a record somewhere, and is uncomfortably aware that Someone reads it. A day will come when no one can blame his sins on society. It is the Christian psychologist's duty, then, to realize the importance of personal responsibility and to impart this realization to anyone he counsels. Again, without the notion of personal responsibility, the whole of Christian psychology collapses like a house of cards.

Conclusion

Throughout this section we have emphasized the importance of the Christian view of human nature in developing a Christian psychology. One's ideas about human nature play an equally critical role in every psychology. However, the Christian view of human nature not only best fits the facts of experience but also is the only view based on divine revelation. In itself, this should be enough to merit serious consideration by every open-minded psychologist, for, as Crabb says, "Selecting a basic position on the nature of man, the universal so badly needed in the field of counseling, resembles a random throw at the dart board unless some objective source of knowledge is available. To find certainty, there is simply no avenue to pursue but revelation."[86] Harvard psychiatrist Robert Coles also believes the Bible provides overwhelming objective psychological wisdom. "Nothing I have discovered about the make-up of human beings," he says, "contradicts in any way what I learn from the Hebrew prophets such as Isaiah, Jeremiah and Amos, and from the Book of Ecclesiastes, and from Jesus and the lives of those he touched. Anything I can say as a result of my research into human behavior is a mere footnote to those lives in the Old and New Testaments."[87]

"There is nothing serious under the sun except love: of fellow mortals and of God."
—M. Muggeridge

The Christian view of human nature is complex; ironically, it logically leads to a simple method for counseling people. This method requires acknowledging one's sinful nature (Romans 3:23), a confession of sin (1 John 1:9), and a willful decision to submit one's own

Notes and Asides

desires to God's will (Romans 12:1-2). An individual can often do this himself; this process does not, by any means, always require a counselor. Schaeffer outlines a simple approach to "positive psychological hygiene:"

> As a Christian, instead of putting myself in practice at the center of the universe, I must do something else. This is not only right, and the failure to do so is not only sin, but it is important for me personally in this life. I must think after God, and I must will after God. To think after God, as he has revealed Himself in His creation and especially as He has revealed Himself in the Bible, is to have an integrated answer to life, both intellectually and in practice.[88]

Clearly, the Christian clergyman is most often in the position to exhort people to confess their sins and submit their wills to God's plan. Menninger recognizes this, stating, "No psychiatrists or psychotherapists, even those with many patients, have the quantitative opportunity to cure souls and mend minds which the preacher enjoys."[89] Thus, it is the clergyman who most often plays the role of Christian psychologist. This is as it should be. Crabb writes, "Counseling therefore belongs ideally in the local church and not in the private professional office."[90]

Of course, Marxist and Humanist psychologists (indeed, almost all "secular" psychologists) believe just the opposite. They see no place for Christianity in psychology. Why? Because Christian psychology operates according to an entirely different view of man and his place in the universe. The choice between Christian psychology and all other psychological schools is clear cut. As Kilpatrick says, "Our choice . . . is really the same choice offered to Adam and Eve: either we trust God or we take the serpent's word that we can make ourselves into gods."[91]

[1] Franz J. Delitzsch, *A System of Biblical Psychology*, 2d ed., trans. Robert Ernest Wallis (Grand Rapids, MI: Baker Book House, [1861] 1966), p. 113, 114.
[2]William Kirk Kilpatrick, *The Emperor's New Clothes* (Westchester, IL: Crossway, 1985), p. 24.
[3]Boris Sokoloff, *The Permissive Society* (New Rochelle, NY: Arlington House, 1971), p. 20.
[4]Kilpatrick, *The Emperor's New Clothes*, pp. 20-21.
[5]William Kirk Kilpatrick, *Psychological Seduction* (Nashville: Thomas Nelson, 1983), p. 14.
[6]Paul Vitz, *Psychology as Religion* (Grand Rapids, MI: Eerdmans, 1985), p. 43.
[7]Rousas John Rushdoony, "Implications for Psychology," in *Foundations of Christian Scholarship*, ed. Gary North (Vallecito, CA: Ross House Books, 1976), p. 42.
[8]Rousas John Rushdoony, *The One and the Many* (Nutley, NJ: The Craig Press, 1971), p. 368.
[9]Kilpatrick, *Psychological Seduction*, pp. 15-16.
[10]Charles L. Allen, *God's Psychiatry* (Westwood, NJ: Revell, 1953), p. 7, emphasis added.
[11]*Epiphenomenon*: a secondary object or fact of experience that accompanies and is caused by, i.e., dependent on, another. Calling the mind an epiphenomenon of the brain means saying that the mind has no independent existence of its own and is merely an appearance (or experience) caused by the functioning of the brain.
[12]David G. Myers and Malcolm A. Jeeves, *Psychology Through the Eyes of Faith* (New York: Harper and Row, 1987), is a recent exception. The authors not only favor the monistic view, but state "mind is not an extra entity that occupies the brain" (pp. 21, 22). The work is a Christian College Coalition selection. The Christian Free University Curriculum work that refutes this monist psychology is Arthur C. Custance's *The Mysterious Matter of Mind* (Grand Rapids, MI: Zondervan, 1980). The Christian Free University Curriculum is sponsored by Probe Ministries, 1900 Firman Drive, #100, Richardson, TX 75081.
[13]See Arthur Koestler and J. R. Smythies, eds., *Beyond Reductionism* (London: Hutchinson, 1969).
[14]Delitzsch, *System of Biblical Psychology*, p. 113, 114.
[15]Custance, *Mysterious Matter of Mind*, p. 79.
[16]Ibid.
[17]Ibid., p. 81.
[18]Ibid., p. 82.
[19]Sir John Eccles, *The Human Psyche* (New York: Springer International, 1980), p. 233.
[20]Paul Weiss in *Beyond Reductionism*, eds. Koestler and Smythies, pp. 251-2.
[21]Arthur C. Custance, *Man in Adam and in Christ* (Grand Rapids, MI: Zondervan, 1975), p. 256.
[22]Wilder Penfield, *The Mystery of the Mind* (Princeton, NJ: Princeton University Press, 1975) is a valuable resource.
[23]Custance, *Mysterious Matter of Mind*, p. 72.
[24]Eccles, *The Human Psyche*, p. 21.
[25]John Eccles and Daniel N. Robinson, *The Wonder of Being Human* (New York: The Free Press, 1984), p. 14.
[26]C. S. Lewis uses this argument masterfully in *Miracles: A Preliminary Study* (New York: Macmillan, 1963), Chapter 3, "The Self-Contradiction of the Naturalist."
[27]Augustine, *On Continence* 14, in *A Select Library of the Nicene and Post-Nicene Fathers of the Christian Church*, twenty-eight volumes, ed. Philip Schaff (Grand Rapids, MI: Eerdmans, 1978 rpt.), First Series, vol. 3, p. 384.
[28]Custance, *Mysterious Matter of Mind*, p. 72.
[29]John Fiske, *Through Nature to God* , p. 82, cited in James Orr, *God's Image in Man* (Grand Rapids, MI: Eerdmans, 1948), p. 60.
[30]Orr, *God's Image in Man*, p. 145.
[31]Ibid., p. 78.
[32]John W. Cooper, *Body, Soul, and Life Everlasting* (Grand Rapids, MI: Eerdmans, 1989), p. 50.
[33]Custance, *Mysterious Matter of Mind*, pp. 21, 22.
[34]Ibid., p. 33.
[35]Eccles and Robinson, *The Wonder of Being Human*, p. 17.
[36]Custance, *Man in Adam and in Christ*, pp. 10-11.
[37]Orr, *God's Image in Man*, pp. 146-7.
[38]Custance, *Man in Adam and in Christ*, p. 268.

[39]Francis Schaeffer, *True Spirituality*, in *The Complete Works of Francis Schaeffer*, five volumes (Westchester, IL: Crossway Books, 1982), vol. 3, p. 329.
[40]Orr, *God's Image in Man*, pp. 56-7.
[41]Custance, *Man in Adam and in Christ*, p. 303.
[42]Orr, *God's Image in Man*, p. 52.
[43]Martin and Deidre Bobgan, *The Psychological Way/The Spiritual Way* (Minneapolis: Bethany House, 1979), p. 144.
[44]Louis Berkhof, *Systematic Theology*, 4th ed. (Grand Rapids, MI: Eerdmans, 1941), pp. 191-5; Charles Hodge, *Systematic Theology*, three volumes (Grand Rapids, MI: Eerdmans, 1973 rpt.), vol. 2, pp. 42-51; James Oliver Buswell, Jr., *A Systematic Theology of the Christian Religion*, two volumes in one (Grand Rapids, MI: Zondervan, 1973 rpt.), vol. 1, pp. 239-41, 243-48; John Calvin, *Institutes of the Christian Religion*, two volumes, trans. Ford Lewis Battles, ed. John T. McNeill (Philadelphia: Westminster, 1977), vol. 1, pp. 184-6 (I.xv.2).
[45]J. Gresham Machen, *The Christian View of Man* (London: Banner of Truth Trust, [1937] 1965), pp. 139-44.
[46]Delitzsch, *A System of Biblical Psychology*, pp. 103-19.
[47]Ibid.
[48]Rushdoony, "Implications for Psychology," p. 43.
[49]Schaeffer, *True Spirituality*, p. 320.
[50]Ibid., p. 330.
[51]John H. Hallowell, cited in Custance's *Man in Adam and in Christ*, p. 9.
[52]Orr, *God's Image in Man*, p. 243.
[53]Ibid., p. 11.
[54]Ibid., pp. 216-17.
[55]Custance, *Man in Adam and in Christ*, p. 34.
[56]Vitz, *Psychology as Religion*, p. 93.
[57]Karl Menninger, *Whatever Became of Sin?* (New York: Hawthorn Books, 1974), p. 48.
[58]Only Christ is capable of providing comfort in the face of such dire pain and fear. Hebrews 2:14, 15 declares, "Since the children have flesh and blood, he [Christ] too shared in their humanity so that by his death he might destroy him who holds the power of death—that is, the devil—and free those who all their lives were held in slavery by their fear of death."
[59]Arnold Toynbee, *Surviving the Future* (Oxford University Press, 1971). Cited in Menninger, *Whatever Became of Sin?* p. 227.
[60]Schaeffer, *True Spirituality*, p. 322.
[61]Ibid.
[62]Jay E. Adams, *Competent to Counsel* (Grand Rapids, MI: Baker Book House, 1970), p. 28.
[63]Ibid., p. 29.
[64]Menninger, *Whatever Became of Sin?* p. 172.
[65]Lawrence Crabb, Jr., *Basic Principles of Biblical Counseling* (Grand Rapids, MI: Zondervan, 1975), pp. 48-9.
[66]Schaeffer, *True Spirituality*, p. 323.
[67]Crabb, *Basic Principles of Biblical Counseling*, p. 44.
[68]Adams, *Competent to Counsel*, p. 33.
[69]Ibid., pp. 32-3.
[70]Menninger, *Whatever Became of Sin?* p. 188.
[71]Crabb, *Basic Principles of Biblical Counseling*, pp. 104-5.
[72]Adams, *Competent to Counsel*, p. 143.
[73]Bobgan and Bobgan, *Psychological Way/Spiritual Way*, p. 175.
[74]Adams, *Competent to Counsel*, p. xiii.
[75]Crabb, *Basic Principles of Biblical Counseling*, p. 102.
[76]Menninger, *Whatever Became of Sin?* pp. 195-6.
[77]Vitz, *Psychology as Religion*, p. 103.
[78]Bobgan and Bobgan, *Psychological Way/Spiritual Way*, p. 163.

[79]Custance, *Man in Adam and in Christ*, p. 200.
[80]Vitz, *Psychology as Religion*, p. 103.
[81]Kilpatrick, *Psychological Seduction*, p. 181.
[82]Custance, *Man in Adam and in Christ*, p. 280.
[83]Hallowell, as quoted in Custance, *Man in Adam and in Christ*, p. 9.
[84]Custance, *Man in Adam and in Christ*, p. 275.
[85]Menninger, *Whatever Became of Sin?* p. 95.
[86]Crabb, *Basic Principles of Biblical Counseling*, pp. 41-2.
[87]Robert Coles, as cited in Philip Yancey's "The Crayon Man," *Christianity Today*, February 6, 1987, p. 20.
[88]Schaeffer, *True Spirituality*, p. 334.
[89]Menninger, *Whatever Became of Sin?* p. 201.
[90]Crabb, "Moving the Couch into the Church," *Christianity Today*, Sept. 22, 1978, p. 18.
[91]Kilpatrick, *Psychological Seduction*, p. 233.

SECTION SIX

SOCIOLOGY

SOCIOLOGY [French: *socio* (social, society) + Greek: *logos* (word)]: The study of social institutions and society.

	SECULAR HUMANISM	MARXISM/ LENINISM	BIBLICAL CHRISTIANITY
SOURCE	*HUMANIST MANIFESTO I & II*	*WRITINGS OF MARX & LENIN*	*BIBLE*
THEOLOGY	ATHEISM	ATHEISM	THEISM
PHILOSOPHY	NATURALISM	DIALECTICAL MATERIALISM	SUPERNATURALISM
ETHICS	ETHICAL RELATIVISM	PROLETARIAT MORALITY	ETHICAL ABSOLUTES
BIOLOGY	DARWINIAN EVOLUTION	DARWINIAN/ PUNCTUATED EVOLUTION	SPECIAL CREATIONISM
PSYCHOLOGY	MONISTIC SELF-ACTUALIZATION	MONISTIC PAVLOVIAN BEHAVIORISM	DUALISM
SOCIOLOGY	NON-TRADITIONAL WORLD STATE ETHICAL SOCIETY	ABOLITION OF HOME, CHURCH AND STATE	HOME CHURCH STATE
LAW	POSITIVE LAW	POSITIVE LAW	BIBLICAL/NATURAL LAW
POLITICS	WORLD GOVERNMENT (GLOBALISM)	NEW WORLD ORDER	JUSTICE FREEDOM ORDER
ECONOMICS	SOCIALISM	SOCIALISM/ COMMUNISM	STEWARDSHIP OF PROPERTY
HISTORY	HISTORICAL EVOLUTION	HISTORICAL MATERIALISM	HISTORICAL RESURRECTION

CHAPTER

18

SECULAR HUMANIST SOCIOLOGY

"Essentially man is internally motivated toward positive personal and social ends; the extent to which he is not motivated results from a process of demotivation generated by his relationships and/or environment."[1]

—Robert Tannenbaum and Sheldon A. Davis

"A socialized and cooperative economic order must be established to the end that the equitable distribution of the means of life be possible. The goal of humanism is a free and universal society in which people voluntarily and intelligently cooperate for the common good. Humanists demand a shared life in a shared world."[2]

—Humanist Manifesto I

SUMMARY

One of Secular Humanism's central tenets is man's inherent goodness or perfectibility. Both *Humanist Manifestos* describe man as a being with unlimited promise. Corliss Lamont says that Humanism has "its ultimate faith in man" and believes "that human beings possess the power or potentiality of solving their own problems, through reliance primarily upon reason and scientific method applied with courage and vision."[3] How, then, does Humanism explain all the evil wrought by mankind throughout recorded history?

Humanists use sociology to explain the discrepancy between their view of perfectible man and the real world of war, crime, drugs, brutality, selfishness, envy, and deceit—man's inhumanity to man. According to their approach to the science of human society, man's civilization and culture shape the individual. Man is primarily evil because his cultural and social environment are evil. Paul Kurtz says that society "is an instrument of both expression and repression. A qualitatively distinct way of life is adopted as the socio-cultural context itself channels patterns of behavior (through the mechanism of conditioned response) along habitual lines."[4] Put more simply, society is largely responsible for the behavior of the individual.

Further, Humanism maintains that present society (like all past societies) is poorly structured, not always encouraging man to express the proper attitudes and often repressing his better tendencies. In short, society and culture have incorrectly influenced man's actions and, therefore, have stifled his inherent goodness. This sociological theory allows the Humanist to explain man's historic tendency toward evil while calling for social reforms to guarantee man's future tendency for good.

Introduction

Humanist sociology and Humanist psychology are basically two sides of the same coin. Both disciplines act on the same premises; the former concentrates on society, the latter on the individual. Thus, John F. Glass and John R. Staude declare: "Humanistic thought has recently had a great impact in psychology where it has become a third force transcending the limitations of the two main schools of psychology, behaviorism and psychoanalysis. . . . It is this fundamental consideration for the

One of the most pressing and serious reforms Humanist sociologists insist on is the restructuring of the family. Humanism believes that traditional views of marriage and the family are too restrictive and that mankind cannot achieve full potential until the unnecessary norms surrounding the institution are abandoned. Thus, Humanist sociology frowns on any worldview with dogmatic restrictions against premarital sex, adultery, homosexuality, pedophilia, incest, divorce, abortion, etc. Indeed, any ethical stance that may limit human potential is considered outdated. Science is left with the dubious task of determining human potential and ethical norms. If, for example, science determines that pedophilia is "biologically determined" at birth, then man/boy love affairs must be sanctioned and given legal rights. Humanist Vern Bullough, in the foreword to Edward Brongersma's book *Loving Boys*, says that pedophilia is "a subject that too often has been ignored or subjected to hysterical statements."[5]

Public school teaching is the Humanist's favorite means for abolishing outdated societal institutions and ensuring the development of a "free" society. Humanists seek to educate the next generation in a manner that frees them to act always in accordance with their inherent goodness. Eventually, through values clarification, "non-religious" sex education, and conscientious instruction regarding globalism, mankind will achieve a new world order. This order, according to the Humanist, will finally grant the human race the freedom to perfect itself by taking away the social shackles binding them to the past, and by unlocking all of mankind's untapped potential.

human person, and the view of man as having a measure of autonomy, choice, and self-determination that is at the root of a humanistic perspective in sociology and other social sciences."[6] Staude elaborates,

> This "humanistic sociology" restores the individual person to his rightful place as the principal agent of action. Similar to the humanistic psychologists, humanistic sociologists place the person at the center of their study. They see man as the creator of his own acts, with all the uncertainty, ambiguity, dread,

Notes and Asides

anxiety, and responsibility that such freedom, choice and decision imply. Humanistic sociologists remind us that we make our society at the same time that we are shaped by it.[7]

Humanist sociologists, by their own admission, are quite similar to Humanist psychologists. And because of this similarity, they face the same basic problem as their psychologist brothers: the unscientific nature of their approach. Just as Humanist psychologists struggled to redefine science in a way that included their approach while excluding a religious approach, Humanist sociology struggles to be respected as a legitimate method of examining the mechanisms of society.

Some Humanist sociologists are willing to admit that their discipline cannot be regarded as science. William Bogard maintains, "[F]or sociological theory inherent difficulties arise in its pursuit of a disinterested and non-contextual knowledge. These difficulties suggest that sociology has never been, is not now, and can never be a truly scientific enterprise in an ideal sense." Bogard goes on, however, to declare that this fact does not "form a basis for the abandonment of sociology." Why not? Because he believes proper sociology to be an art form: "even if it cannot legitimately be considered a science in an ideal sense of that term, sociology is nonetheless a form of knowledge. What follows is intended to elaborate the implication that sociology is an artistic form of knowledge . . ."[8]

Of course, for many Humanists the term *knowledge* is quite subjective, rarely capable of an accurate description of truth. W. Byron Groves and David H. Galaty admit that they "are persuaded . . . that underlying what we call knowledge, no matter how scientific it seems, is an inaccessible morass of personal and social material."[9] Apparently, they view sociology in much the same light as Bogard—as more of an art form than a science.

However, not every Humanist is willing to give up the title *scientific* without a fight. "Supernaturalism in all its forms is dying out," says Read Bain. "Science has been slowly destroying it for over three hundred years, with rapid acceleration during the last century. Its final stronghold is in the psychosocial realm. During the last fifty years the social sciences have made great strides toward becoming natural sciences and most of the former psychosocial mysteries have become matters of rapidly developing scientific knowledge."[10]

Regardless of Bain's unbridled optimism, even a superficial examination of Humanist sociology reveals that it is less than on par with the natural sciences. Most leading Humanist sociologists recognize this and struggle to infuse value into their discipline through other than purely scientific means.

Notes and Asides

Humanist Sociology as a Catalyst

Many Humanist sociologists attempt to give meaning to their work by viewing it as an instrument for actively bettering the world. While sociology is defined simply as "the study of the beliefs, values, etc. of societal groups and of the processes governing social phenomena,"[11] most Humanists believe that this study must be acted on in such a way as to create better social groups. Thus, many Humanist sociologists believe that they must work not only as observers but also as catalysts. In this way, Humanists can ascribe value to their sociology despite its unscientific nature.

Patricia Hill Collins declares that "the discipline of sociology thus is highly political. . . ."[12] She is echoed by Ted George Goertzel, who states,

> Developing a political strategy is a creative process which begins with a good understanding of the realities and limitations of existing social relations. It requires input from a number of people with different experiences and backgrounds. . . . Sociologists can play a part in this process, both in providing information and in facilitating group process.[13]

Note that Goertzel is not content with simply observing and providing information—he is interested in actively instigating political change.

This attitude differs from the attitude of most scientists, who concern themselves more with adding to human knowledge than with politics. However, since the Humanist sociologist is unsure of the scientific nature of his methods for attaining knowledge, he relies on activism to enforce the meaning and validity of his work. A perfect example of this is Humanist historian Vern Bullough's observation that "Politics and science go hand in hand. In the end it is Gay activism which determines what researchers say about gay people."[14] Likewise, Maurice R. Stein is not ashamed to admit that his political beliefs play a significant role in his sociology: "Where the consensual sociologist seeks to segregate his political beliefs, his life history and his emotional hang-ups from his work, the humanistic sociologist tries to explore, expand, and transform these personal dimensions through his work."[15]

In what kind of activism does the Humanist sociologist specifically engage? Curtis W. Reese, in an article entitled "The Social Implications of Humanism," states,

> The concern of the humanist will also carry him into crusades for governmental programs of health insurance, of hospital

Notes and Asides

> care, of medical research and of planned parenthood; for better working conditions; and for more fresh air and sunshine for more people.[16]

How can the Humanist be certain that "crusades" are called for? Why does the Humanist sociologist feel so strongly that society can be changed for the better?

Society as Evil

The answer is that the Humanist sociologist accepts the same basic premises as the Humanist psychologist. As was pointed out in the chapter on Humanist psychology, the Humanist views man as inherently good; therefore he must pin the blame for man's evil actions elsewhere.

Carl Rogers describes man's inherent goodness this way: "I am not in the least blind to the brutality, cruelty, deceit, defensiveness, abnormality, and stupidity of much of human behavior. Yet there is nothing in my experience which would cause me to regard these as the most basic elements in human nature. Indeed I find that when the individual is given even an imperfect opportunity to grow, to develop, to become his potential, it is precisely these characteristics which he tends to leave behind."[17]

Ashley Montagu and Floyd Matson agree with Rogers, claiming that "there is nothing within us or without to prevent an act of self-transformation, an evolutionary leap, if that is what is called for."[18] Man, for the Humanist sociologist, has unlimited potential for good.

But society inhibits and even distorts that potential, according to the Humanist. Erich Fromm, who speaks of "the social process which creates man,"[19] believes, "Just as primitive man was helpless before natural forces, modern man is helpless before the social and economic forces created by himself."[20]

It should be noted that Fromm elsewhere apparently contradicts himself, stating, "Any group consists of individuals and nothing but individuals, and psychological mechanisms which we find operating in a group can therefore only be mechanisms that operate in individuals. In studying individual psychology as a basis for the understanding of social psychology, we do something which might be compared with studying an object under the microscope."[21] By recognizing that society is nothing more than groups of individuals, Fromm seems to debunk the whole myth that inherently good individuals can form an evil society.

Despite an occasional contradiction, however, Fromm's position is

Notes and Asides

clear. In fact, Fromm wrote *The Sane Society*, which is based on the premise that today's society is insane and therefore corrupting the individual. He writes,

> Yet many psychiatrists and psychologists refuse to entertain the idea that society as a whole may be lacking in sanity. They hold that the problem of mental health in a society is only that of the number of "unadjusted" individuals, and not that of a possible unadjustment of the culture itself. This book deals with the latter problem; not with individual pathology, but with the *pathology of normalcy*, particularly with the pathology of contemporary Western society.[22]

This insane society, according to the Humanist sociologist, restricts man's freedom to act correctly. "Humanist sociology," says Joseph A. Scimecca, "is thus an approach that emphasizes the interrelationship of the individual and society, and the tensions produced as the individual attempts to invoke his or her freedom in the face of social constraint."[23]

This negative effect on the individual is obvious to the Humanist sociologist. Allen Wheelis sums up the despair he believes is caused by society: "It's part of being human, we differ from one another only in more or less. A few tranquil ones, with little conflict, suffer less; at the other extreme, stretched by despair to some dreadful cracking point, one goes berserk. In between are the rest of us, not miserable enough to go mad or jump off the bridge, yet never able if we are honest to say that we have come to terms with life, are at peace with ourselves, that we are happy."[24]

> "There will be no true freedom without virtue, no true science without religion, no true industry without the fear of God and love to your fellow-citizens."
>
> —Charles Kingsley

Abandoning the "Old Culture"

The focus of the Humanist sociologist's studies and activism must be the restructuring of society in an effort to do away with the old social order and create a new social order based on Humanist values. The "old culture"—that is, the culture we are a part of right now, is assumed to inhibit man's natural tendency to grow and become a better human being.

Philip E. Slater describes the problem with the old culture this way:

> The old culture is unable to stop killing people—deliberately in the case of those who oppose it, with bureaucratic indifference in the case of those who obey its dictates or consume its products trustingly. However familiar and comfortable it may seem, the

Notes and Asides

> old culture is threatening to kill us, like a trusted relative gone berserk so gradually that we are able to pretend to ourselves he has not changed.[25]

Obviously, Slater is distrustful of society as it operates today, and he expects people to take part in actively changing it. More than fifteen years ago he predicted that "old-culture moderates or liberals will be given the choice, during the next decade or so, between participating in some way in the new culture or living under a fascist regime. The middle is dropping out of things and choices must be made. If the old culture is rejected, the new must be ushered in as gracefully as possible. If the old culture is not rejected then its adherents must be prepared to accept a bloodbath such as has not been seen in the United States since the Civil War, for genocidal weapons will be on one side and unarmed masses on the other."[26]

The Humanist's antagonism toward modern society and desire for change naturally manifest themselves in an outspoken distrust of tradition. This distrust is seldom supported with any more evidence than the assumption that all of society inhibits the individual's moral nature, and therefore all the tradition behind society must be flawed.

Alfred McClung Lee declares that sociology "is the best way we have discovered yet to check, revise, and even reorganize traditional social ideas we learn from childhood in any social status group."[27] It is important to note that implicit in this vaguely harmless statement is the assumption that all traditions eventually must be improved on—that traditions must undergo a cultural evolution.

This attitude becomes much more evident elsewhere in Lee's writing, when he voices his open disdain for any sociologist who supports traditional aspects of society:

> Many a social scientist has turned away from the rocky path of creative individualistic investigation because he cannot endure the travail—the "cultural shock"—of modifying his own intellectual equipment. In turning away from that rocky path, he often finds himself embraced in the lush appreciation and support given to those who are called positive or constructive. *Positive* and *constructive* are double-talk words; they refer to being traditional or protective of vested interest or the status quo—in other words, subservient to established "truth" and authority.[28]

Naturally, this Humanist disdain for tradition carries over to religions as well. Walda Katz Fishman and C. George Benello declare that Humanist sociology "seeks the concrete betterment of humankind and

Notes and Asides

is opposed to theories that seek either to glorify the status quo or to march human beings lockstep into history in the interests of a vision imposed from above."[29] Since the Humanist denies the existence of God and embraces the evolutionary perspective, any traditions still a part of our society are simply traditions created by less-advanced men than modern man, and therefore greatly in need of revision.

The Failure of Traditional Marriage

Humanist sociologists are especially intolerant of the traditional, Biblical family—father, mother, and child (or children). In fact, Humanists often cite the institution of marriage as a prime example of the failure of Christian culture to provide freedom for the individual to grow. Marriage is considered too restrictive, inhibiting "vital inclinations." Monogamy, for the Humanist, epitomizes social slavery.

Thus, Lawrence Casler declares that "marriage and family life have been largely responsible, I suggest, for today's prevailing neurotic climate, with its pervasive insecurity, and it is precisely this climate that makes so difficult the acceptance of a different, healthier way of life."[30] If this is true, and if, as Robert Rimmer claims, "Marriage and the family is the society in microcosm,"[31] then the failure of marriage points to the failure of our entire society.

Humanists have no difficulty accepting this conclusion. Because they believe that the "old culture" is outdated, it follows that the traditions of that culture are outdated. Casler says bluntly,

> Marriage, for most people, has outlived its usefulness and is doing more harm than good. The solution is not to make divorces more difficult to obtain, but to recognize the so-called divorce problem for what it is: a symptom of the marriage problem.[32]

> "Marriage, for most people, has outlived its usefulness and is doing more harm than good."
> —Lawrence Casler

Marriage has outlived its usefulness. Modern evolving mankind no longer requires it.

This notion of marriage having outlived its usefulness arises from the concept of biological and cultural evolution. As the human species and culture progress, old traditions must be traded for new concepts that speed our evolutionary journey. George Simpson sees this happening with the family:

> The doctrine of cultural evolution emphasized the adaptive stages of human development, ways of social living, and forms of group existence. That is, various social forms came to be seen

Notes and Asides

> as selected means for carrying on the struggle for existence. Thus each family form had to be considered as valuable only relative to the adaptation of the people of a particular group. Hence the western family system was not permanent and final but only one of many possible forms.[33]

In the overall evolutionary scheme of things, the western family system is even now losing its struggle for existence.

Why are marriage and the family relics of the past? Largely because they have been used by men to dominate women, according to Humanist sociologists. Alice S. Rossi claims that "movement toward sex equality is restricted by the fact that our most intimate human relation is the heterosexual one of marriage. This places a major brake on the development of sex solidarity among women. . . ."[34] Sol Gordon agrees: "The traditional family, with all its supposed attributes, enslaved woman; it reduced her to a breeder and caretaker of children, a servant to her spouse, a cleaning lady, and at times a victim of the labor market as well."[35]

Gordon and Rossi, of course, are talking the language of feminism—a movement that emerged from the Secular Humanist worldview. "The feminist movement was begun and has been nourished by leading humanist women,"[36] says Paul Kurtz. He specifically mentions Elizabeth Cady Stanton, Betty Friedan, Gloria Steinem, and Simone deBeauvoir. "Humanism and feminism are inextricably interwoven,"[37] according to Kurtz.

Thus, it is appropriate to examine feminists' attitudes toward the traditional family unit when seeking to understand the perspective of Humanist sociologists. "Let's forget about the mythical Jesus," says Annie Laurie Gaylor, "and look for encouragement, solace, and inspiration from real women. . . . Two thousand years of patriarchal rule under the shadow of the cross ought to be enough to turn women toward the feminist 'salvation' of this world."[38] Steinem, editor of *Ms Magazine*, predicted that by the year 2000 Americans would be raising their children to believe in human potential, not God. When she was asked what feminism really wanted, she said, "Oh, we want the whole bag. We want humanism."[39]

To bring women into the humanist/feminist movement, a middle ground of sorts (some would say "cosmic humanism") is being proposed by such voices as Lois Frankel, who suggests that women worship Goddess—a female god. "Goddess religion celebrates the body," Miss Frankel says, "including its sexual and reproductive functions. Rituals typically celebrate menstruation, birth, and the joy of sexuality."[40] Miss Frankel contends that "the values of Goddess religion are largely humanistic."[41] The move to Goddess religion, how-

Notes and Asides

ever, is merely a halfway house to full Humanist theology—atheism. Says Frankel, "If we 'need the Goddess' to break the shackles of the patriarchal God, then once we are free, we can thank her for her assistance and forge our own path toward freedom and independence."[42] Freedom and independence mean freedom from belief in God or Goddess. It means atheism or Secular Humanist theology.

For the Humanist sociologist, marriage and the family are a failing tradition that must be restructured. Rimmer believes that the total breakdown of traditional marriage will occur soon; he writes, "I have a feeling that in another quarter-century the economic forces at work in the world will break down the barriers of privacy inherent in the nuclear, monogamous marriage. As this happens, other marriage styles will become common."[43]

The Family According to Humanist Sociology

Humanism does not expect marriage to be abandoned altogether. Rather, the Humanist sociologist simply wants to expand the boundaries of marriage to create more potential for human growth. The Humanist is quick to defend this attitude as the logical result of the failure of Western civilization. Robert N. Whitehurst writes, "The

CLOSE-UP

Isaac Asimov (1920-)

Isaac Asimov, one of the most popular science fiction authors of our time, has written hundreds of books, including *I, Robot* and *How Did We Find Out About the Beginning of Life?* He is also an avowed Humanist, having served as President of the American Humanist Association. His articles for *The Humanist* magazine include "The Never-ending Fight" and "For Mutual Survival We Must Bring Our World Together." Asimov has devoted a large part of his life to attacking the creationist hypothesis as unscientific, and promoting evolution as factual. He credits his enduring success as an author neither to God nor to his family, but to "a lucky break in the genetic-sweepstakes."

Notes and Asides

search for alternatives grew out of conventional family failures created by a changing and unstable society. Alternatives can thus be perceived less as a threat to the family than as a means of reconstituting it in different forms."[44]

Whitehurst goes on to list a number of possible alternatives to traditional marriage, including modified open marriage (open to adultery), triads, cooperatives, collectives, urban communes, extended intimates, swinging and group marriage, and part-time marriage.[45] Lester Kirkendall, in *A New Bill of Sexual Rights and Responsibilities*, a declaration signed by a number of Humanists including Paul Kurtz and Albert Ellis, advocates a similar list of alternative lifestyles, including homosexuality, bisexuality, pre-and extra-marital sexual relationships ("with the consent of one's partner") and something called "genital associations."[46]

Many other Humanist sociologists support the notion of alternative marriages. Herbert A. Otto speaks of a "New Family" that "seeks to explore alternatives, such as the 'family cluster'—a union of three to five families who have similar interests, values, and objectives, including possible joint parenting. The New Family is conscious of and combats sexism, sex stereotypes, and sex roles, and it practices open communication in seeking to explore the life-affirming qualities of human sexuality. There is an ongoing commitment to experimental living and to the seeking of new experiences."[47]

Indeed, the Humanist sociologist generally views monogamy as poisonous baggage heaped on us by Christian tradition. We explored the Humanist attitude toward sexual morality more fully in the chapter on Humanist ethics; for our purposes now, one statement by Abraham Maslow will suffice: "My guess is that the advanced societies are now moving toward beginning the sex life approximately at the age of puberty without marriage or without other ties."[48] Cultural evolution is leading us away from monogamy; therefore the Humanist sociologist embraces alternative sexual practices, marriage, and family styles.

Besides emphasizing more varied sexual relations, Humanism's new family will focus more on meeting every family member's needs. "The primary thrust of the New Family," states Otto, "is to recognize and nourish the unique strengths, powers, and resources of each member (including possible extrasensory capacities) and to foster the emergence of self-actualizing processes and forces. Emphasis is on creating a growth-centered, not a child-centered, home environment."[49] This new focus on self-actualization will be examined later, but it is important to note that the Humanist sociologist would de-emphasize the family's role in raising children.

In fact, Humanist sociologists go so far as to suggest that the new family in our new culture will no longer have to concern itself with

Notes and Asides

childrearing. Casler proposes a society in which

> there would be no compulsory responsibility for child-rearing, and institutionalization would be completely free of stigma, both for the child and for the parents who avail themselves of this alternative.[50]

Casler believes that this is a better alternative for all involved and that future generations will be more likely to stay in touch with their inherent goodness when raised in institutions. He writes, "It is supposed that the principles of ethical, productive, and happy living will be learned more readily when children are free of the insecurities, engendered chiefly by parents, that ordinarily obstruct the internalization of these modes of thought."[51]

Casler believes that his proposed state-run childrearing institutions would be agreeable to everyone and economically feasible as well. He outlines the specifics of the program this way:

> If relatively few people select options that do not require childrearing, the number of child-care institutions currently in existence would probably be sufficient, although extensive modernization would be desirable. But if (as seems likely) large numbers of men and women decide upon relationships—such as child-free monogamy or temporary liaisons—that do not include child-care responsibilities, then additional institutions would have to be erected. Such a construction program would require tax increases, but this added out-of-pocket expenditure would be far less than the cost of bringing up a child at home.[52]

The Humanist sociologist's disdain for Christian culture and its traditions causes him to suggest radical changes for the brave new world. But suggestions are not enough; most Humanist sociologists believe that they must actively strive to see these suggestions implemented. Sometimes this means using the classroom as a means for swaying student opinion in favor of creating an entirely new social order free of the debilitating restrictions of the present doomed order.

The Power of the Classroom

Most Humanist sociologists are not at all bashful about acknowledging the usefulness of the public school classroom in promoting activism. Collins believes that teachers automatically become activists when they walk into the classroom.

Notes and Asides

> To me, teaching is much more than the passive transfer of technical skills from teacher to learner. Rather, teaching has political implications that reach far beyond the classroom. . . . The following six years that I spent as teacher/curriculum developer at three Black community schools solidified my conviction that by teaching, one becomes an activist, whether by intention or default.[53]

Collins goes on to claim that the classroom "is a primary arena of activism, a place where people deepen their understanding of the interconnections between thought and action and, in doing so, build the foundation of their own power as social actors."[54] Obviously, if this is the case, the classroom is the ideal place for the Humanist to further the "new" faith of Humanism.

John J. Dunphy, in an article in *The Humanist* titled "A Religion for a New Age," insists that teachers in the classroom "will be ministers of another sort." Utilizing the classroom, they will "convey humanist values in whatever subject they teach." He concludes, "The classroom must and will become an area of conflict between the old and the new—the rotting corpse of Christianity, together with its adjacent evils and misery and the new faith of Humanism, resplendent in its promise of a world in which the never-realized Christian idea of 'Love thy Neighbor' will finally be achieved."[55]

John Dewey also recognized the value of the classroom in terms of initiating social changes. "The first great step," said Dewey, "as far as subject-matter and method are concerned, is to make sure of an educational system that informs students about the present state of society in a way that enables them to understand the conditions and forces at work. If only this result can be accomplished, students will be ready to take their own active part in aggressive participation in bringing about a new social order."[56]

Of course, the Humanists are only willing to allow the classroom to be a place of activism for *Humanist* teachers. Any *Christian* activism, even hanging the Ten Commandments on the wall, is violently opposed by the Humanist under the pretense of enforcing the separation of church and state. Thus, the *Humanist Manifesto II* declares, "The separation of church and state and the separation of ideology and state are imperatives. The state should encourage maximum freedom for different moral, political, religious, and social values in society."[57] Paul Blanshard and Edd Doerr write, "With all its shortcomings, the free, nonsectarian public school is the best institution in our civilization, and the separation of church and state is an essential ingredient in its survival."[58]

Why do the Humanists so vehemently support separation of church and state in education? Because this separation excludes the Christian worldview from public schools, but still allows for Humanist activism in the classroom. Separation naturally expels God from the classroom, leaving the students open only to "secular" religious worldviews. Blanshard is alarmingly blunt:

> I think that the most important factor moving us toward a secular society has been the educational factor. Our schools may not teach Johnny to read properly, but the fact that Johnny is in school until he is sixteen tends to lead toward the elimination of religious superstition. The average American child now acquires a high-school education, and this militates against Adam and Eve and all other myths of alleged history.[59]

The Self-Actualizing Society

We have seen that the Humanist sociologist is dissatisfied with Christian culture and is attempting to create a new society through remodeling the family and activism in the classroom. What type of new world order does the Humanist sociologist envision?

The Humanists are necessarily vague about this new society. Fromm defines his "sane society" as "that which corresponds to the needs of man—not necessarily to what he feels to be his needs, because even the most pathological aims can be felt subjectively as that which the person wants most; but to what his needs are *objectively*, as they can be ascertained by the study of man."[60] By "study" Fromm and the Humanists mean "science." Social science, the most controversial of the sciences (remember, some of their own sociologists referred to Humanist Sociology as art, not science), will determine what man's needs are. If science decrees that incest, for example, is a vital, healthy inclination, then incest will be considered a human need—even a right guaranteed by law. Humanists presently believe that science has found homosexuality, bisexuality, premarital sex, and extramarital sex normal and healthy.[61]

Man's highest need, according to Maslow's hierarchy of needs described in the chapter on Humanist psychology, is self-actualization. For the Humanist, a society that creates self-actualized individuals is the ideal society. Fishman and Benello believe, "As humanists and as human beings we have the obligation to evaluate our society and its institutions in terms of their professed ideals, and beyond that in terms of their capacity to contribute to human growth and self-realization."[62] This emphasis on human growth is just another way of speaking about cultural evolution—man should get better, according to an evolution-

Notes and Asides

ary view. Stein puts the ideal society in evolutionary perspective, declaring that "humanist sociology views society as an historically evolving enterprise that can only be understood through the struggle to liberate human potentialities."[63]

This call for human growth and liberating our potential is exactly what Humanist psychologists such as Maslow and Rogers have emphasized. Humanist sociologists simply focus on creating a society that encourages self-actualized behavior—that is, a society in which everyone can get in touch with his true self, his innate goodness. Glass and Staude sum up: "Just as the humanistic psychologist is concerned with individual change in a growthful direction, the humanistic sociologist is concerned with a society which would encourage and sustain such growth—a self-actualizing society, as it were."[64]

Fishman believes that Humanists are entirely capable of ushering in this new world order. She claims that Humanist sociologists, "through their understanding of the totality of social life in its qualitative as well as quantitative aspects, through their criticism of existing knowledge and social organization, and through their dedication to social change can help create new forms of social structures within which individuals as biological and social beings can develop their full potential as human beings."[65] And since the Humanist views man's potential for good as unlimited, it would seem only a matter of time before Humanist sociologists can lead mankind into a utopian world society.

Economics and the New Society

It should be noted here that Humanist sociologists, perhaps because they view society as needing radical changes, hold slightly more radical views than the average Humanist. Thus, virtually all Humanist sociologists favor socialism as the economic order for a self-actualized society, and many endorse a Marxist approach to economics. For various reasons, the Humanist sociologist believes that socialism is more conducive than capitalism to the individual's self-actualization. We will not dwell unnecessarily on the Humanist's economic views (since an entire chapter has been devoted to them), but we will examine the Humanist sociologist's rationale for embracing socialism as the economy for the self-actualized society.

We have already noted that since the Humanist views society as responsible for man's evils, he perceives Christian culture, with all the evil individual actions it causes, as hopelessly flawed. Therefore, all aspects of Western civilization, including capitalism, have serious flaws as well. "It is clear," says Robert Sheak, "that the system of corporate capitalism creates and re-creates domestic poverty in a

Notes and Asides

multitude of ways. . . ."[66] Fromm describes capitalism as tending to alienate men from each other:

> What is modern man's relationship to his fellow man? It is one between two abstractions, two living machines, who use each other. The employer uses the ones whom he employs; the salesman uses his customer. Everybody is to everybody else a commodity, always to be treated with certain friendliness, because even if he is not of use now he may be later.[67]

Victoria Rader also sees capitalism as alienating: "In sum, an economic and social system built on competition, artificial scarcity, and the division of producer and consumer roles cannot help but be reflected in the fabric of our individual lives."[68]

"The only constructive solution is that of Socialism . . ."
—Erich Fromm

The evil created by the alienation caused by capitalism can be eradicated by a socialist system, according to most Humanist sociologists. Fromm sums up this position well, declaring that Democratic Socialism must "concentrate on the human aspects of the social problem; must criticize Capitalism from the standpoint of what it does to the human qualities of man, to his soul and his spirit, and must consider any vision of Socialism in human terms, asking in what way a socialist society will contribute toward ending the alienation of man, the idolatry of economy and of the state."[69]

Humanist sociologists must focus on creating a more humane society, if people are ever to become self-actualized. According to most Humanist sociologists, socialism is the most humane possible economic system. Lee says simply, "The society we can have can thus reflect our collective recognition that a mass society needs to be a humane society of participants, even a society that will frankly be called 'socialistic.'"[70] Fromm also sees socialism as the most humane system. "The only constructive solution is that of Socialism," says Fromm, "which aims at a fundamental reorganization of our economic and social system in the direction of freeing man from being used as a means for purposes outside of himself, of creating a social order in which human solidarity, reason and productiveness are furthered rather than hobbled."[71]

Fromm, however, takes the idea of humane socialism another step, calling for a guaranteed minimum amount of cash even for people who simply *choose* not to work. He insists that the system of social security, as it exists now in Great Britain, must be retained. "But this is not enough. The existing social-security system must be extended to a *universal subsistence guarantee*."[72]

This call for radical change is typical of the Humanist sociologist. Indeed, some Humanist sociologists are willing to embrace Marxism.

Notes and Asides

Goertzel, for example, writes, "Marxism can be viewed as a humanistic theory which helps people organize to shape history."[73]

Humanist sociology expects radical changes in our society, especially in our economic system. It is important to remember that the Humanist sociologist does not stop at looking for these changes; he also works as an activist to cause them to happen.

Conclusion

Humanist sociologists believe in political and social activism partly because it gives more meaning to their discipline, and partly because they genuinely believe that our culture could evolve in such a way as to encourage universal self-actualization. This unbounded optimism is best summed up by Reese, who states, "Social orders are devices invented by man and they will contain only the values that man puts into them. . . . Informed and active people can make of society what they want it to become."[74]

This optimism in turn causes the Humanist sociologist to feel particularly antagonistic toward our present society, because today's social institutions are infinitely inferior to the utopian society the Humanist believes is possible. His disdain for modern society manifests itself in an open distrust for any and all traditions and a desire to abandon or rework all existing social institutions. The Christian institution of the family must be radically remodeled or eliminated altogether. The institution of the church must be kept under wraps by insisting on the separation of church and state (but such separation does not apply to the religion of Secular Humanism). The institution of the state (and especially the judiciary) must be used to establish the Humanist agenda, including child care centers, gay rights, abortion, and animal rights. Humanists call for the eradication of all Christian institutions, traditions, and symbols and a complete overhaul of American society. Only then will America be prepared to merge slowly with other like-minded Humanist states to forge a new world order.

[1]Robert Tannenbaum and Sheldon A. Davis, "Values, Man and Organizations," in *Humanistic Society*, eds. John F. Glass and John R. Staude (Pacific Palisades, CA: Goodyear Publishing, 1972), p. 352.
[2]*Humanist Manifesto I* (Buffalo: Prometheus Books, 1980), p. 10.
[3]Corliss Lamont, *The Philosophy of Humanism* (New York: Frederick Ungar, 1982), p. 13.
[4]Paul Kurtz, *Philosophical Essays in Pragmatic Naturalism* (Buffalo: Prometheus Books, 1990), p. 156.
[5]Edward Brongersma, *Loving Boys: A Multidisciplinary Study of Sexual Relations Between Adult and Minor Males* (Global Academic Publications, 1986), Foreword. Cited in Judith A. Reisman and Edward W. Eichel, *Kinsey, Sex and Fraud* (Lafayette, LA: Huntington House, 1990), p. 212.
[6]*Humanistic Society*, eds. Glass and Staude, p. xi.
[7]John R. Staude, "The Theoretical Foundations of Humanistic Sociology," in *Humanistic Society*, eds. Glass and Staude, p. 263.
[8]William Bogard, "Toward an Artistic Sociology," *Humanity and Society*, August 1986, p. 321.
[9]W. Byron Groves and David H. Galaty, "Freud, Foucault, and Social Control," *Humanity and Society*, August 1986, p. 297.
[10]Read Bain, "Scientific Humanism," *The Humanist*, May 1954, p. 116.
[11]*Webster's New World Dictionary* (New York: Simon and Schuster, 1982).
[12]Patricia Hill Collins, "Perspectivity and the Activist Potential of the Sociology Classroom," *Humanity and Society*, August 1986, p. 341.
[13]Ted George Goertzel, "Radical Sociology and Redemocratization in South America," *Humanity and Society*, May 1986, p. 231.
[14]Cited in Mark Schoofs, "International Forum Debates Treatment of Homosexuality," *Washington Blade*, December 18, 1987, p. 19.
[15]Maurice R. Stein, "On the Limits of Professional Thought," in *Humanistic Society*, eds. Glass and Staude, p. 165.
[16]Curtis W. Reese, "The Social Implications of Humanism," *The Humanist*, July/August 1961, p. 198.
[17]Carl Rogers, "A Humanistic Conception of Man," in *Humanistic Society*, ed. Glass and Staude, p. 30.
[18]Ashley Montagu and Floyd Matson, *The Dehumanization of Man* (New York: McGraw-Hill, 1983), p. 219.
[19]Erich Fromm, *Escape from Freedom* (New York: Holt, Rinehart, and Winston, 1969), p. 12.
[20]Erich Fromm, *The Sane Society* (New York: Holt, Rinehart and Winston, 1955), p. 362.
[21]Fromm, *Escape from Freedom*, p. 137.
[22]Fromm, *The Sane Society*, p. 6.
[23]Joseph A. Scimecca, "Humanist Sociological Theory: The State of an Art," *Humanity and Society*, August 1987, p. 336.
[24]Allen Wheelis, "The Humanistic Ethic—The Individual in Psychotherapy as a Societal Change Agent," in *Humanistic Society*, ed. Glass and Staude, p. 277.
[25]Philip E. Slater "The Postponed Life," in *Humanistic Society*, eds. Glass and Staude, p. 381.
[26]Ibid., p. 385.
[27]Alfred McClung Lee, "On Context and Relevance," in *Humanistic Society*, eds. Glass and Staude, p. 249.
[28]Alfred McClung Lee, *Toward Humanist Sociology* (Englewood Cliffs, NJ: Prentice-Hall, 1973), p. 165.
[29]Walda Katz Fishman and C. George Benello, *Readings in Humanist Sociology* (Bayside, NY: General Hall, 1986), p. 3.
[30]Lawrence Casler, "Permissive Matrimony: Proposals for the Future," *The Humanist*, March/April 1974, p. 5.
[31]Robert Rimmer, "An Interview With Robert Rimmer on Premarital Communes and Group Marriages," *The Humanist*, March/April 1974, p. 14.
[32]Casler, "Permissive Matrimony: Proposals for the Future," p. 4.
[33]George Simpson, *People in Families* (New York: Thomas Y. Crowell, 1960), p. 4.
[34]Alice S. Rossi, "Sex Equality: The Beginnings of Ideology," *The Humanist*, Sept/Oct 1969, p. 5.
[35]Sol Gordon, "The Egalitarian Family is Alive and Well," *The Humanist*, May/June 1975, p. 18.
[36]Paul Kurtz, "Fulfilling Feminist Ideals: A New Agenda," *Free Inquiry*, Fall 1990, p. 21.
[37]Ibid.
[38]Annie Laurie Gaylor, "Feminist 'Salvation,'" *The Humanist*, July/August 1988, p. 37.
[39]Cited in Joan Kennedy Taylor, "Feminism and Humanism," *Free Inquiry*, Fall 1990, p. 24.

[40]Lois Frankel, "Feminist Spirituality as a Path to Humanism," *Free Inquiry*, Fall 1990, p. 31.
[41]Ibid., p. 35.
[42]Ibid.
[43]Rimmer, "An Interview With Robert Rimmer on Premarital Communes and Group Marriages," p. 12.
[44]Robert N. Whitehurst, "Alternative Life-styles," *The Humanist*, May/June 1975, p. 24.
[45]Ibid, pp. 25-6.
[46]Lester Kirkendall, *A New Bill of Sexual Rights and Responsibilities* (Buffalo, NY: Prometheus Books, 1976, p. 9.
[47]Herbert A. Otto, "The New Family," *The Humanist*, May/June 1975, p. 9.
[48]Abraham Maslow, "Some Fundamental Questions that Face the Normative Social Psychologist," in *Humanistic Society*, eds. Glass and Staude, p. 324.
[49]Otto, "The New Family," p. 8.
[50]Casler, "Permissive Matrimony: Proposals for the Future," p. 6.
[51]Ibid., p. 7.
[52]Ibid.
[53]Collins, "Perspectivity and the Activist Potential of the Sociology Classroom," p. 341.
[54]Ibid., p. 355.
[55]John J. Dunphy, "A Religion for a New Age," *The Humanist*, January/February 1983, p. 26.
[56]John Dewey, *Education and the Social Order* (New York: League for Industrial Democracy, 1934), p. 10.
[57]*Humanist Manifesto II* (Buffalo: Prometheus Books, 1980), p. 19.
[58]Paul Blanshard and Edd Doerr, "The Principle of Separation," *The Humanist*, Nov/Dec 1971, p. 17.
[59]Paul Blanshard, "Three Cheers For Our Secular State," *The Humanist*, March/April 1976, p. 17.
[60]Fromm, *The Sane Society*, p. 20.
[61]See Reisman and Eichel, *Kinsey, Sex and Fraud.*
[62]Fishman and Benello, *Readings in Humanist Sociology*, p. 8.
[63]Stein, "On the Limits of Professional Thought," p. 165.
[64]John F. Glass and John R. Staude, "Individual and Social Change," in *Humanistic Society*, eds. Glass and Staude, pp. 271-2.
[65]Fishman and Benello, *Readings in Humanist Sociology*, p. 19.
[66]Robert Sheak, "There's More to Poverty than the 'Feminization of Poverty': The Trends 1959-1983," *Humanity and Society*, May 1988, p. 125.
[67]Erich Fromm, *Beyond the Chains of Illusion* (New York: Simon and Schuster, 1962), cited in Ross Ellenhorn, "Toward a Humanistic Social Work: Social Work for Conviviality," *Humanity and Society*, May 1988, p. 166.
[68]Victoria Rader, "The Social Construction of Life-Cycle Crises," in *Readings in Humanist Sociology*, eds. Fishman and Benello, p. 58.
[69]Fromm, *The Sane Society*, p. 269.
[70]Lee, *Toward Humanist Sociology*, p. 97.
[71]Fromm, *The Sane Society*, p. 277.
[72]Ibid., p. 335.
[73]Goertzel, "Radical Sociology and Redemocratization in South America," p. 230.
[74]Reese, "The Social Implications of Humanism," p. 198.

CHAPTER

19

MARXIST/ LENINIST SOCIOLOGY

"Bourgeois marriage is in reality a system of wives in common and thus, at the most, what the Communists might possibly be reproached with, is that they desire to introduce, in substitution for a hypocritically concealed, an openly legalised community of women." [1]

—Karl Marx

"With the transfer of the means of production into common ownership [communism], the single family ceases to be the economic unit of society. . . . The care and education of the children becomes a public affair; society looks after all children alike, whether they are legitimate or not." [2]

—Frederick Engels

SUMMARY

Marxist/Leninist economic determinism shapes Marxist sociology. Marxists believe that social consciousness is determined by the mode of production extant in a society, so that capitalism is responsible for society's present failings.

This concept of economic determinism is central to the Marxist worldview. Capitalism allegedly has produced a society rife with oppression and crime; therefore, an economic system must be adopted that changes social consciousness for the better. If, as L. P. Bueva claims, "classes form the basis of social structure: their traits and the relations among them determine all social and socio-psychological processes in society and the laws governing them,"[3] then a classless society (communism) is far superior to a society that encourages one class to oppress another (capitalism). Thus, the Marxist sociologist calls for a socialistic system to replace capitalism, believing that this will guarantee the creation of advanced social consciousness.

The Marxist is especially anxious to usher in a communist society because only then will mankind achieve a truly moral social consciousness. "Right," Karl Marx declares, "can never be higher than the economic structure of society and its cultural development conditioned thereby."[4] According to this view, mankind has been living with a stunted notion of morality throughout history, and a society that encourages proper values is long overdue. These "proper values," however, will not be manifest until the proper society is put into place.

Marxist sociology believes that the advent of such a society is inevitable. Man is guaranteed by biological evolution and the laws of the dialectic to progress socially and culturally. Even now, the proletariat and the bourgeoisie are clashing according to the immutable laws of the dialectic. Man can soon expect world socialism, followed by a new social consciousness. This new society, as it gradually leaves behind the contagion of capitalism, will evolve into a new world order—communism. At that point, society will be so radically altered that the individual will be influenced to act responsibly at all times. For example, Marxists believe that the sins

Introduction

Marxist sociologists, like all other Marxists, claim that their approach to their discipline is more scientific than any other approach. While Humanist sociologists are willing sometimes to face the unscientific nature of sociology (some refer to it as an art instead of a science), Marxists dare to compare their sociology with the natural sciences. Maurice Cornforth boldly proclaims, "Marx laid the foundations of

of greed, selfishness, and envy will disappear completely once private property is abolished. From the ashes, new communist man will emerge.

Modern capitalist society, according to Marxist theory, is contributing to its own demise. By oppressing individuals, it encourages each man to revolt and establish a new mode of production and, consequently, a new society that will respect the individual. Karl Marx and Frederick Engels declare,

> In the present epoch, the domination of material relations over individuals, and the suppression of individuality by fortuitous circumstances, has assumed its sharpest and most universal form, thereby setting existing individuals a very definite task. It has set them the task of replacing the domination of circumstances and of chance over individuals by the domination of individuals over chance and circumstances.[5]

In this way, Marxists grant man free will, rather than a determined consciousness, long enough to help evolution and the dialectic usher in world communism.

And what will this perfect society be like? Marxists tell us that world communism will abandon traditional bourgeois morality with all its religious connotations. The church will be consigned to the scrap heap, and the community will assume responsibility for childrearing, thereby effectively disbanding the family. Indeed, even the state will wither away, leaving every individual to govern his own life. Society will become a collection of perfectible individuals with no institutions to hinder their development or lead them astray. Marxist sociologists insist that this type of society will usher in the golden age of humanity. The coming world order will become a reality in which every human being can claim his manhood and womanhood without exploitation or alienation.

social science by finding the right problems to tackle. To find the problems of science is also to define the subject-matter of science. Formulating the problems, Marxism at the same time enables us to define the subject-matter of the inquiry. It thus becomes a true scientific discipline."[6]

V. I. Lenin claims much the same thing: "This idea of materialism in sociology was in itself a stroke of genius. Naturally, *for the time being* it was only a hypothesis, but one which first created the possibility of

Notes and Asides

a strictly scientific approach to historical and social problems."[7] For the Marxist, the application of Marx's dialectical materialism to sociology created the only truly scientific sociological approach.

On what scientific foundation do the Marxists base their sociological approach? Cornforth hints at the answer when he speaks of the "laws of 'social evolution' discovered by Marx."[8] G. V. Plekhanov is more explicit; he claims that Marxism is "Darwinism in its application to social science."[9] Clearly, the Marxist sociologist perceives his social theory as rooted in the scientific "fact" of Darwinism. This Marxist reliance on evolution as a basis for its social theory greatly influences Marxists' perception of the mechanisms of society. Just as man is evolving biologically, so also man is evolving sociologically. And as man improves through the evolutionary chain of being, so also does society. The scientific fact of biological evolution guarantees both the truth of Marxist social theory and the outcome of the process. Hence, Marxist sociology is based on what Marxists consider sound Darwinian evolutionary science.

Society as an Evolving Entity

Whereas Darwin outlined the concept of the evolution of the *species*, Marxism describes the evolution of *society* as a whole. Thus, Marxist sociologists constantly discuss the "development of society." Lenin writes,

> What Marx and Engels called the dialectical method—as against the metaphysical—is nothing else than the scientific method in sociology, which consists in regarding society as a living organism in a state of constant development . . . an organism the study of which requires an objective analysis of the production relations that constitute the given social formation and an investigation of its laws of functioning and development.[10]

It is important to note, first, that Lenin sees this idea of development as scientific, and, second, that he refers to "production relations" as crucial for understanding a society. This emphasis on the economic aspect of society is inherent to Marxism. Such economic determinism assumes that the particular economic system of a society determines its politics, religion, law, and culture, and especially the individual's social consciousness.

We will examine how this economic determinism affects Marxist social theory in a moment. First, however, we must understand the Marxist concept of the evolution of society. Lenin believes that man can

Notes
and
Asides

truly understand society only in the context of this concept of development. He claims, "Marxism indicated the way to an all-embracing and comprehensive study of the process of the rise, development, and decline of socio-economic systems."[11] This process and the forces that maintain it are outlined by Marx. At a certain stage of social development, said Marx, "the material productive forces of society come into conflict with the existing relations of production. . . . From forms of development of the productive forces these relations turn into their fetters. Then begins an era of social revolution. The changes in the economic foundation lead sooner or later to the transformation of the whole immense superstructure."[12] Note that the economic system of any given society plays the preeminent role in shaping that society, according to Marxist theory.

For the Marxist, the stages in the development of society must parallel the economic stages in mankind's history. Marx divides the history of society into four stages: "In broad outline, the Asiatic, ancient, feudal and modern bourgeois modes of production may be designated as epochs marking progress in the economic development of society."[13] Society, however, does not stop developing at the bourgeois stage. Rather, society will develop eventually into a communist stage. This evolution will occur due to specific economic forces.

The Economic System's Influence on Society

Marx, and with him all Marxist/Leninists, maintains that the basic character of any society is determined by its economic organization.

> In the social production of their existence, men inevitably enter into definite relations, which are independent of their will, namely relations of production appropriate to a given stage in the development of their material forces of production. The totality of these relations of production constitutes the economic structure of society, the real foundation, on which arises a legal and political superstructure and to which correspond definite forms of social consciousness.[14]

For example, if the economic system is capitalism, then one expects laws to arise to protect private property. The political and religious systems will also protect private property, profits, contracts, etc. All of society's social institutions follow the economic institution.

Put more simply, man's economic system determines how men must relate to each other in order to operate efficiently within the system. These forms of relation, in turn, dictate the societal norms in

Notes and Asides

general, including the political and legal aspects of society. V. Yazykova sums up the crucial role of economic systems in the Marxist view:

> Material production forms the basis of the life of human society, for it provides people with the essentials for satisfaction of their needs and determines the social structure of society, its ideology and institutions. Changes in material production [e.g., capitalism] effect changes in all spheres of social life.[15]

Indeed, the Marxist view of economics as the foundation for all of society was the central proposition of *The Communist Manifesto*. Frederick Engels writes in the Preface, "That proposition is: that in every historical epoch, the prevailing mode of economic production and exchange, and the social organization necessarily following from it, form the basis upon which is built up, and from which alone can be explained, the political and intellectual history of that epoch. . . ."[16] *The Manifesto*, of course, goes on to declare that the time for a new society has arisen and that a communist economic system will create the new society.

How can this be? How can the Marxist place such an emphasis on economics that it determines the nature of all of society? The answer lies in a "law" described by Cornforth:

> The historical sequence is in fact governed by the law that people always adapt their relations of production to their forces of production.[17]

That is, the relations between individuals are different in a feudal society than in a capitalistic society, and it is precisely the feudalism or the capitalism that determines these relations. These production relations carry over to all day-to-day relations, whether business oriented or not. This carry-over creates politics, law, culture—in fact, all of society.

Cornforth restates the "law" this way: "According to Marx's theory of 'sociological laws' relations of production depend on forces of production; people change their forces of production in the development of their productive intercourse with nature, and so change their relations of production; and so the unique irreversible stage-by-stage development of social-economic formations of human society takes place. This makes good scientific sense and is empirically verifiable in terms of what people do."[18] Again, we find the Marxist sociological notion of "development" hand-in-hand with the theory that economic systems determine the nature of society. For the Marxist, societies evolve as their economic systems evolve.

Some Marxists, however, have carried this concept to its logical conclusion and declared that society has an even more fundamental basis than economics—namely, geography. "The peculiarities of the geographical environment," writes Plekhanov, "determine the evolution of the forces of production, and this, in its turn, determines the development of economic forces and, therefore, the development of all the other social relations."[19] That is, mankind adapts his economic system to his geographic environment, and thus society is determined, in the final estimation, by its location.

Whether the actual foundation for society is its economic system or its geography, however, the key aspect of the Marxist view is that society can be changed by man only if he can change the forces of production. In other words, society is determined by the economic system on which it is based.

Society as Predetermined

On the surface it appears that the Marxist sociologist still perceives the individual as having a hand in the formation of society—man may indirectly influence society by changing the forces of production. Man cannot directly change society, but he can change the economic system on which it is based, thereby restructuring society.

In truth, however, Marx denies man even this marginal control over his own society. "The mode of production of material life" says Marx, "conditions the general process of social, political and intellectual life. It is not the consciousness of men that determines their existence, but their social existence that determines their consciousness."[20] Man is seen by Marx as a helpless automaton whose consciousness is programmed by his society. This consciousness is based strictly on man's social existence, so much so that man cannot step outside his society in order to change it.

Marx believes that this model of man is the obvious choice:

> Does it require deep intuition to comprehend that man's ideas, views, and conceptions, in one word, man's consciousness, changes with every change in the condition of his material existence, in his social relations and in his social life?[21]

Man is a leaf blown by the changing winds of his social life.

According to the Marxist sociologist, the individual is insignificant in the face of the powerful forces of society. Cornforth believes that "individuals acquire their human individuality only in social relations. . . ."[22] Stalin believes that to understand the historical process one must

Notes and Asides

rely "on the concrete conditions of the material life of society, as the determining force of social development; not on the good wishes of 'great men'."[23]

Indeed, Marxists view the changes in society as often contrary to the efforts of even the best of individuals. Thus, Cornforth says, "motives 'cross and conflict' and, as it works out, what happens is, more often than not, what no one intended."[24] Engels says much the same thing, claiming that "the many individual wills active in history for the most part produce results quite other than those they intended—often quite the opposite; their motives therefore in relation to the total result are

CLOSE-UP

Mao Tse-tung (1893-1976)

Mao Tse-tung's role in the history of Marxism was similar to V.I. Lenin's, at least in the practical realm. While Lenin also made vast contributions to Marxism on the theoretical level, he and Tse-tung both played pioneering roles in establishing communism in their respective countries. In China, Tse-tung found himself attempting to change a political situation almost as unstable as Russia's, but in a culture much more opposed to change. Thus, his move to establish communism required much more time, and more hardship. From 1934 to 1935, Tse-tung and his followers had to endure the Long March, a retreat from persecution that carried them some 6,000 miles from their home soviet. Further, Tse-tung's brand of nationalistic communism was consistently opposed by Chinese Marxists sympathetic to the USSR, and his popularity (and, consequently, his power) fluctuated according to Sino-Soviet relations. In 1945, at a high point in his popularity, he succeeded in including his ideology in China's Marxist party's constitution, and this contrived authority provided him with enough stability to survive fluctuations in popularity in the following years. Tse-tung's most important communist experiment, the Great Leap Forward, took place in 1958, and was based on the idealistic notion that the voluntary zeal of the masses would increase production, regardless of incentives and price mechanisms. The Great Leap Forward failed, but Tse-tung held on to power until his death in 1976.

likewise only of secondary significance."[25]

Why is the individual so ineffective in shaping society? According to the Marxist, the evolution of society is a process just too powerful to be affected by the actions of individuals. L. N. Moskvichev describes the magnitude of the evolutionary process: "Moreover, social determination acts not only through the present social being, the so-called existential factors, but also through the past and future of society, that is through something already non-existent empirically and something which has not yet empirically come."[26] Obviously, in such an overarching development, man must play a very limited role.

Man's One Chance to Create His Own Society

In fact, according to Marxist sociology, throughout the history of the development of society so far, man has only been allowed to play the role determined for him by his society. Surprisingly, however, the Marxist sociologist believes that man finally has the opportunity to have a hand in creating a new society—a society founded on socialism.

According to Engels, after the proletarian revolution man will finally be in a position to control society.

> With the seizing of the means of production by society, man's own social organization, hitherto confronting him as a necessity imposed by Nature and history, now becomes the result of his own free action. The extraneous objective forces that have hitherto governed history pass under the control of man himself. Only from that time will man himself, more and more consciously, make his own history—only from that time will the social causes set in movement by him have, in the main and in a constantly growing measure, the results intended by him. It is the ascent of man from the kingdom of necessity to the kingdom of freedom.[27]

Cornforth says that man can only control his own society once he understands the sociological laws discovered by Marx and Engels:

> In studying the laws of development of society . . . and pointing out that their operation explains the results of human actions irrespective of intentions, Marx and Engels made it quite clear that, once these laws are understood, it becomes possible to project plans of action, based on an objective analysis of circumstances, in which the results will be brought more and more, in a controlled way, within the scope of the intentions.[28]

Notes and Asides

Obviously, the plan of action Cornforth is calling for involves society as a whole controlling the means of production. Once socialism becomes the basis for a society, then man can live a life not entirely predetermined. Engels sums up, "Man, at last the master of his own form of social organization, becomes at the same time the lord over Nature, his own master—free."[29] By implication, until mankind embraces socialism and eventually communism, man cannot be considered free.

It is interesting to note how closely Marxist sociology parallels Marxist psychology at this point. As demonstrated in the chapter on psychology, the Marxist grants the individual virtually no free will until this will is necessary for the revolution to overthrow capitalism. The same phenomenon occurs in the sociological arena of Marxist thought. Society determines the individual, until the free will of the individual is required to create a socialistic society. Then the Marxist sociologist finds himself willing to ignore the previously postulated impotency of man, claiming instead that man now has the opportunity to finally rise up and be "free."

Of course, for the Marxist, the advent of communism is viewed as inevitable regardless of the number of individuals who ignore Marx's "sociological laws" or strive against them. Thus, in Marxist theory, the individual is only free to create the next society if he is willing to go along with the evolutionary process and create a communistic society.

In Marxist sociological theory, the individual can only help create a truly free society if he faces the fact that the objective inevitability of revolutionary socialist changes "is predetermined by the economic laws of social development, by the economic law of the correspondence of the relations of production to the level and character of the productive forces, by the law of the uneven development of capitalism, and so on."[30]

The Ultimate Society

The march toward socialism, and eventually communism, will occur eventually regardless of the number of men who oppose it. Those who choose to support this march will be "free," while all others will remain slaves to present-day capitalist society. This inevitable spread of communism will occur largely because this is the script of social evolution, an evolution based on biological conflict and survival of the fittest.

The existence of class divisions is one of the biggest flaws in modern society, according to the Marxist sociologist. Writes Engels,

Notes and Asides

> The division of society into a small, excessively rich class and a large, propertyless class of wage-workers results in a society suffocating from its own superfluity, while the great majority of its members is scarcely, or even not at all, protected from extreme want. This state of affairs becomes daily more absurd and—more unnecessary. It *must* be abolished, it *can* be abolished.[31]

It will be abolished and replaced with a more fit society.

Marxist sociologists also point to the competition inherent to capitalistic societies as a major flaw. Marx believes that "it is a characteristic feature of labour which posits exchange-value that it causes the social relations of individuals to appear in the perverted form of a social relation between things."[32] Engels also sees capitalistic competition as negative: "Present-day society, which breeds hostility between the individual man and everyone else, thus produces a social war of all against all which inevitably in individual cases, notably among uneducated people, assumes a brutal, barbarously violent form—that of crime."[33]

Clearly, the Marxist sociologist takes a dim view of capitalist society. It would seem, according to this view, that the failed structure of today's society does not bode well for future societies. The Marxist would subscribe to this pessimistic perspective were it not for one factor—the saving grace of the Marxist theory of sociology. "If the scientific ideas of socialism and the theory of communism did not exist today," writes Georgi Shakhnazarov, "the growth of mysticism and obscurantism would be inevitable, as would be the final degeneration and destruction of mankind, since the present high level of scientific knowledge cannot be combined with low, backward social ideas for long."[34]

Of course, the "theory of communism" *does* exist today, and it contains a prescription for the ultimate society. Marxist sociologists believe this prescription will begin to be filled when a socialistic economic system is adopted. The ultimate society, the coming world order, will naturally follow.

One of the dominant aspects of this utopian society will be its abolition of classes. "In communist society," says Engels, "where the interests of individuals are not opposed to one another but, on the contrary, are united, competition is eliminated. As is self-evident, there can no longer be any question of the ruin of particular classes, nor of the very existence of classes such as the rich and the poor nowadays."[35] Socialism is seen as the first step toward this utopia. The text *Socialism as a Social System* states, "In historical terms, socialism is the first phase

Notes and Asides

of the classless communist society. It is society's first resolute step towards abolishing classes and class contradictions."[36] This view of socialism results from the Marxist sociologist's emphasis on economics as the very foundation of society. A socialistic economic system can initiate all the other necessary changes to create a classless society, according to the Marxist view.

This ultimate society, writes Engels, will provide a better life for everyone:

> A new social order is possible in which the present class differences will have disappeared and in which—perhaps after a short transitional period involving some privation, but at any rate of great value morally—through the planned utilisation and extension of the already existing enormous productive forces of all members of society, and with uniform obligation to work, the means for existence, for enjoying life, for the development and employment of all bodily and mental faculties will be available in an equal measure and in ever-increasing fullness. . . .[37]

The *Program of the Communist International* echoes Engels: "The development of the productive forces of the world communist society will make it possible to raise the well-being of the whole of humanity and to reduce to a minimum the time devoted to material production and, consequently, will enable culture to flourish as never before in history."[38]

In this way the Marxist sociologist is much like the Humanist sociologist: he believes that mankind can create an earthly paradise. Shakhnazarov writes, "In essence, communism is identical to humanism since it presupposes the *all-round development of the human personality in a perfectly organized society*."[39]

"In essence, communism is identical to humanism . . . "
—G. Shakhnazarov

This "perfectly organized society," once organized, will no longer need a government to keep it running smoothly, according to Marxist theory. "Only in Communist society," declares Lenin, "when the resistance of the capitalists has been completely broken, when the capitalists have disappeared, when there are no classes (that is, there is no difference between the members of society in their relation to the social means of production), only then the State ceases to exist."[40] We will examine the Marxist view of the state more closely in the chapter on Marxist politics. For the remainder of this chapter, we will concern ourselves with the Marxist sociologist's view of the church, the family, and education—their role in modern society, and the changes they will undergo in the transition to the ultimate society.

Notes and Asides

The Church in Marxist Sociology

As demonstrated in the chapter on Marxist theology, Marxists have little patience with religion or any notion of God. Lenin declares, "Every religious idea, every idea of God, even flirting with the idea of God, is unutterable vileness . . . of the most dangerous kind, 'contagion' of the most abominable kind."[41] Indeed, the Marxist sees religion as a stumbling block, slowing the development of the ultimate society:

> The influence of the church promotes the schism of the workers movement. Reactionary churchmen everywhere try to isolate religious workers from their class brothers by attracting them into separate organizations of a clerical nature . . . and thus diverting them from the struggle against capitalism.[42]

The Marxist would like to see the church abolished, since it is a hindrance to the advent of communism. "All religions," writes Engels, "which have existed hitherto were expressions of historical stages of development of individual peoples or groups of peoples. But communism is that stage of historical development which makes all existing religions superfluous and supersedes them."[43] The Marxist sociologist sees the church as an outdated institution that must be abandoned.

In the Soviet Union, Marxists have used many different methods in their effort to abolish religion. In the early days following the October Revolution, the Marxists simply discriminated against priests in an effort to discourage anyone who wanted to be in the clergy. Robert Conquest, who is not a Marxist, tells us, "Priests and clerics were declared, under another article (65) of the 1918 [Soviet] Constitution, to be 'servants of the bourgeoisie' and disfranchised. This involved their receiving no ration cards, or those of the lowest category; their children were barred from school above the elementary grade; and so on."[44]

When this act of discrimination failed to wipe out religion, the Marxists tried to further restrict the church through state controls. Conquest writes,

> A law of 8 April 1929 forbade religious organizations to establish mutual assistance funds; to extend material aid to their members; "to organize special prayer or other meetings for children, youths or women, or to organize general bible, literary, handicraft, working, religious study or other meetings, groups, circles or branches, to organize excursions or children's playgrounds, or to open libraries or reading rooms, or to

Notes and Asides

organize sanatoria or medical aid". In fact, as an official comment put it, church activity was reduced to the performance of religious services.[45]

Peter Babris, a non-Marxist, describes still another state control inflicted on the church: "Throughout the USSR there are only three Russian Orthodox seminaries, one near Moscow, one in Leningrad and the third in Odessa. Enrollment is about 250 students in each. If a student wishes to attend, he must not only apply to the church but also to the state, and it is the latter that makes the final decision on his acceptance. Thus the student who is accepted is under state control from the outset."[46]

"The Church wants to see religion flourish; communism wants its death."
—*Solovky Memorandum*

Marxist sociologists believe that the state must squeeze all life out of the church before a utopian society can exist. This Marxist acceptance of state controls as appropriate is best summed up by A. Zhdanov, who writes,

> Ministers of religion have not the right to open on their own initiative, churches, mosques and houses of prayer without the special permission of the organs of state power nor to hold baptism services at open reservoirs, hold prayer meetings in buildings not specially designed for this. Soviet law does not allow that a threat to people's health should be caused during religious ceremonies nor that actions arousing superstitions should be committed.[47]

Religion, according to Marxist sociologists, is nothing more than a superstition. Naturally, the church is an unhealthy aspect of society and, therefore, can have no place in a communist utopia.

Education in Marxist Sociology

According to the Marxist, education, as a facet of society, follows directly from the means of production extant in that society. Thus, for the Marxist, education in modern bourgeois society reflects all the evils of that mode of production. For example, Madan Sarup believes, "The [modern] educational system thus meshes with capital to ensure the maintenance of women's oppression."[48] An article in the *Peking Review* assumes that bourgeois society's educational system discriminates against the proletariat because "Education of the proletariat is diametrically opposed to that of all the exploiting classes."[49]

What type of education would the Marxist sociologist provide for the proletariat? Prior to the proletarian revolt and the institution of socialism as the new means of production, the proletariat can only be educated in terms of the dialectical struggle, according to Lenin. "The real education of the masses," he writes, "can never be separated from the independent, the political, and particularly from the revolutionary struggle of the masses themselves. Only the struggle educates the exploited class."[50]

Once the struggle is over, however, and the proletariat has ushered in a socialistic economic system, the Marxist sociologist perceives education as playing a different role in creating the ultimate society—communism. Pinkevich writes, "The aim is the indoctrination of the youth in the proletarian philosophy. In the works of accepted program, the school must be not only a vehicle of the principles of communism in general, but also an instrument through which the proletariat may affect the proletarian strata of the laboring masses with a view to training up a generation capable of finally establishing communism."[51]

This new generation, of course, will have been educated to view all religion as superstition. An article in *Bolshevik* claims,

> Education in the spirit of Leninism means instilling in the youth the Marxist-Leninist outlook on the world, on the social life, on the role and position of man and his behavior in society. It means instilling in them a materialistic world outlook based on science and materialist philosophy, alien to any superstitions or mysticism, seeking no escape into the "other world," alien to any diversion from real life and . . . inspiring them with confidence in their own power and with a knowledge of the conditions and means of victory.[52]

This sentiment is also found in the text *People's Education*:

> The basic work in communist education and the overcoming of the survivals of religiousness must be carried out by the school teachers in the process of teaching the foundations of the sciences. The basic task of communist education and overcoming the survivals of religiousness in our present condition is to prove to the pupils the complete contrast and complete irreconcilability between science, the real and correct reflection of the objectively existing world in the consciousness of people—and religion as a fantastic, distorted and, consequently, harmful reflection of the world in the consciousness of the people.[53]

For the Marxist sociologist, education is a valuable tool for shaping the ideology of individuals. This tool must be used to create citizens more likely to cooperate with and fit into the Marxist notion of the

Notes and Asides

ultimate society. Accordingly, the individual must be educated to detest religion and embrace the Marxist materialistic view of the world. Of course, this type of education cannot be totally employed until capitalism is destroyed. When bourgeois society is destroyed, Marxist education will play a key role in ushering in the ultimate society.

The Family in Marxist Sociology

Marxist sociologists see the family as an entity evolving in much the same way as society. Engels claims, "We thus have three principal forms of marriage which correspond broadly to the three principal stages of human development. For the period of savagery, group marriage; for barbarism, pairing marriage; for civilization, monogamy, supplemented by adultery and prostitution."[54]

Engels sees this development as so important, in fact, that he even describes the family as playing a role (along with the means of production) in determining the whole character of a society. He writes,

> According to the materialistic conception, the determining factor in history is, in the final instance, the production and reproduction of the immediate essentials of life. This, again, is of a twofold character. On the one side, the production of the means of existence, of articles of food and clothing, dwellings, and of the tools necessary for that production; on the other side, the production of human beings themselves, the propagation of the species. The social organization under which the people of a particular historical epoch and a particular country live is determined by both kinds of production: by the stage of development of labor on the one hand and of the family on the other.[55]

The family's place in society is of great importance to the Marxist sociologist. If, as the Marxist assumes, the family can play a part in determining the whole nature of society, then the Marxist must hasten the development of the family type that will usher in communism.

Obviously, the family type extant in bourgeois society is not the advanced family necessary for communism. Like religion and bourgeois education, the modern family is viewed by Marxist sociology as a great failure. Thus, Engels declares, "Monogamous marriage was a great historical step forward; nevertheless, together with slavery and private wealth, it opens the period that has lasted until today in which every step forward is also relatively a step backward, in which prosperity and development for some is won through the misery and frustration of others."[56] Marxists believe this misery to be caused by the greed and

Notes and Asides

competition bred in capitalistic society and necessarily infecting capitalistic families. Marx puts it this way: "The bourgeoisie has torn away from the family its sentimental veil, and has reduced the family relation to a mere money relation."[57] But this family relation exists only among the bourgeois, according to Marx and Engels:

> On what foundation is the present family, the bourgeois family, based? On capital, on private gain. In its completely developed form this family exists only among the bourgeoisie. But this state of things finds its complement in the practical absence of the family among the proletarians.[58]

Indeed, according to the Marxist sociologist, proletarians will never enter into family relations as they exist in present society, because the proletariat is destined to usher in a new, utopian society, complete with a higher form of "family." Until this occurs, the proletariat must shun the bourgeois society family type, because, as Aleksandra M. Kollontai says, "The family deprives the worker of revolutionary consciousness."[59]

What type of "family" will evolve when the proletariat seizes the means of production and ushers in the utopian society? Engels predicts,

> With the transfer of the means of production into common ownership, the single family ceases to be the economic unit of society. Private housekeeping is transformed into a social industry. The care and education of the children becomes a public affair; society looks after all children alike, whether they are legitimate or not. This removes all the anxiety about the "consequences," which today is the most essential social—moral as well as economic—factor that prevents a girl from giving herself completely to the man she loves. Will not that suffice to bring about the gradual growth of unconstrained sexual intercourse and with it a more tolerant public opinion in regard to a maiden's honor and a woman's shame?[60]

"No genuine observer can decide otherwise than that the homes of a nation are the bulwarks of personal and national safety."
—J. G. Holland

That is, the new social order will accept, and even encourage, premarital sex and adultery, as long as it is done in a spirit of freedom and responsibility. Indeed, within the context of community where there is no private property and everyone belongs to everyone, premarital sex and adultery cease to have any meaning.

Marx and Engels argued in *The Communist Manifesto* that the idea of a "community of women" is not new; "it has existed almost from time immemorial."[61] In answer to their critics that communists would "introduce a community of women," Marx and Engels respond,

Notes and Asides

Why not have a community of men?

"Bourgeois marriage is in reality a system of wives in common and thus, at the most, what the Communists might possibly be reproached with, is that they desire to introduce, in substitution for a hypocritically concealed, an openly legalised community of women."[62]

It is important to note, too, that Engels believes the care of children should become "a public affair." In the family in the ultimate society, children play an insignificant role, since they are the entire community's responsibility. In fact, children are basically disengaged from the family in socialist society, according to Yazykova. He claims that in Russia,

> For many youngsters school becomes literally a home. Families that have no one to look after their children after school can arrange for them to stay in extended-day groups where they are under the tutelage of teachers until the parents come home from work.[63]

This alienation of children from their parents helps ensure that children formulate their worldviews according to education provided by the Marxist state. This aspect of the new "family" prevents the child from learning the outdated views held by his parents, especially about religion. However, until the child is totally separated from the family in the utopian society, the Marxist must also take legal precautions to prevent families from imposing religious views on the children. Ye Filimonov believes, "Parents must be made to answer for any anti-social, religious education of the children in the family. This responsibility must be not only of a moral but also, if the interests of the state require it, of a legal nature."[64] Of course, these precautions will no longer be necessary in communist society, because by then every individual will believe that all religion is superstition, and every child will be raised by the community. These developments will follow naturally from the evolutionary progress of society and the family.

Conclusion

Marxist sociology perceives all social institutions as determined by the economic system (and, to some extent, the family type) on which the society is based. The economic system and the family are seen as in a process of constant development, and therefore the resultant societies are perceived as constantly evolving as well. This evolution occurs regardless of the actions of individuals—in fact, it often occurs in spite of their actions.

Marxists believe that the next step in this social and cultural

Notes and Asides

evolutionary process will be a world socialist system and that a new world order will emerge as a result of the changed means of production. This society will move toward abandoning religion and develop a proletarian system of education and family type. The Marxist sociologist is confident in this prediction, because he believes that Marx's approach to sociology is the most scientific.

Lenin himself, while outlining the basic principles of Marxist sociology, sums up Marxism's faith in the infallible nature of their approach:

> Just as Darwin put an end to the view of animal and plant species being unconnected, fortuitous, "created by God" and immutable, and was the first to put biology on an absolutely scientific basis by establishing the mutability and the succession of species, so Marx put an end to the view of society being a mechanical aggregation of individuals which allows of all sorts of modification at the will of the authorities (or, if you like, at the will of society and the government) and which emerges and changes casually, and was the first to put sociology on a scientific basis by establishing the concept of the economic formation of society as the sum-total of given production relations, by establishing the fact that the development of such formations is a process of natural history.[65]

[1]Karl Marx and Frederick Engels, *Collected Works*, forty volumes (New York: International, 1976), vol. 6, p. 502.
[2]Frederick Engels, *The Origin of the Family, Private Property and the State* (New York: International, 1942), p. 67.
[3]L. P. Bueva, *Man: His Behaviour and Social Relations* (Moscow: Progress, 1981), p. 112.
[4]Karl Marx, *On Historical Materialism* (New York: International, 1974), p. 165.
[5]Karl Marx and Frederick Engels, *The Individual and Society* (Moscow: Progress,1984), p. 162.
[6]Maurice Cornforth, *The Open Philosophy and the Open Society* (New York: International,1976), p. 165.
[7]V. I. Lenin, *Collected Works*, forty-five volumes (Moscow: Progress, 1977), vol. 1, p. 139.
[8]Cornforth, *The Open Philosophy and the Open Society*, p. 168.
[9]G. V. Plekhanov, *The Role of the Individual in History* (London: 1940), p. 200.
[10]Lenin, *Collected Works*, vol. 1, p. 165.
[11]Lenin, *Collected Works*, vol. 21, p. 57.
[12]Karl Marx and Frederick Engels, *The Individual and Society* (Moscow: Progress, 1984), p. 193.
[13]Ibid., p. 194.
[14]Ibid., p. 193.
[15]V. Yazykova, *Socialist Life Style and the Family* (Moscow: Progress, 1984), p. 7.
[16]Karl Marx and Frederick Engels, *The Communist Manifesto* (Chicago: Henry Regnery, 1965), p. 7.
[17]Cornforth, *The Open Philosophy and the Open Society*, p. 169.
[18]Ibid., p. 170.
[19]Gustav A. Wetter, *Dialectical Materialism* (Westport, CT: Greenwood Press, 1977), p. 107.
[20]Marx and Engels, *The Individual and Society*, p. 193.
[21]Marx and Engels, *Collected Works*, vol. 6, p. 501.
[22]Cornforth, *The Open Philosophy and the Open Society*, p. 166.
[23]Joseph Stalin, *Problems of Leninism* (Moscow: 1947), p. 579. Cited in Wetter, *Dialectical Materialism*, p. 217.
[24]Cornforth, *The Open Philosophy and the Open Society*, p. 171.
[25]Frederick Engels, *Ludwig Feuerbach* (New York: International, 1941), chapter 4. It is amazing how closely this notion parallels the capitalist notion (following Adam Smith, who coined the phrase) of the "invisible hand," the fact that the actual organization and fruits of productive activity necessarily differ significantly from the intentions of any individuals involved in it. Smith, however, founded his views on the assumptions of divine providence, human freedom, and consequent competition and complementarity of economic activity. Marx founded his notion on the absence of freedom. Nonetheless, Marxists criticize capitalism for substituting an "impersonal market" for the will of the free individual, never hinting in the process that what they substitute for personal freedom is an impersonal geographical and economic determinism allegedly manifested in the decrees of the Communist Party.
[26]L. N. Moskvichev, "The Formation of Sociological Theory," *Developments in Marxist Sociological Theory*, ed. A. G. Zdravomyslov (Beverly Hills, CA: Sage Publications, 1986), p. 49.
[27]Marx and Engels, *The Individual and Society*, pp. 217-18.
[28]Cornforth, *The Open Philosophy and the Open Society*, p. 171.
[29]Frederick Engels, *Socialism: Utopian and Scientific* (New York: International, 1935), p. 75.
[30]T. M. Jaroszewski and P. A. Ignatovsky, eds., *Socialism as a Social System* (Moscow: Progress, 1981), p. 22.
[31]Marx and Engels, *The Individual and Society*, p. 245.
[32]Ibid., p. 196.
[33]Ibid., p. 121.
[34]Georgi Shakhnazarov, *The Coming World Order* (Moscow: Progress, 1981), p. 161.
[35]Marx and Engels, *The Individual and Society*, p. 121.
[36]Jaroszewski and Ignatovsky, eds., *Socialism as a Social System*, p. 142.
[37]Marx and Engels, *The Individual and Society*, p. 245.
[38]*Program of the Communist International* (New York: Workers Library, 1936), pp. 31-2.
[39]Shakhnazarov, *The Coming World Order*, p. 273.
[40]V. I. Lenin, *The State and Revolution* (New York: International, 1932), p. 73.
[41]Lenin, *Collected Works*, vol. 35, p. 122.

[42]*Fundamentals of Marxism-Leninism* (Moscow: 1959), p. 310, cited in *A Lexicon of Marxist-Leninist Semantics*, ed. Raymond S. Sleeper (Alexandria, VA: Western Goals, 1983), p. 36.
[43]Marx and Engels, *The Individual and Society*, pp. 168-9.
[44]Robert Conquest, *The Harvest of Sorrow* (New York: Oxford University Press, 1986), p. 201.
[45]Ibid., pp. 202-3.
[46]Peter Babris, *Silent Churches* (Arlington Heights, IL: Research Publishers, 1978), p. 14. For another excellent non-Marxist critique of the Marxist attitude toward the church, see Kent R. Hill, *The Puzzle of the Soviet Church* (Portland, OR: Multnomah, 1989).
[47]A. Zhdanov, *Science and Religion* (Moscow: 1961), no. 9, cited in *A Lexicon of Marxist-Leninist Semantics*, ed. Sleeper, pp. 36-7.
[48]Madan Sarup, *Education, State and Crisis* (London: Routledge and Kegan Paul, 1982), p. 91.
[49]Unnamed students of Peking University, "Transform Schools into Instruments of Proletarian Dictatorship," *Peking Review*, March 12, 1976, p. 6.
[50]V. I. Lenin, *Selected Works* (New York: International, 1937), vol. 3, p. 6. Cited in *A Lexicon of Marxist-Leninist Semantics*, ed. Sleeper, p. 101.
[51]Pinkevich, *The Education in the Soviet Republic* (1929), pp. 29-30, cited in *A Lexicon of Marxist-Leninist Semantics*, ed. Sleeper, p. 102..
[52]"Communist Education," *Bolshevik* (Moscow), Dec. 1946, no. 23-24, pp. 16-17. Cited in *A Lexicon of Marxist-Leninist Semantics*, ed. Sleeper, p. 102.
[53]*People's Education* (Moscow), April 1949, cited in *A Lexicon of Marxist-Leninist Semantics*, ed. Sleeper, p. 101.
[54]Engels, *The Origin of the Family, Private Property and the State*, p. 66.
[55]Ibid., p. 5.
[56]Ibid., p. 58.
[57]Marx and Engels, *Collected Works*, vol. 6, p. 502.
[58]Ibid., p. 501.
[59]Aleksandra M. Kollontai, *Communism and the Family* (New York: 1920), p. 10. Cited in H. Kent Geiger, *The Family in Soviet Russia* (Cambridge: Harvard University Press, 1970), p. 51.
[60]Engels, *The Origin of the Family, Private Property and the State*, p. 67.
[61]Marx and Engels, *Collected Works*, vol. 6, p. 502.
[62]Ibid.
[63]Yazykova, *Socialist Life Style and the Family*, p. 202.
[64]Ye Filimonov,*Young Communist* (Moscow), October 1959, no. 10, cited in *A Lexicon of Marxist-Leninist Semantics*, ed. Sleeper, p. 102.
[65]Lenin, *Collected Works*, vol. 1, p. 142.

CHAPTER

20

BIBLICAL CHRISTIAN SOCIOLOGY

"For this reason a man will leave his father and mother and be united to his wife, and the two will become one flesh."

—Ephesians 5:31

"Nearly everyone knows . . . that the family is rooted in man's and woman's love of their own. And love of one's own is rooted in the exclusiveness of the sexual passion. A man's confidence in his wife's chastity is the foundation of their family. And the integrity of the family is the foundation of all human well-being in society."[1]

—Harry V. Jaffa

"Our ultimate objective in living must be the spiritual welfare of our sons and daughters. If we lose it there, we have lost everything. But isn't that just the point? The kind of sex education program now operating in America's schools is designed as a crash course in relativism, in immorality, and in anti-Christian philosophy. And it has been remarkably successful in recasting the social order."[2]

—James Dobson and Gary Bauer

SUMMARY

Christian sociology is based on the proposition that both the individual and the social order are important to God, mankind, and society. Proper perspective requires neither emphasizing the influence of society too strongly, nor denying the importance of the individual. Christ died and rose again for each person as an individual; God also ordained social institutions to teach love, respect, discipline, work, and community.

Marxism and Humanism make the mistake of treating the community as ultimate reality. Both of these worldviews believe that society determines man's desires and actions; therefore they conclude that society must be changed before the individual can change in any meaningful way. The Marxist takes the more extreme position, believing that the creation of a communist society takes precedence over human rights. Humanists also place their faith in the creation of a world social order. The Christian denies this unbalanced attitude, realizing that a successful community cannot be based on morally bankrupt individuals. "Societies are tragically vulnerable," says Charles Colson, "when the men and women who compose them lack character. A nation or a culture cannot endure for long unless it is undergirded by common values. . . ."[3] Thus, Christian sociology focuses both on society as a means for human cooperation in accordance with God's will, and on the individual as a vital part of various social institutions in society.

Christian sociologists believe that certain social institutions are ordained by God. Family, church, and state are three of the most important. Both the family and the church were intended by God to provide moral and spiritual nurture and the transmission of values for the individual and society. The state was ordained by God primarily to protect the innocent and punish the guilty. These institutions must remain

Introduction

Every sociologist, whether Marxist, Humanist, or Christian, acknowledges the existence of certain social institutions (such as family, church, and government) in society. However, sociologists differ in opinion when describing the origin of these institutions and their relationship to the individual. This difference results from the assumptions inherent to the sociologist's worldview. "Sociology rests upon certain crucial but ultimately 'unprovable' assumptions," says David Lyon, "which are rooted in world views (such as the place of humans in the natural world)."[4]

relatively stable, thus providing the individual with an understanding of the commitment required for long-lasting human relationships. In addition, the church must provide believers in the Lord Jesus Christ with an opportunity to worship, to receive instruction, and to enjoy fellowship with other believers. "But if we walk in the light, as [God] is in the light, we have fellowship with one another . . ." (1 John 1:7).

Christians strive to influence society with Christian principles, ideals, and love, realizing that the more the home, church, and state reflect such principles, the better for society. Unfortunately, the opposite is also true: the more society strays from Christian principles, the less healthy it becomes. "When the righteous rule," says the Bible, "the people rejoice; when the wicked rule, the people mourn" (Proverbs 29:2). Christian men and women are responsible for influencing the moral character of society; contrary to the Humanist and Marxist belief that society is responsible for the character of its members.

Understanding that mankind cannot blame his evil actions on his environment, man must take responsibility for his actions. The Christian does not hold any illusions about the goodness of man. He recognizes man's sinful nature and understands that a perfect, utopian society can never be wrought by man. Instead, the Christian labors to maintain a relatively workable, peaceful, just society that minimizes man's propensity toward evil, and he looks forward to the day when he will reign with the Lord Jesus Christ over a new social order where "He will wipe every tear from their eyes. There will be no more death or mourning or crying or pain, for the old order of things has passed away" (Revelation 21:4).

Obviously, the Christian sees man's place in the world from a different perspective than that of the Humanist or the Marxist. The Christian views mankind as specially created in God's image, while atheistic worldviews see man as simply an emerging animal. Unfortunately, this latter view is the predominant perspective among modern sociologists. God, Adam and Eve, the Garden of Eden, and the sacred character of the family are considered prescientific myths. Christians believe that this erroneous view of man is largely responsible for the many failures in modern sociology (e.g., its inability to suggest proper solutions to drug abuse, crime, poverty, etc.).

The reason for this failure, according to the Christian sociologist, is

Notes and Asides

that most modern sociologists approach their discipline with the inherent assumption that God does not exist and Christianity is a fairy tale. Obviously, if Christianity is true, modern Humanist and Marxist sociologists are developing a social science based on a foundation of shifting sand. S. D. Gaede writes, "the irrelevance of God [for most sociologists] implied that the data (humanity) could be studied apart from any notion of transcendent connections. Thus, the human sciences assumed that the human being was an autonomous 'thing,' unaffected by the influences of a Creator. Such an assumption is not only incorrect from a Christian perspective, but it has also reaped a whirlwind of reductionist methodology."[5] That is, one of the foundational assumptions of an atheistic sociology is that everything is reducible to materialistic explanations—for example, love is reduced to no more than the firing of chemical synapses in the brain.

The Christian sociologist, however, bases his approach to the discipline on the assumption that man has been given special revelation in the form of the Bible and that this revelation affirms the existence of the supernatural, including a triune God. Thus, the Humanist and Marxist sociology is seen as ignorant of God's existence and plan and therefore based on untenable assumptions. This faulty atheistic and evolutionary basis for most of modern sociology destines it to fail.

When Sociology Ignores God

The Christian sociologist views modern sociology and social theory as a failure because it does not allow for the existence of God. The atheistic sociologist's decision to ignore God has many ramifications for his approach to the discipline. First, it causes him to have incorrect ideas about the nature of relationships. It is man, because of his sinful nature, that disrupts society, not society that disrupts man.

This leads to a still worse error on the part of most modern sociologists, according to Gaede:

> [M]ost tragically, the irrelevance of God in the human sciences has set up unnecessary competition between the interpretations of social science and those of the church. Because the objective scientist is compelled to understand aspects of the human condition as if God is irrelevant, traditional insights into the human condition are assumed to be less than scientific (and probably wrong).[6]

And yet, these traditional insights about the home, sinful man, etc., may be entirely in step with the actual workings of the world.

Notes and Asides

However, by ignoring the Bible and tradition as possible sources of wisdom, the secular sociologist abandons any chance of using the most practical approach to his discipline. Instead, he fights an uphill battle all his life, refusing to accept the world as it was created. The atheistic sociologist's plight is spelled out by Rockne McCarthy, Donald Oppewal, Walfred Peterson, and Gordon Spykman in their book *Society, State, and Schools*:

> Biblical religion offers the most practical way of life in the world. It alone conforms to actual experience. That is, as men seek consciously to order their life relationships in keeping with divinely established norms, they experience a certain affinity with the very nature of things. Antinormative ways of structuring society run into resistance. They create anomalies, injustices, inequities. They tend to become self-serving, and in the end self-defeating and self-destructive, because they work at cross purposes with the built-in meaning of life. Biblical religion aims rather to keep the structures *of* society in line with the structures *for* society, and within that framework to work out the functions of a Biblically structured society.[7]

Sociology apart from the Bible is viewed by the Christian as "self-destructive," leading in one of two possible, and equally futile, directions. "In the absence of biblical norms to guide the relationship between humanity and God," declares Gaede, "we can expect knowledge of ultimate reality to move in either a fatalistic or humanistic direction."[8] The futility of these two possibilities tears at society, according to Francis Schaeffer: "As the Jews of Jeremiah's day were hungry for bread and had no comforter, our post-Christian world is hungry in state and society and in the individual longings of the heart, for it too has turned in our own day from the only sufficient Comforter."[9] The Christian sees denial of God as a problem that can ruin not just individuals but whole societies. "The point, of course," writes Gaede, "is that denial in the ultimate context is not simply a personal problem, of concern only to God and the individual sinner. It is a problem that affects whole societies, having an impact on the way the people live, think, and worship."[10]

This denial of Christian truth by Humanist and Marxist sociologists can eventually affect whole societies, which is exactly what the Humanist and Marxist sociologist would like to accomplish. As demonstrated in the respective sociology and psychology chapters, these atheistic worldviews believe society and its institutions are evil and must be changed so that man can perfect his inherent goodness. Thus, Humanist and Marxist sociologists strive to change society (by elimi-

Haiti – a nation dedicated to Satan will not flourish

Notes and Asides

nating capitalism, promoting ethical relativism in the public schools, down playing the role of the family, promoting the sexual revolution, neutralizing the church, etc.) in an effort to free the individual from the constraints of Christian institutions in order to lead him toward an end more in keeping with his evolving, perfectible nature. The Christian sociologist, however, sees this as an improper view of man's place in the world. "There are two basic ways to improve human life," declares William A. Stanmeyer, "change the environment, which presumably makes people better, or change people and they will make their environment better. Secular humanists try to change the environment; Christians must change people's hearts. Those who would change externals can rely upon their own powers and abilities; those who would change men's hearts must rely only on God, for to rely on human skills would be to misconceive the essence of man's problem and make it worse than before."[11]

The Christian sociologist sees unbiblical sociology as making man's problem "worse than before" by ignoring the individual's crucial relationship to God. While the Humanist and the Marxist perceive man as perfectible, the Christian believes that man is a fallen creature. These differing perspectives create vastly different approaches to the study of society or the social order.

Free Will and Society

One of the fundamental ways in which Christian sociology differs from the Humanist and Marxist approaches is Christianity's affirmation of individual free will and individual responsibility. While the atheistic approaches believe that society almost entirely determines man's consciousness and actions, Christianity describes man as a creature with the freedom to choose between right and wrong and capable of shaping his own society (rather than passively being shaped by society).

"While it might be painful," says Brendan Furnish, "by a resolute act of the will we can free ourselves from past patterns of behavior. Thus, there is the possibility of choice and hence the idea of free will remains a viable concept."[12] Stanmeyer says much the same thing:

> Christianity, then, insists on human free will. It insists that humans are capable of good however bad the environment, and equally capable of evil however good the environment—witness Adam and Eve! Indeed, the Christian knows that "evil" and "good" are never matters of environment, but are always matters of the inner human heart.[13]

Notes and Asides

Recommended Reading for Advanced Study

S. D. Gaede, *Where Gods May Dwell* (Grand Rapids, MI: Zondervan, 1985).

James C. Dobson and Gary L. Bauer, *Children at Risk* (Dallas, TX: Word, 1990).

George Gilder, *Men and Marriage* (Gretna, LA: Pelican, 1986).

Rockne McCarthy, et al., *Society, State, and Schools* (Grand Rapids, MI: Eerdmans, 1982).

William Stanmeyer, *Clear and Present Danger* (Ann Arbor, MI: Servant, 1983).

Indeed, the Christian sociologist believes, as Schaeffer claims, that "Determinism leads in the direction of cruelty and inhumanity. . . ."[14]

The Christian view grants individual man much more control over his society, but it also burdens him with much more responsibility. Man, in the Christian perspective, must face the consequences of his decisions. Gaede says that "the fact that God established a volitional relationship with human beings does not mean that human beings were allowed to operate willy-nilly as they chose, without regard to God's purposes. It is clear that with the ability to choose came the necessity of living with the consequences of choices made."[15]

Indeed, this point is made painfully clear in the opening chapters of Genesis, when Adam and Eve bring a curse on the whole human race and are exiled from the Garden of Eden, all because they choose to disobey God. "Another political truth implicit in Christian belief," says Stanmeyer, "is that *man is a free and responsible moral agent.* If man's behavior were somehow conditioned by genetic code or social externals, then no just judge could blame him for the evil he commits. But

Notes and Asides

the scripture teaches unequivocally that God blamed Adam and Eve for succumbing to the temptation to disobedience and punished them accordingly."[16] Schaeffer agrees: "the Bible's emphasis is that man is responsible; his choices influence history."[17]

The Genesis account of Adam and Eve not only demonstrates that man is responsible for his actions, but also describes another key belief for Christians: every human is guilty. Rousas John Rushdoony writes, "The fact of *guilt* is one of the major realities of man's existence. Both personally and socially, it is a vast drain on human energies and a mainspring of human action. Any attempt at assessing either political action or religious faith apart from the fact of guilt is thus an exercise in futility."[18]

Christian sociology attempts to understand society in light of man's free will and the consequences of his freely choosing to turn from God. The Fall caused every society created by man to be marked by alienation. "We are what we are because we have broken away from God's will," writes Robert E. Webber. "And the history of culture, as well as the turmoil of our own times, witnesses to our alienation."[19] To put it bluntly, ever since God gave man free will and the ability to create his own societies, man's record has been one of degeneration, not evolution. History is replete with broken civilizations and societies. The alienation caused by man pervades all relationships. Webber declares,

> Man's break from the will of God is reflected, not only in a broken relationship with God, but also in the perverted relationship that now exists between man and his fellow man and between man and nature, as well as in an inner break that man has made with his original self. Consequently, the variance of man with the whole of his existence finds acute expression in the unfolding of culture.[20]

Obviously, man's alienation from God, the rest of mankind, and himself plays a crucial role in the Christian approach to sociology. A sociologist who believes that man is alienated will interpret data differently from one who believes that man is inherently good but corrupted by society.

It would seem, at this point, that the Christian sociologist is the most pessimistic of all sociologists, since he perceives man as constantly making the wrong decisions. In reality, however, God's saving grace prevents Christian sociology from wallowing in despair—indeed, God makes the Christian position the most optimistic of all. Webber sums up the Christian sociologist's over-all view:

Notes and Asides

> Here the transcendent God creates man and gives him a cultural responsibility—the care of the earth [Genesis 1:28]. But man, rebelling against God and His will, continually seeks to make himself and his own desires central to life. This desire results in confusion, chaos, disorder, and finally judgment. Nevertheless, God is always at work in history, pointing beyond man's disastrous unfolding to new possibilities.[21]

At this point, we have examined three of the principal aspects that set Christian sociology apart from other sociologies, namely: Christianity's view of God at work in society; its insistence on a free will; and its belief in the alienation of man and society as a consequence of man's choosing. These unique aspects can be summed up in two simple statements: Thomas Howard's contention that "there is no Christian view of man in society that omits the notion of sin,"[22] and Schaeffer's claim that "man is not a cog in a machine; he is not a piece of theater; he really can influence history. From the biblical viewpoint, *man is lost, but great*."[23]

Schaeffer's statement also highlights a fourth principle of Christian sociology that sets it apart from the Humanist and Marxist approaches. The Christian perspective believes that every individual is valuable and is capable of making an important contribution to society. While other sociologists view the individual as basically helpless in the face of societal pressures, the Christian sees every individual as free and therefore capable of influencing society. Indeed, to the Christian, the individual is more important than any institution or society. George A. Hillery, Jr., shows this to be Biblically sound: "In the parable of the *Lost Sheep*, Jesus attests to the supremacy of the individual over any 'cause' (Matthew 18:12-14)."[24]

C. S. Lewis also drives this point home by observing that atheists think "nations, classes, civilizations must be more important than individuals," because "the individuals live only seventy odd years each and the group may last for centuries. But to the Christian, individuals are more important, for they live eternally; and races, civilizations and the like, are in comparison the creatures of a day."[25] Elsewhere he tells us,

> "[T]o the Christian, individuals are more important, for they live eternally; and races, civilizations and the like, are in comparison the creatures of a day."
> —C. S. Lewis

> You have never talked to a mere mortal. Nations, cultures, arts, civilization—these are mortal, and their life is to ours as the life of a gnat. But it is immortals whom we joke with, work with, marry, snub, and exploit—immortal horrors or everlasting splendours.[26]

Notes and Asides

Man as a Social Being

The fact that Christians value the individual over the social order, however, does not diminish the importance of sociology in a Christian worldview. The Christian understands that society plays a key role in the history of mankind and the individual's relationship with God. Above all, he recognizes that man was created a social being (Genesis 2:20f).

Gaede stresses the inherent social nature of man, stating,

> The first biblical insight we must come to grips with if we are to pursue an alternative social science is this: God created the human as a *social* being. God designed the human being to be a relational creature. Note this point well. Humankind was created to relate to other beings. It was not an accident. It was not the result of sin. It was an intentional, creational given.[27]

Webber believes much the same thing, claiming "man's cultural responsibility is rooted in the will of God. Man is divinely commissioned to function in culture. To do God's will requires something more than a narrowly conceived personal morality."[28] Howard also agrees: "We cannot live alone. We are social creatures. We need society. Our very attempts to design cities bear witness to this. From the Christian point of view, this is enormously significant. The fountainhead of human life is to be found in the mystery of the Holy Trinity where we find God existing, we are told, not in solitude, but in what can only be called fellowship, or society."[29]

"So God created man in his own image, in the image of God he created him; male and female he created them."
—Genesis 1:27

Of course, the fellowship of the Trinity is perfect, whereas, as a result of the Fall, mankind's relations in this life will always be hindered by feelings of alienation. Gaede believes that because of the Fall "we find ourselves estranged and alienated. This means that our essential need for relationships is to a large degree thwarted. The Fall left us incomplete and unfulfilled. It left us with an aching need to be related but without the knowledge or tools to fully satisfy that need. Moreover, as we will see, it put humanity on a desperate journey to satisfy this relational void."[30] Gaede refers to this problem as the "relational dilemma" and views it as truth that must be recognized by all sociologists who wish to understand society in the proper perspective. For Christian sociologists, this truth should be obvious. "It is my conviction," says Gaede, "that the relational dilemma provides a context for a Christian understanding of social life."[31] In this context, Christians recognize the true cause of alienation in society and can competently study the results and offer a solution to the world.

Man's alienation and imperfection do not disqualify him from

Notes and Asides

sociological discourse. Rather, the Christian's understanding of man's true social creaturehood makes him the most qualified to study man in society. "More specifically," says Lyon, "a Christian perspective in sociology is founded upon a biblical understanding of human sociality. The key assumption is that, because our Maker has told us about himself and ourselves, disclosing his mind to us through a book, that here is the basis for a truly human outlook on the world. As the image of God, people are social creatures, and what the Scriptures tell us about this aspect of our lives pertains directly to the kinds of issues raised in sociological discourse."[32]

Christian Pluralism

Christian sociologists maintain that the individual is more important than any institution in society, and society is important because man was created a social being. This sociological perspective is referred to as a pluralist view, because the sociologist does not perceive society or the individual as the only true reality. The view that society exclusively shapes reality is called collectivism; the view that only individuals can change reality is called individualism.

Pluralism refers to the belief that proper sociology must value both society and the individual in order to achieve an understanding of reality.

Both the Humanist and the Marxist approach sociology from the collectivist perspective. That is, because these worldviews hold that man is inherently good but is caused by society to either deny or embrace his goodness, they perceive society as creating reality and the individual as helpless and insignificant. McCarthy, et al., point out the flaws in collectivism:

> From a pluralist perspective, collectivism also represents a misdirected manifestation of social life. By all means, community is very important, as are human solidarity and enough sense of unity to allow society to function efficiently. But the whole, like the individual, can never itself be the all-important, all-enveloping standard for the rest of life. . . . It tends to make one institution a megastructure and to give it a messianic, trans-historical status, a status which the Judeo-Christian tradition reserves for the Kingdom of God alone. No earthly institution may thus be absolutized or divinized.[33]

Likewise, the Christian sociologist rejects the notion that only the individual is significant. McCarthy, et al., believe that

> individualism represents a serious compromise of the Biblical view of reality. It is Christian in the sense that it takes man

Notes and Asides

> seriously, as Christianity does, viewing man as the image of God. But it is nonetheless a compromise. It takes individual man too seriously, ascribing to him an independence and autonomy which obscures his position of creaturely dependence.[34]

The Apostle Paul clearly states, "For none of us lives to himself alone" (Romans 14:7). And long before Paul we were told, "The Lord God said, 'It is not good for the man to be alone'" (Genesis 2:18).

The proper perspective for the Christian sociologist is a pluralist view of man and society. This perspective ensures that man "can never be reduced to either a mere atomistic individual or a mere integer in some social whole."[35] It also holds both man and society accountable to God. Stanmeyer explains:

> The public order is man living communally. Put another way, each of us as individuals has his or her "public side"; through tradition, custom, mores, and law we share a community life. This life should honor God even as our private life should honor him. This means this public life should, at a minimum, not draw us away from the Lord, should not make it harder to save our individual souls, should not collectively dishonor God.[36]

Thus, the Christian pluralist view does not allow any individual or aspect of society the luxury of not being responsible for its decisions or foundations. Both society and the individual must answer to God (2 Kings 17:7f; Acts 17:31).

"Individualism is a fatal poison. But individuality is the salt of common life. You may have to live in a crowd, but you do not have to live like it, nor subsist on its food."
—Henry van Dyke

By making every member and aspect of society responsible, the Christian sociologist naturally expects each institution in society to focus on governing its own realm of interests properly and to allow other institutions the same freedom. That is, since the family is responsible for governing the family, it must make the appropriate decisions and face the consequences of those decisions rather than expecting the state or the church to make the decisions, thereby alleviating the family's responsibility. McCarthy, et al., simplify: "Concretely this means, for example, that worship belongs to the church, and not the state or business corporations; parenting belongs to the family, and not to the school or a labor association."[37]

Expanding on this concept, the Christian sociologist believes that interference between institutions must be minimized. Rushdoony describes the importance of such a position with regard to the state and the church:

> The state is an important institution, an indispensable and God-ordained institution, but it is not creative, nor is it productive.

Notes and Asides

> Only as the state is limited to its proper jurisdiction (and the same is true of the church), can society be free and productive. Art, science, church, school, family, business, agriculture, everything can then function freely in order that man might fulfill his calling under God. The state cannot give meaning or function; it must itself derive meaning and direction from a free society under God, one able to realize itself in terms of its image mandate. If the state assumes authority and jurisdiction in the various realms, it chokes off their true development. . . .[38]

This development is hindered whenever the state (or church) limits various institutions' responsibilities by constant interference.

From the Christian sociologist's perspective, institutions and all other aspects of society are also answerable to God and, therefore, must govern wisely and responsibly. Indeed, the Christian sociologist believes that all legitimate institutions in society are specifically ordained by God.

Biblically Prescribed Institutions

"God has established," says Gary North, "three institutional monopolies: family, church, and state. Each of these is a God-ordained government. Each of these is a covenant. . . . Each of these three governments is to protect the other, and each deserves protection from the other."[39] Note that North calls for protection, not interference—while none of these institutions should be allowed to become extinct, neither should one be swallowed by another.

The Christian sociologist agrees with North's assertion that family, church, and state are institutions ordained by God. Some Christians, however, believe that God ordained more than just these three. McCarthy, et al., would add work and education to the list, stating,

> Among the original nuclear tasks that we can perceive dimly and from a distance in the Genesis narratives are the following: marrying (cf. Matthew 19:3-9), family living (Adam, Eve, Cain, Abel, and Seth), working (tilling the soil), learning (naming creatures after their kind), governing (guarding the garden), and worshiping (walking with God in the cool of the day). Each task has its own identity and integrity; one is not reducible to another. Each has its own right of existence and reason for existence. This truth is captured in the idea of sphere sovereignty—namely, that each of these spheres of social activity has an inalienable authority and sovereignty of its own.[40]

Notes and Asides

Gene Garrick also adds work to the list of God-ordained institutions. He writes, "For example, understanding that God works (John 5:17) and created His image, man, to work enables the student to develop a positive attitude toward work as a privilege and a service to others. He is responsible not only because he and his family must be provided for, but because he has this mandate from God Himself (Genesis 2:15). Work should have the purposeful end of serving others and should be done as 'unto the Lord' (Ephesians 6:5-8; 1 Corinthians 10:31)."[41]

Dietrich Bonhoeffer casts still another vote for labor alongside family, state, and church as specifically established by God. He goes on to cite these institutions as demonstrative of the fact that man can never truly separate himself from the spiritual realm: "the world is relative to

CLOSE-UP

Dietrich Bonhoeffer (1906-1945)

German theologian Dietrich Bonhoeffer provided the world with an excellent example of the courage of a man who fears God. As a Christian pastor, Bonhoeffer recognized the inherent evil of Nazism even in its early stages, and understood that he must honor God by working with the anti-Nazi movement. When Adolf Hitler gained power in 1933, Bonhoeffer helped organize the Pastors' Emergency League, which was in the forefront of the resistance. In 1935, he founded an underground seminary to teach pastors involved in the anti-Nazi movement. Convinced that his faith required radical action, he became involved in a plot to assassinate Hitler. Bonhoeffer was arrested for his tireless crusade against Nazism in 1943, and he spent the last two years of his life in prison camps, faced every day with the possibility of execution. In spite of his dire surroundings, he continued to write powerful, Christ-centered works which were later published under the title *Letters and Papers from Prison.* Other important books by Bonhoeffer include *Ethics* and *The Cost of Discipleship.* On April 8, 1945, the day before he was hanged, Bonhoeffer sent a final message to a friend: " . . . This is the end, but for me, it is the beginning."

Notes and Asides

Christ, no matter whether it knows it or not. This relativeness of the world to Christ assumes concrete form in certain mandates of God in the world. The Scriptures name four such mandates: labour, marriage, government, and church. . . . It is God's will that there shall be labour, marriage, government, and church in the world; and it is His will that all these, each in its own way, shall be through Christ, directed towards Christ, and in Christ. . . . This means that there can be no retreating from a 'secular' into a 'spiritual' sphere."[42]

This is what even many christians try to do.

This concept is an important one for the Christian sociologist (indeed, for all Christians) to grasp. After examining a list of the social institutions Christians perceive as ordained by God, one might get the impression that some aspects of society are outside the realm of Christianity. This, however, is not the case. All of society, indeed, all of life, is bound up inextricably with God and His plan for mankind—as Bonhoeffer says, "the world is relative to Christ." Arnold Burron and John Eidsmoe state the case this way: "The modern distinction between the sacred and the secular has no basis in Scripture or in Judeo-Christian tradition. The Apostle Paul clearly says that every thought is to be brought into captivity to Christ (2 Corinthians 10:5)."[43]

Thus, it is unimportant whether the Christian sociologist believes there are three, four, or five societal institutions ordained by God. The crucial point for the Christian sociologist to understand is that every institution is answerable to God—for the Christian, every aspect of life is spiritual. Thus, God's commands in the Bible apply to every facet of society and man. McCarthy, et al., provide an example for the sociologist:

> The most comprehensive Word of God is that which covers the entire range of our life relationships: "Love your neighbors as yourself." That universal command, which is central to God's Word, takes on specific form in the directives given for the various spheres in society: a Word of fidelity for families, of justice for the state, of proclamation for churches, and of learning for schools. Social structures therefore find their ordered beginnings and their legitimate existence in the creative acts of God. The social order is not an autonomously functioning reality or an artificial creation of sovereign people. It is a functioning order dependent upon and answerable to the sovereign will of the Creator.[44]

And because social structures are answerable to God, His moral order is as applicable for them as for individuals.

In the remainder of this chapter, we will focus on the Christian view of two social institutions: the family and the church. The state is

Notes and Asides

examined in the chapter on Christian politics, labor under the chapter on Christian economics. We will discuss education only in the context of the family, since a strong case can be built for the belief that responsibility for educating children is inextricably tied to the family (see Proverbs 22:6).

The significance of the church and the family for the modern Christian cannot be overstated. In a very real sense, these are the only institutions that have not been completely overthrown by Marxist and Humanist values. Dobson and Bauer declare,

> The humanistic system of values has now become the predominant way of thinking in most of the power centers of society. It has outstripped Judeo-Christian precepts in the universities, in the news media, in the entertainment industry, in the judiciary, in the federal bureaucracy, in business, medicine, law, psychology, sociology, in the arts, in many public schools and, to be sure, in the halls of Congress. Indeed, the resources available to secular humanists throughout society are almost unlimited in scope, and they are breaking new ground almost every day.[45]

Thus, the Christian must view the family and the church with renewed appreciation, understanding that these institutions are the most powerful vehicles for effecting constructive changes in society.

Marriage and the Family

For the Christian, marriage and the family are ordained by God (Genesis 2:23-25) and will always be the fundamental institution of society. As the family goes, so goes society. The Christian believes that the family and its role are strictly defined in the Bible; as Dobson and Bauer say, the family exists when "husband and wife are lawfully married, are committed to each other for life, and [the family] adheres to the traditional values on which the family is based."[46] The Biblical definition of family excludes "trial marriages" and living together. Thus, J. Howard Kauffman writes, "Both the Old and the New Testament take the view that marriage is ordained of God and that it is a lifetime commitment (Genesis 2:24; Matthew 19:4-6; Romans 7:2)."[47] And Ray Sutton declares that "the family is a sacred covenant, more than a contract. The powerful effect is that God is the author."[48]

George Gilder believes, as do many Christian sociologists, that the condition of marriage and family in any given society describes the condition of the entire society. If the family is troubled, so is society.

Notes and Asides

> As a social institution, marriage transcends all individuals. The health of a society, its collective vitality, ultimately resides in its concern for the future, its sense of a connection with generations to come. There is perhaps no more important index of the social condition. It is the very temperature of a community. A community preoccupied with the present, obsessed with an immediate threat or pleasure, is enfevered.[49]

It is to society's advantage to build and encourage the God-ordained social institution of marriage and the family.

Unfortunately, from the Christian perspective, modern American society does more to discourage marriage and family than to build it up. This disdain for marriage and the family stems largely from the popularity of the Secular Humanist perspective—especially regarding the sexual revolution.[50] Even as you read this, public school children in sex-education courses are being subjected to some of the most bizarre concepts and practices imaginable. Not only is homosexuality being taught as a normal lifestyle (and a means of fighting AIDS), and not only are students given condoms and advised to practice their usage, but also teenage girls are being encouraged to have abortions without parental knowledge or consent. As Dobson and Bauer note, such sex-ed programs are "a crash course in relativism, in immorality, and in anti-Christian philosophy."[51]

> "Round the family do indeed gather the sanctities that separate men from ants and bees. . . . In the practical proportions of human history, we come back to that fundamental of the father and the mother and the child."
>
> —G. K. Chesterton

Educators justify such attacks on the Biblical model of the family by pointing to studies that declare that "the traditional family is dead" and that "less than 10 percent of America's families are traditional." But as Dobson and Bauer point out, this is a contrived argument.[52] Such studies define the traditional family in such a way as to assure the conclusion that the family is withering away. These studies define the "traditional family" as father at work, mother at home with two children in the family. According to such a narrow definition, a family where the father works and the mother stays at home but there is only one child is considered "non-traditional." Such a manipulation of statistics helps justify Humanistic sex-education and makes it easier to sell "non-traditional" marriages (including homosexual unions) and government-sponsored child care services, but it is clearly dishonest.

Attacks on the Christian family unit and its values are all too common. Most feminists, for example, are hostile toward the Biblical concept of family. The November 1971 *Declaration of Feminism* stated,

> Marriage has existed for the benefit of men; and has been a legally sanctioned method of control over women. . . . We must

Notes and Asides

> work to destroy it. The end of the institution of marriage is a necessary condition for the liberation of women. Therefore it is important for us to encourage women to leave their husbands and not to live individually with men. . . . All of history must be re-written in terms of oppression of women. We must go back to ancient female religions like witchcraft.[53]

"Humanism and feminism," says leading Humanist Paul Kurtz, "are inextricably interwoven,"[54] and Humanist Annie Laurie Gaylor adds, "Let's forget about the mythical Jesus and look for encouragement, solace, and inspiration from real women. . . . Two thousand years of patriarchal rule under the shadow of the cross ought to be enough to turn women toward the feminist 'salvation' of this world."[55]

Why this apparent hatred for the traditional family? Because, as Phyllis Schlafly says, the ideology of women's liberation teaches a woman "to rank her own self-fulfillment above every other value including solemn promises, husband, and children."[56] Not only is this a flagrant distortion of priorities, pushed on women by relativistic worldviews, but also it misleads women by making them think they will find more "self-fulfillment" outside of marriage and childrearing. Sadly, many do not discover the deception until they are beyond their childbearing years.

It is not coincidental that these attacks on the traditional family come largely from proponents of relativistic, materialistic worldviews. Indeed, the Christian expects such persecution from views in rebellion against God. Because such persecution exists, however, the Christian must be extremely careful to recognize and avoid all the lies propagated by materialism. While the Humanist and the Marxist disregard the existence of the spirit and the soul and thereby devalue the family's importance for mankind, the Christian recognizes marriage and the family as the institution that nurtures the whole individual. The family should provide an environment that encourages both mental and spiritual growth.

Many Christians believe that the family's role as nurturer of the whole individual includes the responsibility of education. "The family is the basic unit of Christian education," says David L. Hocking. "Of course, the Bible is quite clear on this matter (Proverbs 22:6) and continually stresses the responsibility of the parents (especially the father) to teach and train their children. When our philosophy of education causes us to take that role and responsibility away from the parents, we are definitely in violation of the plain teaching of God's Word."[57] Too often nowadays, the responsibility for children's education rests squarely on the shoulders of the state. From a Christian perspective, the state is overstepping its God-ordained institutional

Notes and Asides

boundaries whenever it becomes responsible for the whole education of the child. Stanmeyer writes,

> The state in modern times wants to resemble the church in medieval times; it would become the basic institutional educator. . . . It does not recognize the fact that God has given the children to their parents and charged parents with the duty to raise the children in his ways.[58]

Not all Christian sociologists would agree that education is the sole responsibility of the family—some view education as an institution distinct from both state and family. The point, however, is that all Christian sociologists recognize the state's constant interference in education as unnecessary, and they understand that most parents do not invest enough time in educating their children.

This need for all institutions of society to take responsibility for their own realms and to avoid interfering with (while continually protecting) other institutions cannot be over-emphasized. "Any time

Used by permission of the *Colorado Springs Sun*

Notes and Asides

you try to argue that someone, or some 'institution,' owns the family," says Sutton, "you will end up viewing the family as just a human creation, a mere contract. If that's all it is, then there's no reason for the State not to violate it, just as it violates all sorts of private contracts. What principle is to prevent the State from taking a family's children, re-educating them, or breaking it up whenever it seems socially or politically expedient?"[59] Clearly, from the Christian perspective, the break-up of the family would be disastrous. As a God-ordained institution, the family must be given sovereignty within its realm and prepared to face the consequences of its decisions. A society without such a family structure denies the total man.

Sex Standards and Family

A society that denies the reality of total man (body, soul, and spirit) cannot help but undermine the Christian family structure. Today, our society encourages sexual permissiveness. Magazines, books, and television programs often stress sex outside of marriage and other deviances from Biblical morality masquerading as "sexual orientation." The Christian sociologist, recognizing the threat such deviance poses for the traditional family, calls for a return to sexual sanity in the form of monogamous heterosexual marriage.

Any other sexual relations are damaging to both men and women, and in the long run to the institutions of marriage and the family. Thus, Joseph Story writes, "If marriage be an institution derived from the law of nature, then, whatever has a natural tendency to discourage it, or to destroy its value, is by the same law prohibited. Hence we may deduce the criminality of fornication, incest, adultery, seduction, and other lewdness. . . ."[60] For the Christian, any deviance from the model of faithful sexuality in marriage is strictly prohibited.

This includes homosexuality. Gilder writes, "Because psychologists cannot explain homosexuality, they discuss it in terms of sickness or mystery. But homosexuality is merely the most vivid and dramatic manifestation of the breakdown of monogamy—an extreme expression of the sexuality of single man."[61] Homosexuality is a physically and spiritually unhealthy manifestation of sexuality that corrupts the total man and wears away at monogamous marriage. The Christian sociologist views homosexuality and all other deviations from faithful monogamous marriage as dangerous to the institutions of family and marriage and, therefore, to society as a whole.[62]

This appears to be a very narrow view of sexuality. But it is really the only view that respects the individual. Kauffman explains the Christian position this way:

CLOSE-UP

George Gilder (1939-)

George Gilder is perhaps the most popular of all American supply-side economists, and a leading Christian sociologist as well. In his early years, he seemed to lack direction—flunking out of Harvard in 1958 and then spending a year in the Marine Corps Reserve, only to return to Harvard—but he managed to graduate in 1962 and rapidly set out making his mark. He worked as a speechwriter for a number of Republicans including Richard Nixon, and then in 1973 published his first important work, *Sexual Suicide*. Gilder later expanded this book and re-titled it *Men and Marriage*, which stands today as a significant apologetic for the Christian model of the family. In 1981, Gilder published his most popular work, *Wealth and Poverty*, in which he stresses the fact that free markets encourage the creation of wealth. Both *Men and Marriage* and *Wealth and Poverty* are significant contributions to the literature of Biblical Christianity's worldview.

> What shall we say, in conclusion, regarding the moral codes that undergird faithful monogamous marriage? Were they established merely to restrict human sexual freedom, or to prevent people from enjoying sex? It may appear so to some. But would removing the moral codes really bring greater happiness and well-being to mankind in the long run? Definitely not. We would not make driving on the highways more pleasant by abandoning traffic laws. Freedom from traffic rules would bring bondage to fear, anxiety, and insecurities in traveling.[63]

The Christian sociologist views faithful monogamous male/female marriage as the only sexual option outside of celibacy and understands the importance of a proper view of sex for the physical and spiritual health of mankind. He also understands that marriage and family must encourage the growth of the whole person, or these institutions will lose their proper place in society, and their collapse will eventually undermine the social structure.

Notes and Asides

The Church in Society

Like all God-ordained institutions, the church and the family often may be integrated. For example, Sutton believes, "The first thing you need to do with your family is join a good Church, and submit your family to the discipline of worship."[64] This does not mean that the church and the family may interfere with each other whenever they please. It simply means that the God who created the family created man in such a way that His families should desire to worship Him.

God also ordained the church to serve specific functions. In order to serve these functions best, the church must never become so obsessed with structure that it forgets the basic message of Christ. "There is a place for the church until Jesus comes," says Schaeffer, "But there must be the balance of form and freedom in regard to the polity and the practicing community within that church. And there must be a freedom under the leadership of the Holy Spirit to change what needs to be changed, to meet the changing situation in the place and in the moment of that situation. Otherwise, I do not believe there is a place for the church as a living church. We will be ossified and we will shut Christ out of the church."[65]

One of the principal roles of the church (a role that would disappear if Christ were shut out) is the proclamation of sin. By making society aware of sin, the church can effect great positive changes. Sutton writes,

> The Church will have to start by telling the world that sin is the issue. America is in great sin. The State is in great sin. The Church is in great sin. Family life is in great sin. And, *it will all be destroyed through disease, war, and any number of appropriate methods if repentance does not come*. If the Church proclaims this message, society will change.[66]

This concept of judgment goes hand-in-hand with the Christian sociologist's belief that society is responsible for its decisions and attitudes. If society does not repent of its sin, it will be judged. But the church can play a critical role in turning a society toward God by explaining that both the individual and society have sinned and are responsible for their actions.

The church also can cause a society to face God by providing an example of true community. If the Christian church could show the rest of society that it is possible to live according to the command "Love your neighbor as yourself," then individuals and society might finally

Notes and Asides

turn to God and acknowledge Him as the initiator of all relations. Schaeffer is adamant about the need for community in the Christian church:

> Unless people see in our churches not only the preaching of the truth but the practice of the truth, the practice of love and the practice of beauty; unless they see that the thing that the humanists rightly want but cannot achieve on a humanist base—human communication and human relationship—is able to be practiced in our communities, then let me say it clearly: They will not listen and they should not listen.[67]

Truth

Elsewhere Schaeffer reiterates this point: "There is no use saying you have community or love for each other if it does not get down into the tough stuff of life. It must, or we are producing ugliness in the name of truth. I am convinced that in the 20th century people all over the world will not listen if we have the right doctrine, the right polity, but are not exhibiting community."[68]

Ephesians 4:11-16 stresses the value of Christians working together in community:

> It was he [Christ] who gave some to be Apostles, some to be prophets, some to be evangelists, and some to be pastors and teachers, to prepare God's people for works of service, so that the body of Christ may be built up until we all reach unity in the faith and in the knowledge of the Son of God and become mature, attaining to the whole measure of the fullness of Christ. Then we will no longer be infants, tossed back and forth by the waves, and blown here and there by every wind of teaching and by the cunning and craftiness of men in their deceitful scheming. Instead, speaking the truth in love, we will in all things grow up into him who is the Head, that is, Christ. From him the whole body, joined and held together by every supporting ligament, grows and builds itself up in love, as each part does its work.

"Bless all the churches, and blessed be God, who, in this our great trial, giveth us the churches."
—Abraham Lincoln

The church is a necessary social institution. Without the church, mankind would not have an ordered means of worshiping God, and society would not be reminded that it must constantly keep its focus on Christ. The church attempts to maintain this focus in a number of ways, most often by proclaiming the reality of sin and of the gospel of Jesus

Notes and Asides

Christ and by practicing true fellowship in a loving and caring community. A church that understands and accepts this role can be a blessing for the entire society.

Conclusion

Christian sociology values both the individual and society. The individual is seen as capable of free choice, though alienated because of man's decision to turn from God. Society is also seen as fallen and imperfect, as well as responsible for its decisions and attitudes. It is in this perspective that both society and the individual gain value: only people and institutions capable of choosing are truly significant—any man or society whose actions are determined by uncontrollable forces has no more value than a tree or a stone.

In this context of responsibility, the Christian sociologist recognizes that man must face the consequences for the choices he makes in creating his society. Man is charged with the duty of protecting and directing the growth of societal institutions ordained by God, including family, state and church. The family is charged with the generational or reproductive responsibilities; the state is charged with justice issues, which primarily involve maintaining law and order; the church is charged with making sure Christian love is the cement of the social institutions. Mankind is answerable to God for the direction in which society is led by these institutions.

Stanmeyer prescribes certain guidelines for society that accurately sum up the Christian sociological perspective:

> First, men should not build a society on atheism; society should be open to, perhaps even encourage, religious influence on public affairs. Second, society should not impede or interfere with the development of individual moral character; it should promote personal accountability for moral choices. Third, society should not rely solely on public arrangements for human betterment. These are intrinsically incomplete and can never reach the essence of the problem, which is spiritual. Rather, society should tolerate human finitude and imperfection. Fourth, society should not think collectively. Rather it should strive to recognize the value of each human being, a value which comes not at the sufferance of the collectivity but from "outside," that is, from God. Fifth, government may never make a legitimate total claim on the individual. It must permit him leisure, privacy, time, and opportunity for pursuits of the spirit.[69]

Notes and Asides

Such applications ensure a healthy society, one largely free of sociological ills like crime, poverty, and drug abuse, and blessed with personal and social liberty, safety, prosperity, and loving community.

[1]Harry V. Jaffa, "A Terrible Disappointment," in *The Proposition*, (Montclair, CA: The Claremont Institute, 1990), cited in James C. Dobson and Gary L. Bauer, *Children at Risk* (Dallas, TX: Word, 1990), p. 54. The Claremont Institute is located at 4645 Arrow Highway, Suite D-6, Montclair, CA 91763.
[2]Dobson and Bauer, *Children at Risk*, p. 55.
[3]Charles Colson, *Against the Night* (Ann Arbor, MI: Servant Publications, 1989), p. 67.
[4]David Lyon, *Sociology and the Human Image* (Downer's Grove, IL: InterVarsity Press, 1983), p. 181.
[5]S. D. Gaede, *Where Gods May Dwell* (Grand Rapids, MI: Zondervan, 1985), pp. 75-6.
[6]Ibid., p. 77.
[7]Rockne McCarthy, Donald Oppewal, Walfred Peterson, and Gordon Spykman, *Society, State, and Schools* (Grand Rapids, MI: Eerdmans, 1982), p. 151.
[8]Gaede, *Where Gods May Dwell*, p. 128.
[9]Francis A. Schaeffer, *Death in the City* (Downers Grove, IL: InterVarsity Press, 1976), p. 21.
[10]Gaede, *Where Gods May Dwell*, p. 132.
[11]William A. Stanmeyer, *Clear and Present Danger* (Ann Arbor, MI: Servant Books, 1983), p. 161.
[12]Brendan Furnish, "The Scientific Approach to Social Research: Some Dilemmas for the Christian," in *A Reader in Sociology: Christian Perspectives*, eds. Charles P. DeSanto, Calvin Redekop, and William L. Smith-Hinds (Scottdale, PA: Herald Press 1980), p. 66.
[13]Stanmeyer, *Clear and Present Danger*, p. 44.
[14]Schaeffer, *Death in the City*, p. 96.
[15]Gaede, *Where Gods May Dwell*, p. 98.
[16]Stanmeyer, *Clear and Present Danger*, p. 42.
[17]Schaeffer, *Death in the City*, p. 81.
[18]Rousas John Rushdoony, *Politics of Guilt and Pity* (Fairfax, VA: Thoburn Press, 1978), p. 1.
[19]Robert E. Webber, *The Secular Saint* (Grand Rapids, MI: Zondervan, 1979), p. 41.
[20]Ibid., p. 50.
[21]Ibid.
[22]Thomas Howard, "Mere Christianity: A Focus on Man in Society," in *The Christian Vision: Man in Society*, ed. Lynne Morris (Hillsdale, MI: Hillsdale College Press, 1984), p. 27.
[23]Schaeffer, *Death in the City*, p. 81.
[24]George A. Hillery, Jr., "A Christian Perspective on Sociology," in *A Reader in Sociology: Christian Perspectives*, eds. DeSanto, Redekop, and Smith-Hinds, p. 161.
[25]C. S. Lewis, *God in the Dock* (Grand Rapids, MI: Eerdmans, 1972), pp. 109-10.
[26]Clyde S. Kilby, ed., *A Mind Awake: An Anthology of C. S. Lewis* (New York: Harcourt Brace Jovanovich, 1980), p. 125.
[27]Gaede, *Where Gods May Dwell*, p. 98.
[28]Webber, *The Secular Saint*, p. 37.
[29]Howard, "Mere Christianity: A Focus on Man in Society," in *The Christian Vision: Man in Society*, ed. Morris, pp. 22-3.
[30]Gaede, *Where Gods May Dwell*, p. 104.
[31]Ibid., p. 107.
[32]Lyon, *Sociology and the Human Image*, p. 193.
[33]McCarthy, et al., *Society, State, and Schools*, p. 24.
[34]Ibid., p. 21.
[35]Ibid., p. 18.
[36]Stanmeyer, *Clear and Present Danger*, p. 194.
[37]McCarthy, et al., *Society, State, and Schools*, p. 19.
[38]Rousas John Rushdoony, *Intellectual Schizophrenia* (Philadelphia: Presbyterian and Reformed, 1961), pp. 61-2.
[39]Publisher's preface to Ray Sutton, *Who Owns the Family?* (Ft. Worth, TX: Dominion Press, 1986), p. ix.
[40]McCarthy, et al., *Society, State, and Schools*, p. 158.
[41]Gene Garrick, "Developing Educational Objectives for the Christian School," in *The Philosophy of Christian*

School Education, ed. Paul A. Kienel (Whittier, CA: Association of Christian Schools International, 1978), p. 85.
[42]Dietrich Bonhoeffer, *Ethics* (New York: Macmillan, 1959), p. 207.
[43]Arnold Burron and John Eidsmoe, *Christ in the Classroom* (Denver, CO: Accent Books, 1987), p. 23.
[44]McCarthy, et al., *Society, State, and Schools*, p. 151.
[45]Ibid., p. 22.
[46]Dobson and Bauer, *Children at Risk*, p. 112.
[47]J. Howard Kauffman, "Marriage and Family Alternatives," in *A Reader in Sociology: Christian Perspectives*, eds. DeSanto, et al., p. 509.
[48]Sutton, *Who Owns the Family?* p. 12.
[49]George Gilder, *Men and Marriage* (Gretna, LA: Pelican, 1986), p. 16. Interestingly, Gilder was led to embrace Christianity by his discovery "that the essential themes of Christian teaching about marriage and family were true." *Christianity Today*, March 6, 1987, p. 35.
[50]See Lester Kirkendall, *A New Bill of Sexual Rights and Responsibilities* (Buffalo, NY: Prometheus Books, 1976).
[51]Dobson and Bauer, *Children at Risk*, p. 55. For an in-depth look at what is transpiring in such classroom instruction we recommend Dobson and Bauer's book, Phyllis Schlafly's *Child Abuse in the Classroom* (Alton, IL: Marquette Press, 1985), and Judith A. Reisman and Edward W. Eichel's *Kinsey, Sex and Fraud* (Lafayette, LA: Huntington House, 1990).
[52]Ibid., pp. 110-12.
[53]Cited in *New Dimensions*, October 1990, p. 43. New Dimensions is published at 111 N.E. Evelyn Ave., Grants Pass, OR 97526.
[54]Paul Kurtz, "Fulfilling Feminist Ideals: A New Agenda," *Free Inquiry*, Fall 1990, p. 21. This particular issue contains numerous articles about feminism.
[55]Annie Laurie Gaylor, "Feminist 'Salvation,'" *The Humanist*, July/Aug. 1988, p. 37.
[56]*The Phyllis Schlafly Report*, April 1990, p. 2. The *Report* is published at Box 618, Alton, IL 62002. We recommend the following works on feminism: Gilder, *Men and Marriage*; Nicholas Davidson, *Gender Sanity* (Lanahm, MD: University Press of America, 1989); and Michael Levin, *Feminism and Freedom* (New Brunswick, NJ: Transaction, 1987). For women thinking no fault divorce was liberation, we recommend Lenore Weitzman, *The Divorce Revolution* (NY: Free Press, 1985).
[57]David L. Hocking, "The Theological Basis for the Philosophy of Christian School Education," in *The Philosophy of Christian School Education*, ed. Kienel, p. 23.
[58]Stanmeyer, *Clear and Present Danger*, p. 120.
[59]Sutton, *Who Owns the Family?* p. 3.
[60]*Encyclopedia Americana* (new ed.; Philadelphia: Desilver, Thomas & Company, 1836), vol. IX, pp. 150-8.
[61]Gilder, *Men and Marriage*, p. 69.
[62]We recommend the following materials on homosexuality: Enrique T. Rueda, *The Homosexual Network* (Greenwich, CT: Devin-Adair, 1983); Frank duMas, *Gay is Not Good* (Nashville, TN: Thomas Nelson, 1979); William Dannemeyer, *Shadow in the Land* (San Francisco: Ignatius, 1989); David A. Noebel, *The Homosexual Revolution* (Manitou Springs, CO: Summit Press, 1984).
[63]Kauffman, "Marriage and Family Alternatives," p. 528.
[64]Sutton, *Who Owns the Family?* p. 130.
[65]Francis A. Schaeffer, *The Church at the End of the 20th Century* (Downers Grove, IL: InterVarsity Press, 1974), p. 77.
[66]Sutton, *Who Owns the Family?* p. 147.
[67]Schaeffer, *The Church at the End of the 20th Century*, p. 40.
[68]Ibid., p. 73.
[69]Stanmeyer, *Clear and Present Danger*, p. 47.

SECTION SEVEN

LAW

LAW [English: *lagu* (code, rules)]: The study of principles of conduct or procedure which are expected to be observed.

	SECULAR HUMANISM	MARXISM/ LENINISM	BIBLICAL CHRISTIANITY
SOURCE	*HUMANIST MANIFESTO I & II*	*WRITINGS OF MARX & LENIN*	*BIBLE*
THEOLOGY	ATHEISM	ATHEISM	THEISM
PHILOSOPHY	NATURALISM	DIALECTICAL MATERIALISM	SUPERNATURALISM
ETHICS	ETHICAL RELATIVISM	PROLETARIAT MORALITY	ETHICAL ABSOLUTES
BIOLOGY	DARWINIAN EVOLUTION	DARWINIAN/ PUNCTUATED EVOLUTION	SPECIAL CREATIONISM
PSYCHOLOGY	MONISTIC SELF-ACTUALIZATION	MONISTIC PAVLOVIAN BEHAVIORISM	DUALISM
SOCIOLOGY	NON-TRADITIONAL WORLD STATE ETHICAL SOCIETY	ABOLITION OF HOME, CHURCH AND STATE	HOME CHURCH STATE
LAW	POSITIVE LAW	POSITIVE LAW	BIBLICAL/NATURAL LAW
POLITICS	WORLD GOVERNMENT (GLOBALISM)	NEW WORLD ORDER	JUSTICE FREEDOM ORDER
ECONOMICS	SOCIALISM	SOCIALISM/ COMMUNISM	STEWARDSHIP OF PROPERTY
HISTORY	HISTORICAL EVOLUTION	HISTORICAL MATERIALISM	HISTORICAL RESURRECTION

CHAPTER

21

SECULAR HUMANIST LAW

"No matter how misperceived as natural they may be, rights . . . are the works of human artifice."[1]

—Delos B. McKown

"There is something in human nature operating at a deeper level than mere theological belief, and it is this that serves as the real prompt for moral behavior. As with laws, so with morals: human beings seem quite capable of making, on their own, sensible and sensitive decisions affecting conduct."[2]

—Frederick Edwords

SUMMARY

Secular Humanists give mixed signals regarding law. Some tend to make the individual the originator and final authority of law, while others nod or wink briefly at natural law, and still others look to the state and positive law as the rational source. However, these three contenders agree on one thing—Humanist law is based on the biological theory of evolution. It is evolutionary law. It may be discovered in evolving man, nature, or even the state, but it is founded on evolution.

The concept of evolution so permeates Humanist legal thinking that it can be stated, without contradiction, that evolution ultimately determines Humanistic legal principles. Man is evolving. Man is becoming. Everything is in flux. Nothing is permanent. There are no absolute legal standards. There are no permanent Ten Commandments; there is no permanent Constitution. And man has become responsible for his social and biological evolution.

The purpose of law is to assure mankind an environment fit for man's continuing evolution and, at the same time, to permit man to enjoy the process. The Ten Commandments are a serious hindrance to the pursuit of the good life and probably to the evolution of man. Hence, however useful they might once have been, they are useless today.

Although many non-Humanists are puzzled as to why some in our society are "soft on criminals," the reason is clear. Humanism believes that crime is more the fault of the social order than of the criminal himself. Therefore, punishment should be inflicted on society, not the criminal. The criminal, if punished, could develop guilt feelings for his crime, which in turn could thwart his chances for self-actualization. The reason capital punishment is looked on with horror is grounded in the evolving nature of man, law, and society. What today is considered just cause for the death penalty may change tomorrow—will change tomorrow. The finality of the penalty speaks against the ever-evolving legal structure envisioned by the Humanists.

Instead of punishment, Humanists insist on re-education. Instead of a fault structure based on the concept of individual responsibility, individual guilt, and individual punishment, Humanist law insists on a no-fault legal structure. Since man is an evolving social animal reflecting his evolving social environment, no-fault makes sense.

Humanists reject the Ten Commandments for two primary reasons: man is placing himself in obedience to something other than himself, and the Ten Commandments "suppress vital inclinations." As Will and Ariel Durant point out, "Man has never reconciled himself to the Ten Commandments."[3] The 1990 Humanist of the Year—Ted Turner—declared the Ten Commandments obsolete[4] and part of a religion for losers. Morality and legality are to be considered biologically, not theologically; they are man-centered, not God-centered. Man is capable of creating his own legal system. Man knows what is best for man. This, however, always means that a few fallible men seem to know what is best for all mankind.

While a few Humanists have toyed with the notion of natural rights and natural law—law somehow discovered in the nature of nature—most have given that theory scant attention. Why? Because concepts of natural law logically demand a cause for their existence. This immediately suggests a law-giver, which suggests God. Humanists do not want to open that door.

On the other hand, Humanists invest the government with too much power to allow the individual to determine his own laws. Perhaps in the self-actualized society each man will be granted this privilege, but until that utopia is achieved the state must guide and shape man.

Hence, positive law becomes the legal theory most consistent with Humanism. The state must create law, enact law, execute law, interpret law. The state determines human rights and grants such rights as it deems beneficial—presumably to assist man in developing his evolutionary tendencies. The state by granting or withholding rights becomes supreme; it becomes god.

While some non-Humanists may consider the loss of particular human rights a tragedy, Humanists are willing to concede some rights if it means accelerating the evolution of man. The most telling example of this is the present move toward world government, which all Humanists consider an advance in the evolution of man. Julian Huxley's role at the United Nations is most appropriate in establishing world government and advancing the evolution of mankind. The present move to remove Christianity from the public square is a move to establish Humanist law in its place and prepare man for his next stage of evolutionary history.

Notes and Asides

Introduction

Most Humanists avoid discussing the approach to law suggested by their worldview. In fact, no Humanist leader has ever written a book specifically addressing the Humanist attitude toward law. On the surface, it appears the Humanist need not adhere to any definite set of legal assumptions. On closer examination, however, we find that the Humanist worldview is compatible with only one legal theory—indeed, basic assumptions of that theory are revealed throughout the works of a number of Humanists.

As with all other aspects of the Humanist worldview, their legal theory is founded on the basic assumptions that God does not exist and that man, as an evolving animal, is perfectible. Any doubts about the Humanist's belief that evolution is enormously significant for his worldview are erased by a single statement by Julian Huxley: "Our present knowledge indeed forces us to the view that the world of reality is evolution—a single process of self transformation."[5] This attitude causes the Humanist to view man's role in the universe differently from those who reject evolutionary theory. Paul Kurtz believes, "If man is a product of evolution, one species among others, in a universe without purpose, then man's option is to live for himself. . . ."[6]

> "If man is a product of evolution, one species among others, in a universe without purpose, then man's option is to live for himself."
>
> —Paul Kurtz

If man should live only for man, his focus must be on creating an environment that causes most men to be satisfied and encourages further evolutionary progress. As already demonstrated in the Humanist sociology chapter, Humanists believe that any evil manifested in man is really caused by a less-than-perfect environment. If the environment could be perfected, then mankind could learn consistently to choose what is morally correct. Thus, Roger E. Greeley writes, "Humanists since [Sigmund] Freud usually view good and evil as the result of environment and education, while allowing for disturbances that are organic in nature."[7] Because the environment is all that hinders man's evolution into an inherently good being, man may control his development simply by controlling his environment. The *Humanist Manifesto II* asserts, "Using technology wisely, we can control our environment, . . . significantly modify our behavior, alter the course of human evolution. . . ."[8]

This attitude greatly influences Humanism's approach to law. In the first place, it causes the Humanist to perceive punishment for violations of the law as unnecessary, since misdeeds are simply caused by an imperfect environment.

Notes and Asides

Crime and Punishment

Gilbert Murray, quoted in *The Best of Humanism*, provides a perfect example of the Humanist attitude toward a system of law that punishes offenders. He states, "The whole supposition that a system of violent and intense rewards and punishments is necessary to induce human beings to perform acts for the good of others is based on a false psychology which starts from the individual isolated man instead of man the social animal. Man is an integral member of his group. Among his natural instincts there are those which aim at group-preservation as well as self-preservation. . . ."[9] Man the evolving animal has developed enough altruistic tendencies that the proper environment would erase all anti-social and illegal behavior, thereby doing away with the need for punishment (and possibly laws).

Humanists believe that society's present system of punishment hinders the creation of the proper environment in which man can excel morally. As long as a system requiring punishment exists, according to Humanism, man will never develop the necessary moral sensibilities, and his further evolution will be hindered. Joel Feinberg states, "Immoral conduct is no trivial thing, and we should hardly expect societies to tolerate it; yet if men are forced to refrain from immorality, their own choices will play very little role in what they do, so that they can hardly develop critical judgment and moral traits of a genuinely praiseworthy kind."[10] Thus, Humanists like Robert and Delorys Blume conclude that punishment "is not only counterproductive but very destructive of the social cohesion we seek in the modern world."[11]

According to the Blumes, a misguided legal system that uses punishment will eventually destroy itself. They write,

> The punished experience the same long-term emotional effects as crime victims: they want to get even; they want retribution from those who have caused them to suffer. A society that has thousands, or possibly millions, of people with these feelings toward its system of social control is a society that will experience more and more crime. We can easily predict that, if increased crime is met with increasingly harsher punishment, the result will be more crime, ad infinitum, until the whole system breaks down.[12]

Punishment can also create a different, equally undesirable re-

Notes and Asides

sponse. The Blumes worry that the punished offender may "feel guilty and worthless and, therefore, deserving of the punishment."[13] Whereas the Christian (or any person who believes man is responsible for his actions) sees guilt feelings as stemming from objective guilt, i.e., as the natural response to behaving irresponsibly, the Humanist believes guilt feelings are unhealthful, since an imperfect environment, not man, is responsible for an individual's violations of the law.

Clearly, a consistent Humanist worldview perceives punishment as an unnecessary, even harmful, aspect of legal theory. Many Humanists believe people who break the law need to be re-educated, not punished. The Blumes declare, "Our response must change from trying to inflict enough pain on this person to deter him or her from repeating the act to trying to change the way this person thinks or fails to think."[14]

Humanism's attitude toward punishment provides an excellent example of how the Humanist's view of man as an evolving, perfectible animal affects his legal theory. We will further examine the effects of this belief on Humanist legal theory after studying some of the implications of the Humanist's denial of God.

If God Does Not Exist

The Humanist, as demonstrated in the Humanist theology and philosophy chapters, is unwilling to believe in anything supernatural. The reason Humanists cite for their disbelief is the lack of positive proof for the existence of the supernatural. But the Humanists also deny the existence of God because they believe man, to be truly free, must obey only his own reason. Erich Fromm writes,

> Obedience to a person, institution or power . . . is submission; it implies the abdication of my autonomy and the acceptance of a foreign will or judgment in place of my own. Obedience to my own reason or conviction . . . is not an act of submission but one of affirmation. My conviction and my judgment, if authentically mine, are part of me. If I follow them rather than the judgment of others, I am being myself. . . .[15]

Thus, Humanists deny not only God but also the existence of an absolute moral code to which they might owe obedience. Indeed, many Humanists see God's commands (which are traditionally viewed as the absolute moral code) as a potentially malignant fiction. Kurtz declares, "The traditional supernaturalistic moral commandments are especially repressive of our human needs. They are immoral insofar as they foster illusions about human destiny and suppress vital inclinations."[16]

Notes and Asides

Humanists have no qualms about rejecting an absolute moral code because they believe man is capable of devising his own code, with regard to both morals and law. Frederick Edwords declares,

> It should be obvious from the most casual observation that human beings are quite capable of setting up systems and then operating within them. Once this is seen, it can be asked what grounds exist for the belief that human beings cannot continue to operate in this fashion when it comes to laws and moral teachings regulating such things as trade and commerce, property rights, interpersonal relationships, sexual behavior, religious rituals, and the rest of those things that theologians seem to feel are in need of a theological foundation.[17]

Specifically, the Humanist believes morality can be derived from his own worldview. Walter Lippmann states, "Yet with all its difficulties, it is to a morality of Humanism that men must turn when the ancient order of things dissolves. When they find that they no longer believe seriously and deeply that they are governed from heaven, there is anarchy in their souls until by conscious effort they find ways of governing themselves."[18]

Obviously, the Humanist method of governing oneself requires a system of man-centered ethics. If ethics are not grounded in God's nature, then they must be discovered in man's relations with man. Edwords claims, "Morality, then, emerges from humanity precisely because it exists to serve humanity."[19]

This man-centered morality evolves right along with the development of man. "Moral behavior of a rudimentary type," says V. M. Tarkunde, "is found in the higher animals and can be traced even to lower forms of life. This fact is enough to establish that the source of morality is biological and not theological."[20] Jacob Bronowski declares, "A rational and coherent system of ethics must grow out of the exploration of the relations between man and society. It will not be a permanent system; it will not teach us what ought to be forever, any more than science teaches us what is forever. Both science and ethics are activities in which we explore relations which, though permanent in the larger sense, are also in constant evolution."[21]

> "Without a notion of a law-maker, it is impossible to have a notion of a law, and an obligation to observe it."
>
> —John Locke

Humanists base this assumption that man can create his own *ethical* code on the fact that man creates his own *legal* code. Edwords believes that "if it is possible for people to develop laws and impose those laws upon themselves, then it is possible to do the same with morality. As in law, so in morals; the governed are capable of rule."[22]

It is interesting to note that the Humanist assumes the same thing about law that Charles Darwin did: that law, like ethics, is man-

Notes and Asides

centered. Darwin writes, "The more efficient causes of progress seem to consist of . . . a high standard of excellence, inculcated by the ablest and best men, embodied in the laws, customs, and traditions of the nation, and enforced by public opinion."[23] This is an evolutionary concept—deny the Creator, and one is left with a moral and legal code that evolves along with, and is centered in, mankind.

Law From the Evolutionary Perspective

Darwin's evolutionary theory affected the Humanist's conception of law. "There proceeded during the 19th Century," says Huxley, "under the influence of the evolutionary concept, a thoroughgoing transformation of older studies like . . . Law. . . ."[24] This transformation of the attitude toward law shines forth in a comment by Oliver Wendell Holmes, Jr.: "I see no reason for attributing to man a significance different in kind from that which belongs to a baboon or a grain of sand."[25] While Holmes could not be described as a card-carrying Humanist, his theory of law is founded on the same assumptions, and often he eloquently describes a position consistent with Humanism. This is true as well of Roscoe Pound, and therefore we will occasionally refer to the opinions of these two famous law theorists to clarify the Humanist position.[26]

Indeed, Pound, following Christopher C. Langdell, summarizes the Humanist belief that laws, like morality, are man-centered and evolve as man evolves. He writes,

> One has but to compare the law of today on such subjects as torts or public utilities or administrative law with the law of a generation ago to see that we are in a new stage of transition; . . . and to see that the jurist of tomorrow will stand in need of some new philosophical theory of law, will call for some new philosophical conception of the end of law, and at the same time will want some new steadying philosophical conception to safeguard the general security, in order to make the law which we hand down to him achieve justice in his time and place.[27]

Langdell, of course, was the key personality behind the evolutionary interpretation of the law.[28] He became dean of Harvard's Law School in 1870 and proceeded to move Harvard from its Christian foundation to law based on the theory of evolution. Instead of law based on the law of nature and of nature's God, law is based on ever-evolving principles determined primarily by judges. Law no longer has an absolute base, but a relative one. Langdell encouraged his students to abandon William Blackstone's *Commentaries* on the Common Law primarily because he could not accept Blackstone's non-evolutionary interpretation of law. "Thus," writes John Eidsmoe,

> the debate over constitutional interpretation is no mere academic or legal matter. Rather it is a major battle between two conflicting philosophies, two conflicting religions and two conflicting worldviews. [Supreme Court] Justice [William] Brennan openly acknowledged this in his Georgetown address ["The Constitution of the United States: Contemporary Ratification," Teaching Symposium, Georgetown University, Washington, D.C., October 12, 1985, p. 51], declaring that our society must continue its upward progress unbounded by the fetters of original intent or the literal words of the Constitution, through an 'evolutionary process [that] is inevitable and, indeed, it is the true interpretative genius of the text'.[29]

CLOSE-UP

Roscoe Pound (1870-1964)

While not a Humanist according to strict definition (he never signed the *Humanist Manifestoes* nor opted to join the American Humanist Association), Roscoe Pound did more to apply the Humanistic worldview to legal theory than any other individual in the twentieth century. After passing the bar exam in 1890, he worked tirelessly (often sixteen hours a day) to develop a man-centered approach to law. He taught law at Northwestern University and the University of Chicago, and eventually moved to Harvard, where he was employed from 1910 to 1947. In the years from 1916 to 1936 he acted as dean of Harvard's law school—a time which later was referred to as the law school's "golden age." Many of the graduates from those years went on to formulate policies for Franklin D. Roosevelt's New Deal, and all graduates were to some extent influenced by Pound's attempt to apply pragmatism to legal theory. Pound's teachings and writings (especially *Jurisprudence*, a five volume work) are largely responsible for America's move from natural law to legal positivism.

Notes and Asides

This Humanist belief that law evolves will become evident shortly, but for now, it is important to realize that, for the Humanist, the source of law is man, not God. Thus, Gordon Gamm, when describing the criteria for law, states, "The law is limited to imposing penalties for conduct that can be judged antisocial by secular, rational criteria."[30]

The source for all of man's rights protected by law is also a strictly human source, according to the Humanist. Kurtz believes "human rights are characteristics that emerge in human transactions; they are not separate from them."[31] Kai Nielsen claims, "The rights we have flow from what we consider to be our vital interests."[32] If those vital interests require disposing of the old, the infirm, the misfit, the mentally ill, the unborn—so be it.

But if man is really an evolving animal, how can the Humanist claim man has rights apart from other animals, especially if the only source of those rights is man's own transactions and interests? Morris B. Storer puts the question this way: "What is there that's different about a human being that dictates the right to life for all humans (unarguably in most circumstances) where most people acknowledge no such right in other animals? That justifies equal right to liberty where we fence the others in, equal justice under law where the other animals are not granted any trial at all."[33]

Such questions and issues seem unanswerable when God is removed from the equation. Still, the Humanist makes many bold claims about, and even champions, "human rights." Kurtz declares, "There are common human rights that must be respected by everyone."[34] Elsewhere he asserts, "The just society will seek to end discrimination based on race, gender, creed, sexual orientation, physical handicap, ethnicity, or economic background and accord all of its citizens equal rights."[35]

The Humanist accepts the existence of certain rights as indisputable. But how can the Humanist be so certain of rights worthy of protection by law, and indeed law itself, when their source is man the evolving animal? What, for the Humanist, grounds rights and law outside the arbitrary whims of the men presently in power in any given government?

Natural Law

Some Humanists attempt to use the concepts of natural law and natural rights to provide a standard that transcends specific men and governments. The concept of natural law assumes that there is one true morality—one proper way for man to behave—and it is discoverable by man. Laws arise from this natural law to enforce adherence to its code. Likewise, natural rights exist independent of man, much like the law of

Notes and Asides

gravity, but mankind may discover them and enact laws in conformity to them.

A belief in natural law and natural rights lets the Humanist off the hook in one sense, because it provides a more stable source for law than does any human interpretation of legal principles. However, the Humanist is faced with the problem of explaining the origins of this natural law. Whereas the Christian believes God implanted law in the universe and inscribed natural law on the hearts of men, the Humanist cannot tolerate such an explanation. Thus, Humanism falls back on evolutionary theory as the source for natural law, which is in turn the source of all rights and laws. Julian Wadleigh declares, "As I see it, natural law is the basic, instinctive sense of fairness and justice which exists in the human mind. . . . We have it, I believe, because we evolved as a species of social animal, like the bees and the beavers."[36]

Natural law refers to the idea that one correct way for men to behave exists, and all men are aware of this code.

Wadleigh goes on to assert that evolution is just as viable an explanation for the existence of natural law as a Creator, thereby claiming natural law for the Humanist worldview and solving many of Humanism's dilemmas in the realm of ethics and law. He writes, "The Declaration [of Independence] speaks of natural law as an endowment by a creator, whereas I speak of it as the result of humankind's evolution as a social animal. There is a difference, but that difference concerns the questions of how and why we have natural law—not whether or not natural law exists. Regardless of its origin, it is the same natural law."[37]

Thus, many Humanists believe natural law provides a stable source for rights and law, even when it is assumed to have evolved. Edwords states, "The existence of certain genetic behaviors, therefore, makes agreement between people on laws, institutions, customs, and morals far less surprising. We humans are not infinitely malleable, and hence our laws and institutions are not as arbitrary as once thought."[38] Thus, according to this view, evolution was responsible for certain genetic behaviors in man that allow him to discover and conform to natural law (which also is a result of evolution). In theory, then, this approach frees Humanism from much of the ethical and legal relativism that often pervades its worldview.

"The Declaration [of Independence] speaks of natural law as an endowment by a creator, whereas I speak of it as the result of humankind's evolution as a social animal."

—Julian Wadleigh

Unfortunately for the Humanist, this explanation ignores the fact that, according to Humanist biology, evolution is a continuous process. Therefore, while natural law may appear concrete today, it is undergoing constant change, just as man's genetic behaviors and understanding of natural law evolve. If this is true, rights or laws recognized by man today may evolve right out of existence. Thus, the Humanist once again is left with an uncertain and unstable source of law.

Wadleigh tries to integrate this uncertainty caused by evolution, stating, "Natural law is not a set of precise rules but a guide that must be followed using plain common sense."[39] As soon as the Humanist

Notes and Asides

concedes this point, however, he nullifies the central precept of natural law theory—natural law becomes simply a relative guide, not a stable foundation for morality.

So once again the Humanist is left without an absolute standard for rights and law. Even Tibor R. Machan, in an essay attempting to defend the position that Humanism is compatible with natural law, seems to concede its inability to develop any real standard for law: "We see that, in human life, the conduct we choose can objectively enhance or hinder human development. Just what are the standards for distinguishing between the two is a complex matter, and I cannot deal with it here."[40] Indeed, Humanists seem unwilling to deal with this matter anywhere. The reason is simple: Humanism is incompatible with the theory of natural law and natural rights. McKown makes this clear when he asks the pointed question, "When, one wonders, in evolutionary history did hominids first acquire natural rights?"[41] Obviously, the Humanist must abandon natural law to develop a legal theory consistent with the basic assumptions of his worldview.

Natural Law Denied

This denial of natural law begins with a denial of natural rights deserving protection under law. "Am I not bringing in a doctrine of natural rights that are prior to political policy?" asks Kurtz. "No, I reject any such fiction."[42] Indeed, Kurtz sees rights as recently evolved through human systems: "Most . . . rights have evolved out of the cultural, economic, political, and social structures that have prevailed."[43] He denies that natural rights could even be grounded in religion by a person who believes in God: "There is no doctrine of human rights to be found in the Bible or the Koran. The concept of inherent human rights is a recent development."[44]

McKown agrees.

> Given the human brain, motivated by egoism, it is natural, no doubt, that some of us, at conducive times in history, should conceptualize, entertain, and even objectify such an idea as that of natural rights. But by what power do the brain functions we call reason guarantee natural immunities, and by what mechanism does thought call into existence natural remedies whenever rights are violated? No such powers or mechanisms are known to science, nor do natural rights, immunities, and remedies seem to be recognized by the rest of nature.[45]

Elsewhere he states, "The conclusion is inescapable: natural human rights have neither meaning nor efficacy among the denizens of

Notes and Asides

subhuman nature nor among humans in a so-called state of nature."[46] This leads McKown to resolve, "There is, however, so little reason for thinking that [natural rights] exist outside of believing minds that we should cease and desist from asserting that they do exist and from drawing up lists of natural entitlements that humans are supposed to enjoy by birthright."[47]

Clearly, the Humanist consistent with his worldview will deny natural rights. This, in turn, leads to a denial of natural law. John Herman Randall, Jr., proclaims, "The Humanist temper has always protested against any subserviences to an external law, whether religious or mechanical, imposed upon man from without."[48] Interestingly, Randall bases his denial of natural law on the concept of freedom—like Fromm, many other Humanists believe man must not be "subservient" to any force other than his own human understanding.

Kurtz also denies the existence of natural law: "How are these principles [of equality, freedom, etc.] to be justified? They are not derived from a divine or natural law, nor do they have any special metaphysical status. They are rules offered to govern how we shall behave. They can be justified only by reference to their results."[49] Here, then, is a statement attempting to create a coherent Humanist approach to law. Kurtz believes that laws are derived not from natural law but from a relative criterion judged by the reason of men. This approach to legal theory leads to a view known as legal positivism.

Humanist Positive Law

In its strict sense, legal positivism claims that the state is the ultimate authority for creating law. That is, since God is a mythical being and natural law is simply legal fiction, man must rely on his reason to discern what is legal—and the men who decide the law are the men in power, in government. At first glance, it seems like an unqualified leap to call the Humanist legal position positivist solely on the basis of Kurtz's statement that rules "can be justified only by reference to their results." However, when one follows the basic assumptions of the Humanist worldview to their logical conclusion, positivism clearly shows itself to be the only legal theory consistent with Humanism. Humanists willing to draw the necessary conclusions will make this point obvious.

Legal positivism, strictly understood, entrusts the state with ultimate authority for creating and interpreting law.

Max Hocutt is one such Humanist. He understands that Humanism must abandon natural law, thereby causing mankind to be responsible for the creation of all laws: "Human beings may, and do, make up their own rules. All existing moralities and all existing laws are human artifacts, products of human society, social conventions."[50] If this is true, then government must be the final source of legal truths—since it is the

Notes and Asides

state, not the individual, that enacts laws.

The Humanist tries to escape this conclusion by calling for all governments to become democracies, thereby putting the power to enact laws in the hands of the people. Thus, the *Humanist Manifesto II* declares, "All persons should have a voice in developing the values and goals that determine their lives. . . . People are more important than decalogues, rules, proscriptions, or regulations."[51] Elsewhere Kurtz adds, "Societies will continue to need to be regulated by laws, but these should be the products of democratic decision-making and should be open to public revision. The goal of democratic societies is to maximize the opportunities for individual autonomy and freedom of choice."[52]

Of course, even if it were possible for the governed to enact every law, the government would still be responsible for interpreting laws—which, in effect, leaves the state as the final source for legal truth. Holmes writes, "The common law is not a brooding omnipresence in the sky, but the articulate voice of some sovereign or quasi-sovereign that can be identified. . . ."[53] The Humanist may wish to allow the governed to be the source of legal truth, but as Holmes points out, law ultimately must be wielded by the recognized authority—namely, the state.

"One of the great delusions in the world is the hope that the evils of this world can be cured by legislation."
—Thomas B. Reed

Thus, the consistent Humanist legal position denies natural law and embraces a positivist view, which grants the state the role of ultimate source of legal truth. "The main ingredients of an effective world order are well-known," says Louis B. Sohn: "to empower international institutions to enact the necessary rules, to make decisions for the interpretation and application of these rules, and to ensure the enforcement of the rules and decisions thus made."[54] The state is granted all power in enacting and interpreting laws.

This positivism spills over into the realm of rights as well. The state becomes the source of all human rights, which no longer are referred to as natural—only constitutional. McKown says, "Natural human rights exist only among human beings; that is, one holds natural rights only against other natural rights holders. Maintaining this point, however, begs the question of natural rights and leaves us wondering how such rights differ from constitutional or legal rights."[55] McKown draws the conclusion that if the concept of natural rights is simply question begging, then constitutional, or legal, rights are all that exist:

> The concept of inherent, natural, human rights was at best a useful myth in the days of yore, but it was a myth, nevertheless, with all the vulnerability that this implies. Accordingly, the idea of natural human rights should be demythologized. . . . Our eyes and our idealism ought to be focused, rather, on the only kind of rights that can be realized: legal rights, both positive and negative. . . .[56]

Notes and Asides

The consistent Humanist position is legal positivism. It would seem, however, that this position (based on the state as the final source of law) would lead to an arbitrary legal code. Indeed, when one combines this positivism with the Humanist position that mankind and his laws are in a constant state of evolution, the Humanist legal theory seems capricious. Just how capricious is made clear by Kurtz, who declares,

> The ideal is for laws to come into being and to become modified by the parliamentary process, and to be applied impartially and humanely. If law is essential to a democracy, it is equally essential that it must not become sacrosanct, that it be responsive to the will of the people, and tested by its consequences in action.[57]

Elsewhere Kurtz states, "Laws, however, provide us only with general guides for behavior; how they work out depends upon the context. . . . Of course provisions must be allowed for equity in interpreting and adjusting them to new situations."[58]

Kurtz's legal relativism is echoed by John Rawls in a book published by Prometheus: "In a democratic society each man must act as he thinks the principles of political right require him to. We are to follow our understanding of these principles, and we cannot do otherwise. There can be no morally binding legal interpretation of these principles, not even by a supreme court or legislature. Nor is there any infallible procedure for determining what or who is right."[59]

This arbitrary nature of Humanist law creates a problem. Says Pound, "From the time when lawgivers gave over the attempt to maintain the general security by belief that particular bodies of human law had been divinely dictated or divinely revealed or divinely sanctioned, they have had to wrestle with the problem of proving to mankind that the law was something fixed and settled, whose authority was beyond question, while at the same time enabling it to make constant readjustments and occasional radical changes under the pressure of infinite and variable human desires."[60] How does one convince citizens to obey laws that have no other foundation than the state? The question seems unanswerable. And this problem becomes even more complex when one examines other logical consequences of Humanist legal theory.

The Humanist approach to law not only creates a legal system too arbitrary to encourage citizens to obey it but also allows the individual to disobey the law whenever it doesn't enhance his freedom. Fromm declares that "freedom and the capacity for disobedience are inseparable; hence any social, political, and religious system which proclaims freedom, yet stamps out disobedience, cannot speak the truth."[61] The

"NEW WORLD ORDER"... WHICH IS IT?

WHERE WE ALL LIVE UNDER THE RULE OF LAW...
FREE WORLD
SADDAM
ASAY ©
COLORADO SPRINGS
GAZETTE TELEGRAPH

...OR WHERE WE ALL LIVE UNDER HIS RULE OF LAW?
BIG BROTHER IS WATCHING!
ONE WORLD ONE GOVERNMENT

Used by permission of the *Colorado Springs Gazette Telegraph*

citizen, in order to remain truly free, must obey his reason, and when his reason conflicts with the law, he may disobey the law. This attitude is supported by Rawls, who writes, "And if in his judgment the enactments of the majority exceed certain bounds of injustice, the citizen may consider civil disobedience."[62] The key words in this sentence, of course, are "in his judgment"—the Humanist's only criterion for whether a law enacted by the government is just or not is his own reason.

The real problem created by Humanist legal theory is not the potential disobedience of citizens; rather, it is the government's potential to take advantage of its position as ultimate source of legal truth. Machan warns, ". . . to argue that legal rights do not represent basic *natural human rights* and are merely 'permissions' by the state implies that government is a paternalist institution—not a *servant* of the citizenry."[63] Elsewhere, Machan is more explicit about the central danger of legal positivism:

> If there were no moral, humanistic foundations for the legal rights we ought to have, we would face the prospect of governments that exist without any limits, without any standards by

Notes and Asides

> which to ascertain whether or not they are just and morally legitimate.[64]

This is the heart of the problem created by Humanist legal theory: the state is given the authority of a god.

Conclusion

Law, while discussed infrequently by Humanists, is nevertheless a very real aspect of Humanism's worldview. The Humanist, to be consistent with his basic assumptions that God does not exist and that man is an evolving, perfectible animal, must embrace specific legal theories. For example, the consistent Humanist frowns on legal systems that punish lawbreakers, since, according to Humanism, the guilty party cannot be held responsible for his actions. Also, the Humanist must deny any source of ethics, rights, or laws that exists outside of man, including natural law. While many Humanists recognize the problems created by denying natural law and attempt to escape them by redefining natural law to fit their worldview, the consistent Humanist understands that he must abandon natural law and embrace legal positivism.

Legal positivism, however, creates a number of dilemmas of its own. Because it is based on evolutionary theory and the whims of the state, it produces an arbitrary legal system that discourages obedience and grants the state virtually unlimited authority. Humanist law faces a bitter choice: an inconsistent legal theory that embraces natural law, or a consistent legal positivism. Alastair Hannay sums up the dilemma faced by a theory of law that rejects the Lawgiver:

> Humanists naturally want to believe that we have moral obligations, duties in some virtually legalistic sense but not the product of arbitrary legislation, to one another. But on what can the belief be based? The divine legislator and guarantor of human value has gone by the board, but the human legislator doesn't seem to have the credentials.[65]

[1]Delos B. McKown, "Demythologizing Natural Human Rights," *The Humanist*, May/June 1989, p. 24.
[2]Frederick Edwords, "The Human Basis of Laws and Ethics," *The Humanist*, May/June 1985, p. 12.
[3]Will and Ariel Durant, *The Lessons of History* (New York: Simon and Schuster, 1968), p. 40.
[4]Julie Lanham, "The Greening of Ted Turner," *The Humanist*, Nov./Dec. 1989, p. 30.
[5]Julian Huxley, "Evolution and Genetics," in *What is Science?* ed. J. R. Newman (New York: Simon and Schuster, 1955), pp. 278.
[6]Paul Kurtz, "Is Everyone a Humanist?" in *The Humanist Alternative*, ed. Paul Kurtz (Buffalo: Prometheus Books, 1973), p. 179.
[7]Roger E. Greeley, in *The Best of Humanism*, ed. Roger E. Greeley (Buffalo: Prometheus Books, 1988), p. 120.
[8]*Humanist Manifesto II* (Buffalo: Prometheus Books, 1980), p. 14.
[9]Cited in *The Best of Humanism*, ed. Greeley, p. 91.
[10]Joel Feinberg, "Hard Cases for the Harm Principle," in *Morality and the Law*, eds. Robert M. Baird and Stuart E. Rosenbaum (Buffalo: Prometheus Books, 1988), p. 55.
[11]Robert and Delorys Blume, "The Crime of Punishment," *The Humanist*, Nov./Dec. 1989, p. 12.
[12]Ibid.
[13]Ibid., p. 13.
[14]Ibid., p. 14.
[15]Erich Fromm, "Disobedience as a Psychological and Moral Problem," in *Morality and the Law*, eds. Baird and Rosenbaum, p. 95.
[16]Paul Kurtz, "Humanism and the Moral Revolution," in *The Humanist Alternative*, ed. Kurtz, p. 50.
[17]Edwords, "The Human Basis of Laws and Ethics," p. 11.
[18]Walter Lippmann, cited in *The Best of Humanism*, ed. Greeley, p. 95.
[19]Edwords, "The Human Basis of Laws and Ethics," p. 13.
[20]V. M. Tarkunde, "Towards a Fuller Consensus in Humanistic Ethics," in *Humanist Ethics*, ed. Morris B. Storer (Buffalo: Prometheus Books, 1980), p. 156.
[21]Jacob Bronowski, cited in *The Best of Humanism*, ed. Greeley, p. 91.
[22]Edwords, "The Human Basis of Laws and Ethics," p. 10.
[23]Charles Darwin, cited in *The Best of Humanism*, ed. Greeley, p. 217.
[24]Cited in John W. Whitehead, *The Second American Revolution* (Elgin, IL: David C. Cook, 1982), p. 46.
[25]Richard Hertz, *Chance and Symbol* (Chicago: University of Chicago Press, 1948), p. 107.
[26]The use of Holmes and Pound to clarify the Humanist position would not be protested by any consistent Humanist. Indeed, Paul Kurtz lauds these two men, crediting them with furthering the cause of democracy and freedom. In the introduction to his *American Philosophy in the Twentieth Century* (New York: The Macmillan Company, 1967), Kurtz writes, "Pragmatism generally has given impetus to the ideals of liberalism, democracy and freedom. Sociological jurisprudence and legal realism were espoused by pragmatic jurists, such as Roscoe Pound and Oliver Wendell Holmes, Jr.; legal decisions were treated not as formal structures, but as related to actual social needs" (p. 22).
[27]Roscoe Pound, *An Introduction to the Philosophy of Law* (New Haven: Yale University Press, 1969), p. 24.
[28]For a complete summary of Langdell's role in moving America's legal system from Christian to positive law we recommend Herbert W. Titus, "God, Evolution, Legal Education and Law," *Journal of Christian Jurisprudence* (Tulsa, OK: O. W. Coburn School of Law/Oral Roberts University, 1980), pp. 11-48; Titus, "Religious Freedom: The War Between the Faiths," *Journal of Christian Jurisprudence* (1984-85), pp. 111-138; and Titus, *God, Man, and Law: The Biblical Principles* (Virginia Beach, VA: CBN University Press, 1983).
[29]John Eidsmoe, "Creation, Evolution and Constitutional Interpretation," *Concerned Women for America*, September 1987, p. 7. For further insight into the conflicting interpretations of law we recommend Robert H. Bork, *The Tempting of America: The Political Seduction of the Law* (New York: The Free Press, 1990).
[30]Gordon Gamm, "Abortion, Catholicism, and the Constitution," *The Humanist*, July/August 1989, p. 25.
[31]Paul Kurtz, *Forbidden Fruit* (Buffalo: Prometheus Books, 1988), p. 182.
[32]Kai Nielsen, "Morality and the Human Situation," in *Humanist Ethics*, ed. Storer, p. 66.
[33]Morris B. Storer, "A Factual Investigation of the Foundations of Morality," in *Humanist Ethics*, ed. Storer, p. 291.

[34]Paul Kurtz, *Eupraxophy: Living Without Religion* (Buffalo: Prometheus Books, 1989), p. 158.
[35]Ibid., p. 48.
[36]Julian Wadleigh, "What is Conservatism?" *The Humanist*, Nov./Dec. 1989, pp. 20-21.
[37]Ibid., p. 21.
[38]Edwords, "The Human Basis of Laws and Ethics," p. 13.
[39]Wadleigh, "What is Conservatism?" p. 21.
[40]Tibor R. Machan, "Are Human Rights Real?" *The Humanist*, Nov./Dec. 1989, p. 36.
[41]McKown, "Demythologizing Natural Human Rights," p. 22.
[42]Paul Kurtz, *The Fullness of Life* (New York: Horizon Press, 1974), p. 162.
[43]Kurtz, *Forbidden Fruit*, p. 196.
[44]Ibid., p. 180.
[45]McKown, "Demythologizing Natural Human Rights," p. 23.
[46]Ibid.
[47]Ibid., p. 24.
[48]John Herman Randall, Jr., "What is the Temper of Humanism?" in *The Humanist Alternative*, ed. Kurtz, p. 59.
[49]Kurtz, *The Fullness of Life*, p. 162.
[50]Max Hocutt, "Toward an Ethic of Mutual Accommodation," in *Humanist Ethics*, ed. Storer, p. 137.
[51]*Humanist Manifesto II*, p. 19.
[52]Kurtz, *Eupraxophy: Living Without Religion*, p. 122.
[53]*South Pacific Co.* vs. *Jensen*, 244 U.S. 205, p. 222 (1917).
[54]Louis B. Sohn, "Steps Toward World Law/World Peace," *The Humanist*, July/August 1968, p. 6.
[55]McKown, "Demythologizing Natural Human Rights," pp. 23-24.
[56]Ibid, p. 34.
[57]Kurtz, *The Fullness of Life*, p. 164.
[58]Ibid., p. 163.
[59]John Rawls, "The Obligation to Obey the Law," in *Morality and the Law*, eds. Baird and Rosenbaum, p. 138.
[60]Pound, *An Introduction to the Philosophy of Law*, p. 3.
[61]Fromm, "Disobedience as a Psychological and Moral Problem," p. 97.
[62]Ibid., p. 130.
[63]Tibor Machan, "Are Human Rights Real?" p. 28.
[64]Ibid.
[65]Alastair Hannay, "Propositions Toward a Humanist Consensus," in *Humanist Ethics*, ed. Storer, p. 187.

CHAPTER

22

MARXIST/ LENINIST LAW

"The bourgeoisie called its state a legal state. Religion and law are the ideologies of oppressing classes, one gradually replacing the other. And if we ought now at the present time to contend with the religious ideology, then we ought to a far greater degree to contend with the legal ideology."[1]

—A. G. Goikhbarg

"Law, morality, religion, are to [the proletariat] so many bourgeois prejudices, behind which lurk in ambush just as many bourgeois interests."[2]

—Karl Marx

SUMMARY

Marxist/Leninist law carries the burden of biological evolution, class warfare, and its own demise. The victory of communism brings with it the end of all class conflicts, the elimination of private property, and paradise on earth. Once paradise is achieved, there is no need for law or the state.

The biological theory of evolution plays a significant role in Marxist legal theory. There are no legal absolutes because mankind is evolving and law is evolving with it. There is no eternal lawgiver, and there are no eternal legal principles. Legal principles that assist man in his evolution are just; all others are unjust.

Marxists generally trace law back to the concept of private property. Thus law has both a biological and an economic heritage. Property, says the Marxist, divides mankind into owners and non-owners—that is, the bourgeoisie and the proletariat. Law was devised by the propertied class to protect its property. Marxists refer to this as bourgeois law. All bourgeois law is considered unjust, since it stifles the proletariat's evolutionary destiny. "Your jurisprudence," said Marx, "is but the will of your class made into law."[3]

While the basis of bourgeois law is to protect private property, the basis of proletarian law is to protect social or state property. Socialist law grants certain human rights but only such rights as assist the advancement of socialism and communism. Socialist law is just law. Bourgeois law is unjust law. Therefore, to violate bourgeois law is proper and not unlawful. To violate bourgeois law on behalf of socialist law is especially proper.

Marxist/Leninists like to think that proletarian law reflects proletarian man and the proletariat. The truth is slightly different. The vanguard of the proletariat is the Marxist/Leninist Party, and the head of the Party is the Dictator of the Proletariat. In the final analysis, socialist law equals proletarian law equals Marxist/Leninist Party law. And since the Party and the state are one, socialist law quickly becomes positive law with an economic twist. "A court," said Lenin, "is an organ of the state." Written into the U.S.S.R. constitution [especially Article 6] is the fact that the Communist Party is the only guide of Soviet society and the only interpreter of its laws. Hence, the Marxist/Leninist Party decrees the law and the Marxist/Leninist Party is the state that enforces the law. Human rights are decreed by the Party, but only such human rights as advance the socialist goal.

Once the full socialist system is victorious, however, the proletariat experiences its victory of communist paradise and law ceases (along with the state), since the initial reason for law—private property—ceases. Once private property ceases, crime ceases, also, and law withers due to the lack of class struggle. All inequality vanishes. Mankind has evolved to a level determined by nature itself, a goal all Marxist/Leninists strive to accomplish.

Notes and Asides

Introduction

As with Humanist law, Marxist law is based squarely on the assumptions that God does not exist and man is an evolving animal. And just as these assumptions cause the Humanist to abandon the concept of an absolute moral code or natural law, they force the Marxist to deny the existence of any law grounded in an authority outside of man.

V. I. Lenin asks, "In what sense do we repudiate ethics and morality?" He answers, "In the sense in which it was preached by the bourgeoisie, who derived ethics from God's commandments. We, of course, say that we do not believe in God. . . ."[4] The Marxist understands well that his denial of the existence of God causes him to deny any supernatural commands as well. "We deny all morality taken from superhuman or non-class conceptions," said Lenin. "We say that this is a deception, a swindle, a befogging of the minds of the workers and peasants in the interests of the landlords and capitalists."[5] Engels is equally adamant: "We therefore reject every attempt to impose on us any moral dogma whatsoever as an eternal, ultimate and forever immutable moral law. . ."[6]

This attitude is echoed by modern-day Marxists. L. S. Jawitsch, a Marxist law theorist, writes, "There are no eternal, immutable principles of law."[7] Elsewhere he clarifies this point:

> the character of the legal backing of social relations, the content of legislation, the state of the rule of law, and the legal status of the individual, like the political system, constitutional authority, and prevailing moral values, are not, from the standpoint of the materialist conception of history, eternal and immutable, not given by a supernatural power, and cannot be deduced from any metaphysical principles of an absolute idea or *a priori* requirement of reason . . . [8]

Since the supernatural does not exist, the Marxist must find another basis for law and ethics.

Naturally, this basis is the same as the Humanist foundation: mankind. Without the supernatural, only the highest animal in nature can be responsible for determining law. Thus, Lenin states, "We repudiate all morality taken apart from human society and classes."[9] The text *Socialism as a Social System* stands with Lenin: "Under socialism, man's ethicalness, happiness, dignity and freedom are the basis of all moral standards. Viewed from this standpoint, man is the yardstick of all values. All is moral that is conducive to man's all-round development."[10]

With man as the yardstick, morality and law must evolve right along

Notes and Asides

with mankind. Howard Selsam declares, "The Ten Commandments are an important landmark in human social and moral progress. . . . But this in no way relieves us of the task and the responsibility of modifying and reinterpreting these moral principles in the light of new experience, new conditions, and new times."[11] Laws and principles are always subject to reinterpretation when man's reason is the only means of determining their validity.

"There is but one law for all, namely, that law which governs all law, the law of our Creator, the law of humanity, justice, equity—the law of nature and of nations."
—Edmund Burke

Marxism also must deny the existence of natural rights—for the same reason Marxists deny God, an absolute moral code, and a natural, fixed law. If man is the only ethical yardstick, then no unchanging principles can exist, including rights. Maurice Cornforth states, "Rights in general are not . . . inherent in men as men, by virtue of their common human essence. They correspond rather to definite social requirements of definite people situated in definite circumstances."[12]

Clearly the Marxist perceives rights and law as arising from mankind and society, rather than from the commands of a supernatural Being. This implies that law arose at a specific point in history, sometime after the emergence of man on the evolutionary scene. Thus, the Marxist must address the question: When and how did law originate?

The Origin of Law

According to the Marxist, as soon as man formed a society and the most rudimentary economic structure involving class distinctions, two things came into existence simultaneously: law and the state. The reason for this is that societies and economies require order to function properly, and so laws had to arise to prescribe the bounds of order, and the state had to evolve to enforce the order.

Engels describes the origin of law and the state this way: "At a certain, very primitive stage of the development of society, the need arises to co-ordinate under a common regulation the daily recurring acts of production, distribution and exchange. . . . This regulation, which is at first custom, soon becomes *law*. With law, organs necessarily arise which are entrusted with its maintenance—public authority, the state."[13]

This regulation must exist in societies divided into classes because, according to the Marxist, class distinctions will always create conflict and disorder and must be kept in check as much as possible by laws and the state. Engels writes, "In order that these . . . classes with conflicting economic interests, may not annihilate themselves and society in a useless struggle, a power becomes necessary that stands apparently above society and has the function of keeping down the conflicts and maintaining 'order.' And this power, the outgrowth of society, but

Notes and Asides

assuming supremacy over it and becoming more and more divorced from it, is the State."[14]

Unfortunately, this state that arises to subdue class conflict actually winds up perpetuating the conflict, since the dominant class always wields the power of the state. Lenin declares, "The State is an organ of class domination, an organ of oppression of one class by another; its aim is the creation of 'order' which legalises and perpetuates this oppression by moderating the collisions between the classes."[15] According to this view, the state must be done away with—and it will be done away with, in the final stage of Marxism, which is communism. This concept has been presented in the chapter on Marxist politics; what is important to understand here is that the Marxist sees law, like the state, as inextricably tied to economic structures that encourage class conflict.

Whence comes this conflict? According to Marxism, class conflict is basically caused by private property. Thus, law and the state arose at the precise point in time when society and the economic structure gave rise to the concept of property. Jawitsch says, "The basis of law is actual possession of a thing, of property, and social relations in connection with that. . . ."[16] Elsewhere he writes, "Law emerges as a special variety of social consolidation of the prevailing mode of production and is therefore linked from the very start with actual property relations. . . ."[17]

Founding law on a specific theory about economics and property relations has powerful ramifications for the Marxist, as Jawitsch admits: "Legal reality constitutes one of the forms of social consciousness conditioned by social being, a legal superstructure on the economic basis; it therefore has only relative independence and cannot be understood by itself alone."[18] Rather, law must be studied with its "class nature," which is caused by unjust property relations, in mind. Law, for the Marxist, cannot be understood fully apart from its origin in an economy marked by class distinctions.

Law as the Will of the Ruling Class

As stated above, the Marxist believes laws are reflections of the desires of the class wielding state power. This belief stems from the Marxist assumption that the dominant class always gains control of the state, which is responsible for framing laws and enforcing them.

Thus, Andrei Y. Vyshinsky writes, "Marxism-Leninism gives a clear definition (the only scientific definition) of the essence of law. It teaches that legal relationships (and, consequently, law itself) are rooted in the material conditions of life, and that law is merely the will of the dominant class, elevated into a statute."[19] And Jawitsch echoes

Notes and Asides

him today: "Laws and statutes most clearly express the will of the ruling classes."[20] The reason for this is simple: "In the law the dominant will, which has been made into a law for all, is manifested in generally acceptable, binding norms of a general character, upheld by the state, and relations in the appropriate conditions."[21]

Today, according to the Marxist, there are only two basic classes that can be in control of the government and creating laws: the bourgeoisie and the proletariat. Selsam declares that "inasmuch as there are no moral principles standing over and above the needs and desires of men, and since these needs and desires are generally torn asunder by the actual conditions of the class divisions of society, there are only two genuine positions upon which moral judgments can be based. These are the positions or standpoints, the needs and interests, of the bourgeoisie and of the proletariat."[22] Naturally, the Marxist believes that all societies that allow the bourgeoisie to make moral decisions and formulate laws are unjust.

Bourgeois Law and the Proletariat

Marx clearly denounces bourgeois law as nothing more than a reflection of the desires of that class. In the *Communist Manifesto*, he tells the bourgeois: "your jurisprudence is but the will of your class made into a law for all, a will, whose essential character and direction are determined by the economic conditions of existence of your class."[23] This law, according to the Marxist, invariably discriminates against the propertyless working class. *The Fundamentals of Marxist-Leninist Philosophy* declares, "Law is the will of the ruling class, say Marx and Engels, embodied in legal acts. Therefore, like the state, law has a class character and in class-divided society is an instrument in the hands of the ruling class for holding down the working people."[24]

The main reason for the oppressive nature of bourgeois law, of course, is that it is based on the concept of private property. Selsam says, "capitalist ethics is based on private property, as is the law in which that ethics is enacted."[25] This basis causes the law to promote unequal rights. Cornforth writes, "The law protects the right of the owner of means of production to buy labour power and direct its employment, of the worker to sell labour power, and of each to organise to get the best terms he can in the bargain. That is the protection of unequal rights. . . ."[26] In truth, there can never be equal rights in a capitalistic society, according to the Marxist, since the very nature of the system creates haves and have-nots. Cornforth sums up, "There cannot be equality between exploiters and exploited. . . ."[27]

Bourgeois law contains another inherent flaw. According to Marx-

Notes and Asides

ism, laws promoting unequal rights breed protest in the form of lawlessness. Says Engels, "The contempt for the existing social order is most conspicuous in its extreme form—that of offences against the law."[28] He is echoed by Jawitsch, who declares,

> A social system that is based on social inequality and injustice, on the exploitation of man by man, and on the contradictions between social and personal interests, is thus the main source of anti-social excesses, and breeds crimes that are breaches of society's conditions of existence.[29]

Accordingly, society is more responsible for lawlessness than the individual. Indeed, the criminal need feel no remorse for his actions, since the unjust bourgeois society leaves no alternative but to lash out against it. "Crime, as a factor of social life, is not the consequence of an eternal contradiction between man's biological and social nature," writes Jawitsch. "It is the result of the defects of a society in which there is social inequality and injustice and class contradictions, and in which there is no harmony between the personal and the social (public) interest."[30]

Marxism proposes a clear-cut solution to injustice and crime: overthrow the bourgeoisie, thereby allowing the proletariat to make the laws. Jawitsch believes, "Complete success in the masses' struggle for their democratic rights and liberties can only be achieved by overcoming monopoly capital's economic and political domination and establishing a state authority that expresses the interests of the working people."[31]

The need for a society in which the proletariat make the laws is so pressing, and the laws of bourgeois society are so unjust, that the Marxist believes the working class is justified in ignoring modern capitalistic laws in their pursuit of equality. Thus, the text *Why Communism?* declares,

> When you fight capitalism you are doing what is right and just and lawful from the point of view of your class interests and of the future of humanity. You are not "outlaws" the way the capitalist world brands revolutionary fighters. You are fighting for a higher morality and a higher law that will forever abolish exploitation—the morality and the law of the social revolution.[32]

Marxist "higher law", of course, is not God's law or even natural law, but another form of positive law: Communist Party law.

Indeed, this need to create a dictatorship of the proletariat is so

Notes and Asides

strong that every hint of bourgeois law may be ignored by the revolutionary in the pursuit of his goal. A. Shishkin states,

> Having tied up ethics with the class struggle of the proletariat, Marxism has rejected all appeals to "an eternal justice" so characteristic of the old moral doctrines. "For us," wrote V. I. Lenin, "justice is subordinated to our interest in overthrowing capitalism."[33]

> "Soviet law is a contradiction in terms. The widespread use of terror as an administrative tool in the Soviet Union justifies this belief."
> —Max Kampelman

Lenin further proclaims,

> The revolutionary dictatorship of the proletariat is rule won and maintained by the use of violence by the proletariat against the bourgeoisie, rule that is unrestricted by any laws.[34]

Judging from the Marxist's disdain for law when attempting to further the cause of the proletariat, it would seem that Marxism would also largely ignore law once the dictatorship of the proletariat is established. This, however, is not the case. The Marxist has specific ideas about law in a socialist society.

Law Reflects Socialist Economics

Naturally, socialist law will reflect the desires of the working people rather than of the bourgeois. "The new type of state brings into being a new type of law. Socialist law serves the interests of the working people and legalises new social relations; it safeguards social property and defines the legal position of the state organs and mass organisations, the rights and duties of individual citizens, etc."[35] By basing law on the will of the proletariat, the Marxist believes he will be creating a less exploitative society. Jawitsch states, "Whereas law in presocialist formations is permeated with ideological and moral principles corresponding to the outlook of the propertied classes on the world, under socialism the lofty ideas stemming from the theory of scientific communism and its grand humanistic scale of values are proper to law. An anti-exploiter tendency is what characterises the special features of all the principles of the law of socialist society in most concentrated form."[36]

The basis in Marxist society for all judgments regarding exploitation, rights, and the law is the will of the proletariat. God, an absolute moral code, and natural law have no bearing on these judgments. "Marxism, which has been so often accused of seeking to eliminate moral considerations from human life and history," writes Selsam, "emphasizes rather the moral issues involved in every situation. It does

Notes and Asides

so, however, not by standing on a false platform of absolute right, but by identifying itself with the real needs and interests of the workers and farmers. . . ."[37] Jawitsch tries to get around this conclusion by stating, "Marxist science's recognition of the class nature of law, the state and morality in no way excludes the need for a concrete historical approach to the appraisal of punishment from the angle of its fairness."[38] But this reliance on the concept of fairness to separate legal decisions from the whims of the proletariat does not erase the fact that the working class provides Marxism's standard for justice. For without absolutes, the standard for fairness can only be grounded in mankind. As we have seen, the Marxist relies on a specific class of mankind, the proletariat, for such judgments.

Obviously, law based on such an unstable foundation will not be consistent. Rather than calling law based on the whims of the proletariat inconsistent, however, Marxism calls it flexible. The Marxist disregards stable capitalist law as an outmoded form, claiming that just law requires elasticity—even to the point of abandoning any comprehensive legal system. E. B. Pashukanis, a Soviet legal theorist, writes, "In bourgeois-capitalist society, the legal superstructure should have maximum immobility—maximum stability—because it represents a firm framework of the movement of the economic forces whose bearers are capitalist entrepreneurs. . . . Among us it is different. We require that our legislation possess maximum elasticity. We cannot fetter ourselves by any sort of system. . . ."[39]

This view is quite consistent with the Marxist evolutionary perspective. Since man is in a constant state of evolution and law is founded on man, law must also be constantly changing. Jawitsch declares,

> The law, just like morality and politics, develops and changes. Since the course of history is inseparable from human activity, and is the result of the creative efforts of men, social groups, classes, peoples, and nations, legal relations, too, arise and are transformed and perfected solely as a consequence of that same human activity.[40]

Elsewhere he states, "The legal system of every country is fluid, of course, and changes in consequence of the evolution of social relations and in connection with the development of new spheres of human activity subject to some kind of legal mediation."[41]

The Marxist openly admits that his theory causes law to be arbitrary. Selsam says,

> Just as it is impossible to find eternal moral principles in the form of commandments and maxims, it is impossible to find eternal justice embodied in statutes and legal codes. Just as a

Notes and Asides

> given maxim becomes obsolete through changing conditions, so does a principle of legal right require reinterpretation in each new epoch, and, in periods of far-reaching social reconstruction, complete overthrow and a replacement by a new principle meeting new situations and needs.[42]

This arbitrary nature of law extends as well to the realm of rights. Jawitsch claims, "Rights, as a legal phenomenon, have deep social roots and in a way reflect mankind's evolution from complete unfreedom to freedom for the few, and eventually to the social freedom of all in the future communist society."[43]

Socialist laws and rights are completely arbitrary, since they are based on the will of the ruling class—which in socialist society is the proletariat. As demonstrated in the chapter on Humanist law, a system basing laws on the decisions of those in power is nothing more than legal positivism.

Legal Positivism

Legal positivism is a theory that bases all legal truth on the decisions of the state. While the Marxist is unwilling to admit that his theory of law is based on positivism, the conclusion becomes inescapable when one combines the Marxist assumptions that no absolutes exist and that law is the will of the ruling class. Indeed, many statements by Marxists betray the positivist nature of their legal theory.

For example, Lenin proclaims, "A court is an organ of state power. Liberals sometimes forget that. It is a sin for a Marxist to forget it."[44] The Soviet Union takes Lenin's advice to heart:

> Since the court is one of the organs through which the dominant class exercises its rule, it cannot be outside of politics; what is more, the activities of the courts are always political activities. In our Soviet state, measures are taken to see to it that the court is in reality a conductor of the policy of the communist party and the Soviet regime.[45]

Obviously, this Marxist attitude toward the courts is legal positivism with a vengeance. Courts are created to dispense justice—and from whence do they derive this justice? From the state, according to the Marxist.

The Marxist betrays his positivist approach to law in other ways, as well. Jawitsch believes, "As a component of the legal superstructure law is closely linked with the political superstructure and with the

Notes and Asides

state."[46] Elsewhere he declares that socialism "creates the premises for effective, scientifically grounded law-giving by the state authorities, capable of reflecting the people's urgent objective needs and will in the highest degree."[47] This seems a reasonably clear admission that justice in socialist society is created by the state, under the guidance of the proletariat (who, in turn, are guided by the Marxist/Leninist party). The

CLOSE-UP

Yuri Andropov (1914-1984)

At first glance, one might conclude that Yuri Andropov had little influence on the modern Marxist worldview. He served as leader of the USSR for just two years before his death, and even those years were largely spent fighting various illnesses. But when one considers that Andropov has been called Mikhail Gorbachev's "mentor," his significance as a Marxist leader becomes readily apparent. Was Gorbachev's mentor a progressive liberal concerned with human rights and mending relations with the United States, as the Marxists would have us believe? Several facts about Andropov suggest the answer is "no." As the USSR's ambassador to Hungary in 1954-57, Andropov misled rebel Hungarians into believing the Soviet Union would withdraw from Hungary if they staged an uprising. Instead, the USSR brutally crushed the rebel forces, causing some Hungarians to dub Andropov "the butcher." In 1967 Andropov became chairman of the KGB (a position he held for fifteen years), and initiated the practice of confining dissident intellectuals to mental hospitals. After gaining control of the USSR in November of 1982, Andropov accomplished very little—perhaps his most significant legacy was the strained U.S.-Soviet relations he created by reacting with disdain to American protest over the flight 007 tragedy. 269 people died when Soviet pilots shot down that flight, and Andropov showed no signs of regret. It would seem, then, that Gorbachev's mentor could have taught him little about humanitarianism or human rights; instead, Andropov provided numerous examples of the practical cruelty of a worldview that believes the ends justify the means.

Notes and Asides

clearest declaration of legal positivism is made by Lenin, who boldly proclaims, "A law is a political instrument; it is politics."[48]

Obviously, if law is politics, then it is safe to assume that the state is the only real source of justice. As with the Humanist, the Marxist must embrace legal positivism to be consistent with his worldview. However, because Marxism bases much of its legal theory on economics, the Marxist version of legal positivism differs in one sense from the Humanist approach.

Law as an Extension of Party Politics

Since the Marxist believes that the proletariat must gain control of the state and formulate new laws to create a truly just society, the Marxist brand of legal positivism takes on a distinctive class character. While the Humanist simply believes that the state is responsible for establishing rights and promoting justice, the Marxist believes that the proletarian state is the only government capable of promoting justice. Thus, Marxist law requires a state led by the proletariat.

Selsam puts this position simply: "But what is the basis of judgments of right and wrong?" Marxism provides an answer "that has elements of both relativism and absolutism. Marx maintains that 'Right can never be higher than the economic structure and the cultural development of society thereby determined,' and yet at the same time he believes absolutely in the rights and justice of the modern proletariat."[49] That is, the proletariat is the only yardstick for determining justice, and therefore Marxist legal positivism rests on transferring state power into the hands of the proletariat.

> "Lenin laid the foundations for the system of law characteristic of totalitarianism, as opposed to the laws of a despotic system."
> —Leszek Kolakowski

As explained in the Marxist politics chapter, however, the Marxist believes his political party must act as the guiding force for the workers once they achieve power—so the actual source for determining all justice becomes not a class, but a political party: the Marxist-Leninist party. Thus, Vyshinsky states,

> The formal law is subordinate to the law of the revolution. There might be collisions and discrepancies between the formal commands of laws and those of the proletarian revolution. . . . This collision must be solved only by the subordination of the formal commands of law to those of party policy.[50]

In the end, Marxist/Leninist party policy becomes the ultimate criterion for determining law.

The Marxist expects every member of society to accept the Marxist party as the true source of justice. Indeed, even lawyers must subordi-

Notes and Asides

nate their clients' needs to those of the party. K. Jankowski claims, "A lawyer cannot be simply a passive executor of the law. He should be a political activist in the realization of party tasks."[51] An article in the *Literary Gazette* declares,

> A Soviet lawyer cannot confine his task merely to the interests of the client, as a separate isolated person, but must always think in the first instance of the interests of the peoples, the interests of the state.[52]

Marxist law adds a new twist to legal positivism. Marxism declares the proletariat to be the only true source of justice and requires the proletariat to gain power to begin to correct old, unjust bourgeois laws. Thus, the state is seen by the Marxist to be the ultimate source of justice only when the dictatorship of the proletariat has been established. This dictatorship, in turn, requires the guidance of the Marxist/Leninist party—thereby making the party the final source for all legal and moral truth.

Marxist Law and the Enemies of the Proletariat

As one might imagine, if the Marxist/Leninist party is the ultimate source of justice, then anyone in Marxist society who disagrees with this view is guilty of lawlessness. Since the party gets to decide what is legal, it can easily condemn any displeasing actions as illegal.

Thus, the 1936 Soviet Constitution affirms that all citizens are granted certain rights "In conformity with the interests of the working people, and in order to strengthen the socialist system. . . ."[53] Citizens in a Marxist society are guaranteed certain rights as long as they never exercise those rights in a way that hinders the advance of communism. However, individuals who act in a way deemed unacceptable by the Marxist/Leninist party will quickly find themselves without any rights protected by law. This has been documented in such works as Alexander Solzhenitsyn's *The Gulag Archipelago*.

> "Soviet law is what the KGB says it is."
> —Arnold Beichman

The new Soviet Constitution, dated 1977, likewise stresses the power of the Marxist/Leninist party to determine the law and guide the actions of its citizens. Article 6 declares, "The leading and guiding force of Soviet society and the nucleus of its political system, of all state organizations and public organizations, is the Communist Party of the Soviet Union. The CPSU exists for the people and serves the people.

"The Communist Party, armed with Marxism-Leninism, determines the general perspectives of the development of society and the course of the home and foreign policy of the USSR, directs the great

Notes and Asides

constructive work of the Soviet people, and imparts a planned, systematic and theoretically substantiated character to their struggle for the victory of communism."[54]

In the same year, Leonid I. Brezhnev made it clear that the socialist state views anti-communist actions as illegal:

> Of course, comrades, the project of the Constitution proceeds from the fact that the rights and freedoms of citizens cannot and must not be used against our social system, to the detriment of the interests of the Soviet people. It is therefore directly stated in the project, for example, that the taking advantage of rights and freedoms by citizens must not be prejudicial to the interests of society and the state and the rights of other citizens, and that political freedoms are granted in accordance with the interests of the toilers and with the aim of fortifying the socialist system.[55]

This legal discrimination by the Marxist/Leninist party against any individual who disagrees with their political agenda should be relentless, according to Vyshinsky: "The task of justice in the USSR is to assure the precise and unswerving fulfillment of Soviet laws by all the institutions, organizations, officials, and citizens of the USSR. This the court accomplishes by destroying without pity all the foes of the people in whatsoever form they manifest their criminal encroachments upon socialism."[56] A law that is created and enforced by a specific ideology will not tolerate actions opposed to its belief system.

Obviously, the class nature of Marxism's version of legal positivism has distinct ramifications for legal theory in socialist society. Not only does it place all power to interpret justice in the hands of the Marxist/Leninist party, but also it creates legal discrimination against people opposed to the party.

Marxism's approach to legal positivism is unique in another way. As demonstrated in the chapter on Marxist politics, Marxism expects the state to wither away as socialist society moves toward communism. But if the state is to wither away, then the source of all justice will disappear as well. A positivist view of law that calls for the disappearance of the state must also call for the disappearance of law.

Law Withers Away

The Marxist is willing to accept the conclusion that law will wither away in communist society, since he views law as arising from class conflicts caused by property. Vyshinsky states, "Law is no 'enigmatic

Notes and Asides

shape' but a living reality expressing the essence of social relationships between classes."[57] Since communism will abolish all classes, the need to promote order between classes will no longer exist; therefore law will become unnecessary. Lenin put it this way:

> Freed from capitalist slavery, from the untold horrors, absurdities and infamies of capitalist exploitation, people will gradually become accustomed to the observation of the elementary rules of social life. . . . They will become accustomed to observing them without force, without coercion, without subordination, without the special apparatus of coercion which is called "the State."[58]

Communist society will cause people to observe laws and rules without anyone enforcing, or even formulating, a system of law. Thus, the state and law wither away.

However, as the state does not wither away the moment a society overthrows the bourgeoisie and begins the march toward communism, law also must remain in existence in socialist society, the first stage of communism. The state and law must still exist because socialism cannot immediately abolish all classes and inequality. Jawitsch writes, "Both Karl Marx in his *Critique of the Gotha Programme* and Lenin in *The State and Revolution* demonstrated a need to retain law in the first phase of communism, because socialism could not yet ensure actual (economic) equality and full social justice in the distribution of material goods. Law is retained so as to control the measure of labour and consumption, and to protect social property and the principle of 'from each according to his ability, to each according to his work.'"[59]

> "Where law ends, tyranny begins."
> —William Pitt

Although the change to a socialistic economic structure does not instantly abolish law, it does begin the process that eventually causes law to wither away. Pashukanis believes that with the move toward communism there will come "the withering away of law in general, that is, the gradual disappearance of the juridical element from human relations."[60] Jawitsch says that "as society develops and historical types of relations of production and state succeed one another, law's essence of each order undergoes changes, but not so great that law ceases to be law. Only the higher stage of communism is associated with such radical changes in the mode of production and distribution as will exclude the objective need for legally binding yardsticks of conduct protected by the state. . . ."[61] *The Fundamentals of Marxist-Leninist Philosophy*, in a statement brimming with legal positivism, echoes this assertion: "Just as the state cannot manage without law, so the law cannot function without the state, which safeguards the legal norms. Law originated together with the state and together with it will wither

Notes and Asides

away when the causes that engendered it have disappeared. For this reason Marx and Engels always regarded the state and legal superstructure on the economic basis as a single institution."[62]

Thus, the Marxist believes that at the highest stage of communism, law will have ceased to exist. This view is summed up by P. I. Stuchka: "Communism means not the victory of socialist law, but the victory of socialism over any law, since with the abolition of classes with their antagonistic interests, law will die out altogether."[63]

It would seem that the disappearance of law in communist society creates a grave problem for the Marxist. How will order be maintained without law? No action, no matter how irresponsible, could be deemed unlawful by society. Would not chaos result?

The Marxist is untroubled by these possibilities. According to his view, when classes are abolished man will live in an environment that promotes harmony. Criminal actions will almost never occur, since injustice and inequality (catalysts for such anti-social activity) will not exist. J. Plamenatz says that in a communist society crime will be "virtually unknown," because "motives will be less urgent and frequent, and the offender will be more easily brought to his senses by the need to regain the good opinion of his neighbours. The assumption is that he lives in a society that is not divided, where men are not one another's victims, where no man is an outcast or an inferior merely because of his position in society. In a society of this kind, crime is much more clearly irrational, much more clearly against the interests of the criminal."[64] In other words, crime becomes "unscientific." Jawitsch echoes this sentiment: "Communists believe that there will be no crime in [communist] society, that anti-social displays will be very rare, easily eliminated excesses, and that observance of the basic rules of any human intercourse will become habitual for every member of society. And that will happen through true flowering of the human personality in social conditions of genuine equality and justice."[65]

The Marxist believes he can create a socialist/communist society that encourages lawful action and allows the individual to be true to his inherently moral nature, thereby eliminating the need for both state and law. This elimination of law does not occur immediately after the revolution by the proletariat, since class divisions will exist for a time. Eventually, however, communist society will cause both state and law to wither away.

Conclusion

Marxist law is very similar to Humanist law in that both views assume that God does not exist and man and his social institutions are evolving. Because of these assumptions, both Marxism and Humanism must rely

Notes and Asides

on some version of legal positivism. However, the Marxist version of legal positivism is unique in that it assigns a class character to the state's role as ultimate source of justice. Since the Marxist believes that law is always the will of the ruling class and that only the proletariat is capable of creating justice, he must call for rule by the proletariat to create a just system of law. Further, since the proletariat must rule under the guidance of the Marxist/Leninist party, the party becomes the final authority on morality and law.

But a system of law determined by individuals adhering to a specific ideology will consistently create laws prejudiced against people with opposing worldviews. Marxist law allows the Marxist/Leninist party to formulate laws and assign rights in any manner it chooses. The Marxist extends this random approach to law to international law as well. Kozhevnikov declares,

> Those institutions in international law which can facilitate the execution of the stated tasks of the USSR are recognised and applied by the USSR, and those institutions which conflict in any manner with these purposes are rejected by the USSR.[66]

Thus, Marxist law, on both the national and international level, is reduced to nothing more than a reflection of the ideology of the members of the Marxist-Leninist party.

[1]A. G. Goikhbarg, *Foundations of Private Property Law* (Moscow: 1924), p. 9. Cited in Harold J. Berman, *Justice in the USSR* (Cambridge, MA: Harvard University, 1978), p. 26.
[2]Karl Marx and Frederick Engels, *Collected Works*, forty volumes (New York: International Publishers, 1976), vol. 6, pp. 494-5.
[3]Ibid., p. 501.
[4]V. I. Lenin, *On Socialist Ideology and Culture* (Moscow: Foreign Languages Publishing House), pp. 51-2, cited in James D. Bales, *Communism and the Reality of Moral Law* (Nutley, NJ: The Craig Press, 1969), p.2.
[5]V. I. Lenin, *Religion* (New York: International Publishers, 1933), pp. 47-8.
[6]Frederick Engels, *Anti-Dühring* (New York: International Publishers, 1935), p. 109.
[7]L. S. Jawitsch, *The General Theory of Law* (Moscow: Progress Publishers, 1981), p. 160.
[8]Ibid., pp. 22-3.
[9]Lenin, *On Socialist Ideology and Culture*, pp. 51-2.
[10]T. M. Jaroszewski and P. A. Ignatovsky, eds., *Socialism as a Social System* (Moscow: Progress Publishers, 1981), p. 249.
[11]Howard Selsam, *Socialism and Ethics* (New York: International Publishers, 1943), p. 41.
[12]Maurice Cornforth, *The Open Philosophy and the Open Society* (New York: International Publishers, 1976), p. 283.
[13]Selsam, *Socialism and Ethics*, p. 44.
[14]Frederick Engels, *The Origin of the Family, Private Property and the State* (Chicago: Kerr, 1902), p. 206.
[15]V. I. Lenin, *The State and Revolution* (New York: International Publishers, 1932), p. 9.
[16]Jawitsch, *The General Theory of Law*, p. 31.
[17]Ibid., p. 28.
[18]Ibid., p. 10.
[19]Andrei Y. Vyshinsky, *The Law of the Soviet State* (New York: 1948), p. 13. Cited in *A Lexicon of Marxist-Leninist Semantics*, ed. Raymond S. Sleeper (Alexandria, VA: Western Goals, 1983), p. 147.
[20]Jawitsch, *The General Theory of Law*, p. 43.
[21]Ibid., p. 97.
[22]Selsam, *Socialism and Ethics*, p. 93.
[23]Marx and Engels, *Collected Works,* vol. 6, p. 501.
[24]*The Fundamentals of Marxist-Leninist Philosophy*, ed. F. V. Konstantinov (Moscow: Progress Publishers, 1982), p. 296.
[25]Selsam, *Socialism and Ethics*, p. 58.
[26]Cornforth, *The Open Philosophy and the Open Society*, p. 289.
[27]Ibid., p. 290.
[28]Frederick Engels, *The Condition of the Working Class in England* (Moscow: 1973), p. 168. Cited in R. W. Makepeace, *Marxist Ideology and Soviet Criminal Law* (Totowa, NJ: Barnes and Noble, 1980), p. 30.
[29]Jawitsch, *The General Theory of Law*, p. 265.
[30]Ibid., p. 270.
[31]Ibid., p. 46.
[32]*Why Communism?* (New York: Workers Library Publishers, 1935), p. 62. Cited in Bales, *Communism and the Reality of Moral Law*, p. 4.
[33]A. Shishkin, *Foundations of Communist Morality* (Moscow: 1955), p. 77. Cited in *A Lexicon of Marxist-Leninist Semantics*, ed. Sleeper, p. 143.
[34]V. I. Lenin, *Collected Works*, forty-five volumes (Moscow: Progress Publishers, 1981), vol. 28, p. 236.
[35]*The Fundamentals of Marxist-Leninist Philosophy*, ed. Konstantinov, p. 304.
[36]Jawitsch, *The General Theory of Law*, p. 160.
[37]Selsam, *Socialism and Ethics*, p. 13.
[38]Jawitsch, *The General Theory of Law*, p. 283.
[39]E. B. Pashukanis in a 1930 speech regarding the Soviet State and the Revolution of Law (Moscow).
[40]Jawitsch, *The General Theory of Law*, p. 23.
[41]Ibid., p. 134.
[42]Selsam, *Socialism and Ethics*, p. 44.

[43]Jawitsch, *The General Theory of Law*, p. 177.
[44]V. I. Lenin, *Works*, 4th ed. (Moscow: 1949-50), vol. 25, p. 155. Cited in John Hazard, *Settling Disputes in Soviet Soceity* (New York: Columbia University, 1960), p. 3.
[45]*Moscow University Herald* (1951), no. 11, cited in *A Lexicon of Marxist-Leninist Semantics*, ed. Sleeper, p. 73.
[46]Jawitsch, *The General Theory of Law*, p. 290.
[47]Ibid., p. 82.
[48]Lenin, *Works*, vol. 23, p. 36.
[49]Selsam, *Socialism and Ethics*, p. 12.
[50]Andrei Y. Vyshinsky, *Judiciary of the USSR*, 2d ed. (Moscow: 1935), p. 32. Cited in Berman, *Justice in the USSR*, pp. 42-3.
[51]K. Jankowski, *Trybuna Ludu* (Warsaw), 9 Nov. 1963, cited in *A Lexicon of Marxist-Leninist Semantics*, ed. Sleeper, p. 149.
[52]*Literary Gazette* (Moscow), 8 June 1951, cited in Ibid.
[53]Cited in John Hazard, *Law and Social Change in the USSR* (London: Stevens and Sons, 1953), p. 79.
[54]A. M. Prokhorov, ed., *The Great Soviet Encyclopedia* (New York: Macmillan, 1982), vol. 31, p. 10.
[55]L. I. Brezhnev, speech at the CPSU Central Committee Plenary Session of 24 May 1977, *Kommunist* (Moscow), May 1977, cited in *A Lexicon of Marxist-Leninist Semantics*, ed. Sleeper, p. 243.
[56]Vyshinsky, *The Law of the Soviet State*, p. 498.
[57]Ibid., p. 38.
[58]Lenin, *The State and Revolution*, pp. 73-4.
[59]Jawitsch, *The General Theory of Law*, p. 32.
[60]Cited in Berman, *Justice in the USSR*, p. 29.
[61]Jawitsch, *The General Theory of Law*, p. 104.
[62]*The Fundamentals of Marxist-Leninist Philosophy*, ed. Konstantinov, pp. 296-7.
[63]P. I. Stuchka, ed., *Encyclopedia of State and Law* (Moscow: 1927), vol. 3, p. 1594. Cited in Berman, *Justice in the USSR*, p. 26.
[64]J. Plamenatz, *Man and Society*, (London: 1966), vol. 2, p. 374. Cited in Makepeace, *Marxist Ideology and Soviet Criminal Law*, p. 35.
[65]Jawitsch, *The General Theory of Law*, p. 287.
[66]Kozhevnikov, *The Soviet State and International Law* (Moscow: 1948), p. 25. Cited in Hazard, *Law and Social Change in the USSR*, p. 275.

CHAPTER

23

BIBLICAL CHRISTIAN LAW

"But we know that the law is good, if a man use it lawfully."

—1 Timothy 1:8

"Law is organized justice."[1]

—Frederic Bastiat

"The Christian . . . sees justice as rooted in the loving will of God, a will directed towards the good of the beings he created and exemplified in his dealings with men."[2]

—Peter A. De Vos

"To cut off Law from its ethical sources is to strike a terrible blow at the rule of law."[3]

—Russell Kirk

SUMMARY

Christian or divine law consists of both natural and Biblical law originating in the very character of a righteous and loving God—Creator of heaven and earth (Genesis 1:1), of male and female (Genesis 1:27). Divine law is eternal because God is eternal. It is permanent because God is permanent. It is so eternal and permanent that someday God will use it to judge the world (Acts 17:31) in a judgment based on natural and revealed law (Romans 2:12-15).

God's law is manifested everywhere in His creation. Everything from the subatomic to the macro-cosmos bears the mark of the lawful hand of God. Following Logos or Mind, law is the avenue God used to create the universe. Law gives the universe its order and design. He rules His universe according to law.

Natural order is dictated by the law invested in it by its Creator. Christians refer to natural law as general revelation (over against Biblical or special revelation). It is available for all to witness and enjoy. There is a designed law principle in all living things. Man is a walking laboratory of law—every cell in his body obeys an orderly and designed code of lawful information called DNA. God has legislated such law by which the universe operates, by which all organic and inorganic matter operates, and has legislated law for mankind's well-being as well.

Unfortunately, mankind's moral and legal rebellion against his Creator has had a profound impact on the way he views God's law. Instead of welcoming God's concern for His creatures, some have declared war on God (Psalm 2:1-4) and mock His lawful ways.

God established human government and the rule of law primarily to keep man's sinful nature and passions in check (Romans 13:1-4). As James Madison pointed out in *The Federalist Papers*, if men were angels there would be no need for government. In this sense, law is a steady reminder of the sinfulness of man; as St. Paul says, "by law is the knowledge of sin" (Romans 3:20).

Because of the Fall, human history reflects a continuing effort by men to substitute man-made law for God's law. The consequences of such an attempt are obvious in the twentieth century. "Man has forgotten God," cried Alexander Solzhenitsyn in his Templeton Address. The human race has recently been confronted with Nazism, Communism, and Secular Humanism, all of which attempt to cut off the Biblical theological/ethical roots of law by substituting a biological base of evolution.

The Christian concept of law has its theological/ethical roots intact. It recognizes, first, the role of law in God's universe; second, the role of law in God's establishment of human government, which St. Paul summarizes in Romans 13 and 1 Timothy 1:8-10; and third, the role of law in convicting men of their sin and preparing them to accept God's remedy for their sin—Jesus Christ.

Christians realize that law cannot save them from their sin (Galatians 3:11). Only

Jesus Christ can save man, since salvation from sin is by grace through faith (Ephesians 2:8-10). Human government's function is not to establish a church or to save the souls of men but to protect individuals and the God-ordained institutions of home, church, and state from anarchy, crime, corruption, and harm from without.

Christians believe that when God's laws are obeyed, men and societies thrive; when God's laws are ignored or trampled, nations rot from within and crumble. Morally corrupt nations have forgotten God and are part of the dustbin of history.

The Christian concept of human rights involves the Biblical doctrine of man's creation in the image of God. Man's significance proceeds from the fact that God is his creator and as such has bestowed on him certain rights. These rights, which carry with them specific responsibilities, are unalienable. They belong to man because of his relationship with his Creator and not because of his relationship with the state. In fact, the state's primary duty is to protect these God-given rights and punish those who violate them.

The fundamental human right is life itself. Human life is precious and meaningful because God created it. It is also precious because God took human flesh on Himself and dwelt among us (John 1:14). Out of this creative image and incarnation of Jesus Christ flows a comprehensive human rights system that includes justice, order, life, liberty, property, and yes, the pursuit of happiness. While evolution is the key to both the Marxist and the Humanist systems of law, creation and incarnation are the keys to Christian law.

The American Declaration of Independence and the U.S. Constitution were based on Christian law concepts, not Marxist or Humanist principles. These documents recognized human rights as based in the Creator. As men and nations move away from that base, the results will be morally and legally bankrupt societies. The supreme irony is that Creator/Creation concepts are generally outlawed in America's public school systems, and most American law schools ignore Christian law concepts. Only Marxist and Humanist evolutionary concepts are permitted—concepts that do not support America's political or legal system.

God's Word and nature's law are sufficient for mankind to establish a legal system that exemplifies man's created image but does not soft-pedal his depravity. It is hoped that mankind will not forget the lesson Israel should have learned as keeper of the law of Moses: men and society need more than law structure. Society needs grace, mercy, love, and truth as well (John 1:17). Humanist Bertrand Russell admits: "What the world needs is Christian love or compassion."[4] Legal structures accenting justice need the cement of love and compassion to make life meaningful and worth living. The Bible says it with profound simplicity—love covers a multitude of sins (1 Peter 4:8).

Notes and Asides

fellowship w/ God

Introduction

Jean Jacques Rousseau, an eighteenth-century philosopher who denied orthodox Christianity, believed mankind incapable of creating a system of law that dispenses anything close to justice. The Christian agrees with Rousseau on this point. Indeed, Rousseau came remarkably close to describing the Christian attitude toward law when he wrote that in order to discover a legal structure best suited to nations, "a superior intelligence beholding all the passions of men without experiencing any of them would be needed." This intelligence, he said, would have to be "wholly unrelated to our nature, while knowing it through and through; its happiness would have to be independent of us, and yet ready to occupy itself with ours; and lastly, it would have, in the march of time, to look forward to a distant glory, and, working in one century, to be able to enjoy in the next. It would take gods to give men laws. . . ."[5]

More accurately it would take the one true God who created mankind to give men laws. Christian law offers Rousseau (and anyone else seeking a genuine source for law) a real Law-giver, more perfect than anything Rousseau imagines. John Warwick Montgomery put it this way: "Rousseau's 'superior intelligence' as legislator is not a mere ideal—and, instead of being coldly 'unrelated to our nature' and without 'experience of the passions of men,' God himself entered our midst, was 'like us yet without sin,' and imparted to us the true nature and fulfillment of eternal law."[6]

The Christian legal theorist believes that only a being superior to mankind could create a truly just system of law answering to mankind's moral and legal needs. Unlike Rousseau, however, the Christian believes that that being exists in the form of the omniscient, omnipotent, omnipresent, loving God. The God presented in the Bible is a legal being, as witnessed by 1 John 2:1: "And if any man sin, we have an advocate [i.e., attorney] with the Father, Jesus Christ the righteous." Fortunately for mankind, God is also the fountainhead of mercy, grace, love, and forgiveness.

The Christian adheres to the view that God has provided laws (and a means of discovering those laws) for mankind. He believes he worships and prays to the one true source of Law. "God is the only Legislator," says Carl F. H. Henry. "Earthly rulers and legislative bodies are alike accountable to Him from whom stems all obligation—religious, ethical and civil."[7] The Bible says, "Be wise now therefore, O ye kings; be instructed, ye judges of the earth. Serve the Lord with fear, and rejoice with trembling. Kiss the Son, lest he be angry, and ye perish from the way, when his wrath is kindled but a little. Blessed are they that put their trust in him" (Psalm 2:10-12).

If all of this is true, it presents serious implications for all of mankind, and not only in the realm of law. This becomes obvious when one examines the assumptions and consequent failings implicit to every man-centered system of law. Systems which deny God as Law-giver ultimately fail and will always adversely affect every individual mired in them. They fail because they recognize neither the dignity of man created in the image of God nor the fallen nature of man—a condition documented in the Bible and in history.

Systems of Man-Centered Law

If God does exist and does create law, then any society that ignores His laws will be out of step with reality. Indeed, a society or state that forgets God will promote strictly arbitrary laws, consequently causing its subjects to lose respect for the legal system. John Whitehead believes that when fundamental principles of law are undermined, "public confidence in law and public willingness to abide by law are also sapped. And when nonfundamental regulations are elevated to the status of solemn, absolutely binding law, public confidence and trust tend to disappear entirely."[8] Robert Bork sees this same danger: "As we move away from the historical rooted Constitution to one created by abstract, universalistic styles of constitutional reasoning, we invite a number of dangers. One is that such styles teach disrespect for the actual institutions of the American nation."[9] The reason public trust disappears is simple: when law is not considered sacred, neither is it considered binding. If fallen man is in charge of creating law, one can rest assured that he will constantly recreate the law to better suit his innate selfish needs or the innate selfish needs of his constituents. This causes disregard for the rule of law.

Man's disregard for manmade law causes the individual to adopt an arbitrary attitude toward other areas in his life, most notably ethics. Without a law that is both unchanging and worthy of obedience, where can the individual discover a moral code apart from mankind? Man quickly realizes that if God does not exist, all things are permissible. Francis Schaeffer notes that Humanist Will Durant saw this point clearly. Says Schaeffer,

> Will Durant and his wife Ariel together wrote *The Story of Civilization*. The Durants received the 1976 Humanist Pioneer Award. In *The Humanist* magazine of February 1977, Will Durant summed up the humanist problem with regard to personal ethics and social order: "Moreover, we shall find it no easy task to mold a natural ethic strong enough to maintain moral restraint and social order without the support of supernatural

Notes and Asides

> consolations, hopes, and fears."
>
> Poor Will Durant! It is not just difficult, it is impossible.[10]

A void in the realm of legal foundations creates a void in the realm of moral foundations as well. Thus, legal systems that deny the reality of God as ultimate Law-giver are both legally and ethically bankrupt. This bodes ill for men in societies based on legal positivism, because such systems unswervingly lead to societal breakdowns. "Good law is limiting," explains Whitehead. "It prevents the exercise of arbitrary power by the state and its agencies. If, however, the foundation undergirding law in a Christian society shifts from a Christian to a humanistic base [legal positivism], then a 'nervous breakdown' occurs. Anarchy may result, and, if it does, history teaches that an imposed order will be inevitable."[11]

Unfortunately, many modern states and the United Nations[12] are based on positive law. As predicted, this absence of a proper legal foundation is creating breakdowns throughout such societies. Indeed, the bankruptcy of the modern world's legal and ethical codes power-

Recommended Reading for Advanced Study

John W. Whitehead, *The Second American Revolution* (Westchester, IL: Crossway, 1988).

John Warwick Montgomery, *Human Rights and Human Dignity* (Dallas, TX: Probe, 1986).

Gary T. Amos, *Defending the Declaration* (Brentwood, TN: Wolgemuth and Hyatt, 1989).

Frederick Bastiat, *The Law* (Irvington-on-Hudson, NY: The Foundation for Economic Education, 1990).

Restoring the Constitution, ed. H. Wayne House (Dallas, TX: Probe, 1987).

fully demonstrates the need for a legal basis outside of and above man. "The horrors of our recent history," writes Montgomery, "[have] forced us to recognize the puerile inadequacy of tying ultimate legal standards to the mores of a particular society, even if that society is our own."[13]

The reigns of V. I. Lenin, Joseph Stalin, Adolph Hitler, and Mao Tse-tung are gruesome examples of societies in which law was twisted by the state to allow for the murder of millions. "You might think," writes Joseph Sobran, "that the 20th century would have made us all anarchists. The modern state has to its credit two world wars, mass murder on a scale never imagined, enslavement, terror, oppression, and, even at its mildest, a steady level of confiscation, corruption and fraud."[14] Most of these evils can be traced back to positive law based on assumptions found in the Humanist and Marxist worldviews. The irresponsible, destructive actions of the leaders of states based on legal positivism demonstrated the need for a system of law founded on absolutes. Edgar Bodenheimer tells us, "After the cataclysmic events of the Nazi period and the collapse of Germany in the Second World War, [Gustav] Radbruch undertook a revision of his former [relativistic] theories. He expressed the view that there exist certain absolute postulates which the law must fulfill in order to deserve its name. Law, he declared, requires some recognition of individual freedom, and a complete denial of individual rights by the state is 'absolutely false law.'"[15] The Christian view provides just such absolutes for law.

An Absolute Standard

What is needed to restore man's proper sense of ethical and legal obedience? An absolute basis for law. Clearly, the weakest aspect of the entire theory of legal positivism is its founding of law on an ever-changing basis: governmental authority. Legal positivists believe a "flexible" system of law is desirable, since man and his laws are caught up in the process of evolution. But the failings of such a system are obvious, as A. E. Wilder-Smith points out:

> Why have law and order deteriorated so rapidly in the United States? Simply because for many years it has been commonly taught that life is a random, accidental phenomenon with no meaning except the purely materialistic one. Laws are merely a matter of human expediency. Since humans are allegedly accidents, so are their laws.[16]

The legal positivist would not put it quite that way. Positivists believe laws are logically formulated by the state to best suit mankind's

Notes and Asides

evolutionary needs. However, this does not erase the fact that laws become arbitrary in such a system. Indeed, it creates a supreme danger: the all-powerful state. "Whenever law, the condition of man's life, is in the power of the state and is the creation of the state and without transcendental reference," says Rousas Rushdoony, "then man too is the creature of the state and in its power, however ostensibly benevolent the purposes of that state."[17]

Thus, whether atheistic legal systems create evolutionary law or totalitarian law, it is clear that they are unstable and destined to fail. The reason is simple: atheistic legal systems must deny the existence of an absolute legal code. Without an absolute code, we cannot expect such systems to develop absolute, morally binding laws. "To arrive at absolute legal standards," says Montgomery, "one would have to disengage himself from the world and its limited standards and go 'outside the world' to a 'transcendental' realm of values. . . . Water does not rise above its own level; why should we think that absolute legal norms will arise from relativistic human situations?"[18]

Society is faced with a choice: ". . . if there is no fixity in law and no reference point," writes Whitehead, "then law can be what a judge says it is. If, however, there is a fixity to law, there is some absolute basis upon which judgment can be made."[19] Society must decide whether an absolute legal standard exists. It does not matter whether society would *prefer* fixed or flexible laws; what matters is whether an absolute code is *real*. If such a code does exist, we, as mortals, must discover and obey it, for it points to a Law-giver worthy of our obedience and worship.

The Christian, of course, believes such law and such a Law-giver exist. "The Christian worldview teaches a unified view of truth," says Whitehead. "Its principles deal in absolutes that do not vary according to circumstances but should, in fact, govern the actions of man as he responds to constantly changing conditions."[20]

"For there are six things the Lord hates—no, seven: haughtiness, lying, murdering, plotting evil, eagerness to do wrong, a false witness, sowing discord among brothers."
—Proverbs 6:16-19

For the Christian, law is grounded on the firmest foundation and therefore does not flex or evolve. Law remains constant, placing the same expectations on every man in every age. Whitehead insists that law in the Christian sense has something more than mere form. "Law has content in the eternal sense. It has a reference point. Like a ship that is anchored, law cannot stray far from its mooring."[21] The Christian legal perspective creates a legal system that does not fluctuate according to the whims of man and, therefore, is more just.

In one sense, the legal theorist *must* accept the Christian doctrine of an absolute foundation if the concept of law is to have any real meaning. Indeed, the Christian perspective invests more meaning in law than any other worldview. This becomes obvious as we witness the problems created in societies based on legal positivism. Henry states,

Notes and Asides

> However offensive to secular humanists, the theological referent gains double relevance through the conspicuous collapse of modern rights theories. It invests law with transcendent awe and objective authority, and it corresponds to the human condition through its explanation of the confusion over law's nature and content by the fact of moral rebellion.[22]

The Christian approach to law not only provides law with an absolute foundation in God as the ultimate Law-giver but also clears up the confusion over law's nature. Whereas legal positivists can explain neither why laws must exist nor why man can never develop a just system of law, the Christian legal theorist provides a simple, logical answer: man is in rebellion against God and His law; earthly laws are required to curb that rebellion; but the implementation of these laws will always be imperfect, since man's fallen nature keeps him from formulating and enforcing a just legal system.

But if man is truly corrupted by sin, how can he discover any of God's laws? If human nature is fallen, and man is no longer in touch with God's will, how can mankind know what God commands him to do? The answer lies in both general and special revelation.

Natural and Biblical Law

God revealed his law to mankind, generally, through natural law. Every man has some inherent sense of right and wrong. The Apostle John says, "That was the true Light, which lighteth every man that cometh into the world" (John 1:9). The Apostle Paul says, "For when the Gentiles . . . do by nature the things contained in the [revealed] law, these . . . are a law unto themselves" (Romans 2:14). Christianity teaches that mankind can, to some extent, perceive the will of God, and that this perceived will is the law of nature. William Blackstone, a Christian and one of the most influential figures in the history of law, describes natural law this way:

> (W)hen the Supreme Being formed the universe, and created matter out of nothing, he impressed certain principles upon that matter. . . . When he put that matter into motion, he established certain laws of motion. . . . If we farther advance to vegetable and animal life, we shall find them still governed by laws. . . . Man, considered as a creature, must necessarily be subject to the laws of his creator, for he is an entirely dependent being. . . . And consequently as man depends absolutely upon his maker

Notes and Asides

> for every thing, it is necessary that he should in all points conform to his maker's will. This will of his maker is called the law of nature.[23]

This view is consistent with the Biblical account of Creator, creation, moral order, and law. The Apostle Paul specifically discusses the concept of natural law in Romans 1-2, claiming that every man has a fundamental knowledge that there is a transcendental law by which he should abide, and yet which he fails to obey. Man's fallen nature does not destroy his awareness of this general revelation. St. Paul, speaking of men and women who had turned away from God, says, "God gave them up unto vile affections: for even their women did change the natural use into that which is against nature's law" (Romans 1:26).

Gary Amos expands on this idea, noting that "to the Apostle Paul, men who have sunk to the lowest possible level of depravity still 'fully understand' the 'righteous ordinance' of God and—as lawbreakers—deserve to die. This is a remarkable claim by Paul in Romans 1:32, for he declares that even the vilest men not only know, but fully know, the . . . 'righteous ordinance' of God. This is a law of God which is everywhere known by all men. They have this law 'by nature,' and the 'requirement of the law' is 'written in their hearts.'"[24] Clearly, the Bible makes the claim that God gave men a natural law that men intuitively understand they should obey.

Some Christians, however, prefer not to discuss the concept of natural law, because modern legal theorists have largely separated the concept of natural law from that of God as divine Law-giver. Obviously, a Christian must deny that natural law somehow exists apart from God. However, as long as we understand the concept of natural law in its traditional sense, as general revelation from God, it plays an important role in Christian legal theory. "The older natural law was not based on nature alone," notes Whitehead, "at least not in the Christian era. It was based on the doctrine of Creation, the conviction that an all-wise Creator had established the world and its order."[25] Or, as Montgomery would say, natural laws "point beyond themselves." This is the context in which we are using the term *natural law*, and it is also the context in which America's founding fathers viewed the term.

Natural law cannot be ignored simply because it is easily misrepresented. Indeed, the theory that natural law is grounded in God as general revelation is crucial for the Christian's entire legal perspective. Understood properly, natural law explains why *all men* are considered accountable to God for their actions: because all men are aware of the existence of a transcendent law and still consciously disobey it. If the Christian legal theorist wishes to remain consistent with the Biblical explanation of law, he must incorporate this truth into his legal theory. Writes Amos,

Notes and Asides

> Paul denounced a mistake of certain legalists who claimed that the only valid "law of God" was the Mosaic legislation in the Pentateuch. They denied God's general revelation in nature. They did not believe that God had written His moral law on the hearts of unbelievers. They tried to honor God's law by making Biblical law the only law of God. The Apostle pointed out that to say this was not to protect God's law, but to deny God's law, because God Himself gives general revelation in nature and in men's hearts. In the name of honoring the law of God, the legalists were in fact repudiating the law of God and consequently attacking God's sovereignty and omnipotence.[26]

Accordingly, Christian law is based on both general and special revelation. God has made His law known to man through special revelation in the Bible. But general revelation also plays an important role in God's scheme of things. For one thing, God is the judge of all men, but not all men have access to the revealed law of God. Those who don't will be judged by the law of nature written in their heart. The Apostle Paul says, "For when the Gentiles, which have not the [revealed] law, do by nature the things contained in the [revealed] law, these having not the law, are a law unto themselves. Which shew the work of the law written in their hearts, their conscience also bearing witness, and their thoughts the meanwhile accusing or else excusing one another" (Romans 2:14-15). "The 'law of nature,' imposed on men by God Himself," says Amos, "is an immutable law of good and evil to which all men are accountable. Men must have the Bible, special revelation, to know it completely. But they know it also through nature, God's general revelation. However, man cannot know the law adequately through general revelation alone because his intellect is corrupted by sin."[27] Thus, the Bible "fills in the gaps" left open by natural law. Montgomery writes that "the vague generalities of Natural Law are made concrete and visible through a specific scriptural revelation of the divine will for man."[28]

"For the truth about God is known to them instinctively; God has put this knowledge in their hearts."
—Romans 1:19

It is only through understanding and applying special revelation in the context of God's general revelation that mankind can develop a legal system consistent with God's will. General law is important because it provides mankind with a general sense of values. C. S. Lewis, who refers to natural law as the moral order or the "Tao," stresses the importance of God's general revelation of values:

> There never has been, and never will be, a radically new judgment of value in the history of the world. What purport to be new systems or (as they now call them) "ideologies," all consist of fragments from the *Tao* itself, arbitrarily wrenched from their context in the whole and then swollen to madness in

Notes and Asides

> their isolation, yet still owing to the *Tao* and to it alone such validity as they possess.[29]

Thus, natural law provides man with a general concept of right and wrong. The Bible fleshes out this skeletal framework so that man may know what God considers lawful. A classic example of this is found in Leviticus 18. God warns Moses about the legal structures of Egypt and Canaan—"neither shall ye walk in their ordinances"—and insists that Israel not legally permit incest, adultery, infanticide (abortion), homosexuality, and bestiality. These practices still intrigue the natural, fallen man, but God considers them an abomination because they are contrary to nature (Romans 1:26-27) and undermine the dignity and sanctity of the God-ordained home.

Together, general and special revelation give man enough information to implement a legal system that need not depend on the wisdom of men. Indeed, this revelation is made available to all men, regardless of their intellectual capacities. General and specific revelation provide all men with the guidance necessary to create a reasonably just system of law. Says Blackstone,

> Upon these two foundations, the law of nature and the law of revelation [the Bible], depend all human laws; that is to say, no human law should be suffered to contradict these.[30]

These two foundations may be called Christian or divine law. The United States was one of the few countries throughout history to attempt to base its legal system on divine law. "It can safely be stated," says Bodenheimer, "that there is no country in the world where the idea of a law of nature, understood as a safeguard of liberty and property against governmental encroachments, gained a higher significance for the political and social development and the molding of all political and legal institutions than in the United States of America."[31]

To understand the impact of Christian law on America's political and legal institutions, one need only consider the influence that the following had on the founding of our legal system: the Biblical concept of covenant, the Magna Charta, the English Common law, John Locke, Charles de Montesquieu, William Blackstone, and the men involved in the Constitutional convention. As we noted in Christian politics, all of these men and events were influenced by Christianity. For example, legal scholar John C. H. Wu says of the English Common law, "The common law has one advantage over the legal system of any country: it was Christian from the very beginning of its history."[32] Then, too, fifty-one of the fifty-five men who made up the framing committee of the Constitution were Christians,[33] as were Locke, Blackstone, and

Notes and Asides

Montesquieu.

This divine law that formed the basis for the U.S. legal system provides mankind with a definite means of judging laws enacted by men. While legal positivists have no criterion for judging the appropriateness of a law other than man's perceived needs, the Christian can (and must) refer to the divine law as his basis for declaring a law just or unjust. This creates certain implications for Christian legal theory.

Divine Law

If God has given man a means of discovering and implementing divine law, then the true and just legal system must be based on this revealed law. Henry says, "One reason law has lost its power in modern life is the failure to recognize divine law as the fundamental law."[34] Without divine law, the individual has no standard for judging any legal system imposed upon him. "If man cannot know, according to a higher law, what is just or right in a given situation," says Whitehead, "he cannot protest and criticize legitimately any particular course of action as unjust."[35]

However, because a higher law does exist, the concept of justice is made clear for mankind, and all we must do is enforce this standard of justice in our legal systems. Thus, government exists not so much to *create* laws as to secure laws, to apply God's laws to general and specific situations, and to act as the impartial enforcer of such laws. Whitehead argues that the very term "legislator" means not one who makes laws but one who *moves* them—moves them "from the divine law written in nature or in the Bible into the statutes and law codes of a particular society. Just as a translator is supposed to faithfully move the meaning from the original language into the new one, so the legislator is to translate laws, not make new ones. When legislation loses sight of its fundamental limitation (the fact that it is to be carried out in reference to the fundamental, higher law) it becomes lawmaking."[36]

> "Our human laws are but the copies, more or less imperfect, of the eternal laws, so far as we can read them."
> —J. A. Froude

As demonstrated in the Christian politics chapter, government, according to God's plan, should concern itself with encouraging people to obey God's will and with punishing lawbreakers or evildoers. It is worthwhile again to examine the Biblical mandate outlining the relationship between the state and law:

> For rulers hold no terror for those who do right, but for those who do wrong. Do you want to be free from fear of the one in authority? Then do what is right and he will commend you. For he is God's servant to do you good. But if you do wrong, be

Used by permission of the *Colorado Springs Gazette Telegraph*

> afraid, for he does not bear the sword for nothing. He is God's servant, an agent of wrath to bring punishment on the wrongdoer. (Romans 13:3-4).

Legal systems should consist of laws conforming to divine law such that wrongdoers are punished by the system and those who walk according to God's will are protected. Paul says in 1 Timothy 1 that the righteous do not fear state law because they already obey nature's law, which is God's eternal law, internally and externally. The unrighteous need the law to keep them within certain boundaries of acceptable behavior, thereby protecting the innocent citizen from lawlessness.

The courts should reflect this attitude. Rather than concerning themselves with creating laws, courts must simply enforce laws so that God's justice is served. In the past, this attitude was implicit to legal theory. The Christian calls for a return to this approach. Thus, "the fact that courts were once seen as institutions of justice (not legislating bodies) cannot be underscored enough," says Whitehead. "The court's function was to arrive at a just result, but in terms of the higher law."[37] Man, in this view, is seen as answerable to divine law.

Notes and Asides

With this understanding that man is under the law, not the creator of law, man's role in the legal system is set right. Man's relationship to law is primarily ministerial, not legislative. He does not create law. "Instead," says Rushdoony, "man seeks, in his law-making, to approximate and administer fundamental law, law in terms of God's law, absolute right and wrong. Neither majority nor minority wishes are of themselves right or wrong; both are subject to judgment in terms of the absolute law of God, and the largest majority cannot make valid and true a law contrary to the word of God. All man's law-making must be in conformity to the higher law of God, or it is false."[38]

False law-making—such as "concessions to the majority" as a basis for the legalization of abortion, homosexuality, pedophilia, or incest will not be tolerated by God. A society that consciously turns away from divine law will suffer the consequences. "Biblically revealed 'higher law,'" says Montgomery, "offers the only reliable guide to personal and national health, and thus to the preservation of individual and corporate life. The clear pattern throughout Scripture is that those who do God's will live and those who flaunt His commands perish."[39]

Thus, it is evident that man must choose whether to rely on divine law or on a shifting positive legal system. "'Higher law,'" says Montgomery, "is needed not only for sound legal decision, but for the very preservation of the legal system itself; flaunting God's law means the simultaneous collapse of society and of the positive law that cements it together."[40]

It is in man's best interests to ground a society's legal system in divine law. Indeed, it is doubly in man's interest, because obedience to divine law is the only true freedom—all disobedience results in personal and/or political enslavement. This is consistent with Paul's assertion, "But now that you have been set free from sin and have become slaves to God, the benefit you reap leads to holiness, and the result is eternal life" (Romans 6:22).

Christian law consists of five basic precepts: (1) The source of all divine law is the character or nature of God. Says Schaeffer, "God has a character, and His character is the law of the universe."[41] Not all things are the same to Him. Some things conform to His character, and some do not. (2) Out of the character of God proceeds the moral order. This order is as real as the physical order and reflects God's character of holiness, justice, truth, love, and mercy. (3) Man is created in the image of God and therefore has significance. Life is not an afterthought. Because man is created in the image of God, human life, human rights and human dignity follow. God established human government to protect human life, rights and dignity (Genesis 9:6). (4) When Jesus Christ took human form (John 1:14), human life took on even greater significance. God the Creator was now God the Redeemer. (5) Chris-

Notes and Asides

tian law is also based on the fact that some day God through Christ will judge the whole human race (Acts 17:31; Romans 2:16) according to a standard of good and evil (2 Corinthians 5:10). Christians, realizing that they stand guilty before such an awesome God, flee to Jesus Christ for safety. The Bible says that Christ is the way, the truth and the life. Psalm 2:12 clearly states our need for Christ's favor: "Kiss the Son, lest he be angry and you be destroyed in your way, for his wrath can flare up in a moment. Blessed are all who take refuge in him."

The extent to which society and the individual acknowledge and obey divine law powerfully affects the entire fabric of their existence. Nowhere is the truth of this assertion more obvious than in the realm of human rights. As Amos points out, "The Biblical model of rights cannot be separated from the Biblical teaching about justice."[42] A people's response to divine law creates a specific attitude about human rights.

Duties and Rights

The Christian response to divine law calls for man to discover human rights in God's revealed Word, the Bible. Indeed, the Christian believes that the Bible is the only true source of rights, since it is the only special revelation of God's truth. If the Christian is correct in this assumption, then under this system man is more certainly guaranteed specific rights than under any other system proposed in any other worldview.

The reason is simple. If, as the Bible claims, man is created in the image of God, then each human life becomes inestimably precious and meaningful. This, in turn, creates a firm foundation on which a system of human rights can be built. Jerome Shestack states that the concept of man being "created in the image of God certainly endows men and women with a worth and dignity from which there can logically flow the components of a comprehensive human rights system."[43] Amos agrees that the idea that man is created in God's image and has lordship over the earth "is the key to the modern notion of subjective rights." Subjective rights, says Amos "are those that are inherent in the individual; they are inseparably part of the human personality. Being made in God's image makes man a being of enormous value and inherent worth."[44]

Montgomery concurs:

> If people's rights were of their own making, they could as easily unmake them. Since rights come as a divine gift from above, their inalienability is sure. "Every good gift and every perfect gift is from above, and cometh down from the Father of lights, with whom is no variableness, neither shadow of turning" (James 1:17). And because our rights come as a gift and not by

Notes and Asides

> merit, the only hope lies in placing ourselves and our society in the hands of the Giver, to be changed into His likeness.[45]

Thus, because man is made in God's image, he is granted certain rights. These rights are tied to the concept of Christian law much more closely than in other legal systems. According to the Christian perspective, God commands men to obey divine law, and this obedience is what guarantees the protection of rights for all humans. God causes man to be responsible for upholding human rights by binding man's duties to human rights. If man lives Biblically, each person will possess the whole range of rights granted by God. But if man disobeys God, then the system of rights revealed in the Bible will suffer.

"In the Christian view," notes Henry, "inalienable rights are creational rights governing the community and individual, rights implicit in the social commandments of the Decalogue."[46] Thus, certain Biblical commands imply certain specific rights for all men. For example, "Thou shalt not murder" implies that life is a specific human right. "Thou shalt not steal" implies that property is a specific human right, etc. "To be sure," says Henry, "many Biblical duties—if not all—imply a corresponding enforceable right. The divine prohibition of theft or of removal of a landmark implies an unstated right to property and possession."[47]

Rights are given to man by God, but mankind needs to acknowledge God's existence and obey His commands to ensure their protection. Amos argues that men's unalienable duties toward God translate into unalienable rights between men. "God," says Amos "gave and commands life, liberty, property, and a life of blessedness or happiness for man. Each man is a steward under an absolute duty to God for these things. As a steward, trustee, and protector under God, a man may resist other men's unlawful interference with the performance of that duty."[48]

Notice that this concept of stewardship also places specific limitations on man's rights. Man may not trumpet, "I've got my rights!" and then act in any way that he pleases. Divine law constantly commands mankind to act according to the true order of the universe, to walk in God's will. Amos provides a fine example:

> Men have rights, such as the right to life. But because a man has a duty to live his life for God, the right is inalienable. He can defend his life against all others, but not destroy it himself. No man has the right to do harm to himself, to commit suicide, or to waste his life. He has a property interest—dominion—in his own life, but not total control.[49]

The Christian believes that divine law and absolute rights based on specific duties revealed in the Bible provide the only workable frame-

"Wherever there is a human being, I see God-given rights inherent in that being, whatever may be the sex or complexion."
—W. L. Garrison

Notes and Asides

work for a just legal system. Writes Montgomery,

> Why should Jews and Blacks and members of other minority groups receive equal protection under the law? Why was Nazi racism juridically damnable? Not because of our current American social values—since these have no more permanence or absolute validity than those of other peoples—but because God almighty has declared once and for all that He has "made of one blood all nations of men to dwell on all the face of the earth" and that "there is neither Jew nor Greek, there is neither bond nor free." Thus are human equality and legal standing regardless of race or color established on the rock of "higher law," above the shifting sands of cultural change.[50]

The classic example in American jurisprudence, of course, was the school segregation issue (*Brown vs. Board of Education*). As Harold O. J. Brown explains, segregation laws were overturned by *Brown* because of mankind's "conviction that racial segregation, even when based on properly enacted law, is in itself unjust and wrong." He says the source of this conviction lay in "moral sentiments formed by Christian doctrine and the natural law," and concludes, "There is a higher law than the law of the land, to which the law of the land must be made to conform: in the words of the Declaration [of Independence], 'the law of nature and of nature's God.'"[51]

Montgomery lists numerous human rights he believes are grounded in special revelation, including:

(1) Procedural due process rights, which involve impartiality of tribunal, fair hearing, speedy trial, confrontation of witnesses, and no double jeopardy. He sees these rights described in passages like 1 Timothy 5:21, Malachi 2:9, Exodus 22:9, Ezra 7:26, Isaiah 43:9, and Nahum 1:9.

> "All must be treated exactly the same."
> —1 Timothy 5:21

(2) Substantive due process rights that involve equality before the law for all races and sexes, rich and poor, citizens and foreigners, rulers and ruled, etc. He finds these rights in Acts 10:34, Galatians 3:28, James 2:1-7, Amos 9:7, Exodus 21:2, and Isaiah 1:16-17.

(3) Fundamental rights, including right to life, right to family life, freedom of religion, right to work, and the right to own property. He sees these rights in such passages as 1 Timothy 5:8, Matthew 5:21-22, Luke

Notes and Asides

1:15, 1 Corinthians 6:19-20, Exodus 20:13-16, John 7:17, Acts 5:1-4, Ephesians 4:28, and Deuteronomy 23:25-26.

Only this view of rights gives man an ultimate source for his rights while granting him a measure of responsibility for ensuring the existence of those rights on earth. As with divine law, the absolute nature of this system of rights sets it apart from all others. "Personal rights and freedoms are God-given and inalienable," writes Amos, "they do not exist merely for civil convenience or at the discretion of those who hold civil power. This is why only Biblical ethics maintain a proper balance between order in public life and individual freedom."[52]

America's Declaration of Independence was built on just such an unchanging basis for rights, and the nineteenth-century French moral philosopher Frederic Bastiat echoes it when he writes, "Each of us has a natural right from God to defend his person, his liberty, and his property. These are the three basic requirements of life, and the preservation of any one of them is completely dependant upon the preservation of the other two."[53] Thomas Jefferson, author of the Declaration, proclaimed the need for such an absolute basis when he asked rhetorically, "Can the liberties of a nation be thought secure when we have removed their only firm basis, a conviction in the minds of the people that these liberties are the gift of God?"[54]

Removing the Christian Base

Even though Jefferson was a deist, he would be shocked by America's replacement of Christian law with positive law. The firm base he thought was essential for placing conviction in the minds of people that their liberties were gifts of God has been replaced with an alien base not at all conducive to liberty. Today, American law makes government godlike, exempting rulers from laws for the ruled, declaring actions proclaimed immoral by general revelation to be legal (including abortion and homosexuality), removing God and the Ten Commandments from the classroom, granting more rights to the guilty than to the victim, and releasing the guilty to prey on the innocent.

America's law schools are virtually devoid of Christian law. Men such as William Blackstone and James Kent, who championed the Christian conception of law, greatly influenced American legal education until the Civil War era. However, shortly after the Civil War, the Christian theological and ethical roots of American law were severed by the acceptance of Darwin's *Origin of Species*. What Russell Kirk warned against when he wrote, "To cut off Law from its ethical sources

Notes and Asides

> **"The fundamental basis of this nation's law was given to Moses on the Mount. The fundamental basis of our Bill of Rights comes from the teachings which we get from Exodus and St. Matthew, from Isaiah and St. Paul. I don't think we emphasize that enough these days. If we don't have the proper fundamental moral background, we will finally wind up with a totalitarian government which does not believe in rights for anybody except the state."**
>
> **—Harry S. Truman**

is to strike a terrible blow at the rule of law,"[55] occurred in America between 1869 and 1909. Modern American legal theory still has a theological base, but now that base is atheism. It still has an ethical base, but now that base is relativism.

One of the men largely responsible for this change in American legal theory was Christopher Langdell, a staunch Darwinist. For Langdell, law was not static nor fixed by God. Law evolved along with man. Thus, Langdell chose to substitute "the operations of the law of evolution for the laws of God."[56] Harvard law professor Harold J. Berman notes that

> With Langdellian legal education, the older idea that law is ultimately dependent on divine providence, that it has a religious dimension, gradually receded, and I think we can say, has ultimately almost vanished.[57]

Virginia Armstrong puts it like this: "Increasingly in modern America, the Western Christian tradition has been replaced by a humanistic system, particularly among America's legal and educational elites. For most of the last 125 years [since Darwin's *Origin of Species*] the 'rational/secular' form has been in ascendancy."[58]

Armstrong says that, generally speaking, law students are taught: (1) There is no transcendent, personal God. (2) Both the world and man result from evolutionary forces, which continue to direct them. (3) Societal institutions like the family and civil law have no theistic

Notes and Asides

origins. (4) Theistically ordained absolute standards do not exist for the guidance of either individuals or institutions. (5) The Bible is false and of no use as a source of guidance for man in his attempt to progress. (6) Man's self-effort is the primary, if not sole, tool available to him in his attempt to progress. "From these basic tenets," says Armstrong, "principles of jurisprudence are logically derived."[59]

Of course, the Christian does not believe that it is "logical" for American legal schools to base their conclusions on the assumption that God does not exist and the Bible is false. The Christian sees man as created in the image of a personal, holy God, and trusts that modern atheistic legal theory is founded on false assumptions. An excellent example of the failure of modern legal theory is provided by modern legal theorists' insistence that the individual is not responsible for his actions. The Christian, on the other hand, proposes a legal theory which grants man the right to be responsible.

Man's Right to Be Responsible

Both the Humanist and the Marxist portray man as a creature of his environment—inherently good and perfectible, yet unable to achieve that goodness or perfection because he lives in a flawed society. As we have seen throughout this text, this view of man absolves the individual of all responsibility for his actions. The Christian, however, believes that man is responsible for his actions and that God gives man the right to be treated as a moral agent, capable of choosing between right and wrong.

As we noted in the chapter on Secular Humanist law, the Humanist carries his view that man is not responsible to its logical conclusion, calling for the replacement of a legal system based on punishment with one that focuses on the re-education of criminals. The Christian, however, believes that this approach to legal theory denies man a fundamental right and is, in a word, inhumane. Lewis states, "My contention is that this doctrine [calling for the abolition of punishment], merciful though it appears, really means that each one of us, from the moment he breaks the law, is deprived of the rights of a human being."[60]

Lewis bases his conclusion on the fact that a system that only re-educates criminals ignores man's moral responsibility, thereby denying a crucial part of human nature.

> To be 'cured' against one's will and cured of states which we may not regard as disease is to be put on a level with those who have not yet reached the age of reason or those who never will; to be classed with infants, imbeciles, and domestic animals. But

Notes and Asides

> to be punished, however severely, because we have deserved it, because we 'ought to have known better', is to be treated as a human person made in God's image.[61]

This is why the Christian embraces a punitive legal system: any other system, even if its aim is to be merciful, dehumanizes man. The Christian also embraces a punitive legal system because it is consistent with God's means of dispensing justice on the final Judgment Day. On that day (Acts 17:31), man must account for his actions to God, "that every one may receive the things done in his body, according that he hath done, whether it be good or bad" (2 Corinthians 5:10; Revelation 20:11-15).

The Christian recognizes that the concepts of justice and mercy are complementary, not mutually exclusive. Lewis says that the Humanist's theory wants simply to abolish justice and substitute mercy. "This," he says "means that you start being 'kind' to people before you have considered their rights, and then force upon them supposed kindnesses which no one but you will recognize as kindnesses and which the recipient will feel as abominable cruelties. You have overshot the mark. Mercy, detached from Justice, grows unmerciful."[62]

This is the key point: a right granted to man by God, the right to possess free will and therefore be held responsible for his decisions, is ignored by the Humanist in an attempt to substitute mercy for justice. The Christian recognizes, however, that justice cannot be overruled. Without justice, the law is meaningless. Rushdoony warns that "when we reduce the law to humaneness and equate justice with it, then we have replaced justice with pity and substituted sentimentality for law."[63] Rather than replacing justice with mercy, we must uphold justice, so as to mercifully protect man's humanity.

This emphasis on justice and man's moral responsibility to God meshes consistently with the Christian concepts of divine law and human rights. Upon these foundations, and with the aid of special revelation found in the Bible, a Christian legal system can be built.

Biblical Applications to Legal Theory

The Bible contains God's guidelines for an earthly system of law. God expects man to devise an ordered legal system, providing him with an example of such a system in Exodus. John Eidsmoe stresses this point, noting that the Bible calls for "an orderly system of justice." Judges were instituted (Exodus 18:13-16; cf. Deuteronomy 1:16-17; 19:15-21), along with a multi-tiered judicial system with (to use modern

Notes and Asides

terminology) a justice of the peace over every ten families, a local magistrate over every fifty families, a district court judge over every hundred families, a circuit court of appeals over every one thousand families, and Moses himself as the Supreme Court. "The judges were commanded to be honest and not to take bribes or favor the rich (Exodus 23:1-8)," says Eidsmoe. "And neither were they to show special favoritism to the poor. 'Neither shalt thou countenance a poor man in his cause' (Exodus 23:3). Everyone was entitled to equal justice before the law—neither more nor less."[64]

From this we can conclude that God's ideal legal system is not only orderly but also equitable. Every man is granted the right to be judged according to the same standard of justice. Gerald R. Thompson says that the Bible insists that equality is a question of legal opportunity, not factual similarity. He quotes Deuteronomy 1:17, "Do not show partiality in judging; hear both small and great alike," and Leviticus 19:15, "Do not pervert justice; do not show partiality to the poor or favoritism to the great, but judge your neighbor fairly," and concludes, "In each case, the command is to judge according to what a person does, not who he is. Each person has the equal opportunity to prove his innocence, and the equal opportunity to pay the penalty for his misdeed."[65]

The Bible has a relevant message for legal theory in the realm of assigning guilt, as well. Simon Greenleaf says, "the importance of extreme care in ascertaining the truth of every criminal charge, especially where life is involved, may be regarded as a rule of law. It is found in various places in the Mosaic Code, particularly in the law respecting idolatry; which does not inflict the penalty of death until the crime 'be told thee,' (viz. in a formal accusation), 'and thou hast heard of it,' (upon a legal trial), 'and inquire diligently, and behold to be true,' (satisfactorily proved), 'and the thing certain,' (beyond all reasonable doubt)."[66]

Christian legal theory recognizes that an earthly judge should not be hasty in condemning any man. Because man is fallen and his reason exists in a less-than-perfect state, it is quite possible for man to err in meting out justice. According to the Christian position, it is better for the earthly judge to err in favor of the defendant than to punish an innocent man, because ultimately all lawbreakers will be judged by God. Where justice may not be served by earthly courts, it will most certainly be served on the final Judgment Day. Montgomery writes,

reassuring thought!

> Our legal systems suffer from the fallibility of the sinful human situation: absurdities are made law; guilty men go free; innocent men are punished. But Holy Scripture promises a Last Assize, when "there is nothing covered that shall not be revealed,

Notes and Asides

> neither hid that shall not be known." The Judge on that Day will be at the same time omniscient and just, and the ambiguities and failures of human justice through history will be rectified.[67]

Thus, justice will be meted out one day, properly and without error—and on that day, how man will long for Christ to shield him from the terrible face of justice! The certainty of Judgment Day ought to deter man from breaking God's law, as Adam Smith notes: "The idea that, however we may escape the observation of man, or be placed above the reach of human punishment, yet we are always acting under the eye, and exposed to the punishment of God, the great avenger of injustice, is a motive capable of restraining the most headstrong passions. . . ."[68]

Unfortunately, modern man has lost his faith in an ultimate Judge and Judgment Day, and many of his "headstrong passions" go unchecked. The Bible clearly indicates how a system of law should respond to such criminal actions: not only with punishment, but with a sincere effort to restore God's order, which is disordered by the criminal act. Rushdoony notes that Biblical law not only requires restitution to the offended person, but even more basic to the law is the demand for the restoration of God's order. "It is not merely the courts of law which are operative in terms of restitution. For Biblical law, restitution is indeed, a), to be required by courts of law of all offenders, but, even more, b), is the purpose and direction of the law in its entirety, the restoration of God's order, a glorious and good creation which serves and glorifies its Creator."[69]

The Christian believes it is proper to attempt to restore God's order in the world. This belief, however, should not cause the Christian to conclude that every sin should be made explicitly illegal.

Is it Possible to Legislate Morality?

In one sense, law and morality are inseparable. When one declares theft illegal, one is making a moral judgment—theft is condemned as immoral, because either (if one believes the Biblical account) it violates divine law, or (if one denies the existence of God) it violates some non-defensible human right. Rushdoony again tackles the issue:

> According to a very popular and dangerous half-truth, "You can't legislate morality." This is true insofar as it refers to the fact that the law cannot govern a man's heart, the fountainhead of true morality, nor can law produce a change of heart. The law cannot regenerate man; it cannot make a bad man good. On the

Notes and Asides

other hand, we must, and do, legislate morality, in that all law is enacted morality or procedural thereto.[70]

This does not mean that all morals must be enforced by specific laws. A system making all sin illegal would, among other things, cause government to become even more bloated in an effort to enact and enforce a vast array of new laws. Thus, man must concentrate on formulating a legal system that legislates morality only to the extent that order is maintained and human rights are protected. Writes Montgomery,

> Our task is not to correct every moral failing by human legislation; we are rather to legislate where provable harm to the body politic will arise in the absence of law. Thus we must prosecute stealing, but not profanity; perjury and misrepresentation of the terms of a contract, but not lying in general; child abuse, but not the teaching of atheism; murder, but not belief in witchcraft. God is still in His heaven, and the evils we are powerless to correct in accord with His Word He will most assuredly remedy on the last day.[71]

CLOSE-UP

Wendell R. Bird (1954-)

W. R. Bird graduated from Yale Law School in 1978 and soon after began practicing law in Atlanta. He has dedicated much of his legal work to promoting justice in the realm of origin science, even arguing an important origins case before the Supreme Court. Further, Bird recently wrote *The Origin of Species Revisited*, a two-volume work which represents the most comprehensive condemnation of evolutionary theory ever published. His efforts to support creationists' right to dissent most recently led him to California, to defend the Institute for Creation Research. His courageous stand against dogmatic evolutionism has made him unpopular in some circles, but even his critics must respect his level of scholarship and his professionalism: he is a member of the American Law Institute (the most prestigious legal organization), and has published articles in the *Yale Law Journal* and the *Harvard Journal of Law and Public Policy*.

Notes and Asides

good reasoning!

"So many laws argue so many sins."
—John Milton

Elsewhere Montgomery says, "The Old Testament prophets insist that God's ethical standards be incorporated into the very fabric of government, and since all law necessarily reflects a moral value system of some kind, there is every reason to have it reflect the proper (absolute, revelational) value system."[72]

The task of earthly law, according to the Christian, is not to cause man always to act morally. No law could ever hope to accomplish this. And yet, if law is tied so closely to morals, it must affect man's moral nature on a deeper level than simply causing him to behave orderly and respect human rights. How, then, does law serve to bring man to a right understanding of God's universe?

The answer is that no man is capable of living a completely lawful life. This inability on man's part always to act morally is made obvious to him by his violations of God's divine law as stated in Scripture or enforced by earthly legal systems. "In brief," says Rushdoony, "the purpose of any law is not to make men good; this law can never do, either for man or for society, for goodness is inner rather than outward restraint, else prisons would best produce morality. Law declares the standard, and the penalty for offense, protects society, undercuts man's moralism, and is a guide to the godly. Character and righteousness must come from a source other than law. Thus, to decry law because it makes no man good is to miss the purpose of the law. In any and every culture, according to Paul, the law brings to men the same conclusions, that there is none righteous, and that all men sin and fall short of the glory of God, and to this all men must give assent (Romans 3:10-18)."[73]

Thus, a Christian system of law, while stabilizing society and promoting justice (by protecting the weak and innocent and punishing the guilty), also leads man to the knowledge that he is a fallen creature desperately in need of a Savior. In a way similar to the general revelation of natural law, plain, faulty, earthly law helps the non-believer to recognize the corrupt nature of man and seek the reasons behind this corruption and the remedy for it. God in His wisdom uses law not only to ensure justice, but also to demonstrate to man that, in his fallen state, it would be folly to demand his just deserts. Rather, man should beg for mercy and turn to Jesus Christ for salvation, thereby becoming a child of God (see Ephesians 2).

Christians and the Law of Moses

When the Christian talks about legislating morality, it invariably leads to a related issue; namely, are morality and law inseparable? Is the Christian morally compelled to obey every law set down in the Old and New Testaments?

Notes and Asides

Certainly not. Many laws of the Old Testament were designed specifically to signify Israel's unique identity as God's chosen people, distinct from all other peoples in the world (for example, circumcision and the dietary laws). These laws are no longer binding, since in Christ the wall of division between Jew and Gentile is taken away (Acts 10:9-16, 28-29; Ephesians 2:11-18). Other laws were designed specifically to signify the future atoning work of Christ on the cross (for example, all of the sacrificial laws). These, too, are no longer binding, since His great sacrifice is now past, and a new symbol has been instituted to point back to it—the Lord's Supper (1 Corinthians 5:7-8; Hebrews 8—10). Even many of the judicial laws, all of which certainly have a moral basis, are limited to certain cultures in their application.

For example, the requirement that one build a parapet around the roof of his house (Deuteronomy 22:8) protected life in a culture that used flat rooftops as places to relax, to entertain, or even to eat or sleep during hot weather; but in northern climes, where roofs are built steep to prevent the buildup of snow, building a parapet around a roof could actually threaten the lives of those sheltering beneath the roof. Again, the prohibition of taking "the lower or the upper millstone in pledge" for a loan (Deuteronomy 24:6) makes sense in the context of a culture in which every household had a small handmill used to grind each day's grain. In that culture, the handmill was essential to sustaining life, and taking it in pledge would mean treating the property secured by the pledge as equal in value to the life endangered by disabling the handmill. But in a modern culture in which ancient handmills would be curiosity pieces with museum value but no utility in sustaining life, we might uphold the same principle (life is more important than property) by prohibiting the taking of a workman's tools in pledge.

In these and similar instances, the Christian is called on to understand the moral foundation of the specific judicial law and then to apply that moral principle prudently in the context of his own culture. In the case of the civil or judicial laws, then, the just principle underlying the specific application should be all that concerns us now. As the *Westminster Confession of Faith* (1647) put it, ". . . God was pleased to give to the people of Israel . . . as a body politic . . . sundry judicial laws, which expired together with the state of that people, not obliging any other, now, further than the general equity thereof may require" (XIX.iii-iv).

Montgomery ably summarizes the proper attitude toward both the ceremonial/national and the judicial laws:

> Because of the unique nature of Israel as the vehicle for the coming of the Messiah, her purely national and ceremonial legislation is not mandatory for other peoples or for the church

Notes and Asides

> of the New Testament. . . . Moreover, even when general principles of Old Testament legislation remain in force because of their absolute moral content (appellate justice, equitable restitution, etc.), their adjectival law aspects (such as a particular appellate court organization) or detailed remedies (e.g., restitution plus one-fifth in specified circumstances) may be so limited to Hebrew national life as not to be binding on the future.[74]

However, we must be careful to distinguish between the judicial laws and the moral laws. The "law of Christ" (Galatians 6:2) *incorporates* God's eternal moral order. As Charles F. Baker has put it, "Many of the moral and spiritual principles contained in the [Old Testament and] sermon on the mount may be applied to the Body of Christ."[75] The *moral* law of the Old Testament, which is reinforced in the New Testament, remains permanently in force. For example, the Apostle Paul essentially reiterates the Ten Commandments in Romans 13:8-10, where he concludes that love itself, which is required of all Christians, is the fullness or fulfillment of the moral law—not its replacement, but what brings it all together completely under one head. The *Westminster Confession* (XIX.v) says the same thing: "The moral law doth forever bind all, as well justified persons as others, to the obedience thereof; and that not only in regard of the matter contained in it, but also in respect of the authority of God the Creator who gave it. Neither doth Christ in the gospel any way dissolve, but much strengthen, this obligation."

Nonetheless, no one may rely on obeying the moral law as a means of salvation: "For as many as are of the works of the law are under the curse; for it is written, 'Cursed is everyone who does not continue in all things which are written in the book of the law, to do them.' But that no one is justified by the law in the sight of God is evident, for 'the just shall live by faith.' Yet the law is not of faith, but 'the man who does them shall live by them.' Christ has redeemed us from the curse of the law, having become a curse for us (for it is written, 'Cursed is everyone who hangs on a tree'), that the blessing of Abraham might come upon the Gentiles in Christ Jesus, that we might receive the promise of the Spirit through faith" (Galatians 3:10-12).

This does not mean that believers can ignore or defy the moral law. Far from it! The grace of God that justifies them through faith (Romans 3:21—4:8) simultaneously works a change in their hearts, breaking their enslavement to sin (Romans 6:6-14), enslaving them to God and righteousness instead (Romans 6:15-22), and so empowering them to fulfill the righteous requirements of the law by walking in the Spirit rather than in the flesh (Romans 8:3-4). Believers are called on to fulfill the whole law by the very fact that Christ calls on them to love God and their neighbors, for the whole law is summed up in the command to love (Matthew 22:37-40; Romans 13:8-10; Galatians 5:13-14). While believers, then, must not see the law as a path to justification before God, they rightly see it as an indispensable and infallible guide to understand what love requires. This, too, the *Westminster Confession* (XIX.vi) affirms:

> Although true believers be not under the law as a covenant of works, to be thereby justified or condemned; yet is it of great use to them, as well as to others; in that, as a rule of life, informing them of the will of God and their duty, it directs and binds them to walk accordingly; discovering also the sinful pollutions of their nature, hearts, and lives; so as, examining themselves thereby, they may come to further conviction of, humiliation for, and hatred against sin; together with a clearer sight of the need they have of Christ, and the perfection of his obedience. It is likewise of use to the regenerate, to restrain their corruptions, in that it forbids sin; and the threatenings of it serve to show what even their sins deserve, and what afflictions in this life they may expect for them, although freed from the curse thereof threatened in the law. The promises of it, in like manner, show them God's approbation of obedience, and what blessings they may expect upon the performance thereof; although not as due to them by the law as a covenant of works: so as a man's doing good, and refraining from evil, because the law encourageth to the one, and deterreth from the other, is no evidence of his being under the law, and not under grace.

The New Hampshire Baptist Confession (1833) summarizes this position clearly:

> We believe that the Law of God is the eternal and unchangeable rule of his moral government; that it is holy, just, and good; and that the inability which the Scriptures ascribe to fallen men to fulfill its precepts arises entirely from their love of sin; to deliver them from which, and to restore them through a Mediator to unfeigned obedience to the holy Law, is one great end of the Gospel, and of the means of grace connected with the establishment of the visible Church. (XII)

Notes and Asides

Conclusion

Christian law is based on God's natural and revealed law in the Bible. This basis creates an absolute foundation for law, which in turn demonstrates Christianity to be better equipped to offer a system of law than all the worldviews that call for flexible, evolutionary, arbitrary laws. Christian law ensures specific, absolute human rights that cannot be ensured by worldviews that deny God's existence. Christian human rights are based on specific duties prescribed in the Bible—thus, God assigns specific rights to all humans, but man becomes responsible for obeying God and protecting those rights for himself and his fellow man. Obviously, one way to protect these rights is the establishment of human government. Another way is to internalize God's will in our hearts.

Some Secular Humanists charge that Christianity is undemocratic and at root is hostile to religious liberty. In reality, the Bible insists that room be made for both believer and non-believer. "The servants said unto him, wilt thou then that we go and gather them up? But he said, nay; lest while ye gather up the tares, ye root up also the wheat with them. Let both grow together until the harvest; and in the time of harvest I will say to the reapers, Gather ye together first the tares, and bind them in bundles to burn them, but gather the wheat into my barns" (Matthew 13:28-30). Alfred North Whitehead understood this passage to be a significant statement favoring religious liberty.

God makes specific provisions in the Bible for earthly legal systems. He expects them to be both orderly and equitable. God further expects man's legal systems to hold man responsible for his actions and to restore God's order whenever and wherever possible. God does not expect, however, every sin to be declared illegal in human government. Rather, He expects a system of law that maintains both order and liberty by promoting justice as much as humanly possible.

> "For the Lord is our Judge, our Lawgiver and our King."
> —Isaiah 33:22

The Bible tells what is good and what God requires of mankind: "to do justly, and to love mercy, and to walk humbly with thy God" (Micah 6:8). The Christian's motivation to "do justly" is knowing that "the Lord is slow to anger, and great in power, and will not at all acquit the wicked" (Nahum 1:3). His motivation to "love mercy" and "walk humbly" is the supreme example of the Law-giver himself—Jesus Christ—who showed mercy and walked humbly and told the woman taken in adultery, "Neither do I condemn thee: go, and sin no more" (John 8:11). As Christians we know we cannot live the perfect life exemplified by Christ, but we may also be assured that, because of God's grace, Christ will speak these same words to His followers on the Day of Judgment.

[1]Frederic Bastiat, *The Law* (Irvington-on-Hudson, NY: The Foundation for Economic Education, 1990), p. 24.
[2]Peter A. De Vos, "Justice," in *Baker's Dictionary of Christian Ethics*, ed. Carl F. H. Henry (Grand Rapids, MI: Baker Book House, 1973), p. 362.
[3]Russell Kirk, "The Christian Postulates of English and American Law," *Journal of Christian Jurisprudence* (Tulsa, OK: O. W. Coburn School of Law/Oral Roberts University, 1980), p. 66.
[4]Bertrand Russell, *Human Society in Ethics and Politics* (New York: Mentor, 1962), p. viii.
[5]Jean Jacques Rousseau, *Contrat Social*, book 2, chapter 7, cited in John Warwick Montgomery, *The Law Above the Law* (Minneapolis: Dimension Books, 1975), pp. 36-7.
[6]Montgomery, *The Law Above the Law*, p. 42.
[7]Carl F. H. Henry, *Twilight of a Great Civilization* (Westchester, IL: Crossway Books, 1988), p. 147.
[8]John W. Whitehead, *The Second American Revolution* (Westchester, IL: Crossway Books, 1988), p. 80.
[9]Robert Bork, *The Tempting of America* (New York: Free Press, 1990), p. 352.
[10]Francis Schaeffer, *A Christian Manifesto*, in *The Complete Works of Francis A. Schaeffer: A Christian Worldview*, five volumes (Westchester, IL: Crossway Books, 1982), vol. 5, p. 439.
[11]Whitehead, *The Second American Revolution*, p. 20.
[12]Montgomery argues, in *Human Rights and Human Dignity*, that the U.N. Universal Declaration of Human Rights (December 10, 1948) was struck by Rene Cassin and based on the Ten Commandments. Montgomery feels that Johannes Morsink's reading of the matter and concluding that the Declaration was based on "twentieth-century secular humanism" goes too far. We think Morsink is closer to the truth, but what is most disturbing is that the enforcement arm of the United Nations is under Marxist/Leninist control and has been since the inception of the U.N. The Department of Political and Security Council Affairs, which controls the Military Staff Committee, the most important department of the U.N. Secretariat, has been headed by the following individuals: 1946-49, Arkady Sobolev (USSR); 1949-53, Konstantin Zinchenko (USSR); 1953-54, Ilya Tchernychev (USSR); 1954-1957, Dragoslav Protitch (Yugoslavia); 1958-60, Anatoly Dobrynin (USSR); 1960-62, Georgy Arkadev (USSR); 1962-63, E. D. Kiselve (USSR); 1963-65, V. P. Suslov (USSR); 1965-68, Alexei E. Nesterenko (USSR); 1968-73, Leonid N. Kutakov (USSR); 1973-78, Arkady N. Shevchenko (USSR); 1978-81, Mikhail D. Sytenko (USSR); 1981-86, Viacheslav A. Ustinos (USSR); 1987-1990, Vasiliy S. Safronchuk (USSR). Our concern over this matter was refueled by President George Bush's September 11, 1990, speech to Congress and the American people, in which he said, "Out of these troubled times, our fifth objective—a new world order—can emerge. . . . We are now in sight of a United Nations that performs as envisioned by its founders." One of its founders was Alger Hiss, a Marxist/Leninist spy in the U.S. State Department—see Whittaker Chambers, *Witness* (Chicago: Regnery-Gateway, 1978) and *Time*, October 22, 1990, p. 73. In 1944, Hiss functioned as the executive secretary of the Dumbarton Oaks conference where practically all of the critical decisions about the United Nations were made. At the U.N.'s founding conference in San Francisco in 1945, Hiss served as acting secretary-general and as an important member of the steering and executive committees charged with writing the U.N. Charter.
[13]Montgomery, *The Law Above the Law*, p. 26.
[14]*Colorado Springs Gazette Telegraph*, Dec. 13, 1990, p. B7.
[15]Edgar Bodenheimer, *Jurisprudence: the Philosophy and Method of the Law* (Cambridge: Harvard University Press, 1974), p. 141.
[16]A. E. Wilder Smith, *The Creation of Life* (Costa Mesa, CA: TWFT Publishers, 1970), p. ix.
[17]Rousas John Rushdoony, *The Politics of Guilt and Pity* (Fairfax, VA: Thoburn Press, 1978), pp. 126-7.
[18]Montgomery, *The Law Above the Law*, pp. 35-6.
[19]Whitehead, *The Second American Revolution*, p. 21.
[20]Ibid., p. 26.
[21]Ibid., p. 73.
[22]Henry, *Twilight of a Great Civilization*, p. 159.
[23]William Blackstone, *Commentaries on the Laws of England*, in *Blackstone's Commentaries with Notes of Reference to the Constitution and Laws of the Federal Government of the United States and of the Commonwealth of Virginia*, five volumes, ed. St. George Tucker (Philadelphia: William Young Birch and Abraham Small, 1803; reprint, South Hackensack, NJ: Rothman Reprints, 1969), vol. 1, pp. 38-9.
[24]Gary T. Amos, *Defending the Declaration* (Brentwood, TN: Wolgemuth and Hyatt, 1989), p. 178.

[25]Whitehead, *The Second American Revolution*, p. 74.
[26]Amos, *Defending the Declaration*, p. 44.
[27]Ibid., pp. 42-3.
[28]Montgomery, *The Law Above the Law*, p. 42.
[29]C. S. Lewis, *The Abolition of Man* (New York: Macmillan, 1973), p. 56.
[30]John Eidsmoe, *Christianity and the Constitution* (Grand Rapids: Baker Book House, 1987), p. 58.
[31]Edgar Bodenheimer, *Jurisprudence*, p. 52.
[32]John C. H. Wu, cited in Virginia Armstrong, "The Flight from America's Foundations: A Panoramic Perspective on American Law," in *Restoring the Constitution*, ed. H. Wayne House (Dallas, TX: Probe Books, 1987), p. 116.
[33]John Eidsmoe, "The Judeo-Christian Roots of the Constitution," in *Restoring the Constitution*, ed. House, p. 77.
[34]Henry, *Twilight of a Great Civilization*, p. 69.
[35]Whitehead, *The Second American Revolution*, p. 88.
[36]Ibid., p. 76.
[37]Ibid., pp. 87-8.
[38]Rushdoony, *Politics of Guilt and Pity*, p. 143.
[39]Montgomery, *The Law Above the Law*, p. 47.
[40]Ibid., p. 48.
[41]Schaeffer, "Joshua and the Flow of Biblical History," *The Complete Works*, Vol. 2, p. 249.
[42]Amos, *Defending the Declaration*, p. 109.
[43]Jerome Shestack, *Essays on Human Rights* (Philadelphia: Jewish Publication Society of America, 1979), p. 76.
[44]Amos, *Defending the Declaration*, pp. 106-7.
[45]Ibid., p. 217-18.
[46]Henry, *Twilight of a Great Civilization*, p. 158.
[47]Ibid., p. 149.
[48]Amos, *Defending the Declaration*, p. 108.
[49]Ibid., p. 117.
[50]Montgomery, *The Law Above the Law*, pp. 46-7.
[51]*The Religion and Society Report*, November 1990, pp. 6-7. This *Report* is edited by Harold O.J. Brown, Trinity Evangelical Divinity School, Deerfield, Illinois 60015.
[52]Amos, *Defending the Declaration*, p. 126.
[53]Bastiat, *The Law*, p. 6.
[54]Rushdoony, *Politics of Guilt and Pity*, p. 135.
[55]Kirk, "The Christian Postulates of English and American Law," p. 66.
[56]Titus, *God, Man, and Law: The Biblical Principles*, p. 13.
[57]Ibid., p. 2.
[58]Armstrong, "The Flight from America's Foundations: A Panoramic Perspective on American Law," p. 122.
[59]Ibid., p. 122-3.
[60]C. S. Lewis, *God in the Dock* (Grand Rapids, MI: Eerdmans, 1972), p. 288.
[61]Ibid., p. 292.
[62]Ibid., p. 294.
[63]Rushdoony, *Politics of Guilt and Pity*, pp. 97-8.
[64]John Eidsmoe, *God and Caesar* (Westchester, IL: Crossway Books, 1985), p. 197.
[65]Gerald R. Thompson, "Legal Equality: No Respecter of Persons," *Journal of Christian Jurisprudence*, 1987, p. 140.
[66]Simon Greenleaf, *A Treatise on the Law of Evidence* (1824), Part V, Section 29, n. 1, cited in Herbert Titus, *God, Man, and Law: The Biblical Principles* (2d temporary ed., 1983), p. 85.
[67]Montgomery, *The Law Above the Law*, p. 53.
[68]Adam Smith, *The Theory of Moral Sentiments* (Indianapolis: Liberty*Press*/Liberty*Classics*, 1982), p. 170.
[69]Rousas John Rushdoony, *The Institutes of Biblical Law* (Nutley, NJ: Craig Press, 1973), p. 13.

[70]Rushdoony, *Politics of Guilt and Pity*, p. 139.
[71]Montgomery, *The Law Above the Law*, pp. 81-2.
[72]Montgomery, *Human Rights and Human Dignity*, p. 180.
[73]Rushdoony, *Politics of Guilt and Pity*, p. 114.
[74]Montgomery, *Humans Rights and Human Dignity*, pp. 165-6.
[75]Charles F. Baker, *A Dispensational Theology* (Grand Rapids, MI: Grace Bible College Publications, 1971), p. 323.

SECTION EIGHT

POLITICS

POLITICS [Greek: *polis* (city)]: The art of governing a city, state, nation, etc.

	SECULAR HUMANISM	MARXISM/ LENINISM	BIBLICAL CHRISTIANITY
SOURCE	*HUMANIST MANIFESTO I & II*	*WRITINGS OF MARX & LENIN*	*BIBLE*
THEOLOGY	ATHEISM	ATHEISM	THEISM
PHILOSOPHY	NATURALISM	DIALECTICAL MATERIALISM	SUPERNATURALISM
ETHICS	ETHICAL RELATIVISM	PROLETARIAT MORALITY	ETHICAL ABSOLUTES
BIOLOGY	DARWINIAN EVOLUTION	DARWINIAN/ PUNCTUATED EVOLUTION	SPECIAL CREATIONISM
PSYCHOLOGY	MONISTIC SELF-ACTUALIZATION	MONISTIC PAVLOVIAN BEHAVIORISM	DUALISM
SOCIOLOGY	NON-TRADITIONAL WORLD STATE ETHICAL SOCIETY	ABOLITION OF HOME, CHURCH AND STATE	HOME CHURCH STATE
LAW	POSITIVE LAW	POSITIVE LAW	BIBLICAL/NATURAL LAW
POLITICS	WORLD GOVERNMENT (GLOBALISM)	NEW WORLD ORDER	JUSTICE FREEDOM ORDER
ECONOMICS	SOCIALISM	SOCIALISM/ COMMUNISM	STEWARDSHIP OF PROPERTY
HISTORY	HISTORICAL EVOLUTION	HISTORICAL MATERIALISM	HISTORICAL RESURRECTION

CHAPTER

24

SECULAR HUMANIST POLITICS

"It is essential for UNESCO to adopt an evolutionary approach . . . the general philosophy of UNESCO should, it seems, be a scientific world humanism, global in extent and evolutionary in background. . . . Thus the struggle for existence that underlies natural selection is increasingly replaced by conscious selection, a struggle between ideas and values in consciousness."[1]

—Julian Huxley

"All those who share the vision of the human community as part of one world should be willing to take any measures that will awaken world opinion to bring it about."[2]

—Lucile W. Green

SUMMARY

Humanist political theory embraces democracy largely because Humanism is concerned with promoting individual freedom. "[O]ur prime concern," says Antony Flew, "is, or should be, for the liberties of individuals."[3] Recognizing that democracy is designed to protect an individual's right to liberty and believing that man can achieve moral perfection if he is free to pursue his own inherently good moral inclinations, the Humanist calls for democratic government with a powerful emphasis on individual autonomy. In fact, this is one of the few significant differences between the Humanist worldview and the Marxist worldview: Marxism concentrates political power in a very few hands, while Humanism rejects such tactics. Flew consistently opposes Marxists because they are not "democrats."[4]

However, while the means of Humanist political theory differ from those of Marxism, both worldviews share the same ultimate goal: a world state. Every Humanist firmly believes that world government is the next step on mankind's evolutionary road to utopia. Thus Paul Kurtz claims, "We need to build an *ethical commitment to the world community as our highest moral devotion*."[5] World government is not just a desirable accomplishment for the Humanist; it is mankind's highest moral calling. Any act by any individual that in some way hampers the move toward globalism is not only folly—it is morally wrong.

Humanists feel this way about world government for one basic reason: they fervently believe in mankind's ability to achieve utopia, and they understand that the state must play a central role in guiding mankind into the promised land. Time plus an enlightened government is Humanism's equation for attaining paradise.

The reason Humanists invest world government with a central role in mankind's march toward utopia is that they believe that the state, when directed properly, becomes a progressive force in the evolution of man. Humanism believes that man has recently become capable of guiding his own evolution, and the most functional guiding institution is government. To promote evolution effectively, governments must subordinate themselves to world government. Julian Huxley explains, "To have any success in fulfilling his destiny as the controller or agent of future evolution on earth, [man] must become one single inter-thinking group, with one general framework of ideas. . . ."[6]

Movement toward a single inter-thinking government has already begun in the form of the United Nations. Humanism trusts that the U.N. will provide a workable framework on which a world state can be built. Indeed, many Humanists have worked with the U.N. in an effort to hasten the advent of one-world government. Most notably, Huxley served as the Director for UNESCO (United Nations Educational, Scientific, and Cultural Organization), a powerful branch of the U.N. Such support for globalism is not surprising when one remembers that Humanists believe activism for world government is their highest ethical calling.

What responsibilities do Christians have concerning the U.N.?

Notes and Asides

Introduction

Virtually every Secular Humanist embraces democracy as the most acceptable form of government. Paul Kurtz declares, "The Humanist is also committed to democracy, particularly in the present epoch, as an ideal and a method for maximizing happiness and achieving the good society."[7] Elsewhere he calls for Humanists "to firmly defend the ideals of political democracy on a worldwide basis, and to encourage the further extensions of democracy."[8] Rudolf Dreikurs says simply, "We believe sincerely in democracy. . . ."[9]

However, the Humanist does not believe in democracy because it might possibly be the form of government most pleasing to God. Corliss Lamont brashly denies the need for a God in developing standards in government: "Humanism, then, urges complete democracy as both an end and a means; and insists that the idea of democracy has developed in history mainly in a humanistic way, needing no support or sanction in supernatural revelations or metaphysical guarantees."[10] Lamont's stand is completely consistent with the Humanist view, which denies the existence of God and therefore any absolute standards.

Democracy is a form of government in which citizens hold the ruling power, so that the majority rules.

The Humanist conception of democracy also differs from the more common attitude toward democracy in another way—for the Humanist, democracy extends far beyond the realm of government. Indeed, the Humanist believes democracy should color every aspect of man's life. Lamont states, "Humanist principles demand the widest possible extension of democracy to all relevant aspects of human living."[11] Dreikurs believes, "Democracy is more than a form of government; it implies a characteristic and fundamental change in human relations."[12]

Dreikurs goes on to explain the changes that must take place in human relations: "In an autocratic order all relations between individuals and between groups are those of superiors and inferiors. One is dominant, the other submissive. In contrast, the process of democratization entails a process of equalization."[13] This call for equalization greatly influences much of the Humanist's political theory. We will examine this influence later; first, we must explore a Humanist concept most relevant to their approach to politics.

Man's Role in Evolution

As stressed in the chapter on Humanist biology, Secular Humanism views man as part of a constant evolutionary process. Indeed, the Humanist perceives man as still evolving, always moving toward becoming a more perfect being. Julian Huxley believes that "all reality

Notes and Asides

is a single process of evolution."[14]

Obviously, with this kind of attitude toward reality, the Humanist sees man's continued evolution as one of his most pressing concerns. This becomes even more evident when one realizes that the Humanist believes man is capable of controlling his own evolutionary development. Huxley writes,

> Today, in twentieth-century man, the evolutionary process is at last becoming conscious of itself and is beginning to study itself with a view to directing its future course. Human knowledge worked over by human imagination is seen as the basis of human understanding and belief, and the ultimate guide to human progress.[15]

H. J. Muller believes the same thing: "Finally, it should be borne in mind that there is no sign of man having reached any limit in the possibilities of his biological evolution, especially if that be given the aid of ever more intelligent and far-seeing conscious guidance. Thus it seems a quite reasonable possibility that, once this corner leading to the path of rational control has been turned, our descendants may have before them a road of progress far outdistancing that which life on this earth has already traveled in its automatic course of trial and error."[16]

If man is truly capable of controlling his own evolution, and the possibilities of this evolution seem virtually limitless, then certainly this is the most important task with which the human race is faced. For the Humanist, then, the political arena becomes very significant, because government is one of mankind's most powerful agents for effecting the type of change necessary to further mankind's evolution. Indeed, Walt Anderson believes the evolutionary perspective

> urges us to see political development *itself* as an advanced form of biological evolution, to look at humanity not as a cog in a vast social machine but rather as (in Julian Huxley's phrase) evolution become conscious of itself.[17]

Anderson outlines three presuppositions that Humanists defend and that he believes "nearly all of us would readily grant to be obvious and true," then draws the necessary conclusion:

> 1. The human race represents a stage in a long evolutionary development which has produced intelligent life on Earth and which is still in progress.
> 2. There is intelligence in the universe, as evidenced by the fact that we are a part of the universe and possess

Notes and Asides

intelligence.

3. Our intelligence has now reached the point, in science and technology, at which we are beginning to be capable of making decisions that will influence future evolution.

None of the above is particularly controversial, yet if they are taken together and consciously applied to the things about which we think, as citizens and social scientists, they form a whole new perspective: a fundamentally different way of looking at human beings and political organizations.[18]

This new way of looking at political organizations perceives them as valuable means of advancing man's evolution. Anderson explains,

If we should choose to seize upon this opportunity, to make the highest development of human beings a deliberate social goal, then the task before us is to think about the growth possibilities of all people, at all social and economic levels, and also to understand fully what it means when a species begins to become responsible for its own evolution. As we consider such questions the humanistic perspective becomes not merely psychological, but political. We are not talking about principles of research or therapy, but about principles of social action and institutional change. Our new vision of the possibilities of human existence becomes a set of guidelines for building a human community. . . .[19]

Obviously, government is the most crucial institution capable of implementing these guidelines, so government plays a significant role in the Humanist's plans for the newly developing human community.

Just what type of community should evolve through political action? The answer again lies in the Humanist's evolutionary perspective. Because man is seen as the highest of all evolved animals and simply one among many parts of the world's single ecosystem, he is viewed as violating his place in nature when he attempts to divide that ecosystem into states and nations.

Timothy J. Madigan sums up,

Humanism holds that the planet Earth must be considered a single ecosystem, which is to say it is no longer feasible to arbitrarily divide it into separate states and hope that each one can satisfactorily manage itself. . . . Quite simply, national borders can no longer be considered sacrosanct when manipulation of the environment can easily lead to worldwide devastation.[20]

Notes and Asides

Abraham Maslow reminds people to be "a little less members of their culture, a little more members of their species,"[21] and Anderson echoes him, stressing that people are "living parts of a single biosphere."[22]

Linus Pauling takes this notion of the unity of mankind one step further:

> Yet a man or woman is not truly an organism, in the sense that a rabbit is, or a lion, or a whale. Instead, he is a part of a greater organism, the whole of mankind, into which he is bound by the means of communication—speaking, writing, telephoning, traveling over long distances, in the way that the cells of a rabbit are interconnected by nerve fibers and hormonal molecular messengers. This great organism, humankind, is now master of the earth, but not yet master of itself; it is immature, irrational; it does not act for its own good, but instead often for its own harm.[23]

Clearly, this notion of mankind as one organism, or even simply as one part of a single ecosystem, has concrete ramifications for the Humanist concept of community. According to Humanism, mankind should live in one community, apart from national borders and differing state policies. As we will see, the Humanist evolutionary view of community greatly influences Humanism's political views.

Globalism

What happens if the world govt that has absolute control becomes evil? Who would have the power to counteract? There would be no govts to defend the rights of the people.

Humanism believes that mankind should evolve into a world community and that such a community necessitates a world government. Lamont declares, "A truly Humanist civilization must be a world civilization."[24] Kurtz writes,

> the Humanist is truly global in his concern for he realizes that no man is a separate island and that we are all part of the mainland of humanity. Thus the idea of mankind as a whole and of one world, is a profound moral vision that sustains and nourishes the Humanist morality. And this can be achieved only by some degree of rule of law, some measure of peace and economic well-being and cultural enrichment for all men, who may share experience and a sense of brotherhood with others. . . . we nevertheless recognize the need for the human race to transform blind social forces into rational control and to build a world community.[25]

Notes and Asides

This sentiment is reiterated in the *Humanist Manifesto II*: "Each person's future is in some way linked to all. We thus reaffirm a commitment to the building of world community, at the same time recognizing that this commits us to some hard choices."[26] One of these hard choices involves calling for a world government. The Manifesto elsewhere expounds, "We deplore the division of humankind on nationalistic grounds. We have reached a turning point in human history where the best option is to *transcend the limits of national sovereignty* and to move toward the building of a world community in which all sectors of the human family can participate. Thus we look to the development of a system of world law and a world order based upon transnational federal government."[27]

Indeed, the Humanist believes that systems of national government are destined to fail and that the world community is a virtually inevitable step up the evolutionary staircase. William G. Carleton painstakingly sums up the Humanist case against the continued existence of nations:

> For nationalism today is truly beset from all directions. Among the dissolving agents are: the cumulative impact of technology and science resulting in the continued drastic elimination of distance and space, the atomic bomb, the release of atomic energy and the overwhelming necessity of having to extend international functionalism to control what in the future will probably be the world's most important source of industrial production; . . . the glaring fact that real national power in the international power conflict is today possessed by only two nations, leaving all other nations as mere outsiders with no important power . . . the body of practical experience in international cooperation gained through the League of Nations and the United Nations.[28]

This Humanist belief in the unavoidable downfall of nationalism bolsters Humanists' confidence in the inevitability of globalism. Kurtz is certain that "today there are powerful forces moving us toward a new ethical global consciousness."[29] Carleton is even more confident: "Whatever method of putting the world together will ultimately prevail is still anybody's guess, but that the world in our time is in painful process of being put together is more than a guess—it is a hypothesis based upon a growing accumulation of evidence."[30] To no one's surprise, the worldview that will most encourage the creation of this world community (according to the Humanist) is Humanism. Kurtz says, "Humanism, we believe, can play a significant role in helping to

Notes and Asides

"My reading of history convinces me that most bad government has grown out of too much government."
—J. Sharp Williams

foster the development of a genuine world community."[31]

Why will Humanism be able to bring about this peaceful world community? Because man is inherently good, and Humanism provides a framework for channeling that inherent goodness. The *Humanist Manifesto II* proclaims, "What more daring a goal for humankind than for each person to become, in ideal as well as practice, a citizen of a world community. It is a classical vision; we can now give it new vitality. Humanism thus interpreted is a moral force that has time on its side. We believe that humankind has the potential intelligence, good will, and cooperative skill to implement this commitment in the decades ahead."[32] Thus, peaceful world government appears to be inevitable, and it will occur because man is constantly evolving to a higher state and is now capable of controlling his own evolution (by following the guidelines set up by the Humanist worldview).

It should be noted, however, that these guidelines are always of a general nature. Humanists are understandably a little wary of outlining specific steps that must be followed in the establishment of a world government. While they view globalism as inevitable and a necessary advancement, they are unwilling to suggest exactly how the change could be implemented or to propose specific political models.

Humanists do seem to agree, however, on the specific need for a world system of law. Kurtz writes, "We believe, however, that *it is necessary to create on a global scale new democratic and pluralistic institutions that protect the rights and freedoms of all people*. As a first step, humankind needs to establish a system of world law and to endow the World Court with enough moral force that its jurisdiction is recognized as binding by all the nation-states of the world."[33] This notion of "world law" will be explored in the Humanist law chapter.

Occasionally a Humanist will suggest a concrete method for instigating a world government, but it is difficult to make this suggestion mesh with the democratic ideal that Humanists espouse. For example, Edith Wynner suggests,

> Our present tragic necessity requires that world government begin with massive emergency authority granted for ten to twenty years. At the end of that period, the question of the extension or abolition of such emergency powers could be subjected to study, discussion, and decision in separate sessions by a world parliament, a world judiciary, and an interparliamentary meeting of delegates of national legislatures.[34]

Wynner does not suggest how such a massive and powerful world government could be abolished if its functionaries wanted to continue in their exalted positions. Furthermore, this call for "massive emer-

Notes and Asides

gency authority" sounds dangerously like the call for an authoritarian government, which should play no role in a democratic world community. Thus, the Humanist prefers to speak in generalizations regarding world government, in order to avoid the difficult specifics involved in its actual implementation.

Disarmament and the United Nations

Humanists usually make only two rather vague suggestions when attempting to specify the steps necessary for the implementation of a democratic world community. Most Humanists call for universal disarmament and expanded power for the United Nations. Lucile W. Green actually lists six "essentials of world government," but only two of them are steps toward the establishment of world government. She calls for "disarmament, effective peacekeeping machinery, financial security for the United Nations, a world court, a world legislature, and a world executive."[35]

Humanists believe, for obvious reasons, that universal disarmament is a crucial intermediate step in establishing world government. "The first steps in avoiding a nuclear cataclysm and preserving democracy," writes Erich Fromm, "are to agree on universal disarmament. . . ."[36] Harold J. Blackham and J. P. van Praag declare, "Negotiations are also called for to halt the arms race and to provide mutual guarantees against surprise attack, as a preliminary to general disarmament. . . ."[37] Pauling believes, "The only hope for the world lies in achieving control of the methods of waging war and ultimately to reach the goal of total and universal disarmament."[38]

Morris Ginsberg believes that the world community cannot even be considered as a possibility until the threat of war is removed. Conversely, disarmament will make globalism an almost certain reality. He writes,

> Once freed from the fear of war, the peoples of the world will be free to develop each in its own way, but in relation to the whole human community, and to deal with the problems that knowledge can deal with, the conquest of disease and poverty and the removal of the barriers that divide men. They will then realize that they have a common positive aim—the unfolding and fulfillment of human faculty. Both sociological analysis and historical survey show that this aim can only be achieved by an organization covering the whole world and by methods which call forth the willing response of all its members.[39]

Notes and Asides

The Humanist believes that this world organization will eventually evolve into a one-world government. At present, however, the only organization that is truly global in its scope is the United Nations, so much of Humanism's hope is pinned on increased power for this institution. Carleton says simply, "Our hopes for political internationalism may have to center around the United Nations. . . ."[40]

Obviously, the United Nations as it exists today does not wield enough power to encourage implementation of world government. Thus, Blackham and van Praag call for increased membership and an improved constitution for the United Nations: "World order requires institutions, and the United Nations exists to provide them, but all nations must be members and all members must have confidence in the constitution and the secretariat before the United Nations and its agencies are fully international and workable for the purposes of international order and co-operation."[41]

Humanists believe that, when it is improved enough to provide the proper leadership, the United Nations can play an essential role in developing a world community. "A successfully functioning United Nations," says Lamont, "with its many specialized agencies, such as the Economic and Social Council, the Food and Agriculture Organization, the World Health Organization, and UNESCO, obviously entails some degree of global planning and could lay the foundation for an integrated world economy and political federation."[42]

The Humanist is encouraged by this possibility of the United Nations developing into the basis for world government. Indeed, Carleton believes this is Humanism's greatest hope for achieving its political goals:

> The evolution of the United Nations into international or supranational federal government is today an alternative to a world state based upon militarism or upon Communist dictatorship. It alone offers international government based on consent. It alone combines strength and democracy.[43]

With this hope in mind, Humanists have consistently worked in conjunction with the United Nations to bring the world closer to globalism. Julian Huxley served as the first Director General of the United Nations Educational, Scientific, and Cultural Organization (UNESCO). Lamont proclaims, "Ever since I was an undergraduate at Harvard, I have been active in endeavors to establish enduring world peace. I backed the League of Nations, and since World War II, I have vigorously supported the United Nations."[44]

Humanists point to both universal disarmament and increased power for the United Nations as two steps necessary for developing

CLOSE-UP

Julian Huxley (1887-1975)

Julian Huxley based his life work on man-centered theories that were the fashion of the day, and as such provides an excellent example of a man whose thinking was rendered obsolete even while he was still living. Because Huxley chose Darwinism as his dogmatic creed (often declaring evolutionary theory to be "fact"), his work loses credibility as Darwinism loses credibility—something that is happening quite rapidly at present. Thus, modern Humanists rarely acknowledge the debt they owe Huxley. This debt, nonetheless, is large: Huxley was one of the first to postulate that man had evolved the capacity to control his future progress, a concept which is foundational to the Humanistic worldview. Huxley then led Humanism a step farther: carrying faith in science and Darwin to its logical extreme, he concluded that mankind could usher in utopia through social engineering. In 1962 in his Galton Lecture, Huxley called for hastening the progress of man through eugenic improvement, specifically through artificial insemination using donors of superior characteristics. Huxley had ample opportunity to impose his Humanistic views on others as director-general of the United Nations Educational and Scientific Organization (UNESCO) from 1946 to 1948, and as a keynote speaker at the International Planned Parenthood Federation Conference in 1959. Though most of his theories are now obsolete, Huxley's legacy lives on, thanks to his powerful impact on Humanism and his role at the United Nations.

globalism. Before Humanism can move beyond these somewhat general recommendations, however, great compromises of both ideology and ethics must be made between nations and worldviews.

Ideologies and Ethics

The *Humanist Manifesto II* plainly demands ideological compromise: "We thus call for international cooperation in culture, science, the arts, and technology *across ideological borders*. We must learn to live

Notes and Asides

openly together or we shall perish together."[45] This Humanist belief in the need for compromise between ideologies is rooted in Humanists' concept of democracy. As noted earlier, democracy (for Humanists) implies not only a form of government but also an overall means of equalization. Yet proponents of specific ideologies do not perceive other ideologies as equal to their own, and Humanists believe this denial of equality creates tensions that cannot exist in a democratic world government. Indeed, for the Humanist, the mere fact that some ideologies perceive themselves as more right than others (and therefore unequal) is contrary to democracy.

This belief can best be understood by exploring Humanists' attitude toward the role of ethics in establishing the world community. Dreikurs believes, "It is the task of our generation to explore the means by which we can reach agreement, the basis for co-operation between equals. No pressure nor 'being right' will accomplish this. . . ."[46] That is, we must stop worrying about which ideology or worldview might be ethically correct and simply agree to begin agreeing. Blackham and van Praag say much the same thing:

> It is necessary to cease to think in black and white terms, for there are no stainless systems standing against devilish ones, and all systems, anyhow, are in a state of development. This consideration should not lead to unlimited relativism, but to that degree of mutual understanding which is a necessary preliminary to really peaceful co-existence.[47]

The doctrine of moral equivalency is based on the idea that all nations have good and bad points; hence, all nations are morally equal.

These statements represent another attempt by the Humanists to "equalize" all aspects of society. According to Humanism, no ethical system holds all the answers, and no system is totally sinister—instead, we are asked to take a more "democratic" view of ideologies and their ethical systems. That is, a modern man cannot rightfully believe that his ideology is the only proper means of viewing the world because this sets one ideology above others in an unequal, "undemocratic" fashion.

This does not mean, however, that Humanists would have us abandon every ideology. In fact, they believe that ideologies evolve continually and that we must simply embrace the newest, most highly-developed ideology. Huxley puts it this way: ". . . major steps in the human phase of evolution are achieved by breakthroughs to new dominant patterns of mental organization, of knowledge, ideas and beliefs—ideological instead of physiological or biological organization."[48]

This highly-developed ideology will have to be capable of handling all the sticky problems presented by a democratic world government, including effecting a compromise between all of the old ideologies and

Notes and Asides

ethical systems. "The central problem of democracy," says Francis Williams, "is that since it is a system of 'rule by the people,' or at the very least one in which 'the people' are persuaded that they are theoretically the rulers, and will be so in practice when one or two necessary adjustments from the old order have been made, it releases such forces of individual and national initiative, inventiveness and hope, that when tried on a world scale it is in danger of becoming self-destructive, unless means can be found to harness it to a philosophy of life which makes co-operation and toleration seem both natural and inevitable."[49]

So which ideology is most highly evolved and capable of promoting tolerance in a world community? "A world organization can not be based on one of the competing theologies of the world," Huxley believes, "but must, it seems, be based on some form of humanism . . . a world humanism . . . a scientific humanism . . . an evolutionary humanism."[50]

Phillip Butler writes, "We therefore must all broaden our visions and understand that we are a world of one species, interdependent brothers and sisters who must replace patriotism with humanism. We must become world-patriots, which simply means we must become humanists."[51]

How can the Humanist justify defending his ideology while viewing other ideologies as opposed to "democracy"? By claiming that Humanism is open-minded, whereas all other ideologies are dogmatic and far too dependent on absolutes. Williams calls for mankind "to stop thinking politically as Capitalists, or Communists, Christians, Muslims, Hindus or Buddhists, and think as Humanists. The world's democratic dialogue can only be conducted in a global humanist frame. A world in which men have both hydrogen bombs and closed minds is altogether too dangerous."[52] World democracy can only truly flourish when every man abandons whatever backward ideology he is embracing and becomes a Humanist.

Morals and Politics

Humanists recognize that politics cannot be separated from ethical considerations. In fact, John P. Anton believes political theory must be expanded to be used as a tool for developing standards: "Once the political conduct is seen as the matrix for all other types of institutional concerns and habits, there would be nothing to prevent the inquiry into this domain from reaching the level of service it had with Aristotle and thus becoming again the supreme practical science, with a normative as well as a descriptive side to it."[53] Anton is saying, in his own ponderous

Notes and Asides

way, that one can refine norms and standards through the proper use of political theory.

Sidney Hook believes the proper means of developing moral codes and re-examining standards lies in the practical application of political theory. Thus, once the democratic world society is established, mankind can go about the business of discovering what is morally acceptable. This business should be totally separated from religious notions about morality. Hook states, "The democratic open society must be neutral to all religious overbeliefs; but no matter how secular it conceives itself to be, it cannot be neutral to moral issues. It seeks to draw these issues into the area of public discussion in the hope that a reasonable consensus may be achieved."[54] This call for public discussion to determine a system of ethics is reiterated in the *Humanist Manifesto II*: "All persons should have a voice in developing the values and goals that determine their lives."[55]

The notion of democratically determining ethics should extend worldwide, according to the Humanist. Kurtz explains, "The basic premise of . . . global ethics is that each of us has a stake in developing a universal moral awareness, each of us has a responsibility to the world community at large."[56]

However, developing this universal moral awareness through the Humanist political system may not be so easy. Mark Reader tells us that "there is no incompatibility between humanism and politics. . . . In the end politics is the place of public happiness. . . ."[57] But when one accepts the premise that politics is the "place of public happiness," one necessarily runs into a dilemma with regard to developing morals or standards. As James R. Simpson points out, "The 'good life' or 'quality of life' is relative to each individual's preferences, desires, and needs."[58] Yet if politics is intrinsically tied to happiness, and happiness is relative to each individual, how can a government develop a proper moral awareness that encourages personal happiness? How can people democratically arrive at standards satisfactory to every world citizen if all morality is relative? Ironically, Hook accurately sums up the whole puzzle faced by a democratic world government that would give every citizen a voice in establishing standards:

"Vain hope, to make people happy by politics!"
—Thomas Carlyle

> A democratic community may recognize—indeed, it must recognize—what is morally evil, but it cannot recognize the category of sin, legislate against it, and punish those for whom the proscribed action is not sinful. One man's sin may be another man's duty and a third man's bliss.[59]

Thus - justice would be unattainable.

Thus, the Humanist political framework, which would do away with all other ideologies and their ethical systems, is unable to offer a

Notes and Asides

satisfactory alternate means of establishing standards. Furthermore, the one-world government it proposes would be incapable of intervening forcefully to protect anyone from anyone else, since "One man's sin may be another man's duty and a third man's bliss." Indeed, all that Humanism seems to be able to offer to a new democratic world community is its open-minded attitude, which is theoretically more conducive to cooperation and equalization. This Humanist push for equalization, as noted earlier, applies to all aspects of life. Before concluding this chapter, we must examine one other area powerfully affected by the Humanist definition of "democracy."

Humanism and "Economic Democracy"

In the Humanist democratic world government, democracy will extend to the economic sphere as well as the political. V. M. Tarkunde believes, "A genuine political democracy is not possible in the absence of economic democracy."[60] As we explore precisely what the Humanist means by *economic democracy*, it will become evident why many Humanists are socialists and favor the redistribution of wealth, as was demonstrated in the Humanist economics chapter.

Many Humanists believe that man's evolution is being hindered by the unequal distribution of material goods in our world. Anderson claims that "when people are deprived of the fundamental necessities, as are millions of Americans and even more millions of human beings in other countries, their capacity for development is frustrated at the most basic level."[61] Logically, then, the redistribution of wealth is a necessary intermediate step in man's struggle to further his evolutionary development.

Lamont agrees with this conclusion, defining *economic democracy* as "the right of every adult to a useful job at a decent wage or salary, to general economic security and opportunity, to an equitable share in the material goods of this life, and to a proportionate voice in the conduct of economic affairs."[62] The *Humanist Manifesto II* supports Lamont's call for a more equitable distribution of material goods, describing this distribution as a moral imperative:

> The problems of economic growth and development can no longer be resolved by one nation alone; they are worldwide in scope. It is the moral obligation of the developed nations to provide—through an international authority that safeguards human rights—massive technical, agricultural, medical, and economic assistance, including birth control techniques, to the developing portions of the globe. World poverty must cease.

Notes and Asides

> Hence extreme disproportions in wealth, income, and economic growth should be reduced on a worldwide basis.[63]

How does the Humanist propose to initiate this economic democracy? Wealth could be redistributed through taxation. "We believe, however," says Kurtz, "that the more affluent nations have a moral obligation to increase technological and economic assistance so that their less developed neighbors may become more self-sufficient. We need to work out some equitable forms of taxation on a worldwide basis to help make this a reality."[64] And what type of system would best promote continued economic democracy? Tarkunde's solution sounds a lot like socialism:

"The future kingdom of socialism will be a terrible tyranny of criminals and murderers. It will throw humanity into a true hell of spiritual suffering and poverty."
—Feodor Dostoevski

> A cooperative economy in which the workers in an undertaking will be the owners of the means of production employed in that undertaking is undoubtedly the most democratic economic institution conceived so far.[65]

Economic democracy, as outlined by the Humanist, meshes well with the Humanist school of thought that supports socialism and the redistribution of material goods. It also meshes perfectly with the goals of Marxism/Leninism to usher in worldwide socialism and a one-world government.

Conclusion

Humanist politics is tied closely to Humanist biology, economics, ethics, and law. Because the Humanist perceives man as the highest rung on the evolutionary ladder, he has concluded that man can use world politics to further his evolution. Also, this evolutionary perspective views man as part of one ecosystem, the world, and consequently supports a one-world government. The Humanist sees universal disarmament and increased power for the United Nations as two crucial intermediate steps that must be taken before world government can be achieved.

What would a Humanist world government be like? Judging from the Secular Humanist movement in the United States, it would work to eradicate the Christian worldview and its symbols from the public square—removing the Ten Commandments from public schools, replacing Christian ethics with "values clarification" and sex education under the auspices of Planned Parenthood, etc. This seems especially likely when one considers that Huxley has already written the UNESCO materials for the future world government educational institutions.

Notes and Asides

In this capacity, Huxley believes he is helping mankind to replace the "struggle for existence that underlies natural selection" with "conscious selection, a struggle between ideas and values in consciousness."[66] That is, the Humanist now perceives mankind as evolving mentally. And if this is the case, the struggle for survival is a struggle of ideas. According to this view, Christian ideas are regressive and do not advance the consciousness of man, while Secular Humanist ideas are capable of guiding man's future evolutionary development.

Because the Humanist believes in the "equalization" of all aspects of living, he cannot support any ideology or worldview that claims to describe the only proper view of man and his place in the world. Rather, Humanism calls for a democracy that abandons absolute standards and encourages moral compromises. The Humanist recognizes this ethical dilemma as the most pressing problem facing a Humanist world order. "Given the new planetary society that is developing," says Kurtz, "it is clear that the ancient faiths and moralities will not fully serve us. Can we marshal the vision and courage required to build a better world for all members of the human family? The essential ingredient in this new world of planetary humanism depends on the cultivation of ethical wisdom."[67] The question remains: can a Humanist political view that compromises traditional morals create its own ethical wisdom?

[1]Julian Huxley, "A New World Vision: Selections from a Controversial Document," *The Humanist*, March/April 1979, p. 35.
[2]Lucile W. Green, "The Call for a World Constitutional Convention," *The Humanist*, July/August 1968, p. 13.
[3]Antony Flew, "Liberty and Democracy, or Socialism?" *Free Inquiry*, Fall 1989, p. 14.
[4]Ibid., p. 15.
[5]Paul Kurtz, *Eupraxophy: Living Without Religion* (Buffalo: Prometheus Books, 1989), p. 48.
[6]Julian Huxley, *Essays of a Humanist* (London: Chatto and Windus, 1964), p. 84.
[7]Paul Kurtz, "Is Everyone a Humanist?" in *The Humanist Alternative*, ed. Paul Kurtz (Buffalo: Prometheus Books, 1973), p. 179.
[8]Paul Kurtz, "A Declaration of Interdependence: A New Global Ethics," *Free Inquiry*, Fall 1988, p. 7.
[9]Rudolf Dreikurs, "The Impact of Equality," *The Humanist*, Sept./Oct. 1964, p. 143.
[10]Corliss Lamont, *The Philosophy of Humanism* (New York: Frederick Ungar, 1982), p. 262.
[11]Ibid., p. 261.
[12]Dreikurs, "The Impact of Equality," p. 143.
[13]Ibid.
[14]Julian Huxley, "The Humanist Frame," in *The Humanist Frame*, ed. Huxley (New York: Harper and Brothers, 1961), p. 15.
[15]Ibid., p. 7.
[16]Cited in ibid., p. 413.
[17]Walt Anderson, *Politics and the New Humanism* (Pacific Palisades, CA: Goodyear Publishing Company, 1973), p. 83.
[18]Ibid., p. 77.
[19]Ibid., p. 145.
[20]Timothy J. Madigan, "Humanism and the Need for a Global Consciousness," *The Humanist*, March/April, 1986, pp. 17-18.
[21]Cited in Anderson, *Politics and the New Humanism*, p. 81.
[22]Ibid., p. 81.
[23]Linus Pauling, "Humanism and Peace," *The Humanist*, 1961, no. 2, p. 69.
[24]Lamont, *The Philosophy of Humanism*, p. 281.
[25]Kurtz, "Is Everyone a Humanist?" pp. 179-80.
[26]*Humanist Manifesto II* (Buffalo: Prometheus Books, 1980), p. 21.
[27]Ibid. This world order, of course, could not be based on the American model of government, since its political documents are founded on the concept of Creator/creation—"We are endowed by our Creator," etc.
[28]William G. Carleton, *Technology and Humanism* (Nashville: Vanderbilt University Press, 1970), pp. 12-13.
[29]Paul Kurtz, *Forbidden Fruit* (Buffalo: Prometheus Books, 1988), p. 146. Among these forces are Marxism/Leninism, the New Age movement, Secular Humanism, and various Internationalist and Transnationalist organizations including the Council on Foreign Relations, Club of Rome, Bilderburgers, Trilateral Commission, and the United Nations. Biblical Christianity constitutes one major opposition to one-world government; Revelation 13 declares that the head of a manmade world government will be the Beast or Anti-Christ. For a fairly complete list of organizations and movements striving for a world order, see Malachi Martin, *The Keys of This Blood* (New York: Simon and Schuster, 1990), pp. 275f.
[30]Carleton, *Technology and Humanism*, p. 13.
[31]Kurtz, "A Declaration of Interdependence: A New Global Ethics," p. 6.
[32]*Humanist Manifesto II*, p. 23.
[33]Kurtz, "A Declaration of Interdependence: A New Global Ethics," p. 6.
[34]Edith Wynner, "Noah, the Flood, and World Government," *The Humanist*, July/Aug. 1975, p. 27. Internationalist Paul M. Mazur certainly agrees with Wynner's suggestion. In his book *Unfinished Business* (1979), Mazur says it will take "the total dictator" to control the diverse bureaucracies required to govern the world.
[35]Green, "The Call for a World Constitutional Convention," p. 12.
[36]Erich Fromm, *May Man Prevail?* (Garden City, NY: Doubleday, 1961), p. 248.
[37]Harold J. Blackham and J. P. van Praag, "A Statement on World Policy," *The Humanist*, Jan./Feb. 1962, p. 13.

[38]Pauling, "Humanism and Peace," p. 75.
[39]Cited in *The Humanist Frame*, ed. Huxley, p. 127.
[40]Carleton, *Technology and Humanism*, p. 22.
[41]Blackham and van Praag, "A Statement on World Policy," p. 13.
[42]Lamont, *The Philosophy of Humanism*, pp. 279-80.
[43]Carleton, *Technology and Humanism*, p. 36.
[44]Corliss Lamont, *Voice in the Wilderness* (Buffalo: Prometheus Books, 1975), p. 318.
[45]*Humanist Manifesto II*, p. 22.
[46]Dreikurs, "The Impact of Equality," p. 146.
[47]Blackham and van Praag, "A Statement on World Policy," p. 13.
[48]Huxley, "The Humanist Frame," p. 16.
[49]Francis Williams, "The Democratic Challenge," in *The Humanist Frame*, ed. Huxley, pp. 98-9.
[50]Julian Huxley, cited in *Humanist Ethics*, ed. Morris B. Storer (Buffalo: Prometheus Books, 1980), p. 2.
[51]Philip Butler, "From Nationalist to Humanist," *The Humanist*, March/April 1986, p. 32.
[52]Huxley, "The Humanist Frame," p. 107.
[53]John B. Anton, "Theory of Political Humanism," in *Humanist Ethics*, ed. Storer, p. 276.
[54]Sidney Hook, *Religion in a Free Society* (Lincoln: University of Nebraska Press, 1967), p. 36.
[55]*Humanist Manifesto II*, p. 19.
[56]Kurtz, "A Declaration of Interdependence: A New Global Ethics," p. 4.
[57]Mark Reader, "Humanism and Politics," *The Humanist*, Nov./Dec. 1975, p. 38.
[58]James R. Simpson, "Toward a Humanist Consensus on Ethics of International Development," in *Humanist Ethics*, ed. Storer, p. 130.
[59]Hook, *Religion in a Free Society*, p. 38.
[60]V. M. Tarkunde, "An Outline of Radical Humanism," *The Humanist*, July/Aug. 1988, p. 13.
[61]Anderson, *Politics and the New Humanism*, p. 141.
[62]Lamont, *The Philosophy of Humanism*, p. 267.
[63]*Humanist Manifesto II*, p. 22.
[64]Kurtz, "A Declaration of Interdependence: A New Global Ethics," p. 6.
[65]Tarkunde, "An Outline of Radical Humanism," p. 13.
[66]Huxley, "A New World Vision: Selections from a Controversial Document," p. 35.
[67]Kurtz, *Forbidden Fruit*, p. 176.

CHAPTER

25

MARXIST/ LENINIST POLITICS

"The art of politics lies in correctly gauging the conditions and the moment when the vanguard of the proletariat can successfully seize power."[1]

—V. I. Lenin

"In reality, however, the State is nothing more than a machine for the oppression of one class by another."[2]

—Frederick Engels

"In essence, communism is identical to humanism since it presupposes the all-round development of the human personality in a perfectly organized society."[3]

—Georgi Shakhnazarov

SUMMARY

Marxist/Leninists are not afraid to talk about dictatorships. In fact, the "dictatorship of the proletariat" is a respectable political Marxist expression. This dictatorship leads the dialectical clash between the bourgeoisie and the proletariat. Eventually, the proletariat throughout the world will rise up, cast off the chains of bourgeois oppression, and seize the means of production as well as political power, thereby establishing a worldwide dictatorship of the proletariat. When this occurs, as it already has in the Soviet Union, the People's Republic of China, and elsewhere, mankind will be taking its next major evolutionary step toward the coming world order.

The dictatorship of the proletariat will signal the beginning of socialism and the end of property class distinctions, according to the Marxist. The government will centrally plan the economy and shatter all bourgeois oppression. Further, the dictatorship of the proletariat will wage war against any shred of bourgeois mentality (which includes the regressive ideas of traditional morality and religion). Lenin declares, "If war is waged by the proletariat after it has conquered the bourgeoisie in its own country, and is waged with the object of strengthening and developing socialism, such a war is legitimate and 'holy.'"[4] Marxist/Leninists not only demand dictatorships—they expect dictatorships based on repression and terror.

Marxists are willing to call for a one-world dictatorship of the proletariat because they expect to control it. In Marxist political theory, the Marxist/Leninist party acts as the guiding force for the working class and, once in power, the enforcer of socialist laws. Thus, Marxists are talking about a dictatorship of the Marxist/Leninist party.

Mikhail Gorbachev, at this writing, acts as this dictator for the Soviet Union,

Introduction

Marxist/Leninists believe politics to be grounded in economics. As demonstrated in the chapter on Marxist economics, Marxism views the struggle to control the forces of production as the dynamic force behind man's development. The economic system in a society determines the other features of that society, including its political structure. "In the social production which men carry on," says Karl Marx, "they enter into definite relations that are indispensable and independent of their will; these relations of production correspond to a definite stage of development of their material forces of production. The sum total of *these*

basing his *perestroika* (reconstruction or reorganization) on "definite [Marxist/Leninist] values and theoretical premises."[5] He makes it very clear that *perestroika* is not merely a revolution but a direct "sequel to the great accomplishments shared by the Leninist Party in the October days of 1917. And not merely a sequel, but an extension and a development of the main ideas of the Revolution. We must impart new dynamism to the October Revolution's historical impulse and further advance all that was commenced by it in our society."[6] Gorbachev refers to such action as "Bolshevik daring."

Whether mankind would like to see this daring revolution usher in a one-world Marxist dictatorship is completely irrelevant. According to Marxism, the establishment of such a government is inevitable; it is guaranteed by dialectical processes and evolutionary forces.

These forces also guarantee that such a state ultimately will wither away. The Marxist believes that once every trace of bourgeois ideology and all the stains of capitalist tradition have been eradicated, i.e., once all classes are eliminated, a fully communist society will exist. In future communist society, every citizen will be capable of governing himself. Thus, communism will be ushered in by the dialectic and social evolution, through the vehicle of the dictatorship of the proletariat (guided by the Marxist/Leninist party). According to the Marxist, his economic and political vision will become reality through the coming world order and will one day redeem all mankind—an idea in keeping with the religious nature of Marxism/Leninism.

relations of production constitutes the economic structure of society—the real foundation on which rise legal and political superstructure and to which definite forms of social consciousness correspond."[7]

It follows from this that certain economic systems give rise to certain political systems. Marxists embrace this conclusion. Leonid I. Brezhnev declares, "Today, we know not only from theory but also from long years of practice that genuine [political] democracy is impossible without [economic] socialism. . . ."[8] Thus, the Marxist believes genuine democracy exists in the socialist Soviet Union. "In the USSR," says A. Andreyevich, "there are no anti-government demonstrations and manifestations. There are not, nor can there be, for after

Notes and Asides

all, the Soviet Government is always with the people."[9]

According to Marxism, socialism lays the foundation for genuine democracy, although an impure form of democracy can exist in capitalist nations. But is genuine democracy the supreme aim of Marxist politics? Not at all. In fact, the Marxist views democracy as little more than a necessary evil. "Democracy is a *state*," explains Lenin, "which recognises the subordination of the minority to the majority, i.e., an organisation for the systematic use of *force* by one class against another, by one section of the population against another."[10] With this attitude toward democracy, the Marxist is naturally unwilling to view democracy as the ultimate goal of man's development. However, this definition of democracy is consistent with Marxist thought when one takes into account Marxism's emphasis on the class struggle.

Class Antagonism

Because the Marxist sees our present world as a battle between the owners of the means of production (the bourgeoisie) and the workers (the proletariat), and because he views economics as the foundation on which the rest of society is built, he logically perceives the state as simply another arena in which the "haves" and the "have-nots" struggle. Thus, forms of government that the Western world would describe as desirable, such as a democracy or a republic, are still perceived by the Marxist as bad, especially if they exist in a capitalist economic system. "But a republic, like every other form of government," writes Engels, "is determined by its content; so long as it is a form of *bourgeois* rule it is as hostile to us as any monarchy (except that the *forms* of this hostility are different)."[11]

In other words, since the government is founded on the existing economic system, and since capitalism is always undesirable, the government overseeing it is undesirable as well. "The modern state, no matter what its form," says Engels, "is essentially a capitalist machine, the state of the capitalists, the ideal personification of the total national capital. The more it proceeds to the taking over of productive forces, the more does it actually become the national capitalist, the more citizens does it exploit."[12] Obviously, for the Marxist, a state so clearly based on exploiting its citizens is unacceptable.

However, as previously noted, the Marxist perceives not only a capitalist democracy, but also a socialist "genuine" democracy as unacceptable. What, then, causes the Marxist to describe the socialist democracy as genuine? Because, the Marxist claims, in socialist society, the mode of production does not exploit any of the citizens, and

Notes and Asides

therefore encourages a less-exploitative political system. The authors of *Socialism as a Social System* put it this way: "*The political system of socialism*—as opposed to the political systems of the preceding societies—*is based on socio-economic relations free from exploitation and antagonism.*"[13] Marxism believes a socialist government will tend to discourage class antagonism, since it will be founded on an economic system that is a step closer to abolishing classes. This less-exploitative nature of the government makes the democracy more "genuine." It makes socialism more appealing than capitalism, but still less appealing than communism.

The reason the Marxist believes socialist democracy is a better form of government is clear. So why doesn't Marxism embrace a socialist democratic state as the ultimate goal of man's development? Even given the Marxist belief that democracy is a system through which the majority oppresses the minority, surely they must admit it to be a better political system than any of the alternatives?

This, however, is precisely the point for the Marxist: no political system is acceptable. In fact, Marxism perceives the state itself, whether a democracy or a dictatorship, as a vehicle for maintaining class antagonism. "Political power," writes Marx, "is merely the organised power of one class for oppressing another."[14] Lenin agrees: "The State is a special organization of force; it is the organization of violence for the suppression of some class."[15]

except for theirs!

From this Marxist perspective, the state exists because class antagonism exists (Engels says, "Society . . . based upon class antagonisms has need of the State . . . "[16]); however, once this antagonism is eradicated, the state will no longer be necessary. Lenin sums up this point:

> According to Marx, the State could neither arise nor maintain itself if a reconciliation of classes were possible. . . . The State is an organ of class domination, an organ of oppression of one class by another; its aim is the creation of "order" which legalises and perpetuates this oppression by moderating the collisions between the classes.[17]

"In moral terms familiar to the Western mind, there is no way to understand the Communist mentality . . . "
—Malachi Martin

The aim of Marxist politics is to create a society in which the state is an outmoded, unnecessary institution. Because Marxism seeks to abolish all class distinctions and the state is simply a tool for enforcing those distinctions, the Marxist believes the state will naturally wither away as mankind evolves into a classless society. We will examine this concept later. First, however, we must understand the specific nature of the government that the Marxist believes should exist under socialism, as society makes the "inevitable" transition to communism.

Notes and Asides

The Dictatorship of the Proletariat

The Marxist view of man's development from feudal government to socialist State is best described by Herbert Aptheker:

> The bourgeoisie takes state power from the feudal lords and then uses the state to further develop an already existing capitalism; the productive masses take state power from the bourgeoisie and then use state power in order to *begin* the establishment of Socialism.[18]

The state is viewed as necessary at this juncture because it is a starting point for creating a socialist society. The proletariat must overthrow the bourgeois government and use the state to enforce socialism in its early stages. "Once the first radical onslaught upon private ownership has been made," writes Engels, "the proletariat will see itself compelled to go always further, to concentrate all capital, all agriculture, all industry, all transport, and all exchange more and more in the hands of the State."[19]

This concentration of all the means of production in the hands of the state, of course, is the first step in the Marxist formula to abolish all classes. Engels writes, "We want the abolition of classes. What is the means of achieving it? The only means is political domination of the proletariat."[20] Marx calls for this political domination as well: "Between capitalist and communist society lies the period of the revolutionary transformation of the one into the other. Corresponding to this is also a political transition period in which the state can be nothing but *the revolutionary dictatorship of the proletariat*."[21] This dictatorship of the proletariat, according to Lenin, is necessary for the good of all society: "The essence of Marx's theory of the state has been mastered only by those who realise that the dictatorship of a single class is necessary not only for every class society in general, not only for the proletariat which has overthrown the bourgeoisie, but also for the entire historical period which separates capitalism from 'classless society,' from communism."[22]

The dictatorship of the proletariat refers to the form of "genuine democracy" which will exist in socialist societies progressing toward communism.

Marxist/Leninists believe the proletariat must seize political power to instigate socialism and set the stage for the abolition of classes (and eventually the state). The puzzle is that Marxists continually speak of a "dictatorship" of the proletariat. Doesn't a "genuine democracy" arise in socialist states? How can Marxism reconcile this call for a dictatorship with their claim that socialist society encourages true democracy?

Marxists reconcile this apparent contradiction simply by pointing to their definition of democracy. As noted earlier, Marxism perceives democracy as simply the oppression of the minority by the majority.

Notes and Asides

Thus, democracy is similar to a dictatorship in that the majority dictates government policy and laws to the minority. In capitalist society, this means the bourgeoisie uses the state to oppress the proletariat. In socialist society, it means precisely the opposite—the proletariat will operate as the authoritarian majority. "In no civilised capitalist country does 'democracy in general' exist," explains Lenin. "All that exists is bourgeois democracy, and it is not a question of 'dictatorship in general,' but of the dictatorship of the oppressed class, i.e., the proletariat, over its oppressors and exploiters, i.e., the bourgeoisie, in order

THE LEADERS OF THE SOVIET UNION

(years in power)

Vladimir Lenin
(1917-1924)

Joseph Stalin
(1924-1953)

Nikita Khrushchev
(1953-1964)

"collective leadership"
(1964-1966)

Leonid Brezhnev
(1966-1982)

Yuri Andropov
(1982-1984)

Konstantin Chernenko
(1984-1985)

Mikhail Gorbachev
(1985-)

Notes and Asides

to overcome the resistance offered by the exploiters in their fight to maintain their domination."[23]

The Fundamentals of Marxist-Leninist Philosophy puts it this way: "The socialist state is, above all, an instrument for uniting the masses and educating them in the spirit of communism, an instrument for building the new society. This state is dictatorial in a new way, because it is directed against the bourgeoisie, and democratic in a new way because it secures democracy for the working people."[24] Put more simply still, "The dictatorship of the proletariat means the replacement of democracy for the exploiters by socialist democracy for the working people. . . ."[25]

Democracy, for the Marxist, is not the noble cause that much of the Western world perceives it to be.[26] Rather, it is simply a means to an end—a necessary tool for maintaining the early stages of socialism. Indeed, democracy has no value at all as an end in itself. Writes Lenin,

> Democracy is of enormous importance to the working class in its struggle against the capitalists for its emancipation. But democracy is by no means a boundary not to be overstepped; it is only one of the stages on the road from feudalism to capitalism, and from capitalism to communism.[27]

Democracy is useful in establishing the dictatorship of the proletariat; but it is this dictatorship, in the guise of a democracy, that is a crucial facet of Marxist political development.

This dictatorship of the proletariat is crucial for a number of reasons. Obviously, it is needed to consolidate the means of production in the hands of the state, which in turn takes society on the first step toward the abolition of classes. But on a more fundamental level, a dictatorship is necessary because the proletariat will have seized power through a revolution and will need a dictatorial state to thwart bourgeois efforts to reclaim power. Lenin bluntly declares, "Whoever expects that socialism will be achieved *without* social revolution and a dictatorship of the proletariat is not a socialist. Dictatorship is state power, based directly upon *force*."[28] Engels is equally adamant about the need for a government concerned strictly with protecting proletariat interests:

> But the anti-authoritarians demand that the authoritarian political state be abolished at one stroke, even before the social conditions that gave birth to it have been destroyed. They demand that the first act of the social revolution shall be the abolition of authority. Have these gentlemen ever seen a revolution? A revolution is certainly the most authoritarian thing there is; it is the act whereby one part of the population imposes

Notes and Asides

> its will upon the other part by means of rifles, bayonets and cannon—authoritarian means, if such there be at all; and if the victorious party does not want to have fought in vain, it must maintain this rule by means of the terror which its arms inspire in the reactionaries.[29]

This "terror" will be inflicted on those people the proletariat believe to be members of the bourgeoisie. Hence, terrorism has become a mainstay of the Soviet effort to spread socialism around the world.[30] The dictatorship of the proletariat will *not* be a democracy for all (as it should be in the Western sense of the word); rather, capitalists will be not only suppressed but also persecuted and eliminated.

The Fate of the Bourgeoisie

The Marxist/Leninist is quite explicit about the need for suppression of the bourgeoisie by the proletariat. "The state is a special organisation of force," writes Lenin, "it is an organisation of violence for the suppression of some class. What class must the proletariat suppress? Naturally only the exploiting class, i.e., the bourgeoisie. The working people need the state only to suppress the resistance of the exploiters, and only the proletariat can direct this suppression, can carry it out."[31]

Remarkably, Marxism is also brash in its admission that the bourgeoisie must be actively oppressed. Consider the words of Lenin:

> Simultaneously with an immense expansion of democracy which for the first time becomes democracy for the poor, democracy for the people, and not democracy for the rich, the dictatorship of the proletariat imposes a series of restrictions on the freedom of the oppressors, the exploiters, the capitalists. We must crush them in order to free humanity from wage-slavery; their resistance must be broken by force.[32]

This breaking of the bourgeoisie by the proletariat includes the confiscation of virtually all property. Lenin believes, "A democratic peace can be concluded only by proletarian governments after they have overthrown the rule of the bourgeoisie and begun to expropriate it."[33]

Forced surrender of property, however, is only the beginning of the oppression the bourgeoisie must face. Marxists believe the proletariat must hound the capitalists at every turn. Again, Lenin voices the Marxist conviction: "The important thing will not be even the confiscation of the capitalists' property, but country-wide, all-embracing workers' control over the capitalists and their possible supporters."[34]

Notes and Asides

As previously noted, this all-embracing oppression of the bourgeoisie is one of the most crucial tasks faced by the dictatorship of the proletariat. Indeed, V. V. Zagladin lists two main aspects of the dictatorship of the proletariat and declares that one of these aspects "is to ensure the victory of the revolution, crush resistance by hostile classes, and establish the proletariat's political domination over the reactionaries in a given country until the reactionary classes (or forces) are liquidated in the course of socialist transformations."[35]

Such a task will not be easy. The proletariat must not only overthrow the bourgeoisie but also crush any resistance that might linger after the revolution. It is difficult to imagine workers organizing so efficiently that they can accomplish this while at the same time initiating socialism. Fortunately for the proletariat, the Marxist/Leninist party has vowed to guide them in establishing and governing their socialist society.

The Role of the Marxist/Leninist Party

The Marxist recognizes the difficulties the workers will face as they attempt to create a dictatorship of the proletariat. The authors of *Socialism as a Social System* admit, "Marxist/Leninist theory and the experience of history show conclusively that the working class can carry out its historic mission only if led by a strong, well-organised party. Only then can the working people cope successfully with the main and most difficult task of the socialist revolution—the task of building."[36]

Of course, these authors have only one "well-organised party" in mind: the Marxist/Leninist party. They proclaim, "The main distinctive feature and simultaneously an objective natural law of the socialist political system is that its political guidance is exercised by the most important political organisation, i.e., the Marxist/Leninist party."[37] Elsewhere they reiterate the importance of this guidance: "The political system of socialist society operates under the guidance of the communist party, integrally uniting state and non-state (public) political organisations."[38]

"Our Party guides the government," writes Joseph Stalin. "The Party supervises the work of the administration, the work of the organs of power, it corrects their errors and shortcomings, which are unavoidable, helps them to carry out the decisions of the government, and tries to secure for them the support of the masses, since there is not any important decision taken by them without the direction of the Party."[39]

This Marxist dogma creates a problem, however. How can the so-

Notes and Asides

cialist state be viewed as a dictatorship of the proletariat if the Marxist/Leninist Party is actually the guiding force behind every important decision made by the government? Wouldn't it be more appropriate to call socialist government the dictatorship of the Marxist/Leninist Party?

Marxism attempts to answer this charge in two ways. First, the Marxist asserts, all members of the Marxist/Leninist Party are members of the working class, or (at the very least) unswervingly dedicated to furthering the cause of the workers. "The party plays a prominent role during the struggle for seizing and consolidating power. It owes its revolutionary strength to the fact that it is backed by a well-developed and tested scientific theory and consists of the more aware representatives of the proletariat and other working people. . . ."[40] Note that these authors carefully use the term *representatives* to describe the members of the Party. The ambiguity of this term allows them to avoid the true question: is every member of the Marxist/Leninist Party a proletarian in the true sense of the word?

Obviously, not every Party member can be described as a proletarian. Engels himself could not accurately be called a member of the working class, and Marx seldom worked, living instead off the largess of Engels. Thus, the Marxist must settle for claiming that every member of the Marxist/Leninist Party is dedicated to furthering the interests of the proletariat. However, this leaves us simply with a "dictatorship of people who support the working class," which is not the same thing as a dictatorship of the proletariat.

Thus, the Marxist must present his second argument to justify the Party as the guiding force of the socialist state's dictatorship of the proletariat: The dictatorship really is a democracy, and the Marxist/Leninist Party works as the guiding force because the majority of the people (the proletariat) desires it to do so. The Marxist claims that this sequence of events has already occurred in socialist Russia, where the bourgeoisie has become a smaller and smaller minority and the call for guidance from the Marxist/Leninist Party has grown louder and louder.

> "My opinion is that power should always be distrusted, in whatever hands it is placed."
> —Sir William Jones

> The one-party system is an essential feature of the political organisation of Soviet society. It emerged in the distinctive historical circumstances of the country's transition from capitalism to socialism. The Great October Socialist Revolution delivered a crushing blow to the parties of the big bourgeoisie. As for the petty-bourgeois parties, they rejected the opportunity to cooperate which was open to them. By engaging in counter-revolution, they lost much of their social support, became isolated, dwindled away and finally came to an end.[41]

Notes and Asides

Which left, of course, only the Marxist/Leninist Party—in theory, the choice of every proletarian.

Thus, according to the Marxist, the dictatorship of the Marxist/Leninist Party is synonymous with the dictatorship of the proletariat. Whatever one calls it, the state in the early stages of socialist society will be the rule of the majority—the proletariat—as guided by the principles of Marxism/Leninism. People opposed to the principles of the Party will be considered bourgeois or reactionary.

Eventually, those opposed to Marxism will disappear, and the dictatorship of the proletariat will be rendered unnecessary. When classes cease to exist, and the entire population is of like mind, no state will be needed to enforce one class's oppression of another. "At the first stage, the socialist state is a state of the dictatorship of the proletariat, and at the second stage it is a state of the whole people."[42] Obviously, when the state is truly a state of the whole people, no formal state need exist. This is Marxism/Leninism's political goal.

The State Withers Away

Marxists view the state as a transitory phenomenon. According to their perception of man's social development, the state arose at a point in history when it was necessary and will cease to exist when it is no longer an important facet of society. Engels says, "The State is . . . simply a product of society at a certain stage of evolution."[43] Elsewhere he explains,

> The state has not existed from all eternity. There have been societies that did without it, that had no conception of the state and state power. At a certain stage of economic development which was necessarily bound up with the cleavage of society into classes, the state became a necessity owing to this cleavage. We are now rapidly approaching a stage in the development of production at which the existence of these classes not only will have ceased to be a necessity, but will become a positive hindrance to production. They will fall as inevitably as they rose at an earlier stage. Along with them the state will inevitably fall. The society that will organize production on the basis of a free and equal association of our producers will put the whole machinery of the state where it will then belong, into the museum of antiquities, by the side of the spinning wheel and the bronze axe.[44]

As Engels suggests, the Marxist expects the state to begin becoming a needless antiquity when the means of production are transferred

Notes and Asides

from the hands of the bourgeois to the hands of the state. Engels spells this out in *Socialism: Utopian and Scientific* when he writes, "The first act by virtue of which the state really constitutes itself the representative of the whole of society—the taking possession of the means of production in the name of society—this is, at the same time, its last independent act as a state."[45]

Marxists believe this to be the case because they perceive capitalism as responsible for maintaining class antagonisms, and they believe the state is necessary only when class antagonisms exist. Thus, as soon as society begins to embrace a socialistic means of production, class antagonisms begin to vanish, and the state begins to be outdated. The *Program of the Third International* states, "The abolition of private property does away with the exploitation of one human being by another. The work done is no longer done for others; differences between rich and poor disappear. At the same time the organs of class rule also vanish, above all state power. State power, which is the embodiment of class rule, vanishes in proportion to the vanishing of the classes."[46] This stand is consistent with the beliefs of the founders of Marxism. "Marx and I, ever since 1845," states Engels, "have held the view that *one* of the final results of the future proletarian revolution will be the gradual dissolution and ultimate disappearance of that political organisation called *the State*; an organisation the main object of which has ever been to secure, by armed force, the economical subjection of the working majority to the wealthy minority. With the disappearance of a wealthy minority the necessity for an armed repressive State-force disappears also."[47]

Lenin adamantly supports this position, stressing the need to erase the bourgeois class from existence: "Only in communist society, when the resistance of the capitalists has been completely crushed, when the capitalists have disappeared, when there are no classes (i.e., when there is no distinction between the members of society as regards their relation to the social means of production), *only* then 'the state . . . ceases to exist,' and '*it becomes possible to speak of freedom*.'"[48] Before these events occur, however, the Marxist believes freedom is only an illusion. Freedom by Marxist definition means no government. "So long as the state exists," insists Lenin, "there is no freedom. When there is freedom, there will be no state."[49]

Thus, according to the Marxist, the only way for mankind to achieve freedom is to embrace a system that causes the state to wither away. And the Marxist believes "only communism makes the state absolutely unnecessary, for there is *nobody* to be suppressed—'nobody' in the sense of a *class*, of a systematic struggle against a definite section of the population."[50] So humanity's only hope for freedom lies in abolishing classes (and eventually the state) through communism.

Obviously, classes and the state cannot be abolished in a single

Notes and Asides

stroke. Rather, they must gradually wither away. "The state is not 'abolished,'" says Engels, "*It dies out*."[51] And Lenin echoes him: "The abolition of the proletarian state, i.e., of all states, is only possible through 'withering away.'"[52]

This withering away of the state must, for Marxism to consider its political ends achieved, occur throughout the world. If the state still exists somewhere in the world, then that means classes still exist and threaten the societies that are well on their way to being classless—therefore there is still exploitation, and consequently an absence of freedom. Therefore, V. Platkovskiy declares, "The final withering away of the state can take place only with the complete victory of communism on a world-wide scale."[53]

New World Order

Marxists believe that the establishment of a new world order—world communism—and the withering away of the state are inevitable steps in mankind's biological and social evolutionary development. Just as man is evolving biologically, so society is evolving socially, economically, and politically. The new world order is an evolutionary advance over nations, states, tribes and other race and class distinctions.

Marxists believe that this process has begun. Georgi Shakhnazarov, a top aide to Soviet President Mikhail Gorbachev, writes,

> Our epoch is the epoch of the revolutionary transformation of capitalist society into communist. In the international arena our epoch therefore presupposes a change in the correlation of forces to the detriment of capitalism and in favour of socialism. This has been the constant feature of all world politics since October 1917.[54]

"[T]here is in the making nothing less than a *world system*, determining relationships between all the nations that constitute human society."
—Malachi Martin

Elsewhere he says, "the building of a new world order began not ten years ago, not twenty years ago, and certainly not with the Marshall Plan and the Alliance for Progress. It was begun in October 1917 by revolutionary Russia, proclaiming socialist principles."[55]

This has been the goal of all Marxist/Leninists since the inception of Marxism. Marx himself vowed, ". . . the rest of my life will be devoted, as have been my past efforts, to the triumph of the social ideas which some day—you may rest assured of it—will lead to the world-wide victory of the proletariat."[56] Engels tells us the communist revolution "is a world revolution and will, therefore, have the whole world as its arena."[57]

Lenin admits that Marxism's goal is world communism. "The aim

Notes and Asides

of socialism," he writes, "is not only to end the division of mankind into tiny states and the isolation of nations in any form, it is not only to bring the nations closer together but to integrate them."[58] Further, Marxism's end is "to break down national barriers, obliterate national distinctions, and to assimilate nations—a tendency which manifests itself more and more powerfully with every passing decade, and is one of the greatest driving forces transforming capitalism into socialism."[59] He believed this socialist/communist world order was near at hand: "It will not be long and we shall see the victory of communism in the entire world, we

CLOSE-UP

Mikhail Gorbachev (1931-)

The Berlin Wall crumbled and Lithuania declared her independence from the USSR during the regime of Mikhail Gorbachev. If nothing else happened during Gorbachev's stint as President of the Soviet Union, he would nonetheless stand in history as one of the USSR's most significant leaders. He is also one of the most important modern proponents of the Marxist worldview, declaring proudly, "I am now, just as I've always been, a convinced communist." Gorbachev began his move to become General Secretary and a Marxist leader in 1978, when he was appointed agriculture secretary of the Central Committee of the Communist party. He became a member of the Politburo in 1980, and was elected General Secretary in 1985—the youngest Soviet leader since Joseph Stalin. Numerous problems faced Gorbachev when he took power: the GNP had only increased 2 percent the previous year, Soviet oil production was falling off, and agricultural output was typically weak. For this reason, he opted to concentrate on domestic problems, but he did not allow this focus to distract him from building solid international relations. Gorbachev extracted unprecedented arms race concessions from United States President Ronald Reagan, and he is often portrayed as the darling of the American media. Gorbachev, however, should not be judged by his popularity, but by his actions--the actions of an adherent to the Marxist/ Leninist worldview.

Notes and Asides

shall see the founding of a World-wide Federal Republic of Soviets."[60]

All Marxist/Leninists are driven toward establishing a world communist order. Shakhnazarov notes that classical Marxist works "make it clear that a prolonged process of integration on a new socialist basis will lead to the fusion of nations, and, as a result of the withering away of the state, a universal system of communist social self-management will become firmly established."[61] Elsewhere he declares, "The requisite for [a future] world order is the *victory of socialism throughout the world*."[62]

For Marxists, world community is not enough. It must be a world community based on communism. Indeed, the Marxist believes that communism is the only proper economic basis for a world community. Shakhnazarov explains why:

> It is only the elimination of private property and class antagonisms, the establishment of social equality and popular rule which can lead to the gradual eradication of the causes of war, and create the requisites for resolving global problems by the organized and single-minded efforts of the whole of the world community.[63]

Only communism puts the means of production in the hands of the people, abolishes classes, abolishes the state, and so leads man into a world of cooperation. Thus, the ultimate political aim of the Marxist is the establishment of world communism (which necessarily results in the abolition of all government).

How is this world community of communism going to be established? Shakhnazarov says it will be established through the United Nations. He believes the U.N. has taken the necessary first steps in this direction by the "Declaration on the Establishment of a New International Economic Order, adopted by the 6th Special Session of the U.N. General Assembly in May 1974."[64] While Shakhnazarov admits this new international economic order is merely a means for mankind to manage "the planet," it is obvious that he believes this new economic order prepares the way for a unified planned economy. He approvingly quotes Michael Hudson to the effect that the establishment of NIEO "implies the end of America's unique foreign-fed affluence. The more the USA retards the emergence of a new system, the more isolated it will become."[65]

The U.N.'s economic system, of course, requires political power to implement the plan and to regulate the world economy. Shakhnazarov believes the U.N. must begin exercising this power to manage the "planet which is the common property of all people." Says Shakhnazarov, "One ought to bear in mind that although the tendency to increase

Notes and Asides

UN authority is slow and difficult, it is proceeding because of such powerful factors as the growing influence of public opinion and the democratization of international relations."[66]

What Shakhnazarov doesn't mention in *The Coming World Order* is that Soviet Marxist/Leninists were given the most important department of the U.N. Secretariat—the Department of Political and Security Council Affairs. Alger Hiss, who was a Marxist/Leninist in the U.S. State Department[67] before functioning as the executive secretary of the

United Nations
Department of Political and Security Affairs
Under Secretaries

1946-49:
A. Sobolev (USSR)

1949-53:
K. Zinchenko (USSR)

1953-54:
I. Tchernychev (USSR)

1954-57:
K. Protitch (Yugoslavia)

1958-60:
A. Dobrynin (USSR)

1960-62:
G. Arkadev (USSR)

1962-63:
E. D. Kiselev (USSR)

1963-65:
V. P. Suslov (USSR)

1965-68:
A. Nesterenko (USSR)

1968-73:
L. N. Kutakov (USSR)

1973-78:
A. Shevchenko (USSR)

1978-81:
M. D. Sytenko (USSR)

1981-86:
V. A. Ustinov (USSR)

1987-90:
V. Safronchuk (USSR)

Notes and Asides

Dumbarton Oaks conference, played an instrumental role in granting Marxists power over this department (which is the enforcement branch of the United Nations). The value of controlling enforcement, from the Marxist perspective, is obvious. This control grants Marxist/Leninists the power to enforce mankind's march toward world communism.

Conclusion

When Marxists envision their ideal society, they do not picture democracies, republics, or dictatorships governing the people. Indeed, for the Marxist, all forms of government are ugly reflections of the fact that class antagonism exists. Marxists do call for a "democracy" known as the "dictatorship of the proletariat" (guided by the Marxist/Leninist Party), but this "democracy" is a necessary evil that exists in the early stages of socialism.

Eventually, when the socialist society evolves into communism, all class distinctions will have been abolished and therefore the state will no longer be necessary. When communist society exists throughout the world, and governments everywhere are outdated, then the ultimate Marxist political aim will have been achieved.

"Most schemes of political improvement are very laughable things."
—Samuel Johnson

Until that end is achieved, the Marxists warn that there necessarily will be conflict between socialist societies (with states in the process of withering away) and capitalist nations. This conflict will arise as an extension of class antagonism. Just as the bourgeoisie and the proletariat clash, so will nations controlled by capitalists clash with nations controlled by workers. Shakhnazarov writes, "In the first place, when the world became divided into two opposing social systems, states began to embody not only national, but also different social qualities. Accordingly, the axis of conflict in the world arena gradually shifted from the national sphere to the *class* sphere."[68]

This class antagonism on a world scale will lead to war, says Lenin:

> We are living not merely in a state but in a system of states, and the existence of the Soviet republic side by side with imperialist states for a long time is unthinkable. One or the other must triumph in the end. And before this end supervenes, a serious frightful collision between the Soviet republic and the bourgeois states will be inevitable.[69]

Elsewhere he proclaims that the victory of socialism in one country must not only create friction, but direct attempts by the bourgeoisie of the other countries "to crush the victorious proletariat of the socialist state. Under these conditions, war on our part would be legitimate and just. It would be a war for socialism, for the liberation of other nations from the bourgeoisie."[70]

In other words, wars fought to advance communism are justified. "Marxists-Leninists distinguish between unjust and just wars," says Zagladin. "The former are waged by the exploiter classes to strengthen their power and amass wealth, to crush and plunder small and weak nations, and to counter movements for social and national liberation, and to offer opposition to the socialist states. In condemning imperialist wars of plunder, Marxists-Leninists give support to just wars waged in defense of the peoples from imperialist aggression and for national liberation wars waged by the revolutionary classes to foil attempts by the reactionary forces to keep or restore their rule with the aid of arms."[71]

The Marxists are not bashful about admitting their political aims. World communism and the abolition of all government are their ultimate goals, and they are willing to suppress, persecute, and wage war against the enemy to achieve these ends. The political/military history of Marxism, from the October Revolution of 1917 to Tianamen Square, is the history of the most ruthless, efficient killing machine mankind has ever witnessed. The death toll of this seventy-year "scientific" march to a new world order exceeds 80 million.

[1]V. I. Lenin, *Selected Works* (New York: International Publishers, 1938), vol. 10, pp. 91-2.
[2]Karl Marx, *Civil War in France* (New York: International, 1937), p. 19.
[3]Georgi Shakhnazarov, *The Coming World Order* (Moscow: Progress Publishers, 1981), p. 273.
[4]V. I. Lenin, *Collected Works*, forty-five volumes (Moscow: Progress Publishers, 1977), vol. 27, p. 332.
[5]Mikhail Gorbachev, *Perestroika* (New York: Harper and Row, 1987), p. xi.
[6]Ibid., p. 36.
[7]Karl Marx, *A Contribution to the Critique of Political Economy* (Chicago: C. H. Kerr, 1911), p. 11.
[8]*Documents and Resolutions. XXVth Congress of the CPSU*, p. 103, cited in *Socialism as a Social System*, eds. T. M. Jaroszewski and P. A. Ignatovsky (Moscow: Progress, 1981), p. 205.
[9]A. Andreyevich, in *Sovetskaya Belorussiya* (Minsk), 13 Sept. 1963. Cited in Raymond Sleeper, ed., *A Lexicon of Marxist/Leninist Semantics* (Alexandria, VA: Western Goals, 1983), p. 83.
[10]Karl Marx, Frederick Engels, and V. I. Lenin, *On the Dictatorship of the Proletariat* (Moscow: Progress Publishers, 1984), p. 243.
[11]Marx, Engels, and Lenin, *On the Dictatorship of the Proletariat*, p. 161.
[12]Ibid., p. 124.
[13]*Socialism as a Social System*, eds. Jaroszewski and Ignatovsky, p. 180.
[14]Marx, Engels, and Lenin, *On the Dictatorship of the Proletariat*, p. 59.
[15]V. I. Lenin, *The State and Revolution* (New York: International, 1932), p. 22.
[16]Frederick Engels, *Socialism: Utopian and Scientific* (New York: International, 1935), p. 69.
[17]Lenin, *The State and Revolution*, p. 9.
[18]Herbert Aptheker, *On the Nature of Revolution* (New York: New Century, 1959), p. 26.
[19]Marx, Engels, and Lenin, *On the Dictatorship of the Proletariat*, p. 46.
[20]Ibid., p. 108.
[21]Ibid., p. 122.
[22]Ibid., p. 213.
[23]Lenin, *Collected Works*, vol. 28, p. 457.
[24]F. V. Konstantinov, ed.,*The Fundamentals of Marxist-Leninist Philosophy* (Moscow: Progress Publishers, 1982), p. 423.
[25]*Socialism as a Social System*, eds. Jaroszewski and Ignatovsky, p. 193.
[26]See footnote 9 in the chapter on Christian politics for a discussion of the two kinds of democracy. Christianity and the West generally support one kind, constitutional democracy. They reject another, strict majoritarianism, which gives unrestricted authority to majorities. The Marxist understanding of democracy, particularly as applied to the dictatorship of the proletariat, is of this second kind.
[27]Marx, Engels, and Lenin, *On the Dictatorship of the Proletariat*, p. 259.
[28]Lenin, "O lozunge 'razoruzheniia,'" October 1916. Cited in Elliot R. Goodman, *The Soviet Design for a World State* (New York: Columbia University Press, 1968), p. 287.
[29]Marx, Engels, and Lenin, *On the Dictatorship of the Proletariat*, p. 119.
[30]Claire Sterling, *The Terror Network: The Secret War of International Terrorism* (New York: Berkley Books, 1982).
[31]Ibid., p. 203.
[32]Lenin, *Selected Works*, vol. 7, p. 81.
[33]Lenin, *Collected Works*, vol. 23, p. 202.
[34]Marx, Engels, and Lenin, *On the Dictatorship of the Proletariat*, p. 269.
[35]V. V. Zagladin, ed., *The World Communist Movement* (Moscow: Progress Publishers, 1973), p. 159.
[36]*Socialism as a Social System*, eds. Jaroszewski and Ignatovsky, p. 185.
[37]Ibid.
[38]Ibid., p. 183.
[39]Joseph Stalin, "Beseda s pervoi amerikanskoi rabochei delegatsiei," Sept. 9, 1927. Cited in Goodman, *The Soviet Design for a World State*, p. 191.
[40]*Socialism as a Social System*, ed. Jaroszewski and Ignatovsky, p. 186.
[41]Ibid., pp. 191-2.
[42]Ibid., p. 193.

[43]Frederick Engels, *The Origin of the Family, Private Property and the State* (Chicago: Kerr, 1902), p. 206.
[44]Marx, Engels, and Lenin, *On the Dictatorship of the Proletariat*, p. 140.
[45]Ibid., p. 127.
[46]*Program of the Third International* (1928), cited in *A Lexicon of Marxist-Leninist Semantics*, ed. Sleeper, p. 270.
[47]Marx, Engels, and Lenin, *On the Dictatorship of the Proletariat*, p. 134.
[48]Ibid., pp. 249-50.
[49]Ibid., p. 256.
[50]Ibid., p. 251.
[51]Ibid., p. 127.
[52]Lenin, *The State and Revolution*, p. 20.
[53]V. Platkovskiy, *Sovetskaia Rossiia* (Moscow), March 1959, cited in *A Lexicon of Marxist-Leninist Semantics*, ed. Sleeper, p. 273.
[54]Shakhnazarov, *The Coming World Order*, p. 18.
[55]Ibid., p. 201.
[56]Marx, Engels, and Lenin, *On the Dictatorship of the Proletariat*, p. 118.
[57]Goodman, *The Soviet Design for a World State*, p. 2.
[58]Marx, Engels and Lenin, *On the Dictatorship of the Proletariat*, p. 192.
[59]Lenin, *Collected Works*, vol. 20, p. 28, cited in Shakhnazarov, *The Coming World Order*, p. 215.
[60]Lenin, "III Communist International," March 31, 1919, cited in Goodman, *The Soviet Design for a World State*, p. 32.
[61]Shakhnazarov, *The Coming World Order*, p. 214.
[62]Ibid., p. 213.
[63]Ibid., p. 204.
[64]Ibid., p. 196.
[65]Ibid., p. 198.
[66]Ibid., p. 216.
[67]*Time*, October 22, 1990, p. 73. *Time* reports, "Hiss moved to the State Department in the autumn of 1936 and was soon delivering documents to [Whittaker] Chambers at intervals of about a week or ten days. Hiss covered his tracks so well that even [Henry Julian] Wadleigh had no idea that he was working for the Russians." Assisting Hiss with the founding of the United Nations were Harry Dexter White, Virginius Frank Coe, Noel Field, Laurence Duggan, Henry Julian Wadleigh, John Carter Vincent, David Weintraub, Nathan Gregory Silvermaster, Harold Glasser, Victor Perlo, Irving Kaplan, Solomon Adler, Abraham George Silverman, William K. Ullman, and William H. Taylor. Each of these individuals was later identified as a Marxist/Leninist.
[68]Shakhnazarov, *The Coming World Order*, p. 21.
[69]Lenin, *Selected Works*, vol. 8, p. 33.
[70]Lenin, "Voennaia programma proletarskoi revoliutsii," autumn 1916, cited in Goodman, *The Soviet Design for a World State*, p. 290.
[71]Zagladin, ed., *The World Communist Movement*, p. 171.

CHAPTER

26

BIBLICAL CHRISTIAN POLITICS

"Everyone must submit himself to the governing authorities, for there is no authority except that which God has established."

—Romans 13:1

"Give to Caesar what is Caesar's and to God what is God's."

—Jesus Christ, Mark 12:17

"Christianity teaches that the state serves a divinely appointed and divinely defined task, although it is not in itself divine. Its authority is legitimate, though limited."[1]

—Charles Colson

SUMMARY

Biblical Christianity recognizes the state as a God-ordained institution (Genesis 9:6; Romans 13:1-7; 1 Peter 2:13-17). Along with the institutions of the family (marriage and home), the church, education, and work, the state occupies an important place in God's order of things. Christianity believes in the wickedness of man (Jeremiah 17:9) and his moral responsibility; therefore it believes that government is a necessary institution—even to the imposition of the death penalty (Genesis 9:6; Romans 13:1-4). However, government has limited obligations, not totalitarian powers. God established government with limited powers to do only certain things in society. The Bible calls for limited government, falling somewhere between no government (anarchy) and total government (totalitarianism). Caesar has his role (Mark 12:17), but God has appointed roles for the family and the church. All-powerful states are not God's perfect will. And states that forget God are "turned into hell" (Psalm 9:17).

The Bible portrays the proper rule of good government as one of administrating justice (Jeremiah 23:5; Amos 5:15): protecting the weak from the bully, the poor from the rich and powerful (Isaiah 3:13-14; Amos 2:6; 5:12), the innocent from the guilty (Romans 13:3); promoting equality before the law (Acts 10:34; Exodus 23:6); working diligently to restrain evil; protecting the body politic from hostile invasion (2 Chronicles 26:9-15); raising revenues; avoiding deficit spending; and so on. Christian politics is nothing more than insisting with moral persuasion, personal example, and Christian participation that government conform to such a model of responsible leadership.

Introduction

Throughout history, mankind has accepted the existence of the state, believing it to be as unavoidable as death and taxes. The Christian believes this certainty arises because government is an institution established by God. That is, the state is sanctioned by God as a social institution necessary for human society (Genesis 9:6). "Christianity teaches," says Charles Colson, "that the state serves a divinely appointed and divinely defined task, although it is not in itself divine. Its authority is legitimate, though limited."[3]

Christians recognize that government as an institution is sacred, not

Christian politics is rooted in Christian law, which is based on Christian ethics, which in turn is based on God's character. Understanding God's character and how it is reflected in a moral and legal order, and translating this moral and legal order into a political format, is Christian politics. The end result of such a union is the glorification of God and the dignity of the individual. "The highest glory of the American Revolution was this," said John Quincy Adams, "it connected in one indissoluble bond the principles of civil government with the principles of Christianity."[2]

Christians hold no illusions of a utopian state ushered in by the efforts of mankind. Whereas some believe government in the hands of capable men and women can solve all problems, create a perfect society, and establish a new political and economic world order, Christians understand the limits of government. These limits are due to man's sinful nature and the reality of free will. Because man is a fallen being, one could never expect him to erect a government completely free of corruption; and because man is free, he will sometimes choose to disobey governmental legislation.

Thus, while the Christian does not espouse a political theory that envisions a state-directed drive toward utopia, he does honor civil government as an institution of law and order for society. Society flourishes under such a system of law and order because each of society's institutions is doing what it does best without constant interference from the others.

secular or man-made, and that its rulers are ministers of God. They obey the state so that the rest of mankind can better understand God's plan for the institution and the concept of justice. "If while evangelizing," says Carl F. H. Henry, "we abandon the sociopolitical realm to its own devices, we shall fortify the misimpression that the public order falls wholly outside the command and will of God, that Christianity deals with private concerns only; and we shall conceal the fact that government exists by God's will as His servant for the sake of justice and order."[4]

It is the Christian's duty to obey the state. "Submit yourselves for the Lord's sake to every authority instituted among men," says Peter,

Notes and Asides

"whether to the king, as the supreme authority, or to governors, who are sent by him to punish those who do wrong and to commend those who do right" (1 Peter 2:13, 14). That is, since government is appointed by God, as long as it is serving the purpose for which God created it, the Christian shows his allegiance to God by submitting himself to God's earthly authority—human government.

Henry believes this call for obedience to just government is sounded throughout the Bible. He hears it in the Lord's Prayer: "In view of the divine ordering of history, to pray 'thy kingdom come; thy will be done on earth as it is in heaven' (Matt. 6:10) means . . . aligning oneself with the powers through which God purposes to commend the right and condemn the wrong (Rom. 13:2-3). One must do so not because rulers are divine or because civil government is inherently authoritative, but rather because God is the Lord of civil authorities; Christians must acknowledge the divine linking of God's will with civil government."[5] It is only through the Christian's acknowledgment of government as God-ordained that the rest of mankind develops a proper view of government, politics, and ultimately God Himself. For example, the justice/judgment role of government is in accordance with God's will because God is always just and one day will judge mankind (Acts 17:31; Romans 2:16).

Human government cannot free men's hearts from sin and death; only Christ's death on the cross can accomplish this. Indeed, Humanists and Marxists make one of their most critical theoretical errors when they invest the state with God-like tendencies and functions (1 Samuel 8:17). "While it has a moral responsibility to restrain evil," says Colson, "government can never change the hearts and minds of its citizens."[6]

Governments, of course, should adhere to the principle, "Let all things be done decently and in order" (1 Corinthians 14:40; Exodus 18:19f) since this is a reflection of God's character, and it should be participatory, so that Christian citizens can better influence the state to conform to God's will as a social institution (Proverbs 11:11). Also, the Christian understands that power tends to corrupt, so that a government that disperses power is better than one that gathers power into the hands of a few. Christianity, however, does not single out any particular form of government as the only acceptable one. Rather, it expects any type of government to conform to Biblical principles, understanding that this is more likely to occur in a representative form of government than in a dictatorship.

"For the Lord is our judge [judicial], the Lord is our lawgiver [legislative], the Lord is our king [executive]; he will save us."

—Isaiah 33:22

The founding of America and the government of the United States provide some examples of the Christian approach to politics, although neither example conforms perfectly to the Christian ideal. Providing procedures for amendments in the U.S. Constitution shows that the founding fathers also understood the imperfections of their attempt to

Notes and Asides

apply Christianity to government. The major concepts, however, were well founded. Religious, political and economic liberty, and human rights and dignity for citizens, were to be protected. Governmental power was divided among the legislative, executive, and judicial branches, using a system of checks and balances. This division of powers not only attempts to protect American citizens from political corruption but also is an open admission that mankind is morally flawed. Further, the Declaration of Independence and the Constitution (based on the Christian Magna Charta and the Christian English common law) assume certain divinely ordained human rights, such as the rights to life, liberty, and property. This recognition of the rights of the individual as God's creation encourages government to protect those rights, effectively maintaining order, promoting justice and freedom, and restraining evil. Such a society is in keeping with God's design for human community. As George C. Roche points out, "In America, equality before the law and liberty for all men would bring forth a radically different nation, where men would be free to escape their animal instincts and rise to spiritual fulfillment."[7] God expects government to allow man the freedom to strive for spiritual fulfillment. Not that government is to supply such fulfillment—this is the duty of the church and family—but that government protects the freedom to carry on the pursuit of spiritual fulfillment, or, as the Declaration of Independence puts it, "the pursuit of happiness."[8]

"Our [U.S.] Constitution was made only for a moral and religious people. It is wholly inadequate for the government of any other."
—John Adams

Christian ethics, law, and politics reflect the following major Biblical truths: (1) God's character of holiness, justice, love, mercy, and truth; (2) the moral order based on the character of God; (3) man's creation in the image of God; (4) man's fall into sin; (5) the coming of Christ as a man and the value he placed on human beings; and (6) the last Judgment.

In order to formulate a Christian political system, the Christian must take into account these six items. This means a Christian must have a knowledge of theology to understand the nature of God; a knowledge of ethics to understand the moral order; a knowledge of man's glory as created in God's image, but also of the terrible consequences of the fall; a knowledge of Christ's work; and belief in life after death.

Creation and Original Sin

The Christian worldview's concepts of creation and original sin play a significant role in Christian politics. Not surprisingly, these Christian beliefs were taken into account by the framers of the Declaration of Independence and the Constitution of the United States.

Notes and Asides

This does not mean that the Declaration and Constitution are the only Christian models or that government as designed by America's founding fathers is the only Christian approach to government. Indeed, because the Christian views the state as more than manmade and understands that God can work through many forms of government, he need not champion any particular political system. Despite the many advantages of a representative system, God is capable of working just as powerfully through an authoritarian state (see the book of Daniel). "Democracy is not prescribed in the Bible," says Charles Colson, "and Christians can and do live under other political systems. But Christians can hardly fail to love democracy, because of all systems it best assures human dignity, the essence of our creation in God's image."[9]

Yet, there can be no denying that the United States was originally founded on Christian principles and values. Jasper Adams, in a sermon preached in 1833, declares, "In perusing the twenty-four constitutions [of the various states] of the United States . . . we find all of them recognizing Christianity as the well known and well established religion of the communities."[10] John Adams, a member of the committee appointed to draft the Declaration and a former president of the United States, says, "Our Constitution was made only for a moral and religious people. It is wholly inadequate for the government of any other."[11] Adams also told Jefferson in 1813 that they had based their immortal document to a great extent on the tenets laid down in the Bible. "The general principles on which the fathers achieved independence," said Adams, "were the general principles of Christianity." One of America's outstanding Supreme Court justices, Joseph Story, was convinced that Christianity and the common law were "the foundations of the Union, liberty and the social order."[12]

The United States was born in an environment in which men held a Christian view of man's fallen nature; but they did not forget that man was created in the image of God. These two beliefs about man have profound implications for a Christian view of politics, which is reflected in America's founding fathers' attempts to tailor a government suited to man's place in God's creative order.

Human government became necessary because of man's fallen nature. "Man's original act of disobedience in the Garden of Eden," write Robert Linder and Richard Pierard, "transformed him into a sinful, corrupt being, motivated by selfishness, greed and lust. These evil impulses had to be restrained in order to prevent those of one social group from taking advantage of others who possess less power. So God provided the principle of government to keep men from destroying themselves in a 'war of all against all.'"[13] Thus, government protects mankind from its own sinful nature. But who protects the society from the sinful inclinations of the men who make up the government? This

Notes and Asides

was the problem America's early leaders grappled with in attempting to create a just political system.

They solved the dilemma by creating a system of checks and balances within the government. That is, America was designed in such a way that each of the three branches of government (legislative, executive, and judicial) has unique powers that prevent the focus of governmental authority from falling into the hands of a select few. By spreading power and responsibility around, the American system attempts to remove much of the temptation of man's sinful nature to misuse political clout.

James Madison describes the system of checks and balances this way:

> But the great security against a gradual concentration of the several powers in the same department, consists in giving to those who administer each department, the necessary constitutional means, and personal motives, to resist encroachments of the others. The provision for defense must in this, as in all other cases, be made commensurate to the danger of attack. Ambition

Recommended Reading for Advanced Study

Charles Colson, *Kingdoms in Conflict* (Grand Rapids, MI: Zondervan, 1987).

Carl F. H. Henry, *Twilight of a Great Civilization* (Westchester, IL: Crossway, 1988).

John Eidsmoe, *Christianity and the Constitution* (Grand Rapids, MI: Baker, 1987).

Richard J. Neuhaus, *The Naked Public Square* (Grand Rapids, MI: Eerdmans, 1984).

Benjamin Hart, *Faith and Freedom* (Dallas, TX: Lewis and Stanley, 1988).

Notes and Asides

> must be made to counteract ambition. The interest of the man must be connected with the constitutional rights of the place. It may be a reflection on human nature, that such devices should be necessary to control the abuses of government. But what is government itself, but the greatest of all reflections on human nature?[14]

Madison goes on to declare that this human nature reflected by government is of a sinful kind. He was not romantic about human nature. He did not look on mankind as inherently good and politically perfectible.

> If men were angels, no government would be necessary. If angels were to govern men, neither external nor internal controls on government would be necessary. In framing a government, which is to be administered by men over men, the great difficulty lies in this: You must first enable the government to control the governed; and in the next place, oblige it to control itself. A dependence on the people is, no doubt, the primary control on the government; but experience has taught mankind the necessity of auxiliary precautions.[15]

This system of checks and balances arose because America's founding fathers believed that human nature was sinful. This Christian understanding of man's nature helped form a more practical government than governments built on a faulty view of human nature. "If our Founding Fathers had been smitten with the idealism of the Enlightenment," says Tim LaHaye, "the check and balance system would never have been written into our Constitution, and we would have established the same unstable form of government experienced by France, which has endured seven different governmental systems during the two hundred years that America has enjoyed only one."[16]

Christians realize that man's fallen nature has severe implications for every aspect of his life, including the political realm. The American system of checks and balances, therefore, is embraced by Christians in their political theory because it is a genuine attempt to curtail man's sinful tendencies not only among the private citizens but also among their governors. John Eidsmoe, speaking in favor of these controls, says, "Do you see the biblical view of man's sin nature at work here? Each branch, jealous of its own power, battles against encroachments of power by the other branches."[17] This extensive distribution of power has worked remarkably well throughout two centuries of United States history, providing a specific example of how the Christian worldview can translate into a practical solution in the political arena.

"It is Religion and Morality alone which can establish the principles upon which freedom can securely stand. A patriot must be a religious man."

—John Adams

Notes and Asides

A Christian worldview is also indispensable for guaranteeing basic human rights for individuals. Because the Christian believes man is *created in the image of God*, he believes that each individual has value. This becomes doubly clear when we remember that Christ took upon Himself human flesh and died for mankind. Each individual is granted by God certain rights founded on an absolute moral standard. This is the second facet of Christian belief that greatly affects Christian political theory.

As noted earlier, this aspect of the Christian view of man was also taken into account by America's forefathers. Thus, in the Declaration of Independence, we find the proclamation that "all men are created equal; that they are endowed by their Creator with certain unalienable rights. . . ." Two assumptions are inherent to this declaration: first, man was created by a supernatural Being; second, this Being is the foundation for all human rights. "The political life and spirit of this country," says James Reston, "were based on religious convictions. America's view of the individual was grounded on the principle, clearly expressed by the Founding Fathers, that man was a symbol of his Creator, and therefore possessed certain unalienable rights which no temporal authority had the right to violate."[18] It should be obvious to everyone that America was not built on the Secular Humanist worldview. Freedom was looked on as a gift of God. The God who gave us the gift of life also gave us the right to life.

"The rights of man come not from the generosity of the state, but from the hand of God."
—John F. Kennedy

The fact that these unalienable rights have an unchanging Source is crucial for Christian politics. If man's rights were not tied inextricably to the character of God, then human rights would be arbitrarily assigned according to the whims of each passing generation. "Think of this great flaming phrase: 'certain unalienable rights,'" writes Schaeffer. "Who gives the rights? The state? Then they are not unalienable because the state can change them and take them away. Where do the rights come from? [America's founding fathers] understood that they were founding the country upon the concept that goes back into the Judeo-Christian thinking that there is Someone there who gave the unalienable rights."[19]

Specifically, these unalienable rights are revealed to us in the Bible. John Eidsmoe identifies three specific unalienable rights:

> [T]he Bible views man as possessing certain basic human rights, bestowed upon him by the God who created him and gave him human dignity. The negative commands of the Bible are based upon positive rights. When the Bible forbids murder, it protects the right to life. When the Bible forbids man-stealing, it protects the right to liberty. When the Bible forbids stealing, it protects the right to property. These rights are absolute and cannot be abridged by government.[20]

Notes and Asides

John Warwick Montgomery catalogs the following classifications of human rights based on the Scriptures: Procedural due process (including fair hearing, speedy trial, and protection from double jeopardy); substantive due process (the just and unjust stand equally before the law; all races, sexes, classes, citizens, aliens, even the ruler, are under the law); basic rights (to life, family, freedom of religion, thought, expression, assembly, etc.).[21]

These rights are not evolving along with mankind as Humanists and Marxists believe; they are absolute. They are rights God gave to His human creation, establishing government to secure these rights. Because God never intended anyone to murder another human being, for example, the state was established to protect its citizens from murderers. The right to life is protected and honored. To murder is not only to destroy another human being, but to attack the image of God in man. "Whoever sheds the blood of man, by man shall his blood be shed; for in the image of God has God made man" (Genesis 9:6).

"Before any man can be considered as a member of civil society, he must be considered as a subject of the Governor of the Universe."
—James Madison

It is no accident that life and liberty are the first two unalienable rights listed in the Declaration of Independence. America's forefathers understood man's proper place in the universe and attempted to design their government accordingly. The two key facts they took into account, man's creation in God's image and his subsequent fall, still play a crucial role in Christian political theory (as well as every other aspect of the Christian worldview). The Christian view—of the state as established by God, of man as a sinful creature, and of man as possessing certain unalienable rights granted by God, in whose image he was created—provides a more clear, specific, and stable purpose for government than can be postulated by any other worldview.

The Purpose of Government

According to the Biblical Christian worldview, human government was instituted by God to protect man's unalienable rights from mankind's sinful tendencies (Genesis 9:6; Romans 13:1-7). Human nature being what it is, man will attempt to infringe on his fellow man's rights in an effort to improve his own life; therefore a political system must exist to protect rights and keep these evil tendencies at bay. "The institution of government is ordained by God as a means of checking the evil tendencies in the behavior of his creatures," writes William C. Johnson, "and for channeling their actions for socially beneficial purposes."[22]

Protecting human rights from evil tendencies, of course, simply means promoting justice. But what is justice? It is a difficult concept to

Notes and Asides

grasp because, like love, mercy, and power, it is a mental construct with material implications. Russell Kirk, for example, defines justice as an idea "implanted in our minds by a Power that is more than human; and our mundane justice is our attempt to copy a perfect Justice that abides in a realm beyond time and space; and the general rule by which we endeavor to determine just conduct and just reward may be expressed as 'To each man, the things that are his own.'"[23] A concrete example of what God means by justice is found in Jeremiah: "Administer justice every morning; and deliver the person who has been robbed from the power of his oppressor, that My wrath may not go forth like fire and burn with none to extinguish it, because of the evil of their deeds" (21:12). E. Calvin Beisner says justice and truth are interrelated, for justice is the practice of truth in human relationships; he concludes that "justice is rendering to each his due according to a right standard."[24] The Christian, then, defines justice as rendering impartially to each his due according to the standard of God's perfect will expressed in His moral law.

The prophet Amos says, "Seek good, and not evil. . . . Hate the evil, and love the good, and establish justice in the gate" (5:14-15). This, for the Christian, is the overarching reason for the existence of government. "The state thus is established in order to extend God's justice,"[25] says Rushdoony. Henry agrees: "God established civil government for the preservation of justice in fallen society (Rom. 13)."[26]

Most everyone believes that furthering justice is an important task of the state, but the Christian sees justice as the principal reason for the state's very existence. Such a view of justice can follow only from a view grounded on an absolute guarantor of unalienable rights. The Christian position declares that it is *always* wrong for a government official to take a bribe to convict the innocent and allow the guilty to go free (1 Samuel 8:3). This is a moral, legal, and political absolute. Why? Because taking a bribe is unjust. Prohibiting bribe-taking is based on a the moral character of God, and it helps to ensure that each receives what he deserves. Because the Christian view is based on such a foundation, justice becomes more important than any other aspect of government—and Rushdoony is correct to assert that whether a man "can vote or not is not nearly as important as the question of justice: does the law leave him secure in his governmental spheres, as an individual, a family, church, school, or business?"[27] Obviously, since justice is the fundamental task of government, Christian politics is bound closely to legal theory.

For now, it is enough to realize that government is ordained by God to promote justice and that justice involves a standard and receiving

Notes and Asides

what is due. This standard is God's perfect will. "The state was instituted by God to restrain sin and promote a just social order," says Colson.

> One of the most common misconceptions in Western political thought is that the role of government is determined solely by the will of the people. When Pilate questioned Jesus on the eve of His execution, Christ told the governor that he would not even hold his office or political authority if it had not been granted him by God. The apostle Paul spoke of civil authority as "God's servant, an agent of wrath to bring punishment on the wrongdoer." Peter used similar language, saying that governments were set by God to "punish those who do wrong and to commend those who do right."[28]

Government was established by God to manifest and preserve His justice on earth. This is government's central purpose; as such, the state should concentrate on enforcing justice and avoid meddling in other institutions' business. Generally speaking, the church was ordained to manifest God's grace on the earth, and the family to manifest God's community and creativity (including procreativity). The government, then, as the institution of justice, should prohibit, prevent, prosecute, and punish injustice. The church, as the institution of grace, should preach the gospel and be the chief vehicle of charitable aid to the needy. And families should have chief responsibility for bearing, raising, and educating children, and for creating, possessing, and disposing of property.

"After all, government is just a device to protect man so that he may earn his bread in the sweat of his labor."
—Hugh S. Johnson

Each of these institutions is limited by its own definition and by the other two. Because government is an institution of justice, not of grace or community or creativity, it should not interfere with freedom of religion, attempt to dispense grace through tax-funded handouts, control family size, interfere in raising children (including education), or control the economy and the disposition of property. Because the church is an institution of grace, not of justice or community or creativity, it should not attempt to control criminal law systems, to garner the support of the state for its work, or to control family size or business. And because the family is an institution of community and creativity, it should not use government or the church for its own ends.

Because of its natural tendency to expand its own power, government should be granted only enough power to protect society and enforce justice in the social order. The institution of the family precedes the institution of the state—that is, God grants authority to the state through the family. Said United States Supreme Court Chief Justice William Rehnquist,

Notes and Asides

> The ultimate source of authority in this Nation is not Congress, not the states, not for that matter the Supreme Court of the United States. The people are the ultimate source of authority; they have parceled out the authority that originally resided with them by adopting the original Constitution and by later amending it. . . . As between the branches of the federal government, the people have given certain authority to the President, certain authority to Congress, and certain authority to the federal judiciary.[29]

Authority or political power diffused among religious and moral citizens is the path of freedom. Authority concentrated in the hands of a few is the path of dictatorship and slavery. It is obvious from 1 Samuel 8 that God is not interested in political slavery.

The family, however, cannot perform every function in society. Each of the institutions has a role to play. The church must not attempt to usurp the government's role. Colson says, "men and women need more than a religious value system. They need civic structures to prevent chaos and provide order. Religion is not intended or equipped to do this; when it has tried, it has brought grief on itself and the political institutions it has attempted to control. An independent state is crucial to the commonweal."[30] In fact, the church as an institution need not be involved in government or politics. But individual Christians must be involved.

This separation of spheres, however, does not mean what the Secular Humanist means by separation of church and state. The Humanist attempt to strip the public square of all Christian and Jewish values and symbols is not what America's founding fathers had in mind regarding the separation doctrine. Not using taxpayers' monies to establish a national church is what they had in mind.[31] Indeed, Jefferson and Madison were responsible for chaplains and religious services in the armed forces and Congress. It seems hard to believe that these men would have supported the forced removal of the Ten Commandments from public schools. Indeed, from the Christian position, such action is perceived as unjust—in direct contradiction to the government's role as ordained by God.

The state, in order to find favor in God's sight, must protect human rights and promote justice. God expects government always to be an instrument for good. Thus, Paul writes, "For [the one in authority] is God's servant to do you good. But if you do wrong, be afraid, for he does not bear the sword for nothing. He is God's servant, an agent of wrath to bring punishment on the wrongdoer. Therefore, it is necessary to submit to the authorities, not only because of possible punishment but also because of conscience" (Romans 13:4-5).

Notes and Asides

Government's reason for existing is to do what God wills it to do when He ordained it: establish God's justice on the earth. Indeed, the Christian believes anything less from government defeats the purpose of the institution.

Responsibility of the Ruler

God places men in positions of political power to keep the social order secure and promote justice. When rulers abuse the responsibilities granted them by God and deny men their unalienable rights of life, liberty, and property, they invite the judgment of God. The ruler is held responsible by God for his governing policies for the reason summed up in Proverbs 29:2: "When the righteous thrive, the people rejoice; when the wicked rule, the people groan."

> "For as, of all the ways of life, but one—/The path of duty—leads to happiness;/So in their duty States must find at length/ Their welfare, and their safety, and their strength."
>
> —Robert Southey

The Bible clearly states that an evil ruler may not shift the blame for an unjust society to the political system he controls. "The New Testament," writes Henry, "speaks of civil government not impersonally in terms of a state or city but in terms of rulers, kings, emperors or other authorities. Rulers are designated 'priests of God' (Rom. 13:6) whom God entrusts to promote his will by advancing good and suppressing evil."[32]

When rulers don't do God's will, they are subject to His wrath. This does not mean that God's will is totally thwarted by an evil regime—the Lord can work through any circumstance—but it does mean that the evil men in power will be held responsible for the suffering they caused. Christians believe that Adolph Hitler, Joseph Stalin, and Mao Tse-tung will be judged for their crimes against humanity. "All political authority is ultimately rooted in God's will (Rom. 13:1-7), but this fact does not automatically bestow his approval on all actions of each individual ruler," says Johnson. "Those who govern are held responsible to him for implementing the divine standards of justice to the extent possible by and among sinful men."[33]

The Use and Misuse of Power

If the state were powerless, no one (except for the those who recognize government as God-ordained) would obey its laws. Thus, the state and its leaders are granted power by God. Colson writes, "God has given power to the state to be used to restrain evil and maintain order."[34] It is unfortunate that power must be wielded by government, but man's sinful nature can only be restrained by force. Mickelsen quotes Romans 13:4—"The man who does evil should certainly fear because the ruler does not carry the sword [in vain]"—and concludes, "Here Paul insists that force is absolutely necessary to maintain justice. But since this force or power is wielded by imperfect men, it can be misused. Nonetheless, without the force of governmental authority, private or personal might would make right. Isolated individuals would not be able to stand up against pressure groups which are out to further their own ends."[35]

Therefore, government requires some measure of authority, even though it can be misused (and man's sinful nature is forever open to such temptations). This description of human nature has been proved true again and again by political leaders who take office with good intentions and then fall prey to the seductive aroma of power.

Such misuse of power may take various forms, all of which incur God's wrath. Often rulers misuse their power in an effort to obtain more personal power. Colson describes one of the forms of this abuse:

> Governments, with rare exceptions, seek to expand their power beyond the mandate to restrain evil, preserve order, and promote justice. Most often they do this by venturing into religious or moral areas. The reason is twofold: the state needs religious legitimization for its policies and an independent church is the one structure that rivals the state's claim for ultimate allegiance.[36]

Many times political leaders will not even respect man's most basic right—the right to life—in their quest for power. Colson notes, "One of the most startling commentaries on this century is the fact that millions more have died at the hands of their own governments than in wars with other nations—all to preserve someone's power."[37]

Clearly, political power is a dangerous thing. It can be a consuming fire. The Christian, because he recognizes his own sinful nature, is especially wary of positions of political leadership. But this does not mean he should avoid such positions; on the contrary, God prefers leaders who know and fear Him. The Christian political leader is capable of serving God honorably in positions of power as long as he understands, as Schaeffer says, that "the goal for the Christian is not power, but justice. . . . God in His sheer power could have crushed Satan in his revolt. . . . Instead . . . Christ died that justice, rooted in what God is, would be the solution."[38]

The proper Christian attitude toward political power is best summed up by Colson:

> Those who accept the biblical view of servant leadership treat power as a humbling delegation from God, not as a right to

Notes and Asides

> control others. Moses offers a great role model. Though he had awesome power and responsibility as the leader of two million Israelites, he was described in Scripture as "a very humble man, more humble than anyone else on the face of the earth." He led by serving—intervening before God on his people's behalf, seeking God's forgiveness for their rebellion and caring for their needs above his own.[39]

Moses was humble in his leadership because he understood that he was accountable to God for any misuse of his power, yet he knew that his sinful nature would never allow him to lead in the flawless manner God required of him. This very awareness of his proper place in a social institution made Moses a leader pleasing to God. People in positions of authority need only understand Moses' view of man's role in God's creation in order to be good, just leaders.

Sovereignty Apart From God

Today, many leaders (both in politics and in other disciplines) do not understand mankind's true place in the universe—indeed, most do not even acknowledge the sovereignty of God. This incorrect perspective results in a major mistake: placing something other than God in the position of sovereignty. Whatever is placed in God's rightful position is granted authority that is not its own to wield.

The Christian position places all ultimate authority in the hands of God. "All authority," says Rushdoony, "is in essence religious authority; the nature of the authority depends on the nature of the religion. If the religion is Biblical, then the authority at every point is the immediate or mediated authority of the triune God."[40] George Grant sums up: "God *rules* everything and everyone, everywhere and at all times. For, 'the Lord has established His throne in the heavens, and His sovereignty rules over all' (Psalm 103:19)."[41]

Men who do not adhere to a Judeo-Christian understanding of God, however, must believe that something other than God has ultimate authority. In this authoritative vacuum, either some individual or some state becomes sovereign. "To assume that man's mind is as ultimate as God's," says Lawrence D. Pratt, "and therefore to conceive of the universe as a world of chance, requires one to posit the locus of sovereignty apart from God somewhere else in a universe that is greater than both man and God. As it happens, men have posited two basic possibilities for the source of sovereignty apart from God: the individual or the state."[42]

Abandoning God and placing one's trust in an individual or the state

Notes and Asides

has severe ramifications. "Without God and His principles," says Tim LaHaye, "governments traditionally have been either too totalitarian and harsh or too permissive and anarchical, either of which extreme will end in the misery and destruction of its own people."[43] Notice that a government always reflects a nation's attitude toward God's sovereignty and always takes advantage of the vacuum created by forsaking God. Even if a particular society grants sovereignty to the individual, the state will eventually usurp that authority. Colson explains, "Excise belief in God and you are left with only two principals: the individual and the state. In this situation, however, there is no mediating structure to generate moral values and, therefore, no counterbalance to the inevitable ambitions of the state."[44] "If we are not governed by God," says William Penn, "then we will be ruled by tyrants."[45]

Many today, including both Secular Humanists and Marxist/Leninists, are calling for a world state to serve as the ultimate political and economic authority and to assist mankind on its evolutionary journey. If the Marxists and Humanists get their way (and there is plenty of movement toward "a new world order"),[46] it will be not only the Kingdom of Man but also the Kingdom of the Anti-Christ.

"O kings and rulers of the earth, listen while there is time. Serve the Lord with reverent fear; rejoice with trembling. Fall down before his Son and kiss his feet before his anger is roused and you perish."

—Psalm 2:10-12

Utopianism

Utopianism is a prime example of man's denial of God, placing absolute sovereignty in the hands of the state. This mistake results not only from willing disregard of God's ultimate authority but also from a misconception about man's nature. As stressed throughout this text, Marxists and Humanists believe in the perfectibility of human nature, and this belief leads them to conclude that once the correct environment is manufactured for mankind and man's mind is programmed correctly, everyone will live properly. The state (with proper input from the Humanists or Marxists, of course) becomes the manufacturer of the correct environment. The state quickly takes on the role of God.

This belief in man's perfectibility (called by Colson "the most subtle and dangerous delusion of our times")[47] is seen in our present society's denial of individual responsibility. "By denying that man's first parents brought evil into the world through their sin," writes Stanmeyer, "a sin which is transferred by inheritance to each successive generation, the secularists excuse man from responsibility for the very real evil in the world."[48] Colson draws the conclusion, "This elimination of individual responsibility has encouraged the corresponding utopian belief in man's collective perfectibility."[49]

Denying individual responsibility, however, separates man from his only possible salvation—a knowledge and acceptance of Christ's

Notes and Asides

sacrifice for the individual's sins—and condemns secular man to an endless search for the "proper utopian environment." "By blaming externals, such as environment, the Secular Humanist absolves himself of any guilt," says Stanmeyer.

> In his thinking, the evils he privately commits—and we are all sinners—have nothing to do with social or political disorder. Wars, conflict, exploitation, brutality are not expressions of God's judgment on sinful men and women. They occur because essentially good human beings have not quite found the correct formula, the right "peace plan," the perfect method of "conflict resolution," the best negotiating technique. Yet by rejecting repentance and conversion, the secularist is left with no plausible way out of our dilemma.[50]

Indeed, utopianism offers no salvation except through the hope that the state will someday create the perfect environment and the perfect man. Colson says, "While Christian teaching emphasizes that each person has worth and responsibility before God, utopianism argues that salvation can only be achieved collectively."[51] This reliance on the state results in the individual's being trampled underfoot. "Utopianism," says Colson, "always spells disaster because 'the utopian holds that, if the goal is goodness and perfection, then the use of force is justified,' as Thomas Molnar writes. In contrast, the Christian, realizing that perfection eludes us in this life resists the tyranny and bloodshed of the dictator who promises a brave new world."[52]

Modern utopian schemes center around the oft-heard expression "new world order." This order is not based on Jesus Christ, but materialism—the dialectical materialism of Marxism/Leninism and the naturalism of Secular Humanism. It is based upon atheistic evolutionary concepts of man and the state. "No one but a fool," says Malachi Martin, "would suggest that the major 'movers and shakers'" of this order are acting "primarily or even secondarily out of purely religious motives."[53]

Utopianism is simply another attempt by man to do the impossible: wrest ultimate authority from the hands of God. This is what the kings and rulers were seeking to do in David's time (Psalm 2:1-3). David says the Lord God was in heaven—laughing (Psalm 2:4). Elsewhere he says nations that forget God are "turned into hell" (Psalm 9:17). The Apostle Peter, quoting Psalm 2:1-2, says that the kings and rulers, including Herod and Pontius Pilate, "conspired" against the Lord and His anointed (Jesus Christ), and the result of such collusion was the destruction of Jerusalem under God's judgment in A.D. 70 (Acts 4:25-27).

Notes and Asides

Placing one's faith in the state or individual as sovereign always leads to such an end. The state or the individual can never provide an absolute, unchanging source for human rights. "If God be God," says Rushdoony, "then man has no rights apart from God, who is the only true source of all right and of all authority. Destroy the authority of God in human society, and the only right which remains is the right of power, the assertion of sheer force, so that might makes right."[54]

Government and Transcendent Law

The lack of legitimate authority caused by the denial of God reinforces the Christian's belief that God must be recognized as Ruler in every sphere, including politics. Infringements on human rights by various governments based on the sovereignty or whim of the state speaks eloquently of the need for a transcendent law. "[E]ither a religious doctrine of authority binds man," says Rushdoony, "or he is not bound, save at his pleasure or convenience, which is no bond at all."[55]

The twentieth century should have taught us that even the most basic of human rights cannot exist consistently apart from an absolute standard. Christians, therefore, call for a return to a transcendent standard. "Not even the right of political self-determination, on which the democracies so vigorously insist," says Henry, "is self-evident; it presupposes objective rights grounded in a transcendent moral order that secular political scientists blur. The entire corpus of human rights is today in peril, because none of the divergent contemporary philosophical theories can sustain fixed and universal rights; yet secular juridical scholars hesitate to return to a Judeo-Christian grounding for rights."[56]

God's transcendent order is necessary for freedom itself. While a sovereign state may choose arbitrarily to revoke freedom at any time, a state that recognizes God as sovereign must constantly respect individual freedom, as God has commanded. "The question of freedom is first of all a question of sovereignty and of responsibility," says Rushdoony.

> Who is sovereign, and to whom is man responsible? This source of sovereignty is also the source of freedom. If sovereignty resides in God and is only held ministerially by men, then the basic responsibility of ruler and ruled is to God, who is also the source of freedom. But if sovereignty resides in the state, whether a monarchy or democracy, man has no appeal beyond the law of the state, and no source of ethics apart from it.[57]

Notes and Asides

Christians desire a government that recognizes God as the ultimate source of all human rights. The suffering caused by political systems that do not acknowledge God is all too real. Christians believe that God's transcendent law provides the only proper guidance for authority. God is sovereign, and the state derives its authority and the individual his rights from the very nature of God. We agree with Henry:

> It may seem difficult to derive model civil laws and legal regulations from a transcendent principle of justice. But without such a transcendent criterion for evaluating the law, despotism becomes the basis of civil government and rulers can spurn human liberties and cancel citizens' rights at will.[58]

It may seem difficult, but according to Benjamin Hart's *Faith and Freedom: The Christian Roots of American Liberty*,[59] deriving model civil laws and legal regulations from a transcendent principle of justice is exactly what the authors of the Declaration of Independence and the U.S. Constitution intended. The transcendent principles of justice moved in the stream of human history from New Testament times through the Magna Charta, the English common law, John Locke, Charles Montesquieu, William Blackstone, and the participants at the Continental Congress and the Constitutional Convention.[60]

The vast majority of the framers of the Constitution were Christians. "At least 51 of the 55 delegates belonged to Christian churches," says John Eidsmoe, "and at most three of the 55 can be identified as Deists."[61] A similar assessment of the religious commitments of the founding fathers was made by M. E. Bradford: ". . . with no more than five exceptions (and perhaps no more than three), they were orthodox members of one of the established Christian communions: approximately twenty-nine Anglicans, sixteen to eighteen Calvinists, two Methodists, two Lutherans, two Roman Catholics, one lapsed Quaker and sometime-Anglican, and one open Deist—Dr. Franklin, who attended every kind of Christian worship, called for public prayer, and contributed to all denominations."[62] Not surprisingly, none of them adhered to Humanist or Marxist theory. In fact, H. Wayne House says,

> An incipient form of socialism and pre-Marxism was rejected by the Founders. Some intellectuals known as levelers suggested a new economics (socialism) and others argued for a "community of goods." Samuel Adams speaks of these theories: "The utopian schemes of leveling and a community of goods are as visionary and impracticable as those which vest all property in the Crown. These ideas are arbitrary, despotic, and, in our government, unconstitutional."[63]

Notes and Asides

The men responsible for our form of government knew what Eastern Europe is only now finding out—socialism does not work because it is contrary to human nature. That was a lesson our Pilgrim fathers learned in 1620 with the dismal failure of what they had called the "Common Course and Condition."[64]

The proof that our founding fathers understood the reality of human nature is substantiated by the fact that America today is the envy of the world. With all her faults, America is still a beacon of light for political, economic, and religious freedom. These blessings result from the fact that the American governmental structure conforms more closely to Christian principles.

A Question of Obedience

The Christian expects a lot from government. The state must recognize man's place in the universe and understand God as the ultimate source of authority and human rights. Conversely, God expects the Christian to respect, obey, and participate in governments that serve His will. "Everyone must submit himself to the governing authorities," says the Apostle Paul, "for there is no authority except that which God has established. The authorities that exist have been established by God. Consequently, he who rebels against the authority is rebelling against what God has instituted, and those who do so will bring judgment on themselves" (Romans 13:1-2). The reason God demands this is simple: government was instituted to promote justice. Obedience to just government is necessary to keep the need for governmental power at a minimum. As Mickelsen notes, "Without government functioning as Paul describes it in [Romans] 13:1-7, there would be anarchy. If everyone does what is right in his own eyes, chaos will result."[65]

Thus, the Christian is called to obey government, to honor justice, and to preserve order. However, this does not mean that Christians must obey government blindly. As previously discussed, the political leader has a responsibility to God, and the Christian must hold him accountable. Grant reminds us,

> Because God *ordains* civil government, the magistrates *have* real authority. But at the same time, because *God* ordains civil government, the magistrates are *under* authority. Caesar *represents* God's rule and so he must be obeyed. But precisely because he represents *God*, he must abide by the constraints that God has placed on him. He is a "servant" (Romans 13:6) or a "minister" (Romans 13:4) of God. He is thus bound to obedience just as the people are bound to obedience.[66]

Notes and Asides

When a political leader or government strays from obedience, the Christian must attempt to correct the deviance so that He will not be forced to disobey the state. God commands man to obey government, but not when the state requires him to disobey God. "All authority, whether in the home, school, state, church, or any other sphere, is subordinate authority and is under God and subject to His word," writes Rushdoony. "This means, *first*, that all obedience is subject to the prior obedience to God and His word, for 'We ought to obey God rather than men' (Acts 5:29; cf. 4:19)."[67]

Thus, a man is obeying God when he challenges a governmental policy that is unjust—indeed, it is his duty to do so. St. Paul challenged the Roman authorities when it was apparent that an injustice was involved (Acts 22:24-25). "Public duty to civil government by the Christian," says Henry, "includes challenging legal injustice and promoting legal justice and equity in the application of civil law. The Christian is to 'submit to the authorities' in good conscience (Rom. 13:5)."[68]

For the Christian, involvement in the political realm is as mandatory as involvement in the other ordained institutions of God. If

CLOSE-UP

Charles Colson (1931-)

Charles Colson made headlines twice, first for his involvement in Watergate, and then for his conversion to Christianity. News media were skeptical of Colson's conversion and attempted to downplay the significant change Christ brought about in his life. This change, however, has become obvious to the most casual observer. Since his conversion, Colson has authored books with powerful messages about Christian politics and Christian culture in general, including *Kingdoms in Conflict* and *Against the Night*. More importantly, in 1976 he began Prison Fellowship, an outreach program which was designed to share the truth of Christianity with inmates. He has worked diligently to expand the influence of this ministry ever since. Colson's life stands as a shining testimony to the transforming power of Christ.

Notes and Asides

"righteousness exalteth a nation" (Proverbs 14:34), then the righteous must be involved. It is through the godly influence of righteous citizens that a city prospers (Proverbs 11:11). The Creator of heaven and earth is also the Creator of social institutions, and He wants His people involved in these institutions. He wants us to bring Him honor and glory by our involvement.

A classic example of such involvement is provided by the Apostle Paul, who was not ashamed to be a Roman citizen. He did not renounce his citizenship, but used it for the glory of God:

> The chief captain commanded [Paul] to be brought into the castle, and bade that he should be examined by scourging; that he might know wherefore they cried so against him. And as they bound him with thongs, Paul said unto the centurion that stood by, Is it lawful for you to scourge a man that is a Roman, and uncondemned? When the centurion heard that, he went and told the chief captain, saying, Take heed what thou doest: for this man is a Roman. Then the chief captain came, and said unto [Paul], Tell me, art thou a Roman? He said, Yes. And the chief captain answered, With a great sum obtained I this freedom. And Paul said, But I was free born. (Acts 22:24-28)

Every Christian should cherish the opportunity, as a citizen, to participate in government. This may involve registering to vote and voting. Some Christians will be called to run for political offices, and others will be called to serve in non-elected offices. Such involvement is a more effective way than civil disobedience or protest to peacefully persuade government to be obedient to God. "As citizens of two worlds," says Henry, "Christians are indeed obliged to participate in political affairs to the limit of their ability and competence; the price of withdrawal is to be ruled by nonbelievers and to forfeit the vocational leadership and service of believers."[69] If the people rejoice when the righteous rule (Proverbs 29:2), the righteous need to rule. Colson bluntly declares, "The real issue for Christians is not whether they should be involved in politics or contend for laws that affect moral behavior. The question is how."[70]

The answer, of course, is that Christians should become involved to the extent of their ability to serve effectively. Some Christians have been granted by God the ability to serve in the highest governmental offices and champion some of the most difficult political causes. William Wilberforce, for example, served in Parliament in England and was largely responsible for the abolition of slavery in that country. Colson writes, "Wilberforce's dogged campaign to rid the British empire of the slave trade shows what can happen when a citizen of the

Notes and Asides

Kingdom of God challenges corrupt structures within the kingdoms of man."[71]

This call for involvement, especially on the level of Wilberforce, is not without its dangers. Colson warns that "the everyday business of politics is power, and power . . . can be perilous for anyone."[72] But power, as Wilberforce and many other godly Christian leaders in politics have demonstrated, does not have to corrupt the Christian, and the Christian need not fear anything other than God. Obedience to God may require serving in political office, and if it does, the Christian must act courageously, realizing that God honors those faithful to Him. This fact is reinforced in the Bible by the accounts of men like Joseph, Moses, David, and Daniel, who, while acting within God's will, found themselves in government service.

But what if a Christian becomes as politically involved as possible and still finds himself faced with certain governmental policies that are unjust and therefore displeasing to God? As noted earlier, the Bible clearly instructs man to obey God even when His commands conflict with those of the state. Acts 4:19 says that when the Sanhedrin commanded Peter and John to stop teaching about Jesus, they replied, "Judge for yourselves whether it is right in God's sight to obey man rather than God." Mickelsen writes, "Jesus pointed out two spheres: the things that belong to the state and the things that belong to God (Matt. 22:15-22; Mark 12:13-17, Luke 20:20-26). Men must function in both spheres. However, if the state begins to arrogate to itself idolatrous powers, then the Christian must assert his loyalty to God. He will listen to and obey God rather than men (Acts 4:5-7; 5:21, 29)."[73]

This obedience to God is required even after the Christian has worked for reform through all possible political channels. If the system remains unjust, it becomes necessary for the Christian to engage in acts of civil disobedience in order to remain obedient to God. Schaeffer declares,

> In this fallen world God has given us certain offices to protect us from the chaos which is the natural result of that fallenness. But when *any office* commands that which is contrary to the Word of God, those who hold that office abrogate their authority and they are not to be obeyed. And that includes the State.[74]

Colson believes the same thing: "On the one hand Scripture commands civil obedience—that individuals respect and live in subjection to governing authorities and pray for those in authority. On the other it commands that Christians maintain their ultimate allegiance to the Kingdom of God. If there is a conflict, they are to obey God, not man. That may mean holding the state to moral account through civil

Notes and Asides

disobedience. This dual citizenship requires a delicate balance."[75] Schaeffer sums up: "The bottom line is that at a certain point there is not only the right, but the duty, to disobey the state."[76] This disobedience may even result in being put to death by the state. In such instances it is better to die than to live. Daniel understood this truth and chose death over worshiping a king. God honors such commitment.

Conclusion

The Christian knows that he must obey God at all times. The state was established to administer God's justice and preserve the peace. When government rules within the proper boundaries of its role in God's plan and man's place in the universe, the Christian submits to the state because God has placed it in authority above him. However, when the state abuses that authority (as can happen when men become power-mad), or claims to be sovereign, the Christian acknowledges the transcendent law of God rather than the state (Daniel 6:10f). This loyalty to God motivates the Christian to become politically involved in an effort to create good and just government. The involvement of righteous people can, as Proverbs 29:2 states, significantly influence government for the better.

This constant battle by the Christian to create or maintain a just state may or may not have an effect on government policy. That's not the important issue. What is important is that the Christian remains obedient to God under all circumstances. For example, Daniel found himself facing desperate circumstances (wars and rumors of war), but he did not resign himself to fate or "the inevitable." Instead, he "took a stand" (Daniel 11:1), supporting and protecting the right side and the right person. Daniel was a godly leader. As such, he was greatly esteemed by God (Daniel 10:11). Colson stresses this need for faithfulness:

> Christians are to do their duty as best they can. But even when they feel that they are making no difference, that they are failing to bring Christian values to the public arena, success is not the criteria. Faithfulness is. For in the end, Christians have the assurance that even the most difficult political situations are in the hands of a sovereign God.[77]

Political participation, for the Christian, requires the same obedience, the same faithfulness, as is demanded by God in our everyday lives. Of course, if every man were faithful to God in his personal life, there would be far less need for government and political reform. "This issue is ultimately personal: our states cannot represent God if we do not

Notes and Asides

represent Him first of all."[78]

Madison was correct when he insisted that government is "the greatest of all reflections on human nature." He rightly perceived man as inherently sinful and therefore in need of restraint. The Humanist and Marxist understanding of human nature is not merely defective but dangerous—it infuses governments with ultimate authority. On the other hand, the Christian understanding of human nature is profound and sufficient for a political order that honors God, recognizes its limits, administers justice, restrains evil, preserves freedom, protects the unborn and the aged, preserves the peace within and without, promotes the general well-being of other social institutions, and respects the rights of all men everywhere as creatures in the image of God.

[1]Charles Colson, *Kingdoms in Conflict* (Grand Rapids, MI: Zondervan, 1987), p. 92.
[2]Cited in Virginia Armstrong, "The Flight from America's Foundations: A Panoramic Perspective on American Law," in *Restoring the Constitution*, ed. H. Wayne House (Dallas, TX: Probe Books, 1987), p. 114.
[3]Colson, *Kingdoms in Conflict*, p. 92.
[4]Carl F. H. Henry, *Twilight of a Great Civilization* (Westchester, IL: Crossway, 1988), p. 20.
[5]Carl F. H. Henry, *God, Revelation and Authority*, six volumes (Waco, TX: Word Books, 1983), vol. 6, p. 446.
[6]Ibid., p. 118.
[7]George C. Roche, *A World Without Heroes* (Hillsdale, MI: Hillsdale College Press, 1987), p. 184.
[8]The "pursuit of happiness" mentioned in the Declaration of Independence must not be mistaken for the pursuit of mere pleasure. The word *happiness* was not commonly used in that sense in the eighteenth century, and a study of how the founding fathers and other influential writers of the time used it indicates that it bore a much higher meaning. Charles Murray summarizes its meaning as "the good-that-one-seeks-as-an-end-in-itself-and-for-no-other-reason." Charles Murray, *In Pursuit of Happiness and Good Government* (New York: Simon and Schuster, 1988), p. 25.
[9]Colson, *Kingdoms in Conflict*, p. 322. It should be noted that Christianity strongly supports one form of democracy but sees another as dangerous. When we use the word *democracy* to refer to a form of government that takes into account the needs and desires of the governed (a government "of the people, by the people, and for the people," as Abraham Lincoln put it) but that has certain constraints on the will even of large majorities of the people, we are speaking of *constitutional democracy* or, to use a better name, a *representative republic*. Ordinarily constitutional democracy takes a representative form: decisions are not made by direct vote of all citizens but by the vote of representatives elected by the citizens. Such a form of democracy finds sanction in Scripture (Deuteronomy 1:9-18). But when the word *democracy* is used to refer to a government ruled directly by the majority vote of citizens without constitutional limits on its authority, so that the will of the majority can become a justification for violating the rights of some (or even all) citizens, then it denotes a form of government that Scripture does not sanction, for even majorities do not make injustice right (Exodus 23:2). This is why, to the surprise of modern readers, America's founding fathers typically spoke disparagingly of democracy (which at the time denoted primarily unlimited rule of the majority) and exalted republican (representative, constitutional) instead. For a penetrating analysis of the relationship between Christianity and democracy, see Lord Percy of Newcastle, *The Heresy of Democracy: A Study in the History of Government* (Chicago: Henry Regnery, 1955).
[10]Cited in James McClellan, *Joseph Story and the American Constitution* (Norman, OK: University of Oklahoma Press, 1971), p. 136. A Sermon preached in St. Michael's Church, Charleston, February 13, 1833.
[11]Cited in Richard John Neuhaus, *The Naked Public Square* (Grand Rapids, MI: Eerdmans, 1984), p. 95.
[12]Cited in McClellan, *Joseph Story and the American Constitution*, p. 119. We recommend this work for students interested in the relationship between Christianity and the Constitution. We also recommend John Eidsmoe, *Christianity and the Constitution: The Faith of our Founding Fathers* (Grand Rapids, MI: Baker Book House, 1987), Tim LaHaye, *Faith of our Founding Fathers* (Brentwood, TN: Wolgemuth and Hyatt, 1987), Peter Marshall and David Manuel, *The Light and the Glory* (Old Tappan, NJ: Revell, 1977), Marshall Foster and Mary-Elaine Swanson, *The American Covenant: The Untold Story* (Thousand Oaks, CA: Foundation for Christian Self-Government, 1981), Benjamin Hart, *Faith and Freedom: The Christian Roots of American Liberty* (Dallas, TX: Lewis and Stanley, 1988), Verna Hall and Rosalie J. Slater, *Teaching and Learning America's Christian History* (Anaheim, CA: Foundation for American Christian Education, 1965), Russell Kirk, *The Roots of American Order* (LaSalle, IL: Open Court, 1974), and *Restoring the Constitution*, ed. House.
[13]Robert D. Linder and Richard V. Pierard, *Politics: A Case for Christian Action* (Downers Grove, IL: InterVarsity Press, 1973), pp. 44-5.
[14]James Madison, *The Federalist Papers*, no. 51 (New York: Pocket Books, 1964), p. 122.
[15]Ibid., pp. 122-3.
[16]LaHaye, *Faith of Our Founding Fathers*, p. 71.
[17]John Eidsmoe, *God and Caesar* (Westchester, IL: Crossway Books, 1985), p. 87.
[18]James Reston, "Faith of Our Fathers: Living Still?" *The New York Times,* April 2, 1969, p. 46.
[19]Francis A. Schaeffer, *A Christian Manifesto* (Westchester, IL: Crossway Books, 1982), p. 32.
[20]Eidsmoe, *God and Caesar*, pp. 84-5.

[21]John Warwick Montgomery, *Human Rights and Human Dignity* (Dallas, TX: Probe Books, 1986), pp. 168-9.
[22]William C. Johnson, "Government," in *Baker's Dictionary of Christian Ethics*, ed. Carl F. H. Henry (Grand Rapids, MI: Baker Book House, 1973), p. 272.
[23]Russell Kirk, *A Program for Conservatives*, rev. ed. (Chicago: Regnery, 1962), p. 166, cited in E. Calvin Beisner, *Prosperity and Poverty: The Compassionate Use of Resources in a World of Scarcity* (Westchester, IL: Crossway Books, 1988), p. 45.
[24]Beisner, *Prosperity and Poverty*, p. 45.
[25]Rousas John Rushdoony, *The Institutes of Biblical Law* (Nutley, NJ: Craig Press, 1973), p. 199.
[26]Henry, *Twilight of a Great Civilization*, p. 148.
[27]Rousas John Rushdoony, *Politics of Guilt and Pity* (Fairfax, VA: Thoburn Press, 1978), p. 339.
[28]Colson, *Kingdoms in Conflict*, p. 91.
[29]Cited in Jeffrey A. Aman and H. Wayne House, "Constitutional Interpretation and the Question of Lawful Authority," in *Restoring the Constitution*, ed. House, p. 202.
[30]Colson, *Kingdoms in Conflict*, p. 47.
[31]For an excellent discussion of the separation of church and state issue we recommend Robert L. Cord, *Separation of Church and State: Historical Fact and Current Fiction* (New York: Lambeth Press, 1982); John W. Whitehead, *The Freedom of Religious Expression in the Public High Schools* (Westchester, IL: Crossway Books, 1983); Russell Kirk, ed., *The Assault on Religion: Commentaries on the Decline of Religious Liberty* (Lanham, MD: University Press of America, and Cumberland, VA: Center for Judicial Studies, 1986); and McClellan, *Joseph Story and the American Constitution.*
[32]Henry, *God, Revelation, and Authority*, vol. 6, p. 446.
[33]Johnson, "Government," in *Baker's Dictionary of Christian Ethics*, ed. Henry, p. 272.
[34]Colson, *Kingdoms in Conflict*, p. 271.
[35]A. Berkeley Mickelsen, "State," in *Baker's Dictionary of Christian Ethics*, ed. Henry, p. 646.
[36]Colson, *Kingdoms in Conflict*, p. 114.
[37]Ibid., p. 270.
[38]Charles Colson, *Who Speaks for God?* (Westchester, IL: Crossway Books, 1988), p. 40.
[39]Colson, *Kingdoms in Conflict*, p. 275.
[40]Rushdoony, *The Institutes of Biblical Law*, p. 212.
[41]George Grant, *The Changing of the Guard: Biblical Principles for Political Action* (Ft. Worth, TX: Dominion Press, 1987), p. 11.
[42]Lawrence D. Pratt, "The Politics of Pragmatism: Threat to Freedom," in *Foundations of Christian Scholarship*, ed. Gary North (Vallecito, CA: Ross House, 1976), p. 121.
[43]LaHaye, *Faith of Our Founding Fathers*, p. 189.
[44]Colson, *Kingdoms in Conflict*, p. 226.
[45]Schaeffer, *A Christian Manifesto*, p. 34.
[46]*Newsweek* November 26, 1990, p. 29, "The civilized world is now in the process of fashioning the rules that will govern the new world order beginning to emerge in the aftermath of the Cold War," says President George Bush.
[47]Colson, *Who Speaks for God?* p. 144.
[48]William A. Stanmeyer, *Clear and Present Danger* (Ann Arbor, MI: Servant Books, 1983), p. 38.
[49]Colson, *Kingdoms in Conflict*, p. 77.
[50]Stanmeyer, *Clear and Present Danger*, p. 40.
[51]Colson, *Kingdoms in Conflict*, p. 77.
[52]Ibid., p. 78.
[53]Malachi Martin, *The Keys of This Blood* (New York: Simon and Schuster, 1990), p. 491.
[54]Rushdoony, *Politics of Guilt and Pity*, p. 322.
[55]Rushdoony, *The Institutes of Biblical Law*, p. 213.
[56]Henry, *Twilight of a Great Civilization*, p. 24.
[57]Rousas John Rushdoony, *This Independent Republic* (Nutley, NJ: Craig Press, 1964), p. 15.
[58]Henry, *God, Revelation and Authority*, vol. 6, p. 446.

[59]Hart, *Faith and Freedom: The Christian Roots of American Liberty*.
[60]Professor John C. H. Wu says the following about the English common law, "The common law has one advantage over the legal system of any country: it was Christian from the very beginning of its history." Cited in Armstrong, "The Flight from America's Foundations: A Panoramic Perspective on American Law," p. 116. John Locke was a Christian who wrote *The Reasonableness of Christianity* and was, as Montgomery says, "simply putting his faith into practice." He accented contract theory, limited government, and affirmation of unalienable human rights. These ideas took root in the U.S. Constitution. Montesquieu and Blackstone were both Christian gentlemen, and, House says, "The Constitution . . . was built upon the theological views of man's depravity and dignity and structured after the thoughts of Blackstone and Montesquieu."
[61]John Eidsmoe, "The Judeo-Christian Roots of the Constitution," in *Restoring the Constitution*, ed. House, p. 77.
[62]M. E. Bradford, *A Worthy Company: Brief Lives of the Framers of the United States Constitution* (Marlborough, NH: Plymouth Rock Foundation, 1982), pp. viii-ix.
[63]H. Wayne House, "Introduction," in *Restoring the Constitution*, ed. House, p. 7.
[64]William Bradford, *Of Plymouth Plantation* (New York: Alfred A. Knopf, 1966), pp. 120-21. Bradford writes, "that the taking away of property and bringing in community into a commonwealth would make them happy and flourishing; as if they were wiser than God."
[65]Mickelsen, "State," in *Baker's Dictionary of Christian Ethics*, ed. Henry, p. 646.
[66]Grant, *The Changing of the Guard*, p. 18.
[67]Rushdoony, *The Institutes of Biblical Law*, p. 214.
[68]Henry, *God, Revelation and Authority*, vol. 6, p. 451.
[69]Henry, *Twilight of a Great Civilization*, p. 32.
[70]Colson, *Kingdoms in Conflict*, p. 280.
[71]Ibid., p. 109.
[72]Ibid., p. 265.
[73]Mickelsen, "State," in *Dictionary of Christian Ethics*, ed. Henry, p. 647.
[74]Schaeffer, *A Christian Manifesto*, pp. 90-91.
[75]Colson, *Kingdoms in Conflict*, p. 246.
[76]Schaeffer, *A Christian Manifesto*, p. 93. An example of the proper time for disobedience recently arose when the American government (through its public health services) advised churches to amend their attitude toward homosexuality. The Bible clearly dictates the proper Christian response to homosexuality (see Romans 1 and Jude 1), and the church must stand firm in her commitment to obey God's dictums even when they conflict with those of the state.
[77]Colson, *Kingdoms in Conflict*, p. 291.
[78]Rushdoony, *Politics of Guilt and Pity*, p. 340.

SECTION NINE

ECONOMICS

ECONOMICS [Greek: *oikos* (house) + *nomia* (rule)]: The rule or management of resources, whether by an individual or a society.

	SECULAR HUMANISM	MARXISM/ LENINISM	BIBLICAL CHRISTIANITY
SOURCE	*HUMANIST MANIFESTO I & II*	*WRITINGS OF MARX & LENIN*	*BIBLE*
THEOLOGY	ATHEISM	ATHEISM	THEISM
PHILOSOPHY	NATURALISM	DIALECTICAL MATERIALISM	SUPERNATURALISM
ETHICS	ETHICAL RELATIVISM	PROLETARIAT MORALITY	ETHICAL ABSOLUTES
BIOLOGY	DARWINIAN EVOLUTION	DARWINIAN/ PUNCTUATED EVOLUTION	SPECIAL CREATIONISM
PSYCHOLOGY	MONISTIC SELF-ACTUALIZATION	MONISTIC PAVLOVIAN BEHAVIORISM	DUALISM
SOCIOLOGY	NON-TRADITIONAL WORLD STATE ETHICAL SOCIETY	ABOLITION OF HOME, CHURCH AND STATE	HOME CHURCH STATE
LAW	POSITIVE LAW	POSITIVE LAW	BIBLICAL/NATURAL LAW
POLITICS	WORLD GOVERNMENT (GLOBALISM)	NEW WORLD ORDER	JUSTICE FREEDOM ORDER
ECONOMICS	SOCIALISM	SOCIALISM/ COMMUNISM	STEWARDSHIP OF PROPERTY
HISTORY	HISTORICAL EVOLUTION	HISTORICAL MATERIALISM	HISTORICAL RESURRECTION

CHAPTER

27

SECULAR HUMANIST ECONOMICS

"We socialists are not ashamed to confess that we have a deep faith in man and in a vision of a new, human form of society. We appeal to the faith, hope and imagination of our fellow citizens to join us in this vision and in the attempt to realize it. Socialism is not only a socioeconomic and political program; it is a human program: the realization of the ideals of humanism under the conditions of an industrial society."[1]

—Erich Fromm

"For example, should one say that the Humanist is a socialist or a believer in free enterprise? . . . Humanists may honestly disagree about . . . these complex issues."[2]

—Paul Kurtz

SUMMARY

Secular Humanism, in the main, adheres to a socialistic economic theory. Because Humanists believe man is an evolving creature progressing toward a world civilization, most Humanists believe that perfectible man will become capable of planning the perfectible economy, i. e., socialism.

Because there are poor people in the world, Humanists believe our present capitalist system has failed. The solution to poverty, for the socialist Humanist, lies in more strict economic controls by an enlightened government. Socialist Humanists believe central planning is capable of creating a better economy than one governed by the free market because man is the highest intellect and has evolved to the level necessary to control his own destiny. Julian Huxley declares that man, for the first time in the long process of evolution, "can truly see something of the promised land beyond."[3] This promised land, according to most Humanists, will have a planned economy, based on the rational, moral decisions of Humanistic government planners.

A highly evolved, intelligent society cannot tolerate the apparently uncontrolled nature of the free market. Besides, under capitalism non-intellectuals can earn greater remuneration than their professors, which proves to the Humanist mind that capitalism is incapable of judging true values and social worth.

Capitalism is also perceived by the socialist Humanist as an unmanageable, often uncooperative economic system that has not been responsive to the need for redistribution of wealth. Erich Fromm complains, "In contrast to most other societies in which social laws are explicit and fixed on the basis of political power or tradition—Capitalism does not have such explicit laws."[4] Clearly, the Humanist requires an economic environment in which laws are specifically legislated by man; government becomes the ultimate lawgiver. Any less powerful form of government, such as the state in capitalistic societies, is portrayed as ineffectual, out of control. Fromm says capitalist systems "are not . . . controlled by man. They run wild, and their leaders are like a person on a runaway horse, who is proud of managing to keep in the saddle, even though he is powerless to direct the horse."[5]

This precarious control by man is inimical to the Humanist worldview. Man, who must "save himself," must be in absolute control of all aspects of his universe. Thus, the world's economic system must be strictly controlled by political man—that is, civil government must be granted sovereignty over man's economic affairs. In free markets, millions of individuals plan their consumption and production, but under socialist Humanism's central planning, only a few educated ones will decide for the many. Eventually, mankind will evolve into a global society with one-world government controlling a one-world economic system.

Notes and Asides

Introduction

While Secular Humanism requires agreement in the areas of theology, philosophy, and biology, it allows for varied opinions in the field of economics. However, because it is a worldview with a dogmatic foundation, Humanism tends to encourage a particular economic approach: socialism. "Many humanists see socialism," writes Robert Sheaffer, "as a vital element of humanism; indeed, at one time, most humanists believed this."[6]

Kai Nielsen, in an article entitled "Making a Case for Socialism," argues for public ownership and control of the means of production (he calls this industrial democracy), a classless society, rational planning, and the prohibition of capitalist acts (buying and selling) "between consenting adults."[7] He goes on to make it clear that socialism is the most consistent Humanist position:

> To be a humanist one need not be a socialist or even a welfare-state liberal. There are even humanists in good standing who are very conservative indeed; but were they to adequately rationalize into a sound political sociology the ideals of the Enlightenment shared by all humanists they would also be socialists.[8]

Still, as Nielsen admits, not every Humanist is a socialist. Marvin Zimmerman writes, "I contend that the evidence supports the view that democratic capitalism is more productive of human good than democratic socialism."[9] Antony Flew is likewise opposed to socialism. Sheaffer is violently opposed to socialism. He says, "no intellectually honest person today can deny that the history of socialism is a sorry tale of economic failure and crimes against humanity."[10] He continues,

> "[T]he history of socialism is a sorry tale of economic failure and crimes against humanity."
> —Robert Sheaffer

> Socialism is simply "envy" writ large, and elevated to a moral ideal. It brands the most productive as criminals, and makes heroes of those who have difficulty achieving anything at all. The full potential of the human race can never be liberated under such a warped ideal.[11]

Also, some Humanists who were formerly socialists have recently recognized the impracticality of such a position. Paul Kurtz has turned from socialism to free enterprise. Sidney Hook, a lifetime socialist, finally acknowledges, "I no longer believe that the central problem of our time is the choice between capitalism and socialism but the defense and enrichment of a free and open society against totalitarianism."[12]

Of course, Hook's disillusionment with socialism has not caused him to abandon it totally, and this in itself has irked some of the

Notes and Asides

Humanists more oriented toward capitalism. Flew asks,

> Why, in a world now having such abundant experience of practical socialism, a world in which so many peoples have for decades lived under total socialism, a world in which total socialism has always been, in practice, totalitarian, and in which the loss of liberty—as he has himself so often and so rightly insisted—has not even been compensated by great gains in prosperity, why, in the face of all this, has Sidney Hook not once and for always put away the socialist longings of his youth?[13]

The reason Hook cannot bring himself to abandon socialism is simply that, in general, socialism is more consistent with the Humanist worldview. Any view that does not accept man's fallen nature and the reality of Original Sin expects man to be able to overcome evil, and evil is, theoretically, the only thing preventing a socialist economy from working. If there were no such thing as greed, envy, or sloth, if man truly wanted nothing more than to be economically equal with his fellow man, then socialism might be one possible vehicle for achieving a more equitable society. For the Humanist, there is no reason to believe that socialism will not bring about a more humane society.

Therefore, Kurtz admits, "Humanists have generally been sympathetic to socialism as the wave of the future and many have believed that in changing the conditions of ownership and the relationship of production many or most of the inequities of life can be ameliorated."[14] Kurtz himself has abandoned this position, but most of the key players in Humanism have not.

Socialism is an economic system based on the abolition of private ownership of the means of production.

Ludwig von Mises, who was not a Humanist but is a recognized authority on the socialist economic system, defines socialism as "a policy which aims at constructing a society in which the means of production [factories, mines, transportation, etc.] are socialized [i.e., taken from their owners and given to central planners]."[15] A more concise and still accurate definition might be "the abolition of private ownership of the means of production."

However, these definitions are not far-reaching enough for some Humanists. Erich Fromm, for instance, believes that according to its basic principles, "the aim of socialism is the abolition of national sovereignty, the abolition of any kind of armed forces, and the establishment of a commonwealth of nations."[16] Obviously some Humanists perceive socialism as much more than simply an economic system. For our purposes, however, when the term *socialism* is used, it is to be understood in the strict economic sense.

Notes and Asides

Humanist Attitudes Toward Socialism

Both the *Humanist Manifesto I* and the *Humanist Manifesto II* contain passages calling for a more equal distribution of wealth. The first *Manifesto* (1933) states,

> The humanists are firmly convinced that existing acquisitive and profit-motivated society has shown itself to be inadequate and that a radical change in methods, controls, and motives must be instituted. A socialized and cooperative economic order must be established to the end that the equitable distribution of the means of life be possible.[17]

The second *Manifesto* (1973) is more cautious, unwilling to specifically endorse socialism:

> It is the moral obligation of the developed nations to provide—through an international authority that safeguards human rights—massive technical, agricultural, medical, and economic assistance, including birth control techniques, to the developing portions of the globe. World poverty must cease. Hence extreme disproportions in wealth, income, and economic growth should be reduced on a worldwide basis.[18]

Of course, the most obvious means of redistributing wealth is socialism, but the second *Manifesto* avoids this conclusion, apparently in an effort to avoid dogma. Whatever the reason, there are many individual Humanists more than willing to voice their support for socialism.

Corliss Lamont has championed socialism since the early 1930s: "I became a convinced believer in socialism as the best way out for America and the world . . . about 1931 or 1932. Since that time, the rise of fascism, the undoubted economic success of socialism in the Soviet Union, the coming of the Second World War, the defeat of international fascism and the postwar developments of 1945-49 in America, Europe and Asia have all deepened and strengthened my socialist convictions."[19] Lamont elsewhere associates socialism directly with Humanism—apparently drawing the conclusion that socialism is a logical extension from Humanist philosophy:

> In my late twenties I developed an affirmative humanist philosophy of life that holds as its chief ethical goal the happiness, freedom and progress of all humanity—irrespective of nation,

Notes and Asides

> race and social origin—upon this earth, where it has its only existence. If we are really serious about achieving this end, I think that intelligence then leads us to work for a planned and democratic socialism on a world scale.[20]

It is important to note that Lamont believes socialism is the proper economic system for every country, including America: "I think it is this feeling for justice and the welfare of all humanity that has led me to the belief in a democratic socialist economy as the best system, not only for countries that are underdeveloped but for countries that are, say, overdeveloped, like the United States."[21]

John Dewey, a former leader of the League for Industrial Democracy, also believed socialism was the best economic system. He claims that "social control of economic forces is . . . necessary if anything approaching economic equality and liberty is to be realized."[22] Indeed, he says, "The only form of enduring social organization that is now possible is one in which the new forces of productivity are cooperatively controlled and used in the interest of the effective liberty and the cultural development of the individuals that constitute society."[23] That is, socialism is the only means for achieving economic equality and, therefore, liberty.

Indeed, Dewey is associated with Karl Marx in the minds of some Humanists. Hook writes,

> Actually I was not the first or last to find a strong philosophical kinship between Karl Marx and John Dewey. Bertrand Russell, among others, had remarked upon it. This could be traced to their Hegelian origins, their acceptance of the Darwinian revolution in biology as a basis for a world view. . . .[24]

And Roy Wood Sellars gently echoes his call for socialism in the *Humanist Manifesto I* by stating, "I agree with Dewey . . . and Marx on the primacy of the community."[25]

Fromm, of course, is another outspoken Humanist supporter of socialism. He says, "We are not forced to choose between a managerial free-enterprise system and a managerial communist system. There is a third solution, that of democratic, humanistic socialism which, based on the original principles of socialism, offers the vision of a new, truly human society."[26] Hook felt much the same way. "In 1945," Flew writes, "Hook believed: that capitalism in Western Europe was finished; and that only collectivist economic planning could save us from 'that chaos, hunger, and chronic unemployment' which are 'the seedbed of totalitarianism'. . . ."[27]

Notes and Asides

In a more limited sense, John Kenneth Galbraith, a former Humanist of the Year, also supports socialism. "In an intelligently plural economy," says Galbraith, "a certain number of industries should be publicly owned. Elementary considerations of public convenience require it. For moving and housing people at moderate cost, private enterprise does not serve. But I had come reluctantly to the conclusion that socialism, even in this modest design, was something I would never see."[28] Elsewhere he calls for public ownership of housing and transportation instead of the "apologetic half-hearted socialism" of public projects and rent controls. He believes, "The Democratic Party must henceforth use the word socialism. It describes what is needed. If there is assumed to be something illicit or indecent about public ownership, it won't be done well. . . ."[29]

Clearly, most leading Humanists embrace socialism in one form or another. Some, such as Lamont and Fromm, are adamant in their support for this economic system, while others, such as Sellars and Galbraith, are more low-key. What is important is that socialism, for the Humanists, logically follows from their foundation. There are Humanists who are opposed to socialism, but the leaders—the men who have played a role in shaping the whole Humanist worldview—generally regard socialism as the more humanistic economic system. This is true of Lamont, Sellars, Dewey, Hook, and Fromm, and has only recently become untrue of Kurtz.

Humanists cite a number of reasons for selecting socialism as the best economic system. The first, most common reason is their belief that it is the most ethical system.

Socialism and Ethics

Most Humanists who embrace socialism claim to do so for purely moral reasons. Hook says, "In my case, as in so many others, allegiance to socialism at first appeared to be primarily the articulation of a feeling of moral protest against remediable evils that surrounded us."[30] More specifically, Hook states, "I believe I can say with justification that I was one of the few American 'Socialist intellectuals' who read Marx's *Capital* closely but was drawn to socialism on ethical grounds rather than economic ones. This I believe was true of all the leading Socialists of our time."[31] Hook, however, recognizes the paradoxical nature of the belief that socialism would bring about good:

> Despite the fact that the most oppressive regimes in the world today call themselves socialist, it still remains true that for me

Notes and Asides

> "For socialism is not merely the labour question, it is before all things the atheistic question, the question of the form taken by atheism today, the question of the tower of Babel built without God . . . "
> —Feodor Dostoevski

> and many of my contemporaries, the socialist ideal was originally embraced because the movement and thought it inspired would, we hoped, strengthen the prospects of human freedom.[32]

Both Lamont and Dewey also chose socialism on ethical grounds. Lamont writes, "My own path to socialism, therefore, was that of analysis through reason, combined with belief in a humanist ethics and a deep attachment to democracy in its broadest sense."[33] Dewey's concept of liberty also implies a moral ground for choosing socialism: "But the cause of liberalism will be lost for a considerable period if it is not prepared to go further and socialize the forces of production, now at hand, so that the liberty of individuals will be supported by the very structure of economic organization."[34] Dewey even goes so far as to adopt an "ends justify the means" approach to economics, stating that "socialized economy is the means of free individual development as the end."[35]

Some Humanists attach other ethical implications to the socialist theory. Fromm writes, "Humanistic socialism is radically opposed to war and violence in all and any forms. It considers any attempt to solve political and social problems by force and violence not only as futile, but as immoral and inhuman."[36]

Why do many Humanists believe socialism is the most ethical economic system? Partly because they perceive it to allow more freedom, but also because they view it as more concerned with the common good. Lamont writes, "Socialist planning would release and coordinate . . . frustrated intelligences and abilities, bringing into action a great community mind operating on behalf of the common good and embodying the life of reason in social-economic affairs."[37] Later he clarifies,

> The socialist economic system together with socialist teaching effects a transformation in human motives, coordinating the altruistic and egoistic impulses so that people find their welfare and happiness in working for the general good instead of always putting their economic self-interest first, as in capitalist theory.[38]

Obviously, Lamont believes in a common good, although he is understandably vague in describing it. In fact, most Humanists in favor of socialism, including Dewey, Hook, and Fromm, seem to have the idea of the common good in the back of their minds.

Why do Humanists view socialism as the best method for achieving the common good? Fromm answers:

Notes and Asides

> The supreme value in all social and economic arrangements is man; the goal of society is to offer the conditions for the full development of man's potentialities, his reason, his love, his creativity; all social arrangements must be conducive to overcoming the alienation and crippledness of man, and to enable him to achieve real freedom and individuality. The aim of socialism is an association in which the full development of each is the condition for the full development of all.[39]

When man, and not God, is used as the yardstick for measuring morality, then the common good becomes basically another name for utilitarianism—the greatest amount of happiness for the greatest number of people. And this, so the argument goes, can best be achieved through the equal distribution of wealth and work. This way, the greatest number of people can be satisfied with their amount of wealth. More people will be able to concentrate on becoming self-actualized.

Socialism, for the Humanist, ties in closely with his ethical beliefs. The Humanist who embraces utilitarianism (or any version of the common good) finds socialism to be most compatible with his worldview. And as we have seen in the chapter on Humanist ethics, every Humanist consistent with his philosophy embraces some form of ethics relative to man's common good. Therefore, the most consistent Humanist worldview embraces socialism as a logical extension of Humanist morality. Most Humanist leaders recognize this and are willing to draw the necessary conclusions and accept socialism.

The Failure of Capitalism

The second major reason Humanists cite for choosing socialism rather than the free enterprise system is the failure of capitalism. Humanists point to perceived evils extant under the capitalist system and assume that these evils will disappear in a socialist economy.

"The giant corporations which control the economic, and to a large degree the political, destiny of the country," writes Fromm, "constitute the very opposite of the democratic process; they represent power without control by those submitted to it."[40] Therefore, Fromm believes socialism is a more democratic economic system. Furthermore, he claims that capitalism has reduced man to a being concerned almost entirely with consumption: "The spirit of consumption is precisely the opposite of the spirit of a socialist society as Marx visualized it. He clearly saw the danger inherent in capitalism. His aim was a society in which man is much, not in which he has or uses much."[41] Fromm, in

Capitalism is an economic system based on private ownership of the means of production.

Notes and Asides

fact, sees capitalism strictly as a system concerned with manipulating man, teaching him to consume more:

> While our economic system has enriched man materially, it has impoverished him humanly. Notwithstanding all propaganda and slogans about the Western world's faith in God, its idealism, its spiritual concern, our system has created a materialistic culture and a materialistic man. During his working hours, the individual is managed as part of a production team. During his hours of leisure time, he is managed and manipulated to be the perfect consumer who likes what he is told to like and yet has the illusion that he follows his own tastes.[42]

Capitalism, for Fromm, strips man of his humanity. Only socialism can restore it.

> "The market steers the capitalistic economy. Supremacy of the market is tantamount to the supremacy of the consumers."
> —Ludwig von Mises

Lamont cites the "tremendous waste inherent in the capitalist system and its wanton exploitation of men and natural resources"[43] as one of his reasons for embracing socialism. His distrust of capitalism runs so deep that he believes, "Since fascism is simply capitalism stripped of all democratic pretenses and other unessentials—capitalism in the nude, as it were—the danger of fascism remains as long as the capitalist system is with us."[44]

In his typically more conservative approach, Sellars says simply, "Our affluent society is limited in area and has in it pockets of poverty. . . . This social situation demands a measure of revitalization."[45] Again, the assumption is that poverty is a result of the capitalist system.

Dewey believes that capitalism must create artificial scarcity to operate successfully, and he views this contrived scarcity as responsible for poverty and hunger. "There is an undoubted objective clash of interests between finance-capitalism that controls the means of production and whose profit is served by maintaining relative scarcity, and idle workers and hungry consumers."[46] He views this as a blatant infringement of liberty, noting that the early liberals

> overlooked the fact that in many cases personal profit can be better served by maintaining artificial scarcity and by . . . systematic sabotage of production. Above all, in identifying the extension of liberty in all of its modes with extension of their particular brand of economic liberty, they completely failed to anticipate the bearing of private control of the means of production and distribution upon the effective liberty of the masses in industry as well as in cultural goods. An era of power possessed

Notes and Asides

> by the few took the place of the era of liberty for all envisaged by the liberals of the early nineteenth century.[47]

He alludes to this loss of liberty again when he says, "Servility and regimentation are the result of control by the few of access to means of productive labor on the part of the many."[48]

The most significant failing of capitalism, at least for Lamont, is its inescapable lust for war. According to him, war is unavoidable while capitalistic countries thrive, but will be rendered nonexistent as soon as socialism becomes the norm. He states, "I oppose Capitalism because of its continuous cycles of prosperity and depression, because of its inability to eliminate unemployment and poverty, because of its plundering of our planet for the sake of financial profit and because of its initiation of wars and immense armaments."[49] He asks us to "consider the untold loss of wealth through . . . the colossal squandering of human beings and goods in capitalist-caused wars."[50] He believes, "A socialist society cuts away the economic roots of war. Public ownership of the instrumentalities of production means that no individuals or groups can make money from manufacturing armaments."[51] He later cites as an example: "the public ownership of the main means of production and distribution in the U.S.S.R. prevents private individuals and groups from profiting financially from armaments or any other war activity."[52]

Lamont goes so far as to blame the warlike nature of present-day capitalist countries for hindering the development of socialism in the Soviet Union:

> If I may spell this out a little further, it has always seemed to me that a conscious part of capitalist efforts to destroy and discredit Soviet socialism has been to put such pressures on the USSR that, even if it did not collapse, it would be forced into a Draconian dictatorship in order to survive. This has certainly been a prime capitalist motive in the Cold War and the armaments race. The intent has been to increase tension within the Soviet Union by compelling it continually to step up the pace in armaments production and so divert effort from general industrial growth and from raising the standard of living by increasing production of consumer goods.[53]

"Under socialism production is entirely directed by the orders of the central board of production management."
—Ludwig von Mises

Clearly, for Lamont, capitalism is synonymous with war, and socialism with peace. Indeed, for most Humanist leaders, capitalism is viewed as a failure, or an evil system, and socialism its solution.

Notes and Asides

Ironically, Hook, in a book published in his eighty-fourth year, alludes to the faulty reasoning inherent in Humanist critiques of capitalism:

> There was something very naive about the Socialist faith of those years. It was based on a highly informed awareness of the evils of the capitalist system. Rarely, if ever, however, did it consider seriously the possible evils of the system that would replace it.[54]

That is, capitalism admittedly has its faults, but this does not automatically prove that socialism is better. Perhaps socialism is worse. This is a point often overlooked by supporters of socialism.

In truth, Humanists rarely voice their support for socialism simply on its own merits. Lamont states, "In my view the fundamental advantages of Socialism lie in its functioning for use instead of profit and its instituting over-all socio-economic planning through public ownership of the main means of production, distribution and finance."[55] But this affirmation of the advantages of socialism is unusual. Much more time is dedicated to underlining the failings of capitalism.

The only advantage of socialism Dewey stresses is the increased interdependence such a system would create. We are told by Donald Clark Hodges, author of *Socialist Humanism*, that Dewey believes

CLOSE-UP

Sidney Hook (1902-1989)

Once dedicated to the cause of Marxism, Sidney Hook mellowed in his old age and revoked all but the most basic tenets of socialism. He remained a Humanist, however, until the bitter end. With John Dewey as his mentor, Hook learned the lesson of naturalistic philosophy well. He passed on this lesson to numerous students, serving as the head of the philosophy department of New York University from 1948-1969 and as professor emeritus from 1969 till his death. Hook authored a number of books, including *Marxism and Beyond* and *The Place of Religion in a Free Society*. In 1985, he was awarded the Presidential Medal of Freedom.

"personal happiness can be found only through sharing the benefits of collective work."[56] Dewey demonstrates this belief when he states,

> From a social standpoint, dependence denotes a power rather than a weakness; it involves interdependence. There is always a danger that increased personal independence will decrease the social capacity of an individual. In making him more self-reliant, it may make him more self-sufficient; it may lead to aloofness and indifference. It often makes an individual so insensitive in his relations to others as to develop an illusion of being really able to stand and act alone—an unnamed form of insanity which is responsible for a large part of the remediable suffering of the world.[57]

Increased interdependence is the basic merit of socialism, according to Dewey. Sellars also sees interdependence as an advantage, although, again, he chooses to demonstrate the failings of the independence of capitalism: "There are signs of unrest. . . . we hear of social alienation and lack of identification. It would seem that some demands of human nature were being ignored. The private sector, business, had been exalted over the public sector, living together and its needs."[58]

Humanists supporting socialism tend to stress the failures of capitalism and downplay any possible disadvantages of socialism. We are told that capitalism promotes materialism, strips man of his humanity, and creates a hunger for war in its societies. However, we are not often told of the benefits of a socialist system; rather, it is simply assumed that socialism is less evil and therefore more good than capitalism.

Socialism in Practice

Lamont lists a third reason Humanists embrace socialism. Although he is infrequently articulate about the advantages of socialism, Lamont is more than willing to point to the "success" of socialism in countries such as the Soviet Union and the People's Republic of China. He views these societies as fine examples of the practicality of socialism.

"I see," says Lamont, "in the very considerable achievements of the Soviet Union a concrete example of what socialism and socialist [central] planning can do. From an economically backward, chiefly agricultural, 70 percent illiterate country under the Tsars, the Soviet Five-Year Plans have transformed Russia into a dynamic, forward-moving economy with highly developed industry and collectivized agriculture."[59] Elsewhere he claims, "it is accurate to say that Soviet planning is carried out on so wide a scale and so successfully that the

Notes and Asides

whole world, including the most conservative capitalists and economists, is taking note and reluctantly recognizing Soviet Russia's extraordinary achievements."[60]

Lamont also points to the People's Republic of China as an example of the success of socialism:

> Now I turn to the socialist economic system in China. Early in the game, Chairman Mao Tse-tung and the Communist leadership decided that agriculture must be given priority, to feed an enormous population that often in the past suffered from hunger and famine. Now practically everyone is well fed and healthy.[61]

"If control of production is shifted from the hands of entrepreneurs, daily anew elected by a plebiscite of the consumers, into the hands of the supreme commanders . . . , neither representative government nor any civil liberties can survive."

—Ludwig von Mises

For Lamont, socialism in practice proves the feasibility of socialism for all countries.

This belief in the success of socialism in the Soviet Union and China, however, is not shared by Lamont's fellow Humanists. Sellars says that "the Communist world is even sicker" than the U.S. because "there is no liberty there and the economic system will not work in the long run."[62]

Hook recognizes the reason Lamont expresses so much optimism about the socialist system in Russia, acknowledging that he and his socialist friends once felt the same: "We uncritically identified the Soviet Union with its declared Socialist ideal and feared that, if we rejected the Soviet Union and the October Revolution out of which it arose, we would be admitting the bankruptcy of socialism and sentencing ourselves to the miseries of disillusion and disbelief."[63]

Hook, however, has now faced the grim fact that the economies of "countries governed by Bolshevik-Leninist regimes . . . are in shambles. . . ."[64] He admits that he and his socialist allies "did not realize what should have been evident even before the Soviet economy confirmed it: that workers could be exploited in a collectivist economy as well as in a free market economy—in the absence of free trade unions even more so—and that the distribution of social wealth could never be adequately accounted for in purely economic terms."[65] Hook recognizes the evils inherent in the Soviet socialist system, and must (regardless of his sympathy for socialism), admit the failures of the system when put into practice.

Indeed, most Humanists in favor of socialism are not as impressed with the socialistic systems of Russia or China as Lamont. Most understand that not one experiment in socialism has been successful. The Christian explanation for this phenomenon is that socialism is unjust—human nature, even in its most flexible moments, is appalled by the use of force (either taxation or robbery) to strip individuals of possessions they have earned. Humanists in favor of socialism, however, cannot accept this answer and therefore must conclude that socialism has never worked in practice because it has never been implemented by the properly evolved man or state.

Specifics For the Transition to Socialism

According to most of Humanism's leaders, many intermediate steps must be taken before the United States can achieve full-fledged socialism. Hook, for example, realizes that each job must be designed in a way that creates inherent value in the task itself: "But until some way can be found to organize a society in which everyone's way of earning a living is at the same time a satisfactory way of living his or her life, there will always be a problem of incentive."[66]

Lamont points out that the Constitution must still be honored, so one intermediate step requires the government's purchasing the means of production from their rightful owners:

> So far as the United States is concerned, in order to smooth the path to socialism and maintain our constitutional guarantees for everyone, I am in favor of the government's buying out the capitalists when it receives the voters' mandate to socialize the natural resources, the factories, the banks, transportation and communication facilities, and so on.[67]

Lamont does not specify which party (the government or the capitalists) will dictate the price or where the government will get the money to pay for the means of production—whether by confiscatory taxation or by inflationary money creation.

Fromm focuses more on control than the actual buying out of the means of production. He expects the capitalists to surrender their companies willingly to every employee so that each individual will have control of the means of production:

> Following the principle that social control and not legal ownership is the essential principle of socialism, its first goal is the transformation of all big enterprises in such a way that their administrators are appointed and fully controlled by all participants—workers, clerks, engineers—with the participation of trade union and consumer representatives. These groups constitute the highest authority for every big enterprise. They decide all basic questions of production, price, utilization of profits,

Notes and Asides

"Were we directed from Washington when to sow and when to reap, we should soon want bread."
—Thomas Jefferson

Notes and Asides

> etc. The stockholders continue to receive an appropriate compensation for the use of their capital, but have no right of control and administration.[68]

Fromm does not mention how stockholders will feel about this new development.

Once the intermediate steps toward socialism in the United States are taken, the socialistic Humanists are largely in agreement regarding the means of assuring a more "equal" society. Lamont, Dewey, Fromm, and Sellars all call for a redistribution of wealth in the form of a "guaranteed income" for every person in the country. Fromm places special emphasis on the intermediate steps, stressing that nothing, not even a guaranteed income, can help the world unless certain measures are taken:

> The great step of a guaranteed income will, in my opinion, succeed only if it is accompanied by changes in other spheres. It must not be forgotten that the guaranteed income can succeed only if we stop spending 10 percent of our total resources on economically useless and dangerous armaments; if we can halt the spread of senseless violence by systematic help to the underdeveloped countries, and if we find methods to arrest the population explosion. Without such changes, no plan for the future will succeed, because there will be no future.[69]

Granted a future, Fromm believes guaranteed income is the best solution for economic woes. He says, "The individual must be protected from fear and the need to submit to anyone's coercion. In order to accomplish this aim, society must provide, free for everyone, the minimum necessities of material existence in food, housing, and clothing. Anyone who has higher aspirations for material comforts will have to work for them, but the minimal necessities of life being guaranteed, no person can have power over anyone on the basis of direct or indirect material coercion."[70]

Dewey is also concerned with the idea that the average man is coerced by the owners of the means of production. He writes, "That the control of the means of production by the few in legal possession operates as a standing agency of coercion of the many, may need emphasis in statement, but is surely evident to one who is willing to observe and honestly report the existing scene."[71] That is, the average worker can be forced to do things he would otherwise choose not to do, because his employer has the ability to fire him and therefore cause him to lose his means of obtaining food, clothing, and shelter. Guaranteed income would, in theory, render coercion useless.

Notes and Asides

Sellars, too, voices support for guaranteed income. "I suggest the following modification of [Marx's] distributive axiom. 'From each according to his ability, to each a justifiable competence, and to society as a whole a touch of magnificence.'"[72] The implication, of course, is that a guaranteed income will make society as a whole a bit more magnificent.

Lamont sees a guaranteed income as a very plausible goal. He claims, "In the United States, an intelligently run economy such as socialism proposes could promptly guarantee to every American family an annual return of goods and services equivalent in value to more than $5,000."[73]

Socialistic Humanists may not agree on all the intermediate steps necessary for the transition to socialism in the United States, but they do generally agree on the method of redistributing wealth. The idea of guaranteed income ties in with Dewey's notion of liberty, because it would (in theory) grant more economic freedom for all. It also ties in with Fromm's notion of the loss of man's humanity, because (presumably) man would gain his humanity back once he escaped the coercion of the capitalists. In fact, guaranteed income is appealing to any Humanist who believes, usually on ethical grounds, that we must find a method of redistributing wealth.

Conclusion

Socialism is not an inescapable tenet for anyone claiming to be a Humanist. In fact, some Humanists, especially in the United States, avidly support the free enterprise system. However, socialism is more consistent with the Humanist worldview than is free enterprise, and most of the men who have played a role in shaping Humanist thought in the last century have been socialists.

If one denies the inherent fallen nature of man, socialism becomes the most attractive economic system for creating a heaven on earth. For the Humanist, there is no original sin to stand in the way of creating a helping, sharing community on earth. Therefore, the economic system best suited to promote the ethics of Humanism and amend the evils of capitalism is socialism—or so the argument goes. Lamont claims this has been proven in the Soviet Union and China.

Regardless of proof, many Humanist leaders are bursting with suggestions to effect the transition to socialism in the United States. The most popular facet of socialism for the Humanist is the redistribution of wealth through guaranteed income. This plan meshes with their ethical belief.

Holding to the evolutionary perspective, some Humanists are

convinced that socialism is the next, proper step in man's evolution to a better social being. Indeed, some Humanists view socialism in the United States as inevitable. Socialism *will* replace capitalism because it is a system better adapted to society's changing needs. "We are in for some kind of socialism," predicts Dewey, "call it by whatever name we please, and no matter what it will be called when it is realized."[74]

[1]Erich Fromm, *On Disobedience and Other Essays* (New York: Seabury Press, 1981), p. 90.
[2]Paul Kurtz, "Is Everyone a Humanist?" *The Humanist Alternative*, ed. Paul Kurtz (Buffalo: Prometheus Books, 1973), p. 180.
[3]Julian Huxley, *Essays of a Humanist* (London: Chatto and Windus, 1964), p. 81.
[4]Erich Fromm, *The Sane Society* (New York: Ballantine Books, 1988), p. 125.
[5]Ibid., p. 126.
[6]Robert Sheaffer, "Socialism is Incompatible with Humanism," *Free Inquiry*, Fall 1989, p. 19.
[7]Ibid., p. 13.
[8]Ibid., p. 14.
[9]Marvin Zimmerman, "Hooked on Freedom and Science," in *Sidney Hook: Philosopher of Democracy and Humanism*, ed. Paul Kurtz (Buffalo: Prometheus Books, 1983), p. 80.
[10]Sheaffer, "Socialism is Incompatible with Humanism," p. 19.
[11]Ibid., p. 20.
[12]Sidney Hook, *Out of Step* (New York: Harper & Row, 1987), pp. 600-601.
[13]Antony G. N. Flew, "The Socialist Obsession," in *Sidney Hook: Philosopher of Democracy and Humanism*, ed. Kurtz, p. 35.
[14]Kurtz, "Is Everyone a Humanist?" p. 181. "In Europe," says Kurtz, "humanists tend to be socialists. In America a growing percentage tend to be libertarians [capitalists]." Paul Kurtz, "Libertarianism or Socialism: Where do Secular Humanists Stand?" *Free Inquiry*, Fall 1989, p. 4.
[15]Ludwig von Mises, *Socialism: An Economic and Sociological Analysis* (Indianapolis: Liberty Classics, 1981), pp. 9-10.
[16]Fromm, *On Disobedience and Other Essays*, p. 82.
[17]*Humanist Manifesto I* (Buffalo: Prometheus Books, 1980), p. 10.
[18]*Humanist Manifesto II* (Buffalo: Prometheus Books, 1980), p. 22.
[19]Corliss Lamont, *Voice in the Wilderness* (Buffalo: Prometheus Books, 1975), p. 163.
[20]Ibid.
[21]Ibid., p. 309.
[22]John Dewey, *Liberalism and Social Action* (New York: G. P. Putnam's Sons, 1935), pp. 36-7.
[23]Ibid., p. 54.
[24]Hook, *Out of Step*, p. 139.
[25]Roy Wood Sellars, *Social Patterns and Political Horizons* (Nashville: Aurora Publishers, Inc., 1970), p. 340.
[26]Fromm, *On Disobedience and Other Essays*, p. 74.
[27]Flew, "The Socialist Obsession," in *Sidney Hook: Philosopher of Democracy and Humanism*, ed. Kurtz, p. 36; citing Hook, *Political Power and Personal Freedom*, 1959, p. 398.
[28]John Kenneth Galbraith, *Economics, Peace and Laughter* (Boston: Houghton Mifflin, 1971), p. 101.
[29]John Kenneth Galbraith, *Who Needs the Democrats and What It Takes to Be Needed* (Garden City: Doubleday and Co., 1970), p. 73.
[30]Hook, *Out of Step*, p. 30.
[31]Ibid., p. 599.
[32]Ibid., p. 4.
[33]Lamont, *Voice in the Wilderness*, p. 164.
[34]Dewey, *Liberalism and Social Action*, p. 88.
[35]Ibid., p. 90.
[36]Fromm, *On Disobedience and Other Essays*, p. 76.
[37]Lamont, *Voice in the Wilderness*, p. 167.
[38]Ibid., p. 168.
[39]Fromm, *On Disobedience and Other Essays*, pp. 75-6.
[40]Ibid., p. 62.
[41]Ibid., p. 33.
[42]Ibid., p. 64.
[43]Lamont, *Voice in the Wilderness*, p. 166.
[44]Ibid., p. 169. Lamont is clearly confused about economic theories. In reality, fascism is more closely akin to

socialism than to capitalism, for while fascism leaves titular ownership of productive property in private hands, it insists that only the central government should *control* productive property. Capitalist philosophy has always held that control was an essential element of ownership. Therefore capitalism regards fascism as allowing private ownership of the means of production in name only, and not in substance. The only difference between fascism and socialism is that the former allows people to hold legal title to capital; neither allows them to *control* it. It is no wonder, therefore, that of the two major fascist movements in this century, one in Italy under Mussolini and the other Germany under Hitler, the latter called itself *National Socialism*, i.e., Nazism.

[45]Sellars, *Social Patterns and Political Horizons*, p. 359.

[46]Dewey, *Liberalism and Social Action*, pp. 79-80.

[47]Ibid., pp. 35-6.

[48]Ibid., p. 38.

[49]Corliss Lamont, *A Lifetime of Dissent* (Buffalo: Prometheus Books, 1988), p. 367.

[50]Lamont, *Voice in the Wilderness*, p. 166.

[51]Ibid., p. 169.

[52]Lamont, *A Lifetime of Dissent*, p. 86.

[53]Lamont, *Voice in the Wilderness*, p. 198.

[54]Hook, *Out of Step*, p. 30.

[55]Lamont, *A Lifetime of Dissent*, p. 367.

[56]Donald Clark Hodges, *Socialist Humanism* (St. Louis: Warren H. Green, 1974), p. 105.

[57]John Dewey, *Democracy and Education* (New York: Macmillan, 1916), p. 44.

[58]Sellars, *Social Patterns and Political Horizons*, p. 391.

[59]Lamont, *Voice in the Wilderness*, p. 167.

[60]Ibid., p. 270.

[61]Lamont, *A Lifetime of Dissent*, p. 321.

[62]Sellars, *Social Patterns and Political Horizons*, p. 367.

[63]Hook, *Out of Step*, p. 124.

[64]Ibid., p. 600.

[65]Ibid., p. 599.

[66]Ibid., p. 600.

[67]Lamont, *Voice in the Wilderness*, pp. 169-70.

[68]Fromm, *On Disobedience and Other Essays*, pp. 79-80.

[69]Ibid., p. 100.

[70]Ibid., p. 80.

[71]Dewey, *Liberalism and Social Action*, pp. 63-4.

[72]Sellars, *Social Patterns and Political Horizons*, p. 393.

[73]Lamont, *Voice in the Wilderness*, p. 167.

[74]John Dewey, *Individualism, Old and New* (New York: 1930), p. 119.

CHAPTER

28

MARXIST/ LENINIST ECONOMICS

"The theory of Communists may be summed up in the single sentence: Abolition of private property."[1]

—Karl Marx

"Communist society means that everything—the land, the factories—is owned in common. Communism means working in common."[2]

—V. I. Lenin

"The economic basis of the new world order must be the establishment of a unified planned system of economy."[3]

—Georgi Shakhnazarov

"I am a convinced socialist. . . . As we dismantle the Stalinist system, we are not retreating from socialism but are moving toward it."[4]

—Mikhail Gorbachev

SUMMARY

The Marxist/Leninist worldview's theology is atheism; its philosophy is dialectical materialism; its economics is socialism/communism. It is probably safe to say that before Karl Marx, people did not view economics and modes of production as crucial to either their consciousness or the quest for utopia. Since Marx, economics has never been the same.

Marx's counterpart, Frederick Engels, best demonstrated the primacy of economic theory in Marxism's worldview when he declared, "the final causes of all social changes and political revolutions are to be sought, not in men's brains, not in man's better insight into eternal truth and justice, but in changes in the modes of production and exchange. They are to be sought, not in the *philosophy*, but in the *economics* of each particular epoch."[5] This claim obviously has far-reaching implications—not only in the economic discipline, but in psychology, sociology, philosophy, ethics, and history. This chapter focuses on the economic aspects of Marxism.

Because the Marxist assumes that the mode of production forms the foundation for society, he concludes that any ills extant in society are the result of imperfect modes of production. Further, societies have been gradually improving because the economic systems on which they have been founded are gradually improving (thanks to the progressive forces of evolution and the dialectic). Slavery was imperfect, so the dialectical process led society into feudalism, which in turn has formed the new synthesis of capitalism. Unfortunately, capitalism, too, has inherent flaws and contradictions that have led to the oppression of the working class by the bourgeois.

Marxists believe that the proletariat (those without property) and the bourgeois (those who own private property and/or the tools of production) are clashing within the framework of dialectical materialism and that their clash eventually will result in a new, more highly evolved synthesis. This synthesis, which has already been achieved in the Soviet Union and the People's Republic of China (among other countries), is known as socialism. With the advent of socialism, a whole new society

Introduction

Economics plays a much larger role in the Marxist worldview than in either Christianity or Secular Humanism. In fact, economics acts as a major portion of the foundation for Marxist sociological, legal, political, and historical views. According to Marx:

> The general conclusion at which I arrived and which, once reached, continued to serve as the leading thread in my studies,

evolves. Marxists argue that all other social institutions follow the economic institution. Socialism removes the means of production from the hands of the minority (the bourgeois) and puts it in the hands of the State, the Party, or the people. Recent reports have revealed that the East German Communist Party, for example, was worth billions of dollars. Thus, in a socialist society, all private property will gradually be abolished and man no longer will oppress his fellow man in an effort to protect his private property. When all private property and, consequently, all class distinctions have withered away, the slow transition from socialism to the highest economic form, communism, will be complete. What economic form will follow communism will be determined by the eternal workings of the dialectic, but Marxists are hoping that once communism finally arrives it will remain for many, many years—some Marxists place the figure at millions of years.

For now, communism is the ultimate economic system because it adheres to the maxim, "From each according to his ability, to each according to his needs."[6] Whereas socialism is tainted by capitalism and thus will still reward resources to workers according to their labor, communism will create a society in which work becomes "life's prime want,"[7] thereby doing away with the need for incentives to work. Man will produce abundantly because he will be freed from coercion, and scarcity will become a distant memory.

The ultimate aim of Marxism/Leninism is the creation of a political world order based on communism that will solve the economic problem of scarcity so efficiently that each individual will see his every need and most of his wants fulfilled. Once communist man evolves, he will not want more than he knows is best for the new world order. Marx pictured the perfect communist society as one that would require a few hours of work each morning, with afternoons free for recreation, and evenings set aside for cultural activities.

may be briefly summed up as follows: In the social production which men carry on they enter into definite relations that are indispensable and independent of their will; these relations of production correspond to a definite stage of development of their material powers of production. The sum total of these relations of production constitutes the economic structure of society—the real foundation on which rise legal and political superstructures and to which correspond definite forms of social consciousness. The mode of production in material life

Notes and Asides

> determines the general character of the social, political, and spiritual processes of life.[8]

For the Marxist, a society's economic system affects the laws enacted, the type of government, and the whole role of society in day-to-day life and throughout history. While every individual would grant that economics affects these realms to some extent, the Marxist claims that economics dictates their precise character. Marxism believes that a nation's economic system controls the direction of every other institution in that society.

Working with this premise, Marxists naturally draw the conclusion that one economic system is superior to all others, because one system must direct society in a more positive manner than any others. They point to the evils in capitalist society and conclude that capitalism is an economic system with inherent problems that poison all of society. Thus, for the Marxist, capitalism must be replaced with a more humane economic system.

According to Marx, *the key problem with capitalism is that it breeds exploitation*. He says that in capitalist society the bourgeoisie has resolved personal worth into exchange value, and "in one word, for exploitation, veiled by religious and political illusions, it has substituted naked, shameless, direct, brutal exploitation."[9] We will examine Marx's explanation for capitalism's inherent tendency to exploit later, but what is important to understand now is that every Marxist perceives capitalism as having outlived its usefulness.

In modern times, L. Leontyev echoes Marx:

> In reality capitalism exposes the bulk of the population, the working people, to exploitation by an insignificant minority. An insecure life, an uncertain future and worsening living conditions, such is the lot of millions of working people in capitalist society. The mechanics of capitalist society is such that the workers constantly remain propertyless proletarians whose only choice is to sell their labour power.[10]

Marx denied every positive aspect of capitalism. He believed that any benefits resulting from private property could not justify tolerating a capitalist system, saying,

> You are horrified at our intending to do away with private property. But in your existing society, private property is already done away with for nine-tenths of the population; its existence for the few is solely due to its nonexistence in the hands of those nine-tenths.[11]

Notes and Asides

Have the Marxists changed their views about capitalism since Marx's time? Not significantly. "The social effects of capitalism," writes Kenneth Neill Cameron, "are clearly still basically the same as when Engels saw them in 1845. The worker is still sold, as in the 1840s, 'like a piece of goods.' The masses are still doped with drink and religion, still fleeced by patent medicine firms, still thrown on the scrap heap when old; families are still riven by conflicts arising inevitably from exploitation and oppression; prostitution is still rife; crime rampant; the prisons full. Workers are still killed or maimed by the thousands in industrial accidents and slowly poisoned by chemicals at their work, probably at a higher rate than in Engels's day. To these horrors, monopoly capitalism had added those of massive war, whose half-human victims are hidden away by the millions in hospitals and psychiatric institutions; and it now threatens humanity with nuclear destruction and chemical and bacteriological warfare."[12]

Yet Marxist attitudes toward capitalism have changed since the time of Engels and Marx in one sense: Marxists in charge of actual socialistic states have shown themselves willing to fall back on capitalistic methods as a practical means of saving their economies. For example, Lenin reversed himself and allowed possession of private property to rejuvenate the Soviet economy in the early 1920s (calling his program "The New Economic Policy"), and Mikhail Gorbachev, still an avowed Leninist[13] and socialist,[14] is trying to use similar methods today under the new name *perestroika*. For both Lenin and Gorbachev—indeed, for Marxists everywhere—it is simply a matter of perspective: capitalism is seen as a necessary evil, a means to an end; the end itself is socialism/communism.

Capitalism's Self-Destruction

According to the Marxist, capitalism is so destructive that it will eventually destroy itself. Marxists believe that the system of exploitation will simply exploit more and more people until virtually everyone is a member of the proletariat. "All the social functions of the capitalist are now performed by salaried employees," says Engels. "The capitalist has no further social function than that of pocketing dividends, tearing off coupons, and gambling on the Stock Exchange, where the different capitalists despoil one another of their capital. At first the capitalistic mode of production forces out the workers. Now it forces out the capitalists, and reduces them, just as it reduced the workers, to the ranks of the surplus population. . . ."[15]

Engels goes on to describe what happens next:

Notes and Asides

> Whilst the capitalist mode of production more and more completely transforms the great majority of the population into proletarians, it creates the power which, under penalty of its own destruction, is forced to accomplish this revolution. Whilst it forces on more and more the transformation of the vast means of production, already socialized, into state property, it shows itself the way to accomplishing this revolution. The proletariat seizes political power and turns the means of production into state property.[16]

This revolt by the proletariat is crucial for assisting the downfall of capitalism. The proletariat must act as the catalyst for the creation of the new system. Moscow's *Political Dictionary* states,

> Capitalism is the last social system founded on the exploitation of man by man. Under capitalism all the resources of society are in the hands of a small group of private owners—capitalists and landowners—who exploit the workers and peasants. The bourgeois state defends the interests of the capitalists and landowners. The church and school, science and art are all put into the service of capitalist exploitation. The extremely sharp class conflict between the exploiters and the exploited constitutes the basic trait of the capitalist system. The development of capitalism inevitably leads to its downfall. However, the system of exploitations does not disappear of itself. It is destroyed only as the result of the revolutionary struggle and the victory of the proletariat.[17]

Under socialism, "It is no longer the consumers, but the government who decides what should be produced and in what quantity and quality."
—Ludwig von Mises

On the surface it would appear that Marxists are not at all certain of the victory of the proletariat and the self-destruction of capitalism. However, once the dialectic is taken into account, this uncertainty vanishes. For Marxist, it is historically inevitable: the thesis (bourgeoisie) and the antithesis (proletariat) *must* clash and create a synthesis—socialism—and socialism guarantees the advent of communism.

The Inevitability of Communism

Nikita Khrushchev had no doubt that communism will eventually succeed. "We are firmly convinced of the full and final triumph of communism," says Khrushchev. "This conviction rests on the knowledge of the laws of development of human society which were discovered by Marx, Engels, and Lenin and which possess a force similar to that of the laws of nature, because they too operated objectively."[18]

Used by permission of the *Colorado Springs Gazette Telegraph*

Georgi Shakhnazarov agrees: "Socialism is not simply the dictate of common sense, nor is it only an expression of the will of the working class. It is the inevitable result of the natural direction that society takes and can be seen as the historically predetermined destiny of mankind."[19] A. I. Mikoyan declares,

> From year to year history directs mankind along the path to socialism. The victory of socialism throughout the world is inevitable, and just as inevitable is the doom of capitalism. This makes the imperialists angry. Let them be enraged. History is with us and history is the first and foremost judge. Revolutions are the locomotives of history. All that is progressive and honest in the world rallies to the banners of socialism.[20]

The Marxists believe this inevitable victory of communism will occur worldwide. Khrushchev says, "We consider the cause of building socialism and communism to be a great international affair."[21] Elsewhere he states, "We are convinced that sooner or later capitalism will perish, just as feudalism perished earlier. The socialist nations are advancing towards communism. All the world will come to communism. History does not ask whether you want it or not."[22] John Strachey believes the same thing, saying in effect that the world has no other choice: "The science of social change, by revealing the determinate curve of capitalist development, on a world scale and over the centuries, gives us an assurance that in the end socialism will be established throughout the globe. For the only alternative to socialism now before the human race is a decline into a new epoch of barbarism, involving the physical destruction of by far the larger part of the population of such advanced, highly integrated capitalist civilisations as those of Britain and America."[23]

According to Marxism, the whole world will soon embrace communism. Is this any different from the prediction that we will soon have a socialist world system? Is there a difference between communism and socialism?

Differences Between Socialism and Communism

There is a subtle difference between communism and socialism, according to the Marxist. Socialism is simply the first phase of communism—it is a step in the transition to total communism. Therefore, Marxists speak consistently when they predict an inevitable global system of socialism and also an inevitable global system of communism. Socialism will precede communism in the transition to the perfect economic system.

The basic difference between the two systems is best summed up by the *Political Dictionary*:

> Socialism is a social system under which, as a result of the socialist revolution and the consolidation of the dictatorship of the proletariat, private ownership of the means of production is abolished, social, socialist ownership is established as the basis of society, and the exploiting classes are eliminated. Under socialism, no longer are there exploiters and exploited. Manufactured products are distributed according to the work in line with the principle: he who does not work, does not eat. . . . Socialism is the first phase of communism. The principle of socialism is: from each according to his abilities, to each according to his work. . . . Under communism the basic principle of society will be: from each according to his abilities, to each according to his needs.[24]

p695

Marx says simply, "the theory of the Communists may be summed up in the single sentence: Abolition of private property."[25] Lenin expands on this statement slightly: "Communist society means that everything—the land, the factories—is owned in common. Communism means working in common."[26] These are both oversimplifications of the goals Marx and Lenin set for the communist state. Joseph Stalin best defines communism:

> The anatomy of communist society may be described as . . . a society in which: a) there will be no private ownership of the means of production but social collective ownership; b) there will be no classes or state but workers in industry and agriculture managing their economic affairs as free associations of toilers; c) national economy organized according to plan will be based on the highest technique in both industry and agriculture; d) there is no antagonism between city and country, between industrial and agricultural economy; e) the products will be distributed according to the principle of the old French communists, "from each according to his ability, to each according to his needs;" f) science and art will enjoy conditions conducive to their highest development; g) the individual, freed from bread-and-butter cares and of the necessity of cringing to the "powers that be" will become really free.[27]

Communism is a more advanced stage of socialism. We will examine the differences between the two systems and the characteristics of the transition from capitalism to communism later, but first we must examine Marx's view of capitalism to understand better why he dismisses it as an evil system.

Notes and Asides

> "[T]he theory of the Communists may be summed up in the single sentence: Abolition of private property."
>
> —Karl Marx

The Evils of Capitalism

For Marx, two flaws necessarily cause capitalism to be a system of exploitation. The first flaw Marx describes as the problem of surplus labor. According to this concept, the bourgeoisie make their profits not by selling their product at a price above the cost of materials plus labor, but rather by paying the worker less than the proper amount for his labor value.

This idea begins with the theory that all commodities are given their relative value by labor. Marx says, "The relative values of commodities are, therefore, determined by the respective quantities or amounts of labor, worked up, realized, fixed in them."[28] Because labor plays such

Notes and Asides

an intricate role in determining value, Marx claims, it is all the more open to exploitation. He writes, “These laborers, who must sell themselves piecemeal, are a commodity, like every other article of commerce, and are consequently exposed to all the vicissitudes of competition, to all the fluctuations of the market.”[29]

This ability of the bourgeoisie to manipulate the workers allows them to devalue labor, thereby creating a profit for themselves by lowering the price they must pay for labor power. Cameron describes it this way: “If, however, goods are ultimately sold at their exchange values and these values are embodied labor, how can we account for profit? The answer, Marx contended, lay in the fact that some of the embodied labor is in fact unpaid—‘surplus labor.’ What the worker sells is not his labor as such but his ‘Laboring Power, the temporary disposal of which he makes over to the capitalist.’”[30]

For the Marxist, capitalism creates a vicious circle, causing the workers to be exploited more and more. Within the capitalist system, said Marx,

> all means for the development of production transform themselves into means of domination over, and exploitation of, the producers; they mutilate the laborer into a fragment of a man, degrade him to the level of an appendage of a machine, destroy every remnant of charm in his work and turn it into a hated toil . . . They transform his life time into working time, and drag his wife and child beneath the wheels of the Juggernaut of capital. But all methods for the production of surplus-value are at the same time methods of accumulation; and every extension of accumulation becomes again the means for the development of those methods. It follows therefore that in proportion as capital accumulates, the lot of the laborer, be his payment high or low, must grow worse.[31]

Elsewhere he says more succinctly, “Accumulation of wealth at one pole is, therefore, at the same time accumulation of misery, agony of toil, slavery, ignorance, brutality, mental degradation, at the opposite pole, i.e., on the side of the class that produces its own product in the form of capital.”[32]

This Marxist conception of capitalism is still prevalent today. “The capitalist, on the other hand, transforms the product of the workers’ surplus labour into cash,” says Leontyev. “This money can again be used as additional capital to produce more surplus value. This being the case, the greed for surplus labour under capitalism knows no limits. The capitalists use all and every means to intensify the exploitation of their wage slaves. Capital, as Marx said, exhibits a truly wolfish greed for

Notes and Asides

surplus labour."[33] For the Marxist, greed breeds more greed in the capitalist system, and this greed always preys upon the worker.

The second flaw in capitalism, according to Marxism, is its chaotic nature. Whereas the state can control every aspect of socialism (from production to distribution), capitalism is controlled by the free market of exchange. Technically, capitalism is known as a market-directed economy, and socialism is referred to as a centrally planned economy, although in practice most economies are a mixture of both. At the very least, we may say that capitalism tends to be market-directed and socialism tends to be centrally planned. In a socialistic system, economic decisions regarding price, production, consumption, etc. are made by central planners affiliated with the government; whereas in capitalism, economic decisions are made by every producer and every consumer—a housewife with a shopping list, for example, is an economic planner in a capitalistic system.

> **"If the market is not allowed to steer the whole economic apparatus, the government must do it."**
>
> **—Ludwig von Mises**

Marxism stresses this difference, claiming that only a planned economy can truly discover the best methods of production, distribution, etc. The capitalist economy not only flourishes in but also relies on crises to stimulate the economy, according to the Marxist. This reliance on crises will create economic havoc in the long run, Marx writes:

> The conditions of bourgeois society are too narrow to comprise the wealth created by them. And how does the bourgeoisie get over these crises? On the one hand by enforced destruction of a mass of productive forces; on the other, by the conquest of new markets, and by the more thorough exploitation of the old ones. That is to say, by paving the way for more extensive and more destructive crises, and by diminishing the means whereby crises are prevented.[34]

This spontaneous, erratic, free-wheeling system must be replaced by a planned economy. "The economic laws of capitalism and of all earlier forms of society," says Leontyev, "operate spontaneously. People cannot control them just as they cannot control lightning. So long as there is private ownership of the means of production people are unable consciously to use the economic laws of social development, which like the forces of nature operate blindly, violently and destructively. Based as it is on public ownership of the means of production,

Notes and Asides

socialism unites the economy into a single whole. Economic development becomes a sphere of conscious and purposeful activity just as production at every individual enterprise."[35]

The Soviet Union is the prime example of a planned economy. The *Political Dictionary* states, "Planned economy exists only in the USSR. The state of workers and peasants, having concentrated in its hands large-scale industry, land, transport, foreign trade, and banks, develops the entire national economy according to a plan; it plans beforehand what means of production and consumption should be produced, at what time, and how they should be distributed."[36]

Marxists would have the coming world order guided by an economic system like the Soviet system, even though it would require a number of adjustments and controls. Shakhnazarov states, "The economic basis of the new world order must be the establishment of a unified planned system of economy. The federal organs must have the right to redistribute resources and to control profits by means of a unified pricing policy, taxation and money system and the creation of funds for resolving global problems."[37]

In theory, this new world order would result in a much more orderly, much more just economic system. No longer would most of the world be faced with a system that relies largely on crises to maintain its mechanisms. Therefore, the second great flaw of capitalism points up one of the "positive" aspects of communism—it is, by definition, a planned economy. Marxists, indeed, believe there are numerous positive aspects to the socialism-turning-communism system.

Positive Aspects of "Scientific" Socialism/Communism

The Marxist believes his economic system has more positive aspects than any other system because it is the only truly "scientific" approach. Engels wrote about "Scientific Socialism" in his book *Socialism: Utopian and Scientific*, and in the contemporary book *Political Economy: Socialism* we read,

> The political economy of socialism is a living, rapidly developing science. Its foundations were laid by Karl Marx and Frederick Engels, who revealed the tendencies in the development of capitalism that were leading inevitably to its downfall and the triumph of the communist mode of production. From their analysis of these tendencies Marx and Engels revealed the main features of the future communist society and especially of its

Notes and Asides

> first phase, socialism, and in so doing transformed socialism from a utopia into a science.[38]

V. Afanasyev expands on the goals of this "science:"

> Scientific communism is a science dealing with the ways and means of destroying capitalism, with the laws governing the creation of the new, communist society, and with the economic, social and spiritual conditions for the all-round development of man; it is a science dealing with communist society as a complex social organism; it is a science dealing with the conscious, purposeful direction of social processes in the interests of man.[39]

As a science, communism purports to have many positive dimensions. Marxists claim that communism provides more freedom than any other system. "Communism assures people freedom from threat of war; it brings lasting peace, freedom from imperialist oppression and exploitation, and from unemployment and poverty. It leads to general prosperity and a high standard of living, freedom from fear of economic crises, and a rapid growth of the productive forces for the benefit of society as a whole."[40]

This freedom arises largely because communism promotes democracy, according to Leontyev. "Socialism effectuates genuine democracy," he says, "Socialist democratism guarantees both political freedoms and social rights: freedom of speech, the press and assembly, including the holding of mass meetings, the right to elect and be elected, the right to work, rest and leisure, education, and maintenance in old age and also in the case of sickness or disability. Socialism ensures the equality of rights of citizens whatever their nationality or race, it accords women all rights on an equal footing with men in all spheres of economic, government and cultural activity, and guarantees genuine freedom of the individual."[41]

> "The bad workmen, who form the majority of the operatives in many branches of industry, are decidedly of opinion that bad workmen ought to receive the same wages as good."
> —John Stuart Mill

Another theoretical benefit of communism lies in the Marxist belief that the redistribution of wealth will solve a great many problems. A. Denisov and M. Kirichenko claim, "Under the socialist system of economy the distribution of the national income, which is the product of free creative labor, is aimed at the expansion of socialist production, steady improvement of the material well-being and cultural level of all working people, consolidation of the independence and defence capacity of the socialist state. Thus, it serves the interests of the people as a whole."[42] Redistribution of wealth is presented as a cure-all in the text

Notes and Asides

Political Economy: Socialism, as well: "Once the exploiting classes with their parasitic consumption have been abolished, the national income becomes wholly at the disposal of the people. Working conditions are radically altered, housing conditions in town and country substantially improved and all the achievements of modern culture made accessible to the working people."[43]

Still another Marxist-perceived advantage of communism lies in its ability to motivate workers. "Can capitalist society with its chronic unemployment ensure each citizen the opportunity to work, let alone to choose the work he likes? Clearly, it cannot. But the socialist system makes the right to work a constitutional right of a citizen, delivering him from the oppressive anxiety and uncertainty over the morrow. Free

CLOSE-UP

Nikita Khrushchev (1894-1971)

Nikita Khrushchev, one of the twentieth century's most powerful Marxist leaders, had humble beginnings. His father worked as a miner in Yuzovka, Russia. At age 15, Khrushchev began work as an apprentice mechanic, and eventually secured a job as a machine repairman in regional coal mines. He joined the Red Army in 1918, and served almost three years before returning to Yuzkova. After graduating from the Donets Industrial Institute in 1925, he began his career as a full-time communist party official by working as a secretary of a district party committee. His loyalty to the party was rewarded in 1949, when he was called to Moscow to serve in the party's Secretariat, directed by Stalin. When Stalin died in 1953, Khrushchev became one of the most powerful eight men in the USSR. In just two years, through shrewd political moves, he was firmly entrenched as both head of the government and the communist party. While his reign was generally characterized by efforts to end the terror inflicted by the Stalin regime, he showed himself to be every bit as dedicated as Stalin to the Marxist ideal of world communism. His dedication to this ideal was manifested in the Cuban missile crisis, when he pushed the world to the brink of nuclear war by placing nuclear weapons in Cuba, and then lying to the United States about their existence.

Notes and Asides

labor becomes not only a means of subsistence, but also the chief measure of the social value of man, a matter of honor and valor for him."[44]

In short, socialism/communism is the only "scientific" economic system capable of affecting society and history for the good. Shakhnazarov sums up: "a just and rational world order can arise only on a socialist basis."[45] The positive advantages of the Marxist economic system, according to the Marxists, will have a positive impact on all aspects of our world, from ethics to politics.

Socialism in Practice

Marxists often point to countries already practicing socialism to prove the advantageous nature of this economic system. "The progressive nature of socialism and communism in history can be proven not only theoretically but also from practical results of the successful development of the world socialist system and of the transition of new countries and peoples to the socialist path."[46] Marxists claim that the success of socialism in these countries demonstrates the positive impact it could have throughout the world.

For example, L. Leontyev declares, "Convincing proof of socialism's decisive superiority over capitalism is offered by the consistent rise in the standard of living in socialist countries."[47] And the text *Political Economy: Socialism* proclaims, "The years of experience of socialist construction in the Soviet Union and a number of other countries have confirmed the correctness of Marxist-Leninist economic doctrine."[48]

When socialism finally achieves all that it is capable of in socialist countries, not even the staunchest supporters of capitalism will be able to deny the need for world socialism, according to Khrushchev, who predicted,

> The victory of the USSR in economic competition with the U.S., the victory of the whole socialist system over the capitalist system, will be the biggest turning point in history, will exert still more powerful, revolutionizing influence on the workers' movement all over the world. Then, even to the greatest skeptics, it will become clear that it is only socialism that provides everything necessary for the happy life of man, and they will make their choice in favor of socialism.[49]

Thus, Marxism believes a world system of socialism/communism will inevitably prevail largely due to its obvious merits, proven by its

Notes and Asides

practice in certain countries, including the Soviet Union. These merits, according to many Marxists, become more and more obvious every day—rapidly paving the way for world communism.

It must be stressed, however, that Marxists believe a communist system does not yet exist anywhere in the world. Many countries now rely on a socialist economic system, but the final stage—pure communism—has not yet been attained anywhere. The world must embrace socialism before it can embrace communism. The differences between the two systems are subtle but real.

Stages in the Transition to Pure Communism

Why must a transitional phase necessarily exist between capitalism and communism? Engels addresses this question by asking, "Will it be possible to abolish private property at one stroke?" and then answering: "No, such a thing would be just as impossible as at one stroke to increase the existing productive forces to the degree necessary for instituting community of property. Hence, the proletarian revolution, which in all probability is impending, will transform existing society only gradually, and be able to abolish private property only when the necessary quantity of the means of production has been created."[50] Therefore, because both the abolition of private property and the refining of the means of production must happen gradually, the move to communism requires a transitional phase.

Marx tells us, "Between capitalist and communist society lies a period of revolutionary transformation from one to the other."[51] This period is usually labelled by the Marxist as "socialism," although it is sometimes referred to as the "dictatorship of the proletariat." *Scientific Communism: A Glossary* spells it out: "The different stages in the development of society based on public ownership of the means of production are the two phases of communism, the lower—socialism, and the higher—complete or developed communism."[52] This view is still espoused by Marxists. Maurice Cornforth states, "Marx quite clearly defined where we have to go in terms of communism, explaining that the socialist organisation of social production which must immediately replace capitalism is only a transitional stage towards a communist society."[53]

This transitional stage of socialism will be a blend between capitalism and communism. "Theoretically," says Lenin, "there can be no doubt that between capitalism and communism there lies a definite transition period which must combine the features and properties of both these forms of social economy. This transition period has to be a period of struggle between dying capitalism and nascent commu-

Notes and Asides

nism—or, in other words, between capitalism which has been defeated but not destroyed and communism which has been born but is still very feeble."[54]

The main difference between socialism and communism is that socialism will not have abolished all the problems created by capitalism, whereas communism will. Strachey tells us, "The socialist system of distribution will, then, abolish social classes. But it will not create equality of income."[55] This inequality of income will result largely because this transitional stage will operate according to the maxim "From each according to his abilities, to each according to his work." Only in pure communism will work become such an integral part of every individual's life that each man can receive "according to his needs."

Marxists also confess that suppression and terror must still exist during the socialist transition. Lenin states,

> Furthermore, during the transition from capitalism to communism suppression is still necessary, but it is now the suppression of the exploiting minority by the exploited majority. A special apparatus, a special machine for suppression, the "state," is still necessary, but this is now a transitional state.[56]

This state is still necessary because not everyone will accept a dictatorship of the proletariat, and so the new economic system must be enforced.

Pure communism, the final phase of society's development, will only result from society's constant maturation in the socialist phase. Engels describes the specifics for the new society's emergence:

> Finally, when all capital, all production, and all exchange are concentrated in the hands of the nation, private ownership will automatically have ceased to exist, money will have become superfluous, and production will have so increased and men will be so much changed that the last forms of the old social relations will also be able to fall away.[57]

This new society, under pure communism, will not require any form of government. Lenin writes, "And so in capitalist society we have a democracy that is curtailed, wretched, false, a democracy only for the rich, for the minority. The dictatorship of the proletariat, the period of transition to communism, will for the first time create democracy for the people, for the majority, along with the necessary suppression of the exploiters, of the minority. Communism alone is capable of providing really complete democracy, and the more complete it is, the sooner it

> "What is a communist? One who has yearnings/ For equal division of unequal earnings."
> —Ebenezer Elliot

Notes and Asides

will become unnecessary and wither away of its own accord."[58] Lenin goes on to explain why the state will become unnecessary under communism: "Lastly, only communism makes the state absolutely unnecessary, for there is nobody to be suppressed—'nobody' in the sense of a class, of a systematic struggle against a definite section of the population."[59]

Another characteristic of the new world order under pure communism will be the individual's new attitude toward work. *Scientific Communism: A Glossary* claims,

> When the psychological repugnance to labor caused by capitalism was overcome, personal and collective material interest began to combine with a selfless interest based on ideals, moral-social incentives, and enthusiasm for work on the part of the popular masses—a result of the socialist revolution. . . . As communist society matures, awareness of the need to toil for the common benefit will turn into a habit for all its members.[60]

Communism, as described by the Marxist, refers to an economic system based on socialism, in which no classes exist and everyone works according to his ability and receives according to his need.

Marx himself provides us with the best summation of the second and final phase of communism. In a higher phase of communist society, says Marx,

> after the enslaving subordination of the individual to the division of labor shall have disappeared, and with it the antagonism between the intellectual and manual labor, after labor has become not only a means of life but also the primary necessity of life, when, with the development of the individual in every sense, the productive forces also increase and all the springs of collective wealth flow with abundance—only then can the limited horizon of bourgeois right be left behind entirely and society inscribe upon its banner: "from each according to his abilities, to each according to his needs."[61]

The Transition in Practice

In 1918, the Marxist effort to rapidly install socialism in Russia resulted in a Soviet Constitution that proclaimed that "all private property in land is abolished, and the entire land is declared to be national property and is to be apportioned among agriculturists without any compensation to the former owners, in the measure of each one's ability to till it."[62] The first phase in the transition to socialism is to take the property from its rightful owners.

Lenin quickly realized, however, that the Russian economy would never survive such a rapid change to socialism. In 1921 he declared, "We are no longer attempting to break up the old social economic order, with its trade, its small-scale economy and private initiative, its capitalism, but we are now trying to revive trade, private enterprise, and capitalism, at the same time gradually and cautiously subjecting them to state regulation just as far as they revive."[63]

Does it seem odd that such a dedicated Marxist would find himself forced to revert back to capitalism? Lenin recognizes the danger of his position and is careful to justify his stance: "Capitalism is an evil in comparison with socialism, but capitalism is a blessing in comparison with medievalism, with small industry, with fettered small producers thrown to the mercy of bureaucracy."[64] Lenin claimed that Russia had not even progressed to an advanced stage of capitalism, and therefore must first undergo such a phase before the move to socialism.

During this move through advanced capitalism to beginning socialism, Lenin was willing to experiment with a number of other social methods to hasten the transition. He suggested experimentation to discover the best means of dealing with people not doing their share of the work, saying,

> Thousands of practical forms and methods of accounting and controlling the rich, the rogues and the idlers should be devised and put to a practical test by the communes themselves, by small units in town and country. Variety is a guarantee of virility here, a pledge of success in achieving the single common aim—to purge the land of Russia of all vermin, of fleas—the rogues, of bugs—the rich, and so on and so forth.

He then suggests some possible methods: imprisonment, forced labor, "one out of every ten idlers will be shot on the spot," etc.[65]

Communism and the Family

Marxists have distinct ideas about the role of the family in a socialist/communist system, as well. As the transition to communism becomes more complete, the family will increasingly fade from the picture.

Engels describes the beginning of the break-up of the family, writing, "With the transfer of the means of production into common ownership, the individual family ceases to be an economic unit of society. Private housekeeping is transformed into a social industry. The care and education of children become a public affair; society looks after all children equally, whether they are born in or out of wedlock."[66] Obviously, under this system the family unit loses much of its impor-

Notes and Asides

tance for society.

The active destruction of a certain type of family is advocated by G. Grigorov and S. Shkotov: "From the moment the family begins to oppose itself to society, enclosing itself in the narrow circle of purely domestic interests, it begins to play a conservative role in the whole social structure of life. This sort of family we are certainly obliged to destroy."[67] The same sentiment is voiced by M. N. Liadov, who writes,

> Is it possible to bring up collective man in an individual family? To this we must give a categorical response: No, a collectively thinking child may be brought up only in a social environment. . . . Every conscientious father and mother must say: If we want our child to be liberated from that philistinism which is present in each of us, he must be isolated from ourselves. . . . The sooner the child is taken from his mother and given over to a public nursery, the greater is the guarantee that he will be healthy.[68]

"The sooner the child is taken from his mother and given over to a public nursery, the greater is the guarantee that he will be healthy."
—M. N. Liadov

The text *The Family and the Way of Life* draws the logical conclusion resulting from these attitudes toward the nuclear family: "In future socialist society, where the obligation for the upbringing, education and maintenance of children will be shifted from the parents to society as a whole, it is clear that the family must wither away."[69] In other words, during the stage of socialism the family will be tolerated, but once communism is achieved the family will cease to exist. Everything will be in common.

Conclusion

Marxists see the world inevitably moving toward a socialistic world system, which will eventually make the transition to a communistic world order. This move is theoretically inevitable for two reasons: (1) dialectical materialism demands it, and (2) the success of scientific socialism in countries around the world is showing socialism to be a more humane and caring system of economics. Marxists also believe that once the world finally accepts capitalism as historically outdated, the traditional nuclear family of father, mother, and children will be an outdated institution as well.

To hasten the rise of socialism/communism, Marxists call for cuts in U.S. military spending and disarmament. Says Victor Perlo,

> The progress of detente and cutting of the military budget will create more favorable conditions for the working class to

Notes and Asides

> struggle for social reforms, to win economic and political concessions, and to conduct the struggle for the transition to socialism. The struggle for disarmament, for detente in the military field, is therefore a crucial struggle for the working people, and first of all in the United States.[70]

These military cuts and calls for disarmament, however, only take place in capitalist countries. The Soviet Union continues to arm in spite of the call for an end to the cold war with the West. *Scientific Communism: A Glossary* calls for increased military defense spending by countries already employing a socialistic system:

> Experience shows that, under present conditions, the victory of the socialist system in a country may be viewed as final and the restoration of capitalism may be considered excluded only if the communist party as the guiding force in society, firmly conducts a Marxist-Leninist policy in all spheres of social life; only if the party untiringly fortifies the defense of the country and protects its revolutionary gains; only if it retains and trains the people to maintain vigilance with regard to the class enemy and implacability toward bourgeois ideology; only if the principles of socialist internationalism are piously observed and unity and fraternal solidarity with other socialist countries are fortified.[71]

When communism becomes the world's economic system, Marxists believe it will remain the system of choice for millions of years. Cameron writes, "Marx and Engels expected that communist society would be the last form of human society, for once the world's productive forces were communally owned no other form could arise. They anticipated that it would last not merely for thousands but for millions of years."[72]

Nothing could be more ideal, from the Marxist point of view. Indeed, nothing else will even allow the human race to survive, according to Lenin. "Outside of socialism," says Lenin, "there is no salvation for mankind from war, hunger and the further destruction of millions and millions of human beings."[73]

[1]Karl Marx and Frederick Engels, *Collected Works*, forty volumes (New York: International Publishers, 1976), vol. 6, p. 498.
[2]V. I. Lenin, *Selected Works* (New York: International Publishers, 1937), vol. 9, p. 479.
[3]Georgi Shakhnazarov, *The Coming World Order* (Moscow: Progress Publishers, 1981), p. 214.
[4]*Time*, June 4, 1990, pp. 27, 31.
[5]Frederick Engels, *Socialism: Utopian and Scientific* (New York: International Publishers, 1935), p. 54.
[6]Karl Marx, *On Historical Materialism* (New York: International Publishers, 1974), p. 165.
[7]Ibid.
[8]Karl Marx, *Critique of Political Economy* (Chicago: Kerr, 1913), p. 11.
[9]Marx and Engels, *Collected Works*, vol. 6, p. 487.
[10]L. Leontyev, *Political Economy* (New York: International Publishers, 1978), p. 52.
[11]Marx and Engels, *Collected Works*, vol. 6, p. 500.
[12]Kenneth Neill Cameron, *Marxism: the Science of Society* (Massachusetts: Bergin & Garvey, 1985), p. 85.
[13]Mikhail Gorbachev, *Perestroika: New Thinking for Our Country and the World* (New York: Harper and Row, 1987), p. 11.
[14]*Time*, June 4, 1990, pp. 27, 31.
[15]Engels, *Socialism: Utopian and Scientific*, p. 67.
[16]Ibid., p. 69.
[17]*Political Dictionary* (Moscow: 1940), p. 245, cited in *A Lexicon of Marxist-Leninist Semantics*, ed. Raymond S. Sleeper (Alexandria, VA: Western Goals, 1983), p. 30.
[18]Nikita Khrushchev, "Interview with Dr. Hans Thirring," Radio Moscow Broadcast, Jan. 2, 1962.
[19]*Pravda*, July 23, 1976.
[20]*Pravda*, Nov. 27, 1962.
[21]Nikita Khrushchev, "Speech," 5th Congress, SED (East Berlin), July 11, 1958.
[22]Nikita Khrushchev, "Interview," *Tass*, June 29, 1957, cited in *A Lexicon of Marxist-Leninist Semantics*, ed. Sleeper, p. 51.
[23]John Strachey, *The Theory and Practice of Socialism* (New York: Random House, 1936), p. 481.
[24]*Political Dictionary*, pp. 528-9, cited in *A Lexicon of Marxist-Leninist Semantics*, ed. Sleeper, p. 249.
[25]Marx and Engels, *Collected Works*, vol. 6, p. 498.
[26]Lenin, *Selected Works*, vol. 9, p. 479.
[27]Joseph Stalin, Interview with American Labor Delegation, Sept. 9, 1927, cited in *A Lexicon of Marxist-Leninist Semantics*, ed. Sleeper, p. 258.
[28]Karl Marx, *Value, Price and Profit* (Chicago: Kerr), p. 57, cited in Harry W. Laidler, *History of Socialism* (New York: Thomas Y. Crowell, 1968), p. 164.
[29]Marx and Engels, *Collected Works*, vol. 6, p. 490.
[30]Cameron, *Marxism: The Science of Society*, p. 74.
[31]Karl Marx, *Capital* (London: Sonnenschein), pp. 660-1, cited in Laidler, *History of Socialism*, pp. 152-3.
[32]Ibid.
[33]Leontyev, *Political Economy*, p. 49.
[34]Marx and Engels, *Collected Works*, vol. 6, p. 490.
[35]Leontyev, *Political Economy*, p. 141.
[36]*Political Dictionary*, pp. 424-5, cited in *A Lexicon of Marxist-Leninist Semantics*, ed. Sleeper, p. 99.
[37]Shakhnazarov, *The Coming World Order*, p. 214.
[38]G. A. Kozlov, ed., *Political Economy: Socialism* (Moscow: Progress Publishers, 1977), p. 13.
[39]V. Afanasyev, *Scientific Communism* (Moscow: 1967), p. 12. Cited in *A Lexicon of Marxist-Leninist Semantics*, ed. Sleeper, p. 51.
[40]*Statement of 81 Communist Workers Parties* (Moscow: 1960), cited in *A Lexicon of Marxist-Leninist Semantics*, ed. Sleeper, p. 51.
[41]Leontyev, *Political Economy*, p. 137.
[42]A. Denisov and M. Kirichenko, *Soviet State Law* (Moscow: 1960), p. 112. Cited in *A Lexicon of Marxist-Leninist Semantics*, ed. Sleeper, pp. 99-100.
[43]Kozlov, ed., *Political Economy: Socialism*, p. 55.

[44]*Fundamentals of Marxism-Leninism* (Moscow: 1961), p. 741. Cited in *A Lexicon of Marxist-Leninist Semantics*, ed. Sleeper, p. 302.
[45]Shakhnazarov, *The Coming World Order*, p. 213.
[46]*Philosophical Encyclopedia* (Moscow: 1967), vol. 4, pp. 381-3. Cited in *A Lexicon of Marxist-Leninist Semantics*, ed. Sleeper, p. 249.
[47]Leontyev, *Political Economy*, p. 238.
[48]Kozlov, ed., *Political Economy: Socialism*, p. 489.
[49]Khrushchev, speech entitled "New Victories in the World Communist Movement," *Kommunist* (Moscow), Jan. 1961.
[50]Marx and Engels, *Collected Works*, vol. 6, p. 350.
[51]Karl Marx, *The Gotha Program,* cited in Cameron, *Marxism: the Science of Society*, p. 97.
[52]*Scientific Communism: A Glossary* (Moscow: 1975), p. 53. Cited in *A Lexicon of Marxist-Leninist Semantics*, ed. Sleeper, p. 50.
[53]Maurice Cornforth, *The Open Philosophy and the Open Society* (New York: International Publishers, 1976), p. 343.
[54]V. I. Lenin, *Collected Works*, forty-five volumes (Moscow: Progress Publishers, 1980), vol. 30, p. 107.
[55]Strachey, *The Theory and Practice of Socialism*, p. 115.
[56]Lenin, *Collected Works*, vol. 25, p. 468.
[57]Marx and Engels, *Collected Works*, vol. 6, p. 351.
[58]Lenin, *Collected Works*, vol. 25, p. 468.
[59]Ibid., p. 469.
[60]*Scientific Communism: A Glossary*, pp. 143-5. Cited in *A Lexicon of Marxist-Leninist Semantics*, ed. Sleeper, p. 52.
[61]Karl Marx, *Capital and Other Writings*, cited in *A Lexicon of Marxist-Leninist Semantics*, ed. Sleeper, p. 50.
[62]Laidler, *History of Socialism*, p. 384.
[63]*Pravda*, Nov. 7, 1921.
[64]Lenin, "Concerning the Food Tax," cited in Laidler, *History of Socialism*, p. 390.
[65]Lenin, *Collected Works*, vol. 26, pp. 414-15.
[66]Frederick Engels, *Works* (Moscow and Leningrad: 1928-48), vol. 16, p. 57.
[67]G. Grigorov and S. Shkotov, *The Old and the New Way of Life* (Moscow and Leningrad: 1927), p. 156. Cited in Igor Shafarevich, *The Socialist Phenomenon* (New York: Harper and Row, 1980), p. 245.
[68]M. N. Liadov, *About the Way of Life* (Moscow: 1925), pp. 25-7. Cited in Ibid., p. 246.
[69]A. Adolpf, B. Bolshevskii, V. Stroev, and M. Shishkevich, *The Family and the Way of Life* (Moscow: 1927), p. 121. Cited in Ibid., p. 245.
[70]*World Marxist Review* (Toronto), Nov. 1976, p. 98.
[71]*Scientific Communism: A Glossary*, p. 270. Cited in *A Lexicon of Marxist-Leninist Semantics*, ed. Sleeper, p. 254.
[72]Cameron, *Marxism: the Science of Society*, p. 107.
[73]Strachey, *The Theory and Practice of Socialism*, title page.

CHAPTER

29

BIBLICAL CHRISTIAN ECONOMICS

"Thou shalt not steal. . . . Thou shalt not covet."

—Exodus 20:15, 17

"While it [land] remained, was it not thine own? and after it was sold was it [money] not in thine own power?"

—Peter, Acts 5:4

"Democratic capitalist societies exhibit the lives of human beings not perhaps as they should be but as they are, for they have been conceived in due recognition of the errant human heart, whose liberty they respect. In this, they follow the example of the Creator who knows what is in humans—who hates sin but permits it for the sake of liberty, who suffers from it but remains faithful to his sinful children."[1]

—Michael Novak

"If socialism were merely an economic system, it would long ago have been heaved aside to be replaced by barter, hunting-and-gathering, or some other more advanced economic system not so given to socialism's shoddy merchandise, shortages, and economic stagnation. . . . But socialism is art, the art of self-delusion."[2]

—R. Emmett Tyrrell, Jr.

SUMMARY

Christians begin their economic theory with an assumption about human nature—one that is diametrically opposed to the Marxist and Humanist assumptions. The Bible declares that man is sinful (Romans 3:23), and Christians believe this apparently irrelevant fact is crucial to economic theory. Another Biblical precept that seems to have little bearing on economics—the concept of justice—also plays an important role for the Christian.

While the Christian disagrees with the Marxist and the Humanist regarding human nature, it seems that all three worldviews agree that justice should play a powerful role in economic theory. However, the Christian concept of justice differs significantly from that of the other worldviews. Biblical justice implies impartiality in protection of human rights, whereas Marxist and Humanist "justice" enforces strict equality. This emphasis on equality strips man of his other rights because it ignores differences in talent and dedication among individuals. Calvin Beisner says, "Justice is rendering to each his due in accord with the standard of God's Law. It demands impartial application of all laws to all people. It respects natural, divinely ordained spiritual and physical differences among men and, respecting these, also respects their inevitable effects: diversity of intellectual, social, economic, and spiritual attainments."[3] The Christian is more interested in an economic system that protects human rights than in one that enforces equality through the redistribution of wealth.

In this sense, the Biblical concept of justice is closely tied to the concept of man's fallen nature. The most desirable economic system, for the Christian, would promote justice by protecting the rights of men from infringement by others. If all men were inherently good, one might not have to worry about individuals denying the rights of others; but people are not inherently good. Therefore, Christians believe the best economic system contains basic checks and balances that can guarantee the protection of human rights.

Applying this criterion, the Christian believes free enterprise is more compatible with his worldview. Free enterprise is a market economy that grants man a measure of freedom in his choices regarding consumption and production. This economic freedom protects the individual from coercion by the state (which is a necessary facet of socialism). Justice requires that man be free from state coercion in order to use his talents to God's glory and, with integrity, to work and reap rewards. Further, capitalism is based on private property—the legitimacy of which is affirmed in the Bible—and on encouragement of responsibility and just reward for work. Only a free economic system can provide this type of justice and protect men from coercion by other men.

If the Christian's beliefs about man's nature and justice are correct, we should expect Christianity's resultant view of economics to conform to reality better than that of other worldviews. This is precisely what we find. In the real world, capitalism creates more wealth than any alternative economic system and distributes it more justly. The free market is also better able to respond to the rapidly changing needs and wants of society because of the information conveyed by its pricing mechanism. Thus it gives rise to a wealthier, less bureaucratic society. Socialism, in contrast, attempts to control all economic decisions through central planning (government) and therefore creates an unresponsive economy ruled by a government without limits to its sovereignty. Property in a socialist society is mistreated because it belongs to everyone and no one at the same time, leaving little incentive to protect it, improve it, or use it productively. Planned economies tend toward poverty and injustice; free markets tend toward more productive, more just societies.

Put bluntly, *the Christian view of economics is less concerned with money than it is with freedom, justice, and responsibility*. Money does not make any person more human or closer to conformity to Christ's image. But economic systems that check injustice and grant men responsibility—in terms both of private property and economic decisions—can allow men the freedom to act with all the dignity of beings created in God's image. This, according to the Christian view, is the important end of economic theory: offering men not riches or luxury but the freedom to seek fulfillment through understanding their role in God's scheme of things. The Apostle Paul sums up this position when he explains that Christ, not wealth, is the only worthy goal: "I have learned the secret of being content in any and every situation, whether well fed or hungry, whether living in plenty or in want. I can do everything through him who gives me strength" (Philippians 4:12-13).

Notes and Asides

Introduction

Christians are divided on the issue of economics. While many Christians believe the Bible encourages a system of private property and individual responsibilities and initiatives (citing Isaiah 65:21-2; Jeremiah 32:43-4; Acts 5:1-4; Ephesians 4:28), many others are adamant in their support for a socialist economy (citing Acts 2:44-45). In fact, some Christians proclaim that the Bible teaches a form of Marxism. These people describe themselves as "liberation theologians." "In its most narrow sense," explains Ronald Nash, "liberation theology is a movement among Latin American Catholics and Protestants that seeks radical changes in the political and economic institutions of that region along Marxist lines."[4] According to these theologians, Christ decreed that His followers must help the poor (true), and that communism is the most effective means of doing so (false). Thus, the liberation theologian believes it is the Christian's duty to work tirelessly for the Marxist cause.

This is a trap of which every Christian must be wary because no economic system—whether communist, socialist or capitalist—is capable of saving mankind. Michael Novak warns, "It is a mistake, I believe, to try to bind the cogency of Scripture to one system merely. The Word of God is transcendent. It judges each and every system, and finds each gravely wanting. Liberation theologians in the Third World today err in binding Scripture to a socialist political economy, and I do not wish to indulge in a parallel mistake."[5] Neither do we. Thus, this chapter will in no way describe an economic system as inherently Christian, but rather seeks to discover the system that is most compatible with God's Word and this fallen world. As the chapter progresses, it will become obvious that only one contemporary economic option meets both requirements.

Socialism or Free Enterprise?

On the most basic level, the Christian is faced with a choice between supporting either socialism or free enterprise. In the real world, neither socialism nor capitalism exists in its "pure" form—that is, all capitalist systems contain certain elements of socialism, and vice versa. But for our purposes, we will discuss these opposing systems in terms of their least diluted states.

The simplest distinction between socialism and the free market system is outlined by Nash:

> One dominant feature of capitalism is economic freedom, the right of people to exchange things voluntarily, free from force,

Notes and Asides

> fraud, and theft. Capitalism is more than this, of course, but its concern with free exchange is obvious. Socialism, on the other hand, seeks to replace the freedom of the market with a group of central planners who exercise control over essential market functions. There are degrees of socialism as there are degrees of capitalism in the real world. But basic to any form of socialism is distrust of or contempt for the market process and the desire to replace the freedom of the market with some form of centralized control.[6]

Christians who believe socialism (or communism) is the more desirable system trust that this centralized control will create a more just means of sharing scarce resources. They believe the Bible supports their call for socialism, often pointing to Acts 2:44-45 as evidence that God's Word calls for such an economic arrangement.

"Men must choose between capitalism and socialism."
—Ludwig von Mises

Rousas J. Rushdoony responds to this claim: "The so-called communism of Acts 2:41-47, also cited by ecclesiastical socialists, was simply a voluntary sharing on the part of some (Acts 5). It was limited to Jerusalem. Because the believers took literally the words of Christ concerning the fall of Jerusalem (Matthew 24:1-28), they liquidated their properties there. The wealthier members placed some or all of these funds at the church's disposal, so that a witness could be made to their friends and relatives before Jerusalem fell."[7]

Indeed, when one studies the Bible as a whole—focusing on foundational principles rather than on verses taken out of context—it is much more supportive of an economic system respecting private property and the work ethic (see especially Isaiah 65:21-2 and Jeremiah 32:43-44). For example, Psalm 112 describes a gracious, compassionate, righteous man. We are told that "wealth and riches are in his house" (verse 3) and that he is generous, conducting "his affairs with justice" (verse 5). We are further told, "He has scattered abroad his gifts to the poor, his righteousness endures forever; his horn will be lifted high in honor" (verse 9). Paul quotes this verse in 2 Corinthians 9:9 in his message about giving, clearly indicating that personal wealth should not be condemned but seen as a blessing that allows for generosity.

Private Property

Christians who adhere to socialism claim that private property encourages greed and envy and that public ownership would remove much temptation to sin. Is this compatible with Scripture? Irving E. Howard doesn't think so: "The commandment 'Thou shalt not steal' is the clearest declaration of the right to private property in the Old Testament."[8]

Notes and Asides

In fact, private ownership and stewardship of property is assumed to be the proper state of affairs throughout the Bible (Deuteronomy 8; Ruth 2; Isaiah 65:21-22; Jeremiah 32:42-44; Micah 4:1-4; Luke 12:13-5; Acts 5:1-4; Ephesians 4:28). Calvin Beisner demonstrates this by asking,

> Why does Scripture require restitution, including multiple restitution, in cases of theft, even if paying the restitution requires selling oneself into slavery (Exodus 22:1ff)? Why does God's Law specifically permit the use of force—even lethal force—to protect private property in case of a break-in at night (Exodus 22:2,3)? And why does God's Law require showing respect for others' property by returning lost animals and helping overburdened animals even if they belong to enemies (Exodus 23:4f)?[9]

Clearly, the answer to these questions is that God has bestowed on mankind a right to property.

This right to property stems from our duty to work. After casting man out of Eden, God decreed that mankind must face a life of toil (Genesis 3:17-19). But God, in His mercy, allowed that men who conscientiously adhere to this duty may be rewarded with private property. Proverbs 10:4 states, "Lazy hands make a man poor, but diligent hands bring wealth." And Proverbs 14:23 declares, "All hard work brings a profit, but mere talk leads only to poverty." Thus, God has designed a world in which the existence of private property encourages men to be fruitful. Beisner puts it this way: "Men have not only the *duty* but also the *right* to work and to rest. As a reward for their work comes a right to property, protected by the Eighth Commandment, which forbids stealing. According to Jesus the laborer is 'worthy of his wages' (Luke 10:7); there is an inherent connection between work and its fruit."[10] Isaiah says that men will build houses and inhabit them, plant vineyards "and eat the fruit of them" and "enjoy the work of their hands" (Isaiah 65:21-2). And this is to be the situation when God has established "new heavens and a new earth" (Isaiah 65:17), indicating that private property is not a mere concession to evil times but a part of God's plan for His mature Kingdom.

> "Our country would become fabulously prosperous if, beginning tomorrow morning, everyone would do a full day's work."
> —Howard Kershner

Further, since God grants man private ownership of certain aspects of His creation, man becomes accountable to God for the way in which he uses his property. In God's wonderfully intricate plan, the duty to work gives rise to the right to property, which in turn creates the duty to use the property wisely. Beisner states,

> Biblical stewardship views God as Owner of all things (Psalm 24:1) and man—individually and collectively—as His steward.

Notes and Asides

Every person is accountable to God for the use of whatever he has (Genesis 1:26-30; 2:15). Every person's responsibility as a steward is to maximize the Owner's return on His investment by using it to serve others (Matthew 25:14-30).[11]

This use of property to serve others can only occur in a society in which property is privately owned. Publicly owned property destroys man's sense of responsibility to use his possessions wisely. "A society that does not respect property," says Beisner, "will not—indeed cannot—prosper, for property will be cared for and enhanced only to the extent that anyone recognizes a benefit from it, and when it can be taken at random by others no one will be able to foresee such benefit."[12] This truth is summarized in an anonymous verse: "Lease a man a garden/ And in time he will leave you/A patch of sand./ Make a man a full owner/Of a patch of sand/And in time he will grow there/A garden on the land."[13]

Recommended Reading for Advanced Study

E. Calvin Beisner, *Prosperity and Poverty: The Compassionate Use of Resources in a World of Scarcity* (Westchester, IL: Crossway, 1988).

Is Capitalism Christian? ed. Franky Schaeffer (Westchester, IL: Crossway, 1986).

Ronald Nash, *Poverty and Wealth: The Christian Debate Over Capitalism* (Westchester, IL: Crossway, 1987).

Michael Novak, *The Spirit of Democratic Capitalism* (New York: Simon and Schuster, 1982).

George Gilder, *Wealth and Poverty* (New York: Basic Books, 1981).

Warren T. Brookes, *The Economy in Mind* (New York: Universe Books, 1982).

Notes and Asides

Thus, private property, from the Christian perspective, actually discourages greed and envy by causing man to focus on the need to work and serve others rather than accumulate more for himself. When one understands property in the context of stewardship, it becomes obvious that private property encourages a more careful attitude toward scarce resources than does public property.

At this point, however, the socialist may argue that we live in an imperfect world and that one cannot expect every man always to have an attitude of stewardship. This, unfortunately, is true. But is the socialist's conclusion—that allowing selfish men to compete in a free market system for limited property leads to counterproductive actions—also necessarily true? Is economic competition inherently evil?

"Let him that stole steal no more: but rather let him labour, working with his hands the thing which is good, that he may have to give to him that needeth."
—St. Paul

Economic Competition

Judging from aforementioned verses such as Proverbs 10:4; 14:23, and Luke 10:7, it would seem that the Bible calls for men to compete with each other in the work place to encourage fruitfulness. Still, if economic competition proves to suffocate man's tendencies to cooperate, perhaps we must admit the socialist's claims to be well founded.

Fortunately, in a free market system the opposite proves to be true. Competition encourages cooperation in a capitalist society, because men in such a system act in accordance with the principle of comparative advantage. This principle basically states that every member of a free market society can produce a valuable good or service by specializing in the area in which he enjoys the least absolute disadvantage.[14] Thus, individuals find that they can be more successful operating in a free market by focusing their energies on production that is more beneficial to society as a whole—that is, by cooperating. This in turn creates more goods and services, making them available to poorer members of society. Beisner explains:

> [E]conomic competition enhances cooperation for the very reason that it helps participants to identify absolute and comparative advantages. Knowing those, they can focus on endeavors in which they have comparative advantages and so increase overall productivity. Since this means making more goods and services available to consumers, it also means reducing the prices of those goods and services (an operation of the law of supply and demand) and thus making them available to consumers with lower incomes.[15]

When viewed from the perspective of comparative advantage, competition creates still another benefit: it promotes the worth of each

Notes and Asides

individual. The free market preserves each man's dignity, as Peter Hill points out:

> Capitalism recognizes the worth of those with little economic and political power and offers them opportunities not readily available under alternative rules. Under a private property, market system, everybody is a "best" producer of some product or service. It is not the case that those with abundant skills or resources can outcompete the unskilled or unproductive across the board. Under the principle of comparative advantage all of us are least-cost producers in some area and thus worthy of attention by others in the society.[16]

This meshes perfectly with the Biblical perspective, which describes each individual as intrinsically valuable because he is made in the image of God.

Competition, when it leads to cooperation and a recognition of the worth of the individual, fits the Christian worldview. Indeed, when one understands that the only alternative to competition is specifically contrary to Biblical revelation, one must admit the value of a capitalist system. Nash explains, "We live as fallen creatures in an imperfect world where scarcity abounds. The alternative to nonviolent competition for these scarce resources is the use of force, violence, and theft."[17]

Tragically, socialism calls for just such a non-Biblical means of allocating scarce resources. Beisner writes, "The sole alternative to free competition—socialism—is allocation by agents with legal power to enforce their decisions regardless of the consent of those affected by them, and this power ultimately amounts to the threat or actual use of violence."[18]

> "As iron sharpens iron, so one man sharpens another."
> —Proverbs 27:17

It would seem evident that the Christian must support some form of a capitalist economic system to be consistent with his worldview. However, Christians who view socialism as the proper economic system have an ace in the hole. They claim that social justice demands that each individual possess an equal share of scarce resources and that this primary principle overrules all other considerations.

The Principle of Social Justice

On the surface, social justice demanding economic equality seems a noble ideal. What could be more fair than every man sharing equally the scarce resources available? But we have already demonstrated that God's Word calls for private property, and further, we are faced with the disturbing words of the Apostle Paul in 2 Thessalonians 3:10: "For even when we were with you, we gave you this rule: 'If a man will not

Notes and Asides

work, he shall not eat.'" How does one reconcile the seemingly noble notion of economic equality with Biblical truth?

The answer, of course, is that one cannot. Beisner quotes from Leviticus 19:15 ("You shall do no injustice in judgment; you shall not be partial to the poor nor defer to the great, but you are to judge your neighbor fairly"), and concludes, "God is not 'on the side of the poor,' despite protests to the contrary. Any law, therefore, that gives an advantage in the economic sphere to anyone, *rich or poor*, violates Biblical justice."[19] Why is this the case? Because justice requires equality before the law, not equality of incomes or abilities.

And indeed, justice will necessarily lead to economic inequality. "Because God equips people unequally," says Beisner, "social justice requires that their roles—and consequently their wealth and many other circumstances—be unequal as well, despite the fact that justice requires equality before law."[20] And elsewhere he states that "the Bible demands impartiality, which—because people differ in interests, gifts, capacities, and stations in life—must invariably result in conditional inequality."[21] This unequal distribution of income is consistent with true justice, as Ernest van den Haag explains:

> "Man is unequal in time allocated for him; talent entrusted to him; and treasure required of him. Man is only equal to man before the bar of justice."
> —Anonymous

> We would not be satisfied if the indolent worker were to get as much as the hard worker, the careless fool as much as a careful and intelligent craftsman. Equal treatment of unequals cannot be just, as Aristotle[22] pointed out. Merits differ.[23]

Justice is based not on equal income but on opportunity equally unhindered by coercive shackles. "Given the diversity and liberty of human life," says Novak, "no fair and free system can possibly guarantee equal outcomes. A democratic system depends for its legitimacy, therefore, not upon equal results but upon a sense of equal opportunity."[24] And equal opportunity means not that everyone must start with the same skills and social contacts, but that no one must be prohibited by law from attempting something morally legitimate in the marketplace. This conforms to the Biblical view. Social justice, from a genuinely Christian perspective, is summed up by Beisner:

> Just as personal justice is individual conformity with the standards of rightness, so social justice is societal conformity with the standards of rightness. Understanding this should prevent our falling into the mistaken idea that social justice has something to do with a particular distribution of goods, privileges, or powers in society. Real social justice, on the contrary, attends only to the question whether goods, privileges, and powers are distributed in conformity with the standards of rightness. Whatever

Notes and Asides

> factual distribution results from conformity with those standards is just regardless how far it strays from conditional equality. . . .[25]

The Christian must call for true social justice—equality under the law providing equal freedom of opportunity—and declare with Proverbs 16:8, "Better a little with righteousness than much gain with injustice."

The Rich and the Poor

Much of the reason the Christian socialist insists upon the need for economic equality lies in his mistaken assumption that the rich take their wealth from the poor. Thus, the socialist believes justice requires returning to the poor what was wrongfully stolen from them. If this view were correct, the socialist call for economic equality would be justified. However, this view is out of touch with reality.

First, the Bible makes it clear that poverty does not always result from exploitation by the rich. "It is certainly true," says Nash, "that Scripture recognizes that poverty sometimes results from oppression and exploitation. But Scripture also teaches that there are times when poverty results from misfortunes that have nothing to do with exploitation. These misfortunes include such things as accidents, injuries, and illness. And of course the Bible also makes it plain that poverty can result from indigence and sloth (Proverbs 6:6-11; 13:4; 24:30-34; 28:19)."[26]

Second, in market economies, the wealthy ordinarily *create* wealth. Socialists would have us view rich individuals as hoarding already scarce resources, but in truth, the wealthy often use the free market effectively to multiply the goods and services available. This in turn creates more opportunity for rich and poor alike. "Under capitalism," explains George Gilder, "when it is working, the rich have the anti-Midas touch . . . turning gold into goods and jobs and art. That is the function of the rich: fostering opportunities for the classes below them in the continuing drama of the creation of wealth and progress."[27]

In this way, the rich aid the poor by constantly expanding the pool of wealth and opportunity. Gilder elsewhere explains that "most real wealth originates in individual minds in unpredictable and uncontrollable ways. A successful economy depends on the proliferation of the rich, on creating a large class of risk-taking men who are willing to shun the easy channels of a comfortable life in order to create new enterprise, win huge profits, and invest them again."[28] The free market encourages the wealthy to invest their wealth in productive enterprises, thus making jobs, goods, and services available to others. But a socialist economy

Notes and Asides

encourages the wealthy to hide their wealth from taxation by hoarding it in the form of foreign bank accounts, superfluous luxuries, non-profit foundations that benefit primarily the rich themselves, and other fundamentally nonproductive uses.

This is a fundamental truth that socialists ignore: wealth comes more from the creativity and hard work fostered by free enterprise than from resources themselves. Indeed, resources are not strictly natural at all; they are all made by the application of human thought and energy to the raw materials around us. Land in and of itself produces only weeds and an occasional berry; land under the guidance of man's creativity and hard work can yield fruit and vegetables for an entire community. (This is why, even under the most hospitable circumstances, hunting and gathering can support only one or two people per square mile of land at mere subsistence level, while a market economy can support hundreds of people per square mile at very high standards of living.)

Thus, it is inaccurate for the socialist to describe the wealthy man as someone who has simply gathered more resources for himself at the expense of the poor. Rather, the rich individual ordinarily is someone who *makes* more resources than others, and the resources he makes benefit more people than just himself.

This principle becomes especially obvious when one examines the economic well-being of specific countries. There is usually little correlation between a country's resources and its prosperity. "Societies can become wealthy through the blessings of nature," observes Novak, "which the Creator distributed unequally. Yet richly endowed nations, like the Middle Eastern oil sheikdoms, can remain in poverty for millennia without awareness of the wealth awaiting their awakening. Societies may lack resources and, nevertheless, become wealthy, like Hong Kong and Japan."[29] Franky Schaeffer agrees: "Clearly the economic and political system of a country itself produces wealth or poverty, and not natural resources, a colonial past, or any other factor."[30]

But the socialist is unwilling to admit this. Rather, he chooses to cite Third World countries as examples of poor people suffering from exploitation by the rich (capitalist countries). This is simply not true. Contact with capitalist countries helps create wealth in the Third World. "In Africa as elsewhere in the Third World," says P. T. Bauer, "the most prosperous areas are those with most commercial contacts with the West."[31] He further declares,

> Far from the West having caused the poverty in the Third World, contact with the West has been the principal agent of material progress there. The materially more advanced socie-

CLOSE-UP

Francis A. Schaeffer (1912-1984)

One of the most outspoken champions of the Biblical Christian worldview, Francis A. Schaeffer dedicated much of his life to exposing the bankruptcy of Humanism and its adverse affect on culture. His message, however, was slow to gain the attention of the general public—Schaeffer spent years in relative obscurity before achieving the popularity he enjoys today. Ordained as a Presbyterian minister in 1938, Schaeffer worked the next ten years in America as a pastor. In 1948, he left his native country and followed God's call to minister in Switzerland, where he established the now-famous L'Abri Fellowship in 1955. L'Abri serves today as one of the finest examples of a Christian community seeking to live according to biblical precepts, but in its early years it afforded Schaeffer little opportunity to widely influence Christian thought. Indeed, Schaeffer did not achieve a broad sphere of influence until he published his first book in 1968, when he was 56 years old. From that point forward, his contribution to Christian worldview analysis grew astronomically. Today, with works such as *The Christian Manifesto* and *How Should We Then Live?* to his credit, Schaeffer stands in the forefront of the Christian move to embrace a Biblical worldview. His wife Edith and son Franky continue his work at L'Abri.

> ties and regions of the Third World are those with which the West established the most numerous, diversified and extensive contacts: the cash-crop producing areas and entrepot ports of South-East Asia, West Africa and Latin America; the mineral-producing areas of Africa and the Middle East; and cities and ports throughout Asia, Africa, the Caribbean and Latin America.[32]

Indeed, it is ridiculous to speak of rich countries as having gained their wealth at the expense of poorer countries:

Notes and Asides

> The recent practice of referring to the poor as deprived or underprivileged again helps the notion that the rich owe their prosperity to the exploitation of the poor. Yet how could the incomes of, for example, people in Switzerland or North America have been taken from, say, the aborigines of Papua, or the desert peoples or pygmies of Africa? Indeed, who deprived these groups and of what?[33]

The facts indicate quite clearly that capitalist systems do not encourage the exploitation of the poor. When one understands that wealth comes more from the creativity of individuals than from resources, one realizes that the system that better promotes creativity (namely, capitalism) is capable of creating more wealth.

Thus, we would expect better gains in living conditions for the poor under systems of free enterprise than under any other economy—and reality meets our expectations. Novak states unequivocally, "Under market economies, the historical record shows unprecedented gains in real incomes for the poor."[34] The socialist states of Eastern Europe and even the Soviet Union, meanwhile, propagate poverty. The Soviet economic system is so bad that its people suffer the constant risk of famine.

From the Christian perspective, the need for economic equality is both unfounded and contrary to Biblical social justice. Wealth is not distributed in a free market system in an inherently unjust manner, and any attempts to forcibly redistribute wealth oppose the Biblical call for equality before the law. Still, most countries' economies redistribute wealth in one way or another—which allows the alert observer to view the results of man's choice to ignore God's Word.

Redistribution in Practice

Why do most countries resort to some form of redistribution? Because they are unwilling to recognize that wealth can be generated in market economies. Hernando de Soto writes,

> A state which does not realize that wealth and resources can grow and be promoted by an appropriate system of institutions, and that even the humblest members of the population can generate wealth, finds direct redistribution the only acceptable approach.[35]

de Soto lived under just such a state in Peru and found (as the Christian would expect) that it destroyed all sense of equality under the law.

Why? Simply because in a system in which some people have their possessions taken away and some have possessions given to them, the law clearly favors the latter group over the former. de Soto puts it this way: "It is simply untrue that, in Peru, we are all equal before the law, because no two people pay the same tax, no two imports are taxed in the same way, no two exports are subsidized in the same way, and no two individuals have the same right to credit."[36]

The injustice of a system based on laws that treat men unequally is best summed up in a hypothetical situation described by Wilford I. King:

> Suppose that, in an isolated valley, there are three men, each working for himself on his own farm. One is very diligent, and when winter arrives, has accumulated a large store of foodstuffs, and has on hand ample feed for his horses, cows and poultry. The others, having taken life easy during the summer, find that long before spring they are short of provisions. If, then, they combine forces, set upon their neighbor, and seize his possessions, both capitalists and collectivists will agree that the two lazy farmers have violated the Eighth Commandment—in other words, they have stolen the diligent farmer's goods. But suppose, instead, that the two insist upon establishing a democratic government for the valley. They hold a "town meeting," and by a vote of two to one adopt a statute requiring that all share equally in the summer's produce. Is this a perfectly legitimate action, falling outside the scope of the Eighth Commandment? If not, just how many persons does it take to establish a government and make the procedure ethical?[37]

This type of injustice, caused by a system of redistribution like the one established in Peru, multiplies into still other problems. Because members of such a society want to be part of the group *receiving* redistributed wealth, they recognize the value of organizing to influence government. Citizens who would otherwise focus their energies on earning income (i.e., creating wealth) in the marketplace now focus on organizing political movements, thereby eliminating themselves as potential sources of wealth for themselves and others. de Soto watched this happen first-hand in Peru:

> In addition to its overall economic impact, however, the redistributive tradition has created in Peru a society where almost all the country's vital forces have organized in political and economic groups, one of whose main aims is to influence government in order to obtain a redistribution which favors them or

Notes and Asides

> their members. This competition for privileges through the lawmaking process has resulted in a widespread politicization of our society. . . .[38]

Incredibly, systems of redistribution don't even accomplish the one goal they seemed certain to achieve: improvement of the living standards of the poverty-stricken. The unjust nature of the system actually leads to the ruin of the country's economy. Writes Bauer,

> Except perhaps over very short periods, redistributive policies are much more likely to depress the living standards of the poor than to raise them. The extensive politicization brought about by large-scale redistribution diverts people's energies and ambitions from productive economic activity to politics and public administration. . . . An even more evident result is that these policies systematically transfer resources from people who are economically productive to others who are less so. Thus such policies inhibit a rise in incomes and living standards, including those of the poor.[39]

Peru opened the door to injustice and economic collapse by employing a system of redistribution. As hinted earlier, however, Peruvians are not alone in their folly—most countries have chosen to ignore Biblical truth. This includes the United States, with its peculiar form of redistribution known as welfare.

The Welfare System

As with all other forms of redistribution, on the surface it seems decidedly unchristian to speak out against the welfare system. After all, how can a Christian, who is commanded to help the poor, oppose a system that gives concrete financial aid to those living in poverty? The answer, of course, is that welfare is based on the unjust system of inequality before the law and perpetuates poverty rather than alleviating it.

The Christian recognizes that God has designed the world in such a way that man has a duty to work and is rewarded with property for his work. Thus, Christians have compassion on those who are incapable of labor, and they will gladly share their wealth with such people. But Christians also understand that it is more compassionate to encourage men capable of work to work than to give them handouts, because the Bible makes it clear that the only way to truly escape poverty is through hard labor. Nash elaborates:

Notes and Asides

> There are certainly times when the poor do require help in the form of cash and noncash benefits in the present, in the short run. But a system of "aid" that encourages people to become dependent on the dole, that robs the poor of any incentive to seek ways of helping themselves, that leads the poor into a poverty trap, is hardly a model of genuine compassion or of wise public policy.[40]

Welfare is not a compassionate system. It encourages the poor to abandon the lifeline of hard work and often undermines the family unit. "As long as welfare is preferable (as a combination of money, leisure, and services) to what can be earned by a male provider," writes Gilder, "the system will tend to deter work and undermine families."[41] This denial of the need for work is "the most serious fraud" of the welfare culture, according to Gilder, who says that for the poor "to live well and escape poverty they will have to keep their families together at all costs and will have to work harder than the classes above them. In order to succeed, the poor need most of all the spur of their poverty."[42] Here Gilder echoes the Bible, which says, "a worker's appetite works for him, for his hunger urges him on" (Proverbs 16:26).

"The laborer's appetite works for him; his hunger drives him on."
—Proverbs 16:26

Welfare removes this spur to hard labor, thereby harming poor people rather than helping them. "Welfare is an enemy of the poor and friend of the vast and expensive bureaucracies which it creates," says Clark Pinnock. "It prevents poor people from taking the only road that leads out of poverty: development through hard work and accumulation."[43] Charles Murray, once a proponent and architect of America's welfare program, has written a devastating critique of the actual impact of welfare on the poor in America, showing that it has both increased the rate of poverty (or in some cases slowed the rate's decline) and helped to perpetuate poverty among recipients.[44]

Welfare does not succeed in its endeavor to help the poor. Why, then, does the United States welfare system continue to grow? Because of the "vast and expensive bureaucracies" mentioned by Pinnock. In systems of redistribution, more government must be created to legislate, regulate, enforce, and perform the taking and giving of wealth. It takes a big, powerful government to take from and give to. But government tends to be self-perpetuating—that is, once men gain political power, they usually attempt to increase, rather than restrict, their power. Thus, the United States, by incorporating the socialist concept of redistribution into its generally capitalist economy, has also opened the door to the increased central control of the state necessary to socialism. This brings our discussion full circle.

Notes and Asides

Freedom and Economics

We began our analysis of capitalism and socialism by noting that capitalism trusts the free market while socialism requires centralized control. From this most fundamental difference between the two systems springs a number of ramifications, including the counterproductive bureaucracies created by the welfare system in the United States. Because socialism requires a planned economy, including control over wealth distribution, pricing, and production, it also requires a powerful central government to initiate the plans. As Bauer points out, "Attempts to minimize economic differences in an open and free society necessarily involve the use of coercive power."[45] Thus, the socialist must rely upon increased political power to achieve his goals of economic equality and a planned economy.

In a capitalist system, in contrast, far less political power is necessary, because the government need not worry about controlling

Used by permission of the *Colorado Springs Gazette Telegraph*

Notes and Asides

incomes, prices, or production. Clearly, there is a relationship between the type of economy a society chooses and the amount of freedom the individual must sacrifice. In a socialist society, the individual must relinquish to the government much of the control over his life. "Every form of political redistributionism widens power differentials in society," explains Edmund A. Opitz; "officeholders have more power, citizens less; political contests become more intense, because control and dispersal of great amounts of wealth is at stake. Every alternative to the market economy—call it socialism, or communism, or fascism, or whatever—concentrates power over the life and livelihood of the many in the hands of a few."[46] Beisner agrees: "The only way to arrive at equal fruits is to equalize behavior; and that requires robbing men of liberty, making them slaves."[47]

Upon examining socialism in practice in specific countries, these assertions prove undeniable. Schaeffer writes, "What ought to be an obvious lesson of the twentieth century is that when economic freedoms are lost, all freedoms atrophy."[48] The reverse also proves to be true—capitalism encourages political freedom. Nash's claim that "Economic freedom aids the existence and development of political liberty by helping to check the concentration of too much power in the hands of too few people"[49] and Novak's declaration that "political democracy is compatible in practice only with a market economy"[50] are justified by a comparison of the socialist states with the capitalist United States.

"The idea that political freedom can be preserved in the absence of economic freedom, and vice versa, is an illusion. Political freedom is the corollary of economic freedom."
—Ludwig von Mises

Judging from the real world, economic freedom and the right to private property are crucial for political freedom. Further, capitalism backs up its supporters' assertion that it can create a better standard of living, in practice, than socialism, not only for the rich but for everyone in society. According to Schaeffer, "America's poverty line is now $1,000 above the average income in the Soviet Union,"[51] and the Soviet Union has one of the highest standards of living among socialist and communist nations! Reality demonstrates that capitalism unquestionably exceeds socialism's ability to improve people's lives, in terms of both economics and freedom. The failure of socialism in the Soviet Union and Eastern European countries in the late 1980s and early 1990s reinforces this point.

Why Socialism in Practice Fails

The basic reason socialism is impractical was outlined by Ludwig von Mises decades ago. This problem stems from the most fundamental aspect of socialism: centralized control. The socialist expects the government to be able to control all economic calculations, but according to von Mises, "socialism can never work because it is an economic

Notes
and
Asides

system that makes economic calculation impossible. And because economic calculation is impossible, socialism turns out to be an economic system that makes rational economic activity impossible."[52]

These economic calculations, when occurring in a capitalist system according to the law of supply and demand, are described by Beisner as incredibly vast and changeable:

> In a free market, economic calculation takes place in the form of billions of tiny, interrelated decisions and actions. These decisions go on constantly, every minute of every day, constantly revising the total economic information in the marketplace.[53]

von Mises recognized that these calculations can only be made by a free market system—that no government could be expected to adequately replicate the market's ability to process economic information.

The practical application of von Mises's refutation of socialism is best outlined by Tom Bethell:

> It is one thing for central planners to draw up a plan of production. It is quite another thing to carry it out. . . . How can you (the planner) know what should be produced, before you know what people want? And people cannot know what they want unless they first know the price of things. But prices themselves can only be established when people are permitted to own things and to exchange them among themselves. But people do not have these rights in centrally planned economies.[54]

"Socialism would kill enterprise . . . Socialism attacks capital . . . "
—Winston Churchill

Socialism, in an attempt to tame the "uncontrollable" free market,[55] suddenly unleashes uncontrollable economic calculations. Thus, socialism is always unworkable in real-life situations.

Yet many people faced with the unswerving logic of von Mises's refutation still adhere to the socialist dream. Why, when socialism has proved to deny individual freedom, to create inequality before the law, and to be completely unworkable in practice, do socialists refuse to abandon their hope?

Human Nature and Economics

The answer lies in the socialist's misbegotten ideas about human nature. Whereas the Christian understands man to be a fallen creature, many other people (including many socialists) hold to the notion that man is inherently good and will flourish in a "positive" society. "In socialist societies," writes Novak, "the enemy of human development is thought to lie in inequalities of economic wealth and power. These being removed, it is imagined that society will be cooperative and the human breast at peace with itself."[56]

Christians, however, recognize that sin always exists in earthly societies—which means the utopian vision of socialism is unfounded. Reinhold Niebuhr, who at one time believed Christianity could be reconciled with Marxism, eventually faced this inescapable conclusion.

> We Christian "prophetic" sympathizers with Marxism were as much in error in understanding the positive program of socialism as we were in sharing its catastrophism. For the positive program was utopian, despite the explicit anti-utopianism of the Marxist. It sought to establish the kingdom of perfect brotherhood or of perfect justice on earth. It completely failed to appreciate the possibility of corruption through self-interest in any structure of society.[57]

Capitalism, on the other hand, takes human corruption into account and seeks to discourage it, or even to harness its energy to encourage unselfish deeds.[58] As previously noted, capitalism uses peaceful competition to allocate scarce resources. In this way, men's greed is channeled into cooperative efforts. Lewis S. Feuer puts it this way:

> The unparalleled achievement of the competitive capitalist society rests on a psychological fact: Previously, aggressive drives were mainly expressed through war, conquest, plunder, and enslavement; these drives always went hand in hand with the destruction of societies, communities, and people.[59]

Capitalism channels men's energies into enterprises that benefit not only themselves but the rest of society as well.

Capitalism also works to stifle man's sinful nature by encouraging political freedom and limited government, writes Nash.

> One of the more effective ways of mitigating the effects of human sin in society is dispersing and decentralizing power. The combination of a free market economy and limited constitutional government is the most effective means yet devised to impede the concentration of economic and political power in the hands of a small number of people. . . . Private ownership of property is an important buffer against any exorbitant consolidation of power by government.[60]

Notes and Asides

For the Christian, capitalism is far more practical than socialism's idealistic denial of man's sinfulness. As Schaeffer says, "Since utopian perfection cannot be achieved in a fallen world, three-quarters of a capitalist loaf is better than the whole loaf promised by Socialist dreamers but never delivered."[61] Novak agrees:

> Whereas socialists frequently promise, under their coercive system, "a new socialist man" of a virtuous sort the world has never seen before, democratic capitalism (although it, too, depends upon and nourishes virtuous behavior) promises no such thing. Its political economy, while depending upon a high degree of civic virtue in its citizens (and upon an especially potent moral-cultural system separated from the state), is designed for sinners. That is, for humans as they are.[62]

Clearly, the only economic system the Christian can accept while remaining practical and consistent with his worldview is free enterprise. While some Christians adhere to socialism, they do so at the expense of their intellectual integrity. Both the real world and Biblical revelation support private property, stewardship, reward for work, giving, etc.

Conclusion

The Christian worldview embraces democratic capitalism for a number of reasons. The Bible not only grants man the right to private property but also calls for man to be a good steward of his property—and the free enterprise system affords man the most opportunity to act as a responsible steward by creating wealth and opportunity. Further, the competition in a free market works according to the principle of comparative advantage, which affirms the inherent worth of every individual.

Capitalism is also more socially just than socialism. While the socialist calls for economic equality, capitalism respects the Biblical requirement of equality before the law. This does not, as the socialist contends, cause the rich to get richer and the poor poorer. Rather, it encourages the rich to create more wealth, thereby aiding all of society. The policies of redistribution, including welfare systems, only multiply the problems for the poor—creating needless bureaucracies and concentrating too much power in the hands of the government. Conversely, capitalism encourages freedom in the political sphere. This removes the danger of granting sovereignty to the state instead of to God.

In practice, capitalism proves the only workable system. Socialism leads to oppression, while capitalism offers unparalleled freedom and

Notes and Asides

economic opportunity. Socialism cannot possibly manage all the economic calculations necessary to maintain a stable economy; the free market shows itself constantly capable. Socialism ignores man's inherent sinfulness; capitalism works to stifle man's sinful tendencies and to turn even selfishness to service. Clearly, the Christian who accepts the Bible must also accept democratic capitalism or free enterprise as the system most compatible with his worldview.

Even Frederick Engels understood that the Bible could in no way be construed to support a socialist system. Said Engels, ". . . if some few passages of the Bible may be favourable to Communism, the general spirit of its doctrines is, nevertheless, totally opposed to it. . . ."[63]

[1]Michael Novak, *The Spirit of Democratic Capitalism* (New York: Simon and Schuster, 1982), pp. 81-2.
[2]R. Emmett Tyrrell, Jr., "The Enthusiasm for Spending," in *Is Capitalism Christian?* ed. Franky Schaeffer (Westchester, IL: Crossway, 1986), pp. 9-10.
[3]E. Calvin Beisner, *Prosperity and Poverty: The Compassionate Use of Resources in a World of Scarcity* (Westchester, IL: Crossway, 1988), p. 73.
[4]Ronald Nash, *Poverty and Wealth: The Christian Debate Over Capitalism* (Westchester, IL: Crossway, 1987), p. 103.
[5]Novak, *The Spirit of Democratic Capitalism*, p. 335.
[6]Nash, *Poverty and Wealth*, p. 63.
[7]Rousas J. Rushdoony, *The Institutes of Biblical Law* (Nutley, NJ: The Craig Press, 1973), p. 451.
[8]Irving E. Howard, *The Christian Alternative to Socialism* (Arlington, VA: Better Books, 1966), p. 43.
[9]Beisner, *Prosperity and Poverty*, p. 66.
[10]Ibid., p. 53.
[11]Ibid., pp. xi-xii.
[12]Ibid., p. 154.
[13]Cited in George Gilder, *The Spirit of Enterprise* (New York: Simon and Schuster, 1984), p. 23.
[14]For an excellent discussion of comparative and absolute advantage, see Beisner, *Prosperity and Poverty*, pp. 93-99.
[15]Ibid., p. 98.
[16]Peter J. Hill, "Private Rights and Public Attitudes: A Christian Defense of Capitalism," unpublished, Department of Economics, Montana State University, pp. 17-18.
[17]Nash, *Poverty and Wealth*, p. 74.
[18]Beisner, *Prosperity and Poverty*, p. 99.
[19]Ibid., p. 52.
[20]Ibid., p. 48.
[21]Ibid, p. 52.
[22]Aristotle's definition of justice may be summarized as "rendering equal things to equals and unequal things to unequals in accord with their relevant inequalities." It should be noted here that Aristotle also recognized the evil nature of man and treated this as a given in his work regarding politics.
[23]Ernest van den Haag, ed., *Capitalism: Sources of Hostility* (New Rochelle, NY: Epoch Books, 1979), p. 25.
[24]Novak, *The Spirit of Democratic Capitalism*, p. 15.
[25]Beisner, *Prosperity and Poverty*, p. 47.
[26]Nash, *Poverty and Wealth*, p. 71.
[27]George Gilder, *Wealth and Poverty* (New York: Basic Books, 1981), p. 63.
[28]Ibid, p. 245. For further discussion of the role of mind in economics, see Warren Brookes's excellent work *The Economy in Mind* (New York: Universe Books, 1982).
[29]Novak, *The Spirit of Democratic Capitalism*, p. 285.
[30]Schaeffer, ed., *Is Capitalism Christian?* pp. xxvii-xxviii.
[31]P. T. Bauer, *Equality, the Third World, and Economic Delusion* (Cambridge, MA: Harvard University Press, 1981), p. 70.
[32]Ibid.
[33]Ibid., p. 74.
[34]Novak, *The Spirit of Democratic Capitalism*, p. 109.
[35]Hernando de Soto, *The Other Path: The Invisible Revolution in the Third World*, trans. June Abbott (New York: Harper and Row, 1989), p. 189.
[36]Ibid., p. 195.
[37]Cited in John R. Richardson, *Christian Economics* (Houston, TX: Thomas Press, 1966), p. 31.
[38]de Soto, *The Other Path*, p. 190.
[39]Bauer, *Equality, the Third World, and Economic Delusion*, p. 23.
[40]Nash, *Poverty and Wealth*, p. 167.
[41]Gilder, *Wealth and Poverty*, p. 122.
[42]Ibid., p. 118.

[43]Clark Pinnock, "A Pilgrimage in Political Theology: A Personal Witness," in *Is Capitalism Christian?* ed. Schaeffer, p. 322.
[44]Charles Murray, *Losing Ground: American Social Policy, 1950-1980* (New York: Basic Books, 1984).
[45]Bauer, *Equality, the Third World, and Economic Delusion*, p. 18.
[46]Edmund A. Opitz, *Religion and Capitalism: Allies, Not Enemies* (New Rochelle, NY: Arlington House, 1970), p. 242.
[47]Beisner, *Prosperity and Poverty*, p. 54.
[48]Schaeffer, ed., *Is Capitalism Christian?* p. xvii.
[49]Nash, *Poverty and Wealth*, p. 78.
[50]Novak, *The Spirit of Democratic Capitalism*, p. 14.
[51]Schaeffer, ed., *Is Capitalism Christian?* p. xxv.
[52]Nash, *Poverty and Wealth*, p. 82.
[53]Beisner, *Prosperity and Poverty*, p. 118.
[54]Tom Bethell, "Why Socialism Still Doesn't Work," *The Free Market*, November 1985, pp. 6-7.
[55]In reality, of course, the free market is "controlled" by millions of individual planners who know their own needs and wants better than a few central planners.
[56]Novak, *The Spirit of Democratic Capitalism*, p. 83.
[57]Cited in *Religion and Culture: Essays in Honor of Paul Tillich*, ed. Walter Leibrecht (New York: Harper and Bros., 1959), p. 51.
[58]For example, a businessman may be a selfish tyrant in his own home, but cannot manifest such qualities in the marketplace and succeed.
[59]Lewis S. Feuer, "Some Irrational Sources of Opposition to the Market System," in *Capitalism: Sources of Hostility*, ed. van den Haag, p. 103.
[60]Nash, *Poverty and Wealth*, p. 68.
[61]Schaeffer, ed., *Is Capitalism Christian?* p. xviii.
[62]Novak, *The Spirit of Democratic Capitalism*, p. 85.
[63]Karl Marx and Frederick Engels, *Collected Works*, forty volumes (New York: International Publishers, 1976), vol. 3, p. 399.

SECTION TEN

HISTORY

Chapter 30: *Secular Humanism*
Chapter 31: *Marxism/Leninism*
Chapter 32: *Biblical Christianity*

HISTORY [Latin: *historia* (information)]: The study of past places, persons, and events.

	SECULAR HUMANISM	MARXISM/ LENINISM	BIBLICAL CHRISTIANITY
SOURCE	*HUMANIST MANIFESTO I & II*	*WRITINGS OF MARX & LENIN*	*BIBLE*
THEOLOGY	ATHEISM	ATHEISM	THEISM
PHILOSOPHY	NATURALISM	DIALECTICAL MATERIALISM	SUPERNATURALISM
ETHICS	ETHICAL RELATIVISM	PROLETARIAT MORALITY	ETHICAL ABSOLUTES
BIOLOGY	DARWINIAN EVOLUTION	DARWINIAN/ PUNCTUATED EVOLUTION	SPECIAL CREATIONISM
PSYCHOLOGY	MONISTIC SELF-ACTUALIZATION	MONISTIC PAVLOVIAN BEHAVIORISM	DUALISM
SOCIOLOGY	NON-TRADITIONAL WORLD STATE ETHICAL SOCIETY	ABOLITION OF HOME, CHURCH AND STATE	HOME CHURCH STATE
LAW	POSITIVE LAW	POSITIVE LAW	BIBLICAL/NATURAL LAW
POLITICS	WORLD GOVERNMENT (GLOBALISM)	NEW WORLD ORDER	JUSTICE FREEDOM ORDER
ECONOMICS	SOCIALISM	SOCIALISM/ COMMUNISM	STEWARDSHIP OF PROPERTY
HISTORY	HISTORICAL EVOLUTION	HISTORICAL MATERIALISM	HISTORICAL RESURRECTION

CHAPTER

30

SECULAR HUMANIST HISTORY

"Man's destiny is to be the sole agent for the future evolution of this planet. He is the highest dominant type to be produced by over two and a half billion years of the slow biological improvement effected by the blind opportunistic workings of natural selection; if he does not destroy himself, he has at least an equal stretch of evolutionary time before him to exercise his agency."[1]

—Julian Huxley

"[T]he laws of biology are the fundamental lessons of history."[2]

—Will and Ariel Durant

SUMMARY

For the Humanist, the basic ingredients of both written and unwritten history are materialism, spontaneous generation, evolution, and an optimistic expectation of a future paradise on earth created by rational, scientific mankind. One of history's major tasks is to record man's ascent through competition and natural selection: "[W]ar is one of the constants of history," say Will and Ariel Durant, "and is the ultimate form of natural selection in the human species."[3] History is also to bear witness to the evolution of a new species fit to inhabit a new world order. Humanists insist that the new species can be evolved only via a humanistic, scientific worldview. It will not come about through divine intervention or "prescientific" worldviews like Christianity. Man must save himself. He must direct his own evolution.

Humanists view early history from a strictly materialistic or naturalistic vantage point. The universe, including our world, is the product of materialistic forces with no supernatural interference. God does not exist. Only matter exists. From a Humanist historical viewpoint, "In the beginning, matter" is the first lesson of history.

The second lesson of history is the slow, methodical evolutionary emergence of all living forms, including man. The move from nonliving to living matter (spontaneous generation) ranks as one of history's most decisive moments, especially since it required billions of years of preparation and performance and will require billions more to play out. Indeed, man is still an evolving, competitive animal. "The laws of biology," say the Durants, "are the fundamental lessons of history."[4] For the Humanist, the laws of biology are the laws of evolution.

Unfortunately, mankind's future is clouded by the Second Law of Thermodynamics, which insists that cold will engulf the earth when the heat of the sun is depleted. But man, insist the Humanists, has approximately two billion years to prepare to handle absolute zero. The task of present-day history, therefore, is to record the evolution of man to withstand such an eventuality and survive. Random nature has brought us this far, and the Humanist believes mankind's reason and scientific genius will direct his future evolution and assure survival.

The history of man and the universe is the history of evolutionary activity, and, though it is propelled by neither purpose nor design but by "blind natural selection" alone, it is a history moving upward to higher and higher forms. During the ascent, history shows no support for the supernatural,[5] and, indeed, the Bible is shown to be a book consisting primarily of myths and legends written by prescientific men who were nonprogressive and primitive in worldview. A progressive man accepts the evolution of man as scientific fact and strives toward a new world order that may ultimately mitigate man's competitive nature. Say the Durants, "Until our states [nations] become members of a large and effectively protective group [world government] they will continue to act like individuals and families in the hunting stage."[6]

The theory of evolution plays the foundational role in Humanist historical analysis and accounts for the Humanist's faith in progress in history. Humanists, however, rarely discuss their blind faith in progress, since progress as a universal law would imply design of sorts, and Humanists cannot tolerate the idea of a Designer. Before the arrival of man on the evolutionary scene, progress was explained as the action of "blind natural selection," but man's emergence allows for man himself to become the guiding principle of progress. Man controls his own evolution. Man creates his own heaven on earth—man as related to science, that is. Elite scientific man shapes the future—if elite scientific man doesn't blow up the world before the new species evolves. The new species presently being considered worthy of evolving is "computer man." Computer man, containing all of mankind's consciousness, is being readied to inherit the cold, cold world for billions of years to come. Such is the essence and agenda of Humanist history. Such is the story of atheistic, materialistic, evolutionary history.

Notes and Asides

Introduction

Humanists argue that their atheistic, evolutionary worldview best fits the facts of recorded and unrecorded history. They contend that their historical interpretation is the scientific, non-mythological, realistic perspective. With this contention in mind, the author of the *Humanist Manifesto II* attempted to paint a more accurate picture of man's history and future than was described in the first *Manifesto*. The more recent text claims that events since the 1933 *Manifesto* make that earlier statement seem far too optimistic. "Nazism," says *Manifesto II*, "has shown the depths of brutality of which humanity is capable. Other totalitarian regimes have suppressed human rights without ending poverty. Science has sometimes brought evil as well as good. Recent decades have shown that inhuman wars can be made in the name of peace."[7]

Judging from this statement, it would seem that Humanists have come to grips with man's inherent sinfulness and recognize that there is little room for optimism about man's future. Assuming a realistic, atheistic stance, the Humanist must view mankind's history as a bumbling, chancy, often immoral enterprise, with little hope for improvement in the future. Apparently, *Humanist Manifesto II* affirms the Humanist's acceptance of just such a true-to-life situation.

Or does it? On the very next page we find a statement of incomparable historical optimism:

> Using technology wisely, we can control our environment, conquer poverty, markedly reduce disease, extend our life-span, significantly modify our behavior, alter the course of human evolution and cultural development, unlock vast new powers, and provide humankind with unparalleled opportunity for achieving an abundant and meaningful life.[8]

How could the first *Manifesto* make a declaration any more optimistic than this? The Humanist claims to have adopted a realistic view of mankind's history, but time and time again he makes statements that betray his unlimited faith in evolving mankind.

Thus, even though Bertrand Russell sensed bad times ahead, he was encouraging: "[W]e should remember while they [bad times] last the slow march of man, chequered in the past by devastations and retrogressions, but always resuming the movement toward progress."[9] This optimism is echoed by John H. Dietrich: "Step by step up the ages man has marched toward a higher civilization. This is the way the world has grown into its present shape; and we are still only in the beginning of our long march. Man is not yet really civilized. It is only the dawn."[10]

Notes and Asides

George Sarton is so optimistic about mankind's history that he perceives man as marching toward a future paradise. In the long run, he believes, "generous ideas will survive ungenerous ones, and justice, injustice. In the long run, beautiful things will outlast ugly ones. In the long run, truth will eradicate error."[11] From a Humanist worldview fashioned by randomness, chance, and accident it appears that the cards are stacked in a particularly beautiful way.

Humanists have not abandoned the notion that man is progressing upward and is basically good. Edwin H. Wilson says that Humanism expresses the belief that man has "potentially the intelligence, good will and co-operative skills to survive on this planet, to explore space and to provide security and an opportunity for growth, adventure, meaning and fulfillment for all men."[12]

Humanist Manifesto II sees this opportunity for growth to include a daring goal for mankind:

> . . . for each person to become, in ideal as well as practice, a citizen of a world community. It is a classical vision; we can now give it new vitality. Humanism thus interpreted is a moral force that has time on its side. We believe that humankind has the potential intelligence, good will, and cooperative skill to implement this commitment in the decades ahead.[13]

> "History is, indeed, little more than the register of the crimes, follies, and misfortunes of mankind."
> —Edward Gibbon

This optimistic view of man's nature allows the Humanist to be optimistic about mankind's history regardless of the millions of atrocities committed by men in this century alone. Corliss Lamont proclaims, "Despite the appalling world wars and other ordeals through which humanity has passed during the twentieth century, despite the unprecedented menace of nuclear annihilation, Humanism takes the long view and remains hopeful of the decades to come."[14] Is this a realistic assessment of man's history and future? What causes the Humanist to make irrationally optimistic statements like this? Why does the Humanist insist that mankind's future will always outshine his past?

Two Reasons Humanists Must Be Optimistic

Despite the Humanist's desire to assume a realistic view of history, he must remain unrealistically optimistic for two reasons. The first and most telling is his belief that all life evolved from non-life. Harry Elmer Barnes, one of the leading Humanist historians, affirms the Humanist faith in evolutionary theory: "While flaws have been revealed in some of the details of the processes regarded by Darwin as fundamental in the evolution of life, the vital principles which he suggested have been

Notes and Asides

established as firmly as any law or process of science."[15] This evolutionary perspective colors the Humanist's attitude toward all history and reality. Thus, Julian Huxley can state, "Evolution in the most general terms is a natural process of irreversible change, which generates novelty, variety, and increase of organization: and all reality can be regarded in one aspect as evolution."[16]

The ramifications of this attitude are clear: if all reality is progressing toward increased organization, if all reality is an evolutionary pattern that has moved upward step by step to create rational thought and morality in the highest species, then mankind's history must also be a progressive march toward a better world. As the evolutionary process continues, so must progress continue. Thus, according to the Humanist, all of history is a development from simple to more complex, from mindless to mind, from amoral to moral. Civilization constantly improves and ultimately carries the human race (or whatever race evolution dictates) into some type of world community.

Dietrich sums up this view: "I need not speak of the progressive development of . . . life into higher and higher forms until at last it reached the stature of man; but let me speak of man who has been on this planet for several hundred thousand years at the very least. There never has been any Garden of Eden, or perfect condition in the past, there never has been any fall, there has been a constant rise. Man has been climbing slowly up the ages from the most primitive condition to the present civilization."[17]

Barnes says much the same thing as he insists that man is no longer to be thought of as striving to regain "his lost estate." Rather, says Barnes, "his 'lost estate' is the one thing which the informed historical student of the present would least desire to recover, as the difference between that and our present condition is what really constitutes progress and civilization."[18] This notion that mankind is constantly on the upward draft, caused by the belief that all reality is in a state of evolution, forces the Humanist to adopt an optimistic view of history.

Thus, the whole process of history is perceived by the Humanist as the evolution of cultures and civilizations into more desirable cultures and civilizations. Huxley declares that machines, works of art, educational systems, agricultural methods, religions, and even men's values and ideals, are "natural phenomena, at once products of and efficient agencies in the process of cultural evolution." He also insists that the "rise and fall of empires and cultures is a natural phenomenon, just as much as the succession of dominant groups in biological evolution."[19] The Humanist feels confident that the future will improve on the past and the present because evolution demands progress.

The second reason Humanists adhere to an optimistic view is best summarized by Huxley: "In the evolutionary pattern of thought there is no longer either need or room for the supernatural."[20] Humanism denies

Notes and Asides

the existence of God. This greatly reduces the importance of men's actions, since in this view, as Russell notes, "The universe is vast and men are but tiny specks on an insignificant planet."[21] Oddly enough, however, this denial of a source of meaning in history pushes the Humanist toward historical optimism. While it seems that such a denial would generate pessimism, it instead spurs the Humanist to pin all his hopes on history and the future, because the progress of mankind becomes the only meaningful goal. Russell, in an odd bit of reasoning, claims that man's overwhelming insignificance makes his achievements throughout history all the more impressive—giving mankind all the more reason for optimism. He writes, "But the more we realize our minuteness and our impotence in the face of cosmic forces, the more astonishing becomes what human beings have achieved."[22] The Humanist's atheism, instead of leading him into the trap of nihilism, make him dependent on the progress of human history to provide meaning for mankind. Thus, the Humanist must believe that progress is inevitable, if he is to believe anything.

Humanism and the Bible

Humanists' belief in progress throughout history is forced on them by their theory of evolution and their disbelief in the existence of God. Ironically, Humanists use the discipline of history to support their atheism. They claim that historians have proven the Bible to consist chiefly of legends and that a scientific approach to history has exposed the mythological nature of the account of Christ's miracles, resurrection, and ascension. Paul Kurtz declares,

> [S]cientific and scholarly biblical criticism has made it abundantly clear that the Bible is a human document, a thousand-year-old record of the experiences of primitive nomadic and agricultural tribes living on the eastern shore of the Mediterranean. There is no evidence that Yahweh spoke to Abraham, Moses, Joseph, or any of the Old Testament prophets. The biblical accounts of their experiences are the records of Hebrew national existence, seeking to sustain itself by the myth of the "chosen people." These books have not been empirically validated; they express an ancient world view and the moral conceptions of a prescientific culture that invoked deities to sanctify its ideological aspirations.[23]

Barnes feels equally distrustful of the accuracy of the Bible: "Biblical criticism, applied to the New Testament, has removed the element of supernaturalism from the biographies of its founders as

Notes and Asides

thoroughly as Old Testament criticism has from those of its heroes."[24]

The case against the Bible is summed up by William Floyd, who concludes that the doctrines of Judaism and Christianity recorded in the Holy Bible "are not established beyond a reasonable doubt." He maintains that the events and persons described in the sacred Scriptures "are not sufficiently well documented to be accepted as literally true or historically authentic. The miraculous occurrences for which the Bible is famous are not consistent with the laws of nature as now understood. It is therefore not surprising that the result of relying upon Biblical Religion has not been satisfactory."[25]

Obviously, if the Bible is inaccurate, then it is foolish to believe that Christ said and did all the things claimed by the New Testament. Floyd agrees: "Jesus obviously never said and did many of the things attributed to him. There is no agreement among Biblical scholars as to which passages are accurate and which misrepresent him. The gospels are not discriminating but are a hopeless melange of truth and falsehood, historical and non-historical writings."[26]

Kurtz agrees:

> The New Testament presents the incredible tale of Jesus, a man of whom we have very little historical knowledge. Obviously this is not an objective historical account. The "divinity" of Jesus has never been adequately demonstrated. . . . The tales of Jesus' life and ministry expressed in the Four Gospels and the letters of Paul were written twenty to seventy years after his death. They are riddled with the contradictions implicit in an oral tradition.[27]

The Humanist clearly regards the Bible, and especially its historical account of Christ's resurrection and ascension, as historically inaccurate. Indeed, Humanists believe every account of the supernatural to be historically inaccurate, because Humanism's atheistic theology and naturalistic philosophy allow for the existence of natural processes alone. But this leaves the Humanist with a major problem: who or what guarantees and directs progress in history?

Who Shapes History?

As we have seen, the Secular Humanist denies the existence of any supernatural guiding force that might direct history. No Humanist believes that God oversees the course of mankind's existence. Barnes declares, "There is no one key to the riddle of historical causation. At times one or another factor may rise to a position of transcendent

Notes and Asides

importance, but no single 'cause' or 'influence' has been dominant throughout all of human history."[28]

Indeed, some Humanists carry this disbelief in any overriding historical influence so far that they even contradict their own optimistic statements about the inevitable progress of civilization. Russell calls it a great evil "when history is regarded as teaching some general philosophical doctrine, such as: Right, in the long run, is Might; Truth always prevails in the end; or, Progress is a universal law of society. All such doctrines require, for their support, a careful choice of place and time, and, what is worse, a falsification of values."[29]

Kurtz also denies that progress is guaranteed throughout history, stating,

> Many Humanists worship the myth of Progress, and judge all programmes by whether they contribute to a progressive view of history. Humanists surely ought to work for progressive improvement without personally believing that progress exists in the womb of nature or that there is an inevitable march of human history.[30]

These two gentlemen are unwilling to declare progress inevitable because they recognize that Humanism has no foundation for such a claim. Because God (or any supernatural guide for history) does not exist, absolute guarantees do not exist, including any guarantee that

CLOSE-UP

Paul Kurtz (1925-)

Few people have done more to advance the cause of Humanism than Paul Kurtz, author of the *Humanist Manifesto II.* As the editor-in-chief of Prometheus Books (Humanism's most important publishing house) and editor of *Free Inquiry* magazine, he has immense opportunity to influence Humanistic thinking. Further, as a prolific writer (recent works include *Forbidden Fruit* and *Philosophical Essays in Pragmatic Naturalism*), he constantly challenges Christian assumptions and asserts the supremacy of his worldview. Kurtz also teaches philosophy at SUNY-Buffalo.

Notes and Asides

civilization must always progress. Still, it is clear that the Humanist may theoretically discard the inevitability of progress while still practically embracing such a notion. As we have noted, there is nothing else on which the Humanist may base his optimism.

At present, we will grant Russell and Kurtz the assertion that there is no overarching guide—whether God or Progress—for history. This leads to the next possibility: perhaps man's environment plays the largest role in shaping history. This assertion would be most consistent with the Humanist worldview, since the Humanist perceives man as an inherently good evolving animal constantly driven to evil by his environment. Clearly, the Humanist views the environment as acting significantly on man and his culture.

And in truth, many Humanists do claim that man's environment shapes history. Barnes writes, "History is a record of man's development as conditioned by his social environment."[31] *Humanist Manifesto I* says, "Humanism recognizes that man's religious culture and civilization, as clearly depicted by anthropology and history, are the product of a gradual development due to his interaction with his natural environment and with his social heritage. The individual born into a particular culture is largely molded to that culture."[32]

> "Progress in substance is refuted by the facts. . . . Cultures were destroyed by barbarians. The physical annihilation of the highest types of men by the oppressive realities of the mass is a fundamental phenomenon of history."
>
> —Karl Jaspers

This attitude is also expressed by the many Humanists who accept some form of economic interpretation of history, thereby assuming that the economic environment at least partially shapes history. Lamont provides a fine example of this perspective when he states, "The realistic Humanist, however, believing in at least a limited economic interpretation of history, will look beyond fine-sounding peace pronouncements and formal peace organizations to those fundamental economic forces and relationships that make for war."[33]

It would seem, at first glance, that the Humanist believes the real force behind history is man's environment. In practice, however, the Humanist cannot accept this conclusion. As soon as the Humanist declares the environment the dynamic force behind history, man is stripped of purpose. The Humanist could not encourage the individual to act nobly or work to change the world, because man, according to this view, is nothing but a leaf swept along by the stream of environmental change. Thus, in order to grant man the power to control his own destiny and maintain an optimistic attitude toward history, the Humanist must abandon his belief in environmental influence and stress man's role in shaping history.

Algernon D. Black, while mulling over this predicament, is cautious about the extent of man's role: "But in the evolution of human life, there is a consciousness and emerging conscience. The key question is whether human beings can rise to a level of awareness of the values and the choices which are within human control."[34] Shortly we will consider

Notes and Asides

the manner in which mankind may rise to this necessary level of awareness. For now, we must understand that Humanism holds the carrot of controlled destiny in front of mankind's nose, in an effort to keep the individual motivated to improve his world. Lamont waves the carrot boldly, stating, "Humanism denies that there is any overarching fate, either in the form of a Divine Providence or a malignant Satanism, that is either helping or hindering man's progress and well-being. Within certain limits prescribed by our earthly circumstances and by scientific law, individual human beings, entire nations, and mankind in general are free to choose the paths that they truly wish to follow. To a significant degree they are the moulders of their own fate and hold in their own hands the shape of things to come."[35] *Humanist Manifesto II* is equally willing to single out mankind as the dynamic force in history: ". . . we can discover no divine purpose or providence for the human species. While there is much that we do not know, humans are responsible for what we are or will become. No deity will save us; we must save ourselves."[36]

By declaring man's actions to be the key force in history, the Humanist maintains both his optimism and his belief in purpose for mankind. However, this concession creates two new problems for Humanism's worldview. First, as we have seen, it is inconsistent with the Humanist assertion that man is a product of his environment. Second, by allowing that man shapes history, the Humanist opens the door for any individual to change the course of history—whether Humanist, Christian, or someone incapable of formulating and adhering to any worldview at all. This seriously hinders the cause of Humanism, because it suggests that any view may bring about equally valuable, or even more valuable, changes in history. The Humanist, however, believes that only his ideology is capable of ushering mankind into a future paradise. How can he convince the rest of humanity to adopt a Humanistic view of history?

Ideologies Shape History

The Humanist solves this dilemma in two steps. First, he clarifies his assertion: men in and of themselves do not shape history; rather, men's *ideologies* are the dynamic force in history. Second, he declares that ideologies evolve, and therefore some ideologies are better suited for effecting change in different periods of history. Huxley claims that "major steps in the human phase of evolution are achieved by breakthroughs to new dominant patterns of mental organization, of knowledge, ideas and beliefs—ideological instead of physiological or biological organization."[37]

Notes and Asides

Elsewhere, Huxley expounds on this theory by insisting that, in man, dominant systems of ideas guide thought and action during a given period of human history, just as dominant types of organisms guide given periods of biological evolution. "After a certain time," says Huxley, "a dominant organization of thought may no longer fit the developing conditions of human life, or may come up against a limit and find that its capacity for interpreting the world and providing comprehension of human destiny is inadequate. Then history has to wait until a new and more appropriate organization of ideas and beliefs is brought to birth and becomes the new dominant system."[38]

The implications of this theory are clear: if man's systems of thought evolve, then some ideologies are hopelessly outdated and unsuited to modern problems, and other ideologies are precisely the solution for a certain era. It takes little imagination to guess which ideologies the Humanist considers outdated—any worldview that accepts the existence of the supernatural is scoffed at by Humanism. Thus, Humanists portray Christianity as a primitive ideology that may have been relevant in ancient history but is useless in addressing modern problems. Barnes states that there has been much discussion of the psychological contrast between primitive man and modern man. "It is more or less generally agreed that the dominating characteristics of primitive thought were an all-pervading belief in supernaturalism, an absence of high-developed logical thinking, and paucity of concrete scientific knowledge. If this be true, then it will be readily conceded that the great majority of Americans were primitive minded a couple of generations back, as indeed many remain to the present day."[39] That is, anyone who still believes in Christianity has a primitive mindset and cannot be expected to have any progressive impact on history today.[40]

So which ideology is most relevant for advancing the evolution of mankind? Huxley suggests a worldview suspiciously similar to Humanism: "Above all, it is necessary to take a scientific look at the historical process in general, as we have successfully begun to do with the general process of biological evolution. In so far as we succeed in this new scientific venture, we shall be able to construct the framework for a new, open-ended, and much more comprehensive pattern or system of ideas, capable of expansion and application in many new fields."[41]

Obviously, Humanists believe Humanism is the dominant ideology—which allows them to claim that man's ideologies influence history while they restrict Christianity and other worldviews from positively affecting the present or the future.

Thus, Humanism becomes the single causal agent for effecting change in mankind's destiny. Neither God, nor the environment, nor any man adhering to any worldview other than Humanism, can lead our

Notes and Asides

world into the future. Not surprisingly, the Humanist also believes that only Humanism can interpret the past properly. This results from the Humanist's beliefs about the relationship between evolutionary ethics and evolutionary history.

The Role of Ethics in the Study of History

Humanists believe that one's value judgments powerfully shape his interpretation of the past. Sidney Ratner declares that all scientific judgments, whether in history, natural sciences, or the social sciences, "are related to and depend upon ethical and moral judgments, and conversely."[42] And since no other worldview has provided the historian with an adequate ethical code (Barnes says, "Two thousand years of religion, philosophy and metaphysics have left us no reliable and definitive body of rules for conduct . . ."[43]), Humanists must provide the historian with the proper moral perspective for interpreting past history.

As explained in the chapter on Humanist ethics, Humanists believe they can create an entire system of ethics founded solely on man's rationality. For this reason, they do not worry that they might be presenting a biased account of history when they judge the past according to their system of morality. Ratner makes it very clear that ethics is as much "a normative science as economics or logic." "Hence," he says, "ethical and moral judgments in history need not be the expression of pure bias and prejudices, but may be based on rational grounds."[44]

The Humanist relies on his rationality, of course, because he believes no other standard for ethics exists. Ratner emphasizes that there "are no absolutes, no values or facts outside space and time, only those ends in view and facts that we help to discover or create."[45] Thus, the Humanist worldview, which Humanists believe is the ideology of the future, creates its own value system and then applies that system to judging history. All of mankind must subscribe to its judgments, because it is the dominant ideology of our time.

What, then, is the criterion by which Humanism would judge history? After addressing the problem of value judgments strictly from a rational standpoint, what has the Humanist deduced? Ratner, after explaining how ethics is relevant to science "because science, in the last analysis, is a human activity and is pursued because it satisfies the desire for knowledge for its own sake, and the desire to use knowledge as a means of satisfying other desires," says, "History, like the natural and social sciences, therefore cannot escape critical evaluation in terms of its contribution to human good."[46] Four words sum up Humanism's

Notes and Asides

criterion for judging the past: "contribution to human good." According to the Humanist, people, eras, and civilizations throughout history can all be judged by rationally examining whether they brought about "good" for humanity. Apparently, the Humanist considers this a better system of ethics (and a better means of judging history) than that of any other worldview. Thus, the Humanist believes that his ideology is not only best suited for meeting the challenges of the present and the future but also most appropriate for judging the past.

Indeed, the Humanist is convinced that the only way mankind can properly understand history and ensure the progress of the human race is by embracing Humanism. We must therefore examine the role Humanism would have mankind play in shaping history.

Man's Role in Creating the Future

As previously demonstrated, the Humanist believes that only men with a Humanistic worldview can play a significant role in promoting progress. It would seem that this would place strict limits on the extent to which man could dynamically affect history. However, the Humanist believes that individuals embracing this ideology can affect history almost limitlessly. Indeed, Humanism believes mankind can redeem itself through the course of history. Lamont bluntly declares, "Humanism assigns to man nothing less than the task of being his own savior and redeemer."[47]

Why? Simply because, as we noted earlier, the Humanist must remain optimistic about history because time is the only variable on which he may pin his hopes of salvation. While the Christian believes God incarnate is man's only Savior, the Humanist denies the supernatural and therefore can only hope for an earthly paradise brought about by mankind's own actions. Thus, the Humanist clings to the vision of progress implied by the evolutionary view. Huxley declares that "the evolutionary vision . . . illuminates our existence in a simple but almost overwhelming way. It exemplifies the truth that truth is great and will prevail, and the greater truth that truth will set us free."[48]

Humanism expects human history to culminate in a utopian society. Indeed, Lamont says that the nonexistence of any heaven to prepare for means there should be plenty of time to create one on earth:

> The philosophy of Humanism, with its conscious limitation of the human enterprise to this existence, sets us free to concentrate our entire energies, without distraction by either hopes or fears of individual immortality, on that building of the good society that has been the dream of saints and sages since the dawn of history.[49]

Notes and Asides

The Humanist remains optimistic about history because he believes he can save himself and mankind by leading the world into a utopian, global society. This also grants the Humanist's life a sense of purpose, since he creates a historic mission for the individual to work for the "human good." Lamont writes, "The individual, under whatever sky and no matter what his work or where he stands on the ladder of achievement, infuses his life with meaning through his devotion and contribution to the larger social good."[50]

What is more, the Humanist contends that he is unconcerned with whether utopia is achieved in his lifetime, because he perceives the individual as only a small fragment of humanity. Sarton claims, "It is worthwhile to interrogate the past as fully as we can, because the race is more important than the individual."[51] In this way, the Humanist believes all of mankind can be redeemed by the creation of a future paradise. History can be manipulated for the salvation of every man. The rationale for this attitude is summed up by Sarton: "I believe that I am only a fragment of humanity, yet that I must try to look at things from the point of view of the whole, and not of the fragment. Hence there is no past, there is no future, simply an everlasting present."[52] An everlasting present, of course, implies that all humanity will some day attain the redemption of having contributed to the progress that finally culminated in "the good society."

If anyone doubts that Humanism deifies man, this attitude toward history should bury such lingering uncertainty. The Humanist view of history portrays man as capable of both creating and redeeming humanity, given ample time. Man is described as Creator by Erich Fromm when he states, "Man creates himself in the historical process. . . ."[53] Later Fromm blatantly portrays man as his own Redeemer: "The messianic time is the next step in history, not its abolition. The messianic time is the time when man will have been fully born. When man was expelled from Paradise he lost his home; in the messianic time he will be at home again—in the world."[54] That is, man (operating from a Humanistic perspective) can create his own paradise on earth, thereby saving all mankind.[55]

> "It is worthwhile to interrogate the past as fully as we can, because the race is more important than the individual."
> —George Sarton

Of course, the Humanist is inconsistent with his own philosophy when he assigns this incredible redemptive power to man. In order to mesh with his naturalistic views, the Humanist should adhere to a strictly behavioristic perspective. Man should be described by the Humanist as controlled by his environment, rather than vice versa. Indeed, some Humanists do seem to embrace behaviorism—for example, Barnes admits that conduct is the inevitable result of a vast set of influences, from the general physical nature of mankind and particular hereditary traits of each individual to the effects of the most recent set of experiences that have operated on his psyche. "Our personality," he says, "at any time is but a cross-section of the habit-complexes which

Notes and Asides

have been built up in the lifelong process of conditioning. Human behavior, then, reveals a process of strict determinism obeying scientific laws as invariable as the law of gravitation."[56]

Despite this clear admission that man is not in control of his own destiny, however, Barnes, as a Humanist, still adheres to the belief that man can redeem himself through history. He justifies this stance by claiming that man is determined by his environment but is now in position to control his environment so that he will always be caused to choose correctly.

Thus, for Barnes and other Humanists who still profess behavioristic attitudes, man's redemptive work in history must focus on changing the environment so that in the future it will always cause man to behave in the correct manner. "From the deterministic point of view," says Barnes,

> we can feel assured that the person who is born with normal qualities and is afforded the opportunity to build up normal social habits is not likely to go wrong. We can thus work with some confidence in the task of improving the human stock biologically and in eliminating those social environments which constitute the breeding-places of bad habits and of anti-social attitudes and actions.[57]

And who will direct this restructuring of environment for the salvation of mankind? Not just anyone, according to Barnes. Rather, an intelligent, informed, experienced, elite class must make the decisions affecting humanity's destiny.

> [T]he vital classification of society should be into that of the able, intelligent, informed and experienced, on the one hand, and the mediocre, stupid, ignorant and incompetent, on the other. There will then be no difficulty in deciding as to which group we shall entrust the future destinies of mankind. More and more, history, biological science, psychology, educational philosophy and social science are uniting upon the position that we can hope for nothing better than the chaos of today unless we discover some more effective way for installing in positions of control and authority the capable minority, while at the same time securing some guaranty that they will not lose their sense of responsibility to the majority.[58]

Barnes's statement should trouble anyone concerned with human rights or individual freedom, if for no other reason than the fact that he makes no allowances for those who don't want to be manipulated into

Notes and Asides

further evolution. Still more troubling is the Humanists' description of the type of "destiny" they foresee being ushered in by a Humanistic approach to creating history. They believe that man's destiny lies in manipulating his environment so that he may further the progress of evolution. Huxley believes that "man's true destiny . . . is to be the chief agent for the future of evolution on this planet."[59] Thus, the Humanist is striving to redeem mankind by creating paradise on earth, but that paradise might be populated by a species more highly evolved than humans. Lamont admits this when he states, "Humanism definitely places the destiny of man within the very broad limits of this natural world. It submits that men can find plenty of scope and meaning in their lives through . . . helping to evolve a new species surpassing Man."[60]

What sort of species could be higher than man? Victor J. Stenger has an idea. He believes man is in the process of creating a greatly improved version of himself, "not by the painfully slow and largely random process of biological evolution," but by rapid and guided advances of technology. "This new form of 'life' I will call, for historical reasons, the *computer*."[61] Stenger is convinced that computers will eventually prove themselves more capable than humans in every meaningful realm of "life:"

> If there is anything we do that computers cannot, be patient. In time they will do it better, if it is worth doing at all.[62]

Further, it stands to reason that computers will have a better chance of withstanding absolute zero when the Second Law of Thermodynamics takes its final toll.

Of course, not every Humanist believes that mankind must focus all his energies on redeeming mankind by speeding up the evolution of the computer. But Stenger's ideas are certainly consistent with the Humanist attitude toward history. Stenger believes man will usher in a future paradise on earth—it's just that his paradise will be populated by computers programmed to preserve the consciousness of humanity. He admits that most of us, "with our deeply embedded anthropocentric traditions," may have very negative initial reactions to these ideas. But think about the question objectively, he insists.

> Given our own severely limited physical bodies, we can never hope to live longer than a century or to explore much beyond the confines of earth. Imagine, however, being part of a collective consciousness of all humankind and computerkind, with mental powers and sensory inputs infinitely superior to the ones we now possess. . . . With our infinitely expanded mental capacity,

"For the love of God they substitute love of humanity; for vicarious atonement the perfectibility of man through his own efforts, and for the hope of immortality in another world the hope of living in the memory of future generations."
—Carl L. Becker

Notes and Asides

> we would be able to think thoughts, to enjoy pleasures of beauty and intellect, beyond our wildest dreams and fantasies.[63]

Why shouldn't this be a possible future reality for the Humanist? It fits nicely with his optimism about the future, his belief that mankind can redeem itself through history, and his conviction that man can now work to control evolution to develop a species higher than himself.

Conclusion

For the Secular Humanist, history is not only about the past, it is also about revealing its ending. While Humanism does not go so far as to predict when the new world order will be achieved, it does declare that man will at some future date redeem himself by creating the ultimate social order. Once this order is perfect, mankind or computerkind will be perfect also. This optimism is a natural offshoot of Humanism's evolutionary perspective and deification of man.

By dethroning God, however, the Humanist removes the most reliable guide for history and must grant this power to some other force. To be consistent with his philosophy, the Humanist should grant it to the environment—but this creates inescapable problems, and therefore the Humanist falls back upon man as guide. More accurately, Humanists declare man's dominant emerging ideology to be the real dynamic force in history, and the elite few who embrace it the proper lords of the path to the future. Naturally, Humanists believe the dominant ideology of today is Secular Humanism. Thus, man working within a Humanistic framework becomes the savior of the world.

Likewise, only Humanists can judge the past properly, evaluating events according to their effect on the "social good." As one might surmise, this view of history allows for a number of "correct" perspectives according to different Humanistic definitions of the "social good." Indeed, this approach to history often denies the existence of any true chronology. Barnes confesses that this is unacceptable for many historians: "The historian may shout in despair that this means insufferable confusion, anarchy and complexity. We must frankly admit that for the time being it does. . . ."[64] But to the Humanist, it is a small price to pay for such large dividends.

[1]Julian Huxley, *Essays of a Humanist* (London: Chatto and Windus, 1964), p. 77.
[2]Will and Ariel Durant, *The Lessons of History* (New York: Simon and Schuster, 1968), p. 18.
[3]Ibid., p. 81. Durant says that in the last 3,421 years of recorded history only 268 years have seen no war. He quotes Heraclitus to the effect that war is the father of all things and peace an "unstable equilibrium."
[4]Ibid., p. 18.
[5]Ibid., p. 46. "Does history support a belief in God?" asks the Durants: "the answer must be a reluctant negative."
[6]Ibid., p. 19.
[7]*Humanist Manifesto II* (Buffalo: Prometheus Books, 1980), p. 13.
[8]Ibid., p. 14.
[9]Robert E. Egner and Lester E. Denonn, eds., *The Basic Writings of Bertrand Russell*(New York: Simon and Schuster, 1961), p. 685.
[10]Roger E. Greeley, ed., *The Best of Humanism* (Buffalo: Prometheus Books, 1988), p. 174.
[11]George Sarton, *The History of Science and the New Humanism* (Bloomington: Indiana University Press, 1962), p. 173.
[12]Edwin H. Wilson, "Humanism's Many Dimensions," in *The Humanist Alternative*, ed. Paul Kurtz (Buffalo: Prometheus, 1973), pp. 18-19.
[13]*Humanist Manifesto II*, p. 23.
[14]Corliss Lamont, *The Philosophy of Humanism* (New York: Frederick Ungar, 1982), p. 282.
[15]Harry Elmer Barnes, *Living in the Twentieth Century* (Indianapolis: Bobbs-Merrill, 1928), p. 32.
[16]Huxley, *Essays of a Humanist*, p. 29.
[17]Greeley, *The Best of Humanism*, p. 173.
[18]Harry Elmer Barnes, *The New History and the Social Studies* (New York: Century, 1925), p. 21.
[19]Huxley, *Essays of a Humanist*, p. 33.
[20]Ibid., p. 78.
[21]Egner and Denonn, eds., *The Basic Writings of Bertrand Russell*, p. 687.
[22]Ibid.
[23]Paul Kurtz, *Eupraxophy: Living Without Religion* (Buffalo: Prometheus, 1989), pp. 33-4.
[24]Barnes, *The New History and the Social Studies*, p. 300.
[25]William Floyd, *Humanizing Biblical Religion* (New York: Arbitrator Press, 1943), p. 253.
[26]Ibid., pp. 232-3.
[27]Kurtz, *Eupraxophy: Living Without Religion*, p. 34.
[28]Barnes, *Living in the Twentieth Century*, p. 361.
[29]Egner and Denonn, eds., *The Basic Writings of Bertrand Russell*, p. 524.
[30]Paul Kurtz, "Is Everyone a Humanist?" in *The Humanist Alternative*, ed. Kurtz, p. 182.
[31]Barnes, *Living in the Twentieth Century*, p. 377.
[32]*Humanist Manifesto I*, p. 8.
[33]Lamont, *The Philosophy of Humanism*, p. 280.
[34]Algernon D. Black, "Our Quest for Faith: Is Humanism Enough?" in *The Humanist Alternative*, ed. Kurtz, p. 75.
[35]Lamont, *The Philosophy of Humanism*, p. 109.
[36]*Humanist Manifesto II*, p. 16.
[37]Huxley, *Essays of a Humanist*, p. 76.
[38]Ibid., p. 51.
[39]Barnes, *Living in the Twentieth Century*, p. 21.
[40]For example, as we demonstrated in the Humanist ethics chapter, Christian morality is seen by the Humanist as a hindrance to the happiness of mankind. Humanist new morality, based on science, provides the only true basis for man's present and future satisfaction.
[41]Huxley, *Essays of a Humanist*, p. 52.
[42]Sidney Ratner, "Facts and Values in History," *The Humanist*, Jan./Feb. 1957, p. 35.
[43]Barnes, *The New History and the Social Studies*, p. 533.
[44]Ratner, "Facts and Values in History," p. 37.
[45]Ibid., p. 38.

[46]Ibid., p. 36.
[47]Lamont, *The Philosophy of Humanism*, p. 283.
[48]Huxley, *Essays of a Humanist*, p. 88. Compare this statement to Russell's assertion on page 729.
[49]Lamont, *The Philosophy of Humanism*, p. 115.
[50]Ibid., pp. 250-1.
[51]Sarton, *The History of Science and the New Humanism*, p. xiv.
[52]Ibid.
[53]Erich Fromm, *You Shall Be as Gods* (New York: Holt, Rinehart, and Winston, 1966), p. 88.
[54]Ibid., p. 123.
[55]It should be noted here that "messianic," "savior," "redeemer," and "saving oneself" are all religious expressions—further evidence that Humanism is a religious worldview. And why shouldn't it be? It takes huge quantities of faith to believe that Humanist ideology can alter the course of evolution for the good of mankind.
[56]Barnes, *Living in the Twentieth Century*, pp. 50-1.
[57]Ibid., p. 52.
[58]Barnes, *The New History and the Social Studies*, p. 596.
[59]Huxley, *Essays of a Humanist*, p. 32.
[60]Lamont, *The Philosophy of Humanism*, pp. 107-8.
[61]Victor J. Stenger, *Not By Design* (Buffalo: Prometheus Books, 1988), p. 186.
[62]Ibid., p. 188.
[63]Ibid., p. 189.
[64]Barnes, *Living in the Twentieth Century*, p. 366.

CHAPTER

31

MARXIST/ LENINIST HISTORY

"The real driving force of history is the revolutionary class struggle." [1]

—V. I. Lenin

"A historian is not just an impartial narrator who sets down facts and arranges them, albeit even in a scientifically based scheme; he is a fighter who sees his aim as bringing history to the service of the struggle for communism." [2]

—B. N. Ponomarev

"Whatever is the mode of production of a society, such in the main is the society itself, its ideas and theories, its political views and institutions. Or, to put it more crudely, whatever is man's manner of life, such is his manner of thought." [3]

—Joseph Stalin

SUMMARY

The Marxist/Leninist interpretation of history consists of one major and a few minor players. The major player is the dialectical nature of matter. All history—all reality—is seen as the outworking of this all-encompassing concept. It isn't just that matter is eternal, but that dialectical matter is eternal. All else follows from this premise. Dialectical matter determines history and all that history encompasses.

Marxist/Leninists understand matter or reality (whether the reality of physics, biology, or the social sciences) to operate through a process of thesis, antithesis, and synthesis. Whether subatomic or atomic, animate matter or inanimate, individual man or society, all live and move dialectically, since dialectics is the essence of matter and matter is ultimately all that is real. The so-called "hidden laws of nature" are the laws of dialectical process, and all nature obeys these laws. These laws were "discovered" by Marx and Engels and are as important to comprehending historical reality scientifically as Darwin's discovery of evolutionary law is to comprehending biology scientifically.

Marxist/Leninists begin with eternal matter and spontaneous generation and view history as a progression of biological and economic evolution that ultimately will result in a society of communist man in a communist paradise. According to Marxists, the future communist society is written into nature itself. The hidden, impersonal laws of nature—dialectical matter—have so determined the outcome. Man is merely the consequence of these impersonal happenings, but man is given a minor role to play, i.e., to nudge history along a little faster toward its predetermined end.

History records that socialist/communist man has been responsible for the death

Introduction

Marxism has developed its interpretation of history much more completely than has Humanism. Indeed, the Marxist view of history is central to the entire theory of Marxism. Karl Marx and Frederick Engels were so confident of the power of their approach to history that they believed it would lead mankind into a classless, perfectly democratic society. Engels, in a preface to *The Communist Manifesto*, declares that

of millions in his attempt to nudge history. Joseph Stalin alone was guilty of "the persecution, imprisonment, torture and death of some fifty million human beings" *prior* to World War II.[4] The historical struggle for communism is looked on as synonymous with the biological struggle for existence. Only the fit will survive, and the Marxists believe that the proletariat are the fit.

The problem, of course, is calling a halt to the historical process once the desired end is accomplished. According to the dialectical interpretation of reality, all syntheses are transitory, that is, all become new theses that, in turn, rouse their particular antitheses. The process never ends; it is eternal. To view history as a move from eternal nonliving matter to living matter, from living matter to man, from man the biological animal to man the economic animal, from the economic to the social, and from the social to the paradise of a communist society—and then call off the dialectical process because the end has been accomplished—is a problem of major proportions.

The whole process of human history is the workings of dialectical matter through biological evolution, economics, and the social order. The struggle between the bourgeoisie and the proletariat on the economic-social level is basically the same struggle involved in the atom and in the evolutionary process of living matter. Historical materialism is dialectical materialism wrought in history. It is historical determinism with a vengeance. While Marxists seek to make man significant in some ways, impersonal, dialectical matter is the only critical aspect of the equation. Life, man, mind, love, ideas, and consciousness are all secondary to the great forces determining nature and history.

the pamphlet's central proposition "is destined to do for history what Darwin's theory has done for biology. . . ."[5]

Marxists believe their historical perspective is based strictly on a scientific view of the world, and that this scientific approach makes their view better suited than any other to interpret history. Naturally, the Marxist works to integrate other conclusions of science with his own approach, including evolutionary theory. V. I. Lenin provides a fine example of the Marxist faith in evolution when he declares, "..."

Notes and Asides

Darwin put an end to the view of animal and plant species being unconnected, fortuitous, 'created by God' and immutable, and was the first to put biology on an absolutely scientific basis by establishing the mutability and the succession of species. . . ."[6]

This belief in evolution shapes the Marxist view of history in much the same way it shaped Secular Humanism's view. The Marxist sees evolution as continuously encouraging development and progress in living things; therefore he assumes that man has been constantly improving himself and will continue to progress in the future. This attitude is summed up in *The Fundamentals of Marxist-Leninist Philosophy*:

> Human history has not been a continuous and straight ascent, always and everywhere expressing the march of progress. It has known reverses, zigzags, disasters such as wars, barbarian invasions, the decline and fall of powerful states, the disappearance of entire nations. But taken as a whole it has been an ascent, from one social-economic formation to another, from lower to higher forms.[7]

"Evolutionism, when it ceases to be simply a theorem in biology and becomes a principle for interpreting the total historical process, is a form of Historicism."
—C. S. Lewis

In this sense, the Marxist/Leninist and Secular Humanist views of history are identical. However, as will become clear, Marxism creates a much stronger framework for its historical perspective.

For now, it is important to note that Marxism's "scientific" approach to biology leaves no room in its worldview for God, especially a God who might influence history. Maurice Cornforth proclaims, "The whole conception of an external influence at work in human affairs—whether it is called the Absolute Spirit, God, Fate, or merely the influence of the stars, makes very little difference—is an idealist conception, totally foreign to science and therefore to Marxism."[8] The scientific approach to history, according to the Marxist, leaves no room for God, or indeed any supernatural entities. For this reason, the Marxist view of history is termed Historical Materialism. In an effort to be consistent with their philosophy, Marxists cling to the "scientific" assumption that only matter exists and only it can influence world events. Stalin writes, ". . . Marx's philosophical materialism holds that the world is by its very nature *material*, that the multifold phenomena of the world constitute different forms of matter in motion, that interconnection and interdependence of phenomena, as established by the dialectical method, are a law of the development of moving matter, and that the world develops in accordance with the laws of movement of matter and stands in no need of a 'universal spirit.'"[9]

This is the crucial proposition for the Marxist view of history and, indeed, for the Marxist worldview. Neither God, nor angels, nor men's

Notes and Asides

souls act as the actual basis for the workings of history; rather, matter obeying specific laws drives the progress of the world. For the Marxist, matter is primary, and anything else (if there is anything else) is but a pale reflection. The questions arise, then: What specific material things form the foundation on which man's societies are based? And do any of the institutions or people in society play any role in charting the course of history?

Matter as the Basis For the Social Superstructure

The central flaw of other worldviews' perceptions of history, according to the Marxist, is that these views do not recognize the root material cause behind all historical movement. Frederick Engels declares, "The inconsistency [in other approaches to history] does not lie in the fact that ideal driving forces are recognized, but in the investigation not being carried further back behind these into their motive causes."[10] That is, the Marxist will admit that sometimes the workings of men's minds influence history, but these workings are ultimately influenced by material forces outside of man. Thus, Marx postulates, "It is not the consciousness of men that determines their existence, but, on the contrary, their social existence determines their consciousness."[11] If one wants to get at the real driving force behind history, he must look beyond the ideas of men to the true reality of the material world.

Historical Materialism is a Marxist theory which states that all of human history results from matter's obedience to the laws of the dialetic.

Specifically, he must examine mankind's means of production and exchange to understand the basis for all historical progress. Marxists believe this material, concrete aspect of man's culture determines the historical development of the species of man. Engels states, "The materialist conception of history starts from the principle that production, and with production the exchange of its products, is the basis of every social order."[12] Put more simply, economics is the driving force of history—as Marx says, "With the change of the economic foundation the entire immense superstructure is more or less rapidly transformed."[13] Engels elaborates:

> The economic structure of society always furnishes the real basis, starting from which we can alone work out the ultimate explanation of the whole superstructure of juridical and political institutions as well as of religious, philosophical and other ideas of a given historical period.[14]

The Marxist believes that economics acts as the foundation for man's whole social superstructure. Judging from Engels's last statement, as well as Marx's prediction that social consciousness is deter-

Notes and Asides

mined by social existence, it would also seem that Marxists believe man's ideas are shaped by the particular economic system extant in his society. A careful reading of Marxist leaders proves this assumption true. Marx and Engels proclaim,

> Morality, religion, metaphysics, all the rest of ideology and their corresponding forms of consciousness . . . no longer retain the semblance of independence. They have no history, no development; but men, developing their material production and their material intercourse, alter, along with this their real existence, their thinking and the products of their thinking.[15]

Elsewhere Engels declares that "in every historical epoch, the prevailing mode of economic production and exchange, and the social organization necessarily following from it, form the basis upon which is built up, and from which alone can be explained, the political and intellectual history of that epoch. . . ."[16]

This attitude is maintained in modern Marxist thought, as well. Cornforth says that "circumstances not only limit what men *can* do, but condition what in practice they *want* to do; people's desires, aims and ideals are conditioned by their circumstances; what one effectively wants to do, or would like to see done, takes its start from the circumstances in which the wish is born. . . . men's ways of thinking—the scope of their ideas, the ways they conceive of themselves and of the world about them—are conditioned by circumstances."[17] *The Fundamentals of Marxist-Leninist Philosophy* sums up:

> In complete accord with the materialist world outlook, historical materialism proceeds from the proposition that social existence is primary in relation to social consciousness. Social consciousness is a reflection of social existence. It may be a more or less correct reflection or it may be false. It is not social consciousness or the ideas of some political leader that determine the system of social life and the direction of social development, as the idealists assume. On the contrary, *it is social existence that ultimately determines social consciousness, the ideas, aspirations and aims of individuals and social classes*.[18]

For Marxism, the economic structure of society proves to be the driving force of history. Governments, courts, philosophies, and religions all are based on this foundation and therefore affect history only to the extent that economics shapes their ability to guide man's development. Thus it appears that, for the Marxist, economics is the only

Notes and Asides

dynamic force in history, and all other aspects of mankind and his society are determined by it. The Marxist, however, attempts to evade this conclusion by claiming that economics, in shaping society's superstructure and man's ideas, does not leave these secondary forces predetermined and powerless. Engels writes, "According to the materialist conception of history the determining element in history is *ultimately* the production and reproduction in real life. More than this neither Marx nor I have ever asserted. If therefore somebody twists this into the statement that the economic element is the *only* determining one, he transforms it into a meaningless, abstract and absurd phrase. The economic situation is the basis, but the various elements of the superstructure . . . also exercise their influence upon the course of the historical struggles and in many cases preponderate in determining their form."[19]

Obviously, Marxists refuse to draw the logically necessary conclusion from historical materialism: that man has no say in the progress of society and thought. Why? Because this conclusion would destroy the need for a Marxist worldview, since (if it were true) it would mean that man is powerless to change the course of history and therefore need not act or adhere to any ideology. But can the Marxist escape this conclusion after placing such an emphasis on the economic basis for history?

Economic Determinism

Marx believes that man can still be viewed as possessing free will, but he carefully distinguishes between being totally free and being free within the constraints placed on man by all outside, material influences. He writes, "Men make their own history, but they do not make it just as they please; they do not make it under circumstances chosen by themselves, but under circumstances directly encountered, given and transmitted from the past."[20] Within the constraint of circumstances, though, man becomes the dynamic force in history. *The Fundamentals of Marxist-Leninist Philosophy* is also optimistic about man's impact on history: "*The people is the chief creator, the real subject of history*—this is the fundamental proposition of historical materialism."[21]

But despite all this optimism, many Marxist claims parade the fact that economics determines the entire course of history, inexorably steamrolling anyone who does not "choose" the course already predetermined by the modes of production and exchange. Marx states,

> In the social production which men carry on they enter into definite relations that are indispensable and independent of their will; these relations of production correspond to a definite

Notes and Asides

> stage of development of their material powers of production. The sum total of these relations of production constitutes the economic structure of society—the real foundation, on which rise legal and political superstructures and to which correspond definite forms of social consciousness. *The mode of production in material life determines the general character of the social, political and spiritual processes of life.*[22]

The key word, of course, is *determines*. If indeed the mode of production determines the general character of all aspects of life, then the specific influences of these aspects can only be extensions of the development of history already set in motion by the economic foundation. That is, man is free to choose, but he can only choose one specific direction if he hopes to influence history. All other directions are fruitless.

Marx seems to admit as much when he says,

> Are men free to choose this or that form of society for themselves? By no means. Assume a particular state of development in the productive forces of man and you will get a particular form of commerce and consumption. Assume particular stages of development in production, commerce and consumption and you will have a corresponding social structure, a corresponding organization of the family, of orders or of classes, in a word, a corresponding civil society. . . . It is superfluous to add that men are not free to choose their *productive forces*—which are the basis of all their history—for every productive force is an acquired force, the product of former activity.[23]

But if man may not choose his society, his society's superstructure, or its mode of production, and if these things in turn determine his mode of thought, then what on earth can man choose? It would seem that man could choose only to go along with the flow of history as determined by the economic structure. Should he choose otherwise, history will sweep him aside.

This conclusion seems even more inescapable in light of the Marxist's belief that history is governed by certain scientifically discoverable laws. Cornforth declares, "In explaining social development and predicting its continuation, therefore, the materialist conception of history does not, as a scientific conception, need to invoke any inexorable 'fate' or 'destiny' brooding over human affairs and directing them. We conduct our affairs without that. And still the conduct of our affairs is, like other things, explicable and predictable."[24] Social development is predictable, according to the Marxist, because it adheres to

Notes and Asides

certain laws. Lenin believes Marx drew attention "to a scientific study of history as a single process which, with all its immense variety and contradictoriness, is governed by definite laws."[25] These laws are independent of mankind's will and desires, as pointed out by a Marxist philosophy text: "The fundamental direction of social development, for example the transition from feudalism to capitalism or the replacement of capitalist by socialist society, is determined by objective laws that do not depend on the will and consciousness of people, even the most outstanding."[26]

If history really develops according to certain inescapable laws, then no man, society, or philosophy can act as the driving force of history, or indeed influence history in any valuable manner. If history is driven by laws toward a certain goal that inevitably will be achieved, then man's efforts toward or away from that goal are insignificant. Engels hints at this conclusion when he writes,

> That which is willed happens but rarely; in the majority of instances the numerous desired ends cross and conflict with one another, or these ends themselves are from the outset incapable of realization or the means of attaining them are insufficient. . . . The ends of the actions are intended, but the results which actually follow from these actions are not intended; or when they do seem to correspond to the end intended, they ultimately have consequences quite other than those intended. Historical events thus appear on the whole to be likewise governed by chance. But where on the surface accident holds sway, there actually it is always governed by inner, hidden laws.[27]

"The third [broad conception of history] is that history as actuality is moving in some direction away from the low level of primitive beginnings, on an upward gradient toward a more ideal order—as imagined by . . . Karl Marx . . . "
—Charles Beard

The sinister implications of belief in such "hidden laws" appear when we realize that they allow Marxists to abandon both morality and reason, since neither will alter the course of development dictated by these laws, and since whatever he does he can justify as predetermined by the "hidden laws" that always govern historical events. Stalin claims, "Hence the practical activity of the party of the proletariat must not be based on the good wishes of 'outstanding individuals,' not on the dictates of 'reason,' 'universal morals,' etc., but on the laws of development of society and on the study of these laws."[28]

Clearly, these laws operate outside the constraints of human influence. Indeed, Marxists believe that these laws create the great men who move history in a specific direction, rather than that great men change the course of history. Engels states,

> That such and such a man and precisely that man arises at a particular time in a particular country is, of course, pure chance.

Notes and Asides

> But if one eliminates him there is a demand for a substitute, and this substitute will be found, good or bad, but in the long run he will be found. That Napoleon, just that particular Corsican, should have been the military dictator whom the French Republic, exhausted by its own warfare, had rendered necessary, was chance; but that, if a Napoleon had been lacking, another would have filled the place, is proved by the fact that a man was always found as soon as he became necessary: Caesar, Augustus, Cromwell, etc.[29]

That is, the development of history according to certain laws chooses the great men in history; men are only great when they work in accordance with these laws.

This is the redemptive aspect of the Marxist interpretation of history. According to this "scientific" approach, mankind is guaranteed development of a future paradise on earth by specific historical laws. These laws will guide history through a series of economic systems to a system on which the perfect society can be built. This redemption is guaranteed, regardless of the action or inaction of individuals. Indeed, the Marxist grants this view of history Godlike powers by including omnipotence. Lenin writes, "The Marxist doctrine is omnipotent because it is true. It is comprehensive and harmonious, and provides men with an integral world outlook irreconcilable with any form of superstition, reaction, or defence of bourgeois oppression."[30]

Like Humanism's philosophy of history, Marxism's view of history as redemptive and Godlike attempts to grant mankind a sense of purpose. The Marxist believes the march toward a perfect society gives the individual's life meaning. Thus, *The Fundamentals of Marxist-Leninist Philosophy* declares, "But taken as a whole, the contemporary historical process is heading towards socialism and communism, and in this lies its profound meaning."[31]

Communism as Inevitable

The paradise to which all of history is leading, Marx discovered, is a socialist/communist society. Salvation, for the Marxist, lies in the consummation of the historical process in a one-world utopia. The Marxist believes that there exist laws of development moving the world ever closer to communism. Lenin proclaims,

> Communists should know that the future belongs to them; therefore we can (and must) combine the most intense passion in the great revolutionary struggle with the coolest and most

> sober estimation of the frenzied ravings of the bourgeoisie. But in all cases and in all countries communism is becoming steeled and is spreading, its roots are so deep that persecution does not weaken it, does not debilitate it, but strengthens it.[32]

As previously demonstrated, the laws leading the world toward communism are inexorable, and no amount of human will can stop the collapse of capitalism, the rise of socialism, and the steady transition from socialism to communism. Cornforth declares,

> From the point of view of the capitalist class, Marx's theory is certainly "fatalistic". It says: You cannot contrive a managed capitalism, you cannot do away with the class struggle, you cannot keep the system going indefinitely. It does not go so far as to say, You can do nothing to block socialist advance; but it does say, You can never block it once for all, but will have to keep on blocking it until finally it blocks you.[33]

"All nations will arrive at socialism—this is inevitable . . ."
—V. I. Lenin

Lenin is equally certain of the future for all mankind: "All nations will arrive at socialism—this is inevitable. . . ."[34] Georgi Shakhnazarov echoes Lenin today, stating, "*Socialism is inevitable and it will constantly improve itself.*"[35]

The Marxist believes that there are scientific laws that direct the evolution of economic systems toward a paradisiacal end. Marxism perceives men's efforts toward any other end as useless and insignificant, declaring that mankind will achieve utopia (a communist society) despite all efforts and desires to the contrary. Surely, this is the ultimate proof that Marxism's economic determinism leaves no room for men's ideas or societies as historical forces. Surely the insignificance of man rings forth in this attitude and in the words of Engels: "The final causes of all social changes and political revolutions are to be sought, not in men's brains, not in man's better insight into eternal truth and justice, but in changes in the modes of production and exchange. They are to be sought, not in the *philosophy*, but in the *economics* of each particular epoch."[36]

The Dialectic Applied to History

As previously noted, the Marxist cannot accept the premise that man and his society are insignificant historical forces, because this erases the need for the Marxist party and discourages the revolution of the proletariat. Thus, the Marxist must distinguish between absolute predetermination and the determination enforced by historical laws:

Notes and Asides

> Historical necessity is, therefore, not the same thing as predetermination. In real life, thanks to the effect of objective laws and various trends of social development, there arise certain possibilities, the realisation of which depends on the activity of the masses, on the course of the class struggle, on the scientifically worked out policies of Marxist parties.[37]

The possibilities that arise, of course, are only the possibilities of recognizing the unalterable course of history and then working to hasten the realization of its end.

Thus, man is free in the sense that he may influence history by striving to achieve communism, but he is determined in the sense that he can affect history in no other way and is headed toward communism whether he likes it or not. Communism is inevitable, as dictated by the laws of history. These laws, in turn, are governed by the dialectic. Engels states, "Dialectics is nothing more than the science of the general laws of motion and development of Nature, human society and thought."[38] That is, the whole process of history can be explained by applying the laws of the dialectic to the evolution of the modes of production of various societies.

Put simply, the dialectic (which has been explained in the chapter on Marxist philosophy) predicts that the initial phase of development (the thesis) will draw to itself its opposite (the antithesis), and these opposing forces will clash, bringing about a new, more developed state of affairs (the synthesis). This synthesis becomes a new thesis for the next stage in historical development, and the dialectical process begins anew. Marxists believe that the dialectic has guided society through certain phases (all based on economic structures) in a constant upward spiral. They believe that human society began with primitive communism, but thesis and antithesis collided and gave birth to societies based on slavery, which in turn developed (thanks to the guidance of the dialectic) into feudalism. This phase progressed into capitalism, which is now moving toward socialism. The continued clash of the bourgeoisie (the present thesis) with the proletariat (the present antithesis) will lead society into a transitional phase—socialism—and when the clash is resolved due to the abolition of classes, society will have achieved communism. Thus, history must obey the laws of the dialectic, and these laws declare that economic structures will eventually evolve into communism, on which the perfect societal superstructure will arise.

The dialectical nature of the Marxist approach to history plays a crucial role in Marxists' theory not only because it is the mechanism that causes history to progress toward redemption for mankind but also because it allows Marxists to suggest that mankind does shape history.

While Marxism's reliance on economic determinism and inexorable laws seems to guarantee mankind's insignificance in the face of the historical process, the dialectic's reliance on the clash of forces to achieve synthesis creates the need for mankind to provide the clash. The individual is still insignificant in the Marxist view of history, but classes of mankind (in modern times, the bourgeoisie and the proletariat) can play a role in the development of mankind. Cornforth states, "Historical development is not determined by the personal decisions of public men, but by the movement of classes."[39]

Thus, the dialectic appears to save the Marxist interpretation of history from elevating man's development to a position totally independent of men's actions. Of course, men's actions only matter with regard to their movements as a class, and even then only if they are working in accordance with the laws of history. In other words, in modern times, only the proletariat can work as a progressive force, and even then only under the guidance of the Marxist party (because only the party truly understands the historical process). Man's ability to shape history according to this view is, to say the least, limited. But the Marxist stresses this ability as much as possible.

Revolution as the Catalyst of History

The Marxist emphasizes the revolutionary periods in history to play up the importance of class action in hastening progress. Marx states, "At a certain stage of their development, the material forces of production in society come in conflict with the existing relations of production, or—what is but a legal expression for the same thing—with the property relations within which they had been at work before. From forms of development of the forces of production these relations turn into their fetters. Then comes the period of social revolution."[40]

This period of social revolution requires classes to mobilize to act as the catalyst for history. Stalin declares,

> Up to a certain period the development of the productive forces and the changes in the realm of the relations of production proceed spontaneously, independently of the will of men. But that is so only up to a certain moment, until the new and developing productive forces have reached a proper state of maturity. After the new productive forces have matured, the existing relations of production and their upholders—the ruling classes—become that "insuperable" obstacle which can only be removed by the conscious action of the new classes, by the forcible acts of these classes, by revolution.[41]

Notes and Asides

When such a time comes, says Stalin, "The spontaneous process of development yields place to the conscious actions of men, peaceful development to violent upheaval, evolution to revolution."[42]

Marxism so desperately requires the participation of the masses (from a practical standpoint) that it often describes the revolutionary's role as the most critical in history. Lenin went so far as to proclaim, "According to the theory of socialism, i.e., of Marxism . . . the real driving force of history is the revolutionary class struggle."[43]

In theory, however, the Marxist should not feel such a desperate need for the classes to act. According to Marxism's theoretical interpretation of history, a revolutionary class can only (at most) hasten the inevitable progress of history—indeed, historical laws guarantee the

CLOSE-UP

Joseph Stalin (1879-1953)

Born Iosif Vissarionovich Dzhugashvili, Joseph Stalin changed his name to the Russian term for "man of steel." This new surname was in many ways appropriate. Not only did Stalin seem indestructible—in his youth, he survived numerous bank robberies committed in support of the Marxist party, and escaped from a Siberian prison camp—but he also proved to be a dictator of the hardest, most unforgiving order. After V.I. Lenin's death in 1924, Stalin and two other men grappled for control of the USSR, and Stalin won the battle at a cost of numerous lives. Officials ideologically opposed to him usually wound up in obscure prison camps or facing firing squads. Once in power, Stalin incorporated his methodology of terror into his governmental policies. Approximately fourteen million peasants died prematurely under Stalin's regime from 1930-1937. His World War II pact with Adolph Hitler and his blatant unwillingness to honor such pacts or to act as a trustworthy ally provides us with a shining example of the practical consequences of adhering to the Marxist belief that the ends justify the means. Indeed, Stalin's entire career serves as a horrifying reminder of the actions which can be justified by a Marxist/Leninist worldview.

eventual achievement of a future paradise whether the proletariat violently and quickly overthrows the bourgeoisie, or the bourgeoisie is slowly crowded out by the increasing mass of the proletariat. Lenin alludes to this fact elsewhere when he explains that "revolutionary periods are mainly such periods in history when the clash of contending social forces, in a comparatively short space of time, decides the question of the country's choice of a direct or a zigzag path of development for a comparatively very long time."[44] The zigzag path is still a path of development—still a move toward communism—it is simply a less direct route.

Naturally, Marxists downplay the possibility of following the zigzag path of development, since it slows down the realization of their goals and destroys any notion of human freedom in determining the course of history. As we have seen, without human freedom there is no need for philosophies or ideologies (including Marxism), since mankind is guaranteed to progress with or without guidance from a worldview. Thus, the Marxist emphasizes the need to follow the direct route to progress: revolution under the guidance of the ideology of the Marxist party. *The Fundamentals of Marxist-Leninist Philosophy* declares, "[P]rogressive, revolutionary ideas and the policies based on them play a great part, particularly when these ideas become widespread among the masses, when they act as a mobilising, organising and transforming historical force. Marxism-Leninism and the policies of the Marxist parties and socialist states that are based upon it play such a role in the present age."[45] Whereas ideas should be written off by a materialist worldview as insignificant reflections of reality, they instead take on great meaning when espoused by Marxists.

Still another inconsistency of the Marxist insistence that man must strive to take the direct path toward communism lies in that it seems to grant classes acting in a revolutionary manner the power to be historical catalysts, thereby achieving a modicum of freedom. But these classes are, according to the Marxist view, determined by economic structures. "These warring classes of society," writes Engels, "are always the products of the modes of production and of exchange—in a word, of the economic conditions of their time."[46] The inconsistency is obvious: if economic conditions determine the character of classes and the individuals who make up these classes, then the people within these predetermined groups cannot be free in any meaningful sense.

Marxism's historical materialism, based on economic determinism and the laws of the dialectic, denies mankind and society any real free agency in acting as a historical force. This would seem to be a major flaw in the Marxist interpretation of history. However, even if the Marxist were able to reconcile these inconsistencies, he is faced with still another difficulty.

Notes and Asides

The Future According to Marx

The dialectic, according to the Marxist, is ultimate reality. It is *the* mechanism that drives history forward. But if we grant the Marxist the premise that classes act as a catalyst for the dialectic (remember that Cornforth tells us, "Historical development is not determined by the personal decisions of public men, but by the movement of classes."[47]), then what becomes of the dialectic when classes cease to exist?

Under communism, the Marxist believes, all class distinctions will be abolished. "The ultimate goal of the class struggle waged by the proletariat is to abolish capitalist society with its inevitable antagonism between classes, and to create the classless communist society."[48] But without classes, what will act as the thesis and the antithesis to drive the dialectic toward a clash and ultimately to a new synthesis? What will keep the wheels of history turning? Engels sums up the problem when he writes, ". . . the whole history of mankind . . . has been a history of class struggles, contests between exploiting and exploited, ruling and oppressed classes; . . . the history of these class struggles forms a series of evolution in which, now-a-days, a stage has been reached where the exploited and oppressed class—the proletariat—cannot attain its emancipation from the sway of the exploiting and ruling class—the bourgeoisie—without, at the same time, and once and for all, emancipating society at large from all exploitation, oppression, class-distinctions and class struggles."[49]

The abolition of classes, then, seems to spell the end of historical development. Without classes, the dialectic has no catalyst. Further, the dialectic has constantly improved mankind's economic structures (and consequently, mankind's societies and ideas) throughout history, but as soon as the dialectic leads the whole world to communism, the ultimate mode of production and exchange will have been achieved, and the need for the dialectic will have been erased. Cornforth states,

> The socialist revolution is different in kind from every previous revolutionary change in human society. In every revolution the economic structure of society is transformed. Every previous transformation has meant the birth and consolidation of a new system of exploitation. The socialist revolution, on the other hand, once and for all ends all exploitation of man by man.[50]

How can the dialectic lead mankind beyond communism? No better economic structure (and therefore, no better basis for society and men's ideas) exists.

Notes and Asides

Indeed, communism seems to be, from the Marxist perspective, the final phase in history—paradise on earth. *The Fundamentals of Marxist-Leninist Philosophy* proclaims,

> The victory of communism on a world scale will provide the necessary material and intellectual preconditions for the merging of nations. A communist economy developing according to a single plan and securing a degree of economic integration never known before will gradually be formed throughout the world. There will emerge a common moral code which will fully absorb all that is best in the character of each nation. There will be a common language, a common means of communication for all people. Mankind will become one united, fraternal community completely free of antagonisms.[51]

This freedom from antagonisms allows the communist society to blossom into paradise. Cornforth believes, "When all mankind is free from exploitation, people will live without want, in security and happiness, and will be fully capable of taking care of the future."[52] And elsewhere he states, "The equality which communism brings is the equal opportunity for everyone to develop all his capacities as a many-sided individual."[53]

Obviously, the Marxist believes that the dialectic is leading mankind into paradise. This is the redemptive aspect of historical materialism: the dialectic will save mankind from the evils of capitalism (and all other forms of oppression) by guiding the world to a communist society. Marx contrasts the evils of capitalism and the perfect nature of communism when he speaks of the transitional phase of socialism: ". . . what we have to deal with here is a communist society, not as if *it had developed on a basis of its own*, but on the contrary as *it emerges from capitalist society*, which is thus in every respect tainted economically, morally and intellectually with the hereditary diseases of the old society from whose womb it is emerging. . . . these deficiencies are unavoidable in the first phase of communist society when it is just emerging after prolonged birthpangs from capitalist society."[54] But these deficiencies will be corrected. And eventually, mankind will be redeemed by the dialectic and live in an earthly paradise.

The only problem, of course, is that the dialectic becomes unnecessary when this utopia is achieved. The dialectic is a mechanism that encourages progress, and when society is perfected there is no need for a progressive mechanism. But the Marxist cannot simply abandon the dialectic once world communism exists because, as we have noted, the

Notes and Asides

dialectic is his ultimate reality. Marxism can no more abandon the dialectic than ignore the law of gravity—it is a process, a series of laws, as fundamental as existence itself. Thus, the Marxist must work under the assumption that the dialectical process continues to occur beyond communism.

Beyond Communism

Stalin admits as much: "Further, if the world is in a state of constant movement and development, if the dying away of the old and the upgrowth of the new is a law of development, then it is clear that there can be no 'immutable' social systems. . . ."[55] It would seem that even a communist utopia must develop into something better. But what?

Wherever the dialectic leads communism, the Marxist is certain it will not be a regression to an old economic structure. Cornforth states,

> Marx's predictions concerned the work of Communist organisations in bringing about first socialism, and then the transition from socialism to communism. It is clear enough that, when the latter goal is realised, the communist organisation will have completed its function. So what people do after that will be up to them. We can certainly predict that the principal causes of present social ills will by then have been finally removed and that, having established social appropriation to match social production, people will not go back again to private appropriation.[56]

But if the dialectic no longer is based on changing modes of production and exchange, then what will fuel the changes wrought by the dialectic?

Stalin hints that, beyond communism, it may be man's ideas that advance the dialectical process. He writes, "New social ideas and theories arise only after the development of the material life of society has set new tasks before society. But once they have arisen they become a most potent force which facilitates the carrying out of the new tasks set by the development of the material life of society, a force which facilitates the progress of society."[57] Indeed, it seems to be the consensus view of Marxists that man will begin governing history once communism is achieved (a view similar to the Humanist belief that man is now capable of controlling his own evolution). Cornforth declares,

> With communism, then, there disappears the last vestige of the domination of man by his own means of production and his own products. Henceforward man is fully the master of his own

> social organisation and increasingly the lord of nature. With this, as Marx said, the prehistory of mankind ends and human history begins.[58]

The Marxist expects the dialectic to further improve on the perfection of communist society as history marches on. In this, the Marxist interpretation of history never wavers from its conviction: history is guided by the dialectic toward a future world order fit for mankind.

Conclusion

There are many similarities between Marxist/Leninist historical materialism and the Secular Humanist interpretation of history. Both Marxists and Humanists view history from an evolutionary perspective, and therefore both believe mankind's history will always progress, just as the development of life constantly progresses. Consequently, both worldviews perceive the historical process as guaranteeing the redemption of mankind through the future establishment of some kind of heaven on earth. Instead of Jesus Christ establishing the Kingdom of God on earth, both Marxists and Humanists insist that evolving man—the new socialist man—will usher in the Kingdom of Man.

Marxism differs from Humanism, however, in that the Marxist establishes a much stronger basis for his faith in the historical process. He believes that history operates according to specific, discoverable laws of the dialectic, changing man's economic structures and thereby revolutionizing men's societies and ideas.

Marxists try to re-establish man as a driving force in history by declaring the revolution of the oppressed classes to be the catalyst for the dialectical process. According to this view, only people who act in accordance with the laws of history and the course of development have any impact. Thus the individual, in the Marxist view of history, is much like the fan at a fixed boxing match. No matter how long and loud the fan cheers, no matter how hard he claps and stomps his feet, the boxer "taking a dive" will undoubtedly lose; one might as well clap and cheer for the predetermined winner, perhaps encouraging him to win the bout more decisively.

Put in Marxist terms, whether mankind takes the direct route or zigzags, the final outcome of history is always the same. The Marxist believes his worldview alone adheres to the scientific conception of history and that natural laws guarantee inevitable progress. Marxism grants all power to the historical process and calls for the individual only to work in submission to this omnipotent force. Says Marx, "History is the judge—its executioner, the proletarian."[59]

[1]V. I. Lenin, *Collected Works*, forty-five volumes (Moscow: Progress Publishers, 1980), vol. 11, p. 71.
[2]B. N. Ponomarev, "Report to the All-Union Historian's Conference" (Moscow), Dec. 18, 1962.
[3]Joseph Stalin, *Dialectical and Historical Materialism* (New York: International, 1977), p. 29.
[4]Malachi Martin, *The Keys of This Blood* (New York: Simon and Schuster, 1990), p. 177.
[5]Frederick Engels, *The Communist Manifesto* (Chicago: Henry Regnery, 1954), p. 5.
[6]Lenin, *Collected Works*, vol. 1, p. 142.
[7]F. V. Konstantinov, ed., *The Fundamentals of Marxist-Leninist Philosophy* (Moscow: Progress Publishers, 1982), pp. 208-9.
[8]Maurice Cornforth, *Historical Materialism* (New York: International, 1972), p. 27.
[9]Stalin, *Dialectical and Historical Materialism*, p. 15.
[10]Frederick Engels, *Ludwig Feuerbach* (New York: International, 1934), p. 59.
[11]Karl Marx, *A Contribution to the Critique of Political Economy* (New York: International, 1904), p. 11. Marx's view here is identical to that of the existentialists, who insist that existence precedes essence. Little wonder that so many existentialists have also been Marxists.
[12]Frederick Engels, *Anti-Dühring* (London: 1934), p. 294. Cited in Gustav A. Wetter, *Dialectical Materialism* (Westport, CT: Greenwood Press, 1977), p. 40.
[13]Marx, *Contribution to the Critique of Political Economy*, p. 12.
[14]Frederick Engels, *Socialism: Utopian and Scientific* (New York: International, 1935), p. 51.
[15]Karl Marx and Frederick Engels, *On Historical Materialism* (New York: International, 1974), p. 23.
[16]Marx and Engels, *The Communist Manifesto*, p. 5.
[17]Maurice Cornforth, *The Open Philosophy and the Open Society* (New York: International, 1976), pp. 133-4.
[18]Konstantinov, ed., *The Fundamentals of Marxist-Leninist Philosophy*, p. 202.
[19]Letter to Block, in Frederick Engels, *Selected Correspondence* (New York: International, 1942), p. 475. Cited in Charles J. McFadden, *The Philosophy of Communism* (Kenosha, WI: Cross, 1963), p. 96.
[20]Marx, *On Historical Materialism*, p. 120.
[21]Konstantinov, ed., *The Fundamentals of Marxist-Leninist Philosophy*, p. 403.
[22]Marx, *Contribution to the Critique of Political Economy*, p. 11.
[23]Karl Marx, *The Poverty of Philosophy* (New York: International, 1936), pp. 152-3.
[24]Cornforth, *The Open Philosophy and the Open Society*, p. 145.
[25]Lenin, *On Historical Materialism*, p. 461.
[26]Konstantinov, ed., *The Fundamentals of Marxist-Leninist Philosophy*, p. 406.
[27]Engels, *Ludwig Feuerbach*, p. 58.
[28]Stalin, *Dialectical and Historical Materialism*, p. 19.
[29]Frederick Engels, letter to W. Borgius (London), Jan. 25, 1894, cited in *The Fundamentals of Marxist-Leninist Philosophy*, ed. Konstantinov, p. 407. One need hardly point out the illogic of Engels's argument. It is completely tautologous, for of course whenever we look back through history we find that what happened, happened, and what didn't happen didn't happen. This no more proves historical determinism than a particular order of cards dealt proves that the dealer intended it.
[30]Lenin, *On Historical Materialism*, p. 452.
[31]Konstantinov, ed., *The Fundamentals of Marxist-Leninist Philosophy*, p. 209.
[32]V. I. Lenin, *Selected Works* (1947), vol. 2, p. 57, cited in *A Lexicon of Marxist-Leninist Semantics*, ed. Raymond S. Sleeper (Alexandria, VA: Western Goals, 1983), p. 121.
[33]Cornforth, *The Open Philosophy and the Open Society*, p. 159.
[34]V. I. Lenin, "A Caricature of Marxism and Imperialist Economism," in *Collected Works*, vol. 23, p. 69.
[35]Georgi Shakhnazarov, *The Coming World Order* (Moscow: Progress Publishers, 1984), p. 275.
[36]Engels, *Socialism: Utopian and Scientific*, p. 54.
[37]Konstantinov, ed., *The Fundamentals of Marxist-Leninist Philosophy*, p. 208.
[38]Engels, *Anti-Dühring*, p. 158.
[39]Cornforth, *Historical Materialism*, p. 68.
[40]Marx, *Contribution to Critique of Political Economy*, p. 12.
[41]Stalin, *Dialectical and Historical Materialism*, p. 43.
[42]Ibid., p. 44.

[43]Lenin, *Collected Works*, vol. 11, p. 71.
[44]Lenin, *On Historical Materialism*, p. 419.
[45]Konstantinov, ed., *The Fundamentals of Marxist-Leninist Philosophy*, p. 207.
[46]Engels, *Socialism: Utopian and Scientific*, p. 51.
[47]Cornforth, *Historical Materialism*, p. 68.
[48]Konstantinov, ed., *The Fundamentals of Marxist-Leninist Philosophy*, p. 274.
[49]Marx and Engels, *The Communist Manifesto*, p. 5.
[50]Cornforth, *Historical Materialism*, p. 76.
[51]Konstantinov, ed., *The Fundamentals of Marxist-Leninist Philosophy*, p. 292.
[52]Cornforth, *Historical Materialism*, p. 145.
[53]Ibid., p. 121.
[54]Marx, cited in Cornforth, *The Open Philosophy and the Open Society*, pp. 368-9.
[55]Stalin, *Dialectical and Historical Materialism*, p. 13.
[56]Cornforth, *The Open Philosophy and the Open Society*, p. 150.
[57]Joseph Stalin, *Problems of Leninism* (Moscow and London: 1947), p. 546. Cited in Wetter, *Dialectical Materialism*, p. 217.
[58]Cornforth, *Historical Materialism*, p. 140.
[59]Marx, *On Historical Materialism*, p. 135.

CHAPTER

32

BIBLICAL CHRISTIAN HISTORY

"But when the fulness of the times was come, God sent forth his Son, made of a woman, made under the law."

—Galatians 4:4

"Christianity claims to be a historical religion not simply in the sense that all world religions are historical, that is, phenomena of human history; it asserts more than this, namely, that the living God decisively grounds divine revelation in specific external events attested in the Judeo-Christian Scriptures."[1]

—Carl F. H. Henry

"Paul regarded the resurrection as an event in history supported by the strongest possible eyewitness testimony, including his own (1 Corinthians 15:5-8). For Paul, the historicity of the resurrection was a necessary condition for the truth of Christianity and the validity of Christian belief."[2]

—Ronald H. Nash

SUMMARY

Christianity and history have always been allies. Leopold Von Ranke's observation that history convinces more people than philosophy is certainly confirmed by the Christian response to this discipline. The Bible contains a great deal more history than philosophy. Christianity is rooted in history and without its historical roots there would be no Christian worldview (1 Corinthians 15:14).

Nearly all history, from the Christian perspective, can be summarized by reference to a few landmark historical events—the revelation of God (primarily His intelligence and power) through the creation of heaven and earth (Genesis 1:1); the special creation of male and female as body, soul, and spirit (Genesis 1:26-27); the rebellion of mankind against his Creator[3] (Genesis 3:1-15); the revelation of God through the patriarchs (Abraham, Isaac, and Jacob) and Israel (primarily Old Testament); the crossing of the Red Sea; the appearance of God in history in the person of Jesus Christ to redeem mankind from sin (1 Timothy 3:16); the resurrection of Jesus Christ (1 Corinthians 15); the revelation of God through His Church, the Body of Christ (primarily New Testament); the judgment of the world (Acts 17:31); and the new heavens, new earth, and new Jerusalem for the redeemed of all ages (Revelation 21). Christian history, like Marxist and Humanist history, has past, present, and future characteristics. Christians adhere to a linear, rather than a cyclical, view.

For Christians the Bible is a work of beauty and truth—a word from God concerning His love for His creation—not a work of myth and legend. The Bible is accurate, describing events that actually occurred in history. Twentieth-century archaeology generally reinforces Biblical history, including the Mosaic authorship of the Pentateuch,[4] the historicity of the patriarchs and the exodus, and the historical background surrounding the virgin birth, sinless life, vicarious death, and physical resurrection of Jesus Christ.

Of course, St. Paul's statement regarding history in 1 Corinthians 10:1f ("I would

Introduction

Christians believe the basis for their entire worldview appeared in human history in the form of Jesus Christ almost two thousand years ago. While "Christ died for our sins" is solid orthodox Christian *theology*, "Christ died" is *history*. In Christianity, doctrine is based on historical events. To shatter Christian doctrine and the Christian

not have you to be ignorant of [history]") is a solid base for a philosophy of history. Christians are certainly exhorted to learn from history (1 Corinthians 10:11). St. Paul also made it very clear that if Christ were not raised from the dead, there would be no Christian faith (1 Corinthians 15:14). Christians view the resurrection of Christ as a historical event occurring in Jerusalem sometime between A.D. 30 and 33.

Stephen's defense of the faith in Acts 7 is a lesson on history. Luke, author of two books of the Bible (Luke and Acts), was a meticulous historian. The historical Bible (the written Word) and Jesus Christ (the living Word) are the two cornerstones of the Christian worldview. If the Bible is not history, or if Jesus Christ is not "God with us" (Matthew 1:23), Christianity crumbles. Therefore, Christians need to invest a great deal of time and effort defending both foundation stones.

Naturally, Marxists and Humanists cannot accept the Bible as an accurate historical document. The character and actions of Christ shatter every basic tenet of an atheistic, naturalistic, evolutionary view of history. Instead of God planning and running His creative and redemptive order (history, in part, being a record of such orders), the Marxist has to trust the dialectic, and the Secular Humanist must trust man's ability to direct future evolution. Neither of these two worldviews can satisfactorily account for the purpose manifest in the world. The Christian, however, has a simple yet profound answer—"In the beginning, God." God gives purpose and order to His creation. We are part of His vast creative order, and God is responsible for us. We cannot save ourselves—even from physical death. But God can, and history tells us He offered His Son as a perfect sacrifice for that special purpose.

It is the Christian position that it takes less faith to believe that God created the heavens and the earth and all things therein than to believe that everything is a result of chance. Christians understand God to have created history when He created time, and they believe God also has the ability to control the universe and bring history to a fitting close.

worldview, one need only shatter its historical underpinnings. "The distinctively Christian understanding of history," explains Kenneth Scott Latourette, "centers upon historical occurrences. It has at its heart . . . a person."[5] The Christian also believes that the Bible is God's revealed Word in the form of a trustworthy book grounded in history. Thus, for the Christian, history is supremely important. Either Christ is a historical figure and the Bible is a historical document that describes

Notes
and
Asides

God's communications with man and records events in the life of Christ, or the Christian faith is bankrupt. As St. Paul says, if Christ is not raised from the dead [historically] then our faith is in vain (1 Corinthians 15:14).

For the Christian, the Bible is a record of concrete, historical fact containing true stories about real events and real people. In 1 Corinthians 10, the Apostle Paul outlines the Christian's attitude toward history when he says, "I would not that ye should be ignorant how that all our fathers were under the cloud, and all passed through the sea" (verse 1). The Exodus was a historical event, and the apostle wants us to learn from it, especially so that we may understand the role of God in human history. "Evangelical Christianity insists that certain specific historical acts are integral and indispensable to Judeo-Christian revelation," says Carl F. H. Henry.

> Biblical Christianity claims to be true not only in its many statements about man's inner life and about the nature of God, but also in a panoply of statements concerning redemptive historical acts. Evangelical Christians maintain that the object of biblical faith can be historically investigated, at least to some extent. Their apologists . . . have emphasized, and rightly, that orthodox theism has nothing in common with a faith that sacrifices either sound historical method or intellectual honesty.[6]

Christianity cannot accept Jesus Christ as a mythical figure or the Bible as allegory any more than any good historian could accept Tiberius Caesar or Pontius Pilate as myths. Our theology must be based on human history, or we have no theology. As Herbert Schlossberg notes, the Bible itself stresses the importance of history, not allegories:

> Mystical visions, ratiocination, and emotional experiences are not central to the biblical epistemology, but history lessons are. When Samuel gave up the office of judge, he charged the people to remain faithful to God and reminded them, in a history lesson, that God had been faithful in leading them out of captivity (1 Sam. 12). When Stephen the martyr appeared before the high priest on charges of blasphemy, he gave the council a history lesson (Acts 7).[7]

History is as important for the Christian worldview as it is for the Marxist/Leninist and the Secular Humanist worldviews. And if the Christian perspective is correct, history has already revealed the worldview that fits the facts of reality. While the Humanist and the Marxist see

Notes and Asides

mankind's salvation in the distant future, the Christian sees redemption offered to mankind almost two thousand years ago and working as powerfully today as it did then. If this is true, then the wise man will discover all he can about Jesus Christ, who Christians believe redeemed mankind. "I am profoundly convinced," said Millar Burrows, "that the historic revelation of God in Jesus of Nazareth must be the cornerstone of any faith that is really Christian. Any historical question about the real Jesus who lived in Palestine nineteen centuries ago is therefore fundamentally important."[8]

The Bible and History

The logical question that arises is this: do we know the record of God's activities, the Bible, to be a reliable historical document? Can we trust the Bible to tell us the truth? If the Bible can be proven to be fictional or inaccurate, then the Christian faith is left clutching at straws. Both the Marxist and the Humanist attack Christianity from this angle, claiming the Bible to be largely myth and legend.

The first area we must explore when judging the historicity of the Bible is the question of authorship. Was the Bible written by eyewitnesses of historical events,[9] or were some books written many years after the fact by men who had only heard vague accounts of the events they attempted to describe? For example, did one of Christ's apostles write the book of Matthew, or did some unknown scribe who had not known Christ write the book in an effort to strengthen the case for Christianity?

Today's scholars have little doubt that the books of the Bible were written largely by eyewitnesses. Historian John Warwick Montgomery concludes,

> On the basis, then, of powerful bibliographic, internal, and external evidence, competent historical scholarship must regard the New Testament documents as deriving from the first century and as reflecting primary-source testimony concerning the person and claims of Jesus.[10]

William F. Albright, a leading twentieth-century archaeologist, writes, "In my opinion, every book of the New Testament was written by a baptized Jew between the forties and the eighties of the first century A.D. (very probably sometime between about A.D. 50 and 75)."[11] Norman L. Geisler points out that even the radical "death of God" theologian Bishop John A. T. Robinson "has become honest with the facts and declared that the New Testament was written between A.D. 40 and 65.

"In my opinion, every book of the New Testament was written by a baptized Jew between the forties and the eighties of the first century A. D. . . . "
—W. F. Albright

Notes and Asides

This would mean that the basic New Testament documents were written by contemporaries only seven years or so after the events and were circulated among other eyewitnesses and/or contemporaries of the events."[12]

Indeed, H. G. Wells, a confirmed atheist, acknowledged that "the four gospels . . . were certainly in existence a few decades after [Christ's] death. . . ."[13] These statements definitely point to the conclusion that the history in the Bible was written by men living in that historical period. At least in this regard, we must trust the Bible to be a reliable historical document.

However, a second objection arises. Perhaps, say the critics, the Bible was an accurate historical document as it was originally written—but it has been copied and re-copied for thousands of years, and so it has been warped by the inevitable mistakes of copyists. At first glance, this objection seems plausible. Yet textual critic William Green claims (regarding the Old Testament) that "it may safely be said that no other work of antiquity has been so accurately transmitted."[14] Indeed, many modern scholars regard the Bible of today as virtually identical to the original text. New Testament scholar Bruce Metzger insists that the Bible has a 99.5 percent rate of accuracy in transmission, compared to 95 percent for Homer's *Iliad*, generally considered one of the best transmitted of ancient texts.[15] How can these scholars be so confident?

The answer lies in an archaeological discovery made nearly half a century ago. Gleason L. Archer, Jr. explains: "Even though the two copies of Isaiah discovered in Qumran Cave 1 near the Dead Sea in 1947 were a thousand years earlier than the oldest dated manuscript previously known (A.D. 980), they proved to be word for word identical with our standard Hebrew Bible in more than 95 per cent of the text. The 5 per cent of variation consisted chiefly of obvious slips of the pen and variations in spelling."[16] That is, a manuscript one thousand years older than the oldest copy of the Bible previously known to exist proved the transmission over that time span to be virtually error free.

In fact, archaeology has consistently supported the assertion that the Bible is a trustworthy historical document. An interesting example is provided by Immanuel Velikovsky in *Ages in Chaos*. Velikovsky explains that archaeologists have discovered an ancient Egyptian papyrus that seems to describe one of the most crucial events in Biblical history: the plagues prior to the Exodus. This ancient manuscript, known as the Papyrus Ipuwer, is incomplete—but the sentences that are decipherable describe events remarkably similar to those documented in the book of Exodus. Thus, where Exodus 7:20 declares, ". . . all the waters that were in the river were turned to blood," the Papyrus Ipuwer 2:10 states, "The river is blood." And where Exodus 10:22 declares, ". . . and there was a thick darkness in all the land of Egypt," the

Notes and Asides

Papyrus 9:11 states, "The land is not light. . . ." These striking similarities exist throughout the Papyrus and have led Velikovsky to conclude, "The description of disturbances in the Papyrus Ipuwer, when compared with the scriptural narrative, gives a strong impression that both sources relate the very same events."[17]

This is not an isolated example. Indeed, archaeology provides massive support for the accuracy of the Bible. "The science of archaeology," says Geisler, "has confirmed the historical accuracy of the Gospel records. This can be dramatically illustrated through the writings of Sir William Ramsay, whose conversion from a skeptical view of the New Testament was supported by a lifetime in the Near Eastern world."[18] Albright states, "Archaeology, after a long silence, has finally corroborated biblical tradition in no uncertain way."[19] Says Herbert Butterfield, "A remarkable factor affecting both classical and Biblical history has been the archaeological discoveries which confirmed the literary documents sometimes in unexpected points of detail."[20] Nelson

Recommended Reading for Advanced Study

God, History, and Historians, ed. C. T. McIntire (New York: Oxford University, 1977).

John Warwick Montgomery, *Where is History Going?* (Minneapolis: Bethany, 1969).

Herbert Butterfield, *Christianity and History* (New York: Charles Scribner's Sons, 1950).

C. S. Lewis, *Miracles* (London: Geoffrey Bles, 1952).

Gary Habermas and Antony Flew, *Did Jesus Rise From the Dead?* (New York: Harper and Row, 1987).

Ronald Nash, *Christian Faith and Historical Understanding* (Dallas, TX: Probe, 1984).

Notes and Asides

Glueck is even more confident: "It may be stated categorically that no archaeological discovery has ever controverted a biblical reference."[21] Burrows, a Yale archaeologist, declares, "On the whole, however, archaeological work has unquestionably strengthened confidence in the reliability of the Scriptural record. More than one archaeologist has found his respect for the Bible increased by the experience of excavation in Palestine."[22]

Further, Montgomery argues that modern archaeological findings are confirming again and again "the reliability of New Testament geography, chronology, and general history."[23] His classic example is Pontius Pilate. Says Montgomery,

> To take but a single, striking example: after the rise of liberal biblical criticism, doubt was expressed as to the historicity of Pontius Pilate, since he is mentioned even by pagan historians only in connection with Jesus' death. Then in 1961 came the discovery at Caesarea of the now famous "Pilate inscription," definitely showing that, as usual, the New Testament writers were engaged in accurate historiography.[24]

Harvard's Simon Greenleaf (the greatest nineteenth-century authority on the law of evidence in the common law) believed "that the competence of the New Testament documents would be established in any court of law."[25] Clearly, the science of archaeology[26] supports both the historical accuracy of the Bible and the accurate transmission of the manuscript through the centuries.

> "There is no body of ancient literature in the world which enjoys such a wealth of good textual attestation as the New Testament."
>
> —F. F. Bruce

As we have noted, this is crucial for the Christian faith. The Bible must be an accurate historical document proclaiming God's special revelation, or the Christian faith is based on mere wishful thinking. The historicity of the Bible is more important for the Christian than anything in the world, because, as Archer points out, "One cannot allow for error in history-science without also ending up with error in doctrine."[27] Thus, the honest Christian must scrutinize the Bible more closely than its harshest critics.

Incredibly, the Bible emerges from this scrutiny as a document singular in its accuracy. Carl F. H. Henry declares that "current scholarship increasingly affirms the reliability of Old Testament historical perspectives."[28] F. F. Bruce writes, "There is no body of ancient literature in the world which enjoys such a wealth of good textual attestation as the New Testament."[29] Geisler says,

> It may seem a gross exaggeration, to one not familiar with the evidence, to claim that there is more documentary evidence for the reliability of the New Testament than for any other book

Notes and Asides

> from the ancient world. But it is true, nonetheless. The evidence for this claim is abundant.[30]

Geisler quotes Bruce to the effect that there exist only nine or ten manuscript copies of Caesar's *Gallic War*, twenty copies of Livy's *Roman History*, two copies of Tacitus's *Annals*, and eight manuscripts of Thucydides's *History*—even Homer's *Iliad*, the best-documented ancient secular writing, has only 643 known copies—but the New Testament has 5,300! Says Geisler, "The New Testament is the most highly documented book from the ancient world."[31] And Albright goes so far as to proclaim, "the excessive skepticism shown toward the Bible by important historical schools of the eighteenth and nineteenth centuries, certain phases of which still appear periodically, has been progressively discredited. Discovery after discovery has established the accuracy of innumerable details, and has brought increased recognition to the value of the Bible as a source of history."[32]

Indeed, the evidence for the historicity of the Bible is so overwhelming that it forces the honest skeptic to acknowledge its veracity. Werner Keller was just such a skeptic, but finally had to admit, "In view of the overwhelming mass of authentic and well-attested evidence now available, as I thought of the skeptical criticism which from the eighteenth century onward would fain have demolished the Bible altogether, there kept hammering in my brain this one sentence: 'The Bible is right after all!'"[33]

One may conclude with confidence that the Bible is an accurate historical document; the events described in the Old and New Testaments did happen. But this poses a problem for every non-Christian, because the Bible states that God became man in Jesus Christ—and if this is true, no other worldview fits the facts of history. Some non-Christians at this point choose a rather illogical means of avoiding the seemingly unavoidable claims of the Bible, suggesting that while the Bible may be true, it does not accurately describe the man known as Jesus Christ. Indeed, some non-Christians go so far as to claim that Jesus Christ never existed.[34] Therefore, we must turn our attention to this aspect of history.

The Historicity of Christ

The obvious problem faced by people who deny that the Bible accurately describes the life of Jesus Christ is that archaeology and modern criticism have revealed the Bible to be historically correct. "What, then, does a historian know about Jesus Christ?" asks Montgomery. "He knows, first and foremost, that the New Testament document can be

Notes and Asides

relied upon to give an accurate portrait of him, and that this portrait cannot be rationalized away by wishful thinking, philosophical presuppositionalism, or literary maneuvering."[35] The modern atheist has no grounds for claiming that man cannot know what Christ did on earth, or if He even existed, because the New Testament provides a historical account of His life. However, for the moment we will ignore this key point and focus on still more evidence for the historicity of Christ.

Christ was treated as a historical figure by early historians other than Christians. Around A.D. 93, the great Jewish historian Josephus referred to Jesus at least twice in his *Antiquities of the Jews*. In one instance, he recorded that the high priest Annas "assembled the sanhedrim of the judges, and brought before them the brother of Jesus, who was called Christ, whose name was James . . ." (*Antiquities* XX.ix.1). In an earlier and more celebrated instance (XVIII.iii.3), Josephus focused attention on Jesus Himself. There is some question about precisely what the original text said, but the most likely reading appears to have been:

> At this time there was a wise man who was called Jesus. And his conduct was good, and [he] was known to be virtuous. And many people from among the Jews and other nations became his disciples. Pilate condemned him to be crucified and to die. And those who had become his disciples did not abandon his discipleship. They reported that he had appeared to them three days after his crucifixion and that he was alive; accordingly, he was perhaps the messiah concerning whom the prophets have recounted wonders.[36]

Despite the questions about the precise wording of the text,[37] there is no serious doubt that Josephus did refer to Jesus Christ and to the movement that stemmed from Him.

Another early historian, Cornelius Tacitus, wrote around A.D. 112 about "the persons commonly called Christians," and also stated, "Christus, the founder of the name, was put to death by Pontius Pilate, procurator of Judea in the reign of Tiberius: but the pernicious superstition, repressed for a time broke out again, not only through Judea, where the mischief originated, but through the city of Rome also."[38]

These references and others provide sufficient evidence for the historicity of Christ, even when the New Testament is ignored. Bruce Metzger writes that "the early non-Christian testimonies concerning Jesus, though scanty, are sufficient to prove (even without taking into account the evidence contained in the New Testament) that he was a historical figure who lived in Palestine in the early years of the first century, that he gathered a group of followers about himself, and that he was condemned to death under Pontius Pilate. Today no competent

Notes and Asides

scholar denies the historicity of Jesus."[39] New Testament scholar Bruce agrees:

> Some writers may toy with the fancy of a "Christ-myth," but they do not do so on the ground of historical evidence. The historicity of Christ is as axiomatic for an unbiased historian as the historicity of Julius Caesar. It is not historians who propagate the "Christ-myth" theories.[40]

Jesus Christ was a historical figure. Furthermore, the honest critic must believe that the New Testament accurately describes His words and actions. In fact, even without modern archaeological support of the New Testament, the character of Christ as presented by the gospel writers is too powerful and unique to be merely an exaggerated account. The words and actions of Christ must be real—they are too incredible to have been fabricated. Humanist Will Durant recognizes this: "That a few simple men should in one generation have invented so powerful and appealing a personality, so lofty an ethic and so inspiring a vision of human brotherhood, would be a miracle far more incredible than any recorded in the Gospels. After two centuries of Higher Criticism the outlines of the life, character, and teaching of Christ, remain reasonably clear, and constitute the most fascinating feature in the history of Western man."[41]

> "Today no competent scholar denies the historicity of Jesus."
> —Bruce Metzger

It would seem that there is no escape for the non-Christian. Not only is Christ a historical figure, but the Bible is a trustworthy historical document and its revealed character of Christ is indisputably genuine. As Montgomery points out, the unbeliever seems trapped by cold, hard facts:

> Now if you are not inclined in the direction of Christianity—as I was not when I entered university—the most irritating aspect of the line of argumentation [based on the historicity of the Bible and Christ] . . . is probably this: it depends in no sense on theology. It rests solely and squarely upon historical method, the kind of method all of us, whether Christians, rationalists, agnostics, or Tibetan monks, have to use in analyzing historical data.[42]

Still, there are learned historians who accept the historicity of the Bible and Christ, and remain atheists. Wells declares, "The gospels and the Acts of the Apostles present a patched and uneven record, but there can be little question that on the whole it is a quite honest record of those early days."[43] He treats the entire New Testament account of Jesus' life as accurate, *except for the miracles performed by Christ*. This is Wells'

Notes and Asides

(and a good many other nonbelievers') reason for sticking to atheistic assumptions: the miracles recorded in the Bible are mythological.

Miracles in History

Oddly enough, Durant is not among those who discount the miracle stories in the Bible. He says, "That [Christ's] powers were nevertheless exceptional seems proved by his miracles."[44] Both C. S. Lewis, in his classic work *Miracles*, and Geisler, in *Miracles and Modern Thought*, present a powerful case for the historicity of miracles in Scripture. Geisler maintains that there are only two basic questions to answer before one can know if New Testament miracles actually occurred: (1) the reliability of the document, and (2) the integrity of the witnesses.[45]

Geisler's first point is the same problem that faces individuals who deny the historicity of Christ—namely, if the Bible is accurate in all other aspects of its historical record, then why should one believe that it is inaccurate in this specific area? Some materialists answer that miracles cannot occur because no supernatural cause for miracles exists, but this simply begs the question. As Montgomery points out, ". . . miracles are impossible only if one so defines them—but such definition rules out proper historical investigation."[46]

Geisler's second point is also easily defended by the Christian historian. The honesty of the witnesses is beyond dispute. New Testament authors were, according to Geisler, "men of the highest integrity."[47] The Apostle John, for example, was "from a cultured background, Paul was highly educated (Acts 22:3), and Luke was a physician (Colossians 4:14)."[48]

> "History after all is the true poetry."
> —Thomas Carlyle

Skeptics, however, do not restrict themselves to these two logical points. Some try to discount miracles by claiming that no one alive has ever witnessed a miracle, and this proves that miracles never occur. But according to Henry, this is based on an unwarranted assumption. "Those who criticize the biblical miracles," he writes, "because of the lack of analogy in present experience assume that present-day empirical science is normative for what may or may not have taken place in the past or may occur in the future."[49] That is, these skeptics assume miracles cannot occur based on a generalization that may or may not be accurate. Such reasoning leads to other illogical conclusions, as pointed out by Geisler: "Most astronomers today believe the universe began with a great explosion (several billions of years ago). But there is nothing like this occurring in the present . . . [thus, applying such faulty reasoning] we would have to reject out of hand this modern scientific understanding of the universe, simply because we have no like events today."[50]

Notes and Asides

Perhaps the strongest argument against the occurrence of miracles is the claim by some skeptics that if God did exist, He would have created a lawful universe and could be expected to adhere to order rather than to bending natural laws capriciously at His pleasure. The Christian agrees that God could and did create a universe that obeys specific laws at all times. The Christian disagrees, however, with the definition of miracles as temporary suspensions or violations of natural laws. Lewis states, "The divine act of miracle is not an act of suspending the pattern to which events conform but of feeding new events into that pattern."[51] In fact, Lewis claims that if one accepts the notion of a supernatural Being active in human affairs, one must expect miracles to occur—that miracles cannot help but happen in a universe truly ordered by a God active in history. He writes,

> The necessary truth of the laws [of nature], far from making it impossible that miracles should occur makes it certain that if the Supernatural is operating they must occur. For if the natural situation by itself, and the natural situation *plus* something else, yielded only the same result, it would be then that we should be faced with a lawless and unsystematic universe. The better you know that two and two make four, the better you know that two and three don't.[52]

Clearly there exist powerful reasons for accepting the miracle stories of the Bible as historical events. Yet, if one accepts the historicity of the Bible and Christ, as well as the truth of Biblical miracle stories, then one can only maintain personal integrity by adhering to the Christian worldview. This is precisely the claim of the Christian historian. Christians base their worldview not on some contrived mythology and a lot of blind faith, but on historical people and events.

The Resurrection and History

The Bible goes out of its way to place its message and major figures in history. Regarding the early ministry of Christ and John the Baptist, Luke writes, "Now in the fifteenth year of the reign of Tiberius Caesar, Pontius Pilate being governor of Judea, and Herod being tetrarch of Galilee, and his brother Phillip tetrarch of Ituraea and of the region of Trachonitis, and Lysanias the tetrarch of Abilene, Annas and Caiaphas being the high priests, the word of God came unto John the son of Zacharias in the wilderness" (Luke 3:1-2). Luke uses other historical figures as reference points to accentuate the fact that the Biblical accounts of the life of John the Baptist and Jesus Christ present their

Notes and Asides

subjects as actually occurring in history.

Further, Luke stresses that Christ's death and resurrection were historical events. He mentions Pilate, Caesar, Herod, Barabbas, "Joseph, counsellor," "Arimathaea, a city of the Jews," and in this historical context says,

> Now upon the first day of the week, very early in the morning, they came unto the sepulchre, bringing the spices which they had prepared, and certain others with them. And they found the stone rolled away from the sepulchre. And they entered in, and found not the body of the Lord Jesus. And it came to pass, as they were much perplexed thereabout, behold two men stood by them in shining garments: And as they were afraid, and bowed down their faces to the earth, they said unto them, Why seek ye the living among the dead? He is not here, but is risen: remember how he spake unto you when he was yet in Galilee, Saying, "The Son of man must be delivered into the hands of sinful men, and be crucified, and the third day rise again." [Luke 24:1-7]

Clearly, Luke believed the resurrection to have occurred in history and described it in its historical context so that it would be verifiable.

Luke was not the only one who witnessed the resurrection in its historical context. More than five hundred people saw the risen Jesus (1 Corinthians 15:6). Geisler lists them:

> Jesus appeared to Mary (John 20:11-18), to the other women (Matt. 28:9-10), to Peter (Luke 24:34), to two disciples going to Emmaus (Luke 24:13-32), to ten apostles (John 20:19-25), to eleven apostles (John 20:26-29), to seven apostles at the Sea of Galilee (John 21:1-14), to the eleven apostles to commission them (Matt. 28:16-20), to more than "five hundred brethren" (1 Cor. 15:6), to his unbelieving brother James (1 Cor. 15:7), and to the disciples at the ascension (Luke 24:50-53; Acts 1:4-11).[53]

These witnesses were so moved by the resurrection that they committed their lives to it and to the One whose divinity and righteousness it vindicated. Josephus wrote, "those who had become [Christ's] disciples did not abandon his discipleship. They reported that he had appeared to them three days after his crucifixion and that he was alive: accordingly, he was perhaps the messiah concerning whom the prophets have recounted wonders."[54] The disciples did not abandon Christ, but were willing to die for the truth they were propagating—including His physical resurrection (Acts 3:15). Indeed, the resurrection of Christ

Notes and Asides

took "a group of scared (Mark 16:8; John 20:19) and skeptical (Luke 24:38; John 20:25) men" and transformed them "into courageous evangels who proclaimed the Resurrection in the face of threats on their lives (Acts 4:21; 5:18)!"[55] If the disciples did not consider the resurrection a historical event, is it really conceivable that they would be willing to die for this kind of testimony? Obviously not. The Apostle Paul certainly would not have wasted his life preaching the resurrection if he thought for one moment that it was a hoax. Says Nash,

> Paul regarded the resurrection as an event in history supported by the strongest possible eyewitness testimony, including his own (1 Cor. 15:5-8). For Paul, the historicity of the resurrection was a necessary condition for the truth of Christianity and the validity of Christian belief (1 Cor. 15:12-19).[56]

The behavior of the disciples and the early Christian Church lends powerful support to the historicity of the resurrection.

When Paul appeared before King Agrippa and told him about the sufferings and death of Christ and "that he should be the first that should rise from the dead" (Acts 26:23), he assured the king that "this thing was not done in a corner" (Acts 26:26). Agrippa's response: "Almost thou persuadest me to be a Christian" (vs. 28).

Gary Habermas, in *Did Jesus Rise From the Dead?* argues that one must establish the veracity of four points to prove the resurrection of Christ: (1) Jesus' death due to crucifixion, (2) the disciples' conviction that they had witnessed genuine appearances of the risen Jesus, (3) the corresponding transformation of these men, and (4) Paul's conversion experience, which he also believed was an appearance of the risen Jesus. Habermas notes that "few scholars dispute these four facts" and claims that this argues powerfully for the literal, physical resurrection of Jesus Christ.[57] Geisler agrees. "The Resurrection is a matter of history open to any who wish to examine the evidence."[58] In other words, the resurrection did not occur in some small corner of the world, but took place among intelligent people at Jerusalem, a city famous in its own right.

> "The Resurrection is a matter of history open to any who wish to examine the evidence."
> —Norman Geisler

At this point, when an individual accepts the complete historical accuracy of the Bible, he is driven to the conclusion that Christ's resurrection is the most important event in all of human history. And this conclusion forms the basis for the Biblical Christian worldview and the Christian philosophy of history. "With the resurrection of Jesus," says Wolfhart Pannenberg, "the end of history has already occurred, although it does not strike us in this way. It is through the resurrection that the God of Israel has substantiated his deity in an ultimate way and is now manifest as the God of all men."[59]

Notes and Asides

It is also through the resurrection that God reveals His plan for mankind by conquering sin and guaranteeing a triumphant end to human history. D. W. Bebbington says that since the battle against evil was won by Jesus on the cross, "The outcome of world history is therefore already assured. God will continue to direct the course of events up to their end when the outcome will be made plain."[60] The Christian learns from history that Christ offered Himself up as a perfect sacrifice for mankind, and this is the most important revelation. But the Christian also discovers another important truth: God is active throughout history and plans to lead it to a triumphant conclusion.

While the course of history may seem tragic to some people, the Christian understands that all history is working together for good. Because God became man and died for man's sins, the final chapter of history will proclaim the conquering of sin. Thus, the Christian is prepared to face a difficult, sometimes pain-filled life, because he understands that the sin that causes pain has been erased from his future. The Christian holds no unreasonable expectations for his earthly lifetime—he doesn't expect to be sheltered from trouble or given any special treatment—but he does expect to be triumphant in the end because God has come into history to save man from his own sinful inclinations. "Providence at least is not a thing to be presumed upon," says Butterfield, "and indeed the Christian knows that it gives him no guarantee against martyrdom for the faith. What it does guarantee so exultantly in the New Testament is a mission in the world and the kind of triumph that may come out of apparent defeat—the kind of good that can be wrested out of evil."[61]

This concept of Providence is simply another way of describing the Christian belief that God works in history in a specific way. Bebbington sums up the concept:

> Christians . . . have normally adhered to these three convictions about history: that God intervenes in it; that he guides it in a straight line; and that he will bring it to the conclusion that he has planned. The three beliefs together form the core of the Christian doctrine of providence.[62]

And the direction in which Providence is leading the people who choose to be led is the direction established by the resurrection: to a society freed from the bonds of sin. The Christian knows that God's movements in history are all ultimately aimed toward breaking the chains of sin and re-establishing a right relationship between God and man. Therefore, the Christian can declare, along with the Apostle Paul, ". . . we know that in all things God works for the good of those who love him, who have been called according to his purpose" (Romans 8:28).

Notes and Asides

And, "If God is for us, who can be against us?" (Romans 8:31).

From the Christian perspective history is a beautiful unfolding of God's ultimate plan for mankind. Does this mean, however, that only the future holds any value for the Christian? Does the Christian worldview destroy the role of the present in history? The answer is a resounding *no*. In the Christian view, God is active throughout history; therefore, this perspective creates more meaning for every moment of time than does any other worldview. "It is always a 'Now,'" writes Butterfield, "that is in direct relation to eternity—not a far future; always immediate experience of life that matters in the last resort—not historical constructions based on abridged text-books or imagined visions of some posterity that is going to be the heir of all the ages."[63] For the Christian, each moment of history is precious because God is the God of history and is directing its course toward the final new Heavens, new Earth and new Jerusalem (Isaiah 65:17; Philemon 3:20; Hebrews 11:16; Revelation 21:1-2).

The central difference between the Christian view of history and that of Marxism and Humanism comes down to this one point. Either human history was ordained by God and is directed by Him toward an ultimate conclusion, or human history began due to a random spark in a prebiotic soup and has only chance to thank for its present course.

> Either you must say that Chance is one of the greatest factors in history and that the whole of the story is in the last resort the product of blind Chance, or you must say that the whole of it is in the hands of Providence—in him we live and move and have our being—even the free will of men and even the operation of law in history, even these are within Providence itself and under it.[64]

"To be ignorant of what happened before you were born is to be ever a child."

—Cicero

Butterfield's statement clearly delineates the differences between the Christian approach to history and the Marxist and Humanist approaches. But it also raises a specific problem faced by the Christian. Put simply: if God directs history, does man have free will? If God decides where history is going, can man choose his actions, or is everything already predetermined?

Man's Role in History

In the first place, the Christian view stresses that if man had never sinned, the issue of man's free will would be a moot point. Since sin may be defined as man's defiance of God's will, one may conclude that man's will would always be in harmony with God's will if man were

Notes and Asides

freed from the bonds of sin. In this instance, the question as to whether God or man were directing history would never arise, since both God and man would always be choosing to work toward the same end. Therefore, one must understand man's sinful nature in order to understand man's role in history, as well as the Christian philosophy of history. For this reason, we will briefly examine man's inherent

CLOSE-UP

Martin Luther (1483-1546)

Martin Luther's most significant contibution to history occurred in 1517 when he nailed the 95 Theses for an academic debate on indulgences on the door of the castle church at Wittenberg. However, one cannot fully appreciate the significance of this event unless one understands the character of Luther—a man wholly concerned with discovering and defending truth. Luther began college in pursuit of his legal degree, but around 1503 became convinced he was called to study theology and in 1505 entered the Reformed Congregation of the Eremetical Order of St. Augustine at Erfurt, a monastery. He made his vows in 1506 and was ordained the following year. After receiving his doctorate in theology in 1512, Luther was appointed professor of theology at Wittenberg, where he quickly discovered his gift for teaching. In these early years, Luther felt himself to be "a sinner with an unquiet conscience," and this attitude caused him to constantly strive to make peace with God. Eventually, it led him to his most famous conclusion: man is saved not by indulgences or through acting perfectly but through faith in God's mercy. Luther incorporated this biblical doctrine in his 95 Theses, thereby inciting the wrath of much of the organized church. The following year the papal legate at Augsburg called for him to renounce his theses, and Luther refused. He refused to renounce them again in 1521, under still stronger papal pressure, declaring, "I cannot and will not retract anything, for it is neither safe nor salutary to act against one's conscience. God help me." Luther's conscience dictated strict adherence to a Biblical Christian worldview and, as such, led him to make one of the most courageous stands in history.

sinfulness and its relation to human history, prior to specifically addressing the question of free will.

The Bible clearly proclaims the sinful nature of man. Romans 3:23 states, "for all have sinned and fall short of the glory of God." Psalm 14:3 declares, "there is no one who does good, not even one." Butterfield describes these sinful tendencies as "that gravitational pull in human nature, which draws the highest things downwards, mixes them with earth, and taints them with human cupidity."[65]

This belief about human nature, if it is true, grants man the proper perspective on history in terms of past, present, and future. With regard to the past, this view provides the historian with a consistent description of human nature—something other worldviews lack. The fallen nature of mankind, while tragic, grants the historian a solid basis for understanding the actions of individuals who lived before him. Montgomery states that the divine revelation

> gives us absolute assurance that man's essential nature does not change. Thus the Christian historian has the assurance that a common ground exists between himself and the men of past ages whom he studies. . . . It should be noted that apart from Biblical testimony in this matter, no historian can possibly be sure that human nature is stable enough to allow for analogous reasoning from the historian's own present to the dim and distant past. Thus the non-Christian historian is unable even to justify his own field of study philosophically![66]

The Christian's belief in man's inherent sinfulness also provides him with the proper perspective of how man's sinfulness can affect history. While other worldviews blame most of the tragedy in history on specific societies created by uncommon madmen such as Mao Tse-tung, Joseph Stalin, Adolph Hitler, or Idi Amin, the Christian understands that human tragedies occur every day due to common human nature. As Butterfield notes, "A civilisation may be wrecked without any spectacular crimes or criminals but by constant petty breaches of faith and minor complicities on the part of men generally considered very nice people."[67] This provides the Christian with the proper perspective for living in the present, because it emphasizes the fact that every man's sin, no matter how apparently insignificant, can contribute to the downfall of society. The Christian understands that he must constantly strive to act morally whether he is a world leader or an unknown, and that he need not worry about devoting his life to redeeming the whole world, because God is the only One who can save mankind. Thus, the Christian may confidently state, as Butterfield does,

Notes and Asides

> Those people work more wisely who seek to achieve good in their own small corner of the world and then leave the leaven to leaven the whole lump, than those who are for ever thinking that life is vain unless one can act through the central government, carry legislation, achieve political power and do big things.[68]

Finally, the Christian doctrine of man's sinful nature allows for a proper perspective with regard to the future, in the sense that it holds no false hopes for man to achieve moral perfection through his own works. The Christian contradicts Humanist and Marxist predictions of future manmade utopias, since, as Schlossberg states, "In contrast with the historicist religion of progress, Christianity foresees no improvement in the moral condition of mankind."[69]

The Christian holds to an understanding of man's nature which allows the historian to develop a consistent philosophy of history, but also stresses the ultimate impossibility of man's ever making a valuable contribution to history on his own. Man's nature is corrupted by sin and therefore unfit for directing the course of history. Lewis says it best:

> Let us not be deceived by phrases about 'Man taking charge of his own destiny.' All that can really happen is that some men will take charge of the destiny of the others. They will be simply men; none perfect; some greedy, cruel and dishonest.[70]

No man is fit to be a leader of all mankind. The Christian yearns not for imperfect human control of history, but for God's direction of the course of events.

"It should certainly be emphasized, for example, how much of our Western aims and ends, humanitarianism, freedom, equality, we owe to the influence of Christianity."
—Karl Popper

Can Man Choose His Role in History?

From this it would seem that the Christian is not interested in the question of free will. If man's freely chosen actions are so damaging to the course of history, perhaps we should just claim that man cannot help himself and that all our actions are predetermined by God. Certainly, the Christian cannot suggest that man has free will in any meaningful sense, since God directs the course of history. Or can he?

Carl Henry declares that "no world view can do justice to reality unless it leaves room for personal agency, both divine and human. . . ."[71] Christianity definitely claims to do justice to reality. Does this mean that the Christian believes man can act freely to affect the course of history? Unquestionably. Francis Schaeffer states, "Because God created a true universe outside of Himself (not as an extension of His essence), there is a true history which exists. Man as created in God's

Notes and Asides

image is therefore a significant man in a significant history, who can choose to obey the commandment of God and love Him, or revolt against Him."[72]

Schaeffer's last sentence is especially relevant for our present discussion. When the Christian speaks of man's ability to choose, he is really delineating only two options: man may either obey or disobey God. As the Apostle Paul put it in Romans 6, there really are only two options: men are either slaves of sin, and so destined for death, or, "Being then made free from sin" they have become "servants of righteousness" (verse 18). Real freedom does not mean the capacity to choose willy-nilly; real freedom means being freed from sin and empowered to act righteously in a warm, vital relationship with God.

Thus, the Christian's belief about free will draws a crucial distinction when understanding man's role in the course of history. When man chooses to do God's will, he is acting on God's direction of history in the proper manner, and history requires no adjustments from God to move in the right direction. But when man chooses to disobey God, he may bring tragedy on the scene and cause God to make adjustments to continue His guidance of history to a triumphant end. Rushdoony describes this type of freedom for man as "liberty of a second cause." He explains, "Man's freedom is the liberty of a second cause; it is genuine liberty, but it is limited because man is a creature, and it is subordinate to the total creation and determination of all things by the triune God."[73]

Thus, in a very real sense, we may say that man is free to affect human history in the short run either for the better or for the worse, but in the long run, "in all things God works for the good of those who love him" (Romans 8:28). That is, man may sin and bring about present evil consequences, but God will not allow man's disobedience to thwart His overall direction of history.

> Yahweh vindicates his holy purpose even amid human actions that defiantly repudiate him and his concerns. All historical events are subject to his overruling omnipotence and inescapably serve his intended ends; even the untoward actions of wicked men are made sovereignly instrumental to God's purposes of redemptive grace and triumphant righteousness. Mankind's self-assertive and rebellious will in no case diminishes the course of events under Yahweh's sovereign control; even the most insolent actions of unregenerate humanity promote a divine overarching purpose.[74]

The prime example of God working through man's disobedience in history is mentioned by Bebbington: "Perhaps most characteristically

Notes and Asides

[God] is represented as overruling human intentions. Thus, for instance, when Joseph has been sold by his resentful brothers to a band of desert merchants but has nevertheless risen to become the right-hand man of the pharaoh of Egypt, he eventually explains to the brothers that 'it was not you who sent me here, but God' (Gen. 45:8)."[75] And, in Genesis 50:20, Joseph says, "But as for you, ye thought evil against me, but God meant it unto good, to bring to pass, as it is this day, to save much people alive."

Men's actions shape history—as Henry says, one does not do justice to reality unless one acknowledges man's free will—but the Christian perspective on history claims that God can guide history in the proper direction regardless of the actions men choose. "A God who guides the course of history but who is opposed on the way will surely bring the process to a triumphant conclusion,"[76] says Bebbington. We may speak of man's free will, but it rapidly becomes apparent that the only will that really matters is God's—and that man would choose wisely if he chose always to subject his will to his Lord. In this way, both God and man would still play a role in history, but it would be cooperative, rather than a rivalry.

Purpose in History

By now it should be obvious that the Christian believes that history has an overarching purpose. A God who directs the course of human events and sends his Son to become the central figure in human history clearly has invested man's reality with meaning. This becomes even more evident on reading Acts 17:26-28a:

> From one man [God] made every nation of men, that they should inhabit the whole earth; and he determined the times set for them and the exact places where they should live. God did this so that men would seek him and perhaps reach out for him and find him, though he is not far from each one of us. For in him we live and move and have our being.

This belief about God's actions in history has vast ramifications for mankind. If the Christian philosophy of history is correct, then not only is the overall story of mankind invested with meaning, but every moment that man lives is charged with purpose. "Where a God who is totally purposive and totally foreseeing acts upon a Nature which is totally interlocked," explains Lewis, "there can be no accidents or loose ends, nothing whatever of which we can safely use the word *merely*. Nothing is 'merely a by-product' of anything else. All results are

Notes and Asides

intended from the first."[77] God's purpose works through the life of every individual at all times.

Indeed, it is through understanding how God works in our individual lives that we can truly understand how God directs the course of history. "If we wish to know how God works in history," writes Butterfield, "we shall not find it by looking at the charts of all the centuries—we have to begin by seeing how God works in our individual lives and then we expand this on to the scale of the nation, we project it on to the scale of mankind. Only those who have brought God home to themselves in this way will be able to see him at work in history, and without this we might be tempted to see history as a tale told by an idiot, a product of blind Chance."[78] Butterfield goes on to outline the specifics of the Christian application of this principle:

> [T]here are some people who bring their sins home to themselves and say that this is a chastisement from God; or they say that God is testing them, trying them in the fire, fitting them for some more important work that he has for them to do. Those who adopt this view in their individual lives will easily see that it enlarges and projects itself onto the scale of all history; it affects our interpretation of national misfortunes as well as personal ones. When we reach this point in the argument we realize that we are adopting the biblical interpretation of history.[79]

That is, how God works in our individual lives can be extrapolated to explain how God works throughout history. Purpose and meaning saturate both individual lives and the life of all mankind.

In order to speak accurately about purpose, however, the Christian must speak not only of God's actions throughout history but also of the ultimate goal toward which He is leading mankind. Purpose implies constant activity by God, a direction for the course of human events, and an ultimate end or goal. This direction has been hinted at and is summed up by Montgomery: "This promise of final, perfectly just judgment at the end of time gives the Christian conception of history a direction and an ultimate meaning."[80] For the Christian, history is moving toward a specific climax: the final Day of Judgment (Acts 17:31; Romans 2:11-16). At this point, Christ's victory over sin will become apparent to all, and Christians throughout history will be allowed to share in His triumph. This is the good news of Christianity, the truth that makes all earthly trials bearable. Paul sums up this faith in two marvelous statements: "I consider that our present sufferings are not worth comparing with the glory that will be revealed in us" (Romans 8:18), and

CLOSE-UP

John Calvin (1509-1564)

French Protestant reformer John Calvin, in the *Institutes of the Christian Religion*, presented the most lucid outline of predestination ever recorded. In that work, which arose largely in response to Martin Luther's teachings that man is justified by faith, Calvin argued that man can in no way participate in his own salvation. This tension between Luther and Calvin has sparked lively debate among Christians throughout the centuries, and Calvin's *Institutes* still stands as the authoritative work regarding the concept of election. Late in life, Calvin had the unique opportunity to put his various ideas about society into practice, acting as the leader of the political council for Geneva from 1541 until his death in 1564. He attempted to create a theocracy, in which the law of the land was based exclusively on the Bible. While not entirely successful, this experiment did restore order in Geneva. Calvin's followers continued to expand his influence after his death.

For we which live are alway delivered unto death for Jesus' sake, that the life also of Jesus might be made manifest in our mortal flesh. So then death worketh in us, but life in you. We having the same spirit of faith, according as it is written, I believed, and therefore have I spoken; we also believe, and therefore speak; knowing that he which raised up the Lord Jesus shall raise up us also by Jesus, and shall present us with you. For all things are for your sakes, that the abundant grace might through the thanksgiving of many redound to the glory of God. *For which cause we faint not; but though our outward man perish, yet the inward man is renewed day by day. For our light affliction, which is but for a moment, worketh for us a far more exceeding and eternal weight of glory; while we look not at the things which are seen, but at the things which are not seen; for the things which are seen are temporal; but the things which are not seen are eternal.* [2 Corinthians 4:11-18]

Notes and Asides

The ultimate direction of history is toward a triumphant close. Even at this very moment, God is moving human history closer to that end—which, in a very real sense, is only the beginning.

The Linear Conception of History

This Christian belief about the direction of history is known as a linear conception of history. That is, Christians believe that human history had a specific beginning (creation) and is being directed by God toward a specific end (the final Day of Judgment), and that historic events follow a nonrepetitive course toward that end. To the individual living in the Western hemisphere, this may not seem to be a unique view of history. Doesn't everyone believe that human history had a beginning and moves along a linear path to its end?

Most of Western society has a linear view of history. But it is founded on the Judeo-Christian perspective. Schlossberg states, "The linearity of Western conceptions of history reflects the conviction that history is what comes between creation and final judgment."[81] Prior to this Christian description of history, Classical thought supported a cyclical view, in which historical events were repeated over and over by consecutive societies. St. Augustine describes the reason the cyclical view is unacceptable to Christians: "far be it, I say, from us [Christians] to believe this [the Classical philosophy of history]. For once Christ died for our sins; and, rising from the dead, He dieth no more."[82]

Thus, the Christian view of history as directional did create a unique conception of the movement of mankind through time. "The importance of the Biblical conception cannot be overstressed," says Montgomery. "Here for the first time Western man was presented with a purposive, goal-directed interpretation of history. The Classical doctrine of recurrence had been able to give a 'substantiality' to history, but it had not given it any aim or direction."[83]

Direction, as always, comes from God. The linear conception of history is simply another way of saying that all of history is meaningful because it is all directed toward a purposeful end. Schlossberg sums up the Christian position:

> Christianity . . . is by its nature historically minded. It rejects both cyclical theories of history and notions of the eternality of the universe. The doctrines of creation and of eschatology are explicit statements that history has both a beginning and an end and that it is possible to say something intelligible about both. Events between the two termini are also intelligible, and, being related to them, have meaning.[84]

Notes and Asides

The fact that God will one day judge every man should cause the individual to see astounding meaning in each decision he makes and renew his understanding of the impact of man's actions on history.

Christianity and Historicism

However, just because the Christian recognizes all of history to be fraught with meaning does not mean that he is capable of discerning God's entire pattern for history. The attempt to understand history as a comprehensive, law-governed whole is known as historicism. Both the Marxist and the Humanist subscribe to a form of historicism when they base their theories of history on the assumption of progress guaranteed by evolution (or the dialectic). "Evolutionism," says Lewis, "when it ceases to be simply a theorem in biology and becomes a principle for interpreting the total historical process, is a form of Historicism."[85] The Christian believes that historicism, in any form, is both foolish and dangerous.

Historicism refers to the attempt to understand history as a comprehensive, law-governed whole.

Historicism is foolish in the sense that it is truly absurd for a mere creature to believe he can discern the pattern established by his Creator. "If, by one miracle," says Lewis, "the total content of time were spread out before me, and if, by another, I were able to hold all that infinity of events in my mind and if, by a third, God were pleased to comment on it so that I could understand it, then, to be sure, I could do what the Historicist says he is doing. I could read the meaning, discern the pattern. Yes; and if the sky fell we should all catch larks. . . . I do not dispute that History is a story written by the finger of God. But have we the text?"[86]

No man should claim to play God and describe the laws that move history. Yet some men try—and therein lies the danger. From a strictly Christian perspective, historicism may cause Christians to act against God's will. Writes Schlossberg,

> The conviction that God is active in history makes historicism especially attractive to the church, tempting it to argue that the resurrection guarantees continual victory over the world, that the Christian consequently can enter into the world's works without worrying about the finer points of scruples, that the lordship of Christ over history guarantees that, when one system replaces another, God's will is being accomplished. The chief consequence of such mistakes is that Christians justify evil political, economic, and social forces.[87]

Clearly, God's will is that Christians oppose corrupt systems, rather than predict how these systems fit into God's pattern of history.

Notes and Asides

From a more general perspective, historicism is dangerous because it allows madmen to justify their actions as conforming to the pattern of history. Lewis says that historicism "encourages a Mussolini to say that 'History took him by the throat' when what really took him by the throat was desire. Drivel about superior races or immanent dialectic may be used to strengthen the hand and ease the conscience of cruelty and greed. And what quack or traitor will not now woo adherents or intimidate resistance with the assurance that his scheme is inevitable, 'bound to come,' and in the direction which the world is already taking?"[88] Historicism is a tool used by manipulators. Christians are called not to be manipulators but rather servants of God.

The Christian attitude toward historicism is summed up by Montgomery: "Because the final evaluation of all historical events rests with God and not with man, and because the final judgment will take place at the end of time, not within time, the Christian historian does not presume to make categorical judgments himself, and is more concerned with understanding than with pontificating."[89] Indeed, the Christian historian should understand better than anyone that God is precisely the element that makes history unpredictable. While secular historians believe they have all the parts of the puzzle and still find themselves unable to discover the pattern of history, the Christian recognizes that God's mind is unfathomable[90] and that this is the precise reason historicism always fails. Christopher Dawson speaks of God's guidance of history as the unpredictable element, pointing out that "the Christian solution is the only one which gives full weight to the unknown and unpredictable element in history; whereas the secular ideologies which attempt to eliminate this element, and which almost invariably take an optimistic view of the immediate future are inevitably disconcerted and disillusioned by the emergence of this unknown factor at the point at which they thought that it had been finally banished."[91]

Conclusion

Christian history centers in the reliability of the Bible, with the events described in Scripture subject to verification. While we have focused on the most significant event in the Biblical Christian worldview, the resurrection of Jesus Christ, the history of the rest of the Bible is also open to close inspection. The Bible's history, as recorded in both Testaments, has stood the test of time—including Old Testament prophecies fulfilled during New Testament times. For example, Micah predicted the birth of Jesus Christ in Bethlehem (5:2); Christ was born in Bethlehem. Daniel (9:24-27) correctly dated the "cutting off" (death) of the Messiah six hundred years before the event took place in history.

Notes and Asides

Luke 19:41f refers to the prophecy in Daniel and bemoans the fact that Jerusalem "did not recognize the time of God's coming" (vs. 44).[92]

Marxism/Leninism and Secular Humanism may believe that man can save himself, but the Christian better understands human nature, and it is this perspective that allows him to form a consistent view regarding the past, the present, and the future. It also helps him to understand man's role in history. Man may freely choose to obey or disobey God, but it is only when he acts in obedience that he can affect history positively. Regardless of how man chooses to affect history, God will work through his actions to direct history toward His ultimate end: the final Day of Judgment. This belief in a climactic conclusion causes the Christian to adopt a linear conception of history. This linear conception reflects the vast meaning with which God has endowed history.

If this historical perspective is correct, then the entire Christian worldview is proved to be true, and it follows that knowing, accepting, and following Jesus Christ as Savior and Lord is the most important thing anyone can do. Wise men still seek him, and for good reason. He gives meaning to history. "If you are not a Christian," says Schaeffer, "remember that you are faced with a choice which will make total differences to you. . . . Your choice is not a piece of theater. You are not thistledown in the wind. There are good and sufficient reasons in history to know that this is the choice you should make, and you are called upon to make it. Choose once for all for justification."[93] This choice has not only eternal significance, but also epistemological significance: Christ opens our eyes to historical reality (Luke 24:31) and eventually to all wisdom and knowledge (Colossians 2:2-3).

[1]Carl F. H. Henry, *God, Revelation and Authority*, six volumes (Waco, TX: Word Books, 1976ff), vol. 2, p. 312.
[2]Ronald H. Nash, *Christian Faith and Historical Understanding* (Dallas, TX: Probe Books, 1984), p. 112.
[3]This event is sometimes called the Fall. While twentieth-century man often speaks disparagingly of the notion of sin, he must ignore the fact that the twentieth century bred two world wars that killed more people than all the previous wars of history. Historian Will Durant, in *The Lessons of History* (New York: Simon and Schuster, 1968), p. 40, states, "History offers some consolation by reminding us that sin has flourished in every age." Durant quotes Voltaire to the effect that history is nothing more than "a collection of the crimes, follies, and misfortunes of mankind." Mankind's capacity for selfishness, pride, envy, idolatry, hatred, murder, lying, deceit, and thievery hasn't changed much since the Fall of mankind.
[4]William F. Albright, *The Archaeology of Palestine* (Baltimore: Penguin Books, 1960), p. 225: "It is, accordingly, sheer hypercriticism to deny the substantially Mosaic character of the Pentateuchal tradition."
[5]Kenneth Scott Latourette, "The Christian Understanding of History," in *God, History, and Historians*, ed. C. T. McIntire, (New York: Oxford University Press, 1977), p. 52.
[6]Henry, *God, Revelation and Authority*, vol. 2, p. 311.
[7]Herbert Schlossberg, *Idols for Destruction* (Nashville, TN: Thomas Nelson, 1983), p. 29.
[8]Millar Burrows, *More Light on the Dead Sea Scrolls* (New York: Viking Press, 1958), p. 55.
[9]With the obvious exception of the early chapters of Genesis, which, according to the Christian view, were based on God's direct revelation of historical events to the author.
[10]John Warwick Montgomery, *Where is History Going?* (Minneapolis: Bethany House, 1969), p. 49.
[11]W. F. Albright, "Toward a More Conservative View," *Christianity Today*, Jan. 18, 1963, p. 4.
[12]Norman L. Geisler, *Miracles and Modern Thought* (Dallas, TX: Probe Books, 1982), p. 145.
[13]H. G. Wells, *The Outline of History* (Garden City, NY: Garden City Publishing, 1921), p. 497.
[14]William Green, *General Introduction to the Old Testament: The Text* (New York: C. Scribner's Sons, 1899), p. 181.
[15]Geisler, *Miracles and Modern Thought*, p. 143.
[16]Gleason L. Archer, Jr., *A Survey of Old Testament Introduction* (Chicago: Moody Press, 1968), p. 19.
[17]Immanuel Velikovsky, *Ages in Chaos* (Garden City, NY: Doubleday, 1952), p. 34.
[18]Geisler, *Miracles and Modern Thought*, p. 145
[19]Albright, *The Archaeology of Palestine*, pp. 123-4.
[20]Herbert Butterfield, *Christianity and History* (New York: Charles Scribner's Sons, 1950), p. 17.
[21]Nelson Glueck, *Biblical Archaeologist*, vol. 22 (Dec. 1959), p. 101.
[22]Millar Burrows, *What Mean These Stones?* (New York: Meridian Books, 1956), p. 1.
[23]Ibid., pp. 143, 144.
[24]Ibid., p. 144.
[25]John Warwick Montgomery, *Human Rights and Human Dignity* (Dallas, TX: Probe Books, 1986), p. 137.
[26]Both the Marxists and the Humanists continually give the impression that their worldview is scientific while the Christian worldview is either prescientific or unscientific. The truth is that science has been very friendly to Christianity, especially the science of archaeology.
[27]Archer, *A Survey of Old Testament Introduction*, p. 21.
[28]Henry, *God, Revelation and Authority*, vol. 2, p. 248.
[29]F. F. Bruce, *The Books and the Parchments* (Westwood, NJ: Fleming H. Revell, 1963), p. 178.
[30]Geisler, *Miracles and Modern Thought*, p. 141.
[31]Ibid.
[32]Albright, *The Archaeology of Palestine*, pp. 127-8.
[33]Werner Keller, *The Bible as History* (New York: William Morrow, 1964), p. xviii.
[34]For example, the second edition of the *Great Soviet Encyclopedia* (Moscow: 1952), a 53-volume series, contains only two lines about Jesus Christ, declaring Him to be "the mythological founder of Christianity;" vol. 17, p. 523.
[35]Montgomery, *Where is History Going?* p. 52.
[36]This is the wording of a tenth-century Arabic manuscript of Josephus's *Antiquities* discovered in late 1971 or early 1972; see New York Times press release, Feb. 12, 1972, published under the title "Christ Documentation: Israeli Scholars Find Ancient Document They Feel Confirms the Existence of Jesus," *Palm Beach Post-Times*,

Feb. 13, 1972, citing Hebrew University (Jerusalem) Professor Shlomo Pines and Hebrew University (New York) Professor David Flusser. Cited in Josh McDowell, *Evidence that Demands a Verdict: Historical Evidences for the Christian Faith* (San Bernardino, CA: Campus Crusade for Christ International, 1972), p. 85. See also "Josephus and Jesus," *Time*, Feb. 28, 1972, p. 55.

[37]The most commonly cited wording of the passage is from *Josephus: Complete Works*, trans. William Whiston (Grand Rapids, MI: Kregel, [1867] 1960):

> Now, there was about this time, Jesus, a wise man, if it be lawful to call him a man, for he was a doer of wonderful works,—a teacher of such men as receive the truth with pleasure. He drew over to him both many of the Jews, and many of the Gentiles. He was [the] Christ; and when Pilate, at the suggestion of the principal men amongst us, had condemned him to the cross, those that loved him at the first did not forsake him, for he appeared to them alive again the third day, as the divine prophets had foretold these and ten thousand other wonderful things concerning him; and the tribe of Christians, so named from him, are not extinct at this time.

Although this wording is cited by the fourth-century Christian historian Eusebius in a manner that makes it certain that at least some manuscript(s) of Josephus contained it before Eusebius wrote (*Ecclesiastical History* [written circa A.D. 324], I.xi.7-8; *Demonstration of the Evangel* [written circa A.D. 310] iii.5.105), the complete lack of reference to it by earlier Christian writers, especially Origen, along with the high improbability that Josephus, who believed that the Roman Emperor Vespasian was the Messiah, would use such language in describing Jesus, make it nearly impossible that this wording is original. It is more likely that Eusebius worked from some manuscript(s) of Josephus that reflected the editing of early Christians who changed Josephus's words to comport better with their faith. Professor Joseph Klausner, of the Hebrew University of Jerusalem, suggested in 1929 that the original wording of the passage might have been:

> Now, there was about this time Jesus, a wise man; for he was a doer of wonderful works; a teacher of such men as receive the truth with pleasure. He drew over to him both many of the Jews and many of the Gentiles. And when Pilate, at the suggestion of the principal men among us, had condemned him to the cross, those that loved him at the first ceased not so to do; and the race of Christians, so named from him, are not extinct even now.

(Joseph Klausner, *Jesus of Nazareth* [London: 1929], pp. 55ff; cited in F. F. Bruce, *Jesus and Christian Origins Outside the New Testament* [Grand Rapids, MI: Eerdmans, 1974], pp. 38-9.)

Historian F. F. Bruce suggests another rendering that, he believes, "probably expresses Josephus's intention more closely," based on linguistic, religious, historical, and contextual arguments:

> Now there arose about this time *a source of further trouble* in one Jesus, a wise man who performed surprising works, a teacher of men who gladly welcome *strange things*. He led away many Jews, and also many of the Gentiles. He was the *so-called* Christ. When Pilate, acting on information supplied by the chief men among us, condemned him to the cross, those who had attached themselves to him at first did not cease *to cause trouble*, and the tribe of Christians, which has taken this name from him, is not extinct even today.

(Bruce, *Jesus and Christian Origins Outside the New Testament*, p. 39.)

Whatever the original wording was, there is little reason to doubt that Josephus did indeed refer to Jesus as a historical figure whose followers, who thought Him to be the Messiah, became known as Christians.

[38]Cornelius Tacitus, *Annals* XV.44; cited in McDowell, *Evidence that Demands a Verdict*, p. 84.

[39]Bruce M. Metzger, *The New Testament: its Background, Growth, and Content* (Nashville: Abingdon Press, 1965), p. 78.

[40]F. F. Bruce, *The New Testament Documents: Are They Reliable?* (Downers Grove, IL: InterVarsity Press, 1972), p. 119.

[41]Will Durant, *Caesar and Christ* (New York: Simon and Schuster, 1944), p. 557.

[42]Montgomery, *Where is History Going?* pp. 53-4.
[43]Wells, *The Outline of History*, p. 510.
[44]Durant, *Caesar and Christ*, p. 562.
[45]Geisler, *Miracles and Modern Thought*, p. 141.
[46]John Warwick Montgomery, *The Shape of the Past* (Minneapolis: Bethany Fellowship, 1975), p. 139.
[47]Ibid., p. 149.
[48]Ibid., p. 151.
[49]Henry, *God, Revelation and Authority*, vol. 2, p. 326.
[50]Geisler, *Miracles and Modern Thought*, p. 93.
[51]C. S. Lewis, *Miracles: A Preliminary Study* (London: Geoffrey Bles, 1952), p. 72. Geisler says of Lewis's work on miracles, "The best overall apologetic for miracles written in this century;" *Miracles and Modern Thought*, p. 167.
[52]Ibid., pp. 70-1.
[53]Geisler, *Miracles and Modern Thought*, p. 149.
[54]Josephus, *Antiquities of the Jews*, XVIII.iii.3, according to the tenth-century Arabic text. (Compare notes 36 and 37 above.)
[55]Geisler, *Miracles and Modern Thought*, p. 149.
[56]Nash, *Christian Faith and Historical Understanding*, p. 112.
[57]Gary Habermas and Antony Flew, *Did Jesus Rise From the Dead?* (New York: Harper and Row, 1987), p. 25. We recommend this work for students wishing to go deeper into the subject.
[58]Ibid., p. 153.
[59]Wolfhart Pannenberg, "Revelation as History," in *God, History, and Historians*, ed. McIntire, p. 127.
[60]D. W. Bebbington, *Patterns in History* (Downers Grove, IL: InterVarsity Press, 1979), p. 169.
[61]Butterfield, *Christianity and History*, p. 112.
[62]Bebbington, *Patterns in History*, p. 43.
[63]Butterfield, *Christianity and History*, p. 66.
[64]McIntire, ed., *God, History, and Historians*, p. 200.
[65]Butterfield, *Christianity and History*, p. 39.
[66]Montgomery, *The Shape of the Past*, p. 148.
[67]Butterfield, *Christianity and History*, p. 37.
[68]Ibid., p. 104.
[69]Schlossberg, *Idols for Destruction*, p. 31.
[70]C. S. Lewis, *God in the Dock: Essays on Theology and Ethics*, ed. Walter Hooper (Grand Rapids, MI: Eerdmans, 1972), p. 316.
[71]Henry, *God, Revelation and Authority*, vol. 2, p. 277.
[72]Francis Schaeffer, *The God Who Is There*, in *The Complete Works of Francis A. Schaeffer*, six volumes (Westchester, IL: Crossway Books, 1982), vol. 1, p. 113.
[73]Rousas John Rushdoony, *The Biblical Philosophy of History* (Nutley, NJ: Presbyterian and Reformed, 1977), p. 6.
[74]Henry, *God, Revelation and Authority*, vol. 2, p. 254.
[75]Bebbington, *Patterns in History*, p. 44.
[76]Ibid., p. 65.
[77]Lewis, *Miracles*, p. 149.
[78]McIntire, ed., *God, History, and Historians*, p. 201.
[79]Ibid.
[80]Montgomery, *Where is History Going?* p. 34.
[81]Schlossberg, *Idols for Destruction*, p. 12.
[82]Whitney J. Oates, ed., *Basic Writings of St. Augustine*, two volumes (Grand Rapids, MI: Baker, 1980), vol. 2, p. 192.
[83]Montgomery, *The Shape of the Past*, p. 42.
[84]Schlossberg, *Idols for Destruction*, p. 5.
[85]C. S. Lewis, *Christian Reflections* (Grand Rapids, MI: Eerdmans, 1971), p. 101.

[86]Ibid., pp. 104-5.
[87]Schlossberg, *Idols for Destruction*, p. 31.
[88]Lewis, *Christian Reflections*, p. 110.
[89]Montgomery, *The Shape of the Past*, p. 146.
[90]Romans 11:34 asks, "Who has known the mind of the Lord?"
[91]Christopher Dawson, "The Christian View of History," in *God, History, and Historians*, ed. McIntire, p. 44.
[92]Robert Anderson, *The Coming Prince* (Grand Rapids, MI: Kregel, 1975) and Josh McDowell, *Daniel in the Critic's Den* (Grand Rapids, MI: Kregel, 1980) cover the Daniel passage in some detail.
[93]Francis A. Schaeffer, *Joshua and the Flow of Biblical History*, in *The Complete Works of Francis A. Schaeffer*, vol. 2, p. 315.

CONCLUSION

"COME NOW, LET US REASON TOGETHER."

"At every stage of religious development man may rebel, if not without violence to his own nature, yet without absurdity. He can close his spiritual eyes against the Numinous, if he is prepared to part company with half the great poets and prophets of his race, with his own childhood, with the richness and depth of uninhibited experience. He can regard the moral law as an illusion, and so cut himself off from the common ground of humanity. He can refuse to identify the Numinous with the righteous, and remain a barbarian, worshipping sexuality, or the dead, or the life-force, or the future. But the cost is heavy. And when we come to the last step of all, the historical Incarnation, the assurance is strongest of all. The story is strangely like many myths which have haunted religion from the first, and yet it is not like them. It is not transparent to the reason: we could not have invented it ourselves. . . . If any message from the core of reality ever were to reach us, we should expect to find in it just that unexpectedness, that wilful, dramatic anfractuosity which we find in the Christian faith. It has the master touch--the rough, male taste of reality, not made by us, or, indeed, for us, but hitting us in the face."[1]

—C. S. Lewis

Notes and Asides

Setting the Stage

The body of this text has established the contours of the Biblical Christian, Marxist/Leninist, and Secular Humanist worldviews, as described by the words and actions of their leaders. We have presented the emerging Cosmic Humanist or New Age worldview in Appendix A. For the most part we have withheld critical comment. Our silence, however, should not be construed as a lack of interest in such discourse.

"Come now, let us reason together," God says (Isaiah 1:18). "Be ready to give an answer to every man that asketh you a reason of the hope that is in you with meekness and fear," says the Apostle Peter (1 Peter 3:15). Acting in accordance with these exhortations, the Christian must meet the challenge posed by non-Christian religious worldviews that claim that Biblical Christianity is irrational, unscientific, and false. We will present our comments from a Christian perspective and use that perspective to highlight the unreasonableness and untruthfulness of Marxism and Humanism when compared to the Christian worldview.

Both Marxism and Humanism, of course, contain truth. Both, for example, acknowledge the existence of the physical universe. Both acknowledge the significance and relevance of science. Both understand the importance of "saving" mankind. However, they differ radically with the Christian model of salvation: Christianity's message is that Jesus Christ is the key to reality—not Karl Marx, V. I. Lenin, John Dewey, or Isaac Asimov. Christianity views Jesus Christ as the way, the truth and the life (John 14:6). Marxism and Humanism reject Jesus Christ—Marxists have been known to deny His very existence. Thus, an insurmountable difference exists between Christianity and these two worldviews.

Did Jesus Christ live on this earth two thousand years ago? Was He God in flesh? Did He come to earth to reveal God's will for man and to save the human race from sin? These are important questions. Biblical Christianity lives or dies on the answers. "If Christ be not risen," says Paul, "your faith is in vain" (1 Corinthians 15:14).

John Warwick Montgomery says that the answer revolves around one key issue—"How good are these New Testament records?" He believes that they are very good, quoting Simon Greenleaf (Harvard's great nineteenth-century authority on the law of evidence) to the effect that "the competence of the New Testament documents would be established in any court of law."[2] Montgomery insists that if one compares the New Testament with universally accepted secular writings of antiquity "the New Testament is more than vindicated."[3] Further, he says,

> Modern archaeological research has confirmed again and again the reliability of New Testament geography, chronology, and

Notes and Asides

general history. To take but a single, striking example: after the rise of liberal biblical criticism, doubt was expressed as to the historicity of Pontius Pilate, since he is mentioned even by pagan historians only in connection with Jesus' death. Then in 1961 came the discovery at Caesarea of the now famous "Pilate inscription," definitely showing that, as usual, the New Testament writers were engaged in accurate historiography.[4]

Yet in spite of overwhelming historical evidence confirmed by the science of archaeology, Secular Humanists and Marxist/Leninists insist that Biblical Christianity is a pre-scientific myth unworthy of serious consideration.

Whether one chooses to accept Marxism/Leninism, Secular Humanism, or Biblical Christianity, that individual is accepting a worldview that describes the opposition as hopelessly distorted. Only one view depicts things as they really are; all other perspectives must be out of step with the nature of man and the universe. Indeed, the Marxists and the Humanists are quick to describe Christians as not only out of step but victims of serious delusion. Marx, of course, viewed all religion as a drug that deluded its adherents—an "opiate of the masses." Humanists often portray Christians as just plain crazy. For example, James J. D. Luce, the assistant executive director of Fundamentalists Anonymous, claims that "the fundamentalist experience can be a serious mental health hazard to perhaps millions of people."[5] His organization works to "heal" Christians of their "mental disorder"—Christianity. Harvard's Edward O. Wilson describes Christianity as "one of the unmitigated evils of the world."[6] Adherents to secular religious worldviews understand that, if their assumptions are correct, any worldview that postulates the supernatural must be dangerous to the health and safety of mankind.

"To [the apostles] also [Christ] showed himself alive after his passion by many infallible proofs, being seen of them forty days, and speaking of the things pertaining to the kingdom of God."
—St. Luke

Likewise, the Biblical Christian must understand that his worldview excludes the possibility that foundational Marxist and Humanist assumptions might provide a helpful insight into reality. Foundational secular assumptions are antithetical to Christian presuppositions. *No compromise can exist between the worldviews on this fundamental level.* Either the Christian correctly describes reality when he speaks of a loving, just, personal God and His incarnation and resurrection, or he is talking nonsense. We cannot blend the basic claims of the Bible with the Humanist and Marxist claims that man is inherently good and requires no savior other than himself. Only one view properly describes the cold hard facts of a universe that Christians believe was created by God. If it turns out that the universe wasn't created, that Christ did not rise again from the grave, and that life is, as Stephen Jay Gould says, "an afterthought," then Christianity may be judged a false worldview.

Two views, those of the Humanist and the Marxist, paint a picture

Notes and Asides

of reality so bleak that even their adherents, in their more lucid moments, recognize the need to cling to artificial hopes to avoid slipping into despair. Humanist Herbert Tonne alludes to the atheist's willingness to abandon sanity at a crucial juncture in his worldview, claiming that

> a truly sane person would be socially insane. Functionally sanity means being deluded sufficiently to believe that life is worth living and that the human race is worth preserving. In our really sane moments we realize that life is but a "poor player that struts and frets his hour upon the stage and then is seen no more"; that "it is a tale told by an idiot full of sound and fury meaning nothing."[7]

This attitude has permeated the mental health field, thanks to the influence Humanism has had on the discipline. In fact, even Humanist Peter R. Breggin admits "it would be hard to find a more unhappy lot than those clustered in the mental health field. Especially among psychiatrists, suicide, depression, drug addiction and alcoholism are notoriously rife. Among non-medical mental health professionals, the situation doesn't seem much better. Not only are many mental health professionals unhappy but they do not live ethically inspired lives."[8]

> "But when the Holy Spirit controls our lives he will produce this kind of fruit in us: love, joy, peace, patience, kindness, goodness, faithfulness, gentleness, and self-control."
>
> —St. Paul

One would expect such a dangerous mindset to be spawned by a worldview inconsistent with reality. Indeed, it always seems that man can expect poor results when applying Humanist or Marxist theory to real life, while the Christian worldview consistently bears good fruit when conscientiously applied.

The Christian position, of course, requires no delusion to convince its adherents that life is worth preserving. Scripture provides mankind with a view of reality that allows the individual to function cooperatively in society without deluding himself. The Christian treats man as "fearfully and wonderfully made" (Psalm 139:14) because his worldview describes man as such.

The Humanist and the Marxist are aware of the complexity and value of mankind, without being able to account for its existence. This is a fundamental flaw of the secular religious worldviews, one that points up the fact that Christianity and other ideologies are mutually exclusive at ground level. We must discern which view is the proper attitude toward life and death, good and evil, design and chance, and then resign ourselves to a life of despair or welcome a life of joy, accordingly.

Because such differences exist, and because there can be no reconciliation between Christianity and opposing worldviews, men and

Notes and Asides

women must examine the evidence and determine the truth. To this end, this chapter will focus on the fundamental concepts of these worldviews. We are not interested in hair-splitting. Secular Humanism, for example does not stand or fall according to its stance regarding gun control. It does stand or fall, however, on its theology, philosophy, ethics, and biology. Our emphasis will be foundational—we desire to examine the concepts on which each worldview is based. Here, in the heart of the ideologies, a student can test the character of the worldviews and separate wheat from chaff, truth from fiction. And here (we believe) Christianity stands tall, looming over its adversaries.

After working our way through a systematic analysis of the ten major components of the three worldviews, our studied conclusions are that:

in **theology**, the evidence for the existence of God, a designed and intelligible universe, and an earth prepared for human life far outweighs any argument for atheism;

in **philosophy**, the notion that mind (logos) precedes matter is far superior to the atheistic stance of matter preceding mind;

in **biology**, the concept of a living God creating life fits the evidence better than any hint of spontaneous generation and evolution;

in **ethics**, the concept that right and wrong are absolutes based on the nature and character of a personal, loving, holy God is far superior both theoretically and practically to any concept of moral relativism;

in **law**, the notion that God always (absolutely) hates the perversion of justice is far superior to any theory of legal relativism or positive law;

in **psychology**, the ingredients of body, soul, spirit and mind far outweigh physical explanations that reduce mind and brain to random chemical explosions in some kind of supercharged matter;

Notes and Asides

in **sociology**, the Biblical family of father, mother, and child far transcends any experiments in homosexuality, trial marriages, etc.;

in **politics**, the Christian belief that human rights are a gift from God protected by government is more logically persuasive, morally appealing, and politically sound than any atheistic theory that maintains that human rights are a largess of the state;

in **economics**, the concept of stewardship of private property and using resources responsibly to glorify God is more noble than the notion of a society in which common ownership destroys individual responsibility and work incentives;

and in **history**, the veracity of the Bible and its promise of a future kingdom ushered in by Jesus Christ is far more credible than any vague, utopian, global schemes dreamed up by sinful, mortal men.

In other words, in every discipline, the Christian worldview shines brighter than its competition, is more realistic, better explains man and the universe, is true to the Bible, is more scientific, is more intellectually satisfying and defensible, and best of all, is in keeping with and faithful to the one person who has had the greatest influence in heaven and on earth—Jesus Christ.

Indeed, we cannot imagine one category in which Humanism or Marxism outshines the Christian position. For example, putting Christian economics into practice results in prosperity and the avoidance of poverty,[9] while all forms of socialism (including the welfare state) guarantee various levels of poverty.[10] Putting Christian sociology into practice results in strong families that discourage societal trends toward drug-use, crime, unemployment, poverty, and disease,[11] whereas Marxist and Humanist experimentation with the family unit (including Humanism's self-proclaimed "important role in the sexual revolution"[12]) causes society to disintegrate. Putting Christian law into practice results in the Magna Charta, the English common law, and the U.S. Constitution, guaranteeing human rights as God-ordained, while the history of positive law—in France for two centuries, in the Soviet Union for seventy years, and in the U.S. for the last half-century—has been a history of blood baths. (Yes, blood baths in the United States: 1.5 million unborn babies killed every year by abortion.) Most importantly, of course, putting Christian theology and philosophy into practice

Notes and Asides

results in salvation of the soul (Matthew 16:26), enlightenment of the mind, and purpose in living.

It should be noted here that this critique does not treat Marxism and Humanism as mutually exclusive, for the simple reason that, as Erich Fromm says, "Marxism is humanism."[13] Georgi Shakhnazarov is even more explicit,

> In essence, communism is identical to humanism since it presupposes the all-round development of the human personality in a perfectly organized society.[14]

We have already pointed out that Humanism is the root and Marxism the branch—that is, Marxism is a subset of Humanism. The body of this text makes it obvious that most of Humanism's and Marxism's foundational or theoretical assumptions are virtually indistinguishable, with the notable exception that Marxism treats economics as primary, while Secular Humanism tends to concentrate on philosophy and biology. Both worldviews are, in the main, atheistic, materialistic (or naturalistic), evolutionary, positivistic, monistic, utopian, and relativistic; but Marxism, thanks to its dialectic and well developed economic theory, provides a better-defined perspective. Thus, there will be places in this critique where we address only the flaws of Marxist theory, but for the most part, our criticism will apply to both worldviews.

> "In essence, communism is identical to humanism since it presupposes the all-round development of the human personality in a perfectly organized society."
> —G. Shakhnazarov

We contend that Marxism and Humanism are profoundly incapable of describing the universe from start to finish. Therefore, we will examine the three worldviews using a model that begins with the beginning of time and works chronologically toward the future. This will reinforce what this text should make clear to all minds concerned with truth and intellectual integrity: only Biblical Christianity presents the proper view of the world and the things contained therein. "I now believe," said the former atheistic philosopher C. E. M. Joad, "that the balance of reasoned considerations tells heavily in favor of the religious, even of the Christian view of the world."[15]

Genesis

In the beginning, one of two things existed: mind or matter. Either a supreme mind has always existed and created matter and the universe at a specific point in time, or matter is eternal and formed the universe by itself. *Either mind created matter, or matter created mind.* Either the mind of God is primary and the material universe is secondary, or matter is primary and mind is secondary.

The Bible, of course, declares that God is eternal and that He created

Notes and Asides

the physical universe and its inhabitants (Genesis 1). It goes on to say that the physical universe was well thought out in the mind of God before creation ever took place (John 1:1-3). The Marxist and the Humanist deny the very possibility that Scripture accurately accounts for the beginning of the universe. They therefore must hold that matter is eternal and has moved from a state of disorder to an ordered state as guided by chance. That is, matter previously packed into a mathematical point and scattered by an incredible bang ordered itself into such remarkable entities as supernovas, diamonds, electrons, DNA—and the mind of man.[16] Further, the non-Christian worldviews believe that the universe was once dead and yet brought forth life—that inorganic matter, given enough time and the proper recipe for primordial soup, brought forth amoebas and hummingbirds, squid and prairie dogs. Further still, the Marxist and the Humanist believe that dead, disordered matter eventually organized man, a being capable of inventing bicycles, jokes, and *Hamlet*. The Christian's faith pales in comparison to the credulity required to believe that such diversity and complexity arose by chance.

> "Through [Christ] all things were made; without him nothing was made that has been made."
>
> —St. John

This is one of the most glaring flaws of Marxist and Humanist theory—it asks man to believe that a reality that currently moves from order to disorder (according to the Second Law of Thermodynamics) moved in exactly the opposite direction for billions of years in the past. Of course, the Marxist and the Humanist ignore, or at least downplay, the teleological nature of the universe and the wonder of man in an effort to mask this inconsistency—Gould describes mankind as an "afterthought"[17]—but they cannot hope to sway any individual with an open mind about the mysteries and manifest intelligence of the universe.

Hillsdale College president George Roche provides an excellent example of the profound design manifested in our universe when he describes the special nature of human beings:

> Man is a very *strange* animal. . . . Not that there is anything particularly queer about our physical equipment; this is all quite reasonable. But gorillas have hands as we do, yet use them for very little, and never to play the piano or skip stones or whittle or write letters. Dolphins have bigger brains than we do, but you seldom hear them discoursing on nuclear physics. Chihuahuas are more hairless than we, but have never thought to wear clothes. . . . Man alone weeps for cause, and "is shaken with the beautiful madness called laughter," as Chesterton put it. . . .[18]

Secular worldview adherents would like to ignore the unmistakably unique character of man, because their ideologies cannot adequately account for it. A worldview that asserts the primacy of matter has a difficult time explaining this unique creature so distant from the rest of the animal kingdom.

Even Marxism, which grants matter God-like qualities, cannot account for the mind and the mystery of human beings. Marxists may criticize other materialistic positions, but what they invest in matter (including an elaborate and highly sophisticated triad of thesis, antithesis, and synthesis) has no scientific backing. To the best of our knowledge, no respectable Western scientist argues for a dialectical behavior of the atom or its subatomic components. To believe that atoms operate according to the dialectic would require belief in a perpetual motion machine.[19]

The Christian worldview, on the other hand, accounts for the unique character of man from the first chapter of Scripture. In Genesis 1:26,

The Solovky Memorandum

(A statement issued by bishops imprisoned in the Soviet Union)

"The Church recognizes spiritual principles of existence; communism rejects them. The Church believes in the living God, the Creator of the world, the leader of its life and destinies; communism denies his existence. . . . The Church sees in religion a lifebearing force which . . . serves as the source for all greatness in man's creativity, as the basis of man's earthly happiness, sanity and welfare; communism sees religion as opium, drugging the people and relaxing their energies, as the source of their suffering and poverty. The Church wants to see religion flourish; communism wants its death. Such a deep contradiction in the very basis of their *Weltanschauungen* [worldviews] precludes any intrinsic approximation or reconciliation . . . as there cannot be any between affirmation and negation . . . because the very soul of the Church, the condition of her existence and the sense of her being, is that which is categorically denied by communism."

Notes and Asides

God declares, "Let us make man in our image, in our likeness, and let them rule over the fish of the sea and the birds of the air, over the livestock, over all the earth, and over all the creatures that move along the ground." Likewise, the Christian view accounts for the rest of the design found in nature, because it begins with a Designer. Whereas the Humanist and the Marxist must rely on chance and matter to explain birds capable of astronomical navigation and bees that communicate through dance, the Christian posits an omniscient God who chose to order the universe into a beautiful symphony of light, life, sound, and color. "The heavens declare the glory of God; the skies proclaim the work of his hands" (Psalm 19:1). "Everywhere we look in nature (whether in living or non-living matter)," say Percival Davis and Dean Kenyon, "design and material organization are on display."[20] Paul Amos Moody sums up the Christian position:

> The more I study science the more I am impressed with the thought that this world and universe have a definite *design*—and design suggests a *designer*. It may be possible to have design without a designer, a picture without an artist, but *my* mind is unable to conceive of such a situation.[21]

It simply comes down to this: did life and intelligence and humor and design come from a living, intelligent God who loves order and joy, or did they arise randomly from dead matter? The Christian believes that a lawfully designed reality demands an origin that provides the groundwork for such attributes. Thus, the Christian finds the key in John 1:1-5:

> In the beginning was the Word, and the Word was with God, and the Word was God. He was with God in the beginning. Through him all things were made; without him nothing was made that has been made. In him was life, and that life was the light of men. The light shines in the darkness, but the darkness has not understood it.

Mind Over Matter?

The ultimate problem faced by the Humanist and Marxist in the area of origins is the existence of mind (the overarching term we will use for all the supernatural qualities of man, including conscience, ideas, soul, and spirit). A naive student might be persuaded that life and order arose

Notes and Asides

from non-living matter, but even the most gullible cannot swallow that the human mind, which has pierced the atom and conceived *The Brothers Karamazov*, came about by the chance workings of matter. It truly is a question of mind creating matter or matter creating mind—did the Supreme mind instill in men reason, appreciation for aesthetic qualities, and a conscience, or did "eternal" nonliving matter?

Clearly, this is a fatal flaw of Marxist and Humanist philosophy. While both secular worldviews claim that matter is primary or ultimate reality and mind is a pale reflection of this reality, they are faced again and again with the magnificent workings of the human mind. Further, experience suggests that mind acts creatively on matter, rather than vice versa. Warren Brookes speaks of the economy in mind as preceding the physical transfer of money, goods, and services. If men conceive things in their minds and then act creatively, doesn't it seem likely that the universe began in a similar fashion? Wouldn't we expect a supreme mind to precede matter?

"There needs not a great soul to make a hero; there needs a God-created soul which will be true to its origin; that will be a great soul."
—Thomas Carlyle

Again, Roche provides us with an excellent example of an insurmountable problem created by the monistic attitude of Marxism and Humanism. "Altruism," he writes, "is not a scientific concept. It is a metaphysical reality that is simply unaccountable to a materialist philosophy."[22] That is, the Christian expects heroism from his fellow man—after all, he is made in the image of the God who sacrificed His own life so that we might live. The secular religious worldviews, on the other hand, can only speak of self-preservation and species-preservation instincts, which provide a pretty poor explanation for a young man diving into an icy river to save an octogenarian. Indeed, the Humanist and the Marxist had best ignore such non-material activity, since it demands more than a materialist explanation. No scientist, including the world's finest neurosurgeon, has ever held the idea of altruism in his hands for inspection or dissection.

The only time the secular worldviews care to treat the mind as important is in reference to the theories devised by their own minds. But as we have stressed throughout this text, it is irrational to consistently portray the mind as random chemical firings of synapses in the brain and a mere reflection of the physical universe, and then expect one's own mind, a product of chance and accident, to comprehend and process reality accurately. No less of an authority than Charles Darwin recognized the problem faced by adherents to atheistic, materialistic explanations of mind:

> With me, the horrid doubt always arises whether the convictions of man's mind, which has been developed from the mind

Notes and Asides

> of lower animals, are of any value or at all trustworthy. Would any one trust in the convictions of a monkey's mind, if there are any convictions in such a mind?[23]

And further—would anyone trust a mind whose ancestral roots trace back beyond monkeys' minds to mindless amoebas and even to mindless, inorganic, chaotic matter?

The answer is obvious. Naturalistic theologies and philosophies that begin with matter are incapable of explaining not only the teleological nature of the universe but also the capabilities of human minds and souls. Perhaps it sounds more manageable to simplify or reduce all reality to an ultimate material substance, but in the end this oversimplified worldview leads to hopeless complications because of its inability to explain reason. As Albert Einstein said, things should be made as simple as possible, but not simpler. It is all well and good to declare, as Carl Sagan does in his book *Cosmos*, that matter (or nature, or the Cosmos) is all that has ever existed or ever will, but it leaves the Humanist and the Marxist with a number of inexplicable phenomena to sweep under the rug. For one thing, science has been arriving at the conclusion that ultimate substance is not matter at all. The further the search into the subatomic world, the more it appears that ultimate reality is something spiritual. Sir Arthur Eddington referred to this reality as "spiritual" or "mind-stuff."[24] Indeed, Eddington writes, "The idea of a universal Mind or Logos would be, I think, a fairly plausible inference from the present state of scientific theory; at least it is in harmony with it."[25] For another thing, what does a materialist do with mind, soul, altruism, creativity, rationality, conscience, song, and laughter? He may try to ignore them, but they face him every day. Indeed, he depends on them. It sounds learned to describe them as secondary, derivative, mere reflections of material reality, but how can the thought processes that formulated the notion of dialectical materialism be described as reflections, as cranial illusions, when they seem to be (at least for the Marxist) the most powerful facet of reality?

> "The idea of a universal Mind or Logos would be, I think, a fairly plausible inference from the present state of scientific theory; at least it is in harmony with it."
> —Arthur Eddington

The questions of origins and ultimate substance provide an excellent starting point for a serious critique of Humanism and Marxism, because they highlight the glaring weaknesses in both worldviews' theology and philosophy. The Christian expects man to be the most intricate part of an infinitely intricate creation, because he begins with a personal God, who specially created a world for male and female.[26] The Humanist and the Marxist should expect very little—should, indeed, be awed by ordered matter—and instead they find that man, an "afterthought" in the universe, is larger than life—and completely inexplicable in materialist terms.

In *Does God Exist? The Great Debate*, Dallas Willard, a professor of philosophy at the University of Southern California, raises an important point. Every great philosopher—Plato, Aristotle, St. Augustine, St. Thomas, William of Occam, Rene Descartes, Baruch Spinoza, Gottfried von Leibniz, John Locke, George Berkeley, Immanuel Kant, and Georg W. F. Hegel—was a theist, in one form or another. Even David Hume, a man Secular Humanists embrace as one of their own, declared,

> The whole frame of nature bespeaks an intelligent author; and no rational enquirer can, after serious reflection, suspend his belief a moment with regard to the primary principles of genuine Theism and Religion.[27]

The conclusion for the Christian worldview is obvious: Christian theology and philosophy are more intellectually defensible than the secular worldviews' versions.[28]

The Evolution of Evolution

Wait a minute. From the perspective of the Secular Humanist and the Marxist/Leninist, our discussion of mankind and all other life forms is premature. While the Biblical Christian can begin talking about mankind virtually from the beginning of time, the secular worldviews must postulate an immense amount of time (ca. 16 billion years) between the formation of the universe and the development of life and man. In order to do justice to Humanism and Marxism's view of mankind and his institutions, we must back up and examine the cornerstone of their worldview: the theory of spontaneous generation and evolution.

We have, of course, discussed the theory of evolution at length in the section on biology. We have noted the scientific fact that no one has ever produced a new species by means of natural selection, and we have acknowledged microbiologist Michael Denton's charge that Darwinism lacks empirical verification: "Neither of the two fundamental axioms of Darwin's macroevolutionary theory . . . has . . . been validated by one single empirical discovery or scientific advance since 1859."[29] Indeed, we have highlighted most of the flaws in evolutionary theory already, because such commentary strengthens the Christian position of creationism (if Darwinian evolution and punctuated equilibrium are scientifically untenable, creation becomes more tenable). Evolutionary theory is marked with more inconsistencies and contradictions than can be discussed here.[30] Thus, for the purpose of this critique, we will focus on two distinct aspects of the theory that were only touched on in the body of the text: the amount of faith required to

Notes and Asides

believe in spontaneous generation, and the evolution of the theory of evolution.

One of the most fundamental beliefs that a Marxist or a Humanist must cling to is that somewhere, somehow, sometime, life arose from non-life. Without spontaneous generation, something living must always have existed, namely an eternal God. Therefore, in order to be a consistent naturalistic atheist, the Humanist and the Marxist must ignore the experiments of Francesco Redi and Louis Pasteur, which disproved spontaneous generation, and trust fervently in the ability of inorganic matter to self-organize toward life.

George Wald provides an excellent example of the dogmatic tenacity with which materialistic evolutionists cling to the concept of spontaneous generation. He speaks of believing in spontaneous generation as a "philosophical necessity" for the scientist and declares,

> Most modern biologists, having reviewed with satisfaction the downfall of the spontaneous generation hypothesis, yet unwilling to accept the alternative belief in special creation, are left with nothing. I think a scientist has no choice but to approach the origin of life through a hypothesis of spontaneous generation.[31]

Wald takes his own advice seriously: "Back of the spontaneous generation of life under other conditions than now obtain upon this planet, there occurred a spontaneous generation of elements of the kind that still goes on in the stars; and back of that I suppose a spontaneous generation of elementary particles under circumstances still to be fathomed, that ended in giving them the properties that alone make possible the universe we know."[32]

In an effort to bolster their faith in spontaneous generation, proponents of the secular religious worldviews have encouraged numerous experiments in which sparks are introduced into carefully concocted primordial soups in an effort to duplicate the first jump from non-life to life. A. I. Oparin made these experiments famous and remains a darling of evolutionists.[33] But the hard fact remains that neither Oparin nor any other scientist has succeeded in coaxing spontaneous generation in his primordial soup. Neither is such a miracle likely to occur. "The step from simple compounds to the complex molecules of life, such as protein and DNA, has proved to be a difficult one," say Davis and Kenyon, "thus far it has resisted all efforts by the scientists working on the problem."[34] Elsewhere these authors state, "Without intelligence using selected chemicals and control conditions, amino acids have not been collected in the laboratory. Doubtless the same is true in nature."[35] Besides, all of these experiments seeking to create life in a test tube were conducted in the absence of oxygen, since oxygen would destroy any organic compounds. "Yet scientists now know," say Davis and Kenyon, "that oxygen was present on the earth from the earliest ages."[36]

Fred Hoyle, for years a leading atheist spokesman, has seen the error of his thinking and now argues that there is a better chance of producing a Boeing 747 via an explosion in a junkyard than there is to arrive at life by accident. He believes there is no way of producing DNA by chance processes, noting that merely lining up the necessary enzymes by chance would consume 20 billion years. Three respected scientists—Charles Thaxton, Walter Bradley, and Roger Olsen—write in *The Mystery of Life's Origin: Reassessing Current Theories* that "the undirected flow of energy through a primordial atmosphere and ocean is at present a woefully inadequate explanation for the incredible complexity associated with even simple living systems, and is probably wrong."[37]

Naturally, this conclusion is unacceptable for both the Marxist and the Humanist. To admit that life cannot arise from non-life would shake their worldviews to the very foundations. Adherents of both secular worldviews are fond of labeling Christians as dogmatic, but they neglect to mention that the doctrine of spontaneous generation is every bit as sacred to the atheist as the doctrine of the Incarnation is to the Christian. Humanist Keith Parsons, for example, states, "With the environment operating to remove nonviable variations, the appearance of life on earth becomes a certainty rather than an extreme improbability."[38] Thus, we discover in Marxism and Humanism a faith more profound and more unfounded than that of the most rudimentary religions.

Further, we find that this blind faith has been extended to encompass the entire discipline of biology. In the introduction to the 1971 edition of Darwin's *The Origin of Species*, L. H. Matthews admits,

> The fact of evolution is the backbone of biology, and biology is thus in the peculiar position of being a science founded on an unproved theory—is it then a science or a faith? Belief in the theory of evolution is thus exactly parallel to belief in special creation—both are concepts which believers know to be true but neither, up to the present, has been capable of proof.[39]

In examining mankind's changing attitude toward evolutionary theory, it becomes obvious that evolution has been reduced to an insupportable dogma embraced by secular religions. But it wasn't always this way. Evolution began as just another scientific theory. Darwin even treated his theory as subject to falsification, believing that unless numerous transitional forms appeared in the fossil record, his theory broke down. He wrote, "The number of intermediate varieties

Notes and Asides

> "Ever since the famous Scopes 'monkey' trial of 1925 . . . the theory of evolution has enjoyed the status of revealed truth for most of the educated public. But there are cracks in the facade. The great body of work deriving from . . . 'On the Origin of Species' is under increasing attack—and not just from the creationists. . . . The editors of a new book assert that when it comes to accounting for life on earth, natural selection should be 'relegated here to the [explanation of] last resort.'"
>
> —*Newsweek*

which have formerly existed on the earth, [must] be truly enormous. Why then is not every geological formation and every stratum full of such intermediate links? Geology assuredly does not reveal any such finely graduated organic chain; and this, perhaps, is the most obvious and gravest objection which can be urged against my theory."[40] Darwin's embarrassment over his theory's conflict with the fossil record is evidenced by the fact that, in *The Descent of Man*, "Darwin did not cite a single reference to fossils in support of his belief in human evolution."[41] Despite Darwin's own reservations, however, Humanists and Marxists and atheists everywhere found that this theory allowed them to avoid the uncomfortable concept of God, so they proclaimed evolution to be fact. Julian Huxley declared around 1960 that Darwin "rendered evolution inescapable as a fact . . . all-embracing as a concept."[42]

Now, perhaps in 1960 one could get away with such a rash claim. Perhaps three decades ago the evidence against evolutionary theory was not quite so damning. But today, as we have demonstrated in this text, it is generous even to label evolution as a scientific theory, and one is sorely tempted to describe it as myth. In modern times, we have entered the third phase of the evolution of the theory of evolution: the theory has

Notes and Asides

become a religious dogma that is counter-rational and therefore demands great resources of faith.

In the beginning, evolution was a theory; later (thanks to Humanists and Marxists) it was championed as fact; today it is still touted as fact. But now it is such a remarkable fact that it can contradict all the factual findings of paleontology, homology, and molecular biology and still be labeled absolute truth. Humanists and Marxists cling to evolution *despite* the findings of modern science,[43] using one of two methods: blinding themselves to all facts that contradict evolution, or abandoning Darwinian evolution and postulating a theory (punctuated equilibrium) that circumvents the absence of supportive facts (i.e., it explains away any need for evidence). The theory of punctuated equilibrium, of course, is the first "scientific" theory ever postulated that claims to be true not because any facts support it but because no fact can be conceived that disputes it. "The newer forms of evolutionary theory may fit the facts better," say Davis and Kenyon, "but their weakness is that they are based upon negative evidence. There is still no positive fossil evidence for evolutionary descent from one taxon to the next. At best, punctuated equilibrium advances an explanation for evolution's lack of evidence."[44] Clearly, this position has all the earmarks of blind faith, since it asks men to believe in occurrences of which no traces exist.

However, the modern evolutionists who choose not to embrace punctuated equilibrium demonstrate the greatest credulity. These evolutionists must actually blind themselves to the entire fossil record in order to maintain their belief in evolution. For example, Humanist Chris McGowan points to a few fossils and concludes, "These intermediate fossils falsify the creationists' claim that transitional fossils linking major groups do not exist, and provide compelling evidence for evolution."[45] The plain fact from which McGowan has shielded his eyes is this: the more honest members of his own camp—*evolutionists*—admit that not one transitional fossil exists.[46] It would be one thing if only a few rabid creationists were proclaiming the absence of transitional fossils—but it is quite another when non-creationist paleontologists declare it. In fact, no less august an authority than Colin Patterson, a paleontologist with the London Museum of Natural History, admits that he does not know of any evidences, "fossil or living," that provide "direct illustration of evolutionary transitions."[47] Elsewhere he writes more definitely: "I will lay it on the line—there is not one such fossil [that is ancestral or transitional] for which one could make a watertight argument."[48]

The flaws in evolutionary theory have become so glaring that evolution is revealed as an unacceptable explanation for the scientific facts of geology and paleontology. Marxists and Humanists are seeing

Notes and Asides

countless reputable evolutionists abandon ship for the simple reason that evolution has been tried and found wanting. Patterson is rapidly falling away from an evolutionary mindset, and his reasoning is sound:

> One of the reasons I started taking this anti-evolutionary view, or let's call it a non-evolutionary view, was that last year I had a sudden realization. For over twenty years I was working on evolution in some way. One morning I woke up and something had happened to me in the night, and it struck me that I had been working on this stuff for more than twenty years, and there was not one thing new about it. It's quite a shock to learn that one can be misled for so long. Either there was something wrong with me or there was something wrong with evolutionary theory. Naturally I know there is nothing wrong with me, so for the last few weeks I've been putting a simple question to various people and groups. Question is: can you tell me anything you know about evolution? Any one thing, any one thing that is true?[49]

"I will lay it on the line—there is not one such fossil [that is ancestral or transitional] for which one could make a watertight argument."
—Colin Patterson

It is startling to realize that evolutionists cannot point to even one aspect of their theory that they know to be true. Clearly, evolution must be abandoned. But few evolutionists can summon the courage to completely break away from their discredited theory. As the *Encyclopedie francaise*, written in cooperation with the leading biologists of France, says, "It follows from this presentation that the theory of evolution is impossible. . . . Evolution is a kind of dogma in which its priests no longer believe but which they keep presenting to their people."[50]

It is our contention that this position will be dominant in the next century. To argue, as Sagan does, that we are the children of the stars may be good poetry, but it is terrible theology and even worse science. We agree with Soren Lovtrup's observation: "I believe that one day the Darwinism myth will be ranked the greatest deceit in the history of science."[51]

But the theory of evolution will die hard. Both the Humanists and the Marxists must trust in it blindly and defend it to the death. Their willingness to cling to such a poor explanation of life should not surprise us; G. K. Chesterton warned long ago that if man will not believe in God, the danger is not that he will believe in nothing, but that he will believe in anything. What should surprise us is that so much of the world and, tragically, so many Christians, swallowed the entire theory and allowed it to gain such ascendancy among worldviews. Even today, member institutions of the Christian College Coalition are accepting a text by Richard T. Wright that presents a Darwinian evolutionary point of view.[52] Theistic evolutionists would do well to listen to Michael Denton:

> The influence of evolutionary theory on fields far removed from biology is one of the most spectacular examples in history of how a highly speculative idea for which there is no really hard scientific evidence can come to fashion the thinking of a whole society and dominate the outlook of an age. Considering its historic significance and the social and moral transformation it caused in western thought, one might have hoped that Darwinian theory was capable of a complete, comprehensive and entirely plausible explanation for all biological phenomena from the origin of life on through all its diverse manifestations up to, and including, the intellect of man. That it is neither fully plausible, nor comprehensive, is deeply troubling. One might have expected that a theory of such cardinal importance, a theory that literally changed the world, would have been something more than metaphysics, something more than a myth.[53]

Christianity offers a worldview that really is capable of changing the world, and yet many Christians turned their backs on special revelation and bought into evolutionary theory, a theory that conflicts with the Bible and gradually is proving to conflict with science. This was a mistake, but it is not too late to turn from it.

Unfortunately, however, much of the damage has already been done. Most of the basic premises of Humanism and Marxism are founded on evolutionary theory (including those in law, ethics, and politics), and, ironically, they gained much of their credibility because of their close association with the "scientific" theory of evolution. Now the science is evaporating and the whole house of cards built on myth could crumble.

The Buck Stops . . . Where?

Marxism and Humanism's assumptions about human nature provide a prime example of the damage done by evolutionism. By accepting an erroneous explanation of man's origin, the secular worldviews also embrace a distorted view of human nature.

The Christian model of human nature is based on the Book of Genesis. We believe that Adam and Eve lived in the Garden of Eden until they chose to disobey God, and that the human race has suffered the consequences of their disobedience ever since, including a universally shared sin nature. Ironically, Sagan acknowledges that the Genesis account explains a number of things, including the fact that "childbirth is generally painful in only one of the millions of species on Earth: human beings."[54] However, his evolutionary preconceptions will not

Notes and Asides

allow him to accept the Bible as a trustworthy document; therefore he explains this phenomenon by postulating, "Childbirth is painful because the evolution of the human skull has been spectacularly fast and recent."[55]

It is our contention that Genesis provides a better over-all explanation for the way humans really are than does Marxism or Humanism. We stress this distinction because one's view of human nature colors one's attitude toward all the disciplines. In fact, Joad's conversion to Christianity resulted largely from his recognition that the Christian explanation of human nature better fits the facts of experience and allows a more comprehensible view of the world. He says his "changed view of the nature of man . . . led to a changed view of the nature of the world."[56] That is, once man understands himself to be sinful, he understands his need for Christ's sacrificial death, and the wonder of His resurrection. Man must first understand himself to be dead in Adam, before he can desire to be alive in Christ. The man who accepts the Christian view of human nature is not far from understanding Romans 5:19: "For just as through the disobedience of the one man the many were made sinners, so also through the obedience of the one man the many will be made righteous." But the theory of evolution, by doing away with Adam and Eve, makes nonsense of this central point of the gospel.

"Yes, all have sinned; all fall short of God's glorious ideal."
—St. Paul

Humanists and Marxists shudder at such a "guilt-ridden" description of man. They view man from an evolutionary perspective and believe that his gradual, tireless ascent implies that man is forever progressing toward perfection. The consistent evolutionist perceives human nature as morally perfect in its pristine state. Unfortunately for these evolutionists, they cannot deny that man acts immorally in the real world, so they must find a scapegoat for man's sinful actions. Their scapegoat is society and its institutions. They claim that man's environment encourages the wrong kind of actions in men and that if only the right society could be created, moral, perfectible man would never sin again.

This method of passing the buck—denying individual responsibility for individual actions—permeates all Marxist and Humanist psychology. K. Platonov, a Marxist psychologist, provides an excellent example of how this attitude dehumanizes man, turning the individual into a machine that must be fine-tuned to fit into a particular set of circumstances extant in society:

> It should be constantly borne in mind that in administering psychotherapy we must consider the individual peculiarities of man, which spring from the enormous complex of intricate and socially conditioned temporary bonds and cortical dynamic

Notes and Asides

> structures of his life's experience. In restoring by methods of psychotherapy the normal state of the higher nervous activity which was disturbed by the ailment the physician must consider the basic peculiarities of the concrete social environment in which the person found himself before the ailment and will find himself after the treatment.[57]

Man is not responsible for his wrong-doings—he is only an automaton that responds to the stimuli forced on him by society.

For this reason, the Humanist and the Marxist believe fervently that the most humane, noble thing they can do is to usher in the proper society. The most desirable goal for the proponents of these worldviews is the creation of a utopian society in which man's perfect nature can flourish. Toward this end, both the Marxists and the Humanists have called for major revisions of the traditional family unit. *The Communist Manifesto* derides the traditional unit of father, mother, and child as bourgeois, and Communist Russia acted on this assumption for a long time, establishing free love associations and sanctioning lax divorce and abortion laws to break down family units based on Christian ideals.[58] Secular Humanism has opted to move the same way, attacking the traditional family and encouraging experimentation, including bisexuality, homosexual marriage, open marriages, pederasty, and abortion as a means of birth control.[59] Further, both secular worldviews often support state-run child care centers.

The Christian position is that just such attacks on the traditional family have formed the groundwork for many of our social ills,[60] including AIDS, poverty, drug abuse, and crime. The family is the glue that holds society together. As the family goes, so goes society. Examples of the cause-and-effect role the family plays in society are everywhere: poverty is epidemic among families headed by single women; young men and women between 17 and 24 years old are far more likely to abuse drugs or commit crimes if they come from fatherless homes; legalized abortion has cheapened human life to the point that Americans are no longer shocked by euthanasia and child abuse rates have risen right along with abortion rates. These tendencies can only be righted in the home, according to the Biblical view. Thus, the Christian calls for a return to the traditional family unit of father and mother (married to each other for life) and children, and traditional family values including love, fidelity and respect,[61] while the Humanist and the Marxist cling to the hope that one day society will have evolved to the point where men and women are "free" of the constraints of such tradition.

> "For from the very first [God] made man and woman to be joined together permanently in marriage . . . "
>
> —Jesus Christ

On that day, according to the secular religious worldviews, society will become perfect, and consequently man, too, will achieve perfec-

Notes and Asides

tion. Yet, isn't this an odd thing for products of evolution to desire? As Carl F. H. Henry points out, "If homo sapiens is essentially but an animal, he can hardly be expected to subordinate self-interest to the good of the community."[62] Why would a being caught up in the evolutionary process dedicate his life toward achieving a goal that he won't live to see realized? How long could one submit to "the Great Soviet Experiment" with faith in a far-off utopia, especially when every day one is faced with the fact that most of its leaders have been charged with corruption, lawlessness, and even "mafia" actions?[63]

Further, and perhaps even more puzzling, how does one know whom to trust as an architect of a perfect society, since all men are theoretically tainted by their present environmental stimuli? Can we trust Karl Marx's conclusions, since his life work was influenced by his living in bourgeois society? Is Corliss Lamont's belief that the perfect society will be socialistic fostered by his inherent goodness, or a reflection of the negative impact American society has had on him? We cannot know. And in these two points, we find two of the most basic inconsistencies of the secular worldviews' belief about human nature: it is irrational for a product of evolution to work toward creating a distant utopia, and it is impossible to find a perfect man to shape a perfect society.

But these are really just asides compared to the most basic flaw in the Humanist and the Marxist's view of man—the flaw that exists in the deepest recess of our being. Because when an individual is really honest with himself, when he asks himself whether his inclinations are really toward good or toward evil and if it is fair to blame society for his urge to steal a candy bar or tell a lie, that individual—each one of us—must face the fact that he has an inherent tendency toward sin. As Joad says,

> Is it not obvious that human arrogance and love of power, that human brutality and cruelty, that, in a word, man's inhumanity to man, are responsible for . . . [tragic events such as the Holocaust]; obvious, too, that it is precisely these characteristics that have written their melancholy record upon every page of human history?[64]

Deep down we all know it; we understand that "our righteous acts are like filthy rags" (Isaiah 64:6). A simple adherence to the ancient admonition "Know thyself" reveals the folly of the Marxist and Humanist view of human nature.

Marxism/Leninism, of course, provides some of the most powerful examples of sinful human nature in this century. The record stretches from Karl Marx's consistent dishonesty and misrepresentation of facts in his writings[65] to the slaughter of millions by Marxist/Leninist

Notes and Asides

dictators. The *Moscow News* speaks of "the horrors of Stalinism" and admits that Stalin was responsible for the mass murder of 15,000 Polish officers in the Katyn forest.[66] Robert Conquest documents Stalin's systematic annihilation of 14.5 million Ukrainians,[67] and Ronald Nash mentions that Rumanian Communist Nicolae Ceausescu ordered the deaths of some 60,000 people during his reign of terror.[68]

Christianity expects man to be capable of such inhumanity. The Bible, in contrast to the Marxists and Humanists, never waxes romantic about human nature; instead, it graphically depicts the utter sinfulness of man (Jeremiah 17:9; Romans 3:10-23). And the historical fruits of both Marxism/Leninism (e.g., Soviet and Chinese atrocities, the Cambodian killing fields) and Secular Humanism (e.g., the murder of 1.5 million unborn children in America alone every year) confirm the Bible's perspective. The Bible is right: the heart of man is deceitful and desperately wicked.

Another Socialist Experiment

Remarkably, however, Marxists and Humanists, blind to the folly of their ways, press fervently on toward utopia. In their quest for the ultimate society, Marxists believe that economics and the forces of production play the primary role, while Humanists trust world government to lead us to the promised land. Both worldviews believe that civilization is evolving from imperfection to perfection, from disorder to order (in direct contradiction to the principle of the Second Law of Thermodynamics). Both want a world order based on atheism, evolution, and socialism.

The Marxist believes that the dialectic has worked throughout history to lead society through a series of syntheses, from primitive communism to slavery to feudalism to capitalism and, recently, to socialism. Socialism itself is a transition between capitalism and communism. Marxist theory trusts that the worker (the antithesis) will clash with the capitalist (the thesis), creating a revolution leading to world socialism and, eventually, communism. A dictatorship of the proletariat (under the guidance of the Marxist/Leninist party) will be necessary initially to enforce such a world order, but it will wither away with the advent of communism. Likewise, law is now necessary to move men toward communism, but eventually the need for law will disappear.

As with the rest of the Marxist worldview, there are a number of inconsistencies in its theories regarding civilization and her institutions. If man is but a helpless pawn of the dialectic, why bother to encourage workers to revolt—won't societal change happen inevitably

Notes and Asides

when the dialectic demands it? Further, does the dialectic just stop working once the perfect society (i.e., communism) is attained? Or will communism draw a new antithesis to itself and clash to form another synthesis? In other words, since the synthesis is transitory, even utopia will be transitory and must logically give way to another social order.

A larger problem is created by the Marxist's insistence that socialism is an improvement over capitalism. Perhaps some credence might have been given to this claim a century ago, before the grand socialist experiment in Soviet Russia, but the constant failings of the Soviet economy have unambiguously demonstrated the impracticality of socialism. As Biblical Christianity declared all along, socialism robs mankind of any incentive to better himself. It is contrary to human nature's built-in sense of justice. Those who are lazy and do not produce—whether grades in school or cars on an assembly line—should not receive an equal result. A student who studies hard and earns an "A" should not be required to share his or her grade with someone who studies little. Socialism discriminates against the competent, the hard-working, the productive, and encourages envy and laziness among poor

Used by permission of the *Colorado Springs Sun*

Notes and Asides

men and women who might, in a capitalist society, achieve productivity and cultivate feelings of self-worth rather than jealousy.

Further, socialism does not hasten the abolition of class distinctions (as Marxists claim it will), but creates a new elite. Hoover Institute Research Fellow Arnold Beichman points out that socialism in the Soviet Union created a class known as the *nomenklatura* (also referred to as the "state bourgeois" or the "class of privileged exploiters"). This class, according to Beichman, is the prime example of the inequality spawned by socialism. Its members "own everything, the auto factories, the dachas, the food markets, the pharmacies, the transport system, the department stores. Everything. Soon they will own what's being shipped from Germany and the United States."[69] Instead of destroying class distinctions, socialism created a completely authoritarian class. Milovan Djilas says, "The Communist revolution, conducted in the name of doing away with classes, has resulted in the most complete authority of any single new class."[70] This elite, founded on political connections and applied communist ideology, has run the Soviet economic sector into the ground.

East Germany provides another telling example of the havoc that can be wrought by a socialistic economy. Steve Hanke, a Johns Hopkins University professor and economic advisor to the vice president of the Socialist Federal Republic of Yugoslavia, reported,

> Since the Berlin Wall came down [November 1989], the ravages of socialism have become clear to even the most casual observer: antiquated factories, crumbling roads and bridges, fouled environments and impoverished workers. It is ironic that socialism, which was violently and ruthlessly imposed in the name of the workers, has left the Eastern European proletariat ill-trained, unmotivated, incapable of making ends meet and disgruntled.
>
> To assess the damage, the nations of Eastern Europe have imported Western accountants in large numbers, since competent members of that profession are nowhere to be found in the East. These shock troops of capitalism are busy examining the industrial corpses. For example, about one-quarter of West Germany's accountants are presently attempting to make sense out of the 8,000 largest enterprises in East Germany. Not surprisingly, "insolvent—must liquidate" has been stamped on most of these operations. Consequently, most of the factories will have to be scrapped—literally. Scrap metal, which represents the remains of socialism, will be one of the East's most significant exports over the next few years.[71]

Notes and Asides

After being confronted with the tragic results of applied socialism, why would anyone be interested in attaining advanced socialism? The Marxist attitude toward private property removes the incentive to work and replaces it with governmental coercion—causing production to grind to a virtual halt—and then wants to remove the coercion! Somehow, we are told, the dialectic will lead mankind into a glorious society in which man works according to his ability, and takes according to his need. But the economies in Russia, China, Cuba and every other Marxist country in the world demonstrate that even the pale shadow of such a society (socialism) creates an environment in which man is less and less willing to demonstrate ability, and more and more willing to demonstrate need.

This is the same problem faced by the Humanists who call for wealth redistribution. They ignore the fact that redistribution encourages recipients to work not to earn a living but to demonstrate need, to get the biggest piece of the redistributive pie. Further, both socialistic Humanists and Marxists refuse to recognize that free enterprise and private property, a New Testament concept (Acts 5:1-4), actually work to produce wealth. In capitalism, property and skills can be used to produce more, thereby creating a wealthier society. In contrast, wealth redistribution programs merely spread wealth around, encouraging a consumptive, rather than productive, mindset. The question becomes not "How can I produce more?" but "How can I get more?" This is evident even in the United States, a country that should have learned from the practical failures of socialism around the world but instead is embracing more and more plans for wealth redistribution.[72]

The greatest flaw in the socialistic schemes of both the Marxist and the Humanist was pointed out by the economist and social philosopher Ludwig von Mises years ago. Socialists expect to replace the precise free market mechanism with central planners. They trust that enough economists can make the proper decisions about what to produce and how much of it to produce, and assign various prices, as efficiently as the constant adjustments made by supply and demand. Not only does this claim appear unworkable in theory, it has been proven totally unworkable in practice in numerous socialist countries. There are not enough smart, moral people to know all the economic factors to make such decisions. Black markets thrive in such settings because they supply the goods and services people actually want—something the central planners have never shown themselves able to accomplish.

Trust in central planners, although impractical, is a logical extension of Marxist and Humanist thought. Because these worldviews believe that man is inherently good, they expect that, given enough control over his environment, man can create the perfect society. Central planners should work better than the free market, according to

Marxist and Humanist thought, because the free market is a part of the society that influences man to act improperly. By reshaping the economy to grant inherently good men more control, we should be moving toward a more desirable society.

The offshoot of such thought is obvious: we need only to grant men more power—to expand government a little more—before we have enough control over our environment to perfect it. One can imagine how bureaucracy swells in a socialistic society, when one considers all the necessary central planners. Then add the men and women responsible for social programs that create more "healthy" families (remember, the Marxists want to remove the burden of child-rearing from the parents),[73] and social engineers such as mental health consultants and sociologists, and you are faced with an enormously complex system of government. Humanists and Marxists consider such a bureaucracy good, since it grants more men control over their environment, enabling men to influence society rather than letting society influence men.

Naturally, both Marxists and Humanists hesitate to discuss this aspect of their political theory, since *bureaucracy* is an unpopular term. The Marxist actually denies the major role that government plays in his worldview, claiming that the state will wither away in communist society. If this is true, of course, we have judged the Marxist too harshly. But is it true? It seems unlikely, given the Marxist fascination with power. Lenin went so far as to name power as the primary goal of the revolution: "The seizure of power is the business of the uprising; its political purpose will become clear after the seizure."[74] These are not the words of a man unconcerned with governmental strength.

This statement, however, was made prior to the emergence of socialism in Russia. Perhaps such fascination with power is only manifested by Marxists in communism's formative years. Perhaps after socialism has been established and allowed to flourish for seventy years we can expect the state to begin to wither away. Certainly, the present Soviet leader, Mikhail Gorbachev, has begun to relinquish power. Or has he? *Newsweek* magazine tells us that, upon establishment of the presidential form of government in the USSR, "Gorbachev will preside over both government and party with more formal authority than even Lenin possessed."[75] His use of military force against independence movements in the Baltic republics in early 1991 showed his willingness to use that power. The question arises, then: When, exactly, can we expect to see the state begin to wither away? Which Marxist leader will show himself willing to abandon power rather than garner more?

These questions are unanswerable for the simple reason that no one who has tasted power is interested in abandoning it. Power, as Lord Acton said long ago, tends to corrupt. The more power one gets, the more it tends to corrupt him. And this problem is by no means restricted

Notes and Asides

to the Marxist worldview—the Humanists must answer variations of the same questions. When will government be big enough? When society becomes perfect? When every man, woman, and child holds a government title?

Until every problem faced by the human race—from famine to slander—is solved, Humanists and Marxists will blame society and cry for more government to correct the flaws of our environment. Their move now is to establish one huge world government to control the whole human race in order to direct human evolution toward some unknown destination.

This call for world government is a cause for much concern among Christians. After witnessing Humanists' systematic eradication of Christianity from the public square in America over the past thirty years, Christians are justified in opposing a world government that, designed by Humanists, would surely work toward the same goal on a global scale. Such an order would be based on materialist, not Christian, values, since everyone promoting world government (Secular Humanists, Marxist/Leninists, New Agers, etc.) is anti-Christian.[76] The roots of globalism smack of Psalm 2:1-3; its trunk and branches of Revelation 13.

"Then the Dragon encouraged [the Beast] to speak great blasphemies against the Lord; and gave him authority to control the earth for forty-two months."
—St. John

The Christian recognizes the false assumptions that form the basis for bloated governmental power. He understands that the blame lies not on faulty societal structures but on the inherent sinfulness of every human heart. Thus, Christianity postulates a cure—the gospel of transformation by Christ—that actually treats the disease. By acknowledging man's responsibility for his actions, the Christian view grants every individual the opportunity to break the bonds of sin rather than saddling him with the quiet desperation of trusting the government to solve the world's problems. "Christianity" says Montgomery, "asserts that man, being radically self-centered, can only be saved and transformed so as to treat his neighbor with proper dignity when he admits that he cannot 'do his duty' or save himself—and relies entirely on God in Christ for salvation."[77] Sociologist Peter Berger also sees the necessity for personal conversion. Says Berger,

> The Christian faith . . . lies in history, not in psychology. It tells us that the God who created the distant nebulae, the God who is other than anything we can imagine, has come to us; that his coming gives redeeming meaning to our finite existence; and that this meaning may be found in the life, death, and resurrection of Jesus Christ. The eyes of the Christian faith look not inward into itself, but outward towards this man Jesus, of whom the New Testament speaks and who asked this question of his early followers: "Who do you say that I am?" Conversion to the

> Christian faith is the answer to this question, the one once given by Simon Peter—the stupendous affirmation that the man asking the question is Christ, the savior. It is the decisive act of God's breaking into history.[78]

Marxism and Humanism's false ideas of politics and economics trace back to their false assumptions of human nature, which in turn stem from their false beliefs about man's origins. By declaring that God does not exist and that matter organized itself into man, the secular worldviews strip sovereignty from God and find themselves forced to bestow sovereignty on the state. Humanists and Marxists are usually unwilling to admit that their views grant sovereignty to government, but the simple fact remains that, barring anarchy, human beings require an absolute basis on which to judge individual actions, and if God is denied, the state must usurp His role. Thus, absolute power falls into the hands of politicians—men who are not, despite the claims of secular worldviews, infallible. Leaders like Hitler, Stalin, and Mao have demonstrated the corrupting nature of states that enjoy unlimited authority.

Ironically, one of the men Humanists most frequently point to as a proponent of Humanist thought, Thomas Jefferson, strongly opposed big government. He believed that good government is government "which shall restrain men from injuring one another, shall leave them otherwise free to regulate their own pursuits of industry and improvement, and shall not take from the mouth of labor the bread it has earned."[79] This portrait of government is remarkably similar to the proper Biblical government described in Romans 13:1-5. It is also common sense, if one understands the true role of government and man's responsibility for his own actions.

The Evolution of Law

But Humanists and Marxists don't understand, and thus they create another problem. When one denies man's responsibility and declares the state sovereign, one also destroys justice. This is perhaps the most dangerous aspect of the utopian vision of Marxism and Humanism. When government becomes the only guide for mankind, then only legal positivism can result. Legal positivism and the sovereignty of the state are inseparable—either theory assumes the other. Gary Amos says that, for Humanists, "The only law in society is positive law, law enacted and enforced by rulers. All that matters is the law of the state and the will of the ruler. That is why most of the humanists were advocates of statism."[80]

Notes and Asides

If we recall that the three most tyrannical dictators of the twentieth century, Hitler, Stalin, and Tse-tung, all advocated statism and practiced positive law, we should find no comfort in knowing that the law on which the "new world order" will be founded is positivist. The legal structures proposed by world government proponents are based on the materialistic interpretation of man and government. Human rights are assigned according to the criteria of what will assist man in his evolutionary climb to perfection. The design of this whole legal and political superstructure, as Malachi Martin points out,

> is built on the presumption that we ourselves are the authors of our destiny. Man is exalted. The God-Man is repudiated; and with him, the idea of man's fallenness is rejected. Evil is a matter of malfunctioning structures, not in any way a basic inclination of man. Behind the godless and un-Christian design of transnationalist and Internationalist there stands man as a Nietzschean figure, a Superman. . . . in the age of Superman there would no longer be any reason to believe in Christian morality, individual liberty, and equality before the law. Attachment to civil rights, to the dignity and welfare and political worth of the individual, would become illusory and pointless.[81]

Why is the only law for Humanists and Marxists positive law? Because God does not exist, and therefore neither does His law. Thus, man must either be a law unto himself or trust the sovereign state to manufacture law. Trusting the state for the foundation of law is a positivist approach.

Trusting the state as the absolute basis in law leads to legal relativism, since government is an ever-changing entity. For law to remain constant, for the word *justice* to mean anything in a rational sense, law must have an unchanging basis—i.e., Jesus Christ, "the same yesterday and today and forever" (Hebrews 13:8). Only such an absolute foundation can create absolute laws like "It is always unlawful and morally wrong for a judge to take a bribe." Other systems of law can only declare, "It is unlawful, in the present circumstances, to take a bribe" or "Thou shalt not commit bribery . . . ordinarily."

Any doubts that the legal theory of Humanism is positivism should be dispelled by reading one statement by Sidney Hook: "The rights of man depend upon his nature, needs, capacities, and aspirations, not upon his origins. Children have rights not because they are our creatures but because of what they are and will become. It is not God but the human community that endows its members with rights."[82] More accurately, it is the state, not the human community, that endows its members with rights—but we won't quibble with that. Look instead at

Notes and Asides

the basis for human rights, according to the secular mindset: man's nature, needs, and capacities. This is the height of relativism! Since man's nature is always in evolutionary flux and every individual differs from his fellow human beings in terms of needs and capacities, it naturally follows that each generation's and each individual's rights must vary in proportion to these differences. Does this mean, then, that I have fewer rights than a concert pianist, since he is more capable than I? Do I have more rights than the needy in Ethiopia? Clearly, it is no good founding rights on human characteristics or governmental policies. Rights and laws must be based on the character of God, or they will be arbitrary.

A prime example of this is provided by some Humanists' recently cultivated concern for animal rights. Kenneth L. Feder and Michael Alan Park write,

> With biological distinctions blurred, there is no objective rationale for elevating our species into a category separate from the rest of the animals with whom we share the presence of a nervous system, the ability to feel pain, and behaviors aimed at avoiding pain. Thus, the fundamental rights we accord ourselves must be equally applicable to any other organism with these same characteristics.[83]

"The sacred rights of man . . . are written as with a sunbeam in the whole volume of human nature by the hand of divinity itself and can never be erased by mortal power."

—A. Hamilton

Consistent with their evolutionary bias, these Humanists see no distinction between humans and the rest of the animal kingdom—men and rats must be viewed as equals, with no favoritism displayed in the realm of rights. But this view strips man of his dignity as created in the image of God and denies God's will for mankind over His creation (Genesis 1:28), thus rendering human rights as transitory and meaningless as the rights we bestow on toads and tasmanian devils. We must seriously consider: will lions have the right, according to the Humanist view, to pursue happiness, even if that entails depriving jackals of their right to life? Will we bestow rights on plants as well (after all, they are also living evolutionary relations), thereby starving the human race for fear of "murdering" a fellow organism? The absurdity is apparent—as obvious as the absurdity of animal rights advocates displaying more affection for bald eagles in the shell than for human babies in the womb. But the absurdity follows necessarily from worldviews that base human rights on temporal, changeable institutions and ideologies.

The danger of legal relativism should be obvious to all. Montgomery warns, "if law is indeed relative, it can be twisted in a totalitarian, revolutionary or anarchical manner according to the desires of those in power, and becomes no more than a tool of the party for effecting social change according to whatever definition of social value or dysvalue

Notes and Asides

happens to be theirs."[84] Humanists and Marxists grant sovereignty to the state and then show themselves willing to use the state in any manner to "improve" society. Thus, law becomes a pawn in man's pursuit of utopia. It is no exaggeration to say that under positivist law, an individual might one day awaken to find that green eyes have been decreed illegal, and be executed that morning for his eye color. When the state is the only basis for law, any law may be conceived.

Examples of this truth may be seen throughout society. Hitler, Mao, Stalin, and many others used positive law to murder millions—passing laws to eliminate Jews, gypsies, the sick, landowners, Christians, or anyone they had an urge to destroy—which fundamentally means anyone who stood in the way of their absolute domination of every person and action in society. In America, laws that many people considered inconceivable a few years ago are now standards by which we must live. Abortion has been legalized because, suddenly, the state decided that a baby in the womb is not a baby. Perhaps, twenty years from now, infanticide will be legalized, because the state will have decided that a baby is not a human being until it can walk or talk. The distinction between right and wrong is tenuous in a society that subscribes to legal positivism.

Conversely, Christian law applied to society results in practical and just legal structures. Based on the character of God, a moral order, man created in the image of God, and the coming of Jesus Christ in flesh, Christian law has produced the concept of common law, the Magna Charta, the Declaration of Independence, and the Constitution of the United States. Legal scholar John C. H. Wu says of the Magna Charta,

> I cannot dismiss the Magna Charta without mention of Cardinal Stephen Langton, Archbishop of Canterbury, who was actually the soul of the whole movement. To me it is not without significance that the father of the Magna Charta was also the author of the magnificent hymn to the Holy Ghost, *Veni Sancte Spiritus*. The same Spirit that inspired that hymn motivated and energized, on a lower plane, the movement which was crowned by the Magna Charta; and I think that the same Spirit has enlivened the common law by breathing into it the liberalizing influence of natural justice and equity.[85]

The Magna Charta resulted in a just government in England; likewise, the application of Christian law to the U.S. Constitution positively shaped America. Because our founding fathers read the nature of man correctly and divided power properly, America boasts a system of law that protects human rights and human dignity and is the envy of the world. "There is no country in the whole world," said Alexis de Tocqueville, "in which the Christian religion retains a greater influence over the souls of men than in America; and there can be no greater proof of its utility, and of its conformity to human nature, than that its influence is most powerfully felt over the most enlightened and free nation of the earth."[86]

Contrast such legal history with the history of positive law: "No half-century ever witnessed slaughter on such a scale," said Robert Jackson, "such cruelties and inhumanities, such wholesale deportations of peoples into slavery, such annihilations of minorities."[87] And Montgomery says, "Socialist states have—predictably—built up one of the very worst records of human rights violations in the modern world."[88]

It should be noted that the legal positivism responsible for these atrocities has been incorporated into the United Nations. This organization's Universal Declaration of Human Rights grants various rights to the people of the world, but explicitly describes these rights as subject to change. Indeed, Article 29 declares, "These rights and freedoms may in no case be exercised contrary to the purposes and principles of the United Nations."[89] Further, the U.N. apparatus established by Alger Hiss, the first acting secretary-general of the U.N.'s founding conference in San Francisco in 1945, to enforce the Declaration (the Department of Political and Security Council Affairs' Military Staff Committee) is weighed heavily in favor of Marxism/Leninism—which should come as no surprise, since Hiss has been identified as a Marxist/Leninist by both Whittaker Chambers and *Time*[90] magazine.

Doubting Thomases

Obviously, granting sovereignty to the state is a dangerous thing. Politics, economics, and law—all closely related disciplines—are all aspects of the Marxist and Humanist worldviews that do not adequately take into account the workings of the real world. Adherents to both worldviews try to circumvent the problems of statism by claiming that the real basis for the state's guidance of society lies in the scientific method. That is, man is able to use science to discern the proper direction for society, and science provides a foundation that is not subject to the whims of man. Science becomes the force that will lead man to utopia. Paul Kurtz says bluntly, "Science (reason in the community) is the ultimate source of our knowledge of value. . . . It discovers and creates ideal systems which contribute to the homeostatic expansion of life. Therefore, the extension of science is perhaps the chief practical good for humankind to achieve. . . ."[91]

This discussion naturally leads us back to philosophy. When one speaks of science as *the* means of discerning knowledge, values, and

Notes and Asides

guidance, one is making an epistemological claim. Both the Humanist and the Marxist rely on science (conveniently ignoring the science of archaeology when it confirms Biblical veracity) as their method of knowing. In this, they believe, they rely on an epistemology far superior to that of the Christian. The Marxist and the Humanist claim to believe only in things that can be observed and that the scientific method can be applied to, whereas the Christian believes even in things he cannot physically see.

For this reason, secular worldviews label Christians unscientific and claim science as their exclusive property. But is it fair to stake such a claim? Indeed, could science even exist today if the Marxist and Humanist descriptions of reality were correct?

Of course not. If the atheistic, materialistic assumptions of these two worldviews were correct, we would live in a disorderly universe that followed no discernible pattern and subscribed to no unalterable laws. We would neither have seasons nor the law of gravity nor swallows that migrate to the same area year after year. Only in the Christian model of the universe—a universe created by a rational, personal God—can one expect to find such magnificent order. And only an ordered and intelligible universe allows room for science.

The fact that science arose at all is powerful testimony to the truth of Christianity. As Louis Victor de Broglie says, "We are not sufficiently astonished by the fact that any science may be possible."[92] This is especially true of the Marxist and the Humanist. They do not understand that science could never have been conceived in a society dominated by their worldviews. Modern science has its roots in Christian thinking. Historian and philosopher of science Stanley Jaki says that "the belief in a personal rational Creator . . . as cultivated especially within a Christian matrix . . . supported the view for which the world was an objective and orderly entity investigable by the mind because the mind too was an orderly and objective product of the same rational, that is, perfectly consistent Creator."[93] Man believed science possible because man believed in a God of reason and order.

Modern science is not an enemy of the Bible, but an ally. It constantly provides the Christian with examples of teleology. Its principles of conservation of matter (Laws of Thermodynamics) perfectly fit the Biblical Christian worldview. The early fathers of modern science worked primarily from the Christian point of view.[94] "The faith in the possibility of science," said Alfred North Whitehead, "generated antecedently to the development of modern scientific theory, is an unconscious derivative from medieval theology."[95] Norman L. Geisler and J. Kerby Anderson quote M. B. Foster to the same effect: "The modern investigators of nature were the first to take seriously in their science the Christian doctrine that nature is created."[96]

In other words, the Christian worldview had a great deal more to do with the founding of modern science than either the Secular Humanist or the Marxist/Leninist worldview. These, for reasons of their own, have simply adopted science as the foundation for their epistemology. They were certainly not responsible for science and, in fact, could not have been. Science requires a rational explanation of the universe, something an atheistic worldview cannot provide.[97] The supreme irony, of course, is that modern science classrooms, using the arbitrary power of positive law, bar the Christian worldview while welcoming both the Marxist and the Secular Humanist perspectives. It is an irony that Thomas Jefferson, the mis-claimed hero of Secular Humanists, would have been quick to spot:

> Was the government to prescribe to us our medicine and diet, our bodies would be in such keeping as our souls are now. Thus in France the emétic was once forbidden as a medicine, and the potato as an article of food. Government is just as infallible, too, when it fixes systems in physics. Galileo was sent to the Inquisition for affirming that the earth was a sphere; the government had declared it to be as flat as a trencher, and Galileo was obliged to abjure his error. This error, however, at length prevailed, the earth became a globe, and Descartes declared it was whirled round its axes by a vortex. The government in which he lived was wise enough to see that this was no question of civil jurisdiction, or we should all have been involved by authority in vortices. In fact, vortices have been exploded, and the Newtonian principle of gravitation is now more firmly established, on the basis of reason, than it would be were the government to step in, and to make it an article of necessary faith. Reason and experiment have been indulged, and error has fled before them. It is error alone which needs the support of government. Truth can stand by itself.[98]

Atheist worldviews have, of course, expanded on the concept of science to the point of distortion, assigning it the ability to grant man knowledge of everything, including value and truth. Tonne declares, "Seeking the nearest approximation to truth that we can attain is an endless struggle. It is probably the most important study we undertake. That is what 'science' is all about."[99] Humanists and Marxists have invested science with an almost supernatural quality—even speaking of its "omnipotence"—trusting the scientific method to provide them with the correct answer to virtually any question.

But such attitudes toward science are false. Science has natural limits, including the fact that it can only provide us with knowledge

Notes and Asides

about the material, observable universe. Any attempt to expand science beyond these natural limits leads not to better science but to scientism. Trusting science for one's entire epistemology leads either to frustration or to methods of obtaining knowledge that are labeled scientific but are unfounded. Humanists and Marxists are usually guilty of the latter error, describing utopian social programs and ethical codes with no basis in science as scientific. This approach actually hinders true scientific progress. Jaki explains, "Scientism is never a genuine reverence for science but a harnessing of science for a nonscientific purpose. Since that purpose is fixed, science can only serve it by remaining fixed, namely, by remaining in its supposedly final stage."[100]

Scientism is yet another flaw that taints both Marxist and Humanist theory. It is unreasonable to demand that science provide mankind with all knowledge. Even Julian Huxley, in one of his more candid moments, recognized the limited nature of the scientific method:

Scientism refers to attempts to apply the scientific method to all categories of life, thereby overstepping science's natural limits.

> Science has removed the obscuring veil of mystery from many phenomena, much to the benefit of the human race: but it confronts us with a basic and universal mystery—the mystery of existence in general, and of the existence of mind in particular. Why does the world exist? Why is the world-stuff what it is? Why does it have mental or subjective aspects as well as material or objective ones? We do not know.[101]

Experimenting With the Ten Commandments

Unfortunately, Humanists and Marxists ignore Huxley's startling admission and cling tenuously to their scientism. Without science for their epistemology, they would have to revert to the "trust the voice within you" mentality of Cosmic Humanism. That is, their theory of knowledge could only be based on individual experience. But by clinging to science, they find themselves trusting an epistemology unqualified to speak to a number of disciplines, including ethics.

Marxists and Humanists apply the theories of evolution and the dialectic to morality and conclude that ethics develops as humanity progresses and that we have not yet established the perfect ethical code that will govern man in utopian society. Indeed, the Marxist goes so far as to declare all present moral codes bourgeois and therefore sinister. Given these beliefs, proponents of Marxism and Humanism must perceive ethics as relative. They must reject all ethical absolutes, and even view claims of unchangeable ethical codes as horrible deceptions. Tonne warns that "the notion that there is an absolute truth etched into the eternal heavens as so many of us were brought up to believe is not only a falsehood, it is a menace to human development."[102]

In reality, Tonne's ideas are the menace to human development. Humanism's ethical stance allows people like Ted Bundy to justify even rape and murder. Harry V. Jaffa, political philosopher at the Claremont Institute, fictionalized the following scenario between Bundy and one of his victims: Bundy told his victim, "a life without raping and murdering is not worth living to me." When his victim pleaded for her life, insisting that her family would pay any ransom, and told Bundy that the Bible says such behavior is wrong, Bundy replied, "What you call wrong, I call attempts to limit my freedom." Bundy then admitted,

> I want you to know that once upon a time I too believed that God and the moral law prescribed boundaries within which my life had to be lived. That was before I took my first college course in philosophy. Then I learned that all moral judgments are "value judgments," that all value judgments are subjective, and that none can be proved to be either "right" or "wrong."

Bundy concluded his conversation before he raped and murdered this young lady,

> Surely, you would not, in this age of scientific enlightenment, declare that God or nature has marked some pleasures as "moral" or "bad." Let me assure you, my dear young lady, that there is absolutely no comparison between the pleasure I might take in eating ham, and the pleasure I anticipate in raping and murdering you. That is the honest conclusion to which my education has led me—after the most conscientious examination of my spontaneous and uninhibited self.[103]

This is powerful testimony both to the practical application of Humanist ethics and to the sinfulness inherent in man.

Trusting science and evolution to provide one with the proper conclusions about modern-day ethics can lead one down a number of paths—all of which are hopelessly twisted. If ethics can be shown to be relative and based on evolutionary theory, then Hitler, Stalin, and Tse-tung are twentieth-century saints. Hitler applied the theory of evolution, especially Darwin's idea of natural selection, to morality and concluded, "There is absolutely no other revolution but a racial revolution. There is no economic, no social, no political revolution. There is only the struggle of lower races against the higher races."[104] Marx and Engels applied science to ethics and concluded that the ends justified the means, which justified Stalin's conclusion that "the dictatorship of the proletariat is the domination of the proletariat over the bourgeoisie,

Notes and Asides

untrammeled by the law and based on violence and enjoying the sympathy and support of the toiling and exploited masses."[105] Mao's first lectures to villagers following his 1949 conquest of China were not about Marxist theory; they were about Charles Darwin. Nowadays, most Marxists and Humanists are quick to condemn Hitler, Stalin, and Mao, but they are hard pressed to explain why. If ethical relativism is true and each culture determines its own moral conduct, Hitler, Mao, and Stalin were morally correct in doing what they did best. And if they moved the evolutionary timetable forward a notch or two, then Humanists and Marxists should applaud them.

Still another frightening conclusion that Humanists must accept when attempting to base their ethics on scientism is summed up by Harry Elmer Barnes. He assumes that an individual with enough brains can use the scientific method to establish morals, and he draws the logical conclusion that

> one can probably say that there is no truly or completely intelligent person who is not at the same time moral in the scientific sense of that term. . . . It should be absolutely clear to any thoughtful and informed person that morality, far from being divorced from intelligence, depends more thoroughly and completely upon intelligence and scientific information than any other phase of human thought. . . .[106]

This theory takes on a sinister character when we realize that it grants those men and women labeled by society as exceptionally intelligent free reign in morals. Further, it allows such persons to dictate right and wrong for every member of society with a lower IQ. Barnes admits as much: "Wide variations in capacity appear to be the most important single fact about the human race. . . . It would seem to follow that there will be certain kinds of conduct which will not be harmful for the abler members of society; which, indeed, may be positively desirable and beneficial. . . ."[107]

This belief that some men will always know better than others, regardless of actual concern with morality, has already severely wounded our world. It allowed dictators to commit unspeakable acts of violence. It encouraged the attitude in America that the mother knows what is right for her unborn baby, even if it means abortion, that doctors know when a fatally ill person would like to die, and that Planned Parenthood knows the proper means of sex education for our children (which doesn't happen to include the Biblical admonition to abstain from sex until marriage). The results of such morality are the slaughter of Ukrainians and the unborn and a raging AIDS epidemic. "The new morality," says William Stanmeyer, "makes it quite possible to be a

Used by permission of the *Colorado Springs Sun*

passionate lover of humanity, like a . . . Marx or a Lenin, and to be a passionate hater of actual human beings."[108] According to such an ethical vision, it makes sense to kill millions of bourgeois or millions of babies, since they are obstacles to mankind's march toward utopia.

The Humanistic attempt to make science produce a new moral order is taking on breathtaking parameters—especially in sexual ethics. "Science" is being used to bolster homosexuality, pedophilia (adult-child sex), and even incest.

Humanist historian and senior editor of *Free Inquiry* Vern Bullough told the *Washington Blade*: "Politics and science go hand in hand. In the end it is Gay activism which determines what researchers say about gay people."[109] This is not science, but scientism. Bullough also wrote in the foreword to *Loving Boys: A Multidisciplinary Study of Sexual Relations Between Adults and Minor Males*, that pedophilia is "a subject that too often has been ignored or subjected to hysterical statements."[110] Pedophilia is seriously being considered "a sexual orientation" along with homosexuality.[111] The idea of child molester and victim is being softened into "adult/child participants in sexual experience."[112]

Notes and Asides

Naturally, Humanists and Marxists do not like to talk about the devastating consequences of their ethics. When discussing morality, they prefer positive terms like *justice*, *love*, and *courage*. But when asked for the specific basis for such concepts, they flounder. Science can no more reveal a meaningful foundation for these terms than it can explain a man and a woman falling in love. So, despite railing against absolute codes and traditional morality, the secular worldviews must fall back on some form of Christian ethics when postulating specific moral suggestions. Humanist H. J. Eysenck warns, "In rejecting religion altogether, Humanism may be throwing out the ethical baby with the supernatural bathwater."[113] Corliss Lamont also tries to borrow Christian ethics while snubbing their foundation: "Any humane philosophy must include such New Testament ideals as the brotherhood of man, peace on earth and the abundant life. There is much ethical wisdom, too, in the Old Testament and its Ten Commandments. Without accepting any ethical principle as a dogmatic dictum never to be questioned, the Humanist certainly adheres in general to a Biblical commandment such as, 'Thou shalt not bear false witness against thy neighbor.'"[114]

That sounds nice, of course, but Lamont surely knows that if God is missing, everything is permissible. Without its foundation in the absolute nature of God, morality flounders. Will Durant admits, "we shall find it no easy task to mold a natural ethic strong enough to maintain moral restraint and social order without the support of supernatural consolations, hopes and fears."[115] Indeed, as Francis Schaeffer says, "It is not just difficult, it is impossible."[116]

Did science have anything to do with forming the foundation for Biblical morality? Certainly not. God's character is the foundation for Christian law and ethics—and as a result, Christian legal and ethical systems fit the facts of reality and provide genuine guidance for the man seeking to act rightly. Schaeffer remarks that one of the distinctive things about God is that "He is a God with character. Everything is not equally right before God, and because of this we have our absolutes. . . ."[117] God is opposed to ethical systems that encourage evil men to destroy human value and dignity, giving rise to Tianamen Square, Buchenwald, Katyn Forest, and the Gulag. Whereas Marxists and Humanists have built their ethical systems on shifting sand and therefore tolerate any action that supposedly causes the human race to progress toward utopia, the Christian bases morality on the unchanging nature of God, a moral order reflecting God's character, and understands that man's highest calling is to servanthood (Mark 10:43-45; Romans 7:4-6).

"Whatever makes men good Christians, makes them good citizens."
—Daniel Webster

Notes and Asides

"I Couldn't Help Myself"

Ethics, however, is not the only realm in which the secular worldviews' scientism creates unsolvable problems. Marxists and Humanists' psychology is also distorted by their theoretical assumptions. Because both worldviews assume that science is the only means of discerning truth, both must abandon all "unscientific" notions like mind, idea, conscience, soul, and spirit. Humanist Edward O. Wilson declares, "A scientific humanist . . . is someone who suggests that everything in the universe has a material basis. And that means everything, including the mind and all its spiritual products."[118] Humanist psychology is ontological monism since mind and brain are considered materialistic events or entities.

We noted many of the inconsistencies of such a belief when discussing man's origins, but the full ramifications can only be examined in the context of the twentieth century, when men like I. P. Pavlov and B. F. Skinner carried the Marxist and Humanist worldviews to their logical conclusion. Before then, or at least before Darwin's *Origin of Species*, mankind would have scoffed at the completely behavioristic theories of Pavlov and Skinner. Many early atheists, of course, had suggested that mind and soul did not exist, but none had the audacity to draw the logical conclusion: without mind, man's actions are but a series of responses to various external stimuli; therefore, they are completely determined.

Such a conclusion shouldn't shock us. Behaviorism is the logical extension of naturalism. What should shock us is that the Marxist and the Humanist expect us to believe that this model accurately describes reality. But a model that strips man of free will can only lead to nonsensical conclusions. As Roche points out, it "means you literally have no choice about reading this book at this moment; your doing so was, as it were, determined by the stars. Nor have I any choice in what I'm writing, being, as it were, merely a stenographer for what is dictated by the dance of the atoms. Consequently, if I were to write that all naturalists were ugly useless cockroaches, the naturalist would have to agree that Nature herself forced me to say so."[119] That is, the naturalist could not blame Roche for such a statement, because behaviorism absolves man of responsibility for his actions. Of course, in real life, Humanists and Marxists do hold people responsible for their actions (when someone steals their car, they demand prosecution), but when they do so they are acting inconsistently. True adherence to secular philosophy, theology, psychology, and biology requires never blaming (or praising) an individual for his actions.

Notes and Asides

Further, true adherence to a behavioristic view of man negates the meaningfulness of the behaviorist's findings. "We must use our will," says Roche, "to study the world. If we conclude that the world is of a character that does not allow free will, we destroy our credentials for saying so."[120] Only if our mind is more than a receptor and processor of stimuli can we trust it to devise meaningful theories. Only if our will is our own, and not slave to the changeable winds of society, can we arrive at a rational conclusion.

Marxists and Humanists understand this. They are embarrassed by it. Thus, they presently downplay the behavioristic aspect of their worldviews. This works to their advantage in a related area as well, because both secular worldviews like to treat man as if he possesses free will when they encourage him to choose to support their particular revolution or utopian vision.[121] In a very real sense, Humanists and Marxists want to have their cake and eat it, too. They desire a universe without God, made entirely of matter, and evolving toward perfection, but they wish to retain concepts negated by these presuppositions, including mind, ideas, and free will. Humanist Wayne L. Trotta provides the perfect example of this mentality:

> It may be prudent to assume that all behavior is governed by causal laws. But reducing human conduct to a set of mechanistic—"if this happens then that happens"—formulae would ultimately reduce therapy to nothing more than a set of techniques.[122]

Basically, Trotta is saying that he still thinks Humanism's behaviorist assumptions are true, but Humanism should ignore them in practice since they don't work. This is the height of inconsistency! Why retain a theory that doesn't fit the facts? If behaviorism doesn't explain the way things really are, then get rid of it—along with its foundational assumptions of atheism, naturalism, evolution, and monism.

In a sense, this is what Marxists and Humanists are forced to do when coping with the real world. Their worldviews describe the universe one way, but they cannot *live* in accordance with their views. Secular worldview proponents leave their atheism and materialism on the shelf and embrace the concept of absolutes and free will when interacting with the community.

For example, Erich Fromm, as a Humanist *and* a Marxist, logically must embrace psychological or ontological monism, denying the existence of mind, soul, etc. But he recognizes that, in order to succeed as a psychologist, he must work within the framework of the world as it really is. He needs, therefore, to acknowledge the existence of supernatural phenomena. He admits that the psychoanalyst "discovers

Notes and Asides

that mental sickness cannot be understood apart from moral problems; that his patient is sick because he has neglected his soul's demands. The analyst is not a theologian or a philosopher and does not claim competence in those fields, but as a physician of the soul he is concerned with the very same problems as philosophy and theology: the soul of man and its cure."[123]

One wonders why the Marxist and the Humanist would continue to cling to worldviews that must be abandoned when faced with cold, hard facts. If, as 1 Timothy 1:5 tells us, love "comes from a pure heart and a good conscience and a sincere faith," which even Erich Fromm seems willing to acknowledge, why do secular worldviews insist on denying the existence of the supernatural? Why, when Marxist regimes are crumbling throughout the world, do American professors still believe that Marxism is a workable worldview?[124] Why do Humanists deny the existence of the conscience and the divinity of Christ and then proclaim, as Bertrand Russell does, that the world needs more "Christian love"? The answer is that both Marxism and Humanism are religions that require an unreasonable faith.[125] The reason people are willing to accept worldviews that require such faith will become clear as we turn our eyes toward the future.

The Kingdom of Heaven or Utopia?

Both the Humanist and the Marxist base their attitudes toward history and the future on the belief that evolution is a fact. Accordingly, all of life is on a grand march forward, progressing toward perfection (Marxism makes doubly sure of this progress by postulating a near-divine, teleological dialectic that moves men through various means of production toward the most desirable society). This belief that evolution virtually guarantees the eventual perfection of life is as old as Darwin, who suggested that since "natural selection works solely by and for the good of each being, all corporeal and mental endowments will tend to progress towards perfection."[126]

Clearly, Marxist and Humanist worldviews offer incentives for their faithful. Not only do they promise an "inevitable" ascent into paradise; they also promise a heaven without the uncomfortable concept of a holy, just God. Man does not have to be responsible for his actions; he can still achieve paradise! This belief about history and the future provides the incentive for men and women to cling to worldviews that are otherwise untenable.

Sadly, even the paradise that provides hope for so many Humanists and Marxists is a pale and inadequate thing. Since nothing supernatural exists, the individual dies when his body dies. Thus, paradise becomes

Notes and Asides

a fleeting state, and all men who have already died will never experience it. William Kirk Kilpatrick points out,

> What good does it do to the billions who have already passed through this life in wretchedness, that scientific humanism will one day create a world without suffering? For that matter what good does it do to those who are right now dying miserable and lonely deaths all over the world? All that a strict humanism has to say to most of the human race living and dead is "Too bad you were born too early" and "Too bad about your suffering." The bulk of the world's pain is written off as a bad expense.[127]

Such a callous, tenuous paradise could hardly be described as paradise at all.

As one might expect, some Humanists and Marxists try to circumvent man's mortality in an effort to create a more appealing notion of utopia. By granting the evolutionary process a state of wisdom usually reserved for God, they claim that progress will one day guide man to an evolutionary form that fosters immortality. For example, Victor Stenger claims that computers are the next step in the evolutionary ladder and says that since their memory banks are basically immortal, mankind "*also can become immortal*. It should be possible in the future to save the accumulated knowledge of an individual human being when he or she dies. Perhaps even those thoughts which constitute consciousness will also be saved, and the collective thoughts of all human beings will be continued in the memory banks of computers."[128]

Even ignoring Stenger's inconsistent belief that it is possible to discuss an immortal consciousness and still deny the existence of the supernatural, one must be appalled by the naivete of his faith in evolution. Such a trust that change always denotes progress is completely unfounded in reality. As Roche says,

> We have to sweep away the trashy modern superstition that history is on some sort of grand, unstoppable march to human betterment. . . . In its thrall, we automatically assume that "new" is better. The ceaseless anti-heroic murmur for "change" is a statement that everything past is evil, and *any* change is better. This is not only idiocy but moral defection. Does anybody really believe Germany was the better for Hitler? Change for the worse, both personal and social, is more the rule than the exception. Humans are born backsliders.[129]

This is one of the biggest flaws in the view of history founded on evolution and the dialectic: There is no evidence that mankind and

Notes and Asides

society are moving toward perfection. In fact, the evidence is to the contrary. Twentieth-century Nazism, Fascism, Communism, world wars, abortion, homosexuality, hedonism, perversion of culture, etc. are examples not of evolution but of devolution. The human race has not produced a playwright the equal of Shakespeare in 400 years. Even more significantly, no man has come close to duplicating the moral character of Jesus Christ, who lived almost 2,000 years ago.

Or can we say that? Is it fair to use Christ as proof of the inconsistency of the Humanist and Marxist worldviews, since they clearly don't believe in Him? Of course it is—because they do believe. Christ's existence acts always as the central proof of the inconsistency of secular worldviews, because virtually all proponents of these views acknowledge that He lived in history,[130] and was the greatest ethical teacher. Will Durant admits,

> That a few simple men should in one generation have invented so powerful and appealing a personality, so lofty an ethic and so inspiring a vision of human brotherhood, would be a miracle far more incredible than any recorded in the Gospels. After two centuries of Higher Criticism the outlines of the life, character, and teaching of Christ, remain reasonably clear, and constitute the most fascinating feature in the history of Western man.[131]

> "[T]here is progress in knowledge, in technology, in the prerequisites for new human possibilities, but not in the substance of humanity. Progress in substance is refuted by the facts."
>
> —Karl Jaspers

But if Humanists are willing to admit that the Bible accurately describes history when it describes the life of Christ (and really they must admit it, for the Bible has been proven historically accurate by the science of archaeology),[132] then they have no basis for denying the historicity of Christ's miracles as described in Scripture.[133] If the Bible is accurate in its account of Christ's life and teachings, why should we assume that it is inaccurate when it describes His miracles? Luke, the author of the third gospel and the Book of Acts, was a first-rate historian.[134] In Luke's references to thirty-two countries, fifty-four cities, and nine islands, there are no errors. If Luke can be this accurate with regard to geography, why would we doubt his accuracy in describing the miracles that Jesus Christ performed? Indeed, if this great ethical teacher really did claim to be the Messiah, then wouldn't we expect Him to prove it with miracles and to conquer death?

Humanists and Marxists cannot answer these questions, but neither can they accept the logical implication of such reasoning: the truth of the Biblical Christian worldview. Because they begin with the assumption that God is not, they must ignore all evidence to the contrary and make not one but numerous irrational leaps of faith to cope with their theology, philosophy, ethics, biology, etc. This necessarily distorts their entire perspective and causes them to discount the one historical

Notes and Asides

Figure who really holds the key to a paradise in mankind's future—"the kingdom of God's dear Son" (Colossians 1: 13), open to anyone who accepts the Lord Jesus Christ (Acts 16:31; Matthew 7:21; Ephesians 2:8-10). By opting for a paradise that does not require man to be responsible to God, the Marxist and the Humanist turn their backs on the One who said He was The Way, The Truth and the Life (John 14:6).

They also turn their backs on reality. They choose to deal in distortions and shadows, advancing theories that deny the most important aspects of existence: God, the soul, mind, conscience, ideas, free will, and altruism. Such denial leads to inhuman theories and concepts, including "survival of the fittest" and the morality of violence against an entire class of people (the bourgeoisie). It leads to moral nonsense like "Thou shalt not commit murder . . . ordinarily," and a whole host of sexual perversions.

A Call to Dedication

The acceptance of many of these distortions by the Christian community is our greatest shame. Countless Christians, thanks to books like *Biology Through the Eyes of Faith*, have accepted evolutionary theory, many so firmly that they treat creationists as unwelcome brethren or worse.[135] Many Christian colleges that have finally recognized the scientific weaknesses of theistic Darwinian evolution still shun special creationism, moving instead toward Marxist[136] Stephen Jay Gould's punctuated equilibrium. Other Christians are embracing various forms of Marxism and socialism, calling it "Liberation Theology."[137] Some have bought into concepts like ontological monism, self-actualization, behaviorism, feminism, abortion, and world government. The Christian College Coalition's *Psychology Through the Eyes of Faith* not only champions psychological monism but embraces homosexuality as biologically determined.

Why do Christians so easily accept inconsistencies into their worldview? In this sense, the Marxist and Humanist are much more consistent. There are no Marxist/Leninist theists. There are no Secular Humanist creationists. It is always the Christian who compromises portions of his worldview; never the other way around. The Christian, who trusts the Scriptures and therefore has access to the one worldview based on eternal truth, should be the first person to recognize the bankruptcy of secular religious views. Yet all too often he is the first to embrace them!

It is our position that too many Christians ignore Paul's admonition that they not be taken captive "through vain and deceitful philosophy" (Colossians 2:8).

This text is an attempt to amend that situation. The superiority of the Christian position in theology, philosophy, ethics, economics, politics, law, biology, history, psychology, and sociology has been elucidated again and again. The Humanists and the Marxists have, in their own words, declared their position to be irreconcilable with Christianity. The battle lines have been drawn. As Christians armed with the truth—indeed, armed with the revelation of Truth Himself (John 14:6)—we are more than equipped to shatter the myths of all opposing worldviews,

> For though we walk in the flesh, we do not war after the flesh: (for the weapons of our warfare are not carnal, but mighty through God to the pulling down of strongholds;) casting down imaginations, and every high thing that exalteth itself against the knowledge of God, and bringing into captivity every thought to the obedience of Christ. (2 Corinthians 10:3-5)

And yet we are not doing the job. Seven million American Secular Humanists are overwhelming 192 million Christians. The Christian worldview is in retreat in nearly every arena of American life—including our universities, media, arts, music, law, business, medicine, psychology, sociology, public schools, and government. "The humanistic system of values has now become the predominant way of thinking in most of the power centers of society,"[138] claim James C. Dobson and Gary L. Bauer. According to Dobson and Bauer, the Christian worldview has only two power centers remaining in America—the church and the family—and both of them are under tremendous pressure to surrender.

What are we to do?

Go on the offensive! Light a candle. Pray (2 Chronicles 7:14; Colossians 1:9-14). Study (2 Timothy 2:15). Understand the times (1 Chronicles 12:32). Rebuild the foundations (Psalm 11:3). Spread the word.[139] Truth is our greatest weapon. Humanism and Marxism are both based on denials, not affirmations. Make this clear and we could see the demise of Humanism in our power centers just as the nations of Eastern Europe have seen the demise of Marxism in theirs. Philosophy students at Charles University in Prague, Czechoslovakia, told their professors they had had enough of Marxist/Leninist dialectics. American students can do the same—casting Humanism out of the classroom. But such a stand will not come easy; it will take a rebirth of morality, a revival of spiritual interests, a renewal of intellectual honesty, and a recovery of courage. It will take a shoring up of the family and a reawakening in our churches. It will take blood, sweat, and tears to re-establish the influence of Christianity on our culture, but it can be done.

> "The humanistic system of values has now become the predominant way of thinking in most of the power centers of society."
> —James C. Dobson

Perhaps most importantly, Christians must shore up our worldview and teach it to young people. We must immerse ourselves and our

Notes and Asides

children in *Christian* theology, *Christian* philosophy, *Christian* ethics, *Christian* politics, *Christian* economics, *Christian* psychology, *Christian* sociology, *Christian* biology, *Christian* law, and *Christian* history.

Some progress has been made in this direction. Alvin Plantinga, a leading Christian philosopher, has challenged the Christian community to discover its worldview. Philosophers like Plantinga, Henry, Willard, J. P. Moreland, William Lane Craig, and Geisler have gone to great lengths to defend Christianity from its Secular Humanist opponents.

Henry Morris, Duane Gish, Ken Cummings, A. E. Wilder-Smith, and a whole host of Christian men of science have demonstrated the veracity of the creationist position. Wendell Bird's *Origin of Species Revisited* contains enough scientific data to sink evolutionary theory. Thaxton, Bradley and Olson's *The Mystery of Life's Origins* and Davis and Kenyon's *Of Pandas and People* encourage the position that science and Christianity are allies. Still, much more needs to be accomplished to remind the world of the truth of Christianity and give encouragement for the future.

We need Christian young people, strong in the faith, to follow the likes of Cal Thomas, Fred Barnes, and Patrick J. Buchanan into the media, to take charge of the universities, to run for Congress and school boards, and to espouse Christian sociology (with a strong emphasis on traditional family values). We need Christian artists challenging us with something that feeds the spirit and fuels the imagination (instead of art, literature, and music fit for the cultural sewer).

> "The true religion is built upon the rock; the rest are tossed upon the waves of time."
>
> —Francis Bacon

Christians can reclaim law, history, politics, economics, and all other disciplines. Understanding themselves to be men and women created to serve God, they can feel the call to excellence more profoundly than proponents of any other worldview (especially because most other worldviews strip man of his dignity and free will). Thus, we join Roche in issuing this challenge:

> If you take the anti-heroic view that there is nothing the individual person can do to control his own destiny, then stand aside. Be the helpless pawn of fate you say you are. But if you long for the sense of life and purpose our era denies; if your mind hungers and your spirit thirsts for something far better than the pursuit of things, or power, or politics, or self, then the time to change is now.[140]

The first and last words Christ spoke to Peter were, "Follow me." He speaks them to us still.

[1]C. S. Lewis, *The Problem of Pain* (London: Geoffrey Bles, 1952), pp. 12-13.
[2]John Warwick Montgomery, *Human Rights and Human Dignity* (Dallas, TX: Probe Books, 1986), p. 137.
[3]Ibid., p. 139.
[4]Ibid., pp. 143-4.
[5]James J. D. Luce, "The Fundamentalists Anonymous Movement," *The Humanist*, Jan/Feb 1986, p. 11.
[6]Edward O. Wilson, "The Relation of Science to Theology," *Zygon*, Sept/Dec 1980, cited in Henry M. Morris, *The Long War Against God* (Grand Rapids, MI: Baker Book House, 1990), p. 34.
[7]Herbert A. Tonne, *Scribblings of a Concerned Secular Humanist* (Northvale, NJ: Humanists of North Jersey, 1988), p. 39.
[8]Peter R. Breggin, "Mental Health Versus Religion," *The Humanist*, Nov/Dec 1987, p. 13.
[9]See E. Calvin Beisner, *Prosperity and Poverty: The Compassionate Use of Resources in a World of Scarcity* (Westchester, IL: Crossway, 1988), and Ronald Nash, *Poverty and Wealth: The Christian Debate Over Capitalism* (Westchester, IL: Crossway, 1987).
[10]See Hernando de Soto, *The Other Path: The Invisible Revolution in the Third World* (New York: Harper and Row, 1989), and Charles Murray, *Losing Ground: American Social Policy, 1950-1980* (New York: Basic Books, 1984).
[11]See George Gilder, *Men and Marriage* (Gretna, LA: Pelican, 1989) for an excellent defense of this point.
[12]Lester Kirkendall, *A New Bill of Sexual Rights and Responsibilities* (Buffalo: Prometheus Books, 1976), p. 1. This claim is supported by the fact that free love advocate and founder of Planned Parenthood Margaret Sanger was named Humanist of the Year in 1957.
[13]Erich Fromm, *On Disobedience and Other Essays* (New York: The Seabury Press, 1981), p. 24.
[14]Georgi Shakhnazarov, *The Coming World Order* (Moscow: Progress Publishers, 1981), p. 273.
[15]C. E. M. Joad, *The Recovery of Belief* (London: Faber and Faber, 1955), p. 22.
[16]It should be noted that the recent discovery of a string of galaxies stretching across the universe for at least a half-billion light years has cast a shadow of doubt over the entire "Big Bang" theory. See *The Denver Post*, January 3, 1991, p. 3.
[17]Cited in Daniel S. Levy, "Interview: Evolution, Extinction and the Movies," *Time*, May 14, 1990, p. 19.
[18]George C. Roche, *A World Without Heroes* (Hillsdale, MI: Hillsdale College Press, 1987), p. 103.
[19]For a more in-depth discussion of the inadequacies of the Marxist dialectic, see Gustav A. Wetter, *Dialectical Materialism* (Westport, CT: Greenwood Press, 1977) and Leszek Kolakowski, *Main Currents of Marxism: Its Origins, Growth and Dissolution*, three volumes, trans. P. S. Falla (Oxford and New York: Oxford University Press, 1982).
[20]Percival Davis and Dean H. Kenyon, *Of Pandas and People* (Dallas, TX: Haughton, 1989), p. 55.
[21]Paul Amos Moody, *Introduction to Evolution* (New York: Harper and Row, 1970), p. 497.
[22]Roche, *A World Without Heroes*, p. 245.
[23]Francis Darwin, ed., *The Life and Letters of Charles Darwin* (London: J. Murray, 1888), vol. 1, p. 316.
[24]Sir Arthur Eddington, *The Nature of the Physical World* (Ann Arbor, MI: The University of Michigan Press, 1968), pp. 275-6. Says Eddington, "Physics may as well admit at once that reality is spiritual."
[25]Ibid., p. 338.
[26]This notion of a world specially created for the human race is termed the "Anthropic Principle."
[27]Cited in Dallas Willard, "Language, Being, God, and the Three Stages of Theistic Evidence," in *Does God Exist? The Great Debate*, ed. J. P. Moreland and Kai Nielsen (Nashville: Thomas Nelson, 1990), p. 211. Willard cites Hume's Introduction to *The Natural History of Religion*.
[28]For further reading, we recommend J. P. Moreland, *Scaling the Secular City: A Defense of Christianity* (Grand Rapids: Baker Book House, 1987).
[29]Michael Denton, *Evolution: A Theory in Crisis* (Bethesda, MD: Adler and Adler, 1986), p. 345.
[30]They are adequately discussed in Wendell R. Bird's mammoth *The Origin of the Species Revisited*, two volumes (New York: Philosophical Library, 1987).
[31]George Wald, "The Origin of Life," *Scientific American*, August 1954, p. 33.
[32]George Wald, *Origins of Life* 5 (1974), p. 26. Cited in Morris, *The Long War Against God*, p. 21.
[33]See Karen Arms and Pamela S. Camp, *Biology* (Philadelphia: Saunders College Publishing, 1982), p. 294.
[34]Davis and Kenyon, *Of Pandas and People*, p. 3.

[35]Ibid., p. 56.
[36]Ibid., p. 4.
[37]Charles Thaxton, Walter Bradley, and Roger Olsen, *The Mystery of Life's Origin: Reassessing Current Theories* (New York: Philosophical Library, 1984), p. 186. Students particularly interested in biological origins should also read Davis and Kenyon, *Of Pandas and People: The Central Question of Biological Origins.*
[38]Keith Parsons, "Is There a Case for Christian Theism?" in *Does God Exist: The Great Debate*, ed. Moreland and Nielsen, p. 185.
[39]L. H. Matthews, "Introduction," in Charles Darwin, *The Origin of Species* (London: J. M. Dent and Sons, 1971), pp. x-xi. Cited in Luther D. Sunderland, *Darwin's Enigma* (San Diego: Master Books, 1984), pp. 30-31.
[40]Cited in Davis and Kenyon, *Of Pandas and People*, p. 94.
[41]Ibid., p. 108.
[42]Julian Huxley, *Essays of a Humanist* (London: Chatto and Windus, 1964), p. 9.
[43]Modern science is finding no new species via natural selection, no macroevolution via microevolution, no fossils to prove a gradual ascent of life, etc. In fact, most species exhibit stasis. "They appear in the fossil record," says Gould, "looking much the same as when they disappear" (cited in Davis and Kenyon, *Of Pandas and People*, p. 96). Johns Hopkins University paleontologist Stephen Stanley says, "Despite the detailed study of the Pleistocene mammals of Europe, not a single valid example is known of phyletic [gradual] transition from one genus to another" (cited in Ibid.).
[44]Davis and Kenyon, *Of Pandas and People*, p. 25.
[45]Chris McGowan, *In the Beginning . . .* (Buffalo: Prometheus Books, 1984), p. 141.
[46]It is this very fact, the absence of transitional fossils, that has caused so many evolutionists to flee into the comforting arms of punctuated equilibrium. For more on this subject, see Duane T. Gish, *Evolution: The Challenge of the Fossil Record* (El Cajon, CA: Creation-Life, 1985) and Denton, *Evolution: A Theory in Crisis*.
[47]Cited in Sunderland, *Darwin's Enigma*, p. 89.
[48]Cited in Davis and Kenyon, *Of Pandas and People*, p. 106.
[49]Cited in Roche, *A World Without Heroes*, p. 277.
[50]Cited in ibid., p. 261.
[51]Soren Lovtrup, *Darwinism: The Refutation of a Myth* (London: Croom Helm, 1987), p. 422.
[52]Richard T. Wright, *Biology Through the Eyes of Faith* (San Francisco: Harper and Row, 1989).
[53]Denton, *Evolution: A Theory in Crisis*, p. 358.
[54]Carl Sagan, *The Dragons of Eden* (New York: Random House, 1977), p. 92.
[55]Ibid., p. 93.
[56]Joad, *The Recovery of Belief*, p. 46.
[57]K. Platonov, *The Word as a Physiological and Therapeutic Factor* (Moscow: Foreign Languages Publishing House, 1959), p. 223.
[58]For a full account of the Marxist/Leninist attitude toward the family, see H. Kent Geiger, *The Family in Soviet Russia* (Cambridge, MA: Harvard University Press, 1970).
[59]See Judith A. Reisman and Edward W. Eichel, *Kinsey, Sex and Fraud* (Lafayette, LA: Huntington House, 1990).
[60]See James C. Dobson and Gary L. Bauer, *Children at Risk* (Dallas, TX: Word, 1990).
[61]See Gilder, *Men and Marriage*.
[62]Carl F. H. Henry, *Christian Countermoves in a Decadent Culture* (Portland, OR: Multnomah Press, 1986), p. 16.
[63]"Where Mafia Used to Rule the Roost," *Moscow News*, March 18, 1990, p. 13.
[64]Joad, *The Recovery of Belief*, p. 64.
[65]There is no doubt that Marx "cooked" the numbers and quotations in *Das Capital*. "What emerges from a reading of *Capital*," says Paul Johnson, "is Marx's fundamental failure to understand capitalism. He failed precisely because he was unscientific; he would not investigate the facts himself, or use objectively the facts investigated by others. From start to finish, not just *Capital* but all his work reflects a disregard for truth which at times amounts to contempt." Paul Johnson, *Intellectuals* (New York: Harper and Row, 1988), p. 69.
[66]*Moscow News*, March 25, 1990.
[67]Robert Conquest, *The Harvest of Sorrow* (New York: Oxford University Press, 1986).

[68]Ronald H. Nash, *The Closing of the American Heart* (Dallas, TX: Probe Books, 1990), p. 153.
[69]Arnold Beichman, "Immune from the Shortages," *The Washington Times*, December 31, 1990, p. G3.
[70]Cited in ibid.
[71]Steve Hanke, "Marxism: A Major Meltdown," *The Washington Times*, September 18, 1990, p. G1.
[72]See Murray, *Losing Ground*.
[73]Frederick Engels claims that in socialistic society, "Private housekeeping is transformed into a social industry. The care and education of the children becomes a public affair; society looks after all children alike. . . ." Karl Marx and Frederick Engels, *Capital, the Communist Manifesto and Other Writings* (New York: 1932), p. 339.
[74]V. I. Lenin, *Collected Works*, forty-five volumes (Moscow: Progress Publishers, 1977), vol. 26, p. 235.
[75]Russell Watson with Fred Coleman, "Life Without Lenin," *Newsweek*, February 19, 1990, p. 21.
[76]For an in-depth look at the anti-Christian nature of the new world order advocates, see Malachi Martin, *The Keys of This Blood* (New York: Simon and Schuster, 1990), pp. 275f.
[77]Montgomery, *Human Rights and Human Dignity*, p. 123.
[78]Cited in Russell Heddendorf, *Hidden Threads: Social Thought for Christians* (Dallas, TX: Probe Books, 1990), p. 244-5.
[79]Cited in Roche, *A World Without Heroes*, p. 186.
[80]Gary T. Amos, *Defending the Declaration: How the Bible and Christianity Influenced the Writing of the Declaration of Independence* (Brentwood, TN: Wolgemuth and Hyatt, 1989), p. 63.
[81]Martin, *The Keys of This Blood*, p. 656.
[82]Sidney Hook, "Solzhenitsyn and Secular Humanism: A Response," *The Humanist*, Nov/Dec 1978, p. 6.
[83]Kenneth L. Feder and Michael Alan Park, "Animal Rights: An Evolutionary Perspective," *The Humanist*, July/August 1990, p. 44.
[84]John Warwick Montgomery, *The Law Above the Law* (Minneapolis, MN: Dimension Books, 1975), p. 56.
[85]Cited in Montgomery, *Human Rights and Human Dignity*, p. 170.
[86]Alexis de Tocqueville, *Democracy in America*, two volumes (New Rochelle, NY: Arlington House, n.d.), vol. 1, p. 294.
[87]Cited in Montgomery, *Human Rights and Human Dignity*, p. 107.
[88]Ibid., p. 99.
[89]Cited in ibid., p. 224.
[90]Christopher Andrew and Oleg Gordievsky, "Inside the KGB: A Double Agent's Tale," *Time*, October 22, 1990, p. 73.
[91]Paul Kurtz, *Philosophical Essays in Pragmatic Naturalism* (Buffalo: Prometheus Books, 1990), p. 163.
[92]Cited in Roche, *A World Without Heroes*, p. 289.
[93]Stanley L. Jaki, *The Road of Science and the Ways to God* (Chicago: University of Chicago Press, 1978), p. 242. We also recommend Norman L. Geisler and J. Kerby Anderson, *Origin Science: A Proposal for the Creation-Evolution Controversy* (Grand Rapids, MI: Baker Book House, 1987), and J. P. Moreland, *Christianity and the Nature of Science* (Grand Rapids, MI: Baker Book House, 1989).
[94]Henry M. Morris, *Men of Science—Men of God* (El Cajon, California: Master Books, 1989), contains mini-biographies of 101 Christian men of science. The Christian origin of science is covered brilliantly in Stanley L. Jaki, *The Savior of Science* (Washington, D.C.: Regnery Gateway, 1988) and Geisler and Anderson, *Origin Science: A Proposal for the Creation-Evolution Controversy*.
[95]Alfred North Whitehead, *Science and the Modern World* (New York: The Free Press, 1925), p. 13.
[96]Geisler and Anderson, *Origin Science*, p. 37.
[97]For more on this aspect of science we suggest Jaki's *The Road of Science and the Ways to God*.
[98]Thomas Jefferson, *Notes on Virginia*, cited in *The Jeffersonian Cyclopedia*, two volumes, ed. John P. Foley (New York: Russell & Russell, [1900] 1967), vol. 1, p. 386.
[99]Tonne, *Scribblings of a Concerned Secular Humanist*, p. 40.
[100]Jaki, *The Road of Science and the Ways to God*, p. 218.
[101]Huxley, *Essays of a Humanist*, p. 107.
[102]Tonne, *Scribblings of a Concerned Secular Humanist*, p. 40.
[103]Cited in Harry V. Jaffa, *Homosexuality and the Natural Law* (Montclaire, CA: The Claremont Institute, 1990), pp. 4-5.

[104]Cited in Roche, *A World Without Heroes*, p. 248.
[105]Joseph Stalin, speech delivered April 24, 1924 (New York: International Publishers, 1934).
[106]Harry Elmer Barnes, *The New History and the Social Studies* (New York: Century, 1925), p. 543.
[107]Ibid., p. 539.
[108]William Stanmeyer, *Clear and Present Danger* (Ann Arbor, MI: Servant Books, 1983), p. 167.
[109]*Washington Blade*, December 18, 1987, p. 19. Cited in Reisman and Eichel, *Kinsey, Sex and Fraud*, p. 212.
[110]Cited in Reisman and Eichel, *Kinsey, Sex and Fraud*, p. 212. *Loving Boys* was published by Global Academic Publications in 1986.
[111]Cited in ibid., p. 206.
[112]Ibid. For students who can't quite make up their minds between the Christian sexual ethic and the Humanist sexual ethic we suggest a thoughtful reading of Dobson and Bauer's *Children at Risk*, Reisman and Eichel's *Kinsey, Sex and Fraud*, Jaffa's *Homosexuality and the Natural Law* (which contains Bundy's bone-chilling conversation with his eighty-ninth victim), and Phyllis Schlafly's *Child Abuse in the Classroom* (Alton, IL: Marquette Press, 1985).
[113]H. J. Eysenck, "Reason With Compassion," in *The Humanist Alternative* ed. Paul Kurtz (Buffalo: Prometheus Books, 1973), p. 92.
[114]Corliss Lamont, *A Lifetime of Dissent* (Buffalo: Prometheus Books, 1988), p. 55.
[115]Cited in Francis A. Schaeffer, *A Christian Manifesto*, in *The Complete Works of Francis A. Schaeffer: A Christian View of the West*, five volumes (Westchester, IL: Crossway Books, 1982), vol. 5, p. 439. Schaeffer cites Durant's article from *The Humanist*, February 1977.
[116]Schaeffer, *Complete Works*, vol. 5, p. 439.
[117]Ibid., vol. 4, p. 30. God's character as the ground of moral absolutes and the only way to avoid complete relativism is a recurrent theme in Schaeffer's writings. It appears again in *The Church Before the Watching World*, where he writes, "God is the Creator and the Judge of the universe; His character is the law of the universe, and when He tells us a thing is wrong, it *is* wrong . . ." (*Works*, vol. 4, p. 137) and "there are some things that conform to His nature and some things that do not. God's holiness, in other words, involves moral content. . . . there are those moral actions which conform to God's character and those that do not" (*Works*, vol. 4, pp. 172-3). In *Death in the City* he writes, "But the Bible is clear: there is a moral law of the universe. And that basic law is the character of God Himself. There is no law behind God that binds God. Rather, God Himself is the law because He is not a contentless God, but a God with a character. His character *is* the law of the universe. When He reveals this character to us in verbalized, propositional form, we have the commands of God for men. Thus there are absolutes and categories; the law which the God who exists has revealed and which is based upon His character is final. . . . Therefore, when men break these commands, they are guilty . . ." (*Works*, vol. 4, p. 267). In *The God Who Is There* he writes, "There is no law behind God, because the furthest thing back *is* God. The moral absolutes rest upon God's character. The creation as He originally made it conformed to His character. Men as created in His image are to lie by choice on the basis of what God is. The standards of morality are determined by what conforms to His character, while those things which do not conform are immoral" (*Works*, vol. 1, p. 115), and ". . . God does exist, and He has a character; there are things which are outside the commandments He has given us as the expression of His character" (*Works*, vol. 1, p. 171). In *He Is There and He Is Not Silent*, "God's character is the moral absolute of the universe. . . . It is not that there is a moral absolute *behind* God that binds man and God, because that which is farthest back is always finally God. Rather, it is God Himself and His character who is the moral absolute of the universe. . . . We need to know who He is, and what His character is, because His character is the law of the universe. He has told us what His character is, and this becomes our moral law, our moral standard. It is not arbitrary, for it is fixed in God Himself, in what has always been. It is the very opposite of what is relativistic. It is either this, or morals are not morals. They become simply sociological averages or arbitrary standards imposed by society, the state or an elite" (*Works*, vol. 1, p. 303). In *Joshua and the Flow of Biblical History* he writes, ". . . God's commands are His propositional statements about His character. They are not arbitrary. God has a character, and His character is the law of the universe" (*Works*, vol. 4, p. 249), and "Because God exists and because He has a character, we live in a true moral universe. . . . God is really there and really has a character. He is really a holy God. Therefore, when I sin, my guilt is real" (*Works*, vol. 4, p. 300). In an unpublished paper delivered to a gathering of legal scholars, Schaeffer made the same point, that "not all things are the same to Him." God's character is such that "some things conform

to his character, and some are opposite to His character" (cited in Montgomery, *Human Rights and Human Dignity*, p. 113).
[118]Edward O. Wilson, "Biology's Spiritual Products," *Free Inquiry*, Spring 1987, p. 14.
[119]Roche, *A World Without Heroes*, p. 116.
[120]Ibid., p. 106.
[121]That is, Marxists attempt to sway the working class to revolt, even though strict adherence to materialistic philosophy dictates that the workers are unable to choose whether to revolt.
[122]Wayne L. Trotta, "Why Psychotherapy Must Be, and Cannot Be, a Science," *The Humanist*, Sept/Oct 1989, p. 42.
[123]Erich Fromm, *Psychoanalysis and Religion* (New Haven: Yale University Press, 1959), p. 7. Elsewhere Fromm confesses, "Without the existence of conscience, the human race would have bogged down long ago in its hazardous course" (*Man for Himself* [New York: Holt, Rinehart and Winston, 1964], pp. 141-2).
[124]For an excellent discussion of Marxism on American campuses, see Roger Kimball, *Tenured Radicals* (New York: Harper and Row, 1990).
[125]Christianity requires faith, too, but it is a faith in a rational God who created a rational universe and revealed Himself and His works in a rational way. That's why the Christian model better explains the real world. Truly superhuman faith is required only of adherents of the secular religious worldviews, who believe irrational claims in an effort to avoid the concept of God.
[126]Cited in Roche, *A World Without Heroes*, p. 238. Elsewhere Darwin proclaimed, "Man may be excused for feeling some pride at having risen, though not through his own exertions, to the very summit of the organic scale; and the fact of his having thus risen, instead of having been aboriginally placed there, may give him hopes for a still higher destiny in the distant future." *The Descent of Man*, cited in Sagan, *The Dragons of Eden*, title page.
[127]William Kirk Kilpatrick, *Psychological Seduction* (Nashville, TN: Thomas Nelson, 1983), p. 185.
[128]Victor Stenger, *Not By Design* (Buffalo: Prometheus Books, 1988), p. 188.
[129]Roche, *A World Without Heroes*, p. 87.
[130]A notable exception is provided by volume 17 of the *Great Soviet Encyclopedia*, 2d ed. (Moscow: 1952), which describes Christ as "the mythological founder of Christianity" (p. 523). Incredibly, a few Secular Humanists are also willing to blind themselves to the findings of archaeology. Gabriel Seabrook, in an article entitled "Christmas: The Birthday of the Sun," writes, "Christians might be . . . amazed to learn that . . . a person by the name of Jesus Christ did not live in historical reality." (*Free Inquiry*, Winter 1990/91, p. 14).
[131]Will Durant, *Caesar and Christ* (New York: Simon and Schuster, 1944), p. 557.
[132]The Christian worldview, contrary to Humanist claims, has a solid historical base and a scientific base—the science of archaeology. This science is not destroying the credibility of the Christian Scriptures, but verifying them. Nelson Glueck, a world-renowned archaeologist and student of William F. Albright, with thirty years of on-site experience, admitted that he never found one item in all his excavations to disprove one verse of the Bible. On the contrary, what he did find confirmed the truth of the Bible—both Old and New Testaments. See Werner Keller, *The Bible as History* (New York: William Morrow, 1956); William F. Albright, *The Archaeology of Palestine* (Gloucester, MA: Peter Smith, 1971); E. M. Blaiklock, *The Archaeology of the New Testament* (Grand Rapids, MI: Zondervan, 1970); and Edwin M. Yamauchi, *The Stones and the Scriptures* (Grand Rapids, MI: Baker Book House, 1981).
[133]See C. S. Lewis, *Miracles: A Preliminary Study* (New York: Macmillan, 1947), and Norman L. Geisler, *Miracles and Modern Thought* (Dallas, TX: Probe Books, 1982).
[134]Geisler, *Miracles and Modern Thought*, p. 146.
[135]For example, Richard T. Wright, a Christian, believes that creationists have "erected a very large stumbling block to belief in the God of the Bible." *Biology Through the Eyes of Faith* (San Francisco: Harper and Row, 1989), p. 81.
[136]Niles Eldredge and Stephen Jay Gould, "Punctuated Equilibria: The Tempo and Mode of Evolution Reconsidered," *Paleobiology*, vol. 3 (Spring 1977), pp. 145-6: "It is not at all surprising that a punctuational view of speciation, much like our own, but devoid (so far as we can tell) of references to synthetic evolutionary theory and the allopatric model, has long been favored by many Russian paleontologists. It may also not be irrelevant to our personal preferences that one of us [Gould] learned his Marxism, literally at his daddy's knee."
[137]Jim Wallis's *Sojourners* is an excellent example of an effort to mix Christianity and Marxism. Wallis's

Marxist stance is outlined in Clark H. Pinnock, "A Pilgrimage in Political Theology," in *Liberation Theology*, ed. Ronald H. Nash (Milford, MI: Mott Media, 1984). Also see Joan Harris, *The Sojourners File* (Washington, DC: New Century Foundation Press, 1983).
[138]Dobson and Bauer, *Children at Risk*, p. 22.
[139]Write Summit Ministries, P. O. Box 207, Manitou Springs, Colorado 80829 for information on how we are placing the course of study "Understanding the Times" in Christian high schools, Christian home schools and other study groups across America.
[140]Roche, *A World Without Heroes*, p. 358.

APPENDIX

A

THE COSMIC HUMANIST WORLDVIEW

As noted in the Introduction, this book deals with views prevalent in the Western hemisphere. It therefore excludes religions such as Buddhism, Taoism, and Islam, and deals with Marxism/Leninism, Secular Humanism, and Christianity—the three dominant worldviews in the West.

In recent years, however, a fourth worldview has begun to gain visibility. Commonly referred to as the New Age movement, it is more accurately described by the term *Cosmic Humanism*. Because it is still in its formative stages and professes a marked disdain for dogma, this worldview is more vaguely defined than the other three. Indeed, some members of the New Age movement go so far as to claim that their worldview "has no religious doctrine or teachings of its own."[1] This

Notes and Asides

attitude results from the New Age belief that truth resides within each individual and, therefore, no one can claim a corner on the truth or dictate truth to another. "The New Age," explains Christian writer Johanna Michaelsen, "is the ultimate eclectic religion of self: Whatever *you* decide is right for you is what's right, as long as you don't get narrow-minded and exclusive about it."[2]

By assuming that truth resides within each individual, however, one lays the cornerstone for a worldview. Granting oneself the power to discern all truth is a facet of theology, and this theology has ramifications that many members of the New Age movement have already discovered. Some have grudgingly begun to consider their movement a worldview. Marilyn Ferguson, author of *The Aquarian Conspiracy* (a book referred to as "The New Age watershed classic"), says the movement ushers in a "new mind—the ascendance of a startling worldview. . . ."[3] This worldview is summed up in its skeletal form, agreeable to virtually every Cosmic Humanist, by Jonathan Adolph: "In its broadest sense, New Age thinking can be characterized as a form of utopianism, the desire to create a better society, a 'New Age' in which humanity lives in harmony with itself, nature, and the cosmos."[4]

This appendix is an attempt to discover the heart of this worldview. The need for such an attempt is pressing. While the New Age movement still appears to be fragmented and without strong leadership, it has grown at a remarkable rate. The Stanford Research Institute estimates that "the number of New Agers in America could be as high as 5 to 10 percent of the population—12 million or more people."[5] Others have put the figure as high as 60 million,[6] although this includes people who merely believe in reincarnation and astrology. John Randolph Price, a world leader of the New Age movement, says, "there are more than half a billion New Age advocates on the planet at this time, working among various religious groups."[7]

Further, people adhering to the Cosmic Humanist worldview are gaining power in our society and around the world. Malachi Martin lists dozens of organizations that are either New Age or New Age sympathetic.[8] Barbara Marx Hubbard, a spokeswoman for the New Age, made a bid for the 1984 Democratic vice presidential nomination. Clearly, Cosmic Humanism is becoming a "fourth force" in the Western hemisphere.

Theology

Like the other worldviews, Cosmic Humanism's theology forms the foundation for all of the other aspects of its worldview. However, the New Age movement differs from these in that it embraces neither theism nor atheism.

Notes and Asides

Cosmic Humanism begins by denying the preeminence of any purported special revelation over any other. That is, Cosmic Humanists believe that the Bible is no more the word of God than is the Koran, or the works of Confucius. David Spangler, who has been described as the "Emerson of the New Age," says, "We can take all the scriptures, and all the teachings, and all the tablets, and all the laws, and all the marshmallows and have a jolly good bonfire and marshmallow roast, because that is all they are worth."[9]

Obviously, if the Bible is valuable only as fuel, this nullifies the significance of the life, death, and resurrection of Jesus Christ. The Cosmic Humanist sees Christ's life as important only in the sense that it showed man to be capable of achieving perfection, even godhood. An article in the publication *Science of Mind* states, "The significance of incarnation and resurrection is not that Jesus was a human like us but rather that *we are gods like him*—or at least have the potential to be."[10] This interpretation of Christ allows the New Age theologian to postulate, as John White does, that "The Son of God . . . is not Jesus but our combined Christ consciousness. . . ."[11] Jesus is looked on as one of a select company, having achieved Christ consciousness. Mankind is encouraged to acquire this same level of consciousness. Christian writer Dean Halverson summarizes the New Age view of Christ this way: "In our true selves, we are each the Christ." That is, "Christ is the principle of divinity or perfection that lies within each person."[12]

> "The equal toleration of all religions . . . is the same thing as atheism."
>
> —Pope Leo XIII

The Cosmic Humanist denies that the Bible is God's special revelation, but he does not totally abandon it. Rather, he reinterprets it to support the claims of the New Age movement. What are these claims? The essence of them is that Cosmic Humanists believe that man and God are ontologically one.

John Bradshaw states: "Each of us has access to a supraconscious, creative, integrative, self-organizing, intuitive mind whose capabilities are apparently unlimited. This is the part of our consciousness that constitutes our God-likeness."[13] Most Cosmic Humanists state the case more forcefully. Ruth Montgomery supposedly channeled a spirit that spoke through her, claiming, ". . . We are as much God as God is a part of us . . . each of us is God . . . together we are God . . . this all-for-one-and-one-for-all . . . makes us the whole of God."[14] White states that "sooner or later every human being will feel a call from the cosmos to ascend to godhood."[15] Meher Baba declares, "There is only one question. And once you know the answer to that question there are no more to ask. . . . Who am I? And to that question there is only one answer—I am God!"[16] Shirley MacLaine recommends that every person should begin each day by affirming his or her own godhood. "You can use *I am God* or *I am that I am* as Christ often did, or you can extend the affirmation to fit your own needs."[17] The conclusion is obvious, as stated by Christian writer Douglas Groothuis: "Kneel to

Notes and Asides

your own self. Honor and worship your own being. God dwells within you as You."[18]

Special revelation need not exist in books or in any other form outside of man, because each man has his own special revelation in his higher consciousness, his ability to get in touch with the part of him that is God. Inner soul searching becomes the only significant means of discovering truth. By asserting that man is God, the Cosmic Humanist grants each individual the power of determining reality by creating or co-creating truth.

It is important to understand that the belief that every individual is God and God is every individual is tied inextricably to the concept of consciousness. Because the Cosmic Humanist has this "all is one" mentality, he necessarily believes that humanity can become attuned to all the powers of its godhood by achieving unity of consciousness. "Once we begin to see that we are all God," says Beverly Galyean, "that we all have the attributes of God, then I think the whole purpose of human life is to reown the Godlikeness within us; the perfect love, the perfect wisdom, the perfect understanding, the perfect intelligence, and when we do that, we create back to that old, that essential oneness which is consciousness."[19] Robert Muller says, "Only the unity of all can bring the well-being of all."[20]

The concept of mankind's unity, the idea that all is one, tends to support the theological concept of reincarnation. Virtually every "orthodox" adherent of the New Age movement believes that each individual's soul was present in other material forms earlier in history and that it will manifest itself in still other forms after its present body dies. The body may pass away, but the soul will continue its quest for godhood or Christ consciousness in other bodies. This belief in reincarnation caused MacLaine, when recalling her daughter's birth, to muse, "When the doctor brought her to me in the hospital bed on that afternoon in 1956, had she already lived many many times before, with other mothers? Had she, in fact, been one herself? Had she, in fact, ever been *my* mother? Was her one-hour-old face housing a soul perhaps millions of years old?"[21]

"Pantheism is said . . . to be merely atheism in disguise."
—M. De Unamuno

Reincarnation, however, is not the only logical consequence of a theology based on the unity of God and man and the concept that all is one. If one cannot delineate between God and man, how can one be certain that he can delineate between other living or dead things and God? Indeed, if all is one, perhaps everything that exists is God. And so it is. Stars are God, water is God, plants are God, trees are God, the earth is God, whales and dolphins[22] are God, everything is God. New Agers have set up elaborate ceremonies to become one with the spirits of lakes, trees, dolphins, etc., in order to help them commune with the creative forces of the universe. Cosmic Humanists worship the creation

Notes and Asides

and the creator at the same time. For them, there is no difference.

The belief that everything is God and God is everything is known as *pantheism*. This ancient concept forms the theological foundation of the New Age movement. "Everything has divine power in it," says Roman Catholic New Ager Matthew Fox, and this divine force is what gives the planet its "sacredness."[23] Shakti Gawain puts her pantheism in plainer language, proclaiming the "great trust I now have in the higher power of the universe [a synonym for God] that is within me and within everyone and everything that exists."[24]

This higher power of the universe is not personal. It is cosmic force. There is no transcendent God "out there" apart from His creation. God is the creation. Says Ferguson, "In the emergent spiritual tradition God is not the personage of our Sunday School mentality. . . . God is experienced as flow, wholeness . . . the ground of being. . . . God is the consciousness that manifests as *Lila*, the play of the universe. God is the organizing matrix we can experience but not tell, that which enlivens matter."[25]

Pantheism is the theological belief that all reality is God or parts of God.

Unlike the Marxist/Leninist and the Secular Humanist, the Cosmic Humanist believes in a supernatural realm consisting of spiritual relationships. However, the New Age version of God differs infinitely from the Christian concept of God. While the Christian believes that God created mankind and all that exists and that man can know His will only through the general revelation of nature and conscience and the special revelation of the Bible, the Cosmic Humanist believes that every person and all reality *is* God, and therefore that any "truth" our inner selves discover is God's truth. This theological pantheism has a powerful impact on New Age philosophy.

Philosophy

The Cosmic Humanist rejects naturalistic and materialistic philosophies because such explanations ignore the all-pervasive supernatural. "From a very early age," says Spangler, "I was aware of an extra dimension or presence to the world around me, which as I grew older I came to identify as a sacred or transcendental dimension."[26] If Spangler's perspective is correct, and if (as pantheism declares) every aspect of existence is sacred, then everything must have a spiritual nature. And since it is the spiritual side of life that leads us to higher consciousness and inner truth, we should view all reality from a supernatural perspective. Thus, the Cosmic Humanist arrives at a philosophy of non-naturalism (there is nothing natural; everything is supernatural), a philosophy that focuses on the spiritual nature of all things, because the spiritual dimension of everything is the important,

Notes and Asides

god-like side of reality.

The Cosmic Humanist believes that all reality is God—from a grain of sand to the Milky Way—and his philosophy reflects this attitude by focusing on such principles as the Gaia hypothesis. This principle (Gaia is sometimes referred to as "Mother Nature") views the planet earth—indeed, the whole universe—as an actual living organism. Fritjof Capra says, "The universe is no longer seen as a machine, made up of a multitude of objects, but has to be pictured as one indivisible, dynamic whole whose parts are essentially interrelated and can be understood only as patterns of a cosmic process."[27]

This non-naturalism affects both the epistemological and the ontological aspects of the Cosmic Humanist philosophy. In terms of their theory of knowledge, proponents of the New Age movement emphasize the importance of getting in touch with one's higher self. When one gets in touch with the God-force within, one can intuitively "know" accurately and without limits. Says Gawain, "When we consistently suppress and distrust our intuitive knowingness, looking instead for [external] authority, validation, and approval from others, we give our personal power away."[28] Each one creates his own truth according to the principle "if it feels like truth to you it is."[29] That is, all knowledge exists in the God-force within each individual, and any individual who connects with that power can tap that knowledge. Indeed, Jack Underhill believes that when the whole world gets in touch with its godhood, "They can turn off the sun and turn it back on. They can freeze oceans into ice, turn the air into gold, talk as one with no movement or sound. They can fly without wings and love without pain, cure with no more than a thought or a smile. They can make the earth go backwards or bounce up and down, crack it in half or shift it around. . . . There is nothing they cannot do."[30]

Non-naturalism is a philosophical school of thought which treats all reality as supernatural.

Similarly, Cosmic Humanists' ontological beliefs stem from their non-naturalistic pantheism. Ultimate being or substance, for a New Ager, is the God-force, the Christ consciousness. God is "the essence of existence, the life force within all things."[31] Everything is God, and God is ultimate reality. Philosophically, Cosmic Humanism is monism: All reality is one. Muller hints at this when he states, "Oh God, I know that I come from you, that I am part of you, that I will return to you, and that there will be no end to my rebirth in the eternal stream of your splendid creation."[32] However, this statement only implies that God is the ultimate essence of man. A more accurate description of New Age ontology is provided by Spangler when he admits that "this worldview encourages us to treat all things not only as ourselves, as the holistic view would see it, but as honored and precious manifestations of God."[33]

Notes and Asides

Philosophically speaking, this ontological perspective might not be entirely satisfactory. What substance, if substance there be, makes up this God-force? Because every individual arrives at his own truth, New Age thinkers often differ in their interpretations. The answer may be "living consciousness," "life force," or "spiritual relationships," but the Cosmic Humanist generally is unconcerned with these questions. Spangler does say, "all life is interrelated and interdependent" and "the formative elements of creation are not bits of matter but relationships."[34] Since the whole of reality is God, whatever this substance may turn out to be will comprise God and, therefore, ultimate reality. Cosmic Humanists prefer to acknowledge this inner God without insisting on dogmatic views of its final nature. Ferguson states, "We need not postulate a purpose for this Ultimate Cause nor wonder who or what caused whatever Big Bang launched the visible universe. There is only the experience."[35]

Ethics

Cosmic Humanism's ethical perspective is based on its theological pantheism and philosophical monism. If each person is God, then all final authority resides within, and individuals must seek the freedom to act in harmony with their inner truth. MacLaine states, "Free will is simply the enactment of the realization you are God, a realization that you are divine: free will is making everything accessible to you."[36] The sacred nature of individual autonomy is the only ethical absolute promoted by the New Age movement.

This autonomy places the authority for judging values squarely within the soul of each human being. Ferguson writes, "Most importantly, when people become autonomous, their values become *internal*."[37] Internalized values are a must for every person seeking higher consciousness; any outside limit or external authority blocks his ability to get in touch with his inner truth. Thus, Vera Alder tells us,

> We should search ourselves very carefully to see if we have any fixed ideas, any great shyness or self-consciousness. If we have, we *must* seek freedom.[38]

Gawain provides us with a practical application of this call for total freedom when she calls for total sexual freedom: "If you're setting limits on your sexual energy, it becomes distorted. If you believe it is something to be hidden, ignored, and controlled, then you learn to hold back completely or act sexually only at certain safe moments."[39]

Notes and Asides

According to the Cosmic Humanist worldview, such limitations sap our personal power and deny our godhood. Man must not acknowledge outside boundaries, especially the boundaries of the Ten Commandments. The Commandments are external authority and, as such, hinder one's evolutionary growth.

Of course, when our values are internalized and we choose to ignore all outside authority and rational boundaries, boundless ethical relativism must result. Ferguson admits as much: "Autonomous human beings can create and invent. And they can change their minds, repudiating values they once held."[40] This relativism means that no one may decide whether another's actions are right or wrong. Ferguson believes that once we have achieved the higher consciousness of the New Age, "There is less certainty about what is right for others. With an awareness of multiple realities, we lose our dogmatic attachment to a single point of view."[41] MacLaine says simply, "It [is] not possible to judge another's truth."[42] Randall Baer, a former Cosmic Humanist who converted to Christianity, translates:

> "It [is] not possible to judge another's truth."
> —Shirley MacLaine

> There's a basic credo that says "create your own reality according to what feels right for you." For example, whether a person chooses to be homosexual, bisexual, monogamous, polygamous or whatever is OK as long as "It's right for me" or "It's done with love and no one's hurt." This is a kind of relativistic, human-founded ethics (or design-your-own ethics). In effect, New Age persons pick and choose from the multitudes of options in each area of life according to their own personal preferences.[43]

Elsewhere Baer says,

> The belief that sex should only take place in marriage (between a man and woman) is considered old-fashion and even "limiting your potential." Concerning ethics, sex outside marriage is exceedingly permissive, morally accepted, and justified as such in many ways. Within marriage, one of the more common excuses for committing adultery is the concept of an "open relationship" in which married mates are free to explore their potential by having sexual relations with others as they desire. . . . *Karma*, as well, is a widely used excuse for sexual dalliances. If two people have some *karma* left over from past lives together, they think, "now's a good time to work out that *karma*."[44]

Notes and Asides

Thus, according to the Cosmic Humanist, we must simply assume that everyone acts morally by following inner truth. Gawain, in fact, absolves Hitler and every other human being of moral responsibility by claiming that everyone is following the shortest path to higher consciousness and therefore acting morally: "I believe that every being chooses the life path and relationships that will help him or her to grow the fastest."[45]

Ethical relativism, as one would expect, has led the Cosmic Humanist to a point where the distinction between good and evil has become hopelessly blurred. No absolute right or wrong exists; only what is right or wrong according to each individual's truth. If everything is one, it is difficult to distinguish between good and evil. What may appear evil in this life could be the reverse in a reincarnated existence. Such a concept involves what New Agers refer to as *karma*.[46] According to MacLaine, *karma* means,

> Whatever action one takes will ultimately return to that person—good and bad—maybe not in this life embodiment, but sometime in the future. And no one is exempt. . . . For every act, for every indifference, for every misuse of life, we are finally held accountable. And it is up to us to understand what those accounts might be.[47]

Unfortunately, since there is no standard by which to judge what may be "an indifference," or "a misuse of life" it is difficult to know if there is any difference between them or, for that matter, if there is any difference between cruelty and non-cruelty.[48] This is an alarming conclusion, but one the Cosmic Humanist is more than willing to accept. This willingness results from the New Age concept of unity. If all is one, then good and evil are one,[49] and so are right and wrong. Ferguson states, "This wholeness unites opposites. . . . In these spiritual traditions [that the New Age draws on] there is neither good nor evil. There is only light and the absence of light . . . wholeness and brokenness . . . flow and struggle."[50] Spangler echoes this view, in more startling language: "Christ is the same force as Lucifer. . . . Lucifer prepares man for the experience of Christhood. . . . Lucifer works within each of us to bring us to wholeness as we move into the New Age."[51] What the world considers evil—war, murder, etc.—is part of the evolutionary flow and struggle of reality as supra-consciousness strives to be born on a higher level.

Recommended Reading for Advanced Study

Randall N. Baer, *Inside the New Age Nightmare* (Lafayette, LA: Huntington House, 1989).

Peter Jones, *The Gnostic Empire Strikes Back* (Phillipsburg, NJ: Presbyterian & Reformed, 1992).

Douglas Groothuis, *Unmasking the New Age* (Downers Grove, IL: InterVarsity Press, 1986).

David Clark and Norman L. Geisler, *Apologetics in the New Age: A Christian Critique of Pantheism* (Grand Rapids, MI: Baker, 1990).

Elliot Miller, *A Crash Course on the New Age Movement* (Grand Rapids, MI: Baker, 1989).

Biology

It would seem that a worldview based on pantheism would embrace a creationist perspective of biology, viewing God as the power that brought all life forms into existence in a single, creative act. However, the Cosmic Humanist instead believes that God acted as the Ultimate Cause of the universe and then allowed evolution to direct it to its present state.

Cosmic Humanists embrace evolutionary theory because evolution provides the best mechanism for ushering in a New Age. While a standard creationist view of biology seems to contradict the concept that man will eventually progress toward a heaven on earth (especially in light of the Laws of Thermodynamics), evolution provides just such a framework. Cosmic Humanists need reassurance that progress will occur because of their belief that mankind is moving upward toward an age of higher consciousness. The "science" of evolution provides the guarantee that all humanity will one day achieve this consciousness.

Notes
and
Asides

This union with the God-force will be collective—that is, man will achieve unity with both his fellow man and God. Collective consciousness means that the "ultimate end of the individual is to expand into the universal oneness, which really means that the individual disappears as a separate person."[52] Because the Cosmic Humanist believes this, he postulates an evolutionary theory that allows for not only individual but also collective development. Ferguson writes, "The proven plasticity of the human brain and human awareness offers the possibility that *individual evolution* may lead to *collective evolution*. When one person has unlocked a new capacity its existence is suddenly evident to others, who may then develop the same capacity."[53] Not every individual in the world will evolve at an even rate toward higher consciousness; rather, when enough people have achieved higher consciousness, other unenlightened individuals will be naturally absorbed (or evolved) into the collective consciousness. Thus, not everyone in the world must embrace the New Age movement before it can become a reality—dedicated Cosmic Humanists can simply act as the catalyst for an evolutionary leap into utopia.

Some New Age thinkers recognize that this view of evolution best fits the specific hypothesis known as punctuated equilibrium. When one speaks in terms of leaps or shifts, one is abandoning Darwinian theory and embracing the "hopeful monster" hypothesis. Spangler, for example, uses the terminology of punctuated equilibrium when he states, "In this [evolutionary] context, civilizations, like individuals, go through profound changes from time to time which represent discontinuities; that is, a jump or shift is made from one evolutionary condition to another. The New Age is such a shift."[54] Cosmic Humanists believe an elite "enlightened" element of the human race will "jump" into this New Age as an evolutionary leap and drag the rest of humanity with it.

Ferguson agrees that her Aquarian conspiracy "requires a mechanism for biological change more powerful than chance mutation." What is biologically necessary is the "possibility of rapid evolution in our own time, when the equilibrium of the species is punctuated by stress. Stress in modern society is experienced at the frontiers of our psychological rather than our geographical limits."[55] Instead of further human physical evolution determined by geography, environment, and natural selection, Cosmic Humanists advocate psychological evolution. This evolution guides mankind to a higher social order, "a New One-World Order, all to occur sometime before the year 2000."[56]

And what will man be like after the evolutionary leap into the New Age has occurred? Armand Biteaux explains, "Every man is an individual Christ; this is the teaching for the New Age. . . . Everyone will receive the benefit of this step in human evolution."[57] Every man will achieve the higher consciousness or godhood. "The final appearance of

Notes and Asides

the Christ will not be a man in the air before whom all must kneel," says White. "The final appearance of the Christ will be an evolutionary event. It will be the disappearance of egocentric, subhuman man and the ascension of God-centered Man. A new race, a new species, will inhabit the Earth—people who collectively have the stature of consciousness that Jesus had."[58] Once this collective higher consciousness is achieved, every human will be perfectly at one with every other human in collective godhood.

Of course, the evolutionary leap into the New Age may bring about even greater progress than connecting man into a unified God-consciousness. Peter Russell believes,

> Evolutionary trends and patterns . . . suggest a further possibility: the emergence of something beyond a single planetary consciousness or Supermind: a completely new level of evolution, as different from consciousness as consciousness is from life, and life is from matter.[59]

Realistically, however, most Cosmic Humanists are willing to settle for achieving divinity. Indeed, as we have seen, most perceive this as the ultimate end of man's existence, guaranteed by the ever upward spiral of evolution.

Psychology

The belief that an individual can hasten the work of evolution and usher in the utopian finale to history by achieving a higher consciousness is tied closely to Cosmic Humanist psychology. Achieving higher consciousness is the central goal for any member of the New Age movement—and only psychology provides the means for unlocking the secrets of this higher mindset. Cosmic humanists sometimes refer to their approach to psychology, with its emphasis on higher consciousness, as "fourth force" psychology. White explains, "Fourth force psychology covers a wide range of human affairs. All of them, however, are aimed at man's *ultimate* development—not simply a return from unhealthiness to normality—as individuals and as a species."[60]

This ultimate development, according to the New Age movement, represents the only truly healthy mindset. Ferguson writes, "Well-being cannot be infused intravenously or ladled in by prescription. It comes from a matrix: the bodymind. It reflects psychological and somatic harmony."[61] One's consciousness affects both body and soul, and only a constant state of higher consciousness can insure mental and physical well-being. Thus, psychology plays a crucial role in Cosmic Humanism's worldview not only because it can hasten the evolution of all mankind to a collective God-consciousness, but also because it works to ensure perfect health for every individual.

The message from Cosmic Humanist psychologists to people suffering health problems is simple: mindset is responsible for health. People suffering through painful sickness or disease are doing so because they have not yet achieved higher consciousness. "Every time you don't trust yourself and don't follow your inner truth," says Gawain, "you decrease your aliveness and your body will reflect this with a loss of vitality, numbness, pain, and eventually, physical disease."[62] This same general failing to contact the "God within" creates criminal tendencies. Vera Alder explains that in the New Age,

> A criminal or an idler will be recognized as a sick individual offering a splendid chance for wise help. Instead of being incarcerated with fellow unfortunates in the awful atmosphere of a prison, the future "criminal" will be in much demand. The finest types of psychologists or religionists will offer him sanctuary and earnest help. . . .[63]

There can be no concept of punishment for wrong behavior, because there is no wrong behavior.

Conversely, if we attain higher consciousness, we can guarantee ourselves excellent physical and mental health. "Health and disease don't just happen to us," says Ferguson. "They are active processes issuing from inner harmony or disharmony, profoundly affected by our states of consciousness, our ability or inability to flow with experience."[64]

What methods does this "fourth force" psychology employ to induce states of higher consciousness in willing individuals? Most often it relies on meditation (often aided by crystals or mantras). An author in *Life Times Magazine* states emphatically, "My message to everyone now is to learn to meditate. It was through meditation that many other blessings came about. . . ."[65] According to the Cosmic Humanist, higher consciousness will naturally flow from meditation as one of its many "blessings." But other "blessings" may manifest themselves as well. For example, meditation often creates in an individual the ability to channel spirits, according to Kathleen Vande Kieft:

> *Almost without exception, those who channel effectively meditate regularly*. The process of channeling itself is an extension of the state of meditation . . . the best way to prepare, then, for channeling is by *meditation*.[66]

Notes and Asides

The Cosmic Humanist believes that spirits will sometimes speak to and through a particularly gifted individual engaged in meditation. Elena, a spirit channeled by John Randolph Price, allegedly describes beings like herself as "angels of light—whether from earth or other worlds. They search, select and guide those men and women who may be suitable subjects."[67]

Not every member of the New Age movement would see much significance in channeling; indeed, some are embarrassed by the channelists in their midst. But every Cosmic Humanist embraces meditation as an important psychological tool for attaining higher consciousness. Channeling and other practices, including astrology, firewalking, ouija boards, and aura readings,[68] are often suggested by various New Age psychologists and practitioners. Generally these are offered only as means of enhancing the higher consciousness achieved through meditation. Regardless of the specific psychological package prescribed by various individual Cosmic Humanists, New Age psychology is based on a simple rule: meditate to commune with the God within. (This is the fundamental difference between New Age [or pantheist] and Christian meditation. New Age meditation focuses on the "God within." Christian meditation focuses on the God outside us, our Maker and Judge and Savior, and on His objective, external revelation of truth to us in the Bible.) The emphasis is always on the supernatural character (what the Christian might describe as the occult side[69]) of psychological health. Ken Carey sums up the basic credo of New Age psychology, "Everyone anywhere who tunes into the Higher Self becomes part of the transformation. Their lives then become orchestrated from other realms."[70]

Channeling is a technique used by New Agers to contact spirit guides.

Sociology

Once every individual has been given the benefit of the evolutionary leap to collective godhood, psychology and sociology will merge—both will study a society unified into one mind (the mind of God). However, until that happens, New Age sociology must concentrate on exploding the limits of our current societies, because modern societies inhibit man's ability to achieve higher consciousness. Ferguson complains, "Every society, by offering its automatic judgments, limits the vision of its members. From our earliest years we are seduced into a system of beliefs that becomes so inextricably braided into our experience that we cannot tell culture from nature."[71]

According to this Cosmic Humanist approach, all of our institutions must be re-worked so as to encourage, rather than discourage, individuals to seek the inner truth of their non-fallen human nature. Specifically, sociologists must adopt a pantheistic perspective. Spangler says that the New Age approach

> is to look at the objects, people, and events in our lives and to say "You are sacred. In you and with you I can find the sacramental passages that reconnect me to the wholeness of creation." It is then to ask ourselves what kind of culture, what kind of institutions—be they political, economic, artistic, educational, or scientific—we need that can honor that universal sacredness.[72]

Most Cosmic Humanists point to marriage and family as examples of outdated, unenlightened institutions. Both marriage and family, in their traditional Judeo-Christian forms, are regarded as too limiting and too hopelessly blind to universal sacredness to be useful in achieving full enlightenment, or God-consciousness. Thus, Alder claims that in the New Age the concept of family will have so evolved that "the idea that an unmarried person of either sex should have to remain childless will seem far-fetched."[73] Gawain believes we need to re-work our attitude about divorce to create a society more conducive to mankind's evolution to godhood: "People who divorce almost inevitably feel that they have failed, because they assume all marriages should last forever. In most such cases, however, the marriage has actually been a total success—it's helped each person to grow to the point where they no longer need its old form."[74]

According to this sociological view, it is counter-evolutionary to attempt to maintain the institutions of marriage and family in the traditional sense. Writes Gawain,

> Relationships and families as we've known them seem to be falling apart at a rapid rate. Many people are panicky about this; some try to re-establish the old traditions and value systems in order to cling to a feeling of order and stability in their lives. It's useless to try to go backward, however, because our consciousness has already evolved beyond the level where we were willing to make the sacrifices necessary to live that way.[75]

Institutions must be restructured to promote this evolution of consciousness. Cosmic Humanists hope to facilitate this restructuring by working within an already existing institution: our educational system. By teaching children the proper attitudes toward themselves and their consciousness, New Age educators believe that they can create a generation capable of re-working all other aspects of society and, potentially, ushering in the New Age. For this reason, many

Notes and Asides

Cosmic Humanists choose careers in education. In fact, Ferguson admits that out of all the New Age professionals she surveyed for *The Aquarian Conspiracy*, "more were involved in education than in any other single category of work."[76] Many of these Cosmic Humanists use their positions to promote their worldview. John Dunphy, in an article entitled "A Religion for the New Age," says the battle for the future will be fought in the classroom:

> I am convinced that the battle for humankind's future must be waged and won in the public school classrooms by teachers who correctly perceive their role as proselytizers of a new faith: a religion of humanity that recognizes and respects the spark of what theologians call the Divinity in every human being. These teachers must embody the same selfless dedication as the most rabid fundamentalist preachers.[77]

With the implementation of Values Clarification,[78] sex education, sex clinics, moral relativism, biological evolution, *Cosmos*, and globalism in most public school curriculum, Dunphy's "proselytizers" have already established the foundation for their new faith.

Politics

The institution Cosmic Humanists would most like to see restructured is national government. Members of the New Age movement believe that national governments must be merged to form a world government. Their call for world government is due in part to their fear of global nuclear annihilation, since they believe that, as Ferencz and Keyes state, "*International governance—something like a United Nations of the World—will rescue us from our deadly predicament*."[79] But most Cosmic Humanists call for world government simply because they see it as the next logical evolutionary step toward godhood and utopia. "I believe the most fundamental thing we can do today," says Robert Muller, a former U.N. assistant secretary-general, "is to believe in evolution."[80]

Cosmic Humanists perceive mankind as evolving toward a collective consciousness. Clearly, this collective consciousness will transcend all material and individual boundaries—thereby rendering national and political boundaries obsolete. World government seems a natural evolutionary step in this dissolution of boundaries. Thus, Ferencz and Keyes claim, "Despite all of the contemporary stresses and strife, an objective analysis of the historical record will show that humankind is experiencing a continuous—though wobbly—move-

Notes and Asides

ment toward a more cooperative world order."[81] Donald Keys is even more optimistic, declaring that humanity is "on the verge of something entirely new, a further evolutionary step unlike any other: the emergence of the first global civilization."[82]

It needs to be stressed here that the New Age call for world government is based less on political theory than on the New Age concepts that all is one and that evolution plus other scientific principles are leading mankind into this unity. World government is important to Cosmic Humanists because it removes barriers that prevent unity, not because of specific mundane political considerations. "Unlike many historical expressions of the one-world idea," says Spangler, "which focus in particular upon the establishment of a world government, the vision of the New Age qua planetary civilization arises less out of politics than out of what is called the holistic vision. This is the awareness that all life is interrelated and interdependent, that the formative elements of creation are not bits of matter but relationships, and that evolution is the emergence of ever more complex patterns and syntheses of relationships."[83]

We have already discussed the role of punctuated equilibrium in the New Age worldview, so we will concentrate here on the other scientific principles New Agers believe will usher in the second "Garden of Eden." Baer was introduced to the New Age movement through *Keys of Enoch*, a book that claimed that science guarantees the advent of a New Age. He says,

> I read that startling advances in such diverse scientific fields as genetic engineering, telecommunications, supercomputers, nuclear fusion technology, artificial intelligence, solid state physics, quantum physics, advanced holography, laser optics, astrophysics, and others were to be combined with New Age spiritual philosophy in creating a utopian New World Order. This "Sacred Science" claims to be a revolutionary super-science capable of linking with the infinite powers of the universe, all applied to completely re-create the planet into a paradise and its populace into gods. Thus, a grand "Second Genesis" would generate a super-Renaissance global utopia.[84]

The specific political nature of the coming world order to be ushered in by evolution and technology is rarely discussed by Cosmic Humanists. Neither democracy nor totalitarianism is offered as a potential system of world government, for the simple reason that New Age thinkers believe that each person is rapidly evolving the capacity for self-government. When mankind achieves a collective consciousness, world government will be synonymous with self-government.

Notes and Asides

"The new political awareness has little to do with parties or ideologies," says Ferguson. "Its constituents don't come in blocs. Power that is never surrendered by the individual cannot be brokered. Not by revolution or protest but by autonomy, the old slogan becomes a surprising fact: *Power to the people*. One by one by one."[85]

Thanks to the higher consciousness presently evolving in all mankind, centralized government will wither away. Autonomy will be the ruling order of the New Age. Oddly enough, however, Cosmic Humanists do not extend autonomy to every realm. One significant aspect of personal freedom—religious preference—will not be tolerated in the New Age. "Religions," says Muller, "must actively cooperate to bring to unprecedented heights a better understanding of the mysteries of life and of our place in the universe. 'My religion, right or wrong,' . . . must be abandoned forever in the Planetary Age."[86] This attitude is based on the knowledge that some religions, such as Christianity, are incompatible with a Cosmic Humanist perspective and therefore would hinder mankind's efforts to achieve collective consciousness in a new world order.

Law

As one might expect, world government requires a system of international law. Ferencz and Keyes believe that "we must establish a world system where international law, courts, and enforcement are a reality."[87] But the question arises: On whose authority will this international law be based? If the individual is to have all authority in future economic and political systems, why shouldn't the individual act as his own authority in legal matters as well?

According to the Cosmic Humanist, all authority does reside within each individual. Since every person is God, and God is every person, man can only decide the legality of an action by getting in touch with this God within. Thus, every individual must act as his own legal authority, because any manifestation of outside authority hinders communion with one's godhood. "The real problem with commitment to an external form," explains Gawain, "is that it doesn't allow room for the inevitable changes and growth of people and relationships. If you promise to feel or behave by a certain set of rules, eventually you are going to have to choose between being true to yourself and being true to those rules."[88] Should one choose to honor a certain set of rules rather than inner truth, one sacrifices his godhood. As we noted earlier, "When we consistently suppress and distrust our intuitive knowingness," writes Gawain, "looking instead for [external] authority, validation, and approval from others, we give our personal power away."[89]

Notes
and
Asides

"Personal power" apparently causes one to act under proper authority (the God within). These actions will be proper because they will conform with the reality we, as part of God, are creating. "As each of us connects with our inner spiritual awareness," says Gawain, "we learn that the creative power of the universe is within us. We also learn that we can create our own reality and take responsibility for doing so."[90] Thus, under the New Age legal perspective, any action man might choose will be perceived as lawful, as long as it is an action true to the God within. Once mankind has achieved collective consciousness, we will all be co-creators of reality; therefore we will all work according to our own authority.

This attitude causes the Cosmic Humanist to view Biblical Christianity with distaste, since the Christian worldview describes both an outside Authority and a specific moral order based on the transcendent nature of God. These concepts are far too restrictive for members of the New Age movement. Spangler (more specifically, a spirit channeled by Spangler) disdains Christians and all others opposed to the New Age worldview, declaring, "Their world (of darkness) is under the law and shall disappear."[91] In stark contrast, Cosmic Humanists are under no outside authority. They create their own reality and their own rules; they are a law unto themselves.

Economics

New Age beliefs about the need for a world system of self-government necessarily shape New Age economic theory. Predictably, some Cosmic Humanists have begun calling for a universal system of exchange. Alder describes the system of the future: "As . . . individual needs would largely be supplied on the ration-card system, the need for handling of money would dwindle. There would, of course, be a universal currency the world over. There would be a central bank. . . ."[92]

However, most Cosmic Humanists don't discuss the specifics of a world economic system for the same reason they avoid concrete political declarations or definitive legal systems: the degree of autonomy the individual will experience in the New Age cannot be bound by the limitations of any present-day economic system. "Both capitalism and socialism," says Ferguson, "as we know them, pivot on material values. They are inadequate philosophies for a transformed society."[93] A transformed society will enjoy so much personal freedom that all concern with the marketplace will be swept away. Future world citizens will not ask themselves, What goods can I produce or services can I perform to meet the needs (or demands) of my neighbors? Rather, they will ask, What is my inner voice calling me to do? Since the inner voice is the voice of God, the inner urge will be to produce and perform unselfishly.

Incredibly, everyone's inner voice will lead him or her in such a way that no member of society will want for anything. Gawain proclaims,

> We make a contribution to the world just by being ourselves in every moment. There are no more rigid categories in our lives—this is work, this is play. It all blends into the flow of following the universe and money flows in as a result of the open channel that's created. You no longer work in order to make money. Work is no longer something you have to do in order to sustain life. Instead, the delight that comes from expressing yourself becomes the greatest reward.[94]

Elsewhere she claims, "The more you are willing to trust yourself, and take the risks to follow your inner guidance, the more money you will have. The universe will pay you to be yourself and do what you really love!"[95]

This concept was also accepted by Baer. In New Age success philosophy, says Baer, "the more attuned a person is to the 'Universal Mind' the more the universe will demonstrate this level of enlightenment by mirroring more 'god-money in action.' The more enlightened a person is, the more money and success will naturally occur in life."[96]

Not all Cosmic Humanists are as eloquent as Gawain and Baer in discussing the economics of the New Age, but their conclusions follow the same vein. When higher consciousness is achieved, paradise follows—and we all know that no one had to toil for food in the original Garden of Eden.

History

Like the Secular Humanist and the Marxist/Leninist, the Cosmic Humanist trusts evolution to guide mankind unswervingly toward perfection. In a very real sense, members of the New Age movement place their faith in evolution as humanity's savior.

This faith in evolution causes the Cosmic Humanist to view human history as an ascent—a constant development, though wobbly at times, from lower to higher levels of consciousness. Each jump of punctuated evolution is a jump upward. It is a jump upward because the God-force within the universe pulls it upward. During the equilibrium or stasis[97] phase of evolution, however, Cosmic Humanists admit that evolution

Notes and Asides

is a history of vicious killings and survival of the fittest. Ferencz and Keyes state, "We have seen that humankind is not simply moving in a vicious killing circle; it is on *an upward climb* toward completing the governmental structure of the world. We are inspired by our great progress toward planethood."[98] Elsewhere they declare that this "*optimism is justified by the facts*."[99] History, according to the Cosmic Humanist, is progressive—thanks to the redemptive force of evolution. Even the Second Law of Thermodynamics does not discourage their optimistic view of history. Indeed, learned physicist Paul Davies writes, "Far from sliding towards a featureless state, the Universe is progressing from featurelessness to states of greater organization and complexity. This cosmic progress defines a global arrow of time that points in the opposite way to the thermodynamic arrow."[100]

Further, this evolutionary force assures mankind of continued development in the future. Faith in this sustained progress into the New Age has been demonstrated by a number of Cosmic Humanists, but it is defended especially by M. Scott Peck:

> God wants us to become himself (or Herself or Itself). We are growing toward godhood. God is the goal of evolution. It is God who is the source of the evolutionary force and God who is the destination. This is what we mean when we say that He is the Alpha and the Omega, the beginning and the end.[101]

"We are growing toward godhood. God is the goal of evolution."
—M. Scott Peck

Human history began because of the actions of an Ultimate Cause, and it has been marked by a steady, though bloody, evolution toward the New Age. During the New Age all mankind will achieve a unity of consciousness with God. What this entails has been revealed through a channeled work *A Course in Miracles*.[102] Every person will be absorbed into a "Divine Abstract," where there are "no distinctions, where no words are communicated, and where there are no events—only a static, eternal now."[103] The jumps of evolutionary history, for some reason, cease. Everything becomes stasis.

Some members of the New Age movement, unsatisfied with the concept of evolution as the redemptive force in history, have postulated the appearance of a spiritual Savior who will guide mankind to higher consciousness and utopia. Thus, Donald H. Yott suggests that a "Savior appears every two thousand years (more or less) for the different ages. Each Savior brings the tone or key-note for the age."[104] A spirit channeled by Levi proclaims, "But in the ages to come, man will attain to greater heights. And then, at last, a mighty Master Soul will come to earth to light the way up to the throne of perfect man."[105] These predictions are not intended to deny the evolutionary force's influence upon man's development. Rather, they simply add a "supernatural"

Notes and Asides

dimension to human progress. While not every Cosmic Humanist would agree with the idea that a new Savior will appear in the future, all would agree with the assertion that man throughout history evolves from lower to higher consciousness.

A historical perspective that embraces evolution as the vehicle for change—that expects that it is only a matter of time until mankind achieves perfection—can be expected to tend toward complacency. If one believes that the evolutionary process will determine how and when man achieves godhood, then why bother working toward godhood in this lifetime? Cosmic Humanists circumvent this apathetic attitude by stressing that man has already achieved a level of consciousness that allows him to work in harmony with evolution to hasten the advent of the New Age.[106] This view not only encourages the Cosmic Humanist to act on his beliefs but also allows those with a higher consciousness to catapult the "backward" part of humanity into godhood. "Every individual's consciousness is connected to, and is a part of, the mass consciousness," explains Gawain. "When a small but significant number of individuals have moved into a new level of awareness and significantly changed their behavior, that change is felt in the entire mass consciousness."[107] This is the goal that all Cosmic Humanists work toward in an effort to hasten the full-blown evolution of all things. Spangler describes this as the "individual's sense of being a co-creator with history, of being involved in a process of conscious and participatory evolution."[108]

Conclusion

The New Age worldview is based on theological pantheism (all is God), philosophical monism (all is one substance), ethical relativism (all is changing), biological punctuated evolution (all is progressing), and psychological higher consciousness (all is perfectible). The Cosmic Humanist believes that perfectible human nature provides the best means for governing under a new world order and that it will create the most just world economic order and legal system—in short, personal freedom will usher man into utopia, where every human being ultimately will experience Christ-consciousness.

If God exists within everything, then mankind must simply get in touch with this higher consciousness to attain collective godhood. Some enlightened men and women are already exploring psychology (especially meditation, channeling, crystals, etc.) in an effort to reach this higher consciousness, while others are stumbling along blindly and must be thrust into utopia by the combined efforts of evolution and the more highly evolved Cosmic Humanists.

Mankind's return to the Garden of Eden is guaranteed by the evolutionary force as viewed through history. The Cosmic Humanist understands history as a progressive development toward a New Age, in which all will be one. The world will be guided into this New Age by the God within, and perhaps by other spirits contacting the human race through channeling, ouija boards, tarot cards, outer space travel, or other means. While Cosmic Humanists rarely provide specific formulas for the coming transition to the New Age, they are more than willing to speculate as to what the New Age will entail: world government, an absence of want, complete personal freedom (except for the freedom to cling to a lower consciousness through unenlightened religions), and collective godhood.

As has been pointed out by numerous scholars, there is very little that is actually "new" in the New Age worldview. The theology of pantheism is virtually as old as mankind, and the ancient Greeks had visions of utopian societies.[109] C. S. Lewis says,

> Pantheism is congenial to our minds not because it is the final stage in a slow process of enlightenment, but because it is almost as old as we are. It may even be the most primitive of all religions. . . . Theosophy and the worship of the life-force are both forms of it; even the German worship of a racial spirit is only Pantheism truncated or whittled down to suit barbarians.[110]

Further, none of the psychological methods suggested by Cosmic Humanists differ significantly from the practices of early fortune-tellers and mystics, and the hunger for total personal freedom has been felt by every adolescent that ever lived. Spangler is forced to admit that "the image of a New Age is not really new at all. Its echoes can be found in many cultures throughout history."[111]

The Apostle Paul addressed "the image of a New Age" two thousand years ago:

> Because that, when they knew God, they glorified him not as God, neither were thankful; but became vain in their imaginations, and their foolish heart was darkened. Professing themselves to be wise, they became fools, And changed the glory of the uncorruptible God into an image made like to corruptible man, and to birds, and fourfooted beasts, and creeping things. Wherefore God also gave them up to uncleanness through the lusts of their own hearts, to dishonor their own bodies between themselves; Who changed the truth of God into a lie, and worshipped and served the creation more than the Creator, who is blessed for ever. Amen. For this cause God gave them up unto

Notes and Asides

> vile affections: for even their women did change the natural use into that which is against nature's law; And likewise also the men, leaving the natural use of the woman, burned themselves out in their lust one toward another; men with men working that which is unseemly, and receiving in themselves that recompense of their error which was right. And even as they did not like to retain God in their knowledge, God gave them over to a reprobate mind, to do those things which are not convenient. (Romans 1:21-28)

The only novel aspect of Cosmic Humanism is its new-found respect: what once was a loose-jointed worldview espoused by eccentric fringes of Western society has rapidly gained acceptance among many mainstream Western intellectuals. Men and women who understand the irrationality of an atheistic explanation for the universe, instead of embracing a theistic interpretation, have embraced pantheism. Davies, for example, has come from an atheistic "Accidental Universe" concept to a universe based on a "Cosmic Blueprint," but in the process he has missed the theistic God of Christianity. He is now talking about a self-emerging, self-generating, self-organizing universe.

NEW AGE-ORIENTED PUBLICATIONS

Brain/Mind Bulletin Newsletter	*The New Times*
East West Journal	*New Age Journal*
The Essential Whole Earth Catalog	*New Realities*
Holistic Health	*Reflections*
Life Times	*Whole Life Magazine*
The Monk	*Yoga Journal*

(Source: Randall N. Baer, *Inside the New Age Nightmare*, Appendix D)

Notes and Asides

Carl Sagan, long known for his atheism—"only nature exists"—wrote a novel titled *Contact* in which the long-sought "perfect circle" reveals that "the universe was made on purpose." Says novelist Sagan, "As long as you live in this universe, and have a modest talent for mathematics, sooner or later you'll find it. It's already here. It's inside everything. You don't have to leave your planet to find it. In the fabric of space and in the nature of matter, as in a great work of art, there is, written small, the artist's signature. Standing over humans, gods, and demons, subsuming Caretakers and Tunnel builders, there is an intelligence that antedates the universe."[112] In his chapter titled "The Artist's Signature" he quotes Nicomachus of Gerasa (ca. A.D. 100): "The universe seems . . . to have been determined and ordered in accordance with number, by the forethought and the mind of the creator of all things; for the pattern was fixed, like a preliminary sketch, by the domination of number pre-existent in the mind of the world-creating God." Is Sagan leaning from Secular Humanism to Cosmic Humanism?

The similarities between the New Age movement and Secular Humanism and Marxism/Leninism are obvious. In virtually every discipline, Cosmic Humanism is in either the Humanist or the Marxist camp. At the foundational level, New Age biology is Marxist biology; New Age psychology is Secular Humanist psychology; New Age politics is Humanist and Marxist politics. While one would think that pantheism would be closer to theism than to atheism, the truth seems to be, "if everything is God; nothing is God." The only realm in which Cosmic Humanism is supportive of Christianity is its insistence that the universe could not happen by chance, and there is more to reality than matter. In most every other respect, Cosmic Humanists, Secular Humanists, and Marxist/Leninists are family.

How closely they are related has only recently become evident. "Fans of harmonic convergences," says *Time* magazine, "have been noting Mikhail Gorbachev's frequent use of phrases associated with the New Age movement, that mystical, universalist philosophy that preaches, as the Soviet President does, of the need for 'a New World Order.' As he said in California: 'All mankind is entering a new age, and world trends are beginning to obey new laws and logic.' More strikingly, he held a private meeting in Canada earlier in the week with one of the leading gurus of the New Age movement, Sri Chinmoy, who read him a 'spiritual song' and gave him a volume of admiring letters."[113]

This sudden ascendancy of the New Age worldview has now made it impossible for the Western world to dismiss Cosmic Humanists as cranks. Indeed, Cosmic Humanism must be viewed with utmost seriousness.

[1]Jonathan Adolph, "What is New Age?" *New Age Journal*, Winter 1988, p. 11. *The New Age Journal* is published at 342 Western Ave., Brighton, MA 02135.
[2]Johanna Michaelsen, *Like Lambs to the Slaughter* (Eugene, OR: Harvest House, 1989), p. 11.
[3]Marilyn Ferguson, *The Aquarian Conspiracy: Personal and Social Transformation in the 1980s* (Los Angeles: J. P. Tarcher, 1980), p. 23.
[4]Adolph, "What is New Age?" p. 6.
[5]Ray A. Yungen, *For Many Shall Come in My Name* (Salem, OR: Ray Yungen, 1989), p. 34.
[6]Randall N. Baer, *Inside the New Age Nightmare* (Lafayette, LA: Huntington House, Inc., 1989), p. 81. This figure is an estimate of Americans "being involved in one aspect of the New Age or another."
[7]Cited in Malachi Martin, *The Keys of This Blood* (New York: Simon and Schuster, 1990), p. 308.
[8]Ibid., pp. 302-8.
[9]David Spangler, *Reflections on the Christ* (Scotland: Findhorn Publications, 1982), p. 73.
[10]*Science of Mind*, October 1981, pp. 40-2, cited in Yungen, *For Many Shall Come in My Name*, p. 164.
[11]John White, "A Course in Miracles: Spiritual Wisdom for the New Age," *Science of Mind*, March 1986, p. 10.
[12]Dean C. Halverson, *Crystal Clear: Understanding and Reaching New Agers* (Colorado Springs, CO: NavPress, 1990), p. 55.
[13]John Bradshaw, *Bradshaw on the Family* (Pompano Beach, FL: Health Communications, 1988), p. 230.
[14]Ruth Montgomery, *A World Beyond* (New York: Ballantine/Fawcett Crest Books, 1972), p. 12.
[15]John White, ed., *What is Enlightenment?* (Los Angeles: J. P. Tarcher, 1984), p. 126.
[16]Meher Baba, cited in Allan Y. Cohen, "Meher Baba and the Quest of Consciousness," in *What is Enlightenment?*, ed. White, p. 87.
[17]Cited in F. LaGard Smith, *Out On a Broken Limb* (Eugene, OR: Harvest House, 1986), p. 181.
[18]Douglas Groothuis, *Unmasking the New Age* (Downers Grove, IL: InterVarsity Press, 1986), p. 21.
[19]Cited in Francis Adeney, "Educators Look East," *Spiritual Counterfeits Journal*, Winter 1981, p. 29. SCP *Journal* is published by Spiritual Counterfeits Project, P. O. Box 4308, Berkeley, CA 94704.
[20]Cited in Benjamin B. Ferencz and Ken Keyes, Jr., *PlanetHood* (Coos Bay, OR: Vision Books, 1988), p. 92.
[21]Cited in Smith, *Out on a Broken Limb*, p. 12.
[22]Baer, *Inside the New Age Nightmare*, p. 118: "The New Age really has gone ga-ga on this one. Quite popular is the belief that dolphins are repositories of virtual libraries of information from super-advanced ancient civilizations (like Atlantis), and can communicate this knowledge telepathically to those tuned in on the New Age wavelength."
[23]Matthew Fox, in an interview with Laura Hagar, "The Sounds of Silence," *New Age Journal*, March/April 1989, p. 55.
[24]Shakti Gawain, *Living in the Light* (San Rafael, CA: New World Library, 1986), p. 8.
[25]Ferguson, *The Aquarian Conspiracy*, p. 382.
[26]David Spangler, *Emergence: The Rebirth of the Sacred* (New York: Delta/Merloyd Lawrence, 1984), p. 12.
[27]Fritjof Capra, *The Turning Point* (Toronto: Bantam, 1982), p. 77-8.
[28]Gawain, *Living in the Light*, p. 69.
[29]Baer, *Inside the New Age Nightmare*, p. 88. He adds, "Here you pick your own truth, your own morals, and your own wisdom."
[30]Jack Underhill, "My Goal in Life," *Life Times Magazine*, Winter 1986/1987, p. 90.
[31]Halverson, *Crystal Clear*, p. 91.
[32]Robert Muller, *The New Genesis: Shaping a Global Spirituality* (New York: Image Books, 1984), p. 189.
[33]Spangler, *Emergence: The Rebirth of the Sacred*, p. 83.
[34]Ibid., p. 42.
[35]Ferguson, *The Aquarian Conspiracy*, p. 383.
[36]Cited in William Goldstein, "Life on the Astral Plane," *Publishers Weekly*, March 18, 1983, p. 46.
[37]Ferguson, *The Aquarian Conspiracy*, p. 327.
[38]Vera Alder, *When Humanity Comes of Age* (New York: Samuel Weiser, 1974), p. 148.
[39]Gawain, *Living in the Light*, p. 128.
[40]Ferguson, *The Aquarian Conspiracy*, p. 331.
[41]Ibid, p. 192.

[42]Cited in Smith, *Out on a Broken Limb*, p. 33.
[43]Baer, *Inside the New Age Nightmare*, p. 88.
[44]Ibid., p. 126.
[45]Gawain, *Living in the Light*, p. 60.
[46]Ibid., p. 112. "Karma: The spiritual and moral law of cause and effect. That which you do in either a previous or present lifetime will come back to you in this lifetime or the next. One's karma determines one's destiny in reincarnation."
[47]Shirley MacLaine, *Out On a Limb* (Toronto: Bantam, 1984), pp. 96, 111.
[48]Evolution, of course, is the most cruel method imaginable to bring about a new species or a new world order. Not only did Jacques Monod admit that natural selection was the "most cruel way of evolving new species," but Bertrand Russell agreed: "We are told that evolution is the unfolding of an idea which has been in the mind of God throughout. It appears that during those ages . . . when animals were torturing each other with ferocious horns and agonizing stings, Omnipotence was quietly waiting for the ultimate emergence of man, with his still more widely diffused cruelty. Why the Creator should have preferred to reach His goal by a process, instead of going straight to it, these modern theologians do not tell us." Bertrand Russell, *Religion and Science* (Oxford University Press, 1961), p. 73.
[49]Francis A. Schaeffer, *How Should We Then Live?* (Old Tappan, NJ: Revell, 1976), p. 177: "In Hindu thought one of the manifestations of God is Kali, a feminine representation of God with fangs and skulls hanging about her neck. Why do Hindus picture God this way? Because to them everything that exists now is part of what has always been, a part of that which the Hindus would call 'God'—and therefore cruelty is equal to non-cruelty. Modern humanistic man in both his secular and his religious forms has come to the same awful place. Both have no final way to say what is right and what is wrong, and no final way to say one should choose non-cruelty instead of cruelty."
[50]Ferguson, *The Aquarian Conspiracy*, p. 381.
[51]David Spangler, *Reflections on the Christ* (Scotland: Findhorn, 1977), pp. 40-44.
[52]Halverson, *Crystal Clear*, p. 77.
[53]Ferguson, *The Aquarian Conspiracy*, p. 70.
[54]Spangler, *Emergence: The Rebirth of the Sacred*, p. 18.
[55]Ferguson, *The Aquarian Conspiracy*, p. 159.
[56]Baer, *Inside the New Age Nightmare*, p. 47.
[57]Armand Biteaux, *The New Consciousness* (Oliver Press, 1975), p. 128. Cited in Yungen, *For Many Shall Come in My Name*, p. 166.
[58]John White, "The Second Coming," *New Frontier Magazine*, December 1987, p. 45.
[59]Peter Russell, *The Global Brain* (Los Angeles: J. P. Tarcher, 1983), p. 99.
[60]John White, *Frontiers of Consciousness* (New York: Julian Press, 1985), p. 7.
[61]Ferguson, *The Aquarian Conspiracy*, p. 248.
[62]Gawain, *Living in the Light*, p. 156.
[63]Alder, *When Humanity Comes of Age*, p. 82.
[64]Ferguson, *The Aquarian Conspiracy*, p. 257.
[65]"The Joys and Frustrations of Being a Healer," *Life Times Magazine*, vol. 1, no. 3, p. 61, cited in Yungen, *For Many Shall Come in My Name*, p. 102.
[66]Kathleen Vande Kieft, *Innersource: Channeling Your Unlimited Self* (New York: Ballantine Books, 1988), p. 114.
[67]John Randolph Price, *The Superbeings* (Austin, TX: Quartus Books, 1981), pp. 51-2.
[68]See Baer, *Inside the New Age Nightmare*, chapter 5, for an in-depth look at these practices.
[69]Unfortunately, an in-depth discussion of these occult tendencies would require an extended digression from our present attempt to understand the New Age as a systematic worldview. This is not meant to suggest, however, that the New Age should be understood as a worldview without occult ties. Indeed, the New Age movement—in part because of its pantheism—is saturated with occult practices (as their interest in meditation and channeling implies). For an excellent discussion of the occult side of the New Age movement, see Michaelsen, *Like Lambs to the Slaughter* and Texe Marrs, *Dark Secrets of the New Age* (Westchester, IL: Crossway Books, 1987).

[70]Ken Carey, in a speech at Whole Life Expo, Los Angeles, Feb. 1987, cited in Yungen, *For Many Shall Come in My Name*, p. 52.
[71]Ferguson, *The Aquarian Conspiracy*, p. 104.
[72]Spangler, *Emergence: The Rebirth of the Sacred*, p. 82.
[73]Alder, *When Humanity Comes of Age*, pp. 83-4.
[74]Gawain, *Living in the Light*, p. 110.
[75]Ibid., p. 103.
[76]Ferguson, *The Aquarian Conspiracy*, p. 280.
[77]John J. Dunphy, "A Religion for the New Age," *The Humanist*, January/February 1983, p. 26.
[78]Merrill Harmin and Sidney Simon admit that Values Clarification is "not based upon the assumption that absolute good exists and can be known. They view values as relative, personal, and situational." Halverson, *Crystal Clear*, p. 91.
[79]Ferencz and Keyes, *PlanetHood*, p. 41.
[80]Cited in Kristin Murphy, "United Nations' Robert Muller . . . A Vision of Global Spirituality," *The Movement Newspaper*, Sept. 1983, p. 10.
[81]Ferencz and Keyes, *PlanetHood*, p. 33.
[82]Donald Keys, *Earth at Omega: Passage to Planetization* (Boston: Branden Press, 1982), p. iii.
[83]Spangler, *Emergence: The Rebirth of the Sacred*, p. 42.
[84]Baer, *Inside the New Age Nightmare*, p. 34.
[85]Ferguson, *The Aquarian Conspiracy*, p. 240.
[86]Muller, *The New Genesis: Shaping a Global Spirituality*, p. 164.
[87]Ferencz and Keyes, *PlanetHood*, p. 147.
[88]Gawain, *Living in the Light*, p. 110.
[89]Ibid., p. 69.
[90]Ibid., p. 3.
[91]David Spangler, *Revelation: The Birth of a New Age* (Middleton, WI: Lorian Press, 1976), p. 65.
[92]Alder, *When Humanity Comes of Age*, pp. 48-9.
[93]Ferguson, *The Aquarian Conspiracy*, pp. 326-7.
[94]Gawain, *Living in the Light*, p. 135.
[95]Ibid., p. 142.
[96]Baer, *Inside the New Age Nightmare*, p. 140.
[97]Stasis refers to the slowing or stoppage of the evolutionary process until the process is punctuated with rapid changes.
[98]Ferencz and Keyes, *PlanetHood*, p. 141.
[99]Ibid., p. 33.
[100]Paul Davies, *New Scientist*, December 17, 1987, pp. 41-2.
[101]M. Scott Peck, *The Road Less Traveled* (New York: Simon and Schuster, 1978), pp. 269-70.
[102]*A Course in Miracles* (Tiburon, CA: Foundation for Inner Peace, 1975).
[103]Halverson, *Crystal Clear*, p. 77.
[104]Donald H. Yott, *Man and Metaphysics* (New York: Weiser, 1980), p. 74.
[105]Levi, *The Aquarian Gospel of Jesus the Christ* (Los Angeles: DeVorss & Co., 1970).
[106]Note the similarity between this view and the view professed by Julian Huxley and others cited in the chapter on Humanist history.
[107]Gawain, *Living in the Light*, p. 179.
[108]Spangler, *Emergence: The Rebirth of the Sacred*, p. 28.
[109]David K. Clark and Norman L. Geisler, in *Apologetics in the New Age: A Christian Critique of Pantheism* (Grand Rapids, MI: Baker Book House, 1990), trace thoroughly the historical roots of New Age theology and philosophy in ancient pantheistic and monistic Japanese, Chinese, Indian, and Greek religions and philosophies. They also delineate sound ways of responding to the various arguments presented as supports for pantheism and monism. We highly recommend the book to those who want to understand the logical weaknesses of Cosmic Humanism and learn how to communicate effectively with New Agers.
[110]C. S. Lewis, *Miracles: A Preliminary Study* (London: Geoffrey Bles, 1952), pp. 100-101.

[111]Spangler, *Emergence: The Rebirth of the Sacred*, p. 19.
[112]Carl Sagan, *Contact: A Novel* (New York: Simon and Schuster, 1985), p. 430.
[113]Paul Gray and David Ellis, "Gorby, the New Age Guru?" *Time*, June 18, 1990, p. 15. For further information on the relationship between the Marxist/Leninists and the New Agers we recommend Malachi Martin's *The Keys of This Blood*, pp. 292-312. Says Martin, "For a long time now, the Pontiff and his advisers have known that the Pontifical Commission for Peace and Justice, though still nominally Roman Catholic, has been taken over by converts to Marxism. Necessarily, too, the Pope and his advisers have concluded that four of the main Mega-Religionist organizations—WCRP [World Conference of Religion for Peace], WCF [World Congress of Faith], UB and TU [Temple of Understanding]—arc under the control of a master puppeteer whose home base is surely that red-gabled building in Moscow's Red Square" (p. 305). Elsewhere Martin says, "Writing in 1948, the Marxist, millionaire, publisher and Mega-Religionist Victor Gollancz said, 'The ultimate aim should be that Judaism, Christianity and all other religions should vanish and give place to one great ethical world religion, the brotherhood of man'" (p. 299).

APPENDIX

B

A MOSCOW ADDRESS

(FORMER PRESIDENT RONALD REAGAN'S MAY 31, 1988 REMARKS TO STUDENTS AND FACULTY AT MOSCOW STATE UNIVERSITY)

The President. Thank you, Rector Logunov, and I want to thank all of you very much for a very warm welcome. It's a great pleasure to be here at Moscow State University, and I want to thank you all for turning out. I know you must be very busy this week, studying and taking your final examinations. So, let me just say *zhelayu vam uspekha* [I wish you success]. Nancy couldn't make it today because she's visiting Leningrad, which she tells me is a very beautiful city, but she, too, says hello and wishes you all good luck.

Let me say it's also a great pleasure to once again have this opportunity to speak directly to the people of the Soviet Union. Before I left Washington, I received many heartfelt letters and telegrams asking me to carry here a simple message, perhaps, but also some of the

Notes and Asides

most important business of this summit: It is a message of peace and good will and hope for a growing friendship and closeness between our two peoples.

As you know, I've come to Moscow to meet with one of your most distinguished graduates. In this, our fourth summit, General Secretary Gorbachev and I have spent many hours together, and I feel that we're getting to know each other well. Our discussions, of course, have been focused primarily on many of the important issues of the day, issues I want to touch on with you in a few moments. But first I want to take a little time to talk to you much as I would to any group of university students in the United States. I want to talk not just of the realities of today but of the possibilities of tomorrow.

Standing here before a mural of your revolution, I want to talk about a very different revolution that is taking place right now, quietly sweeping the globe without bloodshed or conflict. Its effects are peaceful, but they will fundamentally alter our world, shatter old assumptions, and reshape our lives. It's easy to underestimate because it's not accompanied by banners or fanfare. It's been called the technological or information revolution, and as its emblem, one might take the tiny silicon chip, no bigger than a fingerprint. One of these chips has more computing power than a roomful of old-style computers.

As part of an exchange program, we now have an exhibition touring your country that shows how information technology is transforming our lives—replacing manual labor with robots, forecasting weather for farmers, or mapping the genetic code of DNA for medical researchers. These microcomputers today aid the design of everything from houses to cars to spacecraft; they even design better and faster computers. They can translate English into Russian or enable the blind to read or help Michael Jackson produce on one synthesizer the sounds of a whole orchestra. Linked by a network of satellites and fiber-optic cables, one individual with a desktop computer and a telephone commands resources unavailable to the largest governments just a few years ago.

Like a chrysalis, we're emerging from the economy of the Industrial Revolution—an economy confined to and limited by the Earth's physical resources—into, as one economist titled his book, "The Economy in Mind," in which there are no bounds on human imagination and the freedom to create is the most precious natural resource. Think of that little computer chip. Its value isn't in the sand from which it is made but in the microscopic architecture designed into it by ingenious human minds. Or take the example of the satellite relaying this broadcast around the world, which replaces thousands of tons of copper mined from the Earth and molded into wire. In the new

Notes and Asides

economy, human invention increasingly makes physical resources obsolete. We're breaking through the material conditions of existence to a world where man creates his own destiny. Even as we explore the most advanced reaches of science, we're returning to the age-old wisdom of our culture, a wisdom contained in the book of Genesis in the Bible: In the beginning was the spirit, and it was from this spirit that the material abundance of creation issued forth.

But progress is not foreordained. The key is freedom—freedom of thought, freedom of information, freedom of communication. The renowned scientist, scholar, and founding father of this university, Mikhail Lomonosov, knew that. "It is common knowledge," he said, "that the achievements of science are considerable and rapid, particularly once the yoke of slavery is cast off and replaced by the freedom of philosophy." You know, one of the first contacts between your country and mine took place between Russian and American explorers. The Americans were members of Cook's last voyage on an expedition searching for an Arctic passage; on the island of Unalaska, they came upon the Russians, who took them in, and together, with the native inhabitants, held a prayer service on the ice.

The explorers of the modern era are the entrepreneurs, men with vision, with the courage to take risks and faith enough to brave the unknown. These entrepreneurs and their small enterprises are responsible for almost all the economic growth in the United States. They are the prime movers of the technological revolution. In fact, one of the largest personal computer firms in the United States was started by two college students, no older than you, in the garage behind their home. Some people, even in my own country, look at the riot of experiment that is the free market and see only waste. What of all the entrepreneurs that fail? Well, many do, particularly the successful ones; often several times. And if you ask them the secret of their success, they'll tell you it's all that they learned in their struggles along the way; yes, it's what they learned from failing. Like an athlete in competition or a scholar in pursuit of the truth, experience is the greatest teacher.

> "In the beginning was the spirit, and it was from this spirit that the material abundance of creation issued forth."
> —Ronald Reagan

And that's why it's so hard for government planners, no matter how sophisticated, to ever substitute for millions of individuals working night and day to make their dreams come true. The fact is, bureaucracies are a problem around the world. There's an old story about a town—it could be anywhere—with a bureaucrat who is known to be a good-for-nothing, but he somehow had always hung on to power. So one day, in a town meeting, an old woman got up and said to him: "There is a folk legend here where I come from that when a baby is born, an angel comes down from heaven and kisses it on one part of its body. If the angel kisses him on his hand, he becomes a handyman. If he kisses him on his forehead, he becomes bright and clever. And I've

Notes and Asides

been trying to figure out where the angel kissed you so that you should sit there for so long and do nothing." [*Laughter*]

We are seeing the power of economic freedom spreading around the world. Places such as the Republic of Korea, Singapore, Taiwan have vaulted into the technological era, barely pausing in the industrial age along the way. Low-tax agricultural policies in the subcontinent mean that in some years India is now a net exporter of food. Perhaps most exciting are the winds of change that are blowing over the People's Republic of China, where one-quarter of the world's population is now getting its first taste of economic freedom. At the same time, the growth of democracy has become one of the most powerful political movements of our age. In Latin America in the 1970's, only a third of the population lived under democratic government; today over 90 percent does. In the Philippines, in the Republic of Korea, free, contested, democratic elections are the order of the day. Throughout the world, free markets are the model for growth. Democracy is the standard by which governments are measured.

We Americans make no secret of our belief in freedom. In fact, it's something of a national pastime. Every 4 years the American people choose a new President, and 1988 is one of those years. At one point there were 13 major candidates running in the two major parties, not to mention all the others, including the Socialist and Libertarian candidates—all trying to get my job. About 1,000 local television stations, 8,500 radio stations, and 1,700 daily newspapers—each one an independent, private enterprise, fiercely independent of the government—report on the candidates, grill them in interviews, and bring them together for debates. In the end, the people vote; they decide who will be the next President.

But freedom doesn't begin or end with elections. Go to any American town, to take just an example, and you'll see dozens of churches, representing many different beliefs—in many places, synagogues and mosques—and you'll see families of every conceivable nationality worshiping together. Go into any school room, and there you will see children being taught the Declaration of Independence, that they are endowed by their Creator with certain unalienable rights—among them life, liberty, and the pursuit of happiness—that no government can justly deny; the guarantees in their Constitution for freedom of speech, freedom of assembly, and freedom of religion.

Go into any courtroom, and there will preside an independent judge, beholden to no government power. There every defendant has the right to a trial by a jury of his peers, usually 12 men and women—common citizens; they are the ones, the only ones, who weigh the evidence and decide on guilt or innocence. In that court, the accused is innocent until proven guilty, and the word of a policeman or any official

Notes and Asides

has no greater legal standing than the word of the accused.

Go to any university campus, and there you'll find an open, sometimes heated discussion of the problems in American society and what can be done to correct them. Turn on the television, and you'll see the legislature conducting the business of government right there before the camera, debating and voting on the legislation that will become the law of the land. March in any demonstration, and there are many of them; the people's right of assembly is guaranteed in the Constitution and protected by the police. Go into any union hall, where the members know their right to strike is protected by law. As a matter of fact, one of the many jobs I had before this one was being president of a union, the Screen Actors Guild. I led my union out on strike, and I'm proud to say we won.

But freedom is more even than this. Freedom is the right to question and change the established way of doing things. It is the continuing revolution of the marketplace. It is the understanding that allows us to recognize shortcomings and seek solutions. It is the right to put forth an idea, scoffed at by the experts, and watch it catch fire among the people. It is the right to dream—to follow your dream or stick to your conscience, even if you're the only one in a sea of doubters. Freedom is the recognition that no single person, no single authority or government has a monopoly on the truth, but that every individual life is infinitely precious, that every one of us put on this world has been put there for a reason and has something to offer.

America is a nation made up of hundreds of nationalities. Our ties to you are more than ones of good feeling; they're ties of kinship. In America, you'll find Russians, Armenians, Ukrainians, peoples from Eastern Europe and Central Asia. They come from every part of this vast continent, from every continent, to live in harmony, seeking a place where each cultural heritage is respected, each is valued for its diverse strengths and beauties and the richness it brings to our lives. Recently, a few individuals and families have been allowed to visit relatives in the West. We can only hope that it won't be long before all are allowed to do so and Ukrainian-Americans, Baltic-Americans, Armenian-Americans can freely visit their homelands, just as this Irish-American visits his.

Freedom, it has been said, makes people selfish and materialistic, but Americans are one of the most religious peoples on Earth. Because they know that liberty, just as life itself, is not earned but a gift from God, they seek to share that gift with the world. "Reason and experience," said George Washington in his farewell address, "both forbid us to expect that national morality can prevail in exclusion of religious principle. And it is substantially true, that virtue or morality is a necessary spring of popular government." Democracy is less a

"Reason and experience both forbid us to expect that national morality can prevail in exclusion of religious principle."
—G. Washington

Notes and Asides

system of government than it is a system to keep government limited, unintrusive; a system of constraints on power to keep politics and government secondary to the important things in life, the true source of value found only in family and faith.

But I hope you know I go on about these things not simply to extol the virtues of my own country but to speak to the true greatness of the heart and soul of your land. Who, after all, needs to tell the land of Dostoevski about the quest for truth, the home of Kandinski and Scriabin about imagination, the rich and noble culture of the Uzbek man of letters Alisher Navoi about beauty and heart? The great culture of your diverse land speaks with a glowing passion to all humanity. Let me cite one of the most eloquent contemporary passages on human freedom. It comes, not from the literature of America, but from this country, from one of the greatest writers of the 20th century, Boris Pasternak, in the novel "Dr. Zhivago." He writes: "I think that if the beast who sleeps in man could be held down by threats—any kind of threat, whether of jail or of retribution after death—then the highest emblem of humanity would be the lion tamer in the circus with his whip, not the prophet who sacrificed himself. But this is just the point—what has for centuries raised man above the beast is not the cudgel, but an inward music—the irresistible power of unarmed truth."

The irresistible power of unarmed truth. Today the world looks expectantly to signs of change, steps toward greater freedom in the Soviet Union. We watch and we hope as we see positive changes taking place. There are some, I know, in your society who fear that change will bring only disruption and discontinuity, who fear to embrace the hope of the future. Sometimes it takes faith. It's like that scene in the cowboy movie "Butch Cassidy and the Sundance Kid," which some here in Moscow recently had a chance to see. The posse is closing in on the two outlaws, Butch and Sundance, who find themselves trapped on the edge of a cliff, with a sheer drop of hundreds of feet to the raging rapids below. Butch turns to Sundance and says their only hope is to jump into the river below, but Sundance refuses. He says he'd rather fight it out with the posse, even though they're hopelessly outnumbered. Butch says that's suicide and urges him to jump, but Sundance still refuses and finally admits, "I can't swim." Butch breaks up laughing and says, "You crazy fool, the fall will probably kill you." And, by the way, both Butch and Sundance made it, in case you didn't see the movie. I think what I've just been talking about is *perestroika* and what its goals are.

But change would not mean rejection of the past. Like a tree growing strong through the seasons, rooted in the Earth and drawing life from the Sun, so, too, positive change must be rooted in traditional values—in the land, in culture, in family and community—and it must take its life from the eternal things, from the source of all life, which is

Notes and Asides

faith. Such change will lead to new understandings, new opportunities, to a broader future in which the tradition is not supplanted but finds its full flowering. That is the future beckoning to your generation.

At the same time, we should remember that reform that is not institutionalized will always be insecure. Such freedom will always be looking over its shoulder. A bird on a tether, no matter how long the rope, can always be pulled back. And that is why, in my conversation with General Secretary Gorbachev, I have spoken of how important it is to institutionalize change—to put guarantees on reform. And we've been talking together about one sad reminder of a divided world: the Berlin Wall. It's time to remove the barriers that keep people apart.

I'm proposing an increased exchange program of high school students between our countries. General Secretary Gorbachev mentioned on Sunday a wonderful phrase you have in Russian for this: "Better to see something once than to hear about it a hundred times." Mr. Gorbachev and I first began working on this in 1985. In our discussion today, we agreed on working up to several thousand exchanges a year from each country in the near future. But not everyone can travel across the continents and oceans. Words travel lighter, and that's why we'd like to make available to this country more of our 11,000 magazines and periodicals and our television and radio shows that can be beamed off a satellite in seconds. Nothing would please us more than for the Soviet people to get to know us better and to understand our way of life.

Just a few years ago, few would have imagined the progress our two nations have made together. The INF treaty, which General Secretary Gorbachev and I signed last December in Washington and whose instruments of ratification we will exchange tomorrow—the first true nuclear arms reduction treaty in history, calling for the elimination of an entire class of U.S. and Soviet nuclear missiles. And just 16 days ago, we saw the beginning of your withdrawal from Afghanistan, which gives us hope that soon the fighting may end and the healing may begin and that that suffering country may find self-determination, unity, and peace at long last.

It's my fervent hope that our constructive cooperation on these issues will be carried on to address the continuing destruction of conflicts in many regions of the globe and that the serious discussions that led to the Geneva accords on Afghanistan will help lead to solutions in southern Africa, Ethiopia, Cambodia, the Persian Gulf, and Central America.

I have often said: Nations do not distrust each other because they are armed; they are armed because they distrust each other. If this globe is to live in peace and prosper, if it is to embrace all the possibilities of the technological revolution, then nations must re-

Notes and Asides

nounce, once and for all, the right to an expansionist foreign policy. Peace between nations must be an enduring goal, not a tactical stage in a continuing conflict.

I've been told that there's a popular song in your country—perhaps you know it—whose evocative refrain asks the question, "Do the Russians want a war?" In answer it says: "Go ask that silence lingering in the air, above the birch and poplar there; beneath those trees the soldiers lie. Go ask my mother, ask my wife; then you will have to ask no more, 'Do the Russians want a war?'" But what of your one-time allies? What of those who embraced you on the Elbe? What if we were to ask the watery graves of the Pacific or the European battlefields where America's fallen were buried far from home? What if we were to ask their mothers, sisters, and sons, do Americans want war? Ask us, too, and you'll find the same answer, the same longing in every heart. People do not make wars; governments do. And no mother would ever willingly sacrifice her sons for territorial gain, for economic advantage, for ideology. A people free to choose will always choose peace.

Americans seek always to make friends of old antagonists. After a colonial revolution with Britain, we have cemented for all ages the ties of kinship between our nations. After a terrible civil war between North and South, we healed our wounds and found true unity as a nation. We fought two world wars in my lifetime against Germany and one with Japan, but now the Federal Republic of Germany and Japan are two of our closest allies and friends.

Some people point to the trade disputes between us as a sign of strain, but they're the frictions of all families, and the family of free nations is a big and vital and sometimes boisterous one. I can tell you that nothing would please my heart more than in my lifetime to see American and Soviet diplomats grappling with the problem of trade disputes between American and a growing, exuberant, exporting Soviet Union that had opened up to economic freedom and growth. And as important as these official people-to-people exchanges are, nothing would please me more than for them to become unnecessary, to see travel between East and West become so routine that university students in the Soviet Union could take a month off in the summer and, just like students in the West do now, put packs on their backs and travel from country to country in Europe with barely a passport check in between. Nothing would please me more than to see the day that a concert promoter in, say, England could call up a Soviet rock group, without going through any government agency, and have them playing in Liverpool the next night. Is this just a dream? Perhaps. But it is a dream that is our responsibility to have come true.

Your generation is living in one of the most exciting, hopeful times in Soviet history. It is a time when the first breath of freedom stirs the air and the heart beats to the accelerated rhythm of hope, when the accumulated spiritual energies of a long silence yearn to break free. I am reminded of the famous passage near the end of Gogol's "Dead Souls." Comparing his nation to a speeding troika, Gogol asks what will be its destination. But he writes, "There was no answer save the bell pouring forth marvelous sound."

We do not know what the conclusion will be of this journey, but we're hopeful that the promise of reform will be fulfilled. In this Moscow spring, this May 1988, we may be allowed that hope: that freedom, like the fresh green sapling planted over Tolstoi's grave, will blossom forth at last in the rich fertile soil of your people and culture. We may be allowed to hope that the marvelous sound of a new openness will keep rising through, ringing through, leading to a new world of reconciliation, friendship, and peace.

Thank you all very much, and *da blagoslovit vas gospod'*—God bless you.

[This speech was reprinted in *Weekly Compilation of Presidential Documents*, 6 June 1988, vol. 24, no. 22, pp. 703-8.]

APPENDIX

C

"THE GODS OF THE COPYBOOK HEADINGS"

(By Rudyard Kipling)

[*Note*: This insightful poem is unfortunately dated by its reference to "copybook headings." In present times, of course, copybooks are rare—but in the early twentieth century, students learned their ABC's by copying the headings on each page of the "copybook." These headings, in order to further edify the student, were usually sentences containing "eternal truths" such as "Blessed are the meek, for they will inherit the earth." Thus, when Kipling speaks of the "Gods of the Copybook Headings," he is referring to the moral order of the universe—what Christians would call general revelation or natural law. "The Gods of the Market-Place," obviously, refers to many of the "Gods" refuted in this text.]

"THE GODS OF THE COPYBOOK HEADINGS"

As I pass through my incarnations in every age and race,
I make my proper prostrations to the Gods of the Market-Place.
Peering through reverent fingers I watch them flourish and fall,
And the Gods of the Copybook Headings, I notice, outlast them all.

We were living in trees when they met us. They showed us each in turn
That Water would certainly wet us, as Fire would certainly burn:
But we found them lacking in Uplift, Vision and Breadth of Mind,
So we left them to teach the Gorillas while we followed the March of Mankind.

We moved as the Spirit listed. *They* never altered their pace,
Being neither cloud nor wind-borne like the Gods of the Market-Place;
But they always caught up with our progress, and presently word would come
That a tribe had been wiped off its icefield, or the lights had gone out in Rome.

With the Hopes that our World is built on they were utterly out of touch.
They denied that the Moon was Stilton; they denied she was even Dutch.
They denied that Wishes were Horses; they denied that a Pig had Wings.
So we worshipped the Gods of the Market Who promised these beautiful things.

When the Cambrian measures were forming, They promised perpetual peace.
They swore, if we gave them our weapons, that the wars of the tribes would cease.
But when we disarmed They sold us and delivered us bound to our foe,
And the Gods of the Copybook Heading said: "*Stick to the Devil you know.*"

On the first Feminian Sandstones we were promised the Fuller Life
(Which started by loving our neighbor and ended by loving his wife)
Till our women had no more children and the men lost reason and faith,
And the Gods of the Copybook Headings said: "*The Wages of Sin is Death.*"

In the Carboniferous Epoch we were promised abundance for all,
By robbing selected Peter to pay for collective Paul;

But, though we had plenty of money, there was nothing our money could buy,
And the Gods of the Copybook Headings said: "*If you don't work you die.*"

Then the Gods of the Market tumbled, and their smooth-tongued wizards withdrew,
And the hearts of the meanest were humbled and began to believe it was true
That All is not Gold that Glitters, and Two and Two make Four—
And the Gods of the Copybook Headings limped up to explain it once more.

* * * * *

As it will be in the future, it was at the birth of Man—
There are only four things certain since Social Progress began:—
That the Dog returns to his Vomit and the Sow returns to her Mire,
And the burnt Fool's bandaged finger goes wabbling back to the Fire;
And that after this is accomplished, and the brave new world begins
When all men are paid for existing and no man must pay for his sins,
As surely as Water will wet us, as surely as Fire will burn,
The Gods of the Copybook Headings with terror and slaughter return!

[Cited in *Kipling: A Selections of His Stories and Poems*, ed. John Beecroft (Garden City, NY: Doubleday, 1956).]

INDEX